WEST ACADEMIC PUBLISHING'S EMERITUS ADVISORY BOARD

WEST ACADEMIC PUBLISHING'S LAW SCHOOL ADVISORY BOARD

INSURANCE LAW AND PRACTICE

CASES, MATERIALS, AND EXERCISES

Second Edition

■ ■ ■

Christopher C. French
Professor of Practice
Penn State Law

AMERICAN CASEBOOK SERIES®

WEST ACADEMIC PUBLISHING

444 Cedar Street, Suite 700
St. Paul, MN 55101
1-877-888-1330

Printed in the United States of America

ISBN: 978-1-64708-519-3

For Jodi

PREFACE AND ACKNOWLEDGMENTS

This book is the product of my nearly thirty years of teaching and practicing Insurance Law. The book is intended to lend itself to teaching Insurance Law as either a traditional doctrinal course or as an experiential course because it includes numerous practical exercises that can be assigned periodically throughout the course. Unlike many other Insurance Law casebooks, this one also has sections on subjects such as Choice of Law, Personal and Advertising Liability Coverage, Claims-Made Insurance, Proofs of Loss and Examinations under Oath, Concurrent Causation, and Business Interruption Insurance.

In addition to being based upon my own experiences, this book is indebted to Robert H. Jerry, II, Professor Emeritus at the University of Missouri School of Law and Dean Emeritus at the University of Florida School of Law, and Roger C. Henderson, Emeritus Professor and Dean-Emeritus at the University of Arizona School of Law. Professor Jerry edited the first edition of this book, and some of the cases and notes in the book originally were selected or created by Professors Jerry and Henderson. They are both luminaries in the field of Insurance Law.

Finally, I thank current and former Penn State Law students Katrina Feller, Kyle Kenny, Jacob LaFreniere, and Victoria Veatch for their research and editing assistance on the book.

CHRISTOPHER C. FRENCH

University Park, Pennsylvania
August 2020

SUMMARY OF CONTENTS

TABLE OF CONTENTS

TABLE OF CASES

The principal cases are in bold type.

Insurance Law and Practice

Cases, Materials, and Exercises

Second Edition

CHAPTER ONE

INTRODUCTION

■ ■ ■

"Perhaps no modern commercial enterprise directly affects so many persons in all walks of life as does the insurance business. Insurance touches the home, the family, and the occupation or the business of almost every person in the United States."

— Justice Hugo L. Black, in *United States v. South-Eastern Underwriters Association*, 322 U.S. 533, 540 (1943)

I. THE HISTORY AND PURPOSE OF INSURANCE

The world is a very dangerous place.[1] Every day there is a chance that each of us could be in a car accident. Or, we could be the victims of a natural catastrophe such as a tornado, flood or earthquake. Every day someone is diagnosed with a deadly disease. Our properties are in constant peril—houses catch fire every day and trees regularly fall on houses during storms. Any one of these events could have devastating financial consequences, and they are just a few of the many risks that surround our daily lives. There are a number of ways we attempt to reduce these risks. For example, we fasten our seat belts and maintain our vehicles in an attempt to avoid accidents and minimize the consequences of accidents. We cut down trees next to our houses and install smoke alarms in an attempt to prevent damage to our homes and the people in them. In addition to loss prevention measures, however, one of the principal ways we manage risk is by purchasing insurance.

The concept underlying insurance is quite simple. A person or a business transfers the risk of loss to another entity in exchange for the payment of a premium. The principal reason most people and businesses purchase insurance is to avoid uncertain, but potential, future losses. The purchaser of insurance incurs a relatively small certain loss by paying a premium in order to avoid the risk of larger, uncertain future losses. Although the law has sought to diminish insurance's similarity to gambling by requiring, for example, that a person purchasing insurance actually have an "insurable interest" in the object being insured (i.e., a reason to want the person or item insured not to be injured or damaged), a person

[1] Much of this introductory section was taken almost verbatim from Christopher C. French, *The Role the Profit Imperative Plays in Risk Management*, 17 U. Pa. J. Bus. L. 1081, 1083–85, 1089–95 (2015) (citations omitted).

who purchases insurance is hedging against the risk of something terrible happening. As described by one court, a person who buys insurance is attempting to "buy financial protection and peace of mind against fortuitous losses."[2]

The entity that accepts the risk of loss typically spreads the risk of loss across a large number of policyholders. Although it is expected that some people will suffer losses, only a subset of the total pool of people insured will actually incur losses. This concept is known as the "law of large numbers." In essence, the large percentage of fortunate people that pay for insurance but do not suffer a loss receive peace of mind through their purchase of insurance and their premiums subsidize the unfortunate few people who do suffer losses. In short, everyone pays a premium to create a pool of funds from which the unfortunate few who suffer losses will be paid.

In a non-profit context, the insurer simply functions as an intermediary that facilitates this transfer of risk from the individual to the group. For some lines of insurance, such as auto insurance, the insurance industry can predict with great accuracy the likelihood and extent of the actual risk of loss that is transferred because it has collected very detailed and accurate information regarding the likelihood and severity of injuries with respect to various risk classifications. For example, for the year 2017, insurers knew that on average: (1) there would be 16 fatalities for every 100,000 licensed drivers, (2) a driver aged 21 to 24 was almost twice as likely to be involved in a fatal crash while intoxicated as a driver 55 to 64 years old, and (3) the average auto liability claim for property damage would be approximately $3,400. Knowing what each policyholder pays in premiums and the amount of the losses, the insurer is able to predict with great accuracy the expected return it will receive for accepting the transfer of risk. Consequently, insurers can and do use claims data and risk classifications to charge different premium rates to the people in the various risk classifications or to refuse to insure certain people or risks they deem unprofitable or inadequately profitable.

Insurance traces its roots back to Babylonian maritime traders as early as 2250 B.C. The Babylonians developed what were known as contracts of "bottomry," under which investors would loan money or goods to a merchant at a high interest rate with the understanding that the borrower's obligation to pay the interest or the debt would be eliminated if the vessel carrying the goods sank or was pirated. The Phoenicians, Greeks, and Romans subsequently used contracts of bottomry. Centuries later, bottomry contracts evolved into what we know today as insurance contracts with Lloyd's of London being the first formal insurer of vessels and cargo in the late seventeenth century. Following the Great Fire of

---

[2] Jay M. Feinman, Delay, Deny, Defend: Why Insurance Companies Don't Pay Claims and What You Can Do About It 19 (2010) (*quoting Campbell v. State Farm Mut. Auto Ins. Co.*, 98 P.3d 409, 415 (Utah 2004)).

London in 1666, insurers also began selling insurance to cover fire losses for non-marine properties.

As originally conceived and implemented in America in the mid-1700s, insurance functioned as a social safety net through which a community or group as a whole acted for the benefit of the unlucky few who suffered losses. People and businesses each contributed a premium to a "mutual" company or group to create a pool of money from which losses were paid. Essentially, the insurance company acted as a third-party administrator that collected the premiums to create the pool of money from which losses would be paid, and then paid such losses as they arose. Initially, these mutual insurance companies only covered fire losses. Over time, however, insurance expanded to cover the other myriad risks of loss that exist.

The need for insurance is even greater today than it was in the 1700s. Imagine being a homeowner in Oklahoma when tornadoes rip through the state each spring, or on the coast in the Gulf of Mexico, Florida or the East Coast when a hurricane makes landfall. Or, imagine being diagnosed with cancer. Now imagine that the afflicted homeowner or person does not have property insurance or health insurance. What happens to such people? Financial ruin unless they are the beneficiaries of the generosity of strangers or a government bailout.

Not only does insurance provide peace of mind and ensure one's financial security in the event of a catastrophe in ways that hoping for a government bailout or the generosity of strangers do not, but insurance actually has become a necessity to live and function in America today. It is required, for example, in order to legally drive a car to work or to obtain a mortgage for a home. In short, in most parts of this country a person cannot hold a job or be a homeowner today without insurance.

Yet, as the need for insurance has increased, insurers' willingness to cover certain people and risks has decreased. Although the profit imperative began forcing insurers to begin refusing to insure some perils, such as floods, in the 1950s and 1960s, insurers' efforts to avoid insuring certain people and certain risks have accelerated since the 1970s. The reason is simple: profits. The idea of insurance as a social safety net, in which a group of people or businesses as a whole acts for the benefit of the unfortunate few, was lost when the corporate structure of insurance companies shifted from mutual companies to for-profit, publicly traded stock companies. Although this shift had been occurring for some time, it accelerated in the 1980s and 1990s to the point that the vast majority of insurance companies today are for-profit, publicly traded stock companies.

Another reason that insurance has become central to our lives is the public policy concern that innocent victims will go uncompensated in the absence of insurance if they are injured. Many injured people would not be able to pay their medical bills or recover lost wages in the absence of insurance because tortfeasors often do not have sufficient assets to adequately compensate the people they injure. Indeed, ensuring that innocent victims will be compensated is the primary reason automobile insurance is mandatory in this country.

Other public policy concerns are also central to much of insurance law today. Because of the disparity in knowledge and power between the insurers and consumers, legislatures and courts are protective of consumers. For example, much of the regulation of the insurance industry is directed at ensuring that insurers remain solvent so they can pay claims. Similarly, because insurance policies are complex contracts of adhesion drafted by insurers and sold on a take-it-or-leave-it basis, courts apply *contra proferentem* strictly to construe any ambiguities in the policy language in favor of the consumer (aka the policyholder). In addition, many courts have adopted a doctrine known as the "reasonable expectations" doctrine, which allows courts to construe policy language in favor of the policyholder in situations where the policyholder reasonably thought it was obtaining coverage even though the policy language, if read and understood, would not support a finding of coverage. In addition, because insurers control the defense and settlement of most claims in the liability insurance context, many courts treat insurers as quasi-fiduciaries when exercising that control by requiring insurers to consider the interests of the policyholder when deciding how to defend and settle claims. If the insurer does not act reasonably in doing so, then, unlike almost all other types of breach of contract, it can be liable to the policyholder for extra contractual damages, including punitive damages.

Because of its importance to society today, insurance has become a huge industry with global premiums exceeding $4 trillion, with the United States alone accounting for 28% of that amount. Accounting for 7% of the world's gross domestic product, the insurance industry has grown to become one of the largest and most important industries in the world.

NOTES AND QUESTIONS

1. *Responding to Risk.* Purchasing a policy of insurance is only one of a number of ways people respond to risk. Preventing loss, mitigating the effects of loss, diversification, self-insurance through reserves, and transferring risk through insurance are the common methods of risk management. Think about the risks you face on a daily basis. How do you deal with them?

Without risk, there is no need for insurance. If the future were foreseeable with certainty, what would there be to insure? Of course, some things are certain to occur (e.g., death), but what is uncertain about these "certain" occurrences is the timing. Death at a particular time can have very different consequences for survivors than death at some other time. For example, death of a parent with young, dependent children has different implications than if the parent dies when the children are self-supporting adults. How, then, would you describe the risk being protected by life insurance? As we will see, life insurance can also have an investment purpose, but this only means that a different kind of risk is being addressed through purchase of the insurance.

2. *The Determinable Value of Responding to Risk.* Professor A. Mitchell Polinsky has created a useful hypothetical well suited for law students that illustrates that the elimination of risk has a determinable value. Imagine that your only job offer—which you need to accept to pay off student loans—is with a firm that has an unusual proposal. You will work on one case all year, and if you win the case at trial, the firm will pay you $100,000. If you lose, the firm will pay you nothing. The firm knows from its long experience with cases of this kind that the chances of the case being won are 50 percent. How confident are you in your legal skills? The value of the proposal to you is $50,000, because it computes to an expected benefit of $50,000. (This hypo involves a beneficial risk because, from your perspective, it only involves gain. If the hypo were about a possible loss to you, it would involve a negative risk.) The critical question, though, is this: how much would you be willing to accept as a certain payment for your year's work in order to avoid the 50 percent chance of being paid nothing? The difference between that number and $50,000 is the monetary value to you of eliminating the risk of being paid nothing. Do you see an opportunity in this hypo for someone else to make a profit from your desire to receive a certain payment less than $50,000 in order to escape the $100,000-or-nothing, 50/50 proposition? *See* A. Mitchel Polinsky, An Introduction to Law and Economics.

II. KEY INSURANCE CONCEPTS

To understand insurance law and the cases that will be discussed in this book, one must understand several key concepts that either motivate insurers' behavior or serve as part of the theoretical basis for the reasoning of the courts.

Risk Transfer. One of the primary purposes of insurance is the transfer of risk from one entity to another. When an individual or firm encounters the uncertainty of something bad happening, the entity has a *risk of loss.* The usual response to a risk of loss is to attempt to manage it through one or more risk management tools. For example, the entity may invest in safeguards that prevent or reduce the probability that a loss will happen at all. This occurs, to illustrate, when a consumer chooses to buy an automobile equipped with all the available automated collision-avoidance options, such as pedestrian detection, autonomous braking and steering crash-avoidance systems, and audio alerts. To take another example, the entity might invest in safeguards that reduce the amount of damage if an accident should occur. Thus, "surround-the-passenger" air bags and pre-crash, radar-triggered seatbelt tightening systems will not prevent accidents, but they will reduce injuries suffered in an accident if one should occur. When these and other risk management tools are fully utilized or are no longer cost effective because the value of the reduction in risk is less than the cost of acquiring and implementing the risk management tool, entities turn to insurance to manage the risks that remain. The essence of insurance is not to reduce the frequency of loss or its magnitude when it happens, but is instead the transfer of risk from one entity to another—specifically, to an entity whose business purpose is to receive risks that others wish to transfer (and then to distribute them across a large pool of similarly situated individuals or firms, a feature of insurance which is discussed below).

The risks of bad things happening are called *negative risks*. When expected losses are small, individuals and firms may be able to pay for them easily out-of-pocket. This can be understood as *self-insurance*, which is the opposite of risk transfer, and occurs when an entity sets up reserves to deal with the possible losses. With respect to some small losses, entities are *risk neutral*—meaning they are totally ambivalent about whether loss happens or not. When losses are small, insurance is not needed, and when entities are ambivalent about risk, insurance will not be sought, even if it would be wise to do so. With respect to the risk of large losses (including situations where a high frequency of small-loss events are possible), most people are *risk averse*. Thus, as a general proposition, entities prefer to pay relatively small, predictable amounts of money (i.e., premiums) to avoid the possibility of suffering a relatively large loss at an uncertain time.

Entities that seek insurance are comparatively risk averse, which means they would prefer to pay a relatively small amount of money (i.e., a premium) in order to avoid the possibility of suffering a relatively large loss. Most people and businesses are generally risk averse with respect to low-probability but high-magnitude losses. For example, most people do not want to bear the risk of their homes burning down even though the chances of that occurring are low. Thus, people are willing to pay premiums to transfer the risk of their homes burning down to another entity (i.e., an insurer).

The exceptions to this principle of risk aversion involve entities with such extraordinary wealth that they are not impacted by large losses. In other words, wealth reduces risk aversion. For most entities, however, the destruction of a home, the personal losses and liabilities associated with automobile accidents, the loss of income when becoming disabled due to illness or accident, the destruction of a manufacturing plant, the interruption of business activity due to natural disasters, and so on, all involve very severe consequences. Thus, individuals and firms are willing to pay premiums to transfer the risk of loss to other entities, and insurance companies engage in the business of receiving these transfers in exchange for the payment of the premiums. Risk transfer is at the core of the business of insurance.

Risk Pooling (or Risk Distribution). Risk transfer, in and of itself, simply shifts risk; it is when risk transfer is combined with risk pooling that actual risk management occurs. Insurance functions by pooling the risk of loss for individuals into a larger group, which has the effect of distributing the risk across this group. By insuring a large number of similarly situated individuals, an insurer essentially spreads the risk of loss of any individual insured across all members of the group. Although it is unknown whether any individual insured will suffer a loss in any given year, the predictability of losses for the group as a whole increases over time and as the size of the group increases. Consequently, although there may be a high percentage chance (or even a certainty) that some insureds within the group will suffer a loss in any given year, the financial impact of the individual losses becomes predictable when the group is sufficiently large and is relatively minor in the context of the entire insured group.

The key to this phenomenon is a mathematical principle known as the *law of large numbers*. The law describes what happens when the same action with seemingly random results is performed a large number of times. In the long term, the average of the results from a large number of actions will be very close to the expected value, and it will become closer as more actions occur. If, for example, two six-sided dice (with values on each side of 1, 2, 3, 4, 5, and 6) are tossed ten times, the sum of the values on the top of the dice will appear to be randomly distributed between 2 and 12, with a more-likely-than-not concentration around the values of 6, 7, and 8. But if the two dice are tossed 500,000 times, the value 7 will appear 16.66667% of the time. Simply put, the law of large numbers predicts stable long-term outcomes for the averages of a large number of random events.

In insurance, the law of large numbers means that the larger the pool of insureds independently exposed to a loss-producing risk, the more likely it is that the actual number of losses in the pool will equal the expected number of losses. With the relative certainty about the number of losses that will occur in a large group due to the law of large numbers, insurers can accept the transfer of risk with relative confidence that they will charge a sufficient premium to each member of the group to reimburse the losses that occur, cover the expenses of forming and managing the insurance pool, and earn an appropriate profit (if this is the insurer's goal).

Risk Classification. When large groups of individuals are insured over time, insurers are able to understand which characteristics of the insured individuals, such as geographic location and the nature of the activities engaged in by insureds, result in more or less claims of more or less severity. This enables insurers to classify the riskiness of individual insureds and to charge premiums accordingly.

Insurers can also then incentivize insureds to alter their behavior based on the amount of premium charged. For example, if a health insurer charges higher premiums to insureds who smoke because the insurer knows through experiential data that people who smoke generally have more health problems than people who do not smoke, then the insurer can create a financial incentive for insureds who smoke to stop smoking.

Correlated Risks. The law of large numbers, as applied to insurance, will fail in two situations. First, if the pool of insureds is too small, the probability that the actual number of losses in the pool will equal the expected number declines, which means that an insurer that assumes the risk of all losses in the pool is at increased risk of collecting insufficient premiums to cover the actual losses. When the insurer has insufficient reserves to cover losses, the insurer is functionally insolvent, and an insurer at risk of insolvency provides little security to its policyholders. Second, the law of large numbers presumes that policyholders in the pool have exposures to risk independent of each other. If every policyholder in the pool will suffer a loss if a particular covered occurrence happens, then the insurance mechanism fails because the insurer will have to charge a premium to each policyholder sufficient to cover the probability of every policyholder in the pool suffering a loss simultaneously. This is the concept of *correlated risks*.

Sensitivity to the problem of correlated risks explains a significant amount of insurance company underwriting behavior. (*Underwriting* is the process whereby insurers decide whether to issue coverage and, if issued, at what price for selected coverages.) An example of an especially important manifestation of risk correlation is geography.

"Correlated risks are risks of the same type of loss by numerous people in the same geographic area at approximately the same time. Insurers generally attempt to avoid insuring correlated risks of loss due to actuarial and capitalization concerns; they contend they cannot accurately predict the frequency or severity of such losses or collect enough premiums to spread the risk of loss across a large enough pool of policyholders to cover the losses when they occur. Correlated-risk concerns are greatest when an insurer sells insurance only in a limited geographic area because the pool of policyholders is limited, and all of these policyholders are likely to face the same natural hazards at the same time. Namely, people who live in the same neighborhood have similar risks of loss for floods, earthquakes and tornadoes. Consequently, if an insurer sells policies only locally or regionally, correlated-risk concerns regarding natural disasters are well founded."[3]

The concept of correlated risks explains why no insurer sells life insurance only to workers in Chicago's Willis Tower or New York's Freedom Tower. Although we should not underestimate the security

[3] Christopher C. French, *Insuring Landslides: America's Uninsured Natural Catastrophes*, 17 Nev. L. J. 63, 76–77 (2016) (citations omitted).

measures in place to protect these buildings after the lessons learned on 9/11, these buildings remain prominent targets for terrorist activity, which means the personal injury risks in these buildings are correlated. Similarly, insurers largely refuse to insure some natural catastrophes absent special pricing that reduces the amount of risk the insurer assumes. Earthquakes and hurricanes are the two most prominent examples. Absent very large deductibles requiring insureds to bear significant loss personally before proceeds are paid by the insurer, insurance companies are not willing to write such coverage. Flood risk historically has been viewed by insurers as so highly correlated that private insurers have refused to write the coverage at all. Yet, individuals and businesses in flood prone areas will not continue to reside and work in these areas absent insurance. Congress deemed the economic well-being of these areas to be so important that it created a federally subsidized flood insurance program a half-century ago, effectively spreading the risk of flood loss to the limited pool of insureds with the federal government as the guarantor of payment—which essentially means all taxpayers to the extent the program does not generate premiums adequate to cover all of the losses. Earthquakes, hurricanes, and floods can cause extraordinary damage, and thus the largest insured losses—which produces significant challenges for insurance markets because of the correlated nature of the risks. Of course, because natural catastrophes potentially have the most devastating personal and financial consequences for individuals, they are exactly the types of risks for which individuals need insurance the most.

Adverse Selection. Despite the law of large numbers, all insurers face a common problem when setting the criteria for entry into the pools of insureds for which they provide coverage. Despite an insurer's best efforts to classify insureds according to level of risk, every insurance pool contains a disproportionate number of high-risk policyholders. The economic principle underlying this reality is that individuals and firms with the greatest need for insurance—in other words, entities that face the highest risks of loss—are most likely to purchase insurance. For example, individuals who know they are afflicted with a terminal illness will be more interested in purchasing life insurance than individuals who know they are healthy or who lack the knowledge that they are terminally ill. A business with plants built on land vulnerable to sinkholes is more likely to desire to purchase sinkhole insurance than a business located in an area that has never seen a sinkhole. *Adverse selection* describes the tendency of high-risk entities to seek insurance and the reality that risk pools may contain a disproportionate number of such entities.

Many insurer underwriting practices, insurance policy provisions, and insurance law principles can be understood as manifestations of the efforts of insurance companies to combat adverse selection. For example, insurers try to measure risk and then use that information to subdivide risk pools into lower risk and higher risk subgroups. Eventually, the cost of making the measurements will exceed the benefits gained by subdividing the groups and the insurer will stop making the measurements. At that point, there will be some individuals who are riskier than the insurer has classified them. Thus, in whatever subgroups remain after an insurer stops making distinctions among the policyholders, some number of higher risk insureds will populate the groups. If adverse selection operates to excess, the insurer will discover that it is paying more in proceeds for claims than is justified for the premium charged.

Adverse selection is much more likely to occur when the insurance only covers a single risk or peril. Flooding is a good example. People who think they are most likely to suffer flood losses will be more inclined to purchase flood insurance than people who do not think they are at risk for flooding.

"Adverse-selection theory posits that 'a party facing a high risk of loss is more likely to seek insurance than a party facing a low risk.' The theory is premised on the idea that policyholders have an informational advantage over insurers, which enables the policyholders to use that informational advantage to allow people who know they are bad risks to buy more insurance than people who are good risks. When an insurance policy covers only a single peril, then adverse selection is more likely to occur. A person who thinks his house may be damaged by a landslide because he lives on or near a hill or mountain is more likely to want to purchase landslide insurance than someone who lives on flat farmland."[4]

Reverse adverse selection occurs when insurers identify the people most likely to suffer losses and then either charge them higher premiums or completely refuse to insure them. For many lines of insurance, such as auto and life insurance, insurers have much more information regarding the risk of loss for the individuals insured than the individuals themselves do because insurers have been collecting claims data based upon the risk profiles of insureds for decades. Consequently, reverse adverse selection is a bigger problem than adverse selection in many situations.

Moral Hazard. Whereas adverse selection describes the tendency for high-risk entities to join risk pools in disproportionate numbers, *moral hazard* describes what happens inside risk pools once they are formed. As an economics principle, moral hazard refers to the tendency of an economic actor to take more risks if someone else bears the cost of those risks. This principle is very important in insurance, given that the whole point of insurance is to transfer one party's risks to another entity. The idea of moral hazard is that someone who is insured for loss will have less incentive to take precautions against loss—or may even take affirmative steps to cause a loss for the purpose of recovering under the insurance

[4] *Id.* at 74–75 (citations omitted) (quoting Kenneth S. Abraham & Daniel Schwarcz, Insurance Law and Regulation 6 (6th ed. 2015)).

policy. In other words, the existence of insurance has the perverse effect of increasing the probability of loss. To illustrate, if a mechanic knows that in the event her tools are stolen the insurer will reimburse the loss in total, the mechanic may be less likely to endure the inconvenience of putting the tools in a locked storage area at the end of the working day. More pernicious is the tendency for property insurance to induce the unscrupulous insured to commit arson when economic times are hard. As with adverse selection, there is much about insurer practices, insurance policy content, and insurance law that can be understood as the result of insurance company efforts to combat moral hazard.

The presence of moral hazard varies depending upon the type of insurance at issue. For example, in the property insurance context, the concern that a policyholder may destroy the insured property to collect an insurance payout is legitimate if the insurance payout is greater than the value of the insured property or the policyholder is in desperate need of money. On the other hand, in the auto insurance context, there is less concern that a policyholder will intentionally crash in order to recover an insurance payout for the bodily injuries because the policyholder will actually suffer bodily injuries. A person's self interest in avoiding injury, pain and suffering tends to deter such actions. Thus, the existence of auto insurance is less likely to create a disincentive to drive carefully.

In life insurance, the situation where someone takes out a policy on someone else's life with the intention of killing the insured for the purpose of enriching oneself through the proceeds is thankfully rare, but it happens. A number of insurance law rules have developed to eliminate the incentive to devise and implement schemes to profit through the destruction of people or property, and the core rationale for these rules is combatting moral hazard.

Moral hazard concerns also influence how insurance policies are drafted. This is particularly evident with respect to many exclusions found in insurance policies, such as, for example, the "expected or intended" exclusion, which purports to exclude coverage for any injuries or damage expected or intended by the policyholder.

Insurers also attempt to combat moral hazard through the limits of insurance they are willing to underwrite (e.g., by insuring less than the full value of the insured item, the policyholder will be incentivized to preserve the item to avoid suffering a loss for the uninsured amount). Insurers also use deductibles or self-insured retentions to ensure that the policyholder will bear a portion of any loss to again incentivize the policyholder to avoid losses. To illustrate, if the mechanic described earlier has to bear a portion of any loss out of her own pocket, then the probability that she will lock up her tools at the end of the day goes up.

Solidarity Versus Self-Determination. American insurance law largely is based upon the American concept of self-determination—that people generally should be responsible for their own financial well-being—as well as the idea that people should be free to enter or not enter into contracts. Although there has been some erosion of these principles due to public policy concerns regarding the compensation of injured parties and consumer protection, insurance in America is still primarily governed by contract law in most states.

America's approach to insurance law stands in contrast to the way much of the developed world approaches insurance. In China and many European countries, the fortunes of individuals are tied to the fortunes of the community at large. When an individual suffers a loss, the community as a whole shares the loss. This idea of "solidarity" manifests itself in various ways. For example, in many European countries, it is mandatory that insurers cover natural catastrophes such as flooding that U.S. insurers are allowed to, and do, refuse to cover. In other countries, the government either directly covers the losses or reimburses insurers for covering such losses.

America seems to be gradually moving in the direction of solidarity, but the march is slow and proceeds in fits and starts. In addition to the increasing role that public policy plays in the area of insurance law, America actually has adopted a number of "solidarity" insurance programs. Medicare is one example. Social Security disability coverage, which provides payments for disabled people, is another example. Workers' Compensation, a form of no-fault insurance, and unemployment insurance are other examples. The Affordable Care Act, which restricts insurers' ability to employ reverse adverse selection to refuse to insure people who are "bad risks" or already sick, is yet another example.

Although the concepts of risk pooling, risk classification, correlated risks, adverse selection, moral hazard, and solidarity may seem to be abstract concepts as one begins to explore insurance law, one will find these concepts at the heart of insurer conduct when it comes to drafting the language and exclusions in insurance policies, underwriting decisions, and claims handling practices. These concepts implicitly or explicitly also underlie many court decisions. Consequently, these concepts will be worth revisiting at the end of the semester to synthesize how they manifested themselves throughout the course.

NOTES AND QUESTIONS

1. *Insurance as a Product? Or Something Else?* As the reading makes clear, insurance policies generally are treated and analyzed as contracts between policyholders and insurance companies. Is there another way to conceptualize insurance policies? In many recent television and social media advertisements of the Progressive Insurance Company, the background scene

is a store where the shelves contain boxes representing the insurance policies themselves. In at least one commercial, the customer carries the boxes as if proceeding to the checkout counter. Is this advertisement conveying the impression that insurance is a product and not a contract? Few of us understand how an automobile works or know what is inside the engine (do you understand, and can you explain, bore, stroke, rings, cams, displacement, and compression ratio?). We simply rely on a car to provide reliable transportation. Is an insurance policy any different? The question is not a new one. For example, Professor Samuel Williston of contracts and evidence fame understood decades ago that insurance may be something different from a personal contract between insurer and policyholder:

> The typical [insurance] applicant buys "protection" much as he buys groceries. The protection is intangible, to be sure, but he is reassured by the words of the agent and by the fact that agent and company are regulated by the state and licensed to do business there . . . . [F]or most purposes, insurance must still be considered a contract between insurer and insured, but it is a very special type of contract and one currently involved in a prolonged period of popular gestation from which it may well eventually emerge as a new and special form of chattel, or perhaps, quasi chattel.

7 Samuel Williston & Walter H. E. Jaeger, A Treatise on the Law of Contracts § 900, at 34 (3d ed. 1963).

Can you think of other ways to describe an insurance policy? Professor Abraham observes that in recent decades conceptions of public utility/regulated industry and governance (i.e., the idea that insurers "govern" their policyholders as the functional equivalent of a government) have also been proposed in addition to contract and product. He writes:

> Although these conceptions adopt very different perspectives, each is a way of struggling with the two fundamental questions that modern insurance law has continually faced. The first question involves the extent to which the language of an insurance policy should determine its legal effect. This is the insurance law version of the age-old question concerning the validity of one-sided provisions in contracts of adhesion. Because virtually all insurance policies, including high-end corporate insurance policies, are standard-forms, it is a question at the core, not the periphery, of insurance law. The second question involves the proper influence of what are sometimes called "public law" values on the scope of private insurance coverage. This is a question with which much of modern private law struggles. To what extent should private law be about doing justice between two contracting parties, and to what extent should it also be concerned with other, more nearly public law matters? . . . [S]ometimes we do not see through our conceptual structures but instead are led around by them.

Kenneth S. Abraham, *Four Conceptions of Insurance*, 161 U. Pa. L. Rev. 653, 653–54 (2013). As we move through the course, think about some of the different consequences that might flow from viewing an insurance policy as something other than a contract.

2. *Insurance and Social Order*. Professor Lon Fuller (1902–1978) was an influential legal philosopher whose work on sources of law continues to shape modern thinking on the subject. He believed there are two fundamental forms of social ordering: one based on reciprocity or exchange where people tend to deal more or less at arm's length in ordering transactions, and one based on common ends or shared interests, such as when people work together to build a wall against some common problem or threat. *See* Lon L. Fuller, *The Forms and Limits of Adjudication*, 92 Harv. L. Rev. 353, 357–62 (1978). Are the risks against which we seek security through insurance contracts more like the common ends/shared problem situation, or are they more like reciprocal, exchange-type relationships? What does the answer tell us about the nature of the policyholder-insurer relationship and the goals which it might have? Courts often speak of the business of insurance and insurance policies as being clothed with the public interest. When courts say this, do they have a particular kind of social order in mind? Does any of this help explain why a contract of insurance might call for a different judicial approach than a contract for the sale and purchase of carrots? Is the sale of a smartphone more like the sale of a carrot or an insurance policy, or does it fall somewhere in-between?

3. *Tension in the Contract Conception*. It is one thing for courts—or, for that matter, legislatures—to make up the rules of tort law as they go along. Products liability and environmental liability are two areas that arguably serve as examples of the rules being made up as courts or legislatures "go along." Arguably, it is quite another matter to rewrite agreements between parties, especially on a retroactive basis through ex poste adjudication. But, if insurance contracts are genuinely unique, then is it appropriate for courts to engage in judicial regulation of this kind of contract?

Of course, insurance is not the only field in which standardized agreements are used. Is the fundamental problem that the law of contracts is being used to regulate a kind of contracting process that has little resemblance to contract formation as it existed at the time the rules of contract law were developed? In other words, contract law struggles to deal with the problems and issues presented by standardized forms. Are insurance policies simply one example of that problem? Or is there something more in play with insurance?

EXERCISES

1. Consider a homeowner who lives in an area at risk for landslides. All homeowners insurance policies sold in the area contain an "earth movement" exclusion that is worded as follows:

A. We do not insure for loss caused directly or indirectly by . . .

2. Earth Movement [, which] means:

a. Earthquake, including land shock waves or tremors before, during or after a volcanic eruption;

b. Landslide, mudslide or mudflow;

c. Subsidence or sinkhole; or

d. Any other earth movement including earth sinking, rising or shifting.

This Exclusion A.2 applies regardless of whether any of the above, in A.2.a through A.2.d, is caused by an act of nature or is otherwise caused. However, direct loss by fire, explosion or theft resulting from any of the above, in A.2.a through A.2.d, is covered.

Write a 5-page memo that addresses the following questions:

A. What are the arguments for and against requiring insurers to cover landslide losses under homeowners insurance policies?

B. If landslide insurance were sold as stand-alone coverage, which means the insurance policy only covers landslide losses, what concepts that underlie insurance law would be implicated?

C. How could those conceptual concerns be addressed?

2. Write a 5-page memo setting forth the conceptual issues that are raised if homeowners insurance excludes coverage for landslides and insurance coverage for landslide losses generally is not available. The memo should identify the conceptual issues raised and then provide a solution to the issues, including potentially requiring homeowners insurance to cover landslides or offering landslide insurance on a stand-alone basis.

III. TYPES OF INSURERS AND INSURANCE

A. INSURER ORGANIZATIONS

There are many ways to classify insurers. Private insurers run a gamut of business organizations insofar as forms of legal ownership are concerned. Some of the principal organizations are capital stock companies, mutual companies, and Lloyds of London. A brief description of each follows.

Stock and Mutual Companies. A stock company is organized as a profit-making venture, with the stockholders assuming the risks that are transferred by the individual insureds. Of course, the stockholders, who need not be policyholders, receive any profits. A mutual company, on the other hand, is owned by its policyholder members and is not organized for the purpose of making a profit, but rather, for the purpose of providing insurance for the members. Unlike the capital stock company, the mutual company has no paid-in capital as a guard against insolvency. Instead, it relies on accumulated surplus. In a mutual company, any money left after paying all costs of operation, including additions to surplus, is returned to the policyholder members in the form of dividends. Mutual companies have various permutations based on, for example, whether premiums are payable in advance or whether the policyholder members are subject to assessments for losses incurred. Fraternal benefit organizations, sometimes called "mutual aid societies," constitute a special form of mutual insurer. Fraternal societies, lodges, and employee associations organize for a variety of purposes, and sometimes one aspect of their missions is offering insurance to their members.

Lloyds of London. Lloyds of London does not issue policies or underwrite insurance as such. It markets the services of a group of individuals, each of whom is an insurer who issues policies and underwrites risks separately or collectively with other members of the group. These organizations bear the name of the legendary Lloyd's of London, the oldest and, perhaps, the most famous of all insurance organizations in the world. Today, "Lloyds" has taken on a generic meaning, and other organizations that have the name Lloyds in their title are not to be confused with the Lloyd's of London.

Lloyd's of London has been in existence for over three centuries and is one of the major insurance markets in the world. It acquired its name because insurance transactions originally occurred in a place known as Lloyd's Coffee House, where insurance policies consisted of no more than slips of paper that identified the insured party as well as the percentage amounts of the risk each "Name" (i.e., each individual who was insuring the risk) was accepting. Lloyd's of London operates under an Act of Parliament and is governed by a council that establishes standards and rules for its members. From its inception, a distinguishing feature of Lloyd's has been the fact that individuals, each of whom assumes a fraction of the risk, underwrite the insurance. Each underwriter conducts business as an individual proprietor or as a member of one of the many Lloyd's syndicates, and, while liability is several only, each member is personally liable for all the losses he or she underwrites. One interesting legal ramification of this arrangement is that, in theory, a claimant must sue each of the individuals underwriting the insurance policy in the event of a lawsuit. However, in practice, a "lead" underwriter usually serves as the named defendant, a nominee as such, so all underwriters are not actually sued.

Although it is still true that an individual underwriting insurance through Lloyd's is personally liable, Lloyd's now permits corporate members to underwrite risks in an attempt to gain new infusions of capital. In fact, in 1998, for the first time, corporate members made up the majority of the Lloyd's insurance market's capacity to underwrite risk.

Consequently, despite the fact that many policies are still underwritten by individuals, the Lloyd's market is starting to look more like that of the United States where, with rare exception, only corporations are allowed to underwrite insurance.

While Lloyd's of London is licensed to do business in only two American states, Illinois and Kentucky, Lloyd's brokers and agents operate throughout the United States and the rest of the world.

Lloyd's also sells surplus lines insurance in all fifty of the United States. Surplus line insurers are not licensed to do business in a state, but they are allowed to sell insurance if no licensed insurer is willing to sell the insurance policy at issue. The policy provisions of surplus line insurance and the premiums charged therefore are not scrutinized by regulators. Surplus line insurance generally is viewed as less favorable to the consumer than insurance sold by licensed insurers. If no other insurance is available, however, then it often is better than no insurance.

The Lloyd's policies issued in the United States have a clause whereby the underwriter agrees to submit to the jurisdiction of the courts of Illinois, Kentucky, and any other court of competent jurisdiction in the United States.

Government Programs. There are various government-sponsored insurance programs. The largest of the public programs are those administered by the federal Social Security Administration—Federal Old Age, Survivors, Disability, and Medicare. Medicaid and unemployment insurance are joint federal-state undertakings. Although some of these are social programs designed to provide only subsistence levels of support, others are more extensive.

There are other public insurance programs that compete directly with the types of insurance traditionally marketed by private insurance companies. For example, there are government programs for life and crop insurance and for insuring properties against crime, flood, and riots. In some states, workers' compensation insurance is underwritten exclusively by state funds; elsewhere, state funds provide an alternative to, and thus compete directly with, private insurers. As a result of the so-called medical malpractice insurance crises of the 1970s and 1980s, some states created governmental or quasi-governmental insurance programs for this type of errors and omissions insurance. The foregoing list of government sponsored insurance programs is not exhaustive, but it does provide a basis for comparing public insurance mechanisms with the world of private insurance.

B. LINES OF INSURANCE

Historically, insurance has been divided into three basic fields or lines: (1) life, (2) fire and marine, and (3) casualty insurance. Underwriters more or less voluntarily limited themselves in the early period of insurance development by specializing in only one of these lines, but there soon followed regulatory laws which formally segregated the underwriters. These laws were passed largely because of the concern that different lines required unique regulatory provisions to ensure financial qualification and stability and to encourage proficiency through specialization. Various conflagrations, such as the New York City fire of 1835 and the Chicago fire of 1871, were instrumental in keeping fire insurers as "monoline" underwriters. The New York fire resulted in the ruin of twenty-three of the twenty-six fire insurers in the state at the time. Needless to say, the Great Depression also had an impact on life insurers, and the general concern over solvency has influenced the continued segregation of life underwriters to this day.

Despite the early developments regarding monoline underwriting, the reasons for segregating fire and marine insurers (including the allied forms of property insurance) from casualty insurers became less apparent as both of these areas of underwriting grew to include new types of risks that were not distinctly dissimilar. In addition, insurers circumvented the laws by organizing subsidiaries or developing associations with counterparts to meet the needs of the insuring public. As a result, after World War II many states began to enact legislation permitting "multiple line" underwriting by companies in the fields of fire and marine and casualty insurance when the capital and surplus requirements of each line were met. However, for historical and other reasons, many insurers today still use separate companies to underwrite different types of insurance in these fields. In addition, although some states have permitted "all line" underwriting by one company, which permits fire and marine and casualty insurers to write life insurance and vice versa, there has been no great movement to break down the barrier between these types of insurers.

Today, private insurance is now commonly divided into just two groups: (1) life and health, and (2) property and casualty. This break from the earlier trichotomy—life, fire and marine, and casualty insurance—undoubtedly is a result of the multiple line development, and also of the modern prominence of health care insurance.

Numerous lines of insurance fall under the umbrella of property and casualty insurance. Some lines of insurance, such as Commercial General Liability (CGL) and professional liability insurance such as Errors and Omissions (E&O) and Directors and Officers (D&O), only provide coverage for claims asserted against the policyholder. Liability insurance typically provides coverage on either an "occurrence" basis or "claims-made" basis. The distinctions between these two types of liability policies will be covered in Chapter 4.

Other lines of property and casualty insurance, such as "all risk" property insurance, provide coverage only for damage to property owned by the policyholder. There are also specialty lines of property and casualty insurance that cover only a single type of property or peril such as flood insurance, earthquake insurance, and boiler and machinery insurance.

Other lines of property and casualty insurance, such as homeowners insurance and auto insurance, combine coverage for liability claims and property damage claims in a single policy. Consequently, both liability claims asserted against the policyholder and damage to property owned by the policyholder are covered.

There are also numerous specialty lines of property and casualty insurance that are designed to cover specific types of claims, whether for liabilities or property damage, such as environmental and cyber risks. Indeed, if there is a type of loss or risk that is insurable, then there probably is an insurer willing to insure it for the right price.

IV. CHOICE OF LAW

The first question that must be answered before one can begin to analyze any insurance claim is familiar to any law student: What law applies? For historical reasons found in a narrative that dates back almost to the Civil War, state law generally governs insurance disputes. An important part of this story was the enactment by Congress in 1945 of the McCarran-Ferguson Act, in which Congress threw the full weight of its Commerce Clause authority behind state laws regulating the business of insurance. The Act is best understood as a "reverse preemption" statute: Congress declared that to the extent states regulate the business of insurance, inconsistent federal efforts to regulate the business are preempted by state law unless Congress explicitly declares within a future federal statute that its enactment is specifically intended to preempt state insurance law. For more discussion, *see* Robert H. Jerry II & Douglas R. Richmond, Understanding Insurance Law 64–84 (5th ed. 2012). Despite the unifying tendencies provided through model state insurance statutes recommended by the National Association of Insurance Commissioners, insurance law can vary significantly from state to state. Indeed, in many complex insurance coverage disputes, the outcome of the litigation will be heavily dictated by which state's law is applied because of the variations in insurance law from state to state. And, it often is the case that numerous states' laws potentially are applicable to a dispute. Consequently, the choice of law battle is often where a case is won or lost.

Choice of law is the question of which jurisdiction's laws should govern the dispute. The subject of choice of law is covered in Conflicts of Laws courses, but because it is so important in insurance coverage disputes, a quick primer on the subject is appropriate for students who have not taken

Conflicts of Laws, or as a refresher for those who already have studied the subject.

"Insurance policies typically do not contain a choice of law provision that specifies which state's laws will apply, so the court must rely upon state choice of law rules to make this critical decision. In the absence of a contractual mandate, courts typically only apply the law of a single state even if the case involves multiple parties from different states and the interests of multiple states will be impacted by the outcome of the litigation. Courts generally justify the application of a single state's law as an approach that promotes fairness, judicial economy, and consistency in the individual claim's outcome."[5]

The choice of law rules of the state in which the insurance coverage lawsuit is filed typically are applied to determine which state's substantive laws will apply to the dispute. The traditional approach to choice of law for contract disputes was to apply either the law of the place of contracting or the place of performance to resolve dispute. Today, many states have adopted:

> [W]hat is known as the "center of gravity" or the "significant contacts" approach. The "center of gravity" approach gives "the place having the most interest in the problem paramount control over the legal issues arising out of a particular factual context." Under this approach, courts analyze the relative contacts the states have with the dispute to determine which state has the most "significant contacts" that justifies having that state's law applied. Over time, the "center of gravity" approach . . . has been shaped and influenced by the factors considered under the modern choice of law approaches reflected in the Restatement (Second) of Conflicts of Law.
>
> The Second Restatement offers seven general principles "relevant to the choice of applicable rule of law," which include considerations such as the "policies of . . . interested states," "the protection of justified expectations," and "certainty, predictability and uniformity of result." With respect to contracts in particular, if the contract does not specify which state's laws govern, there are five factors to consider when analyzing the seven general overriding principles: "[1] the place of contracting, [2] the place of negotiation of the contract, [3] the place of performance, [4] the location of the subject matter of the contract, and [5] the domicile, residence, nationality, place of incorporation and place of business of the parties." Thus, when determining questions of choice of law,

---

[5] Christopher C. French, *A Battlefield Map for NFL v. Insurance Industry Re: Concussion Liabilities*, 53 San Diego L. Rev. 901, 916–18 (2017) (citations omitted).

> . . . courts typically analyze the significant contacts of the relative states and parties involved in light of these factors.
>
> In addition to the general factors discussed above, the Second Restatement also contains provisions to determine choice of law in disputes that involve liability policies. Specifically, it provides the governing law should be "the local law of the state which the parties understood was to be the principal location of the insured risk during the term of the policy, unless with respect to the particular issue, some other state has a more significant relationship under the principles stated in § 6 to the transaction and the parties, in which event the local law of the other state will be applied."
>
> Thus, for simple insurance disputes, courts often presume that the principal place of the insured risk has the most "significant relationship" and that state's law typically applies to the dispute. A showing that another state has a more significant relationship, however, can defeat that presumption and lead to another state's law being applied.
>
> The approach . . . courts use to determine the law applicable to insurance disputes where the insured risk is spread across multiple states, however, is different and more complex because the Second Restatement recognizes that no single location of the insured risk exists if the insured risk spreads across multiple states. The goal of the analysis in such circumstances is to use the law of the state with the most at stake in the litigation, as opposed to the state that simply has the most contacts associated with the placement of the policies. . . .
>
> In short, the court . . . attempts to determine which state has the most at stake in the resolution of the case and then appl[ies] that state's law.[6]

The next case is an example of a court analyzing the choice of law issue in the context of a complex insurance dispute where the underlying claims and interests of the parties involve multiple states.

---

[6] *Id.* at 918.

CERTAIN UNDERWRITERS AT LLOYD'S, LONDON, ET AL. V. FOSTER WHEELER CORPORATION

822 N.Y.S.2d 30 (App. Div. 2006), aff'd, 876 N.E.2d 500 (N.Y. 2007)

OPINION OF THE COURT

FRIEDMAN, J.P.

The question presented is whether New York law or New Jersey law governs a large number of excess liability insurance policies, under which the insured seeks coverage for a portion of the costs of defending and paying asbestos-related personal injury claims that have been asserted against it since the 1970s. For the reasons discussed below, we conclude that New Jersey law applies.

This declaratory judgment action seeks an apportionment of responsibility for the defense and indemnity costs of hundreds of thousands of asbestos-related personal injury claims (the asbestos claims) among defendant Foster Wheeler Corporation (FW Corp.), its subsidiary, Foster Wheeler Energy Corp. (FW Energy), and their liability insurers. The asbestos claims, which have been asserted in jurisdictions throughout the United States since the 1970s, are based on allegations that the claimants or their decedents were exposed to asbestos contained in boilers and other steam-generating equipment designed and built for industrial customers by FW Corp. (from the early twentieth century until 1973) or by FW Energy (since 1973, when FW Energy took over FW Corp.'s commercial operations). FW Corp. was incorporated under New York law from 1900 until 2001, when it was merged into another entity in a corporate restructuring. FW Energy, which is now a subsidiary of FW Corp.'s successor-by-merger, has been incorporated under Delaware law at all times since its formation in 1973. We use the term "Foster Wheeler" to refer to FW Corp. and FW Energy collectively.

From its founding in 1900 until 1962, Foster Wheeler's principal place of business was located in New York City. From 1962 to the present, Foster Wheeler's principal place of business has been in New Jersey. After the 1962 move to New Jersey, Foster Wheeler continued to maintain a small office in New York City, where only one employee was assigned on a full-time basis. It is undisputed that, at all relevant times, Foster Wheeler's operations relating to the design and building of asbestos-containing products were conducted throughout the United States, and that its customers purchasing such products were similarly widespread.

Before the order appealed from was rendered, Foster Wheeler reached settlements with all of its insurers except for defendants-respondents (the nonsettling insurers). From 1970 to 1981, the nonsettling insurers sold Foster Wheeler certain excess liability policies (the unsettled policies) that covered various periods between February 1, 1970 and October 1, 1982.

Thus, all of the unsettled policies were issued while Foster Wheeler's principal place of business was in New Jersey. The nonsettling insurers (of which there are about 30) had their principal places of business in various states at the times their policies were issued; five were domiciled in New York, three in New Jersey. It is undisputed that almost all of the nonsettling insurers are licensed to do business in both New York and New Jersey.

The parties agree that the underlying asbestos claims are based on injuries that are deemed, for purposes of insurance coverage, to have been suffered continuously over extended periods of time. This makes it necessary to allocate each injury "horizontally" over the period of its occurrence in order to determine the coverage obligation of each nonsettling insurer. The conflict-of-laws issue in this case arises from the circumstance (on which the parties agree, as more fully discussed below) that New York and New Jersey prescribe different mathematical methods of performing such an allocation. The matter is further complicated by the need, once an allocation is made to each year (whichever method is used), to allocate the loss for that particular year "vertically" among the various layers of insurance purchased for that year, with primary policies paying first within each year. Thus, as the nonsettling insurers point out, "the way in which liabilities are allocated to policies in the primary layers will determine when those primary policies are exhausted, and thus when excess layer policies [such as the unsettled policies] are reached, if at all."

Since there is no suggestion that methods of allocating a loss "horizontally" over time can be derived from the terms of the relevant policies, such an allocation method must be supplied by the applicable state law. As the relevant policies do not contain choice-of-law provisions, we are required to make that determination in accordance with our state's established choice-of-law principles.

As previously indicated, the parties agree (and we accept for purposes of this appeal) that New York and New Jersey (the only states suggested as the source of applicable law on the allocation issue) each uses a different mathematical method of effecting a pro rata allocation of an insured loss over the period of its occurrence. The " 'time-on-the-risk' method" that was approved by the New York Court of Appeals in *Consolidated Edison Co. of N.Y. v. Allstate Ins. Co.* (98 NY2d 208, 225 [2002]) derives the portion of the total loss allocable to the term of a given policy "by multiplying the [total loss] by a fraction that has as its denominator the entire number of years of the claimant's injury, and as its numerator the number of years within that period when the policy was in effect" (*Stonewall Ins. Co. v. Asbestos Claims Mgt. Corp.*, 73 F3d 1178, 1202 [2d Cir 1995]).[1] The New

[1] Although the Court of Appeals stated that its approval of the time-on-the-risk method in *Consolidated Edison* was "not the last word on proration" (98 NY2d at 225), for purposes of this

Jersey Supreme Court, on the other hand, has adopted the method of "proration on the basis of policy limits, multiplied by years of coverage" (*Owens-Illinois, Inc. v. United Ins. Co.*, 138 NJ 437, 475, 650 A2d 974, 993 [1994]). Under the New Jersey method (which has been referred to as "time-plus-limits"), the proportion of the total loss allocable to the term of a given policy is the ratio of the total coverage purchased (or risk retained) during the term of that policy to the total coverage purchased (or risk retained) during the entire period of the injury's occurrence (excluding any time during which insurance for the risk was unavailable) (*see Carter-Wallace, Inc. v. Admiral Ins. Co.*, 154 NJ 312, 322–323, 712 A2d 1116, 1122 [1998] [illustrating how the method operates]). It is undisputed that the time-plus-limits method, by "intentionally assign[ing] a greater portion of indemnity costs to years in which greater amounts of insurance were purchased" (154 NJ at 326, 712 A2d at 1123 [internal quotation marks and citation omitted]), would make tens of millions of dollars more coverage available to Foster Wheeler than would the time-on-the-risk method.

In the proceedings before the motion court, Foster Wheeler moved for partial summary judgment declaring all disputed issues to be governed by New Jersey law, while the nonsettling insurers moved for partial summary judgment declaring New York law to govern. In the order appealed from, the motion court ruled that New York law applies. We now reverse and hold that New Jersey law applies.

Under New York's "center of gravity" or "grouping of contacts" approach to choice-of-law questions in contract cases, we are required to apply the law of the state with the "most significant relationship to the transaction and the parties" (*Zurich Ins. Co. v. Shearson Lehman Hutton*, 84 NY2d 309, 317 [1994], quoting Restatement [Second] of Conflict of Laws [hereinafter, Restatement] § 188 [1]). This approach generally dictates that a contract of liability insurance be governed by the law of "the state which the parties understood was to be the principal location of the insured risk . . . unless with respect to the particular issue, some other state has a more significant relationship . . . to the transaction and the parties" (*id.* at 318, quoting Restatement § 193). However, the location-of-the-risk rule obviously cannot be applied without modification in the event the insurance policies in question cover risks that are spread through multiple states. Such is the case here, where the risks covered by the unsettled policies are nationwide or global in scope, and, given Foster Wheeler's widely dispersed operations and customers, there is no contention that, at the time the unsettled policies were issued, the parties would have understood any one state to have constituted, in a literal sense, "the principal location of the insured risk." Accordingly, we turn to broader choice-of-law principles for guidance.

---

appeal, we accept the parties' shared premise that *Consolidated Edison* adopted time-on-the-risk as New York's allocation method.

In adopting the "grouping of contacts" theory to resolve choice-of-law issues in contract cases, the Court of Appeals noted that the merit of this approach "is that it gives to the place having the most interest in the problem paramount control over the legal issues arising out of a particular factual context, thus allowing the forum to apply the policy of the jurisdiction most intimately concerned with the outcome of the particular litigation" (*Auten v. Auten*, 308 NY 155, 161 [1954] [internal quotation marks, brackets and citation omitted]). Thus, although contract cases do not call for use of the pure "interest analysis" employed in tort cases (*see Zurich*, 84 NY2d at 319), the respective "governmental interests" of the competing jurisdictions nonetheless "should be considered" (*Zurich*, 84 NY2d at 319, quoting *Matter of Allstate Ins. Co. [Stolarz—New Jersey Mfrs. Ins. Co.]*, 81 NY2d 219, 226 [1993]).

The governmental interests implicated by an insured's claim against an insurer of risks located in multiple states are those in: (1) regulating conduct with respect to insured risks within the state's borders; (2) assuring that the state's domiciliaries are fairly treated by their insurers; (3) assuring that insurance is available to the state's domiciliaries from companies located both within and without the state; and (4) regulating the conduct of insurance companies doing business within the state's borders (*see Fireman's Fund Ins. Co., Inc. v. Schuster Films, Inc.*, 811 F Supp 978, 984 [SD NY 1993] [applying New York choice-of-law principles]). In the case of a corporate insured seeking coverage under a policy covering risks in multiple states, the foregoing interests, in aggregate, weigh in favor of applying the law of the insured's domicile, notwithstanding that certain other states (e.g., the states of the insurer's domicile, and where negotiation and contracting occurred) may share, to a lesser extent, in the fourth interest enumerated above (*see id.* at 984–985).[2]

Additional goals of choice-of-law analysis are "certainty, predictability and uniformity of result" and "ease in the determination and application of the law to be applied" (Restatement § 6 [2] [f], [g]; *see Zurich*, 84 NY2d at 318 n 5 ["Section 6 of (the) Restatement . . . embodies the general choice of law principles"]). These goals, too, will be furthered by applying the law of the insured's domicile to liability insurance policies covering multistate risks. The state of the insured's domicile is a fact known to the parties at the time of contracting, and (in the absence of a contractual choice-of-law provision) application of the law of that state is most likely to conform to their

[2] The nonsettling insurers, citing *Stolarz* (81 NY2d at 226), argue that New York, as the center of the worldwide insurance industry, has an interest in the issues in dispute, given that the insurance brokers that procured the unsettled policies were located in New York, as more fully discussed below. We acknowledge, of course, that the Court of Appeals has recognized New York's interest in "maintain[ing] its position as a financial capital of the world" (*id.*). While this interest might well warrant applying New York law to determine the authority of the New York-based brokers that procured the policies, we are not persuaded that the involvement of New York brokers gives New York a greater interest than the state of the insured's domicile in the construction of the policies themselves.

expectations. As a Rhode Island federal court addressing a similar choice-of-law issue has observed, "common sense suggests that, knowing of the potential for claims in any number of states and even in foreign countries, the parties would consider the insured's principal headquarters as the one jurisdiction which ties all potential parties together" (*CPC Intl., Inc. v. Northbrook Excess & Surplus Ins. Co.*, 739 F Supp 710, 715 [D RI 1990], *reconsideration granted on other grounds* 839 F Supp 124 [D RI 1993], *affd.* 46 F3d 1211 [1st Cir 1995]; *accord Liggett Group Inc. v. Affiliated FM Ins. Co.*, 788 A2d 134, 138 [Del Super 2001]). Moreover, the state of the insured's domicile can be ascertained in any subsequent litigation without fact-intensive inquiry or unguided weighing of different contacts, and making the insured's domicile the primary factor in selecting applicable law minimizes the likelihood that contemporaneous policies will be deemed governed by the laws of different states. Thus, in addition to rendering the resolution of choice-of-law issues less difficult, adoption of a rule to apply the law of the insured's domicile makes it more likely that consistent and uniform results will be reached in different cases.

What emerges from the foregoing is that, where it is necessary to determine the law governing a liability insurance policy covering risks in multiple states, the state of the insured's domicile should be regarded as a proxy for the principal location of the insured risk. As such, the state of domicile is the source of applicable law. This conclusion accords with prior decisions of this Court and of the Third Department. Most recently, in *Steadfast Ins. Co. v. Sentinel Real Estate Corp.* (283 AD2d 44 [2001]), this Court held that, where the policy in question covered the risks arising from "the nationwide scope of [the insured's] operations, the principal location of the insured risk should be deemed to be the state where [the insured] is incorporated and has its principal place of business" (*id.* at 50), i.e., the insured's domicile.[3] Similarly, in *Munzer v. St. Paul Fire & Mar. Ins. Co.* (203 AD2d 770 [1994]), the Third Department held that the "primary factor" in ascertaining the law governing a liability policy covering risks in multiple states was that the insured was "a Vermont based business" (*id.* at 772), notwithstanding that, among other things, the policy had been procured by a New York broker from the insurer's New York office (*id.* at 771).[4] Finally, in *Regional Import & Export Trucking Co. v. North Riv. Ins. Co.* (149 AD2d 361 [1989]), this Court held that "a policy delivered to a New Jersey corporation to

---

[3] We also noted in our discussion of the choice-of-law issue in *Steadfast* that the insured's domicile in that case was also the place "from which it negotiated the special terms of the Policy, and where the Policy presumably was delivered to it (thus constituting the state where the contract was made)" (283 AD2d at 50). While these factors provided additional support for the choice-of-law ruling in *Steadfast*, for the reasons discussed below, they were not essential to that ruling.

[4] As more fully discussed below, *Munzer*'s holding that the law of the state of the insured's principal place of business should be applied if that state is different from the insured's state of incorporation (203 AD2d at 771, 772) is also of significance to this appeal.

insure against a loss occurring 'anywhere' should be subject to the law of that State" (*id.* at 362).

The foregoing establishes that, "where the insured risk is scattered throughout multiple states, courts still deem the risk to be located principally in one state" (*Maryland Cas. Co. v. Continental Cas. Co.*, 332 F3d 145, 153 [2d Cir 2003] [following *Steadfast*]), namely, in the state of the insured's domicile at the time the policy was issued. It remains for us to discuss whether a corporate insured's domicile is the state of its principal place of business or the state of its incorporation, where, as here, these are not the same state.[5] In the case of such a divergence, the state of the principal place of business takes precedence over the state of incorporation, a point that the nonsettling insurers apparently do not dispute (*see Munzer,* 203 AD2d at 771, 772 [applying the law of Vermont, the state of the insured's principal place of business, rather than the law of New York, the state of incorporation]). Treating the state of the principal place of business as the corporate domicile for these purposes, rather than the state of incorporation, is consistent with the view expressed in the Restatement that, "[a]t least with respect to most issues, a corporation's principal place of business is a more important contact than the place of incorporation" (Restatement § 188, Comment *e,* at 581). We look to the state of incorporation for the law governing the corporation's internal corporate governance and its relations with shareholders, not for the law governing the corporation's contractual relationships in general.

Significantly, our conclusion that New Jersey law applies to the unsettled policies finds further support in the fact that Foster Wheeler, as an insured with a New Jersey principal place of business, will look to the New Jersey insurance guaranty fund for payment of its claims against insolvent insurers (*see* NJ Stat Ann § 17:30A–5; *see also American Employers' Ins. Co. v. Elf Atochem N. Am., Inc.*, 157 NJ 580, 591, 725 A2d 1093, 1099 [1999]; *Eastern Seaboard Pile Driving Corp. v. New Jersey Prop.-Liab. Ins. Guar. Assn.*, 175 NJ Super 589, 594, 421 A2d 597, 600 [App. Div. 1980]). New Jersey's provision of such protection to Foster Wheeler, based on Foster Wheeler's maintenance of its principal place of business in that state, confirms that New Jersey now has, and had at the time the unsettled policies were issued, the greatest interest in the determination of the amount of coverage available to Foster Wheeler.

We recognize that, in contract cases generally, the resolution of a choice-of-law issue involves consideration of five factors enumerated in section 188 of the Restatement (the Restatement factors), viz., the place of contracting, the place of negotiation, the place of performance, the location of the subject

[5] As previously noted, throughout the period in which the unsettled policies were issued (1970–1981), the principal place of business of Foster Wheeler (meaning both FW Corp. and FW Energy) was in New Jersey, while FW Corp. and FW Energy were incorporated, respectively, in New York and Delaware.

matter, and the contracting parties' domiciles (*see Zurich*, 84 NY2d at 317, citing Restatement § 188 [2]). In arguing for the application of New York law, the nonsettling insurers rely heavily on the first three of these factors, emphasizing the role New York City insurance brokerage firms (specifically, Marsh & McLennan and Johnson & Higgins) played in procuring the unsettled policies. In this regard, the nonsettling insurers point to evidence that, among other things: (1) the unsettled policies were generally negotiated and "bound" by these brokers in New York City; (2) many of the unsettled policies were countersigned by the insurers' agents in New York; (3) the insurers generally delivered the policies to the brokers' New York offices; (4) premium invoices were sent by the insurers to, and premium checks remitted to the insurers from, the brokers' offices; and (5) most of Foster Wheeler's premium checks were drawn on a bank account it maintained in New York City. Based on this evidence, the nonsettling insurers argue that New York was the place where the unsettled policies were contracted, negotiated and performed.[6]

Foster Wheeler, for its part, argues that New Jersey was the place of contracting, negotiation and performance for each of the unsettled policies. To this end, Foster Wheeler highlights evidence that, among other things: (1) each of the unsettled policies was either mailed or hand-delivered to Foster Wheeler in New Jersey; (2) Foster Wheeler's internal activities related to obtaining the policies (e.g., setting specifications, preparing applications, giving brokers authority to act, writing premium checks) were performed in New Jersey; (3) the brokers frequently met with Foster Wheeler in New Jersey; and (4) Foster Wheeler received premium invoices in New Jersey.[7]

As previously discussed, in cases involving liability insurance covering multistate risks, we regard the state of the insured's domicile to be a proxy for the principal location of the insured risk, which, under New York law and Restatement § 193, is the controlling factor in determining the law applicable to a liability insurance policy, thereby obviating the need to consider all five Restatement factors. Even if consideration of all five Restatement factors were required, however, we still would conclude that New Jersey law should be applied. Further, we would reach the same conclusion even if, as the nonsettling insurers argue, New York constituted

[6] The nonsettling insurers apparently use the term "performance" to refer only to the insured's payment of the premium. This ignores the fact that the insurer's payment of a claim (which has not yet occurred with regard to any of the unsettled policies) also constitutes the performance of a policy obligation.

[7] Foster Wheeler apparently concedes that it generally remitted premium checks to, and received policies and premium invoices from, the brokers' New York offices. Foster Wheeler argues that this should not affect the choice-of-law analysis because (according to Foster Wheeler) the brokers, in transmitting such material between the parties, were acting as agents of the insurers. Not surprisingly, the nonsettling insurers argue that the brokers were acting as agents of Foster Wheeler. For the reasons discussed below, we find it unnecessary to determine which party the brokers were representing in performing these functions.

the place of contracting, negotiation, and the insured's performance. This is because the Restatement factors "are to be evaluated according to their relative importance with respect to the particular issue" (Restatement § 188 [2]). Stated otherwise, the choice-of-law analysis is not "a mindless scavenger hunt to see which state can be found to have more contacts, but rather . . . an effort to detect and analyze what interest the competing states have in enforcing their respective rules" (*Fireman's Fund*, 811 F Supp at 984). In the case of a liability insurance policy covering risks in multiple states, the state of the insured's principal place of business has a greater concern with issues of policy construction and application bearing on the amount of available coverage than do the states where contracting, negotiation, or payment of the premium happened to occur.

In this case, the nonsettling insurers' argument that the first three Restatement factors point to New York (which the motion court essentially adopted) is based largely on the fact that the unsettled policies were procured by New York-based insurance brokers. As a result of the brokers' involvement, certain of the relevant activities (negotiations, policy delivery, premium collection) occurred in New York. We agree with Foster Wheeler that the nonsettling insurers' approach places too much weight on the location of the broker, who, after all, is not a party to the insurance contract (*see Munzer*, 203 AD2d at 771 [applying the law of Vermont, the state of the policyholder's principal place of business, although the "policies were procured through a New York insurance broker from (the insurer's) New York office"]; *Regional Import & Export*, 149 AD2d at 362 ["(t)he mere fact that the policy was placed through a New York insurance broker which negotiated its terms is not a sufficient contact" to warrant application of New York law, given the insured's New Jersey domicile]; *see also CPC Intl.*, 739 F Supp at 712 ["the locations of the brokers present mere distractions because the brokers acted only as intermediaries"]; *Liggett Group*, 788 A2d at 141 [in choice-of-law analysis, roles of brokers "pale in comparison and significance to the role of the insured" (internal quotation marks, brackets, ellipsis and citation omitted)]). Thus, when the Restatement factors are "evaluated according to their relative importance with respect to the particular issue [presented in this case]" (Restatement § 188 [2]), the conclusion is that the insured's principal place of business should be considered the "primary factor" (*Munzer*, 203 AD2d at 772) in the choice-of-law analysis.

In the alternative, the nonsettling insurers argue that, even assuming that the insured's primary place of business is the primary factor in resolving the choice-of-law issue presented here (as we now hold), the law governing the unsettled policies cannot be chosen without also considering the settled policies, as well as still earlier lost policies that the nonsettling insurers also consider relevant. Many of the settled policies, and all of the lost policies, were issued before 1962, when Foster Wheeler's principal place of business was still in New York. Since these pre-1962 settled and lost policies presumably would have been deemed governed by New York law, the nonsettling insurers contend, considering each policy separately for choice-of-law purposes would result in "applying differing allocation approaches to the same sequence of policies." This, they maintain, "would add insurmountable complexity if not impossibility to the process, undermining the basic principles underlying allocation," which they describe as "divid[ing] responsibility for a continuing liability in a consistent and coordinated way." Accordingly, the nonsettling insurers reason, there should be a blanket choice-of-law determination for all policies covering the asbestos claims, whether issued before or after Foster Wheeler's 1962 move to New Jersey, and whether settled, unsettled, or lost. In their view, the law chosen to govern all implicated policies should be that of New York, on the ground that, even if the insured's principal place of business is the primary factor in choosing the governing law, Foster Wheeler had its principal place of business in New York for the majority of the years the nonsettling insurers regard as relevant (1940 to 1982).

The crux of the nonsettling insurers' concern is that, in determining when their excess layers of coverage are reached, the losses will be allocated to the now-settled primary policies (and lower-level excess policies) in force during the same years (1970 to 1982) in accordance with a state law different from that applicable to the unsettled policies themselves. Specifically, the nonsettling insurers are concerned that the losses will be allocated in accordance with New York law to the policies issued by settled defendant Liberty Mutual Insurance Company (Liberty), which provided underlying primary coverage for all but three years (1972–1975) of the decades of the injuries' occurrence, at the same time that New Jersey law is applied to the unsettled policies.[11] As previously noted, the nonsettling insurers contend that Foster Wheeler was based in New York for most of what they view as the relevant period, and contend, on that basis, that New York law is applicable to the Liberty policies, whenever issued. As also previously discussed, New York law spreads the loss evenly over the entire period of loss occurrence, while New Jersey law shifts more of the loss to periods when more coverage was purchased, i.e., the later years, when the unsettled policies were in force. Therefore, applying New York law to the settled policies underlying the unsettled policies, while applying New Jersey law to the unsettled policies, will result in simultaneously reaching the unsettled policies earlier (through smaller allocations to the lower-level policies) and allocating more of the loss to the unsettled policies.

---

[11] Contrary to the nonsettling insurers' claim that Foster Wheeler has attempted to manipulate the choice-of-law determination by selectively settling with certain insurers rather than others, the record establishes that Liberty, as well as Hartford Accident & Indemnity Company, the primary insurer during Liberty's three-year hiatus, both argued for application of New Jersey law before they settled with Foster Wheeler.

We are not persuaded by the nonsettling insurers' contention that all of the settled policies (and the lost policies, assuming their relevance) must be considered in determining which state's law governs the unsettled policies. Under our choice-of-law analysis, the settled primary and lower-level excess policies underlying the unsettled policies in force from 1970 to 1982 will also be deemed governed by New Jersey law, for the simple reason that all such underlying policies were, like the unsettled policies, issued while Foster Wheeler was based in New Jersey. The pre-1962 settled policies do not underlie the unsettled policies that cover the years 1970 to 1982, and are therefore irrelevant to determining when the layer of coverage afforded by each unsettled policy is reached in the vertical allocation for the year that policy was in force.[12] Thus, the problem posited by the nonsettling insurers, while it might actually be presented in some future case, is illusory here.

. . . .

Accordingly, the order of the Supreme Court, New York County (Barbara R. Kapnick, J.), entered January 10, 2005, which denied defendant-appellant Foster Wheeler Corporation's motion for partial summary judgment declaring that New Jersey substantive law governs all disputed issues in this action, and granted the motions by defendants-respondents for partial summary judgment declaring that New York substantive law governs all disputed issues in this action, should be reversed, on the law, without costs, the motion by Foster Wheeler Corporation granted to the extent of declaring that the liability insurance policies issued by defendants-respondents, and the underlying settled policies providing primary and lower-level excess coverage for the same years, are governed by New Jersey substantive law, and the motions by defendants-respondents denied.

NOTES AND QUESTIONS

1. *Different Courts, Different Tests*. The *Foster Wheeler* case is just one example of a choice of law analysis under New York law in a complex insurance

---

[12] This point is demonstrated by a hypothetical the New Jersey Supreme Court posed to illustrate how vertical allocation within a policy year operates: "Assume that primary coverage for one year was $100,000, first-level excess insurance totaled $200,000, and second-level excess coverage was $450,000. If the loss allocated to that specific year was $325,000, the primary insurer would pay $100,000, the first-level excess policy would be responsible for $200,000, and the second-level excess policy would pay $25,000" (*Carter-Wallace*, 154 NJ at 326–327, 712 A2d at 1124). Given that the primary and lower-level excess insurers have settled with Foster Wheeler, New Jersey apparently requires (subject to the particular terms of each unsettled policy) that, in determining when the nonsettling insurers' layers of coverage are reached, each nonsettling insurer receive a credit for the full amount of the loss allocable to the underlying settled policies (*see Chemical Leaman Tank Lines, Inc. v. Aetna Cas. & Sur. Co.*, 177 F3d 210, 227–228 [3d Cir 1999] [applying New Jersey law]; *UMC/Stamford, Inc. v. Allianz Underwriters Ins. Co.*, 276 NJ Super 52, 68–69, 647 A2d 182, 190–191 [Law Div 1994]; *see also Carpenter Tech. Corp. v. Admiral Ins. Co.*, 172 NJ 504, 517–518, 522, 800 A2d 54, 61–62, 64 [2002] [discussing with apparent approval the *Chemical Leaman* and *UMC/Stamford* holdings on this issue]).

coverage case. One should not read that case to mean that the majority rule is that the domicile state of the policyholder will govern. The "most significant contacts" or "center of gravity" test considers many factors, and various factors can be emphasized to support numerous reasonable choice of law decisions. For example, some courts have concluded the state in which the underlying injury or litigation occurred has the most significant contacts with the parties' dispute even though the policyholder was domiciled in another state and the policy was issued in the policyholder's domicile state. *See, e.g.*, *Am. Guarantee & Liab. Ins. Co. v. U.S. Fid. & Guar. Co.*, 668 F.3d 991, 1000–1002 (8th Cir. 2012) (applying the most significant contacts test for tort claims and concluding that the law of the state in which the underlying litigation occurred had the most significant relationship to the dispute).

2. *The Race to the Courthouse*. The choice of law issue can be critical in complex insurance disputes because of the differences in insurance law from state to state. Courts typically apply the choice of law rules of their own state in resolving the issue. In conducting the choice of law analysis, courts also often conclude that their own state's substantive law should apply to resolve the parties' dispute. Consequently, which party files an insurance coverage lawsuit first and in which state the action is filed can be case dispositive.

This insight is not a secret in the world of sophisticated insurance coverage litigation. Thus, there is a premium on winning the race to the courthouse.

EXERCISE

1. Draft a 2-page memo in which the choice of law rules of Florida and Pennsylvania are compared and contrasted.

CHAPTER TWO

POLICY FORMATION AND SALE

■ ■ ■

"I look, absolutely, like I'm going to sell you insurance."

— Stephen Colbert, quoted in Dave Itzkoff, *Stephen Colbert, the Late Night Hope*, New York Times, Sept. 2, 2015

I. THE DRAFTING AND SALE OF INSURANCE POLICIES

Insurance policies, almost without exception, are lengthy, complex standard form contracts of adhesion drafted by insurers and sold on a take-it-or-leave-it basis with respect to their terms.[1] Indeed, insurance policies were the first type of standardized form agreements to be described as contracts of adhesion. Consequently, purchasers have no input regarding the policy language. The only negotiations between a policyholder and an insurer typically relate to the policy limits, premium, deductible, and endorsements added in some circumstances. Except for clerical matters, even the endorsements are drafted by insurers and use standard form policy language. "Manuscript" policies, which are policy forms typically created by brokers for corporate policyholders and then presented to insurers for adoption, are also effectively drafted by insurers, because brokers merely cut and paste the language from insurers' policy forms to create the manuscript policy. Consequently, even with manuscript policies, the policyholder has no role in the drafting of the terms.

An organization known as the Insurance Services Office, Inc. (ISO) drafts many policy forms. Insurers pay fees for ISO membership. As members of ISO, insurers can, and many do, use the policy forms drafted by ISO.

Many of the terms and conditions contained in standard form ISO policies were drafted many years ago and are reused each time ISO issues new versions of the policy form. For example, the policy language in the 1943 New York Standard Fire Insurance Policy is still used today in some homeowners' insurance policies. Because much of the standard form policy language used today was drafted long ago, the original drafters are often

---

[1] This subchapter is taken verbatim from Christopher C. French, *Understanding Insurance Policies as NonContracts: An Alternative Approach to Drafting and Construing These Unique Financial Instruments*, 89 Temp. L. Rev. 535, 546–553 (2017) (citations omitted).

dead or unknown. Documentation regarding the drafters' intent also rarely exists. Consequently, it is difficult, if not impossible, to discern the drafters' intent if the policy language is ambiguous.

In addition to drafting standard policy forms, ISO also collects claims data and provides actuarial services for its insurer members. Two of the advantages of using ISO's nonnegotiable, standard form policies are (1) it reduces transaction costs because there are no negotiations regarding the policy language, and (2) it increases the predictive power of the claims data for actuarial purposes because of the lack of variation in coverage and exclusions among different companies' policies.

Insurers' use of the same policy forms and the industry-wide sharing of claims data would be considered anticompetitive or even collusive behavior in most industries. Consequently, when the U.S. Supreme Court ruled in 1944 that the insurance industry was subject to the antitrust provisions of the Sherman Act, insurers lobbied hard for exemption and were successful when Congress passed the McCarran-Ferguson Act, which insurer representatives drafted.

Regardless of whether a policy form was drafted by ISO or the insurer itself, the individuals responsible for selling the policies generally do not have authority to make any changes to the policy language. Consequently, purchasers cannot negotiate the language because insurers generally use the same policy forms and the insurer representatives who are in direct contact with purchasers lack the ability or authority to make any changes to the terms.

In addition to having no role in the drafting of insurance policies, policyholders typically do not even get a chance to review the policy they are purchasing prior to payment. Instead, the policy is provided to the policyholder weeks or months (if ever) after the policyholder has paid for the policy or at least the initial premium. If and when policyholders receive a copy, they rarely read it. And if they do, few can understand the policy's terms and conditions because of its length and complexity. At no point in the sales process does the insurer explain the terms of coverage to the policyholder. And the policyholder never signs the policy to indicate agreement to its terms and conditions.

The insurance policies drafted by ISO and sold by insurers have become more complex over time. As an illustration of the complexity, consider ISO's 2010 standard form homeowners policy. It is twenty-four pages long, contains thirteen sections of coverage provisions, thirty-one exclusions, and thirty-seven conditions. In addition to the confusing language, the length and complex organization of the terms, conditions, and exclusions make such insurance policies incomprehensible to most consumers.

The incomprehensibility of today's insurance policies to the average policyholder has prompted the Supreme Court of South Carolina to describe insurance policies as "impenetrable thicket[s] of incomprehensible verbosity":

> Ambiguity and incomprehensibility seem to be the favorite tools of the insurance trade in drafting policies. Most are a virtually impenetrable thicket of incomprehensible verbosity. It seems that insurers generally are attempting to convince the customer when selling the policy that everything is covered and convince the court when a claim is made that nothing is covered. The miracle of it all is that the English language can be subjected to such abuse and still remain an instrument of communication. But, until such time as courts generally weary of the task we have just experienced and strike down the entire practice, we feel that we must run with the pack and attempt to construe that which may well be impossible of construction.[2]

The Supreme Court of New Hampshire similarly has described insurance policies as "inexplicable riddle[s]":

> [I]nsurance policies are weighted with such a prolixity of complex verbiage that "they would not be understood by men in general, even if [the policies were] subjected to a careful and laborious study. . . . [The policy] if read by him, would, unless he were an extraordinary man, be an inexplicable riddle, a mere flood of darkness and confusion. Some of the most material stipulations were concealed in a mass of rubbish on the back side of the policy and the following page . . . where scarcely any one would think of looking for information so important. . . . As if it were feared that, notwithstanding these discouraging circumstances, some extremely eccentric person might attempt to examine and understand the meaning of the involved and intricate net in which he was to be entangled, it was printed in such small type, and in lines so long and crowded, that the perusal of it was made physically difficult, painful, and injurious."[3]

Because the policyholder has no role in the drafting of the insurance policy and typically does not even get a copy of it prior to purchase, a policyholder's understanding of the coverage typically is based upon the type of insurance at issue, the statements of the broker and the insurer's agents during the sales process, and insurer advertisements. In advertisements, insurers seek to create the impression that their policies

---

[2] *South Carolina Ins. Co. v. Fidelity and Guar. Ins. Underwriters*, 489 S.E.2d 200, 206 (S.C. 1997) (*quoting Universal Underwriters Ins. Co. v. Travelers Ins. Co.*, 451 S.W.2d 616, 622–23 (Ky. Ct. App. 1970)).

[3] *Storms v. U. S. Fid. & Guar. Co.*, 388 A.2d 578, 580 (N.H. 1978) (*quoting DeLancy v. Ins. Co.*, 52 N.H. 581, 587–88 (1873)).

provide broad coverage and that policyholders' claims will be paid promptly—messages conveyed by using scenes of devastation followed by marketing phrases like "you're in good hands" and "like a good neighbor" to describe the coverage provided and the insurers' claims payment practices.

So, how effective are insurer advertisements and statements by insurance brokers and agents in informing purchasers about the scope of policy coverage? Not very. For example, recent studies by the National Association of Insurance Commissioners (NAIC) and other institutions have revealed that purchasers of homeowners insurance have very little understanding of the losses their policies actually cover. Set forth below are the percentages of consumers who mistakenly believed that their homeowners insurance covered the following losses:

- 68%—cars, boats, and motorcycles stolen from, or damaged on, their property;
- 51%—a break in their water supply line;
- 37%—a break in the sewer line on their property connecting to the municipal sewer system;
- 35%—damage from earthquakes;
- 31%—damage from termites, rats, mice, and other infestations;
- 33%—flood damage, even after Hurricane Katrina, when it was widely reported that homeowners policies do not cover flood losses.

In short, many homeowners mistakenly believe that many types of losses are covered when, in fact, they are not.

In addition, more than 70% of homeowners did not understand that they would be compensated at actual cash value, meaning the value after depreciation, not replacement cost, for damage to personal property. In other words, most homeowners did not know that they would receive only pennies on the dollar for most of their covered personal property that is damaged or destroyed.

Even though most consumers cannot negotiate the terms of policies and do not even understand the scope of coverage they are receiving when they buy an insurance policy, they do not really have a choice whether to purchase many types of insurance in today's complex world. For example, automobile insurance is mandatory. Homeowners insurance is also essentially mandatory because a homeowner must have insurance if the mortgage for the house is federally guaranteed, which is the case for the vast majority of houses. Workers' compensation insurance is also mandatory for businesses in every state except Texas.

Because policyholders cannot negotiate policy language but are required to purchase many types of insurance sold by insurers using the same policy form, states have the power to regulate insurers to account for this discrepancy in power. This power to regulate insurers includes (1) ensuring their solvency, (2) approving premium rates to ensure the rates are not excessive, (3) approving premium rates to ensure the rates are not unfairly discriminatory, and (4) approving policy forms. With respect to policy forms, regulators have the power to reject policy language or terms that are unfair, ambiguous, unreasonable, contrary to public policy, or some combination of these broadly stated standards.

Unfortunately, states' regulation of the insurance industry generally, and their approval of policy forms specifically, is a classic example of regulatory capture. Regulatory capture is the phenomenon whereby the regulation of an industry is dominated by the industry itself such that the industry is actually regulated for its own benefit.

State insurance regulators, despite express statutory authority to do so, generally do not exercise their power to reject policy language that could be considered unfair, ambiguous, unreasonable, or contrary to public policy. Instead, insurance regulators typically only require insurers to submit policy forms for approval when insurers change the language, which means that policy language that may be decades old is not reviewed. Furthermore, insurance regulators' review of policy forms generally focuses on making sure that insurers cannot cancel or refuse to renew policies without providing adequate notice and on ensuring that policies meet minimum readability requirements, based on the length of words and sentences rather than the overall complexity or comprehensibility. During the policy form review process, only insurers are represented by attorneys, and the state regulators are typically former employees of insurers (who will return to work for insurers after serving as regulators). In short, insurance regulators do not rigorously scrutinize or police policy language. Consequently, the approval process essentially amounts to a rubber stamp.

In sum, policyholders (1) have no ability to change the language contained in insurance policies, (2) do not get copies of the policies before they buy them, (3) do not have the ability to understand them even if they read them because policies are so complex, and (4) do not have a choice whether to buy certain critical types of insurance. Despite the gross disparity in power, knowledge, and resources between the sellers and buyers of insurance, state insurance regulators are essentially the only check on insurers' power over the terms and conditions in policies—but regulators do not review and revise the language contained in standard form policies to ensure fairness to consumers or comprehensibility due to regulatory capture.

II. WARRANTIES AND MISREPRESENTATIONS

Although insurers draft the policies they sell and have a significant amount of claims data regarding most types of risks they insure, they lack information about the specific individuals who present themselves to the insurer as potential insureds—in other words, as individuals seeking to purchase insurance. Consequently, to determine whether they even want these individuals as customers and what premiums to charge them if they do, insurers need to obtain information about these individual applicants. With unlimited resources, insurers could conduct an unlimited investigation, acquire unlimited information, and make absolutely perfect decisions. But resources are not unlimited, and investigating potential policyholders before deciding whether to insure them is a cost that insurers must account for, one way or another, on their balance sheets. Thus, although insurers strive to get the best information possible at a reasonable cost, insurers cannot acquire perfect information about the riskiness of individual policyholders.

Moreover, some information is simply inaccessible to insurers. Consider, for example, an insurer who is asked to insure a building against loss by fires, windstorms, hurricanes, tornados, etc. With respect to the weather-related risk, the insurer can learn about the frequency of damaging winds, tornados, and hurricanes by investigating weather patterns. As a result, a policyholder in Florida will pay more for protection against the risks posed by hurricanes than a policyholder in Michigan. With respect to the fire risk, however, the behavior of the policyholder is a material factor affecting the likelihood of damage to the building due to fire. For example, whether the policyholder installs and adequately maintains a sprinkler system is highly relevant to the amount of damage that would occur if a fire should break out. Thus, a policyholder who installs and maintains a sprinkler system will pay less for the insurance. The insurer can check on whether the system has been installed easily enough. But how is the insurer to know whether the policyholder leaves the system on all the time? Obviously, the insurer cannot cost-effectively post one of its agents at the policyholder's building to make sure that the sprinkler system is always properly maintained and functional.

To deal with this lack of information, an insurer seeks information regarding the policyholder through the insurance application process. But gaps in the insurer's information will remain, and the insurer may ask the policyholder to "warrant" that a sprinkler system will be properly maintained and fully functional at all times. Alternatively, the insurer may seek to "condition" the coverage on the presence of a functional sprinkler system. If the insurer does not wish to continually inspect the inside of the building (after all, the inspection is a cost to the insurer and it would be extremely costly to conduct continuous inspections of every building or house it is insuring to check for the presence of an operational sprinkler system), the insurer may ask the policyholder to "represent" that the building has an operational sprinkler system. To that end, the application for insurance may ask, "Do the premises for which insurance is sought have a sprinkler system?" If the applicant answers the question incorrectly, then this misrepresentation may have consequences for coverage in the future.

In sum, insurers respond to the problem of obtaining adequate information about the risks associated with individual policyholders by requiring warranties and representations from their policyholders and by limiting coverage. A fair amount of older insurance law addressed the extent that insurers can limit their coverage obligations in these ways. Consequently, the history of insurance law regarding warranties and misrepresentations is a story about the extent to which courts and legislatures have allowed insurers to rely on a policyholder's breach of a warranty or misrepresentation as a basis for refusing to provide coverage to the policyholder. The seminal article on the history of warranties in the early common law was written by Professor William R. Vance, and all subsequent treatments of the subject heavily depend on Professor Vance's insights. *See* William R. Vance, *The History of the Development of the Warranty in Insurance Law*, 20 Yale L. J. 523 (1911).

A. WARRANTIES

Prior to the late eighteenth century, warranties in insurance law were indistinguishable in legal effect from warranties in any other type of contract. A warranty was merely an agreed upon condition, set forth in the contract itself, that had to be strictly satisfied (which sometimes required performance). If it was not strictly satisfied, then the policy was voidable by the underwriter. In this early time, warranties and representations were similar in all important respects. Both required a material relation to the risk transferred in order for noncompliance or nonsatisfaction to have an effect on the insurance contract. Thus, both the nonsatisfaction of an immaterial warranty and an immaterial noncompliance with an otherwise material warranty were inconsequential.

All of this changed by the late eighteenth century, and Lord Mansfield deserves most of the credit (or blame, depending on your perspective) for these changes. First, in a line of cases beginning in 1763 with *Woolmer v. Muilman*, 1 W. Bl. 427, Burr, 1419, and culminating in 1786 with *De Hahn v. Hartley*, 1 T.R., 343, Lord Mansfield eliminated the materiality requirement for warranties. Professor Vance describes the effect of the latter case:

> But it is not until 1786 that we find the fully developed warranty really in action. In *De Hahn v. Hartley*, a vessel was insured for a voyage from Africa to the West Indies. The vessel was described as "warranted copper sheathed, and sailed from Liverpool with

> fourteen six pounders, . . . fifty hands or upwards." The vessel having been captured during the period covered by the policy, the underwriter paid the loss. Subsequently, learning that the vessel had sailed from Liverpool with only forty six hands, although it had, six hours later, taken on six additional men at Anglesea, thus sailing from that island with fifty two men, the broker brought his action to recover the money paid on the ground that the insurance was void for breach of warranty. It is very clear that the risk assumed for the voyage from Africa to the West Indies was in no wise enhanced by the fact that the vessel had only forty six hands during the short voyage on inland waters from Liverpool to Anglesea, yet it was held that the policy was avoided by the breach of the warranty. In his opinion, Lord Mansfield stated the law in this characteristic fashion: "There is a material distinction between a warranty and a representation. A representation may be equitably and substantially answered; but a warranty must be strictly complied with. Supposing a warranty to sail on the first of August, and the ship did not sail till the second, the warranty would not be complied with. A warranty in a policy of insurance is a condition or a contingency, and unless that be performed, there is no contract. It is perfectly immaterial for what purpose a warranty is introduced; but being inserted, the contract does not exist unless it be literally complied with. Now, in the present case, the condition was the sailing of the ship with a certain number of men; which not being complied with, the policy is void."

William R. Vance, *The History of the Development of the Warranty in Insurance Law*, 20 Yale L. J. 523, 529–30 (1911).

Professor Vance also describes how the change wrought by *De Hahn* and its progeny necessitated a further distinction:

> Since the court had decided that the distinction between warranties and representations was accompanied by such striking and surprising legal consequences, it naturally was a matter of great interest to the underwriters to know when a statement descriptive of a risk was a warranty and when a representation. Lord Mansfield very quickly decided that a statement written in the policy was a warranty, while one written anywhere else, or not written at all, was only a representation. Then the question arose, How must it be written in the policy? It was determined that a statement should bear the magical potency of the warranty if it was written anywhere on the face of the policy as on the margin, straight or obliquely; but if the written statement was inscribed on a different paper folded within the policy, or even fastened by a wafer to the policy, it was no more than a representation, which could not destroy the rights of the insured or enable the

> underwriter to escape his liability, unless it had really prejudiced the underwriter. It will be observed that the mere fact that a stipulation or a descriptive term was written in the policy was of itself sufficient to determine its character as a warranty. No other evidence of the intention of the parties to make it a warranty was deemed necessary.

Id. at 530.

Although the strict compliance rule left the policyholder with a high risk that coverage might be forfeited, the rule had a significant commercial purpose in marine insurance in eighteenth century England. Recurrent wars of that period made it highly desirable that ships sail in a convoy. Therefore, a policyholder might be asked to warrant that the ship would not sail alone. Additionally, sailing at certain times of the year was more dangerous. Thus, a policyholder might be asked to warrant that the ship would sail at a particular time. *See* Edwin W. Patterson, Essentials of Insurance Law 274 (2d ed. 1957). Insurers were not, of course, in a position to monitor the ship's compliance with the warranty after it had left port, particularly given the primitive methods of communication in that era. Thus, warranties were important to marine insurers as a method of dealing with inadequate information. At least initially, underwriters sought to limit their exposure to certain risks, and the warranties they inserted in policies pertained to matters that materially affected the risk. However, as Professor Patterson described it, things soon got out of hand:

> These decisions [about warranties] were deemed necessary by Lord Mansfield and other English judges in order to protect the "infant industry," marine insurance, which was a valuable aid to British overseas commerce. Hence the adoption of the rule, after a long period of development, that the materiality of a breach of warranty will not be inquired into, because the expert underwriter took the risk on the assumption that certain facts (warranted to be so) existed or would exist, and no judge or jury should be allowed to substitute his or its judgment for the underwriter's. . . .
>
> The earlier warranties were few in number, and were drawn for each individual contract between persons of equal bargaining power. If anything, the shrewd shipowner or trader, often insuring a ship "lost or not lost" long after she had sailed and after she had last been heard from, was in a better position to know the risk than the underwriter at Lloyds. In the nineteenth century this English doctrine of warranty was transferred to the popular forms of insurance in the United States, especially life insurance and above all fire insurance, with warranties drawn by insurance company lawyers to guard against every potential hazard, multiplied by the printing press into an array of formal and stilted

> clauses which the insured could not understand even if he tried to read them. Thus, as a New York court said in a notable opinion [*Van Schroick v. Niagara Fire Ins. Co.*, 68 N.Y. 434 (1877)], a fact well known to both the insured and the insurer's agent might create a defense for the insurer "by force of some condition, crouched unseen in the jungle of printed matter with which a modern policy is overgrown."

Patterson, *supra*, at 274–75.

This kind of forfeiture suffered by policyholders led courts, and eventually legislatures, to find ways to mitigate the potentially harsh effects of warranties. Beginning in the Nineteenth Century, courts began mitigating the impact of warranties on policyholders. *See* Vance, *supra*, at 534. One approach that courts began adopting that continues to dominate today was to treat warranties as representations by the policyholder rather than guarantees. Under this approach, a misrepresentation only allows the other party to void the contract if it was fraudulent or involved a matter material on which the other party reasonably relied. *See* Restatement (Second) of Contracts, § 164(1) ("If a party's manifestation of assent is induced by either a fraudulent or a material misrepresentation by the other party upon which the recipient is justified in relying, the contract is voidable by the recipient."). For a more thorough discussion regarding courts' approaches to the problem, *see* John F. Dobbyn & Christopher C. French, Insurance Law In A Nutshell 330–32 (5th ed. 2016); Robert H. Jerry II & Douglas R. Richmond, Understanding Insurance Law 725–28 (5th ed. 2012).

Today, warranty law in the insurance context is almost exclusively governed by state statutes. Nearly every state has adopted a statute that governs warranties in the context of insurance. *See* John F. Dobbyn & Christopher C. French, Insurance Law In A Nutshell 332–35 (5th ed. 2016); Robert H. Jerry II & Douglas R. Richmond, Understanding Insurance Law 752–54 (5th ed. 2012). Although there are variations from statute to statute, they generally collapse the distinction between warranties and representations so breaches of warranties are treated like incorrect information provided by the policyholder. Consequently, a breach of warranty only results in a forfeiture of coverage if it is material or fraudulent *and* the insurer detrimentally relied upon it by either selling the policy when the insurer would not have done so if the insurer had possessed accurate information, or the insurer would have charged a higher premium if it had possessed accurate information.

The biggest exception to the general rule under which states have collapsed warranties into representations is marine insurance. In many respects, marine insurance is still governed by historic common law insurance rules, unlike all other lines of insurance where modern rules have largely replaced the old ones. For marine insurance, some states still use traditional warranty law, which treats warranties as guarantees immune to judicial inquiry on whether the warranty is actually material to the insured risk. Thus, in those states, strict compliance with warranties in marine insurance is required and a breach of a warranty can lead to the voiding of the policy.

B. MISREPRESENTATIONS

As noted above, state statutes now govern warranties and misrepresentations in the insurance context. Although the exact wording of the statutes and specific requirements that allow misrepresentations to result in the rescission of a policy vary, such statutes generally require that the representation or warranty be: 1) material, and 2) false or misleading. Some statutes also require that the misrepresentations relate to the loss that actually occurs or be made with the intent to deceive. As three examples, the warranty and misrepresentation statutes in Utah, New York and Pennsylvania will be considered.

Utah Insurance Code § 31A–21–105. Representations, warranties, and conditions

. . . .

(2) Except as provided in Subsection (5), no misrepresentation or breach of an affirmative warranty affects the insurer's obligations under the policy unless:

(a) the insurer relies on it and it is either material or is made with intent to deceive; or

(b) the fact misrepresented or falsely warranted contributes to the loss.

(3) No failure of a condition prior to the loss and no breach of a promissory warranty affects the insurer's obligations under the policy unless it exists at the time of the loss and either increases the risk at the time of the loss or contributes to the loss. This Subsection (3) does not apply to failure to tender payment of premium.

(4) Nondisclosure of information not requested by the insurer is not a defense to an action against the insurer. Failure to correct within a reasonable time any representation that becomes incorrect because of changes in circumstances is misrepresentation, not nondisclosure.

(5) If after issuance of a policy the insurer acquires knowledge of sufficient facts to constitute a general defense to all claims under the policy, the defense is only available if the insurer notifies the insured within 60 days after acquiring the knowledge of its intention to defend against a claim if one should arise . . . .

BERGER V. MINNESOTA MUTUAL LIFE INSURANCE CO.

723 P.2d 388 (Utah 1986)

PER CURIAM:

Plaintiff Anna Marie Berger appeals from the judgment entered on a jury verdict that denied her recovery of the proceeds of her husband's credit life insurance policy issued by defendant Minnesota Mutual Life Insurance Co. ("Minnesota Mutual"). Minnesota Mutual declined coverage under the policy, claiming that plaintiff's deceased husband materially misrepresented his medical condition when he submitted his insurance application form.

In a 1974 pre-employment physical examination at Kennecott Copper Corporation, David Berger was diagnosed as afflicted with mild diabetes mellitus. The physician discussed with Berger the diabetes tests given him and any past family history of the disease. Medication was prescribed for Berger, and the doctor noted that the diabetes could be controlled as long as Berger continued with prescribed medication and dietary restrictions. When Kennecott was advised that Berger's diabetes could be controlled if treated, Berger was hired by the company.

On subsequent occasions between 1975 and 1979, Berger had several contacts with medical clinics and doctors who examined and discussed his diabetic condition and medication. In connection with another employment physical in June 1976, Berger listed his diabetes on his medical history form. There was also evidence that he often ignored the medication and dietary restrictions imposed to control his diabetes, which required more extensive medical treatment for his condition.

In April 1979, Berger applied for and received group credit life insurance from Minnesota Mutual to satisfy his home mortgage in the event of his death. On the insurance application concerning his medical history, he wrote that in the past three years he had only consulted with a physician regarding an earache and sore throat and that he had never been treated for or advised that he had diabetes. The jury found these representations to be false but not fraudulently made.

In February 1981, Berger was admitted to the hospital to bring his diabetes under control. A few weeks after his release, on March 8, 1981, he died of an acute codeine overdose. When a claim was made on the life policy, Minnesota Mutual undertook an independent investigation of the death. Discovering the preexisting diabetic condition, the insurer refused payment under its policy, claiming that the misrepresentation on the policy application was material to Berger's insurability and that Minnesota Mutual would not have issued the policy had the truth been disclosed at the time the application for insurance was made.

Under our statute enacted in 1963, a misrepresentation, omission, or concealment of facts shall not prevent recovery under an insurance policy unless:

> (a) fraudulent; or
>
> (b) material either to the acceptance of the risk, or to the hazard assumed by the insurer; or
>
> (c) the insurer in good faith either would not have issued the policy, . . . or would not have issued . . . a policy or contract in as large an amount, or would not have provided coverage with respect to the hazard resulting in the loss, if the true facts had been made known to the insurer as required either by the application for the policy or contract or otherwise.

U.C.A., 1953, § 31–19–8(1) (1974 ed.). The statutory alternatives are stated in the disjunctive, not the conjunctive. In order to invalidate a policy because of a misrepresentation by the insured, an insurer need prove applicable only one of the above provisions.

The court submitted the matter to the jury under instructions setting forth the alternative provisions of section 31–19–8(1). Responding to special interrogatories, the jury found, *inter alia*, that:

a. David Berger failed to disclose to Minnesota Mutual that he had been treated for and/or advised that he had diabetes;

b. David Berger's diabetic condition was material either to the acceptance of the risk or the hazard assumed by Minnesota Mutual under the policy;

c. Had David Berger disclosed his diabetic treatment, Minnesota Mutual, in good faith, either would not have issued the policy, or would not have issued the policy at the same rate or in as large an amount, or would not have provided coverage with respect to the hazard resulting in the loss.

d. David Berger's diabetes did not cause or contribute to his death.

e. The plaintiff was not entitled to recover on the policy.

Consistent with these findings, the trial court entered judgment for defendants, voiding the policy.

On appeal, we view the record in a light most favorable to the jury's findings and special verdict, which are entitled to a presumption of validity and will not be disturbed if supported by substantial evidence. We find a reasonable basis in the evidence to support the jury's verdict.

Regardless of section 31–19–8, plaintiff claims that our prior decisions require that in order to defeat coverage, a misrepresentation by an insured must be made with a knowing and willful intent to deceive. However, our prior cases, cited by plaintiff to support this requirement, were decided under the statute which existed prior to 1963 and which allowed avoidance of a policy only if the misrepresentations materially affected the acceptance of the risk assumed *and* were made with an intent to deceive. *See* U.C.A., 1953, § 31–19–8 (repealed 1963 Utah Laws ch. 45, § 3).

When a statutory defense is asserted, a defendant is entitled to rely upon the language of the existing statute for the requisite elements of that defense. The jury was properly instructed regarding the statutory elements required to determine whether the misrepresentation was sufficient to avoid the policy.

The evidence supports the conclusion that, although not fraudulent, Berger's concealment of his diabetic condition was knowing and intentional. The misrepresentation was not merely considered as an expression or representation of his general health condition, but was a falsehood and a concealment of a significant medical illness. *See* 43 Am. Jur. 2d *Insurance* § 1055, at 1059–61 (1982).

We also reject plaintiff's second argument, that in order for the misrepresentation to be material, the insurer must prove that the fact misrepresented resulted in the insured's death. Again, plaintiff relies upon decisions under our prior statute. Under our present statute, a misrepresentation may prevent recovery under an insurance contract when it is material to the risk of death assumed by the insurer. There is substantial evidence to support the jury's verdict that Berger's diabetic condition was material to his insurability and to the acceptance by Minnesota Mutual of the risk of death. The materiality of a fact misrepresented or withheld is determined by the probable and reasonable effect that a truthful disclosure would have had upon the insurer in determining the advantages of the proposed contract.

Because the materiality of a misrepresentation by the insured is determined by the extent to which it initially influenced the insurer to assume the risk of coverage, materiality is measured at the time that the risk is assumed and not at the subsequent death. Therefore, the misrepresentation in an insurance application may be material if it diminishes the insurer's opportunity to determine or estimate its risk. By withholding facts relevant to his insurability, the decedent prevented Minnesota Mutual from appraising its risk on the basis of the facts as they truly existed at the time the contract was made.

According to the medical testimony, diabetes is associated with an acceleration of arthrosclerosis and heart and circulatory complications, resulting in a lower average life expectancy. There is also a greater risk of dangerous side effects from the controlling medication, particularly when used with alcohol and codeine. A finding that Berger did not die from diabetes does not necessarily determine the immateriality of the misrepresentation. Because the materiality of a misrepresentation is related to the insurer's willingness to initially accept the risk, the ultimate cause of death may be a factor considered by the jury, but is not of itself necessarily determinative. Other jurisdictions have also held that the concealment or misrepresentation by the insured of a diabetic condition is material to the risk assumed by the insurer, even though the insured's death or injury results from other causes.

The materiality of the misrepresentation in this case was for the jury to determine on the basis of what a reasonable and prudent insurer would do in the industry. The evidence was unrebutted that a truthful representation by Berger of his diabetic condition would have caused rejection of this type of credit life policy. The jury was entitled to conclude that Minnesota Mutual's practice to deny group life insurance to applicants with diabetes was reasonable and prudent. Therefore, we decline to disturb the jury's determination that the misrepresentation by the insured was material to the risk of death assumed by Minnesota Mutual and that it would not have issued the policy to Berger under truthful circumstances. . . .

The verdict and judgment below in favor of defendants are affirmed.

NOTES AND QUESTIONS

1. *Utah Then, Utah Now.* Utah's current statute regarding the misrepresentation defense, quoted above, is different than at the time *Berger* was decided. How is it different? Would the result in the case be the same under the current statute?

2. *New York, New York (Then and Now).* Consider the current New York statute on misrepresentation:

> **New York Insurance Law § 3105. Representations by the insured**
>
> (a) A representation is a statement as to past or present fact, made to the insurer by, or by the authority of, the applicant for insurance or the prospective insured, at or before the making of the insurance contract as an inducement to the making thereof. A misrepresentation is a false representation, and the facts misrepresented are those facts which make the representation false.
>
> (b)(1) No misrepresentation shall avoid any contract of insurance or defeat recovery thereunder unless such misrepresentation was material. No misrepresentation shall be deemed material unless knowledge by the insurer of the facts misrepresented would have led to a refusal by the insurer to make such contract. . . .
>
> (c) In determining the question of materiality, evidence of the practice of the insurer which made such contract with respect to the acceptance or rejection of similar risks shall be admissible.

Now consider the following case decided under the New York statute.

MUTUAL BENEFIT LIFE INSURANCE CO. v. JMR ELECTRONICS CORP.

848 F.2d 30 (2d Cir. 1988)

Opinion

PER CURIAM:

JMR Electronics Corporation ("JMR") appeals from a judgment of the District Court for the Southern District of New York (Robert W. Sweet, Judge) ordering recission of a life insurance policy issued by plaintiff-appellant The Mutual Benefit Life Insurance Company ("Mutual") and dismissing JMR's counterclaim for the policy's proceeds. Judge Sweet ruled that a misrepresentation made in the policy application concerning the insured's history of cigarette smoking was material as a matter of law. Appellant contends that the misrepresentation was not material because Mutual would have provided insurance-albeit at a higher premium rate-even if the insured's smoking history had been disclosed. We agree with the District Court that summary judgment was appropriate and therefore affirm.

The basic facts are not in dispute. On June 24, 1985, JMR submitted an application to Mutual for a $250,000 "key man" life insurance policy on the life of its president, Joseph Gaon, at the non-smoker's discounted premium rate. Mutual's 1985 Ratebook provides: "The Non-Smoker rates are available when the proposed insured is at least 20 years old and has not smoked a cigarette for at least twelve months prior to the date of the application." Question 13 of the application inquired about the proposed insured's smoking history. Question 13(a) asked, "Do you smoke cigarettes? How many a day?" Gaon answered this question, "No." Question 13(b) asked, "Did you ever smoke cigarettes?" Gaon again answered, "No." Based on these representations, Mutual issued a policy on Gaon's life at the non-smoker premium rate.

Gaon died on June 22, 1986, within the period of contestability contained in the policy, *see* N.Y. Ins. Law § 3203(a)(3) (McKinney 1985). Upon routine investigation of JMR's claim for proceeds under the policy, Mutual discovered that the representations made in the insurance application concerning Gaon's smoking history were untrue. JMR has stipulated that, at the time the application was submitted, Gaon in fact "had been smoking one-half of a pack of cigarettes per day for a continuous period of not less than 10 years." Mutual brought this action seeking a declaration that the policy is void. Judge Sweet granted Mutual's motion for summary judgment, dismissed JMR's counterclaim for the proceeds of the policy, and ordered recission of the insurance policy and return of JMR's premium payments, with interest.

Under New York law, which governs this diversity suit, "[i]t is the rule that even an innocent misrepresentation as to [the applicant's medical history], if material, is sufficient to allow the insurer to avoid the contract of insurance or defeat recovery thereunder." *Process Plants Corp. v. Beneficial National Life Insurance Co.,* 53 A.D.2d 214, 216, 385 N.Y.S.2d 308, 310 (1st Dep't 1976), *aff'd mem.,* 42 N.Y.2d 928, 397 N.Y.S.2d 1007, 366 N.E.2d 1361 (1977). A "misrepresentation" is defined by statute as a false "statement as to past or present fact, made to the insurer . . . at or before the making of the insurance contract as an inducement to the making thereof." N.Y. Ins. Law § 3105(a) (McKinney 1985). A misrepresentation is "material" if "knowledge by the insurer of the facts misrepresented would have led to a refusal by the insurer to make such contract." *Id.* § 3105(b). Case law has somewhat broadened the materiality inquiry: "The question . . . is not whether the company *might have issued* the policy even if the information had been furnished; the question in each case is whether the company has been induced to accept an application which it *might otherwise have refused.*" *Geer v. Union Mutual Life Insurance Co.,* 273 N.Y. 261, 269, 7 N.E.2d 125 (1937) (emphasis in original). The materiality determination normally presents an issue of fact for the jury, but "where the evidence concerning the materiality is clear and substantially uncontradicted, the matter is one of law for the court to determine." *Process Plants Corp. v. Beneficial National Life Insurance Co., supra,* 53 A.D.2d at 216, 385 N.Y.S.2d at 310–11.

In the present case JMR has stipulated that Gaon's smoking history was misrepresented in the insurance application. However, JMR disputes that this misrepresentation is material as a matter of law. JMR argues that under New York law a misrepresentation is not material unless the insurer can demonstrate that, had the applicant provided complete and accurate information, coverage either would have been refused or at the very least withheld pending a more detailed underwriting examination. In JMR's view summary judgment was inappropriate on the facts of this case because a jury could reasonably have found that even "had appellee been aware of Gaon's smoking history, a policy at the smoker's premium rate would have been issued," Appellant's Br. at 4 (emphasis omitted). JMR takes the position that the appropriate remedy in this situation is to permit recovery under the policy in the amount that the premium actually paid would have purchased for a smoker.

We agree with Judge Sweet that this novel theory is without basis in New York law. The plain language of the statutory definition of "materiality," found in section 3105(b), permits avoidance of liability under the policy where "knowledge of . . . the facts misrepresented would have led to a refusal by the insurer to make *such contract.*" (Emphasis added). Moreover, numerous courts have observed that the materiality inquiry under New York law is made with respect to the particular policy issued in reliance upon the misrepresentation. In *Barrett v. State Mutual Life Assurance Co.*, 58 A.D.2d 320, 396 N.Y.S.2d 848 (1st Dep't 1977), *aff'd*, 44 N.Y.2d 872, 407 N.Y.S.2d 478, 378 N.E.2d 1047 (1978), *cert. denied*, 440 U.S. 912, 99 S.Ct. 1226, 59 L.Ed.2d 461 (1979), for example, the Court found that misrepresentations concerning the insured's medical history contained in his application for life insurance were material as a matter of law, notwithstanding a jury's verdict granting recovery under the policy. The evidence conclusively demonstrated, said the Court, that "had [the insurer] known the truth, the policy in evidence, *whatever may have been done about a possible higher premium rate*, would not have issued in the form found here." *Id.* at 323, 396 N.Y.S.2d at 851 (emphasis added). *See also Cohen v. Mutual Benefit Life Insurance Co.*, 638 F.Supp. 695, 697 (E.D.N.Y.1986) ("A determination of materiality as a matter of [New York] law may be based on evidence . . . that the insurer would not have issued the particular contract it did had the facts been disclosed."); *L. Smirlock Realty Corp. v. Title Guarantee Co., supra*, 70 A.D.2d at 462, 421 N.Y.S.2d at 237 (asking whether "insurer would not have issued the particular contract it did at the same premium had the facts been disclosed"); *Johnson v. United States Life Insurance Co.*, 4 A.D.2d 825, 825, 164 N.Y.S.2d 748, 749 (4th Dep't 1957) ("[T]he question of materiality depend[s] upon whether the insurer would have issued the standard policy at the standard rate."); *North Atlantic Life Insurance Co. v. Rothman*, No. 561/87, slip op. at 2 (Sup.Ct. Nassau Cty. Feb. 22, 1988) (misrepresentation concerning insured's smoking history in application for "non-smoker's" life insurance policy material as a matter of law, "[w]hether or not a smoker policy would have been issued at a higher premium") (citing Judge Sweet's opinion in pending case); *cf. Equitable Life Assurance Society of the United States v. O'Neil*, 67 A.D.2d 883, 884, 413 N.Y.S.2d 714, 716 (1st Dep't 1979) (misrepresentations material as matter of law because "had [the insurer] been aware of the true facts the disability premium waiver provision would not have been included in the policy"). Our conclusion is supported as well in case law from other jurisdictions and by the commentators.[2]

. . . .

There is no doubt that Mutual was induced to issue the non-smoker, discounted-premium policy to JMR precisely as a result of the misrepresentations made by Gaon concerning his smoking history. That Mutual might not have refused the risk on *any* terms had it known the undisclosed facts is irrelevant. Most risks are insurable at some price. The purpose of the materiality inquiry is not to permit the jury to rewrite the

---

[2] "[T]he test of materiality [is] whether knowledge of the facts would have influenced the insurer in determining whether to accept the risk or in fixing the amount of premiums. . . ." 45 C.J.S. *Insurance* § 595, at 406 (1946); *see also* 7 G. Couch, *Cyclopedia of Insurance Law* § 35:79, at 127 (2d ed. 1985) ("[T]he test of materiality is: Did the fact or circumstance represented or misrepresented operate to induce the insurer to accept the risk, or to accept it at a lower premium?").

terms of the insurance agreement to conform to the newly disclosed facts but to make certain that the risk insured was the risk covered by the policy agreed upon. If a fact is material to the risk, the insurer may avoid liability under a policy if that fact was misrepresented in an application for that policy whether or not the parties might have agreed to some other contractual arrangement had the critical fact been disclosed. As observed by Judge Sweet, a contrary result would reward the practice of misrepresenting facts critical to the underwriter's task because the unscrupulous (or merely negligent) applicant "would have everything to gain and nothing to lose" from making material misrepresentations in his application for insurance. Such a claimant could rest assured not only that he may demand full coverage should he survive the contestability period, N.Y. Ins. Law § 3203(a)(3), but that even in the event of a contested claim, he would be entitled to the coverage that he might have contracted for had the necessary information been accurately disclosed at the outset. New York law does not permit this anomalous result. The judgment of the District Court is affirmed.

NOTES AND QUESTIONS

1. *The Meaning of "Such Contract" in the New York Statute.* New York's statute regarding the misrepresentation defense, quoted above, expressly states the misrepresentation must have been such that the insurer would not have issued the policy if the insurer had accurate information. Was there any evidence in the record that the insurer would have refused to issue the life insurance policy to Gaon if the insurer had known he was a smoker? How did the Second Circuit address that point? Is the Second Circuit's analysis persuasive?

2. *And Then There's Pennsylvania.* Consider the Pennsylvania misrepresentation statute, which was applied in the case following it:

> **Pennsylvania Insurance Code § 757. False statements in applications**
>
> The falsity of any statement in the application for any policy covered by subdivision (b) of this article shall not bar the right to recovery thereunder, unless such false statement was made with actual intent to deceive, or unless it materially affected either the acceptance of the risk or the hazard assumed by the insurer.

ALUMINUM CO. OF AMERICA V. AETNA CAS. & SUR. CO.

998 P.2d 856 (Wash. 2000)

Opinion

We are asked in this case to apply the law of Pennsylvania to resolve disputes between the Aluminum Company of America, its subsidiary Northwest Alloys, Inc. (Alcoa), and 167 insurers regarding insurance coverage for environmental damage under comprehensive general liability (CGL) policies and property insurance policies called differences in conditions (DIC) policies. We accepted direct interlocutory review in this case. We generally affirm the trial court's disposition of the issues in the case, but we reverse the trial court with respect to its treatment of the issues of fortuity, the contractual limitation periods, and the allocation of damages.

Facts

Alcoa is a large, multinational aluminum producing company with industrial locations across the United States and the world. In the ordinary course of its business over the years, Alcoa generated waste products that were stored in on-site disposal facilities, landfills, and lagoons; and sometimes discharged into the property of others. In recent years, federal and state environmental agencies and private parties made claims against Alcoa for the cleanup of groundwater, surface water, and soil contamination at disposal sites, lagoons, landfills, and other such facilities in Washington and around the country, all stemming from Alcoa's disposal of its waste products. Alcoa paid for investigation and remediation of the environmental harm. Alcoa's claims for coverage in this case involved 35 different facilities in 11 different states. Raising a variety of defenses, the insurers denied coverage. Alcoa hereafter filed this declaratory judgment action in the King County Superior Court in December 1992 against 167 insurers seeking coverage for the cost of pollution damage, investigation, and remediation.

In order to streamline pretrial and trial procedure, the trial court designated 3 of the 35 sites at issue—Vancouver, Washington; Massena, New York; and Point Comfort, Texas—as test sites for the trial. Original damage estimates against the DIC insurers for these three sites alone approached $850 million.

The trial involving the three sites was called Phase I; the future Phase II trial is intended to resolve issues arising from the remaining 32 sites. The Phase I trial consisted of two stages. Stage 1 was designed to determine whether the policy jackets the DIC insurers added to the insurance policy Alcoa drafted were part of the insurance contract. That trial lasted three weeks. The jury returned a complete verdict concerning the applicability of policy jackets to the insurance contract. The Stage 2 trial lasted 10 weeks and the jury deliberated for 3 months before returning an incomplete verdict; the jury answered only about one-half of the interrogatories submitted it.

The trial court then certified the case for appeal pursuant to CR 54(b), setting out in detail all of the jury's findings of fact and the trial court's extensive summary judgment orders containing conclusions of law. The trial court certified the case for reasons of judicial economy, concluding, "there must be resolution of the legal standards that will apply" before continuing with trial on the remaining 32 sites. We accepted direct review.

Issues

. . . .

2. Did Alcoa's alleged misrepresentations or failure to disclose relevant information to its insurers render the policies void ab initio?

. . . .

Analysis

Background to the Insurance Coverages

To understand the issues in this case fully, it is necessary to describe how the parties agreed to the insurance coverage provided and the nature of the coverage obtained. As befits a large, sophisticated, multinational enterprise, Alcoa had its own internal insurance or risk management department. Wishing to procure property insurance for its far-flung operations for the periods 1977–80, 1980–83, and 1983–84, Alcoa prepared "submissions" that described the nature of Alcoa's business, its properties, and the insurance coverages Alcoa sought. Attached to the submissions were "manuscript forms," actual proposed insurance policies prepared by Alcoa and its insurance brokers. The manuscript forms included both CGL and DIC coverages. Large insurance brokerage firms shopped the submissions and manuscript forms to various insurers. The insurers responded with price quotations for the layers of coverage they offered to Alcoa. Upon the placement of coverage, the insurers sent "policy jackets," standard policy language, to the brokers for inclusion in the formal policies.

Ultimately, the first layer of CGL coverage for the period 1977–84 was placed with Commercial Union. Lexington covered the first layer of DIC coverage for 1977–80, but various other insurers provided the initial coverage for 1980–84. Numerous insurers provided excess layers of coverage.

In the mid-1980s, pressed by state and federal regulators to clean up environmental hazards on its own property and elsewhere, Alcoa incurred substantial expenses to remediate these hazards. The essence of the problem with Alcoa's insurance coverage claims here rested with the retroactive liability imposed on potentially responsible parties by CERCLA (Comprehensive Environmental Response, Compensation, and Liability Act of 1980), 42 U.S.C. § 9607(a)(2). *See, e.g., Combined Properties/ Greenbriar Ltd. Partnership v. Morrow*, 58 F.Supp.2d 675 (E.D.Va.1999) (retroactive application of CERCLA does not violate due process). At the time the coverages were placed in this case, it is unlikely any of the parties anticipated CERCLA's imposition of retroactive liability on Alcoa. To compound the complexity of the issues here, a significant portion of the harm was to Alcoa's own property.

Central to understanding the insurers' defenses is recognition of the two different types of insurance involved in this case: CGL insurance (third-party insurance), and a special type of property coverage known as DIC insurance (first-party insurance). Some of the insurers issued both types of policies to Alcoa.

"Third party insurance involves protection for the policyholder for liability it incurs to someone else, while first party insurance involves protection for losses to the policyholder's own property." *Olds-Olympic, Inc. v. Commercial Union Ins. Co.*, 129 Wash.2d 464, 479, 918 P.2d 923 (1996). Generally, a CGL policy insures against injury or damage to a third party; the insurer agrees to defend and indemnify the insured against liability for risks identified in the policy. A DIC policy, by contrast, is generally a first-party insurance policy that indemnifies the insured for damage to its own property. Harold Meeks, a former manager of Alcoa's casualty and property insurance division, testified Alcoa purchased DIC insurance to cover damage to Alcoa's property not covered by other property damage policies Alcoa had in place. In particular, the DIC policies were "all-risk" policies that acted either as excess coverage to risks covered by other Alcoa property damage policies, or primary coverage for property damage not covered by Alcoa property damage policies. Trial Ex. 431 at 6 ("perils insured"), 10 ("other insurance"). According to the trial court, DIC policies were written for only a short period of time (the late 1970s to the early 1980s), so there is either no authority or only sparse authority for their interpretation. Clerk's Papers at 050753.

The trial court granted summary judgment dismissing Alcoa's claims against the CGL insurers. The DIC policies presented many issues that were not, like the CGL policies, susceptible to summary judgment. Consequently, the case was tried in the King County Superior Court on issues relating to the DIC coverage.

Misrepresentation

The insurers argued to the jury Alcoa omitted material facts in its application for DIC insurance, and, as a result, the policies should be void ab initio under Pennsylvania law. "Pennsylvania common law has long recognized that contracts for insurance, procured by fraud, are void *ab initio*." Washington law is the same. The insurers argued Alcoa was aware of significant environmental damage to the property it sought to insure and failed to inform them of that damage.

The jury rejected the insurers' argument after the trial court submitted the following special verdict question to the jury: "In obtaining the DIC policies, did Alcoa make any material misrepresentations to the insurers?" The jury answered "No" as to all 52 policies the jury considered. The insurers then moved the trial court to enter a judgment notwithstanding the verdict of the jury (JNOV), pursuant to CR 50(b) and for a new trial pursuant to CR 59, alleging four improper arguments by Alcoa's counsel in closing argument. The trial court denied both motions. Finally, the insurers contend the trial court erred in ruling its denial of the misrepresentation defense is preclusive as to the remaining 32 sites.

Turning first to the motion for JNOV, the standard of review we apply for a trial court's ruling on a CR 50(b) motion is the following: In reviewing a JNOV, this court applies the same standard as the trial court. . . . A JNOV is proper only when the court can find, "as a matter of law, that there is neither evidence nor reasonable inference therefrom sufficient to sustain the verdict." A motion for a JNOV admits the truth of the opponent's evidence and all inferences that can be reasonably drawn therefrom, and requires the evidence be interpreted most strongly against the moving party and in the light most favorable to the opponent. No element of discretion is involved.

"Under Pennsylvania law an insurance policy is void for misrepresentation when the insurer establishes three elements: (1) that the representation was false; (2) that the insured knew that the representation was false when made or made it in bad faith; and (3) that the representation was material to the risk being insured." This is the common law rule that has been in effect since *Evans v. Penn Mut. Life Ins. Co.,* 322 Pa. 547, 186 A. 133 (1936). The rule is simply a version of the well-known common law principle, "Fraud renders a contract voidable by the innocent party." False applications for casualty insurance have also been a matter of statutory law in Pennsylvania since 1921:

> The falsity of any statement in the application for any policy covered by subdivision (b) [casualty insurance] of this article shall not bar the right to recovery thereunder, unless such false statement was made with actual intent to deceive, or unless it materially affected either the acceptance of the risk or the hazard assumed by the insurer.

PA. STAT. ANN. tit. 40, § 757 (footnote omitted) (West 1999) (originally enacted as 1921 Pa. Laws 682, art. VI, § 622). The insurers make no reference to this statute.

The Pennsylvania Superior Court (the intermediate level appellate court in Pennsylvania) has recently explained the rule for proving fraud in the context of an insurance contract: "It is well established that "where the execution of a contract of insurance has been induced by fraudulent misrepresentations of the insured, the insurer may secure its cancellation[.]" The burden of proving fraud is on the insurer who must prove, by clear and convincing evidence, that on the application, the insured knowingly made false statements or knowingly failed to disclose information which was material to the risk against which the insured sought to be protected. In order to show a policy is void *ab initio* on the basis of fraud, the insurer must prove that the intent to deceive was deliberate.

Mere mistakes, inadvertently made, even though of material matters, or the failure to furnish all details asked for, where it appears that there is no intention of concealing the truth, does not work a forfeiture, and a forfeiture does not follow where there has been no deliberate intent to deceive, and the known falsity of the answer is not affirmatively shown.

The clear and convincing standard of proof is sufficiently met if the evidence presented was "so clear, direct, weighty, and convincing as to enable the jury to come to a clear conviction, without hesitancy, of the truth of the precise facts in issue." Nonetheless, "fraud . . . is never proclaimed from the housetops nor is it done otherwise than surreptitiously with every effort to conceal the truth of what is being done. So fraud can rarely if ever be shown by direct proof. It must necessarily be largely inferred from the surrounding circumstances." *Rohm & Haas Co. v. Continental Cas. Co.*, 732 A.2d 1236, 1251–52 (Pa.Super.1999).

The insurers argue Alcoa's actions satisfied all three prongs. First, they contend Alcoa did not reveal in its applications for DIC coverage its land had already been contaminated by industrial wastes. They treat this omission as a false representation. That there was damage to some of Alcoa's property prior to the time Alcoa requested insurance coverage from the insurers had been established by pretrial orders. Jury Instruction No. 20 detailed as much:

> As a result of rulings made prior to trial, I instruct you that, as a matter of law, you must take as established the following:
>
> (a) Land and groundwater are real property covered under the DIC policies.
>
> (b) Prior to July 1, 1977, Alcoa was aware that mercury, cyanide, and PCBs, in certain forms, under certain conditions, at some concentration, and through certain biological pathways, could be considered hazardous or toxic.
>
> (c) Prior to July 1, 1977, Alcoa knew that it sustained mercury-related property damage at the Point Comfort facility in the following areas: the portion of Lavaca Bay leased by Alcoa, in the four Bauxite Residue Lakes, Dredge Island, and the Dredge Spoil Lake.
>
> (d) No later than July 1, 1980, Alcoa knew that it sustained PCB-related property damage at the Massena facility in the following waste management units: The Lubricating Waste Oil Lagoon and the Soluble Oil Lagoon.

> (e) As of December 1978, Alcoa knew that cyanide had damaged the groundwater under the SPL pile at the Vancouver facility.
>
> (f) Prior to July 1, 1977, Alcoa knew that fluoride had damaged the Settling Lagoons at the Vancouver facility. As of the start of the Vancouver Sludge Pond's operation in 1978, Alcoa was also aware of the fluoride-related damage to the pond.

Clerk's Papers at 049132. Question No. 4 on the Special Verdict Form asked, "When did Alcoa know of the property damage in each area or become substantially certain that such damage would occur [?]" In its answer, the jury indicated Alcoa knew of many areas where damage had occurred before Alcoa applied for insurance. Clerk's Papers at 049392–95. Thus, the insurers appear to meet the first test for misrepresentation.

Second, the insurers contend Alcoa did not inform them of this damage when it applied for insurance. Alcoa disputes this contention. Alcoa asserts it did not knowingly or in bad faith fail to inform the insurers of the damage. The crux of Alcoa's argument is it was not aware the insurers needed information from Alcoa about environmental damage to its own property. This contention blends into the third prong, materiality, and does not refute the insurers' argument Alcoa did not inform them of environmental damage to its own property. The insurers appear to meet the second test for misrepresentation.

Third, the insurers contend Alcoa's omission of information about damage to its property from industrial wastes was material. Under Pennsylvania law, "Information is said to be material if knowledge or ignorance of it would naturally influence the judgment of the insurer in issuing the policy, in estimating the degree and character of the risk, or in fixing the premium rate." *A.G. Allebach, Inc. v. Hurley,* 373 Pa.Super. 41, 540 A.2d 289, 295 (1988). The insurers assert, "[A]ny information pertaining to this property and insured-risk would, *a fortiori,* be material." Br. of Cross-Appellants at 25. But the insurers decline to confront the crucial question regarding misrepresentation: was information of damage material?

The trial court held it was not. In its order denying the motion for JNOV, the trial court said:

> As of 1977, when the Lexington policies were negotiated, there were no statutory requirements that the owner of an industrial facility clean up its own property, there was no indication that Alcoa had ever or would ever incur costs to remedy pollution-related damage on its own property, there was no indication that Alcoa was contemplating making claims for such damage, and there is no evidence that Alcoa had made pollution-related claims in the past. The jury could conclude that, as of 1977, the fact that the operation of Alcoa's waste management units had damaged its

> own property, where no claim had ever been made or was ever likely to be made regarding such damage, would not have been material to either party. The jury's findings of no material misrepresentations were, therefore, appropriate as to the Lexington policies.

Clerk's Papers at 050067.

The trial testimony of insurance company representatives is important regarding materiality. One representative testified the damage Alcoa did not report was not material because he did not believe the DIC policies covered environmental damage:

> Q. Well, today, [are] environmental assessment[s] . . . done in connection with underwriting property policies?
>
> A. DICwise, I don't believe so.
>
> Q. They are not done?
>
> A. They are not done.
>
> Q. I take it, then, that they weren't done in the 1977 to the 1984 time period either?
>
> A. I don't think so.
>
> Q. Mr. Daly, if environmental assessments are not done today, in connection with the issuance of the DIC policies, then that information is not material in determining whether or not to underwrite the DIC policies. Isn't that correct?
>
> A. The information is not material to not write them?
>
> Q. You testified that environmental assessments are not being done today?
>
> A. I said I think so.
>
> Q. You said that you think that they weren't being done in the 1977 to the 1984 time period either in connection with the issuing of the DIC policies; right?
>
> A. Right.
>
> Q. So that the information that one might get from the environmental assessments might not be material at the time of writing DIC policies?
>
> A. Maybe so. I don't know for sure.
>
> Q. If environmental assessments are not being done today in connection with the DIC policies, do you think that the information that an environmental assessment might generate would be material to issuing those policies today?

A. Yes.

Q. Why aren't they, why aren't environmental [assessments] done?

A. Because to this day I don't think that contamination and pollution are covered as a specific peril.

Report of Proceedings at 10972–73 (testimony of John Daly, a property underwriter with 22 years of experience. Report of Proceedings at 2499). Another insurance company executive was even more definite about the immateriality of environmental damage to Alcoa's property to the decision to insure:

Q. Now, similarly, at the time that you were underwriting these policies, in 1983, these DIC policies, you didn't think that the policies covered contamination of land by waste generated by Alcoa; isn't that right?

A. I still don't.

Q. You still don't. All right. Now, Mr. York, at the time that you underwrote these policies, you really didn't know much about Alcoa's waste generation activities; isn't that right?

A. No, I did not.

Q. You don't recall really asking about any information about Alcoa's waste handling or generation activities; isn't that right?

A. I could see no relation to that to the subject of our property policies.

Q. You weren't really that concerned about Alcoa's waste generation, or about hazardous chemicals contaminating land, because you didn't think that contamination of the land was covered under those DIC policies through the underwriting. Isn't that right?

A. Correct.

Q. So that type of information was not really a primary consideration for you, when you were underwriting the policies. You were focused more on the flood exposures and the earthquake exposures and information relating to those types of exposures; isn't that right?

A. Yes.

Q. You don't recall having any particular concern at that time about any contamination or pollution exposures of Alcoa; isn't that right?

A. No. We would have, I testified earlier that how we would have approached underwriting to cover land and we just didn't really have a good feeling about that. We wouldn't have done it.

Q. I am asking you not to speculate what you would have done or thought, if you had known land was covered under these policies. I am talking about what you did think and what you were focused on at the time that you underwrote these policies at the time that you didn't think that land was covered under them; that is, that you weren't that focused or concerned about exposures relating to contamination for pollution. Isn't that right? . . .

A. I don't think that it is a very direct question, either. I am afraid you are kind of putting words into my mouth. You are not asking me what I thought. You are saying, "yada, yada, yada, is that a fair statement?"

Q. Well, let me try it again, Mr. York. I won't use "yada, yada, yada" in this sentence. At the time that you underwrote these Commonwealth policies, you don't recall having any particular concern about Alcoa's exposures relating to contamination or pollution; isn't that correct?

A. No, I don't recall any such concerns.

Report of Proceedings at 11095–97 (testimony of Hugh York, manager of the United States Property Underwriting Division of Commonwealth Insurance). Thus, the jury heard testimony that allowed it to conclude the information Alcoa omitted about damage to its property was not material to the decision to issue insurance.

Because we are addressing a defense, a species of fraud in the inducement, that voids the insurance contract in its entirety from the outset, we are careful in applying this most extreme of remedies. Under Pennsylvania law, the test is, as it should be, a very rigorous one with a high burden on the insurers. Pennsylvania law abhors forfeitures. Although Alcoa did not inform the insurers about pollution damage to Alcoa's property at the time Alcoa applied for insurance, the trial court was correct in holding pollution damage was not a material factor in the insurers' decision to insure because nobody considered pollution damage to be covered by the DIC policies in the first instance. Failing of this third prong of the test for misrepresentation, the insurers have not met their burden to sustain a motion for JNOV.

We hold, therefore, there was sufficient evidence before the jury to sustain its verdict, and conclude the trial court did not err in denying the insurers' motion for JNOV.

. . . .

Conclusion

This case presents numerous complex factual and legal issues arising under Pennsylvania law. We both affirm and reverse the trial court, as noted above.

NOTES AND QUESTIONS

1. *Choice of Forum.* Why did Alcoa, a Pittsburgh-based company with its principal place of business in Pennsylvania, file the lawsuit in Seattle, Washington?

2. *Pennsylvania's Misrepresentation Standard.* Is Pennsylvania's common law with respect to the requirements to successfully assert a misrepresentation defense the same as Pennsylvania's statutory law? To the extent there are discrepancies between the two, how did the Washington Supreme Court resolve them?

3. *Restatement of the Law of Liability Insurance.* In 2019, the American Law Institute published the Restatement of the Law of Liability Insurance. Because insurance law generally is governed by state law, it is difficult to state a black letter of the law regarding many issues. For that reason, the Restatement is a blend of descriptive and prescriptive aspects of insurance law. With respect to the misrepresentation defense, the Restatement provides:

> **§ 7 Misrepresentation**
>
> (1) Any statement of fact made by a policyholder in an application for an insurance policy is a representation by the policyholder.
>
> (2) Subject to the rules governing defense obligations, an insurer may deny a claim or rescind the applicable insurance policy on the basis of an incorrect representation made by a policyholder in an application for an insurance policy (hereinafter referred to as a misrepresentation) only if the following requirements are met:
>
> (a) The misrepresentation was material as defined in § 8; and
>
> (b) The insurer reasonably relied on the misrepresentation in issuing or renewing the policy as specified in § 9.
>
> (3) When the policy is rescinded under subsection (2), the insurer must return all of the premiums paid for the policy.

4. *Test for Materiality.* The test for materiality can vary, but in many states the information sought is material if it would significantly affect the decision of the underwriter in issuing the policy at all or in fixing the amount of premium to be charged for the coverage. *See, e.g., Grande v. St. Paul Fire & Marine Ins. Co.*, 436 F.3d 277, 282 (1st Cir. 2006) (applying Maine law) ("[A]n insurance contract is ordinarily voidable if a false statement in the application was "material"—materiality meaning something that affects the risk and might lead either to a higher premium or a refusal of insurance."); *Oade v. Jackson Nat. Life Ins. Co. of Michigan*, 632 N.W.2d 126, 131 (Mich. 2001) ("[A]

fact or representation in an application is 'material' where communication of it would have had the effect of 'substantially increasing the chances of loss insured against so as to bring about a rejection of the risk or the charging of an increased premium.' "). The Restatement also reflects this standard. *See* Restatement of the Law of Liability Insurance § 8 ("A misrepresentation by an insured during the application for, or renewal of, an insurance policy is material only if, but for the misrepresentation, a reasonable insurer in this insurer's position would not have issued the policy or would have issued the policy only under substantially different terms.").

5. *Duty to Investigate.* Does an insurer have a duty to investigate or confirm the accuracy of the information contained in an application? Generally, courts hold that no duty exists. Insurers use applications so that they do not have to investigate every fact potentially relevant to the applicant's risk. In some states, however, an insurer does have a duty to investigate under the "inquiry notice" rule, which provides that an insurer has a duty to conduct a reasonable investigation if the information provided by the policyholder is patently incomplete or suspicious such that a reasonably prudent insurer would conduct a follow up investigation. *See, e.g.*, *W. Coast Life Ins. Co. v. Hoar*, 558 F.3d 1151, 1159 (10th Cir. 2009) ("an insurer is chargeable with knowledge of undisclosed information only where it 'had sufficient information that would have put a prudent man on notice and would have caused him to start an inquiry, which would have uncovered the truth.' ") (quoting *Major Oil Corp. v. Equitable Life Assurance Soc'y*, 457 F.2d 596, 604–05 (10th Cir.1972)). In short, an insurer cannot simply turn a blind eye to suspicious or incomplete information in an application and then seek to void the policy only if a claim is tendered.

6. *Omissions.* Other than for marine insurance, where the policyholder has an affirmative obligation to disclose information material to the risk, the policyholder generally does not have to disclose material information that is not requested by the insurer. The reason for this rule is that insurers are in a better position to know what information is important in making an underwriting decision, and they can ask for such information during the application process. Thus, a policyholder's failure to provide requested information is simply a type of misrepresentation.

7. *"Post-Claim Underwriting."* The practice of some insurers of going back to the application and attempting to find some basis for voiding a policy once a claim is tendered is known as "post-claim underwriting." *See* Thomas C. Cady & Georgia Lee Gates, *Post Claim Underwriting*, 102 W. Va. L. Rev. 809 (2000). It is not an unusual practice, as insurers typically use every means at their disposal to deny claims to the extent legally permissible. The *Alcoa* case is an example of post-claim underwriting.

8. *Misrepresentation by Applicant or by Agent?* Simply because an application is attached to the policy does not necessarily mean that the insurer will prevail when the application contains inaccurate or false information. It is very common for agents to fill out the application based on the applicant's oral

answers to questions posed by the agent. Thus, in many instances, the policyholder will assert that the insurer's agent was correctly informed but mistakenly recorded or even intentionally omitted information supplied by the applicant. Despite the policyholder's opportunity to read the application and point out any misinformation, courts have held that the insurer is deemed to have knowledge of facts known to its agent and therefore have estopped the insurer from asserting the defense of misrepresentation, except where there is collusion between the agent and the policyholder. *See, e.g.*, *Bunn v. Monarch Life Ins. Co.*, 478 P.2d 363 (Or. 1970); *Ward v. Durham Life Ins. Co.*, 368 S.E.2d 391 (N.C. Ct. App. 1988).

9. *Duty to Update Information.* Does an applicant for insurance have any obligation to inform the insurer of material information coming to light after the application is submitted but before the insurer has accepted the risk? If the time of completion of the application is the critical date for determining acceptance of the risk, then changes in the applicant's condition after this date are irrelevant. But what about situations where the insurer allows itself the option to make a decision to accept a risk at any time up to and until the application is accepted? Needless to say, the scope of the applicant's duty, if any, has been the subject of considerable dispute in a number of cases. The general rule is that for personal lines of insurance, such as life insurance, an applicant has a duty to disclose changes in his health occurring between the date of his application and the delivery of policy. For a more complete discussion of these issues, *see* John F. Dobbyn & Christopher C. French, Insurance Law In A Nutshell 322–23 (5th ed. 2016); Robert H. Jerry, II & Douglas R. Richmond, Understanding Insurance Law § 102[j] (5th ed. 2012).

10. *Incontestability.* As will be discussed more fully in Chapter 7, in the life and disability contexts, insurers have a limited period of time, usually two years, in which to conduct an investigation of the policyholder and seek to rescind the policy on the basis that false information was provided in the application. The idea is that the policy is "contestable" during the first two years after issuance, but if the insurer does not act to rescind the policy during that period of time, the policy becomes "incontestable." If a claim is made during the first two years, the claim is contestable.

11. *Post-Loss Misrepresentations.* In most states, a material misrepresentation by a policyholder regarding a loss is not grounds for voiding the policy, but it may be a basis for denying the claim. In some states, however, post-loss material misrepresentations can be grounds for voiding a policy. *See, e.g.*, *Longobardi v. Chubb Ins. Co. of New Jersey*, 582 A.2d 1257, 1261 (N.J. 1990) ("[A]n insured's commitment not to misrepresent material facts extends beyond the inception of the policy to a post-loss investigation.").

III. ESTOPPEL AND WAIVER

REPUBLIC INSURANCE CO. V. SILVERTON ELEVATORS, INC.

493 S.W.2d 748 (Tex. 1973)

DANIEL, JUSTICE.

This suit was brought by Respondents, Silverton Elevators, Inc. and Carl L. Tidwell, against Petitioner, Republic Insurance Company, to recover under a Texas Standard Fire Policy issued to Silverton Elevators by Republic covering a residential dwelling and household goods contained therein. In a non-jury trial, Silverton was awarded $3,000 "for the use and benefit" of Carl L. Tidwell for the loss of the household goods. The Court of Civil Appeals affirmed. We affirm.

Carl L. Tidwell was at all times material to this controversy, an officer, director and the general manager of Silverton Elevators, Inc. Silverton owned and furnished to Tidwell a house near its elevators, together with the insurance on the house and on Tidwell's household goods, as part of his compensation as general manager. Since 1964, Republic's local agent had issued and renewed insurance policies in the name of Silverton covering the dwelling and its household goods. It is undisputed that the local agent, who had authority to issue the policies and receive the premiums, knew that the household goods belonged to Tidwell and that Silverton was carrying the insurance for the benefit of Tidwell. On April 17, 1970, a tornado destroyed the house and the household goods.

On the date of the tornado there was in effect a Texas Standard Fire Policy with Extended Coverage on DWELLING & HOUSEHOLD GOODS in the sum of $10,000 issued by Republic to Silverton for the period of April 20, 1969 to April 20, 1972, insuring against loss from windstorm the specifically described "occupied dwelling" for $7,000 and "household goods . . . while in the described building" for $3,000.00. It is undisputed that Silverton paid the $227.00 premium, and the local agent admitted that at the time he issued the policy he knew the facts heretofore mentioned with respect to actual ownership of the insured property. He testified that he wrote the policy to cover Tidwell's household goods located in the dwelling which Tidwell and his family occupied; that he knew Silverton was carrying the policy on the household goods for the benefit of Tidwell; that when he issued the policy he did not think it made any difference that it was in the name of Silverton because "they were paying the premium"; and that he told Tidwell that the policy covered his household goods both before and after the tornado.

Republic acknowledged coverage on the house and paid Silverton $7,000 for its damage, but it denied any liability to Silverton or Tidwell on the household goods. Thereupon, Silverton and Tidwell brought this suit against Republic claiming coverage to the limit of the policy ($3,000) on the household goods owned by Tidwell. Republic defended on the grounds that Silverton had no ownership and therefore no insurable interest in the household goods and that the policy as written was limited by its terms to household goods owned by Silverton Elevators, Inc., the named insured.

Silverton and Tidwell's pleadings asserted that they both had insurable interests; that the insurance was purchased by Silverton and extended to Tidwell as part of his compensation as manager and as "a legal representative of Silverton Elevators, Inc.," and that when Republic issued its policy and accepted premiums with full knowledge of the true ownership and relations between Silverton and Tidwell, it waived the right to complain about any lack of ownership or insurable interest of the named insured and was estopped from denying coverage on behalf of Tidwell. As heretofore indicated, the trial court awarded Silverton Elevators $3,000 "for the use and benefit of Carl L. Tidwell."

Since the policy refers to and clearly purports to cover the household goods located in the specifically described dwelling, we agree with the Court of Civil Appeals that the knowledge of Tidwell's ownership of the household goods by Republic's local agent and his actions with respect thereto were imputed to and binding upon Republic. Issuance of the policy and collection of the premiums with such knowledge operates as a waiver of any requirement that the named insured own or possess a beneficial interest in the insured property. *National Fire Ins. Co. of Hartford v. Carter,* 257 S.W. 531 (Tex. Comm'n App. 1924, jdgmt adopted); *Continental Ins. Co. v. Cummings,* 98 Tex. 115, 81 S.W. 705 (1904); *Wagner v. Westchester Fire Ins. Co.,* 92 Tex. 549, 50 S.W. 569 (1899); *Liverpool and London and Globe Insurance Company v. Ende,* 65 Tex. 118 (1885); *Old Colony Insurance Company v. S.D. Messer,* 328 S.W.2d 335 (Tex. Civ. App. 1959, writ ref., n.r.e.); *Germania Mutual Aid Association v. Trotti,* 318 S.W.2d 918 (Tex. Civ. App. 1958, no writ).

In the above cases, the named insureds were not the owners or sole owners of the insured properties. In each case, the true owner was known to the insurance agent and was allowed direct recovery, or recovery for his benefit, on the grounds that the insurance company had waived warranties of sole ownership or lack of insurable interest. There is no conflict between the above cases and those which hold that waiver and estoppel cannot operate to bring within the terms of a policy liabilities or benefits which were expressly excepted therefrom, such as liability from injuries due to gunshot wounds; loss for injuries while in military service in time of war; or payment of benefits beyond a specified termination date at age 65. The latter cases recognize that waiver and estoppel may operate to avoid forfeiture of coverage and benefits stated in the policy, but not to add specifically excluded risks or to enlarge the benefits or risks therein set forth. In the present case, plaintiffs seek to recover only on the risk assumed by Republic under the terms of the written policy. Republic's policy insured against the destruction of precisely the same household goods identified in its policy and for which it collected its premiums. There is no evidence that its risk was enlarged because the household goods were owned by Tidwell rather than Silverton.

. . . .

It has been suggested, but not by Republic, that the building item provision contained in the "Mortgage or Trustee" clause at the bottom of the face of the policy, and particularly the last sentence thereof, limits liability for compensation to the "interest of the insured," and that this applies to personal property.[3] Even though the provision does not speak of "named insured," and for all practical purposes Tidwell was the "insured" because the policy as to household goods was written for his benefit, there are other more compelling reasons why this provision is inapplicable to the personal property involved in this case. Clearly, the entire clause refers to loss on "building items," their value at the time of loss less depreciation, repair, replacement and reconstruction, etc. None of the language refers to personal property. Furthermore, the last sentence begins with the words, "Subject to Article 6.13 of the Texas Insurance Code," and this Article contains the specific provision that: "The provisions of this article shall not apply to personal property."

The above clause has been a part of the Texas Standard Fire Policy form prescribed by the Insurance Commission since 1943. Since then we have found no case involving a claim of an actual owner for whose benefit a policy was taken out with full knowledge by the insurance company of the true ownership, in which this clause has been applied to deny recovery by or on behalf of the true owner. In the later case the clause was specifically raised as a defense and overruled on the grounds (1) that the company was estopped by its knowledge that the named insured was not the true owner and (2) that one for whose benefit a policy is issued under such circumstances is entitled to recover thereon. The latter reason was based on a well-established rule of contract law which is applicable to insurance contracts.

---

[3] The clause reads:

Loss on building items shall be payable to ASSURED ONLY

Address as Mortgagee or Trustee, as their interest may appear at time of loss, subject to Mortgage Clause (without contribution) printed elsewhere in this policy. Subject to Article 6.13 of the Texas Insurance Code, 1951, liability hereunder shall not exceed the actual cash value of the property at the time of loss, ascertained with proper deduction for depreciation; nor shall it exceed the amount it would cost to repair or replace the property with material of like kind and quality within a reasonable time after the loss, without allowance for any increased cost of repair or reconstruction by reason of any ordinance or law regulating construction or repair, and without compensation for loss resulting from interruption of business or manufacture; nor shall it exceed the interest of the insured, or the specific amounts shown under "Amount of Insurance."

Whether applicable to personal property or not, we hold that the portion of the clause relating to limitation of liability to "the interest of the insured" falls within the category of ownership provisions which may be waived; the insurer may be estopped from denying liability to the true owner on policies issued in the names of third parties covering the risks on identified property with full knowledge by the company that the property is actually owned by the one for whose benefit the policy was written or maintained.

Republic insists that reformation of the policy is the only proper remedy, if any, for recovery by Silverton on behalf of Tidwell, because of failure of the written policy to identify the household goods as belonging to Tidwell. We disagree. As heretofore indicated, under the undisputed facts, the household goods described in the policy belonged to Tidwell and were insured by Silverton for his benefit in a policy drawn by Republic's agent for such purpose, with assurances from the agent that it would cover Tidwell's furniture. If this was a mistake, it was made by Republic's agent, and it was mutual, because Tidwell and Silverton took the agent's word that it expressed the true agreement. With this evidence being fully developed in the present record, there is no reason to require another trial for reformation of the written policy. It has been held that even without a plea for reformation, when the facts show the true agreement intended and a mutual mistake, or mistake of the agent, in preparing the written policy, the agreement intended will be enforced without going through the formal proceedings of reformation.

Silverton and Tidwell made every proof in this case that would entitle recovery on the policy as written. Under the above cited authorities, the trial court and Court of Civil Appeals have properly held that Silverton is entitled to recover for the benefit of Tidwell on the written policy without seeking a reformation thereof.

Accordingly, the judgments of the lower courts are affirmed.

Dissenting Opinion by WALKER, J., joined by GREENHILL, C.J., and POPE and REAVLEY, JJ.

WALKER, JUSTICE (dissenting).

I respectfully dissent. . . .

The provision limiting liability to the interest of the insured obviously applies to both real and personal property. Since the Court does not hold otherwise, no purpose will be served by a discussion of the point. According to the majority opinion, the provision limiting liability "falls within the category of ownership provisions which may be waived; the insurer may be estopped from denying liability to the true owner on policies issued in the names of third parties *covering the risks on identified property* with full knowledge by the company that the property is actually owned by one for whose benefit the policy was written and maintained." (Emphasis supplied)

It will be noted that the Court there assumes that the policy covered Tidwell's property, and that is the question presented for decision. There is no contention and has been no suggestion that the limitation of liability would, in itself and under the facts of this case, deprive respondents of a recovery to which they might otherwise be entitled under the provisions of the policy. It is, however, one of the provisions that should be considered in determining the coverage afforded by the policy as written. It must be eliminated in some way before the policy can be said to cover all household goods, regardless of by whom owned, located in the described dwelling. This the Court attempts to do by holding that the limitation of liability provision has been waived. I do not agree.

The net effect of the majority holding is to extend the policy coverage and create an entirely different contract by waiver or estoppel. That is contrary, of course, to the established rule in Texas and most other jurisdictions.

As pointed out by the Supreme Court of Michigan in *Ruddock v. Detroit Life Ins. Co.*, 209 Mich. 638, 177 N.W. 242, "to apply the doctrine of estoppel and waiver here would make this contract of insurance cover a loss it never covered by its terms, to create a liability not created by the contract and never assumed by the defendant under the terms of the policy." Neither doctrine can properly be made to serve that purpose. In *Great American Reserve Ins. Co. v. Mitchell*, Tex. Civ. App., 335 S.W.2d 707 (wr. ref.), the court reviewed the authorities and correctly stated the Texas rule as follows:

. . . Waiver and estoppel may operate to avoid a forfeiture of a policy, but they have consistently been denied operative force to change, re-write and enlarge the risks covered by a policy. In other words, waiver and estoppel cannot create a new and different contract with respect to risks covered by the policy. This has been the settled law in Texas since the decision in *Washington Nat. Ins. Co. v. Craddock*, 130 Tex. 251, 109 S.W.2d 165, 113 A.L.R. 854. . . .

None of the cases cited in support of the waiver holding is pertinent here. Most of them involved the so-called sole and unconditional ownership clause, which provided that the entire policy would be void if the interest of the insured was other than sole and unconditional ownership. Others involved a stipulation that the policy would be void in case of a change of ownership unless otherwise provided by agreement endorsed on the policy. The policy in *Old Colony Insurance Co. v. Messer*, Tex. Civ. App., 328 S.W.2d 335 (wr. ref. n.r.e.) covered the dwelling that was damaged by fire, but it contained a provision limiting liability to the interest of the insured and another making the policy void if the insured had concealed any material fact. These provisions as well as lack of insurable interest were pled by the insurance company in bar. Although the jury made findings tending to support an estoppel theory, the Court of Civil Appeals affirmed the trial court's judgment in favor of the true owner on the basis of its holding that the provisions in question had been waived by issuance of the policy and acceptance of the premiums with knowledge of the ownership of the property. Be that as it may, there was no question of coverage in the case, and the decision does not stand for the proposition that the limitation of liability may be waived out of the policy for the purpose of determining coverage.

There is no sole and unconditional ownership or similar provision involved in the present case. Petitioner does not urge lack of insurable interest and, contrary to the suggestion in the majority opinion, we are not concerned with a "requirement that the named insured own or possess a beneficial interest in the insured property." The provision limiting liability to the interest of the insured is not a requirement, warranty or representation. It is not a condition of forfeiture, but it is of considerable importance here in determining the property covered by the policy. So far as I am able to determine, the present case is the first in which our Court has held, albeit somewhat circuitously, that an insurance company may "waive" itself into liability for a loss not covered by the policy.

It is my opinion that respondents are not entitled to recover on the policy as written, and that is all they have attempted to do thus far. Tidwell may show his right to recover by offering evidence and obtaining findings that establish mutual mistake and the terms of the true agreement. The trial court would then be in position to enter a judgment based on the coverage actually agreed upon and intended by the parties. It would also be in position to insure that petitioner receives the appropriate premium for the risk actually assumed. I would reverse the judgments of the courts below and remand the cause in the interest of justice.

GREENHILL, C.J., and POPE and REAVLEY, J.J., join in this dissent.

NOTES AND QUESTIONS

1. *Role of Waiver and Estoppel in Insurance.* The doctrines of waiver and estoppel have come to play a formidable role in insurance litigation. Next to claims that the policy contains an ambiguity, these doctrines probably are advanced more often by claimants than any other legal theory. Much of this has to do with the way insurance contracts are marketed. With hundreds and sometimes thousands of agents negotiating on behalf of insurers, the field is fertile for claims by insureds that they obtained something more than what the insurer intended to sell. Professor Clarence Morris theorized nearly fifty years ago that "waiver and estoppel are two of several guises that cloak the courts' part in changing insurance from a service safely bought only by sophisticated businessmen to a commodity bought with confidence by untrained consumers" and that "[j]udges, at the urging of policyholders' advocates, have used waiver and estoppel to convert insurance from a custom-made document designed in part by knowing buyers to a brandname staple sold over the counter by mine-

run salesmen to the trusting public." Clarence Morris, *Waiver and Estoppel in Insurance Policy Litigation*, 105 U. Pa. L. Rev. 925 (1957). No doubt there are many cases where the facts justify a finding of waiver or estoppel, but one can hardly avoid the impression that the technical requirements of the doctrines are not always strictly enforced.

2. *Elements of Waiver*. Waiver is the voluntary and intentional relinquishment of a known right. First, did the agent in *Silverton Elevators* have the authority, actual or apparent, to waive policy provisions? Second, did the agent understand that he was relinquishing the right of the insurance company to enforce the policy as written? Assuming the answers to these questions are "yes," if the agent had thought through what he was doing, is it not more plausible that he would have written the insurance in a way to make it clear that Mr. Tidwell's interest was covered? The parties probably never really focused on the point. If that is true, then how could the agent have intended to waive anything?

3. *Elements of Estoppel*. Estoppel differs from waiver. Estoppel is available where one with knowledge of the facts has acted in a particular manner so that she ought not to be allowed to assert a position inconsistent with the former acts to the prejudice of others who have relied thereon. One key difference between estoppel and waiver is that detrimental reliance is required in the former, but not in the latter. Another difference is that waiver involves consent on the part of the waiving party, whereas in most instances the party sought to be estopped did not actually agree or consent to give up anything by taking the earlier position. There is a very practical consequence to this difference, aside from the different burden of proof that is placed upon the person asserting either waiver or estoppel. As Judge Keeton and Professor Widiss point out:

> When a claimant bases a claim for rights at variance with policy provisions on the conduct of persons alleged to have acted on behalf of an insurer, the difference between estoppel and waiver can be particularly significant if agency concepts are also invoked. Estoppel often is more compatible than waiver with applying a relatively "broad" agency concept that precludes an insurer from objecting to the actions of the insurer's representative, and this is especially the case when the individual has exceeded the scope of authority prescribed by express provisions in the contractual relationship between the insurer and agent.

Robert E. Keeton, Alan I. Widiss, & James M. Fischer, Insurance Law 520 (2017). In other words, under estoppel, it may be argued that the insurer-principal should be liable on a *respondeat superior* basis, as occurs in tort law when the agent acts within the course and scope of the employment. *See* Restatement (Second) of Agency § 8B, cmt. *a* (1958). In contrast, the theory of waiver seems to lend itself more to an analysis based on contract law, i.e., a determination as to whether the agent had the authority to relinquish the right. Because agents seldom have the authority to waive policy provisions, or at least the ones that insureds typically assert were waived, the difference between waiver and estoppel can be crucial to many insureds' cases.

Based on these observations, what would you argue as plaintiff's counsel in the *Silverton Elevators* case regarding estoppel? Do you have a better case based on estoppel as compared to waiver?

4. *Restatement of the Law of Liability Insurance*. The Restatement has adopted rules regarding waiver and estoppel that are similar to those set forth in *Silverton Elevators*:

§ 5 Waiver

A party to an insurance policy waives a right under the policy if:

(1) that party, with actual or constructive knowledge of the facts giving rise to that right, expressly relinquishes the right, or engages in conduct that would reasonably be regarded by the counterparty as an intentional relinquishment of that right, and

(2) the relinquishment or conduct is communicated or known to the counterparty.

§ 6 Estoppel

A party to an insurance policy who makes a promise or representation that can reasonably be expected to induce detrimental reliance by another party to the policy is estopped from denying the promise or representation if the other party does in fact reasonably and detrimentally rely on that promise or representation.

5. *What Remedy Was Most Appropriate in Silverton Elevators?* After considering the above observations concerning waiver and estoppel, do you agree with the dissent in *Silverton Elevators* that reformation was the appropriate remedy? If you had the opportunity to plead the case anew, how would you proceed?

6. *Creating Coverage by Waiver or Estoppel*. Most courts continue to adhere to the position, mentioned by the court in *Silverton Elevators*, that neither waiver nor estoppel may be employed to expand coverage not otherwise provided in an insurance contract. *See, e.g.*, *Laidlaw Environmental Services (TOC), Inc. v. Aetna Casualty & Surety Co.*, 524 S.E.2d 847, 852 (S.C. Ct. App. 1999) (waiver cannot create coverage that does not otherwise exist); *Martin v. United States Fidelity and Guaranty Co.*, 996 S.W.2d 506, 511 (Mo. 1999) (estoppel cannot be used to create coverage); *Shepard v. Keystone Insurance Co.*, 743 F. Supp. 429, 433 (D. Md. 1990) (under Maryland law, "waiver and estoppel cannot be used to create liability where none previously existed, or to extend coverage beyond what was originally intended"); *Fli-Back Co., Inc. v. Philadelphia Manufacturers Mutual Insurance Co.*, 502 F.2d 214, 216 (4th Cir. 1974) (same under North Carolina law). An example of a case for the minority view is *Harr v. Allstate Insurance Co.*, 255 A.2d 208 (N.J. 1969):

Although we have not previously passed upon the question here involved, we have no hesitation in deciding, in line with the rationale just outlined, that, speaking broadly, equitable estoppel is available to bar a defense in an action on a policy even where the estopping conduct arose before or at the inception of the contract, and that the parol evidence rule does not apply in such situations.

. . . .

However, many jurisdictions which have long followed this view nevertheless hold that equitable estoppel is not available to broaden the coverage of a policy so as to protect the insured against risks not included therein or expressly excluded therefrom, as distinct from alleviation of other limitations or conditions of the contract. . . . While there is a clear split of authority, with the decisions holding estoppel not available to broaden coverage presently representing the majority view, many of the cases so stating are confusing and not clear cut. Estoppel and waiver are often interchangeably and improperly used, and in many cases where estoppel is held unavailable the necessary elements have not been made out anyway, or the insured by reason of his own conduct is clearly not entitled to relief. The reasons generally advanced in support of the majority view are that a court cannot create a new contract for the parties, that an insurer should not be required by estoppel to pay a loss for which it charged no premium, and perhaps that a risk or peril should not be imposed upon an insurer which it might have declined.

We are more impressed with the decisions in those jurisdictions which hold that equitable estoppel is utilizable to bar a defense of non-coverage of the loss claimed, *i.e.,* the minority rule.

These decisions all proceed on the thesis that where an insurer or its agent misrepresents, even though innocently, the coverage of an insurance contract, or the exclusions therefrom, to an insured before or at the inception of the contract, and the insured reasonably relies thereupon to his ultimate detriment, the insurer is estopped to deny coverage after a loss on a risk or from a peril actually not covered by the terms of the policy. The proposition is one of elementary and simple justice. By justifiably relying on the insurer's superior knowledge, the insured has been prevented from procuring the desired coverage elsewhere. To reject this approach because a new contract is thereby made for the parties would be an unfortunate triumph of form over substance. The fact that the insurer has received no premium for the risk or peril as to which the loss ensued is no obstacle. Any additional premium due can be deducted from the amount of the loss. If the insurer is saddled with coverage it may not have intended or desired, it is of its own making, because of its responsibility for the acts and representations of its employees and agents. It alone has the capacity to guard against such a result by the

> proper selection, training and supervision of its representatives. Of course, the burden of proof of equitable estoppel rests on the insured and, since evidence of representations is almost always oral, a trial court must be convinced that the requisite elements have been established by reliable proof and that the insured has met his burden by a fair preponderance of the evidence.
>
> We agree with the Appellate Division that New Jersey should adopt the view that equitable estoppel is available, under appropriate circumstances, to bring within insurance coverage risks or perils which are not provided for in the policy or which are expressly excluded.

255 A.2d at 218–19.

Although *Silverton Elevators* may still represent the majority rule on this point, the position is eroding, as a number of states have followed the line of reasoning represented in *Harr. See, e.g., Bill Brown Construction Co. v. Glens Falls Insurance Co.*, 818 S.W.2d 1 (Tenn. 1991); *Crown Life Insurance Co. v. McBride*, 517 So. 2d 660 (Fla. 1988); *Darner Motor Sales, Inc. v. Universal Underwriters Insurance Co.*, 682 P.2d 388 (Ariz. 1984); *Martini v. Lafayette Studios Corp.*, 676 N.Y.S.2d 808 (N.Y. App. Div. 1998). In *Potesta v. United States Fidelity & Guaranty Co.*, 504 S.E.2d 135 (W. Va. 1998), the Supreme Court of West Virginia affirmed the rule that waiver and estoppel may not be used to extend coverage, but then allowed that the rule is subject to exceptions—such as when the insurer's or agent's misrepresentation at the policy's inception prevented the insured from getting the coverage she desired, the insurer defends the insured without a reservation of rights, or the insurer acts in bad faith. 504 S.E.2d at 147–50. With which position do you agree?

7. *What About Promissory Estoppel?* Is it at all relevant that the doctrine of promissory estoppel, as compared to estoppel in pais, had not been fully recognized at the time most of the early cases espousing the majority view were decided? Indeed, is it possible to follow the majority view with respect to equitable estoppel but allow coverage to be created under the doctrine of promissory estoppel? In *Verschoor v. Mountain West Farm Bureau Mutual Insurance Co.*, 907 P.2d 1293 (Wyo. 1995), the court stated: "Estoppel and waiver will not operate to create additional coverage in an existing contract of insurance . . . . However, no retreat from [that rule] is required to make room for the possibility that [the insurer's agent's] promises to Chad [an employee under a policy of group health insurance] resulted in the formation of an entirely new contract of insurance, not under a theory of equitable estoppel but by virtue of promissory estoppel." *Id.* at 1298.

EXERCISES

1. Mary Smith is from State College, Pennsylvania, but she goes to school in New York City. She applies for auto insurance and states in the application that she lives in State College, Pennsylvania. Write a 2-page memo arguing that the information Mary provided regarding where she lives should

not be grounds for voiding the policy in the event she is involved in a car accident in Pennsylvania.

2. Assume the same facts set forth in Exercise 1 except that the accident occurs in New York City while Mary is at school. Write a 2-page memo arguing that the information Mary provided should be grounds for voiding the policy.

3. Assume the same facts set forth in Exercise 1 except that Mary has not yet been accepted to school when she applies for auto insurance and the policy is issued. Assume she later moves to New York City during the policy period but she does not inform the insurer that she has moved to New York City. Also assume that she has an accident in New York City. Write a 2-page memo arguing the insurer should not be permitted to void the policy when the loss related to the accident is tendered.

4. Assume the same facts set forth in Exercise 1 except that the insurer discovers Mary goes to school in New York City. Also assume the insurer does not seek to void the policy until Mary has an accident three months after the insurer learned Mary moved to New York City. Draft a 2-page memo arguing the insurer should not be permitted to void the policy.

IV. INTERMEDIARY (BROKER OR AGENT) LIABILITY

As the preceding materials demonstrate, insurance policies are generally issued and sold by corporations, with the exceptions being those policies underwritten by individuals through a Lloyd's association, such as Lloyd's of London. Individuals, corporations, and other organizations are the consumers and buyers of insurance. In the great majority of these transactions, the contracting parties never see or deal with each other directly. Although insurance is sometimes purchased directly from the insurer, a practice that has become more common in the Internet age, usually the parties—even if the transaction begins or ends on the Internet—deal through agents, brokers, and other intermediaries. Thus, the role of these intermediaries and the law governing their relationships with insurers and policyholders are extremely important. The most important body of law governing insurance intermediaries and their relationships is agency law. This section introduces some of the rules regarding the principal/agent relationship and the common kinds of legal problems arising in the context of insurance marketing.

ADEN V. FORTSH

776 A.2d 792 (N.J. 2001)

Opinion

The question presented in this appeal is whether a policyholder's failure to read his policy may be asserted as comparative negligence in a professional malpractice action against an insurance broker. In a published opinion, the Appellate Division reversed a jury verdict in favor of the insureds and held that the trial court should have instructed the jury on comparative negligence for the failure to read the policy. *Aden v. Fortsh,* 327 *N.J.Super.* 360, 743 *A.*2d 371 (App.Div.2000). We reverse.

In New Jersey, the comparative fault defense traditionally "will not apply in a plaintiff's suit alleging a professional's malpractice, at least in those cases in which the defendant argues that the plaintiff was at fault in failing to understand or to perform the task for which the professional was hired." Brian E. Mahoney, *New Jersey Comparative Fault and Liability Apportionment* § 6:2–10 at 119 (2001). We now hold that the comparative negligence defense is unavailable to a professional insurance broker who asserts that the client failed to read the policy and failed to detect the broker's own negligence. It is the broker, not the insured, who is the expert and the client is entitled to rely on that professional's expertise in faithfully performing the very job he or she was hired to do.

Facts

In September 1994, Benjamin and Beatrice Aden purchased a $48,000 condominium in Sussex County. Prior to closing, Benjamin Aden (Aden), a retiree, contacted Robert Fortsh, an insurance broker, to request insurance coverage for the new condominium. Fortsh had been the Adens' broker since about 1979, selling them a variety of insurance policies, including auto insurance, life insurance, health insurance, and homeowners' insurance for their previous home. Although Aden and Fortsh agree that they spoke on two occasions regarding the new policy, the parties dispute the substance of those conversations.

Aden testified that he asked Fortsh for "a policy that would cover any losses I might have in my condo" and told Fortsh he wanted the equivalent of "a homeowners' policy which happened to be [for] a condo." Aden further testified that Fortsh asked him two questions regarding the policy during their first conversation in the beginning of August 1994: first, the amount Aden paid for the condominium, which Aden told him was $48,000; and, second, the worth of his personal contents in the condominium, which Aden estimated at $16,000.

Aden testified that in their second conversation Fortsh offered him a policy with an annual premium of $98. Aden stated that Fortsh neither explained what the policy covered nor advised Aden to verify that his condominium association insurance policy provided coverage for losses that the policy issued by Fortsh did not. Aden accepted the policy but testified that he did not read it when he received it.

Fortsh's description of events was markedly different. He testified that when Aden first contacted him about insuring the new condominium, Aden asked for the "minimum policy requirements." Fortsh also testified that he instructed Aden to contact his condominium association to discover what type of coverage the association provided because, in Fortsh's experience, some association policies cover damages to both the exterior of the condominium and the interior or "dwelling," obviating the need for unit owners to purchase dwelling coverage. He then offered Aden a policy with a $120 annual premium from Prudential. According to Fortsh, Aden rejected that policy as too expensive after he consulted with his neighbors in the condominium development. Because of his longtime business relationship with the Adens, Fortsh testified that he tried to obtain a cheaper policy from a different insurer, the Hartford Insurance Company, through a different broker, Johl & Company. Fortsh noted that ordinarily he would not have made additional efforts because the initial quote of $120 was relatively inexpensive. Fortsh also indicated that he would have received a slightly higher commission if he provided a Prudential policy rather than a Hartford policy.

Nevertheless, Fortsh contacted Aden and offered him the Hartford policy with the $98 annual premium. Fortsh testified that he then read a computer printout containing the policy limits and again advised Aden to consult the condominium association policy to ensure that anything not covered under the Hartford policy would be covered under the association policy. Although the Hartford policy was less expensive than the initial Prudential policy offered to Aden, Fortsh testified that the coverage was the same.

There is no dispute that in September 1994, Aden sent Fortsh a check for $98 for the Hartford premium, as well as written authorization for Fortsh to apply for the policy on behalf of Aden. Fortsh completed the application for the Hartford policy and signed it with Aden's permission. Aden was not sent a copy of the application. The policy issued to the Adens provided $1,000 in coverage in the event of damages to their dwelling.

On cross-examination, Fortsh conceded that he did not verbally review with Aden the specific amount of dwelling coverage. Rather, Fortsh testified that when he returned the application for the Hartford policy, he left the box for dwelling coverage blank. The record is unclear with respect to how the amount of dwelling coverage became $1,000 under the policy since Fortsh left that portion of the application blank and the application itself is not included in the parties' appendices. In any event, Fortsh's deposition testimony, read to the jury during trial, indicated that he believed that dwelling coverage under the Hartford policy would be unnecessary because there should have been adequate coverage through Aden's condominium association policy. Fortsh testified that he himself never reviewed the condominium association policy to verify that belief. Fortsh also testified that he "assumed" that Aden read his association policy. The policy was renewed after a year.

In June 1996, a fire damaged the Adens' condominium. The damage caused to the exterior of the building was covered by the insurance provided under the condominium association policy. Nevertheless, Aden paid about $20,000 in repairs for damage to the interior of the building because, as noted, the Hartford policy provided for only $1,000 in dwelling coverage. Aden testified that he discovered the limited amount of coverage after the fire occurred, when he read his policy for the first time.

In October 1996, the Adens filed a complaint in the Law Division against Fortsh and Johl & Company for negligently failing to procure adequate insurance on the condominium. Prior to trial, the Adens settled with Johl & Company.

A two-day trial commenced in August 1998. In addition to the testimony of Aden and Fortsh, the jury heard from two expert witnesses. Plaintiffs' expert, Debra Stanton, an insurance agent, testified that the generally-accepted procedure by which an insurance broker procures a condominium insurance policy for a client is to review the insured's condominium association policy beforehand to determine what "the condominium association is agreeing to cover versus what they're making the unit owner responsible to cover." To that end, according to Stanton, a broker either should ask the client to obtain a copy of the condominium's master deed, or should directly contact the association to obtain the master deed which would indicate the coverage contained in the association policy.

Stanton testified that many, if not the majority of association policies will provide coverage for the exterior of the condominium but not the dwelling. If a copy of the association policy was not readily available, Stanton testified that her company would require the insured to purchase at least $10,000 worth of coverage. Because Fortsh did not review the Adens' master deed before procuring the policy, it was Stanton's opinion that he did not act in conformance with industry standards.

Defendant's expert, Armando Castellini, a licensed broker, testified that Fortsh acted in conformance with industry standards. Castellini testified that by advising Aden to review the master deed to find out whether there were any further insurance requirements, as Fortsh claimed to have done, Fortsh did what was expected of him. Furthermore, Castellini stated that it was not a prerequisite for a broker such as Fortsh to review the Adens' master deed prior to securing coverage for them. Had Fortsh failed to advise Aden to review the master deed, Castellini conceded that Fortsh would not have met industry standards. Conversely, if Fortsh attempted to review the master deed, Castellini claimed that would have been an inappropriate "attempt to interpret legal documents." Castellini also testified that if the dwelling coverage limits of the Adens' policy were increased to $48,000, the annual premium would have risen to $296 per year.

At the conclusion of the trial, the court charged the jury in part that the law imposes on the insurance broker the duty or obligation to have and to use that degree of skill and knowledge which insurance brokers of ordinary ability and skill possess and exercise in the representation of a client, such as the plaintiff Aden in this case. This is the standard by which to judge the defendant Fortsh in his placement and advice as to the insurance on this dwelling, condominium dwelling unit.

To find proximate cause it is not necessary that the negligence of the defendant Fortsh be the sole cause of the plaintiff Aden's harm. The law recognizes that in the case of insurance malpractice, there may be any number of factors that led to the plaintiff's harm. However, in order for the defendant Fortsh's conduct to be considered a proximate cause of the plaintiff Aden's harm, the negligence of the defendant Fortsh must have been a substantial factor in bringing about that harm or loss.

Now, defendant has offered testimony that the plaintiff Aden's own actions or inactions were the sole proximate cause of having virtually no interior structural and fixture insurance coverage for the fire damage to his condominium. If you find that defendant has proven by a preponderance of evidence that plaintiff was the sole proximate cause of this lack of insurance coverage, you will find in favor of defendant and dismiss plaintiff's case.

On the other hand, if you find that the plaintiff has proven by a preponderance of evidence the negligence of the defendant in providing inadequate and incomplete advice and procurement of insurance coverage, and that that was a substantial factor in bringing about the losses that occurred, and that some harm to the plaintiff was foreseeable from the defendant Fortsh's negligence, then you will find in favor of plaintiff.

Defense counsel had requested the court to charge the jury that "an insured is chargeable with knowledge of the contents of a policy" and that "an insured is chargeable with knowledge of the contents of a policy in the absence of fraud or inequitable conduct on the part of the insurer." The court, however, declined to accept that recommended charge. We accept, for purposes of this appeal, defense counsel's assertion that the recommended charge represented a request for an instruction in respect of comparative negligence.

During deliberations, the jury requested clarification on the meaning of proximate cause. In response, the court read back that portion of its instructions. The jury ultimately returned a unanimous 7–0 verdict in favor of the Adens. The parties had stipulated damages in the amount of $18,566. After calculating pre-judgment interest, the trial court entered judgment in the amount of $20,877.

The Appellate Division reversed, holding that the trial court erred in refusing to instruct the jury with respect to Aden's failure to read the policy. This Court granted certification. We now reverse the judgment of the Appellate Division and reinstate the verdict.

Analysis

Our Legislature abolished contributory negligence in favor of the doctrine of comparative fault by adopting the Comparative Negligence Act, *L.* 1973, *c.* 146. Section two of the Act currently states that in all negligence actions jurors are responsible for determining "[t]he extent, in the form of a percentage, of each party's negligence or fault." *N.J.S.A.* 2A:15–5.2. The Act applies to strict liability and negligence actions, including "civil actions for damages based upon theories of negligence, products liability, [and] professional malpractice whether couched in terms of contract or tort and like theories." *Ibid.* However, unlike the comparative negligence statutes of other states, our Legislature decided against requiring jurors, *and only jurors,* to resolve allegations of the plaintiff's negligence. Rather, the Legislature allowed our courts to retain the authority to establish a "policy-based preclusion" of the factfinder's consideration of the plaintiff's conduct. Mahoney, *supra,* § 5:7–1a at 86.

In recent years, the application of that policy-based preclusion has been most apparent in professional malpractice cases. Actions involving a breach of professional duty are not everyday negligence claims—they involve obligations arising from special relationships. Five years ago, a unanimous Court in *Conklin v. Hannoch Weisman,* 145 *N.J.* 395, 412, 678 *A.*2d 1060 (1996), observed that, "when the duty of the professional encompasses the protection of the client or patient from self-inflicted harm, the infliction of that harm is not to be regarded as contributory negligence on the part of the client." The view that comparative or contributory negligence generally may not be charged when a professional breaches his or her duty to a client reflects our heightened expectations of professional services in this State. *See, e.g., Conklin, supra,* 145 *N.J.* at 412, 678 *A.2d* 1060 (holding injured party's negligence not relevant in attorney malpractice action).

That is not to say that the conduct of the client in a professional malpractice action is irrelevant in other respects. Illustratively, *Conklin* noted that in an attorney malpractice action, "if a client or patient deliberately violates the professional's instructions with respect to self-care or heedlessly enters a transaction regardless of any instructions on the part of the professional, the trier of fact may find that there is no causal connection between the fault and the harm, or that the plaintiff failed to mitigate her damages as she should have. *See, e.g., McLister v. Epstein & Lawrence, P.C.,* 934 *P.2d* 844, 846–47 (Colo.App.1996) (noting that client's alleged negligence in professional malpractice action "relevant to the issue of causation, but would not present a proper basis for a comparative negligence instruction"). Thus, if the conduct of the client, rather than that of the professional, was the sole proximate cause of the alleged tort, a jury may conclude that the professional is not liable.

Similarly, comparative negligence principles may be applied in professional malpractice claims in which the client's alleged negligence, although not necessarily the sole proximate cause of the harm, nevertheless contributed to or affected the professional's failure to perform according to the standard of care of the profession. *Scioto Mem. Hosp. Ass'n. v. Price Waterhouse,* 74 *Ohio St.*3d 474, 659 *N.E.*2d 1268, 1274 (1996) (Cook, J. concurring) (noting that in accounting malpractice action "comparative negligence may be applied only to negligent acts of a client that contribute to the accountant's failure to perform according to the standards of the accounting profession. Other negligence by the client . . . is to be considered in the context of whether [the] damages proximately resulted from its own conduct. . . ."). *Cf. Rosenblum v. Adler,* 93 *N.J.* 324, 350–51, 461 *A.2d* 138 (1983) (observing in professional malpractice action that "[n]egligence of the injured party could bar or limit the amount of recovery under the Comparative Negligence Act"). Thus, if a client impedes the professional in his or her performance by, for example, withholding or failing to provide certain information to the professional concerning the matter for which the professional was hired that could have reduced a portion of the harm committed, the client's conduct may constitute comparative negligence unless the professionals' scope of employment included an obligation to prevent such conduct on the part of the client. *See* Hawkins, *Professional Negligence Liability of Public Accountants,* 12 *Vand. L.Rev.* 797, 811 (1959) (noting that in accountant malpractice actions "[t]here can be nothing unreasonable about plaintiff's conducting his affairs on the assumption that defendant is doing his job properly" but that plaintiff's conduct is relevant if it "goes beyond passive reliance and actually affects defendant's ability to do his job with reasonable care") (footnote omitted). A policy-based preclusion of the comparative negligence defense also may be unavailable depending on the level of knowledge the client has in the field of expertise of the particular professional. Moreover, the Comparative Negligence Act further serves to allocate fault among multiple defendants in professional malpractice cases.

Nevertheless, professionals may not diminish their liability under the Comparative Negligence Act when the alleged negligence of the client relates to the task for which the professional was hired. That rule is premised on the heightened responsibilities of professionals in this State. Otherwise, the fiduciary relationship between the professional and the client may be undermined and professionals may be allowed to escape liability for their malpractice. As one commentator has accurately summarized our law, "[i]n general, the comparative fault defense will not apply in a plaintiff's suit alleging a professional's malpractice, at least in those cases in which the defendant argues that the plaintiff was at fault in failing to understand or to perform the task for which the professional was hired." Mahoney, *supra,* § 6:2–10 at 119.

The import of the fiduciary relationship between the professional and the client is no more evident than in the area of insurance coverage. Insurance intermediaries in this State must act in a fiduciary capacity to the client " '[b]ecause of the increasing complexity of the insurance industry and the specialized knowledge required to understand all of its intricacies.' " *Walker v. Atl. Chrysler Plymouth, Inc.,* 216 *N.J.Super.* 255, 260, 523 *A.*2d 665 (App.Div.1987) (quoting *Sobotor v. Prudential Prop. & Cas. Ins. Co.,* 200 *N.J.Super.* 333, 341, 491 *A.*2d 737 (App.Div.1984)); *see also N.J.A.C. 11:17A–4.10* ("An insurance producer acts in a fiduciary capacity in the conduct of his or her insurance business."). The fiduciary relationship gives rise to a duty owed by the broker to the client "to exercise good faith and reasonable skill in advising insureds." *Weinisch v. Sawyer,* 123 *N.J.* 333, 340, 587 *A.*2d 615 (1991).

Accordingly, an insurance broker who agrees to procure a specific insurance policy for another but fails to do so may be liable for damages resulting from such negligence. *Rider v. Lynch,* 42 *N.J.* 465, 476, 201 *A.*2d 561 (1964). Liability resulting from the negligent procurement of insurance is premised on the theory that a broker "ordinarily invites [clients] to rely upon his expertise in procuring insurance that best suits their requirements." *Id.* at 477, 201 *A.*2d 561. The concept is essentially one of professional malpractice. A broker engaged to obtain insurance must exercise reasonable skill and "is expected to possess reasonable knowledge of the types of policies, their different terms, and the coverage available in the area in which his principal seeks to be protected." *Id.* at 476, 201 *A.*2d 561. Furthermore, if a broker "neglects to procure the insurance or if the policy is void or materially deficient or does not provide the coverage he undertook to supply, because of his failure to exercise the requisite skill or diligence, he becomes liable to his principal for the loss sustained thereby." *Ibid.; see also Restatement (Second) of Agency,* § 401 (1957) ("An agent is subject to liability for loss caused to the principal by any breach of duty.").

Before the advent of comparative fault in New Jersey, this Court held that an insured's failure to read the policy did not constitute contributory negligence in an action seeking damages because of a broker's failure to procure appropriate insurance coverage. *Rider v. Lynch, supra,* 42 *N.J.* at 482, 201 *A.*2d 561. In *Rider,* an eighteen-year-old with a limited ability to read English told a broker that she needed auto insurance for a car owned by her fiancé who gave her permission to use the car while he was out of state. 42 *N.J.* at 470–71, 201 *A.*2d 561. The broker issued a nonowner's insurance policy to her but did not explain the limitations under such a policy, namely, that the policy covered only automobiles not regularly used by the insured or any relative. *Id.* at 473–74, 201 *A.*2d 561. The coverage therefore was worthless to the woman and her family who planned to use the car on a regular basis, a fact the broker knew or should have known. *Id.* at 474, 201 *A.*2d 561. Neither the woman nor her step-father read the policy. *Id.* at 482, 201 *A.*2d 561. After her step-father was involved in an accident, the insurer denied coverage and the step-father brought suit on behalf of the daughter against the insurer and the broker. *Id.* at 468, 201 *A.*2d 561.

This Court reversed the dismissal of the plaintiff's claim against the broker, concluding that a factual question existed with regard to whether the broker breached his duty of care. The Court noted that because of the nature of the principal-agent relationship the broker was charged with the knowledge that the policy did not fit his client's need and, even if the broker was not aware of the limited policy coverage, he was under a duty to examine and reject the policy himself before delivering it to the woman. *Id.* at 481, 201 *A.*2d 561. The Court also observed:

> In passing, it should be said that failure of [the daughter] or the plaintiff to read the policy will not estop either of them from prosecuting a cause of action in negligence against [the broker]. Nor will such failure support a defense of contributory negligence. *In view of the relationship of principal and agent between [the daughter and the broker], she and her father were entitled to rely upon and believe that the broker had fulfilled his undertaking to provide the coverage impliedly agreed upon, and that the policy sent to them represented accomplishment of that undertaking.*

Id. at 482, 201 A.2d 561 (emphasis added).

The *Rider* decision is based on the sound policy that an insured in this State is entitled to assume that a broker has performed his or her fiduciary duty. That duty is not diminished when a policyholder fails to detect the broker's breach of that duty. *Ibid.; see also Winans-Carter Corp. v. Jay & Benisch*, 107 *N.J.Super.* 268, 272, 258 *A.2d* 131 (App.Div.1969) (holding that plaintiff's failure to read fire insurance endorsement did not contribute to defendant-broker's nonperformance).

Authoritative commentators on insurance law, leading jurisprudence encyclopedias, and other jurisdictions are in accord with that view. 12 Holmes, *Appleman on Insurance* 2d, § 87.3 (noting that allegations of failure to read policy "not really appropriate to insurance agency and brokerage liability where the question is fundamentally whether, considering all the facts, did the insured have the right to rely on the agent or broker?"); 3 *Couch on Insurance* § 46:69 (3d ed.) ("The insured's failure to read the policy has traditionally been held not to be a defense to an action against the agent for failure to procure insurance, on the reasoning that the principal is entitled to assume that the agent performed his or her duty. . . ."); 43 *Am.Jur.*2d Insurance § 141 ("[I]f an insurance agent or broker has failed to procure a policy which in terms and coverage is of the type specified by the insured, and the insured consequently suffers an uninsured loss, the agent or broker cannot successfully contend that he is relieved of liability by reason of any contributory negligence on the part of the insured in not having read and familiarized himself with the contents of the policy.").

In view of New Jersey's tradition of holding insurance professionals and other fiduciaries to higher standards, we conclude that Aden's failure to read the insurance policy cannot be asserted as comparative negligence in an action against the broker for negligent failure to procure insurance. As the *Rider* Court recognized, insureds are "entitled to rely upon and believe that the broker had fulfilled his undertaking to provide the coverage . . . agreed upon, and that the policy sent to them represented accomplishment of that undertaking." 42 *N.J.* at 482, 201 *A.*2d 561. To hold that an insured must read the policy, and therefore is not entitled to rely on the broker's expertise, is directly contrary to *Rider*. Such a holding also contradicts *Conklin* because it would make the insured responsible for "self-inflicted harm," despite the broker's express obligation to protect the insured from that harm.

This case demonstrates why a comparative negligence charge places undue emphasis on Aden's behavior rather than on Fortsh's negligence. By contacting Fortsh, Aden elected to obtain the services of a professional licensed by this State. Aden could have purchased his policy directly from the insurer. Brokers such as Fortsh, however, hold themselves out as having more knowledge than members of the public with regard to the insurance policies and coverage they procure. A broker is not an "order taker" who is responsible only for completing forms and accepting commissions. The expert testimony at trial, for instance, indicated that an insurance broker who elects to procure policies relating to condominiums has a duty to be aware that there is a strong possibility that the insured's condominium association may not provide coverage for the interior of the condominium. Aden's expert testified that it was Fortsh's duty, not Aden's, to ensure that the policy he was procuring for Aden provided a sufficient amount of dwelling coverage for the condominium. It was undisputed that Fortsh failed to meet that standard.

Our disposition does not prevent brokers from contending during trial that an insured's failure to read the policy severed the causal connection between the broker's fault and the insured's harm. That is precisely the argument defense counsel made in this case. The trial court did not preclude Fortsh from presenting evidence to attempt to prove that Aden's admission that he did not read the policy until after the fire was the proximate cause of the harm. The jury, however, rejected defense counsel's argument, a rejection supported by the evidence. Aden, *even had he read the policy,* would have been entitled to assume that the $1,000 in dwelling coverage was sufficient coverage in light of Fortsh's professional obligation to ensure that the condominium association policy and the policy he was procuring for Aden, in the aggregate, provided adequate coverage. Aden's failure to read the policy could not logically have been termed the direct cause of the malpractice.

Furthermore, we are of the view that the Legislature has intended the Comparative Negligence Act to apply to the conduct of victims of professional malpractice, but only to the extent that such conduct substantially contributed to the defendant's nonperformance. *Winans-Carter, supra,* 107 *N.J.Super.* at 272, 258 *A.*2d 131. In this case, for instance, had Aden told Fortsh that his personal contents were worth less than they actually were, or had he provided wrong or inadequate information to Fortsh, a comparative negligence charge would have been appropriate to allow the jury to apportion fault or reduce the amount that Aden could recover as a result of such conduct. Here, however, Aden's conduct was sufficiently remote to preclude Fortsh from raising it as an affirmative defense. Further, there is no evidence that Aden possessed any specialized knowledge in the area of insurance.

. . . .

Insurance consumers who instruct their brokers to provide coverage are entitled to have those instructions followed without regard to the insured's failure to detect the broker's negligent conduct.

Reversed.

NOTES AND QUESTIONS

1. *A Concise Review of Agency Law.* More attention to the law of agency is usually given in the standard law school course on business associations or introductory corporate law. The following discussion is a quick primer on the subject.

The principal/agent relationship involves the power of the former to affect the legal relationship of the latter with third parties. This power may be express; that is, it may arise from an agreement whereby the agent is expressly authorized to act on behalf of the principal. In the world of insurance, this agreement is usually in writing, but it can be oral. The principal/agent relationship also may be implied from the acts of the parties even though there is no express agreement. Whether the relationship is express or implied, the agent must reasonably believe she has the authority to act on behalf of the principal. Finally, implied authority also may be incidental to express authority because it is not always possible to cover every detail of the agent's power in the agreement. Whether the agent's authority is explicit or implicit, this authority constitutes actual authority and is to be distinguished from apparent authority. Apparent authority results from a manifestation by a person that another person is his agent. If the agent has neither actual nor apparent authority, as a general rule the agent cannot bind the insurer.

2. *Agents Versus Brokers.* Although the terminology is used loosely in common parlance, in the insurance industry the words "agent" and "broker" have distinct meetings. An "agent" usually refers to someone who has exclusive actual authority from *one* insurer, whereas a "broker" has actual authority, typically more limited with respect to each insurer, to act on behalf of *multiple* insurers. Because the insurance broker is a person who solicits and negotiates contracts of insurance on behalf of the consumer, the broker may have an agency relationship with the policyholder. In other words, the broker is a classic example of the dual agency in action. This is true even though the broker is compensated through a commission from the insurer.

3. *Agency Law Applied in Aden.* What kind of agency relationship existed in *Aden*? Did the agent's duties sound in contract, tort, or both? Does the answer make a difference when the argument that the policyholder did not read the policy is being asserted? Whatever the theory, the law is clear that an agent who undertakes to procure coverage may be liable for failing to do so. What is the standard of care, and does it make a difference if the underlying theory is contract or tort?

4. *Failure to Procure or Failure to Advise?* Suppose an agent recommends at the time of a policy's renewal that the policyholder delete a particular coverage on the ground that it is not needed. The policyholder follows the recommendation. The policyholder then suffers a loss that would have been covered but for the deletion. Should the policyholder be able to pursue a claim for negligent failure to procure insurance? Or, is the appropriate theory breach of a "duty to advise?" Is there a difference?

5. *Causation.* When the agent or broker fails to procure the "correct" coverage and the policyholder fails to read the policy, one question is whether the policyholder's failure breaks the causal connection between the agent or broker's breach of duty and the loss under the reasoning that the policyholder could have (and should have) prevented the problem. If the policyholder reads the policy and understands that it does not provide the expected coverage, should the policyholder lose the ability to make a winning claim against the broker?

Another causation question is lurking in some of the cases. In order to recover for a failure to procure, must the prospective policyholder prove that a policy substantially similar to what was applied for would have been issued but for the default of the agent? What if coverage like what the policyholder claims was expected is not available anywhere in the market at any price? Does it matter whether the cause of action is one for breach of contract or negligence? Further, must the proof show that an insurer which the agent had authority to bind would have issued the policy, or just that it was more probable than not that the policyholder would have obtained the type of policy or coverage applied for from some insurer?

A. SUING BOTH THE INSURER AND BROKER

As another example of how a policyholder can sue its broker if it is unclear whether the insurer or broker were at fault in failing to issue the proper coverage, consider the following lawsuit that was filed in state court in New Jersey.

COMPLAINT, JURY DEMAND AND DESIGNATION OF TRIAL COUNSEL

Plaintiffs International Fund Services (N.A.), L.L.C. ("IFS North America") and International Fund Services (Ireland) Limited ("IFS Ireland"), by and through their attorneys, K&L Gates LLP, bring this complaint against Defendants Atlantic Risk Specialists, Inc. ("ARS") and American International Specialty Lines Insurance Company ("AIG"), and allege as follows:

NATURE OF THE ACTION

1. This is an action to recover, from either its insurance broker, ARS, or its insurer, AIG, in excess of $2.75 million in defense costs that IFS Ireland has incurred in defending itself in a lawsuit related to a failed hedge fund.

2. In early 2003, IFS North America and IFS Ireland engaged their insurance broker, ARS, to procure an errors and omissions ("E&O") insurance policy to cover themselves and related entities. IFS North America and IFS Ireland provided a policy application to ARS that explicitly stated IFS North America and all of its related affiliates and subsidiaries, including IFS Ireland, were to be insured under the policy. ARS procured an E&O policy from AIG.

3. In February 2004, IFS Ireland was named a defendant in a lawsuit brought by investors in a hedge fund that IFS Ireland administered. When ARS tendered the lawsuit to AIG on behalf of IFS Ireland, AIG denied coverage on the grounds that IFS Ireland allegedly was not an insured under the policy issued by AIG.

4. Consequently, this action is being brought to adjudicate whether ARS or AIG is liable for the defense costs IFS Ireland incurred in the underlying actions related to the hedge fund. In short, because ARS was specifically instructed to procure an E&O policy that covered, among other entities, IFS Ireland, and an application for such coverage was submitted to and accepted by AIG, either AIG failed to list IFS Ireland as an insured under the E&O policy and improperly has denied coverage under the E&O policy or ARS is liable for IFS Ireland's defense costs due to its failure to procure an E&O policy that covers IFS Ireland.

PARTIES

5. Plaintiff International Fund Services (N.A.), L.L.C. is a Delaware limited liability company that maintains its principal place of business at 1290 Avenue of the Americas, New York, New York, and is authorized to conduct business in the State of New Jersey.

6. Plaintiff International Fund Services (Ireland) Limited is an Irish company that maintains its principal place of business at Bishop's Square, Redmond's Hill, Dublin 2, Ireland.

7. Defendant Atlantic Risk Specialists, Inc. is a New York corporation that maintains its principal place of business at I International Boulevard, Mahwah, New Jersey, and is licensed to conduct business, and is engaged in the business of acting as a commercial insurance broker, in the State of New Jersey.

8. Defendant American International Specialty Lines Insurance Company is an Alaska corporation that maintains its principal place of business at 70 Pine Street, New York, New York, and conducts business in the State of New Jersey.

JURISDICTION AND VENUE

9. This Court has personal jurisdiction over ARS because it is licensed to do business in this jurisdiction, transacts business in this jurisdiction, and/or contracts to supply services in this jurisdiction, including but not limited to, the procurement of policies of insurance.

10. This Court has personal jurisdiction over AIG because it transacts business in this jurisdiction and/or contracts to underwrite policies of insurance issued in this jurisdiction.

11. By virtue of the facts alleged in Paragraphs 7 and 8, venue is proper in Middlesex County.

FACTUAL BACKGROUND

ARS's Procurement of the E&O Policy

12. ARS is a commercial insurance broker.

13. ARS represents itself as "a full service wholesaler and managing general agent with offices in New Jersey, New York, and Florida. Our insurance professionals have many years of experience in all aspects of program management, underwriting, and brokerage sales. And, they're able to use these skills to develop innovative solutions for individual areas."[1]

14. ARS held itself out to IFS North America and IFS Ireland as a trusted advisor and a competent, highly skilled, and experienced insurance

---

[1] http://www.arspecialists.com (visited March 3, 2010).

brokerage company that would provide professional services to them in connection with the procurement of the Policy, intended for them to rely on such expertise and services, and understood that they were reasonably relying on its expertise and services.

15. IFS North America and IFS Ireland engaged ARS to be their insurance broker in connection with the procurement of insurance coverage, including the policy at issue.

16. ARS was paid a fee for these services.

17. At the time ARS was engaged as their insurance broker, IFS North America and IFS Ireland did not have their own insurance department, and consequently, they relied on ARS's expertise and services to procure the insurance requested.

18. ARS knew or should have known that IFS North America and IFS Ireland reasonably relied on ARS to provide its expertise and services, including the procurement of insurance coverage for all entities that they intended to have insured.

19. In connection with the procurement of the E&O policy at issue, and at ARS's direction, IFS North America and IFS Ireland completed and signed an Investment Management Insurance Renewal Application ("Application") on or about March 14, 2003.

20. On the line of the Application marked "Name of applicant," IFS North America and IFS Ireland wrote "INTERNATIONAL FUND SERVICES (NA) LLC & AFFILIATES."

21. IFS North America and IFS Ireland also attached to the Application a Schedule of Affiliates that were intended to be covered by the policy, which listed, among other entities, "International Fund Services (NA) LLC" and "International Fund Services (Ireland) Limited."

22. ARS understood at the time the E&O policy at issue was purchased that IFS North America and IFS Ireland intended for IFS Ireland to be covered under the policy.

23. Upon information and belief, AIG also understood at the time the E&O Policy was purchased that IFS North America and IFS Ireland intended to procure E&O insurance coverage for IFS Ireland.

24. In response to IFS North America and IFS Ireland's Application for E&O coverage, AIG issued Policy No. 324–33–89 for the policy period April 30, 2003, to April 30, 2004 (the "E&O Policy").

25. IFS North American and IFS Ireland paid a premium of $314,361 for the E&O Policy.

26. IFS North America and IFS Ireland did not, however, receive a copy of the E&O Policy until after the complaint was filed in the underlying actions at issue.

The E&O Policy

27. The E&O Policy states that the Named Insured is "INTERNATIONAL FUND SERVICES (N.A.), LLC (F/K/A INVESTMENT MANAGEMENT SERVICES, INC.)."

28. The E&O Policy states that the Application "and its attachments and the material incorporated therein" form a part of the Policy. E&O Policy, p.1.

29. The E&O Policy provides up to $10 million in insurance coverage in excess of a $200,000 self-insured retention.

30. Under the Policy, AIG promised, among other things, to indemnify the insured(s) with respect to defense costs, including the costs of investigation, adjusting, and administration, in connection with claims alleging liability because of the insured's rendering or failing to render administration services for others for compensation in the course of IFS Ireland's business as a hedge fund administrator. See E&O Policy, Insuring Agreement, pp. 2–3.

The Underlying Actions

31. On February 12, 2004, a lawsuit captioned *Pension Committee of the University of Montreal Pension Plan, et al. v. Banc of America Securities, LLC, et al.*, was filed against, among other parties, IFS Ireland, in the United States District Court for Southern District of Florida and subsequently transferred to the United States District Court for the Southern District of New York. On August 25, 2006, a Second Amended Complaint was filed.

32. On August 19, 2004, another lawsuit captioned *John Bruhl, et al v. PricewaterHouseCoopers International Limited II, et al.*, was filed against, among other parties IFS Ireland, in the United States District Court for the Southern District of Florida. On April 28, 2006, a Consolidated Second Amended Securities Class Action Complaint was filed in the case. The claims against IFS Ireland in this case subsequently were severed and transferred to the United States District Court for the Southern District of New York. (Collectively, the two underlying lawsuits are referred to hereinafter as the "Underlying Actions").

33. The plaintiffs in the Underlying Actions are a group of investors who purchased shares in a hedge fund, Lancer, Inc. ("Fund"). IFS Ireland served as the administrator of the Fund from September 2002 until July 2003. As the administrator of the Fund, IFS Ireland published the net asset

value of the Fund and disseminated such information to the Fund's investors on a monthly basis.

34. The underlying plaintiffs allegedly lost nearly all of their investments in the Fund.

35. In an attempt to recover their losses, the underlying plaintiffs asserted various claims in the Underlying Actions against IFS Ireland, alleging that (i) IFS Ireland had been required to value the Fund's portfolio properly and report the Fund's net asset value based on those valuations; (ii) IFS Ireland did not perform an independent valuation of the Fund's net asset value but instead relied on fraudulent valuations provided by others, which IFS Ireland then distributed to the plaintiffs; (iii) IFS Ireland received false documentation regarding the Fund's portfolio; and (iv) IFS Ireland should have noticed numerous problems with reports provided to it but used these false valuations to prepare net asset value statements that it distributed to the Fund's investors. See Second Amended Complaint, ¶¶ 376–83.

36. On October 29, 2008, following the close of discovery, the court in the Underlying Actions granted IFS Ireland's motion for summary judgment regarding all of the claims against IFS Ireland. The court determined that IFS Ireland could not have caused the plaintiffs' damages because (i) IFS Ireland became the administrator of the Fund only after the Fund had become worthless; (ii) no material change occurred in the Fund's portfolio after IFS Ireland became the administrator; and (iii) even if IFS Ireland had uncovered and disclosed the Fund's alleged scheme, the plaintiffs still would have been able to recover only pennies on the dollar.

37. Thus far, IFS Ireland has incurred costs in excess of $2.75 million in its defense of the Underlying Actions.

AIG's Denial of Coverage for the Lancer Claim

38. Following receipt of the complaint in the Underlying Actions, on behalf of IFS Ireland, ARS tendered the Underlying Actions to AIG for coverage under the E&O Policy.

39. After the Underlying Actions were tendered to AIG, AIG denied coverage and took the position that IFS Ireland is not a named insured under the E&O Policy and therefore no coverage is available to IFS Ireland for the Underlying Actions.

40. Notwithstanding AIG's denial of coverage, ARS contended that IFS Ireland was intended to be, and is, insured under the E&O Policy and that the E&O Policy provides insurance coverage to IFS Ireland for the Underlying Actions. Consequently, until December 2008, ARS, on IFS Ireland's behalf continued to negotiate with AIG in an attempt to resolve this coverage dispute.

41. Notwithstanding ARS's and IFS Ireland's requests for coverage for the Underlying Actions, AIG continues to deny that it has any coverage obligations to IFS Ireland and refuses to provide coverage for the Underlying Actions.

42. On March 10, 2009, ARS, IFS North America and IFS Ireland entered a one-year tolling agreement to toll and suspend all applicable statutes of limitations and repose periods relating to this matter.

43. As a result of ARS's failure to obtain coverage for IFS Ireland under the E&O Policy and/or AIG's refusal to perform its obligations under the E&O Policy, IFS Ireland has suffered substantial damages, including but not limited to all of the amounts it has expended defending itself in the Underlying Actions.

44. IFS Ireland has complied with all conditions precedent to recovery under the E&O Policy or, alternatively, all conditions precedent have been waived.

FIRST CAUSE OF ACTION

Broker Malpractice v. ARS

45. IFS North America and IFS Ireland incorporate by reference the allegations contained in the previous paragraphs in this Complaint as if fully set forth herein.

46. ARS provided professional insurance brokering and consulting services to IFS North America and IFS Ireland in connection with procurement of the E&O Policy.

47. ARS acted as IFS North America's and IFS Ireland's insurance broker in connection with the procurement of the E&O Policy.

48. ARS had an obligation to deal with IFS North America and IFS Ireland professionally and competently. This obligation arises out of the law as well as the contractual relationship between ARS and IFS North America and IFS Ireland.

49. ARS holds itself out as a trusted advisor and a competent, highly skilled, and experienced insurance brokerage company with the expertise to provide IFS North America and IFS Ireland with valuable and competent advice regarding their insurance coverage.

50. Under New Jersey law, as a professional with expertise in the field of insurance brokerage and consulting, ARS had a duty to act with the degree of skill and knowledge required of a reasonably prudent professional in the insurance brokerage field in order to procure the insurance requested and required by IFS North America and IFS Ireland.

51. IFS North America and IFS Ireland did not have their own insurance department at the time the E&O Policy was purchased and therefore, they relied on ARS's expertise and services.

52. IFS North America and IFS Ireland specifically applied for, and instructed ARS to procure, E&O insurance coverage for those entities listed on the Application, including IFS Ireland.

53. ARS understood at the time the E&O Policy was purchased that IFS North America and IFS Ireland intended to purchase E&O insurance coverage for IFS Ireland.

54. ARS owed IFS North America and IFS Ireland the duty to use reasonable diligence to make certain that the E&O Policy insured IFS Ireland.

55. ARS is a sophisticated insurance brokerage company and is or reasonably should be aware that the lack of insurance coverage for IFS Ireland under the E&O Policy would necessitate the purchase of other E&O insurance coverage for IFS Ireland.

56. At no time prior to the filing of the Underlying Actions did ARS inform IFS North America or IFS Ireland that IFS Ireland was not insured under the E&O Policy.

57. To the contrary, even after the filing of the Underlying Actions, despite AIG's contention that IFS Ireland was not insured under the E&O Policy, ARS contended that IFS Ireland was intended to be, and was, insured under the E&O Policy.

58. IFS North America and IFS Ireland have at all times been justified, and have acted reasonably, in relying upon ARS's insurance policy procurement services.

59. In the event that it is determined IFS Ireland is not an insured under the E&O Policy, then ARS failed to act with the degree of skill and knowledge required of a reasonably prudent professional in the insurance brokerage field in order to procure the insurance requested and required by IFS North America and IFS Ireland. Such acts and omissions of ARS constitute broker malpractice, as that term is understood in law, and have caused IFS North America and IFS Ireland to suffer substantial losses.

60. In the event that it is determined IFS Ireland is not an insured under the E&O Policy, then ARS engaged in broker malpractice, through acts and omissions, by and through its agents, servants, and/or employees, acting in the course and scope of their employment

61. As a direct and proximate result of ARS's broker malpractice, IFS North America and IFS Ireland have suffered damages.

WHEREFORE, IFS North America and IFS Ireland request judgment in their favor against ARS and awarding:

(1) Actual money damages including, but not limited to, all of the costs IFS Ireland has incurred and will incur defending itself in the Underlying Actions according to proof at trial;

(2) Reasonable attorneys' fees and costs incurred in this suit, pre-judgment and post-judgment interest; and

(3) Such other and further relief as the Court may deem just and proper.

. . . .

THIRD CAUSE OF ACTION

Breach of Contract v. ARS

73. IFS North America and IFS Ireland incorporate by reference the allegations contained in the previous paragraphs of this Complaint as if fully set forth herein.

74. Through a series of oral and written communications, IFS North America and IFS Ireland entered into a valid and binding contract with ARS under which ARS agreed to procure insurance coverage for IFS North America and IFS Ireland.

75. In return for providing these services, ARS was paid a substantial fee.

76. IFS North America and IFS Ireland specifically applied for, and instructed ARS to procure, E&O insurance coverage for those entities listed on the Application, including IFS Ireland.

77. At no time prior to the filing of the Underlying Actions did ARS inform IFS North America or IFS Ireland that IFS Ireland was not insured under the E&O Policy.

78. To the contrary, even after the filing of the Underlying Actions, despite AIG's contention that IFS Ireland was not insured under the E&O Policy, ARS contended that IFS Ireland was intended to be, and was, insured under the E&O Policy.

79. In the event that it is determined IFS Ireland is not an insured under the E&O Policy, then ARS breached its contractual and other obligations to IFS North America and IFS Ireland including, but not limited to, its duty to procure E&O insurance coverage for IFS Ireland.

80. As a direct and proximate result of ARS's breach of contract, IFS North America and IFS Ireland have suffered damages. ARS is liable to IFS North America and IFS Ireland for all damages in an amount to be proven at trial caused by ARS's breaches, including all incidental and consequential damages, together with costs and disbursements of this action, including, but not limited to, reasonable attorneys' fees, and pre- and post-judgment interest.

WHEREFORE, IFS North America and IFS Ireland request judgment in their favor against ARS and awarding:

(1) Actual money damages including, but not limited to, all of the costs IFS Ireland has incurred and will incur defending itself in the Underlying Actions according to proof at trial;

(2) Reasonable attorneys' fees and costs incurred in this suit, pre-judgment and post-judgment interest; and

(3) Such other and further relief as the Court may deem just and proper.

FOURTH CAUSE OF ACTION

Breach of Contract v. AIG

81. IFS North America and IFS Ireland incorporate by reference the allegations contained in the previous paragraphs of this Complaint as if fully set forth herein.

82. Thus far, IFS Ireland and has incurred costs in excess of $2.75 million in defending itself in the Underlying Actions

83. The Underlying Actions allege claims against IFS Ireland that are covered under the E&O Policy.

84. In material breach of the E&O Policy, AIG has refused to pay IFS Ireland's defense costs with respect to the Underlying Actions.

85. As a direct and proximate result of AIG's breach of contract, IFS Ireland has suffered damages.

WHEREFORE, Plaintiffs IFS North America and IFS Ireland request judgment in their favor against AIG and awarding:

(1) Specific performance of the E&O Policy issued by AIG;

(2) Compensatory damages including, but not limited to, reimbursement of all costs, including attorneys' fees, consultants' fees, and supplemental expenses, incurred by IFS Ireland in the investigation and defense of the Underlying Actions;

(3) Reasonable attorneys' fees, pursuant to R 4:42–9(a)(6), and costs incurred in this suit, pre-judgment and post-judgment interest; and

(4) Such other and further relief as the Court may deem just and proper.

FIFTH CAUSE OF ACTION

Declaratory Judgment v. AIG

86. IFS North America and IFS Ireland incorporate by reference the allegations contained in the previous paragraphs of this Complaint as if fully set forth herein.

87. An actual, present, and justiciable controversy exists between IFS Ireland and AIG with respect to IFS Ireland's rights and benefits, and AIG's duties and obligations under the E&O Policy with respect to the Underlying Actions. Specifically, IFS Ireland contends that AIG is obligated to pay IFS Ireland's defense and indemnity costs that IFS Ireland incurs in connection with the Underlying Actions under the E&O Policy.

88. AIG disputes that the E&O Policy provides insurance coverage to IFS Ireland for the Underlying Actions.

89. Declaratory relief from this Court will terminate some or all of the existing controversy between the parties.

90. A judicial declaration is necessary as to IFS Ireland's rights under the E&O Policy and the duties and obligations of AIG under the E&O Policy with respect to the Underlying Actions.

WHEREFORE, Plaintiffs IFS North America and IFS Ireland request judgment declaring that:

(1) IFS Ireland is an insured covered under the E&O Policy;

(2) AIG has a duty to pay IFS Ireland's defense and indemnity costs related to the Underlying Actions;

(3) AIG has a duty and obligation to pay all of IFS Ireland's attorneys' fees, consultants' fees, and supplemental expenses, incurred by IFS Ireland in the investigation and defense of the Underlying Actions;

(4) IFS Ireland is entitled to its reasonable attorneys' fees, pursuant to R 4:42–9(a)(6), and costs incurred in this suit, pre-judgment and post-judgment interest; and

(5) Such other and further relief as the Court may deem just and proper.

The relevant policy provisions provided:

Named Insured

International Fund Services (NA), LLC (F/N/A Investment Management Services, Inc.)

Preamble to Policy

"In consideration of the payment of the premium, and in reliance upon the statements made to American International Specialty Lines Insurance Company (herein called the "Company") by application forming a part hereof and its attachments and the material incorporated therein, the Company agrees as follows . . . ."

Additional Undisputed Facts

The insurance application contained an attachment that listed the requested "Insureds." International Fund Services (Ireland) Limited was included on the list.

The insurer's position was that it did not make a mistake in failing to include IFS Ireland as an insured under the policy, while the broker contended the insurer did make a mistake in failing to include IFS Ireland as an insured.

The policyholder was not provided a copy of the policy before the underlying claims were asserted against it.

The insurer would be liable to the policyholder under the policy if the policyholder was an insured under the policy.

NOTES AND QUESTIONS

1. Why did the policyholder sue both the insurer and broker instead of just the broker?

2. Why was the lawsuit filed in New Jersey instead of New York even though all of the parties had a New York connection?

3. How strong is the argument that the application was incorporated into the policy by reference (and thus IFS Ireland was an additional insured because it was listed as an insured for whom coverage was sought)?

4. Whose responsibility was it to make sure IFS Ireland was listed as an insured in the policy (e.g., the broker, the policyholder, or the insurer)?

5. The parties agreed to litigate the dispute with only limited discovery (i.e., just the production of documents and interrogatories). Why would each party in the case agree to such an approach?

6. What do you think was the just outcome of the dispute: A) the insurer and the broker are equally liable, B) the insurer is solely liable, C) the broker is solely liable, or D) neither the insurer nor the broker are liable?

EXERCISES

1. Draft a 3-page memo setting forth the policyholder's best arguments under New Jersey law regarding why the broker should be liable.

2. On behalf of the insurer, draft a 2-page memo in response to the arguments set forth in Exercise 1.

V. RULES OF INSURANCE POLICY INTERPRETATION

Despite the fact that insurance policies are not mutually drafted and the policyholder essentially has no input into the language contained in insurance policies, the rules of contract interpretation still generally apply to insurance policies. That being said, contract law, as a general body of law, has struggled with legal issues arising out of the use of standardized forms—essentially since those forms first appeared on the scene. Nowhere is that struggle more evident or acute than in the field of insurance law. When the social importance of insurance contracts is added to the mix, and when the reality sinks in that some kinds of insurance are mandatory due to powerful public policy considerations (compulsory auto liability insurance is the most prominent example), the pressures that exist on traditional rules of insurance policy interpretation are neither surprising nor especially hard to discern—at least when one is looking for them. These aspects of insurance contracts undermine the legal fiction that insurance policies are arm's length transactions negotiated by two willing parties, but courts generally treat insurance policies as a species of standardized contracts of adhesion.

There are exceptions to this general rule in areas where the government is providing the insurance and the insurance functions more like a benefit, such as is the case with Social Security, Medicare and Medicaid, and unemployment compensation. In these areas, administrative law plays a significant role. Similarly, if the insurance is provided as a benefit of employment, as is the case with most private health insurance and a great deal of life and disability insurance, then ERISA (the Employee Retirement Income Security Act of 1974) applies, and it differs some from the common law contract laws that apply when the insurance is sold by private companies outside the employment context even though the insurance in question is sold by a private company that is not a party to the employer-employee relationship. ERISA will be discussed more fully in Chapter 9.

Outside of these limited contexts, courts apply state common law rules regarding the interpretation of contracts to insurance policies with two notable exceptions: 1) courts typically apply a strict liability version of *contra proferentem*, and 2) the reasonable expectations doctrine. These two nuanced doctrines have led to some counterintuitive case results which we will explore in the remainder of this chapter.

A. GENERAL RULES

The basic principles regarding the interpretation of insurance policies are generally the same as the rules of contract interpretation:

> The interpretation of insurance policies is a question of law. The provisions of a policy that grant coverage are construed broadly, while the provisions that exclude or limit coverage are construed narrowly. Exclusions should not be interpreted in a way that allows them to swallow the basic coverage provided. The insurer

> has the burden of proving that exclusions eliminating or reducing coverage apply. Courts construe policy language with the purpose of the insurance in mind as a layman would understand the terms. Consequently, when interpreting policies, courts often refer to standard dictionaries, as opposed to technical insurance industry understandings or definitions of the terms.
>
> Another basic rule of insurance policy interpretation is that, if possible, the various provisions in the policy should be interpreted to reconcile them and give effect to all of them. In essence, this rule means that courts should give effect to all of the policies' provisions if possible and should do so in a way that is consistent with the general purpose of the policy as a whole.

Christopher C. French, *Understanding Insurance Policies as Non-Contracts: An Alternative Approach to Drafting and Construing These Unique Financial Instruments*, 89 Temp. L. Rev. 535, 553–54 (2017) (citations omitted).

The next case is an example of a court applying these general rules of contract interpretation in the insurance context.

FIREMAN'S FUND INSURANCE CO. V. ALLSTATE INSURANCE CO. ET AL.

234 Cal. App. 3d 1154 (1991)

Opinion

NICHOLSON, ASSOCIATE JUSTICE.

. . . .

Plaintiff Fireman's Fund Insurance Company (Fireman's) appeals from a judgment entered in favor of defendants Allstate Insurance Company (Allstate) and Northbrook Property and Casualty Insurance Company (Northbrook) following a court trial in Fireman's declaratory relief action. Fireman's issued a commercial automobile liability policy to a group of independent truckers. Although the truckers discontinued Fireman's coverage and substituted other insurance at the same policy limits, Fireman's failed to give the required notice of cancellation to the PUC. Thus, we conclude Fireman's policy was in full force and effect on the date of the accident giving rise to damage claims. . . . We also conclude the trial court properly found the Allstate and Northbrook policies did not cover the highway carrier as an additional insured. Accordingly, we affirm the judgment.

FACTUAL AND PROCEDURAL BACKGROUND

Lisa DeNoon and her passenger, Stephanie White, were seriously injured on May 29, 1985, when a tractor-trailer rig jumped the center divider on the Yolo Causeway and collided with DeNoon's vehicle. Ultimately, a personal injury action was filed on behalf of the two women against shipper Spring Air Mattress (owner of the trailer), carrier Better Home Deliveries, Leaseway Transportation Corporation (Better Home's parent company), sub-carrier Richardson Trucking (owner of the tractor), Timothy Gerk (the truck driver), and various entities involved in construction work being done on the Yolo Causeway at the time of the accident. A coverage dispute developed among three of six insurers involved in the personal injury litigation and resulted in the declaratory relief action now before us on appeal. DeNoon settled for more than $6 million. White settled for $267,500.

. . . .

On the date of the accident, Leaseway and Better Home were insured by a $1 million primary policy issued by Allstate and a $5 million excess policy issued by Northbrook.

Richardson Trucking secured insurance through a program administered by Better Home and Leaseway for truckers who contracted with Better Home. Richardson Trucking was covered by a $1 million primary policy, No. KLA 321 44 96, issued by Fireman's to "Independent Contractors of Better Home Deliveries, Inc.," for two policy periods beginning July 1, 1983, and ending July 1, 1985. Harold Lang, the insurance and risk manager for Leaseway, discontinued Fireman's policy and replaced it with a $1 million primary policy issued by Central National Insurance Company to "Specified Independent Contractors of Leaseway," effective November 1, 1984. Central National defended Richardson Trucking, paid its policy limits, and has not contested coverage.

Although Fireman's filed a certificate of insurance with the PUC on August 27, 1984, shortly after the beginning of the second policy period, certifying its policy, KLA 321 44 96, was effective July 1, 1984, until cancelled, it did not notify the PUC of cancellation. There is no record of Central National filing a certificate of replacement insurance with the PUC. . . .

Fireman's filed this action seeking a declaration Richardson Trucking had no coverage under its policy, No. KLA 321 44 96, for claims arising from the DeNoon/White personal injury action. Fireman's alleged the policy was terminated on November 1, 1984, and replaced by the Central National policy which became effective on that same date. Allstate and Northbrook filed a cross-complaint alleging Fireman's failure to comply with PUC cancellation requirements resulted in the policy, No. KLA 321 44 96, remaining in effect to its $1 million limits. The cross-complaint also alleged the Allstate and Northbrook policies never covered Richardson Trucking or its driver, Timothy Gerk. Allstate and Northbrook maintained they were entitled to recover $750,000 from Fireman's.

Fireman's moved for summary judgment and summary adjudication of issues. Allstate and Northbrook filed a similar cross-motion. The trial court denied Fireman's motion in its entirety. It ruled Fireman's policy provided $1 million in coverage to Richardson Trucking on May 29, 1985, as excess above the Central National policy. The court also found Fireman's policy limits would have to be exhausted before the Allstate and Northbrook policies would come into effect.

. . . .

The case proceeded to trial. In an 18-page ruling, the trial court found "[t]he provisions of the Public Utilities Code, General Order 100–K and the certificate of insurance itself, provide that the policy and the Certificate of Insurance are not cancelable and remain in full force and effect until the required notice is given to the Public Utilities Commission." In its order the court determined:

> "1. The policy of insurance of FIREMAN'S FUND INSURANCE COMPANY, policy No. KLA 321 44 96 was in full force and effect on May 29, 1985.
>
> 2. The policy limits of the FIREMAN'S FUND policy in effect on May 29, 1985 were $1,000,000.
>
> 3. The FIREMAN'S FUND insurance policy was obligated to indemnify Richardson Trucking for any damages that may have been awarded against Richardson Trucking in the action filed by Lisa Renee DeNoon, by and through her Guardians ad Litem, Ray DeNoon and Stephanie White, and its obligation extended to the full policy limits of $1,000,000.
>
> 4. The FIREMAN'S FUND policy provided primary coverage.
>
> 5. The policies of insurance from ALLSTATE INSURANCE COMPANY, policy No. 05009501, and NORTHBROOK PROPERTY AND CASUALTY INSURANCE COMPANY, policy No. UEL0310283, do not provide coverage to Richardson Trucking for the damages arising out of the May 29, 1985 accident. . . ."

Fireman's appeals and contends its policy did not provide coverage on May 29, 1985, and, if it did provide coverage, that coverage was (1) excess to all other coverage available to Richardson Trucking, (2) co-excess with the Northbrook policy, or (3) limited to the minimum PUC requirement. It therefore asserts Richardson Trucking was covered by the Allstate and Northbrook policies. . . .

DISCUSSION

. . . .

III. *The Allstate and Northbrook Policies*

Fireman's also challenges the trial court's determination the Allstate and Northbrook policies issued to Better Home and Leaseway did not provide coverage to Richardson Trucking for damages arising from the DeNoon/ White accident. . . .

The parties agree the Allstate policy defines coverage provided by the $5 million excess policy issued by Northbrook. Endorsement 3 of the Northbrook policy provides Northbrook coverage is "at least as broad" as the coverage provided by the $1 million primary policy issued by Allstate. Because "[a]n insurance policy is, fundamentally, a contract between the insurer and the insured. . . ." (*Stein v. International Ins. Co.* (1990) 217 Cal.App.3d 609, 613, 266 Cal.Rptr. 72), we must first examine the language of the Allstate policy to determine the obligations the parties have assumed.

" 'The interpretation of an insurance policy, like any other contract, is a matter of law as to which a reviewing court must make its own independent determination.' " (*State Farm Fire & Casualty Co. v. Lewis* (1987) 191 Cal.App.3d 960, 963 [236 Cal.Rptr. 807].) " 'As a general rule, ambiguities and uncertainties in a policy of insurance are resolved in favor of the insured.' " (*Gray v. Zurich Insurance Co.* (1966) 65 Cal.2d 263, 269 [54 Cal.Rptr. 104, 419 P.2d 168].) An insurance policy is not rendered ambiguous or uncertain, however, because of a strained or grammatically incorrect reading of the policy's terms. (*Atlas Assurance Co. v. McCombs Corp.* (1983) 146 Cal.App.3d 135, 144 [194 Cal.Rptr. 66].) "Although we construe all provisions, conditions, or exceptions that tend to limit liability strictly against the insurer [citation], strict construction does not mean strained construction. We may not, under the guise of strict construction, rewrite a policy to bind the insurer to a risk that it did not contemplate and for which it has not been paid." (*Safeco Ins. Co. v. Gilstrap* (1983) 141 Cal.App.3d 524, 532–533 [190 Cal.Rptr. 425].) The words used in a policy of insurance are to be construed according to the plain meaning a layman would ordinarily attach to them, and the policy is to be construed as a whole, each clause helping to interpret the other. (*McBride v. Farmers Ins. Group* (1982) 130 Cal.App.3d 258, 260–261 [181 Cal.Rptr. 539].) "In short, an insurance contract is to be construed in a manner which gives meaning to all its provisions in a natural, reasonable, and practical manner, having reference to the risk and subject matter and to the purposes of the entire contract." (*Barrett v. Farmers Ins. Group* (1985) 174 Cal.App.3d 747, 750–751 [220 Cal.Rptr. 135].)

The Allstate policy must also be considered in light of the expectations of Leaseway, Better Home, and Allstate as to the extent of coverage. "[T]he intent and meaning of the parties is far more important than the strict literal sense of the words used in the contract. For that reason it is equally important to consider the subject matter of insurance and the purpose or object which the parties had in view at that time. *It is also proper to consider the business of the parties, the circumstances surrounding the making of a contract, the situation of the property,* and all other conditions which have a legitimate bearing upon the intention of the parties." (*Dart Transportation Service v. Mack Trucks, Inc.* (1970) 9 Cal.App.3d 837, 847, 88 Cal.Rptr. 670) (emphasis added).

Here, Leaseway's insurance and risk manager said he had many discussions with people at Leaseway and Allstate about the effect the Allstate policy would have on subhaulers. Leaseway's insurance premium was based on actual losses with retroactive premiums charged if money had to be paid to claimants such as DeNoon. Thus, it was never Leaseway's intent to cover subhaulers, such as Richardson Trucking, which provided their own insurance. Dennis Richardson, owner of Richardson Trucking, knew he carried the $1 million in liability insurance required by his contract with Better Home, but was unaware he was covered by any other insurance policies at the time of the accident.

The language of the Allstate policy is consistent with Leaseway's intent to exclude Richardson from coverage. Under "Who Is Insured," the truckers's endorsement reads:

> 1. *You* are an *insured* for any covered *auto.*
>
> 2. Anyone else is *insured* while using with *your* permission a covered *auto you* own, hire or borrow except:
>
> a. The owner of a covered *private passenger type auto you* hire or borrow from one of *your* employees or agents or a member of his or her household;
>
> b. Someone using a covered *auto* while he or she is working in a business of selling, servicing, repairing or parking *autos* unless that business is *yours.*
>
> c. Anyone other than *your* employees, a lessee or borrower or any of their employees, while moving property to or from a covered *auto.*
>
> 3. The owner or anyone else from whom *you* hire or borrow a covered *auto* which is a *trailer* is an *insured* while the *trailer* is connected to another covered *auto* which is a power unit, or, if not connected:
>
> a. Is being used exclusively in *your* business as a *trucker,* and
>
> b. Is being used pursuant to operating rights granted to *you* by a public authority.

> 4. The owner or anyone else from whom *you* hire or borrow a covered *auto* which is not a *trailer* is an *insured* while the covered *auto*:
>
> a. Is being used exclusively in *your* business as a *trucker,* and
>
> b. Is being used pursuant to operating rights granted to *you* by a public authority."

(Italics in original.)

. . . .

Here, Leaseway intended to exclude subhaulers from coverage. We may not infer the insureds granted Richardson Trucking permissive use of its own fully insured vehicle.

This view of the policy is reinforced by an examination of paragraphs 3 and 4, quoted above. These paragraphs speak to hirings from the owner of a covered auto. They discuss coverage for the owner or anyone else from whom the carrier hires or borrows trailers (par. 3) or autos that are not trailers (par. 4). Paragraph 4 speaks precisely to the situation where a carrier hires a covered auto, which is not a trailer, from the owner. In our view, this provision, not paragraph 2, reasonably applies to the present situation since, as has been said, we would not expect the carrier to grant permission to the owner to use the owner's own covered auto.

Under paragraph 4, the owner of the vehicle, Fireman's argues, is covered by Better Home and Leaseway's Allstate policy (Richardson) as an insured only "while the covered auto: a. Is being used exclusively in your business as a trucker, and b. Is being used pursuant to operating rights granted to you by a public authority." Richardson fulfills neither of these conditions. The trial court had before it evidence that Richardson was free to use the tractor for any other business. Moreover, Richardson was operating under its own PUC permit, not that of Better Home or Leaseway. For these reasons, we affirm the trial court's finding Richardson Trucking was not an additional insured under the Allstate and Northbrook policies.

. . . .

For these reasons, we affirm the trial court's finding Richardson Trucking was not an additional insured under the Allstate and Northbrook policies.

. . . .

DISPOSITION

The judgment is affirmed.

B. *CONTRA PROFERENTEM*

The doctrine of *contra proferentem* provides that any language in a contract that is unclear or ambiguous should be construed against the drafter of the language.[4] In the insurance context, because insurers draft the policies, any ambiguities should be construed against them. The test in many states for determining whether policy language is ambiguous is whether the provisions at issue are reasonably or fairly susceptible to different interpretations or meanings. If the policyholder and insurer both offer reasonable interpretations, then the policy language is ambiguous and should be construed in favor of coverage. Where the controversy involves a term or phrase that has generated many lawsuits with inconsistent results, many courts view the inconsistent results as indicia that the policy language is ambiguous.

Unlike in typical contract disputes where *contra proferentem* essentially serves as a tiebreaker when ambiguous policy language cannot be conclusively clarified by extrinsic evidence, most courts simply construe any ambiguities in the policy language against the insurer and in favor of coverage. For this reason, the application of *contra proferentem* to ambiguous policy language in insurance cases has been described as strict liability for the insurer.

To initially determine whether policy language is ambiguous, courts in some states will consider extrinsic evidence as opposed to just the policy language itself. If the court determines that the policy language is ambiguous, either on its face or when applied to the facts of the case, then it also will consider extrinsic evidence, if it exists, to clarify the meaning of the policy language. If the extrinsic evidence does not clarify the meaning, then the court will resolve the ambiguities in favor of the policyholder. Under the last step of this approach, the courts treat insurance policies like traditional contracts and the doctrine essentially serves as a tiebreaker to resolve ambiguities. In the absence of extrinsic evidence regarding the drafting intent, which is typically the case, the language is construed against the insurer.

The next case is an example of a court applying *contra proferentem* in the insurance context.

HECLA MINING CO. V. NEW HAMPSHIRE INSURANCE CO.

811 P. 2d 1083 (Colo 1991)

Opinion

JUSTICE ERICKSON delivered the Opinion of the Court.

We granted certiorari to review *New Hampshire Insurance Co. v. Hecla Mining Co.,* 791 P.2d 1154 (Colo.App.1989), which held that a

[4] The introduction to this subchapter regarding *contra proferentem* is taken verbatim from Christopher C. French, *Understanding Insurance Policies as Non-Contracts: An Alternative Approach to Drafting and Construing These Unique Financial Instruments,* 89 Temp. L. Rev. 535, 555–57 (2017) (citations omitted).

comprehensive general liability insurance policy did not require an insurer to defend an action for damages for pollution resulting from the insured's mining activities. We reverse and remand with directions.

In 1983, the state of Colorado (state) filed suit in federal district court under the Comprehensive Environmental Response, Compensation and Liability Act of 1980 (CERCLA), 42 U.S.C. §§ 9601, 9607 (1983 & 1990 Supp.), against Asarco, Inc., Resurrection Mining Company, and the Res-Asarco Joint Venture.[1] The state alleged that the defendants were jointly and severally liable under the strict liability provisions of CERCLA, and under common-law negligence theories, for the cleanup costs and other damages resulting from the discharge of heavy metals and other contaminants into California Gulch from the Yak Tunnel. The state filed an amended complaint in April 1985, seeking compensation for the cleanup costs for the entire California Gulch drainage basin system.

The state's CERCLA complaint was initiated after employees of Asarco caused a surge of yellow sedimentary sludge to emit from the Yak Tunnel when shoring timbers and accumulated debris were removed that had impounded the contaminated water.[3] The yellow sedimentary sludge emitted from the Yak Tunnel was a limonitic precipitate, formed by ferric hydroxide and a variety of ferric sulfates, that accumulated on the bottom of the drainage tunnel. The surge of contaminated water turned a twenty-mile stretch of the Arkansas River orange.

In January 1985, Resurrection, Asarco, and Res-Asarco Joint Venture filed a third-party complaint against Hecla Mining Company. The complaint against Hecla seeks contribution for alleged discharges into the Yak Tunnel that occurred from 1938 to 1953 when Hecla was a shareholder and had a one-third ownership interest in the Resurrection Mining Company. The Resurrection Mining Company mined gold, silver, and lead ore at the Resurrection mine. Two of Resurrection's mine shafts connect with and drain into the Yak Tunnel. From 1981 to 1985, Hecla also held a lease interest in a mill and several tailings impoundments located in the lower California Gulch.

---

[1] CERCLA creates statutory liability for present and former owners of hazardous waste disposal sites, transporters of hazardous wastes, and those who arrange for the transport and disposal of hazardous waste. 42 U.S.C. § 9607. Under CERCLA, any party with an ownership interest in the site responsible for the release of contaminants can be held strictly liable regardless of fault or intent. *Id.* The liability under CERCLA is joint and several, regardless of each party's degree of fault or responsibility for the creation of the hazardous condition. *Id.*

[3] A "surge" is a sudden release of water that has been impounded in a mine tunnel. A surge is of short duration and generally produces a high flow of water. When a tunnel is properly maintained as part of the ongoing mining operations, surges do not occur, although once maintenance stops, roof rock and timbers collapse, creating debris barriers, impounding water that has seeped into the tunnel. When the hydraulic pressure becomes high enough, the impounded water bursts the debris barrier and a surge results. Flow rates and volumes of a surge are unpredictable.

Industrial Indemnity Company provided a series of comprehensive general liability (CGL) insurance policies covering Hecla from January 1, 1974, through January 1, 1982. New Hampshire Insurance Company provided a series of one year CGL insurance policies for Hecla from January 1, 1980, through January 1, 1985. Hecla requested that both Industrial and New Hampshire provide a defense against the joint venture's third-party complaint. Industrial denied coverage and filed a declaratory judgment action in Denver District Court to obtain a judicial determination of whether it had a duty to defend the third-party claim, and whether it had a duty to indemnify Hecla for any liability resulting from the lawsuit. New Hampshire originally agreed to defend Hecla, subject to a reservation of its right to deny coverage. New Hampshire later denied coverage and intervened in the declaratory judgment action brought by Industrial.

The district court entered summary judgment in favor of Hecla, finding that Industrial and New Hampshire had a duty to defend Hecla in the CERCLA action, and that the issue of the duty to indemnify was not ripe for resolution. The court of appeals reversed the district court, holding that Hecla knew or should have known of a substantial probability that its mining activities would result in environmental damage, and therefore the resulting damage was not an unexpected and unintended occurrence and was thus outside the scope of Hecla's coverage. The court of appeals concluded that neither Industrial, nor New Hampshire, had a duty to defend or to indemnify Hecla for liability resulting from pollution generated by its mining activities. We hold that under the terms of Hecla's CGL policies, both Industrial and New Hampshire have a duty to defend Hecla against the state's CERCLA action. The issue of Industrial's or New Hampshire's duty to indemnify Hecla can only be determined after liability of Hecla has been determined, and is therefore not ripe for resolution at this stage of the proceedings.

I.

The CGL insurance policies issued to Hecla by Industrial and New Hampshire limit defense and liability coverage to property damage caused by an occurrence. The word "occurrence" is defined in Hecla's policies as: "an accident, including continuous or repeated exposure to conditions, which result in bodily injury or property damage, neither expected nor intended from the standpoint of the insured." *See* Fire Casualty & Surety Bulletin, Aat-1 (1986) (commenting on CGL coverage forms and interpretations of occurrence and claims-made trigger provisions). Hecla's policies also contain exclusions that limit the scope of coverage as defined in the insuring agreement. The pertinent exclusion at issue here is: "*This insurance does not apply* . . . to bodily injury or property damage arising out of the discharge, dispersal, release or escape of smoke, vapors, soot, fumes, acids, alkalis, toxic chemicals, liquids or gases, waste materials or other irritants, contaminants, pollutants into or upon land, the atmosphere or any water course or body of water; *but this exclusion does not apply if such discharge,* dispersal, release or escape *is sudden and accidental* . . . ." (Emphasis added). This CGL policy provides defense and liability coverage for damage that results from an unexpected and unintended occurrence, not including damage caused by the discharge of pollution, unless that discharge is sudden and accidental.

Hecla contends that the discharge of heavy metals into California Gulch was neither an expected, nor intended, consequence of its mining activity, and that although the discharge of heavy metals constitutes pollution, the discharge was sudden and accidental. Hecla therefore contends that both Industrial and New Hampshire are liable for defense and indemnification costs associated with the state's CERCLA action.

Industrial and New Hampshire both contend that the contamination of California Gulch was reasonably foreseeable and thus was expected and not an occurrence under the terms of Hecla's policies. Industrial and New Hampshire argue that even if this court determines that the damage was unexpected and unintended, the discharge of pollution was not sudden and accidental and is therefore not covered under the CGL insurance policies.

A.

The court of appeals concluded that the damage caused by Hecla's mining operations was not unexpected, and therefore was not an occurrence covered by Hecla's insurance policies. The court of appeals reasons were that:

> The results of one's intentional acts cannot be unexpected if they are the ordinary consequences of those acts. Here, Hecla knew or should have known of a substantial probability that its mining activities would result in environmental damage. The Colorado Mined Land Reclamation Act, § 34–32–101, 14 C.R.S. (1984), expresses the General Assembly's intent to "aid in the protection of wildlife and aquatic resources . . . and promote the health, safety, and general welfare of the people of this state." Section 34–32–102, 14 C.R.S. (1984). . . . Thus, absent a contrary showing, the Act provides constructive notice to all mine operators that their activities could cause environmental damage. . . . Accordingly, the damage that occurred was an ordinary consequence of Hecla's actions. As a matter of law, it was not unexpected.

New Hampshire Ins. Co. v. Hecla Mining Co., 791 P.2d at 1157 (citations omitted).

The court of appeals reasoning is in error. The Colorado Mined Land Reclamation Act does not provide notice to all mine operators that mining could cause environmental damage. The court of appeals, in interpreting the Mined Land Act, failed to consider the entire section on which it relied for its holding. Section 34–32–102, 14 C.R.S. (1984), begins:

> It is declared to be the policy of this state that the extraction of minerals and the reclamation of land affected by such extraction are both *necessary and proper activities*. It is further declared to be the policy of this state that *both such activities should be and are compatible*. It is the intent of the general assembly by the enactment of this article to allow for the continued development of the mining industry of this state, while requiring those persons involved in mining operations to reclaim land affected by such operations. . . .

(Emphasis added). Contrary to the court of appeals analysis, the Mined Land Act proclaims that mining is a necessary and proper activity, and should be promoted by the state of Colorado.

Hecla's CGL insurance policies provide that an occurrence is an accident that is neither expected nor intended from the standpoint of the insured. In *City of Johnstown v. Bankers Standard Insurance Co.*, 877 F.2d 1146 (2nd Cir.1989), the Second Circuit held that damages are only intended if the insured knew that they would flow directly and immediately from the insured's intentional act. The Second Circuit said:

> In general, what make injuries or damages expected or intended rather than accidental are the knowledge and intent of the insured. It is not enough that an insured was warned that damages might ensue from its actions, or that, once warned, an insured decided to take a calculated risk and proceed as before. Recovery will be barred only if the insured intended the damages, or if it can be said that the damages were, in a broader sense, "intended" by the insured because the insured knew that the damages would flow directly and immediately from its intentional act . . . .

Id. at 1150 (citations omitted). We are persuaded by the Second Circuit and hold that the phrase "neither expected nor intended" should be read only to exclude those damages that the insured knew would flow directly and immediately from its intentional act.

The state's CERCLA complaint contains claims asserting strict liability. The third-party complaint against Helca does not allege that Hecla expected or intended environmental damage to result from its mining operations. There is no allegation and no proof that the damage caused by Hecla was expected or intended. The incident therefore must be deemed an occurrence under the terms of the CGL policies for the purposes of determining the insurers' duty to defend.

B.

Indemnity and New Hampshire contend that even if the discharge is an occurrence covered by the policies, the discharge is subject to the exclusionary clause because it was not a sudden and accidental discharge, but rather occurred continuously for a period of many years. Hecla contends that because the phrase sudden and accidental is ambiguous, it must be construed against the insurance carriers to mean unexpected and unintended.

. . . .

In order to avoid policy coverage, an insurer must establish that the exemption claimed applies in the particular case, and that the exclusions are not subject to any other reasonable interpretations. *City of Johnstown v. Bankers Standard Ins. Co.*, 877 F.2d at 1149. *See also Koncilja v. Trinity Universal Ins. Co.*, 35 Colo.App. 27, 528 P.2d 939, 941 (1974) (having affirmatively expressed coverage through broad promises, the insurer assumes a duty to define any limitations upon that coverage in clear and explicit terms). The insurer has a duty to defend unless the insurer can establish that the allegations in the complaint are solely and entirely within the exclusions in the insurance policy. *Id.* An insurer is not excused from its duty to defend unless there is no factual or legal basis on which the insurer might eventually be held liable to indemnify the insured.

The determination of a duty to defend in this case depends on the terms in the insurance policy, and the interpretation of those terms based upon the principles of contract interpretation. Hecla's CGL insurance policies do not define the meaning of the phrase "sudden and accidental." The interpretation of the phrase "sudden and accidental" is therefore dependent on whether the phrase is used ambiguously in the context of the policy's exclusionary clause.[12] Ambiguous language must be construed in favor of the insured and against the insurer who drafted the policy. Terms used in a contract are ambiguous when they are susceptible to more than one reasonable interpretation.

A majority of the courts addressing the meaning of the phrase "sudden and accidental" as used in CGL insurance policies have determined that the phrase is ambiguous and therefore must be construed against the insurer to mean unexpected and unintended. Other courts have determined that "sudden and accidental" has a temporal quality and means immediate, unexpected, and unintended.

When determining the plain and ordinary meaning of words, definitions in a recognized dictionary may be considered. In doing so, we find that a number of recognized dictionaries differ on the meaning of the term

[12] Some courts have determined that the terms "sudden and accidental" are ambiguous by the mere fact that they are not defined in the insurance policy. *See Buckeye Union Ins. v. Liberty Solvents & Chem.*, 17 Ohio App.3d 127, 477 N.E.2d 1227 (1984).

"sudden." Webster's Third New International Dictionary 2284 (1986) attaches a number of definitions to "sudden." Webster's first defines "sudden" as "happening without previous notice . . . occurring unexpectedly . . . not foreseen." Webster's then lists synonyms for "sudden" that include "prompt" and "immediate." Random House Dictionary of the English Language 1900 (2 ed. 1987) defines the word "sudden" in a temporal sense as "happening, coming, made, or done quickly." Black's Law Dictionary 1284 (5th ed.1979) defines "sudden" as "[h]appening without previous notice or with very brief notice; coming or occurring unexpectedly; unforeseen; unprepared for."

In *Claussen v. Aetna Casualty & Surety Co.*, 259 Ga. 333, 335, 380 S.E.2d 686, 688 (1989), the Georgia Supreme Court stated:

> Perhaps, the secondary meaning is so common in the vernacular that it is, indeed, difficult to think of "sudden" without a temporal connotation: a sudden flash, a sudden burst of speed, a sudden bang. But, on reflection one realizes that, even in its popular usage, "sudden" does not usually describe the duration of an event, but rather its unexpectedness: a sudden storm, a sudden turn in the road, sudden death. Even when used to describe the onset of an event, the word has an elastic temporal connotation that varies with expectations: Suddenly, it's spring. *See also* Oxford English Dictionary, at 96 (1933) (giving usage examples dating back to 1340, e.g., "She heard a sudden step behind her"; and, "A sudden little river crossed my path As unexpected as a serpent comes.").

Although "sudden" can reasonably be defined to mean abrupt or immediate, it can also reasonably be defined to mean unexpected and unintended. Since the term "sudden" is susceptible to more than one reasonable definition, the term is ambiguous, and we therefore construe the phrase "sudden and accidental" against the insurer to mean unexpected and unintended.[13]

If we were to construe "sudden and accidental" to have a solely temporal connotation, the result would be inconsistent definitions within the CGL policies. In the portion of the policies defining occurrence, accident is defined to include "continuous or repeated exposure to conditions, which result in bodily injury or property damage, neither expected nor intended from the standpoint of the insured." If "sudden" were to be given a temporal connotation of abrupt or immediate, then the phrase "sudden and accidental discharge" would mean: an abrupt or immediate, and continuous

---

[13] The determination that "sudden and accidental" is an ambiguous phrase is supported by a large amount of conflicting authority. Although the mere existence of conflicting authority does not establish the ambiguity of a contract term, *see Allstate Insurance Co. v. Troelstrup*, 789 P.2d 415 (Colo.1990), "this type of comprehensive debate dispels the insurer's contention that the exclusionary language is clear." *Just v. Land Reclamation, Ltd.*, 456 N.W.2d at 578.

or repeated discharge. The phrase "sudden and accidental" thus becomes inherently contradictory and meaningless. *City of Northglenn v. Chevron, U.S.A., Inc.*, 634 F.Supp. 217, 222 (D.Colo.1986); *United States v. Conservation Chem. Co.*, 653 F.Supp. 152, 203–04 (W.D.Mo.1986); *Van's Westlake Union, Inc.*, 34 Wash.App. at 711–15, 664 P.2d at 1265–66.

Neither the state's CERCLA complaint, nor the third-party complaint contains claims asserting that Hecla expected or intended the discharge of pollutants into the California Gulch as a result of its mining operations.

Hecla's CGL policies extend coverage to a sudden and accidental occurrence. The trial court resolved the duty to defend issue by entering a summary judgment. No allegations were made in either the CERCLA complaint or in the third-party complaint that the damage caused by Hecla's discharge of the contents of the Yak tunnel was either expected or intended. No proof was offered by either Indemnity or New Hampshire, discovery proceedings had not been completed, and the factual issues had not been determined. Accordingly, the trial court did not err in concluding that Indemnity and New Hampshire had the duty to defend Hecla.

We reverse and remand to the court of appeals with directions to reinstate the judgment entered by the trial court against Indemnity and New Hampshire.

NOTES AND QUESTIONS

1. *Determining Ambiguity.* In the context of insurance policy interpretation under the doctrine of *contra proferentem*, it generally does not matter whether the insurer's interpretation of the policy language at issue is reasonable so long as the policyholder's interpretation is reasonable. Courts do not determine which party has the better interpretation and then apply that interpretation. The insurer's interpretation must be the only reasonable interpretation in order for the insurer's interpretation to prevail. Consequently, *contra proferentem* essentially creates strict liability for insurers for ambiguous policy language.

2. *Use of Extrinsic Evidence to Clarify Ambiguity.* For obvious reasons, insurers almost always claim the policy language at issue is unambiguous. They also typically refuse to produce drafting history documents or other documents regarding insurers' interpretation of policy language. Courts are not in agreement regarding the discoverability of extrinsic evidence with respect to the drafting history or meaning of policy language. Some courts allow it, but many do not. Other courts will allow such discovery if there appears to be an ambiguity in the policy language as applied to the facts of the case or inherently in the language itself. Even if a policyholder is successful in obtaining a court order requiring the production of extrinsic evidence regarding the drafting history or meaning of policy language, it often is the case that little or no documentation currently exists to be produced or can be located by the insurers for production.

3. *Theoretical Justifications for a Strict Liability Version of Contra Proferentem*. "There are numerous theoretical justifications for the strict liability version of *contra proferentem* used in insurance cases. First, by construing ambiguous language against the drafter, the drafter has an incentive to make sure the language is clear. Second, allowing the court to construe ambiguous language against the drafter rather than making its meaning a question of fact to be resolved by the factfinder based upon extrinsic evidence saves judicial resources by avoiding trials. Third, there is a great disparity in knowledge and expertise regarding insurance matters between insurers and policyholders. Fourth, some courts view insurance policies as an extreme type of contract of adhesion because many insurers use the exact same policy form, sold on a take-it-or-leave-it basis. Therefore, not only do policyholders lack input regarding the policy language, but oftentimes, they cannot even shop around for different terms. This problem is further exacerbated by the fact that many types of insurance are mandatory, requiring policyholders to purchase insurance with terms they cannot choose or negotiate. Fifth, because there are no negotiations regarding policy language, and the policyholder does not even see the policy before purchase, there is no mutual intent to discern regarding the meaning of the policy's terms. Consequently, it is pointless to attempt to clarify the parties' mutual intent regarding ambiguous policy language through the use of extrinsic evidence. Sixth, because state insurance regulators do not actually edit the policy language, *contra proferentem* serves as a judicial restraint on overreaching by insurers. Collectively, these justifications have resulted in the application of *contra proferentem* to create strict liability for insurers whenever policy language is subject to multiple reasonable interpretations." Christopher C. French, *Understanding Insurance Policies as Non-Contracts: An Alternative Approach to Drafting and Construing These Unique Financial Instruments*, 89 Temp. L. Rev. 535, 557–58 (2017) (citations omitted).

4. *Other Perspectives*. For other perspectives regarding the doctrine of *contra proferentem*, particularly in the context of insurance cases, *see, e.g.*, Restatement (Second) of Contracts § 206 (1979); Jeffrey E. Thomas, 1–5 New Appleman on Insurance Law § 5.02; Michelle E. Boardman, *Contra Proferentem: The Allure of Ambiguous Boilerplate*, 104 Mich. L. Rev. 1105, 1121 (2006); Ethan J. Leib & Steve Thel, *Contra Proferentem and the Role of the Jury in Contract Interpretation*, 87 Temp. L. Rev. 773, 774 (2015).

C. REASONABLE EXPECTATIONS DOCTRINE

Another staple of policy interpretation doctrine is that a policy should be construed to fulfill the reasonable expectations of the policyholder.[5] Over forty years ago, then-Professor Robert Keeton wrote a seminal article regarding the reasonable expectations doctrine. *See* Robert Keeton,

[5] The introduction to this subchapter regarding the reasonable expectations doctrine is taken almost verbatim from Christopher C. French, *Understanding Insurance Policies as NonContracts: An Alternative Approach to Drafting and Construing These Unique Financial Instruments*, 89 Temp. L. Rev. 535, 558–60 (2017) (citations omitted).

Insurance Law Rights at Variance with Policy Provisions, 83 Harv. L. Rev. 961, 966 (1970). In his subsequent treatise, Judge Keeton summarized the doctrine as follows:

> In general, courts will protect the reasonable expectations of applicants, insureds, and intended beneficiaries regarding the coverage afforded by insurance contracts even though a careful examination of the policy provisions indicates that such expectations are contrary to the expressed intention of the insurer.

Robert E. Keeton, Alan I. Widiss, & James M. Fischer, Insurance Law, §§ 6.3(a)(5), at 538 (2017).

Stated differently, under Judge Keeton's view of the reasonable expectations doctrine, "even when the policy language unambiguously precludes coverage, under certain circumstances, courts will hold that coverage exists." Francis J. Mootz III, *Insurance Coverage of Employment Discrimination Claims*, 52 U. Miami L. Rev. 1, 22 (1997). In short, the policyholder receives the coverage that he reasonably expected, even when policy language or an exclusion credibly can be argued to defeat coverage of a claim.

Although numerous courts have adopted Judge Keeton's version of the reasonable expectations doctrine, it is not the only version of the doctrine courts employ. Some courts only apply the reasonable expectations doctrine if the exclusion or limitation in the policy is concealed or difficult to find. Thus, under this version, courts implicitly resort to equitable principles when interpreting the policy.

Other courts only apply the reasonable expectations doctrine if they conclude the policy language is ambiguous. In such jurisdictions, the reasonable expectations doctrine becomes duplicative of *contra proferentem* and is arguably unfavorable from the policyholders' perspective. Courts that employ this version of the reasonable expectations doctrine reduce the policyholder-friendly effect of *contra proferentem* because the ambiguous language is construed in a manner that a reasonable policyholder would expect, as opposed to simply against the insurer. The basic reasoning of such courts is that it cannot be reasonable, as a matter of law, for a policyholder to expect coverage for a claim under a policy that unambiguously excludes it.

The next two cases are examples of courts applying the reasonable expectations doctrine.

NATIONAL MUTUAL INSURANCE CO. V. MCMAHON & SONS, INC.

356 S.E.2d 488 (W. Va. 1987)

Opinion

MCGRAW, CHIEF JUSTICE:

This is an appeal from a declaratory judgment order entered by the Circuit Court of Jefferson County. The circuit court ruled that the plaintiff-appellee, National Mutual Insurance Company, had no obligation to defend or pay any liability of the defendant-appellant, McMahon and Sons, Inc. Following the entry of this order, Farmers and Mechanics Mutual Fire Insurance Company was allowed to intervene and joins as an appellant in this action.

This appeal presents peculiarly convoluted relationships combined with sparse factual development below. The circuit court made its ruling based on eleven stipulations of fact, the wording of the insurance policy exclusion involved, and taking judicial notice of two related civil actions. For the reasons detailed below, we find that the record in this case contains insufficient information to support the circuit court's rulings. We, therefore, reverse and remand this case for further development.

The stipulated facts reveal that appellee National Mutual issued a general business liability policy to appellant McMahon and Sons on May 7, 1981 to insure its general contracting and real estate development activities. One month later, appellant McMahon and Sons entered into a contract to build a house for Harry J. McMahon, Jr. and Linda Fike. Harry J. McMahon, Jr. signed the contract both as the president of appellant McMahon and Sons and as the home owner. The contract provided that the owner would "carry fire and other associated lines of insurance." Appellant Farmers and Mechanics wrote a fire policy for McMahon and Fike as the home owners.

Sometime after the appellant McMahon and Sons began work on the house, a fire broke out while the contractor's workers were present. The partially built house was destroyed. Appellant McMahon and Sons does not deny negligence in connection with the fire's origin.

In Civil Action No. 82–C–149, McMahon and Fike secured a judgment against appellant Farmers and Mechanics. They have since accepted payment in full satisfaction and compromise of that judgment. Farmers and Mechanics, as subrogee, has since filed a negligence suit, Civil Action No. 83–C–48, in the name of McMahon and Fike against appellant McMahon and Sons. An answer has been filed to the complaint in that action, but the record is not clear as to any further proceedings therein. The instant case is the third lawsuit rising from the ashes of the fire. Appellee National Mutual contends that an exclusionary clause in the general liability policy relieves it of any liability to appellant McMahon and

Sons regarding Civil Action No. 83–C–48. Appellant McMahon and Sons argues that there was coverage under the policy . . . .

III.

We now turn to the primary issue in this case-whether an exclusionary clause in the general liability policy should operate to relieve the appellee of any obligation to defend or pay any liability of appellant McMahon and Sons arising from the pending Civil Action No. 83–C–48. The language of the policy promises that the appellee will defend the insured against any suit for bodily injury or property damage and pay all sums which the insured becomes legally obligated to pay, up to the dollar limits of the policy. This insuring agreement, however, is followed by sixteen exclusions, including the one at issue here, which provides that the insurance does not apply:

(j) to property damage to

(1) property owned or occupied by or rented to the insured,

(2) property used by the insured, or

(3) property in the care, custody or control of the insured or as to which the insured is for any purpose exercising physical control but parts (2) and (3) of this exclusion do not apply with respect to liability under a written sidetrack agreement and part (3) of this exclusion does not apply with respect to property damage (other than to elevators) arising out of the use of an elevator at premises owned by, rented to or controlled by the named insured.

Unlike the circuit court, we do not find the language of this exclusion to be plain and unambiguous, especially when, as in the instant case, the exclusion is asserted in relation to real property. . . . "It is well settled law in West Virginia that [ambiguous terms in] insurance contracts are to be strictly construed against the insurance company and in favor of the insured." *West Virginia Public Employees Insurance Board v. Blue Cross Hospital Service, Inc.*, ___ W.Va. ___, 328 S.E.2d 356, 359 n. 3 (1985). This rule applies in this case not only because the appellee chose the policy language, but because where the policy language involved is exclusionary, it will be strictly construed against the insurer in order that the purpose of providing indemnity not be defeated.

While we have not previously had occasion to examine a care, custody, and control exclusionary clause, a review of the relevant decisions in other jurisdictions quickly reveals that whether the clause acts to relieve the insurer from providing coverage depends heavily upon the facts presented in each case. Mustachio, *Manufacturers' and Contractors' Liability Insurance Policy: The Care, Custody, or Control Exclusion Clause,* 6 Hous.L.Rev. 359, 374 (1968); 43 Am.Jur.2d *Insurance* § 720 (1982); *see*

Estrin Construction Co. v. Aetna Casualty and Surety Co., 612 S.W.2d 413, 421 (Mo.Ct.App.1981). After the circuit court has developed on the record the necessary facts and considered each of the factors discussed below, it will be in a better position to determine if the exclusion should apply in this case. The circuit court should consider the purpose of the exclusionary clause, whether it may appropriately be applied in this case, and the role of appellant McMahon and Sons' reasonable expectations.

A primary purpose of the care, custody, and control exclusion is to prevent the general liability insurer from becoming the guarantor of the insured's workmanship. . . . From the stipulated facts, it is clear that the workmanship of appellant McMahon and Sons is not involved here, and so this reason for allowing the exclusion to operate does not apply.

In determining whether to apply such an exclusion several courts have utilized a multi-factor analysis with regard to the property involved. . . . We adopt a similar test and in determining whether a care, custody, and control exclusion applies, this Court begins its analysis by examining (1) whether the property is personalty or realty, (2) the location, size, and other characteristics of the property, and (3) the insured's relationship to the property, including the insured's duties with respect to the property, the nature and extent of the insured's control over the property, and any interest the insured may have in the property.

In this case, the property involved is realty, a factor which favors coverage. . . . The stipulated facts provided us yield little information regarding the other two tests. We note, however, that several courts have refused to apply the exclusion when it was shown that the insured did not have exclusive control of the property, especially when noninsured owners and tenants continued to exercise some control. If, on remand, the appellee could show[5] exclusive control in appellant McMahon and Sons, this would be a factor militating toward application of the exclusion. However, proof of this issue is complicated by the identity between the insured and one of the home owners.

The final matter to be considered in examining the applicability of the exclusion is whether appellant McMahon and Sons had a reasonable expectation of coverage under the general liability policy. This Court has adopted the doctrine of reasonable expectations. "An insurance contract should be given a construction which a reasonable person standing in the shoes of the insured would expect the language to mean." *Soliva v. Shand, Morahan & Co.*, 176 W.Va. 430, 345 S.E.2d 33, 35–36 (1986). . . . With respect to insurance contracts, the doctrine of reasonable expectations is that "[t]he objectively reasonable expectations of applicants and intended beneficiaries regarding the terms of insurance contracts will be honored

[5] An insurance company seeking to avoid liability through the operation of an exclusion has the burden of proving the facts necessary to the operation of that exclusion.

even though painstaking study of the policy provisions would have negated those expectations." Keeton, *Insurance Law Rights at Variance with Policy Provisions,* 83 Harv.L.Rev. 961 (1970).[6]

In West Virginia, the doctrine of reasonable expectations is limited to those instances, such as the present case, in which the policy language is ambiguous. *Soliva,* 176 W.Va. at ___, 345 S.E.2d at 36.[7] Where ambiguous policy provisions would largely nullify the purpose of indemnifying the insured, the application of those provisions will be severely restricted. *Linden Motor Freight Co. v. Travelers Insurance Co.,* 40 N.J. 511, 193 A.2d 217 (1963); *see* Keeton, 83 Harv.L.Rev. at 976. An exclusion in a general business liability policy should not be so construed as to "strip the insured of protection against risks incurred in the normal operation of his business," especially when the insurer was aware of the nature of the insured's normal operations when the policy was sold.

Where an insured has a reasonable expectation of coverage under a policy, he should not be subject to technical encumbrances or to hidden pitfalls. *Gerhardt v. Continental Insurance Co.,* 48 N.J. 291, 225 A.2d 328 (1966). An insurer wishing to avoid liability on a policy purporting to give general or comprehensive coverage must make exclusionary clauses conspicuous, plain, and clear, placing them in such a fashion as to make obvious their relationship to other policy terms, and must bring such provisions to the attention of the insured. Of course, the insurer may avoid liability by proving that the insured read and understood the language in question, or that the insured indicated his understanding through words or conduct.

On remand, the circuit court should develop a sufficiently detailed record to allow it to decide whether the care, custody, and control exclusion may equitably be allowed to operate under all the facts of this case.

---

[6] The doctrine is also recognized by other authorities. "[C]ourts in construing and applying a standardized contract seek to effectuate the reasonable expectations of the average member of the public who accepts it." Restatement (Second) of Contracts § 237 comment e. "[T]he construction adopted is that which a reasonable person in the position of the insured would have understood the language used to mean." 2 *Couch on Insurance 2d* § 15.16, p. 174 (1984). In applying the doctrine of reasonable expectations to standardized insurance contracts, we must reject that portion of the reasoning in *Soliva* which is based on the general rule that a party to a contract has a duty to read the instrument. While this rule may equitably be enforced with regard to a contract negotiated at arm's length between parties of reasonably equivalent bargaining power and signed by each, it would be unfair to apply the general rule in the case of the modern insurance contract. These policies are contracts of adhesion, offered on a take-it-or-leave-it basis, often sight unseen until the premium is paid and accepted, full of complicated, almost mystical, language. "It is generally recognized the insured will not read the detailed, cross-referenced, standardized, mass-produced insurance form, nor understand it if he does." *C & J Fertilizer, Inc. v. Allied Mutual Insurance Co.,* 227 N.W.2d 169, 174 (Ia.1975); *accord,* 3 *Corbin on Contracts* § 559 (1960); Keeton, 83 Harv.L.Rev. at 968. The majority rule is that the insured is not presumed to know the contents of an adhesion-type insurance policy delivered to him, 7 *Williston on Contracts* § 906 B (1963), and we hereby adopt the majority view.

[7] The requirement of ambiguity is based on the fact that the doctrine of reasonable expectations is essentially a rule of construction, and unambiguous contracts do not require construction by the courts.

Reversed and Remanded.

ATWATER CREAMERY CO. V. WESTERN NATIONAL MUTUAL INSURANCE CO.

366 N.W.2d 271 (Minn. 1985)

Opinion

WAHL, JUSTICE.

Atwater Creamery Company (Atwater) sought a declaratory judgment against its insurer, Western National Mutual Insurance Company (Western), seeking coverage for losses sustained during a burglary of the creamery's storage building. . . . The trial court then dismissed the jury for lack of disputed issues of fact and ordered judgment in favor of the insurer, concluding that the burglary insurance policy in effect defined burglary so as to exclude coverage of this burglary. We . . . reverse as to the policy coverage.

Atwater does business as a creamery and as a supplier of farm chemicals in Atwater, Minnesota. It was insured during the time in question against burglary, up to a ceiling of $20,000, by Western under Merchantile Open Stock Burglary Policy SC10–1010–12, which contained an "evidence of forcible entry" requirement in its definition of burglary. The creamery had recovered small amounts under this policy for two separate burglaries prior to the events in this case.

Atwater built a separate facility, called the Soil Center, a few blocks away from its main plant in 1975 for the purpose of storing and selling chemicals. The Soil Center is a large rectangular building with two regular doors along the north side and two large, sliding doors, one each on the east and west sides. There are no other entrances or exits to or from the building itself. One of the doors on the north side leads into the office in the northwest corner of the building. It is secured by a regular dead bolt lock, opened with a key. There is no access into the main portion of the building from the office. Persons entering the main area must use the other door on the north side which is secured by a padlock after hours. The large sliding doors on the east and west are secured by large hasps on each side of each door which are held tight by turnbuckles that must be loosened before the doors can be opened.

Inside the main area of the building, along the north wall, is a large storage bin with three separate doors, each of which is secured by a padlock. Between the storage bin and the office is an "alleyway," entered through the large sliding doors, which runs east and west the length of the building. Trucks are stored in the alleyway when not in use.

Sometime between 9:30 p.m., Saturday, April 9, and 6 a.m., Monday, April 11, 1977, one or more persons made unauthorized entry into the building, took chemicals worth $15,587.40, apparently loading them on the truck that had been parked inside and driving away after loosening the turnbuckles on the east door and closing it. The truck was later found parked near the town dump, with the key still in the ignition.

Larry Poe, the plant manager at the Soil Center, had left at 9:30 p.m. on Saturday, after making sure everything was properly secured. On Monday morning, the north side doors were locked securely, but two of the three doors to the storage bin were ajar. Their padlocks were gone and never found. The turnbuckles had been loosened on the east sliding door so that it could be easily opened or closed.

An investigation by the local police, the Kandiyohi County Sheriff's Department, and the Minnesota Bureau of Criminal Investigation determined that no Atwater Creamery employees, past or present, were involved in the burglary. Suspicion settled on persons wholly unconnected with the creamery or even with the local area, but no one has been apprehended or charged with the crime.

Atwater filed a claim with Western under the burglary policy. Western denied coverage because there were no visible marks of physical damage to the exterior at the point of entrance or to the interior at the point of exit, as required by the definition of burglary in the policy. The creamery then brought suit against Western for the $15,587.40 loss, $7,500 in other directly related business losses and costs, disbursements and reasonable attorney fees.

Charles H. Strehlow, the owner of the Strehlow Insurance Agency in Willmar, Minnesota, and Western's agent, testified that he is certain he mentioned the evidence-of-forcible-entry requirement to Poe and members of the Atwater Board of Directors but was unable to say when the discussion occurred. Poe and the board members examined do not remember any such discussion. None of the board members had read the policy, which is kept in the safe at the main plant, and Poe had not read it in its entirety. He stated that he started to read it but gave up because he could not understand it.

The issues on appeal are:

. . . .

2. whether the reasonable expectations of the insured as to coverage govern to defeat the literal language of the policy;

. . . .

2. APPLICATION OF THE POLICY DEFINITION OF BURGLARY.

The definition of burglary in this policy is one used generally in burglary insurance. Courts have construed it in different ways. It has been held ambiguous and construed in favor of coverage in the absence of visible marks of forceable entry or exit. *United States Fidelity & Guaranty Co. v. Woodward,* 118 Ga.App. 591, 164 S.E.2d 878 (1968). We reject this analysis because we view the definition in the policy as clear and precise. It is not ambiguous.

In determining the intent of the parties to the insurance contract, courts have looked to the purpose of the visible-marks-of-forcible-entry requirement. These purposes are two: to protect insurance companies from fraud by way of "inside jobs" and to encourage insureds to reasonably secure the premises. *See* 5 Appleman § 3176 at 517. As long as the theft involved clearly neither an inside job nor the result of a lack of secured premises, some courts have simply held that the definition does not apply. *Limberis v. Aetna Casualty & Surety Co.,* 263 A.2d 83 (Me.1970); *Kretschmer's House of Appliances, Inc. v. United States Fidelity & Guaranty Co.,* 410 S.W.2d 617 (Ky.1966).

In the instant case, there is no dispute as to whether Atwater is attempting to defraud Western or whether the Soil Center was properly secured. The trial court found that the premises were secured before the robbery and that the law enforcement investigators had determined that it was not an "inside job." To enforce the burglary definition literally against the creamery will in no way effectuate either purpose behind the restrictive definition. We are uncomfortable, however, with this analysis given the right of an insurer to limit the risk against which it will indemnify insureds.

At least three state courts have held that the definition merely provides for one form of evidence which may be used to prove a burglary and that, consequently, other evidence of a burglary will suffice to provide coverage. *Ferguson v. Phoenix Assurance Co. of New York,* 189 Kan. 459, 370 P.2d 379 (1962); *National Surety Co. v. Silberberg Bros.,* 176 S.W. 97 (Tex.Civ.App.1915); *Rosenthal v. American Bonding Co. of Baltimore,* 124 N.Y.S. 905 (N.Y.Sup.Ct.1910). The Nebraska Supreme Court recently rejected this argument in *Cochran v. MFA Mutual Insurance Co.,* 201 Neb. 631, 271 N.W.2d 331 (1978). The *Cochran* court held that the definition is not a rule of evidence but is a limit on liability, is unambiguous and is applied literally to the facts of the case at hand. We, too, reject this view of the definition as merely a form of evidence. The policy attempts to comprehensively define burglaries that are covered by it. In essence, this approach ignores the policy definition altogether and substitutes the court's or the statute's definition of burglary. This we decline to do, either via the conformity clause or by calling the policy definition merely one form of evidence of a burglary.

Some courts and commentators have recognized that the burglary definition at issue in this case constitutes a rather hidden exclusion from coverage. Exclusions in insurance contracts are read narrowly against the insurer. Running through the many court opinions refusing to literally enforce this burglary definition is the concept that the definition is surprisingly restrictive, that no one purchasing something called burglary insurance would expect coverage to exclude skilled burglaries that leave no visible marks of forcible entry or exit. Professor Robert E. Keeton, in analyzing these and other insurance cases where the results often do not follow from the rules stated, found there to be two general principles underlying many decisions. These principles are the reasonable expectations of the insured and the unconscionability of the clause itself or as applied to the facts of a specific case. Keeton, *Insurance Law Rights at Variance with Policy Provisions,* 83 Harv.L.Rev. 961 (1970). Keeton's article and subsequent book, *Basic Text on Insurance Law,* (1971), have had significant impact on the construction of insurance contracts.

The doctrine of protecting the reasonable expectations of the insured is closely related to the doctrine of contracts of adhesion. Where there is unequal bargaining power between the parties so that one party controls all of the terms and offers the contract on a take-it-or-leave-it basis, the contract will be strictly construed against the party who drafted it. Most courts recognize the great disparity in bargaining power between insurance companies and those who seek insurance. Further, they recognize that, in the majority of cases, a lay person lacks the necessary skills to read and understand insurance policies, which are typically long, set out in very small type and written from a legalistic or insurance expert's perspective. Finally, courts recognize that people purchase insurance relying on others, the agent or company, to provide a policy that meets their needs. The result of the lack of insurance expertise on the part of insureds and the recognized marketing techniques of insurance companies is that "[t]he objectively reasonable expectations of applicants and intended beneficiaries regarding the terms of insurance contracts will be honored even though painstaking study of the policy provisions would have negated those expectations." Keeton, 83 Harv.L.Rev. at 967.

The traditional approach to construction of insurance contracts is to require some kind of ambiguity in the policy before applying the doctrine of reasonable expectations. Several courts, however, have adopted Keeton's view that ambiguity ought not be a condition precedent to the application of the reasonable-expectations doctrine.

As of 1980, approximately ten states had adopted the newer rule of reasonable expectations regardless of ambiguity. *Davenport Peters Co. v. Royal Globe Insurance Co.,* 490 F.Supp. 286, 291 (D.Mass.1980). Other states, such as Missouri and North Dakota, have joined the ten since then. Most courts recognize that insureds seldom see the policy until the premium is paid, and even if they try to read it, they do not comprehend it. Few courts require insureds to have minutely examined the policy before relying on the terms they expect it to have and for which they have paid.

The burglary definition is a classic example of a policy provision that should be, and has been, interpreted according to the reasonable expectations of the insured. *C & J Fertilizer, Inc. v. Allied Mutual Insurance Co.,* 227 N.W.2d 169 (Iowa 1975). *C & J Fertilizer* involved a burglary definition almost exactly like the one in the instant case as well as a burglary very similar to the Atwater burglary. The court applied the reasonable-expectations-regardless-of-ambiguity doctrine, noting that "[t]he most plaintiff might have reasonably anticipated was a policy requirement of visual evidence (abundant here) indicating the burglary was an 'outside' not an 'inside' job. The exclusion in issue, masking as a definition, makes insurer's obligation to pay turn on the skill of the burglar, not on the event the parties bargained for: a bona fide third party burglary resulting in loss of plaintiff's chemicals and equipment." *Id.* at 177. The burglary in *C & J Fertilizer* left no visible marks on the exterior of the building, but an interior door was damaged. In the instant case, the facts are very similar except that there was no damage to the interior doors; their padlocks were simply gone. In *C & J Fertilizer,* the police concluded that an "outside" burglary had occurred. The same is true here.

Atwater had a burglary policy with Western for more than 30 years. The creamery relied on Charles Strehlow to procure for it insurance suitable for its needs. There is some factual dispute as to whether Strehlow ever told Poe about the "exclusion," as Strehlow called it. Even if he had said that there was a visible-marks-of-forcible-entry requirement, Poe could reasonably have thought that it meant that there must be clear evidence of a burglary. There are, of course, fidelity bonds which cover employee theft. The creamery had such a policy covering director and manager theft. The fidelity company, however, does not undertake to insure against the risk of third-party burglaries. A business that requests and purchases burglary insurance reasonably is seeking coverage for loss from third-party burglaries whether a break-in is accomplished by an inept burglar or by a highly skilled burglar. Two other burglaries had occurred at the Soil Center, for which Atwater had received insurance proceeds under the policy. Poe and the board of the creamery could reasonably have expected the burglary policy to cover this burglary where the police, as well as the trial court, found that it was an "outside job."

The reasonable-expectations doctrine gives the court a standard by which to construe insurance contracts without having to rely on arbitrary rules which do not reflect real-life situations and without having to bend and stretch those rules to do justice in individual cases. As Professor Keeton points out, ambiguity in the language of the contract is not irrelevant under this standard but becomes a factor in determining the reasonable expectations of the insured, along with such factors as whether the insured was told of important, but obscure, conditions or exclusions and whether the particular provision in the contract at issue is an item known by the public generally. The doctrine does not automatically remove from the insured a responsibility to read the policy. It does, however, recognize that in certain instances, such as where major exclusions are hidden in the definitions section, the insured should be held only to reasonable knowledge of the literal terms and conditions. The insured may show what actual expectations he or she had, but the factfinder should determine whether those expectations were reasonable under the circumstances.

We have used the reasonable-expectations-of-the-insured analysis to provide coverage where the actual language interpreted as the insurance company intended would have proscribed coverage. *Canadian Universal Insurance Co. v. Fire Watch, Inc.,* 258 N.W.2d 570 (Minn.1977). Western correctly points out that the issue there concerned a special endorsement issued subsequent to the policy which reduced coverage without notice to the insured. While the issue is somewhat different in the instant case, it is not so different that the general concept is made inapplicable.

. . . .

We hold that where the technical definition of burglary in a burglary insurance policy is, in effect, an exclusion from coverage, it will not be interpreted so as to defeat the reasonable expectations of the purchaser of the policy. Under the facts and circumstances of this case, Atwater reasonably expected that its burglary insurance policy with Western would cover the burglary that occurred. Our holding requires reversal as to policy coverage.

NOTES AND QUESTIONS

1. *Counting Courts.* Some version of the reasonable expectations doctrine has been adopted in most states. *See* Barry R. Ostrager & Thomas R. Newman, Handbook on Insurance Coverage Disputes § 1.04[b] (18th ed. 2017) (identifying courts in forty-two states that have expressed support for, or applied a form of, the reasonable expectations doctrine). For commentary regarding the reasonable expectations doctrine and the various iterations of it, *see* Daniel Schwarcz, *A Products Liability Theory for the Judicial Regulation of Insurance Policies*, 48 Wm. & Mary L. Rev. 1389, 1395 (2007) (criticizing the reasonable expectations doctrine and arguing that the case law endorsing the doctrine is "confused and inconsistent"); Robert H. Jerry II, *Insurance, Contract, and the Doctrine of Reasonable Expectations*, 5 Conn. Ins. L.J. 21 (1998) (discussing the doctrine as conceptualized by Keeton); Roger C. Henderson, *The Doctrine of Reasonable Expectations in Insurance Law After Two Decades*, 51 Ohio St. L.J. 823 (1990) (providing a detailed historical account of the doctrine and asserting that the doctrine is principled and can be applied within justifiable guidelines); William A. Mayhew, *Reasonable Expectations: Seeking a Principled Application*, 13 Pepp. L. Rev. 267, 287–96 (1986) (formulating standards for applying the doctrine); Mark C. Rahdert, *Reasonable Expectations Reconsidered*, 18 Conn. L. Rev. 323, 392 (1986)

(arguing for refinements to the doctrine in response to the fading appeal that the doctrine holds for courts and commentators and contending that courts should "discard their unfortunate tendency to speak the platitudes of reasonable expectations without undertaking a careful and systematic analysis"); Jeffrey W. Stempel, *Unmet Expectations: Undue Restriction of the Reasonable Expectations Approach and the Misleading Mythology of Judicial Role*, 5 Conn. Ins. L.J. 181, 182–83, 191 (1998) (describing the various judicial approaches to the doctrine and noting both liberal and narrow approaches among the numerous states that have adopted the doctrine).

2. *Theoretical Justifications for Reasonable Expectations Doctrine.* Theoretically, several grounds justify the reasonable expectations doctrine.[6] Many of them overlap with the justifications for use of the strict liability version of *contra proferentem* in the insurance context. First, there is a great disparity between insurers and policyholders, both in knowledge and expertise regarding insurance matters and in economic power generally. Thus, vulnerable policyholders need protection against insurers overreaching.

Second, policyholders have no input into the policy language. Policyholders also do not receive the policies until after purchase and they generally cannot understand the terms and conditions due to their complexity. Consequently, the policy language does not serve as the source of policyholders' understanding regarding the scope of coverage. Other considerations necessarily must come into play when determining the scope of coverage provided once it is accepted that, unlike in traditional contract disputes where the goal is to determine the parties' mutual intent, mutual intent does not exist in insurance policies. Such considerations include the type of insurance at issue, insurer ads, and agents' and brokers' statements, all of which shape a policyholder's beliefs regarding coverage.

Third, the Restatement (Second) of Contracts specifically contemplates that courts can refuse to enforce terms contained in standardized insurance policies that the insurer knows policyholders would not accept if they were aware of the terms and could reject them: "Where the other party has reason to believe that the party manifesting [assent to a written agreement] would not do so if he knew that the writing contained a particular term, the term is not part of the agreement." The official comment to this section of the Restatement specifically states:

> [C]ustomers . . . are not bound to unknown terms which are beyond the range of reasonable expectation. . . . [A] party who adheres to the other party's standard terms does not assent to a term if the other party has reason to believe that the adhering party would not have accepted the agreement if he had known that the agreement contained the particular term. Such a belief or assumption may be shown by the prior negotiations or inferred from the circumstances.

[6] This Note is taken almost verbatim from Christopher C. French, *Understanding Insurance Policies as Non-Contracts: An Alternative Approach to Drafting and Construing These Unique Financial Instruments*, 89 Temp. L. Rev. 535, 560–62 (2017) (citations omitted).

> Reason to believe may be inferred from the fact that the term is bizarre or oppressive, from the fact that it eviscerates the non-standard terms explicitly agreed to, or from the fact that it eliminates the dominant purpose of the transaction. The inference is reinforced if the adhering party never had an opportunity to read the term, or if it is illegible or otherwise hidden from view. This rule is closely related to the policy against unconscionable terms and the rule of interpretation against the draftsman.

Thus, the Restatement specifically recognizes courts' authority to employ interpretive tools such as the reasonable expectations doctrine when construing insurance policies.

Fourth, because state insurance regulators have the power to reject policy terms that are unreasonable, unfair, ambiguous, or contrary to public policy, courts likewise have the power to refuse to enforce terms that insurance regulators arguably should not have approved.

Fifth, insurers are in a quasi-fiduciary relationship with policyholders under liability policies because of their ability to control the defense and settlement of claims asserted against policyholders. Thus, policyholders need greater protection by the courts than parties who enter arm's-length contracts and have the ability to control the defense and settlement of claims asserted against them.

Sixth, policyholders are also vulnerable because they already have performed their end of the bargain by paying the premium and, unlike parties in a typical contract dispute, they cannot get another insurer to replace the breaching insurer after a loss occurs. Stated differently, unlike typical breach of contract situations where the nonbreaching party has the ability to "cover" the subject of the contract by hiring another party to perform in the event of a breach, the policyholder has no ability to obtain replacement coverage once a loss has occurred.

Seventh, public policy can trump policy language. Public policies in play include (1) ensuring that injured parties are compensated, and (2) fulfilling the purpose of insurance as a social safety net that is intended to prevent the financial ruin of individual policyholders.

Some commentators have described these theoretical justifications for the reasonable expectations doctrine as an amalgamation of the doctrines of waiver, estoppel, unconscionability, reformation, and rescission. Regardless of which theoretical justifications may apply, the reasonable expectations doctrine is not really a rule of contract interpretation. Rather, it is a judicially created rule that many courts have employed in their attempts to reach fair and equitable results where insurers may be relying upon policy language to defeat coverage in a way that is at odds with the general purpose of insurance.

EXERCISE

1. A policyholder has an "all risk" property policy that insures "against all risk of physical loss or damage to property described herein." The phrase "physical loss or damage" is not defined in the policy. The policyholder's place of business was included in the "property described herein." The policyholder's business was the victim of a cyber attack that caused its website to stop working for 12 hours. The policyholder lost $50,000 in profits due to lost sales that day, but the website became fully functional again once the cyber attacker was blocked from accessing the website.

Do one of the following:

A. Draft a 2-page memo making the argument that the loss is covered under the rules of insurance policy interpretation; or

B. Draft a 2-page memo making the argument that the loss is not covered under the rules of insurance policy interpretation.

D. SOPHISTICATED PURCHASERS

A few courts have recognized an exception to *contra proferentem* in the insurance context—the "sophisticated purchaser" or "sophisticated policyholder" exception. The sophisticated purchaser exception is premised upon the idea that sophisticated purchasers of insurance—typically large corporations with vast resources and access to attorneys, risk managers, and insurance brokers—are not at a negotiating disadvantage when it comes to purchasing insurance. Thus, under the doctrine, they should not receive the benefit of *contra proferentem*. Despite vigorous advocacy on behalf of the doctrine by insurers, however, it has not gained widespread acceptance by the courts. *See, e.g., Armstrong World Indus., Inc. v. Aetna Cas. & Sur. Co.*, 52 Cal. Rptr. 2d 690, 697 (Cal. Ct. App. 1996) ("A policy should not be read as it might be analyzed by an attorney or an insurance expert. This is so even if the policyholder is a sophisticated insured."); *Boeing Co. v. Aetna Cas. & Sur. Co.*, 784 P.2d 507, 514 (Wash. 1990) ("[T]hese standard rules of construction are no less applicable merely because the insured is itself a corporate giant.").

Commentators have explained the rationale for the sophisticated purchaser exception as follows:

> [T]he general rule requiring construction of an insurance policy against the insurer should have no application in the context of business insurance policies that have been negotiated by parties with substantially equal bargaining power. . . . [T]he contra-insurer rule of construction developed as a judicial response to the unequal bargaining power of the average personal insurance consumer in relation to his insurer, particularly in cases involving

> 'standard form' personal insurance policies drafted by the insurer and marketed to insureds on a 'take it or leave it' basis. . . . [B]usiness insureds, by contrast, have considerable sophistication and bargaining power, and . . . business insurance policies are typically negotiated (and often drafted) on behalf of the business by corporate risk managers, independent insurance brokers and/or attorneys. . . .

Barry R. Ostrager & David W. Ichel, *The Role of Bargaining Power Evidence in the Construction of the Business Insurance Policy: An Update*, 18 Forum 577 (1983).

The exception has been around for a while even though few courts have adopted it. In 1976, the Fifth Circuit, explained its reasoning for applying it in a 1976 case:

> We do not feel compelled to apply, or, indeed, justified in applying the general rule that an insurance policy is construed against the insurer in the commercial insurance field when the insured is not an innocent but a corporation of immense size, carrying insurance with annual premiums in six figures, managed by sophisticated business men, and represented by counsel on the same professional level as the counsel for insurers. In substance the authorship of the policy is attributable to both parties alike. Significantly, the policy in question is not the usual printed form but is what is known as a "manuscript" policy, containing some standard printed clauses but confected especially for Olin. It is true, of course, as the trial judge observed, 'scriveners of insurance policies are acutely aware of the meaning and effect of the language.' We comment: So too, are counsel for large companies carrying fleet insurance with annual premiums in six figures. There is no purpose in following a legal platitude that has no realistic application to a contract confected by a large corporation and a large insurance company each advised by competent counsel and informed experts.

Eagle Leasing Corp. v. Hartford Fire Ins. Co., 540 F.2d 1257, 1261 (5th Cir. 1976).

In essence, a sophisticated purchaser is 1) a policyholder with wealth, knowledge, legal or broker representation, and substantial bargaining power, and 2) a policyholder who participates in the negotiation and drafting of the policy language. The most important factor from an analytical perspective concerning the application of *contra proferentem* is whether the policyholder or its representatives actually participated in the drafting of the policy language. The conceptual foundation of *contra proferentem* is that ambiguous contractual language should be construed against the drafter of the language, but if the drafting is essentially a shared responsibility or a shared process, then the foundation for applying *contra proferentem* arguably disappears.

The next case is an example from one of the minority of jurisdictions that has applied the doctrine.

EASTERN ASSOCIATED COAL CORP. V. AETNA CAS. & SUR. CO.

632 F.2d 1068 (3rd Cir. 1980)

Opinion

This diversity case involves cross-appeals from a partial grant of the defendants' motion for judgment notwithstanding the verdict. The jury awarded Eastern Associated Coal Corporation (Eastern) $4,736,377 under a business interruption insurance policy held with the defendant insurers for losses incurred due to the closing of Eastern's Joanne Mine after an underground fire. The defendants moved for judgment n. o. v. on two grounds. First, the defendants' motion argued that there was insufficient evidence to support the plaintiff's theory concerning the sales value of a portion of the coal which would have been mined by Eastern during the interruption covered by the policy. The trial judged granted this portion of the motion and reduced the jury's award by $890,744. Eastern appeals from this action. Second, the defendants' motion argued that the insurance policy did not cover any expenses incurred by Eastern in obtaining alternative coal to fulfill its contractual obligation to supply metallurgical coal from the Joanne Mine to Sharon Steel Corporation. The trial court, 475 F.Supp. 586, denied this portion of the motion and entered judgment for $3,845,633. We affirm the trial court's grant of judgment n. o. v. with regard to the first portion of the motion and reverse the trial court's denial of judgment n. o. v. with regard to the second portion of the motion. The case will be remanded for entry of judgment against the defendant insurers in the amount of $287,277.

Facts

Eastern, a West Virginia corporation with offices in Pittsburgh, Pennsylvania, operates a number of underground soft coal mines in Pennsylvania and West Virginia. In 1969, Eastern purchased the Joanne Mine, located near Rachel, West Virginia, from Sharon Steel Corporation. Some of the coal in the mine was metallurgical coal; the balance was classified as steam coal. Sulphur content is the distinguishing factor between the classifications. Metallurgical coal has a low sulphur content, and accordingly burns at high temperatures. It is required in the production of steel. Steam coal has a higher sulphur content, burns at lower temperatures, and is not suited to use in steel production. The purchase agreement with Sharon provided in part for a coal supply contract, under which Eastern agreed to furnish the metallurgical coal requirements of

Sharon's Fairmont Coke Works, estimated at 250,000 tons annually, for a ten-year period. The contract contained base prices for coal and an escalator clause to cover increases in the cost of production. It also provided that the coal supplied would come from the Joanne Mine until its metallurgical coal reserves were exhausted. As the seam was estimated to contain 1,125,000 tons of metallurgical coal, the Joanne Mine was expected to supply Sharon for approximately four and one-half years. After exhaustion of the Joanne metallurgical area, Eastern was obligated under the contract to obtain metallurgical coal from other sources for the remainder of the term of the contract. The contract also contained a provision which required all metallurgical coal to have a sulphur content of less than 1.6%. Sharon could reject any coal which did not comply with this specification.

In 1972 Eastern bought the business interruption insurance policy under which it is currently suing. The policy was part of a four-policy package which covered all of Eastern's mines in Pennsylvania and West Virginia for business interruption insurance. Eastern's protection under the total package was $20,000,000. Each layer insured $5,000,000. The first policy covered losses up to $5,000,000. sustained from the closing of any mine. The second policy covered losses from $5,000,000 to $10,000,000., the third up to $15,000,000., and the fourth up to $20,000,000. These policies were produced by Eastern's insurance broker, Marsh & McLennan, Inc., which selected the form, prepared the policies, and sent the policies to the insurers and underwriters for signature. Several insurers helped to underwrite each policy.

On January 14, 1974, a fire broke out as the result of an underground accident involving the derailment of a mine locomotive in the metallurgical section of the Joanne Mine. Within 24 hours the mine was totally sealed as a means of extinguishing the fire by depriving it of oxygen. This fire, however, terminated all mining operations for a 12-month period, which was the term of coverage under the policy.

During the year after the closing, Eastern's coal production at the mine was essentially zero. However, it was estimated that Eastern could have mined approximately 181,000 tons of metallurgical coal and 434,000 tons of steam coal during the year of coverage, if there had been no interruption. In determining recovery under the policy, the value of this lost production to Eastern is an important factor. The recovery increases directly in proportion to the value of lost production.

. . . Eastern claims that the policy covered the expenses Eastern incurred in obtaining alternative coal to fulfill its contractual obligation to supply metallurgical coal from the Joanne Mine to Sharon Steel. After the fire, Eastern contended that due to a force majeure clause in its contract with Sharon, it was relieved of its obligation to supply Sharon with metallurgical coal. Sharon disagreed, and the dispute was brought to arbitration. The arbiter held that Eastern's obligation to Sharon continued despite the fire, and Eastern was accordingly forced to continue supplying Sharon with metallurgical coal.

This arbitration award exposed Eastern to a substantial new expense. Due to the oil embargo in 1973, the price of coal began to rise steadily. However, during the year of interruption the escalator clause in the contract with Sharon did not keep pace with the increase in market price. Under the contract with Sharon, Eastern was being paid $13.00 to $18.00 a ton for metallurgical coal, while the market price ranged from $50.00 to $75.00. During the interruption, Eastern obtained much of the coal for Sharon from its other mines. Such coal has been denominated "substitute coal." In selling the substitute coal to Sharon, Eastern was deprived of the profit it could have made by selling such coal on the market. Eastern calculated its loss during the year on substitute coal to be $1,599,461. Eastern met the remaining requirements under the Sharon contract by buying coal on the open market and reselling it to Sharon at the lower contract price. Coal bought on the market has been denominated "brokerage coal," and Eastern calculated its loss on brokerage coal to be $2,175,240. Totaled, Eastern determined its loss on its contract with Sharon to be $3,774,701, thus bringing the full liability claimed against the insurers to $9,952,722. The insurers disputed Eastern's right to recover any money for the expense incurred in complying with Sharon's contract. This presents the second issue we must resolve.

. . . .

The trial judge denied the defendant insurers' motions for summary judgment and a directed verdict and submitted [the] issues to a jury. The jury returned a verdict against the insurers in the amount of $4,736,377, which is $216,345 less than the total demanded by Eastern. Post-trial motions for judgment n. o. v. were filed by the insurers. The trial judge granted judgment n. o. v. against Eastern on [one] issue. He found the evidence supporting this claim to be speculative and reduced the recovery by $890,744. The judge denied the motion on the second issue and entered judgment against the defendant insurers for $3,845,633. The parties appeal from the grant and denial of judgment n. o. v., respectively.

Analysis

. . . .

Issue No. 2

The insurers appeal from the district court's entry of judgment on the second issue. They argue that the insurance policy is unambiguous and makes no provision for recovery of new expenses which an insured may incur due to an interruption. Accordingly, they argue that as a matter of law Eastern's loss incurred in selling substitute and brokerage coal to Sharon under the contract is not insured under the policy. Eastern, however, argues that the policy is ambiguous, and that the language should be construed to afford recovery. Eastern contends that recovery is assured under two separate provisions in the policy. The district court charged the jury in accordance with Eastern's theories. To determine whether this was error, we must analyze the policy.

The rules relating to the analysis of insurance policies in Pennsylvania are well established. Since the policy is a contract, the court's duty is to ascertain the intent of the parties as manifested in the language of the agreement. The court should read policy provisions so as to avoid ambiguities, if the plain language of the contract permits. A court should not torture the language of the policy in order to create ambiguities. If the language is unambiguous, interpretation of the contract is a matter of law for the court. If an ambiguity does exist and if the insurer wrote the policy or is in a stronger bargaining position than the insured, the ambiguity is generally resolved in favor of the insured and against the insurer. However, the principle that ambiguities in policies should be strictly construed against the insurer does not control the situation where large corporations, advised by counsel and having equal bargaining power, are the parties to a negotiated policy.

As pointed out above, Eastern's insurance broker selected the policy forms, prepared the policies, and sent them to the insurance companies for execution. Under these circumstances, the Pennsylvania cases indicate that conflicts over the interpretation of an insurance contract should be resolved against the party preparing the contract. *See Sykes v. Nationwide Mutual Insurance Co.*, 413 Pa. 640, 643, 198 A.2d 844, 845 (1964) ("where ambiguity clouds interpretation the contract in controversy must be interpreted against its authors"); *Cadwallader v. New Amsterdam Cas. Co.*, 396 Pa. 582, 586, 152 A.2d 484, 487 (1959) ("if there be any ambiguity in the contract of insurance it must be resolved in favor of the insured since it was the insurer who wrote the contract."). At a minimum, the above cited cases require that we not construe the language against the defendants.

These legal principles are fully applicable to the interpretation of business interruption insurance. With these legal principles in mind, we turn to the language of the policy in controversy. The policy sets out a general statement of its coverage and then addresses the determination of the value of the loss insured. It reads as follows:

> "3. COVERING ON:
>
> (B) This policy also insures against loss of earnings (as defined herein) resulting from damage to, or destruction of any of the property of the Assured occurring during the term of this policy.

"10. VALUATION:

b. Business Interruption-Recovery in the event of loss hereunder shall be the ACTUAL LOSS SUSTAINED by the Assured directly resulting from such interruption of business, but not exceeding the reduction in earnings less charges and expenses which do not necessarily continue during the interruption of business, for only such length of time as would be required with the exercise of due diligence and dispatch to rebuild, repair or replace such part of the property herein described as has been damaged or destroyed, commencing with the date of such damage or destruction and not limited by the date of expiration of this policy. Due consideration shall be given to the continuation of normal charges and expenses, including payroll, expense, to the extent necessary to resume operations of the Assured with the same quality of service which existed immediately preceding the loss.

"EARNINGS DEFINED: For the purpose of this insurance "Earnings" are defined as . . .:

"(a) Total net sales value of production,

. . . In determining "Earnings" due consideration shall be given to the experience of the business before the date of damage or destruction and the probable experience thereafter had no loss occurred.

"EXPENSES INCURRED TO REDUCE LOSS: Any and all expense incurred by the Assured to reduce loss hereunder is covered by this insurance to the extent only of the loss which would have been sustained had such expense not been incurred."

As noted above, the insurers argue that this policy is unambiguous and makes no provision for recovery of new expenses. Eastern disagrees and contends, first, that the language in paragraph 10-b defining recovery is ambiguous and hence the rule of construction that ambiguous language should be interpreted against the insurer and in favor of coverage should be applied. We agree with the insurers and find this language unambiguous. For this reason, the rule that contracts are construed strictly against the insurer cannot apply. As will be explained below, the language of paragraph 10-b itself is an adequate guide to interpretation. . . . Accordingly, we need not resort to rules of construction.

Paragraph 10-b sets forth a formula precisely limiting the scope of recovery. The policy states that the business interruption loss shall not exceed "the reduction in earnings less charges and expenses which do not necessarily continue during the interruption." A close analysis of the terms of this formula demonstrates that it is subject to only one reasonable interpretation.

The first element of the formula is "the reduction in earnings." To understand this element, the term "earnings" must first be understood. On the facts of this case, earnings are the "total net sales value of production." This phrase refers to the value of the coal which Eastern would have mined during the period of interruption, if operations had continued. In light of this definition of "earnings," the phrase "the reduction in earnings" can only refer to the difference between expected earnings and actual earnings-in mathematical language, the expected value of production if no interruption had occurred minus the actual value of production from mining operations. As the mine was totally closed after the fire, the actual value of production in this case was zero. Accordingly, "the reduction in earnings" in this case equals the value of lost production.

The second element of the formula is the phrase "charges and expenses which do not necessarily continue during the interruption." This language refers to expenses that the insured business incurs during normal operations which, because of the work stoppage, it does not need to incur during the interruption, such as fuel to run machinery in the mine. Thus, the second element of the formula refers to expenses which could properly be discontinued during the interruption.

The formula directs that the recovery may not exceed the first element less the second element. Thus, in fuller terms, the formula provides that discontinued expenses be subtracted from the value of lost production. Recovery may not exceed the resulting figure. Eastern's initial claim filed with the insurers followed this formula precisely, demonstrating that this provision of the policy was understood by both parties to the contract. This fact further buttresses our conclusion that the language is not ambiguous and that its terms should be strictly followed.

From this review of the formula used to calculate recovery under the policy, we believe it is apparent that the policy makes no provision for recovery of an expense which is newly created by the interruption, such as Eastern's substitute and brokerage coal cost. The policy merely insures that the interrupted business will receive the amount of money which continued operation would have produced reduced by the amount of any routine costs which the business avoided by closing. If new expenses are produced by the interruption, the formula under paragraph 10-b makes no allowance for their recovery.

Despite the failure of the language of paragraph 10-b to insure against new expenses, Eastern argues that coverage for new expenses must be provided on the basis that business interruption insurance should protect insureds from all loss due to business interruptions. Eastern bases this assertion on the generally accepted statement that business interruption insurance "is designed to do for the insured in the event of business interruption caused by fire, just what the business itself would have done if no interruption had occurred . . ." *National Union Fire Ins. Co. v. Anderson-Prichard Oil Corp.*, 141 F.2d 443 (10th Cir. 1944). Eastern extrapolates from this general statement that the recovery must leave the insured in the same financial position it would have been in at the end of the policy's term had no interruption taken place. Eastern argues that, because it is in a worse financial position after the interruption, due to the new expenses, than it would have been in if no interruption had occurred, new expenses must be covered.

Eastern's argument based on this general statement fails because the policy makes no provision for recovery of new expenses and because the clear language of the policy limits recovery to the amount derived from the formula discussed above. If new expenses are to be compensated, the express language limiting recovery would have to be ignored. Since there is no ambiguity, there is no basis for ignoring this language.

Moreover, there is no support in the case law for Eastern's argument. *National Union Fire Ins. Co. v. Anderson-Prichard Oil Corp., supra,* and the many other cases citing the general statement concerning business interruption insurance quoted above do not address the problem of whether to award recovery for new expenses produced by an interruption. They simply note in situations where new expenses have not been incurred, that the recovery under a business interruption insurance policy is likely to return the insured to the financial status it would have been in if no interruption had occurred. In situations where no new expenses are incurred, this statement is correct. In light of the lack of ambiguity in the policy, the absence of any provision compensating new expenses in paragraph 10-b's formula, and Eastern's failure to uncover any cases in which recovery for new expenses was obtained under a business interruption policy, we hold that new expenses produced by the interruption are not covered by the formula for recovery provided in paragraph 10-b of this policy. In charging the jury in accordance with Eastern's theory of paragraph 10-b, the district court erred.

Issue No. 3

The district judge also charged the jury with a second theory of recovery for the substitute and brokerage coal expense under the policy. The court charged that these additional expenses could be compensated under the "Expenses Incurred to Reduce Loss" provision of paragraph 10-b of the policy. This charge was also incorrect.

The provision provides as follows:

> "EXPENSES INCURRED TO REDUCE LOSS: Any and all expense incurred by the Assured to reduce loss hereunder is

> covered by this insurance to the extent only of the loss which would have been sustained had such expense not been incurred."

Here, again, the words of the policy are not sufficiently ambiguous to necessitate the application of rules of construction. As noted above, Pennsylvania cases hold that a clause must be ambiguous before a court applies rules of construction.

Eastern argues that its substitute and brokerage coal expense was "incurred by the Assured to reduce loss" caused by the interruption and, therefore, is covered by the policy. We do not doubt that Eastern's liability to Sharon was reduced by its resort to substitute and brokerage coal. However, Eastern fails to take account of the exact words of the policy. The provision compensates insureds for expenses incurred "to reduce loss hereunder" (emphasis added). We believe the phrase "loss hereunder" plainly refers to loss compensated under the policy. As was established above in discussing the formula for recovery under paragraph 10-b, the new brokerage and substitute coal expenses resulting from the interruption are not losses compensated under this policy. Accordingly, such new expenses cannot serve to "reduce loss hereunder."

Our interpretation is consistent with the clear intent of the "Expenses Incurred to Reduce Loss" provision. The provision is designed to encourage insureds to undertake new expenses which will result in an overall reduction of the insurer's liability. Support for our interpretation can be found in the Sixth Circuit's case of *American Alliance Ins. Co. v. Keleket X-Ray Corp., supra*. In Keleket the district court had awarded recovery under a provision of a business interruption insurance policy substantially similar to the one at bar for expenses incurred in decontaminating a building which had been contaminated by radioactive material in a small explosion inside the building. The court reversed the district court's award under the provision, and explained that:

> "(T)he insured (has not) introduced any evidence of expenses necessarily incurred to reduce the business interruption losses. Had the plaintiff shown that the period of interruption had been shortened by use of overtime labor at premium wages, for example, then the premium wages would be allowable up to the amount by which the liabilities of the insurers under the business interruption policies had been reduced. The record is devoid of evidence to this effect. In the absence of evidence showing that the expenditures had actually reduced the business interruption losses, the district court was in error in allowing any decontamination expense as an expense incurred to reduce the loss under the business interruption policies."

Id. at 930–31.

As the brokerage and substitute coal expense in no way served to reduce the insurer's liability under the policy, it cannot be compensated under the "Expenses Incurred to Reduce Loss" provision. Eastern's interpretation, which renders the word "hereunder" meaningless, is plainly at odds with the unambiguous meaning of the provision.

Our review of the pertinent case law and the language of this policy convinces us that Eastern is not entitled to recover new expenses produced by the closing of the Joanne Mine. Accordingly, the insurer's motion for judgment n. o. v. should have been granted.

Conclusion

In conclusion, we hold that the district court did not err in entering judgment n. o. v. against Eastern based on the speculative nature of the evidence concerning the [first issue] . . . . We further hold that the district court erred in denying the motion for judgment n. o. v. against Eastern with respect to the brokerage and substitute coal expenses. Accordingly, the case will be affirmed in part, reversed in part, and remanded to the district court for entry of judgment against the insurers for $287,277, the amount conceded to be owed by defendants.

NOTE

1. *A Tool for Your Toolbox.* Although the sophisticated purchaser defense has not been adopted in many states, it is an argument that could allow insurers to escape the strict liability version of *contra proferentem*, so one should expect counsel representing insurers to continue advancing it. For a further understanding of the defense, *see* Jeffrey W. Stempel, *Reassessing The Sophisticated Policyholder Defense in Insurance Coverage Litigation*, 42 Drake L. Rev. 808, 829, 833, 840, 849–52 (1993); Hazel Glenn Beh, *Reassessing the Sophisticated Insured Exception*, 39 Tort & Ins. L.J. 85, 94 (2003).

CHAPTER THREE

POLICYHOLDER/LIABILITY INSURER RELATIONSHIP

■ ■ ■

> *"Most people don't give the risk of a lawsuit a second thought. But with liability law suits on the rise and attorneys seeking larger awards, the risk is very real. . . . In a lawsuit, where damages can run to millions of dollars, . . . [y]ou can lose your life's savings . . . and the equity in your home in a large claim. . . . [You need] protection beyond your capacity to pay for legal defense and claims."*
>
> — Ray Martin, *Moneywatch*, CBS News, May 30, 2013

Every liability insurance policy contains a variety of provisions setting forth the insurer's and the policyholder's rights and responsibilities when claims are asserted against the policyholder. Sequentially, the first responsibility is the policyholder's—giving notice to the insurer of the claim asserted against the policyholder. The policyholder has other responsibilities during claims processing, too, including cooperating with the insurer, giving examinations under oath when requested, etc. These will be discussed in later chapters. Once the insurer receives notice of a claim, the insurer's obligations commence, and two of these constitute the core of the security the policyholder seeks when purchasing liability insurance: 1) defending claims asserted against the policyholder, and 2) paying any settlements or judgments entered against the policyholder with respect to covered claims. These two insurer obligations are known as the defense and indemnity obligations. Insurers have these rights and obligations because it is the insurers' money that ultimately is used to fund the defense, as well as settlements and judgments. The content of these obligations is the product of a complex mix of policy language, court-made rules interpreting and applying this language, occasionally statutes, and the rules of professional conduct that govern the actions of attorneys retained to fulfill the insurer's defense responsibility. This chapter examines this mix and some of the challenging questions arising out of it.

I. THE DUTY TO DEFEND

Under many policies, including policies sold in the consumer lines, the duty to defend and the duty to indemnify are independent in the sense that money spent defending a case does not erode the policy limits. The duties to defend and indemnify, however, do share a very important characteristic: both are tied to coverage. In most states, if a single claim asserted against the policyholder is potentially covered, then the insurer's defense obligation can be limitless, whereas the indemnity obligation will be capped by the policy limits. In some lines of insurance, insurers sell what are commonly called "defense within limits" policies (also known as "wasting" policies or "burning limits" policies), under which every dollar spent defending the policyholder (i.e., on defense costs) reduces the funds available to pay a settlement or judgment. In these kinds of policies, essentially one limit exists which can be used for defense costs or indemnity. If, for example, the limits are exhausted for defense costs, then nothing is available for the indemnity obligation.

Most older policies stated an insurer's duty to defend extends to covered claims even when the allegations against the policyholder were "groundless, false, or fraudulent." Even though most current iterations of liability policies do not contain that phrase, it continues to accurately reflect the fact that the duty to defend is broader than the duty to indemnify. An insurer's duty to indemnify is triggered only if a claim is reduced to a settlement or a judgment against the policyholder. But, in most states, if a single claim asserted against the policyholder potentially is covered, then all claims—even if the policyholder wins the case or no settlement is ever reached—must be defended. Thus, the universe of claims that must be defended is larger than the universe of claims that must be indemnified.

Today, the insuring agreement in the standard liability insurance policy has language stating that the insurer has a "right and a duty to defend the insured against any 'suit.'" What does this phrase mean, and what is the scope of the obligation? What are the consequences for an insurer that breaches the duty to defend? The next three cases illustrate some courts' views regarding the answers to those questions.

A. DETERMINATION OF THE DUTY TO DEFEND AND ITS IMPACT ON THE INDEMNIFICATION OBLIGATION

BRESEE HOMES, INC. V. FARMERS INS. EXCHANGE

293 P.3d 1036 (Or. 2012)

Opinion

DURHAM, J.

Plaintiff, Bresee Homes, Inc. (Bresee), seeks review of a Court of Appeals decision that affirmed a trial court judgment in favor of defendant, Farmers Insurance Exchange (Farmers). *Bresee Homes, Inc. v. Farmers*

Ins. Exchange, 227 Or.App. 587, 206 P.3d 1091 (2009). The dispute concerns the correct interpretation of the commercial general liability (CGL) policy that Farmers sold to Bresee. For the reasons explained below, we reverse.

. . . .

On July 15, 2005, the Joneses filed an action against Bresee for breach of contract and negligence regarding the construction of their home. The Joneses alleged that, on April 2, 1999, they had contracted with Bresee, a contractor, for the construction of a custom home in Salem. They alleged that Bresee had failed to install flashing properly and that the exterior synthetic stucco, known as the Exterior Insulated Finish System (EIFS), leaked water into the interior and failed. They sought $52,580 in damages from Bresee, consisting of both the cost to repair the siding work and damages arising from the failure of the siding.

According to Bresee, Farmers had sold a CGL policy to Bresee that was in effect over various successive periods from the late 1980s to June 17, 2003. When Bresee received the Joneses' complaint, Bresee tendered the Joneses' claims to Farmers and requested a defense and indemnification under the CGL policy. When Bresee tendered the Joneses' claims, Farmers, acting through its lawyer, denied the tender, citing the "products—completed operations hazard" exclusion in the policy. We discuss the pertinent provisions of the CGL policy and the exclusion below.

Bresee filed this action against Farmers for breach of contract and for a declaratory judgment, asserting, as noted above, that Farmers had contractual obligations to provide a defense against the Joneses' action and to indemnify Bresee for any liability to the Joneses. Farmers filed a motion for summary judgment and argued that the "products—completed operations hazard" endorsement to the CGL policy precluded any liability to Bresee. Bresee filed a cross-motion for partial summary judgment and argued that the endorsement did not apply and that, even if it did, the court should conclude that the Joneses' complaint, reasonably construed, could be read to include a covered loss, *i.e.,* property damage occurring before completion of construction and damages arising from the failure of a product installed by a subcontractor.

. . . .

The trial court . . . granted Farmers's motion for summary judgment and denied Bresee's cross-motion for partial summary judgment. The trial court determined, as an initial matter, that the property damage claimed by the Joneses was included within the coverage portion of the Farmers CGL policy. However, the court ultimately concluded that the "products—completed operations hazard" policy provision defeated any claim for coverage. The trial court also determined that Bresee's claim for a defense was not well taken because Bresee, in submitting evidence on summary judgment, had not established when Bresee's subcontractor had completed the work and when the alleged damage had occurred.

The Court of Appeals did not separately analyze Bresee's claims for a defense against the Joneses' claim and for coverage under Farmers's CGL policy. That court concluded, however, that the trial court was correct in deciding that the policy was unambiguous and afforded no coverage to Bresee. The Court of Appeals affirmed the trial court's decision to grant summary judgment against Bresee. This court granted Bresee's petition for review.

Bresee's claims for a defense and for coverage under the CGL invoke separate contractual obligations governed by different legal standards. We begin with Bresee's claim for a defense against the Joneses' action.

This court examines two documents to determine whether an insurer has a duty to defend an action against its insured: the insurance policy and the complaint in the action against the insured. *Marleau v. Truck Insurance Exchange,* 333 Or. 82, 89, 37 P.3d 148 (2001). As this court has explained:

> An insurer has a duty to defend an action against its insured if the claim against the insured stated in the complaint could, without amendment, impose liability for conduct covered by the policy.
>
> In evaluating whether an insurer has a duty to defend, the court looks only at the facts alleged in the complaint to determine whether they provide a basis for recovery that could be covered by the policy[.] * * * An insurer should be able to determine from the face of the complaint whether to accept or reject the tender of the defense of the action.
>
> The insurer has a duty to defend if the complaint provides *any basis* for which the insurer provides coverage. Even if the complaint alleges some conduct outside the coverage of the policy, the insurer may still have a duty to defend if certain allegations of the complaint, without amendment, could impose liability for conduct covered by the policy. Any ambiguity in the complaint with respect to whether the allegations could be covered is resolved in favor of the insured.

Ledford v. Gutoski, 319 Or. 397, 399–400, 877 P.2d 80 (1994) (emphasis in original; citations omitted).

Regardless of the presence of ambiguity or unclarity in the complaint, the key question is whether the court can reasonably interpret the allegations to include an incident or injury that falls within the coverage of the policy. *Blohm et al v. Glens Falls Ins. Co.,* 231 Or. 410, 416, 373 P.2d 412 (1962). As this court observed *in Marleau,* "[N]either the failure to identify correctly the claims nor the failure to state them separately defeats the duty to defend." 333 Or. at 91, 37 P.3d 148. As long as the complaint contains allegations that, without amendment, state a basis for a claim covered by the policy, the duty to defend arises. *Id.* The inclusion in the complaint of other allegations describing claims that fall outside the policy's coverage is immaterial. *See Abrams v. General Star Indemnity Co.*, 335 Or. 392, 400, 67 P.3d 931 (2003) (if the complaint contains allegations of covered conduct, the insurer has a duty to defend even if the complaint also contains allegations of excluded conduct). Any ambiguity concerning potential coverage is resolved in favor of the insured. *Ledford,* 319 Or. at 400, 877 P.2d 80.

We turn now to the provisions of the CGL policy that Farmers issued to Bresee. The parties agree that the following policy terms were in effect between June 17, 1998, and June 17, 2003; that the parties renewed the policy annually; and that the policy pertains to the claim that the Joneses filed against Bresee.

The policy, as pertinent to this dispute, consists of a broad insuring agreement stating the insurer's promise to pay specified damages and to defend the insured against claims brought against the insured to recover those damages. A list of exclusions from coverage follows the insuring agreement. Finally, the policy sets out a list of definitions of terms and phrases in the policy. We set out below those relevant parts of the policy:

> "Throughout this policy the words 'you' and 'your' refer to the Named Insured shown in the Declarations, and any other person or organization qualifying as a Named Insured under this policy.
>
> "* * * *
>
> "SECTION I—COVERAGES
>
> "COVERAGE A. BODILY INJURY AND PROPERTY DAMAGE LIABILITY
>
> "1. Insuring Agreement
>
> "a. We will pay those sums that the insured becomes legally obligated to pay as damages because of 'bodily injury' or 'property damage' to which this insurance applies. We will have the right and duty to defend the insured against any 'suit' seeking those damages. However, we will have no duty to defend the insured against any 'suit' seeking damages for 'bodily injury' or 'property damage' to which this insurance does not apply. * * *
>
> "* * * *
>
> "2. Exclusions
>
> "This insurance does not apply to:
>
> "* * * *

"j. Damage to Property

" 'Property damage' to:

"(1) Property you own, rent, or occupy;

"* * * *

"(5) That particular part of real property on which you or any contractors or subcontractors working directly or indirectly on your behalf are performing operations, if the 'property damage' arises out of those operations; or

"(6) That particular part of any property that must be restored, repaired or replaced because 'your work' was incorrectly performed on it.

"* * * *

"Paragraph (6) of this exclusion does not apply to 'property damage' included in the 'products—completed operations hazard.'

"* * * *

"1. Damage to Your Work

" 'Property damage' to 'your work' arising out of it or any part of it and included in the 'products—completed operations hazard.'

"This exclusion does not apply if the damaged work or the work out of which the damage arises was performed on your behalf by a subcontractor.

" * * * *

"SECTION V—DEFINITIONS

" * * * *

"14. 'Products—completed operations hazard':

"a. Includes all 'bodily injury' and 'property damage' occurring away from premises you own or rent and arising out of 'your product' or 'your work' except:

"(1) Products that are still in your physical possession; or

"(2) Work that has not yet been completed or abandoned. However, 'your work' will be deemed completed at the earliest of the following times:

"(a) When all of the work called for in your contract has been completed.

"(b) When all of the work to be done at the job site has been completed if your contract calls for work at more than one job site.

"(c) When that part of the work done at a job site has been put to its intended use by any person or organization other than another contractor or subcontractor working on the same project.

"Work that may need service, maintenance, correction, repair or replacement but which is otherwise complete, will be treated as completed.

"* * * *

"15. 'Property damage' means:

"a. Physical injury to tangible property, including all resulting loss of use of that property. All such loss of use shall be deemed to occur at the time of the physical injury that caused it; or

"b. Loss of use of tangible property that is not physically injured. All such loss of use shall be deemed to occur at the time of the 'occurrence' that caused it.

. . . .

The policy was accompanied by a separate form labeled as the "EXCLUSION—PRODUCTS—COMPLETED OPERATIONS HAZARD" endorsement, which states:

"This endorsement modifies insurance provided under the following: COMMERCIAL GENERAL LIABILITY COVERAGE Part.

"This insurance does not apply to 'bodily injury' or 'property damage' included within the 'products—completed operations hazard.' "

Several aspects of the insurance policy are noteworthy. First, the coverage agreement, and specifically the duty to defend Bresee, would apply to the Joneses' claims if the property damages that their complaint sought constitutes "property damage" to which the policy applied.

Second, the policy incorporates qualifying wording for some property damage exclusions that has the effect of limiting or cancelling the particular exclusion. For example, in the coverage portion of the policy, paragraph 2.j. (6) excludes property damage to property "that must be restored, repaired or replaced because 'your work' was incorrectly performed on it." However, the policy declares that that exclusion is inapplicable "to 'property damage' in the 'products—completed operations hazard.' Similarly, paragraph 2.1. excludes " '[p]roperty damage' to 'your work' arising out of it or any part of it and included in the 'products—completed operations hazard[,]' " but then declares that that exclusion is inapplicable "if the damaged work or the work out of which the damage arises was performed on your behalf by a subcontractor."

. . . .

In construing the policy to determine whether it gives rise to a duty to defend, we construe the text of the policy as a whole, rather than view particular parts of the policy in isolation. *Hoffman Construction Co. v. Fred S. James & Co.,* 313 Or. 464, 836 P.2d 703 (1992). That principle applies with equal force to the construction of policy endorsements, exclusions, and exceptions. We may conclude, after construction of the policy as a whole, that a particular provision nullifies or limits coverage or that one policy provision controls over another. That conclusion, however, must result from the application of familiar principles of interpretation to the policy as a whole, not from an attempt to give particular weight or effect to one provision because it is an exclusion or exception to the policy's coverage.

Some aspects of the Joneses' complaint are noteworthy. The allegations do not state whether the claimed damages from the alleged breach of contract and negligence occurred before or after the completion of Bresee's work. From all that appears from a reading of the complaint, the described property damage occurred, or could have occurred, when Bresee's work was neither completed nor "deemed complete" under the "products—completed operations hazard," as defined in the policy.

Farmers argues that this court should conclude that the property damage alleged in the Joneses' complaint occurred after Bresee completed its work, in part because that complaint was filed in 2005 and used verbs in their past tense (*e.g.,* "flashing was not properly installed," "the exterior synthetic stucco system failed") to describe the alleged deficient performance. We are not persuaded. The allegations describe events and damage that occurred in the past, but which could have occurred at any time after contract execution. The allegations describing past deficient performance and damage do not necessarily say anything about the date Bresee completed its work.

The Joneses' allegations also do not permit this court to conclude that the alleged damage arose from Bresee's work that "may [have] need[ed] service, maintenance, correction, repair or replacement but which is otherwise complete" within the meaning of the "products—completed operations hazard" definition. The allegations say nothing about whether Bresee's work was "otherwise complete," or whether Bresee's work might need service, maintenance, etc., to be regarded as completed.

Farmers also argues that Bresee bore the burden of demonstrating that the work was *not* completed when the alleged property damage occurred, in order to avoid the effect of the "products—completed operations hazard" exclusion. That is not correct. With regard to the duty to defend, Bresee has no burden to come forth with facts beyond those alleged in the Joneses' complaint. Those allegations stated the pertinent facts when Bresee tendered the Joneses' claims to Farmers and requested a defense. Our analysis of the duty to defend focuses on those allegations whether or not different or additional facts might be adduced at trial.

The Court of Appeals applied a different analysis of Farmers's motion for summary judgment, and we take this opportunity to correct it. As noted, the Court of Appeals observed that Farmers had presented some evidence in support of its motion for summary judgment indicating that Bresee had completed work on the Joneses' home in 1999, and that Bresee had presented no contradictory evidence that the claimed damage had occurred before Bresee had completed its work. The Court of Appeals concluded, as a result, that the record contained no issue of fact on that question and that Farmers was entitled to summary judgment. The court reasoned that Bresee had a specific burden to produce evidence that an exception (*i.e.*, damage arising out of uncompleted work) to the exclusion—the "products—completed operations hazard"—applied. *See Bresee*, 227 Or.App. at 593, 206 P.3d 1091.

The Court of Appeals was mistaken in that analysis. Farmers relied on facts concerning the completion of Bresee's work that were not alleged in the Joneses' complaint. Farmers could discern from facts alleged by the Joneses and from its policy that the Joneses potentially could prove that the claimed damage arose before Bresee completed its work. When Bresee tendered the Joneses' complaint for defense, the factual question of whether the claimed damages had occurred before or after the completion of Bresee's work was an issue that the litigation between the Joneses and Bresee might determine, and, once established, could affect Farmers's duty to indemnify Bresee. The potential factual determinations in that litigation, however, are not the facts that governed Farmers's duty to defend Bresee. When Bresee tendered the Joneses' claims, only the facts alleged by the Joneses and the terms of the Farmers policy governed Farmers's duty to provide a defense.

Farmers also posits that the court's analytical focus in this context is not confined strictly to the insurance policy and the underlying complaint, because this court's cases have left the door open for consideration of other "compelling evidence of no coverage" outside the complaint that would nullify a duty to defend. *See Casey v. N.W. Security Ins. Co.*, 260 Or. 485, 489, 491 P.2d 208 (1971) (applying that criterion); *Marleau,* 333 Or. at 91, 37 P.3d 148 (quoting that criterion in *Casey*). However, the qualification that *Casey* recognized is a narrow one and has no application here.

In *Casey,* the insured drove his automobile into Shelton, causing injuries. Shelton sued the insured, alleging assault and battery. He then amended his complaint to also allege negligence. Ordinarily, the alleged facts would have been sufficient to state a claim covered by the insured's automobile liability policy, and thus, the facts would have given rise to the insurer's duty to defend the insured against Shelton's claim. This court, however, considered other evidence in the record. That evidence demonstrated that, before Shelton filed his complaint, the insured had been criminally prosecuted for his conduct and had been convicted of intentionally injuring Shelton with his automobile. The court held that that evidence was available for consideration because it established beyond dispute that the insured was estopped to assert that he did not act intentionally in injuring Shelton. 260 Or. at 490–92, 491 P.2d 208. The court declined to permit the insured to relitigate a key factual issue that the criminal prosecution already had conclusively resolved against him. The incontrovertible determination that the insured had intentionally injured Shelton established that the insured had no insurance coverage, and thus, the insurer had no duty to defend. *Id.* at 492, 491 P.2d 208.

This case involves no court determination that precludes coverage like the criminal court adjudication considered in *Casey*. This court has consistently focused its analysis on the policy and the underlying complaint,[1] *Marleau,* 333 Or. at 91, 37 P.3d 148, and we adhere to that approach in this case.

The foregoing discussion indicates that the "products—completed operations hazard" exclusion does not eliminate Farmers's duty to defend Bresee against the Joneses' claims. We conclude that the Farmers policy provides a basis for coverage of property damage claims that the "products—completed operations hazard" exclusion does not eliminate. Under the facts alleged in the Joneses' complaint, Bresee could have liability for conduct covered by the policy. Under this court's standard, as discussed in *Marleau* and *Ledford,* Farmers owed a duty to defend Bresee. The trial court erred in granting Farmers's motion for partial summary judgment and in denying Bresee's cross-motion for summary judgment on the issue of the duty to defend.

The parties have submitted additional arguments regarding Farmers's ultimate duty to pay the benefits of its policy to Bresee. We cannot determine the answer to that question at this point. Bresee informed the trial court that the underlying case involving the Joneses had been settled.

---

1 *Casey* explained why the court, in the absence of a judicial determination that precluded coverage, confines its analysis of a claim based on the duty to defend to the insurance policy and the complaint against the insured:

> The insurer has a duty to defend only if the claim made against the insured is one covered by the insurer. *MacDonald v. United Pacific Ins. Co.,* 210 Or. 395, 399, 311 P.2d 425 (1957). The difficulty arises when there is doubt as to coverage. This doubt sometimes cannot be resolved until a judgment is entered in litigation between the insured and the insurer. This is too late; the lawsuit by the injured party has been filed and probably gone to judgment before this time. The insurer has contracted with its insured to defend him. This benefit to the insured would be curtailed if it could be withheld in the event of a dispute about coverage. *For this reason we have adopted the rule that in the absence of any compelling evidence of no coverage, the insurer owes a duty to defend if the injured claimant can recover under the allegations of the complaint upon any basis for which the insurer affords coverage.*

260 Or. at 489, 491 P.2d 208 (emphasis added).

However, neither party disclosed to the trial court the cost of indemnifying Bresee as a consequence of that agreement. Neither party advised the Court of Appeals or this court of the terms of the settlement or how they may affect any issue concerning indemnification. As Bresee correctly argued, whether Farmers has a duty to pay must be determined on the basis of the ultimate facts proven at trial or, as in this case, the facts that formed the basis for the settlement. We cannot determine, from the record made below, whether the policy affords a basis for indemnification. We conclude that neither party was entitled to summary judgment on the issue of indemnification.

The decision of the Court of Appeals is reversed. The judgment of the circuit court is reversed and the case is remanded to that court for further proceedings.

NOTES AND QUESTIONS

1. *Who Is Claiming Against Whom?* The Joneses have a claim against Bresee. Is it groundless? Apparently not, because at the end of the opinion we learn that Bresee settled with the Joneses. Why might the disputed question of coverage matter to the Joneses? Note that in this case the policyholder is suing the insurer. It is often said that if you want to know what is happening, then "follow the money." What are the possible ways the money may be flowing in this set of disputes?

2. *Groundless Versus Non-Covered Claims.* As noted in the test prior to the case, the language often found in older liability insurance policy forms that triggers the duty to defend even "groundless, false, or fraudulent" suits means that the insurer has a duty to defend even though there may be no factual or legal basis for the suit, or even that the claimant's suit is predicated on false or fraudulent grounds. Even if, however, the quoted phrase is not contained in a policy because newer policy forms omit the "groundless, false, or fraudulent" phrase, the essential nature of the coverage is unchanged—the insurer agrees to defend any claim filed against the insured potentially within the policy's coverage, regardless of the claim's merit, and even if the claim is specious.

Some policies, such as professional liability or errors and omissions policies, contain an exclusion providing that "[t]his policy does not apply to any dishonest, fraudulent, criminal or malicious act or omission of any insured, partner or employee." Some courts view the exclusionary language as eliminating the insurer's obligation to defend where false or fraudulent conduct is alleged against the insured; that is, such conduct is outside the policy's coverage. This is to be distinguished from allegations that fall within the coverage but which are falsely or fraudulently brought. *See, e.g., Chipokas v. Travelers Indemnity Co.*, 267 N.W.2d 393 (Iowa 1978); *National Union Fire Insurance Co. v. Shane and Shane Co.*, 605 N.E.2d 1325 (Ohio Ct. App. 1992). *But see Conner v. Transamerica Insurance Co.*, 496 P.2d 770 (Okla. 1972).

3. *The "Potentially Covered" Rule*. A majority of courts apply the potentially covered (or "possibility of coverage") rule used by *Bresee Homes*. For other examples, *see McCormack Baron Management Services, Inc. v. American Guarantee & Liability Insurance Co.*, 989 S.W.2d 168 (Mo. 1999) (en banc); *Shoshone First Bank v. Pacific Employers Insurance Co.*, 2 P.3d 510 (Wyo. 2000); *Maine Mutual Fire Insurance Co. v. Gervais*, 745 A.2d 360 (Me. 1999). As explained by one court in an oft-quoted passage, the duty to defend "rests primarily on the possibility that coverage exists. This possibility may be remote but if it exists[,] the [insurer] owes the insured a defense." *Spruill Motors, Inc. v. Universal Underwriters Insurance Co.*, 512 P.2d 403, 407 (Kan. 1973).

4. *Restatement of the Law of Liability Insurance*. The Restatement reflects the general rule regarding the duty to defend:

§ 13 Conditions Under Which the Insurer Must Defend

(1) An insurer that has issued an insurance policy that includes a duty to defend must defend any legal action brought against an insured that is based in whole or in part on any allegations that, if proved, would be covered by the policy, without regard to the merits of those allegations.

5. *Who Is the Insured?* The short answer to the question, "to whom is the duty to defend owed," is "the named insured and any additional insureds." Suppose that Tortfeasor negligently operates Owner's vehicle in a manner that injures Pedestrian. Pedestrian sues Tortfeasor and alleges that Tortfeasor was operating Owner's vehicle with Owner's permission. Tortfeasor submits the claim to Owner's insurer and requests a defense. If Tortfeasor were operating Owner's car with Owner's permission, then the insurer would be obligated to provide a defense and indemnify Tortfeasor. If Owner, however, claims that Tortfeasor stole the vehicle, must the insurer provide a defense? *See Colon v. Aetna Life and Casualty Insurance Co.*, 494 N.E.2d 1040 (N.Y. 1985); *Holland American Insurance Co. v. National Indemnity Co.*, 454 P.2d 383 (Wash. 1969).

6. *Ambiguous Claims*. If the complaint is ambiguous on a point determinative of coverage, does the insurer have an obligation to defend? The *Bresee Homes* case answers this question in the affirmative. Suppose, for example, like in *Bresee Homes*, that the plaintiff sues the insured for negligence, alleging that the insured's actions caused the plaintiff an injury in July or August of 2017. The policyholder's policy terminated, however, on July 31, 2017. Is the insurer obligated to provide a defense? *See, e.g.*, *Trizec Properties v. Biltmore Construction Co.*, 767 F.2d 810 (11th Cir. 1985); *Howard v. Russell Stover Candies, Inc.*, 649 F.2d 620 (8th Cir. 1981); *Monfils v. Charles*, 575 N.W.2d 728 (Wis. Ct. App. 1998). Does the insurer have a duty to investigate the facts to see if coverage might exist? *See Dairy Road Partners v. Island Insurance Co.*, 992 P.2d 93 (Haw. 2000).

7. *Discovery of Facts Negating Coverage*. If the insurer undertakes the defense of a claim which is not clearly within or clearly outside the coverage, what is the effect of the discovery of facts that unequivocally and absolutely

negate coverage? The majority rule is that an insurer has a duty to defend "until it [can] confine the claim to a recovery that the policy [does] not cover." *See Lee v. Aetna Casualty & Surety Co.*, 178 F.2d 750, 753 (2d Cir. 1949) (opinion by Judge Learned Hand). *See also Meadowbrook, Inc. v. Tower Insurance Co.*, 559 N.W.2d 411, 416 (Minn. 1997) ("[A]n insurer who undertakes an insured's defense under a reservation of rights can withdraw its defense once all arguably covered claims have been dismissed with finality"). If the insurer must defend whenever there is a "potentiality" of coverage, should the insurer be allowed to disclaim the duty when it is clear that there is no potential for coverage based on extrinsic evidence? *See Dairy Road Partners v. Island Insurance Co.*, 992 P.2d 93, 113–14 (Haw. 2000) (discussing split of authority but noting the majority rule is that insurers cannot rely upon disputed extrinsic evidence to defeat the duty to defend).

If, as a general rule, the insurer is allowed to withdraw from the defense when no potentially covered claims remain in the case, can an insurer withdraw if the only potentially covered claim is eliminated on the eve of trial? *See Raymond v. Monsanto Co.*, 329 F. Supp. 247 (D.N.H. 1971). In general, an insurer cannot withdraw from the defense if the timing of doing so would prejudice the policyholder's defense.

8. *Premature Termination of the Duty to Defend?* Since the 1980s, the ISO CGL policy form has read, in pertinent part, as follows: "Our [the insurer's] right and duty to defend end when we have used up the applicable limit of insurance in the payment of judgments or settlements under Coverages A [bodily injury and property damage liability] or B [personal and advertising injury or liability] or medical expenses under Coverage C." The vast majority of courts take note of the words "judgments" and "settlements" and reason that if the insurer has paid out the policy limits pursuant to judgments or settlements, then the duty to defend no longer exists. *See, e.g., Utah Power & Light Co. v. Federal Insurance Co.*, 711 F. Supp. 1544 (D. Utah 1989); *Samply v. Integrity Insurance Co.*, 476 So. 2d 79 (Ala. 1985). This does not mean, however, that in circumstances where the plaintiff has a claim against the insured for much more than the policy limits, the insurer can simply tender the policy limits and refuse to defend. Such a payment would not be made pursuant to a "judgment" or "settlement." *See, e.g., Continental Insurance Co. v. Burr*, 706 A.2d 499 (Del. 1998) (insurer that tendered policy limits in interpleader action against multiple persons injured by insured in accident had not satisfied duty to defend); *California Casualty Insurance Co. v. State Farm Mutual Automobile Insurance Co.*, 913 P.2d 505 (Ariz. Ct. App. 1996) (primary insurer not relieved of duty to defend insured by paying policy limits to tort claimant).

9. *Pre-Tender Defense Costs.* As explored in more detail in Chapter 4, the policyholder must notify the insurer in a timely fashion that an event which may give rise to liability has transpired. If the policyholder has already begun defending itself before notice of the claim is provided to the insurer, should pre-tender defense costs be reimbursable by the insurer? *See, e.g., Nagel v. Kentucky Central Insurance Co.*, 894 S.W.2d 19 (Tex. App. 1994). Note that the

ISO CGL policy form provides in the Section IV conditions that "[n]o insureds will, except at their own cost, voluntarily . . . incur any expense, other than for first aid, without [the insurer's] consent." Consequently, some courts have held that defense costs incurred prior to tender of the defense may not be reimbursable under the "voluntary payment" provision. *See, e.g., Lafarge Corp. v. Hartford Casualty Co.*, 61 F.3d 389 (5th Cir. 1995); *Faust v. Travelers Insurance Co.*, 55 F.3d 471 (9th Cir. 1995). What is the difference, however, between a "voluntarily" incurred defense cost and an "involuntarily" incurred defense cost? Are defense costs incurred in response to legal process and to protect one's legal interests "involuntary" or "voluntary"? *See Fiorito v. Superior Court*, 226 Cal. App. 3d 433 (1990).

10. *A Duty to Prosecute Appeals?* Suppose the insurer provides a defense for the insured and a judgment adverse to the insured is entered in the trial court. What are the insurer's obligations? It is generally accepted that the insurer is not obligated to prosecute appeals where it would be plainly futile to do so. Beyond this principle, there are different tests for the boundary between situations where the insurer must appeal and situations where an appeal is not necessary. *See, e.g., Hawkeye-Security Insurance Co. v. Indemnity Insurance Co.*, 260 F.2d 361 (10th Cir. 1958) (insurer's failure to appeal is breach of duty to defend if failure is fraudulent or in bad faith); *Delmonte v. State Farm Fire and Casualty Co.*, 975 P.2d 1159, 1169 (Haw. 1999) ("[A]s a general proposition, . . . the insurer's duty to defend includes a duty to appeal where reasonable grounds for an appeal exist."); *Guarantee Abstract & Title Co. v. Interstate Fire & Casualty Co. Inc.*, 618 P.2d 1195 (Kan. 1980) (insurer has duty of good faith and fair dealing, which sometimes requires the insurer to appeal).

Does the "reasonable grounds" test mean that the insurer must appeal whenever there are non-frivolous grounds for doing so? If a judgment is entered against the insured in excess of the policy limits, is the insurer required to appeal? If the judgment is within the policy limits, should the insurer have a right to appeal? Does it matter if a possible outcome of a successful appeal is a new trial which may expose the insured to the risk of an excess judgment? *See generally* Robert H. Jerry, II & Douglas R. Richmond, Understanding Insurance Law § 113 (5th ed. 2012).

11. *Mixed Actions: Covered and Non-Covered Claims in the Same Complaint.* If the plaintiff in the underlying action alleges a combination of covered and non-covered claims, must the insurer defend all the claims? As reflected in the *Bresee Homes* case, the insurer has an obligation to defend the entire action. If covered claims and non-covered claims are alleged in the same complaint, what problems might arise in connection with the conduct of the defense if the insurer were only obligated to defend the covered claims?

What about counterclaims? Does the insurer have an obligation to cover the costs associated with prosecuting counterclaims on behalf of the insured? Does it matter whether the costs associated with prosecuting the counterclaims can be segregated from the defense costs? *See, e.g., Shoshone*

First Bank v. Pacific Employers Ins. Co., 2 P.3d 510, 517 (costs associated with prosecuting counterclaims are not covered, but the insurer has the burden of proving such costs can be segregated from the defense costs as a practical matter).

12. *A Right to Reimbursement for Costs Incurred in Defending Non-Covered Claims?* If an insurer opts to defend under a reservation of rights and it is later determined no claims were covered, can the insurer recoup its defense costs? The traditional rule has been that an insurer which defends under a reservation of rights is only reserving the right to contest coverage and disclaim the indemnity obligation, not to recoup litigation costs. *See, e.g., Terra Nova Insurance Co. v. 900 Bar, Inc.*, 887 F.2d 1213 (3d Cir. 1989). The Restatement also adopts this traditional rule. *See* Restatement of the Law of Liability Insurance § 21 ("Unless otherwise stated in the insurance policy or otherwise agreed to by the insured, an insurer may not obtain recoupment of defense costs from the insured, even when it is subsequently determined that the insurer did not have a duty to defend or pay defense costs."). *But see Buss v. Superior Court*, 939 P.2d 766, 775–77 (Cal. 1997) (when an insurer is obligated to defend a mixed action (i.e., an action which alleges both covered and non-covered claims), the insurer is entitled to reimbursement of defense costs incurred in defending non-covered claims but not in defending potentially covered (and, of course, covered) claims).

GRAY V. ZURICH INS. CO.

419 P.2d 168 (Cal. 1966)

TOBRINER, JUSTICE.

This is an action by an insured against his insurer for failure to defend an action filed against him which stemmed from a complaint alleging that he had committed an assault. The main issue turns on the argument of the insurer that an exclusionary clause of the policy excuses its defense of an action in which a plaintiff alleges that the insured intentionally caused the bodily injury. Yet the language of the policy does not clearly define the application of the exclusionary clause to the duty to defend. Since in that event we test the meaning of the policy according to the insured's reasonable expectation of coverage and since the language of the policy would lead the insured here to expect defense of the third party suit, we cannot exonerate the carrier from the rendition of such protection.

Plaintiff, Dr. Vernon D. Gray, is the named insured under an insurance policy issued by defendant. A 'Comprehensive Personal Liability Endorsement' in the policy states, under a paragraph designated 'Coverage L,' that the insurer agrees '(T)o pay on behalf of the insured all sums which the insured shall become legally obligated to pay as damages because of bodily injury or property damage, and the company shall defend any suit against the insured alleging such bodily injury or property damage and seeking damages which are payable under the terms of this endorsement, even if any of the allegations are groundless, false or fraudulent; but the company may make such investigation and settlement of any claim or suit as it deems expedient.' The policy contains a provision that '(T)his endorsement does not apply' to a series of specified exclusions set forth under separate headings, including a paragraph (c) which reads, 'under coverages L and M, to bodily injury or property damages caused intentionally by or at the direction of the insured.'

The suit which Dr. Gray contends Zurich should have defended arose out of an altercation between him and a Mr. John R. Jones.[1] Jones filed a complaint in Missouri alleging that Dr. Gray 'wilfully, maliciously, brutally and intentionally assaulted' him; he prayed for actual damages of $50,000 and punitive damages of $50,000. Dr. Gray notified defendant of the suit, stating that he had acted in self-defense, and requested that the company defend. Defendant refused on the ground that the complaint alleged an intentional tort which fell outside the coverage of the policy. Dr. Gray thereafter unsuccessfully defended on the theory of self-defense; he suffered a judgment of $6,000 actual damages although the jury refused to award punitive damages.

Dr. Gray then filed the instant action charging defendant with breach of its duty to defend. . . . [T]he court rendered judgment in favor of defendant. We must decide whether or not defendant bore the obligation to defend plaintiff in the Missouri action.

Defendant argues that it need not defend an action in which the complaint reveals on its face that the claimed bodily injury does not fall within the indemnification coverage; that here the Jones complaint alleged that the insured committed an assault, which fell outside such coverage. Defendant urges, as a second answer to plaintiff's contention, that the contract, if construed to require defense of the insured, would violate the public policy of the state and that, indeed, the judgment in the third party suit upholding the claim of an intentional bodily injury operates to estop the insured from recovery. Defendant thirdly contends that any requirement that it defend the Jones suit would embroil it in a hopeless conflict of interest. Finally it submits that, even if it should have defended the third party suit, the damages against it should encompass only the insured's expenses of defense and not the judgment against him.

We shall explain our reasons for concluding that defendant was obligated to defend the Jones suit, and our grounds for rejecting defendant's remaining propositions. Since the policy sets forth the duty to defend as a primary one and since the insurer attempts to avoid it only by an unclear

---

[1] Immediately preceding the altercation Dr. Gray had been driving an automobile on a residential street when another automobile narrowly missed colliding with his car. Jones, the driver of the other car, left his vehicle, approached Dr. Gray's car in a menacing manner and jerked open the door. At that point Dr. Gray, fearing physical harm to himself and his passengers, rose from his seat and struck Jones.

exclusionary clause, the insured would reasonably expect, and is legally entitled to, such protection. As an alternative but secondary ground for our ruling we accept, for purposes of argument, defendant's contention that the duty to defend arises only if the third party suit involves a liability for which the insurer would be required to indemnify the insured, and, even upon this basis, we find a duty to defend.

In interpreting an insurance policy we apply the general principle that doubts as to meaning must be resolved against the insurer and that any exception to the performance of the basic underlying obligation must be so stated as clearly to apprise the insured of its effect.

These principles of interpretation of insurance contracts have found new and vivid restatement in the doctrine of the adhesion contract. As this court has held, a contract entered into between two parties of unequal bargaining strength, expressed in the language of a standardized contract, written by the more powerful bargainer to meet its own needs, and offered to the weaker party on a 'take it or leave it basis' carries some consequences that extend beyond orthodox implications. Obligations arising from such a contract inure not alone from the consensual transaction but from the relationship of the parties.

Although courts have long followed the basic precept that they would look to the words of the contract to find the meaning which the parties expected from them, they have also applied the doctrine of the adhesion contract to insurance policies, holding that in view of the disparate bargaining status of the parties we must ascertain that meaning of the contract which the insured would reasonably expect. Thus as Kessler stated in his classic article on adhesion contracts: "In dealing with standardized contracts courts have to determine what the weaker contracting party could legitimately expect by way of services according to the exterpriser's 'calling', and to what extent the stronger party disappointed reasonable expectations based on the typical life situation." (Kessler, *Contracts of Adhesion* (1943) 43 Colum.L.Rev. 629, 637.)

. . . .

Thus we held in *Steven v. Fidelity & Casualty Co., supra*, 58 Cal.2d 862, 27 Cal.Rptr. 172, 377 P.2d 284, that we would not enforce an exclusionary clause in an insurance contract which was unclear, saying: "If (the insurer) deals with the public upon a mass basis, the notice of non-coverage of the policy, in a situation in which the public may reasonably expect coverage, must be conspicuous, plain and clear." P. 878, 27 Cal.Rptr. p. 182, 377 P.2d p. 294.)

When we test the instant policy by these principles we find that its provisions as to the obligation to defend are uncertain and undefined; in the light of the reasonable expectation of the insured, they require the performance of that duty. At the threshold we note that the nature of the obligation to defend is itself necessarily uncertain. Although insurers have often insisted that the duty arises only if the insurer is bound to indemnify the insured, this very contention creates a dilemma. No one can determine whether the third party suit does or does not fall within the indemnification coverage of the policy until that suit is resolved; in the instant case, the determination of whether the insured engaged in intentional, negligent or even wrongful conduct depended upon the judgment in the Jones suit, and, indeed, even after that judgment, no one could be positive whether it rested upon a finding of plaintiff's negligent or his intentional conduct. The carrier's obligation to indemnify inevitably will not be defined until the adjudication of the very action which it should have defended. Hence the policy contains its own seeds of uncertainty; the insurer has held out a promise that by its very nature is ambiguous.

Although this uncertainty in the performance of the duty to defend could have been clarified by the language of the policy we find no such specificity here. An examination of the policy discloses that the broadly stated promise to defend is not conspicuously or clearly conditioned solely on a nonintentional bodily injury; instead, the insured could reasonably expect such protection.

The policy is a 'comprehensive personal liability' contract; the designation in itself connotes general protection for alleged bodily injury caused by the insured. The insurer makes two wide promises: '(1.) To pay on behalf of the insured all sums which the insured shall become legally obligated to pay as damages because of bodily injury or property damage, and (2.) the company shall defend any suit against the insured alleging such bodily injury or property damage and seeking damages which are payable under the terms of this endorsement, even if any of the allegations of the suit are groundless, false, or fraudulent': clearly these promises, without further clarification, would lead the insured reasonably to expect the insurer to defend him against suits seeking damages for bodily injury, whatever the alleged cause of the injury, whether intentional or inadvertent.

But the insurer argues that the third party suit must seek 'damages which are Payable under the terms of this endorsement'; it contends that this limitation modifies the general duty to defend by confining the duty only to actions seeking damages within the primary coverage of the policy. Under 'Exclusions' the policy provides that it 'does not apply * * * under coverage L and M to bodily injury * * * caused intentionally by * * * the insured.'

The very first paragraph as to coverage, however, provides that 'the company shall defend any such suit against the insured alleging such bodily injury' although the allegations of the suit are groundless, false or fraudulent. This language, in its broad sweep, would lead the insured reasonably to expect defense of any suit regardless of merit or cause. The relation of the exclusionary clause to this basic promise is anything but clear. The basic promise would support the insured's reasonable expectation that he had bought the rendition of legal services to defend against a suit for bodily injury which alleged he had caused it, negligently, nonintentionally, intentionally or in any other manner. The doctrines and cases we have set forth tell us that the exclusionary clause must be 'conspicuous, plain and clear.' (*Steven v. Fidelity & Casualty Co.*, supra, 58 Cal.2d 862, 878, 27 Cal.Rptr. 172, 377 P.2d 284.) This clause is not 'conspicuous' since it appears only after a long and complicated page of fine print, and is itself in fine print; its relation to the remaining clauses of the policy and its effect is surely not 'plain and clear.'

A further uncertainty lurks in the exclusionary clause itself. It alludes to damage caused 'intentionally by or at the direction of the insured.' Yet an act of the insured may carry out his 'intention' and also cause unintended harm. When set next to the words 'at the direction of the insured' the word 'intentionally' might mean to the layman collusive, wilful or planned action beyond the classical notion of intentional tort.[11] This built-in ambiguity has caused debate and refined definition in many courts; in any event, the word surely cannot be 'plain and clear' to the layman.

The insured is unhappily surrounded by concentric circles of uncertainty: the first, the unascertainable nature of the insurer's duty to defend; the second, the unknown effect of the provision that the insurer must defend even a groundless, false or fraudulent claim; the third, the uncertain extent of the indemnification coverage. Since we must resolve uncertainties in favor of the insured and interpret the policy provisions according to the layman's reasonable expectations, and since the effect of the exclusionary clause is neither conspicuous, plain nor clear, we hold that in the present case the policy provides for an obligation to defend and that such obligation is independent of the indemnification coverage.

. . . .

Our holding that the insurer bore the obligation to defend because the policy led plaintiff reasonably to expect such defense, and because the insurer's exclusionary clause did not exonerate it, cuts across defendant's answering contention that the duty arises only if the pleadings disclose a cause of action for which the insurer must indemnify the insured. Defendant would equate the duty to defend with the complaint that pleaded a liability for which the insurer was bound to indemnify the insured. Yet even if we accept defendant's premises, and define the duty to defend by measuring the allegations in the Jones case against the carrier's

---

[11] Thus Prosser points out: 'The defendant who acts in the belief or consciousness that he is causing an appreciable risk of harm to another may be negligent and if the risk is great his conduct may be characterized as reckless or wanton, but it is not classed as an intentional wrong. In such cases the distinction between intent and negligence obviously is a matter of degree.' (Prosser, Law of Torts (3d ed. 1965) p. 32.)

liability to indemnify, defendant's position still fails. We proceed to discuss this alternative ground of liability of the insurer, accepting for such purpose the insurer's argument that we must test the third party suit against the indemnification coverage of the policy. We point out that the carrier must defend a suit which potentially seeks damages within the coverage of the policy; the Jones action was such a suit.

Defendant cannot construct a formal fortress of the third party's pleadings and retreat behind its walls. The pleadings are malleable, changeable and amendable. Although an earlier decision reads: 'In determining whether or not the appellant was bound to defend * * * the language of its contract must first be looked to, and next the allegations of the complaints * * *' (*Lamb v. Belt Casualty Co.*, *supra*, 3 Cal.App.2d 624, 630, 40 P.2d 311, 314), courts do not examine only the pleaded word but the potential liability created by the suit. Since the instant action presented the potentiality of a judgment based upon nonintentional conduct, and since liability for such conduct would fall within the indemnification coverage, the duty to defend became manifest at the outset.

To restrict the defense obligation of the insurer to the precise language of the pleading would not only ignore the thrust of the cases but would create an anomaly for the insured. Obviously, as *Ritchie v. Anchor Casualty Co.*, *supra*, 135 Cal.App.2d 245, 286 P.2d 1000, points out, the complainant in the third party action drafts his complaint in the broadest terms; he may very well stretch the action which lies in only nonintentional conduct to the dramatic complaint that alleges intentional misconduct. In light of the likely overstatement of the complaint and of the plasticity of modern pleading, we should hardly designate the third party as the arbiter of the policy's coverage.

Since modern procedural rules focus on the facts of a case rather than the theory of recovery in the complaint, the duty to defend should be fixed by the facts which the insurer learns from the complaint, the insured, or other sources. An insurer, therefore, bears a duty to defend its insured whenever it ascertains facts which give rise to the potential of liability under the policy. In the instant case the complaint itself, as well as the facts known to the insurer, sufficiently apprised the insurer of these possibilities; hence we need not set out when and upon what other occasions the duty of the insurer to ascertain such possibilities otherwise arises.

Jones' complaint clearly presented the possibility that he might obtain damages that were covered by the indemnity provisions of the policy. Even conduct that is traditionally classified as 'intentional' or 'wilful' has been held to fall within indemnification coverage.[16] Moreover, despite Jones'

---

[16] See cases collected in fn. 12, *supra*. As the court said in *Russ-Field Corp. v. Underwriters at Lloyd's* (1958) 164 Cal.App.2d 83, 96, 330 P.2d 432, 439, 'A 'wilful act' as used in this statute connotes something more blameworthy than the sort of misconduct involved in ordinary

pleading of intentional and wilful conduct, he could have amended his complaint to allege merely negligent conduct. Further, plaintiff might have been able to show that in physically defending himself, even if he exceeded the reasonable bounds of self-defense, he did not commit wilful and intended injury, but engaged only in nonintentional tortious conduct. Thus, even accepting the insurer's premise that it had no obligation to defend actions seeking damages not within the indemnification coverage, we find, upon proper measurement of the third party action against the insurer's liability to indemnify, it should have defended because the loss could have fallen within that liability.

. . . .

Nor can we accept defendant's argument that the duty to defend dissolves simply because the insured is unsuccessful in his defense and because the injured party recovers on the basis of a finding of the assured's wilful conduct. Citing *Abbott v. Western Nat. Indem. Co.* (1958) 165 Cal.App.2d 302, 331 P.2d 997, the insurer urges that if the judgment in a third party suit goes against the insured it operates as 'res judicata or collateral estoppel in the insured's action or proceeding against the insurer.'

We have explained that the insured would reasonably expect a defense by the insurer in all personal injury actions against him. If he is to be required to finance his own defense and then, only if successful, hold the insurer to its promise by means of a second suit for reimbursement, we defeat the basic reason for the purchase of the insurance. In purchasing his insurance the insured would reasonably expect that he would stand a better chance of vindication if supported by the resources and expertise of his insurer than if compelled to handle and finance the presentation of his case. He would, moreover, expect to be able to avoid the time, uncertainty and capital outlay in finding and retaining an attorney of his own. 'The courts will not sanction a construction of the insurer's language that will defeat the very purpose or object of the insurance.' (*Ritchie v. Anchor Casualty Co., supra,* 135 Cal.App.2d 245, 257, 286 P.2d 1000, 1007.)

Similarly, we find no merit in the insurer's third contention that our holding will embroil it in a conflict of interests. According to the insurer our ruling will require defense of an action in which the interests of insurer and insured are so opposed as to nullify the insurer's fulfillment of its duty of defense and of the protection of its own interests. For example, the argument goes, if defendant had defended against the Jones suit it would have sought to establish either that the insured was free from any liability or that such liability rested on intentional conduct. The insured, of course, would also seek a verdict holding him not liable but, if found liable, would attempt to obtain a ruling that such liability emanated from the

negligence, and something more than the mere intentional doing of an act constituting such negligence.'

nonintentional conduct within his insurance coverage. Thus, defendant contends, an insurer, if obligated to defend in this situation, faces an insoluble ethical problem.

Since, however, the court in the third party suit does not adjudicate the issue of coverage, the insurer's argument collapses. The only question there litigated is the insured's liability. The alleged victim does not concern himself with the theory of liability; he desires only the largest possible judgment. Similarly, the insured and insurer seek only to avoid, or at least to minimize, the judgment. As we have noted, modern procedural rules focus on whether, on a given set of facts, the plaintiff, regardless of the theory, may recover. Thus the question of whether or not the insured engaged in intentional conduct does not normally formulate an issue which is resolved in that litigation.[18]

In any event, if the insurer adequately reserves its right to assert the noncoverage defense later, it will not be bound by the judgment. If the injured party prevails, that party or the insured will assert his claim against the insurer. At this time the insurer can raise the noncoverage defense previously reserved. In this manner the interests of insured and insurer in defending against the injured party's primary suit will be identical; the insurer will not face the suggested dilemma.

Finally, defendant urges that our holding should require only the reimbursement of the insured's expenses in defending the third party action but not the payment of the judgment. Defendant acknowledges the general rule that an insurer that wrongfully refuses to defend is liable on the judgment against the insured. (*Arenson v. Nat. Automobile & Cas. Ins. Co.* (1955) 45 Cal.2d 81, 84, 286 P.2d 816; Civ.Code, s 2778.) Defendant argues, however, that the instant situation should be distinguished from that case because here the judgment has not necessarily been rendered on a theory within the policy coverage. Thus defendant would limit the insured's recovery to the expenses of the third party suit.

We rejected a similar proposal in *Tomerlin v. Canadian Indemnity Co., supra*, 61 Cal.2d 638, 649–650, 39 Cal.Rptr. 731, 394 P.2d 571. In that case, as we have noted, the insurer's obligation to defend arose out of estoppel. The insurer contended that we should apply a 'tort' theory of damages to its wrongful refusal to defend. Such a theory, we explained, would impose upon the insured 'the impossible burden' of proving the extent of the loss caused by the insurer's breach. As this court said in an analogous situation in *Arenson v. National Auto. & Cas. Ins. Co.* (1957) 48 Cal.2d 528, 539, 310 P.2d 961, 968: 'Having defaulted such agreement the company is manifestly bound to reimburse its insured for the full amount of any

[18] In rare cases the issue of punitive damages or a special verdict might present a potential conflict of interests, but such a possibility does not outweigh the advantages of the general rule. Even in such cases, however, the insurer will still be bound, ethically and legally, to litigate in the interests of the insured.

obligation reasonably incurred by him. It will not be allowed to defeat or whittle down its obligation on the theory that plaintiff himself was of such limited financial ability that he could not afford to employ able counsel, or to present every reasonable defense, or to carry his cause to the highest court having jurisdiction, * * *. Sustaining such a theory * * * would tend * * * to encourage insurance companies to similar disavowals of responsibility with everything to gain and nothing to lose.'

In summary, the individual consumer in the highly organized and integrated society of today must necessarily rely upon institutions devoted to the public service to perform the basic functions which they undertake. At the same time the consumer does not occupy a sufficiently strong economic position to bargain with such institutions as to specific clauses of their contracts of performance, and, in any event, piecemeal negotiation would sacrifice the advantage of uniformity. Hence the courts in the field of insurance contracts have tended to require that the insurer render the basic insurance protection which it has held out to the insured. This obligation becomes especially manifest in the case in which the insurer has attempted to limit the principal coverage by an unclear exclusionary clause. We test the alleged limitation in the light of the insured's reasonable expectation of coverage; that test compels the indicated outcome of the present litigation.

The judgment is reversed and the trial court instructed to take evidence solely on the issue of damages alleged in plaintiff's complaint including the amount of the judgment in the Jones suit, and the costs, expenses and attorney's fees incurred in defending such suit.

NOTES AND QUESTIONS

1. *A Windfall for Dr. Gray?* In the underlying action, Dr. Gray was found by the jury to have committed a willful assault on Jones. If you were a member of the pool of insureds which included Dr. Gray, would you have been pleased if the insurer raised your next premium to help pay for Dr. Gray's defense? If you, as the victim of a willful assault, inflicted physical harm on the perpetrator in self-defense, and if you were later sued by the perpetrator for alleged intentionally-inflicted injuries suffered at your hands, would you be pleased if your liability insurer refused to defend you? In this last scenario, suppose you decided that, although you are certain of your defense, the simplest way to be rid of the nuisance suit would be to pay a modest amount in settlement of the claim. Does the insurer's argument in *Gray* imply that the insured who settles such an action automatically forfeits coverage?

2. *Defending Without a Reservation of Rights or a Non-Waiver Agreement.* "A reservation of rights notice is simply a unilateral notice sent by the insurer to the insured stating that the insurer reserves the right to contest coverage despite its undertaking to investigate the claim and defend the insured." Robert H. Jerry, II & Douglas R. Richmond, Understanding

Insurance Law § 114[c][3], at 874 (5th ed. 2012). "A non-waiver agreement is a contract between the insurer and insured in which the insurer agrees to continue with the defense, while the insured agrees that the insurer shall have the right to contest any issues relating to coverage in the event the insured is found liable in the underlying action. . . . In effect and often in form, it is a reservation of rights letter to which the insured has consented." *Id.* at 873. Because an insurer does not have a right to demand that a policyholder enter a non-waiver agreement, why would a policyholder ever agree to do so?

As noted in *Gray*, where a liability insurer improperly refuses to defend an insured or defends without a reservation of rights notice or non-waiver agreement, many courts hold that the insurer has waived its right, or is estopped, to assert coverage defenses later. *See, e.g.*, *Knox-Tenn Rental Co. v. Home Insurance Co.*, 2 F.3d 678 (6th Cir. 1993); *Peavey Co. v. M/V ANPA*, 971 F.2d 1168 (5th Cir. 1992); *Steptore v. Masco Construction Co.*, 643 So. 2d 1213 (La. 1994).

What could the insurer have done differently in *Gray* to avoid the outcome it received?

3. *Recovery of Attorney's Fees Incurred in Coverage Action.* In addition to recovering the defense costs incurred defending the underlying lawsuit when an insurer breaches its duty to defend, in many states the policyholder can also recover the attorneys' fees it incurs when it is required to sue its insurer to establish the breach of the duty to defend. *See* Restatement of the Law of Liability Insurance § 47(3), cmt. *c. Liability-insurance-law exceptions to the American rule regarding attorneys' fees* ("Courts in about half the states award attorneys' fees to an insured that prevails in an ordinary insurance-coverage action, without requiring a finding of bad faith. Most often, the source of the legal rule authorizing courts to award fees in liability-insurance-coverage actions is statutory, but there are many states in which the liability insurance exceptions to the American Rule are common-law rules.").

4. *Self-Defense.* Dr. Gray alleged in the underlying action that the injury he inflicted on the underlying plaintiff was in self-defense. The insurer's contention was that injuries inflicted in self-defense are nevertheless intentional and are therefore excluded from coverage under the intentional act exclusion. Today, many liability policies, such as standard form homeowners policies, contain an exception for injuries intentionally committed as a matter of self-defense. *See, e.g.*, Exclusion 2.a of the Sample CGL Policy in Chapter 4 ("This exclusion does not apply to 'bodily injury' resulting from the use of reasonable force to protect persons or property.").

5. *Strategic Pleading.* Suppose your client suffers serious injury in a wanton, unprovoked attack by a neighbor wielding a shovel. You understand that the neighbor lacks personal assets to pay any judgment of significant size. The neighbor does have, however, a homeowners policy and an umbrella policy with combined limits of $1 million. Should you file a complaint against the neighbor on your client's behalf alleging the neighbor negligently injured your client with a shovel? You realize you could never establish a negligence claim

at trial, but you hope to get at least some insurer-funded settlement of the claim. Should you do so? *See Boyles v. Kerr*, 855 S.W.2d 593 (Tex. 1993). For more discussion, *see* Ellen S. Pryor, *The Stories We Tell: Intentional Harm and the Quest for Insurance Funding*, 75 Tex. L. Rev. 1721 (1997).

6. *Four (or Eight) Corners Rule.* In *Gray*, the court did not restrict its analysis regarding whether there was a duty to defend to just the allegations in the complaint. To the contrary, the court considered Dr. Gray's potential liability under the basic facts alleged and then concluded that Dr. Gray could have been held liable for negligent, as opposed to intentional, conduct. Thus, the insurer had a duty to defend. Other courts similarly have held that if an insurer is aware of facts outside the complaint that would give rise to a covered claim, then the insurer must defend. *See, e.g., Fitzpatrick v. Am. Honda Motor Co.*, 575 N.E.2d 90, 93 (N.Y. 1991) ("[R]ather than mechanically applying only the 'four corners of the complaint' rule . . . the sounder approach is to require the insurer to provide a defense when it has actual knowledge of facts establishing a reasonable possibility of coverage."). Many courts, however, still apply what is known as the "four corners" or "eight corners" rule, which provides that the duty to defend is determined based solely upon the allegations in the complaint and the policy language. *See, e.g., Kvaerner Metals Div. of Kvaerner U.S., Inc. v. Commercial Union Ins. Co.*, 908 A.2d 888, 896 (Pa. 2006) (trial court's ruling regarding the duty to defend was reversed because the trial court considered evidence outside the four corners of the complaint); *see also* Barry R. Ostrager & Thomas R. Newman, Handbook on Insurance Coverage Disputes § 5.02[b] (19th ed. 2019).

EXERCISE

1. On behalf of the insurer in *Gray*, draft a reservation of rights letter that is no longer than 2 pages.

B. TRIPARTITE RELATIONSHIP AND CONFLICTS OF INTEREST

SAN DIEGO NAVY FEDERAL CREDIT UNION, ET AL. V. CUMIS INS. SOCIETY, INC.

162 Cal. App. 3d 358 (Cal. Ct. App. 1984)

Opinion

GAMER, ASSOCIATE JUSTICE.

Cumis Insurance Society, Inc. (Cumis) appeals a judgment requiring Cumis to pay the San Diego Navy Federal Credit Union, J.W. Jamieson and Larry R. Sharp (insureds) all reasonable past and future expenses of their independent counsel retained for the defense of a lawsuit filed against the insureds by Magdaline S. Eisenmann (Eisenmann action).

The issue presented to this court by the appeal is whether an insurer is required to pay for independent counsel for an insured when the insurer provides its own counsel but reserves its right to assert noncoverage at a later date. We conclude under these circumstances there is a conflict of interest between the insurer and the insured, and therefore the insured has a right to independent counsel paid for by the insurer.

The Eisenmann action against the insureds seeks $750,000 general and $6.5 million punitive damages for tortious wrongful discharge, breach of the covenant of good faith and fair dealing, wrongful interference with and inducing breach of contract, breach of contract and intentional infliction of emotional distress. Under insurance policies issued by Cumis, the insureds tendered the defense of the Eisenmann action to Cumis. Cumis associate counsel Willis E. McAllister reviewed the complaint in the Eisenmann action and concluded Cumis had a duty to provide a defense to the insureds. McAllister selected and retained, at Cumis' expense, the San Diego law firm of Goebel & Monaghan to represent the interests of the insureds in the Eisenmann action. McAllister informed Goebel & Monaghan it was to represent the insureds as to all claims in the Eisenmann action, including the punitive damages claim. He also told Goebel & Monaghan Cumis was reserving its right to deny coverage at a later date and the insurance policies did not cover punitive damages.

. . . .

McAllister believed if the Eisenmann action resulted in a finding of wilful conduct or an award of punitive damages, the Cumis policies did not provide coverage for those damages. Moreover, his view was if the Eisenmann action resulted in a finding of breach of contract as against any of the insureds, there might be no coverage under the relevant Cumis policies. Accordingly, on behalf of Cumis, McAllister notified each insured by letter Cumis was reserving its rights to disclaim coverage and denying any coverage for punitive damages.[2]

---

[2] The reservation of rights letter explained:

"Because of the nature of the case and the present lack of factual information relative to the allegations of the plaintiff, it is necessary for CUMIS Insurance Society, Inc. to reserve its rights to disclaim coverage on the ground that the actions complained of by the plaintiff are not covered under the Directors and Officers Endorsement to the CUMIS Discovery Bond, or any other coverage provided by CUMIS to you. CUMIS specifically denies any coverage for punitive damages in the above-mentioned legal action.

"On behalf of CUMIS Insurance Society, Inc., we will conduct an investigation of this case, and provide the defense to you under a full reservation of the Society's rights. In addition, if CUMIS settles the above-mentioned legal action, CUMIS reserves its right to seek reimbursement from you for such settlement amount if noncoverage by CUMIS is subsequently established. Such investigation, defense or settlement shall not prejudice the rights of CUMIS Insurance Society, Inc. to disclaim coverage at a later date.

"Although CUMIS is not now denying coverage, we are sending this Reservation of Rights letter to you so that we may proceed to investigate the case, defend you or arrange settlement of this suit pending a decision of whether or not the actions complained of by

The Credit Union retained the San Diego law firm of Saxon, Alt & Brewer (independent counsel) to provide independent representation to protect the insureds' interests. Independent counsel notified Cumis it was retained to act as co-counsel with Goebel & Monaghan and presented Cumis a claim for its attorneys' fees and costs. McAllister was persuaded California law required Cumis to pay the fees, and he agreed to pay the fees and costs incurred by independent counsel as co-counsel for the insureds. Cumis paid two separate invoices for legal services of independent counsel but additional invoices were not paid. After independent counsel sent a demand letter to Cumis and further discussed the matter with McAllister, McAllister sought a separate opinion on the question from Cumis' home office and asked Goebel & Monaghan if it felt there was a conflict of interest in representing the insureds such that Cumis would be required to pay the expenses of separate counsel. Goebel & Monaghan told McAllister it did not see a conflict of interest. Cumis' home office came to the same conclusion and McAllister notified independent counsel Cumis would pay no further invoices.

. . . .

In this action, the trial court ruled Cumis is required to pay for the insureds' hiring of independent counsel, rejecting Cumis' argument the court was bound by *Gray v. Zurich Insurance Co.* (1966) 65 Cal.2d 263, 54 Cal.Rptr. 104, 419 P.2d 168, and reasoning:

> . . . .
>
> "The Carrier is required to hire independent counsel because an attorney in actual trial would be tempted to develop the facts to help his real client, the Carrier Company, as opposed to the Insured, for whom he will never likely work again. In such a case as this, the Insured is placed in an impossible position; on the one hand the Carrier says it will happily defend him and on the other it says it may dispute paying any judgment, but trust us. The dictum in *Gray* [that there is no conflict of interest for defense counsel when a complaint asserts potentially inconsistent claims against the policyholder—some of which are covered and some of which are not covered] flies in the face of the reality of insurance defense work. Insurance companies hire relatively few lawyers and concentrate their business. A lawyer who does not look out for the Carrier's best interest might soon find himself out of work."

In the usual tripartite relationship existing between insurer, insured and counsel, there is a single, common interest shared among them. Dual representation by counsel is beneficial since the shared goal of minimizing or eliminating liability to a third party is the same. A different situation is

the plaintiff are covered by CUMIS. In the meantime, your rights and interests are being protected as though coverage does extend to the fact situation involved."

presented, however, when some or all of the allegations in the complaint do not fall within the scope of coverage under the policy. In such a case, the standard practice of an insurer is to defend under a reservation of rights where the insurer promises to defend but states it may not indemnify the insured if liability is found. In this situation, there may be little commonality of interest.[3] Opposing poles of interest are represented on the one hand in the insurer's desire to establish in the third party suit the insured's "liability rested on intentional conduct" (*Gray, supra,* 65 Cal.2d 263, 279, 54 Cal.Rptr. 104, 419 P.2d 168), and thus no coverage under the policy, and on the other hand in the insured's desire to "obtain a ruling . . . such liability emanated from the nonintentional conduct within his insurance coverage" (*ibid.*). Although issues of coverage under the policy are not actually litigated in the third party suit, this does not detract from the force of these opposing interests as they operate on the attorney selected by the insurer, who has a dual agency status (see *Tomerlin v. Canadian Indemnity Co.* (1964) 61 Cal.2d 638, 647, 39 Cal.Rptr. 731, 394 P.2d 571).

Here, it is uncontested the basis for liability, if any, might rest on conduct excluded by the terms of the insurance policy. Goebel & Monaghan will have to make certain decisions at the trial of the Eisenmann action which may either benefit or harm the insureds. For example, it will have to seek or oppose special verdicts, the answers to which may benefit the insureds by finding nonexcluded conduct and harm either Cumis' position on coverage or the insureds by finding excluded conduct. These decisions are numerous and varied. Each time one of them must be made, the lawyer is placed in the dilemma of helping one of his clients concerning insurance coverage and harming the other.

The conflict may appear before trial. Goebel & Monaghan represented the insureds in the Eisenmann action settlement conference and the case did not settle although a demand was made within policy limits. Before and during the settlement conference, Goebel & Monaghan was in contact with Cumis but had no contact with the insureds about settlement until after the conference ended. The insureds then wrote a letter to counsel:

> "You should know that the Credit Union desires the lawsuit to be settled without trial. Our insurance coverages, duly paid and contracted for, are precisely for such cases and any settlement liability that may arise therefrom. Your confidence in the defensibility of the case is appreciated. Should trial prove you

[3] *See Purdy v. Pacific Automobile Insurance Co.* (1984) 157 Cal.App.3d 59, 76, 203 Cal.Rptr. 524, which states in part: "[T]he 'triangular' aspect of the representation afforded the insured by the insurer's lawyers is described as a coalition for a common purpose, a favorable disposition of the claim—with the attorney owing duties to both clients. As a practical matter, however, there has been recognition that, in reality, the insurer's attorneys may have closer ties with the insurer and a more compelling interest in protecting the insurer's position, whether or not it coincides with what is best for the insured."

> wrong, however, and the jury awards damages, the insurance may no longer cover the Credit Union's possible losses. As you know, such losses would considerably exceed any possible settlement amount. It is clear that trial in lieu of settlement in this case subjects the Credit Union to a considerably additional risk while possibly lowering or eliminating a claim payout by CUMIS. Such is not the basic premise upon which we contracted for insurance with CUMIS.
>
> I urge you to work for an appropriate settlement before trial in this case so that CUMIS will have provided the risk protection for which the Credit Union has contracted."

On the advisability of settlement, Goebel & Monaghan represented clients with conflicting interests (*Tomerlin v. Canadian Indemnity Co., supra,* 61 Cal.2d 638, 647, 39 Cal.Rptr. 731, 394 P.2d 571). No matter how honest the intentions, counsel cannot discharge inconsistent duties.

The potential problems may develop during pretrial discovery which must go beyond simple preparation for a favorable verdict to develop alternate strategies minimizing exposure. Goebel & Monaghan was bound to investigate all conceivable bases on which liability might attach. These investigations and client communications may provide information relating directly to the coverage issue. Furthermore, counsel may form an opinion about the insureds' credibility. As between counsel's two clients, there is no confidentiality regarding communications intended to promote common goals (Evid.Code, § 962). But confidentiality is essential where communication can affect coverage. Thus, the lawyer is forced to walk an ethical tightrope, and not communicate relevant information which is beneficial to one or the other of his clients.

The ABA Code Ethical Considerations 5–1 reads:

> "The professional judgment of a lawyer should be exercised, within the bounds of the new law, solely for the benefit of his client and free of compromising influences and loyalties. Neither his personal interests, the interests of other clients, nor the desires of third persons should be permitted to dilute his loyalty to his client."

ABA Code Ethical Considerations 5–15 states, in pertinent part:

> "If a lawyer is requested to undertake or to continue representation of multiple clients having potentially differing interests, he must weigh carefully the possibility that his judgment may be impaired or his loyalty divided if he accepts or continues the employment. He should resolve all doubts against the propriety of the representation. A lawyer should never represent in litigation multiple clients with differing interests,

> and there are few situations in which he would be justified in representing in litigation multiple clients with potentially differing interests. If a lawyer accepted such employment and the interests did become actually differing, he would have to withdraw from employment with likelihood of resulting hardship on the clients; and for this reason it is preferable that he refuse the employment initially."

The standard of care expressed in the ABA canons underscores the existing conflict.

Cumis contends *Gray v. Zurich Insurance Co., supra,* 65 Cal.2d 263, 54 Cal.Rptr. 104, 419 P.2d 168, is controlling and asserts Cumis fully met its duty to defend when it retained counsel at its expense and instructed counsel to defend the insureds in the underlying action.

. . . .

[Although the *Gray* court held there was not a conflict of interest in that case that allowed the insurer to avoid its duty to defend,] the court recognized, in the footnote . . . "[i]n rare cases the issue of punitive damages or a special verdict might present a potential conflict of interests, but such a possibility does not outweigh the advantages of the general rule. Even in such cases, however, the insurer will still be bound, ethically and legally, to litigate in the interests of the insured." (*Gray, supra,* 65 Cal.2d at p. 279, fn. 18, 54 Cal.Rptr. 104, 419 P.2d 168.)

Gray found the insurer's contractual duty to defend cannot be avoided by creating a conflict of interest. *Gray* is not controlling here because it does not address whether the scope of the duty to defend includes payment for the insured's independent counsel where a conflict of interest exists.

We find authority for that proposition in an earlier case, *Tomerlin v. Canadian Indemnity Co., supra,* 61 Cal.2d 638, 39 Cal.Rptr. 731, 394 P.2d 571, which involved a coverage problem arising out of a third party complaint alleging conduct partially excluded under the policy. *Tomerlin* stated:

> "Similarly, in cases involving multiple claims against the insured, some of which fall within the policy coverage and some of which do not, the insurer may be subject to substantial temptation to shape its defense so as to place the risk of loss entirely upon the insured. . . .
>
> It is true, of course, that defendant's attorney owes to the insured a legal duty to defend in good faith, but as Professor Keeton points out 'On the other hand [the] company has no duty to sacrifice its own interests when they conflict with those of the insured.' (Keeton, *Liability Insurance & Responsibility for Settlement, supra,* 67 Harv.L.Rev. 1136, 1170.)

> Customarily, insurers, in cases involving tort claims in excess of policy limits, notify the insured that he may employ his own attorney to participate in the defense. (*Id.* at p. 1169.) A like duty must arise in the instant case in which potential conflict stemmed not only from the multiple theories of the Villines complaint and the propriety of settlement, but from the total absence in defendant of any economic interest in the outcome of the suit." (*Tomerlin, supra,* 61 Cal.2d at p. 647, 39 Cal.Rptr. 731, 394 P.2d 571.)

Thus, the California Supreme Court recognized where, as here, multiple theories of recovery are alleged and some theories involve uncovered conduct under the policy, a conflict of interest exists. *Tomerlin* concluded: "In actions in which . . . the insurer and insured have conflicting interests, the insurer may not compel the insured to surrender control of the litigation. [Citations.]" (*Tomerlin, supra,* 61 Cal.2d at p. 648, 39 Cal.Rptr. 731, 394 P.2d 571.) Although *Tomerlin* did not expressly state the insurer had to pay for the insured's independent counsel under such circumstances, this is necessarily implicit in the decision. If the insurer must pay for the cost of defense and, when a conflict exists, the insured may have control of the defense if he wishes, it follows the insurer must pay for such defense conducted by independent counsel.

. . . .

The lawyer's duties in the conflict of interest situation presented here are correlative to the insurer's contractual duty to pay for an independent lawyer when it reserves its rights to deny coverage under the policy. California Rules of Professional Conduct rule 5–102(B) states: "A member of the State Bar shall not represent conflicting interests, except with the written consent of all parties concerned."

Counsel representing the insurer and the insured owes both a high duty of care (*Lysick v. Walcom, supra,* 258 Cal.App.2d 136, 146, 65 Cal.Rptr. 406) and unswerving allegiance (*Betts v. Allstate Ins. Co.* (1984) 154 Cal.App.3d 688, 715–716, 201 Cal.Rptr. 528). When two clients have diverging interests, counsel must disclose all facts and circumstances to both clients to enable them to make intelligent decisions regarding continuing representation (*Ishmael v. Millington* (1966) 241 Cal.App.2d 520, 528, 50 Cal.Rptr. 592). The ABA Model Code EC 5–14, 5–15, 5–16 and 5–17 reinforce these constrictions, EC 5–16 stating in part: "[B]efore a lawyer may represent multiple clients he should explain fully to each client the implications of the common representation and should accept or continue employment only if the clients consent."

One commentator analyzing these Ethical Considerations concluded:

> "The emphasis of the . . . Rules suggests a functional means of resolving the conflicts which confront counsel hired by an insurer

> to defend its insured. The best course is for an attorney to beware of the potential for conflict at the outset. . . . Where a question exists as to whether an occurrence is within coverage, independent counsel representing the insured's interests is required. The insurer is contractually obligated to pay for insured's independent counsel." (Dondaville, 1982, *Defense Counsel Beware: The Perils of Conflicts of Interest,* 26 Trial Lawyer's Guide, 408, 415.)

. . . .

We conclude the Canons of Ethics impose upon lawyers hired by the insurer an obligation to explain to the insured and the insurer the full implications of joint representation in situations where the insurer has reserved its rights to deny coverage. If the insured does not give an informed consent to continued representation, counsel must cease to represent both. Moreover, in the absence of such consent, where there are divergent interests of the insured and the insurer brought about by the insurer's reservation of rights based on possible noncoverage under the insurance policy, the insurer must pay the reasonable cost for hiring independent counsel by the insured. The insurer may not compel the insured to surrender control of the litigation (*Tomerlin v. Canadian Indemnity Co., supra,* 61 Cal.2d 638, 648, 39 Cal.Rptr. 731, 394 P.2d 571; and see *Nike, Inc. v. Atlantic Mut. Ins. Co.* (1983) 578 F.Supp. 948, 949). Disregarding the common interests of both insured and insurer in finding total nonliability in the third party action, the remaining interests of the two diverge to such an extent as to create an actual, ethical conflict of interest warranting payment for the insureds' independent counsel.

Judgment affirmed.

NOTES AND QUESTIONS

1. *The Tripartite Relationship.* Exactly what obligation the insurer owes the policyholder when a conflict of interest arises was vigorously debated for years, but it is now settled in most jurisdictions. To understand what the debate was about and what the conclusions to it mean, it is useful to remember that the insurer's obligation to the policyholder is created by a contract between insurer and policyholder. When the insurer is obligated to provide a defense, it contracts with an attorney to provide the representation. The contract between insurer and attorney may be formal (i.e., a retention agreement) or may be informal (i.e., oral and lacking in detail). When the attorney appears for and undertakes the defense of the insured, the attorney also establishes her own professional relationship with the insured. This relationship might (should) have its own retainer agreement. The substance of the relationship is also informed by the law of agency, the professional and ethical obligations that attach whenever a lawyer-client relationship is created, and fiduciary considerations. Because the defense of a third-party's

claim under a liability policy involves three different relationships (insurer-insured, insurer-attorney, and insured-attorney), the package of relationships is often labeled a "tripartite relationship."

2. *Post-Cumis.* After *Cumis* was decided, in 1987 the California Legislature passed a statute that largely accepted the *Cumis* right to independent counsel. *See* California Civil Code § 2860 (West 1994). The clear weight of authority outside of California also holds that when an irreconcilable conflict arises, the insurer must appoint or allow the insured to select independent counsel whose expenses will be paid by the insurer. *See, e.g., Allstate Insurance Co. v. Campbell*, 639 A.2d 652 (Md. 1994); *White Mountain Construction Co. v. Transamerica Insurance Co.*, 631 A.2d 987 (N.H. 1993). If the insurer defends under a reservation of rights, is this by itself enough to create a conflict? *Compare CHI of Alaska, Inc. v. Employers Reinsurance Corp.*, 844 P.2d 1113 (Alaska 1993) (when insurer defends under reservation of rights, policyholder has right to independent counsel) *and Moeller v. American Guarantee and Liability Insurance Co.*, 707 So.2d 1062 (Miss. 1996) (when defending under reservation, policyholder must be given opportunity to select independent counsel, with reasonable legal fees to be paid by the insurer), *with Delmonte v. State Farm Fire and Casualty Co.*, 975 P.2d 1159, 1172 (Haw. 1999) (sending reservation of rights letter does not, by itself, require appointment of independent counsel). Many courts take the position that a reservation, in and of itself, does not create a conflict. In jurisdictions that do view it as creating a conflict, however, what are the potential consequences to an insurer if the policyholder rejects the insurer's defense under reservation?

3. *Restatement of the Law of Liability Insurance.* The Restatement reflects the majority rule that an insurer has an obligation to provide an independent defense when a conflict arises:

> **§ 16 The Obligation to Provide an Independent Defense**
>
> When an insurer with the duty to defend provides the insured notice of a ground for contesting coverage under § 15 and there are facts at issue that are common to the legal action for which the defense is due and to the coverage dispute, such that the action could be defended in a manner that would benefit the insurer at the expense of the insured, the insurer must provide an independent defense of the action.

4. *Other Kinds of Conflicts.* The situations presented in *Gray* and *Cumis* are not the only kinds of conflict that can arise between the policyholder and insurer. How should the following situations be resolved?

> a. Suppose the policyholder, who operates a business, negligently injures one of his key customers, who then sues the insured for damages. The policyholder desires that the insurer settle the claim in order to protect the business relationship the policyholder has with its customer. The insurer believes the claim is meritless and should be vigorously defended. *See Charter Oak Fire Insurance Co. v. Color Converting Industrial Co.*, 45 F.3d 1170 (7th Cir. 1995).

b. Suppose the policyholder, a prominent local politician, negligently injures a third party, who sues the policyholder. Fearing that the adverse publicity will cause her to lose an election she is contesting and otherwise damage her reputation, the policyholder desires a quick, confidential settlement. The insurer believes the claim is meritless and should be vigorously defended. *Cf. Gibson v. Western Fire Insurance Co.*, 682 P.2d 725 (Mont. 1984) (involving physician-insured).

c. Suppose Ron, the policyholder, is a law student who shares an off-campus apartment with three others. The law students carpool to school and take turns providing transportation in their own vehicles. One day while Ron is driving, the four have a particularly spirited discussion of the parol evidence rule. Ron becomes distracted and runs a red light. The car is broad-sided, and all four suffer injury. The three passengers sue Ron for negligence. Ron feels guilty about the accident and is not particularly interested in the insurer's position that the three passengers were not seriously injured, as they allege. *See Dietz v. Hardware Dealers Mutual Fire Insurance Co.*, 276 N.W.2d 808 (Wis. 1979).

d. Suppose a thief steals the policyholder's car. While driving the stolen car away, the thief hits a pedestrian, who is injured. The thief is insolvent, and the policyholder's auto policy provides no coverage in this instance. (Why? The answer will become clear when auto insurance is covered later in the book.) The pedestrian sues the policyholder under the policyholder's homeowners policy under the novel theory of "negligent storage of an automobile." The policyholder desires that a settlement offer by the pedestrian be accepted to make the case go away. The insurer wishes to vigorously defend the suit for the purpose of establishing a precedent that the theory of "negligent storage of an automobile" is meritless.

5. *Conflicts Under "Defense-Within-Limits" Policies?* The introductory text in this chapter described defense-within-limits policies. Does this kind of policy increase the possibility that there will be an insurer and policyholder conflict of interest? *See* Shaun M. Baldwin, *Legal and Ethical Considerations for "Defense Within Limits" Policies*, 61 Def. Couns. J. 89 (1994); Daniel Dorsch, *Insurance Defense Costs and the Legal Defense Cost Containment Program: Is the Free Ride Over?*, 53 Ins. Couns. J. 580 (1986).

EXERCISE

1. Imagine that you represent a manufacturing corporation that has been sued in a tort class action in which independent contractors who visited the manufacturing operations allege they have contracted cancer as a result of exposure to dangerous substances while at the policyholder's plant. The underlying complaint pleads both negligence claims and intentional tort claims (premised upon allegations that the policyholder knew that people would get

cancer if exposed to the substances used at the plant but failed to warn or protect them). The insurer for the policyholder is defending the action subject to a reservation of rights and seeks to intervene in the underlying action in order to propound special interrogatories that ask the jury to answer a question regarding whether the policyholder expected or intended to cause the alleged injuries to the underlying plaintiffs in order to create a defense to coverage based upon an "expected or intended" exclusion contained in the policy.

Draft a 3-page memo that discusses the issues associated with the insurer's actions as well as potential strategies the policyholder could employ in response to the insurer's actions.

II. SETTLEMENT

Unlike the duty to defend, which is a contractual obligation owed by the insurer to the policyholder whenever there is a claim potentially within coverage, insurers are not required to settle claims brought against insureds but instead have the right to control settlement decisions under most liability policies. (As will be discussed in Chapter 4, professional liability policies, however, typically allow the policyholder to make the settlement decisions subject to the insurer's consent, which cannot be unreasonably withheld.) Under the policy language, insurers reserve for themselves the right to control if and when to settle, as well as the amount of the settlement. Realizing that settlements up to the policy limits are made with the insurer's funds (as are the costs of defending claims), insurers have an interest in retaining control of how those funds are spent. Under older policies, the insurers retained the right to settle as they "deemed expedient." In more recent policies, insurers typically retain the right to settle at their "discretion."

When the policyholder has a stake in the settlement, as is the case when the plaintiff's claim exceeds the policy limits, the possibility may arise that the insurer and the policyholder will have different positions with regard to the appropriate response to a settlement offer made by the plaintiff. Consider this example: If a policyholder has $100,000 in insurance but faces a potential judgment of $1 million, the policyholder has a potentially uninsured liability of $900,000 ($1 million less the $100,000 of insurance). If the insurer believes there is a 50/50 chance of obtaining a defense verdict, it has a 50-percent chance of having $0 in liability and a 50-percent chance of having $100,000 in liability (the policy limits). Consequently, based solely on the measures of forecasted judgments, it has little incentive to settle for more than $50,000 because that is the amount of its expected liability (.5 × $100,000). The policyholder, on the other hand, has a 50-percent chance of owing $900,000, which computes to an expected liability of $450,000. Consequently, the policyholder prefers to settle the case for an amount much larger than the insurer's expected loss, particularly if a settlement could be achieved below, near, or at the policy limits, as the policyholder would owe nothing under that scenario. In this situation, the insurer's and policyholder's interests are different. Under the literal policy language regarding settlement, the insurer has no obligation to consider the policyholder's interests because the insurer has "discretion" whether to settle.

Courts have long recognized this problem, and they have articulated rules to deal with it. The next case is the "chestnut" case regarding an insurer's "duty" to settle.

CRISCI V. SECURITY INS. CO.

426 P.2d 173 (Cal. 1967)

PETERS, JUSTICE.

In an action against The Security Insurance Company of New Haven, Connecticut, the trial court awarded Rosina Crisci $91,000 (plus interest) because she suffered a judgment in a personal injury action after Security, her insurer, refused to settle the claim. Mrs. Crisci was also awarded $25,000 for mental suffering. Security has appealed.

June DiMare and her husband were tenants in an apartment building owned by Rosina Crisci. Mrs. DiMare was descending the apartment's outside wooden staircase when a tread gave way. She fell through the resulting opening up to her waist and was left hanging 15 feet above the ground. Mrs. DiMare suffered physical injuries and developed a very severe psychosis. In a suit brought against Mrs. Crisci the DiMares alleged that the step broke because Mrs. Crisci was negligent in inspecting and maintaining the stairs. They contended that Mrs. DiMare's mental condition was caused by the accident, and they asked for $400,000 as compensation for physical and mental injuries and medical expenses.

Mrs. Crisci had $10,000 of insurance coverage under a general liability policy issued by Security. The policy obligated Security to defend the suit against Mrs. Crisci and authorized the company to make any settlement it deemed expedient. Security hired an experienced lawyer, Mr. Healy, to handle the case. Both he and defendant's claims manager believed that unless evidence was discovered showing that Mrs. DiMare had a prior mental illness, a jury would probably find that the accident precipitated Mrs. DiMare's psychosis. And both men believed that if the jury felt that the fall triggered the psychosis, a verdict of not less than $100,000 would be returned.

An extensive search turned up no evidence that Mrs. DiMare had any prior mental abnormality. As a teenager Mrs. DiMare had been in a Washington mental hospital, but only to have an abortion. Both Mrs. DiMare and Mrs. Crisci found psychiatrists who would testify that the accident caused Mrs. DiMare's illness, and the insurance company knew of this testimony.

Among those who felt the psychosis was not related to the accident were the doctors at the state mental hospital where Mrs. DiMare had been committed following the accident. All the psychiatrists agreed, however, that a psychosis could be triggered by a sudden fear of falling to one's death.

The exact chronology of settlement offers is not established by the record. However, by the time the DiMares' attorney reduced his settlement demands to $10,000, Security had doctors prepared to support its position and was only willing to pay $3,000 for Mrs. DiMare's physical injuries. Security was unwilling to pay one cent for the possibility of a plaintiff's verdict on the mental illness issue. This conclusion was based on the assumption that the jury would believe all of the defendant's psychiatric evidence and none of the plaintiff's. Security also rejected a $9,000 settlement demand at a time when Mrs. Crisci offered to pay $2,500 of the settlement.

A jury awarded Mrs. DiMare $100,000 and her husband $1,000. After an appeal (*DiMare v. Cresci,* 58 Cal. 2d 292, 23 Cal. Rptr. 772, 373 P.2d 860) the insurance company paid $10,000 of this amount, the amount of its policy. The DiMares then sought to collect the balance from Mrs. Crisci. A settlement was arranged by which the DiMares received $22,000, a 40 percent interest in Mrs. Crisci's claim to a particular piece of property, and an assignment of Mrs. Crisci's cause of action against Security. Mrs. Crisci, an immigrant widow of 70, became indigent. She worked as a babysitter, and her grandchildren paid her rent. The change in her financial condition was accompanied by a decline in physical health, hysteria, and suicide attempts. Mrs. Crisci then brought this action.

The liability of an insurer in excess of its policy limits for failure to accept a settlement offer within those limits was considered by this court in *Comunale v. Traders & General Ins. Co.,* 50 Cal. 2d 654, 328 P.2d 198, 68 A.L.R.2d 883. It was there reasoned that in every contract, including policies of insurance, there is an implied covenant of good faith and fair dealing that neither party will do anything which will injure the right of the other to receive the benefits of the agreement; that it is common knowledge that one of the usual methods by which an insured receives protection under a liability insurance policy is by settlement of claims without litigation; that the implied obligation of good faith and fair dealing requires the insurer to settle in an appropriate case although the express terms of the policy do not impose the duty; that in determining whether to settle the insurer must give the interests of the insured at least as much consideration as it gives to its own interests; and that when "there is great risk of a recovery beyond the policy limits so that the most reasonable manner of disposing of the claim is a settlement which can be made within those limits, a consideration in good faith of the insured's interest requires the insurer to settle the claim." (50 Cal. 2d at p. 659, 328 P.2d at p. 201.)

In determining whether an insurer has given consideration to the interests of the insured, the test is whether a prudent insurer without policy limits would have accepted the settlement offer.

Several cases, in considering the liability of the insurer, contain language to the effect that bad faith is the equivalent of dishonesty, fraud, and concealment. Obviously a showing that the insurer has been guilty of actual dishonesty, fraud, or concealment is relevant to the determination whether it has given consideration to the insured's interest in considering a settlement offer within the policy limits. The language used in the cases, however, should not be understood as meaning that in the absence of evidence establishing actual dishonesty, fraud, or concealment no recovery may be had for a judgment in excess of the policy limits. *Comunale v. Traders & General Ins. Co., supra,* 50 Cal. 2d 654, 658–659, 328 P.2d 198, makes it clear that liability based [on] an implied covenant exists whenever the insurer refuses to settle in an appropriate case and that liability may exist when the insurer unwarrantedly refuses an offered settlement where the most reasonable manner of disposing of the claim is by accepting the settlement. Liability is imposed not for a bad faith breach of the contract but for failure to meet the duty to accept reasonable settlements, a duty included within the implied covenant of good faith and fair dealing. Moreover, examination of [our prior opinions indicating that bad faith is the equivalent of dishonesty, fraud, and concealment] makes it abundantly clear that recovery may be based on unwarranted rejection of a reasonable settlement offer and that the absence of evidence, circumstantial or direct, showing actual dishonesty, fraud, or concealment is not fatal to the cause of action.

Amicus curiae argues that, whenever an insurer receives an offer to settle within the policy limits and rejects it, the insurer should be liable in every case for the amount of any final judgment whether or not within the policy limits. As we have seen, the duty of the insurer to consider the insured's interest in settlement offers within the policy limits arises from an implied covenant in the contract, and ordinarily contract duties are strictly enforced and not subject to a standard of reasonableness. Obviously, it will always be in the insured's interest to settle within the policy limits when there is any danger, however slight, of a judgment in excess of those limits. Accordingly the rejection of a settlement within the limits where there is any danger of a judgment in excess of the limits can be justified, if at all, only on the basis of interests of the insurer, and, in light of the common knowledge that settlement is one of the usual methods by which an insured receives protection under a liability policy, it may not be unreasonable for an insured who purchases a policy with limits to believe that a sum of money equal to the limits is available and will be used so as to avoid liability on his part with regard to any covered accident. In view of such expectation an insurer should not be permitted to further its own interests by rejecting opportunities to settle within the policy limits unless it is also willing to absorb losses which may result from its failure to settle.

The proposed rule is a simple one to apply and avoids the burdens of a determination whether a settlement offer within the policy limits was reasonable. The proposed rule would also eliminate the danger that an insurer, faced with a settlement offer at or near the policy limits, will reject it and gamble with the insured's money to further its own interests. Moreover, it is not entirely clear that the proposed rule would place a burden on insurers substantially greater than that which is present under existing law. The size of the judgment recovered in the personal injury action when it exceeds the policy limits, although not conclusive, furnishes an inference that the value of the claim is the equivalent of the amount of the judgment and that acceptance of an offer within those limits was the most reasonable method of dealing with the claim.

Finally, and most importantly, there is more than a small amount of elementary justice in a rule that would require that, in this situation where the insurer's and insured's interests necessarily conflict, the insurer, which may reap the benefits of its determination not to settle, should also suffer the detriments of its decision. On the basis of these and other considerations, a number of commentators have urged that the insurer should be liable for any resulting judgment where it refuses to settle within the policy limits.

We need not, however, here determine whether there might be some countervailing considerations precluding adoption of the proposed rule because, under *Comunale v. Traders & General Ins. Co., supra,* 50 Cal. 2d 654, 328 P.2d 198, and the cases following it, the evidence is clearly sufficient to support the determination that Security breached its duty to consider the interests of Mrs. Crisci in proposed settlements. Both Security's attorney and its claims manager agreed that if Mrs. DiMare won an award for her psychosis, that award would be at least $100,000. Security attempts to justify its rejection of a settlement by contending that it believed Mrs. DiMare had no chance of winning on the mental suffering issue. That belief in the circumstances present could be found to be unreasonable. Security was putting blind faith in the power of its psychiatrists to convince the jury when it knew that the accident could have caused the psychosis, that its agents had told it that without evidence of prior mental defects a jury was likely to believe the fall precipitated the psychosis, and that Mrs. DiMare had reputable psychiatrists on her side. Further, the company had been told by a psychiatrist that in a group of 24 psychiatrists, 12 could be found to support each side.

The trial court found that defendant "knew that there was a considerable risk of substantial recovery beyond said policy limits" and that "the defendant did not give as much consideration to the financial interests of its said insured as it gave to its own interests." That is all that was required. The award of $91,000 must therefore be affirmed.

We must next determine the propriety of the award to Mrs. Crisci of $25,000 for her mental suffering. In *Comunale v. Traders & General Ins. Co., supra,* 50 Cal. 2d 654, 663, 328 P.2d 198, 203, it was held that an action of the type involved here sounds in both contract and tort and that "where a case sounds both in contract and tort the plaintiff will ordinarily have freedom of election between an action of tort and one of contract. An exception to this rule is made in suits for personal injury caused by negligence, where the tort character of the action is considered to prevail, but no such exception is applied in cases, like the present one, which relate to financial damage [citations]."[3] Although this rule was applied in *Comunale* with regard to a statute of limitations, the rule is also applicable in determining liability. Insofar as language in *Critz v. Farmers Ins. Group, supra,* 230 Cal. App. 2d 788, 799, 41 Cal. Rptr. 401, might be interpreted as providing that the action for wrongful refusal to settle sounds solely in contract, it is disapproved.

Fundamental in our jurisprudence is the principle that for every wrong there is a remedy and that an injured party should be compensated for all damage proximately caused by the wrongdoer. Although we recognize exceptions from these fundamental principles, no departure should be sanctioned unless there is a strong necessity therefor.

The general rule of damages in tort is that the injured party may recover for all detriment caused whether it could have been anticipated or not. In accordance with the general rule, it is settled in this state that mental suffering constitutes an aggravation of damages when it naturally ensues from the act complained of, and in this connection mental suffering includes nervousness, grief, anxiety, worry, shock, humiliation and indignity as well as physical pain. The commonest example of the award of damages for mental suffering in addition to other damages is probably where the plaintiff suffers personal injuries in addition to mental distress as a result of either negligent or intentional misconduct by the defendant. Such awards are not confined to cases where the mental suffering award was in addition to an award for personal injuries; damages for mental distress have also been awarded in cases where the tortious conduct was an interference with property rights without any personal injuries apart from the mental distress.

---

[3] *Comunale v. Traders & General Ins. Co., supra,* 50 Cal. 2d 654, 328 P.2d 198, was mainly concerned with the contract aspect of the action. This may be due to the facts that the tort duty is ordinarily based on the insurer's assumption of the defense and of settlement negotiations (*see* Keeton, *Liability Insurance and Responsibility for Settlement* (1954) 67 Harv. L. Rev. 1136, 1138–1139; Note (1966), *supra,* 18 Stan. L. Rev. 475), and that in *Comunale* the insurer did not undertake defense or settlement but denied coverage. In any event *Comunale* expressly recognizes that "wrongful refusal to settle has generally been treated as a tort." (50 Cal. 2d at p. 663, 328 P.2d at p. 203.)

We are satisfied that a plaintiff who as a result of a defendant's tortious conduct loses his property and suffers mental distress may recover not only for the pecuniary loss but also for his mental distress. No substantial reason exists to distinguish the cases which have permitted recovery for mental distress in actions for invasion of property rights. The principal reason for limiting recovery of damages for mental distress is that to permit recovery of such damages would open the door to fictitious claims, to recovery for mere bad manners, and to litigation in the field of trivialities. (Prosser, Torts (3d ed. 1964) § 11, p. 43.) Obviously, where, as here, the claim is actionable and has resulted in substantial damages apart from those due to mental distress, the danger of fictitious claims is reduced, and we are not here concerned with mere bad manners or trivialities but tortious conduct resulting in substantial invasions of clearly protected interests.

Recovery of damages for mental suffering in the instant case does not mean that in every case of breach of contract the injured party may recover such damages. Here the breach also constitutes a tort. Moreover, plaintiff did not seek by the contract involved here to obtain a commercial advantage but to protect herself against the risks of accidental losses, including the mental distress which might follow from the losses. Among the considerations in purchasing liability insurance, as insurers are well aware, is the peace of mind and security it will provide in the event of an accidental loss, and recovery of damages for mental suffering has been permitted for breach of contracts which directly concern the comfort, happiness or personal esteem of one of the parties.

It is not claimed that plaintiff's mental distress was not caused by defendant's refusal to settle or that the damages awarded were excessive in the light of plaintiff's substantial suffering.

The judgment is affirmed.

NOTES AND QUESTIONS

1. *How Much Discretion?* In typical cases, the discretion afforded insurers to settle claims under the policy language is considerable. It may even extend to permitting the insurer to settle claims without obtaining the policyholder's consent. *See Caplan v. Fellheimer Eichen Braverman & Kaskey*, 68 F.3d 828 (3d Cir. 1995); *Shuster v. South Broward Hospital District Physicians' Professional Liability Insurance Trust*, 591 So. 2d 174 (Fla. 1992). Should the insurer have this much discretion if the claim is entirely within the deductible? *See, e.g., Western Polymer Technology, Inc. v. Reliance Insurance Co.*, 38 Cal. Rptr. 2d 78 (Cal. Ct. App. 1995). What if most, but not all, of the claim is within the deductible? *See United Capitol Insurance Co. v. Bartolotta's Fireworks Co.*, 546 N.W.2d 198 (Wis. Ct. App. 1996) (insurer decides to settle claim for $35,000 in circumstances where the self-insured retention was $25,000).

The seminal article on the liability insurer's duties regarding settlement is Robert E. Keeton, *Liability Insurance and Responsibility for Settlement*, 67 Harv. L. Rev. 1136 (1954). For a more recent discussion, *see* Kent Syverud, *The Duty to Settle*, 76 Va. L. Rev. 1113 (1990).

2. *Policyholder's Settlement Without Insurer's Consent*. Ordinarily, the standard liability policy prohibits the policyholder from settling any claims, voluntarily assuming a liability, or interfering in a legal proceeding or settlement negotiation without the insurer's consent.

Suppose an insurer is defending an insured under a reservation of rights and the policyholder has retained his own separate counsel. If the policyholder, through his own counsel, settles with the tort victim without the insurer's consent, does this action breach the cooperation clause of the policy? If so, should the insurer be bound by the settlement regarding the basis of liability or the amount of the settlement? *See United Services Automobile Ass'n v. Morris*, 741 P.2d 246 (Ariz. 1987).

3. *Strict Liability for Refusal to Settle Within Policy Limits?* Should an insurer be strictly liable for failing to accept offers within policy limits? The *Crisci* court pondered the question, but it did not answer the question because of its holding in favor of the policyholder on other grounds. Even though no court has adopted such a rule, a few states have decisions that adopted fairly close standards. *See Rova Farms Resort, Inc. v. Investor Insurance Co. of Am.*, 323 A.2d 495, 509–10 (N.J. 1974) (considered adopting strict liability standard but ultimately concluded it was unnecessary to do so under the facts of the case); *Shamblin v. Nationwide Mut. Ins. Co.*, 396 S.E. 2d 766 (W. Va. 1990) (insurer is strictly liable for judgments in excess of policy limits unless insurer can prove by clear and convincing evidence that its failure to settle was based upon "reasonable and substantial" grounds); *Asermely v. Allstate Insurance Co.*, 728 A.2d 461, 464 (R.I. 1999) ("If the insurer declines to settle the case within the policy limits, it does so at its peril in the event that a trial results in a judgment that exceeds the policy limits, including interest. If such a judgment is sustained on appeal or is unappealed, the insurer is liable for the amount that exceeds the policy limits, unless it can show that the insured was unwilling to accept the offer of settlement. The insurer's duty is a fiduciary obligation to act in the best interests of the insured.").

Suppose the plaintiff sues a policyholder for a claim covered by a $250,000 liability insurance policy. The plaintiff asserts damages of $300,000. The insurer values the claim at $25,000. The plaintiff offers to settle the claim for $200,000. What considerations are important to the insurer's assessment of whether this offer should be accepted? If the insurer refuses the offer and the case is tried, what are the ramifications of each of the following jury verdicts under a strict liability rule? (a) $15,000; (b) $25,000; (c) $200,000; (d) $300,000.

4. *The "Reasonable Offer" Test*. The duty to settle is not absolute. In other words, an insurer does not have to accept each and every settlement offer made by a plaintiff. If the duty to settle is not absolute and a strict liability rule is rejected, there is still a need to articulate a standard which

distinguishes between settlement offers that must be accepted and offers which can be rejected. A variety of tests have been articulated by different courts: the insurer must give equal consideration to the insured's interests; the insurer must act non-negligently; the insurer must act in good faith; the insurer must act reasonably based on a totality of the circumstances. What appears to be the most widely favored rule in the courts is the "reasonable offer test," which is akin to the tort concept of negligence as opposed to bad faith. *See, e.g.*, Ellen S. Pryor & Charles Silver, *Defense Lawyers' Professional Responsibilities, Part I—Excess Exposure Cases*, 78 Tex. L. Rev. 599, 656–57 (2000) ("[A]ll jurisdictions require carriers to make reasonable settlement decisions."). Although most courts allow the factfinder to consider the totality of the circumstances in making this determination, many states use the "disregard the limits" rule that the *Crisci* court employed when analyzing whether the settlement offer was reasonable.

5. *Restatement of the Law of Liability Insurance.* The basic holding in the *Crisci* case is memorialized in the Restatement, which provides:

> **§ 24 The Insurer's Duty to Make Reasonable Settlement Decisions**
>
> (1) When an insurer has the authority to settle a legal action brought against the insured, or the insurer's prior consent is required for any settlement by the insured to be payable by the insurer, and there is a potential for a judgment in excess of the applicable policy limit, the insurer has a duty to the insured to make reasonable settlement decisions.
>
> (2) A reasonable settlement decision is one that would be made by a reasonable insurer that bears the sole financial responsibility for the full amount of the potential judgment.
>
> (3) An insurer's duty to make reasonable settlement decisions includes the duty to make its policy limits available to the insured for the settlement of a covered legal action that exceeds those policy limits if a reasonable insurer would do so in the circumstances.
>
> **§ 27 Remedies for Breach of the Duty to Make Reasonable Settlement Decisions**
>
> (1) An insurer that breaches the duty to make reasonable settlement decisions is subject to liability for any foreseeable harm caused by the breach, including the full amount of damages assessed against the insured in the underlying legal action, without regard to the policy limits.
>
> . . . .

6. *Tort or Contract Claim (or Both)?* Consider what the court in *Crisci* says about the nature of the claim for breach of the duty to settle. Is the duty to settle simply a subset of the duty to defend, in that settling claims is simply one way insurers defend lawsuits against policyholders? By that thinking, the breach of the duty to settle feels like a breach of contract. Yet, for courts that use a "reasonableness" standard to evaluate whether the insurer has breached the duty to settle, it is understandable why the breach of the duty is often

viewed as "sounding" in tort, particularly given that the typical liability insurance policy lacks a specific contractual provision imposing the duty.

If the duty to settle comes from the implied obligation of good faith and fair dealing, does it follow that the duty to settle is a tort-based duty? The Restatement (Second) of Contracts § 205 provides that every party to a contract owes the other a duty of good faith and fair dealing in contract performance. If the duty of good faith is a contract duty, does it not follow that a breach of the duty to settle is a contract breach? Is it possible for an insurer to "fail to exercise good faith in responding to a settlement offer" without committing the "tort of bad faith?" (The tort of bad faith receives more attention in the next section). Why does it matter whether the theory of the action is tort or contract?

7. *The $91,000 Question*. Whether the theory of Mrs. Crisci's action was tort or contract, once the breach of the duty to settle was found, the insurer was liable for the amount of the judgment against Mrs. Crisci above the policy limits. Do you agree that if the theory is contract, the excess judgment is foreseeable at the time of contracting, thereby falling within the range of awardable consequential damages for breach of contract? Does the tort theory take us to the same answer?

Suppose the theory of the action for breach of the duty to settle sounds in tort. After the excess judgment is entered, the insurer voluntarily pays the entire amount of the excess judgment. Should this payment then insulate the insurer from a claim that the insurer exercised bad faith in refusing to settle? *See* David R. Anderson & John W. Dunfee, *No Harm, No Foul: Why a Bad Faith Claim Should Fail When an Insurer Pays the Excess Verdict*, 33 Tort & Ins. L. J. 1001 (1998).

8. *Damages for Mental Anguish*. Contract law generally does not award damages for mental anguish, but it has long recognized special, exceptional classes of contracts where emotional distress damages can be awarded for the breach of contract if it is particularly foreseeable at the time of contracting that mental distress will accompany a breach due to the nature of the contract. *See, e.g., Flores v. Baca*, 871 P.2d 962 (N.M. 1994); *Wilson v. Houston Funeral Home*, 42 Cal. App. 4th 1124 (1996). Should insurance policies be considered one of the special, exceptional classes of contracts where mental anguish is foreseeable if the insurer breaches? Most courts do not. *Crisci* is actually a minority decision with respect to the award of non-economic damages for an insurer's breach of the duty to settle.

9. *Settlement and Multiple Plaintiffs/Multiple Claims*. A liability insurer may settle with some claimants in a multiple claims situation even though such settlements deplete or exhaust the policy limits of liability so that the remaining claimants have little or no recourse against the insurer. However, the insurer must act in good faith. *See, e.g., Castoreno v. Western Indemnity Co.*, 515 P.2d 789 (Kan. 1973). Where there is a discriminatory payment made in bad faith, the insurer may be liable for amounts in excess of

the policy limits. *See Hartford Casualty Insurance Co. v. Dodd*, 416 F. Supp. 1216 (D. Md. 1976).

10. *A Duty to Initiate Settlement Discussions?* If the plaintiff-tort victim never makes an offer to settle within the policy limits or any offer at all, does this mean that the liability insurer has no obligation to conduct settlement negotiations? *See Coleman v. Holecek*, 542 F.2d 532 (10th Cir. 1976) (applying Kansas law); *Fulton v. Woodford*, 545 P.2d 979 (Ariz. Ct. App. 1976). Although the case law is mixed regarding whether insurers have an affirmative obligation to seek to settle within policy limits in the absence of a settlement demand within policy limits, prudent plaintiffs' counsel should affirmatively offer to settle for the full policy limits quickly if the prospects of recovering an excess verdict from the policyholder are poor or the policy has "wasting" limits.

III. INSURER BAD FAITH

Although the plaintiff recovered in *Crisci* due to the insurer's failure to settle when it had a reasonable opportunity to do so, *Crisci* also can be viewed as a bad faith case. Judicial formulations of what constitutes bad faith vary widely, but the common descriptions point to unreasonable insurer conduct that rises to a level of egregious behavior, reckless disregard of the policyholder's interests, or deliberate elevation of the insurer's interests over the policyholder's. In theory, bad faith involves more than making a mistake. A reasonable, but mistaken, judgment is ordinarily not held to be bad faith. The ways in which insurers can find themselves in the hot water of bad faith are myriad. For example, insurer bad faith can be based on an unreasonable denial of coverage. It might arise out of an unreasonable delay in investigating or paying a claim. It might be an unreasonable refusal to defend or an unreasonable refusal to settle. Virtually anything that an insurer does, or is expected to do, in the normal course of business has the potential to become the basis for a bad faith claim.

Insurer bad faith claims are viewed as tort claims in most states, contract claims (breach of the implied duty of good faith and fair dealing) in some states, and in some states they are treated as both. Although many courts state that a viable bad faith claim requires something more than mere negligence by the insurer, as a practical matter, bad faith claims sound a lot like a type of a negligence claim because they are based upon unreasonable insurer behavior, which is the hallmark of a tort negligence claim.

The advantages of asserting a bad faith claim from the policyholder's perspective (and disadvantages from the insurer's perspective) are the additional damage remedies potentially available, such as an award of the attorneys' fees incurred to prosecute the claim, an award of emotional distress damages in some states (such as California, as reflected in the *Crisci* case), and an award of punitive damages if the insurer's behavior warrants it. In some states, statutory extra-contractual remedial schemes exist in place of the common law bad faith remedies.

The next two cases applying Pennsylvania law provide an example of one state's approach to insurer bad faith.

KLINGER V. STATE FARM MUT. AUTO. INS. CO.

115 F.3d 230 (3rd Cir. 1997)

Opinion

Mark Klinger and Linda Neyer appeal from the decision of the district court denying them costs, attorney's fees and the full amount of pre-judgment interest they sought in their otherwise successful bad faith action against State Farm Mutual Automobile Insurance Company. . . . We . . . affirm.

Facts

In August 1992, Klinger and Neyer were seriously injured in a head-on collision while riding in Klinger's van, which was one of two vehicles owned by him and insured by State Farm. The other driver's insurance was inadequate to compensate them for their injuries, so Klinger and Neyer filed underinsured motorist claims against the two State Farm policies.

State Farm disputed the amount of coverage available under these insurance policies, and the parties agreed to bifurcate the issues of coverage and damages and to arbitrate them separately. Attorney Richard Wix represented State Farm. Attorney David L. Lutz represented Klinger and Neyer.

In October 1993, the arbitrators determined that the coverage available under Klinger's two policies was $115,000. That established, in November, Attorney Lutz sent two letters to Wix demanding that State Farm tender the policy limits to his clients. Wix, however, never apprised State Farm of either of these letters. State Farm contends that it did not know the results of the arbitration because its attorney, Wix, did not answer his phone calls. A State Farm claims representative, however, did not personally visit Wix's office until March 1994. Nonetheless, in January 1994, Attorney Lutz told Timothy Spader, a State Farm claims representative, the results of the arbitration and of his demand letters, when Spader happened to be talking to Lutz about another matter.

Spader then contacted Attorney Wix, who promised him a letter documenting the status of the case. After receiving nothing, Spader finally visited Wix's office personally in March 1994 and obtained some medical records and documentary data. Only then did Spader contact Attorney Lutz, who had earlier written that he was considering a bad faith claim and stated that he would provide State Farm with whatever information it needed to evaluate the extent of damages.

Still State Farm did nothing. In March 1994, the arbitrators scheduled the damages arbitration for June 28. Again Lutz demanded that State Farm pay the policy limits. Again, State Farm's attorney apparently failed to forward this request to State Farm. In April, Lutz went around State Farm's attorney, writing directly to Spader, and inquired whether State Farm was interested in settling the case. Still State Farm offered its insureds nothing.

In June, although the hearing was scheduled for less than a week later, and even though Wix himself now recommended that State Farm tender them the policy limits, State Farm made no offer to pay the appellants anything. Instead, State Farm sought a stay of the hearing. Attorney Lutz refused, and they arbitrated damages. The arbitrators awarded $115,000 to Klinger and $70,000 to Neyer. Finally, on August 2, 1994, a full two years after the accident, and months after State Farm had all the information necessary to evaluate Klinger and Neyer's claims, State Farm paid them.

Klinger and Neyer filed suit in the Dauphin County Court of Common Pleas, alleging that State Farm's delay in paying their claims was a display of bad faith under 42 Pa.C.S.A. § 8371. State Farm removed the case to federal court based on diversity of citizenship. The case was tried before a jury, which awarded punitive damages to each plaintiff in the amount of $150,000. State Farm then filed a motion for judgment as a matter of law, or, in the alternative, for a new trial, under Fed.R.Civ.P. 50(b) and 59(a). The district court denied this motion. . . . These appeals followed.

Discussion

Bad Faith Standard

State Farm first argues that the evidence was insufficient to support the jury's verdict of bad faith. It also asserts that the jury was improperly instructed on the test to be applied in determining the existence of bad faith under Pennsylvania law. It is wrong on both points.

The standard for bad faith claims under § 8371 is set forth in *Terletsky v. Prudential Property & Cas. Ins. Co.,* 437 Pa.Super. 108, 649 A.2d 680, 688 (1994), *appeal denied,* 540 Pa. 641, 659 A.2d 560 (1995). There, the Pennsylvania Superior Court applied a two-part test, both elements of which must be supported with clear and convincing evidence: (1) that the insurer lacked a reasonable basis for denying benefits; and (2) that the insurer knew or recklessly disregarded its lack of reasonable basis. The district court instructed the jury accordingly. The *Terletsky* court also stated, however, that:

> "Bad faith" on part of insurer is any frivolous or unfounded refusal to pay proceeds of a policy; it is not necessary that such refusal be fraudulent. For purposes of an action against an insurer for failure to pay a claim, such conduct imports a dishonest purpose and means a breach of a known duty (i.e., good faith and fair dealing), through some motive of self-interest or ill will; mere negligence or bad judgment is not bad faith.

Id. (quoting Black's Law Dictionary 139 (6th ed. 1990)). From this, State Farm argues that a third element must be satisfied, to wit, that the insurer was motivated by an improper purpose such as ill will or self-interest.

We reject that reading of *Terletsky*. Although the definition the court recited did advert to a "dishonest purpose" such as "self-interest or ill will [,]" this is dictum. Moreover, State Farm's self-interest is the only plausible explanation for its delay. Nonetheless, we need not reach that issue: A page later the court actually applied the two-part test:

> To recover under a claim of bad faith, the Terletskys were required to show that Prudential lacked a reasonable basis for partially denying payment . . . and that Prudential recklessly disregarded a lack of reasonable basis in denying the payment. Prudential's actions, however, were reasonably based.

Id. 649 A.2d at 689–90. In our prediction of how the Pennsylvania Supreme Court would measure bad faith claims, we will rely on the actual test that *Terletsky* applied and refrain from creating a third part based only on dictum quoted from *Black's Law Dictionary*. Accordingly, we conclude that the district court did not err when it instructed the jury.

Sufficiency of Evidence

We also believe that the evidence was sufficient for a jury to conclude that State Farm lacked a reasonable basis for refusing to pay the appellants, and knew or recklessly disregarded that fact. State Farm acknowledged at oral argument that it is chargeable with the actions of its attorney. As such, it is also chargeable with his inactions. Moreover, Mr. Spader testified that, as early as March 1994, he knew that liability was clear and that State Farm had received a demand package indicating that both Klinger and Neyer had sustained serious injuries. Next, Wix himself testified that he advised State Farm to tender the policy limits before the damages arbitration. Yet, State Farm never offered to pay Klinger and Neyer anything beyond the early and clearly inadequate offer it made before the coverage arbitration. Finally, plaintiffs' expert testified that State Farm acted recklessly and unreasonably. Hence there is ample evidence from which a reasonable jury could have concluded that State Farm knew or recklessly disregarded the fact that it had no reasonable basis for refusing to pay its insureds' claims.[2] We will not disturb its verdict.

. . . .

Punitive Damages

State Farm also takes issue with the jury's decision to impose punitive damages. It argues that the evidence was insufficient to support such an award and that, in any event, the matter should have been decided by the court rather than the jury. Again, we disagree.

We will look to Pennsylvania law governing punitive damages to determine whether the award was proper. Pennsylvania has adopted section 908 of the Restatement (Second) of Torts governing punitive damages. *Delahanty v. First Pa. Bank, N.A.*, 318 Pa.Super. 90, 464 A.2d 1243, 1263 (1983). They are awarded to punish a defendant for outrageous conduct, which is defined as an act which, in addition to creating "actual damages, also imports insult or outrage, and is committed with a view to oppress or is done in contempt of plaintiffs' rights." *Id.* Both intent and reckless indifference will constitute a sufficient mental state. *See id.*

Here, the district court concluded that the jury could have reasonably found that State Farm's conduct, to wit, relying on its counsel despite his non-performance and never making an offer to pay its insureds before the damages arbitration, was egregious enough to warrant punitive damages. We agree. Insurance contracts create affirmative duties: The insured must pay premiums; the insurer must pay when its insured suffers an insured event. There was testimony from plaintiffs' expert that State Farm's conduct was in reckless disregard of plaintiffs' rights because it "didn't have a good reason for not making an offer[ ]" and because State Farm was not "considering the interests of their—of Klinger and Neyer who were their insureds." He added that "[t]hey made them no offer when there was no reason for not doing this. There was clear liability and serious injuries." When asked how he would characterize that type of conduct, he answered, "I think that's disregarding, recklessly disregarding the rights of their insured." He then stated that, in his opinion, this conduct was outrageous.

[2] State Farm argues that it reasonably relied upon its counsel. We would never opine to the contrary, at least for certain advice and representation. Nonetheless, because this point is argued we find it necessary to remark that representation is not an excuse for the insurer's failure to perform its obligations under the policy it issued to the insured. Here, State Farm's attorney would not even answer his phone calls. With admittedly clear liability, serious injuries and Mr. Klinger on welfare because he could no longer work, it was incumbent upon State Farm to do more. And because counsel for the insureds cannot simply make an "end-run" around the insurer's attorney to deal directly with the insurer, the insurer may not hide behind this relationship to argue that it reasonably ignored its obligations under the insurance policy to its insureds, one of which is to pay them compensation if injured. Otherwise, an insurer could simply hire counsel, bury its head in the sand, pay when ordered to do so, retain the use of the insured's money in the meantime, and escape without adverse consequences.

This testimony provided the jury a sufficient basis to award punitive damages.

State Farm also argues that the issue of punitive damages was required by the terms of § 8371 to be decided by the court and not placed before the jury because the statute provides that "the court" may impose, *inter alia,* punitive damages. Frankly, we fail to see the harm. Clearly, the court can ask for an advisory verdict. Second, the court could have rejected the verdict. Finally, it was the court that entered judgment on the verdict. Hence, it had control at all stages.

Moreover, as State Farm acknowledges, the Seventh Amendment itself provides the right to trial by jury in suits at common law. *See Curtis v. Loether*, 415 U.S. 189, 192, 94 S.Ct. 1005, 1007, 39 L.Ed.2d 260 (1974). Arguing, however, that the Seventh Amendment provides no right to a jury trial on punitive damages in a § 8371 case, State Farm relies on *Tull v. United States,* 481 U.S. 412, 107 S.Ct. 1831, 95 L.Ed.2d 365 (1987). In that case, the Supreme Court held that the amount of a statutory civil penalty under the Clean Water Act could be decided by the trial court, *id.* at 427, 107 S.Ct. at 1840, even though the issue of liability implicated the right to trial by jury under the Seventh Amendment. *Id.* at 423, 107 S.Ct. at 1838. It reasoned that, because "Congress itself may fix the civil penalties, it may delegate that determination to trial judges[,]" *id.* at 427, 107 S.Ct. at 1840, noting that calculations of civil penalties involve exercises of discretion "traditionally performed by judges." *Id.*

We find *Tull* inapposite. Rather, we believe that the appropriate precedent is *Curtis,* in which the Court held that a "damages action under [42 U.S.C. § 3612] . . . is analogous to a number of tort actions recognized at common law. More important, the relief sought here—actual and punitive damages—is the traditional relief offered in the courts of law." *Id.* at 195–96, 94 S.Ct. at 1009. Thus, we conclude that the punitive damages remedy in a statutory bad faith action under § 8371 triggers the Seventh Amendment jury trial right, a result consistent with several cases that have decided the issue.

Accordingly, we will affirm the jury's award of punitive damages.

. . . .

NOTES AND QUESTIONS

1. *Pennsylvania's Bad Faith Statute.* Pennsylvania's bad faith law is fairly consistent with most states' bad faith laws, but it has some differences. In particular, it has a statute that specifically authorizes bad faith claims and specifies the relief available, 42 Pa.C.S.A. § 8371. This statute provides:

§ 8371. Actions on insurance policies

In an action arising under an insurance policy, if the court finds that the insurer has acted in bad faith toward the insured, the court may take all of the following actions:

(1) Award interest on the amount of the claim from the date the claim was made by the insured in an amount equal to the prime rate of interest plus 3%.

(2) Award punitive damages against the insurer.

(3) Assess court costs and attorney fees against the insurer.

What does "bad faith" mean under this statute? As the *Klinger* court noted, the term is undefined in the statute. Consequently, Pennsylvania courts have defined the term as a matter of common law.

2. *Right to a Jury Trial?* The Third Circuit held in *Klinger* that there is a right to a jury trial for bad faith claims in federal court under the Seventh Amendment to the U.S. Constitution. The Pennsylvania Supreme Court has held there is no right to a jury trial under Pennsylvania's bad faith statute, 42 Pa.C.S.A. § 8371. *See Mishoe v. Erie Ins. Co.*, 824 A.2d 1153 (Pa. 2003) (the bad faith statute uses the term "court," and the state constitutional right to a jury trial only applies to causes of action that existed at the time the constitution was adopted). The inconsistent approaches by federal courts and Pennsylvania state courts creates a strategic dilemma for policyholders regarding whether to sue in federal court (assuming there is jurisdiction) or state court. What are the advantages and disadvantages of trying a bad faith claim? As a plaintiff, would you prefer to bring an insurance lawsuit in state or federal court?

3. *When Does the Basis for a Bad Faith Claim End?* In *O'Donnell ex rel. Mitro v. Allstate Ins. Co.*, 734 A.2d 901 (Pa. Super. Ct. 1999), the court held that the insurer has a duty to act in good faith toward its policyholder even after it has been sued by its policyholder. *See also Hollock v. Erie Ins. Exchange*, 842 A.2d 409 (Pa. Super. Ct. 2004), *appeal granted*, 893 A.2d 66 (Pa. 2005), *appeal dismissed*, 903 A.2d 1185 (Pa. 2006) (bad faith verdict was based, in part, on insurer representatives' testimony in the litigation wherein they tried to cover up improper claims handling conduct). Is it fair to require insurers to continue to act in good faith after a policyholder has sued the insurer and accused the insurer of acting in bad faith? What conduct after the commencement of litigation constitutes bad faith?

4. *The Unfair Insurance Practices Act.* The Unfair Insurance Practices Act is a model act drafted by the National Association of Insurance Commissioners. Although the Act has a different name in some states, the Act, or some variation of it, has been adopted in almost all states. The Act sets forth, among other things, claims settlement practices that are unlawful. Pennsylvania's version of the Act, the Unfair Insurance Practices Act (40 Pa.C.S.A. § 1171.5(a)(10)), provides as follows:

> Any of the following acts if committed or performed with such frequency as to indicate a business practice shall constitute unfair claim settlement or compromise practices.
>
> . . . .
>
> (ii) Failing to acknowledge and act promptly upon written or oral communications with respect to claims arising under insurance policies.
>
> (iii) Failing to adopt and implement reasonable standards for the prompt investigation of claims arising under insurance policies.
>
> (iv) Refusing to pay claims without conducting a reasonable investigation based upon all available information.
>
> . . . .
>
> (vi) Not attempting in good faith to effectuate prompt, fair and equitable settlements of claims in which the company's liability under the policy has become reasonably clear.
>
> (vii) Compelling persons to institute litigation to recover amounts due under an insurance policy by offering substantially less than the amounts due and ultimately recovered in actions brought by such persons.
>
> (viii) Attempting to settle a claim for less than the amount to which a reasonable man would have believed he was entitled by reference to written or printed advertising material accompanying or made part of an application.
>
> . . . .
>
> (xiii) Failing to promptly settle claims, where liability has become reasonably clear, under one portion of the insurance policy coverage in order to influence settlements under other portions of the insurance policy coverage or under other policies of insurance.
>
> (xiv) Failing to promptly provide a reasonable explanation of the basis in the insurance policy in relation to the facts or applicable law for denial of a claim or for the offer of a compromise settlement.

Some states provide a private cause of action under the Act (*see, e.g.*, Fla. Stat. § 624.155(1)(a)(1)), while most states reserve enforcement of the Act to the state insurance commissioner. Pennsylvania does not provide a private cause of action under the Act, but Pennsylvania courts have interpreted violations of the Act to constitute bad faith conduct under Pennsylvania's bad faith statute, 42 Pa.C.S.A. § 8371. *See, e.g.*, *Romano v. Nationwide Mut. Fire Ins. Co.*, 646 A.2d 1228, 1233 (Pa. Super. Ct. 1994). Thus, contrary to conventional wisdom, a bad faith claim can be premised upon a variety of insurer misconduct other than just an insurer's wrongful denial of coverage or failure to settle a case.

BIRTH CENTER V. ST. PAUL COMPANIES, INC.

787 A.2d 376 (Pa. 2001)

Opinion

The St. Paul Companies, Inc. ("St. Paul") appeals from an Order of the Superior Court that reversed the Order of the Court of Common Pleas of Delaware County ("trial court"), which granted St. Paul's motion for judgment notwithstanding the verdict. The jury found, by clear and convincing evidence, that St. Paul acted in bad faith when it refused to settle a civil action against The Birth Center ("Birth Center"), and that St. Paul's bad faith conduct was a substantial factor in causing The Birth Center to incur compensatory damages in the amount of $700,000.00.

We affirm the decision of the Superior Court. Where an insurer refuses to settle a claim that could have been resolved within policy limits without "a bona fide belief . . . that it has a good possibility of winning," it breaches its contractual duty to act in good faith and its fiduciary duty to its insured. *Cowden v. Aetna Casualty and Surety Company,* 389 Pa. 459, 134 A.2d 223, 229 (1957). Therefore, the insurer is liable for the known and/or foreseeable compensatory damages of its insured that reasonably flow from the bad faith conduct of the insurer. The fact that the insurer's intransigent failure to engage in settlement negotiations forced it to pay damages far in excess of the policy limits so as to avoid a punitive damages award, does not insulate the insurer from liability for its insured's compensatory damages where the insured can prove that the insurer's bad faith conduct caused the damages.[2]

Factual and Procedural History

The Underlying Action—Norris v. The Birth Center

This claim arose out of St. Paul's bad faith refusal to engage in settlement negotiations in the underlying action, *Norris*. In that case, Gerald and Denise Norris ("Parents") filed suit on November 16, 1986 against Birth Center[3] alleging that its negligence during the birth of their daughter Lindsey, caused her to suffer severe physical injury and permanent brain damage. After service of the complaint, The Birth Center turned to St. Paul, its professional liability insurance carrier, for its legal defense.[4] St.

---

[2] St. Paul could have easily avoided liability by engaging in good faith settlement negotiations. Instead, St. Paul patently disregarded the interests of its insured by refusing to negotiate. For example, after the trial began but before the jury announced its $4,500,000.00 verdict, St. Paul refused to offer any money. For an insurer to refuse to offer any money and to state that it tries "all of these bad baby cases" (N.T. 5/6/96 at 16) regardless of the impact that decision might have on its insured invites a bad faith case.

[3] The Parents also sued two doctors (who Birth Center employed) and the attending midwife.

[4] St. Paul insured Birth Center under a professional liability policy with a $1,000,000.00 policy limit.

Paul hired counsel to defend The Birth Center and undertook an investigation of the Parents' claim.

On August 2, 1991, the Parents proposed, on behalf of Lindsey, to settle the case within the limits of The Birth Center's professional liability insurance policy with St. Paul. The Birth Center notified St. Paul that it was making a firm demand to settle the case within its policy limits. On August 7, 1991, St. Paul refused to settle or to even make an offer of settlement.

During the course of an August 8, 1991 pre-trial conference, the presiding judge recommended settlement of *Norris* within the limits of The Birth Center's insurance policy. Again, St. Paul refused. At a second pre-trial conference, a second judge assigned to the case also recommended settlement within Birth Center's policy limits. The Birth Center demanded settlement in accordance with the judge's recommendation; but St. Paul refused to negotiate or offer any money.

In January of 1992, St. Paul requested the defense attorneys for The Birth Center and one of the doctors involved in Lindsey's delivery to prepare pre-trial reports for St. Paul's consideration. In her report to St. Paul, defense counsel for The Birth Center stated that The Birth Center had, at best, a fifty-percent chance of successfully defending the lawsuit at trial. Furthermore, she advised that the jury verdict could range from $1,250,000.00 to $1,500,000.00. The doctor's defense counsel advised St. Paul that he believed that The Birth Center had a thirty-five percent chance of winning at trial and predicted a jury verdict of $5,000,000.00 to $6,000,000.00.

On January 27, 1992, the executive director of The Birth Center put St. Paul on written notice of the potential for compensatory damages and expressed her deep concerns regarding the possibility of a verdict in excess of Birth Center's policy limits. She explained that such a verdict would have devastating effects upon The Birth Center and could risk its continued existence. When expressing the same concerns to the St. Paul claims representative assigned to the case, the claims representative informed her that St. Paul tries "*all of these bad baby cases, and we're going to trial.*" (N.T. 5/6/96 at 16) (emphasis added).

Before the commencement of the *Norris* trial, a third judge, who ultimately presided over that trial, held another conference and recommended settlement within The Birth Center's policy limits. St. Paul refused to make any offer whatsoever. Then, on February 12, 1993, the Parents made a high/low offer of settlement, in which St. Paul would pay a non-refundable $300,000.00 amount regardless of the verdict. If, however, the jury returned a verdict in excess of Birth Center's policy limits, the Parents agreed to accept the policy limits as total satisfaction of the verdict. Finally, the settlement offer provided that if the jury returned a verdict lower than

The Birth Center's maximum coverage, but higher than the low figure of $300,000.00, then the Parents would accept such verdict as full satisfaction of The Birth Center's liability. St. Paul refused this offer of settlement and made no counter-offer.

On February 16, 1993, the day of trial, a final pre-trial conference took place in the robing room of the trial judge. At this time, the Parents reasserted their high/low offer of settlement. The Birth Center expressed its desire that St. Paul agree to the Parents' proposal; but, a representative of St. Paul, present during the discussion in the robing room, rejected the high/low offer of settlement on the record. Following St. Paul's rejection, the judge stated that he believed that St. Paul's actions were in bad faith and that it was putting its interests ahead of those of its insured. (N.T., 2/16/93, at 15–19).

The *Norris* trial ensued. After the start of the trial, but before the jury returned a verdict, the trial judge instructed defense counsel for The Birth Center to contact St. Paul to see if it intended to make any offer of settlement. When counsel returned from her telephone conversation with St. Paul, she stated to those present in the robing room: "They must be crazy. They're not offering a dime. They won't give me authority to offer any money in this case, you know I can't believe it." (N.T., 5/3/96, at 69).

On March 4, 1993, the jury returned a verdict in favor of the Parents for $4,500,000.00, with The Birth Center liable for sixty percent of that amount. The final verdict was molded to include delay damages and interest and totaled $7,196,238. The Birth Center's ultimate liability amounted to $4,317,743.00. St. Paul agreed to indemnify The Birth Center for the entire verdict and the parties settled the case for $5,000,000. Before St. Paul paid the excess verdict, it requested that The Birth Center sign a release in exchange for the payment, but The Birth Center refused to sign the release. St. Paul paid on September 20, 1993.

The Birth Center v. St. Paul—The Bad Faith Action

On June 3, 1994, The Birth Center sued St. Paul, alleging that St. Paul breached its fiduciary duty to The Birth Center, its implied covenant of good faith, and its contract. The Birth Center also claimed that St. Paul's failure to settle *Norris* within its policy limits constituted negligence, reckless disregard for the rights of Birth Center, willful and wanton behavior and bad faith pursuant to the Bad Faith Statute, 42 Pa.C.S.A. § 8371.

On May 3, 1996, the trial began. The Birth Center claimed that St. Paul's refusal to engage in reasonable settlement negotiations damaged "its business, reputation and credit." Appellee's Br. at. 11. After the trial, the jury found, by clear and convincing evidence, that St. Paul acted in bad faith and that its actions were a substantial factor in bringing about harm to The Birth Center totaling, $700,000.00 in compensatory damages. The jury did not award punitive damages.

St. Paul moved for judgment notwithstanding the verdict. On February 7, 1997, the trial court granted St. Paul's motion. The trial court concluded that St. Paul's payment of the excess verdict nullified Birth Center's bad faith claim, that compensatory damages are not available pursuant to 42 Pa.C.S.A. § 8371, and that, because it believed that it had not charged the jury on the breach of contract claim, that The Birth Center could not recover compensatory damages based on that theory. *See The Birth Center v. St. Paul Companies, Inc.,* No. 94–6492, slip op. at 9 (C.P. Delaware County Aug 11, 1997). The trial court denied The Birth Center's motion for reconsideration. On June 10, 1997, the trial court entered judgment in favor of St. Paul.

On appeal, the Superior Court determined that the payment of the excess verdict did not preclude the award of compensatory damages and that the trial court had charged the jury on breach of contract. Therefore, it reversed the decision of the trial court, reinstated the jury award, and remanded the case for a determination of The Birth Center's entitlement to interest, attorney's fees and costs pursuant to 42 Pa.C.S.A. § 8371.

St. Paul appealed the Superior Court's decision to this Court.

Discussion

St. Paul's Arguments in Opposition to the Award of Compensatory Damages

St. Paul sets forth [several] reasons why it is not liable for Birth Center's compensatory damages. First, it asserts that its payment of the excess verdict barred Birth Center's bad faith claim. St. Paul argues that allowing bad faith claims despite an insurer's "voluntary" excess payment would discourage insurance companies from satisfying future excess verdicts. Second, St. Paul contends that *D'Ambrosio v. Pennsylvania National Mut. Ins.,* 494 Pa. 501, 431 A.2d 966 (1981) bars The Birth Center's claim. Third, St. Paul points to 42 Pa.C.S.A. § 8371, which authorizes the award of punitive damages, attorneys fees and costs when an insurer is found to have acted in bad faith, and asserts that because the statute does not mention compensatory damages, none are available. . . .

. . . .

A court may not vacate a jury's finding unless "the evidence was such that no two reasonable minds could disagree that the outcome should have been rendered in favor of the movant." *Moure,* 604 A.2d at 1007 quoting *Cummings v. Nazareth Borough,* 427 Pa. 14, 233 A.2d 874 (1967). . . . [T]he jury was the finder of fact. It found that based upon all of the evidence that The Birth Center proved "by clear and convincing evidence that [St. Paul] acted in bad faith in handling the underlying case of *Norris v. The Birth*

Center." We also note that Judge Clouse, who tried the underlying case, stated, the day of trial, that he believed that St. Paul's settlement posture was in bad faith and inconsistent with its fiduciary duty to the Birth Center. Specifically, Judge Clouse expressed his opinion that:

> There is a clear indication of *bad faith* here. I think the insurance company is not proceeding in a responsible manner and is *not discharging its fiduciary obligation to its insureds* in this case . . . I think this insurance company has operated in a highly irresponsible manner. I want it clear that they have turned this high/low offer of $300,000.00 down in which [sic] I think is a *breach of their fiduciary responsibility* to their insureds. And I want that clear on this record.

(N.T., 2/16/93, at 15–19, emphasis added). While Judge Clouse's opinion is arguably irrelevant to the jury's determination that St. Paul acted in bad faith, it is a compelling indication of how a reasonable jury could have come to a similar conclusion that St. Paul acted in bad faith.

While a judge may disagree with a verdict, he or she may not grant a motion for J.N.O.V. simply because he or she would have come to a different conclusion. Indeed, the verdict must stand unless there is no legal basis for it. Without agreeing or disagreeing with . . . Judge Clouse, we view the evidence in the light most favorable to Birth Center, the verdict winner, and give it the benefit of every reasonable inference arising therefrom while rejecting all unfavorable testimony and inferences. From that perspective, we are unable to conclude that no reasonable jury could have found that St. Paul acted in bad faith. Therefore, although, . . . we may not have reached the same verdict as the jury, there was sufficient evidence to sustain the verdict and a reasonable basis for the jurors to have found, from the evidence-that St. Paul acted in bad faith. Consequently, the trial court should not have granted the motion for a directed verdict based on St. Paul's argument that it did not act in bad faith.

Payment of the Excess Verdict

Next, we address St. Paul's arguments that the trial court properly granted its motion for a judgment notwithstanding the verdict because of its contentions that: (1) an insurer's payment of an excess verdict precludes all bad faith claims, and (2) allowing The Birth Center to recover additional compensatory damages would discourage insurance companies from satisfying excess verdicts. St. Paul states:

> The effect of the Superior Court's holding is to discourage insurance companies from satisfying excess verdicts unless they are required to do so. If an insurance company can still be exposed to a bad faith suit even *after* voluntarily satisfying an excess verdict, the company has no incentive to pay the excess.

* * *

> If it remains exposed to the bad faith claim and punitive damages anyway, the obvious course for the insurance company is to stand its ground, defend the bad faith claim, and leave its insured to its own devices.

Appellant's Br. at 15.

While St. Paul's argument has facial appeal, it does not stand up to closer examination. St. Paul did not pay the excess verdict out of the goodness of its heart. It had reason to believe that The Birth Center was going to sue for bad faith[9] and it knew that if it were found to have acted in bad faith, it would be liable for punitive damages as well as the amount of the excess verdict. 42 Pa.C.S.A. § 8371. It, therefore, appears that St. Paul paid the excess in an attempt[10] to avoid a punitive damages award.

The purpose of damages in contract actions is to return the parties to the position they would have been in but for the breach. *Gedeon,* 188 A.2d at 322 n. 5. The relationship and dispute between The Birth Center and St. Paul flow from their contract. *Gray,* 223 A.2d at 12. "Breach of . . . [the] obligation [to act in good faith] constitutes a breach of the insurance contract for which an action in assumpsit will lie." *Id.* Therefore, where an insurer acts in bad faith, the insured is entitled to recover such damages sufficient to return it to the position it would have been in but for the breach. St. Paul's payment of the excess verdict does not bar The Birth Center's claim for compensatory damages because The Birth Center was able to prove that St. Paul's bad faith conduct was a substantial factor in The Birth Center suffering damages in addition to the excess verdict.

Furthermore, there is no reason to limit damages to the amount of the verdict where the insured can show that the insurer's bad faith conduct caused it additional damages. The insurer's conduct is not the subject of the underlying court action against the insured and, except for the amount of the excess verdict, damages stemming from the insurer's bad faith conduct are not resolved by the action against the insured. Where, as here, the insured can prove that it sustained damages in excess of the verdict, the insurer's payment of the excess has little to do with the insured's damages. Accordingly, the insurer's payment of the excess should not free it from other known or foreseeable damages it has caused its insured to incur.

---

[9] St. Paul does not appear to dispute the contention of The Birth Center that its private attorney sent St. Paul "dozens" of written threats stating that if St. Paul did not pay the excess verdict, Birth Center would sue St. Paul for its bad faith conduct. Appellee's Br. at 10.

[10] It was a successful one. The jury did not award punitive damages.

D'Ambrosio Does Not Bar The Birth Center's Claim

Next, St. Paul contends that *D'Ambrosio,* 494 Pa. 501, 431 A.2d 966, bars Birth Center's claim for compensatory damages. We disagree. Our holding in *D'Ambrosio* was a narrow one. *D'Ambrosio* involved a claim by an insured that his insurer acted in bad faith by failing to explain why it was declining to pay a property damages claim. The insured asserted that the insurer was implicitly stating that the claim was fraudulent. We described the insured's bad faith claim as "dubious." *Id.* at 971. We held that where the allegations in the complaint failed to show how the insurer acted in bad faith, we would not allow the insured to recover punitive damages or damages for emotional distress on his *trespass* cause of action. The contractual cause of action was never before the Court. In fact, we expressly stated that, in an appropriate case, an insured could recover compensatory damages based on a contract cause of action, because of an insurer's bad faith conduct. We explained:

> The possibility cannot be ruled out that emotional distress damages may be recoverable on a *contract* where, for example, the *breach* is of such a kind that serious emotional disturbance was a particularly likely result. . . . The present record falls far short of establishing such conduct.

431 A.2d at 970 (internal citations, quotations omitted and emphasis added). Similarly, in Chief Justice Nix's concurring opinion, he stated:

> In addition to the deterrent provisions of the Unfair Insurance Practices Act . . . appellant was also in a position to seek relief under a theory of *breach of contract,* or by pursuing the common law tort of deceit. . . . I do not accept the dissent's implicit premise that these existent remedies are inadequate to make appellant whole.

Id. at 973–974 (internal citations omitted emphasis added). Because nothing in *D'Ambrosio* bars a party bringing a bad faith action sounding in contract from recovering damages that are otherwise available to parties in contract actions, we reject St. Paul's argument that *D'Ambrosio* bars Birth Center's claim.[12]

42 Pa.C.S.A. § 8371 Does Not Prohibit the Award of Compensatory Damages

In St. Paul's third argument, it incorrectly asserts that compensatory damages may not be awarded when an insurer's bad faith conduct causes the insured to incur actual damages, because the damages are not

---

[12] Justice Cappy, in his concurring opinion in *Johnson v. Beane,* 541 Pa. 449, 664 A.2d 96 at 101–102 (1995), correctly examined this issue and observed that at least since this Court's 1957 decision in *Cowden,* 389 Pa. 459, 134 A.2d 223 common law contract rights permit an insured to recover compensatory damages in bad faith actions.

mentioned in 42 Pa.C.S.A. § 8371. While The Birth Center may not recover compensatory damages based on Section 8371, that Section does not alter The Birth Center's common law contract rights. We begin with the words of the statute. Section 8371 provides:

> § 8371. Actions on insurance policies
>
> In an action arising under an insurance policy, if the court finds that the insurer has acted in bad faith toward the insured, the court may take all of the following actions:
>
> (1) Award interest on the amount of the claim from the date the claim was made by the insured in an amount equal to the prime rate of interest plus 3%.
>
> (2) Award punitive damages against the insurer.
>
> (3) Assess court costs and attorney fees against the insurer.

42 Pa.C.S.A. § 8371.

The statute does not prohibit the award of compensatory damages. It merely provides an additional remedy and authorizes the award of additional damages.[14] Specifically, the statute authorizes courts, which find that an insurer has acted in bad faith toward its insured, to award punitive damages, attorneys' fees, interest and costs. *Id.* The statute does not reference the common law, does not explicitly reject it, and the application of the statute is not inconsistent with the common law. Consequently, the common law remedy survives. *Metropolitan Property and Liability Insurance Co. v. Insurance Commissioner of Pennsylvania,* 525 Pa. 306, 580 A.2d 300 (1990). In *Metropolitan Property,* we rejected an insured's argument that the Unfair Insurance Practices Act abrogated the insurer's contractual, common law right of rescission. *Id.* at 302–303. We explained that because the statute did not refer to the common law remedy of rescission and its concurrent application was not inconsistent with the statute that the legislature did not intend to preclude the remedy. *Id.* We determined that:

> Under the . . . [Statutory Construction Act. 1 Pa.C.S. § 1921 et seq] an implication alone cannot be interpreted as abrogating existing law. The legislature must affirmatively repeal existing law or specifically preempt accepted common law for prior law to be disregarded.
>
> * * *
>
> [Because 40 Pa.C.S. § 1171.5 (the provision at issue in *Metropolitan Property*)] makes no reference to the common law

[14] This case does not require that we resolve the question of whether Section 8371 creates an independent cause of action or an additional remedy. We make no comment on that issue here because the issue is not squarely before us.

> right to rescission . . . [s]much an omission cannot be interpreted as an intention to foreclose such a long-standing right.

Id. at 311, 580 A.2d 300.

Similarly, in *Rahn v. Hess,* 378 Pa. 264, 106 A.2d 461 (1954), we stated: "statutes are never presumed to make any innovation in the rules and principles of the common law or prior existing law beyond what is expressly declared in their provisions." *Id.* at 270, 106 A.2d 461. Indeed, in the context of determining whether 42 Pa.C.S.A. 8371 altered the burden of proof, the Third Circuit applied Pennsylvania law and explained that because the legislature did not expressly alter prior law, it did not intend to change it. *Polselli v. Nationwide Mutual Fire Insurance Co.,* 23 F.3d 747, 752 (3d Cir. 1994). There, the court observed that:

> In enacting a statute, the legislature is presumed to have been familiar with the law, as it then existed and the judicial decisions construing it. *See Raymond v. School Dist.,* 186 Pa.Super. 352, 142 A.2d 749 (1958). Had the legislature intended to make changes in the law with respect to the burden of persuasion necessary to prove bad faith, it could have done so expressly. *See Harka v. Nabati,* 337 Pa.Super. 617, 487 A.2d 432, 435 (1985). By failing to articulate any changes, the legislature implicitly acknowledged that the existing standards remain applicable.

23 F.3d at 751. The same reasoning applies where, as here, the legislature did not expressly prohibit the continued award of compensatory damages when an insurer's bad faith conduct causes them.

Therefore, contrary to St. Paul's contention, Section 8371 does not prohibit courts from awarding compensatory damages that are otherwise available.[15] In Section 8371, the legislature granted the court additional

---

[15] Before the enactment of Section 8371, courts could award compensatory damages in contract cases when the damages were known or foreseeable and subject to calculation. *R.I. Lampus Co. v. Neville Cement Products Corp.,* 474 Pa. 199, 378 A.2d 288 (1977); *Cowden,* 389 Pa. 459, 134 A.2d 223. In *R.I. Lampus,* we quoted Professor Corbin for the following proposition of law:

> All that is necessary, in order to charge the defendant with the particular loss, is that it is one that ordinarily follows the breach of such a contract in the usual course of events, or that reasonable men in the position of the parties would have foreseen as a probable result of breach.

378 A.2d at 291, quoting 5 A. Corbin, *Corbin on Contracts* § 1010 at 79 (1964). The same year the legislature enacted Section 8371 we were not breaking new ground when we stated, "in addition to allowing compensatory damages under [the Uniform Commercial C]ode, Pennsylvania allows compensatory damages in the form of lost profits to be recovered." *AM/PM Franchise Association v. Atlantic Richfield Co.,* 526 Pa. 110, 584 A.2d 915, 920 (1990). Indeed, by the time that the legislature enacted Section 8371, it had long been axiomatic that compensatory damages were available in contract actions where the damages were the foreseeable result of the breach. *Delahanty v. First Pennsylvania Bank N.A.,* 318 Pa.Super. 90, 464 A.2d 1243 (1983). The *Delahanty* court observed that:

> It is well settled law in Pennsylvania that loss of profits are recoverable upon proper proof in contract . . . The general rule of law applicable for loss of profits in both contract and tort actions allows such damages where (1) there is evidence to establish them with

authority to award punitive damages, interest, costs and attorneys' fees. The fact that the statute authorized courts to award these damages does not prohibit them from granting other remedies that they theretofore had the power to award without the grant of additional authority.

Finally, St. Paul's argument that damages not mentioned by Section 8371 are not available is inconsistent with St. Paul's admission that other damages, not listed in Section 8371, remain viable. Appellant's Reply Br. at 3. Notwithstanding that Section 8371 does not provide that courts may require an insurer to pay an excess verdict when it refuses, in bad faith, to settle a case, St. Paul admits, as it must,[16] that such an award is permissible. St. Paul states:

> It has long been held in this Commonwealth that when an insurance company fails to settle a third-party claim against its insured, the insurer can be liable for the full amount of any excess verdict, if the decision not to settle was made in bad faith. [St. Paul also admits that] this right has been held to be contractual in nature; it can be enforced by an action in assumpsit; and it is assignable to the injured third party.

Appellant's Reply Br. at 3. St. Paul, thereby, concedes that an insurer who acts in bad faith may be subject to damages other than those set forth in Section 8371. Accordingly, just as courts may require an insurer to pay an excess verdict even though Section 8371 does not mention excess verdict liability, the absence of compensatory damages from Section 8371 does not alter the authority of courts to award compensatory damages.

Requiring insurers, who act in bad faith, to pay excess verdicts protects insured from liability that, absent the insurer's bad faith conduct, the insured would not have incurred.[17] The insured's liability for an excess

---

> reasonable certainty, (2) there is evidence to show that they were the proximate consequence of the wrong; and, in the contract actions, that they were reasonably foreseeable.

Id. at 1258. Because compensatory damages were available at the time the legislature enacted Section 8371, and that Section does not provide that the court may no longer award compensatory damages, those damages remain available.

[16] An insurer, who acts in bad faith by unreasonably refusing to settle a case, may be liable for the full amount of a verdict notwithstanding that the verdict exceeds the insured's policy limits. *Cowden,* 389 Pa. 459, 134 A.2d 223. In *Cowden,* we stated that an insurer:

> may be liable for the entire amount of a judgment secured by a third party against the insured, regardless of any limitation in the policy, if the insurer's handling of the claim, including a failure to accept a proffered settlement, was done in such a manner as to evidence bad faith on the part of the insurer in the discharge of its contractual duty.

Id. at 224. See also *Gray v. Nationwide Insurance Co.,* 422 Pa. 500, 223 A.2d 8 (1966).

[17] The rationale for requiring an insurer to pay an excess verdict derives from the insurer's right to control the defense of an action. *Cowden,* 134 A.2d at 228. Where the insurance company takes control of the decision to settle or litigate actions brought by third parties, the insurance company owes its policyholder a fiduciary duty, among other things, to engage in good faith settlement negotiations. *Gedeon v. State Farm Mutual Automobile Insurance Company,* 410 Pa. 55, 188 A.2d 320 (1963). In *Gedeon,* we stated that:

verdict is a type of compensatory damage for which this court has allowed recovery. Therefore, when an insurer breaches its insurance contract by a bad faith refusal to settle a case, it is appropriate to require it to pay other damages that it knew or should have known the insured would incur because of the bad faith conduct.

. . . .

Conclusion

Today, we hold that where an insurer acts in bad faith, by unreasonably refusing to settle a claim, it breaches its contractual duty to act in good faith and its fiduciary duty to its insured. Therefore, the insurer is liable for the known and/or foreseeable compensatory damages of its insured that reasonably flow from the insurer's bad faith conduct. Accordingly, we affirm the decision of the Superior Court, reinstate the jury's verdict and remand this case to the trial court for a determination of The Birth Center's entitlement to interest, reasonable attorneys' fees and costs pursuant to 42 Pa.C.S.A. § 8371.

NOTES AND QUESTIONS

1. *Tort or Contract Claim (Reprise)?* Is a bad faith claim under Pennsylvania law a tort or a contract claim? Are different damage remedies available depending upon whether the claim is a tort or a contract claim? Although the dominant approach is to treat bad faith claims as tort claims, some states treat them as contract claims, or both tort and contract claims, such as Pennsylvania in the *Birth Center* case.

2. *Widespread Recognition of Bad Faith Claims.* The tort of bad faith breach of an insurer's obligation was first recognized by a court of last resort

---

> by asserting in the policy the right to handle all claims against the insured, including the right to make a binding settlement, the insurer assumes a fiduciary position towards the insured and becomes obligated to act in good faith and with due care in representing the interests of the insured.

Id. at 322. Because of the insurer's controlling role in the litigation, the insurer enters a fiduciary relationship with its insured and accepts the responsibility to protect the interests of its insured. *Gray v. Nationwide Mutual Insurance Company,* 422 Pa. 500, 223 A.2d 8 (1966) (holding that an insured's right to recover an award in excess of his policy limits from his insurer, when the insurer refuses to settle a claim against the inured in bad faith, was assignable). Notwithstanding the insurer's contractual duty to its insured, the interests of insurers and their insureds are not always consistent and are frequently in conflict with one another. Indeed, an insured's interests are particularly at risk when a plaintiff expresses a willingness to settle for the policy limits. When it becomes clear that an insurer could settle a third-party claim against its insured for the limits of the policy, and thereby release its insured from any worry about an excess verdict, the insurer must be vigilant to ensure that it has a reasonable basis to try the case and that it is not breaching its fiduciary duty to its insured, based upon a small chance of a defense verdict. *Cowden,* 134 A.2d at 228. An insured's interests are particularly in jeopardy under the forgoing facts because whether the insurer settles for the policy limits or loses at trial, its risk is the same; in both instances, and absent bad faith, all it would have to pay would be the policy limits. *Id.* In such a situation, a faithless insurer would have nothing to lose by trying the case; it might as well take the risk and hope for a defense verdict. At the same time, the insured would have no reason to risk a trial. *Cowden,* 134 A.2d at 223.

in 1973 in the landmark case of *Gruenberg v. Aetna Insurance Co.*, 510 P.2d 1032 (Cal. 1973). Today, most states allow bad faith claims against insurers, whether based upon the common law or a statute. *See, e.g.*, Barry R. Ostrager & Thomas R. Newman, Handbook on Insurance Coverage Disputes § 12.09[b] (18th ed. 2017) (50-state survey reflecting the statutory or common law basis for the claim and whether it is a tort or a contract claim); Jeffrey W. Stempel & Erik Knutsen, Stempel and Knutsen on Insurance Coverage § 10.02[A] (4th ed. 2017) ("[A] majority of states treat the insurance contract as imposing a duty of good faith, the breach of which comprises a tort supporting punitive damages."); *see also* Roger C. Henderson, *The Tort of Bad Faith in First-Party Insurance Transactions After Two Decades*, 37 Ariz. L. Rev. 1153, 1153–55 (1995). For concise summaries of the history of bad faith, *see* Stephen S. Ashley, *One Hundred Years of Bad Faith*, 15 Bad Faith L. Rpt. 207 (1999); John H. Bauman, *Emotional Distress Damages and the Tort of Insurance Bad Faith*, 46 Drake L. Rev. 717, 732–45 (1998).

3. *The Bad Faith Standard (Reprise).* As noted at the beginning of this section, defining what constitutes bad faith is not a simple matter. Generally, it must be more than mere nonperformance of the contract. Otherwise, the cause of action is nothing more than a breach of contract claim. Early cases referred to conscious or deliberate wrongdoing, such as where the insurer knows the claim is valid but declines to pay it anyway, perhaps hoping to extort a settlement for less than the contract obligation. *See Gruenberg v. Aetna Insurance Co., supra*; *Christian v. American Home Assurance Co.*, 577 P.2d 899 (Okla. 1978). This kind of intentional wrongdoing fits easily within the traditional notions of what constitutes a tort. It was not long, however, before some courts began to view "bad faith" as involving less capricious kinds of insurer behavior. A watershed of sorts was the decision of the Supreme Court of Wisconsin in *Anderson v. Continental Insurance Co.*, 271 N.W.2d 368 (Wis. 1978), where the court held that an insurer could be liable for bad faith not only where it denies a claim knowing that it has no legitimate basis for doing so, but also where it "recklessly" disregards the rights of the policyholder. *Anderson* also recognized a safe harbor of sorts for the insurer. In the court's words, "when a claim is 'fairly debatable,' the insurer is entitled to debate it, whether the debate concerns a matter of fact or law." 271 N.W.2d at 376. This means that when the policyholder's claim is "fairly debatable," the insurer that denies coverage cannot be held liable for bad faith. *See, e.g.*, *Radecki v. Mutual of Omaha Insurance Co.*, 583 N.W.2d 320 (Neb. 1998); *Bushey v. Allstate Insurance Co.*, 670 A.2d 807 (Vt. 1995); *Morgan v. American Family Mutual Insurance Co.*, 534 N.W.2d 92 (Iowa 1995); *First Wyoming Bank, N.A., v. Continental Insurance Co.*, 860 P.2d 1094 (Wyo. 1993). What, though, makes a claim "fairly debatable?" Is an insurer's position on coverage "fairly debatable" if it has some legal support, even if it lacks clear supporting authority? Is the insurer's position on any issue of first impression automatically "fairly debatable?" Is the test simply one of asking whether the insurer has a "reasonable" legal argument?

Currently, many states apply the "fairly debatable" test, but the emerging predominant test is the "reasonableness" test, which asks whether the insurer acted "reasonably" in investigating the claim, denying the claim, refusing to settle, etc., and either knew or recklessly disregarded the lack of reasonableness of its position. *See, e.g.*, *Nardelli v. Metro Grp. Pro. & Cas. Ins. Co.*, 277 P.3d 789, 795 (Ariz. Ct. App. 2012) ("An insurer acts in bad faith when it unreasonably investigates, evaluates, or processes a claim (an 'objective' test), and either knows it is acting unreasonably or acts with such reckless disregard that such knowledge may be imputed to it (a 'subjective' test).").

4. *Restatement of the Law of Liability Insurance.* The Restatement also has adopted the reasonableness test:

> **§ 49 Liability for Insurance Bad Faith**
>
> An insurer is subject to liability to the insured for insurance bad faith when it fails to perform under a liability insurance policy:
>
> (a) Without a reasonable basis for its conduct; and
>
> (b) With knowledge of its obligation to perform or in reckless disregard of whether it had an obligation to perform.

5. *Punitive Damages.* Punitive damages can be awarded in bad faith claims, but typically the insurer misconduct required to support a punitive damage award must be greater than the conduct necessary to satisfy a finding of insurer bad faith. The something "greater" required to support a punitive damage award is commonly described as insurer misconduct that is "aggravated, outrageous, malicious, or fraudulent." *See, e.g.*, *Rawlings v. Apodaca*, 726 P.2d 565 (Ariz. 1986). In some states, reckless indifference is enough to satisfy the something "greater" requirement. *See, e.g.*, *Klinger v. State Farm Mut. Auto. Ins. Co.*, 115 F.3d 230, 235 (3rd Cir. 1997) ("Both intent and reckless indifference will constitute a sufficient mental state.") (*citing Delahanty v. First Pa. Bank, N.A.*, 464 A.2d 1243, 1263 (Pa. Super. Ct. 1983)).

6. *Impact of Bad Faith Claims.* In the absence of a bad faith claim, insurers have little legal incentives to pay claims timely and in full because their only liability for failing to do so is payment of the claim in full plus whatever, if any, prejudgment interest is allowed in the particular state. The availability of bad faith claims changes this dynamic because such claims create downside risk for insurers if they lose insurance disputes in which a bad faith claim is also asserted. Some commentators have concluded the existence of bad faith claims has increased the settlement amount of insurance claims. *See, e.g.*, Mark J. Browne, Ellen S. Pryor, & Bob Puelz, *The Effect of Bad-Faith Laws on First-Party Insurance Claims Decisions*, 33 J. Legal Stud. 355 (2004); Daniel P. Asmat & Sharon Tennyson, *Does the Threat of Insurer Liability for "Bad Faith" Affect Insurance Settlements?*, 81 J. Risk & Ins. 1 (2014).

7. *"Reverse" or "Comparative" Bad Faith?* If the insurer can be held liable to the policyholder for the tort of bad faith, what about the policyholder's reciprocal obligations to the insurer? In other words, is "bad faith" a one-way or two-way street? Is a two-way street more attractive if good faith is deemed

a contract duty and not a tort duty? Independent of the question of whether the insurer should have a bad faith cause of action against the policyholder, should the policyholder's bad faith offset the insurer's bad faith under comparative or contributory fault principles?

Notwithstanding a kind of "symmetric appeal" of the two-way street position, the clear weight of authority, excluding some isolated cases to the contrary, is that the tort of bad faith is a one-way street. *See Kransco v. Am. Empire Surplus Lines Ins. Co.*, 2 P.3d 1 (Cal. 2000) (rejecting comparative bad faith defense asserted by insurer); *Stephens v. Safeco Insurance Co. of Am.*, 852 P.2d 565 (Mont. 1993) (disapproving doctrine); *Tokles & Son, Inc. v. Midwestern Indemnity Co.*, 605 N.E.2d 936 (Ohio 1992) (disapproving doctrine). For more discussion, *see* Ellen Smith Pryor, *Comparative Fault and Insurance Bad Faith*, 72 Tex. L. Rev. 1505 (1994); Douglas R. Richmond, *Insured's Bad Faith as Shield or Sword: Litigation Relief for Insurers?*, 77 Marq. L. Rev. 41 (1993). Given the strong consumer protection overtones running throughout insurance law, is this a surprising answer?

CHAPTER FOUR

LIABILITY INSURANCE

■ ■ ■

"[T]he existence of affordable and readily available liability insurance is vital to the operation of the economy. Without such coverage, consumers pay higher prices for essential goods and services; those with legitimate claims are left uncompensated; professional services are curtailed; jobs are lost, and taxes go up as local governments are forced to pay higher premiums for their municipal liability insurance. Moreover, the lack of affordable and available insurance hinders the development of new enterprises and technology and weakens the Nation's position in world trade."

— Sen. Comm. on Commerce, Science, and Transportation, *Risk Retention Amendments of 1986*, S. Rep. No. 294, 99th Cong., 2d Sess. 5 (1986)

I. COMMERCIAL GENERAL LIABILITY INSURANCE

Commercial General Liability Insurance (CGL) is a type of liability insurance sold to businesses.[1] The CGL policy, which was renamed the "Commercial" General Liability insurance policy by insurers in 1986 in order to avoid the broad coverage implications of the word "comprehensive," was first created in the 1940s. Although the first CGL policy was sold in 1941, the policy form that became widely used was first issued in 1943. The two rating bureaus that initially created the CGL policy eventually merged and became the Insurance Services Office, Inc. (ISO).

Prior to 1943, there were numerous different lines of liability insurance available to cover specific risks such as Public Liability Insurance and Premises Operations Insurance that were issued by various insurers with varying policy language. Due to the numerous specific lines of insurance available, policyholders were able to purchase only the specific lines of insurance they needed, which meant insurers had a customer base of only policyholders who believed they had a meaningful risk of loss under each of the selected lines of insurance. The CGL policy was created to

[1] This introduction regarding CGL insurance was taken verbatim from Christopher C. French, *The Role of the Profit Imperative in Risk Management*, 17 U. Pa. J. Bus. L. 1081, 1096–99 (2015) (citations omitted).

broaden the insurance pool and to address other problems associated with splintered lines of coverage such as insurers' use of differing terms and conditions in their policies. As is still the case today with almost all insurance policies, the terms of CGL policies were drafted by insurers, set forth in lengthy, complex contracts of adhesion, and then sold on a take-it-or-leave-it basis.

When created, the CGL policy became the broadest form of liability coverage that could be purchased because the insurer agrees under CGL policies to pay "all sums" for which the policyholder becomes liable for "bodily injuries" or "property damage" caused by an accident. Despite the expansive coverage grant, insurers embraced the CGL policy because they were able to charge higher premiums and could avoid situations where policyholders only purchased the lines of coverage under which the policyholders thought they most likely would have claims. In addition, because insurers often would not have to pay claims until many years after the premiums for such policies had been paid, insurers would be able to earn investment income on the premiums until funds were needed to pay claims. The insurers' profits created by this delay are referred to as the "float." Warren Buffett has famously acknowledged that Berkshire-Hathaway earns most of its profits from the "float," as opposed to underwriting profits (i.e., the amount of premiums collected that exceed the amount paid for claims). Indeed, in [2015], for example, insurers made $49 billion in investment income.

Under the CGL policy forms used between 1943 and 1966, the policies covered liabilities "caused by accident." The term "accident" was not defined, and thus courts were left to determine what constituted an "accident." As the case law developed, courts increasingly concluded that "accidents" were not confined in time and space to a single event and could include injury-producing events that took place over longer spans of time.

As a result of the judicial trend in the case law, among other reasons, the CGL policy form was revised in 1966 to substitute the term "occurrence" for the term "accident." The term "occurrence" was defined as "an accident, including continuous or repeated exposure to conditions which results in bodily injury or property damage neither expected nor intended from the standpoint of the insured." Significantly, the change to the "occurrence" form meant that it became undisputed that insurance coverage was provided not only for events, but also for gradual, ongoing or continuous injury situations.

The CGL has undergone many revisions through the years, with the most significant ones occurring in 1966, 1973, 1985, and 2004. As of 2020, the most recent changes were made in 2013. When the CGL that provides occurrence-based coverage goes through a revision, the older versions of the CGL do not lose relevance. In many areas of the policies, the language is not changed. Further, sometimes claims are brought today for injuries or damages that were incurred many years ago (subject only to the preclusive effects of relevant statutes of limitations, which under some circumstances are subject to being tolled), and the older policies may be the ones under which the coverage is provided that pays a claim today. Thus, some familiarity with the older versions of the forms is important, and it is always important to read the policy that applies to the particular claim at issue.

A. SAMPLE COMMERCIAL GENERAL LIABILITY POLICY

A Sample Commercial General Liability Policy is reproduced below. As you read it, consider its complexity. It contains multiple sections that set forth the coverage provided for "bodily injuries" and "property damage," multiple sections that set forth definitions and exclusions, and multiple "Conditions" sections.

COMMERCIAL GENERAL LIABILITY COVERAGE FORM

Various provisions in this policy restrict coverage. Read the entire policy carefully to determine rights, duties and what is and is not covered.

Throughout this policy the words "you" and "your" refer to the Named Insured shown in the Declarations, and any other person or organization qualifying as a Named Insured under this policy. The words "we", "us" and "our" refer to the company providing this insurance.

The word "insured" means any person or organization qualifying as such under Section **II** – Who Is An Insured.

Other words and phrases that appear in quotation marks have special meaning. Refer to Section **V** – Definitions.

SECTION I – COVERAGES

COVERAGE A – BODILY INJURY AND PROPERTY DAMAGE LIABILITY

1. Insuring Agreement

a. We will pay those sums that the insured becomes legally obligated to pay as damages because of "bodily injury" or "property damage" to which this insurance applies. We will have the right and duty to defend the insured against any "suit" seeking those damages. However, we will have no duty to defend the insured against any "suit" seeking damages for "bodily injury" or "property damage" to which this insurance does not apply. We may, at our discretion, investigate any "occurrence" and settle any claim or "suit" that may result. But:

(1) The amount we will pay for damages is limited as described in Section **III** – Limits Of Insurance; and

(2) Our right and duty to defend ends when we have used up the applicable limit of insurance in the payment of judgments or settlements under Coverages **A** or **B** or medical expenses under Coverage **C**.

No other obligation or liability to pay sums or perform acts or services is covered unless explicitly provided for under Supplementary Payments – Coverages **A** and **B**.

b. This insurance applies to "bodily injury" and "property damage" only if:

(1) The "bodily injury" or "property damage" is caused by an "occurrence" that takes place in the "coverage territory";

(2) The "bodily injury" or "property damage" occurs during the policy period; and

(3) Prior to the policy period, no insured listed under Paragraph **1.** of Section **II** – Who Is An Insured and no "employee" authorized by you to give or receive notice of an "occurrence" or claim, knew that the "bodily injury" or "property damage" had occurred, in whole or in part. If such a listed insured or authorized "employee" knew, prior to the policy period, that the "bodily injury" or "property damage" occurred, then any continuation, change or resumption of such "bodily injury" or "property damage" during or after the policy period will be deemed to have been known prior to the policy period.

c. "Bodily injury" or "property damage" which occurs during the policy period and was not, prior to the policy period, known to have occurred by any insured listed under Paragraph **1.** of Section **II** – Who Is An Insured or any "employee" authorized by you to give or receive notice of an "occurrence" or claim, includes any continuation, change or resumption of that "bodily injury" or "property damage" after the end of the policy period.

d. "Bodily injury" or "property damage" will be deemed to have been known to have occurred at the earliest time when any insured listed under Paragraph **1.** of Section **II** – Who Is An Insured or any "employee" authorized by you to give or receive notice of an "occurrence" or claim:

(1) Reports all, or any part, of the "bodily injury" or "property damage" to us or any other insurer;

(2) Receives a written or verbal demand or claim for damages because of the "bodily injury" or "property damage"; or

(3) Becomes aware by any other means that "bodily injury" or "property damage" has occurred or has begun to occur.

e. Damages because of "bodily injury" include damages claimed by any person or organization for care, loss of services or death resulting at any time from the "bodily injury".

2. Exclusions

This insurance does not apply to:

a. Expected Or Intended Injury

"Bodily injury" or "property damage" expected or intended from the standpoint of the insured. This exclusion does not apply to "bodily injury" resulting from the use of reasonable force to protect persons or property.

b. Contractual Liability

"Bodily injury" or "property damage" for which the insured is obligated to pay damages by reason of the assumption of liability in a contract or agreement. This exclusion does not apply to liability for damages:

(1) That the insured would have in the absence of the contract or agreement; or

(2) Assumed in a contract or agreement that is an "insured contract", provided the "bodily injury" or "property damage" occurs subsequent to the execution of the contract or agreement. Solely for the purposes of liability assumed in an "insured contract", reasonable attorneys' fees and necessary litigation expenses incurred by or for a party other than an insured are deemed to be damages because of "bodily injury" or "property damage", provided:

(a) Liability to such party for, or for the cost of, that party's defense has also been assumed in the same "insured contract"; and

(b) Such attorneys' fees and litigation expenses are for defense of that party against a civil or alternative dispute resolution proceeding in which damages to which this insurance applies are alleged.

c. Liquor Liability

"Bodily injury" or "property damage" for which any insured may be held liable by reason of:

(1) Causing or contributing to the intoxication of any person;

(2) The furnishing of alcoholic beverages to a person under the legal drinking age or under the influence of alcohol; or

(3) Any statute, ordinance or regulation relating to the sale, gift, distribution or use of alcoholic beverages.

This exclusion applies even if the claims against any insured allege negligence or other wrongdoing in:

(a) The supervision, hiring, employment, training or monitoring of others by that insured; or

(b) Providing or failing to provide transportation with respect to any person that may be under the influence of alcohol;

if the "occurrence" which caused the "bodily injury" or "property damage", involved that which is described in Paragraph **(1)**, **(2)** or **(3)** above.

However, this exclusion applies only if you are in the business of manufacturing, distributing, selling, serving or furnishing alcoholic beverages. For the purposes of this exclusion, permitting a person to bring alcoholic beverages on your premises, for consumption on your premises, whether or not a fee is charged or a license is required for such activity, is not by itself considered the business of selling, serving or furnishing alcoholic beverages.

d. Workers' Compensation And Similar Laws

Any obligation of the insured under a workers' compensation, disability benefits or unemployment compensation law or any similar law.

e. Employer's Liability

"Bodily injury" to:

(1) An "employee" of the insured arising out of and in the course of:

(a) Employment by the insured; or

(b) Performing duties related to the conduct of the insured's business; or

(2) The spouse, child, parent, brother or sister of that "employee" as a consequence of Paragraph **(1)** above.

This exclusion applies whether the insured may be liable as an employer or in any other capacity and to any obligation to share damages with or repay someone else who must pay damages because of the injury.

This exclusion does not apply to liability assumed by the insured under an "insured contract".

f. Pollution

(1) "Bodily injury" or "property damage" arising out of the actual, alleged or threatened discharge, dispersal, seepage, migration, release or escape of "pollutants":

(a) At or from any premises, site or location which is or was at any time owned or occupied by, or rented or loaned to, any insured. However, this subparagraph does not apply to:

(i) "Bodily injury" if sustained within a building and caused by smoke, fumes, vapor or soot produced by or originating from equipment that is used to heat, cool or dehumidify the building, or equipment that is used to heat water for personal use, by the building's occupants or their guests;

(ii) "Bodily injury" or "property damage" for which you may be held liable, if you are a contractor and the owner or lessee of such premises, site or location has been added to your policy as an additional insured with respect to your ongoing operations performed for that additional insured at that premises, site or location and such premises, site or location is not and never was owned or occupied by, or rented or loaned to, any insured, other than that additional insured; or

(iii) "Bodily injury" or "property damage" arising out of heat, smoke or fumes from a "hostile fire";

(b) At or from any premises, site or location which is or was at any time used by or for any insured or others for the handling, storage, disposal, processing or treatment of waste;

(c) Which are or were at any time transported, handled, stored, treated, disposed of, or processed as waste by or for:

(i) Any insured; or

(ii) Any person or organization for whom you may be legally responsible; or

(d) At or from any premises, site or location on which any insured or any contractors or subcontractors working directly or indirectly on any insured's behalf are performing operations if the "pollutants" are brought on or to the premises, site or location in connection with such operations by such insured, contractor or subcontractor. However, this subparagraph does not apply to:

(i) "Bodily injury" or "property damage" arising out of the escape of fuels, lubricants or other operating fluids which are needed to perform the normal electrical, hydraulic or mechanical functions necessary for the operation of "mobile equipment" or its parts, if such fuels, lubricants or other operating fluids escape from a vehicle part designed to hold, store or receive them. This exception does not apply if the "bodily injury" or "property damage" arises out of the intentional discharge, dispersal or release of the fuels, lubricants or other operating fluids, or if such fuels, lubricants or other operating fluids are brought on or to the premises, site or location with the intent that they be discharged, dispersed or released as part of the operations being performed by such insured, contractor or subcontractor;

(ii) "Bodily injury" or "property damage" sustained within a building and caused by the release of gases, fumes or vapors from materials brought into that building in connection with operations being performed by you or on your behalf by a contractor or subcontractor; or

(iii) "Bodily injury" or "property damage" arising out of heat, smoke or fumes from a "hostile fire".

(e) At or from any premises, site or location on which any insured or any contractors or subcontractors working directly or indirectly on any insured's behalf are performing operations if the operations are to test for, monitor, clean up, remove, contain, treat, detoxify or neutralize, or in any way respond to, or assess the effects of, "pollutants".

(2) Any loss, cost or expense arising out of any:

(a) Request, demand, order or statutory or regulatory requirement that any insured or others test for, monitor, clean up, remove, contain, treat, detoxify or neutralize, or in any way respond to, or assess the effects of, "pollutants"; or

(b) Claim or suit by or on behalf of a governmental authority for damages because of testing for, monitoring, cleaning up, removing, containing, treating, detoxifying or neutralizing, or in any way responding to, or assessing the effects of, "pollutants".

However, this paragraph does not apply to liability for damages because of "property damage" that the insured would have in the absence of such request, demand, order or statutory or regulatory requirement, or such claim or "suit" by or on behalf of a governmental authority.

g. Aircraft, Auto Or Watercraft

"Bodily injury" or "property damage" arising out of the ownership, maintenance, use or entrustment to others of any aircraft, "auto" or watercraft owned or operated by or rented or loaned to any insured. Use includes operation and "loading or unloading".

This exclusion applies even if the claims against any insured allege negligence or other wrongdoing in the supervision, hiring, employment, training or monitoring of others by that insured, if the "occurrence" which caused the "bodily injury" or "property damage" involved the ownership, maintenance, use or entrustment to others of any aircraft, "auto" or watercraft that is owned or operated by or rented or loaned to any insured.

This exclusion does not apply to:

(1) A watercraft while ashore on premises you own or rent;

(2) A watercraft you do not own that is:

(a) Less than 26 feet long; and

(b) Not being used to carry persons or property for a charge;

(3) Parking an "auto" on, or on the ways next to, premises you own or rent, provided the "auto" is not owned by or rented or loaned to you or the insured;

(4) Liability assumed under any "insured contract" for the ownership, maintenance or use of aircraft or watercraft; or

(5) "Bodily injury" or "property damage" arising out of:

(a) The operation of machinery or equipment that is attached to, or part of, a land vehicle that would qualify under the definition of "mobile equipment" if it were not subject to a compulsory or financial responsibility law or other motor vehicle insurance law where it is licensed or principally garaged; or

(b) The operation of any of the machinery or equipment listed in Paragraph **f.(2)** or **f.(3)** of the definition of "mobile equipment".

h. Mobile Equipment

"Bodily injury" or "property damage" arising out of:

(1) The transportation of "mobile equipment" by an "auto" owned or operated by or rented or loaned to any insured; or

(2) The use of "mobile equipment" in, or while in practice for, or while being prepared for, any prearranged racing, speed, demolition, or stunting activity.

i. War

"Bodily injury" or "property damage", however caused, arising, directly or indirectly, out of:

(1) War, including undeclared or civil war;

(2) Warlike action by a military force, including action in hindering or defending against an actual or expected attack, by any government, sovereign or other authority using military personnel or other agents; or

(3) Insurrection, rebellion, revolution, usurped power, or action taken by governmental authority in hindering or defending against any of these.

j. Damage To Property

"Property damage" to:

(1) Property you own, rent, or occupy, including any costs or expenses incurred by you, or any other person, organization or entity, for repair, replacement, enhancement, restoration or maintenance of such property for any reason, including prevention of injury to a person or damage to another's property;

(2) Premises you sell, give away or abandon, if the "property damage" arises out of any part of those premises;

(3) Property loaned to you;

(4) Personal property in the care, custody or control of the insured;

(5) That particular part of real property on which you or any contractors or subcontractors working directly or indirectly on your behalf are performing operations, if the "property damage" arises out of those operations; or

(6) That particular part of any property that must be restored, repaired or replaced because "your work" was incorrectly performed on it.

Paragraphs **(1)**, **(3)** and **(4)** of this exclusion do not apply to "property damage" (other than damage by fire) to premises, including the contents of such premises, rented to you for a period of seven or fewer consecutive days. A separate limit of insurance applies to Damage To Premises Rented To You as described in Section **III** – Limits Of Insurance.

Paragraph **(2)** of this exclusion does not apply if the premises are "your work" and were never occupied, rented or held for rental by you.

Paragraphs **(3)**, **(4)**, **(5)** and **(6)** of this exclusion do not apply to liability assumed under a sidetrack agreement.

Paragraph **(6)** of this exclusion does not apply to "property damage" included in the "products-completed operations hazard".

k. Damage To Your Product

"Property damage" to "your product" arising out of it or any part of it.

l. Damage To Your Work

"Property damage" to "your work" arising out of it or any part of it and included in the "products-completed operations hazard".

This exclusion does not apply if the damaged work or the work out of which the damage arises was performed on your behalf by a subcontractor.

m. Damage To Impaired Property Or Property Not Physically Injured

"Property damage" to "impaired property" or property that has not been physically injured, arising out of:

(1) A defect, deficiency, inadequacy or dangerous condition in "your product" or "your work"; or

(2) A delay or failure by you or anyone acting on your behalf to perform a contract or agreement in accordance with its terms.

This exclusion does not apply to the loss of use of other property arising out of sudden and accidental physical injury to "your product" or "your work" after it has been put to its intended use.

n. Recall Of Products, Work Or Impaired Property

Damages claimed for any loss, cost or expense incurred by you or others for the loss of use, withdrawal, recall, inspection, repair, replacement, adjustment, removal or disposal of:

(1) "Your product";

(2) "Your work"; or

(3) "Impaired property";

if such product, work, or property is withdrawn or recalled from the market or from use by any person or organization because of a known or suspected defect, deficiency, inadequacy or dangerous condition in it.

o. Personal And Advertising Injury

"Bodily injury" arising out of "personal and advertising injury".

p. Electronic Data

Damages arising out of the loss of, loss of use of, damage to, corruption of, inability to access, or inability to manipulate electronic data.

However, this exclusion does not apply to liability for damages because of "bodily injury".

As used in this exclusion, electronic data means information, facts or programs stored as or on, created or used on, or transmitted to or from computer software, including systems and applications software, hard or floppy disks, CD-ROMs, tapes, drives, cells, data processing devices or any other media which are used with electronically controlled equipment.

q. Recording And Distribution Of Material Or Information In Violation Of Law

"Bodily injury" or "property damage" arising directly or indirectly out of any action or omission that violates or is alleged to violate:

(1) The Telephone Consumer Protection Act (TCPA), including any amendment of or addition to such law;

(2) The CAN-SPAM Act of 2003, including any amendment of or addition to such law;

(3) The Fair Credit Reporting Act (FCRA), and any amendment of or addition to such law, including the Fair and Accurate Credit Transactions Act (FACTA); or

(4) Any federal, state or local statute, ordinance or regulation, other than the TCPA, CAN-SPAM Act of 2003 or FCRA and their amendments and additions, that addresses, prohibits, or limits the printing, dissemination, disposal, collecting, recording, sending, transmitting, communicating or distribution of material or information.

Exclusions **c.** through **n.** do not apply to damage by fire to premises while rented to you or temporarily occupied by you with permission of the owner. A separate limit of insurance applies to this coverage as described in Section **III** – Limits Of Insurance.

COVERAGE B – PERSONAL AND ADVERTISING INJURY LIABILITY

1. Insuring Agreement

a. We will pay those sums that the insured becomes legally obligated to pay as damages because of "personal and advertising injury" to which this insurance applies. We will have the right and duty to defend the insured against any "suit" seeking those damages. However, we will have no duty to defend the insured against any "suit" seeking damages for "personal and advertising injury" to which this insurance does not apply. We may, at our discretion, investigate any offense and settle any claim or "suit" that may result. But:

(1) The amount we will pay for damages is limited as described in Section **III** – Limits Of Insurance; and

(2) Our right and duty to defend end when we have used up the applicable limit of insurance in the payment of judgments or settlements under Coverages **A** or **B** or medical expenses under Coverage **C**.

No other obligation or liability to pay sums or perform acts or services is covered unless explicitly provided for under Supplementary Payments – Coverages **A** and **B**.

b. This insurance applies to "personal and advertising injury" caused by an offense arising out of your business but only if the offense was committed in the "coverage territory" during the policy period.

2. Exclusions

This insurance does not apply to:

a. Knowing Violation Of Rights Of Another

"Personal and advertising injury" caused by or at the direction of the insured with the knowledge that the act would violate the rights of another and would inflict "personal and advertising injury".

b. Material Published With Knowledge Of Falsity

"Personal and advertising injury" arising out of oral or written publication, in any manner, of material, if done by or at the direction of the insured with knowledge of its falsity.

c. Material Published Prior To Policy Period

"Personal and advertising injury" arising out of oral or written publication, in any manner, of material whose first publication took place before the beginning of the policy period.

d. Criminal Acts

"Personal and advertising injury" arising out of a criminal act committed by or at the direction of the insured.

e. Contractual Liability

"Personal and advertising injury" for which the insured has assumed liability in a contract or agreement. This exclusion does not apply to liability for damages that the insured would have in the absence of the contract or agreement.

f. Breach Of Contract

"Personal and advertising injury" arising out of a breach of contract, except an implied contract to use another's advertising idea in your "advertisement".

g. Quality Or Performance Of Goods – Failure To Conform To Statements

"Personal and advertising injury" arising out of the failure of goods, products or services to conform with any statement of quality or performance made in your "advertisement".

h. Wrong Description Of Prices

"Personal and advertising injury" arising out of the wrong description of the price of goods, products or services stated in your "advertisement".

i. Infringement Of Copyright, Patent, Trademark Or Trade Secret

"Personal and advertising injury" arising out of the infringement of copyright, patent, trademark, trade secret or other intellectual property rights. Under this exclusion, such other intellectual property rights do not include the use of another's advertising idea in your "advertisement".

However, this exclusion does not apply to infringement, in your "advertisement", of copyright, trade dress or slogan.

j. Insureds In Media And Internet Type Businesses

"Personal and advertising injury" committed by an insured whose business is:

(1) Advertising, broadcasting, publishing or telecasting;

(2) Designing or determining content of web sites for others; or

(3) An Internet search, access, content or service provider.

However, this exclusion does not apply to Paragraphs **14.a., b.** and **c.** of "personal and advertising injury" under the Definitions section.

For the purposes of this exclusion, the placing of frames, borders or links, or advertising, for you or others anywhere on the Internet, is not by itself, considered the business of advertising, broadcasting, publishing or telecasting.

k. Electronic Chatrooms Or Bulletin Boards

"Personal and advertising injury" arising out of an electronic chatroom or bulletin board the insured hosts, owns, or over which the insured exercises control.

l. Unauthorized Use Of Another's Name Or Product

"Personal and advertising injury" arising out of the unauthorized use of another's name or product in your e-mail address, domain name or metatag, or any other similar tactics to mislead another's potential customers.

m. Pollution

"Personal and advertising injury" arising out of the actual, alleged or threatened discharge, dispersal, seepage, migration, release or escape of "pollutants" at any time.

n. Pollution-related

Any loss, cost or expense arising out of any:

(1) Request, demand, order or statutory or regulatory requirement that any insured or others test for, monitor, clean up, remove, contain, treat, detoxify or neutralize, or in any way respond to, or assess the effects of, "pollutants"; or

(2) Claim or suit by or on behalf of a governmental authority for damages because of testing for, monitoring, cleaning up, removing, containing, treating, detoxifying or neutralizing, or in any way responding to, or assessing the effects of, "pollutants".

o. War

"Personal and advertising injury", however caused, arising, directly or indirectly, out of:

(1) War, including undeclared or civil war;

(2) Warlike action by a military force, including action in hindering or defending against an actual or expected attack, by any government, sovereign or other authority using military personnel or other agents; or

(3) Insurrection, rebellion, revolution, usurped power, or action taken by governmental authority in hindering or defending against any of these.

p. Recording And Distribution Of Material Or Information In Violation Of Law

"Personal and advertising injury" arising directly or indirectly out of any action or omission that violates or is alleged to violate:

(1) The Telephone Consumer Protection Act (TCPA), including any amendment of or addition to such law;

(2) The CAN-SPAM Act of 2003, including any amendment of or addition to such law;

(3) The Fair Credit Reporting Act (FCRA), and any amendment of or addition to such law, including the Fair and Accurate Credit Transactions Act (FACTA); or

(4) Any federal, state or local statute, ordinance or regulation, other than the TCPA, CAN-SPAM Act of 2003 or FCRA and their amendments and additions, that addresses, prohibits, or limits the printing, dissemination, disposal, collecting, recording, sending, transmitting, communicating or distribution of material or information.

COVERAGE C – MEDICAL PAYMENTS

1. Insuring Agreement

a. We will pay medical expenses as described below for "bodily injury" caused by an accident:

(1) On premises you own or rent;

(2) On ways next to premises you own or rent; or

(3) Because of your operations;

provided that:

(a) The accident takes place in the "coverage territory" and during the policy period;

(b) The expenses are incurred and reported to us within one year of the date of the accident; and

(c) The injured person submits to examination, at our expense, by physicians of our choice as often as we reasonably require.

b. We will make these payments regardless of fault. These payments will not exceed the applicable limit of insurance. We will pay reasonable expenses for:

(1) First aid administered at the time of an accident;

(2) Necessary medical, surgical, X-ray and dental services, including prosthetic devices; and

(3) Necessary ambulance, hospital, professional nursing and funeral services.

2. Exclusions

We will not pay expenses for "bodily injury":

a. Any Insured

To any insured, except "volunteer workers".

b. Hired Person

To a person hired to do work for or on behalf of any insured or a tenant of any insured.

c. Injury On Normally Occupied Premises

To a person injured on that part of premises you own or rent that the person normally occupies.

d. Workers' Compensation And Similar Laws

To a person, whether or not an "employee" of any insured, if benefits for the "bodily injury" are payable or must be provided under a workers' compensation or disability benefits law or a similar law.

e. Athletics Activities

To a person injured while practicing, instructing or participating in any physical exercises or games, sports, or athletic contests.

f. Products-Completed Operations Hazard

Included within the "products-completed operations hazard".

g. Coverage A Exclusions

Excluded under Coverage **A.**

SUPPLEMENTARY PAYMENTS – COVERAGES A AND B

1. We will pay, with respect to any claim we investigate or settle, or any "suit" against an insured we defend:

a. All expenses we incur.

b. Up to $250 for cost of bail bonds required because of accidents or traffic law violations arising out of the use of any vehicle to which the Bodily Injury Liability Coverage applies. We do not have to furnish these bonds.

c. The cost of bonds to release attachments, but only for bond amounts within the applicable limit of insurance. We do not have to furnish these bonds.

d. All reasonable expenses incurred by the insured at our request to assist us in the investigation or defense of the claim or "suit", including actual loss of earnings up to $250 a day because of time off from work.

e. All court costs taxed against the insured in the "suit". However, these payments do not include attorneys' fees or attorneys' expenses taxed against the insured.

f. Prejudgment interest awarded against the insured on that part of the judgment we pay. If we make an offer to pay the applicable limit of insurance, we will not pay any prejudgment interest based on that period of time after the offer.

g. All interest on the full amount of any judgment that accrues after entry of the judgment and before we have paid, offered to pay, or deposited in court the part of the judgment that is within the applicable limit of insurance.

These payments will not reduce the limits of insurance.

2. If we defend an insured against a "suit" and an indemnitee of the insured is also named as a party to the "suit", we will defend that indemnitee if all of the following conditions are met:

a. The "suit" against the indemnitee seeks damages for which the insured has assumed the liability of the indemnitee in a contract or agreement that is an "insured contract";

b. This insurance applies to such liability assumed by the insured;

c. The obligation to defend, or the cost of the defense of, that indemnitee, has also been assumed by the insured in the same "insured contract";

d. The allegations in the "suit" and the information we know about the "occurrence" are such that no conflict appears to exist between the interests of the insured and the interests of the indemnitee;

e. The indemnitee and the insured ask us to conduct and control the defense of that indemnitee against such "suit" and agree that we can assign the same counsel to defend the insured and the indemnitee; and

f. The indemnitee:

(1) Agrees in writing to:

(a) Cooperate with us in the investigation, settlement or defense of the "suit";

(b) Immediately send us copies of any demands, notices, summonses or legal papers received in connection with the "suit";

(c) Notify any other insurer whose coverage is available to the indemnitee; and

(d) Cooperate with us with respect to coordinating other applicable insurance available to the indemnitee; and

(2) Provides us with written authorization to:

(a) Obtain records and other information related to the "suit"; and

(b) Conduct and control the defense of the indemnitee in such "suit".

So long as the above conditions are met, attorneys' fees incurred by us in the defense of that indemnitee, necessary litigation expenses incurred by us and necessary litigation expenses incurred by the indemnitee at our request will be paid as Supplementary Payments. Notwithstanding the provisions of Paragraph **2.b.(2)** of Section **I** – Coverage **A** – Bodily Injury And Property Damage Liability, such payments will not be deemed to be damages for "bodily injury" and "property damage" and will not reduce the limits of insurance.

Our obligation to defend an insured's indemnitee and to pay for attorneys' fees and necessary litigation expenses as Supplementary Payments ends when we have used up the applicable limit of insurance in the payment of judgments or settlements or the conditions set forth above, or the terms of the agreement described in Paragraph **f.** above, are no longer met.

SECTION II – WHO IS AN INSURED

1. If you are designated in the Declarations as:

a. An individual, you and your spouse are insureds, but only with respect to the conduct of a business of which you are the sole owner.

b. A partnership or joint venture, you are an insured. Your members, your partners, and their spouses are also insureds, but only with respect to the conduct of your business.

c. A limited liability company, you are an insured. Your members are also insureds, but only with respect to the conduct of your business. Your managers are insureds, but only with respect to their duties as your managers.

d. An organization other than a partnership, joint venture or limited liability company, you are an insured. Your "executive officers" and directors are insureds, but only with respect to their duties as your officers or directors. Your stockholders are also insureds, but only with respect to their liability as stockholders.

e. A trust, you are an insured. Your trustees are also insureds, but only with respect to their duties as trustees.

2. Each of the following is also an insured:

   a. Your "volunteer workers" only while performing duties related to the conduct of your business, or your "employees", other than either your "executive officers" (if you are an organization other than a partnership, joint venture or limited liability company) or your managers (if you are a limited liability company), but only for acts within the scope of their employment by you or while performing duties related to the conduct of your business. However, none of these "employees" or "volunteer workers" are insureds for:

      (1) "Bodily injury" or "personal and advertising injury":

      (a) To you, to your partners or members (if you are a partnership or joint venture), to your members (if you are a limited liability company), to a co-"employee" while in the course of his or her employment or performing duties related to the conduct of your business, or to your other "volunteer workers" while performing duties related to the conduct of your business;

      (b) To the spouse, child, parent, brother or sister of that co-"employee" or "volunteer worker" as a consequence of Paragraph **(1)(a)** above;

      (c) For which there is any obligation to share damages with or repay someone else who must pay damages because of the injury described in Paragraph **(1)(a)** or **(b)** above; or

      (d) Arising out of his or her providing or failing to provide professional health care services.

      (2) "Property damage" to property:

      (a) Owned, occupied or used by;

      (b) Rented to, in the care, custody or control of, or over which physical control is being exercised for any purpose by;

      you, any of your "employees", "volunteer workers", any partner or member (if you are a partnership or joint venture), or any member (if you are a limited liability company).

   b. Any person (other than your "employee" or "volunteer worker"), or any organization while acting as your real estate manager.

   c. Any person or organization having proper temporary custody of your property if you die, but only:

      (1) With respect to liability arising out of the maintenance or use of that property; and

      (2) Until your legal representative has been appointed.

   d. Your legal representative if you die, but only with respect to duties as such. That representative will have all your rights and duties under this Coverage Part.

3. Any organization you newly acquire or form, other than a partnership, joint venture or limited liability company, and over which you maintain ownership or majority interest, will qualify as a Named Insured if there is no other similar insurance available to that organization. However:

   a. Coverage under this provision is afforded only until the 90th day after you acquire or form the organization or the end of the policy period, whichever is earlier;

   b. Coverage **A** does not apply to "bodily injury" or "property damage" that occurred before you acquired or formed the organization; and

   c. Coverage **B** does not apply to "personal and advertising injury" arising out of an offense committed before you acquired or formed the organization.

No person or organization is an insured with respect to the conduct of any current or past partnership, joint venture or limited liability company that is not shown as a Named Insured in the Declarations.

SECTION III – LIMITS OF INSURANCE

1. The Limits of Insurance shown in the Declarations and the rules below fix the most we will pay regardless of the number of:

   a. Insureds;

   b. Claims made or "suits" brought; or

   c. Persons or organizations making claims or bringing "suits".

2. The General Aggregate Limit is the most we will pay for the sum of:

   a. Medical expenses under Coverage **C**;

   b. Damages under Coverage **A,** except damages because of "bodily injury" or "property damage" included in the "products-completed operations hazard"; and

   c. Damages under Coverage **B.**

3. The Products-Completed Operations Aggregate Limit is the most we will pay under Coverage **A** for damages because of "bodily injury" and "property damage" included in the "products-completed operations hazard".

4. Subject to Paragraph **2.** above, the Personal And Advertising Injury Limit is the most we will pay under Coverage **B** for the sum of all damages because of all "personal and advertising injury" sustained by any one person or organization.

5. Subject to Paragraph **2.** or **3.** above, whichever applies, the Each Occurrence Limit is the most we will pay for the sum of:

   a. Damages under Coverage **A**; and

   b. Medical expenses under Coverage **C**

   because of all "bodily injury" and "property damage" arising out of any one "occurrence".

6. Subject to Paragraph **5.** above, the Damage To Premises Rented To You Limit is the most we will pay under Coverage **A** for damages because of "property damage" to any one premises, while rented to you, or in the case of damage by fire, while rented to you or temporarily occupied by you with permission of the owner.

7. Subject to Paragraph **5.** above, the Medical Expense Limit is the most we will pay under Coverage **C** for all medical expenses because of "bodily injury" sustained by any one person.

The Limits of Insurance of this Coverage Part apply separately to each consecutive annual period and to any remaining period of less than 12 months, starting with the beginning of the policy period shown in the Declarations, unless the policy period is extended after issuance for an additional period of less than 12 months. In that case, the additional period will be deemed part of the last preceding period for purposes of determining the Limits of Insurance.

SECTION IV – COMMERCIAL GENERAL LIABILITY CONDITIONS

1. Bankruptcy

Bankruptcy or insolvency of the insured or of the insured's estate will not relieve us of our obligations under this Coverage Part.

2. Duties In The Event Of Occurrence, Offense, Claim Or Suit

a. You must see to it that we are notified as soon as practicable of an "occurrence" or an offense which may result in a claim. To the extent possible, notice should include:

(1) How, when and where the "occurrence" or offense took place;

(2) The names and addresses of any injured persons and witnesses; and

(3) The nature and location of any injury or damage arising out of the "occurrence" or offense.

b. If a claim is made or "suit" is brought against any insured, you must:

(1) Immediately record the specifics of the claim or "suit" and the date received; and

(2) Notify us as soon as practicable.

You must see to it that we receive written notice of the claim or "suit" as soon as practicable.

c. You and any other involved insured must:

(1) Immediately send us copies of any demands, notices, summonses or legal papers received in connection with the claim or "suit";

(2) Authorize us to obtain records and other information;

(3) Cooperate with us in the investigation or settlement of the claim or defense against the "suit"; and

(4) Assist us, upon our request, in the enforcement of any right against any person or organization which may be liable to the insured because of injury or damage to which this insurance may also apply.

d. No insured will, except at that insured's own cost, voluntarily make a payment, assume any obligation, or incur any expense, other than for first aid, without our consent.

3. Legal Action Against Us

No person or organization has a right under this Coverage Part:

a. To join us as a party or otherwise bring us into a "suit" asking for damages from an insured; or

b. To sue us on this Coverage Part unless all of its terms have been fully complied with.

A person or organization may sue us to recover on an agreed settlement or on a final judgment against an insured; but we will not be liable for damages that are not payable under the terms of this Coverage Part or that are in excess of the applicable limit of insurance. An agreed settlement means a settlement and release of liability signed by us, the insured and the claimant or the claimant's legal representative.

4. Other Insurance

If other valid and collectible insurance is available to the insured for a loss we cover under Coverages **A** or **B** of this Coverage Part, our obligations are limited as follows:

a. Primary Insurance

This insurance is primary except when Paragraph **b.** below applies. If this insurance is primary, our obligations are not affected unless any of the other insurance is also primary. Then, we will share with all that other insurance by the method described in Paragraph **c.** below.

b. Excess Insurance

(1) This insurance is excess over:

(a) Any of the other insurance, whether primary, excess, contingent or on any other basis:

(i) That is Fire, Extended Coverage, Builder's Risk, Installation Risk or similar coverage for "your work";

(ii) That is Fire insurance for premises rented to you or temporarily occupied by you with permission of the owner;

(iii) That is insurance purchased by you to cover your liability as a tenant for "property damage" to premises rented to you or temporarily occupied by you with permission of the owner; or

(iv) If the loss arises out of the maintenance or use of aircraft, "autos" or watercraft to the extent not subject to Exclusion **g.** of Section **I** – Coverage **A** – Bodily Injury And Property Damage Liability.

(b) Any other primary insurance available to you covering liability for damages arising out of the premises or operations, or the products and completed operations, for which you have been added as an additional insured.

(2) When this insurance is excess, we will have no duty under Coverages **A** or **B** to defend the insured against any "suit" if any other insurer has a duty to defend the insured against that "suit". If no other insurer defends, we will undertake to do so, but we will be entitled to the insured's rights against all those other insurers.

(3) When this insurance is excess over other insurance, we will pay only our share of the amount of the loss, if any, that exceeds the sum of:

(a) The total amount that all such other insurance would pay for the loss in the absence of this insurance; and

(b) The total of all deductible and self-insured amounts under all that other insurance.

(4) We will share the remaining loss, if any, with any other insurance that is not described in this Excess Insurance provision and was not bought specifically to apply in excess of the Limits of Insurance shown in the Declarations of this Coverage Part.

c. Method Of Sharing

If all of the other insurance permits contribution by equal shares, we will follow this method also. Under this approach each insurer contributes equal amounts until it has paid its applicable limit of insurance or none of the loss remains, whichever comes first.

If any of the other insurance does not permit contribution by equal shares, we will contribute by limits. Under this method, each insurer's share is based on the ratio of its applicable limit of insurance to the total applicable limits of insurance of all insurers.

5. Premium Audit

a. We will compute all premiums for this Coverage Part in accordance with our rules and rates.

b. Premium shown in this Coverage Part as advance premium is a deposit premium only. At the close of each audit period we will compute the earned premium for that period and send notice to the first Named Insured. The due date for audit and retrospective premiums is the date shown as the due date on the bill. If the sum of the advance and audit premiums paid for the policy period is greater than the earned premium, we will return the excess to the first Named Insured.

c. The first Named Insured must keep records of the information we need for premium computation, and send us copies at such times as we may request.

6. Representations

By accepting this policy, you agree:

a. The statements in the Declarations are accurate and complete;

b. Those statements are based upon representations you made to us; and

c. We have issued this policy in reliance upon your representations.

7. **Separation Of Insureds**

Except with respect to the Limits of Insurance, and any rights or duties specifically assigned in this Coverage Part to the first Named Insured, this insurance applies:

a. As if each Named Insured were the only Named Insured; and

b. Separately to each insured against whom claim is made or "suit" is brought.

8. **Transfer Of Rights Of Recovery Against Others To Us**

If the insured has rights to recover all or part of any payment we have made under this Coverage Part, those rights are transferred to us. The insured must do nothing after loss to impair them. At our request, the insured will bring "suit" or transfer those rights to us and help us enforce them.

9. **When We Do Not Renew**

If we decide not to renew this Coverage Part, we will mail or deliver to the first Named Insured shown in the Declarations written notice of the nonrenewal not less than 30 days before the expiration date.

If notice is mailed, proof of mailing will be sufficient proof of notice.

SECTION V – DEFINITIONS

1. "Advertisement" means a notice that is broadcast or published to the general public or specific market segments about your goods, products or services for the purpose of attracting customers or supporters. For the purposes of this definition:

a. Notices that are published include material placed on the Internet or on similar electronic means of communication; and

b. Regarding web sites, only that part of a web site that is about your goods, products or services for the purposes of attracting customers or supporters is considered an advertisement.

2. "Auto" means:

a. A land motor vehicle, trailer or semitrailer designed for travel on public roads, including any attached machinery or equipment; or

b. Any other land vehicle that is subject to a compulsory or financial responsibility law or other motor vehicle insurance law where it is licensed or principally garaged.

However, "auto" does not include "mobile equipment".

3. "Bodily injury" means bodily injury, sickness or disease sustained by a person, including death resulting from any of these at any time.

4. "Coverage territory" means:

a. The United States of America (including its territories and possessions), Puerto Rico and Canada;

b. International waters or airspace, but only if the injury or damage occurs in the course of travel or transportation between any places included in Paragraph **a.** above; or

c. All other parts of the world if the injury or damage arises out of:

(1) Goods or products made or sold by you in the territory described in Paragraph **a.** above;

(2) The activities of a person whose home is in the territory described in Paragraph **a.** above, but is away for a short time on your business; or

(3) "Personal and advertising injury" offenses that take place through the Internet or similar electronic means of communication;

provided the insured's responsibility to pay damages is determined in a "suit" on the merits, in the territory described in Paragraph **a.** above or in a settlement we agree to.

5. "Employee" includes a "leased worker". "Employee" does not include a "temporary worker".

6. "Executive officer" means a person holding any of the officer positions created by your charter, constitution, bylaws or any other similar governing document.

7. "Hostile fire" means one which becomes uncontrollable or breaks out from where it was intended to be.

8. "Impaired property" means tangible property, other than "your product" or "your work", that cannot be used or is less useful because:

a. It incorporates "your product" or "your work" that is known or thought to be defective, deficient, inadequate or dangerous; or

b. You have failed to fulfill the terms of a contract or agreement;

if such property can be restored to use by the repair, replacement, adjustment or removal of "your product" or "your work" or your fulfilling the terms of the contract or agreement.

9. "Insured contract" means:

a. A contract for a lease of premises. However, that portion of the contract for a lease of premises that indemnifies any person or organization for damage by fire to premises while rented to you or temporarily occupied by you with permission of the owner is not an "insured contract";

b. A sidetrack agreement;

c. Any easement or license agreement, except in connection with construction or demolition operations on or within 50 feet of a railroad;

d. An obligation, as required by ordinance, to indemnify a municipality, except in connection with work for a municipality;

e. An elevator maintenance agreement;

f. That part of any other contract or agreement pertaining to your business (including an indemnification of a municipality in connection with work performed for a municipality) under which you assume the tort liability of another party to pay for "bodily injury" or "property damage" to a third person or organization. Tort liability means a liability that would be imposed by law in the absence of any contract or agreement.

Paragraph **f.** does not include that part of any contract or agreement:

(1) That indemnifies a railroad for "bodily injury" or "property damage" arising out of construction or demolition operations, within 50 feet of any railroad property and affecting any railroad bridge or trestle, tracks, road-beds, tunnel, underpass or crossing;

(2) That indemnifies an architect, engineer or surveyor for injury or damage arising out of:

(a) Preparing, approving, or failing to prepare or approve, maps, shop drawings, opinions, reports, surveys, field orders, change orders or drawings and specifications; or

(b) Giving directions or instructions, or failing to give them, if that is the primary cause of the injury or damage; or

(3) Under which the insured, if an architect, engineer or surveyor, assumes liability for an injury or damage arising out of the insured's rendering or failure to render professional services, including those listed in **(2)** above and supervisory, inspection, architectural or engineering activities.

10. "Leased worker" means a person leased to you by a labor leasing firm under an agreement between you and the labor leasing firm, to perform duties related to the conduct of your business. "Leased worker" does not include a "temporary worker".

11. "Loading or unloading" means the handling of property:

a. After it is moved from the place where it is accepted for movement into or onto an aircraft, watercraft or "auto";

b. While it is in or on an aircraft, watercraft or "auto"; or

c. While it is being moved from an aircraft, watercraft or "auto" to the place where it is finally delivered;

but "loading or unloading" does not include the movement of property by means of a mechanical device, other than a hand truck, that is not attached to the aircraft, watercraft or "auto".

12. "Mobile equipment" means any of the following types of land vehicles, including any attached machinery or equipment:

a. Bulldozers, farm machinery, forklifts and other vehicles designed for use principally off public roads;

b. Vehicles maintained for use solely on or next to premises you own or rent;

c. Vehicles that travel on crawler treads;

d. Vehicles, whether self-propelled or not, maintained primarily to provide mobility to permanently mounted:

(1) Power cranes, shovels, loaders, diggers or drills; or

(2) Road construction or resurfacing equipment such as graders, scrapers or rollers;

e. Vehicles not described in Paragraph **a., b., c.** or **d.** above that are not self-propelled and are maintained primarily to provide mobility to permanently attached equipment of the following types:

(1) Air compressors, pumps and generators, including spraying, welding, building cleaning, geophysical exploration, lighting and well servicing equipment; or

(2) Cherry pickers and similar devices used to raise or lower workers;

f. Vehicles not described in Paragraph **a., b., c.** or **d.** above maintained primarily for purposes other than the transportation of persons or cargo.

However, self-propelled vehicles with the following types of permanently attached equipment are not "mobile equipment" but will be considered "autos":

(1) Equipment designed primarily for:

(a) Snow removal;

(b) Road maintenance, but not construction or resurfacing; or

(c) Street cleaning;

(2) Cherry pickers and similar devices mounted on automobile or truck chassis and used to raise or lower workers; and

(3) Air compressors, pumps and generators, including spraying, welding, building cleaning, geophysical exploration, lighting and well servicing equipment.

However, "mobile equipment" does not include any land vehicles that are subject to a compulsory or financial responsibility law or other motor vehicle insurance law where it is licensed or principally garaged. Land vehicles subject to a compulsory or financial responsibility law or other motor vehicle insurance law are considered "autos".

13. "Occurrence" means an accident, including continuous or repeated exposure to substantially the same general harmful conditions.

14. "Personal and advertising injury" means injury, including consequential "bodily injury", arising out of one or more of the following offenses:

a. False arrest, detention or imprisonment;

b. Malicious prosecution;

c. The wrongful eviction from, wrongful entry into, or invasion of the right of private occupancy of a room, dwelling or premises that a person occupies, committed by or on behalf of its owner, landlord or lessor;

d. Oral or written publication, in any manner, of material that slanders or libels a person or organization or disparages a person's or organization's goods, products or services;

e. Oral or written publication, in any manner, of material that violates a person's right of privacy;

f. The use of another's advertising idea in your "advertisement"; or

g. Infringing upon another's copyright, trade dress or slogan in your "advertisement".

15. "Pollutants" mean any solid, liquid, gaseous or thermal irritant or contaminant, including smoke, vapor, soot, fumes, acids, alkalis, chemicals and waste. Waste includes materials to be recycled, reconditioned or reclaimed.

16. "Products-completed operations hazard":

a. Includes all "bodily injury" and "property damage" occurring away from premises you own or rent and arising out of "your product" or "your work" except:

(1) Products that are still in your physical possession; or

(2) Work that has not yet been completed or abandoned. However, "your work" will be deemed completed at the earliest of the following times:

(a) When all of the work called for in your contract has been completed.

(b) When all of the work to be done at the job site has been completed if your contract calls for work at more than one job site.

(c) When that part of the work done at a job site has been put to its intended use by any person or organization other than another contractor or subcontractor working on the same project.

Work that may need service, maintenance, correction, repair or replacement, but which is otherwise complete, will be treated as completed.

b. Does not include "bodily injury" or "property damage" arising out of:

(1) The transportation of property, unless the injury or damage arises out of a condition in or on a vehicle not owned or operated by you, and that condition was created by the "loading or unloading" of that vehicle by any insured;

(2) The existence of tools, uninstalled equipment or abandoned or unused materials; or

(3) Products or operations for which the classification, listed in the Declarations or in a policy Schedule, states that products-completed operations are subject to the General Aggregate Limit.

17. "Property damage" means:

a. Physical injury to tangible property, including all resulting loss of use of that property. All such loss of use shall be deemed to occur at the time of the physical injury that caused it; or

b. Loss of use of tangible property that is not physically injured. All such loss of use shall be deemed to occur at the time of the "occurrence" that caused it.

For the purposes of this insurance, electronic data is not tangible property.

As used in this definition, electronic data means information, facts or programs stored as or on, created or used on, or transmitted to or from computer software, including systems and applications software, hard or floppy disks, CD-ROMs, tapes, drives, cells, data processing devices or any other media which are used with electronically controlled equipment.

18. "Suit" means a civil proceeding in which damages because of "bodily injury", "property damage" or "personal and advertising injury" to which this insurance applies are alleged. "Suit" includes:

a. An arbitration proceeding in which such damages are claimed and to which the insured must submit or does submit with our consent; or

b. Any other alternative dispute resolution proceeding in which such damages are claimed and to which the insured submits with our consent.

19. "Temporary worker" means a person who is furnished to you to substitute for a permanent "employee" on leave or to meet seasonal or short-term workload conditions.

20. "Volunteer worker" means a person who is not your "employee", and who donates his or her work and acts at the direction of and within the scope of duties determined by you, and is not paid a fee, salary or other compensation by you or anyone else for their work performed for you.

21. "Your product":

a. Means:

(1) Any goods or products, other than real property, manufactured, sold, handled, distributed or disposed of by:

(a) You;

(b) Others trading under your name; or

(c) A person or organization whose business or assets you have acquired; and

(2) Containers (other than vehicles), materials, parts or equipment furnished in connection with such goods or products.

b. Includes:

(1) Warranties or representations made at any time with respect to the fitness, quality, durability, performance or use of "your product"; and

(2) The providing of or failure to provide warnings or instructions.

c. Does not include vending machines or other property rented to or located for the use of others but not sold.

22. "Your work":

a. Means:

(1) Work or operations performed by you or on your behalf; and

(2) Materials, parts or equipment furnished in connection with such work or operations.

b. Includes:

(1) Warranties or representations made at any time with respect to the fitness, quality, durability, performance or use of "your work"; and

(2) The providing of or failure to provide warnings or instructions.

Page 16 of 16 **CG 00 01 04 13**

NOTES AND QUESTIONS

1. *All Risk Coverage?* Does the Sample Commercial General Liability Policy provide "all risk" coverage? If it is an "all risk" policy, why is it 16 pages long with 22 definitions, 9 conditions, a 2-page explanation of who is insured, and 39 exclusions (not including subparts)?

2. *Bodily Injury or Property Damage?* Does the policy require "bodily injury" or "property damage" in order to trigger coverage under Coverage B? If not, what types of injury are compensable?

3. *Conditions.* What are "Conditions" under the policy? Should a policyholder be required to comply with all of the conditions in the policy in order to recover?

B. THE MEANING OF "OCCURRENCE," "PROPERTY DAMAGE," "BODILY INJURY," AND "DAMAGES"

In order to obtain coverage under a CGL policy, the policyholder has the initial burden of proving the claim is at least potentially covered under the policy's "insuring agreement." In general, this means the policyholder must prove an "occurrence" caused either "property damage" or "bodily injury" for which someone is seeking "damages." The first three of these terms are defined in CGL policies, but "damages" is not. The next three cases are examples of courts interpreting and applying these terms.

UNITED STATES FIDELITY & GUARANTY CO. V. WILKIN INSULATION CO.

578 N.E.2d 926 (Ill. 1991)

Opinion

JUSTICE BILANDIC delivered the opinion of the court:

We are called upon to interpret certain provisions of comprehensive general liability insurance policies dealing with the duty of insurance companies to defend their insureds. This litigation originates as a result of underlying lawsuits instituted by school districts and public building owners against a multitude of defendants that collectively make up the "asbestos industry." The defendant herein, Wilkin Insulation Company (Wilkin), is alleged to be a part, although relatively insignificant, of the "asbestos industry." The underlying lawsuits seek reimbursement of costs incurred in asbestos abatement procedures from Wilkin and its codefendants. The events giving rise to the underlying litigation coincide with the periods of coverage of one or more of the comprehensive general liability insurance policies issued by plaintiff insurance companies to Wilkin.

Wilkin promptly notified its insurers of these asbestos-related cases and asked plaintiffs to defend it and to pay the resulting damages, if any, within the policy limits. Plaintiff United States Fidelity & Guaranty Company (USF & G) refused to defend Wilkin and denied all coverage. The other plaintiffs, Commercial Union Insurance Company and Employers Fire Insurance Company (collectively, Commercial Union), Argonaut Insurance Company and Argonaut Midwest Insurance Company (collectively, Argonaut), Aetna Casualty & Surety Company (Aetna) and Zurich

Insurance Company (Zurich), undertook Wilkin's defense under a reservation of rights.

USF & G instituted the instant declaratory judgment action, in the circuit court of Cook County, against Wilkin Insulation Company, Wilkin Properties, Inc., and Architectural Sales, Inc., the named insureds under its comprehensive general liability policy (collectively, Wilkin). USF & G sought a determination that it had no duty to defend or indemnify Wilkin in the underlying lawsuits. Thereafter, Commercial Union, Argonaut, Aetna and Zurich intervened in this action as party plaintiffs, seeking the same declarations with regard to their duties to defend and indemnify Wilkin.

During consecutive policy terms between 1964 and 1985, Wilkin was insured under comprehensive general liability insurance policies issued at varying times by plaintiffs. Under the terms of these policies, each plaintiff agreed to defend and provide coverage for Wilkin in any action seeking damages on account of "property damage" caused by an "occurrence."

Wilkin is a small, family-run operation, whose business is the installation of insulation products in buildings under construction. From 1958 to 1970, a small percentage of Wilkin's business was the contract installation of spray-on fireproofing products which contained asbestos. Wilkin would act as a sub-contractor, applying the fireproofing products in accordance with the specifications and requirements of the general contractors, architects and engineers of various construction projects located in Indiana and Illinois.

Until roughly the mid-1970s, the use of asbestos-containing material for fireproofing and soundproofing was an accepted, and often required, specification in building construction. In the last decade, however, the well-recognized utility of these products has been overshadowed by the potential health hazard to human beings exposed to asbestos fibers. Concern over the effects of exposure to asbestos fibers has resulted in a maze of Federal and State regulations requiring local educational facilities and other public building owners to identify the presence of asbestos in their buildings and take corrective measures to contain or remove the asbestos products from their buildings. See, *e.g.*, 20 U.S.C. § 3601 *et seq.* (1988); 40 C.F.R. § 763 (1990); Ill.Rev.Stat.1985, ch. 122, par. 1401 *et seq.*

These regulations have resulted in mass litigation brought by these building owners against the whole "asbestos industry" to recover the costs associated with the inspection, removal from and/or replacement of asbestos in their buildings. Wilkin has found itself a named defendant in this asbestos-related litigation brought against an enormous defendant class, made up of the entire chain of miners, manufacturers, distributors, sellers, architects, engineers, contractors and installers of asbestos-containing products. The instant action involves nine of these asbestos-related lawsuits, brought by various building owners against over 60 named defendants, including Wilkin.

In the case at bar, plaintiffs moved for summary judgment on the issues of their duty to defend and indemnify Wilkin in the underlying lawsuits. Wilkin responded with its cross-motion for summary judgment against plaintiffs, contending that each plaintiff had a duty to defend and indemnify Wilkin under the terms of their respective comprehensive general liability policies. (Aetna made no motion for summary judgment but agreed to be bound by the trial court's determination.) The trial court granted plaintiffs' motions for summary judgment and denied Wilkin's summary judgment motion, finding that plaintiffs had no duty to defend Wilkin in the underlying lawsuits. . . .

In granting plaintiffs' motions for summary judgment, the trial court determined that the underlying complaints did not allege "property damage" caused by an "occurrence" under the terms of the various insurance policies. . . .

Wilkin appealed the trial court's order granting summary judgment in favor of plaintiffs. The appellate court reversed, finding that the underlying complaints sufficiently alleged "property damage" caused by an "occurrence" to bring the cases within coverage by plaintiffs' insurance policies. . . . We granted plaintiffs' petitions for leave to appeal (134 Ill.2d R. 315) and consolidated these actions for review. . . .

At the time of this appeal, no determination of Wilkin's liability in the underlying lawsuits has been made. Therefore, any determination of plaintiffs' duty to indemnify Wilkin with respect to the underlying lawsuits is premature. (*Maryland Casualty Co. v. Chicago & North Western Transportation Co.* (1984), 126 Ill.App.3d 150, 81 Ill.Dec. 289, 466 N.E.2d 1091.) The issue presented is whether the appellate court correctly determined that plaintiffs have a duty to defend Wilkin in the underlying lawsuits under the terms of their comprehensive general liability policies. We affirm.

. . . .

We must determine whether the underlying complaints allege potentially covered "property damage" caused by an "occurrence" . . . .

II.

PROPERTY DAMAGE

We have reviewed each of the nine underlying complaints pursuant to the liberal duty to defend standard. . . . Each complaint alleges that asbestos-containing products were installed in the buildings. The complaints further allege that, upon deterioration of the asbestos-containing product itself or upon disturbance from an outside force, asbestos fibers are released into the air. These fibers are extremely durable and lasting. The asbestos fibers are of the size and shape that permit them to remain airborne for periods of time, settle, and then become resuspended in the air to later settle at different locations throughout the buildings. Thus, the buildings and their contents (*e.g.,* carpets, upholstery, drapery, etc.) are virtually contaminated or impregnated with asbestos fibers, the presence of which poses a serious health hazard to the human occupants. Finally, under various theories of recovery, the underlying complaints seek damages in the form of the costs of inspecting their buildings and the contents therein for the presence of asbestos fibers. The complaints further seek to recover from all defendants, including Wilkin, any costs associated with the containment, removal and/or replacement of the asbestos-containing products.

Turning to the definitions of property damage contained in plaintiffs' insurance policies, we note that these definitions vary somewhat. However, for purposes of our review, we will use the strictest definition of property damage. The post-1973 standard form policy, issued by Aetna, Zurich and USF & G, defines property damage as:

> "1) physical injury to or destruction of tangible property, which occurs during the policy period, including the loss of use thereof at any time resulting therefrom."

All plaintiffs essentially argue that the underlying complaints do not allege *physical* injury to *tangible* property. Rather, plaintiffs contend that the presence of health-threatening, asbestos-containing products results only in intangible economic loss in the form of diminished market values of the buildings.

This court, however, has already found that asbestos fiber contamination constitutes physical injury to tangible property, *i.e.,* the buildings and their contents. (*Board of Education v. A.C. & S, Inc.* (1989), 131 Ill.2d 428, 137 Ill.Dec. 635, 546 N.E.2d 580.) In *Board of Education,* we rejected the same argument that the instant plaintiffs now make. There this court found:

> [I]t would be incongruous to argue there is no damage to other property when a harmful element exists throughout a building or an area of a building which by law must be corrected * * *. The view that asbestos fibers may contaminate a building sufficiently to allege damage to property has been recently adopted in a number of cases. * * *
>
> The essence of the allegations [of the complaints] is that the buildings have been contaminated by asbestos to the point where corrective action, under the law, must be taken. Thus, the buildings have been damaged.

(*Board of Education v. A.C & S, Inc.* (1989), 131 Ill.2d 428, 446–49 [137 Ill.Dec. 635, 546 N.E.2d 580] (citing *City of Greenville v. W.R. Grace & Co.* (4th Cir.1987), 827 F.2d 975; *City of Manchester v. National Gypsum Co.* (D.R.I.1986), 637 F.Supp. 646; *Town of Hooksett School District v. W.R. Grace & Co.* (D.N.H.1984), 617 F.Supp. 126; *Shooshanian v. Wagner* (Alaska 1983), 672 P.2d 455).)

In the instant action, the underlying complaints allege that the buildings and the contents therein were contaminated by toxic asbestos fibers. Therefore, the underlying complaints allege physical injury to tangible property. Thus, we find that the underlying complaints allege potentially covered property damage.

III.

OCCURRENCE

To determine whether the insurers have a duty to defend Wilkin in the underlying lawsuits, we must further determine whether the contamination of the buildings resulted from an "occurrence." Generally, the policies define occurrence as:

> "an accident, including continuous or repeated exposure to conditions which result in property damage * * * neither expected nor intended from the standpoint of the insured."

Plaintiffs argue that there is no "occurrence" because (1) there is no event or accident which results in property damage and (2) the property damage was either expected or intended by Wilkin.

First, plaintiffs argue that the only event which precedes the alleged property damage is Wilkin's intentional act of installing the asbestos-containing products in the buildings. Therefore, plaintiffs reason that the property damage was not the result of any preceding "accident."

The insurance policies' definition of "accident," however, includes the "continuous or repeated exposure to conditions." In the instant action, the underlying complaints all allege that the asbestos-containing products continuously release toxic asbestos fibers into the air. This continuous release of asbestos fibers constitutes a harmful condition. By virtue of the "continuous or repeated exposure to the condition" of asbestos fiber release, the buildings and their contents became contaminated. It is the continuous exposure of the buildings and their contents to released asbestos fibers which constitutes the "accident," as defined by the insurance policies. This "accident" results in "property damage." Therefore, the "property damage" alleged in the underlying complaints is caused by an "occurrence," as defined within the insurance policies.

Next, plaintiffs contend that Wilkin either expected or intended the threat to human health posed by the asbestos-containing product. Plaintiffs point to several theories of recovery within the underlying complaints which allege intentional torts. Plaintiffs argue that the underlying complaints allege that Wilkin intentionally installed asbestos-containing products in the buildings with knowledge of the products' threat to human health. Therefore, plaintiffs conclude that the resulting health threat "was expected or intended from the standpoint of Wilkin."

Plaintiffs misread the definition of "occurrence" contained in the policies. Under this definition, it is the "property damage" which must be "neither expected nor intended from the standpoint of the insured." Therefore, it is the contamination of the buildings and their contents that must be neither expected nor intended by Wilkin. We have reviewed the underlying complaints and are unable to find any allegations that Wilkin "expected or intended" to contaminate the buildings and the contents therein with toxic asbestos fibers.

Moreover, . . . an insurer has a duty to defend its insured if *any* theory of recovery alleges potential coverage. Each underlying complaint alleges, *inter alia,* a theory of recovery sounding in negligence. These negligence counts allege that Wilkin *knew or should have known* of the propensity of the product to release toxic asbestos fibers. Since we are required to liberally construe the pleadings and the insurance policies in favor of the insured, we conclude that the underlying complaints do not allege that Wilkin *expected or intended* to contaminate the buildings and the contents therein with toxic asbestos fibers.

Therefore, we conclude that the underlying complaints allege potential coverage for "property damage" caused by an "occurrence."

. . . .

V.

CONCLUSION

We therefore conclude that the underlying complaints allege potentially covered "property damage" caused by an "occurrence" . . . . Therefore, plaintiffs have the duty to defend Wilkin in the underlying lawsuits.

Accordingly, for the foregoing reasons, we affirm the judgment of the appellate court.

NOTES AND QUESTIONS

1. *What Is an "Occurrence"?* "For many years, 'occurrence' was defined in ISO's standard form CGL policies as 'an accident, including continuous or repeated exposure to conditions, which results in bodily injury or property damage neither expected nor intended from the standpoint of the insured . . . .' Under this definition, to determine whether there was an occurrence, the analysis focused on whether there was an accident that resulted in bodily injury or property damage that the policyholder did not expect or intend. In

short, the question amounts to: did unexpected and unintended bodily injury or property damage result from the policyholder's actions? Beginning in 1986, and continuing today in the current version of ISO's standard form CGL policy, 'occurrence' is defined as 'an accident, including continuous or repeated exposure to substantially the same general harmful conditions.' As courts were already treating the 'expected or intended' language in the definition of an 'occurrence' as an exclusion, in 1986 the language was formally moved to the exclusions section of CGL policies: "This insurance does not apply to. . . '[b]odily injury' or 'property damage' expected or intended from the standpoint of the insured. . . ." This move, however, did not change the analysis of whether there has been an occurrence. The question to be answered still remains whether the policyholder did something that resulted in property damage or bodily injury that the policyholder did not expect or intend to cause." Christopher C. French, *Revisiting Construction Defects as "Occurrences" under CGL Insurance Policies,* 19 U. Pa. J. Bus. L. 101, 105–06 (2016).

2. *Courts' Interpretations of "Property Damage."* As reflected in the *Wilkin Insulation* case, the term "property damage" has been interpreted broadly to include situations where property may be functioning as intended, but it nevertheless must be removed or remediated because it is creating an unexpected hazard. *See, e.g., Dayton Indep. Sch. Dist. v. National Gypsum Co.*, 682 F. Supp. 1403, 1407 (E.D. Tex. 1988), *rev. sub nom. W.R. Grace & Co. v. Continental Cas. Co.*, 896 F.2d 865 (Tex. 1990); *Eljer Mfg. Co. v. Liberty Mut. Ins. Co.*, 972 F.2d 805 (7th Cir. 1992). A more difficult question arises when a defective product is incorporated into another product. Has the finished product suffered "property damage"? Courts have reached conflicting conclusions. *Compare, e.g., Pittsburgh Plate Glass Co. v. Fid. and Cas. Co.*, 281 F.2d 538 (3d Cir. 1960) (holding that defective paint that chipped after applied to blinds was "property damage"), *with Federated Mut. Ins. Co. v. Concrete Units, Inc.*, 363 N.W. 2d 751 (Minn. 1985) (defective concrete used in the construction of a grain elevator that diminished the value of the grain elevator was not "property damage").

3. *Is Lost Data "Property Damage"?* In recent years, there has been some litigation regarding the issue of whether hacking events cause "property damage" when there is a loss of electronic data. Courts have reached mixed conclusions on the issue. *Compare, e.g., Retail Systems, Inc. v. Cas. Ins. Cos.*, 469 N.W.2d 735 (Minn. Ct. App. 1991) (data stored on computer tapes and lost was "property damage"), *with America Online Inc. v. St. Paul Mercury Ins. Co.*, 207 F. Supp. 2d 459 (E.D. Va. 2002), *aff'd*, 347 F.3d 89 (4th Cir. 2003) (damaged computer data was not "property damage"). The issue may be becoming moot under CGL policies because, in 2014, ISO introduced several endorsements to CGL policies that address the access or disclosure of confidential or personal information, including a number of exclusion endorsements, with one that excludes coverage for losses of electronic data: "This insurance does not apply to . . . The loss of, loss of use of, damage to, corruption of, inability to access, or inability to manipulate electronic data." To provide coverage for cyber risks,

new lines of cyber risk insurance have been created. In fact, cyber insurance is one of the fastest growing new lines of insurance.

LAVANANT V. GENERAL ACC. INS. CO. OF AMERICA

595 N.E.2d 819 (N.Y. 1992)

OPINION OF THE COURT

KAYE, JUDGE.

This appeal by an insurer presents an issue that has divided courts in other jurisdictions but remains open here: whether coverage for "bodily injury" includes emotional distress resulting from the insured's negligent conduct, where no physical injury or contact is involved. We conclude that in the circumstances presented, mental injury alone is covered.

I.

Plaintiffs are the owner and managing agent of a four-story brownstone located on East 24th Street in Manhattan. The property was insured under two policies. The first, a comprehensive general liability policy issued by defendant General Accident Insurance Company of America, provided coverage of up to $500,000 for each occurrence. The second, an umbrella policy issued by defendant Federal Insurance Company, provided excess liability coverage of $10,000,000 over General Accident's occurrence limit.

General Accident's policy—the one directly in issue in this case—provided coverage for bodily injury and property damage. "Bodily injury" was defined as "bodily injury, sickness or disease."

In 1984, during renovation of the premises, a portion of the ceiling collapsed in the apartment rented by Emilio Belliti and Victor Rizika. In a single action, they sought damages from plaintiffs for personal injury and property damage, alleging negligence, intentional infliction of emotional distress, assault, and breach of warranty of habitability. The complaint did not allege any physical injury or contact.

Upon receiving notification of the action, General Accident undertook the defense, reserving its rights on certain questions of coverage. Federal took no action until 1988, when it acknowledged the negligence cause of action and disclaimed liability as to the remaining claims.

Concerned with assigned counsel's handling of the case, plaintiffs substituted their own counsel. On the day of the substitution, and over plaintiffs' objection, General Accident settled the property damage claim under the first cause of action for $50,000. The second and third causes of action—based on intentional conduct—were dismissed by the trial court prior to submission to the jury. In 1988, the jury awarded the tenants $400,000 for personal injuries—including emotional distress—on their negligence claim and $5,226 on the breach of warranty claim; a punitive damage award of $2,500,000 was set aside by the trial court. Judgment was entered in the amount of $410,738, which was affirmed on appeal.

While the tenants' appeal was pending, plaintiffs commenced this action against General Accident seeking indemnity for the judgment and attorneys' fees. In response to plaintiffs' motion for partial summary judgment, General Accident argued both that the damages award was based on intentional conduct and thus outside the scope of coverage, and that there was no coverage for emotional distress in the absence of physical injury or contact. Supreme Court granted plaintiffs partial summary judgment, to the extent of requiring General Accident to indemnify them for the judgment in the tenants' action, plus interest, attorneys' fees and costs incurred in defending that action; it severed plaintiffs' claims for punitive damages and attorneys' fees incurred in the present action, which remain pending in the trial court. The court based its holding on the intentional conduct issue and did not reach the question of coverage for purely mental injury.

While noting that the issue appeared to present a case of first impression in New York, the Appellate Division rejected General Accident's assertion that coverage would not attach without physical injury or contact, and held that "bodily injury" includes "the emotional and psychological effects of incidents that are otherwise covered by the policy." In a separate order, the Appellate Division affirmed Supreme Court's award of $104,624 for attorneys' fees and costs incurred by plaintiffs in defending the tenants' action.

General Accident appeals both determinations, arguing that emotional distress without physical injury or contact does not constitute "bodily injury" under the terms of its policy, and that Supreme Court erred in calculating attorneys' fees. Both the order affirming the attorneys' fees award and the prior nonfinal order granting partial summary judgment are reviewable by this Court, but on the merits the insurer's arguments must be rejected.

. . . .

III.

The principles governing interpretation of insurance contracts are well settled. Unambiguous provisions of a policy are given their plain and ordinary meaning. But where there is ambiguity as to the existence of coverage, doubt must be resolved in favor of the insured and against the insurer.

The legal question whether the term "bodily injury" is ambiguous has been extensively litigated in other jurisdictions and has engendered lively debate throughout the country. Some courts have found the term ambiguous (*see, e.g., Lees v. Smith*, 363 So.2d 974, 980 [La.App. 3rd

Cir.1978]; *NPS Corp. v. Insurance Co.,* 213 N.J.Super. 547, 517 A.2d 1211), while others have found no ambiguity (*see, e.g., Allstate Ins. Co. v. Diamant,* 401 Mass. 654, 658, 518 N.E.2d 1154; *Farm Bur. Mut. Ins. Co. v. Hoag,* 136 Mich.App. 326, 356 N.W.2d 630).

We conclude that the key term "bodily injury," as used in the policy before us, is ambiguous.

On its face, the policy purchased by plaintiff property owners is one of comprehensive general liability insurance. It specified as "coverages" "bodily injury liability and property damage liability," suggesting one covered category of injury to the person and a second covered category of injury to property. There is at least an ambiguity in this respect. The ambiguity is heightened, not eliminated, by the policy's explicit definition of "bodily injury" as "bodily injury, sickness or disease." The categories "sickness" and "disease" in the insurer's definition not only enlarge the term "bodily injury" but also, to the average reader, may include mental as well as physical sickness and disease.

We decline General Accident's invitation to rewrite the contract to add "*bodily* sickness" and "*bodily* disease," and a requirement of prior physical contact for compensable mental injury. General Accident could itself have specified such limitations in drafting its policy, but it did not do so.

We note that the definition proposed by plaintiffs—one that includes coverage for purely emotional distress—is consistent with recent case law in this State allowing recovery for such injuries in a variety of contexts (*see, e.g., Matter of Wood v. Laidlaw Tr.,* 77 N.Y.2d 79, 564 N.Y.S.2d 704, 565 N.E.2d 1255; *see also, Kennedy v. McKesson Co.,* 58 N.Y.2d 500, 504, 462 N.Y.S.2d 421, 448 N.E.2d 1332). In upholding such claims, we have recognized that emotional trauma may be as disabling as physical injury, and that whether a person suffers one form of injury or the other may be a fortuity determined solely by the particular vulnerability of an individual. In a given situation "one person may be susceptible to a heart attack while another may suffer a depressive reaction." (*Matter of Wolfe v. Sibley, Lindsay & Curr Co.,* 36 N.Y.2d 505, 510, 369 N.Y.S.2d 637, 330 N.E.2d 603; *see also, NPS Corp. v. Insurance Co.,* 213 N.J.Super., at 552–553, 517 A.2d, at 1214, supra.)

This development of the law is relevant to the present controversy. Recognition of the compensability of purely mental injuries for claimants brings with it increased exposure to liability for insureds. This underscores that the reasonable expectation of property owners purchasing a comprehensive policy such as plaintiffs' would be that their liability for purely mental injury would fall within their insurance coverage (*see, Thomas J. Lipton, Inc. v. Liberty Mut. Ins. Co.,* 34 N.Y.2d 356, 361, 357 N.Y.S.2d 705, 314 N.E.2d 37).

Thus, we conclude that "bodily injury" in General Accident's policy is ambiguous and that, resolving the doubt in favor of insured and against the insurer, General Accident is obligated to indemnify plaintiffs.

. . . .

Accordingly, the order of the Appellate Division should be affirmed, with costs.

NOTES AND QUESTIONS

1. *Easy Cases.* Whether a "bodily injury" has occurred is not an issue that is litigated as frequently as the issue of whether "property damage" has occurred. This is primarily due to the fact that it is clear in most cases whether someone has been injured, and the case law is well established that emotional injuries accompanied by a physical manifestation of distress are "bodily injuries." *See, e.g.*, Peter J. Kalis, Thomas M. Reiter & James R. Segerdahl, Policyholder's Guide to the Law of Insurance Coverage § 7.02[B] (1st ed. 1997 & Supp. 2017) ("There is general agreement that 'bodily injury' includes physical injury resulting from emotional distress.").

2. *Divided Courts.* Courts are divided, however, on the issue of whether mental or emotional distress constitutes "bodily injury" under CGL policies, particularly in cases where there is no physical manifestation of the distress. *Compare, e.g.*, *Maine State Academy of Hair Design, Inc. v. Commercial Union Fire Ins. Co.*, 699 A.2d 1153 (Me. 1997), *with Rolette County v. Western Cas. & Sur. Co.*, 452 F. Supp. 125 (D. N.D. 1978) ("bodily injury" under CGL policies does not include "non-physical harm to the person").

AETNA CAS. & SUR. CO. V. COMMONWEALTH OF KENTUCKY

179 S.W.3d 830 (Ky. 2005)

Opinion

Opinion of the Court by JUSTICE SCOTT.

This appeal is from the judgment of the Court of Appeals, affirming the decision of the Jefferson Circuit Court . . . .

Six separate issues were raised on appeal and cross-appeal by the various parties. These include: . . . (3) whether the costs of site measures are paid "as damages because of property damages" within the meaning of the ANI policies. . . .

We shall address all six issues argued, but first set forth the following summary of facts, taken largely from the list of sixty-eight stipulations compiled by the parties and the Court of Appeals Opinion:

Maxey Flats is a chemical and nuclear waste disposal facility located in eastern Fleming County which accepted waste from 1963 to 1977. Over this time period, approximately 4.75 million cubic feet of low-level radioactive waste was received and buried at the Maxey Flats facility. The waste originated from power plants, hospitals, universities, various industries, and government installations. Most of the waste transported to the Maxey Flats facility consisted of solid materials that were deposited in containers constructed of various materials including cardboard, wood and steel. Liquid wastes, including tritium, were also accepted at Maxey Flats from 1963 to 1972. Both solid and liquid radioactive waste was buried in trenches at Maxey Flats.

The use of trenches to bury waste was a permissible practice for disposing of low-level radioactive waste during the time period the Maxey Flats facility was open for the receipt of commercial waste.

Unfortunately, rain water penetrated the large, unlined trenches, mixed with the radioactive waste, and leached out underneath the trenches and beyond the facility.

In December, 1977, the Commonwealth of Kentucky ("Commonwealth"), as the primary regulatory authority with respect to the use and disposal of radioactive material in Kentucky, became alarmed at the level of radioactive contaminants migrating off-site. Accordingly, it issued an order suspending the facility's license to accept additional waste. Thus, no commercial waste was received at the Maxey Flats facility after December 1977.

Atcor, Inc., Chem-Nuclear Systems, Inc. ("Chem-Nuclear") and Hittman Nuclear & Development Corporation ("Hittman") were in the business of transporting and/or arranging for the transportation of low level radioactive waste to licensed waste disposal sites throughout the United States. Hittman was acquired by Westinghouse Electric Corporation in 1982. In 1984, the name of the corporation was changed to Westinghouse Hittman Nuclear Incorporated.

Atcor and Chem-Nuclear never owned or operated the Maxey Flats facility. Neither Hittman, Westinghouse Electric Corporation nor Westinghouse Hittman Nuclear Incorporated (collectively "Hittman") owned or operated the Maxey Flats facility while it was open and accepting commercial waste.

Aetna Casualty and Surety Company, and the other involved insurance companies (36 companies altogether) are members of the American Nuclear Insurers, or "ANI." ANI is an unincorporated underwriting association, formed by conventional insurance carriers, which issues nuclear liability insurance policies.

. . . .

In 1986, the Environmental Protection Agency ("EPA") placed the Maxey Flats facility on the National Priorities List. Pursuant to the Comprehensive Environmental Response, Compensation and Liability Act ("CERCLA"), 42 U.S.C. § 9601 *et seq.*, the EPA instituted administrative proceedings against the insureds for the cleanup of the contaminated site and the abatement of the effects of the contamination. The initial step in such proceedings took place November 26, 1986 when the EPA sent notices by certified mail to approximately 832 Potentially Responsible Parties ("PRPs") who had owned or operated the Maxey Flats facility, or who had transported or arranged for the transportation of waste to the facility. These entities included Atcor, Chem-Nuclear, U.S. Ecology, the Kentucky Natural Resources and Environmental Protection Cabinet and Westinghouse Electric Corporation on behalf of Hittman.

When the insureds notified ANI of the EPA's PRP notices, ANI refused to defend or indemnify them in the CERCLA action. Therefore, the insureds were forced to deal with the EPA on their own. Subsequently, in 1987 the PRPs agreed to a consent order with the EPA obligating them to perform a "Remedial Investigation and Feasibility Study" ("Feasibility Study") to determine the nature and extent of the property damage, and to evaluate alternative remediation programs for its correction or containment. The study was completed at a cost of over $5,000,000. Following submission of the Feasibility Study, the EPA issued a Record of Decision which incorporated parts of this Feasibility Study in a clean-up remedy for the insureds to implement at Maxey Flats. The remedial plan had an estimated cost of implementation in excess of $57,000,000. The insureds ultimately settled the EPA's claims and the settlement is contained in a consent decree filed with the United States District Court for the Eastern District of Kentucky in July 1995.

Meanwhile, in April 1987, ANI, having refused to defend, filed a declaratory judgment action in the Jefferson Circuit Court seeking to establish no coverage liability. Counterclaims were made by the insureds for coverage under the policies and money damages for ANI's breach of contractual duties to defend and indemnify them.

Following discovery, all parties filed cross-motions for summary judgment. On January 4, 1995, the Jefferson Circuit Court entered a partial summary judgment in favor of the insureds, holding (1) the response costs required to remediate the site were "damages" within the meaning of the policy and (2) the contamination of off-site property constituted "property damage" as defined by the policies. Thereafter, the Court summarily ruled that ANI's duty to defend the appellees had been triggered by the EPA's notice of CERCLA proceedings (the PRP notice letters).

. . . .

The Court of Appeals affirmed the circuit court's summary judgment ruling. . . . This Court granted discretionary review.

. . . .

c. ***Whether the costs of site measures are paid "as damages because of property damages" within the meaning of the ANI policies.***

Appellants, ANI, argue the costs of site measures are not paid "as damages because of property damage." They contend: (1) none of the insureds' Maxey Flats response cost liability was spent to compensate third parties for a "compensable loss;" (2) no third party has "sued" any of the insureds alleging bodily injury or property damage to its property because of the nuclear energy hazard at Maxey Flats; and (3) the CERCLA liability was imposed for purely "prophylactic" measures for which ANI's policies do not provide coverage.

Appellees, Hittman and Chem-Nuclear (position also adopted by Commonwealth) argue the response costs at issue are damages for three reasons: (1) the plain and ordinary meaning of the term "damages" encompasses any monetary liability for property damage, without regard to the form of action in which the liability is imposed, (2) 15 of 17 state supreme courts that have addressed this issue have held that legally mandated environmental remediation costs are "damages," and (3) the term "damages" is at least ambiguous and must be construed in favor of coverage.

In its policies, ANI promises "to pay on behalf of the insured. . . all sums which the insured shall become legally obligated to pay as damages because of . . . property damage . . . ."

CERCLA expressly permits responsible parties to insure against the costs of relief under this legislation. See 42 U.S.C. § 9607(e). Therefore, our task is to decide whether ANI's policies do provide coverage according to their terms despite "damages" being undefined within the policy language.

. . . .

As damages are not defined within ANI's policies, and various authorities from dictionaries to court opinions define the term to encompass diverse aspects of monetary awards, we find the term ambiguous and subject to the reasonable expectations of the insureds.

We believe the policy language, "all sums which the insured shall become legally obligated to pay as damages because of property damage," can reasonably be interpreted to cover any claim asserted against the insured arising out of property damage, which requires the expenditure of money, regardless of whether the claim can be characterized as legal or equitable in nature. This interpretation is supported by the dictionary definition of "damages" which makes no distinction between damages at law and actions in equity. *See* Webster's Third New International Dictionary 571 (P. Gove ed.1961).

We agree with the majority of state appellate courts that hold the ordinary meaning of "damages" is broad enough to, and does include, government mandated response or cleanup costs under CERCLA and similar state environmental protection statutes: as long as the purpose is to rectify, correct, control, lessen or stop ongoing injury of the premises. This purpose is met in this action.

We are further persuaded by the reasoning of the Wisconsin Supreme Court in *Johnson Controls, Inc. v. Employers Insurance of Wausau,* 264 Wis.2d 60, 665 N.W.2d 257 (2003), wherein the Court explained:

> [T]he nature of relief in CERCLA response cost actions is not confined to future injuries; it includes legal recompense for injuries sustained. . . . Thus, there is both a prospective and remedial element to an insured's response cost liability. Because CERCLA proceedings seek the costs of repairing damaged property, rather than the cost of conforming one's future conduct, the nature of the relief is, at least in part compensatory.

Id. at 274.

The Sixth Circuit Court of Appeals has also explained its interpretation of the term "damages" in the case of *Anderson Development Co. v. Travelers Indem. Co.,* 49 F.3d 1128 (6th Cir.1995), wherein the Court wrote:

> The fact that the insured cooperates and assumes the obligation to conduct the clean-up, rather than forcing the EPA to incur the expenses of a clean-up and then bring a coercive suit, does not change the bottom line that a legal obligation exists. Accordingly, we. . . hold. . . government imposed environmental clean-up costs constitute "damages."

Id. at 1133.

We would add, also, that if ANI intended a narrow technical definition of "damages," it was their duty to define the term clearly within their policies. See *Minnesota Min. & Mfg. Co. v. Travelers Indem. Co.,* 457 N.W.2d 175, 181 (Minn.1990).

The second question we must answer before concluding ANI's policies provide coverage for the cost of site measures incurred by the insureds, is whether these costs are "damages because of property damage" within the meaning of the policies.

Unlike standard form general liability policies, ANI's policies expressly define "property damage" to include "radioactive contamination" and also contemplate within the definition, the "imminent danger of such contamination." Because radioactive contamination of property has unquestionably occurred at, in, and around Maxey Flats, we find "property damage" has occurred as the term is defined within the policies.

We think the trial court explained its reasoning well when it wrote:

> The EPA response costs were triggered by, and can be seen by the ordinary insured to have been imposed "because of" the radionuclide levels which were discovered on the adjacent property. Since the radionuclide levels on the adjacent property triggered the liability, they were "property damage" from the standpoint of the insureds. The ambiguity of the provision allows nontechnical construction, and application in the insureds' favor.

Thus, we affirm the Court of Appeal's decision that the insureds' costs of site measures are "damages because of property damage" as defined within ANI's policies.

. . . .

COOPER, JUSTICE, dissenting in part.

I dissent from the majority opinion because . . . the insurance policies issued by American Nuclear Insurers (ANI) are third-party liability policies that do not provide coverage either for property damage to the insured site or for capital improvements to the site itself (referred to as "site measures"). . . .

(2) Property damage.

It was asserted in the PRP letters and found by the trial court that some radionuclides had, in fact, migrated from the Maxey Flats site to adjacent property. The majority opinion characterizes that assertion as proof that " 'property damage' has occurred as the term is defined within the policies." *Ante,* at 839. However, the Department of Health regulations governing Maxey Flats authorized the migration of minimal amounts of radioactivity from the site so long as such releases did not exceed prescribed limits, which, consistent with Kentucky's "Agreement State" status with the EPA, were identical to permissible discharge limits established under federal regulations. The mere presence of radioactive particles on property does not *ipso facto* constitute "property damage." *Wilhite v. Rockwell Int'l Corp.,* 83 S.W.3d 516, 520–21 (Ky.2002).

I would note in passing that, while the PRP letters recited that elevated levels of radionuclides have been detected off-site and that studies have shown higher-than-normal tritium levels in trees adjacent to the site, the findings of fact in the Administrative Order By Consent prepared four months later recited only that elevated levels of radionuclides have been detected "on the site outside the restricted area." *In re Maxey Flats Nuclear Disposal Site,* U.S. EPA Docket No. 87–08–C, Finding of Fact D, at 3 (Envtl. Prot. Agency, Region IV, Mar. 24, 1987). None of the remediation or site measures involved any off-site clean-up or construction. As of this writing, the Maxey Flats nuclear disposal site has been closed for twenty-eight years and no adjacent property owner has yet made a claim for damages for property damage alleged to have been caused by migration of radionuclides from the site.

. . . .

(3) "Damages."

The majority opinion attempts to satisfy the "damages" requirement of ANI's coverage provisions by likening the cost of the site improvement measures to "damages," because they were supposedly "ordered" by the EPA pursuant to CERCLA. *Ante,* at 839. However:

> "Damages," as distinguished from claims for injunctive or restitutionary relief, includes only payments to third persons when those persons have a legal claim for damages. . . . The general comprehensive liability policy between the parties covers "damages," but not the expenditures which result from complying with the directives of regulatory agencies.

Md. Cas. Co. v. Armco, Inc., 822 F.2d 1348, 1352 (4th Cir.1987).

> [T]he insurer's duty to indemnify the insured for "all sums that the insured becomes legally obligated to pay as damages" under the standard comprehensive general liability insurance policy is limited to money ordered by a court. . . . For it is in a "suit" that "damages" are sought in some amount through the court's order.

Certain Underwriters at Lloyd's of London v. Superior Court, 24 Cal.4th 945, 103 Cal.Rptr.2d 672, 16 P.3d 94, 103–04 (2001). Improvements to one's own property, even at the behest of an administrative agency, are not "damages." The majority opinion resorts to Webster's dictionary to ascertain the ordinary meaning of damages. *Ante,* at 837. However, while "[v]iewed outside the insurance context, the term 'damages' is ambiguous . . . the term 'damages' is not ambiguous in the insurance context and . . . the plain meaning of the term 'damages' used in the CGL policies refers to legal damages and does not cover cleanup costs." *Cont'l Ins. v. Northeastern Pharm. & Chem. Co.,* 842 F.2d 977, 985 (8th Cir.1988) (en banc) (construing Missouri law). *See also Grisham v. Commercial Union Ins. Co.,* 951 F.2d 872, 875 (8th Cir.1991) (same) (construing Arkansas law); *Mraz v. Canadian Universal Ins. Co., Ltd.,* 804 F.2d 1325, 1329 (4th Cir.1986) (as evidenced by CERCLA provisions, response costs are an economic loss, not damages); *Patrons Oxford Mut. Ins. Co. v. Marois,* 573 A.2d 16, 18–19 (Me.1990) ("There may be a substantial difference between these remedial costs and the amount of damages the Maroises would have to pay to property owners for damages to their property. It is the latter expenditure upon which the parties have contracted and upon which the insurance premium is based."); *Coakley v. Me. Bonding and Cas. Co.,* 136 N.H. 402, 618 A.2d 777, 784–85 (1992) (containment costs, including related investigatory costs, of insured's landfill were preventive in nature and not "damages," thus not covered by insured's CGL policy); *Weyerhaeuser,* 874 P.2d at 150 ("[T]he term 'damages' does not cover safety measures or other preventive costs taken in advance of any damage to property.").

> The narrow construction of the term "damages" is consistent with the statutory scheme of CERCLA, which differentiates between clean-up costs and damages. Clean-up or response costs are recoverable by the government or by private parties. 42 U.S.C. § 9607(a)(4)(A), (B). *Additionally, the government may sue for "damages* for injury to, destruction of, or loss of natural resources . . . ." 42 U.S.C. § 9607(a)(4)(C). To date, most government actions have sought recovery of response costs, rather than damages.

Verlan, Ltd. v. John L. Armitage & Co., 695 F.Supp. 950, 954–55 (N.D.Ill.1988) (emphasis added).

. . . .

In summary, the cost of the site-improvement measures is not within the coverage of the ANI policies because they were not sums that the insureds were "legally obligated to pay as damages because of . . . property damage". . . .

> [I]nsurance policies are construed strictly against the insurer and liberally in favor of the insured so as not to defeat the intended purpose of the policy. But this does not mean that courts in giving a liberal construction to a policy can ascribe to it a meaning not coming within the limits of the language of the contract of insurance. Nor can courts read into it conditions and terms not incorporated therein.

Cal. Union Ins. Co. v. Spade, 642 S.W.2d 582, 583–84 (Ky.1982) (internal citations and quotations omitted).

As a last resort to justify finding coverage, the majority opinion relies on that old standby, the "doctrine of reasonable expectations," (though it cites a case in which resort to the doctrine was rejected). *Ante,* at 837. "The doctrine of reasonable expectations is used in conjunction with the principle that ambiguities should be resolved against the drafter in order to circumvent the technical, legalistic and complex contract terms which limit benefits to the insured." *Simon v. Cont'l Ins. Co.,* 724 S.W.2d 210, 212–13 (Ky.1986) (quoting R.H. Long, *The Law of Liability Insurance* § 5.10(B)). However:

> [C]ourts should resort to the doctrine of reasonable expectations only when the phrasing of the policy is so confusing that the average policyholder cannot make out the boundaries of coverage. When the terms of an insurance contract are clear, [as in this case,] it is the function of a court to enforce it as written and not to make a better contract for either of the parties.

Signo Trading, 612 A.2d at 938. Appellees are not unsophisticated, uneducated, "run-of-the-mill" policyholders. They are specialists in the field of nuclear waste disposal who purchased policies of public liability insurance specially tailored to the nuclear energy industry for the purpose of providing coverage for potential third-party liability damages as required by 42 U.S.C. § 2210(a). Their efforts to convert them into first-party policies are both unconvincing and disingenuous.

. . . .

NOTES AND QUESTIONS

1. *The Fight Was Intense, but Now It Is over.* The question of what constitutes "damages" was repeatedly litigated in environmental liability insurance cases from the 1980s through the 2000s. Under the federal Comprehensive Environmental Response, Compensation and Liability Act of 1980 ("CERCLA"), 42 U.S.C. § 9601 et seq., commonly known as the "Superfund Act," the Environmental Protection Agency (EPA) can order the cleanup of toxic waste sites or spills and can even order an abatement of environmental threats prior to the occurrence of any damage. *See* 42 U.S.C. § 9607(a). Thousands of "Superfund sites" were in remediation throughout the country, and the environmental statutory liability scheme created retroactive, strict, and joint and several liability for any waste hauler, waste generator, and owner of a waste site, regardless of the size of an individual co-owner's share or the length of time of involvement (as long as it was at or during the time the site was in existence). Thus, there was much at stake for the "potentially responsible parties" (as they were called), and litigation was, to put it mildly, intense.

2. *Response Costs as "Damages."* Are these so-called "response costs" a type of "damages" covered by CGL policies? At first, courts were sharply divided, but most courts ultimately concluded that "damages" includes government-ordered "response costs." *See, e.g.,* Peter J. Kalis, Thomas M. Reiter & James R. Segerdahl, Policyholder's Guide to the Law of Insurance Coverage § 5.03 (1st ed. 1997 & Supp. 2017) ("Courts overwhelmingly have rejected insurers' arguments. Of the 19 state courts of last resort to address the issue, 18 have held that government-mandated environmental remediation costs are 'damages.' Reaching the same decision are numerous federal appellate decisions."). What if the policyholder, knowing that an EPA cleanup order is certain to be issued at some point, and wanting to solve the problem sooner rather than later, perhaps in the hope of reducing the clean-up costs, voluntarily cleans up a toxic waste site? In other words, what if the policyholder cleans up the site in anticipation of government-ordered response costs? Are those expenses "damages" under the CGL? Can it be said that the insured is "legally obligated to pay" those expenses? *Compare Weyerhauser Co. v. Aetna Casualty & Surety Co.*, 874 P.2d 142 (Wash. 1994), *with City of Edgerton v. General Casualty Co. of Wis.*, 517 N.W.2d 463 (Wis. 1994). *See generally* Jordan S. Stanzler & Charles A. Yuen, *Coverage for Environmental*

Cleanup Costs: History of the Word "Damages" Under CGL Policies, 16 Colum. J. Envtl. L. 73 (1991).

3. *Non-Environmental Claims.* Outside of the environmental context, the issue of whether the costs associated with complying with an injunction constitute "damages" is not well developed. Courts in a couple of older cases held that such costs are not "damages." *See Aetna Cas. & Sur. Co. v. Hanna*, 224 F.2d 499 (5th Cir. 1955); *Desrochers v. New York Cas. Co.*, 106 A.2d 196 (N.H. 1954). Thus, it remains to be seen whether these older precedents will hold sway or if the environmental cases will be applied in other contexts.

C. TRIGGER AND ALLOCATION

Asbestos bodily injury and environmental property damage claims are typical long-tail claims.[2] [The "long tail" reference reflects the fact that the injuries or damages may not appear until many years—even decades—after exposure.] Asbestos was used in numerous products—from gloves to insulation—because of its heat-retardant qualities. Consequently, an individual's exposure to asbestos historically may have occurred in numerous places over the course of many years. Once asbestos fibers enter an individual's lungs, a progressive disease process can begin that progresses over many years and ultimately can result in deadly diseases such as mesothelioma and lung cancer.

Similarly, a typical environmental property damage claim arises as follows: a policyholder operated a manufacturing plant for decades that resulted in the release of contaminants at and around the plant site itself or in waste sites such as landfills. Once the contaminants entered the soil or groundwater, they continuously spread through the soil and groundwater over many years until they were discovered and remediated. The policyholder then faces liability to a governmental entity or to a private party for the cleanup of the contaminated property.

Thus, two key questions face policyholders, liability insurers, and courts when determining insurers' coverage responsibility for these types of long-tail claims. One, which policy years are implicated by the covered loss? This is known as the "trigger issue." Two, how much of the covered loss should each insurer whose policy has been triggered pay? This is known as the "allocation issue." The next two cases represent the courts' divergent approaches to these two issues.

---

[2] This introduction to the concepts of trigger and allocation was taken verbatim from Christopher C. French, *The "Non-Cumulation Clause": an "Other Insurance Clause" by Another Name*, 60 U. Kan. L. Rev. 375, 380–81 (2012) (citations omitted).

COMMERCIAL UNION INS. CO. V. SEPCO CORP.

765 F.2d 1543 (11th Cir. 1985)

Opinion

LEWIS R. MORGAN, SENIOR CIRCUIT JUDGE:

Sepco Corporation, an Alabama company, manufactured asbestos insulation products between 1970 and 1979. Its general liability insurance coverage during that time and until the filing of this suit consisted of a series of successive policies, each of which was issued by one of several carriers. A defendant in hundreds of recent lawsuits seeking recovery for asbestos-related illnesses, Sepco has called upon these carriers to defend the suits and to pay any resulting liabilities. One of those insurers, Commercial Union Insurance Company, filed this suit, seeking a declaration that it is not obligated to defend or pay any claim based upon an asbestos-related illness that failed to become manifest while a Commercial Union policy was in effect. Sepco counterclaimed and impleaded the other companies that had provided its primary liability insurance coverage since 1970. These insurers argued before the district court that insurance coverage under a particular policy should be triggered by the exposure of the plaintiff victim to asbestos hazards during the policy period rather than by the manifestation of the subsequent illness during the policy period. *Ducre v. Executive Officers of Halter Marine, Inc.*, 752 F.2d 976, 994 (5th Cir.1985); *Porter v. American Optical Corp.*, 641 F.2d 1128, 1145 (5th Cir.) (approving and adopting *Insurance Co. of North America v. Forty-Eight Insulations, Inc.*, 633 F.2d 1212, 1226 (6th Cir.1980), *cert. denied,* 454 U.S. 1109, 102 S.Ct. 686, 70 L.Ed.2d 650 (1981)), *cert. denied,* 454 U.S. 1109, 102 S.Ct. 1649, 71 L.Ed.2d 878 (1981). Sepco offered still a third theory: each insurer on the risk at any time between the initial exposure and the manifestation of the disease should be liable to Sepco for indemnification and defense costs. *See Keene Corp. v. Insurance Co. of North America*, 667 F.2d 1034, 1047 (D.C.Cir.1981), *cert. denied,* 455 U.S. 1007, 102 S.Ct. 1644, 71 L.Ed.2d 875 (1982). Sepco alternatively supported adoption of the exposure theory.

On Sepco's motion for partial summary judgment, the district court held that *Porter,* as binding precedent (*see Bonner v. City of Prichard, Alabama*, 661 F.2d 1206, 1207 (11th Cir.1981) (en banc)) dictates that the insurance obligations imposed by the policies issued to Sepco be determined according to the injurious exposure theory. Thus, concluded the court, the costs of defense and settlement incurred in each case filed against Sepco should be prorated among those insurers that provided coverage during the periods of the plaintiff's exposure to asbestos hazards created by Sepco. *See Porter*, 641 F.2d at 1145. The court subsequently certified the issue pursuant to 28 U.S.C. § 1292(b), and we permitted the appeal. The parties agree that the sole issue before us is whether the district court erred in holding that the injurious exposure theory controls the construction of the insurance policies issued to Sepco.

The district court found that all of the policies have the following general coverage provisions in virtually the same or identical language:

> The Company will pay on behalf of the insured all sums which the insured shall become legally obligated to pay as damages because of
>
> (A) Bodily Injury or,
>
> (B) Property Damage
>
> to which this insurance applies, caused by an occurrence and the Company shall have the right and duty to defend any suit against the insured seeking damages on account of such bodily injury or property damage, even if any of the allegations of the suit are groundless, false or fraudulent. . . .

The policies define the key terms as follows:

> "bodily injury" means bodily injury, sickness or disease sustained by any person which occurs during the policy period, including death at any time resulting therefrom;
>
> "occurrence" means an accident, including continuous or repeated exposure to conditions, which results in bodily injury or property damage neither expected nor intended from the standpoint of the insured.

Unfortunately, these provisions are not dispositive of the case before us. *See Keene*, 667 F.2d at 1041. The District of Columbia Circuit has succinctly stated the problem as follows:

> The language of each policy at issue in this case clearly provides that an "injury," and not the "occurrence" that causes the injury, must fall within a policy period for it to be covered by the policy. Most suits brought under this type of policy involve an injury and an occurrence that transpired simultaneously, or, at least, in close temporal proximity to one another. In cases involving asbestos-related disease, however, inhalation—the "occurrence" that causes the injury—takes place substantially before the manifestation of the ultimate injury—asbestosis, mesothelioma, or lung cancer. Furthermore, although it is not known how little exposure is required to cause disease, inhalation may occur over a long period of time. As a result, inhalation may continue through numerous policy periods, the disease may develop during subsequent policy periods, and manifestation may occur in yet another policy period. For an insured such as Keene, different insurers are likely to be on the risk at different points in the

> development of each plaintiff's disease. Moreover, part of the development may occur at a time when no insurer was on the risk. Asbestos-related diseases, which are certainly covered by the policies, therefore differ from most injuries and hence present a difficult problem of contractual interpretation.

Id. at 1040. The task before is therefore to determine the point at which a victim of an asbestos-related illness suffers "bodily injury." *Cf. United States Fidelity & Guaranty Co. v. Warwick Development Co.*, 446 So.2d 1021, 1024 (Ala.1984) ("[A]s a general rule the time of an 'occurrence' of an accident within the meaning of an indemnity policy is not the time the wrongful act was committed but the time the complaining party was actually damaged."). *Porter* characterized the medical evidence as indicating that each inhalation of asbestos fibers into the victim's lungs is "bodily injury." 641 F.2d at 1144.

. . . .

Commercial Union . . . contends that the medical evidence in this case, unlike that in *Porter,* contradicts the essential tenet of the exposure theory, which Commercial Union states to be that "each inhalation of asbestos fibers results in bodily injury." It proffers in support of this contention expert testimony to the effect that not everyone exposed to asbestos contracts an asbestos-related disease such as asbestosis and that exposure to asbestos does not produce instantaneous sub-clinical cellular changes in the lungs. We believe that the exposure theory is more accurately analyzed as positing not that each inhalation of asbestos fibers results in bodily injury, but rather that every asbestos-related injury results from inhalation of asbestos fibers. Because such inhalation can occur only upon exposure to asbestos, and because it is impossible practically to determine the point at which the fibers actually imbed themselves in the victim's lungs, to equate exposure to asbestos with "bodily injury" caused by the inhalation of the asbestos is the "superior interpretation of the contract provisions." *Forty-Eight Insulations,* 633 F.2d at 1223; *see Ducre,* 752 F.2d at 992 (*Porter* characterized as equating "bodily injury" with exposure). The district court correctly held that *Porter* dictates the adoption of the exposure theory in this case.

. . . .

Sepco, although it agrees that *Porter* is binding, argues that the district court erred in holding that *Porter* precludes the adoption in this case of the theory established by the District of Columbia Circuit in *Keene.* The court in that case held that inhalation exposure, exposure in residence, and manifestation all trigger coverage under insurance policies such as those now before us. *Keene,* 667 F.2d at 1047. This contention is not properly before us because Sepco failed to timely file a petition for permission to appeal. *Aparacio v. Swan Lake,* 643 F.2d 1109, 1111 & n. 3 (5th Cir.1981).

We note, however, that the Sixth Circuit in *Forty-Eight Insulations* considered and rejected a theory similar to that enunciated in *Keene. See Forty-Eight Insulations,* 633 F.2d at 1226.

AFFIRMED.

NOTES AND QUESTIONS

1. *Exposure Equals Injury?* In *Sepco*, the Eleventh Circuit concluded that exposure to asbestos constituted an "occurrence." Was the court's conclusion based upon medical evidence or something else?

2. *Pro Rata Allocation*. The *Sepco* court adopted pro rata allocation. What is pro rata allocation? Is pro rata allocation based upon any particular policy language? If so, what specific provisions in the Sample CGL Policy at the beginning of this chapter support the use of pro rata allocation?

J.H. FRANCE REFRACTORIES CO. V. ALLSTATE INS. CO.

626 A.2d 502 (Pa. 1993)

Opinion

This case was before us in 1989 to determine the jurisdiction of the trial court when it was alleged that all indispensable parties were not joined in the action. Our opinion in that appeal is helpful in understanding the background of the case.

Factual Background

The factual background of the case is that J.H. France Refractories Company (hereinafter J.H. France) and its now wholly-owned subsidiary, the Van Brunt Company, between 1956 and 1972 manufactured and marketed a product containing asbestos. J.H. France also marketed and continues to market products containing silica, which, like asbestos, is claimed to cause physical injury to those who breathe it. On April 19, 1979, Gladys Temple, administratrix of the estate of Charles Temple, filed suit against J.H. France, claiming that her decedent, Charles Temple, suffered from asbestos-related diseases contracted through exposure to J.H. France's asbestos-containing products from 1948 through 1978.

J.H. France was insured during various time periods relevant to this action by the Pennsylvania Manufacturers Association, St. Paul, Allstate, U.S. Fire, Wausau, and Rockwood Insurance Companies. Upon receipt of this suit, J.H. France presented the Temple claim to Allstate, St. Paul and PMA for defense and indemnity, the insurers who had provided coverage between 1967 and 1979. None of these insurers agreed to defend or indemnify, and J.H. France undertook its own defense. In 1981 J.H. France filed this declaratory judgment action for the purpose of determining the insurers' duty to defend and indemnify against the Temple claim. Subsequent to the filing of this declaratory judgment action, additional asbestos and silica-related lawsuits were filed against J.H. France. Apparently because these actions were for injuries allegedly sustained during a time period which went beyond 1979 (into the 1980's), additional insurance companies became involved. In 1984, Allstate filed its own declaratory judgment action, naming PMA, St. Paul, U.S. Fire, Wausau and Rockwood Insurance Companies, as well as fourteen individuals who had filed asbestos or silica-related lawsuits after J.H. France filed its original declaratory judgment action. Still other asbestos or silica-related claims against J.H. France were filed after Allstate's declaratory judgment actions were consolidated, and the carriers who insured J.H. France during the relevant time periods have taken differing positions with respect to their duty to indemnify and defend. If a defense has been provided, it has been provided subject to reservation of rights.

The issues at trial were whether the various insurance companies were liable for the defense and indemnification of J.H. France for claims based on exposure to its products containing asbestos and silica, and if they were liable, how the liability was to be apportioned among the insurers. The various insurance contracts could be adjudicated in one action because the relevant language was virtually identical in all of the contracts. The trial court . . . worked out a scheme . . . in which the various insurers were required to defend and indemnify against asbestos or silica related claims made against J.H. France and determined that the insurers had not acted in bad faith in failing to defend or indemnify at an earlier time.

Multiple appeals were filed in Superior Court challenging the substance of the trial court's determination. . . .

Some additional facts are necessary to resolve the detailed issues under review. The six insurers which are parties to this action provided comprehensive liability insurance coverage to J.H. France at all times relevant to this action. All the policies contained identical language insofar as the relevant clauses are concerned:

> [The Insurer] will pay on behalf of the Insured all sums which the Insured shall become legally obligated to pay as damages because of bodily injury . . . to which this insurance applies, caused by an occurrence, and [the Insurer] shall have the right and duty to defend any suit against the Insured seeking damages on account of such bodily injury. . . .
>
> "Bodily injury" means bodily injury, sickness or disease sustained by any person which occurs during the policy period, including death at any time resulting therefrom. . . .
>
> "Occurrence" means an accident, including continuous or repeated exposure to conditions, which result in bodily injury . . . neither expected nor intended from the standpoint of the Insured.

Pursuant to the stipulation of all parties, the medical evidence at trial included the testimony of Dr. John E. Craighead, an anatomical and clinical pathologist who is an expert in pneumoconiosis and asbestos-related disease. In summary, he testified that "injury" is a "process which alters structure," and the term is applicable in reference to a cell, a tissue, an organ, or the entire body. "Disease" means "an injury and a response to that injury." The presence of asbestos in the lungs stimulates a wide range of reactions, which Dr. Craighead divides into three responses.

First, characterized as "direct injury," asbestos fibers in the respiratory tract interact with the membranes of the cells lining the trachea and cause the release of enzymes and superoxides which either damage or kill individual cells. If sufficient cells are damaged, tissue (an accumulation of cells) is damaged or destroyed. This injury occurs within minutes after asbestos fibers enter the cells.

Second, characterized as "indirect injury," the presence of asbestos fibers stimulates macrophages to accumulate. Macrophages are scavenger cells which attempt to envelope foreign particles. As microphages attempt to ingest the fibers, there is a release of enzymes which have a damaging effect on tissue. There is also a chemical reaction which scars the injured tissue. The accumulation of scar tissue in the respiratory system prevents the lung from performing its normal oxygen-carbon dioxide gas exchange. The process of macrophage accumulation, tissue scarring, and functional impairment of the lungs begins to occur within a month of exposure.

The third response in the asbestosis process is a change in the form of the cells lining the bronchial tree. The normal lining, designed to move dust particles out of the body, is replaced by cells lacking cilia, resulting in a tendency toward accumulation of asbestos particles.

The asbestosis process continues to progress even after exposure to asbestos ceases. Medical authorities differ on the reasons for this fact. Substantial authority regards this as the nature of the asbestosis pathogenesis. Another view theorizes that disease progression may be attributable to the eventual, and inevitable, decrease in the respiratory function involved in aging, and also to other factors such as cigarette smoking or infection. In either view, the injury process continues after exposure and may culminate in "manifestation," such severe functional impairment that asbestosis is finally diagnosed, and of course, the disease may be fatal.

Based on the foregoing record, the Superior Court held that liability of each insurer was triggered if any one of the three-exposure, progression, or manifestation-occurred during the term of its policy. The court prorated the obligations of all insurers whose policies were in effect throughout the development of the disease, including J.H. France as a self-insurer during periods when it did not purchase liability insurance. Although the Superior

Court did not explicate this point, it seems implicit in its reasoning that the obligations to defend would be allocated pro rata in the same way as the obligations to indemnify; presumably J.H. France would bear a proportionate share of defense costs for periods when it did not purchase liability insurance. Finally, the Superior Court affirmed the trial court's ruling that the insurers were not guilty of bad faith in contesting their duty to defend so that J.H. France was not entitled to attorneys fees in this declaratory judgment action.

Analysis

Trigger

The first issue is whether the Superior Court was correct in applying the "multiple-trigger" theory of determining liability of the insurers-that is, in deciding that liability results if any one of the following occurred during the time an insurer was on the risk: exposure to asbestos or silica, progression of the pathology, or manifestation of the disease. The Superior Court concluded that the medical evidence of discrete cellular injuries occurring upon exposure to asbestos justifies the conclusion that exposure to asbestos causes immediate "bodily injury" in the terms of the insurance policies, triggering the insurers' duty to indemnify. With this analysis and conclusion, we agree. In similar fashion, the Superior Court reached the conclusion that the term "bodily injury" also encompasses the progression of the disease throughout and after the period of exposure until, ultimately, the manifestation of recognizable incapacitation constitutes the final "injury," and that these stages in the pathogenesis of asbestos- and silica-related diseases also trigger the liability of J.H. France's insurance carriers. We find no error in this analysis and conclusion. The insurance policy language and the evidence of the etiology and pathogenesis of asbestos-related disease compel us to reach this result.

The insurance policies obligate the insurers to "pay on behalf of the Insured all sums which the Insured shall become legally obligated to pay as damages because of bodily injury . . . to which this insurance applies, caused by an occurrence." Whether the claimants' diseases are "bodily injury to which this insurance applies" depends on the definition of bodily injury. The policies define bodily injury as "bodily injury, sickness or disease which occurs during the policy period." The injuries at issue are caused by an "occurrence," which the policies define as "an accident, *including continuous or repeated exposure to conditions,* which result in bodily injury . . . neither expected nor intended" by the insured. The medical evidence in this case unequivocally establishes that injuries occur during the development of asbestosis immediately upon exposure, and that the injuries continue to occur even after exposure ends during the progression of the disease right up until the time that increasing incapacitation results in manifestation as a recognizable disease. If any of these phases of the pathogenesis occurs during the policy period, the insurer is obligated to indemnify J.H. France under the terms of the policy.

Abundant authority supports this result. In the surfeit of litigation spawned by asbestos-related disease, many courts have recognized that mere exposure to asbestos causes injury within the meaning of the same policy language which controls this case. *See, e.g., Porter v. American Optical Corp.*, 641 F.2d 1128 (5th Cir.), *cert. denied,* 454 U.S. 1109, 102 S.Ct. 686, 70 L.Ed.2d 650 (1981); *Insurance Co. of North America v. Forty-Eight Insulations, Inc.,* 633 F.2d 1212 (6th Cir.1980), *clarified,* 657 F.2d 814, *cert. denied,* 454 U.S. 1109, 102 S.Ct. 686, 70 L.Ed.2d 650 (1981). Other courts have recognized that manifestation, likewise, constitutes an injury which triggers the insurers' obligation to indemnify. *See, e.g., Eagle-Picher Industries, Inc. v. Liberty Mutual Insurance Co.,* 682 F.2d 12 (1st Cir.1982), *cert. denied,* 460 U.S. 1028, 103 S.Ct. 1280, 75 L.Ed.2d 500 (1983). Rather than selecting one or another of the phases as the exclusive trigger of liability, it seems more accurate to regard all stages of the disease process as bodily injury sufficient to trigger the insurers' obligation to indemnify, as all phases independently meet the policy definition of bodily injury. This multiple-trigger approach, as well, has been adopted by other courts. *See, e.g., Vale Chemical Co. v. Hartford Accident and Indemnity Co.,* 340 Pa.Super. 510, 490 A.2d 896 (1985), *rev'd on other grounds,* 512 Pa. 290, 516 A.2d 684 (1986); *AC and S, Inc. v. Aetna Casualty and Surety Co.,* 764 F.2d 968 (3d Cir.1985); *Keene Corp. v. Insurance Co. of North America,* 667 F.2d 1034 (D.C.Cir.1981), *cert. denied,* 455 U.S. 1007, 102 S.Ct. 1644, 71 L.Ed.2d 875 (1982). We therefore affirm the Superior Court's approval of the so-called multiple-trigger theory of liability adopted by the trial court.

Thus, every insurer which was on the risk at any time during the development of a claimant's asbestos-related disease has an obligation to indemnify J.H. France.

Allocation

The second question is how to allocate the liability of each insurer when, as is commonly the case, more than one insurer was on the risk at one time or another during the development of a claimant's disease.

As we have intimated above, the Superior Court adopted a scheme whereby the several insurers on the risk during a given claimant's development of a disease would share the obligation to indemnify on a pro rata basis apportioned upon the amount of time each policy was in effect, including an obligation of J.H. France to act as a self-insurer during periods when it was uninsured. There are several reasons we decline to adopt this approach.

First, and most compelling, is the language of the policies themselves. Each insurer obligated itself to "pay on behalf of the Insured *all sums* which the

Insured shall become legally obligated to pay as damages because of bodily injury to which this insurance applies." We have already ascertained that any stage of the development of a claimant's disease constitutes an injury "to which this insurance applies" under each policy in effect during any part of the development of the disease. Under any given policy, the insurer contracted to pay *all sums* which the insured becomes legally obligated to pay, not merely some pro rata portion thereof. As another court stated, each policy has a built-in trigger of coverage. Once triggered, each policy covers [the manufacturer's] liability. There is *nothing* in the policies that provides for a reduction of the insurer's liability if an injury occurs only in part during a policy period. As we interpret the policies, they cover [the manufacturer's] entire liability once they are triggered. *Keene, supra,* 667 F.2d at 1048. (Emphasis in original.)

Second, there is no medical evidence in this case to substantiate the assumption that the progression of asbestos-related disease is linear in character. There is, instead, good reason to believe otherwise. *See INA v. Forty-Eight Insulations, Inc., supra,* 633 F.2d at 1214. To apportion liability among the insurers on a strictly temporal basis in direct proportion to the length of time each insurer was on the risk, however, notwithstanding its surface attractiveness, assumes a linearity of disease progression which this record does not support.

Third, although it is superficially attractive to include J.H. France in the pro rata apportionment of liability for periods during which it was uninsured, to do so is to create a judicial fiction which cannot be supported, viz., that J.H. France was self-insured under a policy the terms of which are ascertainable so that J.H. France may be included among the insurers in apportionment of liability. Faced with the same argument, the United States Court of Appeals for the District of Columbia Circuit stated:

> We have no authority upon which to pretend that [the manufacturer] also has a "self-insurance" policy that is triggered for periods in which no other policy was purchased. Even if we had the authority, what would we pretend that the policy provides? What would its limits be? There are no self-insurance policies, and we respectfully submit that the contracts before us do not support judicial creation of such additional insurance policies.

Keene, supra, 667 F.2d at 1048–49.

Fourth, the definition of an "occurrence" which constitutes a risk against which the insurance was provided leads us to reject the pro rata allocation ordered by the Superior Court. The definition suggests that any insurance policy triggered under the "multiple-trigger" concept with respect to any specific claim is potentially liable for the entire amount of any judgment or settlement of that claim. An "occurrence" includes "continuous or repeated exposure to conditions which result in bodily injury." The insurers which drafted the definition obviously contemplated the possibility of injury resulting from continuous or repeated exposure to conditions, and specified that the process of exposure was to constitute one occurrence. If prolonged exposure, constituting one occurrence, resulted in injury, and if the injury occurred during the time a given policy was in effect, then the injury is an insurable risk under the terms of that policy. Being defined as one "occurrence," the entire injury, and all damages resulting therefrom, fall within the indemnification obligation of the insurer. In other words, once the liability of a given insurer is triggered, it is irrelevant that additional exposure or injury occurred at times other than when the insurer was on the risk. The insurer in question must bear potential liability for the entire claim.

In keeping with this analysis, we conclude that each insurer which was on the risk during the development of an asbestosis-related disease is a primary insurer. In order to accord J.H. France the coverage promised by the insurance policies, J.H. France should be free to select the policy or policies under which it is to be indemnified.

This analysis was also used in *Keene, supra,* to implement the multiple-trigger approach to liability. The court stated:

> In any suit against Keene for an asbestos-related disease, it is likely that the coverage of more than one insurer will be triggered. Because each insurer is fully liable, and because Keene cannot collect more than it owes in damages, the issue of dividing insurance obligations arises. The only logical resolution of this issue is for Keene to be able to collect from any insurer whose coverage is triggered, the full amount of indemnity that it is due, subject only to the provisions in the policies that govern the allocation of liability when more than one policy covers an injury. That is the only way that Keene can be assured the security that it purchased with each policy. Our holding each insurer fully liable to Keene is also consistent with other courts' allocation of liability when more than one insurer covers an indivisible loss.
>
> This does not mean that a single insurer will be saddled with full liability for any injury. When more than one policy applies to a loss, the "other insurance" provisions of each policy provide a scheme by which the insurers' liability is to be apportioned.

Keene, 667 F.2d at 1050 (citation omitted).

When the policy limits of a given insurer are exhausted, J.H. France is entitled to seek indemnification from any of the remaining insurers which was on the risk during the development of the disease. Any policy in effect during the period from exposure through manifestation must indemnify the insured until its coverage is exhausted. We believe this resolution of the allocation of liability issue to be most consistent with the multiple-trigger theory of liability.

This conclusion does not alter the rules of contribution or the provisions of "other insurance" clauses in the applicable policies. There is no bar against an insurer obtaining a share of indemnification or defense costs from other insurers under "other insurance" clauses or under the equitable doctrine of contribution.

. . . .

Defense Costs

The fourth issue is how to allocate the insurers' duty to defend when liability under more than one policy is triggered with regard to a claim based on asbestos-related disease. The obligation to defend is based on the policies which state that "the company shall have the right and duty to defend any suit against the insured seeking damages on account of such bodily injury . . . [until] the applicable limit of the company's liability has been exhausted by payment of judgments or settlements." It is well established that the duty to defend and to pay the costs of defense is broader than the duty to indemnify. *Erie Insurance Exchange v. Transamerica Insurance Co.,* 516 Pa. 574, 533 A.2d 1363 (1987).

The defense of a claim is a right, as well as a duty, falling upon the insurer. In order to effectuate that right, we hold that the selection of the insurer or insurers to undertake a defense is to be made by the insurers. In the event that the insurers are unable to agree as to the conduct of the defense, then J.H. France shall be entitled to select an insurer.

. . . .

Conclusion

The order of the Superior Court is reversed insofar as it is inconsistent with this opinion. Reversed in part and affirmed in part.

NOTES AND QUESTIONS

1. *Different Trigger Approaches*. The central focus of the trigger inquiry is whether an injury or damage took place during the policy period. How courts determine whether an injury occurred during the policy period varies. There are four primary approaches to the trigger issue: exposure; injury-in-fact; manifestation; and triple- or continuous-trigger, which combines the other three triggers. Some courts have adopted an "exposure" trigger, which means those insurers whose policies provided coverage at the time of exposure are triggered. *See, e.g., Cont'l Ins. Cos. v. Ne. Phar. & Chem. Co., Inc.*, 811 F.2d 1180, 1189 (8th Cir. 1987) ("Environmental damage occurs at the moment that hazardous wastes are improperly released into the environment[,] and [the] liability policy in effect at the time this damage is caused provides coverage."), *aff'd in part,* 842 F.2d 977 (8th Cir. 1988). Other courts have adopted an "injury

in fact" trigger, which means the liability policies on the risk when the injury actually occurs are triggered. *See, e.g.*, *Abex Corp. v. Md. Cas. Co.*, 790 F.2d 119, 122 (D.C. Cir. 1986) (holding that the "insurer's obligation to indemnify . . . arises when the asbestos causes real bodily injury during the policy period"). Other courts have adopted a "manifestation" trigger, which means the policies on the risk when the injury or disease manifests—that is, when a medical diagnosis is made or adverse health symptoms first appear—are triggered. *See, e.g.*, *Eagle-Picher Indus., Inc. v. Liberty Mut. Ins. Co.*, 523 F. Supp. 110, 118 (D. Mass. 1981) (applying manifestation trigger), *modified*, 682 F.2d 12 (1st Cir. 1982). Finally, other courts have adopted a "continuous" trigger, which means all of the policyholder's liability policies on the risk from the time of initial exposure until the injury or disease manifests are triggered. *See, e.g.*, *Keene Corp. v. Ins. Co. of N. Am.*, 667 F.2d 1034, 1041 (D.C. Cir. 1981) ("[E]ach insurer on the risk between the initial exposure and the manifestation of disease is liable to [the insured] for indemnification and defense costs."). *See* Christopher C. French, *The "Non-Cumulation Clause": an "Other Insurance Clause" by Another Name*, 60 U. Kan. L. Rev. 375, 382–83 (2012).

Because the injury is presumed to have occurred during all of the policy periods between initial exposure and manifestation, the continuous trigger approach eliminates a significant evidentiary burden for policyholders of proving actual injury during each of the policy periods in some jurisdictions. *See, e.g.*, *State v. Cont'l Ins. Co.*, 281 P.3d 1000, 1005 (Cal. 2012) (noting that it is appropriate to use continuous trigger for long-tail claims because "[i]t is often 'virtually impossible' for an insured to prove what specific damage occurred during each of the multiple consecutive policy periods in a progressive property damage case").

2. *Different Allocation Approaches*. Similarly, courts' answers to the allocation question—the amount of liability paid by each triggered policy—also has varied by jurisdiction. Because long-tail claims may trigger numerous policies, some courts such as the *J.H. France* court, relying upon the "all sums" language in commercial general liability policies that provides that the insurer agrees to pay "all sums" for which the policyholder is liable, have held that the policyholder can select which of the triggered policy years will cover the liability subject only to the limits of coverage provided by the policies selected. *See, e.g.*, *Keene Corp.*, 667 F.2d at 1050 (policyholder may "collect from any insurer whose coverage is triggered, the full amount of indemnity that it is due, subject only to the provisions in the policies that govern the allocation of liability when more than one policy covers an injury"). Other jurisdictions have adopted pro rata allocation, which essentially divides the liability equally among the policy years triggered. *See, e.g.*, *Ins. Co. of N. Am. v. Forty-Eight Insulations, Inc.*, 633 F.2d 1212, 1225 (6th Cir. 1980) (holding each of manufacturer's insurers issuing policies covering various time periods liable for its pro rata share). Finally, New Jersey applies a variation of pro rata allocation that divides the liability among the triggered insurance policies based upon the percentage amount of the limits of each policy issued in relation to all of the insurance triggered by the claim. *See, e.g.*, *Carter-Wallace, Inc. v.*

Admiral Ins. Co., 712 A.2d 1116, 1124 (N.J. 1998) (allocating coverage among multiple liability insurers in proportion to the degree of the risks transferred or retained during the years of exposure). *See* Christopher C. French, *The "Non-Cumulation Clause": an "Other Insurance Clause" by Another Name*, 60 U. Kan. L. Rev. 375, 384–85 (2012). Courts are almost evenly divided in adopting "all sums" versus pro rata allocation, with a few more courts adopting pro rata allocation over "all sums."

3. *Allocation and Self-Insurance Features.* The allocation issue can have a significant impact on a policyholder's total recovery. Corporate policyholders often have multiple layers of coverage, with the lowest layer called primary insurance and the layers above that called excess insurance. The primary insurance typically has a self-insurance feature such as a self-insured retention (SIR) or a deductible. These deductible amounts can be quite significant—e.g., in the millions or tens of millions of dollars for particularly large companies. If the policyholder has high SIRs or deductibles, then "all sums" allocation, as opposed to pro rata allocation, can result in significantly more recovery. Why? Also, it is not unusual for high layer excess insurers to prefer pro rata allocation while primary insurers prefer "all sums" allocation. Why?

4. *Uninsured Years and Insurer Insolvencies.* What happens if the occurrence spans years in which the policyholder is uninsured? This can occur in situations where insurance simply is not available for purchase, as was the case when beginning in 1986 insurers began excluding coverage for asbestos claims, thereby making it impossible for a policyholder to purchase CGL insurance covering asbestos claims after 1986. Should some of the loss be allocated to the uninsured years? Many courts have answered that question "no." *See, e.g., Keene Corp.*, 667 F.2d at 1048–49 ("We have no authority upon which to pretend that Keene also has a 'self-insurance' policy that is triggered for periods in which no other policy was purchased."). On the other hand, some courts have allocated some portion of the loss to uninsured years. *See, e.g., Ins. Co. of N. Am. v. Forty-Eight Insulations, Inc.*, 633 F.2d 1212, 1225 (6th Cir. 1980), *decision clarified on reh'g*, 657 F.2d 814 (6th Cir. 1981) ("Were we to adopt [the policyholder's] position on defense costs a manufacturer which had insurance coverage for only one year out of 20 would be entitled to a complete defense of all asbestos actions the same as a manufacturer which had coverage for 20 years out of 20. Neither logic nor precedent support such a result."). What about situations in which there are significant gaps in coverage in some layers of some policy years due to insurer insolvencies? In that circumstance, would a policyholder prefer pro rata or "all sums" allocation?

5. *Restatement of the Law of Liability Insurance.* Allocation was one of many hotly contested areas of insurance law during the drafting of the Restatement. Ultimately, the Restatement adopted pro rata allocation, but noted that many jurisdictions use the "all sums" approach:

§ 41 Allocation in Long-Tail Harm Claims Covered by Occurrence-Based Policies

(1) Except as stated in subsection (2), when indivisible harm occurs over multiple policy periods, the amount of any judgment entered in or settlement of any liability action arising out of that harm is subject to pro rata allocation under occurrence-based liability insurance policies as follows:

(a) For purposes of determining the share allocated to an occurrence-based liability insurance policy that is triggered by harm during the policy period, the amount of the judgment or settlement is allocated equally across years, beginning with the first year in which the harm occurred and ending with the last year in which the harm would trigger an occurrence-based liability insurance policy; and

(b) An insurer's obligation to pay for that pro rata share is subject to the ordinary rules governing any deductible, self-insured retention, policy limit, or exhaustion terms in the policy.

. . . .

Comment:

c. *Theories of allocation for long-tail harms*. . . . . There is some disagreement over the precise number of jurisdictions that have adopted each position. . . . Although the all-sums approach has been adopted by a significant number of courts and many courts have not yet taken a position, a clear majority of the jurisdictions that have addressed the question have adopted the pro rata approach. . . . This Restatement follows the pro rata by years default rule for allocation in the case of long-tail harms, because that approach is the most consistent, simplest, and fairest solution to this problem.

EXERCISES

1. Draft a 2-page memo based upon the language contained in the Sample CGL Policy at the beginning of this chapter that supports the argument that insurers' liabilities should be prorated equally among triggered policy years.

2. Draft a 2-page memo based upon the language contained in the Sample CGL Policy at the beginning of this chapter that supports the argument that the insurers in any policy year triggered should be liable, without proration, for the entire loss subject to the policy's limits.

D. NUMBER OF OCCURRENCES

Another issue that can have a significant impact on the size of a policyholder's recovery is the number of occurrences that give rise to the policyholder's loss or losses. "The number of occurrences issue is the question of how many claims should be lumped together for purposes of the deductibles/SIRs and the policies' limits of liability. In simple cases such as a car accident, there is only one occurrence—the car accident that causes bodily injuries, property damage, or both—so the number of occurrences issue is not important. In long-tail claims . . . on the other hand, where the injured parties were exposed to multiple injury-causing events over a long period of time, determining the number of occurrences could be a significant issue in determining the amount of the [policyholder's] insurance recovery. In situations where a policyholder faces multiple claimants/claims with large liabilities associated with each claim and the available insurance has high per occurrence limits with low deductibles/ SIRs, the policyholder often prefers that each claim be treated as a separate occurrence to increase the amount of its recovery. Conversely, if the applicable insurance has high deductibles/SIRs and the value of each claim separately is relatively small, then the policyholder may prefer to lump all of the claims together as a single occurrence to minimize the number of deductibles/SIRs it must satisfy. And, of course, the insurers will take the opposite view depending upon which approach is more favorable to them. Consequently, policyholders and insurers often disagree about the method to determine the number of occurrences."[3]

The next case represents the majority approach to the issue.

STONEWALL INS. CO. V. E.I. DU PONT DE NEMOURS & CO.

996 A.2d 1254 (Del. 2010)

Opinion

Stonewall Insurance Company and E.I. du Pont deNemours & Company appeal from a series of summary judgment rulings arising out of disputed insurance policy language affecting the amount DuPont may recover under two excess insurance policies. Stonewall contends that the motion judge erroneously determined the number of occurrences triggering coverage as a matter of law . . . . Stonewall further complains that the motion judge awarded prejudgment interest from the wrong date.

With the exception of the prejudgment interest award, which we now REVERSE, we find the motion judge correctly determined the number of occurrences. . . . Accordingly, we AFFIRM in part and REVERSE in part.

Factual and Procedural Background

E.I. du Pont de Nemours and Company developed an acetal resin product to "bridge the gap between metals and plastics." Between 1983 and 1989, DuPont sold that innovative product for use in polybutylene plumbing systems. After allegations surfaced that inherent defects in the product caused leaks in those systems, with resulting property damage and loss of

[3] Christopher C. French, *A Battlefield Map for NFL v. Insurance Industry Re: Concussion Liabilities*, 53 San Diego L. Rev. 901, 937 (2016).

property, DuPont stopped selling the product to polybutylene manufacturers.

During the relevant time period, DuPont maintained a comprehensive general liability insurance plan that utilized a $50 million self-insurance retention and multiple excess insurance policies to cover losses exceeding the SIR. There were four separate "towers" of insurance, one for each year, as follows:

> 1983: $50 million SIR, $145 million excess insurance ($165m);
>
> 1984: $50 million SIR, $145 million excess insurance ($195m);
>
> 1985: $50 million SIR, $115 million excess insurance ($165m);
>
> 1986: $50 million SIR, $195 million excess insurance ($245m).

DuPont defended and settled thousands of claims involving the leaking plumbing systems, incurring liabilities exceeding $239 million. In 1999, DuPont filed a complaint against multiple insurance carriers, seeking a declaration of rights and obligations, including a designation of which of the fifty excess insurance policies issued by sixteen different carriers should respond and indemnify DuPont. Ultimately, DuPont settled and recovered approximately $111.7 million from fifteen carriers. As a result, DuPont's sole remaining recourse was to seek indemnification from Stonewall Insurance Company.

In an August 4, 2006 letter, DuPont demanded recovery under Stonewall's 1985 policies that provided a total of $5 million in excess coverage.[1] Stonewall denied coverage, contending that . . . DuPont's liabilities from the degradation of the acetal resin product constituted multiple occurrences, thereby triggering multiple per-occurrence self-insured retentions.

In a series of summary judgment rulings, the motion judge decided that: (1) the product liabilities arose out of one single occurrence. . . . A Final Judgment Order dated August 5, 2009 directed the Prothonotary to enter judgment in favor of DuPont and against Stonewall for $9,790,982, consisting of Stonewall's policy limits of $5 million and prejudgment interest for $4,790,982. This appeal and cross-appeal followed.

Claims on Appeal

The parties' coverage dispute turns on three issues. The first is whether the product liabilities arose out of a single occurrence so that DuPont only had to contribute one $50 million SIR before seeking coverage from the excess insurers or whether the product liabilities arose out of multiple occurrences, triggering multiple SIRs. . . . The third issue focused on

---

[1] Stonewall participated in the 1985 tower and provided $1 million of coverage in the first layer of excess policies and $4 million of coverage in the second layer of excess policies.

whether prejudgment interest began accruing from the date of DuPont's complaint or from the date of DuPont's specific letter demand.

Discussion

I. The Number of Occurrences

Stonewall's policies provide that:

> The term 'Occurrence,' wherever used herein, shall mean an accident or a happening or event or a continuous or repeated exposure to conditions which unexpectedly and unintentionally results in personal injury, property damage or advertising liability during the policy period. All such exposure to substantially the same general conditions existing at or emanating from one premises location shall be deemed one occurrence.

Stonewall contends that the motion judge erroneously invaded the jury's province by resolving the number-of-occurrences question as a matter of law, where several issues of material fact were in dispute. Stonewall identifies two purportedly disputed facts. The first concerns how many separate causes of system failure gave rise to the polybutylene system liability claims. DuPont claims that the liabilities arose from the product's susceptibility to chemical degradation alone (inside-out cracks). Stonewall claims that fault lies with two separate and independent causes-chemical degradation *and* the product's inability to resist mechanical stresses (outside-in cracks).

Stonewall's "two independent causes" contention misguidedly attempts to turn the number-of-occurrences analysis into a number-of-conditions question. Whether the failure resulted from the product's susceptibility to chemical degradation from the inside of the pipe or from its inability to withstand mechanical stress from the outside, or both, the *product* itself was the source of the leaking polybutylene systems and the resultant property damage. Indeed, both sides' experts agreed that the product was unsuitable for use in that type of system. Whether it was one condition or two that made the product unsuitable for use in polybutylene systems, is of no legal significance.

The second alleged factual dispute arises from the second sentence of the "occurrence" definition in Stonewall's policies; namely that "[a]ll such exposure to substantially the same general conditions existing at or emanating from one premises location shall be deemed one occurrence." Stonewall queries whether there was only one occurrence, because the relevant "premises location" was a plant in West Virginia where DuPont manufactured the product; or whether each of the 469,000 plus liability claims constituted a separate occurrence because each claim involved an individual building where polybutylene systems failed and damage occurred. Not surprisingly, Stonewall argues that the latter interpretation is the correct one.

In *E.I. du Pont de Nemours & Co. v. Admiral Ins. Co.*, a Superior Court judge analyzed how other jurisdictions treated the number-of-occurrences issue and concluded that "generally, an occurrence is determined by the cause or causes of the resulting injury." Following that conclusion, the court adopted the "commonly accepted [cause] test" and reaffirmed the principle that "where a single event, process or condition results in injuries, it will be deemed a single occurrence even though the injuries may be widespread in both time and place and may affect a multitude of individuals."

Consistent with *Admiral,* the motion judge here correctly identified and applied the cause test to the facts set forth by Stonewall and DuPont. Specifically, the judge held that when determining the number of occurrences in a products liability case, the "[p]roper focus is . . . on production and dispersal-not on the location of injury or the specific means by which injury occurred." Therefore, DuPont's production of an unsuitable product triggered only one single occurrence under the policies.

Despite the judge's application of the reasoning in *Admiral* to the set of facts before him, Stonewall (relying on non-Delaware cases) contends that product manufacturers are subject to multiple occurrences findings in the property damage context. We note that the courts in Stonewall's cases reached that result based on their interpretation of the specific policies at issue. Those cases did not apply the cause test, did not involve substantially similar policy language, and did not concern the same type of products liability issue facing DuPont.[7]

Further, if Stonewall's interpretation of the occurrence provision is correct, then each separate claim would constitute its own separate occurrence. As a consequence, DuPont must first expend $50 million per occurrence for a total of approximately $23,450,000,000,000 before being entitled to look to its excess insurers. It is inconceivable to imagine 469,000 occurrences generating almost $24 trillion in damages. Such an interpretation would produce an absurd, unacceptable result that would render meaningless the excess insurance purchased by DuPont and deprive DuPont of the protection for which it paid.

Stonewall's policies are, by definition and by choice, occurrence-based policies, not claims-made policies. The use of the former instead of the latter signifies that neither DuPont nor Stonewall intended to base coverage on individual accidents that gave rise to claims. Rather, they

---

7 The authority cited by Stonewall involves cases applying the "effects" test, environmental liabilities disputes (asbestos and lead paint), products liability cases involving marketing defects (i.e. improper labeling of products), and nuisance-noise cases involving loss of hearing.

intended to base coverage on the underlying circumstances (or occurrences) that resulted in the claims for damages.

Even if Stonewall's interpretation of the deemer clause was somehow tenable, the motion judge correctly declined to require a jury trial, because Stonewall's argument does not involve any issues of fact. Whether the relevant premises location for purposes of determining the number of occurrences was the plant in West Virginia or each individual building where damage occurred, is not a factual issue. Rather, it involves the interpretation of policy language that is generally a question of law for the court and not a factual dispute for a jury to decide.

Accordingly, we hold that the motion judge correctly concluded that only a single "occurrence" triggered the Stonewall policies.

. . . .

III. Amount of Prejudgment Interest

. . . .

Discussion

The parties do not dispute DuPont's entitlement to prejudgment interest; rather, Stonewall questions on what date interest should have begun to accrue. As a general rule, interest accumulates from the date payment was due to a party. For insurance claims, interest accumulates from the date a party actually demands payment. Where it is difficult to determine to a reasonable degree of certainty when an insured demanded payment, we often rely on the date that the insured filed the complaint. Here, the motion judge awarded prejudgment interest from the date DuPont filed its complaint, December 30, 1999.

We disagree with the chosen accrual date. Prejudgment interest is an extraordinary award that applies when a party unjustifiably refuses to live up to its obligation after payment is due. Although DuPont's initial 1999 complaint may in the abstract be construed as a demand for payment, DuPont amended that complaint to make demand against the 1983 insurers. After settling with the 1983 insurers, DuPont then changed its strategy and made claims against the 1985 insurers, including Stonewall, in an August 4, 2006 demand letter. Therefore, Stonewall could not have unjustifiably refused to pay until DuPont demanded payment on August 4, 2006. Accordingly, the motion judge erred by awarding prejudgment interest from December 30, 1999.

Conclusion

For the foregoing reasons, we **AFFIRM** the Superior Court's judgment in part, **REVERSE** the prejudgment interest award and **REMAND** for a modification of the award of prejudgment interest.

NOTES

1. *Cause Test Versus Effects Test.* "Courts typically apply one of two competing approaches in determining the number of occurrences: the 'cause' test or the 'effects' test. The cause test essentially considers how many 'causes' of the damage or injuries there are. [*See, e.g.*, Peter J. Kalis, Thomas M. Reiter & James R. Segerdahl, Policyholder's Guide to the Law of Insurance Coverage § 3.03[B][1] (1st ed. 1997 & Supp. 2017); Robert H. Jerry II & Douglas R. Richmond, Understanding Insurance Law 518 (5th ed. 2012).] Under the cause test, a single cause can give rise to hundreds or thousands of injuries and claims. The effects test looks at how many effects or injuries resulted. [*See, e.g.*, Kalis et al., *supra*, at § 3.03[B][2]; Jerry & Richmond, *supra*, at 519]. Thus, a court could treat an accident that gives rise to multiple injuries and claims as multiple occurrences under the effects test, but a single occurrence under the cause test. Both tests are subject to manipulation, and commentators have noted that some courts have a tendency to apply the tests in such a way as to maximize the policyholder's recovery. [*See, e.g.*, Kalis et al., *supra*, at § 3.03[B][3] ("[S]ome courts have even acknowledged explicitly that the amount a policyholder will recover is a factor to be considered in the number of occurrences determination.")]." Christopher C. French, *A Battlefield Map for NFL v. Insurance Industry Re: Concussion Liabilities*, 53 San Diego L. Rev. 901, 937–38 (2016).

2. *Restatement of the Law of Liability Insurance.* The Restatement concluded the cause test is the majority rule and adopted it:

> **§ 38 Number of Accidents or Occurrences**
>
> For liability insurance policies that have per-accident or per-occurrence policy limits, retentions, or deductibles, all bodily injury, property damage, or other harm caused by the same act or event constitutes a single accident or occurrence.
>
> **Comment:**
>
> *c.* *The cause test(s)*. . . . .[A] substantial majority of courts that have addressed the number-of-accidents-or-occurrences issue look to the cause of the loss rather than the effect. . . . Courts have concluded that the cause test fits more closely than the effects test with the language of the policies and also with the expectations of the parties. . . .

3. *Counting the Occurrences.* Consider, for example, *American Red Cross v. Travelers Indemnity Co.*, 816 F. Supp. 755 (D. D.C. 1993). The insured was sued for allegedly distributing HIV contaminated blood. Under a cause analysis, how many occurrences were there? Notice the variety of plausible answers: one occurrence based on the policyholder's general, negligent practice of handling blood products; or multiple occurrences, which can be calculated in different ways, such as by each decision involved in handling blood (i.e., whether to screen a donor, whether to test the blood, etc.), each shipment of contaminated blood, each packet of contaminated blood in a shipment, or

something else we might identify as a basis for counting. What factors should help decide such cases?

In *Maurice Pincoffs Co. v. St. Paul Fire & Marine Ins. Co.*, 447 F.2d 204 (5th Cir. 1971), the policyholder sold contaminated bird seed to eight dealers who in turn sold the feed to 100 bird owners, each of whom filed a claim for damages. The court held the sale of the contaminated bird seed to each of the dealers was a separate occurrence for a total of eight occurrences. Was *Pincoffs* decided correctly? *See Champion International Corp. v. Continental Casualty Co.*, 546 F.2d 502 (2d Cir. 1976), *cert. denied*, 434 U.S. 819 (1977); *Industrial Steel Container Co. v. Fireman's Fund Insurance Co.*, 399 N.W.2d 156 (Minn. Ct. App. 1987). Is it possible to distinguish contaminated bird seed from the contaminated blood involved in the *American Red Cross* case, *supra*? What if the 100 bird owners now have 3000 dead birds?

What if a manufacturer ships a plaster ingredient that is appropriate only for use on the exterior of houses and not on the interiors, but the packages of the ingredient contain no warning label such as "for exterior use only"? The direct recipient of the product knows of the limitation, but contractors who purchase the product from the first buyer do not. The product is used in the interior of 28 homes, with property damage resulting. How many occurrences are there? One—the failure to warn? Twenty-eight—the 28 incorrect uses? Or some number in between? *See Chemstar, Inc. v. Liberty Mutual Insurance Co.*, 41 F.3d 429 (9th Cir. 1994), cert. denied, 517 U.S. 1219 (1996).

4. *Pattern of Conduct Cases.* Where a pattern of conduct causes injury to one or more persons, it can be difficult to determine the number of occurrences. Suppose, for example, a pattern of company decisionmaking leads to discriminatory employment practices. Is the company-wide policy one occurrence? Is each distribution of the policy to company offices an occurrence? Is each act of discrimination an occurrence? *See Appalachian Insurance Co. v. Liberty Mutual Insurance Co.*, 676 F.2d 56 (3d Cir. 1982); *Transport Insurance Co. v. Lee Way Motor Freight*, 487 F. Supp. 1325 (N.D. Tex. 1980). If the policyholder's pattern of sexual misconduct causes injury to one person over a period of time, is the pattern "one occurrence," or is each separate act of misconduct an "occurrence"? What if there are multiple victims of the same policyholder's repeated misconduct? *Compare Lee v. Interstate Fire & Casualty Co.*, 826 F. Supp. 1156 (N.D. Ill. 1993), *with Society of the Roman Catholic Church of the Diocese of Lafayette and Lake Charles, Inc. v. Interstate Fire & Casualty Co.*, 26 F.3d 1359 (5th Cir. 1994).

5. *Policy Limits and SIRs/Deductibles.* As the *DuPont* case reflects, it would be a mistake to assume that the policyholder is always benefitted by a finding of multiple occurrences. When the policies contain high per-occurrence SIRs/deductibles, then the policyholder's recovery could be consumed by satisfying the SIRs/deductibles. Indeed, in the *DuPont* case, if each claim was a separate occurrence, then the policyholder would have received no insurance despite having hundreds of millions of dollars of insurance. As an additional example, assume that a policyholder's liability was established at $100,000,

and assume that the City's policy had a $10,000 per occurrence deductible. If ten occurrences were found to have created the $100,000 liability, then the insurer would not be obligated to pay for any portion of the loss.

6. *"Batching" or "Deemer" Clauses.* The policy at issue in the *DuPont* case had what is known as a "batching" or "deemer" clause, which provided: "All such exposure to substantially the same general conditions existing at or emanating from one premises location shall be deemed one occurrence." These clauses purport to aggregate all claims arising from a single premises location into a single occurrence. What are the advantages and disadvantages of such a clause?

7. *First-Party Insurance.* Although our focus in this chapter is liability insurance, the same issue can arise in property insurance. The most notorious example involved the property damage claim under the leaseholder's insurance binder for the destruction of the World Trade Center (WTC) twin towers on September 11, 2001. The question was whether it was one occurrence or two, as there was one terrorist plot, but two planes hit the two towers at two different times. At the time of the attack, the final insurance coverage on the WTC was still being negotiated, and temporary binders were in force (except for one policy that had been finalized), as the policyholders (the Silverstein parties) had only recently entered into a long-term lease for the WTC. The binders left the term "occurrence" undefined, but the binder had a per occurrence limit that was insufficient to cover all damage. Thus, at stake on the question of one or two occurrences was whether $3.5 billion or $7 billion of coverage was available under the binders. In *World Trade Center Properties, LLC v. Hartford Fire Insurance Co.*, 345 F.3d 154 (2d Cir. 2003), the court affirmed the district court's single-occurrence conclusion under one of the forms, but for the other insurers, the court held that summary judgment was inappropriate and that the jury needed to decide the question. In the trial which followed, the jury decided that the attacks constituted two occurrences. The court in *SR Int'l Bus. Ins. Co. v. World Trade Ctr. Props., LLC*, 467 F.3d 107 (2d Cir. 2006) found no basis for disturbing this verdict.

8. *An "Insurance" Movie You Must See.* The widely acclaimed and enormously successful movie *Bridge of Spies* is the true story of insurance lawyer James Donovan, who in 1962 negotiated, at the behest of the U.S. government, the release of U-2 spy plane pilot Gary Powers, who was shot down over and captured by the Soviet Union in 1960. The movie introduces Mr. Donovan (played by Tom Hanks) in a scene where he is negotiating with opposing counsel for five persons injured by Prudential Insurance's driver-insured, represented by Donovan. The plaintiffs' attorney argues that when Prudential's insured hit "five guys" when he lost control of his car on a highway, "five things" happened, which triggered five policy limits, not "one accident" with one policy limit, as Mr. Donovan argues. Here is the relevant script from the movie's scene: https://www.youtube.com/watch?v=hrn6EpjNTRg.

Scene: The Harvard Club

Two middle-aged men sit in club chairs facing each other.

Each holds a tumbler of scotch.

DONOVAN
Don't say "my guy." He's not "my guy."

BATES
Yes he's your guy. Who're we talking about?

DONOVAN
We're talking about a guy who is insured by my client. So don't make him "my guy."

BATES
Okay, fine, my point is he—the guy insured by your client—he doesn't deny any of these things happened—

DONOVAN
"These things?"

BATES
Yes. These five things.

DONOVAN
Wait. Hold it, hold it, hold it. Not five things, one thing.

BATES
Clearly, it's five things.

DONOVAN
Well—I'm sorry—it's not clear to me. Five things? Explain it to me.

BATES
It's self-evident.

DONOVAN
Okay, then tell me what happened, tell me the story in a way that makes sense. For five things.

BATES
Fine. Absolutely. Your guy—

DONOVAN
Not my guy. Insured by my client.

BATES
The guy insured by your client—is driving down State Highway 19 when he loses control of his car, hits my five guys. The five guys who hired me to represent them because you're not honoring your claim.

DONOVAN
You mean my client is not honoring the claim. The insurance company.

BATES
Mr. Donovan: we're all clear on who's who here.

DONOVAN
Except, my client honors every claim. They do, Mr. Bates, every single legitimate claim. Up to the limit of their liability, which is $100,000 per accident in the case of this man's policy. And this is one claim, according to your description. "He hit my five guys." The guy insured by my client had one accident, one one one, losing control of the car and hitting five motorcyclists.

BATES
From their point of view, five things happened.

DONOVAN
Look Bob—may I? Bob? (gestures to self) Jim. If I go bowling and I throw a strike, one thing happened. Ten things didn't happen.

BATES
Jim. My clients are not bowling pins. As much your guy might have treated them so—

DONOVAN
Lemme finish. If your house is insured to $100,000 and a tornado carries it away, it carried away one house. It didn't pick up every stick of furniture and destroy it in a separate incident. If that's what you're saying, well, then there is never any limit to our liability and that is the end of the insurance business. And then, Bob, nobody is safe.

. . . .

The negotiation is not completed in the movie because the next scene involves Mr. Donovan's senior partner telling him that something very important has come up. Assume the negotiation in the insurance case in this early scene ultimately fails and the case goes to trial—is it one occurrence/ accident or five?

For more on the interesting career of New York insurance lawyer James Donovan, *see* Randy Maniloff, *Bridge of Spies: Tom Hanks as James B. Donovan—The Most Interesting Coverage Lawyer in the World*, 4 Coverage Opinions, Iss. 10 (Oct. 28, 2015), available at http://coverageopinions.info/Vol4 Issue10/BridgeofSpys.html (visited July 14, 2017).

E. EXCLUSIONS AND INSURER DEFENSES

1. Expected or Intended, Known Losses and Fortuity

Although there are exceptions that will be discussed in Section II of this chapter, insurance generally is intended to cover losses that are not certain to occur or that have not already occurred. This concept is known as the "fortuity" doctrine. Although the term "fortuity" does not appear in insurance policies, many courts have held that there is as an implied exclusion of coverage for non-fortuitous losses. Some states also have codified the fortuity doctrine. For example, Section 533 of the California Insurance Code provides, "An insurer is not liable for a loss caused by the willful act of the insured; but he is not exonerated by the negligence of the insured, or of the insured's agents or others."

In addition to case law creating an implied exclusion for non-fortuitous losses, liability policies contain express provisions precluding coverage for such losses. The fortuity doctrine first appeared in CGL policies in the definition of an "occurrence," which only allowed coverage for losses that were "neither expected nor intended from the standpoint of the insured." Then, in 1986, the expected or intended language was transferred from the definition of "occurrence" to the exclusions section of the policy as a separate exclusion.

The "expected or intended" exclusion and the fortuity doctrine were among the insurers' primary defenses to environmental claims when policyholders began tendering such claims for coverage following the enactment of the Superfund laws in the 1980s. The next case also was included in the materials on misrepresentation in Chapter 2. The facts in the case relating to the fortuity defense and misrepresentation defense were closely related.

ALUMINUM CO. OF AMERICA V. AETNA CAS. & SUR. CO.

998 P.2d 856 (Wash. 2000)

Opinion

We are asked in this case to apply the law of Pennsylvania to resolve disputes between the Aluminum Company of America, its subsidiary Northwest Alloys, Inc. (Alcoa), and 167 insurers regarding insurance coverage for environmental damage under comprehensive general liability (CGL) policies. . . . We accepted direct interlocutory review in this case. We generally affirm the trial court's disposition of the issues in the case, but we reverse the trial court with respect to its treatment of the issue[ ] of fortuity . . . .

Facts

Alcoa is a large, multinational aluminum producing company with industrial locations across the United States and the world. In the ordinary course of its business over the years, Alcoa generated waste products that were stored in on-site disposal facilities, landfills, and lagoons; and sometimes discharged into the property of others. In recent years, federal and state environmental agencies and private parties made claims against Alcoa for the cleanup of groundwater, surface water, and soil contamination at disposal sites, lagoons, landfills, and other such facilities in Washington and around the country, all stemming from Alcoa's disposal of its waste products. Alcoa paid for investigation and remediation of the environmental harm. Alcoa's claims for coverage in this case involved 35 different facilities in 11 different states. Raising a variety of defenses, the insurers denied coverage. Alcoa hereafter filed this declaratory judgment action in the King County Superior Court in December 1992 against 167 insurers seeking coverage for the cost of pollution damage, investigation, and remediation.

In order to streamline pretrial and trial procedure, the trial court designated 3 of the 35 sites at issue—Vancouver, Washington; Massena, New York; and Point Comfort, Texas—as test sites for the trial. Original damage estimates against the DIC insurers for these three sites alone approached $850 million.

The trial involving the three sites was called Phase I. . . . That trial lasted three weeks. The jury . . . answered only about one-half of the interrogatories submitted it.

The trial court then certified the case for appeal pursuant to CR 54(b), setting out in detail all of the jury's findings of fact and the trial court's extensive summary judgment orders containing conclusions of law. The trial court certified the case for reasons of judicial economy, concluding, "there must be resolution of the legal standards that will apply" before continuing with trial on the remaining 32 sites. We accepted direct review.

Issues

. . . .

5. Did the trial court correctly apply the known risk or fortuity defense to the [insurance] policies?

. . . .

Analysis

Background to the Insurance Coverages

. . . .

In the mid-1980s, pressed by state and federal regulators to clean up environmental hazards on its own property and elsewhere, Alcoa incurred substantial expenses to remediate these hazards. The essence of the problem with Alcoa's insurance coverage claims here rested with the retroactive liability imposed on potentially responsible parties by CERCLA (Comprehensive Environmental Response, Compensation, and Liability Act of 1980), 42 U.S.C. § 9607(a)(2). *See, e.g., Combined Properties/ Greenbriar Ltd. Partnership v. Morrow*, 58 F.Supp.2d 675 (E.D.Va.1999) (retroactive application of CERCLA does not violate due process). At the time the coverages were placed in this case, it is unlikely any of the parties anticipated CERCLA's imposition of retroactive liability on Alcoa. To compound the complexity of the issues here, a significant portion of the harm was to Alcoa's own property.

. . . .

Fortuity

The largest issue in the case was the fortuity issue, which consumed at least half the trial time and at least half of the jury deliberation period. "Implicit in the concept of insurance is that the loss occur as a result of a fortuitous event not one planned, intended, or anticipated." LEE R. RUSS & THOMAS F. SEGALLA, 7 COUCH ON INSURANCE 3D § 101:2, at 101–8 (1997). "The fortuity principle is central to the notion of what constitutes insurance. The insurer will not and should not be asked to provide coverage for a loss that is reasonably certain or expected to occur within the policy period." ERIC MILLS HOLMES & MARK S. RHODES, 1 APPLEMAN ON INSURANCE 2D § 1.4, at 26 (1996).

In Washington, we call the fortuity principle the known risk principle, and first enunciated it in *Public Util. Dist. No. 1 v. International Ins. Co.,* 124 Wash.2d 789, 805, 881 P.2d 1020 (1994): "The known risk defense is premised on the principle that an insured cannot collect on an insurance claim for a loss that the insured subjectively knew would occur at the time the insurance was purchased." *Accord Hillhaven Properties Ltd. v. Sellen Constr. Co.*, 133 Wash.2d 751, 767, 948 P.2d 796 (1997) (extending known risk principle to first-party insurance). Moreover, "The knowledge that some loss may occur in the future is the driving force behind the purchase of insurance." *Public Util. Dist. No. 1,* 124 Wash.2d at 808, 881 P.2d 1020. "The known risk, known loss, and loss in progress defenses are generally considered to be part of the 'fortuity' requirement that runs throughout insurance law." 7 COUCH § 102:9, at 102–24.

Oddly, the fortuity principle never appears in insurance contracts. The principle is rooted in common law and in the statutes of at least six states. M. Elizabeth Medaglia, et al., *The Status of Certain Nonfortuity Defenses in Casualty Insurance Coverage,* 30 TORT & INS. L.J. 943, 986 (1995) (listing state statutes). The fortuity principle has the effect of an exclusion. That is, an all-risk policy might provide coverage for all risks minus named exclusions, but never provides coverage for nonfortuitous events, even though nonfortuitous events are not named exclusions in the policy. For this reason, the fortuity principle is sometimes called the unnamed exclusion. Stephen A. Cozen & Richard C. Bennett, *Fortuity: The Unnamed Exclusion,* 20 FORUM 222, 222 (1985).

From the outset, the . . . insurers raised lack of fortuity as an affirmative defense. For instance, Columbia Casualty Company alleged in its answer:

> Plaintiffs' claims are barred to the extent that the Plaintiffs were aware of alleged contamination to its property prior to the

> inception of this Defendant's policies as there was no "risk of loss" or no fortuitous loss.

Clerk's Papers at 000294. The policies at issue all incepted in 1977 and later. The . . . insurers assert Alcoa knew long before 1977 its disposal and handling of toxic chemicals were causing damage to Alcoa's property. For instance, the insurers claim Alcoa knew as early as 1969 it was losing 305 pounds of mercury a day. They also claim Alcoa knew about the hazards of polychlorinated biphenyls (PCBs) by the mid-1970s. Because of this alleged knowledge by Alcoa, the . . . insurers contend the fortuity principle prevents coverage. Certain of the DIC insurers moved for summary judgment on fortuity grounds.

The difficulty for the trial court, and now this Court on appeal, is deciding what legal principles to apply to the facts, which are not in dispute. While Pennsylvania law applies in this case, there was no Pennsylvania law on the fortuity defense or known loss doctrine at the time of the trial court's decision. "The 'known loss' doctrine has not been tested in the state courts of Pennsylvania." *UTI Corp. v. Fireman's Fund Ins. Co.*, 896 F.Supp. 362, 375 (D.N.J.1995). The trial court had to predict what rules of law governing fortuity a Pennsylvania court would apply.

The trial court selected the following legal principles to inform its decision:

> [A] loss or damage is no longer fortuitous, and therefore no longer insurable:
>
> 1. when the insured knows or is substantially certain that it has on its property specific substances; and
>
> 2. when the insured knows or is substantially certain that these substances had or were going to "damage" the insured property. Knowledge of "damage" to real property for fortuity purposes can arise in various ways, including, but not limited to:
>
> a. knowledge of a hazard to the reasonably apparent or anticipated flora and fauna that could be exposed on the insured premises (employees, wildlife, plants, vegetation, organisms); or
>
> b. knowledge that the property is unfit or unusable for reasonably foreseeable uses of the property; or
>
> c. knowledge of circumstances or facts which Alcoa *believed* constituted harm or damage to its property; or
>
> d. knowledge of circumstances or facts from which an ordinary person would conclude that the property had been damaged.

Clerk's Papers at 042650. The trial court held it must look to the *subjective* knowledge of the insured as to damage to the insured's property. In other words, what did the insured know at the time it purchased a policy, and when did it know it? In the trial court's view, if the evidence supported a finding the insured knew a loss was the substantially probable result of the insured's intentional conduct, there was no fortuity, and hence no coverage.

The trial court's summary explication of the fortuity principle appears at Jury Instruction No. 14:

> If you find that there is damage, as described in Instruction No. 12, in the various areas at Vancouver, Massena, and Point Comfort, you must then determine when Alcoa learned of such damage.
>
> The . . . policies provide coverage for property damage suffered by Alcoa only if such damage was "fortuitous"—that means so long as the damage was unknown, accidental, unintended, or the result of a chance event. Damage is not accidental if Alcoa intended to cause such damage, knew it had already occurred, or knew that there was a substantial certainty that its business conduct would result in such damage. Any damage that was known to Alcoa prior to the policy period, or intended or known by Alcoa to be substantially certain to occur before or during the policy period, is not covered by a . . . policy. Once known, or known to be substantially certain, damage is not fortuitous for any subsequent policy.
>
> Alcoa has the burden of showing, by the preponderance of the evidence, that it did not know, at the time of inception of each policy year, that the losses for which it seeks recovery under the policies had occurred or were occurring and that it did not intend to cause the losses or know that the losses were the substantially certain result of its conduct. For any damage which you find to be fortuitous as of July 1, 1977, you will still need to determine if Alcoa knew that such damage had occurred, was then occurring, or was substantially certain to occur between 1977 and 1984.

Clerk's Papers at 049126.

Applying these principles to the facts relating to Alcoa's subjective knowledge, the trial court entered mixed rulings of law on summary judgment as to the various pollutants at the three test sites. With regard to mercury contamination, the trial court ruled as a matter of law Alcoa knew mercury can pose hazards to workers and the environment. Moreover, because Alcoa had learned from the Texas Water Quality Board in 1970 that its mercury discharges into Lavaca Bay at Point Comfort, Texas had injured aquatic life and made the waters of the bay harmful and potentially toxic, the trial court ruled as a matter of law Alcoa had knowledge of damage there. The trial court did find issues of fact concerning Alcoa's knowledge of soil contamination, and therefore granted only in part the . . . insurers' motion for summary judgment based on fortuity with respect to mercury.

With respect to PCB contamination, the trial court ruled as a matter of law Alcoa knew prior to the inception of the earliest policy PCBs posed a threat to both the environment and living organisms. There was no consensus, however, until 1979 on the level of PCB contamination that would cause harm. In 1979, the Environmental Protection Agency decided on 50 ppm as a new threshold level below which, if industry were forced to comply, industry would be unreasonably injured. The trial court fastened on this standard as the level above which, as a matter of law, real property is damaged. Thus, for all the disposal sites at Massena, New York, where sampling had shown concentrations above 50 ppm in 1979, policies issued for those sites in 1980, 1981, and 1983 failed the fortuity principle, and the . . . insurers were granted summary judgment for those policies. As to other areas that could not show contamination levels above 50 ppm, the trial court denied the insurers' summary judgment motion.

With regard to cyanide contamination, the trial court held there was no question Alcoa knew before 1977 of the harm cyanide could cause to humans, aquatic life, and the environment if it were discharged directly into water. It held as matter of law damage from cyanide contamination was not fortuitous for the cyanide that had not moved, and was not fortuitous after 1978 for the cyanide that had moved and reached groundwater, because Alcoa learned of this fact in 1978. Clerk's Papers at 042658–59.

All of these rulings were pretrial rulings on motions for summary judgment.

Question No. 4 of the Special Verdict Form asked the jurors, "When did Alcoa know of the property damage in each area or become substantially certain that such damage would occur" (dates should be stated as "pre-7/1/77," a policy year between 7/1/77 and 7/1/84, or "post-7/1/84")? Clerk's Papers at 050803–06. Out of 85 total subareas at the three test sites, the jury was unable to establish Alcoa's knowledge for 33 of them. At the conclusion of the trial, the trial court set out in concise form all of the claims it had dismissed because of lack of fortuity, identified by area and policy, as well as the areas where the damage was fortuitous.

While the trial court placed the burden of proving fortuity on Alcoa, it failed to note that on motions for summary judgment, "One who moves for summary judgment has the burden of proving that there is no genuine issue of facts, irrespective of whether he or his opponent would, at the trial, have the burden of proof on the issue concerned." *Preston v. Duncan,* 55 Wash.2d 678, 682, 349 P.2d 605 (1960). Thus, because the insurers moved for summary judgment, they had the burden of proving there was no issue of fact with respect to lack of fortuity. The insurers did, in fact, come forward with facts tending to show Alcoa had the requisite knowledge to eliminate fortuity.

The issue on appeal, however, is who bears the burden of proof at trial. The trial court certified the case under CR 54(b), inter alia, specifically to obtain a determination of that issue. In assigning the burden of proof to Alcoa, the trial court was predicting what a Pennsylvania court would do. The trial court observed:

> Where the facts surrounding the claim are not clearly fortuitous, it is fair and equitable to place the burden on the insured to provide additional evidence tending to show that its losses were in fact the type of unexpected and unintended injuries that satisfy the fortuity doctrine. Since the fortuity inquiry revolves around the subjective knowledge of the insured, plaintiffs are in the best position to explain how seemingly foreseeable results of intentional business decisions could have been unexpected and unintended from their point of view. Contrarily, defendants have no access to plaintiffs' state of mind and would be hard pressed to show subjective intent or knowledge.

Clerk's Papers at 050761. Subsequent to the Phase I trial, however, the Court of Appeals for the Third Circuit, predicting Pennsylvania law, held it was *an insurer's* burden to prove lack of fortuity. *Koppers Co. v. Aetna Cas. & Sur. Co.,* 98 F.3d 1440, 1446 (3d Cir.1996) (insurer has burden to prove applicability of exclusions, which act as affirmative defenses). While this decision is not, of course, binding on a Pennsylvania court, a Pennsylvania court is likely to consider it as strong persuasive authority. The *Koppers* court said: "As with exclusions stated in an insurance policy itself, when an insurer relies on public policy [i.e., the fortuity principle] to deny coverage of a claim, the insurer must bear the burden." *Koppers,* 98 F.3d at 1447. A district court, following *Koppers,* said:

> Under Pennsylvania law, the insured bears the burden of proving that its claim falls within the policy's affirmative grant of coverage. *See Koppers Co., Inc. v. Aetna Cas. and Sur. Co.*, 98 F.3d 1440, 1446 (3d Cir.1996). The burden of proving the applicability of any exclusions or limitations on coverage, however, lies with the insurer, as those are affirmative defenses. *See id.* Moreover, the court must construe policy exclusions strictly against the insurer.

Ehrgood v. Coregis Ins. Co., 59 F.Supp.2d 438, 442 (M.D.Pa.1998).

We agree with the *Koppers* court on the burden of proof, and are persuaded it is a better predictor of Pennsylvania law than the trial court's holding. Alcoa can show its damage falls within the insuring clause, as the ... policies cover "all risks of direct physical loss or damage." Trial Ex. 1578–B, at 2. In the ordinary course, it should then be up to the insurer to come forward with some reason why an exclusion applies. Fortuity is, in effect, an exclusion, and it logically should be the burden of the insurer to plead and prove the exclusion, as *Koppers* directed.

Additionally, Alcoa, in opposing the motions for summary judgment, presented the trial court with voluminous testimony from its employees and various experts to the effect it did not know contamination from PCBs and mercury was causing damage at the time it purchased the . . . policies. Alcoa's argument is persuasive under the law the trial court predicted would obtain, but a recent Pennsylvania appellate court case has addressed Pennsylvania law on fortuity questions. The case establishes an *objective* test for knowledge, not the *subjective* test the trial court employed.

In *Rohm and Haas Co. v. Continental Cas. Co.,* 732 A.2d 1236 (Pa.Super.1999), the court noted first the known loss doctrine was a matter of first impression in Pennsylvania, and thus the court had to decide whether to construe it narrowly or broadly. *Id.* at 1256–57. After discussing other court's writings on the known loss doctrine, the court adopted the following rule:

> [W]e think that the appropriate standard for the "known loss" defense in Pennsylvania should not be knowledge of certainty of damages and liability, but whether the evidence shows that the insured was charged with knowledge which reasonably shows that it was, or should be, aware of a likely exposure to losses which would reach the level of coverage. It should not be necessary that the insured have [sic] already been met with a tabulation of losses sufficient to reach the excess coverage, as that would implicate a standard tantamount to criminal fraud. Rather, when a sophisticated insured, such as Rohm & Haas, is faced with mounting evidence that it will likely incur responsibilities to the extent of the insurance which is sought, the known loss defense should intervene. Otherwise, the issue is one not of insurance, but of pure indemnity.

Id. at 1258. The "charged with the knowledge" language imports an objective test into the fortuity question in Pennsylvania.

Thus, in light of these decisions on Pennsylvania law that postdated the trial court's decision here, we reverse the trial court and hold the burden of proof of lack of fortuity lies with the asserting parties, the . . . insurers. On remand, with respect to the trial court's Order Granting in Part and Denying in Part Defendants' Motion for Summary Judgment re: Mercury, PCBs, Cyanide, and Waste Management Units, filed March 8, 1996, the trial court should conform its order to apply Pennsylvania's law on fortuity as set forth in the *Rohm and Haas* case, unless that case is superseded by subsequent Pennsylvania law.

NOTES AND QUESTIONS

1. *An Express or Implied Exclusion?* In the *Alcoa* case, the policies at issue did not contain an "expected or intended" exclusion; thus, the court held there was an implied "expected or intended" exclusion in the policies. The legal standard applied to the fortuity defense typically does not change depending upon whether the exclusion is express or implied.

2. *The Majority Rule?* The *Alcoa* case does not represent the majority rule with respect to every aspect of the fortuity defense. The majority rule is that the insurer has the burden of proving the applicability of the defense, and a subjective, not objective, test regarding the policyholder's knowledge or expectation is applied. *See, e.g.*, *SCSC Corp. v. Allied Mut. Ins. Co.*, 536 N.W.2d 305, 313 (Minn. 1995) (stating that the insurer has burden of proving the applicability of an exclusion as an affirmative defense); *U.S. Fid. & Guar. Co. v. Armstrong*, 479 So. 2d 1164, 1167 (Ala. 1985) ("[T]he legal standard to determine whether the injury was either expected or intended . . . is a purely subjective standard."); *Fire Ins. Exch. v. Berray*, 694 P.2d 191, 194 (Ariz. 1984) (explaining that the court looks "from the standpoint of the insured" to determine whether the insured "expected or intended" to cause injury); *Great Am. Ins. Co. v. Gaspard*, 608 So. 2d 981, 985 (La. 1992) ("[T]he subjective intent of the insured is the key and not what the average or ordinary reasonable person would expect or intend.").

3. *Must the Act or Injury Be Intentional?* What must be expected or intended for the policyholder to lose coverage—the *act* that causes the injury or damage or the *injury or damage itself*? The majority rule is that the injury or damage must be expected or intended, not the act giving rise to it. *See, e.g.*, *Hanover Ins. Co. v. Talhouni*, 604 N.E.2d 689, 690 (Mass. 1992) ("The focus in these cases is whether the insured 'intended' the injury, not whether the insured 'intended' the act."); *Cont'l Cas. Co. v. Rapid-Am. Corp.*, 609 N.E.2d 506, 510 (N.Y. 1993) ("Resulting damage can be unintended even though the act leading to the damage was intentional. A person may engage in behavior that involves a calculated risk without expecting that an accident will occur.").

4. *Restatement of the Law of Liability Insurance and the "Expected or Intended" Exclusion*. The Restatement concluded the subjective test is the appropriate test and that the harm, not the act, must be intentional in order for the expected or intended exclusion to apply:

> **§ 32 Exclusions**
>
> . . . .
>
> (4) Unless otherwise stated in the insurance policy, words in an exclusion regarding the expectation or intent of the insured refer to the subjective state of mind of the insured.
>
> **Comment:**
>
> *d. The default rule in favor of a subjective standard for expectation and intent.* . . . . Under the subjective standard, an insured intends harm when

such harm is the object of the insured's action, and an insured expects harm when the insured foresees that harm is practically certain to occur as the result of the insured's intentional act, even if that harm was not the object of the action. . . .

5. *Whose Expectations?* "In the context of corporate policyholders, determining who must expect or intend the injury or damage is a more complex issue. Corporations act through people. Thus, whose knowledge or expectation should dictate whether the corporation expected or intended the injury or harm? In many instances, an employee of the corporation may have expected or intended the injury or damage, but the management or executives of the corporation had no knowledge of the employee's actions, and therefore, they did not expect or intend any harm. For example, consider a situation in which a seasonal, hourly employee of a roofing subcontractor, unbeknownst to the corporation's management, intentionally fails to install ice shield on a roof because he forgot to put the ice shield on his truck that day and he did not want to drive back to the shop to retrieve it. Subsequently, during a harsh winter, ice dams form on the roof and water infiltrates the house, causing substantial damage. Did the corporation expect or intend to cause the damage in light of the fact that its employee knowingly failed to install the ice shield? In other contexts, courts have answered questions like this in the negative because the knowledge or intent of the corporation's management should be considered instead of the seasonal employee's knowledge or intent. [*See, e.g.*, *Olin Corp. v. Ins. Co. of N. Am.*, 762 F. Supp. 548, 564 (S.D.N.Y. 1991) (concluding that, in determining whether the corporation expected or intended the harm, the dispositive facts were "what [the policyholder's] executives knew, when they knew it, and what conclusions they drew from their knowledge"), *aff'd*, 966 F.2d 718 (2d Cir. 1992); *Bituminous Cas. Corp. v. Kenway Contracting, Inc.*, 240 S.W.3d 663, 639 (Ky. 2007) (explaining that coverage analysis involves determining the intentions and expectations of corporate officers, not lower level employees)]." Christopher C. French, *Construction Defects: Are They "Occurrences"?*, 47 Gonz. L. Rev. 1, 21 (2012).

6. *Restatement of the Law of Liability Insurance and Known Losses.* The Restatement adopts the majority rule that known losses are not covered by liability policies, using a subjective standard regarding the policyholder's knowledge:

§ 46 Insurance of Known Liabilities

(1) Unless otherwise stated in the policy, a liability insurance policy provides coverage for a known liability only if that liability is disclosed to the insurer during the application or renewal process for the policy.

. . . .

Comment:

d. A subjective standard. The known-liability standard is subjective: the known-loss doctrine avoids coverage only if the policyholder knows, prior to the policy period, that it is substantially certain to be held liable in a specific legal action, absent a settlement of that action. The subjective standard best fits the anti-fraud purpose of the known-loss doctrine. . . .

2. Criminal Acts Exclusion

In many situations, the "expected or intended" exclusionary language, whether appearing in the insuring agreement or as an exclusion itself, will serve to preclude coverage for criminal conduct. There are some situations, however, where the policyholder may not intend the harm that results from his criminal conduct. For example, imagine a person is burglarizing someone's home in the belief that no one was home. When confronted by the homeowner, the burglar accidentally kills the homeowner while attempting to escape. A wrongful death claim against the burglar would not necessarily be barred from coverage under the "expected or intended" exclusion because the burglar arguably did not expect or intend to harm or kill the homeowner.

As will also be discussed in Chapter 10, insurance coverage for claims resulting from criminal conduct often is not permitted as a matter of public policy. However, in a world where public policy is uncertain and shifting, to ensure that they are not liable for claims resulting from unintentional injuries that result from criminal conduct, insurers include a "criminal acts" exclusion in many types of liability policies, including CGL policies. For example, the "criminal acts" exclusion in the Sample CGL policy included at the beginning of this chapter provides: "This insurance does not apply to 'Personal and Advertising injury' arising out of a criminal act committed by or at the direction of the insured."

How have courts interpreted and applied such exclusions? Consider the courts' analyses in the next two cases.

ALLSTATE INS. CO. V. BURROUGH

120 F.3d 834 (8th Cir. 1997)

Opinion

MAGILL, CIRCUIT JUDGE.

In response to an Arkansas state court action brought by Garnette Bell on behalf of herself and her son, Kenyatta Williams, Allstate Insurance Company (Allstate) brought this declaratory judgment action against its insured, Joel Mark Burrough, and against Bell in order to ascertain Allstate's obligation to provide coverage to Burrough. Burrough was named as one of the defendants in Bell's state court action for tort damages because of Burrough's involvement in the accidental shooting of Williams. The district court granted summary judgment in favor of Allstate, ruling that a criminal acts exclusion in the policy underwritten by Allstate excluded coverage. *Allstate Ins. Co. v. Burrough,* 914 F.SUPP. 308, 310, 314 (W.D.ARK.1996). Bell appeals, and we affirm.

. . . .

The shooting occurred on October 22, 1993. On that day, Williams was on foot in the parking lot of a Harvest Foods grocery store in Fort Smith, Arkansas. In that same parking lot, Beck and Hauser were in a car driven by Beck. On the floorboard of Beck's car was the .22 caliber handgun that Burrough had stolen from his grandfather. As Beck and Hauser drove by Williams, Beck "flashed" the .22 caliber handgun towards Williams. The handgun accidentally discharged, shooting Williams in the neck. The bullet severed Williams's spinal cord and left him a quadriplegic.

Beck, who was sixteen years old at the time of the shooting, had received the .22 caliber handgun from Hauser. Hauser, who was fifteen or sixteen years old at the time of the shooting, had obtained the handgun from Burrough approximately two weeks prior to the shooting. Burrough was fourteen years old when he gave the gun to Hauser.

. . . .

Bell filed her Arkansas state court action on behalf of herself and Williams, naming Beck, Hauser, and Burrough as defendants. In her complaint, Bell alleged that Beck negligently and recklessly shot Williams, proximately causing damage to her and Williams. She further alleged that Hauser and Burrough acted negligently and recklessly in providing Beck with the .22 caliber handgun, which also proximately caused damage to her and Williams. Allstate subsequently filed this declaratory judgment action in the district court against Burrough and Bell. Allstate seeks a declaration that, under the terms of a homeowner's insurance policy purchased by Burrough's father, Allstate has no obligation to provide coverage for Burrough's acts and that Allstate consequently has no duty to defend Burrough in the state court action.

The parties agree that at all relevant times Burrough was covered by the Allstate homeowner's insurance policy purchased by Burrough's father. The policy obligates Allstate to pay, "[s]ubject to the terms, conditions and limitations of this policy, . . . damages which an **insured person** becomes legally obligated to pay because of **bodily injury** or **property damage** arising from an **occurrence** to which this policy applies. . . ." Allstate Deluxe Plus Homeowners Policy, § II, Coverage X Family Liability Protection (Policy), *reprinted in* Appellee's App. at 6 (emphasis in original). The policy further provides that "[i]f an **insured person** is sued for these damages, **we** [Allstate] will provide a defense with counsel of **our** choice, even if the allegations are groundless, false or fraudulent." *Id.* (emphasis in original).

In its declaratory judgment action, Allstate moved for summary judgment, asserting that, although Burrough was insured under the policy at the time of Williams's shooting, coverage was excluded by operation of the policy's criminal acts exclusion. The criminal acts exclusion provides that:

> **Losses We Do Not Cover Under Coverage X:**
>
> 1. **We** [Allstate] do not cover any **bodily injury** or **property damage** intended by, or which may reasonably be expected to result from the intentional or criminal acts or omissions of, any **insured person**. This exclusion applies even if:
>
> a) such **insured person** lacks the mental capacity to govern his or her conduct;
>
> b) such **bodily injury** or **property damage** is of a different kind or degree than that intended or reasonably expected; or
>
> c) such **bodily injury** or **property damage** is sustained by a different person than intended or reasonably expected.
>
> This exclusion applies regardless of whether or not such **insured person** is actually charged with, or convicted of a crime.

Id., reprinted in Appellee's App. at 6–7 (emphasis in original).

The district court concluded that, although the state of Arkansas never pressed criminal charges or adjudged Burrough to be a juvenile delinquent, Burrough committed a criminal act under Arkansas law. *Burrough,* 914 F.Supp. at 311–12. Specifically, the district court found that Burrough had committed the offense of furnishing a deadly weapon to a minor, in violation of Arkansas Code Annotated § 5–73–109. *Burrough,* 914 F.Supp. at 311–12. In addition, the district court concluded that "[Burrough] should have reasonably expected that someone might be killed or injured when [Burrough] committed the criminal act of providing a minor[, Hauser,] with a firearm." *Id.* at 314. Accordingly, the district court held that Allstate is not obligated to provide coverage for Burrough's role in the accidental shooting incident. *Id.* The district court also held that Allstate has no duty to defend Burrough in the action brought by Bell. *Id.* Bell appeals.

II.

. . . .

Under Arkansas law, "an insurance policy, having been drafted by the insurer without consultation with the insured, is to be interpreted and construed liberally in favor of the insured and strictly against the insurer." *Noland v. Farmers Ins. Co.,* 319 Ark. 449, 892 S.W.2d 271, 272 (1995). However, the Arkansas Supreme Court has cautioned that "[t]he terms of an insurance contract are not to be rewritten under the rule of strict construction against the company issuing it so as to bind the insurer to a risk which is plainly excluded and for which it was not paid." *Smith v. Shelter Mut. Ins. Co.,* 327 Ark. 208, 937 S.W.2d 180, 182 (1997) (quotations and citations omitted). Rather, we must "adhere to the longstanding rule that, where the terms of the policy are clear and unambiguous, the policy language controls. . . ." *Id.* 937 S.W.2d at 181.

Under Arkansas law, "absent statutory strictures to the contrary, exclusionary clauses are generally enforced according to their terms." *Id.* Although ambiguous language in an exclusionary clause "should be construed in favor of the insured," *State Farm Fire & Cas. Co. v. Midgett,* 319 Ark. 435, 892 S.W.2d 469, 471 (1995) (quotations omitted), such "ambiguity exists . . . only when a provision is susceptible to more than one reasonable interpretation." *Id.* "The initial determination of whether a contract is ambiguous rests with the court, and when a contract is unambiguous, its construction is a question of law for the court." *Hartford Fire Ins. Co. v. Carolina Cas. Ins. Co.,* 52 Ark.App. 35, 914 S.W.2d 324, 326 (1996).

To prevail on its summary judgment motion in this declaratory judgment action, Allstate had the burden of proving as a matter of law that Burrough fell within the criminal acts exclusion. *See Arkansas Farm Bureau Ins. Fed'n v. Ryman,* 309 Ark. 283, 831 S.W.2d 133, 134–35 (1992) (holding that an insurer has the burden of proving that an insured fell within an insurance policy exclusion). To fit within the terms of the criminal acts exclusion, Allstate needed to prove (1) that Burrough committed a "criminal act" and (2) that Burrough could have reasonably expected Williams's injury to have resulted from that criminal act.[4] Bell first presents two related arguments that challenge the first prong of this two-part analysis.

A.

Bell argues that, although furnishing a gun to a minor is a criminal act under Arkansas law when committed by an adult, it is merely a delinquent act when committed by a minor. According to Bell, it is therefore unclear whether Burrough, a minor when he gave the handgun to Hauser, committed a criminal act for purposes of Allstate's criminal acts exclusion. Bell thus argues that the criminal acts exclusion is ambiguous and should be construed against Allstate to find coverage for Burrough's act of furnishing a handgun to Hauser. We disagree.

Under § 5–73–109(a) of the Arkansas Criminal Code, Ark.Code Ann. §§ 5–1–101 to 76–106 (Michie 1993 & Supp.1995), "[a] person commits the offense of furnishing a deadly weapon to a minor when he sells, barters, leases, gives, rents, or otherwise furnishes a firearm or other deadly weapon to a minor without the consent of a parent, guardian, or other

[4] Allstate has not argued that Williams's injuries were the intended or expected result of an intentional act committed by Burrough.

person responsible for general supervision of his welfare." Ark.Code Ann. § 5–73–109(a) (Michie 1993). A minor is "any person under eighteen (18) years of age." Ark.Code Ann. § 5–73–101(2) (Michie 1993).

In the present action, it is undisputed that Burrough furnished a .22 caliber handgun to Hauser, who at the time was a minor. It is also undisputed that no responsible adult consented to the transfer. Consequently, Burrough's act of giving the handgun to Hauser satisfied all the elements of the criminal offense of furnishing a deadly weapon to a minor.

We recognize that Burrough, who was fourteen years old when he handed over the handgun to Hauser, could not be charged with or convicted of a § 5–73–109(a) offense in a criminal proceeding. Arkansas's juvenile courts would have exclusive jurisdiction over Burrough with respect to a § 5–73–109(a) offense. *Compare State v. Gray*, 319 Ark. 356, 891 S.W.2d 376, 377 (1995) (holding that the "jurisdiction of the juvenile court is exclusive and original with respect to all offenses charged against a juvenile who is *fourteen* years old at the time of the commission of those offenses, with the exception of certain offenses enumerated in Ark.Code. Ann. § 9–27–318(b)(1) (Repl.1991)" (emphasis in original)) *with* Ark.Code Ann. § 9–27–318(b)(1) (Michie 1993) (granting prosecutorial discretion to charge fourteen-year-olds as adults with certain enumerated offenses, not including § 5–73–109(a)). Therefore, for the act of furnishing a deadly weapon to Hauser, Burrough could only be adjudged a juvenile delinquent in a juvenile court. *See* Arkansas Juvenile Code of 1989, Ark.Code Ann. § 9–27–301 to –352 (Michie 1993) (setting forth provisions dealing with juvenile delinquency).

Although Burrough's status as a juvenile prevents him from being tried as an adult, the offense he committed is still a criminal act. Neither § 5–73–109(a) nor the provisions dealing with juvenile delinquency incorporate an age-based exception to the offense of furnishing a deadly weapon to a minor. Instead, § 5–73–109(a) applies to any "person" who furnishes a deadly weapon to a minor, *see* § 5–73–109(a), and the Arkansas Criminal Code recognizes that a minor, such as Burrough, is a "person." *See* § 5–73–101(2).

Regardless of whether he could be tried as an adult or be adjudged a juvenile delinquent, under the plain language of the Arkansas Criminal Code, Burrough committed an act defined as criminal. Hence, he committed a criminal act for purposes of Allstate's criminal acts exclusion. . . .

. . . .

Finally, it makes no difference whether Burrough was, or ever will be, adjudged a juvenile delinquent or criminally convicted. Under the terms of the criminal acts exclusion, coverage for bodily injury reasonably expected to result from a criminal act is excluded "regardless of whether or not such insured person is actually charged with, or convicted of a crime." Policy, *reprinted in* Appellee's App. at 7 (emphasis omitted). Thus, as long as Williams's injury was the reasonably foreseeable result of Burrough's criminal act, coverage is excluded regardless of whether the state of Arkansas ever takes action against Burrough.

B.

Bell also argues that a reasonable insured, in purchasing a homeowner's insurance policy from Allstate, would not understand or realize that the criminal acts exclusion contained in that policy excluded coverage for the act of furnishing a handgun to a minor. Consequently, Bell argues that the criminal acts exclusion should be construed against Allstate. We disagree.

As a party to a contract governed by Arkansas law, a reasonable insured would understand that a criminal acts exclusion would exclude coverage for acts defined as criminal by the Arkansas Criminal Code. Under the Arkansas Criminal Code, moreover, a violation of § 5–73–109(a) is not such a minor offense that an insured could not reasonably understand that offense to be criminal. At the time Burrough gave the .22 caliber handgun to Hauser, a violation of § 5–73–109(a) was defined as a Class A misdemeanor, *see* Ark.Code Ann. § 5–73–109(b), punishable by up to one year in prison. Ark.Code Ann. § 5–4–401(b)(1) (Michie 1993). Although Burrough, as a minor, would not have faced the same sentence if he had been adjudged a delinquent, the juvenile court could at its discretion have committed him to a youth services center, *see* Ark.Code Ann. § 9–27–330(3) (Michie 1993), or placed him on probation. *See* Ark.Code Ann. § 9–27–330(4) (Michie 1993).

Given the potential loss of liberty for furnishing a handgun to a minor, a reasonable insured would realize that such an act is a criminal act. Any other interpretation of the criminal acts exclusion by this Court would rewrite the clear terms of Allstate's policy and force Allstate to bear a risk "which is plainly excluded and for which it was not paid." *Smith,* 937 S.W.2d at 182 (quotations and citations omitted).

III.

Bell argues that Allstate did not meet its burden of proving as a matter of law that Burrough could have reasonably expected Williams's injury to have resulted from his act of furnishing a handgun to Hauser. We disagree.

To determine whether Allstate met its burden, we must determine whether a reasonable person would find that Williams's injuries were the natural, probable, and foreseeable consequence of Burrough's actions. *Cf.* . . . *Allstate Ins. Co. v. Brown,* 16 F.3d 222, 225 (7th Cir.1994) (holding that, under Indiana law, an objective standard must be applied to interpret a criminal acts exclusion nearly identical to the criminal acts exclusion at issue in the present action and that "[t]he phrase ['reasonably expected'] is meant to ensure that the policy's exclusions apply only to those injuries most likely to result from the insured's intentional or criminal conduct.").

The undisputed material facts demonstrate that a reasonable person would have expected Williams's injuries to result from the act of furnishing Hauser with a loaded .22 caliber handgun that had previously misfired. Based on past experience, Burrough knew that Hauser and Beck were likely to cruise up and down Grand avenue where teenagers hang out in the parking lots, drink beer, smoke marijuana, and get into fights. Furthermore, Burrough knew that, on at least one previous occasion, Burrough and his friends had been harassed by teenagers believed to be involved in gangs. Finally, Burrough knew that the gun had misfired on at least one previous occasion and that the gun was loaded when he handed it over to Hauser.

Given this knowledge, a reasonable insured would have expected that something would go awry after handing over a loaded, malfunctioning handgun to Hauser. A reasonable insured would find Williams's injuries to be the natural, probable, and foreseeable consequence of furnishing Hauser with a loaded, malfunctioning handgun. We reach this conclusion, notwithstanding the fact that Beck, rather than Hauser, was the one who accidentally fired the gun. Regardless of which one of Burrough's friends held the gun when it misfired, once Burrough handed over a loaded, malfunctioning gun to Hauser, Burrough should have reasonably expected that an incident like the one that took place would happen.

IV.

For the foregoing reasons, we affirm.

ALLSTATE INS. CO. V. MCCARN

683 N.W.2d 656 (Mich. 2004)

OPINION

AFTER REMAND

TAYLOR, J.

This case is before us for the second time. In *Allstate Ins. Co. v. McCarn,* 466 Mich. 277, 645 N.W.2d 20 (2002) (*McCarn I*), we held that the shooting death of Kevin LaBelle was "accidental" and, thus, an "occurrence" within the meaning of the insurance policy at issue. Because the shooting was an "occurrence" covered under the policy, it gave rise to Allstate's potential liability. However, because the Court of Appeals had not addressed whether the criminal-acts exception in the policy precluded coverage, we remanded the matter to that Court. On remand, the Court of Appeals held that the criminal-acts exception precludes coverage in this case. We disagree and reverse the decision of the Court of Appeals. We remand to the trial court for further proceedings.

I. FACTS AND PROCEEDINGS

We set forth the facts in our previous opinion, *McCarn I* at 279–280, 645 N.W.2d 20.

This case arises out of the death of sixteen-year-old Kevin LaBelle on December 15, 1995, at the home of defendants Ernest and Patricia McCarn, where their grandson, then sixteen-year-old defendant Robert McCarn, also resided. On that day, Robert removed from under Ernest's bed a shotgun Robert's father had given him the year before. The gun was always stored under Ernest's bed and was not normally loaded. Both Robert and Kevin handled the gun, which Robert believed to be unloaded. When Robert was handling the gun, he pointed it at Kevin's face from approximately one foot away. Robert pulled back the hammer and pulled the trigger and the gun fired, killing Kevin.

Nancy LaBelle, representing Kevin's estate, brought the underlying action against Robert and his grandparents, Ernest and Patricia McCarn, who had a homeowners insurance policy with plaintiff Allstate. Allstate brought the present action, seeking a declaratory judgment that it had no duty to indemnify defendants Robert, Ernest, or Patricia McCarn.

Plaintiff and defendants moved for summary disposition in the declaratory action. The trial court granted defendants' motions for summary disposition and denied plaintiff's, holding that the events constituted an "occurrence" within the meaning of Allstate's policy. The trial court also held that Robert McCarn's conduct was not intentional or criminal within the meaning of Allstate's policy.

Allstate appealed to the Court of Appeals, which reversed the trial court in an unpublished opinion. The Court attempted to apply our recent decisions in *Nabozny v. Burkhardt* and *Frankenmuth Mut. Ins. Co. v. Masters* and concluded that "Robert's intentional actions created a direct risk of harm that precludes coverage."

This Court reversed the decision of the Court of Appeals, holding that the "accident" was an "occurrence" as defined in the insurance policy at issue, thus giving rise to Allstate's potential liability. *Id.* at 291, 645 N.W.2d 20. Once a court decides that liability may exist under an insurance policy, it may then determine whether coverage is precluded by an exception. *Allstate Ins. Co. v. Freeman,* 432 Mich. 656, 668, 443 N.W.2d 734 (1989). Because the Court of Appeals originally found no liability, it did not determine whether the criminal-acts exclusion precluded coverage under the policy. Because the Court of Appeals had not addressed this exclusion, we remanded the issue to that Court to determine if it applied. *McCarn I* at 291, 645 N.W.2d 20.

On remand, the Court of Appeals, in a split opinion, applied the two-pronged test from *Freeman* and concluded that Robert acted criminally under the first prong of the test because his actions constituted manslaughter under M.C.L. § 750.329. Slip op. at 2–4. The Court of Appeals determined that the applicability of the exclusionary clause "turns on whether LaBelle's death was reasonably expected to result from Robert's criminal act." Slip op. at 3. The panel then concluded that "a person who points a gun at another person's face and intentionally pulls the trigger without checking to see whether the gun is loaded can reasonably expect that injury will result." Slip op. at 4. . . . We granted defendants' application for leave to appeal. 469 Mich. 947, 671 N.W.2d 54 (2003).

. . . .

III. ANALYSIS

When this case was last before us, in interpreting the following language, "Allstate will pay damages . . . arising from an occurrence," we concluded that, on the basis of undisputed facts, the shooting was an accident triggering Allstate's liability. Justice Cavanagh, writing for the Court, said:

> [T]his case does not present a question of fact. The fact that Robert believed the gun was unloaded is a matter about which there is no genuine issue of material fact. This is because there is nothing in the record to reasonably support a conclusion that, contrary to Robert's testimony that he believed the gun was unloaded, he consciously believed the gun was loaded, or even contemplated that there was any possibility that it was loaded when he pulled the trigger. Even plaintiff, the insurer, acknowledged that Robert believed the firearm was unloaded when he pulled the trigger. . . .

[*McCarn I, supra* at 285–286, 645 N.W.2d 20.]

To this set of facts we then applied the requisite subjective test and concluded that Robert's expectation that no bodily harm would result from an unloaded gun was reasonable. *Id.* at 291, 645 N.W.2d 20. The wisdom of shooting even an unloaded gun at another in the first place was, and is, not before us.

In this case, we deal with other policy language, which is commonly described as the criminal-acts exclusion. It states:

> We do not cover any bodily injury or property damage intended by, or which may reasonably be expected to result from the intentional or criminal acts or omissions of, any insured person. This exclusion applies even if:
>
> a) such insured person lacks the mental capacity to govern his or her conduct;

> b) such bodily injury or property damage is of a different kind or degree than intended or reasonably expected; or
>
> c) such bodily injury or property damage is sustained by a different person than intended or reasonably expected.
>
> This exclusion applies regardless of whether or not such insured person is actually charged with, or convicted of a crime.

This language directs us to apply a two-pronged test. There is no insurance coverage if, first, the insured acted either intentionally or criminally, and second, the resulting injuries were the reasonably expected result of an insured's intentional or criminal act. We agree with the Court of Appeals that the first prong of this test—that there was an intentional or criminal act—has been met.

Answering the second prong of the test, whether the resulting injury was the reasonably expected result of this criminal act, requires this Court to engage in an objective inquiry. *Allstate Ins. Co. v. Freeman,* 432 Mich. 656, 688, 443 N.W.2d 734 (1989) (opinion by Riley, J.). That is, we are to determine whether a reasonable person, possessed of the totality of the facts possessed by Robert, would have expected the resulting injury. This requirement to base the objective reasonability test on all the facts has been discussed by scholars of tort law: "The conduct of the reasonable person will vary with the situation with which he is confronted. The jury must therefore be instructed to take the circumstances into account. . . ." Prosser & Keeton, Torts (5th ed.), § 32, at 175. We have held similarly in our cases, "[T]he reasonable person standard examines the totality of the circumstances to ensure a fair result." *Radtke v. Everett,* 442 Mich. 368, 391, 501 N.W.2d 155 (1993). This means that here we must consider not just that Robert, as the Court of Appeals described it, "point[ed] a gun at another person's face and intentionally pull[ed] the trigger," but also, as Allstate itself acknowledges, that Robert thought the gun that he pointed was unloaded. Thus, we are called on to determine if a reasonable person would have expected bodily harm to result when the gun, in the unloaded state Robert believed it to be, was "fired." The answer is no because, obviously, an unloaded gun will not fire a shot. As this Court explained in *McCarn I, supra* at 290–291, 645 N.W.2d 20:

> [No] bodily harm could have been foreseen from Robert's intended act, because he intended to pull the trigger of an unloaded gun, and, thus, it was not foreseeable, indeed it was impossible, under the facts as Robert believed them to be, that shot would be discharged.

To recapitulate, the proper test is that we are to first determine what Robert actually believed about the gun being loaded, not what a reasonable third party would have believed on that issue. Then, using that belief as a starting point, we are to determine in the second step if a reasonable person, possessed of Robert's belief, would have expected bodily harm to result from pulling the trigger. In fact, because reasonable minds could not differ that an unloaded gun will not fire a shot, it is appropriate under MCR 2.116(C)(10) to grant summary disposition to defendants.

IV. RESPONSE TO DISSENTS

The dissent[s] . . . [are] predicated on the notion that insurance policies should not cover the acts of foolish, reckless, or even lawless people. This is a peculiar view because these are among the very people that society wishes to be insured and, in some circumstances, such as motor vehicle insurance, even requires to be insured. M.C.L. § 500.3101. She seems to regard insurance as solely benefiting the insured and thus when it pays out it is a form of reward. This overlooks, however, the societal benefit that insurance provides to those injured or damaged by the acts of insured but otherwise uncollectible individuals. The true beneficiary of liability insurance is not the insured, but his injured victim. The Court of Appeals said this aptly twenty years ago:

> [I]t is unlikely that [an] insured [is] induced to engage in the unlawful conduct by reliance upon the insurability of any claims arising therefrom or that allowing insurance coverage . . . would induce future similar unlawful conduct. . . . Nor does it appear that the policy was obtained in contemplation of a violation of the law. Furthermore, coverage does not allow the wrongdoer unjustly to benefit from his wrong. It is not the insured who will benefit, but the innocent victim who will be provided compensation for her injuries.

[*Vigilant Ins. Co. v. Kambly,* 114 Mich.App. 683, 687, 319 N.W.2d 382 (1982) (citations omitted).]

. . . .

The dissents' approaches would eviscerate insurance policies of much of their value to insureds, leaving only "occurrences that were truly unexplainable" covered. *McCarn I, supra* at 289, 645 N.W.2d 20. Yet, unforeseen, unfortunate consequences of explicable or even intentional acts are "the very purpose of insurance. . . ." *Id.* at 288, 645 N.W.2d 20. As this Court stated in *McCarn I, supra* at 288, 645 N.W.2d 20, "We must be careful not to take the expectation of harm test so far that we eviscerate the ability of parties to insure against their own negligence." "Otherwise, liability insurance coverage for negligence would seem to become illusory." *Id.* "The problem, as we see it, with the dissent's opinion is that it undermines the ability of insureds to protect themselves against their own foolish or negligent acts." *Id.* "However, the impetus for insurance is not merely, or even principally, to insure oneself for well thought out and reasoned actions that go wrong, but to insure oneself for foolish or negligent actions that go wrong. Indeed, it is obviously the latter that are more likely to go astray and to precipitate the desire for insurance." *Id.* To the extent that the dissents would erode the ability of insureds to protect themselves against theirs—or their family members'—foolish or stupid acts, they would eviscerate insurance contracts of much of their purpose and value. This is simply to say that with [the dissents'] approach there would be seemingly no coverage for any intentional or criminal act where there was injury resulting from the act. This would narrow those having insurance in such circumstances greatly and perhaps entirely. This disturbing outcome cannot be what this policy provision intended, nor is it what the policy language calls for.

V. CONCLUSION

We hold that there is no question of fact whether Kevin's death was the reasonably expected result of Robert's act. Accordingly, we reverse the judgment of the Court of Appeals and remand to the trial court for further proceedings.

WEAVER, J. (dissenting).

I would hold that the intentional and criminal acts exclusion of the homeowner's insurance policy at issue excludes coverage in this case. . . .

Freeman . . . correctly identified the first question under policy language before the Court as whether "the insured acted *either* intentionally *or* criminally." I agree with the lead opinion that the policy requirement that McCarn acted intentionally or criminally is met. McCarn acted intentionally when he pulled the trigger of a gun while pointing it at LaBelle's face. As correctly explained by the Court of Appeals, McCarn's actions were also criminal. Regarding whether it was reasonable to expect injury or property damage would result from the intentional or criminal act, it is the consensus of this Court *Freeman* correctly employed an objective inquiry. The dispositive question under the language of this policy and the facts of this case should be, therefore, whether a reasonable person would expect bodily injury or property damage to result when a person points a gun at another person's face without determining whether the gun was loaded and then pulls the trigger.

While the lead opinion acknowledges that the language "may reasonably be expected" dictates an objective standard, the lead opinion's rationale only pretends to be objective. By focusing on McCarn's belief that the gun was unloaded, the lead opinion abandons the objective standard in favor of the subjective belief of a teenager under the influence of marijuana. . . . The lead opinion twists the objective standard required by the policy exclusion at issue in this case into a subjective standard in order to justify holding "an insurer liable for a risk it did not assume."

. . . .

The intentional and criminal acts exclusion of the homeowner's insurance policy at issue in this case plainly and unambiguously excludes coverage under these facts since bodily injury can reasonably be expected to result when, without first determining that a gun is unloaded, a person points the gun at another person and pulls the trigger.

For these reasons, I dissent from the lead opinion and would affirm the decision of the Court of Appeals excluding coverage under the intentional and criminal acts exclusion of the homeowner's policy at issue.

NOTES AND QUESTIONS

1. *Reconcilable Holdings?* Are the holdings in *Burrough* and *McCarn* reconcilable? If so, how?

2. *Reasonably Foreseeable Standard.* Notice that both courts applied a two-prong test when determining the applicability of the "criminal acts" exclusion. The first prong considers whether the policyholder subjectively intended to cause harm or acted criminally, while the second prong considers whether the resulting injury was reasonably foreseeable as a result of the conduct (i.e., an objective test). What is the source of the reasonably foreseeable prong of the two-prong test both courts apply?

3. *Public Policy.* Which way does public policy cut with respect to the "criminal acts" exclusion? How does the public policy that favors compensating victims weigh against the public policy of deterring crimes? Do you think people consider whether they have insurance before committing crimes? If not, then how strong is the argument that the presence of insurance creates a moral hazard to commit crimes and the presence of insurance undermines the public policy of deterring crime?

Burrough and *McCarn* reflect a search for the appropriate balance between these two opposing public policies. What considerations do you think are important in finding that balance? The criminal acts exclusion tilts the balance in favor of no coverage, although insurers do not always succeed in eliminating coverage in cases where criminal misbehavior is involved, as the *McCarn* case demonstrates.

4. *Really Bad Criminal Acts Versus Bad Criminal Acts.* Should a distinction be made between an adult giving a handgun to a minor and an adult committing a sexual assault upon a minor? The utter repugnance of the behavior in sexual abuse cases has caused most courts to put this kind of conduct outside the coverage of liability insurance, despite the negative impact on compensation for victims. What kind of principled legal standard explains this result relative to the handgun case, given that the sex abuser will probably have expert testimony opining that the abuser did not intend to hurt the victim?

Also consider the example of drunk drivers. Should "criminal acts" exclusions even be allowed in auto insurance policies? If they are, does that mean anyone who causes an accident while under the influence of drugs or alcohol forfeits coverage? If so, how can that result be reconciled with the public policy that favors compensating injured parties, which is the reason why auto insurance is mandatory?

5. *A Different and Difficult Kind of Criminal Act*. Beginning in the early 1990s through 2001, a Kansas City pharmacist named Robert Courtney diluted (according to law enforcement estimates) 98,000 prescriptions involving 72 different kinds of drugs given to 4,200 patients. Many of his highest profits in the dilution scheme came from chemotherapy drugs, which evidence garnered in the sting operation that caught him showed were diluted to concentrations ranging from zero to 39 percent. In 2002, Courtney pleaded guilty to 20 counts of tampering with and adulterating two chemotherapy drugs, conspiring to traffic in stolen drugs, and filing false Medicare claims. He was sentenced to 30 years in federal prison. *See* Robert Draper, *The Toxic Pharmacist*, New York Times Magazine, June 8, 2003. In the civil actions against Courtney, how do you balance victim compensation and excluding criminal acts? Courtney testified he never intended to hurt anyone, and that his cancer patients were destined to die anyway. Should Courtney's malpractice insurer be required to provide coverage that would be used to compensate those who received diluted medications and the families of the "toxic pharmacist's" deceased patients? If you were the insurer's attorney, what advice would you give on coverage?

3. Owned Property Exclusion

CGL policies are intended to protect the policyholder from liabilities imposed by third parties upon the policyholder. Conversely, CGL policies are not intended to protect the policyholder from damage to the policyholder's own property. For coverage of damages to an insured's own property, the insured is expected to purchase property insurance, which we will be covering in the next chapter. Consequently, CGL policies include an "owned property" exclusion, which is designed to make it clear that CGL policies do not cover damage to property owned by the policyholder. Until 2001, ISO's CGL policy form phrased the exclusion as follows: "This insurance does not apply to: . . . property you own, rent, or occupy." Is this wording ambiguous?

As was the case with many provisions in CGL policies, the environmental litigation of the 1980s and 1990s tested the boundaries of the "owned property" exclusion. The next case, which we also covered earlier in this chapter with respect to the meaning of the term "damages," is representative of many courts' interpretation of the "owned property" exclusion.

AETNA CAS. & SUR. CO. V. COMMONWEALTH OF KENTUCKY

179 S.W.3d 830 (Ky. 2005)

Opinion

Opinion of the Court by JUSTICE SCOTT.

This appeal is from the judgment of the Court of Appeals, affirming the decision of the Jefferson Circuit Court . . . .

Six separate issues were raised on appeal and cross-appeal by the various parties. These include: . . . (4) whether exclusion (f) [the "owned property exclusion] applies and therefore precludes coverage; . . . .

We shall address all six issues argued, but first set forth the following summary of facts, taken largely from the list of sixty-eight stipulations compiled by the parties and the Court of Appeals Opinion:

Maxey Flats is a chemical and nuclear waste disposal facility located in eastern Fleming County which accepted waste from 1963 to 1977. Over this time period, approximately 4.75 million cubic feet of low-level radioactive waste was received and buried at the Maxey Flats facility. The waste originated from power plants, hospitals, universities, various industries, and government installations. Most of the waste transported to the Maxey Flats facility consisted of solid materials that were deposited in containers constructed of various materials including cardboard, wood and steel. Liquid wastes, including tritium, were also accepted at Maxey Flats from 1963 to 1972. Both solid and liquid radioactive waste was buried in trenches at Maxey Flats.

The use of trenches to bury waste was a permissible practice for disposing of low-level radioactive waste during the time period the Maxey Flats facility was open for the receipt of commercial waste.

Unfortunately, rain water penetrated the large, unlined trenches, mixed with the radioactive waste, and leached out underneath the trenches and beyond the facility.

In December, 1977, the Commonwealth of Kentucky ("Commonwealth"), as the primary regulatory authority with respect to the use and disposal of radioactive material in Kentucky, became alarmed at the level of radioactive contaminants migrating off-site. Accordingly, it issued an order suspending the facility's license to accept additional waste. Thus, no commercial waste was received at the Maxey Flats facility after December 1977.

Atcor, Inc., Chem-Nuclear Systems, Inc. ("Chem-Nuclear") and Hittman Nuclear & Development Corporation ("Hittman") were in the business of transporting and/or arranging for the transportation of low level radioactive waste to licensed waste disposal sites throughout the United States. Hittman was acquired by Westinghouse Electric Corporation in

1982. In 1984, the name of the corporation was changed to Westinghouse Hittman Nuclear Incorporated.

Atcor and Chem-Nuclear never owned or operated the Maxey Flats facility. Neither Hittman, Westinghouse Electric Corporation nor Westinghouse Hittman Nuclear Incorporated (collectively "Hittman") owned or operated the Maxey Flats facility while it was open and accepting commercial waste.

Aetna Casualty and Surety Company, and the other involved insurance companies (36 companies altogether) are members of the American Nuclear Insurers, or "ANI." ANI is an unincorporated underwriting association, formed by conventional insurance carriers, which issues nuclear liability insurance policies.

. . . .

In 1986, the Environmental Protection Agency ("EPA") placed the Maxey Flats facility on the National Priorities List. Pursuant to the Comprehensive Environmental Response, Compensation and Liability Act ("CERCLA"), 42 U.S.C. § 9601 *et seq.*, the EPA instituted administrative proceedings against the insureds for the cleanup of the contaminated site and the abatement of the effects of the contamination. The initial step in such proceedings took place November 26, 1986 when the EPA sent notices by certified mail to approximately 832 Potentially Responsible Parties ("PRPs") who had owned or operated the Maxey Flats facility, or who had transported or arranged for the transportation of waste to the facility. These entities included Atcor, Chem-Nuclear, U.S. Ecology, the Kentucky Natural Resources and Environmental Protection Cabinet and Westinghouse Electric Corporation on behalf of Hittman.

When the insureds notified ANI of the EPA's PRP notices, ANI refused to defend or indemnify them in the CERCLA action. Therefore, the insureds were forced to deal with the EPA on their own. Subsequently, in 1987 the PRPs agreed to a consent order with the EPA obligating them to perform a "Remedial Investigation and Feasibility Study" ("Feasibility Study") to determine the nature and extent of the property damage, and to evaluate alternative remediation programs for its correction or containment. The study was completed at a cost of over $5,000,000. Following submission of the Feasibility Study, the EPA issued a Record of Decision which incorporated parts of this Feasibility Study in a clean-up remedy for the insureds to implement at Maxey Flats. The remedial plan had an estimated cost of implementation in excess of $57,000,000. The insureds ultimately settled the EPA's claims and the settlement is contained in a consent decree filed with the United States District Court for the Eastern District of Kentucky in July 1995.

Meanwhile, in April 1987, ANI, having refused to defend, filed a declaratory judgment action in the Jefferson Circuit Court seeking to establish no coverage liability. Counterclaims were made by the insureds for coverage under the policies and money damages for ANI's breach of contractual duties to defend and indemnify them.

Following discovery, all parties filed cross-motions for summary judgment. On January 4, 1995, the Jefferson Circuit Court entered a partial summary judgment in favor of the insureds, holding (1) the response costs required to remediate the site were "damages" within the meaning of the policy and (2) the contamination of off-site property constituted "property damage" as defined by the policies. Thereafter, the Court summarily ruled that ANI's duty to defend the appellees had been triggered by the EPA's notice of CERCLA proceedings (the PRP notice letters).

. . . .

The Court of Appeals affirmed the circuit court's summary judgment ruling. . . . This Court granted discretionary review.

. . . .

d. Whether exclusion (f) applies and therefore precludes coverage

The ANI "Facility" and "S & T" policies contain what are referred to as "Facility Exclusions" [a type of "owned property" exclusion] that preclude coverage for property damage to Maxey Flats. ANI's Facility Form Exclusion (f) provides that coverage does not apply "to property damage to any property at the location designated in [Maxey Flats] . . . ."

The ANI S & T Forms NS-230 and NS-266, at Exclusion f, state that those policies do not apply "to property damage to any property at any nuclear facility or any property threat arising out of the possession, handling, use, storage or disposal of nuclear material at such nuclear facility. . . ."

Kentucky law mandates that exclusions in insurance policies should be narrowly construed as to effectuate insurance coverage. We find in accordance with the Court of Appeal's opinion that the weight of authority favors coverage under liability policies for remediation expenses when the primary intent is to prevent additional harm to the property of others or to public waters. *See, e.g., Intel Corporation v. Hartford Acc. & Indem. Co.*, 952 F.2d 1551 (9th Cir.1991); *Gerrish Corp. v. Universal Underwriters Ins. Co.*, 947 F.2d 1023 (2d Cir.1991). We recognize also that common sense would mandate in this scenario the most effective method of preventing additional harm to the property of others or to public waters would be to target the site of the harm, though it may be on-site, to prevent further contamination via run off to off-site locations.

Plus, we find the parties stipulation that only 2.6% of the total response costs were designed to clean up damage confined to the insured facility determinative of our decision whether exclusion (f) applies to exclude ANI's liability for the insureds' response costs. Accordingly, we affirm the lower court's finding that only 2.6% of the response costs are subject to exclusion (f), a ruling undisturbed by the Court of Appeal's opinion.

COOPER, JUSTICE, dissenting in part.

I dissent from the majority opinion because (1) the insurance policies issued by American Nuclear Insurers (ANI) are third-party liability policies that do not provide coverage either for property damage to the insured site or for capital improvements to the site itself (referred to as "site measures"). . . .

All of these policies are third-party liability policies that pay on behalf of the insureds *damages* arising out of *damage* to property owned by others caused by activities on the insured site, *e.g.,* migration of radionuclides from the insured site to other properties. Because they specifically exclude coverage for property damage to the insured site, itself, and do not purport to pay for capital improvements to the insured site, they are not first-party policies. *Allstate Ins. Co. v. Dana Corp.,* 759 N.E.2d 1049, 1054 (Ind.2001) ("Because there is no liability coverage for damage to Dana's own property, reference to the 'owned property' exclusion in these policies is unnecessary."). First-party policies, sometimes referred to as "Differences in Conditions" (DIC), "All Risks," or Casualty Insurance policies, are conceptually similar to collision coverage in a standard automobile policy or fire coverage in a standard homeowner's policy.

Third party insurance involves protection for the policyholder for liability it incurs to someone else, while first party insurance involves protection for losses to the policyholder's own property. Generally, a CGL [Comprehensive General Liability] policy insures against injury or damage to a third party; the insurer agrees to defend and indemnify the insured against liability for risks identified in the policy. A DIC [Differences in Conditions] policy, by contrast, is generally a first-party insurance policy that indemnifies the insured for damage to its own property. *Aluminum Co. of America ["ALCOA"] v. Aetna Cas. & Sur. Co.,* 140 Wash.2d 517, 998 P.2d 856, 863 (2000) (applying Pennsylvania law and holding that ALCOA's DIC policies, but not its CGL policies, provided coverage for CERCLA clean-up costs incurred with respect to ALCOA's own property).

. . . .

A. Clean-up Costs.

Exclusion (f) in the Facility Form excludes coverage for "property damage to any property at the location designated in Item 3," *i.e.,* Maxey Flats. Exclusion (f) in the S & T Form excludes coverage for "property damage to any nuclear facility" and for "any property threat." The "any nuclear facility" language obviously anticipates that some insured waste haulers will haul waste to more than one nuclear facility. The language includes the Maxey Flats facility and, in that respect, is identical to Exclusion (f) in the Facility Form. Both of these exclusions are akin to the "owned property" exclusion found in virtually all comprehensive general liability (CGL) policies and apply to the clean-up costs required by the EPA pursuant to CERCLA.

. . . .

The site measures, *i.e.*, improvement of the site's containment features, were performed to alleviate the "threat to human health and the environment posed by the site in the future." Obviously, the exclusion in the S & T Form policy of "any property threat" excludes coverage for the cost of implementing the recommended site measures. Furthermore, "threatened harm" is not within the coverage of either policy.

. . . .

None of the remediation or site measures involved any off-site clean-up or construction. As of this writing, the Maxey Flats nuclear disposal site has been closed for twenty-eight years and no adjacent property owner has yet made a claim for damages for property damage alleged to have been caused by migration of radionuclides from the site.

NOTES AND QUESTIONS

1. *Ambiguity?* Was the language in the "owned property" exclusion at issue in *The Commonwealth of Kentucky* case ambiguous? If not, what was the court's reasoning in support of its conclusion that the exclusion did not apply, given that it was the nuclear waste site itself—not third parties' property—that was being cleaned up?

2. *Crazy Counsel?* The parties in *The Commonwealth of Kentucky* case stipulated that only 2.6 percent of the remediation work was designed solely to clean up the nuclear waste site itself, as opposed to preventing the spread of contamination offsite. Why would the insurers' counsel agree to that?

3. *Who Owns Groundwater?* What if there is contamination of groundwater? Is groundwater owned by the policyholder? Does the "owned property" exclusion apply to groundwater remediation? Although the case law is not uniform, most courts have held that the "owned property" exclusion does not apply to groundwater, either because the property owner does not actually own the groundwater or because of a state's *parens patriae* interest in groundwater or interest as a trustee for the people. *See, e.g.*, *United Co-op. v. Frontier FS Co-op.*, 738 N.W.2d 578, 584 (Wis. 2007) ("[G]roundwater is owned by the public."); *see also* Peter J. Kalis, Thomas M. Reiter & James R. Segerdahl, Policyholder's Guide to the Law of Insurance Coverage § 10.03[A][1] (1st ed. 1997 & Supp. 2017).

4. *Majority Rule.* The *Aetna* decision represents the majority rule. If some off-site contamination exists and the on-site remediation is intended to prevent further off-site contamination, then the "owned property" exclusion does not apply. *See, e.g.*, Kalis et al., *supra*, at 10.03[A][2]. If, however, the

property damage, and its remediation, is restricted to just the policyholder's property, then most courts hold that the exclusion applies. *See, e.g.*, *Boardman Petroleum, Inc. v. Federated Mut. Ins. Co.*, 498 S.E.2d 492, 496 (Ga. 1998) ("[W]e hold that the plain language of the owned or rented property exclusion bars coverage for indemnification for the cost of a state-ordered contamination clean-up when that clean-up involves soil . . . contamination to property owned or rented by the insured, and does not involve property of a third party, and poses no immediate or imminent threat of off-site contamination.").

4. Pollution Exclusions

A property owner's liability for environmental contamination can be enormous. In the early 1970s, in response to some widely reported environmental events, insurers created what is referred to as the "qualified pollution exclusion" or the "sudden and accidental" pollution exclusion. The 1973 version of the CGL policy form phrased the exclusion as follows:

> This insurance does not apply. . . (f) to bodily injury or property damage arising out of the discharge, dispersal, release or escape of smoke, vapors, soot, fumes, acids, alkalis, toxic chemicals, liquids or gases, waste materials or other irritants, contaminants or pollutants into or upon land, the atmosphere or any water course or body of water; but this exclusion does not apply if such discharge, dispersal, release or escape is sudden and accidental. . . .

Between 1976 and 1986, Congress passed the Resource Conservation and Recovery Act (RCRA), the Comprehensive Environmental Response Compensation and Liability Act (CERCLA), and the Superfund Amendments and Reauthorization Act (SARA) (collectively, CERCLA and SARA are known as the "Superfund" laws). These three statutes, which are only a portion of at least ten major federal statutes dealing with protection of the environment and the public's health (from environmental contamination), combined to impose retroactive, strict, and joint and several liability for the cleanup of environmental damage on several entities: (1) the current owners and operators of waste sites, (2) the owners or operators of waste sites during the time of the disposal, (3) the entities that arranged for the disposal or treatment of hazardous materials, and (4) the transporters of hazardous materials. These laws combined to create hundreds of billions of dollars of liabilities for policyholders. Not surprisingly, when these liabilities were placed on policyholders, the policyholders turned to their CGL insurers and demanded that they defend the claims and pay the liabilities.

In what became one of the most significant waves of big-dollar commercial litigation in the 1980s and 1990s, policyholders and insurers locked horns regarding the meaning of the "sudden and accidental" pollution exclusion. Insurers took the position that "sudden" meant "abrupt," which meant that liability for environmental contamination was excluded unless the contamination resulted from abrupt events. Policyholders, on the other hand, contended that "sudden" also could mean "unexpected and unintended," from which it arguably followed that the policy language was ambiguous and should be construed against insurers.

In Chapter 2, we covered *Hecla Mining Co. v. New Hampshire Insurance Co.*, 811 P.2d 1083 (Colo. 1991). In that case, the Colorado Supreme Court held that the "sudden and accidental" pollution exclusion was ambiguous. Accordingly, the court construed it against the insurers and required the insurers to defend the policyholder. Not all courts, however, agreed with the *Hecla* decision. Consider the following case.

HYBUD EQUIP. CORP. V. SPHERE DRAKE INS. CO., LTD.

597 N.E.2d 1096 (Ohio 1992)

Facts

Industrial Excess Landfill, Inc. ("IEL") is a corporation that, before 1978, owned and operated the Industrial Excess Landfill, a licensed landfill in Uniontown, Ohio. IEL still owns the site of the landfill; however, the landfill no longer accepts any waste.

Hybud Equipment Corporation ("Hybud") is a corporation with its principal place of business in Akron, Ohio. In addition to building and leasing equipment, compactors, and containers for solid waste, Hybud owns a number of vehicles. These vehicles are employed to collect and transport the waste material of various local commercial and industrial entities. Hybud has taken waste to the Industrial Excess Landfill and the Montville Landfill. The latter landfill is located in Medina County, Ohio.

Hyman Budoff is an officer and director of both IEL and Hybud. Over the years, IEL and Hybud have purchased insurance coverage from a number of companies. From July 30, 1985 until June 30, 1987, IEL, Hybud and Budoff were each covered under two policies issued by the Sphere Drake Insurance Company, Ltd. Sphere Drake is authorized to transact business in Ohio through the Ostrov Corporation, an independent insurance agency.

Under the comprehensive general liability insurance provisions of both policies, Sphere Drake agreed to pay on behalf of IEL, Hybud and Budoff any sums which they would become legally obligated to pay as a result of bodily injury or property damage caused by an "occurrence." These provisions also stated that Sphere Drake "shall have the right and duty to defend any suit against the insured seeking damages on account of such bodily injury or property damage, even if any of the allegations of the suit are groundless, false or fraudulent * * *."

Each policy then listed a number of exclusions to the foregoing coverage, including the so-called "Standard Pollution Exclusion." In the second policy, which covered the period from June 30, 1986 until June 30, 1987, this exclusion was set forth as exclusion (f):

> This insurance does not apply:
>
> . . . .
>
> (f) to bodily injury or property damage arising out of the discharge, dispersal, release or escape of smoke, vapors, soot, fumes, acids, alkalis, toxic chemicals, liquids or gases, waste materials or other irritants, contaminants or pollutants into or upon land, the atmosphere or other water course or body of water; but this exclusion does not apply if such discharge, dispersal, release or escape is *sudden and accidental*[.] (Emphasis added).

The relevant exclusion in the first policy, which covered the period from July 30, 1985 until July 30, 1986, was worded in virtually the same manner.

After the second policy expired, three environmental lawsuits were brought, each involving one or more of the three insureds. . . .

The first action that involved each of the three insureds was initiated in November 1987 in an Ohio federal district court. In that complaint, the plaintiff, Linda Putinski, alleged that she had suffered bodily injury and property damage as a result of the leakage of certain pollutants from the Industrial Excess Landfill. Specifically, she alleged that as a result of damage to storage containers, various chemicals had escaped into the air, soil, and groundwater over a fourteen-year period.

The second action against each of the three insureds also involved the Industrial Excess Landfill. This action was brought by the United States in October 1989 in the same Ohio federal district court. The complaint was predicated on an administrative order issued by the Environmental Protection Agency in December 1987, and then superseded in January 1988.

In the order, the agency found that the landfill had accepted various waste materials over a twelve-year period, even though IEL had failed to install an impermeable liner to halt any leakage of waste. Consequently, certain contaminants had migrated into residential water wells near the landfill. Based upon this, the complaint alleged that IEL, Hybud and Budoff, along with other named defendants, were jointly and severally liable for any costs incurred by the United States in remedial actions.

The third action was originally filed by the state of Ohio in the Medina County Court of Common Pleas. There, the state sought the cleanup of the Montville Landfill. The complaint alleged that as a result of the manner in which the waste had been handled, a leachate had been generated and was seeping into the local ground and surface waters along with other hazardous waste. The complaint further alleged that this had been occurring since the late 1970s.

. . . .

After receiving service in each of the aforementioned actions, the three insureds notified Sphere Drake of each action, and asked the company to defend them in the litigation. In each instance, Sphere Drake refused.

Accordingly, the three insureds initiated the instant declaratory judgment action in the Summit County Court of Common Pleas. For relief, the insureds requested that the trial court declare that under the terms of the two policies, Sphere Drake was required to defend them in each of the foregoing cases. The insureds also claimed damages covering the costs they had incurred as a result of having to defend themselves. In response, Sphere Drake argued, *inter alia,* that it did not have a duty to defend in any of the actions because coverage was excluded by the pollution exclusion clause in both policies.

. . . . After a bench trial, the trial court rendered its first judgment, holding that Sphere Drake was required by the policies to provide a defense to the actions and indemnify the insureds from liability. . . .

. . . . As to the issue of liability, the Ninth Appellate District affirmed the judgment of the trial court. Relying upon its earlier decision in *Buckeye Union Ins. Co. v. Liberty Solvents & Chemicals Co.* (1984), 17 Ohio App.3d 127, 17 OBR 225, 477 N.E.2d 1227, the appellate court rejected Sphere Drake's contention that coverage was barred by the pollution exclusion. . . .

Both sides appealed to this court. In July 1991, this court granted the motion and cross-motion to certify the record.

Opinion

. . . .

For the reasons which follow, this court finds that it is not necessary for us to address the [any other] issues, since the determination of the following single issue will control the outcome in this case. Specifically, we conclude that Sphere Drake was not under an obligation to defend the insureds in the three underlying actions because the claims in those actions were excluded from coverage by the pollution exclusion in each of the two policies. Accordingly, the judgments of both the trial and appellate courts are reversed.

I.

As previously noted, in rejecting Sphere Drake's argument as to the application of the pollution exclusion in this case, the appellate court relied heavily upon its prior decision in *Buckeye Union, supra.* In that case, Liberty Solvents, the insured, was named as a defendant in an action involving the cleanup of a hazardous waste facility. The complaint in the underlying lawsuit alleged that Liberty Solvents had contracted with Chem-Dyne to dispose of its waste, and that this waste had escaped from containers and filtered into the surface water, soil, and groundwater of the surrounding area.

As in the instant case, Liberty Solvents requested that its insurer, Buckeye Union, defend it in the lawsuit. In response, Buckeye Union initiated a declaratory judgment action, seeking a determination that it was not obligated to defend under the policy. In reversing the summary judgment in favor of Buckeye Union, the Ninth Appellate District . . . turned its attention to the pollution exclusion in the policy. The language of that provision was virtually identical to the exclusion in the policy now before this court. Essentially, the exclusion stated that the coverage did not apply to any bodily harm or property damages resulting from the release or escape of pollutants into or upon land, air or water. The final clause in the exclusion then stated that the exclusion did not apply if the release or escape is "sudden and accidental."

In analyzing the exception to the exclusion, the court began by concluding that the phrase "sudden and accidental" was ambiguous, and accordingly had to be construed against the insurer. The court then quoted from other decisions which had determined that the word "sudden" should not be interpreted as being limited to an instantaneous happening, but should cover any release or escape which was unexpected by the insured. By following this interpretation, the court read "sudden and accidental" as having the same meaning as the phrase "neither expected nor intended" in the definition of occurrence:

" 'When viewed in light of the case law cited, the clause can be interpreted as simply a restatement of the definition of "occurrence"—that is, that the policy will cover claims where the injury was "neither expected nor intended." It is a reaffirmation of the principle that coverage will not be provided for intended results of intentional acts, but will be provided for the unintended results of an intentional act.' " *Id.* at 133, 17 OBR at 232, 477 N.E.2d at 1234, quoting *Jackson Twp. Mun. Util. Auth. v. Hartford Acc. & Indemn. Co.* (1982), 186 N.J.Super. 156, 164, 451 A.2d 990, 994.

Applying this logic to the facts of that case, the *Buckeye Union* court held that the exception to the pollution exclusion applied, since the release of pollutants had been unexpected and unintended by the insured. Accordingly, that court found that the insured was entitled to a defense and indemnity in the underlying lawsuit.

II.

During its discussion of the pollution exclusion, the *Buckeye Union* court stated that the "overwhelming authority from other jurisdictions" supported its interpretation of the "sudden and accidental" phrase. While this may have been true in 1984, recent decisions have rejected the holding of *Buckeye Union*.

A prime example of this recent trend is the decision of the North Carolina Supreme Court in *Waste Mgt. of Carolinas, Inc. v. Peerless Ins. Co.* (1986), 315 N.C. 688, 340 S.E.2d 374. There, the insured was engaged in the business of hauling waste materials and disposing of them in a local landfill. When the owners of the landfill were sued by the United States, the insured was added as a third-party defendant. As in the instant case, when its insurer refused to defend it, the insured brought a declaratory judgment action.

Upon reviewing the language of the pollution exclusion and the definition of "occurrence," the Supreme Court of North Carolina held that the provisions were not ambiguous because the language could reasonably be interpreted in only one manner:

> We do not perceive these provisions to be either ambiguous or, except for the repeated appearance of "accident," redundant. In our view, this is an instance where nontechnical words (except for "occurrence," which is defined in the policy) can be given the same meaning they usually receive in ordinary speech. Nor does their context require us to do otherwise.

Id. at 694, 340 S.E.2d at 379.

The North Carolina court then went on to conclude that the word "sudden" had to be interpreted as having a *temporal* aspect, and that it could not be read to include releases which occur over a long period of time: "The exception also describes the event—not only in terms of its being unexpected, but in terms of its happening instantaneously or precipitantly." *Id.* at 699, 340 S.E.2d at 382.

. . . .

Other state supreme courts have also held that the word "sudden" in the exception must be interpreted as having a temporal aspect. *See, e.g., Upjohn Co. v. New Hampshire Ins. Co.* (1991), 438 Mich. 197, 476 N.W.2d 392; *Lumbermens Mut. Cas. Co. v. Belleville Indus., Inc.* (1990), 407 Mass. 675, 555 N.E.2d 568.

In addition to the plain and ordinary meaning of the word, some courts have placed heavy emphasis upon the fact that "sudden" *would not have any* meaning in the exception if it were not interpreted to also mean "quick" or "abrupt." These courts have recognized that the word "accidental" also means unexpected:

> For the word "sudden" to have any significant purpose, and not to be surplusage when used generally in conjunction with the word "accidental," it must have a temporal aspect to its meaning, and

> not just the sense of something unexpected. We hold, therefore, that when used in describing a release of pollutants, "sudden" in conjunction with "accidental" has a temporal element. The issue is whether the release was sudden. The alternative is that it was gradual. If the release was abrupt and also accidental, there is coverage for an occurrence arising out of the discharge of pollutants.

Id., 407 Mass. at 680, 555 N.E.2d at 572.

In addition to state courts, many federal courts have rejected the *Buckeye Union* interpretation of the word "sudden." Of particular interest is a series of decisions of the Sixth Circuit Court of Appeals. In applying state principles of contract interpretation, the circuit court has consistently interpreted the word in the same manner as in *Waste Mgt., supra. See Grant-Southern Iron & Metal Co. v. CNA Ins. Co.* (C.A.6, 1990), 905 F.2d 954; *FL Aerospace v. Aetna Cas. & Sur. Co.* (C.A.6, 1990), 897 F.2d 214; *United States Fid. & Guar. Co. v. Star Fire Coals, Inc.* (C.A.6, 1988), 856 F.2d 31.

. . . .

Besides the Sixth Circuit, other federal appellate courts have followed this interpretation of the word "sudden." *See, e.g., A. Johnson & Co., Inc. v. Aetna Cas. & Sur. Co.* (C.A.1, 1991), 933 F.2d 66; *New York v. Amro Realty Co.* (C.A.2, 1991), 936 F.2d 1420.

Finally, at least one court has predicted that this court would not follow *Buckeye Union*. In *Borden, Inc. v. Affiliated FM Ins. Co.* (S.D.Ohio 1987), 682 F.Supp. 927, the court reviewed our previous pronouncements concerning the proper manner of interpreting insurance contracts, and then rejected the *Buckeye Union* analysis on the ground that the exclusion was unambiguous. The court went on to conclude that in its common usage, "sudden" means "happening without previous notice or with very brief notice." *Id.* at 930.

III.

As the *Borden* court correctly noted, this court has consistently held that insurance contracts must be construed in accordance with the same rules as other written contracts. *Universal Underwriters Ins. Co. v. Shuff* (1981), 67 Ohio St.2d 172, 21 O.O.3d 108, 423 N.E.2d 417; *Rhoades v. Equitable Life Assur. Soc. of the United States* (1978), 54 Ohio St.2d 45, 8 O.O.3d 39, 374 N.E.2d 643.

In applying these rules, we have stated that the most critical rule is that which stops this court from rewriting the contract when the intent of the parties is evident, *i.e.*, if the language of the policy's provisions is clear and unambiguous, this court may not "resort to construction of that language." *Karabin v. State Auto. Mut. Ins. Co.* (1984), 10 Ohio St.3d 163, 167, 10 OBR

497, 499, 462 N.E.2d 403, 406. In *Tomlinson v. Skolnik* (1989), 44 Ohio St.3d 11, 12, 540 N.E.2d 716, 717–718, this court expounded upon this rule further:

> Thus, in reviewing an insurance policy, words and phrases used therein "must be given their natural and commonly accepted meaning, where they in fact possess such meaning, to the end that a reasonable interpretation of the insurance contract consistent with the apparent object and plain intent of the parties may be determined." (*Quoting Gomolka v. State Auto. Mut. Ins. Co.* [1982], 70 Ohio St.2d 166, 167–168, 24 O.O.3d 274, 275–276, 436 N.E.2d 1347, 1348.)

. . . .

Applying these rules of construction to policy language in this case, this court concludes that the analysis of the exception to the pollution exclusion in *Buckeye Union* is incorrect. Specifically, we hold that the word "sudden" in the exception is *not* synonymous with the word "unexpected" in the typical definition of "occurrence"; instead, the word also has a *temporal* aspect. We reach this conclusion for three reasons.

First, and foremost, like the courts in *Borden* and *Waste Mgt.,* this court finds that the word "sudden," as well as the remainder of the exception, is not ambiguous in the context of the entire exclusion. As it is most commonly used, "sudden" means happening quickly, abruptly, or without prior notice. This is the plain and ordinary meaning of the word, and the context in which it is employed does not indicate that it should be given any other meaning.

Second, we agree with the court in *Belleville Indus., supra,* that unless "sudden" is interpreted to have a temporal aspect, the word does not add anything to the phrase "sudden and accidental." In its common, ordinary use, the word "accidental" means unexpected, as well as unintended. Under the *Buckeye Union* interpretation, "sudden" has the same meaning, and accordingly serves no purpose in the phrase. However, "[i]n construing a written instrument, effect should be given to all of its words, if this can be done by any reasonable interpretation." *Wadsworth Coal Co. v. Silver Creek Mining & Ry. Co.* (1884), 40 Ohio St. 559.

Third, if "sudden" were interpreted to be synonymous with "unexpected," then the entire pollution exclusion would not serve the purpose for which it was clearly included. This is because, under *Buckeye Union,* the pollution exclusion would exclude only bodily injury or property damage that was already excluded by the common definition of "occurrence."

. . . [T]he typical definition of "occurrence" in an insurance policy is an accident that results in injury or damage which the insured did not intend or expect. That definition also states that an accident includes continuous or repeated exposure to a condition. Accordingly, under this definition, it does not matter whether the accident happened quickly or gradually; it would still be considered an "occurrence" if it resulted in bodily injury or property damage.

From this broad coverage, the pollution exclusion then excluded those injuries or damages which resulted from pollution or contamination. In doing so, the exclusion did not distinguish between damages caused by a gradual release or discharge and those damages caused by an abrupt release or discharge.

Under the definition of "sudden" now adopted by this court in the present case, the exception to the exclusion covers only those damages in the latter category, *i.e.,* those caused by an abrupt release. However, if "sudden" were construed so that it could also mean "unexpected" and the exception were construed to be just a restatement of the definition of "occurrence," then the exception would cover both categories, *i.e.,* gradual and abrupt. Because such an interpretation would render the entire exclusion meaningless, it is neither acceptable nor desirable under the normal rules of contract construction. *Farmers Natl. Bank v. Delaware Ins. Co.* (1911), 83 Ohio St. 309, 94 N.E. 834.

As an aside, we note that public policy also supports our interpretation of the word "sudden." Under the *Buckeye Union* interpretation, only an intentional polluter was excluded from coverage. Such an interpretation might encourage the polluter to be less than diligent, as merely negligent acts would be covered under the policy. *See Waste Mgt., supra,* 315 N.C. at 697–698, 340 S.E.2d at 381. In contrast, today's holding encourages diligence by placing the financial burden for gradual or long-term pollution upon the entity best able to foresee and stop it.

However, we reiterate that the primary basis for our holding is the lack of ambiguity in the wording of the exception. The inclusion of the word "sudden" readily indicates that the exception was not intended to apply to a release that occurred over an extended time. As one court has noted, the intent behind the "sudden and accidental" exception was to *limit* coverage for pollution-related damages to those events in which "damages are caused by sudden pollution incidents involving equipment malfunctions, explosions and the like." *Claussen v. Aetna Cas. & Sur. Co.* (S.D.Ga.1987), 676 F.Supp. 1571, 1580. Any other interpretation conflicts with the clear language and intent of the provision.

IV.

The application of the foregoing holding to the facts of this case is a relatively simple exercise. The first two complaints related to the operation of the Industrial Excess Landfill. Both complaints alleged that over an extended period of time, the insureds had either disposed of or accepted a variety of wastes in the landfill. The third complaint, which applied only to

Hybud, stated that the insured had deposited various wastes into the Montville Landfill over an extended period of time.

Clearly, each of the three complaints alleged that the resulting injuries and damages had been caused by the deposited waste. These allegations accordingly brought the causes of action within the scope of the pollution exclusion.

Moreover, a review of the complaints shows that there was never any allegation that the release or discharge of the waste happened abruptly or instantaneously. Thus, the exception to the exclusion was not invoked. Under these circumstances, the three insureds were not entitled under the two policies to a defense from Sphere Drake. Thus, the specific allegations of the complaints precluded coverage for the resulting damage.

. . . .

VI.

For the foregoing reasons, Sphere Drake was not obligated to provide a defense for the three insureds in the underlying complaints. The judgment of the court of appeals is reversed.

Judgment reversed.

NOTES AND QUESTIONS

1. *One Meaning?* Does "sudden" only have a temporal meaning that essentially means "abrupt," as the *Hybud* court ruled, or does it also mean "unexpected and unintended," as the *Hecla* court ruled?

2. *The Origins of the "Sudden and Accidental" Pollution Exclusion.* In 1966, the CGL policy form was revised from a policy that covered "accidents" to a policy that covers "occurrences." The change to an "occurrence" form meant that insurance coverage was provided not only for accidental events, but also for gradual, ongoing or continuous injury situations. Consequently, insurers initially marketed occurrence-based CGL insurance as covering pollution claims regardless of whether the damage occurred gradually over time (e.g., due to "continuous or repeated exposure to conditions") or abruptly (e.g., due to a spill) so long as the damage was not expected or intended by the policyholder. *See* Christopher C. French, *The Role of the Profit Imperative in Risk Management*, 17 U. Pa. J. Bus. L. 1081, 1099–1101 (2015). With the creation of strict liability in the 1960s and several subsequent disastrous pollution events, insurers did not want to be viewed as covering intentional polluters, so they created the "sudden and accidental" pollution exclusion, which was incorporated into the ISO CGL policy form in 1973. At the time insurers sought approval of the exclusion from state insurance commissioners, insurers represented that it was not a restriction on the existing coverage for environmental damage under the CGL policy form. Thus, they did not reduce premiums in exchange for approval of the exclusion. *See Morton International, Inc. v. General Acc. Ins. Co.*, 629 A.2d 831, 848–53 (N.J. 1993) (discussing the

insurance industry's explanatory memoranda of the pollution exclusion clause); *Joy Techs., Inc. v. Liberty Mut. Ins. Co.*, 421 S.E.2d 493, 498–99 (W. Va. 1992) (same). This explanation by insurers made sense at the time because the phrase "sudden and accidental" previously had been used by insurers in other liability policies, such as Boiler and Machinery policies. In those policies, the phrase had a judicially established meaning: "courts uniformly had construed the phrase to mean unexpected and unintended." *New Castle Cty. v. Hartford Accident & Indem. Co.*, 933 F.2d 1162, 1197 (3d Cir. 1991), *abrogated by N. Ins. Co. of N.Y. v. Aardvark Assocs., Inc.*, 942 F.2d 189 (3d Cir. 1991). *See also* Steven Plitt et al., 10A Couch on Insurance § 150:30 (3d ed. 2017) ("When coverage is limited to a sudden 'breaking' of machinery, the word 'sudden' should be given its primary meaning as a happening without previous notice or as something coming or occurring unexpectedly as unforeseen or unprepared for. That is, 'sudden' is not to be construed as synonymous with instantaneous.").

3. *Regulatory Estoppel.* As a result of insurers' representations to state insurance commissioners regarding the meaning of the "sudden and accidental" pollution exclusion at the time insurers sought approval for it, some courts held that insurers were estopped from arguing "sudden" means "abrupt." *See, e.g., Morton, supra,* at 874–75.

4. *Majority Rule?* As the meaning of "sudden and accidental" was repeatedly litigated throughout the 1980s and 1990s due to the extraordinary dollars at stake, courts split between the *Hecla* and *Hybud* courts' approaches.

5. *"Absolute" Pollution Exclusion.* In 1986, after losing many times in court regarding the meaning of "sudden and accidental" (and owing billions to their policyholders as a result), insurers created what is known as the "absolute" pollution exclusion. The text of this exclusion does not contain any reference to allowing coverage for "sudden and accidental" releases. This broadly worded exclusion purports to exclude coverage for "pollution" claims regardless of whether the damage occurred "abruptly" or gradually. Is the "absolute" pollution exclusion absolutely unambiguous? Does it apply only to environmental claims? Consider the next case as you think about those questions.

STONEY RUN CO. V. PRUDENTIAL LMI COMMERCIAL INS. CO.

47 F.3d 34 (2d Cir. 1995)

ALTIMARI, CIRCUIT JUDGE:

Plaintiffs appellants Stoney Run Company and Larrymore Organization (collectively, "Plaintiffs") appeal from a judgment of the United States District Court for the Northern District of New York (McAvoy, J.), granting defendant appellee Prudential LMI Commercial Insurance Company's ("Prudential") motion to dismiss two claims for relief in Plaintiffs' complaint. Plaintiffs sought a declaration that Prudential was obliged to defend and/or indemnify them in connection with three civil actions filed against Plaintiffs for damages due to carbon monoxide poisoning in their apartment buildings. The district court dismissed the two claims for relief on the grounds that they fell unambiguously within a "pollution exclusion" clause contained in the policies issued by Prudential to Plaintiffs. Because we conclude that under New York law, the pollution exclusion clause at issue does not unambiguously apply to the underlying civil actions, we reverse the judgment of the district court.

BACKGROUND

Stoney Run Company is a partnership that owns the Stoney Run Apartments, a real estate complex in Kingston, New York. Larrymore Organization is a Virginia corporation that acts as the real estate agent for Stoney Run. Prudential issued two general commercial liability policies to Plaintiffs in connection with the Stoney Run Apartments. During the effective dates of these policies, several tenants at the Stoney Run Apartments were killed or injured by the inhalation of carbon monoxide emitted into their apartments due to a faulty heating and ventilation system.

Subsequently, three civil actions were commenced against Plaintiffs by the injured persons or their legal representatives [for death or injury due to defendant's negligence. . . .]

Prudential declined to defend or provide coverage for [two of the actions, the Gruner and Schomer claims]. . . . Prudential relied on the following exclusion clause contained in its policies:

> This insurance does not apply to: (f)(1) "Bodily injury" or "property damage" arising out of the actual, alleged or threatened discharge, dispersal, release or escape of pollutants: (a) [a]t or from premises you own, rent or occupy[.] Pollutants means any solid, liquid, gaseous or thermal irritant or contaminant, including smoke, vapor, soot, fumes, acids, alkalis, chemicals and waste. Waste includes materials to be recycled, reconditioned or reclaimed.

This clause (hereinafter the "pollution exclusion clause") is a standard industry clause used in general commercial liability policies.

. . . .

Plaintiffs now appeal the district court's dismissal of the claims for relief in their complaint relating to the [two] actions.

DISCUSSION

The sole issue on appeal is whether the claims for relief alleged in the [two] actions fall unambiguously within the pollution exclusion clause under New York law. Prudential argues that the district court correctly held that the injuries caused by carbon monoxide poisoning clearly fell within the pollution exclusion clause: there was a "discharge, dispersal, release or escape" of carbon monoxide, a "pollutant," "at or from the premises" owned by Plaintiffs. Plaintiffs, on the other hand, contend that the district court should have considered the purpose of the pollution exclusion clause in determining whether or not the clause was subject to another reasonable interpretation. The purpose of this standard clause, Plaintiffs maintain, is to exclude coverage only for environmental pollution, not damages due to routine commercial hazards such as a faulty heating and ventilation system. We conclude that the pollution exclusion clause at issue is ambiguous as applied to the [two] actions because it is reasonable to interpret that clause as applying only to environmental pollution.

. . . .

An insurer . . . may negate coverage by virtue of an exclusionary clause if the insurer establishes that the clause "is stated in clear and unmistakable language, is subject to no other reasonable interpretation, and applies in the particular case." *Continental Casualty Co. v. Rapid American Corp.*, 80 N.Y.2d 640, 593 N.Y.S.2d 966, 972, 609 N.E.2d 506, 512 (1993). When construing an insurance policy, the tests applied are "common speech" and the "reasonable expectation and purpose of the ordinary businessman." *Ace Wire & Cable Co. v. Aetna Casualty & Surety Co.*, 60 N.Y.2d 390, 469 N.Y.S.2d 655, 658, 457 N.E.2d 761, 764 (1983). Any ambiguity is to be construed against the insurer, particularly when the ambiguity is in an exclusionary clause. An exclusionary clause, moreover, can be ambiguous in one context and not in another.

As a threshold matter, we believe that it is appropriate to construe the standard pollution exclusion clause in light of its general purpose, which is to exclude coverage for environmental pollution. New York courts have consistently considered this purpose in determining whether an insurer is obliged to defend. In *Continental Casualty*, for example, the Court of Appeals considered an insurer's duty to defend actions for personal injuries suffered by assorted contractors who were exposed to asbestos products. The pollution exclusion clause before the court, which differs slightly from the one we now consider, applied to the discharge, dispersal, release, or escape of irritants, contaminants, or pollutants "into or upon land, the atmosphere or any water course or body of water." The court held that the pollution exclusion clause did not apply, stating that the term "atmosphere" was ambiguous as applied to the inhalation of asbestos. *See* 593 N.Y.S.2d at 972 73, 609 N.E.2d at 512 13. The court then noted that "[a]mbiguity is further revealed by examining the purpose of the clause, meant to exclude coverage for environmental pollution." *Id.* at 973, 609 N.E.2d at 513. In addition, the court stated that terms such as "discharge" and "dispersal" were terms of art of environmental law used in reference to injuries caused by "disposal or containment of hazardous waste." *Id.*

Subsequent decisions of New York courts have also construed pollution exclusion clauses as applying only to environmental pollution. For example, in *Karroll v. Atomergic Chemetals Corp.*, 194 A.D.2d 715, 600 N.Y.S.2d 101 (1993), the court held that the pollution exclusion clause did not apply to injuries suffered by a bulldozer operator who was accidentally sprayed with sulfuric acid. In so holding, the court stated that the clause could be "reasonably interpreted to apply only to instances of environmental pollution." *Id.*, 600 N.Y.S.2d at 102.

Prudential claims that *Continental Casualty* is inapplicable because that decision interpreted a different pollution exclusion clause. In contrast, Prudential argues, the clause in this case refers more broadly to the discharge of pollutants at or from the premises owned by the insured. *See Oates v. State of New York*, 157 Misc. 2d 618, 597 N.Y.S.2d 550, 553 (Ct. Cl. 1993) (injuries suffered by child due to insured's negligent failure to remove lead paint from apartment falls within pollution exclusion clause; court notes that "only reasonable interpretation [of clause] is that it 'is just what it purports to be—absolute' ") (citations omitted). We reject this argument.

Although the Court of Appeals in *Continental Casualty* did base its decision in part on the ambiguous term "atmosphere," it also clearly relied on the general purpose of the pollution exclusion clause. Moreover, in its discussion of this purpose, the Court of Appeals relied on two decisions construing pollution exclusion clauses nearly identical to the clause in the case at bar. *See West Am. Ins. Co. v. Tufco Flooring East, Inc.*, 104 N.C. App. 312, 409 S.E.2d 692, 699 (1991) (court concludes that change in language of pollution exclusion clause was not intended "to expand the scope of the clause to non environmental damage" and that "a discharge into the environment is necessary for the clause to be applicable"); *Atlantic Mut. Ins. Co. v. McFadden*, 413 Mass. 90, 595 N.E.2d 762, 764 (1992) ("We conclude that an insured could reasonably have understood the provision at issue to exclude coverage for injury caused by certain forms of industrial pollution, but not coverage for injury allegedly caused by the presence of leaded materials in a private residence.").

Prudential also argues that *Continental Casualty* and the cases Plaintiffs rely upon are distinguishable because the alleged damages in those cases resulted from direct contact with useful products, such as asbestos, chemicals, or lead paint, intentionally placed into areas where they caused harm. By contrast, Prudential argues, carbon monoxide is a toxic byproduct without a useful purpose that unintentionally was released into the Stoney Run Apartments.

Even if several of the cases cited by Plaintiffs do involve so called direct contact with useful products, courts have not focused on this distinction as the basis for their decisions. The issue remains whether the pollution exclusion clause unambiguously includes injuries caused by exposure to carbon monoxide within an apartment. As set forth above, a reasonable interpretation of the pollution exclusion clause is that it applies only to environmental pollution, and not to all contact with substances that can be classified as pollutants. We hold that the release of carbon monoxide into an apartment is not the type of environmental pollution contemplated by the pollution exclusion clause.

An examination of the manner in which other jurisdictions interpret pollution exclusion clauses further bolsters our conclusion that the clause is ambiguous as applied to the facts presented on this appeal. Two courts addressing nearly identical factual situations have deemed pollution exclusion clauses ambiguous. In a recent decision, the United States Court of Appeals for the Tenth Circuit held that a standard pollution exclusion clause did not exclude coverage for injuries tenants sustained due to carbon monoxide emissions from a faulty wall heater. *See Regional Bank of Colo., N.A. v. St. Paul Fire and Marine Ins. Co.*, 35 F.3d 494 (10th Cir. 1994). The court found the exclusion clause ambiguous, reasoning that:

> While a reasonable person of ordinary intelligence might well understand carbon monoxide is a pollutant when it is emitted in an industrial or environmental setting, an ordinary policyholder would not reasonably characterize carbon monoxide emitted from a residential heater which malfunctioned as "pollution." It seems far more reasonable that a policy holder would understand the exclusion as being limited to irritants and contaminants commonly thought of as pollution and not as applying to every possible irritant or contaminant imaginable.

Id. at 498.

Similarly, another court held that a standard pollution exclusion clause did not apply to injuries caused by carbon monoxide emissions from a leaking gas heater in a home. *See Thompson v. Temple*, 580 So. 2d 1133, 1135 (La. Ct. App. 1991) ("intent of the insurance industry in adding pollution exclusion clauses . . . was to exclude coverage for entities which knowingly pollute the environment over a substantial period of time").

We need not decide the precise scope of the pollution exclusion clause contained in Plaintiffs' policies. Instead, we need only determine whether the clause is ambiguous as applied to the facts of this case and subject to no other reasonable interpretation than the one advanced by Prudential. As noted above, the pollution exclusion clause can be reasonably interpreted as applying only to environmental pollution. A reasonable policyholder might not characterize the escape of carbon monoxide from a faulty residential heating and ventilation system as environmental pollution. Accordingly, we find the pollution exclusion clause ambiguous as applied to the [two] actions.

CONCLUSION

Because the pollution exclusion clause is ambiguous as applied to the facts presented, we reverse the judgment of the district court to the extent that it granted Prudential's motion to dismiss the [two] actions. The district court is directed to enter judgment consistent with this opinion.

NOTES AND QUESTIONS

1. *How Absolute Is "Absolute"?* The pollution exclusion at issue in *Stoney Run* is the version found in the 1986 CGL policy form. How does it differ from the "sudden and accidental" pollution exclusion? Is its meaning absolutely clear with respect to environmental damage? Most courts to consider this last question have answered "yes." *See, e.g., United States Liability Insurance Co. v. Bourbeau*, 49 F.3d 786 (1st Cir. 1995); *Park Ohio Industries, Inc. v. Home Indemnity Co.*, 975 F.2d 1215 (6th Cir. 1992); *Western World Insurance Co. v. Stack Oil, Inc.*, 922 F.2d 118 (2d Cir. 1990). What if the environmental damage is the result of a tanker truck carrying toxic materials overturning and spilling? What if a container of toxic materials falls off a truck and spills? *See Red Panther Chemical Co. v. Insurance Co. of State of Pa.*, 43 F.3d 514 (10th Cir. 1994).

2. *Too Broad or Too Specific?* In one sense, the 1986 exclusion is more specific, in that it takes off the table the difficult "sudden and accidental" issue and it gives a seemingly precise list of items that constitute "pollutants." In another sense, the 1986 exclusion is broader because the sum total of items listed in the definition of "pollutants" represents a fairly large slice of the earth and its atmosphere. For example, lots of things can be an "irritant" in a particular context. Because the exclusion seems to pull in different directions simultaneously, courts have not found the exclusion easy to apply in all settings. One court described the situation this way:

> Unfortunately, despite the abundance of opinions construing the exclusion, courts have not reached a clear consensus as to its proper interpretation. This is true even within the fairly rare context of carbon monoxide poisoning. Some courts have construed the exclusion in favor of the insured, holding that the exclusion is vague and ambiguous. . . . Other courts, however, have denied coverage on the grounds that the exclusion is plain an unambiguous. . . . Still other courts have largely ignored the language of the exclusion and have found coverage on the basis of the reasonable expectations of the insured. . . . Meanwhile, courts have also considered the exclusion in the context of other types of 'pollutants.' They, too, have failed to achieve a consistent interpretation of the clause.

American States Insurance Co. v. Koloms, 687 N.E.2d 72, 78 (Ill. 1997). Although the *Koloms* court ultimately came down on the side of coverage in a situation where tenants suffered carbon monoxide poisoning due to a faulty furnace in their building, a number of courts have disagreed with this position.

See, e.g., *Assicurazioni Generali v. Neil*, 160 F.3d 997 (4th Cir. 1998) (applying Maryland law) (no coverage in a case where hotel guests suffered carbon monoxide poisoning); *Longaberger Co. v. United States Fidelity & Guaranty Co.*, 31 F. Supp. 2d 595 (S.D. Ohio 1998), *aff'd*, 201 F.3d 441 (6th Cir. 1999) (table) (no coverage for carbon monoxide poisoning of a tenant); *Essex Insurance Co. v. Tri Town Corp.*, 863 F. Supp. 38 (D. Mass. 1994) (no coverage for injuries from a carbon-monoxide-emitting Zamboni machine at a hockey game); *Bernhardt v. Hartford Fire Insurance Co.*, 648 A.2d 1047 (Md. Ct. App. 1994), *cert. granted* (Md. 1995), *appeal dismissed prior to oral argument*, 659 A.2d 296 (Md. 1996) (no coverage for an injury to tenants from the build-up of carbon monoxide).

Is the kind of liability incurred by the insured in *Stoney Run* the reason the policyholder purchased liability insurance in the first place? Imagine the same exclusion being included in a homeowners policy. Would the policyholder have a reasonable expectation of coverage if she were sued for negligent maintenance of a basement heater that malfunctioned and caused the death due to carbon monoxide poisoning of an overnight visitor? Would you describe this event as "the guest died in an accident" or "the guest was killed by a pollutant?" *See Western Alliance Insurance Co. v. Gill*, 686 N.E.2d 997 (Mass. 1997) (restaurant customer exposed to carbon monoxide fumes released by tandoori ovens at Indian restaurant). Why should the commercial policy be treated differently? Yet, if a policyholder does not like the constriction of coverage required by the strict language of the exclusion, is the policyholder's only recourse to appeal to the legislature, which could be asked to ban the absolute exclusion? Would banning the exclusion be a good idea?

3. *Lead Paint and Other Situations*. Did the court in *Stoney Run* deal with the lead paint cases adequately? Is lead paint contamination distinguishable from carbon monoxide contamination? Courts have divided on the question of whether the chipping, flaking, or deterioration of lead-based paint into dust or fumes is a "discharge, dispersal, release, or escape" within the meaning of the pollution exclusion clause. *See, e.g.*, *Peace v. Northwestern National Insurance Co.*, 596 N.W.2d 429 (Wis. 1999) (no coverage); *United States Liability Insurance Co. v. Bourbeau*, 49 F.3d 786 (1st Cir. 1995) (no coverage); *Byrd v. Blumenreich*, 722 A.2d 598 (N.J. Super. Ct. App. Div. 1999) (absolute pollution exclusion does not bar coverage for child's ingestion of flaking and peeling lead paint chips).

Exposures to carbon monoxide and to lead paint chip dust are two prominent categories of injuries that have prompted debate over the scope of the 1986 pollution exclusion. There are, of course, other examples. *See, e.g.*, *Garfield Slope Housing Corp. v. Public Service Mutual Insurance Co.*, 973 F. Supp. 326 (E.D.N.Y. 1997) (alleged injury due to fumes from new hallway carpet in apartment); *Meridian Mutual Insurance Co. v. Kellman*, 197 F.3d 1178 (6th Cir. 1999) (fumes from toxic chemical used by construction contractor to seal floor of school). Should the pollution exclusion's field of operation be confined to "traditional" environmental damage? Does the text of the absolute pollution exclusion forbid this interpretation?

EXERCISE

1. You are an insurer that sold a CGL policy to a small restaurant owner. The policy contains an "absolute" pollution exclusion that is worded the same as the one in *Stoney Run*. The restaurant has a fire, and several customers sue the restaurant owner claiming they were injured due to smoke inhalation. Draft a 2-page memo denying coverage for the claims and explaining why the "absolute" pollution exclusion should apply to the claims.

5. Business Risk Exclusions

CGL policies contain several exclusions collectively known as "business risk" exclusions even though they do not carry that label in the policies themselves. The basic idea behind such exclusions is that insurers are not the guarantors of the quality of the work, services, or products sold by business owners, as the quality of the work, services, or products sold by a business owner should be the responsibility of the business owner. As is the case with many policy provisions, the application of the "business risk" exclusions is not always straightforward.

Any discussion of the business risk exclusions must start with the seminal case on the issue, *Weedo v. Stone-E-Brick, Inc.*, 405 A.2d 788, 792 (N.J. 1979).[4] In *Weedo*, a subcontractor was hired to pour a concrete floor on a veranda and to apply stucco to the exterior of a home. Soon after the job was completed, cracks in the stucco appeared and "other signs of faulty workmanship" manifested such that the homeowner had to replace the stucco. The homeowner sued the contractor, and the contractor tendered the claim to its CGL insurer. The insurer denied coverage on the basis that CGL policies allegedly do not cover claims for faulty workmanship.

The CGL policy at issue stated that the insurer agreed to pay "on behalf of the insured all sums which the insured shall become legally obligated to pay as damages because of * * * bodily injury * * * or property damage to which this insurance applies, caused by an occurrence * * *." The policy also contained the 1973 standard form business risk exclusions:

> This insurance does not apply:
>
> (n) to property damage to the named insured's products arising out of such products or any part of such products;
>
> (*o*) to property damage to work performed by or on behalf of the named insured arising out of the work or any portion thereof, or out of materials, parts or equipment furnished in connection therewith.

---

[4] The following discussion of the *Weedo* case was taken verbatim from Christopher C. French, *Revisiting Construction Defects as "Occurrences" under CGL Insurance Policies*, 19 U. Pa. J. Bus. L. 101, 117–19 (2016) (citations omitted).

In rejecting the contractor's claim for coverage, the court reasoned:

> Regardless of the existence of express warranties, the insured's provision of stucco and stone "generally carries with it an implied warranty of merchantability and often an implied warranty of fitness for a particular purpose." . . . Where the work performed by the insured-contractor is faulty, either express or implied warranties, or both, are breached. As a matter of contract law the customer did not obtain that for which he bargained . . . . [A] principal justification for imposing warranties by operation of law on contractors is that these parties are often "in a better position to prevent the occurrence of major problems" in the course of constructing a home than is the homeowner . . . . The consequence of not performing well is part of every business venture; the replacement or repair of faulty goods and works is a business expense, to be borne by the insured-contractor in order to satisfy customers.

To support its decision, the court cited to and relied on a 1971 law review article by a law professor at the University of Nebraska, Roger C. Henderson, regarding the changes made in 1966 to the standard CGL policy form with respect to the business risk exclusions for products liability and completed operations. In particular, the court quoted the portion of the article in which Professor Henderson opined:

> The risk intended to be insured is the possibility that the goods, products or work of the insured, once relinquished or completed, will cause bodily injury or damage to property other than to the product or completed work itself, and for which the insured may be found liable.

The court also pointed to the business risk exclusions in the policy at issue in the case and stated that "given the precise and limited form of damages which form the basis of the claims against the insured, either exclusion is, or both are, applicable to exclude coverage. In short, the indemnity sought is not for 'property damage to which this insurance applies.' "

Since *Weedo* was decided, the business risk exclusions have been revised. The next case is one the leading cases that has interpreted and applied the current version of the "business risk" exclusions.

U.S. FIRE INS. CO. V. J.S.U.B., INC.

979 So. 2d 871 (Fla. 2007)

Opinion

J.S.U.B., Inc. seeks review of the decision of the Second District Court of Appeal in *J.S.U.B., Inc. v. United States Fire Insurance Co.*, 906 So.2d 303

(Fla. 2d DCA 2005), which is in express and direct conflict with the decision of the Fourth District Court of Appeal in *Lassiter Construction Co. v. American States Insurance Co.*, 699 So.2d 768 (Fla. 4th DCA 1997). The conflict issue is whether a post-1986 standard form commercial general liability (CGL) policy with products-completed operations hazard coverage, issued to a general contractor, provides coverage when a claim is made against the contractor for damage to the completed project caused by a subcontractor's defective work.

We answer this question in the affirmative. We conclude that defective work performed by a subcontractor that causes damage to the contractor's completed project and is neither expected nor intended from the standpoint of the contractor can constitute "property damage" caused by an "occurrence" as those terms are defined in a standard form commercial general liability policy. Accordingly, a claim made against the contractor for damage to the completed project caused by a subcontractor's defective work is covered under a post-1986 CGL policy unless a specific exclusion applies to bar coverage. In this case, the terms of the policy included an exception to the "Your Work" exclusion for faulty workmanship by a subcontractor and did not include a breach of contract exclusion. We therefore approve the Second District's decision in *J.S.U.B.* and disapprove the Fourth District's decision in *Lassiter*.

Facts and Procedural History

J.S.U.B., Inc., and Logue Enterprises, Inc., as partners of First Home Builders of Florida ("J.S.U.B."), contracted to build several homes in the Lehigh Acres area of Lee County, Florida. After completion and delivery of the homes to the homeowners, damage to the foundations, drywall, and other interior portions of the homes appeared. It is undisputed that the damage to the homes was caused by subcontractors' use of poor soil and improper soil compaction and testing. The homeowners demanded that J.S.U.B. repair or remedy the damages, asserting breach of contract, breach of warranty, negligence, strict liability, and violation of the Florida Building Code.

During the period in which the homes were built, J.S.U.B. was insured under a commercial general liability policy and renewal policy issued by United States Fire Insurance Company ("U.S. Fire"). The policies provide coverage for the "sums that the insured becomes legally obligated to pay as damages because of 'bodily injury' or 'property damage' " caused by an "occurrence" within the "coverage territory" during the policy period. As defined in the policies, an "occurrence" is "an accident, including continuous or repeated exposure to substantially the same general harmful conditions," and "property damage" includes "[p]hysical injury to tangible property, including all resulting loss of use of that property." The policies also contain "products-completed operations hazard" coverage that:

> Includes all "bodily injury" and "property damage" occurring away from premises you own or rent and arising out of "your product" or "your work" except:
>
> . . . . (2) Work that has not yet been completed or abandoned.

The coverage provisions are limited by numerous exclusions. Of particular relevance are those exclusions, with their exceptions, that exclude coverage for damage to the insured's property and work:

> **j. Damage To Property**
>
> "Property damage" to:
>
> . . . .
>
> (5) That particular part of real property on which you or any contractors or subcontractors working directly or indirectly on your behalf are performing operations, if the "property damage" arises out of those operations; or
>
> (6) That particular part of any property that must be restored, repaired or replaced because "your work" was incorrectly performed on it.
>
> . . . .
>
> *Paragraph (6) of this exclusion does not apply to "property damage" included in the "products-completed operations hazard".*
>
> . . . .
>
> ***l.* Damage To Your Work**
>
> "Property damage" to "your work" arising out of it or any part of it and included in the "products-completed operations hazard".
>
> *This exclusion does not apply if the damaged work or the work out of which the damage arises was performed on your behalf by a subcontractor.*

J.S.U.B. sought coverage under the policies for the structural damage to the homes and the damage to the homeowners' personal property. U.S. Fire agreed that the policies provided coverage for damage to the homeowners' personal property, such as the homeowners' wallpaper. However, U.S. Fire asserted that there was no insurance coverage for the costs of repairing the structural damage to the homes, such as the damage to the foundations and drywall.

J.S.U.B. made the necessary repairs to the homes and filed a declaratory judgment action to determine whether coverage existed for the cost of repairing the structural damage. The circuit court entered judgment in favor of U.S. Fire. . . .

J.S.U.B. appealed and the Second District Court of Appeal reversed. . . . The Second District . . . concluded that the policies contained "broad policy language" that provided coverage to J.S.U.B. . . . and that none of the exclusions in the policies applied. *See J.S.U.B.*, 906 So.2d at 309, 311.

Construing a CGL policy similar to those at issue in this case, the Fourth District Court of Appeal came to a contrary conclusion in *Lassiter*. In that case, the contractor argued that because exclusions (j)(6) and (*l*) "do not exclude work performed by subcontractors, there is coverage for the defective work performed by subcontractors." *Lassiter,* 699 So.2d at 770. The Fourth District disagreed, summarily concluding that "[t]he insured has failed to demonstrate that there are any provisions in the coverage section of the policy which would provide coverage for this defective work." *Id.* We accepted jurisdiction to resolve the conflict between *J.S.U.B.* and *Lassiter*.

Analysis

The issue we decide is whether a post-1986 standard form commercial general liability policy with products-completed operations hazard coverage, issued to a general contractor, provides coverage when a claim is made against the contractor for damage to the completed project caused by a subcontractor's defective work. This is an issue of insurance policy construction, which is a question of law subject to de novo review. *See Fayad v. Clarendon Nat'l Ins. Co.*, 899 So.2d 1082, 1085 (Fla.2005).

. . . .

B. The Origin and Evolution of CGL Policies

. . . .

Like the insuring language, the exclusions in standard CGL policies have been modified over the years. *See generally* 21 Holmes, *supra,* § 132.1–132.9, at 5–158. The exclusions that are of significance to our analysis in this case are the "business risk" exclusions, including the "your work" and "your product" exclusions. The 1973 standard CGL policy interpreted in [in earlier cases] contained broad exclusions for damage to "your work" and "your product" stating that the insurance did not apply:

> (n) to property damage to the named insured's products arising out of such products or any part of such products;
>
> (*o*) to property damage to work *performed by or on behalf of the named insured* arising out of the work or any portion thereof, or out of materials, parts or equipment furnished in connection therewith.

390 So.2d at 326, 21 Holmes, *supra,* § 132.1, at 11 (emphasis supplied).

Beginning in 1976, the insured could purchase a Broad Form Property Endorsement. *See Am. Family Mut. Ins. Co. v. Am. Girl, Inc.*, 268 Wis.2d

16, 673 N.W.2d 65, 83 (2004). This endorsement replaced exclusion (*o*), set forth above, and exclusion (k), which excluded damage to property owned by or within the control of the insured. As to exclusion (*o*), the endorsement replaced it with more specific exclusions and also differentiated between property damage that occurred before and after operations were completed. The endorsement provided that the insurance did not apply:

> (d) to that particular part of any property . . .
>
> > (i) upon which operations are being performed by or on behalf of the insured at the time of the property damage arising out of such operations, or
> >
> > (ii) out of which any property damage arises, or
> >
> > (iii) the restoration, repair or replacement of which has been made or is necessary by reason of faulty workmanship thereon by or on behalf of the insured; . . .
>
> (3) *with respect to the completed operations hazard* and with respect to any classification stated in the policy or the company's manual as "including completed operations," to property damage to work *performed by the named insured* arising out of such work or any portion thereof, or out of such materials, parts or equipment furnished in connection therewith.

21 Holmes, *supra,* § 132.9, at 149 (emphasis supplied). Thus, with regard to completed operations, the endorsement eliminated the exclusion for "work performed on behalf of the named insured."

When the CGL policy was revised again in 1986, it contained new provisions that incorporated and clarified the Broad Form Property Endorsement. *See id.* at 149, 153. New exclusion (j)(6) and the exception to this exclusion clearly stated that the exclusion for faulty workmanship did not apply to work within the products-completed operation hazard:

This insurance does not apply to:

> **j. Damage to Property**
>
> "Property damage" to: . . .
>
> (6) That particular part of any property that must be restored, repaired or replaced because "your work" was incorrectly performed on it. . . .
>
> *Paragraph (6) of this exclusion does not apply to "property damage" included in the "products-completed operations hazard."*

Id. at 145, 153 (emphasis supplied). The 1986 policy also added new exclusion (*l*), the "your work exclusion," with an express exception for subcontractor work as follows:

> This insurance does not apply to: . . .
>
> *l.* **Damage To Your Work**
>
> "Property damage" to "your work" arising out of it or any part of it and included in the "products-completed operations hazard."
>
> *This exclusion does not apply if the damaged work or the work out of which the damage arises was performed on your behalf by a subcontractor.*

Id. at 145, 152 (emphasis supplied). The reason for this 1986 revision that added the subcontractor exception has been explained as follows:

> [T]he insurance and policyholder communities agreed that the CGL policy should provide coverage for defective construction claims so long as the allegedly defective work had been performed by a subcontractor rather than the policyholder itself. This resulted both because of the demands of the policyholder community (which wanted this sort of coverage) and the view of insurers that the CGL was a more attractive product that could be better sold if it contained this coverage.

See 2 Jeffrey W. Stempel, *Stempel on Insurance Contracts* § 14.13[D] at 14–224.8 (3d ed. Supp.2007). Moreover, the Insurance Services Office promulgated a circular on July 15, 1986, confirming that the 1986 revisions to the standard CGL policy not only incorporated the "Broad Form" property endorsement but also specifically "cover[ed] damage caused by faulty workmanship to other parts of work in progress; and damage to, or caused by, a subcontractor's work after the insured's operations are completed." Insurance Services Office Circular, Commercial General Liability Program Instructions Pamphlet, No. GL–86–204 (July 15, 1986). Of course, the subcontractor's exception to the general exclusion for a contractor's defective work becomes important only if there is coverage under the initial insuring provision.

. . . .

[Earlier Florida case law regarding "business risk" exclusions] adopted in full the reasoning and analysis of the New Jersey Supreme Court's decision in *Weedo v. Stone-E-Brick, Inc.,* 81 N.J. 233, 405 A.2d 788, 792 (1979), which was based on the same exclusions at issue in *LaMarche;* specifically, the "insured products" (exclusion "(n)") and "work performed" (exclusion "(*o*)") exclusions. The *Weedo* court explained that the insuring provisions "set forth, in fundamental terms, the general outlines of coverage," while "[t]he limitations on coverage are set forth in the exclusion clauses of the policy, whose function it is to restrict and shape the coverage otherwise afforded." *Id.* at 790. The court then noted that the insurer conceded that:

> But for the exclusions in the policy, coverage would obtain. Hence we need not address the validity of one of the carrier's initially-offered grounds of non-coverage, namely, that the policy did not extend coverage for the claims made even absent the exclusions.

Id. at 790 n. 2.

The New Jersey Supreme Court concluded that coverage was lacking, not due to the insuring provisions, but because faulty workmanship by a contractor was specifically excluded based on the clear and unambiguous "business risk" exclusionary clauses. *Id.* at 792–95 (concluding that the language of these "business risk" exclusions was clear and rejecting the argument that these exclusions were rendered ambiguous when read in conjunction with exclusion (a)). Additionally, the Court reinforced that it was looking to the exclusions to determine if coverage existed by stating the principle that "[t]he limitations on coverage are set forth in the exclusion clauses of the policy, whose function it is to restrict and shape the coverage otherwise afforded." *Id.* at 790. Thus, it is clear that [earlier Florida precedent] relied on the exclusions to determine that no coverage existed in that case.

. . . .

We conclude that [earlier Florida precedent] which relied on *Weedo* and involved the issue of whether there was coverage for the contractor's own defective work, was dependent on the policy language of pre-1986 CGL policies, including the relevant insuring provisions and applicable exclusions. The Minnesota Supreme Court, the Tennessee Supreme Court, and the Wisconsin Supreme Court reached the same conclusion regarding prior state court decisions that relied on *Weedo* and interpreted pre-1986 CGL policies. *See Wanzek Constr., Inc. v. Employers Ins. of Wausau*, 679 N.W.2d 322, 327 (Minn.2004); *Moore & Assocs., Inc.*, 216 S.W.3d at 307; *Am. Girl*, 673 N.W.2d at 77.

. . . .

[W]here the policies and underlying facts are different, then a previous decision should not be binding. We recognized this principle in *Travelers Indemnity Co. v. PCR, Inc.*, 889 So.2d 779, 791 n. 13 (Fla. 2004) (questioning the applicability of a previous decision's definition of a policy term in a subsequent case where the exclusionary clauses were materially different).

. . . .

D. *Whether Faulty Workmanship Can Constitute an "Occurrence"*

The question of whether faulty workmanship can constitute an "occurrence" is a matter governed by the actual terms of the policy and Florida law interpreting insurance contracts. The policy and renewal policy in this case define an "occurrence" as an "accident" but leave "accident" undefined. Thus, under our decision in *CTC Development,* these policies provide coverage not only for " 'accidental events,' but also injuries or damage neither expected nor intended from the standpoint of the insured." 720 So.2d at 1076.

U.S. Fire nevertheless argues that a subcontractor's faulty workmanship that damages the contractor's own work can never be an "accident" because it results in reasonably foreseeable damages. We expressly rejected the use of the concept of "natural and probable consequences" or "foreseeability" in insurance contract interpretation in *CTC Development* when we receded from prior case law. *See id.* at 1074–77.

Further, we fail to see how defective work that results in a claim against the contractor because of injury to a third party or damage to a third party's property is "unforeseeable," while the same defective work that results in a claim against the contractor because of damage to the completed project is "foreseeable." This distinction would make the definition of "occurrence" dependent on which property was damaged. For example, applying U.S. Fire's interpretation in this case would make the subcontractor's improper soil compaction and testing an "occurrence" when it damages the homeowners' personal property, such as the wallpaper, but not an "occurrence" when it damages the homeowners' foundations and drywall. As the Tennessee Supreme Court explained, in rejecting this distinction:

> A shingle falling and injuring a person is a natural consequence of an improperly installed shingle just as water damage is a natural consequence of an improperly installed window. If we assume that either the shingle or the window installation will be completed negligently, it is foreseeable that damages will result. If, however, we assume that the installation of both the shingle and the window will be completed properly, then neither the falling shingle nor the water penetration is foreseeable and both events are "accidents." Assuming that the windows would be installed properly, Moore could not have foreseen the water penetration. Because we conclude the water penetration was an event that was unforeseeable to Moore, the alleged water penetration is both an "accident" and an "occurrence" for which there is coverage under the "insuring agreement."

Moore & Assocs., 216 S.W.3d at 309.

We also conclude that U.S. Fire's argument that a breach of contract can never result in an "accident" is not supported by the plain language of the policies. The Wisconsin Supreme Court came to the same conclusion in *American Girl*:

> [T]here is nothing in the basic coverage language of the current CGL policy to support any definitive tort/contract line of

> demarcation for purposes of determining whether a loss is covered by the CGL's initial grant of coverage. "Occurrence" is not defined by reference to the legal category of the claim. The term "tort" does not appear in the CGL policy.

673 N.W.2d at 77. The Kansas Supreme Court followed *American Girl's* reasoning in holding that a subcontractor's defective work can constitute an "occurrence" under Kansas law. *See Lee Builders, Inc. v. Farm Bureau Mut. Ins. Co.*, 281 Kan. 844, 137 P.3d 486, 491 (2006).

If U.S. Fire intended to preclude coverage based on the cause of action asserted, it was incumbent on U.S. Fire to include clear language to accomplish this result. *See Container Corp. of Am. v. Maryland Cas. Co.*, 707 So.2d 733, 736 (Fla.1998) ("Had Maryland wished to limit Container's coverage to vicarious liability, it could have done so by clear policy language."). In fact, there is a breach of contract endorsement exclusion, not present in the CGL policies at issue in this case, that excludes coverage for breach of contract claims. *See B. Hall Contracting Inc. v. Evanston Ins. Co.*, 447 F.Supp.2d 634, 639 (N.D.Tex.2006). The endorsement provides:

> This insurance does not apply to claims for breach of contract, whether express or oral, nor claims for breach of an implied in law or implied in fact contract, whether "bodily injury," "property damage," "advertising injury," "personal injury" or an "occurrence" or damages of any type is alleged; this exclusion also applies to any additional insureds under this policy.

Id.

Furthermore, ISO has begun to issue an endorsement that may be included in a CGL policy, which entirely eliminates the subcontractor exception to the "your work" exclusion. *See* ISO Properties, Inc., Endorsement CG 22 94 10 01, http://www.lexis.com; *see also Lamar Homes, Inc. v. Mid-Continent Cas. Co.*, 242 S.W.3d 1, 12 (Tex.2007) ("More recently, the Insurance Services Office has issued an endorsement that may be included in the CGL to eliminate the subcontractor exception to the 'your work' exclusion."). The fact that these additional endorsements may be included in CGL policies highlights that the ultimate analysis is governed by the actual language contained in the applicable insurance contract.

U.S. Fire's assertion that damage resulting from a breach of contract must be presumed to be expected is also unpersuasive. As with U.S. Fire's foreseeability argument, this position makes the definition of "occurrence" dependent on whether the property damaged is part of the construction contract or the homeowner's separate property. Under *CTC Development,* the appropriate consideration is whether the damage was expected or intended from the standpoint of the insured, not whose property was damaged. 720 So.2d at 1076; *see also Lamar Homes*, 242 S.W.3d at 9 ("The CGL policy, however, does not define an 'occurrence' in terms of the ownership or character of the property damaged by the act or event. Rather, the policy asks whether the injury was intended or fortuitous, that is, whether the injury was an accident."). As the amici Florida Home Builders Association and National Association of Home Builders assert in arguing that CGL policies issued to their members do not distinguish between the property damaged for purposes of defining "occurrence:"

> If a defective masonry wall falls outward and damages a parked car, no one disputes the "occurrence" of "property damage," but if it falls inward and damages the floor, the insurers label that a non-occurrence or not property damage. Likewise, if the wall falls the day before the home buyer resells to a new owner, they contend it is not covered as a contract claim, but if it falls the day after resale, it is covered as a tort claim.

In sum, we reject a definition of "occurrence" that renders damage to the insured's own work as a result of a subcontractor's faulty workmanship expected, but renders damage to property of a third party caused by the same faulty workmanship unexpected. There is simply nothing in the definition of the term "occurrence" that limits coverage in the manner advanced by U.S. Fire, and we decline to read the broad "business risk" exclusions at issue in [earlier precedent] into the definition of "occurrence" used in the coverage provisions of the post-1986 standard CGL policies at issue in this case. We agree with the Wisconsin Supreme Court's observation that:

> CGL policies generally do not cover contract claims arising out of the insured's defective work or product, but this is by operation of the CGL's business risk exclusions, not because a loss actionable only in contract can never be the result of an "occurrence" within the meaning of the CGL's initial grant of coverage. This distinction is sometimes overlooked, and has resulted in some regrettably overbroad generalizations about CGL policies in our case law.

Am. Girl, 673 N.W.2d at 76; *accord Moore & Assocs.*, 216 S.W.3d at 307 (agreeing with *American Girl* that "[r]eliance upon a CGL's 'exclusions' to determine the meaning of 'occurrence' has resulted in 'regrettably overbroad generalizations' concerning CGLs").

. . . .

Even if there was any ambiguity in the policies as to whether a subcontractor's faulty workmanship can constitute an "occurrence," we would interpret the ambiguity against the insurer and in favor of coverage. *See Taurus Holdings*, 913 So.2d at 532. In addition, our interpretation of the term "occurrence" is guided by a view of the policy as a whole. *See Anderson*, 756 So.2d at 34. As we explained in *CTC Development,* "[a]lthough exclusionary clauses cannot be relied upon to create coverage, principles governing the construction of insurance contracts dictate that when construing an insurance policy to determine coverage the pertinent provisions should be read *in pari materia*." 720 So.2d at 1074–75 (citations, alteration, and internal quotation marks omitted).

In this case, if the insuring provisions do not confer an initial grant of coverage for faulty workmanship, there would be no reason for U.S. Fire to exclude damage to "your work:"

> If . . . losses actionable in contract are never CGL "occurrences" for purposes of the initial coverage grant, then the business risk exclusions are entirely unnecessary. The business risk exclusions eliminate coverage for liability for property damage to the insured's own work or product-liability that is typically actionable between the parties pursuant to the terms of their contract, not in tort. If the insuring agreement never confers coverage for this type of liability as an original definitional matter, then there is no need to specifically exclude it. Why would the insurance industry exclude damage to the insured's own work or product if the damage could never be considered to have arisen from a covered "occurrence" in the first place?

Am. Girl, 673 N.W.2d at 78; *accord Lamar Homes, Inc.*, 242 S.W.3d at 12 ("By incorporating the subcontractor exception into the 'your-work' exclusion, the insurance industry specifically contemplated coverage for property damage caused by a subcontractor's defective performance.")

In addition, a construction of the insuring agreement that precludes recovery for damage caused to the completed project by the subcontractor's defective work renders the "products-completed operations hazard" exception to exclusion (j)(6) and the subcontractor exception to exclusion (*l*) meaningless. *See Lee Builders*, 137 P.3d at 494 (stating that "the 'Damage to Your Work' business risk exclusion in the CGL policy in the instant case supports the determination of an occurrence" because "[i]f there can be no occurrence, the exclusion—and its exception—appear to be superfluous"); *Lennar Corp. v. Great Am. Ins. Co.,* 200 S.W.3d 651, 673 (Tex.App.2006) ("[F]inding no occurrence for defective construction resulting in damage to the insured's work would render the subcontractor exception superfluous and meaningless."), *petition for review filed,* No. 06–287 (Tex. May 11, 2006). Paragraph (j)(6) specifically excludes from coverage that "particular part of any property that must be restored, repaired or replaced because 'your work' was incorrectly performed on it." However, the policy goes on to provide an exception by stating that "[p]aragraph (6) of this exclusion does not apply to 'property damage' included in the 'products-completed operations hazard.' " Exclusion (*l*) excludes damage to " 'your work' arising out of it or any part of it and included in the 'products-completed operations-hazard' " but then provides an exception that states that this "exclusion *does not apply* if the damaged work or the work out of which the damage arises was performed on your behalf by a subcontractor." (Emphasis supplied.) We simply cannot ignore the exception that has now been incorporated into exclusion (*l*), an exception that clearly applies to damages to the insured's own work arising out of the work of a subcontractor. Reading these provisions *in pari materia* with the insuring agreement supports the conclusion that a subcontractor's defective work that results in damage to the completed project can constitute an "occurrence."

Finally, we reject U.S. Fire's contention that construing the term "occurrence" to include a subcontractor's defective work converts the policies into performance bonds. "The purpose of a performance bond is to guarantee the completion of the contract upon default by the contractor." *Am. Home Assur. Co. v. Larkin Gen. Hosp., Ltd.*, 593 So.2d 195, 198 (Fla.1992). Thus, unlike an insurance policy, a performance bond benefits the owner of a project rather than the contractor. *Cf. School Bd. of Palm Beach County v. Vincent J. Fasano, Inc.*, 417 So.2d 1063, 1065 n. 3 (Fla. 4th DCA 1982) ("On private construction projects performance bonds are usually secured for the benefit of the owner. . . ."). Further, a surety, unlike a liability insurer, is entitled to indemnification from the contractor. *See Western World Ins. Co. v. Travelers Indem. Co.*, 358 So.2d 602, 604 (Fla. 1st DCA 1978); *see also Fidelity & Deposit Co. of Md. v. Hartford Cas. Ins. Co.*, 189 F.Supp.2d 1212, 1218 (D.Kan.2002) (rejecting the argument that "if the structural damage caused by faulty workmanship constitutes an 'occurrence,' then the CGL and umbrella policies will be transformed into a performance bond" because the bond "in no way" protected the contractor or subcontractor from liability).

The Texas Court of Appeals explained the salient differences between a liability policy and a performance bond:

> [A]lthough defective construction may constitute an "occurrence," the insurer indemnifies the insured only for resulting "property damage" arising after the project is completed. In contrast, a performance bond is broader than a CGL policy in that it guarantees "the completion of a construction contract upon the default of the general contractor." Therefore, a "variety of deficiencies that do not constitute 'property damage' may be covered by a performance bond, and not all deficiencies cause additional property damage." Consequently, allowing coverage for some "property damage" resulting from defective construction does not transform a CGL policy into a performance bond and require a CGL carrier to pay anytime an insured fails to complete, or otherwise comply with, its contract.

Lennar Corp., 200 S.W.3d at 673–74 (footnote and citations omitted) (quoting *Black's Law Dictionary* 1158 (7th ed.1999) and *O'Shaughnessy v. Smuckler Corp.*, 543 N.W.2d 99, 105 (Minn.Ct.App.1996)); *accord Lamar Homes, Inc.*, 242 S.W.3d at 10 & n. 7 ("[T]he protection afforded by a performance bond is, in fact, different from that provided by [a] CGL insurance policy. . . . [A]n insurance policy spreads the contractor's risk while a bond guarantees its performance. An insurance policy is issued based on an evaluation of risks and losses that is actuarially linked to premiums; that is, losses are expected. In contrast, a surety bond is underwritten based on what amounts to a credit evaluation of the particular contractor and its capabilities to perform its contracts, with the expectation that no losses will occur. Unlike insurance, the performance bond offers no indemnity for the contractor; it protects only the owner."). . . .

We hold that faulty workmanship that is neither intended nor expected from the standpoint of the contractor can constitute an "accident" and, thus, an "occurrence" under a post-1986 CGL policy. In this case, we conclude that the subcontractors' defective soil preparation, which J.S.U.B. did not intend or expect, was an "occurrence." However, in order to determine whether the policies provide coverage for J.S.U.B.'s losses, we must next address whether the "occurrence" caused "property damage" within the meaning of the policies.

E. Whether the Subcontractors' Improper Soil Preparation Caused "Property Damage"

The CGL policies define "property damage" as "[p]hysical injury to tangible property, including all resulting loss of use of that property." U.S. Fire and the amici that argue in favor of its position assert that faulty workmanship that injures only the work product itself does not result in "property damage." However, just like the definition of the term "occurrence," the definition of "property damage" in the CGL policies does not differentiate between damage to the contractor's work and damage to other property.

We further reject U.S. Fire's contention that there can never be "property damage" in cases of faulty construction because the defective work rendered the entire project damaged from its inception. To the contrary, faulty workmanship or defective work that has damaged the otherwise nondefective completed project has caused "physical injury to tangible property" within the plain meaning of the definition in the policy. If there is no damage beyond the faulty workmanship or defective work, then there may be no resulting "property damage."

. . . .

Other courts have also recognized that there is a difference between a claim for the costs of repairing or removing defective work, which is not a claim for "property damage," and a claim for the costs of repairing damage caused by the defective work, which is a claim for "property damage." *See, e.g., Cincinnati Ins. Co. v. Venetian Terrazzo, Inc.*, 198 F.Supp.2d 1074, 1079 n. 1 (E.D.Mo.2001) (concluding that costs of repair and replacement of an improperly installed floor was not covered "property damage"); *Lennar Corp.*, 200 S.W.3d at 679–80 (distinguishing between costs to remove and replace defective stucco as a preventative measure, which were not "damages because of . . . property damage," and the costs to repair water damage that resulted from the application of the defective stucco, which were "damages because of . . . property damage"). As the Supreme Court of Tennessee explained:

> [A] "claim limited to faulty workmanship or materials" is one in which the sole damages are for replacement of a defective component or correction of faulty installation.
>
> We conclude that Hilcom's claim is not limited to faulty workmanship and does in fact allege "property damage." Moore's subcontractor allegedly installed the windows defectively. Without more, this alleged defect is the equivalent of the "mere inclusion of a defective component" such as the installation of a defective tire, and no "property damage" has occurred. The alleged water penetration is analogous to the automobile accident that is caused by the faulty tire. Because the alleged defective installation resulted in water penetration causing further damage, Hilcom has alleged "property damage." Therefore, we conclude that Hilcom has alleged damages that constitute "property damage" for purposes of the CGL.

Moore & Assocs., 216 S.W.3d at 310; *see also Am. Girl*, 673 N.W.2d at 74–75 ("The sinking, buckling, and cracking of the [warehouse] as a result of soil settlement qualifies as 'physical injury to tangible property.' ").

Like the Tennessee case, *Moore & Assocs.*, and the Wisconsin case, *American Girl*, this case does not involve a claim for the cost of repairing the subcontractor's defective work, but rather a claim for repairing the structural damage to the completed homes caused by the subcontractor's defective work. Specifically, it was the subsequent soil settlement due to the subcontractor's faulty workmanship that caused the structural damage to the homes. Because there was "physical injury to tangible property," we conclude that the structural damage to the homes is "property damage" within the meaning of the policies.

In reaching this conclusion, we discern no public policy reason for precluding coverage. A subcontractor's defective work that is neither intended nor expected from the standpoint of the insured is not the type of intentional wrongful act that we have held was uninsurable as a matter of public policy. *See Ranger Ins. Co. v. Bal Harbour Club, Inc.*, 549 So.2d 1005, 1009 (Fla.1989) (holding that public policy prohibits the insured from being indemnified for a loss resulting from intentional employment discrimination). Even if a "moral hazard" argument could be made regarding the contractor's own work, the argument is not applicable for the subcontractors' work:

> Providing coverage for claims arising out of the subcontractor work also made sense in terms of meeting the moral hazard and adverse selection problems associated with faulty workmanship claims. Although it may be unwise to provide liability coverage for a builder directing its own crews, who may be tempted to cut corners if insured, the same rationale did not as readily apply to modern construction that depends heavily on subcontractors on whom general contractors depend. . . . Particularly if the subcontractor does soil, concrete, or framing work, it is as a practical matter very difficult for the general contractor to control the quality of the subcontractor work. Only if the contractor has a supervisor at the elbow of each subcontractor at all times can quality control be relatively assured—but this would be prohibitively expensive. Because the general contractor depends on the subcontractor to a large degree, the general contractor is not tempted by moral hazard to the degree that makes the consequences of faulty subcontractor work more expensive to insure.

Stempel, *supra,* § 14.13[D], at 14–224.8. Further, the argument that indemnity will create a windfall for the contractor is speculative. As the amici point out, the contractor gains nothing if insurance reimburses the costs of repairing the damage caused by the defective work. Moreover, if the insurer decides that this is a risk it does not want to insure, it can clearly amend the policy to exclude coverage, as can be done simply by either eliminating the subcontractor exception or adding a breach of contract exclusion.

Conclusion

We conclude that faulty workmanship that is neither intended nor expected from the standpoint of the contractor can constitute an "accident" and thus an "occurrence" under a post-1986 standard form CGL policy. We further conclude that physical injury to the completed project that occurs as a result of the defective work can constitute "property damage" as defined in a CGL policy. Accordingly, we hold that a post-1986 standard form commercial general liability policy with products completed-operations hazard coverage, issued to a general contractor, provides coverage for a claim made against the contractor for damage to the completed project caused by a subcontractor's defective work provided that there is no specific exclusion that otherwise excludes coverage. In so holding, we distinguish but do not recede from *LaMarche* because that case concluded, based on the policy exclusions, that there was no coverage under a pre-1986 CGL policy for the repair and replacement of the contractor's own defective work.

In this case, because there are no exclusions that bar coverage, we agree with the Second District's conclusion that the CGL policies issued by U.S. Fire to J.S.U.B. provide coverage for the costs to replace the homeowner's personal property, such as their wallpaper, as well as the costs to repair the structural damage to the homes, such as the walls, both of which were caused by the subcontractors' improper soil preparation. Accordingly, we approve the Second District's decision in *J.S.U.B.* and disapprove the Fourth District's decision in *Lassiter* to the extent that it held that CGL policies can never provide coverage for a claim made against the contractor for damage to the completed project caused by a subcontractor's faulty workmanship.

It is so ordered.

NOTES AND QUESTIONS

1. *Tort Versus Contract Claims.* Conventional wisdom says CGL policies only cover tort claims. Is the conventional wisdom correct? If not, why not?

2. *"Property Damage."* Does the definition of "property damage" make any distinctions between damage to the contractor's work versus damage to other property?

3. *What Was Injured or Damaged?* One of the central questions to consider when determining the applicability of business risk exclusions is: "What was injured or damaged?" When the answer is that the only injury or damage is the defective workmanship or product itself, most courts hold there is no coverage. *See, e.g., Town & Country Prop., LLC v. Amerisure Ins. Co.*, 111 So. 3d 699 (Ala. 2011) (holding that damage to property separate from the faulty workmanship itself is covered but not the faulty work itself); *Shane Traylor, LLC v. Am. Res. Ins. Co.*, 126 So. 3d 163 (Ala. 2013) (same); *Owners Ins. Co. v. Jim Carr Homebuilder, LLC*, 157 So. 3d 148 (Ala. 2014) (same); *Capstone Bldg Corp. v. Am. Motorists Ins. Co.*, 67 A.3d 961 (Conn. 2013) (same). As a practical matter, however, it often is not possible to repair damage caused by defective workmanship without also repairing the defective workmanship itself.

4. *Weedo Is Dead.* On August 4, 2016, the New Jersey Supreme Court effectively overruled *Weedo* in *Cypress Point Condominium Assoc. v. Adria Towers, LLC*, 143 A.3d 273 (N.J. 2016).[5] In reaching its holding, the court noted there were a number of differences between the 1973 CGL policy form at issue in *Weedo* and the policy form at issue in the case before it, including the

[5] This Note was taken almost verbatim from Christopher C. French, *Revisiting Construction Defects as "Occurrences" under CGL Insurance Policies*, 19 U. Pa. J. Bus. L. 101, 120–21 (2016) (citations omitted).

subcontractor exception to the business risk exclusions, which the New Jersey Supreme Court previously had not considered. The court also noted that the *Weedo* court had not addressed the issues of whether construction defects could constitute "occurrences" or cause "property damage" because the *Weedo* court based its ruling on the 1973 business risk exclusions that were replaced in 1986. The court also reviewed the existing non-New Jersey case law on the issues, which "represent 'a strong recent trend in the case law [of most federal circuit and state courts] interpet[ing] the term "occurrence" to encompass unanticipated damage to nondefective property resulting from poor workmanship.' " *Id.* at 285. The court then concluded that damage caused by defective workmanship is "property damage":

> [P]ost-construction consequential damages resulted in loss of use of the affected areas by [the] residents and, we hold, qualify as "[p]hysical injury to tangible property including all resulting loss of use of that property." Therefore, on the record before us, the consequential damages to [the residents] were covered "property damage" under the terms of the policies.

Id. at 286. With respect to the issue of whether construction defects could be "occurrences," the court concluded:

> [T]he insurers' argument fails to recognize that Weedo and its progeny were decided based upon exclusions contained within the pre-1986 CGL policy, rather than an interpretation of the policy's terms granting coverage in the first instance . . . . In any event, under our interpretation of the term "occurrence" in the policies, consequential harm caused by negligent work is an "accident." Therefore, because the result of the subcontractors' faulty workmanship here—consequential water damage to the completed and nondefective portions of Cypress Point—was an "accident," it is an "occurrence" under the policies and is therefore covered so long as the other parameters set by the policies are met.

Id. at 288–89.

5. *The New Majority Rule. J.S.U.B.* represents the emerging majority rule on the issue of whether construction defects can be covered by CGL policies. As of 2020, the supreme courts of twenty states have held that construction defects can constitute occurrences and be covered under CGL policies despite the presence of "business risk" exclusions where a subcontractor did the work at issue. Most of these states have adopted the rule set forth in Note 3, which allows coverage for the damage caused by the defective workmanship, but not for the defective workmanship itself. Four additional states—Arkansas, Colorado, Hawaii, and South Carolina—have passed statutes that effectively provide that construction defects are occurrences. As of 2020, under existing state supreme court precedent, there are only three states—Kentucky, Ohio, and Pennsylvania—in which construction defects generally cannot be "occurrences" under CGL policies. *See* Christopher C. French, *Revisiting Construction Defects as "Occurrences" under*

CGL Insurance Policies, 19 U. Pa. J. Bus. L. 101, 123–26 (2016) (citing cases and statutes); *Ohio Northern University v. Charles Construction Services, Inc.*, 120 N.E. 3d 762 (Ohio 2018); *see also* Christopher C. French, *Construction Defects: Are They "Occurrences"?*, 47 Gonz. L. Rev. 1, 32–34 (2012).

6. *Performance Bonds and CGL Insurance.* As noted by the *J.S.U.B.* court, performance bonds and CGL policies have different functions and insure different entities. Performance bonds ensure that the property owner will receive a completed project. CGL insurance protects the contractor from liabilities. Also, under performance bonds, the surety has an indemnification right against the contractor and a subrogation claim against the contractor, while an insurer does not have an indemnification right, or a subrogation claim, against the contractor.

SOKOL AND CO. V. ATLANTIC MUT. INS. CO.

430 F.3d 417 (7th Cir. 2005)

Opinion

SYKES, CIRCUIT JUDGE.

This is an insurance coverage dispute involving spoiled peanut butter. The peanut butter in question was contained in sealed packets supplied by plaintiff Sokol and Company ("Sokol") to its customer Continental Mills ("Continental") for inclusion in boxes of Continental's cookie mix. When Continental discovered that the peanut butter had gone bad, it retrieved the cookie mix, substituted fresh peanut butter packets, and sought reimbursement from Sokol for the costs associated with the replacement. Sokol filed notice of Continental's claim with Atlantic Mutual Insurance Company ("Atlantic"), its Comprehensive General Liability ("CGL") insurer. Atlantic denied coverage, citing a number of the policy's "business risk" exclusions. Sokol then paid Continental's claim itself and sought indemnification from Atlantic under the policy. Atlantic again denied coverage and this litigation ensued.

The district court granted summary judgment for Atlantic, holding that the insurer had no duty to defend under the policy. . . . We affirm. . . . The claim at issue here does not involve "property damage" within the meaning of the policy, and even if it did, coverage is excluded under certain of the policy's "business risk" exclusions. Summary judgment in favor of the insurer was therefore appropriate.

I. Background

Sokol is an Illinois food products manufacturer that supplied sealed packets of peanut butter paste to Continental for inclusion in boxes of Continental's cookie mix. In late August 2001 Sokol sent a shipment of peanut butter paste to Continental. In October 2001, after the paste packets were incorporated into the cookie mix boxes and shipped to customers-but before, it seems, any cookie mix was sold to the consuming public-Continental discovered that the peanut butter was rancid. (Sokol denied the peanut butter was rancid, asserting it was simply "off taste," but this disagreement is irrelevant to the present appeal.) Continental retrieved all of the affected boxes, removed the packets of spoiled peanut butter, and substituted new paste that it acquired from a different vendor. In November 2001 Continental demanded payment from Sokol for these costs. Sokol notified Atlantic, its CGL insurer, of Continental's claim, requesting a defense and indemnification. Sokol sent Atlantic a preliminary claim summary indicating that Continental's loss was $61,910 but that additional expenses would likely accrue. Indeed, Continental eventually sought payment from Sokol in the amount of $75,441.20.

In letters to Sokol dated April 5, 2002, and June 10, 2002, Atlantic took the position that while Continental's claim amounted to "property damage" caused by "an occurrence" under the policy's main Insuring Agreement, coverage was excluded by certain of the "business risk" exclusions in the policy. Atlantic reserved its right to rely on other policy provisions or exclusions and expressly stated it was not waiving its rights or obligations under the policy. Sokol then paid Continental's demand in full and filed a claim for indemnification with Atlantic. Atlantic again declined coverage.

Sokol then sued Atlantic in Cook County Circuit Court. Atlantic, a New York corporation, removed the case to district court; shortly thereafter the parties filed cross-motions for summary judgment. The district court granted summary judgment for Atlantic. . . . Sokol appealed.

II. Discussion

. . . .

B. Indemnification Coverage Under Insuring Agreement

. . . . The policy provides that Atlantic "will pay those sums that the insured becomes legally obligated to pay as damages because of 'bodily injury' or 'property damage' to which this insurance applies." The question of indemnification coverage thus turns on whether the payment Sokol made to Continental qualifies as a sum that Sokol became "legally obligated to pay as damages because of 'bodily injury' or 'property damage.' "

The spoiled peanut butter did not cause "bodily injury" to anyone; only "property damage" is potentially implicated here. The policy defines "property damage" as:

> a. Physical injury to tangible property, including all resulting loss of use of that property. All such loss of use shall be deemed to occur at the time of the physical injury that caused it; or

b. Loss of use of tangible property that is not physically injured. All such loss of use shall be deemed to occur at the time of the "occurrence" that caused it.

Sokol's peanut butter paste, whether rancid or merely "off taste," did not cause "physical injury to tangible property." The paste was sealed in individual packets, and those packets were simply removed from the boxes of cookie mix. There has been no allegation that the spoilage of the peanut butter affected the other food products contained within the boxes. Sokol suggests weakly that when Continental opened the boxes to remove and replace the spoiled paste, the opening itself constituted "property damage" within the meaning of the policy. The act of opening and resealing cookie mix boxes can scarcely be characterized as an "injury" to the boxes.

At oral argument Sokol also suggested that Continental's claim represents a "loss of use" of the cookie mix boxes. The policy defines "property damage" to include the loss of use of tangible property, even if the property is not physically injured. The delay in getting the cookie mix to market, Sokol argues, constitutes a "loss of use" under the policy definition and is therefore within the scope of the coverage grant. But nothing in the record bears this out. The itemized list of expenses that Continental sent to Sokol includes costs for the peanut butter packets, as well as shipping, storage, and handling, and "third-party reconditioning fees." These are not "loss of use" costs; they are costs incurred in swapping Sokol's spoiled peanut butter for fresh substitute.

Because Sokol's payment to Continental was not a sum Sokol was legally obligated to pay for "property damage" as that term is defined in policy, Atlantic had no duty to indemnify Sokol.

C. Exclusions to Coverage

Even if Sokol's payment to Continental could be characterized as one for "property damage," two of the policy's exclusions would operate to preclude coverage. Atlantic bears the burden of establishing that Sokol's claim falls within a provision that limits or excludes coverage.

1. Exclusion m: Damage to Impaired Property

In its letters denying coverage, Atlantic invoked the exclusion for damage to "impaired property," one of the so-called "business risk" exclusions that are standard fare in contemporary CGL policies. Exclusion m states in full:

> This insurance does not apply to:
>
> "Property damage" to "impaired property" or property that has not been physically injured, arising out of:
>
> (1) A defect, deficiency, inadequacy or dangerous condition in "your product" or "your work"; or

(2) A delay or failure by you or anyone acting on your behalf to perform a contract or agreement in accordance with its terms.

This exclusion does not apply to the loss of use of other property arising out of sudden and accidental physical injury to "your product" or "your work" after it has been put to its intended use.

The term "impaired property" is defined in the policy as:

[T]angible property, other than "your product" or "your work", that cannot be used or is less useful because:

a. It incorporates "your product" or "your work" that is known or thought to be defective, deficient, inadequate or dangerous; or

b. You have failed to fulfill the terms of a contract or agreement;

if such property can be restored to use by:

a. The repair, replacement, adjustment or removal of "your product" or "your work"; or

b. Your fulfilling the terms of the contract or agreement.

Sokol's peanut butter paste is "your product" under the terms of the policy, and this product was incorporated into property "other than your product," that is, Continental's cookie mix. It is undisputed that the paste became defective, deficient, or inadequate. Sokol's payment of Continental's claim thus falls within the "impaired property" exclusion under the terms of the policy.

Sokol argues that if Exclusion m applies to this claim, coverage is restored by an exception to the exclusion for "loss of use of other property arising out of sudden and accidental physical injury to 'your product' or 'your work' after it has been put to its intended use." We do not agree. First, as we have noted, Continental's claim was not one for "loss of use" of impaired property. In addition, the exception to Exclusion m applies only to "sudden and accidental" injuries to property. From the record it is not clear exactly when or how the peanut butter paste went bad. Sokol insists it was good when it left the plant in late August 2001; Continental discovered the problem in October 2001. These facts are consistent with the gradual deterioration of a food product. Whether or not the rancidity or bad taste was "accidental" (we express no opinion on that), the situation appears anything but sudden. Sokol cannot survive summary judgment merely by averring that the paste went bad suddenly and accidentally. And that is all Sokol does. The exception to the "impaired property" exclusion does not apply here.

2. Exclusion n: Recall of Products, Work or Impaired Property

Atlantic also invoked Exclusion n, which states in full:

> This insurance does not apply to:
>
> Damages claimed for any loss, cost or expense incurred by you or others for the loss of use, withdrawal, recall, inspection, repair, replacement, adjustment, removal or disposal of:
>
> (1) "Your product";
>
> (2) "Your work"; or
>
> (3) "Impaired property";
>
> if such product, work, or property is withdrawn or recalled from the market or from use by any person or organization because of a known or suspected defect, deficiency, inadequacy or dangerous condition in it.

Exclusion n applies straightforwardly to the facts of this case. As we have noted, Sokol's peanut butter paste qualifies as "your product" under the policy. The peanut butter was withdrawn from the market, replaced, and disposed of after Continental discovered it was rancid or "off taste," an obvious "inadequacy" (if not worse). Even if the Insuring Agreement provided coverage here, Exclusion n applies to knock it out.

D. Other Coverage Issues

1. Products-Completed Operations Hazard

Sokol argues that its payment to Continental was covered under the policy's Products-Completed Operations Hazard. This provision is one of the policy's defined terms rather than a separate grant of coverage. It does not operate to provide coverage that is not otherwise extended by the policy. By virtue of references to the Products-Completed Operations Hazard definition, the policy's underlying coverage for "bodily injury" and "property damage" is extended to include occurrences that take place off the premises of the insured. Although Sokol's peanut butter paste may have gone bad after it left Sokol's premises, the absence of "property damage" within the meaning of the policy precludes coverage here.

2. Product Recall Expense Endorsement

Sokol contends that its payment is covered under the Product Recall Expense Endorsement, a separate rider that operates to modify Exclusion n (Recall of Products, Work or Impaired Property). The Endorsement extends coverage to "Covered Recalls," which are defined as "recall[s] made necessary because the insured or a government body has determined that a known or suspected defect, deficiency, inadequacy or dangerous condition in 'your product' has resulted in or will result in 'bodily injury' or 'property damage.' "

By its terms, this endorsement is limited to recalls initiated by "the insured or a government body." Here, *Continental*-not Sokol or the government-initiated the removal and replacement of the peanut butter paste. Accordingly, the Product Recall Expense Endorsement does not supply coverage.

For the foregoing reasons, the decision of the district court is AFFIRMED.

NOTES AND QUESTIONS

1. *Continuing Vitality of "Business Risk" Exclusions.* As the *Sokol* case reveals, the "business risk" exclusions still apply in a wide variety of circumstances. Unless the policyholder pays a higher premium in order to opt out of the business risk exclusions through an endorsement to the policy, many types of claims relating to defective products, such as warranty claims and product recalls, generally are excluded.

2. *Product Recall?* In *Sokol*, the policyholder had an endorsement that provided coverage for product recalls. Why did the court hold that coverage was inapplicable? Were you persuaded by the court's reasoning?

3. *Loss of Use?* If a product cannot be used due to a defect, does that constitute a "loss of use," which is included in the definition of "property damage"? In *Sokol*, the court held there was no "loss of use" due to the rancid peanut butter. Do you agree?

4. *Majority Rule?* In cases where a defective product is incorporated into another product, courts are divided regarding whether the business risk exclusions apply. *Compare, e.g., Sokol, supra* (business risk exclusions applied) *with Shade Foods, Inc. v. Innovative Prod. Sales & Mktg., Inc.*, 78 Cal. App. 4th 847 (2000), *as modified on denial of reh'g* (Mar. 29, 2000) (business risk exclusions did not apply where nut clusters contaminated with wood were included in boxed cereal). Although the decisions in these cases are driven by the specific facts and policy language at issue, in general, if a defective or contaminated product is incorporated into another product such that the finished product is unusable and the contaminated or defective part cannot be removed or neutralized, then the exclusions do not apply. *See, e.g.*, Peter J. Kalis, Thomas M. Reiter & James R. Segerdahl, Policyholder's Guide to the Law of Insurance Coverage § 10.02[C] (1st ed. 1997 & Supp. 2017).

6. Late Notice

Liability insurance policies contain notice of loss provisions. The sample policy at the beginning of this chapter lists the notice requirement as a policy "condition." It provides, "You must see to it that we are notified as soon as practicable of an 'occurrence' or an offense which may result in a claim. . . ." Older policies required the policyholder to give "prompt" notice. The notice requirement is included in an insurance policy primarily for the benefit of the insurer because the insurer is the party that is required to defend and indemnify the policyholder against claims, and notice is necessarily a prerequisite to the insurer knowing that it may need to perform these duties. Prompt notice is also important to insurers because insurers want to investigate claims before critical evidence is lost or altered. Insurers also want to avoid a situation where a default judgment is entered against their policyholders because the policyholder was sued but failed to defend the case.

Not surprisingly, then, insurers usually urge strict enforcement of these provisions, sometimes describing them as conditions precedent to a policyholder bringing an action on the policy. From the policyholder's perspective, however, much can be lost from failing to comply with the provision. Indeed, forfeiture of all coverage for a loss is a possible consequence. Generally speaking, however, courts abhor forfeitures. Thus, the issue for the courts is whether strict, literal compliance with the policy's notice provisions is required or whether something short of literal compliance is sufficient. Stated differently, should the insurer prevail even where a policyholder's failure to comply causes no harm? Consider the following case, which arose under the older policy language.

JONES V. BITUMINOUS CAS. CORP.

821 S.W.2d 798 (Ky. 1991)

LEIBSON, JUSTICE.

[Bituminous Casualty Corporation, the insurer respondent, filed a declaratory judgment action in which it sought to establish that it had "no obligation or duty to appear and defend . . . or to indemnify" under a liability policy it issued to Huston Partin and others doing business as S & J Mining Company. The injury giving rise to the insureds' potential liability was suffered by John Jones in an explosion on the mining company's premises on February 7, 1988.]

At one point John Jones had been a partner in the enterprise, but at the time of the explosion he was no longer associated with it. He testified that he was revisiting the premises to check on some equipment and to see when the mine would be reopened. He suffered serious injuries when a fire barrel kept on the premises exploded while in use. At the time of the explosion Huston Partin was either the principal party or the sole owner in S & J Mining Company.

The insurance carrier, Bituminous Casualty, was not notified of the occurrence for six and one half months. The trial court rendered summary judgment in favor of the insurance carrier, declaring "the policy in question is voided because of the insured's breach of the policy requirement of prompt notice." Jones argued the insurance carrier suffered "no prejudice" from the delay in providing notice, but the trial court made its decision on the basis that prejudice is not required. The Court of Appeals has affirmed.

We have accepted discretionary review, and we reverse for reasons that follow.

Huston Partin testified by deposition that he purchased the public liability insurance policy at issue because he was required by government authorities to do so in order to obtain his mining permit. Kentucky Administrative Regulation, 405 KAR 10:030, Sec. 4, requires a public liability insurance policy to cover personal injury and property damage to others, including damage caused by the use of explosives.

The policy in question is designated "Commercial General Liability Coverage." The policy period was from June 11, 1987 to June 11, 1988. Throughout the time span of coverage the partners in S & J Mining changed, continually, except for Huston Partin. John Jones became a partner in December 1987, and remained one until the mine was shut down two weeks before the explosion on February 7, 1988.

According to his deposition, Jones went back to the premises to see if the mine owner, Huston Partin, had any plans to reopen in the near future and to check on equipment owned by a different company, Nan Belle Corporation, where Jones was also employed, which was still located at the mine site. Jones and others who had come to the site to see if the mine was going to be reopened started a fire in a fire barrel located on the premises to provide warmth. Some time later Jones went back to the barrel to poke up the fire and the barrel exploded. His right leg was amputated and his hearing and eyesight were permanently impaired as a result of the explosion. Huston Partin testified by deposition that state and federal investigators had reported the explosion was caused by powder (explosives) in the barrel. Subsequently he was cited by the government as the mine operator for a violation generated by his mishandling of explosives.

John Jones testified that he had no idea as to the cause of the explosion, and for some time thought someone had intentionally tried to blow him up. It was only after completion of the investigation that John Jones considered the explosion might have been an accidental occurrence and the subject of a liability insurance claim.

Huston Partin learned of the explosion and injury to Jones on the day it occurred, but he seems to have been unaware he had insurance that might cover Jones' injury. Thus he failed to notify his insurance carrier of the injury. Indeed, for whatever reason, whether because his financial circumstances render him judgment proof or otherwise, Partin has shown little interest in these proceedings, having failed to respond to his insurance carrier's motion for summary judgment or to appeal the declaratory judgment denying him coverage. Nevertheless, it is quite evident that the real party in interest in the coverage question is Jones, the victim of the explosion.

The insurance carrier, Bituminous Casualty, first became aware of the occurrence through a letter sent to Partin by Jones' attorney, dated August 20, 1988, with a copy to Partin's insurance agent, Energy Insurance Agency, advising Jones intended to pursue a claim. This agency in turn reported the potential claim to Bituminous Casualty on August 24, 1988.

The particular provision in the policy with which we are concerned is in "Section IV—COMMERCIAL GENERAL LIABILITY CONDITIONS." This Section includes multiple, diverse conditions pertaining to obligations of both the insurer and the insured. The one in question is:

> "2. Duties In The Event Of Occurrence, Claim Or Suit.
>
> a. You must see to it that we are notified promptly of an 'occurrence' which may result in a claim."
>
> "Section V" of the policy covers "DEFINITIONS" and provides:
>
> "9. 'Occurrence' means an accident, including continuous or repeated exposure to substantially the same general harmful conditions."

The trial court decided this prompt notice clause of the policy was breached by the six and one half months' delay between the date of the occurrence and the date the occurrence was first reported to the insurance carrier, and further, that this breach was fatal to the coverage without regard to whether the liability insurer sustained prejudice from the delay in giving notice. The trial court cited as authority the view that such "prompt notice" requirements are strictly a matter of contract law, and, as such, "a condition precedent to recovery on the policy." *Reserve Ins. Co. v. Richards, Ky.*, 577 S.W.2d 417, 419 (1979). . . .

However, although the leading case, *Reserve Ins. Co. v. Richards*, expressed the view that notice is a condition precedent and prejudice from the delay is not material, as Justice Wintersheimer pointed out in his dissent in *Shipley* [*v. Kentucky Farm Bureau Ins.*, Ky., 747 S.W.2d 596 (1988)], in fact "[i]n *Richards, supra*, the liability carrier did not receive notice until after judgment was entered against the insured which denied the insurance company any opportunity to defend." 747 S.W.2d at 599. The three judge dissent in *Shipley* took the position there was a factual question involving both whether the insured had exercised "reasonable diligence" in providing notice considering the circumstances, and whether the delay in providing notice had prejudiced the insurer.

A recent annotation on the subject in 32 A.L.R.4th 141 addresses the "Modern Status of Rules Requiring Liability Insurer[s] to Show Prejudice to Escape Liability Because of [the] Insured's Failure or Delay in Giving Notice of Accident or Claim, or in Forwarding Suit Papers." It seeks to cover all the more recent cases on this subject from all jurisdictions, including those following a "traditional" view that the "liability insurer need not show that it was prejudiced by an insured's unreasonable and unexcused omission or delay in giving notice," *id.* at 146, and those "representing a modern trend away from the traditional that prejudice to a liability insurer is immaterial" to a new position that "a liability insurer is required to show that it was prejudiced by the insured's omission or delay." *Id.* at 157. Kentucky, citing Reserve Ins. Co. v. Richards, supra, is listed among those states still using the so called "traditional" view.

[While] . . . acknowledging that there are various gradations in adherence to both the "traditional view" and the "modern trend," it suffices to say that a substantial majority now supports the modern trend, holding that an insurer cannot withdraw coverage on the ground that a notice condition has not been met unless the insurer can show that it was prejudiced by the act of the insured. Allowing for certain difficulties in doing the accounting, the ALR Annotation and its Supplement provide cases from some 29 other states now holding that the insurer must show prejudice, and only about 20 still adhering to the view that the presence or absence of prejudice is immaterial. The traditional view has become the minority view, and the view requiring proof of prejudice before invoking a forfeiture now represents the mainstream of American jurisprudence on this subject.

The time has come for Kentucky to reconsider whether failure to provide prompt notice should automatically defeat liability insurance coverage regardless of circumstances. . . .

There are at least four major features in the status of insurance law as it has presently evolved in Kentucky (utilized in varying degrees by the cases from other jurisdictions rejecting the rule of strict contractual construction) which make it unreasonable to follow *Reserve Ins. Co. v. Richards, supra,* in present circumstances. They are:

1) Contracts of Adhesion. Standard form insurance policies such as this are recognized as contracts of adhesion because they are not negotiated; they are offered to the insurance consumer on essentially a "take it or leave it" basis without affording the consumer a realistic opportunity to bargain. As to contracts of adhesion, we stated in Wolford v. Wolford, Ky., 662 S.W.2d 835, 838 (1984): "If the contract has two constructions, the one most favorable to the insured must be adopted . . . . If the contract language is ambiguous, it must be liberally construed to resolve any doubts in favor of the insured . . . ."

A strict forfeiture interpretation of the prompt notice requirement excludes from the equation both the reasons why the insured failed to give prompt notice, such as whether a layman would realize that there was a covered occurrence, and the question whether the insurance carrier suffered any substantial prejudice from the delay. Absent language in the contract clearly spelling out the meaning and parameters of prompt notice and automatic forfeiture consequences, the reach of the term and the consequences are vague. The policy has a latent ambiguity which is subject to the rule of construction that applies to a contract of adherence.

2) The "doctrine of reasonable expectations." In *Woodson v. Manhattan Life Ins. Co. of New York*, Ky., 743 S.W.2d 835, 839 (1987), we summarized from R.H. Long's "The Law of Liability Insurance," Sec. 5.10B:

> "The gist of the doctrine is that the insured is entitled to all the coverage he may reasonably expect to be provided under the policy. Only an unequivocally conspicuous, plain and clear manifestation of the company's intent to exclude coverage will defeat that expectation."

While recognizing that the policy language clearly imposes a duty on the insured to promptly notify the company, by failing to define prompt notice or to warn of a forfeiture, this result falls beyond the reasonable expectations of the ordinary insurance consumer.

3) Statutory coverage. Huston Partin purchased this policy of public liability insurance because it was required by law in order to obtain a mining permit for the benefit of those who would be exposed to the risk involved by the mining operations. The insurance was required by administrative regulations enacted pursuant to statute, and as such a declaration of public policy. In *Bishop v. Allstate Ins. Co.*, Ky., 623 S.W.2d 865, 867 (1981), we struck down the "household" exclusion clause in an automobile liability insurance contract "to the extent that [such exclusions] dilute or eliminate the minimum coverage requirements of the MVRA." *Bishop v. Allstate* has become a leading case on interpreting policies purchased to provide statutory coverage. We have recently cited and applied it in different but similar circumstances. . . . This case presents a similar problem.

While we recognize that insurance carriers have the right to impose reasonable conditions and limitations on their insurance coverage even where coverage is required by law, nevertheless the question then becomes the reasonableness of the condition as a limitation on public policy as opposed to one of strict contract considerations between private parties where no public interest is involved. Recognizing this, whereas a clause requiring prompt notice is reasonable, and a clause defeating coverage where notice unreasonably delayed causes prejudice to the insurer is appropriate, a clause working a strict forfeiture regardless of prejudice unreasonably interferes with coverage required by mine safety regulations.

4) Premiums. The insurance carrier has argued that such clauses are essential from an actuarial standpoint in order to price the insurance according to the risk. Whereas this argument is valid with reference to imposing on the insurer risks which are unreasonable and unforeseeable, such is not the case with this clause in this policy. Where there has been no prejudice to the insurer from the delay in notice, there has been no

increase in the risk. On the contrary, in the absence of prejudice a strict forfeiture clause simply provides the insurance company with a windfall. By adopting a rule requiring proof of prejudice from a delay in notification, all the insurance company is being required to do is to take the risk it was paid to take rather than escape liability for coverage otherwise provided.

Our decision in this case is not without precedent. In *Newark Ins. Co. v. Ezell*, Ky., 520 S.W.2d 318 (1975), a policy condition pertaining to uninsured motorist coverage required the insured to obtain written consent of the company before prosecuting an action against the uninsured motorist. Absent such consent in advance the judgment could not be enforced against the insurer. We held this condition of the policy should not be subject to "strict enforcement." We stated:

> In the field of insurance law recognition frequently has been given to the principle that an insurance company may not rely upon a noncompliance by the insured with a condition of the policy if the company has sustained no prejudice by reason of the noncompliance.

Id. at 321.

This principle was applied because, though the insurance carrier had not been asked nor had it given "written consent" as was specified as a condition of the coverage, the facts showed that the insurance carrier's attorney was aware of the suit in progress against the uninsured motorist and failed to object or to seek to participate in the action.

Thus, Kentucky has already evidenced support for the "modern trend" against strict forfeiture regardless of prejudice in a situation markedly similar to present circumstances. For the reasons stated we overrule *Reserve Ins. Co. v. Richards*, Ky., 577 S.W.2d 417 (1979), [and other cases in accord with *Richards*].

Two unanswered questions remain: (1) Should the insurance carrier have the burden of proving prejudice from the delay, or should the burden be on the claimant to prove lack of prejudice to the insurance carrier? (2) Should prejudice be measured in terms of actual prejudice or probable prejudice?

There are two reasons for imposing the burden on the insurance carrier to prove prejudice, rather than imposing on the claimant the burden to prove no prejudice resulted. The first is the obvious one: it is virtually impossible to prove a negative, so it would be difficult if not impossible for the claimant to prove the insurance carrier suffered no prejudice. Secondly, the insurance carrier is in a far superior position to be knowledgeable about the facts which establish whether prejudice exists. Indeed, it is difficult to imagine where the claimant would look for evidence that no prejudice exists. Thus we hold that the burden is on the insurance carrier to prove there was in fact some substantial prejudice caused by the delay in reporting the occurrence.

Finally, with reference to whether the insurance company's burden to prove prejudice should be stated in terms of actual prejudice or probable prejudice, we recognize that proof of actual prejudice is an unreasonable burden. We view the question of prejudice in terms of whether it is reasonably probable that the insurance carrier suffered substantial prejudice from the delay in notice. If the evidence on this issue is in conflict, or if reasonable minds could differ as to what the evidence proves in this regard, the issue is one for the trier of fact. The issue is ripe for summary judgment only where the proof is conclusive, or there has been a failure of proof, on this subject.

We reverse the Court of Appeals and the trial court. We vacate the summary judgment and remand this case to the trial court for further proceedings consistent with this Opinion.

. . . .

STEPHENS, CHIEF JUSTICE, Dissenting

I respectfully dissent.

This Court rewrites the insurance contract by adopting the rule that the insurer, in order to escape liability for coverage, must prove probable prejudice from a delay in notification. Section IV of said contract, clearly and unambiguously requires the insured to promptly notify the carrier of any "occurrence which may result in a claim."

The insured's untimely notice fails to comply with the condition precedent of the contract (Section IV), thus relieving the carrier of liability under the policy, because six and one half months elapsed between movant's injury and notice to the insurance company of movant's claim. Richards, supra.

. . . .

It is jurisprudentially sound to leave departure from our present established rule in *Richards, supra,* to the General Assembly. The majority's new rule based on the concept of prejudice negates the purpose of the contract conditions, rendering them meaningless and in effect rewrites the insurance policy, contrary to the intent of the parties clearly expressed by the language of the contract. This new rule changes legislative and executive policies implicitly expressed by the insurance department's approval of respondent's insurance contract.

. . . .

NOTES AND QUESTIONS

1. *Timely Notice and Prejudice.* In most states, a two-prong test applies to the late notice issue. First, under the totality of the circumstances, was

notice provided timely? Second, if notice was untimely, was the insurer materially prejudiced by the late notice? *See* Peter J. Kalis, Thomas M. Reiter & James R. Segerdahl, Policyholder's Guide to the Law of Insurance Coverage § 24.02[G] (1st ed. 1997 & Supp. 2017) (listing the late notice rules in a 50-state survey).

Many courts have recognized a variety of extenuating circumstances that excuse the insured's obligation to give notice promptly or within a reasonable time. *See, e.g., Sparacinio v. Pawtucket Mutual Insurance Co.*, 50 F.3d 141 (2d Cir. 1995) (under New York law, labor union's delay in notifying liability insurer was excused where union had a reasonable belief that it was not liable and that there was no coverage); *West American Insurance Co. v. Bank of Isle of Wight*, 673 F. Supp. 760 (E.D. Va. 1987) (policyholder did not know of loss); *Royal Globe Insurance Co. v. Craven*, 585 N.E.2d 315 (Mass. 1992) (policyholder excused from 24-hour notice requirement during time policyholder was in intensive care, but delay for three months after release from hospital was not excused); *Finstad v. Steiger Tractor, Inc.*, 301 N.W.2d 392 (N.D. 1981) (policyholder did not know of policy's existence).

Although some states presume prejudice occurs if notice is particularly late, most states require insurers to prove actual prejudice. *See, e.g., Fund for Animals, Inc. v. Nat'l Union Fire Ins. Co. of Pittsburgh, PA.*, 130 A.3d 1155, 1166–67 (Md. Ct. Spec. App. 2016) ("Proof of harm to the insurer resulting from the late notice is essential. '[P]ossible, theoretical, conjectural, or hypothetical prejudice is not enough to satisfy section 19–110; prejudice cannot be surmised or presumed from the mere fact of delay.' "); *Aetna Casualty & Surety Co. v. Dow Chemical Co.*, 10 F. Supp. 2d 800 813 (E.D. Mich. 1998) ("An insurer must do more than simply claim that evidence was lost, physically altered, or has otherwise become unavailable and that witnesses have died, disappeared, or their memories have faded. It must establish what is in fact lost by the missing evidence, how this prejudices its position, and why information available from other sources is inadequate.").

2. *Restatement of the Law of Liability Insurance*. The Restatement also has adopted the test that requires the insurer to prove it was prejudiced by the timing of the notice in order for a forfeiture of coverage to result:

> **§ 35 Notice and Reporting Conditions**
>
> (1) Except as stated in subsection (2), the failure of the insured to satisfy a notice-of-claim condition excuses an insurer from performance of its obligations under a liability insurance policy only if the insurer demonstrates that it was prejudiced by the failure.

3. *What Constitutes Prejudice?* If the insured fails to give notice of a suit against him or her until after a default judgment has been entered in the plaintiff's favor and the judgment has become final and non-appealable, it seems obvious that the insurer has been prejudiced. Other situations are not so obvious. Is it necessary that the late notice cause the irretrievable loss of a substantial defense? Or is it only necessary that the insurer's ability to defend

the claim be diminished? Or is the threshold for prejudice something in between those two tests? *See Weaver v. State Farm Mutual Automobile Insurance Co.*, 936 S.W.2d 818 (Mo. 1997) (affidavit of insurer's claim superintendent stating that uninsured motorist insurer could not get medical records due to one-year delay in receiving notice did not establish prejudice to insurer).

4. *Notice in Writing?* Many policies require that the notice to the insurer be in writing. That is how the notice was communicated in *Jones*. Some courts have held that oral notice is insufficient to satisfy a requirement that the notice be in writing. *See, e.g., Putney School, Inc. v. Schaaf*, 599 A.2d 322 (Vt. 1991). If the notice in *Jones* had been oral, would it have mattered? How would the insurer have demonstrated prejudice from oral notice?

5. *Manner of Notice*. It was, apparently, undisputed that the insurer did not learn of the occurrence until Jones' attorney's letter of August 20, 1988. What if, however, the explosion that injured Jones had been a major mining disaster, with significant loss of life and substantial attendant publicity in national media? Is common knowledge of the disaster enough to constitute "notice"? *See Frankenmuth Mutual Insurance Co. v. Williams*, 645 N.E.2d 605 (Ind. 1995) (insurer could not be said to lack notice of suit where insurer was aware of accusation, had investigated incident, and had sent reservation of rights letter). What if the information received by an insurer about its insured's potential liability is in the nature of "general neighborhood gossip"? *Compare Bantz v. Bongard*, 864 P.2d 618 (Idaho 1993) (information provided to insurer by someone else, other than insured, involved in the accident), *with Allstate Insurance Co. v. Kepchar*, 592 N.E.2d 694 (Ind. Ct. App. 1994) ("general neighborhood gossip"). Jones was the injured victim, not the policyholder. Should it matter who actually conveys the information about a possible loss to the insurer? Is it prudent or advisable for a victim of a tort to notify the policyholder's liability insurance carrier?

6. *Compulsory Insurance and Late Notice*. Mining is one of those highly dangerous activities which has risks to the well-being not only of those who do it but also those who are in the vicinity. The court in *Jones* thought it relevant that Partin was required by state statute to purchase liability insurance for his mining operation. When insurance is compulsory, what additional public values are implicated when an insurer successfully asserts a defense to coverage based on late notice (or some other related condition)?

7. *Agents and Notice*. Suppose the policyholder negligently operates his vehicle and injures a pedestrian. The policyholder has a liability policy covering the loss. The policy was secured by a broker, an independent entity, from one of the insurers the broker represents. The policyholder notifies the broker of the accident, but the broker leaves on a six-month cruise the next day without forwarding the notice to the insurer. Does this present any problem for the policyholder? *See Met Coil Systems Corp. v. Columbia Casualty Co.*, 524 N.W.2d 650 (Iowa 1994). If the policy provides that the policyholder or beneficiary is to give notice to "the insurer or any authorized agent," should it

suffice if the beneficiary under a group accidental death policy provided by the decedent's employer gives notice to the employer? *See Golt v. Aetna Life Ins. Co.*, 186 F.3d 1184, 1185 (9th Cir. 1999), *certified question answered*, 2 P.3d 841 (Mont. 2000).

8. *Timing Issues*. Where notice of "injury," "loss," or "accident" (or whatever is identified as the triggering event in the policy) must be given, from what moment does the time period run? There must be a minimum of knowledge on the part of the policyholder concerning the event before the notice obligation is triggered. The issue can be complex in some situations. Is the triggering event for giving notice the fact that the policyholder is aware that he or she has been involved in an accident, or that the policyholder believes that a tort claim may be filed, or that the policyholder believes he or she may be liable? Part of the difficulty in liability insurance is that the policyholder may not be aware at the time of the accident that she is potentially liable. In some kinds of insurance, such as automobile insurance, the potential liability will often be apparent. But in other kinds of insurance, such as malpractice insurance, the policyholder may be unaware of the insured event until a claim is filed. The policyholder's reasonable belief that she is not liable may excuse the insured's delay in giving notice to the insurer, but as the court explained in *State v. Glens Falls Insurance Co.*, 365 A.2d 243 (Vt. 1976), this exception presupposes more than a cursory investigation, discussion with the claimant, interviewing witnesses, and, according to some cases, consultation with counsel. The court in *Glens Falls* stated:

> The duty to notify arises with the advent of circumstances calculated to instill in the reasonable person belief in the possibility of an impending claim. Reduced to its illogical conclusion, the State's contention would eliminate forever the need for any notice to the insurer, if the prospect of a claim was not apparent at the very time of the occurrence. Even a subsequent notice of claim would not, under this view, trigger the duty. . . . Supervening circumstance cannot, it is true, give rise *retroactively* to a duty to notify; the duty does not arise until circumstances exist which would be a caveat to a reasonable person. But when such circumstances arise, the duty to notify arises with them. (emphasis in original).

Does it matter how significant the policyholder's SIR or deductible is? For example, in the *DuPont* case discussed earlier in this chapter, DuPont had a $50 million SIR. Should it be required to give notice to an insurer at the $100 million layer when a claim worth $1 million is asserted against it?

F. PERSONAL AND ADVERTISING LIABILITY COVERAGE

An often overlooked but extremely important type of insurance coverage offered under various lines of liability insurance is Personal and Advertising Liability Coverage. This coverage is found in a number of widely used forms, including the Commercial General Liability (CGL) policy and the Personal Umbrella Liability policy. For example, under the 2012 standard form version of the CGL policy (the Sample CGL Policy at the beginning of this chapter), the basic insuring agreement language in the personal injury and advertising liability section is worded as follows:

> **Coverage B—Personal and Advertising Injury Liability**
>
> Insuring Agreement
>
> We will pay those sums that the insured becomes legally obligated to pay as damages because of "personal and advertising injury" to which this insurance applies. We will have the right and duty to defend the insured against any "suit" seeking those damages. . . .
>
> "Personal and advertising injury" is defined as follows:
>
>> "Personal and advertising injury" means injury, including consequential "bodily injury", arising out of one or more of the following offenses:
>>
>> a. False arrest, detention or imprisonment;
>>
>> b. Malicious prosecution;
>>
>> c. The wrongful eviction from, wrongful entry into, or invasion of the right of private occupancy of a room, dwelling or premises that a person occupies, committed by or on behalf of its owner, landlord or lessor;
>>
>> d. Oral or written publication, in any manner, of material that slanders or libels a person or organization or disparages a person's or organization's goods, products or services;
>>
>> e. Oral or written publication, in any manner, of material that violates a person's right of privacy;
>>
>> f. The use of another's advertising idea in your "advertisement"; or
>>
>> g. Infringing upon another's copyright, trade dress or slogan in your "advertisement."

Under this language, many types of intellectual property infringement claims are covered, which is of obviously increasing importance in the "IP age." But one of the arguably counterintuitive aspects of the Personal and Advertising Injury coverage is its reach into the realm of intentional torts. As a general proposition, an individual who intentionally brings about damage to persons or property cannot recover insurance proceeds for the loss suffered, and an individual who intentionally causes injury or damage to a third party cannot look to liability insurance to shield him from the consequences of this deliberate conduct. Covering intentional torts is at odds with both the fortuity doctrine and the "expected or intended" exclusion found in many lines of liability insurance. Yet, many liability policies, including the 2012 CGL policy quoted above, simultaneously contain an "expected or intended" exclusion in the Bodily Injury and Property Damage coverage section of the policy while expressly providing coverage for many types of intentional torts and intellectual property infringement claims in the Personal and Advertising Liability section of the policy. The next few cases are examples of how courts have interpreted and applied the language contained in the Personal and Advertising Injury coverages.

1. Coverage for Intentional Torts

BAILER V. ERIE INS. EXCHANGE

687 A.2d 1375 (Md. 1997)

Opinion

RODOWSKY, JUDGE.

This appeal involves the construction of a personal catastrophe liability policy when the claim against the insured alleges invasion of privacy. The policy expressly covers invasion of privacy as "personal injury," but the policy then excludes "personal injury . . . expected or intended" by the insured. Because of this ambiguity, and as more fully explained below, we shall hold that the policy covers.

The appellants, Byron C. Bailer and Victoria Bailer, husband and wife, own, as their primary residence, a dwelling in Rockville, Maryland. At all times relevant to the instant matter the Bailers were insured under three policies issued by the appellee, Erie Insurance Exchange (Erie): a basic homeowner's policy, an automobile liability policy, and the personal catastrophe liability policy at issue here.

The Bailers hired through an agency a Danish national, Majbrit Meier, as an au pair. In consideration of salary, room, and board Ms. Meier assisted the Bailers with household chores and child care. She was furnished her own room and private bath in the Bailers' home.

In the fall of 1993 Ms. Meier, who apparently had laundry drying in her bathroom at the time, asked Mr. Bailer's permission for her to shower in the bathroom that adjoined the Bailers' bedroom. Before giving Ms. Meier access to that bath, Mr. Bailer concealed there a video camera, focused it on the shower area, and turned on the camera. Ms. Meier used the shower and at some point learned that she had been video taped. Ms. Meier left the Bailers' home and employment and sued both of them in the Circuit Court for Montgomery County for invasion of privacy. The Bailers called upon Erie to defend and to indemnify, but Erie declined to do either. The

Bailers then engaged counsel to defend Ms. Meier's action against them, and they then brought the instant action against Erie in the Circuit Court for Montgomery County.

In the Bailers' action against Erie all parties moved for summary judgment, and the court granted Erie's motion. The Bailers appealed to the Court of Special Appeals, and this Court, on its own motion, issued the writ of certiorari prior to consideration of the matter by the Court of Special Appeals. The action against the Bailers by Ms. Meier was settled sometime prior to the Bailers' filing of their brief as appellants in the instant appeal.

I.

. . . .

Count I sought a judgment "declaring that [the Bailers] are entitled to insurance coverage including defense. . . ." Count II sought damages for breach of the insurance contract, measured by any judgment in favor of Ms. Meier, by attorney's fees and costs incurred in defense of the claim by Ms. Meier, and by attorney's fees and costs incurred in the prosecution of the action of the Bailers against Erie.

. . . .

It appears, however, that the action of Ms. Meier against the Bailers was settled prior to appellate briefing. Consequently, the need for a declaration of the rights of the parties, in order for it to operate prospectively, has become moot. All of the relief now available to the Bailers consists of damages that have accrued, including counsel fees in the instant action. Recovery of the damages, accrued and unaccrued, is available under Count II, the breach of contract claim. This Court recognizes the recoverability of counsel fees and expenses incurred by an insured in successfully prosecuting or defending a coverage issue with a liability insurer. That aspect of the Bailers' claim against Erie is part of their breach of contract claim. *Collier v. MD-Individual Practice Ass'n,* 327 Md. 1, 13–17, 607 A.2d 537, 543–45 (1992) (recovery of counsel fees and expenses incurred by an insured in successfully prosecuting or defending a coverage issue with liability insurer is an exception to the American rule disallowing counsel fees as part of expectation interest damages in breach of contract actions).

Accordingly, we proceed to address the merits of Count II of the Bailers' amended complaint.

II.

In this Court the Bailers rest their breach of contract claim exclusively on Erie's personal catastrophe policy. That policy states Erie's promise as follows:

> We will pay the ultimate net loss which anyone we protect becomes legally obligated to pay as damages because of personal

> injury or property damage covered by this policy. This applies only to damages in excess of the underlying limit or Self-Insured Retention.

"Personal injury" as defined in the policy means:

> (1) bodily injury;
>
> (2) libel, slander or defamation of character;
>
> (3) false arrest, wrongful detention or imprisonment, malicious prosecution, wrongful entry or eviction, *invasion of privacy,* or humiliation caused by any of these.

(Emphasis added). It is this insuring agreement on which the Bailers rely.

Under the section of the policy headed "What we do not cover—Exclusions," appears the following:

> We do not cover:
>
> . . . .
>
> (2) personal injury or property damage expected or intended by anyone we protect. We do cover reasonable acts committed to protect persons or property.

Erie relies on this exclusion, and the circuit court based its grant of summary judgment on this exclusion.

The major contentions are these:

A. The Bailers submit that, even if the injury were expected or intended by Mr. Bailer, the policy literally covers, or, at a minimum, becomes ambiguous because it expressly insures against liability for invasion of privacy.

B. Erie submits that there is no ambiguity in the policy because it should be construed to cover negligent invasions of privacy and to exclude only intentional invasions.

C. Erie submits, and the circuit court agreed, that intentional conduct and intentional results must be distinguished. Hence, says Erie, even if invasion of privacy is exclusively an intentional tort and even if the policy covers intended conduct that produces unintended results, the injury here was intended by the insured so that the exclusion applies.

D. Erie submits that a construction that permits insurance of an intentional injury is contrary to public policy.

No extensive review is required of the legal principles governing the construction of insurance policies. Under Maryland law, "[i]nsurance policies, being contractual, are construed as other contracts." As such, a court interpreting an insurance policy is to examine the instrument as a whole, focusing on the character, purpose, and circumstances surrounding the execution of the contract. "[W]e accord words their ordinary and accepted meanings. The test is what meaning a reasonably prudent layperson would attach to the term." *Id.* Unlike the law of some states which construes insurance contracts against the insurer, this Court holds that an insurance contract will be construed against the insurer only when an ambiguity remains after considering the intentions of the parties from the policy as a whole and, if necessary, after admitting and considering any relevant parol evidence.

A review of the subject catastrophe policy as a whole reveals that its coverage is integrated with the underlying automobile and homeowner's liability coverages. That interrelationship reinforces the Bailers' contention that the parties intended for the policy to cover liability for invasion of privacy.

The catastrophe policy requires the Bailers "to maintain in full effect during the policy period, without alteration, the policies shown on the Declarations . . . as underlying insurance. . . ." The schedule of underlying insurance lists the Bailers' basic homeowner's policy and the Bailers' automobile liability policy. With respect to claims that are covered by the underlying insurance, the catastrophe policy "applies only to damages in excess of the underlying limit. . . ."

The Bailers do not contend that the underlying homeowner's policy covers Ms. Meier's claim against them. Under § II of that policy, dealing with, "Home and Family Liability Protection," Erie agrees to:

> [P]ay all sums up to the amount shown on the Declarations, which anyone we protect becomes legally obligated to pay as damages because of bodily injury or property damage resulting from an occurrence during the policy period. We will pay for only bodily injury or property damage covered by this policy.

Under that policy bodily injury is "physical harm, sickness or disease, including mental anguish, and includes care, loss of services, or resulting death." Under that policy an "occurrence" is "an accident, including continuous or repeated exposure to the same general harmful conditions." The liability protection provisions of the basic homeowner's policy also contain substantially the same exclusion as found in the catastrophe policy for "[b]odily injury or property damage expected or intended by anyone we protect."

The types of tort liabilities such as malicious prosecution, slander, and invasion of privacy which are specifically included within the insuring provision of the catastrophe policy ordinarily are not covered under insuring provisions of the type found in Erie's basic homeowner's policy. This is because these torts typically do not involve bodily injury, *see Allstate Ins. Co. v. LaPore,* 762 F. Supp. 268, 270–71 (N.D.Cal.1991) (defamation); *Washington v. State Farm Fire & Casualty Co.,* 629 A.2d 24, 27 (D.C.1993) (defamation); *Cantrell v. Allstate Ins. Co.,* 202 Ga.App. 859, 860, 415 S.E.2d 711, 712–13 (1992) (false imprisonment and malicious prosecution); *Weaver v. Motorists Mut. Ins. Co.,* 62 Ohio App.3d 836, 839–41, 577 N.E.2d 703, 705–06 (1989) (defamation); or because these torts do not involve an accident, *see Metropolitan Property & Casualty Co. v. Murphy,* 896 F.Supp. 645, 647–48 (E.D.Tex.1995) (invasion of privacy by voyeurism); *Argonaut Southwest Ins. Co. v. Maupin,* 500 S.W.2d 633, 635–36 (Tex.1973) (property damage); or because the damages were expected or intended by the insured, *see Snakenberg v. Hartford Casualty Ins. Co.,* 299 S.C. 164, 383 S.E.2d 2, 6–8 (1989).

The insuring provision in the Bailers' catastrophe policy differs from that in their underlying homeowner's policy and from those in the foregoing cases. The catastrophe policy enlarges the coverage from "bodily injury" to "personal injury" and then defines the latter term specifically to include certain enumerated torts among which is invasion of privacy. Further, the subject catastrophe policy makes plain that it is intended not simply to operate as excess insurance over the limit of the required underlying insurance but also to operate as primary coverage for certain risks that are not covered at all by the underlying policy. In the latter instances, the catastrophe policy pays in excess of the "Self-Insured Retention." "Self-Insured Retention" means:

> The amount shown on the Declarations which is retained and payable by anyone we protect with respect to each occurrence not covered by underlying insurance but which is covered by this policy. All expenses incurred by us, or by anyone we protect with our consent, in the investigation or defense of a claim or suit within the self-insured retention shall be payable by us.

Per their Declaration, the Bailers' Self-Insured Retention is $500 for each occurrence.

Consequently, the policy clearly seems to have been drafted to provide some insurance against liability for claims based on invasion of privacy, under which Erie would pay the damages above the Self-Insured Retention of $500 up to the catastrophe policy limit per occurrence, as well as paying all costs of defense.

Indeed, it appears that personal umbrella liability policies are marketed as providing coverage for the torts enumerated in the Bailers' policy. In an article by W.A. Mueller, C.P.C.U., "Insurance Quiz: Personal Umbrella Liability Insurance," appearing in *American Agent & Broker,* Nov. 1988, at 50, the author points out that "agents and brokers sometimes overlook the coverage enhancements included in [personal umbrella liability policies]." Mueller states that "[g]enerally, these policies provide insuring agreements" for "[p]ersonal injury liability," which includes "[f]alse arrest, [i]nvasion of privacy, [d]efamation of character, [s]lander, [l]ibel,

[h]umiliation, [m]alicious prosecution, [w]rongful detention [and] [w]rongful entry." *Id.* Then, listing that which "usually is excluded in personal umbrellas," the author includes "[i]ntentional injury," without any attempt at reconciling the two statements. *Id.* at 52. *See also* J. Novak, "Leaky Umbrellas," Vol. 157, *Forbes,* Mar. 11, 1996, at 174.[3]

The complexity in the case before us lies in the exclusion. If the exclusion totally swallows the insuring provision, the provisions are completely contradictory. That is the grossest form of ambiguity, and Erie, unquestionably, would be obliged to defend and indemnify. We turn then to Erie's arguments that undertake to resolve the patent ambiguity.

B.

Erie's attempt to split the tort alleged by Ms. Meier into intentional or negligent invasions of privacy has no merit. This Court recognized the tort of invasion of privacy in *Carr v. Watkins,* 227 Md. 578, 586–88, 177 A.2d 841, 845–46 (1962), and subsequent cases have approved the definition of the term set out in Restatement (Second) of Torts § 652A (1977) (Restatement):

> General Principle
>
> (1) One who invades the right of privacy of another is subject to liability for the resulting harm to the interests of the other.
>
> (2) The right of privacy is invaded by:
>
> (a) unreasonable intrusion upon the seclusion of another . . .; or
>
> (b) appropriation of the other's name or likeness . . .; or
>
> (c) unreasonable publicity given to the other's private life . . .; or
>
> (d) publicity that unreasonably places the other in a false light before the public. . . .

See Household Fin. Corp. v. Bridge, 252 Md. 531, 535–38, 250 A.2d 878, 881–83 (1969). In *Household Fin. Corp.* we agreed with the analysis of

---

[3] The article in *Forbes* was inspired by the author's understanding that President William Jefferson Clinton's insurers are defending under a reservation of rights in the litigation reported as *Jones v. Clinton,* 869 F.Supp. 690 (E.D.Ark.1994), *aff'd in part, rev'd in part and remanded,* 72 F.3d 1354 (8th Cir.), *cert. granted,* 518 U.S. 1016, 116 S.Ct. 2545, 135 L.Ed.2d, 1066 (1996). The article describes State Farm as the nation's largest umbrella writer. J. Novak, "Leaky Umbrellas," *Forbes,* Mar. 11, 1996, at 174. The author states:

> The State Farm umbrella, as is typical, raises the personal liability limits of coverage you already have on your auto and home policies and provides coverage for some liabilities that wouldn't be covered at all in a homeowner policy. For example, it provides protection for suits charging you with invasion of privacy, malicious prosecution, defamation and false imprisonment. . . .

Id.

Professor Prosser in his *Handbook of the Law of Torts* (3d ed. 1964), Ch. 22, at 832, that invasion of privacy:

> [I]s not one tort, but a complex of four. The law of privacy comprises four distinct kinds of invasion of four different interests of the plaintiff, which are tied together by the common name, but otherwise have almost nothing in common except that each represents an interference with the right of the plaintiff "to be let alone."

Id. at 537, 250 A.2d at 882 (emphasis omitted).

Ms. Meier alleged that form of invasion of privacy consisting of "unreasonable intrusion upon the seclusion of another, as stated in § 652B." Restatement § 652A(2)(a). Restatement § 652B states the rule to be that:

> One who *intentionally* intrudes, physically or otherwise, upon the solitude or seclusion of another or his private affairs or concerns, is subject to liability to the other for invasion of his privacy, if the intrusion would be highly offensive to a reasonable person.

(Emphasis added).

Snakenberg v. Hartford Casualty Ins. Co., 299 S.C. 164, 383 S.E.2d 2, is instructive on the intent element of "Intrusion Upon Seclusion" described in Restatement § 652B. In that case the insured induced teenage females to model bathing suits at his home. Unknown to the "models," the insured videotaped them while they were using a bedroom to change into and out of the swimsuits. When the insured was sued for invasion of privacy, the insurer refused to defend under a homeowner's policy that was substantially similar to the Bailers' underlying homeowner's policy. Rejecting the insured's argument that he sought only to guard the swimsuits from theft by videotaping the women, and applying the exclusion "for damages intended or expected by the insured," 383 S.E.2d at 4, the court held:

> [W]rongful intrusion into private affairs always involves an intentional act. It is mistaken to conclude, as [the insured] does, that if malice is not an element of invasion of privacy, neither is intent. The tort cannot be committed by unintended conduct amounting merely to lack of due care. Intentional conduct is a necessary element of the cause of action.

Id. at 7. The homeowner's policy in *Snakenberg* did not expressly insure against damages for liability for invasion of privacy.

Erie has not briefed whether forms of invasion of privacy, other than "Intrusion Upon Seclusion" under Restatement § 652B, can be committed unintentionally, and Erie does not argue that its policy, properly construed, insures against liability for some other form of that tort. Consequently, we express no opinion on such a possible construction. It is sufficient for present purposes to hold that the tort in the form alleged here does not accommodate Erie's proffered distinction between negligent and intentional conduct. That proposed distinction does not resolve the intrinsic contradiction in the policy.

C.

. . . .

A personal liability umbrella policy was also involved in *Knowles v. United Servs. Auto. Ass'n,* 113 N.M. 703, 832 P.2d 394 (1992). That policy included coverage for wrongful eviction and excluded coverage for an injury that was expected or intended by the insured. The insured was sued by a neighbor for interfering with the neighbor's easement over the insured's property by having erected a locked gate across a road. 832 P.2d at 395. In its analysis the court first reviewed the line of cases which interpret the exclusion to operate only where the harm was intended, as opposed to the insured's performing an intended act that gives rise to some unexpected harm. The New Mexico court concluded that the insured "intended or expected harm of the same general type as was alleged by the [neighbor's] complaint." *Id.* at 398. The court also found that "the effect of the exclusionary clause at issue in the instant case is to nullify a broad grant of coverage." *Id.* Consequently the court held that "[t]he exclusion of coverage for acts intended or expected by [the insured] is repugnant to the insuring clause that promises broad coverage for injuries arising from wrongful eviction. The reasonable expectations of the insured can be upheld only if the repugnant clause is not given effect." *Id.* at 399.

A policy construction issue similar to that before us arose under a Law Enforcement Officers' Comprehensive Liability Policy in *Lincoln Nat'l Health & Casualty Ins. Co. v. Brown,* 782 F.Supp. 110 (M.D.Ga.1992). Manifesting no reluctance to express its frank opinion, the court said:

> [T]here is an inconsistency in the policy. The policy defines 'personal injury' to mean not only 'bodily injury' but also 'false arrest,' 'malicious prosecution,' and 'assault and battery.' When this definition is read with the provision that only unintentional and unexpected 'personal injury' is covered, then the policy only applies to unintentional false arrest, unintentional malicious prosecution, and unintentional assault and battery. This is complete nonsense.

Id. at 112–13.

The court applied the rule that "when two provisions in an insurance policy are repugnant to one another, the provision most favorable to the insured will be applied." *Id.* at 113.

In a periodical circulated in the insurance industry there is an incisive presentation of the problem now before us. D.S. Malecki, C.P.C.U., "Risk Management: Separation of Coverages in Underlying CGL Forms Deserves Attention," *Rough Notes,* Apr. 1990, at 34. The author begins by observing that "bewildering problems often are raised by the way personal injury and advertising injury coverages are structured under umbrella liability policies." *Id.* Malecki says:

> One of the problem areas is that commercial umbrella policies, unlike primary policies, sometimes provide no clear division between the unintentional tort coverage of bodily injury and the intentional tort coverages of personal injury and advertising injury.
>
> In other words, the insuring agreements of some umbrella policies substitute personal injury in place of bodily injury, but then make coverage contingent on the happening of an occurrence or a result that is unexpected or unintended.

Id.

The author, whose column in the periodical is headed, "Risk Management," gives the following advice: "Commercial umbrella policies that combine the unintentional tort coverage of bodily injury with the intentional tort coverage of personal injury and make both subject to unexpected or unintended results should be avoided." *Id.* Unfortunately, it is too late to apply Mr. Malecki's advice in the instant matter.

We conclude that Erie's suggested reconciliation of the conflict in the policy terms does not apply to the claim asserted against the Bailers by Ms. Meier. The subject policy is a personal, and not a commercial, liability policy. To the reasonable person the promise to pay damages for liability for invasion of privacy, at the time of contracting and under the circumstances presented here, refers to an intrusion upon seclusion. In other words, in an excess policy designed for owners of at least one house and at least one automobile, the contracting parties would not contemplate that the term, "invasion of privacy," primarily relates to such relatively exotic and usually commercial-context torts as appropriation of another's name or likeness, unreasonable publicity, or false light publicity.

Intrusion upon seclusion must always be intentional in order to be tortious, and it is the intrusion that constitutes the harm against which that form of invasion of privacy is intended to protect. Here, Ms. Meier alleged an intentional intrusion. There is no basis for contending that the policy will insure for intentional intrusions upon seclusion that do not result in intended or expected harm, but that the policy will not insure for intentional intrusions upon seclusion that do result in expected or intended harm. The insured's conduct, the invasion, and the claimant's harm, the invasion, are one and the same. Erie's proposed distinction in the context of this specific claim against the Bailers postulates that the policy insures and does not insure for the same conduct, at the same time, and in the same respect. The policy is at least ambiguous, and Erie was obliged to defend and indemnify.

D.

The circuit court entered summary judgment in favor of Erie for the additional reason that "it would be against public policy to allow an insurance company to indemnify someone for a wrongful act or crime committed with deliberate intention." Erie submits that the reasoning applied by the circuit court is a correct statement of the law, but Erie does not cite to us any cases involving insurance policies.

When Erie moved for summary judgment it predicated the motion exclusively on the legal construction of the policy language. Erie did not seek to submit any factual material designed to clarify the intent of the parties in the event the policy were determined to be ambiguous. From the underwriting standpoint this personal catastrophe policy is designed for persons who own their own homes, own one or more automobiles, and are sufficiently concerned about protecting their assets that they insure for excess and enhanced coverage in addition to their underlying liability coverage. Erie presented no evidence that persons to whom personal catastrophe policies are marketed become motivated by the insuring agreement intentionally to invade the seclusion of others or that Mr. Bailer was so motivated to video tape Ms. Meier.

The Bailers submit that the public policy argument was resolved adversely to Erie in *First Nat'l Bank of St. Mary's v. Fidelity Deposit Co.,* 283 Md. 228, 389 A.2d 359 (1978). We agree. There, we held that it was not contrary to public policy to insure against liability for punitive damages awarded in a civil action for malicious prosecution, even though the punitive damages in legal theory are predicated upon malice. *Id.* at 241–43, 389 A.2d at 366–67. In the instant matter the Bailers seek to be made whole for compensatory damages and legal expenses. The instant case is an even weaker one for voiding the insuring agreement on public policy grounds than was the case presented in *First Nat'l Bank of St. Mary's, supra.*

For the foregoing reasons we shall reverse the judgment of the Circuit Court for Montgomery County in favor of Erie Insurance Exchange, and we shall remand this case for the entry of a summary judgment on liability in favor of the Bailers who, on further proceedings in the circuit court, may prove their damages under Count II of their amended complaint.

NOTES AND QUESTIONS

1. *Type of Policy*. What type of insurance policy was at issue in *Bailer*? How did the coverage provided under the policy differ from the liability coverage provided under a homeowners policy?

2. *The Expected or Intended Exclusion.* Why did the *Bailer* court conclude the "expected or intended" exclusion did not apply?

3. *Negligent Invasion of Privacy.* Why did the *Bailer* court reject the insurer's argument that its policy only covered negligent, not intentional, invasion of privacy claims?

4. *Public Policy.* What about public policy? Should insurance policies be permitted, as a matter of public policy, to cover intentional torts such as invasion of privacy?

2. Coverage for Unfair Competition

LIBERTY LIFE INS. CO. V. COMMERCIAL UNION INS. CO.

857 F.2d 945 (4th Cir. 1988)

Opinion

WIDENER, CIRCUIT JUDGE:

The plaintiff, Liberty Life Insurance Company (Liberty), appeals from the district court's order granting summary judgment to the defendants, former insurance carriers of Liberty. Finding this stage of the proceeding to be premature for the dismissal of any of the defendants, we vacate and remand for further proceedings.

This suit was brought by Liberty against its insurance carriers based upon their refusal to defend Liberty in a series of lawsuits brought against Liberty by Metropolitan Life Insurance Company (Metropolitan). The Metropolitan lawsuits all involved an alleged scheme by Liberty to destroy Metropolitan's business. Metropolitan charged that Liberty had enticed Metropolitan's agents away, induced the agents to disparage Metropolitan's policies, and appropriated Metropolitan's customer lists and trade secrets. As the district court noted, the Metropolitan complaints were replete with allegations of intentional misconduct on the part of Liberty.

The theories of recovery alleged in the various Metropolitan lawsuits were as follows:

> North Carolina—Nov. 1983—Unfair competition, tortious interference with contractual relations, willful and malicious appropriations of trade secrets, common law misappropriation of trade secrets.
>
> South Carolina—Nov. 1983—Antitrust violations (Sherman Act, conspiracy in restraint of trade, monopolistic practices), state antitrust violations and unfair trade practice violations, common law unfair competition, wrongful appropriation of trade secrets, breach of duty of loyalty.

> Florida—Nov. 1983—Conspiracy (unfair interference with customer business relations).
>
> Minnesota—June 1984—Conspiracy, misappropriation of confidential information and trade secrets, violations of the Uniform Trade Secrets Act, unfair competition, tortious interference with employment relations, breach of loyalty, commercial disparagement, tortious interference with contractual relations, breach of contract.
>
> Missouri—June 1984—Misappropriation of trade secrets and confidential information, breach of fiduciary duty, conversion, tortious interference with contracts and business relations, tortious interference with employment relations, trade disparagement, civil conspiracy, *prima facie* tort.

During the time frame of the Metropolitan lawsuits, Liberty carried a comprehensive general liability insurance policy through defendants, American Employer's Insurance Company (American) and Home Indemnity Company (Home). While the insurance policies were not identical, they were substantially the same standardized form with respect to terms and definitions. The defendants contracted to provide coverage for property damage, bodily injury, personal injury and advertising injury. In addition to these comprehensive policies, Liberty obtained excess umbrella coverage for the relevant period from defendants, Mission National Insurance Company (Mission) and United States Fire Insurance Company (U.S. Fire). As with the primary policies, the umbrella policies were not identical. They were, however, similar in that both were policies designed to incorporate substantially the terms of the primary policies.

For property damage and bodily injury, each of the four policies at issue predicates some of the duties of the insurance company upon the happening of an occurrence. While the term occurrence is defined in similar fashion in each of the four policies, certain distinctions in these definitions require that each definition be set forth. With respect to the two primary policies, both defined occurrence as (American and Home):

> [A]n accident, including continuous or repeated exposure to conditions, which results in *bodily injury or property damage* neither expected nor intended from the standpoint of the insured.

(Emphasis supplied).

. . . .

The policy of U.S. Fire defined occurrence as:

> (a) With respect to Bodily Injury Liability or Property Damage Liability, injurious exposure to conditions which results in Bodily Injury or Property Damage neither expected nor intended from

the standpoint of the insured. All damages arising out of such exposure to substantially the same general conditions shall be considered as arising out of one occurrence.

(b) With respect to Personal Injury Liability, an offense which results in Personal Injury, other than an offense committed with actual malice or the willful violation of a penal statute or ordinance committed by or with the knowledge or consent of the insured. All damages arising out of such exposure to substantially the same general conditions shall be considered as arising out of one occurrence.

(c) With respect to Advertising Liability, all damages involving the same injurious material or act regardless of the frequency or repetition thereof, the number or kind of media used, and the number of claimants and all such damages shall be considered as arising out of the same occurrence.

Each policy also contained a specific definition of what constituted advertising liability as covered by the individual policies. Again, these definitions were quite similar. American and Home, the primary carriers, defined advertising injury as:

> "Advertising injury" means injury arising out of an offense committed during the policy period occurring in the course of the named insured's advertising activities, if such injury arises out of libel, slander, defamation, violation of right of privacy, piracy, unfair competition or infringement of copyright, title or slogan.

. . . .

Finally, U.S. Fire, the other excess carrier, defined advertising injury as:

> "Advertising Liability" means libel, slander, defamation, infringement of copyright, title or slogan, piracy, unfair competition, idea misappropriation or invasion of rights of privacy committed, or alleged to have been committed in any advertisement, publicity article, broadcast or telecast and arising out of the Named Insured's advertising activities.

While in the process of defending the Metropolitan lawsuits, and in some cases after a settlement had been reached with Metropolitan, Liberty gave notice to each of the defendant insurance companies by forwarding copies of the complaints. None of the defendant insurance companies attempted to defend Liberty in any of the Metropolitan suits, nor did they offer to reimburse Liberty for the expenses associated with those suits. Liberty then brought the instant lawsuit. Although Liberty asserts a variety of theories of recovery, and prays for punitive damages, the gist of this action is the attorneys fees and expenses expended by Liberty in defense of the

Metropolitan suits.[7] Upon cross-motions for summary judgment, the district court entered judgment in favor of all the defendants. The district court based its decision entirely upon the finding that an occurrence (defined in each of the policies) had not taken place, that an occurrence was required under each policy to trigger a duty to defend, and therefore no duty to defend ever existed. Since the district court found no duty to defend on the part of any defendant, it found in favor of the liability carriers on the balance of Liberty's claims, all of which related to the inaction of the liability carriers. This appeal followed.

The district court was correct in determining that there had been no occurrence as that term is defined in any of the policies with respect to property damage or bodily injury. In each of the policies, as heretofore discussed, occurrence was defined in such manner as to require an unintended or unexpected result from the standpoint of the insured. However, this definition is expressly linked only to property damage and bodily injury in the policies of American, Home and U.S. Fire. . . .

The duty of a liability insurer to defend an action brought against the insured is generally determined by the allegations in the complaint.[8] *Employers Mut. Liability Ins. Co. v. Hendrix,* 199 F.2d 53, 56 (4th Cir.1952) (applying South Carolina law); *R.A. Earnhardt Textile Mach. Div., Inc. v. South Carolina Ins. Co.,* 277 S.C. 88, 282 S.E.2d 856 (1981). If the facts alleged in the complaint raise a reasonable possibility that the insured may be held liable for some act or omission covered by the policy, then the insurer must defend. If no such possibility is raised, no duty of defense is owed. *Id.* Hence, whether a duty to defend exists is determined by comparing the allegations of the complaint to the terms of the policy.

The injuries that Metropolitan alleged were inflicted by Liberty, and cannot reasonably be considered to be accidental, unintentional, or unexpected from the standpoint of Liberty. Each complaint alleges a conscious scheme by Liberty to destroy Metropolitan's business, entice its agents away and cause its agents to steal Metropolitan's materials and secrets. The Supreme Court of South Carolina has construed similar occurrence clauses to exclude from coverage injuries caused by the intentional conduct of the insured, including breach of contract, fraud and unfair trade practices. *R.S. Earnhardt Textile Mach. Division, Inc. v. South Carolina Ins. Co.,* 277 S.C. 88, 282 S.E.2d 856 (1981). The district court was correct in finding no occurrence as such term was defined for the property damage and bodily injury risk categories. Significantly, in the

---

[7] All of the suits were eventually settled and dismissed without payment by Liberty of any damages.

[8] Because jurisdiction is based upon diversity of citizenship, 28 U.S.C. § 1332, we look to the law of South Carolina to determine the issues in this case. *Erie R. Co. v. Tomkins,* 304 U.S. 64, 58 S.Ct. 817, 82 L.Ed. 1188 (1938).

South Carolina cases cited, *supra,* the insurance policies covered only property damage and bodily injury. Advertising liability was not an issue.

The district court, however, erred in dismissing the primary carriers, Home and American, and excess carrier, U.S. Fire, from the lawsuit. All three of those policies insured Liberty for claims arising out of unfair competition and disparagement in its advertising activities under sections entitled personal injury and advertising liability coverage. As shown above, many of the claims by Metropolitan alleged unfair competition and disparagement. While conceding as much in their arguments, the defendant carriers assert that these claims did not arise in connection with Liberty's, the insured's, advertising activities. This point, however, was not addressed by the district court and requires consideration upon remand. In this connection, we note that the policies themselves are silent as to what constitutes advertising activity. When these policies are construed against the drafter, it is arguable, for example, that the activities of Liberty's agents, as alleged in the Metropolitan complaints, could be termed advertising. This is particularly so where, as here, we are dealing with the duty to defend, when we remember that the duty to defend in South Carolina is broader than the duty to indemnify. *See Sloan Const. Co., Inc. v. Central Nat. Ins. Co. of Omaha,* 269 S.C. 183, 236 S.E.2d 818, 820 (1977). Additionally, we address this issue at the summary judgment stage where all factual doubt must be resolved in favor of the non-moving party. In all events, we express no opinion upon that question.

We do not agree with the district court that there was a requirement of an unexpected or unintended result from an occurrence to trigger coverage under the advertising liability section of each policy. . . . The two primary policies, American and Home, did not include advertising liability in those policies' restricted definitions of occurrence, and the U.S. Fire policy defined occurrence separately for advertising liability as shown above. Although those three policies (American, Home and U.S. Fire) required such an occurrence to invoke coverage for property damage and property damage was alleged in the Metropolitan lawsuits, ". . . an insurer is not excused from defending suits against the policyholder by the joinder in the same suits of causes of action covered by the policy with the other causes of action beyond its scope. . . ." *Employers Mut. Liability Co. of Wisconsin v. Hendrix,* 199 F.2d 53, 59 (4th Cir.1952).

. . . .

The district court based its dismissal of Liberty's remaining causes of action on its finding that no defendant owed Liberty a duty to defend the Metropolitan lawsuits. Since the ultimate liability of the defendant carriers must await further proceedings in the district court, we reinstate these counts in order to allow the district court to judge their worth anew in light of our decision. Likewise, the district court should consider in the first instance the other defenses raised by the carriers.

We again stress that we are not establishing or apportioning liability. We only hold that liability has been prematurely foreclosed. The judgment of the district court order is vacated, and the case is remanded for further proceedings not inconsistent with this opinion.

VACATED AND REMANDED.

NOTES AND QUESTIONS

1. *Coverage for Unfair Competition.* The policies in *Liberty Life* covered claims for "libel, slander, defamation, infringement of copyright, title or slogan, piracy, unfair competition, idea misappropriation or invasion of rights of privacy committed" during advertising activities. Notably, all of these torts typically are intentional. How did the court in *Liberty Life* reconcile the definition of "occurrence," which only covers accidents that cause bodily injury or property damage, with coverage for these intentional torts?

2. *Advertising Activities.* Why is the restriction that limits coverage for unfair competition claims to only claims based upon activities that occur during "advertising activities" an almost meaningless limitation on coverage?

3. Coverage for Disparagement

BANKWEST V. FIDELITY & DEPOSIT CO. OF MARYLAND

63 F.3d 974 (10th Cir. 1995)

HENRY, CIRCUIT JUDGE.

Plaintiff-appellant Bankwest appeals the district court's order granting summary judgment to defendant-appellee Fidelity Deposit Company of Maryland (Fidelity). The district court ruled that Fidelity had no duty to defend or indemnify Bankwest in conjunction with a lawsuit filed by two customers who alleged Bankwest had damaged their reputation. *See Bankwest v. Fidelity & Deposit Co.,* 832 F.Supp. 313 (D.Kan.1993) We exercise jurisdiction under 28 U.S.C. § 1291, reverse the decision of the district court, and remand for further proceedings.

I. BACKGROUND

In 1987, Harlan Dale House and Cora House sued Bankwest (then known as the Goodland State Bank & Trust Company) in Kansas state court alleging that, in 1985, Bankwest orally agreed to extend them an $800,000 line of credit. The Houses alleged that in exchange for that line of credit they agreed to grant Bankwest a $1,000,000 "fourth Deed of Trust" on real estate they owned in Vail, Colorado. Applt's App. at 237. According to the Houses, they had previously granted three deeds of trust on the same Colorado property: a $40,000 first deed of trust to the First National Bank of Windsor, a $100,000 second deed of trust to the same bank, and a $100,000 third deed of trust to the First Bank of Vail. As part of the alleged oral contract, Bankwest agreed not to interfere with the Houses' existing lines of credit with these other banks.

The Houses' petition further alleged that, approximately sixty days after negotiation of the oral agreement, Bankwest's president sent letters to the Windsor and Vail banks stating that both banks were "estopped from making any future advancements" to the Houses. *Id.* at 238. The Houses also maintained that, from October 1985 until April 1986, Bankwest refused to honor its promise to extend them the $800,000 line of credit.

According to the Houses, in May 1986, Bankwest "renewed its prior agreement to extend a full [$800,000] line of credit to plaintiffs and not to impair or interfere with plaintiffs' existing lines of credit with First National Bank of Windsor and First Bank of Vail, as consideration for plaintiffs' pledge of the fourth Deed of Trust." *Id.* at 239. Subsequently, the Windsor bank sent a proposed agreement to Bankwest's president acknowledging the subordination of Bankwest's fourth deed of trust to the prior deeds of trust. Bankwest's president refused to sign the agreement. As a result, the Houses alleged, the Windsor bank initiated foreclosure proceedings against the Vail property, and they were compelled to file bankruptcy in order to avoid a forced sale.

The Houses' petition asserted three causes of action: (1) a claim that Bankwest breached the agreement to extend the $800,000 line of credit and not to interfere with the Houses' existing lines of credit with other banks; (2) a claim that Bankwest's actions as to the Houses' lines of credit with other banks "were intentional and with malice, and amounted to an interference with the business relationship and interference with contract," *id.* at 241; and (3) a claim that Bankwest obtained the fourth deed of trust by false pretenses in that Bankwest had no intention of honoring the conditions upon which the Houses had tendered it. The Houses sought compensatory and punitive damages, as well as a declaratory judgment that the fourth deed of trust was void.

At the time of the filing of the Houses' lawsuit, Fidelity had issued several liability insurance policies to Bankwest. Only one of these policies is relevant to this appeal: Fidelity's Special Multi-Peril Policy for Financial Institutions (the multi-peril policy). The multi-peril policy provided coverage for bodily injury, property damage, and personal injury. The personal injury section stated, in part:

> The company will pay on behalf of the insured all sums which the insured shall become legally obligated to pay as damages because of injury (herein called "personal injury") sustained by any person or organization and *arising out of one or more of the following*

> *offenses* committed in the conduct of the named insured's business:
>
> . . . .
>
> B. *the publication or utterance of a libel or slander or of other defamatory or disparaging material . . .*;
>
> . . . .
>
> if such offense is committed during the policy period within the United States of America, its territories or possessions, or Canada, and the Company shall have the right and duty to defend any suit against the insured seeking damages on account of such personal injury even if any of the allegations of the suit are groundless, false or fraudulent, and may make such investigation and settlement of any claim or suit as it deems expedient, but the company shall not be obligated to pay any claim or judgment or to defend any suit after the applicable limit of the company's liability has been exhausted by payment of judgments or settlements.

Id. at 292–93 (emphasis added).

Shortly after receiving the Houses' petition, Bankwest's attorney sent a letter to Fidelity's insurance agent requesting Fidelity to defend the action. On October 5, 1987, Fidelity acknowledged receipt of the Houses' petition. However, in a letter dated May 31, 1988, Fidelity stated to Bankwest that it would not defend the lawsuit. Bankwest made several subsequent requests for a defense, but Fidelity refused. In September 1990, the Houses and Bankwest reached a settlement. The Houses received $400,000 in cash from Bankwest and forgiveness of a debt in the amount of $53,993.49. In turn, the Houses dismissed the suit against Bankwest.

In June 1992, Bankwest filed this diversity action, alleging that Fidelity had breached the insurance contract by refusing to defend the Houses' lawsuit and indemnify it for the settlement. Bankwest sought to recover the costs incurred in defending the Houses' suit, the amount paid to the Houses under the terms of the settlement, attorneys' fees, costs, and prejudgment interest.

Both parties filed motions for summary judgment. Bankwest argued that the multi-peril policy's reference to "the publication or utterance of a libel or slander or of other defamatory or disparaging material" was broad enough to include the Houses' lawsuit because the Houses alleged that they had been disparaged by Bankwest's letters to the Colorado banks and sought damages for loss of reputation. Fidelity responded that the policy covered only the specific claims listed and that, because none of the claims in the Houses' lawsuit were listed in the multi-peril policy, it had no duty to defend or indemnify Bankwest.

In granting summary judgment to Fidelity, the district court reasoned that the House lawsuit did not involve the publication of defamatory or disparaging material. The court stated that the only possible defamatory or disparaging publications were the letters that Bankwest sent to the Colorado banks. However, it concluded:

> While those foreclosure proceedings may have been precipitated by the "letters of estoppel," it cannot be argued that those letters were disparaging to the Houses. Even construing the terms "disparaging material" in favor of plaintiff, the court is constrained to conclude that the letters, which merely stated that the Colorado banks were estopped from advancing the Houses any additional money, were not, by any stretch of the meaning, disparaging.

Bankwest, 832 F.Supp. at 318. The court also rejected Bankwest's argument that Fidelity's delay in responding to Bankwest's requests for a defense estopped it from asserting that the policies did not cover the lawsuit.

On appeal, Bankwest renews its argument that the reference in Fidelity's multi-peril policy to "the publication or utterance of a libel or slander or of other defamatory or disparaging material" encompasses the Houses' claim for intentional interference with contract and business relations. As a result, Bankwest maintains, Fidelity had a duty to defend the Houses' lawsuit and to indemnify it on the Houses' intentional interference claim. Bankwest also argues that Fidelity should be estopped from denying coverage.

II. DISCUSSION

. . . .

Under Kansas law, an insurer's duty to defend arises "whenever there is a 'potential of liability' under the policy." *State Farm Fire & Casualty Co. v. Finney,* 244 Kan. 545, 770 P.2d 460, 466 (1989) (quoting *Spruill Motors, Inc. v. Universal Underwriters Ins. Co.,* 212 Kan. 681, 512 P.2d 403, 407 (1973)). The insurer must determine whether there is a potential of liability under the policy by examining the allegations of the complaint as well as any additional facts that have been brought to its attention. *Id.* The relevant determination for the insurer is whether there is "a possibility that under the facts of the case the insured may be found legally obligated to pay damages because of an occurrence that was an insured risk; that is, a possibility that there may be a duty to indemnify arising out of the facts of the case." *American Fidelity Ins. Co. v. Employers Mut. Casualty Co.,* 3 Kan.App.2d 245, 593 P.2d 14, 19–20 (1979).

. . . .

We have discovered no Kansas or Tenth Circuit decisions construing the disputed phrase in the multi-peril policy. However, several other courts have construed the identical phrase, or a similar one, in analogous circumstances. For example, in *Liberty Bank v. Travelers Indem. Co. of America,* 870 F.2d 1504, 1506 (9th Cir.1989), the Ninth Circuit held that a liability insurance policy providing coverage for "a publication or utterance . . . of a libel or slander or other defamatory or disparaging material" did not require the insurer to defend claims for fraudulent misrepresentation, negligent misrepresentation, or breach of an implied covenant of good faith and fair dealing. Although the plaintiff in the underlying action had alleged that employees of the insured bank had written to other banks about the plaintiff's delinquent loan payments, the Ninth Circuit noted that the plaintiff had not alleged that the bank employees' statements were false. "Because falsehood is an element of defamation," the court reasoned, "facts which set forth some element of defamation but not falsehood, when construed in light of a complaint which does not include a cause of action for defamation, do not trigger a duty to defend." *Id.* at 1508; *see also Aetna Casualty & Sur. Co. v. First Sec. Bank,* 662 F.Supp. 1126, 1132 (D.Mont.1987) (holding that the insurer was not required to defend claims for breach of an implied covenant of good faith and fair dealing and for wrongful termination of employment because underlying complaint did not allege that the defendant made a false statement to a third party); *Western Commerce Bank v. Reliance Ins. Co.,* 105 N.M. 346, 732 P.2d 873, 876 (1987) (holding that identical policy language did not require insurer to defend counterclaim for interference with contractual relations because "[t]here were no allegations that the Bank published or uttered anything involving [the plaintiff's] reputation or disparaging [the plaintiff's] property" and because the counterclaim did not necessarily imply such allegations); *American & Foreign Ins. Co. v. Church Sch.,* 645 F.Supp. 628, 634 (E.D.Va.1986) (holding that identical policy language did not require insurer to defend claims for assault, battery, and intentional and negligent infliction of emotional distress in spite of alleged damage to reputation and noting that "coverage must be determined based on the claims under which relief is sought").

In contrast, several other courts have construed the identical or similar policy language more broadly. In *Boston Symphony Orchestra, Inc. v. Commercial Union Ins. Co.,* 406 Mass. 7, 545 N.E.2d 1156 (1989), the court held that a liability insurance policy containing the same personal injury provision as Fidelity's multi-peril policy required the insurer to defend a breach of contract claim in which the actress Vanessa Redgrave alleged that the Boston Symphony's cancellation of a performance with her had "led others to refrain from hiring" her. *Id.,* 545 N.E.2d at 1157. The court reasoned that the essence of Ms. Redgrave's claims was that the Boston Symphony "somehow spoke slightingly of her and damaged her reputation." *Id.,* 545 N.E.2d at 1159. Because "disparage" means, among other things, " 'to lower in rank and estimation by actions or words,' " the court said, the policy could reasonably be construed to cover Ms. Redgrave's claim. *Id.* (quoting *Webster's New International Dictionary of the English Language* 750 (2d ed. 1959)); *see also City of Cape May v. St. Paul Fire & Marine Ins. Co.,* 216 N.J.Super. 697, 524 A.2d 882, 883–86 (Ct.App.Div.1987) (policy covering "the publication or utterance of a libel or slander or other defamatory or disparaging material" required insurer to defend claim for malicious interference with business interests in which plaintiff alleged that insured's false statements damaged his reputation); *CNA Casualty v. Seaboard Sur. Co.,* 176 Cal.App.3d 598, 222 Cal.Rptr. 276, 281 (1986) (holding that policy covering libel, slander, and the publication or utterance of other defamatory or disparaging material required insurer to defend antitrust claim alleging that the insured misrepresented property rights in order to disrupt plaintiff's business relationships).

Bankwest maintains that the latter line of cases establishes that the phrase "the publication or utterance of a libel or slander or of other defamatory or disparaging material" can be reasonably read to encompass claims other than libel or slander that involve the publication of "defamatory or disparaging material." Bankwest's argument is supported by the language of the policy. By listing the "offense" of "the publication or utterance of . . . defamatory or disparaging material" separately, the multi-peril policy appears to cover more than just libel and slander claims.

In fact, there are several torts distinct from libel or slander that one might reasonably describe as the publication or utterance of defamatory or disparaging material. One such tort is " 'called by various names such as 'disparagement of property,' 'slander of goods,' 'commercial disparagement,' and 'trade libel.' " *Bacchus Indus., Inc. v. Arvin Indus., Inc.,* 939 F.2d 887, 892 (10th Cir.1991) (quoting W. Page Keeton et al., *Prosser and Keeton on the Law of Torts* § 128, at 963–64 (5th ed. 1984)). The tort is "now generally referred to as 'injurious falsehood.' " *Id.* The *Restatement (Second) of Torts* § 623A (1979) describes this tort as follows:

> One who publishes a false statement harmful to the interests of another is subject to liability for pecuniary loss resulting to the other if:
>
> (a) he intends for publication of the statement to result in harm to the interests of the other having a pecuniary value, or either recognizes or should recognize that it is likely to do so, and
>
> (b) he knows that the statement is false or acts in reckless disregard of its truth or falsity.

The tort has been broadly interpreted to include the publication of "other falsehoods harmful to any legal interest of another that has pecuniary value." *Id.* § 623A introductory note; *see also* Keeton et al., *supra,* § 128, at

967 (noting that the "cause of action probably is as broad as any injurious falsehood which disturbs prospective advantage, and it is not necessarily confined even to commercial relations"); *Ruiz v. Varan,* 110 N.M. 478, 797 P.2d 267, 269–70 (1990) (discussing elements of injurious falsehood).

The multi-peril policy's reference to "the offense" of the publication of other defamatory or disparaging material is also broad enough to include certain claims for intentional interference with contract. "There is no technical requirement as to the kind of conduct that may result in interference with the third party's performance of the contract," *Restatement (Second) of Torts* § 766 cmt. k (1979), and as a result there are a variety of ways in which interference with another's contractual rights may constitute a tort, *see id.* § 766 cmts. k–n. Making false representations is one such method of tortious interference. *Id.* § 767 cmt. c; Keeton et al., *supra,* § 129, at 992; *see also Ball Corp. v. Xidex Corp.,* 967 F.2d 1440, 1445 (10th Cir.1992) (analyzing claims for "intentional interference with protected property interests, intentional interference with prospective business relationships, and unfair competition" by considering whether the defendant intentionally made false statements or made statements recklessly or with gross negligence as to their truth); *City of Brady v. Bennie,* 735 S.W.2d 275, 279 (Tex.Ct.App.1987) (discussing intentional interference with contract claim involving publication of a letter).

In the instant case, the Houses' claim for intentional interference with contract does allege that Bankwest interfered with their contractual rights and business relations by publishing such false statements. In particular, the letters of estoppel that Bankwest allegedly sent to the Colorado banks asserted that those banks were "estopped" from advancing any additional funds to the Houses. Viewed in conjunction with the other allegations of the Houses' petition, Bankwest's assertion of the limitations on the Colorado banks' lending authority was not true: because Bankwest had no right to interfere with the lines of credit that the Houses' had established with the Colorado banks there was no basis for such an estoppel. Moreover, according to the Houses' petition, Bankwest's false statements about the Colorado banks' lending authority caused the Houses to suffer pecuniary loss.

In reaching the contrary conclusion, the district court appears to have read the phrase "other defamatory or disparaging material" too narrowly. Although the estoppel letters sent by Bankwest did not directly attack the Houses' character, the Houses did allege that these letters harmed a "legal interest . . . that ha[d] pecuniary value." *See Restatement (Second) of Torts* § 623A introductory note; *see also Hurlbut,* 749 S.W.2d at 766 (contrasting action for defamation with action for injurious falsehood and noting that "[t]he action for defamation is to protect the personal reputation of the injured party, whereas the action for injurious falsehood or business disparagement is to protect the economic interests of the injured party against pecuniary loss"); *Georgia Soc. of Plastic Surgeons, Inc. v. Anderson,* 257 Ga. 710, 363 S.E.2d 140, 143 (1987) (stating that action for injurious falsehood protects economic interests).

This is a close case. But Kansas law-as does the law in most states-assists with the resolution of such cases. As discussed earlier, we must construe the multi-peril policy in favor of the insured, Bankwest. Thus we conclude that "the publication of . . . other defamatory or disparaging material" is susceptible of a construction supporting coverage of the Houses' claim that Bankwest interfered with their contractual and business relations by sending the estoppel letters. Accordingly, under the terms of the personal injury section of the multi-peril policy, Fidelity was obligated to defend Bankwest in the Houses' lawsuit.[4] *See Spivey v. Safeco Ins. Co.,* 254 Kan. 237, 865 P.2d 182, 188 (1993) (concluding that when a petition alleges both acts that are covered and acts that are not, "these alleged facts give rise to the potential for liability, and the duty to defend arises"). The district court erred in granting summary judgment to Fidelity on the duty to defend issue.

As to the question of whether Fidelity is obligated to indemnify Bankwest, we conclude that further development of the record is necessary. When a case is settled, the duty to indemnify " 'must be determined [o]n the basis of the settlement.' " *American Motorists,* 946 F.2d at 1488 (quoting *Travelers Ins.,* 883 F.2d at 1099) (alteration in original). Here, the settlement agreement in the Houses' lawsuit specifies neither the claims settled nor the amounts paid to settle each claim. Whether any of the settlement constituted payment for the Houses' claim alleging intentional interference with contractual and business relations is a question we leave for the district court's determination on remand.

In summary, we conclude that the personal injury section of the multi-peril policy obligated Fidelity to defend the Houses' lawsuit and that further development of the record is necessary to determine whether Fidelity is obligated to indemnify Bankwest. The district court's order granting summary judgment to Fidelity and denying summary judgment to Bankwest is reversed and remanded for proceedings consistent with this opinion.

REVERSED and REMANDED

---

[4] We emphasize that it is not the Houses' allegation of damage to reputation that brings their lawsuit within the coverage provided by the personal injury section of the multi-peril policy. Instead, it is Houses' assertion of a claim that, in light of all of its elements, can reasonably be described as the publication of defamatory or disparaging material (*i.e.,* the claim for intentional interference with contractual and business relations) that is dispositive.

NOTES AND QUESTIONS

1. *Disparagement?* What was the "disparagement" in the *Bankwest* case that triggered the insurer's duty to defend?

2. *Limits to Coverage?* Under the *Bankwest* case, are there really any limits to the types of business tort claims that insurers must defend? Can you articulate the boundaries of the duty to defend business tort claims?

4. Coverage for Intellectual Property Infringement

AMAZON.COM INTERNATIONAL, INC. V. AMERICAN DYNASTY SURPLUS LINES INS. CO.

85 P.3d 974 (Wash. Ct. App. 2004)

Opinion

ELLINGTON, J.

In a lawsuit against Amazon.com International, Inc., a software manufacturer alleged that Amazon infringed upon its patents by misappropriating its software for use on Amazon's website to market goods for sale to the public. Because the allegations conceivably amounted to an advertising injury covered by Amazon's policy with Atlantic Mutual Insurance Company, Atlantic Mutual had a duty to defend. We therefore reverse summary judgment in favor of Atlantic Mutual, and remand for entry of summary judgment in favor of Amazon's excess carrier, American Dynasty Surplus Lines.

FACTS

This insurance dispute originated with a lawsuit filed in March 2000 by Intouch Group. Intouch holds patents for interactive music preview technology, which enables customers to listen to samples of music products at kiosks and over the Internet. Intouch alleged Amazon and other defendants had infringed upon those patents; specifically, Intouch alleged Amazon used the Intouch technology to enable customers to preview music products available for sale via Amazon's website.

Amazon tendered its defense to two insurers: Atlantic Mutual Insurance Company, its commercial general liability carrier; and American Dynasty Surplus Lines Insurance Company, an excess carrier. The Atlantic Mutual policy does not expressly cover patent infringement, but does cover advertising injury. The American Dynasty policy covers patent infringement, but only as excess coverage.

Both insurers refused to defend. Amazon initiated a declaratory judgment action against American Dynasty. The parties settled. American Dynasty reimbursed Amazon for its costs in the Intouch litigation, and Amazon assigned its rights against Atlantic Mutual to American Dynasty.

American Dynasty then brought this action, alleging that Atlantic Mutual should have provided a defense because Intouch's allegations amounted to an advertising injury.

Both parties sought summary judgment. The trial court granted summary judgment for Atlantic Mutual. American Dynasty appeals.

DISCUSSION

The duty to defend is broader than the duty to indemnify, and arises whenever a complaint contains any factual allegation which could render the insurer liable to the insured under the policy. "Only if the alleged claim is clearly not covered by the policy is the insurer relieved of its duty to defend. If the complaint is ambiguous, it will be liberally construed in favor of triggering the insurer's duty to defend." When the duty to defend cannot be ascertained from the complaint alone, the insurer must consider facts outside the complaint.

Amazon's Atlantic Mutual policy covers advertising injury "caused by an offense committed in the course of advertising [its] goods, products or services." Coverage thus exists for advertising injury only if the allegations satisfy the policy definition for advertising injury, and there is a causal connection between the allegations and the insured's advertising activities.

According to Intouch's complaint, Intouch holds patents for technology that "provides a method by which consumers can download and listen to portions of pre-selected music over the Internet." The samples are compressed or otherwise digitally altered. Intouch alleged Amazon used Intouch's technology to enable consumers to preview music available for purchase: "Each of the Defendants has at least one network web site, which allows consumers to preview pre-selected portions of pre-recorded music over the internet. . . . Intouch contends that each of the Defendants' web sites . . . infringe upon the Patents."

Advertising Injury

The Atlantic Mutual policy defines "advertising injury" as injury arising from one or more of the following:

> a. Oral or written publication of material that slanders or libels a person or organization or disparages a person's or organization's goods, products or services;
>
> b. Oral or written publication of material that violates a person's right of privacy;
>
> c. *Misappropriation of advertising ideas* or style of doing business; or
>
> d. Infringement or copyright, title or slogan.

Misappropriation of an advertising idea may be accomplished by the "wrongful taking of another's manner of advertising," by "the wrongful taking of an idea concerning the solicitation of business and customers"; or by "the wrongful taking of the manner by which another advertises its goods or services." The misappropriation must occur "in the elements of the advertisement itself—in its text, form, logo, or pictures—rather than in the product being advertised."

Patent infringement arising from the manufacture of an infringing product is not an advertising injury even if the infringing product is used in advertising. But patent infringement may constitute an advertising injury "*where an entity uses an advertising technique that is itself patented.*" That was the essence of Intouch's allegation against Amazon. Giving the required liberal construction to the pleadings, Intouch alleged that its patented music preview technology was an element of Amazon's advertisement. The Intouch complaint thus conceivably alleged misappropriation of an idea concerning the solicitation of business and customers.

Course of Advertising

An advertising injury must occur in the course of advertising goods for sale. "Advertising" normally refers to " 'any oral, written, or graphic statement made by the seller in any manner in connection with the solicitation of business.' " It may also involve the "widespread distribution of promotional material to the public at large." Amazon's website exists for the purpose of promoting products for sale to the public. This is advertising. Intouch's complaint thus implicitly alleged that Amazon used its product in its course of advertising.

Causal Connection Between Advertising and Injury

An advertising injury must also have a causal connection with the insured's advertising activities. That is, the advertising activities must cause the injury, not merely expose it; an injury that could have occurred independent and irrespective of any advertising is not an advertising injury.

This causal requirement is the reason most patent infringement claims do not constitute advertising injuries. The basis of such claims is typically the sale of infringing products, not their advertisement. Nor does an advertising injury occur where the injury is caused by the subsequent advertising of an already infringing product.

Atlantic Mutual contends that a software program embedded in a website cannot satisfy the causation requirement for an advertising injury. Atlantic relies particularly upon *Microtec Research v. Nationwide*. But the facts and issues there were different. In *Microtec,* a software company allegedly passed off a competitor's software as its own, misleading customers "into thinking [it] was capable of writing leading edge compiler code as good as [the competitor's]." As the circuit court noted, however, there was no allegation that Microtec used the stolen code in its advertising. Injury resulted from Microtec's misappropriation of the code, not from any advertising, and there was thus no advertising injury under the policy.

By contrast here, the alleged injury derived not merely from misappropriation of the code, but from *its use as the means to market goods for sale*. In other words, the infringement occurred in the advertising itself. Intouch's allegations therefore satisfied the causation requirement for a potential advertising injury.

Atlantic Mutual had a duty to defend Amazon unless the injuries alleged by Intouch were clearly not covered by the policy. Because the injuries were conceivably covered, Intouch's complaint triggered Atlantic Mutual's duty to defend. As Amazon's assignee, American Dynasty was entitled to summary judgment in its favor.

. . . .

Reversed and remanded for entry of summary judgment in favor of American Dynasty, and for a fees award.

NOTES AND QUESTIONS

1. *Patent Infringement Coverage?* It is important to note that the coverage claim in the *Amazon.com* case was for the use of another party's patented idea in advertising activities, as opposed to simply seeking coverage for a patent infringement claim. Claims for patent infringement, as well as copyright and trademark infringement, outside the advertising context, generally are excluded from coverage under current CGL policy forms. *See, e.g.*, Exclusion i. of Sample CGL Policy at the beginning of this chapter.

2. *Intentional Torts and the "Expected or Intended" Exclusion*. Although the case law is not uniform or unanimous, courts in most states generally enforce coverage for the intentional torts specifically set forth in Personal and Advertising Liability insurance despite the presence of an "expected or intended" exclusion in the "Bodily Injury" and "Property Damage" coverage section of the same policy. *See generally* Christopher C. French, *Debunking the Myth that Insurance Coverage is Not Available or Allowed for Intentional Torts or Damages*, 8 Hastings Bus. L. J. 65 (2012); *Lincoln Nat'l Health & Cas. Ins. Co. v. Brown*, 782 F. Supp. 110, 112–13 (M.D. Ga. 1992) (where the policy specifically includes malicious prosecution as a covered claim, a provision limiting coverage to unintentional acts does not apply); *McCormack Baron Mgmt. Services Inc. v. Am. Guar. & Liab. Ins Co.*, 989 S.W.2d 168, 170 (Mo. 1999) (recognizing in a defamation case that so long as "the complaint merely alleges facts that give rise to a claim potentially within the policy's coverage, the insurer has a duty to defend"); *Fluke Corp. v. Hartford Accident & Indem. Co.*, 34 P.3d 809, 814 (Wash. 2000) (concluding that coverage for malicious prosecution does not violate public policy); *Atl. Mut. Ins. Co. v. J. Lamb, Inc.*,

123 Cal. Rptr. 2d 256, 269 (Cal. Ct. App. 2002) ("Whether characterized as a trade libel or product disparagement, an injurious falsehood directed at the organization or products, goods, or services of another falls within the coverage of the [policy]."); *Century Sur. Co. v. Seductions, LLC*, 349 F. App'x 455, 459 (11th Cir. 2009) (recognizing insurance coverage for wrongful eviction but noting split in authority regarding the necessity of a possessory interest in order to assert claim). Consequently, policyholder and insurer counsel alike should be familiar with this often-overlooked area of insurance coverage.

3. *Exclusions.* There also are numerous exclusions in Personal and Advertising Liability insurance, such as for "knowing" violations of another party's rights, the publication of information known to be false, and criminal acts. *See, e.g.*, Exclusions a., b., and d. of the Sample CGL Policy at the beginning of this chapter. Consequently, as with other types of coverage, the analysis of whether a claim is covered does not end once it has been determined a claim is covered under the insuring agreement.

4. *Specialty Policies That Cover Other Types of Intentional or Unlawful Misconduct.* Although not encompassed by Personal and Advertising Liability insurance, various lines of specialty insurance are also available to cover other types of misconduct that often is intentional and unlawful, such as improper employment practices. Indeed, since the early 1990s, Employment Practices Liability insurance has been available to cover improper employment practices such as racial discrimination, wrongful termination, sexual discrimination, and retaliatory discharge. Courts that allow such insurance despite the fortuity doctrine and the public policy of deterring intentional misconduct give greater weight to the competing public policy of honoring the parties' rights to enter contracts and in recognition of insurers' ability to exclude claims for intentional misconduct if they want to do so. *See, e.g.*, *School District for Royal Oak v. Continental Casualty Co.*, 912 F.2d 844, 849 (6th Cir. 1990). For various commentators' thoughts regarding issues related to insurance coverage for wrongful employment practices and a discussion of the case law in that area, *see, e.g.*, Douglas R. Richmond, *Insurance Coverage for Wrongful Employment Practices*, 48 Okla. L. Rev. 1 (1995); Francis J. Mootz III, *Insurance Coverage of Employment Discrimination Claims*, 52 U. Miami L. Rev. 1 (1997); Jeffrey W. Stempel, *Judge-Made Insurance That Was Not on the Menu: Schmidt v. Smith and the Confluence of Text, Expectation, and Public Policy in the Realm of Employment Practices Liability*, 21 W. New Eng. L. Rev. 283 (1999); Richard A. Bales and Julie McGhahy, *Insuring Title VII Violations*, 27 S. Ill. U. L. J. 71 (2002).

EXERCISES

1. Write a 5-page memo that attempts to reconcile the apparent inconsistency between the "expected or intended" exclusion and the coverage provisions for intentional torts under Personal and Advertising Liability insurance. In your memo, address whether adverse selection, moral hazard, and correlated risks are relevant to the analysis.

2. The saying "when you throw dirt, you lose ground" is often described as a "Texas proverb," but an internet search will show that the phrase is popular throughout the country. An internet search will also confirm that many scorned spouses, partners, significant others, and best friends have paid insufficient attention to this axiom. Consider a situation in which a "scorned ex" posts text messages from or inappropriate (e.g., sexually explicit) photos of that person's ex (the "aggrieved ex") on Facebook or Instagram.

Write a 5-page memo addressing whether there is—and should be—coverage under Personal and Advertising Injury insurance for the invasion of privacy claim that the aggrieved ex subsequently brings against the scorned ex. In your discussion, consider the relevance of the fact that the scorned ex likely does not have any assets that could satisfy a money judgment if the claim against the scorned ex is successful.

II. "CLAIMS-MADE" PROFESSIONAL LIABILITY INSURANCE

Although thus far we have focused on the occurrence-based form of liability insurance, many lines of liability insurance are written as "claims-made" insurance. Claims-made insurance for professional liability policies emerged in the 1940s. Today, although Commercial General Liability and homeowners insurance are still occurrence-based policies, most new lines of liability insurance written are claims-made. For example, the various lines of professional liability insurance, such as Directors and Officers (D&O), Medical and Legal Malpractice, and Errors & Omissions (E&O), are claims-made insurance, as well as Employment Practices, Cyber, and Environmental Liability insurance.

Unlike occurrence-based insurance, where coverage is triggered by injury or damage occurring during the policy period that is caused by the policyholder's acts or omissions (regardless of whether the act or omission giving rise to the injury or damage is before or during the policy period), claims-made insurance is triggered when a claim is asserted against the policyholder during the policy period. Under occurrence-based insurance, claims for which the insurer is liable can be asserted years or even decades after the policy period ends, subject only to the running of the relevant statute of limitations. This makes it difficult for insurers to accurately predict their liabilities and to charge appropriate premiums up front for the insurance. This is especially problematic for "all risk" types of insurance, such as Commercial General Liability insurance, which covers all property damage and bodily injuries caused by an occurrence unless specifically excluded. New types of liabilities are always emerging, and insurers cannot account for them at the time of underwriting. This was especially evident in the late 1970s and through the 1980s when massive liabilities for asbestos bodily injury and environmental property damage claims emerged with highly disruptive impacts.

Insurers prefer to sell claims-made liability insurance. Claims-made insurance creates more certainty regarding their liabilities because, with a few exceptions, the covered claims must be asserted prior to the end of the policy period. This allows insurers to charge more actuarially accurate premiums, which also tend to be lower for the policyholder than premiums for occurrence-based insurance. Claims-made insurance also typically attempts to prevent a policyholder from accessing multiple policy years of coverage for a single injury-causing event or an injury-causing event that is ongoing during multiple policy years. In other words, bodily injury or property damage can be continuous in the sense that it "occurs" over a long period of time, but a claim is only filed once. The rules regarding "late notice" are also much more favorable to insurers because, unlike occurrence-based insurance, insurers do not need to prove they were prejudiced by the timing of the notice in many states. Consequently, the insurance industry made a push in the 1980s to replace occurrence-based Commercial General Liability insurance with claims-made insurance. That effort resulted in an antitrust lawsuit being filed by numerous states and policyholders against certain insurers that ultimately was decided against the insurers by the United States Supreme Court in *Hartford Fire Ins. Co. v. California*, 509 U.S. 764 (1993) (in refusing to recognize antitrust immunity for the insurer-defendants due to the "boycott" exception to the McCarran-Ferguson Act with respect to the alleged conspiracy to change from occurrence-based CGL insurance to claims-made CGL insurance, the Court discussed some of the differences between the two types of insurance).

In order to force policyholders to buy separate claims-made insurance policies to cover certain liabilities such as professional errors and omissions, insurers typically exclude coverage for such risks under occurrence-based policies. Consequently, one of the issues that commonly then arises in the context of claims-made insurance is whether the injury causing activity constituted the rendering of "professional services." The next section addresses that issue.

A. SAMPLE D&O POLICY

Attached is a sample D&O policy, which is a common type of claims-made insurance that most companies purchase to cover their own liabilities and the liabilities of their officers and directors for claims asserted against them for "wrongful acts." D&O insurance is very valuable because the potential damages in shareholder claims against corporations commonly totals in the hundreds of millions or even billions of dollars for large corporations. D&O insurance becomes an important asset in situations where the corporation becomes insolvent or the officers and directors are judgment proof, which is not unusual if the damages sought are for tens of millions of dollars or more. As you read the policy, consider how the coverage provided under a claims-made policy differs from occurrence-based insurance such as the Sample CGL Policy.

TRAVELERS

<Brand Name>
DIRECTORS, OFFICERS, AND ORGANIZATION LIABILITY COVERAGE DECLARATIONS

POLICY NO. XXXXXXXXXX

<Travelers Casualty and Surety Company of America>
Hartford, Connecticut
(A Stock Insurance Company, herein called the Company)

THIS LIABILITY COVERAGE IS WRITTEN ON A CLAIMS-MADE BASIS. THIS LIABILITY COVERAGE COVERS ONLY CLAIMS FIRST MADE AGAINST INSUREDS DURING THE POLICY PERIOD. THE LIMIT OF LIABILITY AVAILABLE TO PAY SETTLEMENTS OR JUDGMENTS WILL BE REDUCED BY DEFENSE EXPENSES, AND DEFENSE EXPENSES WILL BE APPLIED AGAINST THE RETENTION. THE COMPANY HAS NO DUTY TO DEFEND ANY CLAIM.

ITEM 1	**NAMED INSURED:** <enter named insured> Principal Address: <enter address>
ITEM 2	**POLICY PERIOD:** Inception Date: <enter date> Expiration Date: <enter date> 12:01 A.M. local time both dates at the Principal Address stated in ITEM 1.
ITEM 3	**ADDRESS INFORMATION FOR NOTICES TO THE COMPANY:** <Email: BSIclaims@travelers.com FAX: 888-460-6622 Travelers Bond & Specialty Insurance Attn: Claim Department 385 Washington St. – MC 9275-NB08F St. Paul, MN 55102>
ITEM 4	**COVERAGE INCLUDED AS OF THE INCEPTION DATE IN ITEM 2:** Directors, Officers, and Organization Liability Coverage
ITEM 5	**DIRECTORS, OFFICERS, AND ORGANIZATION LIABILITY COVERAGE** **Directors, Officers, and Organization Limit of Liability:** $<enter amount> for all **Claims** **Investigation Expense Limit of Liability:** $<enter amount> for all **Investigation Expense**, which amount is part of, and not in addition to, the Directors, Officers, and Organization Limit of Liability **Supplemental Independent Director Limit of Liability:** $<enter amount> for all **Independent Director Claims**, which amount is in addition to, and excess of, the Directors, Officers, and Organization Limit of Liability

PCDO-15001 Ed. 03-16 Page 1 of 2

	Retention: Not applicable to non-indemnifiable **Loss** or Insuring Agreement D $<enter amount> for all **Securities Claims** $<enter amount> for all other **Claims** **Prior or Pending Proceeding Date:** <enter date>
ITEM 6	**PREMIUM FOR THE POLICY PERIOD:** $<enter amount> Policy Premium
ITEM 7	**EXTENDED REPORTING PERIOD:** Additional Premium Percentage: Additional Months: <enter percentage> % 12 <enter percentage> % 24 <enter percentage> % 36 <enter percentage> % <enter number of months>
ITEM 8	**FORMS AND ENDORSEMENTS ATTACHED AT ISSUANCE:** <enter form number/edition date> <enter form number/edition date> <enter form number/edition date> <enter form number/edition date> <enter form number/edition date> <enter form number/edition date> <enter form number/edition date> <enter form number/edition date>

THE DECLARATIONS, THE APPLICATION, THE DIRECTORS, OFFICERS, AND ORGANIZATION LIABILITY COVERAGE, AND ANY ENDORSEMENTS ATTACHED THERETO, CONSTITUTE THE ENTIRE AGREEMENT BETWEEN THE COMPANY AND THE INSURED.

IN WITNESS WHEREOF, the Company has caused this policy to be signed by its authorized officers.

Executive Vice President

Corporate Secretary

PCDO-15001 Ed. 03-16

TRAVELERS

DIRECTORS, OFFICERS, AND ORGANIZATION LIABILITY COVERAGE

THIS IS A CLAIMS-MADE COVERAGE WITH DEFENSE EXPENSES INCLUDED IN THE LIMIT OF LIABILITY. PLEASE READ THE POLICY CAREFULLY.

CONSIDERATION CLAUSE

IN CONSIDERATION of the payment of the premium, subject to the Declarations, and pursuant to all terms, conditions, exclusions, and limitations of this **Policy**, the Company and the **Insureds** agree as follows:

I. INSURING AGREEMENTS

A. DIRECTORS AND OFFICERS INDIVIDUAL LIABILITY COVERAGE

The Company will pay, on behalf of an **Insured Person**, **Loss** that is not indemnified by the **Insured Organization** and that such **Insured Person** becomes legally obligated to pay on account of a **Claim** first made against such **Insured Person** during the **Policy Period** or any applicable **Extended Reporting Period**.

B. ORGANIZATION INDEMNIFICATION LIABILITY COVERAGE

The Company will pay, on behalf of an **Insured Organization**, **Loss** of an **Insured Person** that such **Insured Organization** indemnifies and that such **Insured Person** becomes legally obligated to pay on account of a **Claim** first made against such **Insured Person** during the **Policy Period** or any applicable **Extended Reporting Period**.

C. ORGANIZATION SECURITIES CLAIM LIABILITY COVERAGE

The Company will pay, on behalf of an **Insured Organization**, **Loss** that such **Insured Organization** becomes legally obligated to pay on account of a **Securities Claim** first made against such **Insured Organization** during the **Policy Period** or any applicable **Extended Reporting Period**.

D. SECURITY HOLDER DERIVATIVE DEMAND OR ACTION INVESTIGATION EXPENSE COVERAGE

The Company will pay, on behalf of an **Insured Organization**, **Investigation Expenses** on account of a **Security Holder Derivative Action** or **Security Holder Derivative Demand** first made during the **Policy Period** or any applicable **Extended Reporting Period**.

II. ADDITIONAL BENEFITS

A. SUPPLEMENTAL INDEPENDENT DIRECTOR LIABILITY COVERAGE

If the Directors, Officers, and Organization Limit of Liability set forth in ITEM 5 of the Declarations and any other insurance or indemnification available to an **Independent Director** are completely exhausted, the Company will pay, on behalf of such **Independent Director**, **Loss** covered under Insuring Agreement A.

This **Policy** will not be subject to the terms, conditions, exclusions, or limitations of any other insurance; provided, if an insurance policy written as specific excess insurance over this **Policy** is more favorable with respect to section III. DEFINITIONS, **Claim**, **Defense Expenses**, **Loss**, or **Wrongful Act**, or section IV. EXCLUSIONS, then coverage under this section will be amended to follow form to such more favorable corresponding definitions or exclusions.

B. INTERVIEW REQUEST COVERAGE

1. The Company will pay, on behalf of an **Insured Person**, **Interview Expenses** that are not indemnified by the **Insured Organization** incurred by such **Insured Person** in responding to an **Interview Request** first made against such **Insured Person** during the **Policy Period** or any applicable **Extended Reporting Period**.
2. The Company will pay, on behalf of an **Insured Organization**, **Interview Expenses** of an **Insured Person** that such **Insured Organization** indemnifies and that such **Insured Person** incurred in responding to an **Interview Request** first made against such **Insured Person** during the **Policy Period** or any applicable **Extended Reporting Period**.

C. **RETIREE COVERAGE**

If, after the Inception Date of this **Policy**, or the first primary policy continuously written by the Company of which the coverage provided by this **Policy** is a renewal or replacement, and before the end of the **Policy Period**:

1. an **Insured Person** retires and no longer serves in his or her capacity as an **Insured Person**;
2. the Company or **Named Insured** does not renew this **Policy**, or the **Named Insured** terminates this **Policy**; and
3. this **Policy** is not replaced by any other directors and officers liability coverage,

then coverage granted by this **Policy** under Insuring Agreement A for such **Insured Person** is extended for a six-year period from such **Insured Person's** official retirement date, but only with respect to a **Claim** for a **Wrongful Act** occurring before such **Insured Person's** official retirement date.

No coverage is available under this section if the **Named Insured** is entitled to elect an extension of coverage pursuant to section V. CONDITIONS, M. CHANGE OF CONTROL.

III. DEFINITIONS

Wherever appearing in this **Policy**, either in the singular or plural, the following words and phrases appearing in bold type have the following meanings:

Application means: (i) all applications submitted during the 12 months preceding the **Policy Period**, including any written materials attached thereto, or submitted to the Company, for the purpose of underwriting this **Policy**; and (ii) all public documents filed by the **Insured Organization** with the Securities and Exchange Commission (SEC) or any similar domestic or foreign regulatory body during the 12 months preceding the **Policy Period**. All such applications, materials, and public documents are deemed attached to, and incorporated into, this **Policy**.

Claim means:

1. a written demand, other than a **Security Holder Derivative Demand**, against an **Insured**, commenced by such **Insured's** receipt of such demand for monetary damages or non-monetary relief, including arbitration, mediation, or other formal alternative dispute resolution, injunctive relief, or a request to toll or waive any statute of limitations;
2. a proceeding, other than an administrative or regulatory proceeding or investigation, against an **Insured**, commenced by: (i) service of a civil complaint or similar pleading; or (ii) the filing of charges, or the return of an indictment, information, or similar document, solely with respect to a criminal proceeding;
3. an administrative or regulatory proceeding, other than an investigation, against an: (i) **Insured Person**; or (ii) **Insured Organization**, provided that such proceeding is initially made and continuously maintained against an **Insured Person** identified by name, commenced by such **Insured's** receipt of a notice of filed charges or similar document;
4. a formal investigation of an **Insured Person** identified by name, commenced by such **Insured Person's** receipt of a formal order of investigation or similar document, or written notice identifying such **Insured Person** as a target of an investigatory authority, including a Wells Notice from the SEC indicating that it may commence an enforcement action against such **Insured Person**;
5. a request for **Extradition**, commenced by receipt of such request;
6. a **Security Holder Derivative Demand**, solely with respect to Insuring Agreement D, commenced by an **Insured's** receipt of such demand; or
7. a subpoena identifying an **Insured Person** by name, commenced by service upon such **Insured Person** pursuant to an SEC formal investigative order against an **Insured**,

for a **Wrongful Act** occurring before or during the **Policy Period**, including any appeal therefrom; or

8. an **Interview Request**, solely with respect to section II. ADDITIONAL BENEFITS, B. INTERVIEW REQUEST COVERAGE, provided notice has been given to the Company pursuant to section V. CONDITIONS, E. NOTICE, 1. Notice of Claim, commenced by receipt of such **Interview Request**.

Defense Expenses mean:

1. the reasonable costs, charges, fees, or expenses, including any premium or origination fee for a bond, loan, or similar financial instrument, incurred: (i) defending, investigating, or appealing a **Claim**, other than an **Interview Request**; (ii) lawfully opposing, challenging, or resisting any request for, or any effort to obtain, **Extradition**; or (iii) lawfully seeking release of any arrest or confinement of an **Insured Person** to a specific residence or a secure custodial facility by or on behalf of any law enforcement authority;

2. **Event Study Expenses**; or
3. **Nominal Defendant Expenses**;

provided, **Defense Expenses** do not include any: (i) regular or overtime wages, salaries, or fees of any director, officer, **Manager**, or employee of an **Insured Organization** or **Outside Entity**; (ii) **Interview Expenses**; (iii) **Investigation Expenses**; or (iv) the principal of, collateral or interest on collateral for, or interest on, a bond, loan, or similar financial instrument.

Enforcement Body means any domestic or foreign governmental regulatory authority, including the U.S. Department of Justice, the SEC, any state attorney general, or the enforcement unit of any securities exchange, or any foreign enforcement body that is the functional equivalent thereof.

Event Study Expenses mean the reasonable costs, charges, fees, or expenses of an expert witness consented to by the Company, such consent not to be unreasonably withheld, incurred by the **Insured** to conduct an event study regarding issues of price impact relevant to the court's decision whether to grant class certification in a **Securities Claim**.

Executive Officer means any natural person who was, is, or becomes the chief executive officer or chief financial officer, or any functional equivalent position, of the **Insured Organization**.

Extended Reporting Period means the period of time set forth in ITEM 7 of the Declarations following the effective date of any nonrenewal or termination of the **Policy**.

Extradition means a formal process by which an **Insured Person** located in any country is surrendered, or sought to be surrendered, to any other country to answer any criminal accusation, including the execution of an arrest warrant where such execution is an element of such process.

Financial Insolvency means the: (i) court appointment of an examiner, receiver, conservator, liquidator, trustee, or rehabilitator, or any functional equivalent position, to take control of, supervise, manage, or liquidate the **Insured Organization** or **Outside Entity**; or (ii) **Insured Organization** or **Outside Entity** becoming a debtor in possession under the U.S. Bankruptcy Code, Chapter 11, or its foreign equivalent.

Financial Interest means the **Named Insured's** insurable interest in an **Insured Organization** that is domiciled in a country or jurisdiction in which the Company is not licensed to provide this insurance, as a result of the **Named Insured's**:

1. ownership of the majority of the outstanding securities or voting rights of such **Insured Organization** representing the present right to elect, appoint, or exercise a majority control over such **Insured Organization's** board of directors, board of trustees, board of managers, natural person general partner, or functional foreign equivalent;
2. indemnification of, or representation that it has an obligation to indemnify, such **Insured Organization** for **Loss** incurred by such **Insured Organization**; or
3. election or obligation to obtain insurance for such **Insured Organization**.

Independent Director means an **Insured Person** who is a "Non-Employee Director" of the **Insured Organization** as such term is defined in Rule 16b-3 promulgated under the Securities Exchange Act of 1934; provided, that the term "issuer" as referenced in such rule is deemed to refer to the **Insured Organization**.

Insured means the **Insured Persons** and the **Insured Organizations**.

Insured Organization means any **Named Insured** or **Subsidiary**, including such entity as a debtor in possession under the U.S. Bankruptcy Code, Chapter 11, or its foreign equivalent.

Insured Person means any natural person:

1. who was, is, or becomes a duly elected or appointed director, officer, **Manager**, risk manager, or in-house general counsel, or any functional equivalent position, of the **Insured Organization**, or such natural person while serving in an **Outside Position**;
2. who was, is, or becomes a shadow director of the **Insured Organization** pursuant to the United Kingdom Companies Act of 2006, or equivalent statute; or
3. not described in 1. who was, is, or becomes a full or part-time employee of the **Insured Organization**, with respect to: (i) a **Securities Claim**; or (ii) any other **Claim**, but only if such **Claim** is made and maintained against both such natural person and any natural person described in 1.

Interview Expenses mean the reasonable costs, charges, fees, or expenses, incurred by an **Insured Person**, or the **Insured Organization** pursuant to its indemnification of an **Insured Person**, in responding to an **Interview Request**. **Interview Expenses** do not include: (i) the regular or overtime wages, salaries, or fees of any director, officer, **Manager**, or employee of an **Insured Organization** or **Outside Entity**, or any other compensation of an **Insured Person**

associated with an **Interview Request**; or (ii) costs, charges, fees, or expenses incurred in responding to requests for the production of documents, records, or electronic information that are in the possession, custody, or control of the **Insured Organization**, an **Enforcement Body**, or any party other than the **Insured Person**.

Interview Request means a written request for an **Insured Person** to appear for an interview or meeting, or to produce documents or records, concerning matters or circumstances occurring before or during the **Policy Period**, made by:

1. an **Enforcement Body** in connection with an investigation of: (i) the **Insured Organization**; or (ii) an **Insured Person**, in his or her capacity as such; or
2. an **Insured Organization** in connection with: (i) an investigation by an **Enforcement Body** against such **Insured Organization**, or (ii) a **Security Holder Derivative Demand**;

provided, **Interview Request** does not include any routine or regularly scheduled examination, inspection, compliance, oversight, interview, or audit conducted pursuant to the **Enforcement Body's** or **Insured Organization's** ordinary review or compliance procedures.

Investigation Expenses mean the reasonable costs, charges, fees, or expenses incurred in connection with investigating or evaluating whether it is in the best interests of the **Insured Organization** to prosecute the claims alleged in a **Security Holder Derivative Demand** or **Security Holder Derivative Action** by: (i) the **Insured Organization**; (ii) the board of directors or board of managers, or any functional equivalent board, of the **Insured Organization**; or (iii) any committee of such board; provided, **Investigation Expenses** do not include regular or overtime wages, salaries, or fees of any director, officer, **Manager**, or employee of an **Insured Organization** or **Outside Entity**.

Joint Venture means any incorporated joint venture, other than a **Subsidiary**, if the **Insured Organization**: (i) owns or controls at least 33% of the outstanding voting securities representing the present right to vote for the election or appointment of the directors or officers, or any functional equivalent position, of such joint venture; or (ii) has the present right to elect or appoint at least 33% of the directors or officers, or any functional equivalent position, of such joint venture.

Loss means: (i) damages, judgments, settlements, prejudgment and postjudgment interest, and **Defense Expenses**; provided, with respect to the multiple portion of any multiplied damage award or punitive or exemplary damages incurred by any **Insured**, **Loss** only includes such damages to the extent they are insurable under the law of a jurisdiction that is most favorable to the insurability of such damages, and has a substantial relationship to the **Insured**, **Claim**, Company, or this **Policy**; (ii) **Investigation Expenses**, with respect to Insuring Agreement D only; (iii) **Interview Expenses**, with respect to section II. ADDITIONAL BENEFITS, B. INTERVIEW REQUEST COVERAGE only; and (iv) **Non-Monetary Resolution Fees**. **Loss**, other than **Defense Expenses**, does not include:

1. any amount that an **Insured** is absolved from paying;
2. taxes, fines, or penalties; provided, **Loss** includes:
   a. civil penalties assessed against an **Insured Person** pursuant to the Foreign Corrupt Practices Act of 1977 §§ 15 U.S.C. 78dd-2(g)(2)(B) and 78ff(c)(2)(B) and the United Kingdom Bribery Act of 2010 (Eng.) § 11(1)(a); or
   b. taxes assessed against an **Insured Person** pursuant to applicable federal, provincial, or territorial statutory law imposing liability upon the **Insured Person** in his or her capacity as such where the **Insured Organization** has failed to deduct, withhold, or remit such amounts as required by law and is financially unable to do so;
3. any cost of complying with any order for, grant of, or agreement to provide, injunctive or non-monetary relief;
4. any cost incurred testing for, monitoring, cleaning up, removing, containing, treating, detoxifying, neutralizing, or assessing the effects of, any **Pollutant**;
5. any amount of damages, judgments, or settlements that represents, or is substantially equivalent to, an increase in the price or consideration paid, or proposed to be paid, for: (i) an actual or attempted acquisition of all, or substantially all, of the ownership interest in, or assets of, an entity; or (ii) merger with any entity;
6. disgorgement or other loss that is uninsurable under the law pursuant to which this **Policy** is construed; provided, the Company will not assert that any amount of a judgment or settlement in a **Securities Claim** for a violation of the Securities Act of 1933 §§ 11, 12, or 15 constitutes disgorgement or other uninsurable loss; or
7. the amount required to be repaid, returned, or refunded pursuant to Dodd-Frank § 954(b)(2), SOX § 304(a), or similar statute or regulation requiring the return of incentive-based compensation.

Manager means, with respect to an **Insured Organization** that is a limited liability company, political action committee, or non-profit entity, any natural person who was, is, or becomes a: (i) member of the board of managers, the board of governors, management committee, or advisory committee, or any functional equivalent position, of such **Insured Organization**; or (ii) trustee, other than a bankruptcy trustee, or any functional equivalent position, of any non-profit entity.

Named Insured means the entity named in ITEM 1 of the Declarations.

Nominal Defendant Expenses mean the reasonable costs, charges, fees, or expenses incurred by an **Insured Organization** in its capacity as a nominal defendant while seeking to dismiss a **Security Holder Derivative Action** for lack of jurisdiction or failure to allege demand futility.

Non-Monetary Resolution Fees mean the reasonable plaintiff's attorney's fees awarded or approved by a court in connection with a judgment in, or settlement of, a **Securities Claim** as defined in subpart (i) of **Securities Claim**, wherein no monetary consideration would be received by such security holders or **Insured Organization**.

Outside Entity means any: (i) non-profit entity, other than a **Subsidiary**; or (ii) **Joint Venture**.

Outside Position means any natural person serving in the position of director, officer, manager, or trustee, or any functional equivalent position, in an **Outside Entity**, but only if service in such position is with the knowledge and consent of, at the direction or request of, or part of the duties regularly assigned to such natural person by the **Insured Organization**.

Policy means, collectively, the Declarations, the **Application**, this coverage form, and any endorsement attached thereto.

Policy Period means the period of time set forth in ITEM 2 of the Declarations, subject to prior termination in accordance with section V. CONDITIONS, P. TERMINATION OF POLICY.

Pollutant means: (i) a solid, liquid, gaseous, or thermal irritant or contaminant; (ii) an electric, magnetic, or electromagnetic field; (iii) an odor or noise; (iv) oil or oil products; or (v) the actual or alleged presence, or actual, alleged, or threatened dispersal of, asbestos, asbestos fibers, or products containing asbestos; including materials to be recycled, reconditioned, or reclaimed.

Related Interview Requests means all **Interview Requests** that have as a common nexus, or are causally connected by reason of, any fact, circumstance, situation, event, or decision.

Related Wrongful Acts means all **Wrongful Acts** that have as a common nexus, or are causally connected by reason of, any fact, circumstance, situation, event, or decision.

Securities Claim means any **Claim**, in whole or in part, that is: (i) brought and maintained by one or more security holders of the **Insured Organization**, in their capacity as such; (ii) based upon or arising out of the purchase or sale of, or offer to purchase or sell, any equity or debt securities of, and issued by, the **Insured Organization**, whether such purchase, sale, or offer involves a transaction with the **Insured Organization** or occurs in the open market, including any such **Claim** brought by the SEC or any other claimant; or (iii) based upon or arising out of the violation of any securities law, rule, or regulation, whether statutory or common law, involving the purchase or sale of, or offer to purchase or sell, any equity or debt securities of, and issued by, the **Insured Organization**. **Securities Claim** does not include a **Claim** brought by an **Insured Person** based upon or arising out of any compensation to such **Insured Person** in the form of securities of the **Insured Organization**.

Security Holder Derivative Action means a civil proceeding brought and maintained on behalf of, or in the name or right of, an **Insured Organization** by one or more security holders of such **Insured Organization** in their capacity as such.

Security Holder Derivative Demand means a written demand on behalf of an **Insured Organization** made by a security holder of such **Insured Organization** and made upon the board of directors or board of managers, or any functional equivalent board, of such **Insured Organization** to bring a civil proceeding in a court of law against an **Insured Person** for a **Wrongful Act** committed by such **Insured Person**.

Spouse means any natural person who qualifies as a legal spouse, domestic partner, or party to a civil union, under the provisions of any applicable domestic or foreign law or regulation, or under the provisions of any formal program established by the **Insured Organization**.

Subsidiary means any:

1. entity while the **Named Insured**, directly or indirectly, owns more than 50% of the outstanding voting securities or other equity ownership, representing the present right to vote for the election or appointment of directors or officers, **Managers**, or any functional equivalent position; or
2. corporation, limited liability company, or non-profit entity while the **Named Insured**, directly or indirectly, has the right, pursuant to a written contract or the by-laws, charter, operating agreement, or similar documents of such entity, to elect or appoint a majority of directors or officers, **Managers**, or any functional equivalent position,

on or before the Inception Date set forth in ITEM 2 of the Declarations or subject to section V. CONDITIONS, K. ACQUISITIONS, during the **Policy Period**.

Wrongful Act means:

1. an actual or alleged error, misstatement, misleading statement, act, omission, neglect, or breach of duty committed or attempted: (i) by an **Insured Person** in his or her capacity as such; or (ii) by an **Insured Organization**, solely with respect to Insuring Agreement C; or
2. any matter claimed against an **Insured Person** solely because of his or her serving in such capacity.

Solely with respect to determining whether a **Security Holder Derivative Action** that names the **Insured Organization** as a nominal defendant is a **Securities Claim** against such **Insured Organization** for purposes of Insuring Agreement C, any **Wrongful Act** as defined in 1.(i) will also be deemed to be a **Wrongful Act** of such **Insured Organization**; provided, this provision will only be deemed to create coverage for **Non-Monetary Resolution Fees** and **Nominal Defendant Expenses**.

Wrongful Act does not include any conduct committed or attempted by any **Insured Person** in his or her capacity as a director, officer, manager, trustee, or employee of any entity other than the **Insured Organization** or **Outside Entity**, even if service in such capacity is with the knowledge and consent of, at the direction or request of, or part of the duties regularly assigned to such **Insured Person** by the **Insured Organization**.

IV. EXCLUSIONS

A. EXCLUSIONS APPLICABLE TO ALL INSURING AGREEMENTS AND ADDITIONAL BENEFITS

1. PRIOR NOTICE

The Company will not be liable for **Loss** on account of a **Claim** based upon or arising out of any fact, circumstance, situation, event, **Wrongful Act**, or **Related Wrongful Act** that has been the subject of any written notice given by or on behalf of any **Insured** and accepted under any directors and officers liability policy of insurance.

2. PRIOR OR PENDING PROCEEDING

The Company will not be liable for **Loss** on account of a **Claim** based upon or arising out of any: (i) prior or pending written demand, suit, or other proceeding against any **Insured** or **Outside Entity** as of, or prior to, the applicable Prior or Pending Proceeding Date set forth in ITEM 5 of the Declarations; or (ii) **Wrongful Act**, or **Related Wrongful Act** underlying or alleged in such written demand, suit, or other proceeding.

3. ENTITY VERSUS INSURED

The Company will not be liable for **Loss** on account of a **Claim** that is brought or maintained by or on behalf of: (i) an **Insured Organization** against an **Insured**; or (ii) an **Outside Entity**, or an entity that has an ownership interest in a **Joint Venture**, against an **Insured Person** for a **Wrongful Act** while serving in his or her capacity in an **Outside Position** with such **Outside Entity**; provided, this exclusion will not apply to a **Claim** brought and maintained:

a. in the form of a security holder derivative action or **Security Holder Derivative Demand**, without the active participation, solicitation, or assistance of an **Insured Person**, or a natural person who is a director, officer, manager, trustee, or functional equivalent position of such entity identified in 3.(ii), unless such person has not served in such capacity for at least three years preceding the date the **Claim** is first made, or is acting pursuant to any whistleblower statute;

b. by the **Insured Organization** pursuant to section II. ADDITIONAL BENEFITS, B. INTERVIEW REQUEST COVERAGE;

c. by a court-appointed examiner, receiver, creditors' committee, conservator, liquidator, trustee, or rehabilitator of such entity, or a similar official serving in the same legal capacity, in a bankruptcy proceeding by or against the entity;

d. outside of the United States (including any U.S. territory, possession, or protectorate), Canada, the United Kingdom, Australia, or any other jurisdiction governed by a common law legal system, but only if the laws where such **Claim** is brought and maintained require that such **Claim** be brought by or on behalf of such entity; or

e. pursuant to Dodd-Frank § 954.

4. ERISA

PCDO-16001 Rev. 12-17 Page 6 of 14

The Company will not be liable for **Loss** on account of a **Claim** for a violation of the responsibilities, obligations, or duties imposed by the Employee Retirement Income Security Act of 1974, or similar provisions of any domestic or foreign law or regulation.

5. **BODILY INJURY, PROPERTY DAMAGE, OR PERSONAL INJURY**

The Company will not be liable for **Loss** on account of a **Claim** for: (i) bodily injury, mental anguish, emotional distress, sickness, disease, or death of any person; (ii) damage to, or destruction of, any tangible property, including loss of use of such property; or (iii) libel, slander, defamation of character, disparagement, or violation of a person's right of privacy; provided, this exclusion will not apply with respect to: (a) any mental anguish, emotional distress, libel, slander, defamation of character, disparagement, or violation of a natural person's right of privacy in any **Claim** brought and maintained by a past, present, or prospective employee of the **Insured Organization** for an employment-related **Wrongful Act**; (b) **Loss** on account of a **Securities Claim**; or (c) **Defense Expenses** for a **Claim** against an **Insured Person** for violation of the United Kingdom Corporate Manslaughter and Corporate Homicide Act of 2007, or any similar statute.

B. **EXCLUSIONS APPLICABLE TO INSURING AGREEMENTS A AND C, AND TO ADDITIONAL BENEFITS A, B.1., AND C**

CONDUCT

The Company will not be liable for **Loss** on account of that portion of a **Claim** based upon or arising out of:

1. a deliberate fraudulent or deliberate criminal act by an:
   a. **Insured Person**, with respect to Insuring Agreement A and section II. ADDITIONAL BENEFITS, A. SUPPLEMENTAL INDEPENDENT DIRECTOR LIABILITY COVERAGE, B. INTERVIEW REQUEST COVERAGE, 1., and C. RETIREE COVERAGE; or
   b. **Executive Officer** or **Insured Organization**, with respect to Insuring Agreement C; or
2. an **Insured** gaining any profit, remuneration, or financial advantage to which such **Insured** was not legally entitled,

if a final, nonappealable adjudication adverse to such **Insured** in the underlying proceeding establishes that such conduct occurred.

Exclusion B.2. will not apply to that portion of: (i) a **Securities Claim** for a violation of the Securities Act of 1933 §§ 11, 12, or 15, to the extent such amount is insurable under the law pursuant to which this **Policy** is construed; or (ii) **Defense Expenses** incurred in connection with a **Claim** made pursuant to Dodd-Frank § 954, SOX § 304(a), or similar statute or regulation requiring the return of incentive-based compensation.

C. **SEVERABILITY OF EXCLUSIONS**

No **Wrongful Act** of, or knowledge possessed by, an **Insured** will be imputed to any other **Insured Person** for purposes of applying section IV. EXCLUSIONS. Only **Wrongful Acts** of, or knowledge possessed by, an **Executive Officer** will be imputed to the **Insured Organization** for purposes of applying section IV. EXCLUSIONS.

V. CONDITIONS

A. **LIMITS OF LIABILITY**

The applicable Limits of Liability set forth in ITEM 5 of the Declarations are the maximum amounts the Company will pay under this **Policy** for all **Loss**, including **Defense Expenses**, regardless of the number of **Claims** or **Insureds**, and regardless of when payment is made by the Company, or when an **Insured's** legal obligation with regard to a **Claim** arises or is established.

The Company's maximum liability for all **Loss** for all **Claims** first made during the same **Policy Period**, whether covered under one or more Insuring Agreements, is the Directors, Officers, and Organization Limit of Liability for the **Policy Period** set forth in ITEM 5 of the Declarations.

The Company's maximum liability under Insuring Agreement D for all **Investigation Expenses** for all **Security Holder Derivative Actions** and **Security Holder Derivative Demands** first made during the same **Policy Period** is the Investigation Expense Limit of Liability set forth in ITEM 5 of the Declarations. Such Investigation Expense Limit of Liability is part of, and not in addition to, the Directors, Officers, and Organization Limit of Liability under this **Policy**.

The Company's maximum liability under section II. ADDITIONAL BENEFITS, A. SUPPLEMENTAL INDEPENDENT DIRECTOR LIABILITY COVERAGE for all **Loss** for all **Claims** first made during the same **Policy Period** is the Supplemental Independent Director Limit of Liability set forth in ITEM 5 of the Declarations. Such Supplemental Independent Director Limit of Liability is in addition to, and excess of, the Directors, Officers, and Organization Limit of Liability under this **Policy**.

All **Claims** arising out of the same **Wrongful Act** and all **Related Wrongful Acts** are deemed one **Claim**, and such **Claim** is deemed to be first made on the date the earliest of such **Claims** is first made against any **Insured**, regardless of whether such date is before or during the **Policy Period**.

All **Related Interview Requests** for which notice has been provided to the Company are deemed one **Interview Request**, and such **Interview Request** is deemed to be first made on the date the earliest of such **Interview Requests** is first made to any **Insured**, regardless of whether such date is before or during the **Policy Period**.

Any **Claim** arising out of the same or substantially similar facts or circumstances as an **Interview Request** for which notice has been provided to the Company is deemed to be first made on the date the earliest of such **Interview Requests** is first made to any **Insured**, regardless of whether such date is before or during the **Policy Period**.

The Limits of Liability for any applicable **Extended Reporting Period** are part of, and not in addition to, the Limits of Liability for the **Policy Period**. The purchase of an **Extended Reporting Period** will not increase or reinstate the Limits of Liability set forth in ITEM 5 of the Declarations.

The Limits of Liability for any applicable coverage extension under section II. ADDITIONAL BENEFITS, C. RETIREE COVERAGE are part of, and not in addition to, the Limit of Liability for the **Policy Period**. Such coverage extension will not increase or reinstate the Limits of Liability set forth in ITEM 5 of the Declarations.

The Limits of Liability for any applicable coverage extension under section V. CONDITIONS, M. CHANGE OF CONTROL are part of, and not in addition to, the Limits of Liability for the **Policy Period**. The election of such coverage extension will not increase or reinstate the Limits of Liability set forth in ITEM 5 of the Declarations.

B. RETENTION

The Company's liability with respect to **Loss** on account of each **Claim** applies only to that portion of **Loss** that is excess of each applicable Retention set forth in ITEM 5 of the Declarations. If a **Claim** is subject to more than one Retention, the largest applicable Retention is the maximum Retention applicable to all **Loss** for such **Claim**. Such Retentions will be borne by the **Insured Organization** uninsured, at its own risk, and in satisfaction of **Loss**.

Regardless of the number of **Claims**, the largest Retention set forth in ITEM 5 of the Declarations is the maximum sum of such Retentions that must be satisfied.

No Retention applies to that portion of **Loss**: (i) incurred as **Event Study Expenses**; or (ii) covered under Insuring Agreements A or D or sections II. ADDITIONAL BENEFITS, A. SUPPLEMENTAL INDEPENDENT DIRECTOR LIABILITY COVERAGE or B. INTERVIEW REQUEST COVERAGE, 1.

C. INDEMNIFICATION AND ADVANCEMENT OF LOSS WITHIN RETENTION

Regardless of whether **Loss** on account of a **Claim** against an **Insured Person** is actually indemnified, the applicable Retention set forth in ITEM 5 of the Declarations will apply to **Loss** that the **Insured Organization** or **Outside Entity** is legally permitted to indemnify, unless such **Insured Organization** or **Outside Entity** fails to provide indemnification solely because of **Financial Insolvency**.

If the **Insured Organization** or **Outside Entity** fails to indemnify an **Insured Person** for **Loss** within the applicable Retention, then the Company will advance such amounts on behalf of the **Insured Person** and such **Insured Person** will not be liable for amounts within the applicable Retention. Such advancement of **Loss** is subject to the following:

1. advancement of **Loss** will reduce, and may exhaust, the Limits of Liability set forth in ITEM 5 of the Declarations;
2. advancement of **Loss** does not relieve the **Insured Organization** or **Outside Entity** of its obligation to provide indemnification to such **Insured Person**, or the **Insured Organization's** obligation to satisfy the applicable Retention on behalf of such **Insured Person**; and
3. the Company will be subrogated to the **Insured Person's** rights of recovery against the **Insured Organization** or **Outside Entity** for any amounts it owes to the **Insured Person** and that the Company has advanced under this section.

The **Insured Organization** or **Outside Entity's** failure to indemnify an **Insured Person** occurs if the **Insured Organization** or **Outside Entity** fails or refuses to pay **Loss** on behalf of the **Insured Person** within 60 days of the **Insured Person's** written demand to the **Insured Organization** or **Outside Entity** for such indemnification payment.

D. **EXTENDED REPORTING PERIOD COVERAGE**

If the Company or **Named Insured** does not renew this **Policy**, or if the **Named Insured** terminates this **Policy**, the **Named Insured** has the right, upon payment of the additional premium described below in this section, to elect an extension of coverage granted by this **Policy** for the **Extended Reporting Period**, but only with respect to: (i) a **Claim**, other than an **Interview Request**, for a **Wrongful Act** occurring before or during the **Policy Period**; or (ii) an **Interview Request** based upon or arising out of matters or circumstances that occurred before or during the **Policy Period**.

The premium due for the **Extended Reporting Period** will equal that percent set forth in ITEM 7 of the Declarations of the original annualized premium, and the fully annualized amount of any additional premium, charged by the Company for or during the **Policy Period**. The entire premium for the **Extended Reporting Period** will be deemed fully earned and non-refundable upon payment.

This right of extension will lapse unless the **Named Insured** provides written notice of such election, together with payment of the additional premium due, to the Company within 60 days following the effective date of such nonrenewal or termination.

The **Named Insured** will not be entitled to elect the **Extended Reporting Period** under this section if an extension of coverage is elected pursuant to section V. CONDITIONS, M. CHANGE OF CONTROL.

E. **NOTICE**

1. Notice of Claim

As a condition precedent to exercising rights under this **Policy**, the **Insured** must give the Company written notice of any **Claim**, other than an **Interview Request**, made against any **Insured** as soon as practicable after the in-house general counsel, risk manager, or any functional equivalent position of the **Named Insured**, first becomes aware of such **Claim**, but in no event later than:

a. 180 days after the Expiration Date of the **Policy Period** as set forth in ITEM 2 of the Declarations, if the **Named Insured** elects to renew this **Policy**; or

b. 60 days after: (i) the Expiration Date of the **Policy Period** as set forth in ITEM 2 of the Declarations; or (ii) the expiration of any applicable **Extended Reporting Period**.

With respect to any **Claim**, other than an **Interview Request**, the **Insured** must give to the Company such other information and cooperation as the Company may reasonably request.

If an **Insured** elects to seek coverage for **Interview Expenses**, the **Insured** must:

a. give the Company written notice of the **Interview Request** as soon as practicable after such **Insured Person** first becomes aware of such **Interview Request**, but in no event later than: (i) 60 days after the Expiration Date of the **Policy Period** as set forth in ITEM 2 of the Declarations; or (ii) the expiration of any applicable **Extended Reporting Period**;

b. include with any notice of an **Interview Request**, the name of the **Enforcement Body** making the request and, to the best of the **Insured's** knowledge, a description of the nature and subject matter identified by the **Enforcement Body** in its **Interview Request**; and

c. provide to the Company such other information and cooperation as the Company may reasonably request, including additional information about the subject matter and nature of the **Interview Request** as it is learned.

2. Notice of Circumstance

If an **Insured**: (i) becomes aware of any circumstance that could give rise to a **Claim** for a **Wrongful Act** occurring before or during the **Policy Period**; and (ii) gives written notice of such circumstance, including the anticipated **Wrongful Act** and other allegations, the reasons for anticipating such **Claim**, the nature of the alleged or potential damage, and the names of potential claimants and **Insureds** involved, to the Company during the **Policy Period** or any applicable **Extended Reporting Period**, then any **Claim** subsequently arising from such circumstance will be deemed made during the **Policy Period**.

3. Notice Requirements

All notices under this section must be sent or delivered to the Company, at the address set forth in ITEM 3 of the Declarations, and will be deemed received and effective upon the earliest of actual receipt by the addressee, or one day following the date such notice is sent. The failure of the **Insured** to give the Company timely notice of any **Claim** will not, for purposes of this **Policy**, result in a forfeiture of coverage under this **Policy**, unless and to the extent that the Company is materially prejudiced by such delay.

F. DEFENSE AND SETTLEMENT

The Company has no duty under this **Policy** to defend any **Claim**. The **Insureds** have the duty to defend **Claims** made against them.

The **Insureds** agree not to settle or offer to settle any **Claim**, or incur any **Defense Expenses** or **Interview Expenses** in connection with any **Claim**, without the Company's written consent; provided, that if the **Insureds** are able to fully and finally settle or otherwise dispose of any **Claim**, for an amount, including **Defense Expenses** or **Interview Expenses**, not to exceed the applicable Retention, the Company's consent will not be required. The Company is not liable for any settlement, **Defense Expenses**, or **Interview Expenses** to which it has not consented.

The **Insureds** also agree not to assume any contractual obligation, stipulate to any judgment, or admit any liability with respect to any **Claim** without the Company's written consent, and the Company will not be liable for any such assumed obligation, stipulated judgment, or admission without such written consent.

With respect to any **Claim** submitted for coverage under this **Policy**, the Company has the right, and will be given the opportunity, to effectively associate with, and be consulted in advance by, the **Insured** regarding the investigation, defense, and settlement of such **Claim**, including the selection of appropriate defense counsel and any settlement negotiations.

The **Insured** agrees to provide the Company with all information, assistance, and cooperation that the Company reasonably requests. Failure of an **Insured Person** to provide the Company with such information, assistance, or cooperation will not impair the rights of another **Insured Person** under this **Policy**.

In the event of a **Claim**, the **Insureds** will do nothing to prejudice the Company's position or its potential or actual rights of subrogation or recovery. The Company may make any investigation it deems necessary.

The Company will advance, on behalf of the **Insureds**, **Defense Expenses**, **Interview Expenses**, or **Investigation Expenses** that the Company believes to be covered under this **Policy** and are incurred in connection with a **Claim** first made against them during the **Policy Period**, or any applicable **Extended Reporting Period**; provided, that to the extent it is finally established that any such **Defense Expenses**, **Interview Expenses**, or **Investigation Expenses** are not covered under this **Policy**, the **Insureds**, severally according to their interests, agree to repay the Company such **Defense Expenses**, **Interview Expenses**, and **Investigation Expenses**. Such **Defense Expenses**, **Interview Expenses**, or **Investigation Expenses** will be advanced within 90 days of the date when the Company's Claims department receives: (i) the invoices documenting that such **Defense Expenses**, **Interview Expenses**, or **Investigation Expenses** have been incurred; and (ii) any additional information or documentation reasonably requested by the Company related to such **Defense Expenses**, **Interview Expenses**, or **Investigation Expenses**.

The Company may, with the written consent of the **Insured**, settle any **Claim** for a monetary amount that the Company deems reasonable.

The Company and the **Insureds** will not unreasonably withhold any consent referenced in this section.

G. ALLOCATION

If, in any **Claim**, an **Insured** incurs **Loss** jointly with others (including an **Insured Person** incurring **Loss** jointly with the **Insured Organization** for any **Claim** not covered under Insuring Agreement C) or incurs an amount consisting of both **Loss** covered by this **Policy** and loss not covered by this **Policy** because the **Claim** includes both covered and uncovered matters, then the **Insureds** and the Company will use their best efforts to allocate such amount between covered **Loss** and uncovered loss based upon the relative legal and financial exposures of the parties to covered and uncovered matters.

If there can be no agreement on an allocation of **Defense Expenses** or **Interview Expenses**, the Company will advance **Defense Expenses** or **Interview Expenses** that the Company believes to be covered under this **Policy** until a different allocation is negotiated, arbitrated, or judicially determined. The Company will advance **Defense Expenses** or **Interview Expenses** allocated to covered **Loss** on a current basis and prior to disposition of the **Claim**. Any negotiated, arbitrated, or judicially determined allocation of **Defenses Expenses** or **Interview Expenses** in connection with a **Claim** will apply retroactively to all **Defense Expenses** or **Interview Expenses** in connection with such **Claim**, notwithstanding any prior advancement to the contrary. Any allocation or advancement of **Defense Expenses** or **Interview Expenses** in connection with a **Claim** will not apply to, or create any presumption with respect to, the allocation of other **Loss** for such **Claim** or any other **Claim**.

H. OTHER INSURANCE

If **Loss** arising from any **Claim** made against an **Insured** is insured under any other valid and collectible insurance, then this **Policy** covers such **Loss** only to the extent that the amount of such **Loss** is in excess of the amount of such other insurance, whether such other insurance is stated to be primary, contributory, excess, contingent, or otherwise, unless such other insurance is a personal umbrella liability policy, personal directors and officers liability policy purchased by an **Insured Person**, or is written as specific excess insurance over this **Policy**. Any payment by an **Insured** of a retention or deductible under any such other insurance issued by the Company or any of its affiliated companies will reduce, by the amount of such payment that would otherwise have been covered under this **Policy**, any applicable Retention under this **Policy**. This **Policy** is not subject to the terms, conditions, exclusions, or limitations of any other insurance, except as provided in section II. ADDITIONAL BENEFITS, A. SUPPLEMENTAL INDEPENDENT DIRECTOR LIABILITY COVERAGE.

This **Policy** covers **Loss** for any **Claim** made against any **Insured Person** serving in an **Outside Position** only to the extent that the amount of such **Loss** exceeds any indemnity and other insurance available from, or provided by, the applicable **Outside Entity**. Payment by the Company, or any of its affiliated companies, under another policy as a result of a **Claim** made against an **Insured Person** in an **Outside Position** reduces the Company's Limits of Liability under this **Policy** with respect to such **Claim**, by the amount of such payment.

I. ORDER OF PAYMENTS

If **Loss** covered under Insuring Agreement A or section II. ADDITIONAL BENEFITS, B. INTERVIEW REQUEST COVERAGE, 1. and any other **Loss** are concurrently due under this **Policy**, the Company will first pay **Loss** covered under Insuring Agreement A or section II. ADDITIONAL BENEFITS, B. INTERVIEW REQUEST COVERAGE, 1.

Except as provided in this section, the Company may pay **Loss** as it becomes due without regard to the potential for other future payment obligations.

J. ESTATES, LEGAL REPRESENTATIVES, AND SPOUSAL LIABILITY COVERAGE

Subject to the applicable Insuring Agreement, this **Policy** will afford coverage for **Claims** for **Wrongful Acts** of any **Insured Person** made against: (i) any estate, heir, legal representative, or assignee of the **Insured Person** in the event of death, incapacity, insolvency, or bankruptcy of such **Insured Person**; or (ii) the **Insured Person's Spouse** solely because of such **Spouse's** legal status as a **Spouse**, or because of such **Spouse's** ownership interest in property that the claimant seeks as recovery for alleged **Wrongful Acts** of the **Insured Person**.

All loss that such estate, heir, legal representative, assignee, or **Spouse** of such **Insured Person** becomes legally obligated to pay for such **Claim** will be treated as **Loss** that the **Insured Person** is legally obligated to pay for such **Claim**. The coverage afforded by this section will not apply to the extent the **Claim** alleges any wrongful act or omission by the estate, heir, legal representative, assignee, or **Spouse** of the **Insured Person**.

K. ACQUISITIONS

If, during the **Policy Period**, an **Insured Organization** acquires or creates a **Subsidiary**, or acquires an entity by such entity's merger into, or consolidation with, an **Insured Organization**, and the **Insured Organization** is the surviving entity, then such **Subsidiary** or acquired entity and its **Insured Persons** will be covered under this **Policy** as follows:

a. If the total assets of any such **Subsidiary** or acquired entity are less than 30% of the total assets of all **Insured Organizations**, as reflected in the **Insured Organizations'** most recent financial statements as of the inception of the **Policy Period**, then it and its **Insured Persons** will be covered automatically under this **Policy**, but only with respect to **Claims** for **Wrongful Acts**, or **Interview Requests** based upon or arising out of matters or circumstances, occurring after such acquisition or creation, unless the Company agrees after presentation of a complete **Application** and all appropriate information to provide coverage by endorsement for **Wrongful Acts** or matters or circumstances occurring prior to such acquisition or creation.

b. With respect to all acquisitions or creations other than as described in K.a., such **Subsidiary** or acquired entity and its **Insured Persons** will be covered automatically under this **Policy**, but only for the lesser of the remainder of the **Policy Period** or 90 days, following the effective date of such acquisition or creation (Automatic Coverage Period), and only with respect to **Wrongful Acts**, or **Interview Requests** based upon or arising out of matters or circumstances, occurring after such acquisition or creation. As a condition precedent to further coverage with respect to such **Subsidiary** or acquired entity and its **Insured Persons** after such Automatic Coverage Period, the **Named Insured** must give written notice of such acquisition or creation to the Company as soon as practicable, but in no event later than 90 days following the effective date of such acquisition or creation, and must promptly provide the Company such information as the Company may reasonably request. Upon receipt of such notice and other information, the Company will provide the **Named Insured** a quotation for such coverage under this **Policy** for the remainder of the **Policy Period**. If the **Named Insured** fails to comply with such condition precedent, or if within 90 days following receipt of such quotation the **Named Insured** fails to pay any additional premium or fails to agree to any additional coverage terms, conditions, exclusions, or limitations set forth in such quotation, coverage otherwise afforded by this section for such **Subsidiary** or acquired entity and its **Insured Persons** will terminate upon expiration of such Automatic Coverage Period.

L. CESSATION OF SUBSIDIARIES

If, before or during the **Policy Period**, an entity ceases to be a **Subsidiary**, coverage with respect to such **Subsidiary** and its **Insured Persons** will continue until termination of this **Policy**, but only with respect to **Claims** for **Wrongful Acts**, or **Interview Requests** based upon or arising out of matters or circumstances, occurring during the time that such entity was a **Subsidiary**.

M. CHANGE OF CONTROL

If, during the **Policy Period**:

1. the **Named Insured** merges into, or consolidates with, another entity such that the **Named Insured** is not the surviving entity; or
2. another entity, person, or affiliated group of entities or persons acting in concert, acquires more than 50% of the outstanding securities or voting rights representing the present right to vote for the election or appointment of directors, officers, **Managers**, or functional equivalent positions, of the **Named Insured**,

then coverage under this **Policy** will continue until termination of this **Policy**, but only with respect to **Claims** for **Wrongful Acts**, or **Interview Requests** based upon or arising out of matters or circumstances, occurring before such event. As of the effective date of such event, all premiums paid or due at any time under this **Policy** are deemed fully earned and non-refundable.

Upon the occurrence of such merger, consolidation, or acquisition, at the **Named Insured's** request, the Company will provide the **Named Insured** with a quotation for a six-year, or shorter period as may be negotiated, extension of coverage from such merger, consolidation, or acquisition. Such quotation will be conditioned upon the **Named Insured** providing any information the Company may request.

Any coverage extension will be conditioned upon the **Named Insured** completing the following within 60 days after receipt of such quotation: (i) providing written notice to the Company of the election of such coverage extension; (ii) paying any additional premium required by the Company, which is deemed fully earned upon inception of such coverage extension; and (iii) accepting any additional terms, conditions, exclusions, and limitations required by the Company. If the **Named Insured** elects such coverage extension, then it is not entitled to elect coverage under section V. CONDITIONS, D. EXTENDED REPORTING PERIOD COVERAGE.

N. REPRESENTATIONS AND SEVERABILITY

In consideration of issuing this **Policy**, the Company has relied upon the statements and representations in the **Application**. The **Insureds** represent and agree that all such statements and representations are true and accurate and are the basis of the **Policy**. This **Policy** is issued in reliance upon the truth of all such statements and representations.

The **Application** will be construed as a separate **Application** for each **Insured** and, with respect to all statements and representations contained in the **Application**, no knowledge possessed by any one **Insured Person** will be imputed to any other **Insured Person**.

The Company will not, under any circumstance, rescind this **Policy** with respect to any **Insured**. However, the **Insureds** agree that in the event any such statements or representations in the **Application** are: (i) untrue or inaccurate, and (ii) are either made with the intent to deceive or materially affect either the acceptance of the risk or the hazard assumed by the Company, then no coverage will be afforded under this **Policy** with respect to the following **Insureds** for any **Claim** based upon or arising out of the information that was not truthfully or accurately disclosed in the **Application** with respect to any of the following **Insureds**:

1. any **Insured Person**, under Insuring Agreements A, who knew the information that was not truthfully or accurately disclosed in the **Application**;
2. the **Insured Organization**, under Insuring Agreement B, to the extent it indemnifies any **Insured Person** referenced in N.1.; and

3. the **Insured Organization**, under Insuring Agreements C or D, if any **Executive Officer** knew the information that was not truthfully or accurately disclosed in the **Application**,

whether or not such **Insured** or **Executive Officer** knew the **Application** contained such untruthful or inaccurate information.

O. TERRITORY AND VALUATION

1. This **Policy** applies anywhere in the world; provided, this **Policy** does not apply to **Loss** incurred by an **Insured** residing or domiciled in a country or jurisdiction in which the Company is not licensed to provide this insurance, to the extent that providing this insurance would violate the laws or regulations of such country or jurisdiction.
2. In the event that an **Insured Person** residing in a country or jurisdiction in which the Company is not licensed incurs **Loss** referenced in O.1. under Insuring Agreement A, such **Loss** will be paid in a country or jurisdiction mutually acceptable to such **Insured Person** and the Company, to the extent that doing so would not violate any applicable laws or regulations.
3. In the event an **Insured Organization** incurs **Loss** referenced in O.1. to which this insurance would have applied, the Company will reimburse the **Named Insured** for its **Loss**, on account of its **Financial Interest** in such **Insured Organization**. As a condition precedent to such reimbursement, or any rights under this **Policy**, the **Named Insured** will cause the **Insured Organization** or its **Insured Persons** to comply with the conditions of this **Policy**.
4. All premiums, Limits of Liability, Retention, **Loss**, and other amounts under this **Policy** are expressed and payable in U.S. dollars. If a judgment is rendered, settlement is denominated, or another element of **Loss** under this **Policy** is stated in a currency other than U.S. dollars, payment under this **Policy** will be made in U.S. dollars at the rate of exchange published in *The Wall Street Journal* on the date the final judgment is reached, the amount of the settlement is agreed upon, or any other element of **Loss** is due, respectively.

P. TERMINATION OF POLICY

This **Policy** terminates at the earliest of the following times:

1. the effective date of termination specified in a prior written notice by the **Named Insured** to the Company; provided, this **Policy** may not be terminated after the effective date of any merger, consolidation, or acquisition of the **Named Insured** as described in section V. CONDITIONS, M. CHANGE OF CONTROL;
2. upon expiration of the **Policy Period** set forth in ITEM 2 of the Declarations;
3. 20 days after receipt by the **Named Insured** of a written notice of termination from the Company for failure to pay a premium when due, unless the premium is paid within such 20 day period; or
4. at such other time as may be agreed upon by the Company and the **Named Insured**.

The Company may not terminate this **Policy** prior to expiration of the **Policy Period**, except as provided above for non-payment of premium. In the event this **Policy** is terminated prior to the expiration of the **Policy Period** set forth in ITEM 2 of the Declarations, the Company will refund any unearned premium computed on a pro rata basis. Payment or tender of any unearned premium by the Company is not a condition precedent to the effectiveness of such termination, but such payment must be made as soon as practicable.

Q. SUBROGATION

In the event of payment under this **Policy**, the Company will be subrogated to all of the **Insureds'** rights of recovery against any person or entity, including the **Insured Persons'** rights to indemnification or advancement from any entity, to the extent of such payment.

The Company will not exercise any available rights of subrogation against an **Insured Person** unless section IV. EXCLUSIONS, B. EXCLUSIONS APPLICABLE TO INSURING AGREEMENTS A, C AND TO ADDITIONAL BENEFITS A AND B.1., CONDUCT applies to such **Insured Person**.

The **Insured** must execute and deliver instruments and papers, and do all that is necessary to secure such rights, and must do nothing to prejudice such rights.

R. APPLICATION OF RECOVERY OF AMOUNTS PAID

In the event the Company recovers amounts it paid under this **Policy**, such amounts will be used to reimburse the Company for amounts paid under this **Policy**; provided, the Company will reinstate the applicable Limits of Liability of this **Policy** to the extent of such recovery, less any recovery costs incurred by the Company. Recoveries do not include any recovery from insurance, suretyship, reinsurance, security, or indemnity taken for the Company's benefit. The Company assumes no duty to seek a recovery of any amounts paid under this **Policy**.

S. BANKRUPTCY

Bankruptcy or insolvency of an **Insured**, or an **Insured's** estate, will not relieve the Company of its obligations, nor deprive the Company of its rights or defenses, under this **Policy**.

In the event a liquidation or reorganization proceeding is commenced by or against an **Insured Organization** pursuant to the U.S. Bankruptcy Code, or any similar domestic or foreign law, and there is **Loss** arising from a covered **Claim** for which payment is due under the provisions of this **Policy**, the **Insureds** must: (i) make a request to waive and release any automatic stay or injunction that may apply to this **Policy** or its proceeds in such proceeding, to the extent permitted under the applicable law; and (ii) agree not to oppose, or object to, any efforts by the Company or any **Insured** to obtain relief from any such stay or injunction.

T. ACTION AGAINST THE COMPANY

No action will lie against the Company unless, as a condition precedent, there has been full compliance with all the provisions of this **Policy**. No person or entity will have any right under this **Policy** to join the Company as a party to any action against any **Insured** to determine such **Insured's** liability, nor may the Company be impleaded by any **Insured** or their legal representative.

U. AUTHORIZATION

By acceptance of this **Policy**, the **Named Insured** agrees to act on behalf of all **Insureds** with respect to the giving and receiving of notice of a **Claim** or termination, nonrenewal, change of coverage, or the payment of premiums and the receiving of any return premiums that may become due under this **Policy**, and each **Insured** agrees that they have, individually and collectively, delegated such authority exclusively to the **Named Insured**; provided, that nothing in this section relieves any **Insured** from giving any notice to the Company required under this **Policy**.

V. ALTERATION AND ASSIGNMENT

No change in, modification of, or assignment of interest under this **Policy** will be effective except when made by the Company by written endorsement to this **Policy**.

W. SANCTIONS

This **Policy** will provide coverage, or otherwise will provide any benefit, only to the extent that providing such coverage or benefit does not expose the Company or any of its affiliated or parent companies to any trade or economic sanction under any law or regulation of the United States or any other applicable trade or economic sanction, prohibition, or restriction.

PCDO-16001 Rev. 12-17 Page 14 of 14

NOTES AND QUESTIONS

1. *Sides A, B, and C Coverages*. Which entities are covered under Coverages A, B, and C (known as Sides A, B, and C coverages in the insurance industry), respectively?

2. *Wrongful Acts.* Does the definition of "wrongful act" include misleading statements? Does the definition make a distinction between intentionally misleading and negligently misleading statements?

3. *Expected or Intended Exclusion.* Are injuries intentionally caused by a policyholder covered under the policy?

4. *Duty to Defend and Settlement.* Who controls the defense and settlement of claims under the policy? We will cover defense and settlement obligations under claims-made insurance in more detail later in this chapter.

B. WHAT CONSTITUTES "PROFESSIONAL SERVICES"

MILLERS CAS. INS. CO. OF TEXAS V. FLORES

876 P.2d 227 (N.M. 1994)

OPINION

BACA, JUSTICE.

Defendant-Appellant, Estefana Flores ("Flores") appeals from a trial court order denying her motion for summary judgment and granting summary judgment in favor of Plaintiff-Appellee, Millers Casualty Insurance Company of Texas ("Millers"). The trial court concluded that an insurance policy issued by Millers to Dr. Harry Winkworth ("Dr. Winkworth") excluded coverage for injuries that Flores suffered at the hands of Dr. Winkworth's assistant. On appeal, we address whether the trial court erred in granting summary judgment in favor of Millers. We review this case under SCRA 1986, 12–102(A)(1) (Repl.Pamp.1992), and affirm.

I.

Flores, a patient of Dr. Winkworth, suffered a debilitating stroke after Florence Curtis ("Curtis"), Dr. Winkworth's unsupervised and untrained assistant, gave Flores a contraindicated injection of estrogen. In September of 1989, Flores brought suit against Dr. Winkworth, his professional corporation, and Curtis. On May 2, 1990, Millers, having sold Dr. Winkworth a Deluxe Businessowners Policy, filed a declaratory judgment action against Flores, Dr. Winkworth, and Curtis. Based on an exclusion in the policy, Millers sought a declaration that it had no duty to defend or indemnify Dr. Winkworth or his corporation for the claims raised in Flores's lawsuit.

On April 1, 1991, Flores made a motion for summary judgment in Millers's declaratory judgment action. Flores contended that the insurance policy sold by Millers to Dr. Winkworth required Millers to defend Dr. Winkworth, and obligated Millers to satisfy any judgment or settlement in her case against Dr. Winkworth. On April 9, 1991, Millers filed a response to Flores's summary judgment motion and a cross-motion for summary judgment. Millers claimed that the policy issued to Dr. Winkworth "unambiguously excluded liability for injury arising out of 'professional services,'" and thus, did not provide coverage for Flores's medical malpractice claims against Dr. Winkworth and Curtis.

The trial court held a hearing on the summary judgment motions on August 27, 1991. Following argument of counsel, the trial court denied Flores's motion for summary judgment and granted Millers's cross-motion. Flores appeals the trial court's ruling to this Court.

II.

On appeal, we address whether the trial court correctly granted summary judgment in favor of Millers. Summary judgment is properly granted in a case when no genuine issues of material fact are presented and the moving party is entitled to judgment as a matter of law. Both parties agree that no issues of material fact are presented. Thus, we determine whether the trial court correctly concluded that Millers was entitled to judgment as a matter of law.

The Deluxe Business Owners Policy that Millers sold to Dr. Winkworth stated:

> [Millers] will pay on behalf of the insured all sums which the insured shall become legally obligated to pay as damages because of bodily injury, property damage or personal injury caused by an occurrence to which this insurance applies. . . .

[T]his policy does not apply:

> * * *
>
> 8. to bodily injury or property damage due to rendering of or failure to render any professional service, including but not limited to:
>
> (a) legal, accounting, advertising, engineering, drafting, architectural, and
>
> (b) medical, dental, pharmacological, cosmetic, hearing aid, optical, or ear piercing services. . . .

(emphasis omitted). In granting summary judgment for Millers, the trial court concluded that Flores's claims sounded in medical malpractice, and that the insurance policy's professional services exclusion—by including medical services in the definition of "professional service"—precluded coverage for such claims.

Flores raises several arguments to assert that the professional services exclusion should not preclude coverage for her claims. Flores concedes that the primary purpose of the Businessowners policy was to cover against liability arising from premises liability, and that Curtis's act of giving her the contraindicated injection constituted the rendering of a medical service for which coverage was excluded. Flores argues, however, that the professional services exclusion does not apply to her claims that Dr. Winkworth negligently hired, failed to train and inadequately supervised Curtis.[1] Flores contends that Dr. Winkworth's decision to hire an underqualified employee, and his failure to adequately train and supervise Curtis, were administrative decisions rather than the rendition of medical services, and that these decisions were removed in time from Curtis's act of failing to render adequate medical care. Flores contends that Dr. Winkworth's bad administrative decisions—rather than constituting the rendition of injury-causing medical services—gave rise to a 'deficiency in the premises' for which coverage under the Businessowners policy must apply.

We find Flores's arguments unpersuasive. Although this case presents an issue of first impression in New Mexico, numerous cases have upheld professional services exclusions on a variety of grounds. In one case, *Mason v. Liberty Mutual Insurance Co.,* 370 F.2d 925, 926 (5th Cir.1967), the plaintiff sued after suffering injuries as the result of an injection administered by a student nurse. After losing summary judgment at the trial court level, the plaintiff appealed, arguing that "there was administrative, as distinguished from professional, negligence in permitting a student nurse to administer the treatment." *Id.* The Fifth Circuit Court of Appeals upheld the professional services exclusion clause, applying the rule that when determining what constitutes professional services, "we should look not to the title or the character of the party performing the act but to the act itself." *Id.* (quoting *D'Antoni v. Sara Mayo Hosp.,* 144 So.2d 643, 646 (La.Ct.App.1962)); *cert. denied*); *see also Multnomah County v. Oregon Auto. Ins. Co.,* 256 Or. 24, 470 P.2d 147, 150 (1970) (excluding coverage under a professional services exclusion, and holding that when "determining whether a particular act or omission is of a professional nature, the act or omission itself must be looked to and not the title or character of the party who performs or fails to perform the act").

Other cases have upheld the effectiveness of professional services exclusions by holding that while nonprofessional personnel may perform some duties that lead to liability, the physician bears ultimate responsibility for the duty performed, and thus the duty is part of rendering professional services. *See Alpha Therapeutic Corp. v. St. Paul Fire & Marine Ins. Co.,* 890 F.2d 368, 370–71 (11th Cir.1989); *Northern Ins. Co. of N.Y. v. Superior Court,* 154 Cal.Rptr. 198, 200 (Cal. App. 1979). One court, in construing a policy that excluded coverage for "professional services" and "business pursuits," noted that all the allegations, regardless of the

---

[1] At the time Curtis was employed by Dr. Winkworth, she had no training as a nurse or medical assistant. While she had worked briefly for another physician and was trained as a phlebotomist, the majority of her work experience was in retail and clerical work. On September 11, 1991, the trial court entered judgment ratifying a mediated agreement whereby Flores was awarded $500,000 for her malpractice claims.

underlying legal theories, arose out of the same professional activity. *See Fire Ins. Exch. v. Alsop,* 709 P.2d 389, 390–91 (Utah 1985). Because the professional activity was conceded to be a "business pursuit," and was also considered to be the rendering of "professional services," coverage under the policy was excluded. *Id.* at 391.

In the instant case, we find the rationale employed in *Northern Insurance Co. of New York* compelling. The fact that a physician utilizes a nonphysician assistant to perform a professional duty does not "alter the professional nature of that nondelegable duty." 154 Cal.Rptr. at 200. It is undeniable that the injury to Flores occurred "as a direct result of the performance of professional services" for which Dr. Winkworth had ultimate responsibility. *Id.* Coverage for injuries caused by the performance of these professional services is excluded under Dr. Winkworth's policy.

Flores contends that "Dr. Winkworth's failure to provide competent personnel in his practice cannot reasonably be seen as 'an integral part of the rendering of medical care.' " We disagree. In our view, Dr. Winkworth was in the business of providing medical services to patients. The hiring and supervision of employees to assist in giving care to his patients constituted an integral part of providing medical services to these patients. *See Perkins v. Kearney,* 155 A.D.2d 191, 553 N.Y.S.2d 552, 553 (1990) (stating that the actions of those personnel assisting a physician are a central part of the process of rendering medical treatment). Dr. Winkworth's failure to hire a competent assistant, as well as his failure to adequately train and supervise her, was a failure to render adequate medical services. *Cf. Bell v. Sharp Cabrillo Hosp.,* 212 Cal.App.3d 1034, 260 Cal.Rptr. 886, 896–97 (1989) (noting that "a hospital has a professional responsibility to insure the competence of its medical staff," and holding that failure to fulfill "that responsibility constitutes 'professional negligence' involving conduct necessary to the rendering of professional services"). Under the policy at issue in this case, coverage for Dr. Winkworth's failure to render adequate medical services, which gave rise to Flores's injuries, was excluded from coverage under the "professional services" clause.

Flores relies heavily on *Guaranty National Insurance Co. v. North River Insurance Co.,* 909 F.2d 133 (5th Cir.1990), in arguing that Dr. Winkworth's decisions regarding the hiring, training and supervision of Curtis were administrative in nature, and did not require professional judgment. In *Guaranty National,* a patient admitted to a hospital for psychiatric care jumped from a fourth floor window to her death. 909 F.2d at 134. A jury awarded the patient's survivors $968,985.82 in damages against the hospital. *Id.* In a subsequent dispute between the hospital's insurers, North River Insurance Company ("North River") denied coverage for the hospital's liability, contending that a professional services clause in the hospital's comprehensive general liability insurance policy excluded coverage for the patient's death. *Id.* at 134–35. The trial court found North River liable for the judgment, and North River appealed. *Id.* at 135. On appeal, the Fifth Circuit Court of Appeals affirmed, holding that:

> The decision to protect the . . . patient[ ] through screws in the window sashes rather than through fixed, protective screens over the windows was an administrative, business decision and was not a professional, medical decision. We conclude, therefore, that the professional services exclusion in the North River policy does not reach the error for which the hospital was found to be liable.

Id. at 136. Flores argues that under *Guaranty National,* Dr. Winkworth's hiring, training, and supervising decisions should not trigger the professional services exclusion in his policy.

We find the case at bar distinguishable from *Guaranty National.* In that case, the Court focused on how the windows were secured and characterized the decision about securing the windows as administrative. In contrast, we believe that Dr. Winkworth's decision to allow Curtis to administer care to his patients, unlike the administrative decision about securing windows, involved an exercise of professional judgment. As a physician, Dr. Winkworth had to rely on his professional judgment to decide whether Curtis was adequately trained and competent enough to provide care to his patients. Under these circumstances, Dr. Winkworth's hiring, training, and supervising decisions involved professional judgment, and the professional services exclusion in Dr. Winkworth's policy applies to bar coverage.

Citing cases that distinguish between ordinary negligence and medical malpractice, *see, e.g., DeLeon v. Hosp. of Albert Einstein College of Medicine,* 566 N.Y.S.2d 213, 215–17 (1991), Flores argues that the decisions Dr. Winkworth made in hiring, training, and supervising Curtis amounted to ordinary negligence, which was not excluded under the policy. These cases, which, for the most part, address whether asserted claims sound in negligence or medical malpractice for the purpose of determining the applicable statute of limitations, are not on point and therefore, not very helpful in resolving this appeal. The case at bar does not require us to define the distinction between medical malpractice and ordinary negligence. Instead we are required to decide whether the hiring, training and supervision of Curtis was part of the medical services Dr. Winkworth offered to his patients. We conclude that the hiring, training, and supervising of employees who rendered care to patients comprised one aspect of the medical services Dr. Winkworth offered to his patients. The injuries resulting from these services are excluded under Dr. Winkworth's policy.

Finally, both Flores and the New Mexico Trial Lawyers Association ("Amicus"), filing an amicus brief on Flores's behalf, argue that the professional services exclusion is ambiguous and, consequently, must be construed against Millers to provide coverage for Flores's injuries. Both Flores and Amicus rely on *Williams v. Herrera,* 83 N.M. 680, 496 P.2d 740 (Ct.App.1972), to argue that the policy's professional services exclusion is ambiguous. In *Williams,* the Court of Appeals concluded that a professional services exclusion in a medical payments insurance policy was ambiguous where the policy failed to define the words "professional services," and New Mexico law did not otherwise define these words. 83 N.M. at 684–85, 496 P.2d at 744–45.

The policy in the instant case, unlike the policy in *Williams,* defined the term "professional service" by enumerating thirteen activities that constitute professional services, and included within this definition "medical" services. Nevertheless, Flores maintains that the exclusion is ambiguous because the exclusion "does nothing to define the scope of what is included within those [medical] services." We think it would be unreasonable to require Millers to provide an exhaustive list of noncovered activities for each of the thirteen professional activities listed in the professional services clause in order for the clause to be considered unambiguous. It is sufficient that the professional services clause includes medical services among the itemized list of professional services for which coverage is excluded. *See Vihstadt v. Travelers Ins. Co.,* 709 P.2d 187, 188 (N.M. 1985) (holding that the trial court erred by ruling that an insurance policy was ambiguous "because it lacked a definition for the term 'accidental injury or sickness.' "); *Security Mut. Cas. Co. v. O'Brien,* 99 N.M. 638, 641, 662 P.2d 639, 642 (1983) (holding that exclusion clauses were unambiguous even though certain terms were not defined). We hold that the exclusion clause in Dr. Winkworth's policy is not ambiguous.

For the foregoing reasons, we conclude that Millers was entitled to judgment as a matter of law. We hold that the trial court did not err in granting summary judgment in favor of Millers. The judgment of the trial court is affirmed.

IT IS SO ORDERED.

ZURICH AMERICAN INS. CO. V. O'HARA REGIONAL CENTER FOR REHABILITATION

529 F.3d 916 (10th Cir. 2008)

Opinion

TYMKOVICH, CIRCUIT JUDGE.

The question presented in this consolidated case is whether general liability insurance policies trigger a duty to defend false billing claims made by the United States and the State of Colorado. O'Hara Regional Center for Rehabilitation argues that its insurance carriers should defend and indemnify it against the government's lawsuit under the False Claims Act and state common law claims. We hold that the applicable insurance policies do not cover these types of claims.

Having jurisdiction pursuant to 28 U.S.C. § 1291, and finding no error, we AFFIRM.

I. Background

Factual Background

O'Hara is a long-term care facility in Denver that has been operated by various corporate entities. O'Hara was licensed by the State of Colorado as a Class V rehabilitation nursing center, meaning it was certified to provide care to residents requiring a substantially greater quantity and quality of skilled nursing care compared to residents at ordinary nursing homes.

O'Hara entered into provider agreements with the United States and the State of Colorado under the Medicare and Medicaid programs. Pursuant to the provider agreements at issue here, Medicaid paid O'Hara for the specialized care almost twice the reimbursement rate it paid other long-term care facilities in Colorado.

Following an audit of O'Hara's billing practices, the government concluded that O'Hara had submitted inflated invoices for patient services. Specifically, the government claimed O'Hara was inadequately staffed to meet the statutory and regulatory requirements provided for in the provider agreements. To recover the overpayments, it sued O'Hara in 2004, alleging that from September 1, 1997 through December 31, 2000, O'Hara "knowingly presented or caused to be presented claims for payment to the Medicare and Medicaid programs, for care, goods or services not rendered, that were inadequate or worthless, or that were rendered in violation of applicable statutes, regulations, and guidelines with a nexus to payment." R., Vol. 30, at 4940, ¶ 12. The government also claimed that O'Hara "systematically and routinely understaffed [the facility]" in violation of the provider agreements. R., Vol. 30, at 4940, ¶ 11. The government, however, did not seek damages on behalf of any patients who might have been harmed by the allegedly inadequate staffing levels.

The government brought a federal cause of action under the False Claims Act, 31 U.S.C. § 3729(a), and also asserted common law claims under Colorado law, including: payment by mistake of fact, unjust enrichment, common law fraud, restitution and disgorgement of illegal profits, and recoupment of overpayments. Following the commencement of the lawsuit, O'Hara tendered its defense to three of its general liability insurance carriers for the years in question: Zurich,[3] Valley Forge,[4] and Lloyd's.[5] O'Hara's theory of coverage was that the allegations of billing irregularities were encompassed by the "professional services" provision in each policy, which covered liability caused by errors and omissions in the furnishing or failure to furnish professional services—in this case, O'Hara's billing and staffing practices.

Valley Forge and Zurich accepted O'Hara's tender of defense under a reservation of rights, while Lloyd's disclaimed coverage altogether.

Procedural Background

While the government's lawsuit proceeded in federal court, all three insurers filed separate complaints against O'Hara, seeking a declaratory judgment that they had no duty to defend or indemnify O'Hara. The insurers claimed the professional services provisions did not provide coverage for the claims of fraud made by the government in the underlying lawsuit. The district court consolidated the cases, and all parties filed cross-motions for summary judgment.

---

[3] *Zurich Policy.*

> We will pay on behalf of any "insured" . . . [damages] that any "insured" becomes legally obligated to pay . . . because of injury to which this insurance applies. *The injury must be caused by a "medical incident"*. . . . "Medical incident" means *any act or omission in . . . the rendering or failing to render* . . . medical, surgical, dental, x-ray, or *nursing service* or treatment, or the furnishing of food or beverage in connection therewith; *any service* or treatment conducive to health or *of a professional nature*. . . .

R., Vol. 27, at 4667, 4757 (emphasis added).

[4] *Valley Forge Policy.* Valley Forge denies that its umbrella policy includes professional liability coverage. O'Hara asserts, however, that the umbrella policy should be reformed to correspond to the coverage provided in the professional liability section of the Resident Health Care Package Policy. For the purposes of this appeal, we assume that the umbrella policy has been reformed to include the following professional liability provisions:

> We will pay those sums that the insured becomes legally obligated to pay as damages *because of a "professional incident"* in the course of performing professional services for your resident health care facility. . . . *"Professional Incident" means . . . [a]ny act or omission in the furnishing or failure to furnish professional services* including the furnishing of food, beverages, medications or appliances in connection with such services and the postmortem handling of human bodies.

R., Vol. 28, at 4813, 4815 (emphasis added).

[5] *Lloyd's Policy.*

> We will pay those sums that you become legally obligated to pay as damages because of injury to which this insurance applies. . . . This insurance applies to injury only if . . . *[t]he injury is caused by a "medical incident"* . . . and [t]he injury arises out of the individual insured's profession as a licensed health care provider. . . . "Medical incident" means *any act or omission . . . [a]rising out of the providing of or failure to provide professional health care services*. . . .
>
> * * *
>
> We will pay those sums that you become legally obligated to pay as damages because of injury to which this insurance applies. . . . This insurance applies to injury only if . . . *[t]he injury is caused by a "business entity incident"*. . . . "Business entity incident" means *any act or omission arising out of the providing of or failure to provide professional health care services*. . . .

R., Vol. 29, at 4906–07, 4912 (emphasis added).

The district court granted the insurers summary judgment, and subsequently certified the judgment as final and appealable. This timely appeal followed. . . .

Because this case arises under our diversity jurisdiction, Colorado insurance law applies.

III. Discussion

O'Hara primarily makes two arguments in support of its theory that the professional services provisions of the insurance contracts provide coverage. First, it claims that the misconduct alleged by the government arose from O'Hara's negligent design and implementation of health care practices—namely, its failure to provide professionally adequate nursing or medical services. Second, it claims that its billing practices pursuant to the Medicare and Medicaid provider agreements also constitute professional services covered by the policies.

We find neither argument persuasive.[6]

A. Duty to Defend and Indemnify

Before turning to the specific language of the policies, several broad principles guide our assessment of the insurers' duty to defend and indemnify. Under Colorado law, an insurer's duty to defend is broader than the duty to indemnify. If there is no duty to defend, then there is no duty to indemnify. *See Cyprus Amax Minerals Co. v. Lexington Ins. Co.,* 74 P.3d 294, 299 (Colo.2003) ("Because the duty to defend encompasses any potential claims raised by the facts and the duty to indemnify relates to the actual liability imposed, this court has considered the duty to defend to be a broader concept than the duty to indemnify.").

When determining whether a duty to defend exists, a court applying Colorado law "look[s] no further than the four corners of the underlying complaint." *Id.* The facts alleged in the complaint, not the legal claims asserted by the plaintiff, determine the insurer's duty. *Gerrity Co. v. CIGNA Property & Cas. Ins. Co.,* 860 P.2d 606, 607 (Colo.Ct.App.1993). If the complaint "alleges any facts that might fall within the coverage of the policy," then the insurer has a duty to defend the insured. *Hecla Mining Co. v. New Hampshire Ins. Co.,* 811 P.2d 1083, 1089 (Colo.1991).

B. Application

O'Hara argues the insurers have a duty to defend the company against the government's lawsuit because the government's allegations fall within the policies' broad coverage for professional nursing and medical services. The

[6] O'Hara additionally contends the district court did not analyze the express language of the insurance policies at issue. The insurers and O'Hara also disagree about whether various policy exclusions bar coverage. Because we interpret the "professional services" language of the applicable policies as not covering the activities alleged in the government's complaint, it is unnecessary for us to address these arguments.

relevant coverage provisions are roughly the same for each of the insurers. They provide coverage where the insured causes injury by negligently (1) providing nursing or medical services or treatment; or (2) generally, providing professional services.

In O'Hara's view, these policies provide coverage because the government's complaint is premised on negligence in either (1) providing professional nursing or medical services, or (2) processing and submitting Medicare and Medicaid forms.

1. Professional Nursing or Medical Services

No one disputes the insurance policies at issue cover errors or omissions made in the furnishing or failing to furnish professional nursing or medical services. The dispute centers on O'Hara's view that the government's case is predicated on O'Hara's failure to provide *adequate* professional nursing services. According to O'Hara, the thrust of the government's argument is that it failed to adequately staff the facility, thus breaching the staffing requirements of the provider agreements. But for the inadequate staffing levels, O'Hara would otherwise have been in compliance with the provider agreements.

We disagree. The government's injury was not caused by O'Hara's failure to provide professional services, but instead resulted from O'Hara's submission of false and fraudulent claims for reimbursement. Specifically, the crux of the government's claim is that O'Hara promised to provide a certain level of patient care; it represented to the government it provided the contractually agreed levels of care; but, in fact, it did not provide the agreed services. As we read the government's cause of action, the problem was not the actual level of services provided to O'Hara's patients, but rather that O'Hara billed for services it did not provide—namely, enhanced services. This violates the provider agreements.

Several cases support this analysis. The insurers, for example, point to a substantially similar case in which the court rejected a nursing home's argument that inadequate staffing could be covered under the professional services provision. *Horizon West, Inc. v. St. Paul Fire & Marine Ins. Co.*, 214 F.Supp.2d 1074 (E.D.Cal.2002), *aff'd*, 45 Fed.Appx. 752 (9th Cir.2002). In that case, the insurance policy stated, "[w]e'll pay amounts you and others protected under this agreement are legally required to pay to compensate others for injury or death resulting from . . . the providing or failure to provide professional services while this agreement is in effect." *Horizon West*, 214 F.Supp.2d at 1076. As in the present case, the plaintiff alleged the facility falsely and fraudulently submitted Medicare and Medicaid claims for services it did not provide. In concluding the insurer did not have a duty to defend, the court found the insured's "injuries"—the possible reimbursement of fraudulent payments it received—were caused by the company's billing practices rather than its nursing services.

The decision in *Horizon West* is consistent with the approach followed in other jurisdictions that have considered whether liability policies cover claims under the False Claims Act or related causes of action. For example, in *M/G Transport Services, Inc. v. Water Quality Insurance Syndicate*, 234 F.3d 974 (6th Cir.2000), a subcontractor signed a contract with the United States government agreeing to transport coal to the Tennessee Valley Authority. As a condition of the contract, the subcontractor agreed to comply with the Clean Water Act. *Id.* at 975–76. A False Claims Act suit was subsequently filed against the subcontractor, alleging it falsified records to hide violations of the Clean Water Act so it could obtain payment from the United States. The subcontractor then sued its insurer, alleging the insurer had a duty to defend the company against the lawsuit because the policy covered any amounts paid "by reason of or with respect to" liability to the United States for violations of the Clean Water Act. *Id.* at 977–78. The Sixth Circuit rejected the subcontractor's arguments for the following reasons:

> M/G's arguments are *thinly disguised attempts to bootstrap liability for FCA violations into the coverage provided by the environmental pollution policies.* Under these circumstances, we cannot conclude that M/G's liability . . . was by reason of, or with respect to, liability to the United States for cleanup costs under the Clean Water Act. An FCA action is not converted into a Clean Water Act action simply because a violation of the Clean Water Act is a predicate to establishing the falsity of a claim, or may be used as a measure of damages under the FCA.

Id. at 978.

We similarly reject O'Hara's attempt to bootstrap liability for False Claims Act violations into the coverage provided by the professional liability policies issued by Zurich, Valley Forge, and Lloyd's. *See also Hampton Med. Group v. Princeton Ins. Co.*, 366 N.J. Super. 165, 840 A.2d 915, 917–18 (N.J.Super.Ct.App.Div.2004) (holding insurer—which provided psychiatrists a professional liability policy covering "injur[ies] caused by a 'medical incident' arising out of your supplying or failure to supply professional services"—did not have a duty to defend the psychiatrists against a lawsuit alleging they billed Blue Cross/Blue Shield for services they never provided).

O'Hara nonetheless makes additional arguments suggesting the insurance policies should be broadly interpreted to cover the government's fraud allegations. In essence, O'Hara argues that even if it received sums of money for services it never provided, the insurance companies should be on the hook when it is required to disgorge the payments. After reviewing the language of the three applicable policies, we disagree. The logic of *Horizon,*

M/G Transport Services, and *Hampton Medical Group* applies equally here.

Zurich's Policies

O'Hara argues Zurich's policies provide especially expansive coverage because the language covers injuries *related* to the rendering of nursing services, not just injuries *caused* by the failure to furnish such services. The policies explain, "Any such act or omission, together with all *related acts or omissions* in the furnishing of or failing to furnish such services to any one person shall be considered as one 'medical incident.' " R., Vol. 27, at 4667, 4757 (emphasis added). Based on this language, O'Hara argues Zurich has a duty to defend because the government's suit is related to its facility's alleged failure to provide adequate nursing services.

But in making this argument, O'Hara takes the phrase "related acts or omissions" out of context. When the sentence is read in its entirety, it is clear that the purpose of the cited clause is not to define or expand the scope of the policy's coverage to include any activity related to the failure to furnish professional services—such as billing the government for services not provided. Instead the clause merely clarifies that one "medical incident" can involve several covered acts or omissions.

Valley Forge's Policy

O'Hara also argues Valley Forge's policy provides broad coverage for inadequate staffing. In particular, the policy "extends coverage to professional services performed *for your resident health care facility*." Aplt. Opening Br. 34. O'Hara's description of the policy, however, is incomplete. The policy requires a causal connection between the injury alleged and a covered activity. The policy states "we will pay those sums that the insured becomes legally obligated to pay as damages *because of* a 'professional incident' in the course of performing professional services for your resident health care facility." R., Vol. 28, at 4813 (emphasis added).

Because no causal connection exists between the failure to perform nursing services and the damages alleged by the government—i.e., over-billing—Valley Forge's policy does not cover the underlying lawsuit.

Lloyd's Policy

Finally, O'Hara argues Lloyd's policy should be interpreted broadly because it includes the phrase "arising out of" within the definitions of "medical incident" and "business entity incident." O'Hara suggests the Colorado Supreme Court has interpreted the phrase as creating a "but-for" test. *See, e.g., Northern Ins. Co. v. Ekstrom,* 784 P.2d 320, 323 (Colo.1989). Because the injury alleged by the government would not have occurred but for the nursing facility's substandard care, the argument goes, this test is satisfied.

This argument is misplaced. The Colorado Supreme Court subsequently clarified that the phrase "arising out of" requires more than a mere "but for" relation between the injury and the covered activity. *See State Farm Mut. Auto. Ins. Co. v. Kastner,* 77 P.3d 1256, 1264 (Colo.2003). "[T]he claimant must [also] show that the [covered activity] and the injury are directly related or inextricably linked so that no independent significant act or [omission] interrupted the 'but for' causal chain between the covered [activity] and the injury." *Id.* O'Hara's false representations to the government here constituted an independent act that interrupted the causal chain between O'Hara's failure to furnish adequate nursing services and the government's injury—the overpayment of claims.

Because the alleged failure to furnish adequate nursing services is not "directly related" or "inextricably linked" to the injury claimed by the government, O'Hara failed to demonstrate that the insurers had a duty to defend.

2. *Billing Practices*

O'Hara alternatively argues the insurers had a duty to defend the company because its billing practices constitute professional services covered by the policies.

Professional liability policies do not insure against all liability incurred by the insured. Instead, such policies often use the term "professional services" or an equivalent phrase to describe the scope of the coverage. 23 *Appleman on Insurance* § 146.3[A]. Zurich's policies refer to "any service . . . of a professional nature." R., Vol. 27, at 4667, 4757. Valley Forge's policy uses the phrase "professional services." R., Vol. 28, at 4815. And, Lloyd's policy refers to "professional health care services." R., Vol. 29, at 4912–13. The terms are not defined in any of the policies, and Colorado courts have not clarified the meaning of the phrase.

The definition of professional services most frequently relied on by courts was first set forth in *Marx v. Hartford Accident & Indemnity Co.,* 183 Neb. 12, 157 N.W.2d 870, 871–72 (1968); 23 *Appleman on Insurance* § 146.3[A]. "A 'professional' act or service is one arising out of a vocation, calling, occupation, or employment involving specialized knowledge, labor, or skill, and the labor or skill involved is predominantly mental or intellectual, rather than physical or manual." *Marx,* 157 N.W.2d at 872; *see also Noyes Supervision, Inc. v. Canadian Indem. Co.,* 487 F.Supp. 433, 438 (D.Colo.1980) (applying Colorado law) (relying in part on *Marx* to determine the meaning of the term "professional services" in an insurance contract); *cf. Titan Indem. Co. v. Travelers Prop. Cas. Co. of Am.,* 181 P.3d 303, 307–08 (Colo.Ct.App.2007) (declining to rely on *Marx* and other cases in determining the meaning of the term "professional services" because the phrase was defined in the policy).

Although processing Medicare and Medicaid claims may be difficult and time consuming, the activity does not characterize a "professional service." The court in *Horizon West* reached a similar conclusion. *Horizon West,* 214 F.Supp.2d at 1079 ("Horizon West . . . fails to offer any legal authority that submission of Medicare and Medicaid claims constitutes anything other than 'ordinary activities achievable by those lacking the relevant professional training and expertise.' ") (quoting *Medical Records,* 142 F.3d at 514 (applying Massachusetts law)).

In fact, courts generally have concluded the preparation of bills or invoices does not qualify as professional services. 23 *Appleman on Insurance* § 146.3 [B] (collecting cases); *see, e.g., Medical Records,* 142 F.3d at 515–16; *see also Cohen v. Empire Cas. Co.,* 771 P.2d 29, 31 (Colo.Ct.App.1989). For example, in *Medical Records,* a law firm sued a medical records processing business, alleging the company overcharged for copies. The company referred the claim to its insurer, arguing the applicable policy covered "[l]oss which the Insured shall become legally obligated to pay . . . by reason of any actual or alleged negligent act, error or omission committed in the rendering or failure to render the Professional Services stated in the Declarations." *Medical Records,* 142 F.3d at 514. The Declarations only identified the professional services as "Medical Records Processor." *Id.*

In determining whether the policy covered the underlying lawsuit, the court relied in part on the definition of professional services articulated in *Marx. Id.* at 515 (citing *Marx,* 157 N.W.2d at 872). It concluded the insurer did not have a duty to defend the company because setting a price for photocopies and producing accurate invoices did not require the level of particularized knowledge necessary to be characterized as a professional service. *See id.* at 516, 157 N.W.2d 870. The processing of Medicare and Medicaid claims likewise does not require a specialized professional service.

Nor does Colorado law support a professional malpractice theory. For example, in a case involving a claim of a lawyer refusing to pay for the legal services of co-counsel, the Colorado Court of Appeals considered whether such a claim could be covered as "arising out of any act or omission of the Insured in rendering or failing to render *professional services* for others in the Insured's capacity as a lawyer." *Cohen,* 771 P.2d at 30 (emphasis added). Although the court did not define the phrase "professional services," it explained billing practices were not covered by the policy,

> Expenses incurred by a lawyer for maintaining his office, hiring secretaries, investigators, consultants, expert witnesses, and associates are incidental to a lawyer's *business*. His failure to pay either the cost of, or the reasonable value for, such *business* expenses cannot rationally be deemed a failure to provide legal

> advice or assistance to others *in his professional capacity as a lawyer.*

Id. at 31.

In much the same way, O'Hara's billing practices are incidental to its business as an operator of a nursing facility. O'Hara's failure to file accurate reimbursement claims with the government is not a failure to provide services in its professional capacity.

Because the underlying lawsuit does not allege an injury caused by an activity covered by the insurance policies at issue in this case, the insurers do not have a duty to defend or indemnify O'Hara.

. . . .

V. Conclusion

For the reasons stated above, we AFFIRM. The case is remanded to the district court for further proceedings consistent with this opinion.

NOTES AND QUESTIONS

1. *Related to Professional Services?* Why did the court in *O'Hara* conclude that the billing for professional services that had not been rendered was not related to and/or arising from the rendering of professional services? Do you agree with the holding? Why or why not?

2. *A Better Outcome?* What could the policyholder have done differently in *Flores* in order to avoid the situation where it was uninsured for claims brought against it related to its business?

3. *Majority Rule.* The *O'Hara* court cited *Marx v. Hartford Accident & Indemnity Co.*, 157 N.W.2d 870, 871–72 (Neb. 1968) for the definition of "professional services." *Marx* represents the majority view on the definition of the term: "A 'professional' act or service is one arising out of a vocation, calling, occupation, or employment involving specialized knowledge, labor, or skill, and the labor or skill involved is predominantly mental or intellectual, rather than physical or manual." *Marx,* 157 N.W.2d at 872.

C. LATE NOTICE

SPARKS V. ST. PAUL INSURANCE CO.

495 A.2d 406 (N.J. 1985)

STEIN, J.

In this case, as in *Zuckerman v. National Union Fire Ins. Co.,* 100 N.J. 304, 495 A.2d 395 (1985), which the Court also decides today, we consider the enforceability of certain coverage limitations contained in a "claims made" professional liability insurance policy issued by appellant St. Paul Insurance Company (St. Paul). The trial court and the Appellate Division refused to enforce the policy provision limiting coverage to claims and potential claims reported to St. Paul during the policy period. We granted the insurance company's petition for certification, 99 N.J. 211, 491 A.2d 706 (1984), in order to resolve the apparent conflict between the unreported Appellate Division decision in this case and the Appellate Division decision in *Zuckerman, supra,* 194 N.J. Super. 206, 476 A.2d 820 (1984), enforcing a similar provision in the "claims made" policy at issue in that case.

I.

The material facts are not in dispute. In November, 1978, respondents, John and Carolyn Sparks, retained A. Raymond Guarriello, a New Jersey attorney, to represent them in connection with the sale of their residence. That transaction resulted in litigation between respondents and the prospective purchasers. In the course of that litigation, apparently due to Guarriello's negligence, Mr. and Mrs. Sparks failed to answer interrogatories. This resulted in an order entered in mid-October, 1979, suppressing the Sparks' answer and counterclaim. A default judgment for specific performance was entered against Mr. and Mrs. Sparks in February, 1980, and a money judgment for $18,899.08 was entered against them in May, 1981. It is not disputed that Guarriello's negligence was the proximate cause of the judgments against Mr. and Mrs. Sparks.

On November 6, 1976, appellant, St. Paul, issued Guarriello a one-year professional malpractice policy that was renewed for successive one-year periods, terminating on November 6, 1979. On September 27, 1979, St. Paul issued a substitute policy for one additional year that was to take effect on November 6, 1979. Guarriello failed to pay the premium and appellant sent Guarriello a notice canceling the substitute policy, effective January 21, 1980. Between June and August of 1980, substituted counsel for respondents notified St. Paul of the underlying facts and demanded that the insurance company provide malpractice coverage with respect to Guarriello's negligence.

The policy issued to Guarriello in 1976 was denominated a "claims made" policy. A "Schedule" attached to the declaration page of the policy bore the following notice:

TO OUR POLICYHOLDERS

> This is a "claims made" Coverage Form. It only covers claims arising from the performance of professional services *subsequent to the retroactive date indicated* and then only to claims first made within the provisions of the Policy while this Coverage Form is in force. No coverage is afforded for claims first made after the termination of this insurance unless and to the extent that Reporting Endorsements are purchased in accordance with Condition 3 of this Coverage Form. Please review the Policy carefully.

(emphasis added).

The retroactive date set forth in the policy was November 6, 1976, the same date as the effective date of coverage. Therefore, unlike the standard "claims made" policy that was involved in our decision in *Zuckerman, supra,* 100 N.J. at 307–309, 495 A.2d 395, St. Paul's policy provided no retroactive coverage whatsoever during its first year. In that year, the coverage provided by the policy applied only to errors and omissions that occurred during the policy year and were reported to the company within the policy year. During the two renewal years beginning November 6, 1977 and November 6, 1978, the policy afforded "retroactive" coverage for negligence that occurred subsequent to November 6, 1976.

In April, 1981, St. Paul rejected respondent's demand that it provide coverage for Guarriello's malpractice since the company received notice of the claim after the termination of the second renewal policy in November, 1979 and after the January, 1980 cancellation of the replacement policy for nonpayment of the premium.[1] In June, 1981, Mr. and Mrs. Sparks obtained a $42,968.08 judgment against Guarriello based upon his malpractice.

The present action commenced in October, 1981. Mr. and Mrs. Sparks sought a declaratory judgment that the liability insurance policy issued by St. Paul was valid and enforceable to pay the judgment obtained against Guarriello. In August, 1983, St. Paul's motion for summary judgment was denied and in September, 1983, summary judgment was granted in favor of Mr. and Mrs. Sparks. That judgment was affirmed by the Appellate Division, which held "claims made" policies to be unenforceable as violative of public policy.

II.

In our decision in *Zuckerman, supra,* 100 N.J. at 309–313, 495 A.2d at 398–400, we summarized the origins of "claims made" or "discovery" liability policies and emphasized the distinction between such policies and the more traditional "occurrence" policies. That distinction warrants reiteration in view of the unusual provisions of the policy issued to Guarriello by St. Paul:

> [T]here are two types of Errors and Omissions Policies: the "discovery" policy and the "occurrence" policy. In a discovery policy the coverage is effective if the negligent or omitted act is discovered and brought to the attention of the insurance company during the period of the policy, no matter when the act occurred. In an occurrence policy the coverage is effective if the negligent or

---

[1] Although St. Paul's Notice of Cancellation stated that it would be effective January 21, 1980, the insurance company now maintains that its effect was to cancel the replacement policy *ab initio* as of November 6, 1979. As discussed *infra* at 415–416 & n. 5, the effective date of the cancellation is not material.

> omitted act occurred during the period of the policy, whatever the date of discovery.

[*Samuel N. Zarpas, Inc. v. Morrow,* 215 F. Supp. 887, 888 (D.N.J. 1963).]

Another court characterized "claims made" policies as "provid[ing] unlimited retroactive coverage and no prospective coverage at all," as distinguished from "occurrence" policies which "provide unlimited prospective coverage and no retroactive coverage at all." *Brander v. Nabors,* 443 F. Supp. 764, 767 (N.D. Miss.), *aff'd,* 579 F.2d 888 (5th Cir. 1978).

The distinction between the two types of policies has also been described in terms of the peril insured:

> In the "occurrence" policy, the peril insured is the "occurrence" itself. Once the "occurrence" takes place, coverage attaches even though the claim may not be made for some time thereafter. While in the "claims made" policy, it is the making of the claim which is the event and peril being insured and, subject to policy language, regardless of when the occurrence took place.

[S. Kroll, "The Professional Liability Policy 'Claims Made,'" 13 Forum 842, 843 (1978).]

In *Zuckerman, supra,* 100 N.J. at 311–313, 495 A.2d at 399, we discussed in detail the significant social utility of the "claims made" policy that has led to its supplanting the occurrence policy in the professional liability field. We noted that since the insurance company that issues an "occurrence" policy is exposed to a "tail"—that is, the lapse of time between the occurrence and the date on which the claim is made—there is considerable difficulty in accurately calculating underwriting risks and premiums with respect to perils that typically lead to long tail exposure. Moreover, claims asserted in the fields of professional malpractice, products liability, and environmental law often present the added difficulty of determining precisely when the actuating event "occurred" for the purpose of defining coverage. From the standpoint of the insured, there is the danger of inadequate coverage in cases in which claims are asserted long after the error or omission occurred, because inflationary factors lead to judgments that are higher than those originally contemplated when coverage was purchased years earlier.

From the insurer's perspective, the clear advantage derived from a "claims made" policy is the limitation of liability to claims asserted during the policy period. This limitation enables insurers to calculate risks and premiums with greater precision. Although "claims made" policies provide coverage for errors and omissions occurring prior to the policy's inception, the elimination of exposure to claims filed after the policy expiration date enables companies to issue these policies at reduced premiums. J. Parker,

"The Untimely Demise of the 'Claims Made' Insurance Form? A Critique of *Stine v. Continental Casualty Co.*," 1983 Det. C.L. Rev. 25, 73.

In *Zuckerman,* we observed that Courts throughout the country have upheld the validity of "claims made" policies. Although "claims made" policies have regularly been challenged on public policy grounds, the vast majority of courts that have considered these challenges have enforced the policies as written.[2]

The courts that have declined to enforce "claims made" policies have based their decisions on special factual circumstances. *J.G. Link & Co. v. Continental Cas. Co.,* 470 F.2d 1133 (9th Cir. 1972), *cert. denied,* 414 U.S. 829, 94 S. Ct. 55, 38 L. Ed. 2d 63 (1973) (policy covered claims made during policy period but due to certain ambiguities in policy language, court could not determine if policy was intended to provide "occurrence" or "claims made" coverage); *Gyler v. Mission Ins. Co.,* 10 Cal. 3d 216, 514 P. [2d] 1219, 110 Cal. Rptr. 139, (1973) (policy insuring against "claims which *may* be made" during the policy period found to be too ambiguous to allow enforcement of "claims made" coverage limitation) (emphasis added).

We also reviewed in *Zuckerman, supra,* the commercial utility of "claims made" policies and scrutinized the terms of the policy at issue in that case. We concluded that there were "no considerations of public policy that would inhibit . . . enforcement of the 'claims made' policy issued to appellant [Zuckerman]." Similarly, we would not hesitate to enforce St. Paul's policy in this case if it comported with the generally accepted expectations of "claims made" insurance. The coverage provided by St. Paul's policy, however, materially diverges from customary "claims made" coverage in terms of its retroactive protection. It provides neither the prospective coverage typical of an "occurrence" policy, nor the retroactive coverage typical of a "claims made" policy. During the first policy year, coverage was limited to acts of malpractice that occurred, were discovered, and were reported to the insurance company during the same year. Although there was slight retroactive coverage during the second and third renewal years of the policy, the retroactive coverage was significantly more limited than that contemplated in the standard "claims made" policy.

III.

Jones v. Continental Cas. Co., 123 N.J. Super. 353, 303 A.2d 91 (Ch. Div. 1973), is the only reported case in which a "claims made" policy was invalidated because of its lack of retroactive coverage. Jones was a professional engineer who was insured against errors and omissions under a policy that took effect in February, 1965, and was renewed annually until its termination in April, 1970. In August, 1971, a contractor sued Jones for malpractice based upon engineering services he had performed during the

[2] For a more complete list of cases enforcing "claims made" policies, see *Zuckerman, supra,* 100 N.J. 313–314, 495 A.2d at 400.

policy period. Jones' insurance carrier declined coverage because it did not receive notification of the claim during the policy period. Jones, seeking to compel coverage, sued the carrier.

The retroactive coverage provided for in Jones' policy was unusual in that it was limited "to errors, omissions or negligent acts which occur[red] . . . prior to the effective date of this policy *if . . . insured by this Company under [a] prior policy.*" *Id.* at 356, 303 A.2d 91 (emphasis added). The court concluded that this retroactive coverage impermissibly inhibited plaintiff's freedom of contract because he would be deprived of coverage if he did not continue to renew his policy with the same insurance company. The court also held that the total absence of prospective coverage violated this State's public policy in favor of extending time for making a claim or bringing suit for latent injuries. Accordingly, the court declined to enforce the coverage limitations in defendant's policy, concluding, on public policy grounds, that such limitations were inconsistent with the plaintiff's "reasonable expectations" of coverage and that plaintiff's notice to defendant was sufficiently timely to invoke coverage under the policy.

Other state and federal courts confronted with "claims made" policies providing limited or no retroactive coverage have declined to follow *Jones.*[3] But at least one proponent of "claims made" policies has acknowledged the unique limitations of the coverage afforded by the "claims made" policy in *Jones:*

> Indeed, the *Jones* [*sic*] policy was peculiarly narrow in its coverage; it required the insured to have been covered by prior policies issued *only* by the insurer as a condition precedent to being covered for errors and omissions accruing prior to the effective date of the policy. . . . Consequently, because the insured did not have prior policies with CNA, the *Jones* policy afforded the insured coverage only for acts occurring during the term of insurance and then only if the policy was maintained; in effect, it only provided "occurrence" coverage without the prospective benefits of the same.

[J. Parker, *supra,* 1983 Det. C.L. Rev. at 36 n. 38.]

Similarly, in *Brander v. Nabors, supra,* 443 F. Supp. 764, a federal district court in Mississippi considered a "claims made" policy that provided no retroactive coverage but afforded prospective coverage for a three-year period beyond the policy expiration date. Although, in the context of that policy, the court found no necessity for retroactive protection, it conceded

---

[3] The cases rejecting *Jones* reasoned that because unambiguous provisions of the policies clearly restricted retroactive coverage, and premiums were presumably reduced to reflect the limited protection, there was no basis on which to invalidate the limitations on coverage. Other cases have enforced "claims made" policies that afforded significantly limited or no retroactive coverage without expressly discussing that issue.

that a more significant problem would be presented by a policy affording neither prospective nor retroactive coverage:

> We would be confronted with a more serious question of public policy if a "claims made" policy with neither a period of retroactive coverage nor a period of prospective coverage, but requiring notice to the insured within the policy period, were involved; in that event, the insurance coverage would be effective only for the time premiums are paid, and during which notice of the claim would have to be given to the insurer. Such a policy would necessitate closer scrutiny from the standpoint of what period of coverage is reasonable in light of public policy. That precise issue is, however, not before us, and we express no opinion as to the validity of a policy structured on such narrow grounds.

[*Id.*, 443 F. Supp. at 773.]

IV.

Although it is a well-established principle that insurance contracts will not be enforced if they violate public policy, the application of that principle has been limited in order that freedom of contract is not impaired unreasonably:

> [P]ublic policy" is that principle of law which holds that "no person can lawfully do that which has a tendency to be injurious to the public or against public good . . ." even though "no actual injury" may have resulted therefrom in a particular case "to the public." It is a question of law which the court must decide in light of the particular circumstances of each case.
>
> . . . .
>
> . . . Men of "full age and competent understanding" have the "utmost liberty of contracting." Contracts so freely and voluntarily made, in the absence of express or implied prohibition, are sacred and are enforced by courts of justice. And courts do "not lightly interfere with this freedom of contract." Lord Jessel, in *Printing Registering Co. v. Sampson,* 19 Eq. 462, 465; 21 E.R. Co. 696, 699 (cited in *Driver v. Smith, supra* ([89 N.J. Eq.] at p. 359 [104 A. 717]). Or in the words of the late Mr. Justice Butler, "The principle that contracts in contravention of public policy are not enforceable should be applied with caution and only in cases plainly within the reasons on which the doctrine rests." *Twin City Pipe Line Co. v. Harding Glass Co., supra,* 283 U.S. 353 (at p. 356 [51 S. Ct. 476, at p. 477, 75 L. Ed. 1112 (1931)]); 75 L. Ed. 1116.

[*Allen v. Commercial Cas. Ins. Co., supra,* 131 N.J.L. at 477–478, 37 A.2d 37.]

The doctrine that courts do not lightly interfere with freedom of contract must be applied cautiously and realistically with regard to complex contracts of insurance, since such contracts are highly technical, extremely difficult to understand, and not subject to bargaining over the terms. They are contracts of adhesion, prepared unilaterally by the insurer, and have always been subjected to careful judicial scrutiny to avoid injury to the public. For example, in *Gaunt v. John Hancock Mut. Life Ins. Co.*, 160 F.2d 599 (2d Cir.), *cert. denied,* 331 U.S. 849, 67 S. Ct. 1736, 91 L. Ed. 1858 (1947), Judge Learned Hand rejected an insurance company's contention that the language set forth on a receipt for a life insurance premium postponed commencement of coverage until the insurer approved the application:

> An underwriter might so understand the phrase, when read in its context, but the application was not to be submitted to underwriters; it was to go to persons utterly unacquainted with the niceties of life insurance, who would read it colloquially. It is the understanding of such persons that counts; and not one in a hundred would suppose that he would be covered, not "as of the date of completion of Part B," as the defendant promised, but only as of the date of approval.

[*Id.* at 601 (footnote omitted).]

The recognition that insurance policies are not readily understood has impelled courts to resolve ambiguities in such contracts against the insurance companies.

This recognition has also led courts to enforce unambiguous insurance contracts in accordance with the reasonable expectations of the insured. . . .

. . . .

The interpretation of insurance contracts to accord with the reasonable expectations of the insured, regardless of the existence of any ambiguity in the policy, constitutes judicial recognition of the unique nature of contracts of insurance. By traditional standards of contract law, the consent of both parties, based on an informed understanding of the terms and conditions of the contract, is rarely present in insurance contracts. W.D. Slawson, "Standard Form Contracts and Democratic Control of Lawmaking Power," 84 Harv. L. Rev. 529, 539–41 (1971); R. Keeton, Insurance Law 350–52 (1971). Because understanding is lacking, the consent necessary to sustain traditional contracts cannot be presumed to exist in most contracts of insurance. Such consent can be inferred only to the extent that the policy language conforms to public expectations and commercially reasonable standards. *See* W.D. Slawson, *supra,* 84 Harv. L. Rev. at 566; *R. Keeton, supra,* at 350–52. In instances in which the insurance contract is inconsistent with public expectations and commercially accepted standards, judicial regulation of insurance contracts is essential in order to prevent overreaching and injustice. *R. Keeton, supra,* at 350–52; R. Keeton, "Insurance Law Rights at Variance with Policy Provisions," 83 Harv. L. Rev. 961, 967 (1970). One commentator has stated the principle as follows:

> The objectively reasonable expectations of applicants and intended beneficiaries regarding the terms of insurance contracts will be honored even though painstaking study of the policy provisions would have negated those expectations.

[*R. Keeton, supra,* at 351; R. Keeton, *supra,* 83 Harv. L. Rev. at 967.]

We find that the contract of insurance sold by St. Paul to Guarriello does not conform to the objectively reasonable expectations of the insured with respect to the scope of the insured and is violative of the public policy of this State. Although we held today in *Zuckerman v. National Union Fire Ins. Co., supra,* 100 N.J. 304, 495 A.2d 395 (1985), that a "claims made" policy that fulfills the reasonable expectations of the insured with respect to the scope of coverage is valid and enforceable, the policy at issue here is substantially different from the standard "claims made" policy. Indeed, St. Paul's policy combines the worst features of "occurrence" and "claims made" policies and the best of neither. It provides neither the prospective coverage typical of an "occurrence" policy, nor the "retroactive" coverage typical of a "claims made" policy. During the first year that the policy was in force, it provided no retroactive coverage for occurrences prior to the effective date of the policy. Thus, it afforded the insured only minimal protection against professional liability claims. Only claims asserted during the policy year, based on negligence that occurred during the policy year, and that were subsequently communicated to the company during the policy year were under the umbrella of coverage.

The realities of professional malpractice, however, suggest that it would be the rare instance in which an error occurred and was discovered with sufficient time to report it to the insurance company, all within a twelve-month period. The victims of professional malpractice are frequently unaware of any negligence until their injury becomes manifest long after the error or omission was committed.

Our review of the use of "claims made" policies in the professional liability field demonstrates that a policy that defines the scope of coverage so narrowly is incompatible with the objectively reasonable expectations of purchasers of professional liability coverage. We assume that there are vast numbers of professionals covered by "claims made" policies who are unaware of the basic distinction between their policies and the traditional "occurrence" policy. However, those professionals covered by "claims made" policies who do understand how their policies differ from "occurrence" policies would expect that in return for the loss of prospective coverage provided by "occurrence" policies, they would be afforded reasonable retroactive coverage by their "claims made" policies. A leading proponent of "claims made" coverage has characterized this *quid pro quo*—the relinquishment of prospective coverage in return for retroactive coverage—as "*the essential* trade-off inherent in the concept of 'claims-made' insurance." S. Kroll, *supra,* 13 Forum at 854 (emphasis added); *see* J. Parker, *supra,* 1983 Det. C.L. Rev. at 27 & n. 3.

We do not decide in this case the precise standard by which the reasonableness of retroactive coverage is to be measured. We hold, however, that where there has been no proof of factual circumstances that would render such limited retroactive coverage both reasonable and expected,[4] a "claims made" policy that affords no retroactive coverage whatsoever during its initial year of issuance does not accord with the objectively reasonable expectations of the purchasers of professional liability insurance. The fact that subsequent renewals of that policy provide minimal retroactive coverage, *i.e.,* to the effective date of the original policy, does not cure the significant deficiency inherent in the underlying policy.

To enforce policies that provide such unrealistically narrow coverage to professionals, and, derivatively, to the public they serve, would in our view cause the kind of broad injury to the public at large contemplated by the doctrine that precludes the enforcement of contracts that violate public policy. Put another way, were we to uphold the validity of St. Paul's policy in this case, the likely result would be the perpetuation in the professional liability insurance market of "claims made" policies offering comparably limited coverage. Because insurance contracts are contracts of adhesion, the terms of which are not customarily bargained for, courts have a special responsibility to prevent the marketing of policies that provide unrealistic and inadequate coverage.

Because in our view the policy sold by respondent is not a true "claims made" policy, we hold that the provisions in the policy that limit coverage to claims asserted only during the policy period are unenforceable. In view of its peculiar, absolute limitations on retroactive coverage, we construe the policy, despite its denomination, as one analogous to an "occurrence" policy. We therefore impute into the policy's provisions a right of prospective notification in order that the policy, as construed by us, provide a scope of coverage commensurate with the reasonable expectations of the insured as to "occurrence" policy coverage. Thus construed, we hold that the actual notice afforded to St. Paul by the attorneys for respondents between June and August, 1980 was furnished as soon as possible under

---

[4] "Claims made" policies with no retroactive coverage might be appropriate in certain contexts. For example, such policies might properly be offered at a reduced premium to the professional in his very first year of practice, or to the professional who changes from "occurrence" to "claims made" protection. Nothing in the record before us suggests that this is such a case.

the circumstances.[5] We follow in this limited and special factual setting the doctrine of *Cooper v. Government Employees Ins. Co.*, 51 N.J. 86, 237 A.2d 870 (1968), and find that there is no necessity to consider whether the insurance company is exposed to prejudice if the notice has been provided within a reasonable time. We emphasize, as we noted in *Zuckerman, supra,* 100 N.J. at 323–324, 495 A.2d at 405–406, the total inapplicability of the *Cooper* doctrine to a true "claims made" policy, but we apply its principle here because of our conclusion that this policy should be construed as a traditional "occurrence" form rather than as a "claims made" policy.

Accordingly, we hold that under these circumstances, the claim asserted by respondents against Guarriello, to the extent that it is based upon negligence that occurred during the policy period, is within the coverage afforded by appellant's policy. The notice to appellant between June and August, 1980, is sufficient to invoke that coverage. Accordingly, we modify and affirm the judgment of the Appellate Division and remand the matter to the trial court to consider, in accordance with the principles set forth in this opinion, any unresolved issues with respect to the specific coverage afforded by St. Paul's policy for the money judgment recovered against Guarriell.[6] We do not retain jurisdiction.

NOTES AND QUESTIONS

1. *The "Retro" Date.* Would an earlier retroactive date in the insured's policy in *Sparks* have changed the fact that the claim was made after the policy's expiration? Note that the problem concerning the court was not the

---

[5] New attorneys for Mr. and Mrs. Sparks were substituted in place of Guarriello on April 8, 1980. They provided St. Paul with official notice of the claim against Guarriello between June and August, 1980. Under the circumstances, we cannot say that the timing of such notice was unreasonable.

We are cognizant that had St. Paul's policy contained adequate retroactive coverage, Mr. and Mrs. Sparks would not have been afforded coverage. See *Zuckerman, supra,* 100 N.J. 304, 495 A.2d 395. An alternative construction of the policy would impute into it reasonable retroactive coverage and sustain the enforceability of the notice requirement. We reject this approach. It would be inequitable to hold an insurance policy void as against public policy and yet, when deciding between two plausible constructions of that policy, adopt the construction that is favorable to the drafter of the offensive document.

[6] This Court has not ruled previously that "claims made" policies without adequate retroactive coverage are contrary to the public policy of this State. In note 4, *supra,* we referred to the narrow circumstances in which such policies might be appropriate and valid. Accordingly, on remand the trial court should not be precluded from considering evidence tending to prove that the terms of this policy were specifically understood and bargained for by Guarriello and that, although a policy with adequate retroactive coverage was available to him from St. Paul, he specifically elected to purchase this policy with no retroactive coverage in the first year. Our holding is based on the record before us and on the assumption that, had any such evidence existed, it would have been offered in opposition to the motion for summary judgment.

If such evidence is offered, and the trial court concludes that the evidence is sufficient to prove that although insurance contracts are normally contracts of adhesion, good faith bargaining in this instance took place between the parties; that the terms of this policy were specifically bargained for and understood by [Guarriello]; and that the policy was purchased by him in preference to a policy with adequate retroactive coverage, the trial court would then be justified in enforcing the policy as written.

"tail" of the claim, but was instead the "nose." When would a policyholder need coverage for claims arising out of occurrences prior to the effective date of the claims-made coverage? If, for example, the insured is switching from occurrence to claims-made coverage, would not the prior occurrence policy(ies) cover any pre-claims-made policy claims? Is the concern over the retroactive coverage much ado about nothing? *See* Richard D. Catenacci, *Sparks Revisited: Sparks v. St. Paul Insurance Co.*, 23 Tort & Ins. L.J. 707 (1988).

2. *Unfair Surprise?* If the real issue with the requirement that a claim be asserted against the policyholder during the policy period under claims-made insurance is one of unfair surprise to the policyholder regarding the nature of the coverage, then what is the unfair surprise in light of the fact the policy clearly stated it was a claims-made policy that only covered claims made during the policy period? In *Concord Hospital v. New Hampshire Medical Malpractice Joint Underwriting Ass'n*, 633 A.2d 1384 (N.H. 1993), the court said that "the layperson of average intelligence does not know what 'claims made' refers to and cannot be expected to read crucial provisions into the term." 633 A.2d at 1386. Should the fact that Mr. Guarriello in *Sparks* was an attorney matter? Should only attorneys who have had a course in insurance law be expected to understand their policies?

THORACIC CARDIOVASCULAR ASSOCIATES, LTD. V. ST. PAUL FIRE AND MARINE INSURANCE COMPANY

891 P.2d 916 (Ariz. 1994)

OPINION

TOCI, JUDGE.

Thoracic Cardiovascular Associates, Ltd. and Thomas J. Trahan (collectively, "Thoracic") sued St. Paul Fire and Marine Insurance Company ("St. Paul") seeking a declaratory judgment requiring St. Paul to provide coverage on a claims made professional liability insurance policy. St. Paul appeals from the trial court's grant of summary judgment in favor of Thoracic.

We must decide whether coverage exists under a claims made professional liability insurance policy when a claim is not reported to the insurer within the policy period. In order to resolve this question, we must also decide whether the doctrine of impossibility excuses untimely reporting of a claim under a claims made policy.

We conclude that the trial court erred in granting summary judgment against St. Paul. We hold that because notice of a claim within the policy period is a material part of the consideration for a claims made policy, to invoke coverage a claim must be made and reported to the insurer during the policy period. We further hold that the doctrine of impossibility does not excuse late reporting of claims under claims made policies. Accordingly, we reverse the trial court's grant of summary judgment against St. Paul and remand with directions to enter judgment for St. Paul.

I. FACTS AND PROCEDURAL HISTORY

St. Paul issued a claims made professional liability insurance policy to Thoracic for the period from November 1, 1987 through May 1, 1988. The policy stated two requirements for coverage: (1) "the professional service must have been performed (or should have been performed) after [the] retroactive date that applies,"[2] and (2) "[t]he claim must also first be made while this agreement is in effect." Under the policy, a "claim is made on the date [the insured] first report[s] an incident or injury to" St. Paul or its agent.

The policy also contained a provision allowing Thoracic to purchase an optional extension of coverage, referred to as a "reporting endorsement." This endorsement would have allowed Thoracic to report claims to St. Paul after the policy term and before the end of the term of the reporting endorsement. The policy provided that St. Paul would sell the reporting endorsement to Thoracic for a premium based on the rules and rating plans being used on the day coverage would begin. According to the policy, the reporting endorsement must be requested in writing within thirty days after the end of the policy term.

On February 16, 1988, before the end of the policy term, Thoracic canceled the liability policy issued by St. Paul. On March 4, 1988, sixteen days after the policy was canceled, St. Paul's underwriting department sent a certified letter to Thoracic advising Thoracic that its policy covered only claims made within the policy term. The letter warned that unless Thoracic purchased the optional reporting endorsement coverage within the time stated in the policy or obtained coverage under a replacement policy, it would not be covered for claims arising out of acts performed prior to the termination date that were not reported until after the termination date. Specifically, the letter stated:

> This is a "claims made" form of coverage. This means you do *not* have coverage for claims arising out of acts performed prior to the termination for which a claim may be made after the termination date, unless you purchase reporting endorsement coverage.
>
> Reporting endorsement coverage extends the time in which a claim may be made for acts which occurred before the termination date. . . .
>
> You may not need this endorsement extension if you have obtained a replacement policy providing coverage for prior acts.

[2] According to the policy in this case, the retroactive date is September 1, 1979.

> IF YOU DO NOT PURCHASE THE OPTIONAL REPORTING ENDORSEMENT WITHIN THE TIME PERIOD STATED IN YOUR POLICY, OR IF YOU DO NOT OBTAIN COVERAGE UNDER A REPLACEMENT POLICY, THEN *YOU DO NOT HAVE COVERAGE* FOR CLAIMS ARISING OUT OF ACTS PERFORMED *PRIOR* TO THE TERMINATION DATE FOR WHICH A CLAIM MAY BE MADE *AFTER* THE TERMINATION DATE.

This letter clearly indicated that St. Paul would not provide coverage for claims reported after termination of the policy unless the reporting endorsement was purchased. Despite this warning, Thoracic neither purchased the endorsement nor obtained a replacement policy.

To further ensure that Thoracic understood the effect of its decision to cancel the policy and decline the reporting endorsement coverage, on March 21, 1988, Jacque Cumbie, an authorized insurance broker for St. Paul, sent another letter to Thoracic. The letter again addressed the effect of the cancellation:

> You had advised our office that you did not want to buy the Extended Reporting Period Endorsement from St. Paul. The policy was on a "claims made" form of coverage. This means that you will note [sic] have coverage from claims arising out of acts performed prior to the termination date for which a claim may be made after termination date, unless you purchase Reporting Period Endorsement coverage.
>
> Please sign the paper attached stating you understand "Claims Made" form of coverage and did not wish to purchase endorsement, and return to our office.

As requested, Thoracic signed and returned the form. By signing the form, Thoracic acknowledged that it understood "the 'Claims Made' form of coverage and did not wish to purchase endorsement."

On October 15, 1987, Alfonso and Linda Grimaldi filed a medical malpractice suit against Thoracic. The Grimaldi complaint alleged that Thoracic negligently provided professional health care services in 1985. When the Grimaldi lawsuit was filed, Thoracic was covered by the claims made professional liability insurance policy issued by St. Paul. Thoracic was not served with the summons and complaint in the Grimaldi suit, however, until July 12, 1988, approximately five months *after* it canceled its policy with St. Paul. Prior to that date, Thoracic was not aware of the existence of the Grimaldi claim.

On August 30, 1988, more than six months after terminating coverage, Thoracic notified St. Paul of the Grimaldi lawsuit. Thoracic requested that St. Paul confirm coverage and provide legal representation to defend against the Grimaldi claim. St. Paul denied coverage and refused to provide legal representation because the claim had not been reported to St. Paul during the policy period as required under the claims made policy.

On August 31, 1990, Thoracic filed the present lawsuit seeking, among other things, declaratory judgment that St. Paul's coverage extended to the Grimaldi claim. St. Paul moved for summary judgment, arguing that under Division Two's decision in *Sletten v. St. Paul Fire & Marine Ins. Co.,* 780 P.2d 428 (Ariz. App. 1989), it did not breach the insurance contract. In response, Thoracic argued that *Sletten* did not control because Thoracic had no knowledge of the Grimaldi claim within the policy period. Consequently, according to Thoracic, it was unable to inform St. Paul of the claim within the policy period. The trial court agreed, granting summary judgment in favor of Thoracic. In rendering its decision, the trial court stated:

> The Court finds that when insureds under a "claims made" policy, ha[ve] a lawsuit filed against them, and it is undisputed that the insureds have no way of knowing that the suit has been filed and but for the failure of the Plaintiff in that lawsuit to serve the complaint within the policy period, the claim would have been made to the insurer, there is coverage under a "claims made" policy even though notice is given after the policy ends.

St. Paul appeals.

II. DISCUSSION

A. Background

We initially consider the difference between an "occurrence" policy and a "claims-made" policy. An "occurrence" policy of professional liability insurance covers an act or omission that occurs within the policy period, regardless of the date of discovery or the date the claim is made or asserted. This type of policy requires that notice be given to the insurer "within a specified time after the insured event." *Stine v. Continental Casualty Co.,* 349 N.W.2d 127, 134 (Mich. 1984). Because injuries from professional malpractice claims may not manifest themselves for years after the occurrence policy has expired, however, an exposure time, or a "tail," is created. A tail is the time lapse between the date of the negligent act or omission and the time when a claim is made. *Gulf,* 433 So.2d at 515.

Thus, occurrence policies with a "tail" that extends beyond the policy period are historically associated with certain difficulties. One problem with occurrence policies is that the insurer cannot calculate the premium for the risk with any certainty. The insurer must compute premiums for occurrence professional liability policies at current rates while claims must be resolved at market rates, sometimes long after the premiums have been paid. Gerald Kroll, Comment, *The "Claims Made" Dilemma in Professional Liability Insurance,* 22 UCLA L.Rev. 925, 928 (1975). Another difficulty with occurrence policies is that when professional negligence continues over a period of time, and an insured changes from one occurrence carrier to another, uncertainty exists about which insurer will provide coverage. *Id.* at 930.

Consequently, to reduce exposure to an unpredictable and lengthy "tail" of lawsuits filed years after the occurrence they agreed to protect against, underwriters shifted to the "claims made" policy. *Pacific Employers Ins. Co. v. Superior Court,* 270 Cal.Rptr. 779, 784 (Cal. App. 1990). An insurer who knows that claims will not arise under the policy after its expiration can underwrite a risk and calculate premiums with greater certainty. *Id.* 270 Cal.Rptr. at 785. The insurer can establish its reserves "without having to consider the possibilities of inflation beyond the policy period, upward-spiralling jury awards, or later changes in the definition and application of negligence." *Id.*

The "claims made" policy differs from an "occurrence" policy in several important aspects. Because it triggers coverage, transmittal of the notice of the claim to the insurer is the most important aspect of the claims made policy. A claims made policy extends coverage if " 'the negligent or omitted act is discovered and brought to the attention of the insurer within the policy term.' " *Id.* (quoting 7A John Alan Appleman, *Insurance law and Practice* § 4504.01, at 312 (Berdal ed. 1979)). "The timing of the making of the claim in such policies stands in equal importance with the error or omission as the insured event." *Stine,* 349 N.W.2d at 134. Notice to the insurer of a claim made against the insured is generally required to be given during the policy period or within a specified amount of time after the policy period. "The essence, then, of a claims-made policy is *notice to the carrier within the policy period.*" *Gulf,* 433 So.2d at 514 (emphasis added).

B. Analysis

Against this backdrop, we turn to the insurance policy in this case. It is clearly a claims made policy. The coverage summary that is attached to the policy provides: "This Coverage Summary shows the limits and extent of coverage under your Physicians' Professional Liability Protection—Claims Made." Further, the reporting language in the policy provides:

> **When you're covered**
>
> *To be covered* the professional service must have been performed (or should have been performed) after your retroactive date that applies. *The claim must also first be made while this agreement is in effect.*
>
> **When is a claim made?**
>
> *A claim is made on the date you first report an incident or injury to us or our agent.* You must include the following information:

- Date, time and place of the incident.
- What happened and what professional service you performed.
- Type of claim you anticipate.
- Name and address of injured party.
- Name and address of any witness.

(Emphasis added). We find that this plain and unambiguous language requires that the insured report a claim to the insurer while the policy is in effect. *See Sletten*, 161 Ariz. at 596–97, 780 P.2d at 429–30 (claims made professional liability policy unambiguously required claims to be reported to insurer during policy period); *Slater v. Lawyers' Mut. Ins. Co.,* 227 Cal.App.3d 1415, 278 Cal.Rptr. 479, 482 (1991) (same). Such a report to the insurer within the policy period is an express condition precedent to coverage. *See Gulf,* 433 So.2d at 515 (coverage depends on claim being made and reported to the insurer during policy period); *Zuckerman v. National Union Fire Ins. Co.,* 100 N.J. 304, 495 A.2d 395, 406 (1985) ("event that invokes coverage under a 'claims made' policy is transmittal of notice of the claim to the insurance carrier").

Here, the negligence upon which the Grimaldis' medical malpractice lawsuit is based occurred in 1985, during the term of Thoracic's policy with St. Paul. And, when the Grimaldis filed their lawsuit in superior court on October 15, 1987, the policy was still in effect. Thoracic, however, did not report the claim to St. Paul until August 30, 1988, approximately six months after cancellation of the policy. Thus, the report was too late to trigger coverage.

Thoracic cites several cases that establish a general rule that when a delay in notice is found to be based upon a reasonable excuse, such excuse restores the timeliness of the notice. While properly acknowledging that this general rule is a product of cases involving occurrence policies, Thoracic contends that "there is no logical reason" why this general rule should not be extended to claims made policies. Based on the distinction between the two types of policies and Division Two's decision in *Sletten,* we disagree.

In *Sletten,* Division Two of this court held that even if an insurer is not prejudiced by late reporting, it need not provide coverage under a medical malpractice claims made insurance policy where the insured reports the claim to the insurer after the policy term has ended. 780 P.2d at 430. There, the insured failed to notify the insurer of a potential claim within the policy period. As in this case, the insured in *Sletten* had been offered extended reporting coverage, which it declined. The insured argued "that so long as [the insurer] was not prejudiced by the late reporting, coverage should exist," even under a claims made policy. *Id.* The court rejected this argument, noting that the late notice/prejudice rule "was developed with respect to 'occurrence' policies which provide coverage for negligent conduct occurring during the policy period regardless of when the claim is made." *Id.* Division Two then quoted extensively from the Florida Supreme Court's decision in *Gulf:*

> Claims-made policies, likewise, require that notification to the insurer be within a reasonable time. Critically, however, claims-made policies require that notice be given *during the policy period* itself. When an insured becomes aware of any event that could result in liability, then it must give notice to the insurer, and that notice must be given "within a reasonable time" or "as soon as practicable"—at all times, however, during the policy period.
>
> . . . Coverage depends on the claim being made and reported to the insurer during the policy period. Claims-made or discovery policies are essentially *reporting* policies. . . . If a court were to allow an extension of reporting time after the end of the policy period, such is tantamount to an *extension of coverage* to the insured gratis, something for which the insurer has not bargained. This extension of coverage, by the court, so very different from a mere condition of the policy, in effect rewrites the contract between the two parties. This we cannot and will not do.

Id.

Thus, the *Sletten* court found the *Gulf* rationale compelling and refused to extend the late notice/prejudice rule to claims made policies. *Id.* It agreed with the Florida court that the effect of allowing late notice "would be to convert claims made policies into occurrence policies" because, in the absence of actual prejudice from late reporting, all negligence during the policy period would be covered. *Id.* Further, in *Sletten,* Division Two said that it could "discern no public policy that mandates that only occurrence coverage be sold in Arizona," especially where an insured was offered, but declined, extended reporting coverage by the insurer that would have protected the insured. 780 P.2d at 430–31. We find *Sletten* dispositive.

Nevertheless, Thoracic argues that *Sletten* and *Gulf* are distinguishable from the present case. In both *Sletten* and *Gulf,* the insured became aware of a liability-triggering event during the policy period, but failed to report such claim to the insurer. *Sletten,* 780 P.2d at 429; *Gulf,* 433 So.2d at 513. Thoracic argues, therefore, that these cases have no application to the situation presented in this case because Thoracic had no knowledge of the Grimaldi claim during the policy period. Thoracic contends that since "this is a case in which an insured, through no fault of his own, had no knowledge of a lawsuit that had been filed against him . . . coverage in this case does not rest merely on the absence of prejudice to St. Paul, but on the fact that the required notification was impossible under the circumstances." We reject this argument.

Because the essence of a claims made policy is notice to the insurer within the policy period, *Gulf,* 433 So.2d at 514, the reasoning of *Sletten* and *Gulf* applies equally where an insured has no knowledge of the claim and, therefore, cannot report the claim to the insurer. To hold that the reporting requirement should be excused any time that the claim was not discovered during the policy period is to essentially convert claims made policies into occurrence policies in those cases. This we will not do. *See Sletten,* 161 Ariz. at 597, 780 P.2d at 430.

Rather, we agree with the rationale of the New Jersey Supreme Court in *Zuckerman,* 495 A.2d at 406, "that an extension of the notice period in a 'claims made' policy constitutes an unbargained-for expansion of coverage, *gratis,* resulting in the insurance company's exposure to a risk substantially broader than that expressly insured against in the policy." Such a change in the coverage provided by claims made policies would significantly affect both the basis upon which premiums have been calculated and the cost of claims made insurance. *Id.* "So material a modification in the terms of this form of insurance widely used to provide professional liability coverage both in this State and throughout the country would be inequitable and unjustified." *Id.*

Our decision is buttressed by the California Court of Appeals decision in *Slater*. There, a lawsuit was filed against an insured during the period his claims made insurance policy was in effect. The insured, however, did not become aware of the claim until after his policy had expired; thus, he did not notify his insurer until after the policy period had expired. The insurer denied coverage, due to late reporting. 278 Cal.Rptr. at 480.

As in this case, in *Slater,* the insured had been "offered the opportunity to protect himself against unknown claims by purchasing an extended reporting period endorsement, which he declined." *Id.* at 484. The *Slater* court concluded that the provisions of the policy requiring that a claim be made and reported to the insurer during the policy period were plain and unambiguous. *Slater,* 278 Cal.Rptr. at 482. Further, the court concluded that the late notice/prejudice rule was not applicable. *Id.* at 482–83. The court held that because the insured failed to report the claim within the policy period, the insurer was not required to provide coverage under the policy. *Id.* at 484.

Notwithstanding, Thoracic argues that the doctrine of impossibility or impracticability should excuse its failure to comply with the notice requirement as a condition precedent to coverage. Thoracic contends that had the insured in *Slater* raised the defense of impossibility, the outcome of the case may have been different. Thoracic believes that the defense of impossibility should be available where it is impossible for the insured to give the required notice because he had no knowledge of the claim. We disagree.

The Colorado Court of Appeals addressed a similar issue in *St. Paul Fire & Marine Ins. Co. v. Estate of Hunt,* 811 P.2d 432 (Colo. Ct. App. 1991). There, a medical malpractice claim was filed during the period when the claims made policy was in effect, but was not reported to the insurer until after the policy had expired. After a jury verdict against the insurer, the trial court entered judgment finding that the doctor's failure to provide timely notice was excused by his mental impairment. The Colorado Court of Appeals reversed, holding that the policy did not provide coverage for an untimely reported claim. The court stated:

> Impracticability excuses the non-occurrence of a condition *if the occurrence of the condition is not a material part of the agreed exchange* and forfeiture would otherwise result.
>
> . . . .
>
> It is because of [the] significant role of notice in "claims-made" policies that numerous courts have held that excusing a delay in notice beyond the policy period should not be done, because to do so would alter a basic term of the insurance contract which expresses the parties' agreement.
>
> Here, we conclude that the condition requiring the insured to provide notice of a claim during the policy period was a material part of the agreed exchange. Therefore, impracticability cannot serve as an excuse for the non-occurrence of such a material condition.

Id. at 434–35 (citations omitted). We find this reasoning persuasive.

Thoracic argues that the *Hunt* decision is flawed because that court incorrectly and "[w]ithout any reasoned or persuasive analysis," determined that the notice requirement of a claims made policy was "material" to the coverage. As we discuss above, however, the condition requiring the insured to provide notice of a claim during the policy period is a material part of the agreed exchange. No coverage exists unless notice is given during the policy term. As recognized by the court in *Hunt,* there can be no excuse for the nonperformance of a material provision of the contract between St. Paul and Thoracic. *See Hunt,* 811 P.2d at 435.

Furthermore, "[i]mpossibility does not excuse nonperformance where the promisor has indicated an intent to assume the risk thereof." *Wiggins v. Warrior River Coal Co.,* 696 F.2d 1356, 1359 (11th Cir.1983); 17A Am.Jur.2d *Contracts* § 684 (1991); *see generally,* 6 Arthur Linton Corbin, *Corbin on Contracts* § 1328 (1962). Where, as here, an insured elects to purchase a claims made policy and does not elect to purchase occurrence coverage, the insured assumes the risk that claims will not be covered unless they are *both* discovered *and* reported during the policy period.

St. Paul was entitled to limit its coverage by clear and unambiguous language. "[I]n the absence of conflict with statute or public policy, insurers may by unambiguous and clearly noticeable provisions limit their liability and impose such reasonable conditions as they wish upon the obligations they assume by their contract." *Livingston Parish Sch. Bd. v. Fireman's Fund Am. Ins. Co.,* 282 So.2d 478, 481 (La.1973); *see also Slater,* 278 Cal.Rptr. at 483–84 (insurance company has right to limit coverage of policy issued by it and when it does so, the plain language of the limitation must be respected). "[T]he insured received what [it] paid for by the present policy, with premiums presumably reduced to reflect the limited coverage." *Livingston Parish,* 282 So.2d at 483; *see also Gulf,* 433 So.2d at 516 (same). Here, St. Paul has limited its risk by clearly stating that no coverage exists unless the insured complies with the requirement of discovering and reporting the claim within the policy period.

. . . .

III. CONCLUSION

For the foregoing reasons, we reverse the judgment of the trial court and remand for entry of judgment in favor of St. Paul, determining that there is no coverage for the Grimaldi claim.

NOTES AND QUESTIONS

1. *The "Notice Prejudice" Rule.* Earlier in this book, we explored the policyholder's obligation to give notice of a loss, including the rule that has developed in many states that forecloses the insurer from denying coverage in the absence of some showing of prejudice on account of the late notice. Why does this general proposition not control the issue presented in both *Sparks* and *Thoracic*? Consider *Lexington Insurance Co. v. St. Louis University,* 88 F.3d 632 (8th Cir. 1996). In that case, "Both [occurrence and claims-made] policies require the insured to promptly notify the insurer of possible covered losses. With a claims made policy, however, that notice is not simply part of the insured's duty to cooperate. It defines the limits of the insurer's obligation—if there is no timely notice, there is no coverage . . . . [E]xcusing tardy notice 'would alter a basic term of the insurance contract.' " 88 F.3d at 634. *See also Home Insurance Co. of Illinois v. Adco Oil Co.*, 154 F.3d 739 (7th Cir. 1998) (under Illinois law, claims-made policy provided no coverage for claim first reported to insurer after expiration of policy). Are courts acting inconsistently with respect to late notice under occurrence-based and claims-made policies? Are the issues distinguishable under the two types of insurance?

2. *Restatement of the Law of Liability Insurance.* The Restatement embraces the holdings of both *Sparks* and *Thoracic*:

§ 35 Notice and Reporting Conditions

. . . .

(2) With respect to claims first reported after the conclusion of the claim-reporting period in a claims-made-and-reported policy, the failure of the insured to satisfy the claim-reporting condition in the policy excuses an insurer from performance under the policy without regard to prejudice, except when:

(a) The policy does not contain an extended reporting period;

(b) The claim at issue is made too close to the end of the policy period to allow the insured a reasonable time to satisfy the condition; and

(c) The insured reports the claim to the insurer within a reasonable time.

3. *Avoiding the Whipsaw.* If a policyholder ceases doing business, as reflected in *Thoracic*, under claims-made insurance the policyholder typically would still need to purchase insurance to protect itself against future claims that may be asserted after the business operations cease (i.e., purchase "Extended Reporting" or "Tail" coverage). On the other hand, under occurrence-based insurance, the policyholder would not need to purchase post-closure insurance because the triggering event is when the injury occurs, which typically would be prior to the cessation of the policyholder's business when the policyholder still has insurance.

The same problem arises if a policyholder switches from occurrence-based to claims-made insurance or between claims-made insurers in subsequent policy periods because a gap in coverage could be created for claims that are asserted against the policyholder for the first time during the policy period of a subsequent insurer, but are the result of the policyholder's conduct during the occurrence-based policy period or during a prior claims-made policy period. Although less common, the same problem can arise if the policyholder switches from claims-made insurance to occurrence-based insurance because an injury may predate the purchase of the occurrence-based insurance but not be asserted against the policyholder until the occurrence-based insurance commences, in which case both the claims-made insurer and the occurrence-based insurer likely would deny the claim. What does the policyholder need to avoid being whipsawed in such a situation?

4. *Professional Liability Insurance Versus CGL Insurance.* The policies in *Sparks* and *Thoracic* involve a kind of "errors and omissions" coverage, or what is more commonly referred to as professional liability or malpractice insurance. Most lay people have a casual understanding of medical and legal malpractice insurance. It is less well known that such policies are also common in the professions of dentistry, accounting, engineering, pharmacy, and architecture. Even insurance agents and brokers can obtain errors and omissions coverage. As discussed above with respect to what constitutes "professional services," these policies are generally limited to providing coverage for liability arising from those acts involving the performance or rendition of services customarily performed by the particular profession. For

example, if a patient slips and falls in the waiting room of a doctor's office due to the negligence of the doctor's employees, the doctor's malpractice policy would not cover the claim. It could be covered, however, under a policy providing liability insurance for premises and operations, such as a CGL policy. *See Foremost Insurance Co. v. Hartford Insurance Group*, 385 So. 2d 110 (Fla. Ct. App. 1980).

5. *Typical Exclusions in Professional Liability Policies*. Malpractice policies typically exclude coverage for dishonest, fraudulent, criminal, or malicious acts or omissions. Not surprisingly, such exclusions have been the subject of much litigation. *Compare Conner v. Transamerica Insurance Co.*, 496 P.2d 770 (Okla. 1972) (holding that there was a duty under the legal malpractice policy to defend the attorney insureds who allegedly engaged in fraudulent, deceitful, and dishonest conduct such as false affidavits, forgery, and deliberate misrepresentations), *with St. Paul Insurance Co. v. Bonded Realty, Inc.*, 578 S.W.2d 191 (Tex. Civ. App.), *affirmed*, 583 S.W.2d 619 (Tex. 1979) (holding that there was no coverage under real estate agent's errors and omissions policy where insured agent was found to have violated the Texas Deceptive Trade Practices Consumer Protection Act by making representations which were known by the insured to be false). In *Brooks, Tarlton, Gilbert, Douglas & Kressler v. U.S. Fire Insurance Co.*, 832 F.2d 1358 (5th Cir. 1987), the court held that the exclusion in question did not operate to preclude coverage where the client alleged that her attorneys violated their ethical obligations, reasoning that these claims amounted only to constructive fraud, which is not the same as a "fraudulent" act under the policy language. The court said that the latter requires dishonesty of purpose or intent to deceive, whereas the former involves a breach of some legal or equitable duty that the law declares to be fraudulent because of its tendency to deceive others, to violate confidence, or to injure public interest.

D. RELATED CLAIMS OR ACTIONS

FEDERAL INS. CO. V. RAYTHEON CO.

426 F.3d 491 (1st Cir. 2005)

Opinion

This is an insurance coverage dispute. On May 19, 2003, a class action was filed against Raytheon Company ("Raytheon") under the Employee Retirement Income Security Act of 1974 ("the ERISA action"). At that time, Raytheon was insured under a liability insurance policy issued by Federal Insurance Company ("Federal") and an excess policy issued by Axis Surplus Insurance Company ("Axis"). Raytheon requested coverage from the insurers. In response, the insurers filed suits for declaratory judgment of non-coverage, invoking the district court's diversity jurisdiction. The insurers contended that the ERISA action was excluded from coverage under the pending and prior litigation exclusions of the policies because there were overlapping allegations between the ERISA action and an earlier securities lawsuit brought against Raytheon in 1999, before the effective dates of the policies.

The district court held that coverage was excluded under the prior and pending litigation exclusion clauses of both policies. We hold that coverage for both insurers is excluded under the Federal policy. We accordingly affirm the judgment of the district court.

Factual Background

Raytheon provides products and services in the areas of defense and commercial electronics. It is a public company listed on the New York Stock Exchange. On October 12, 1999, the Wall Street Journal published an article reporting that Raytheon, unbeknownst to investors, experienced cost overruns and was behind schedule on many defense-related contracts. Later that day, Raytheon reported one-off charges totaling $638 million and reduced earnings expectations. The charges and reduced earnings forecast caused a sharp decline in Raytheon's stock price.

On October 19, 1999, a class action invoking section 10 the Securities Exchange Act of 1934, 15 U.S.C. § 78j (2000), and Rule 10b–5, 17 C.F.R. § 240.10b–5 (2005), was filed in the District of Massachusetts against Raytheon and several of its senior officers ("the Securities action"). *In re Raytheon Co. Sec. Litig.,* No. 99–CV–12142 (D. Mass. June 12, 2000) (amended complaint). The lead plaintiff was the New York State Common Retirement Fund, which sought to represent a class of persons who purchased Raytheon stock from October 7, 1998, to October 12, 1999 (the date of the Wall Street Journal article). The complaint in the Securities action alleged that during the class period, Raytheon issued materially false and misleading statements regarding its financial performance. Briefly, the Securities complaint alleged that (1) Raytheon's Engineering & Constructors division ("RE & C") failed to disclose losses on major contracts; (2) RE & C misleadingly reported revenues on existing and anticipated contracts; (3) Raytheon failed to disclose that projects relating to the P–3 Orion aircraft and other defense equipment were over budget and behind schedule; and (4) Raytheon failed to disclose that the Joint Primary Aircraft Training System was over budget and behind schedule. The Securities action apparently settled in December 2004.

In May 2003, a second class action was filed against Raytheon and several of its officers and employees in the District of Massachusetts, this time based on the Employee Retirement Income Security Act of 1974, 29 U.S.C. § 1001 et seq. *In re Raytheon ERISA Litig.,* No. 03–CV–10940 (D.Mass. Apr. 20, 2004) (amended complaint). The lead plaintiffs were Benjamin Wall and Joseph Duggan III, former Raytheon employees who sought to represent a class of persons who were participants in or beneficiaries of Raytheon's Savings and Investment Plan (the "Plan") at any time between October 7, 1998, and date of the complaint. In contrast to the Securities complaint, the ERISA complaint alleged that the defendants were ERISA fiduciaries of the Plan; that the defendants regularly communicated to Plan participants during the all relevant times; and that the defendants had financial interests tied to the Raytheon stock price at all relevant times. It then charged the defendants with four counts of breach of fiduciary duty, specifically (1) imprudent investment; (2) failure to monitor other fiduciaries; (3) misrepresentation and failure to disclose information to beneficiaries; and (4) failure to avoid conflicts of interest. The ERISA litigation is ongoing.

Apart from differences in parties and legal theories, the factual allegations of the ERISA complaint were in many respects nearly identical to the Securities complaint, but in other respects were different from the Securities complaint. With respect to alleged misdeeds by Raytheon occurring prior to October 12, 1999 (the cut-off date for the Securities class action), the factual allegations of the ERISA complaint mirrored those of the Securities complaint; including (1) RE & C failed to disclose and improperly accounted for losses on major contracts; (2) RE & C misleadingly recognized revenues on existing and anticipated contracts; and (3) Raytheon failed to disclose material cost overruns and delays affecting projects related to the P–3 Orion aircraft. With the exception of allegations concerning several Raytheon Systems Corporation projects and the Joint Primary Aircraft Training System, it is fair to say that all the allegations of Raytheon misdeeds made in the Securities complaint were also included in the ERISA complaint.

However, in two major respects the ERISA complaint included allegations not found in the Securities complaint. First, there were substantial allegations of misdeeds pertaining to the post-October 12, 1999, period in the ERISA complaint that were not alleged in the Securities complaint. For example, the ERISA complaint alleged the existence of "recurring indications of accounting and control irregularities. . . ." J.A. at 194. It alleged that "Defendants' misleading, inaccurate, and incomplete statements regarding the Company's fiscal health extended from 1998 through 1999, and beyond." *Id.* at 195. Other post-October 12, 1999, events alleged included (1) the SEC commenced an investigation into Raytheon's accounting practices in 2003; (2) Raytheon made material misrepresentations in selling the RE & C division to Washington Group International ("WGI"), leading to litigation by WGI and its shareholders; and (3) the SEC commenced proceedings against Raytheon and its former CFO relating to violations of SEC regulations.

Second, to support the different legal theories asserted under ERISA in contrast to the Securities Exchange Act, relevant facts not contained in the Securities complaint were alleged in the ERISA complaint. The complaint alleged that the defendants were ERISA plan fiduciaries. To support the imprudent investment charge, the ERISA complaint alleged that at "[a]ll relevant times, Defendants knew or should have known that Raytheon was engaged in the questionable business practices detailed above which made Raytheon stock an imprudent Plan investment." *Id.* at 215. To support the failure to disclose and misrepresentation charge, the complaint alleged that "Raytheon regularly communicated with employees, including Plan participants, about Raytheon's performance" and failed to disclose and misrepresented material information to Plan beneficiaries. *Id.* at 217. To support the conflict of interest charge, the complaint alleged that the defendants' "compensation was [ ] closely tied to the price of Raytheon Stock" and that the defendants had failed to avoid improper conflicts of interest. *Id.* at 218.

After the ERISA action was filed, Raytheon sought coverage from the insurers. The insurers denied coverage and filed suit in the District of Massachusetts, seeking a declaratory judgment of non-coverage. The insurers contended that coverage was excluded under the prior and pending litigation clause in the Federal Insurance policy, which states:

> The Company [Federal] shall not be liable for Loss on account of any Claim made against any Insured . . . based upon, arising from, or in consequence of any demand, suit or other proceeding pending, or order, decree or judgment entered against any Insured, on or prior to [September 15, 2000], or the same or any substantially similar fact, circumstance or situation underlying or alleged therein.

J.A. at 32–33.

As an excess policy, the Axis policy has a clause stating, "In no event shall this Policy grant broader coverage than would be provided by the most restrictive policy constituting part of the applicable Underlying Insurance." J.A. at 54. Thus, if coverage is excluded under the Federal policy, it is also excluded under the Axis policy. The Axis policy also has its own prior and pending litigation exclusion, which is worded somewhat differently, stating:

> the Insurer [Axis] shall not be liable for any amount in any Claim . . . based upon, arising from, or attributable to:
>
> > (a) any demand, suit or other proceeding pending, or order, decree or judgment entered, against any Insured on or prior to September 15, 2000 or any wrongful act, fact, circumstance or situation underlying or alleged therein; or
> >
> > (b) any other wrongful act, fact, circumstance or situation whenever occurring, which together with a wrongful act, fact, circumstance or situation described in (a) above are causally or logically interrelated by a common nexus.

J.A. at 62.

The insurers moved for judgment on the pleadings. In an oral decision, the district court construed the language "based upon . . . the same or any substantially similar fact, circumstance or situation underlying or alleged" to mean that "if the prior complaint contains any overlapping claims made against any Insured, the exclusion is triggered." Applying this test, the district court found that "Raytheon has not, and cannot, credibly argue that the core allegations of the prior litigation complaint and the ERISA complaint do not overlap." Instead, the district court found that the complaints in the Securities action and the ERISA action revealed "numerous allegations of substantially similar facts, circumstances or situations." Thus, the district court concluded that coverage was excluded, i.e. there was neither a duty to defend nor liability for any loss. Raytheon appeals from the final judgment of the district court.

Analysis

As a preliminary matter, Raytheon submits that the case should be stayed pending the outcome of the ERISA litigation, and in the interim the insurers must defend Raytheon. According to Raytheon, whether a subsequent lawsuit is "based upon . . . any substantially similar fact, circumstance or situation underlying or alleged" in a prior lawsuit cannot be determined until both lawsuits are over. We disagree.

Under Massachusetts law, as a general matter, "the question of the initial duty of a liability insurer to defend third-party actions against the insured is decided by matching the third-party complaint with the policy provisions." *Cont'l Cas. Co. v. Gilbane Bldg. Co.*, 391 Mass. 143, 461 N.E.2d 209, 212 (1984). In this inquiry, "if the allegations of the complaint are 'reasonably susceptible' of an interpretation that they state or adumbrate a claim covered by the policy terms, the insurer must undertake the defense." *Id.* (quoting *Sterilite Corp. v. Cont'l Cas. Co.*, 17 Mass.App.Ct. 316, 458 N.E.2d 338, 340 (1983)). The duty to defend is triggered even if the allegations of the complaint are baseless. *Mt. Airy Ins. Co. v. Greenbaum*, 127 F.3d 15, 18–19 (1st Cir.1997). "However, 'when the allegations in the underlying complaint lie expressly outside the policy coverage and its purpose, the insurer is relieved of the duty to investigate or defend the claimant.' " *Herbert A. Sullivan, Inc. v. Utica Mut. Ins. Co.*, 439 Mass. 387, 788 N.E.2d 522, 531 (2003) (quoting *Timpson v. Transamerica Ins. Co.*, 41 Mass.App.Ct. 344, 669 N.E.2d 1092, 1095 (1996)).

Raytheon cites a line of cases holding that even if an insurer has an initial duty to defend based on the complaints alone, it may be absolved of the duty to defend and liability for loss by subsequent developments in the litigation. *See, e.g., Lumbermens Mut. Cas. Co. v. Belleville Indus., Inc.*, 407 Mass. 675, 555 N.E.2d 568, 575 (1990); *Sterilite Corp.*, 458 N.E.2d at 343–44. This line of cases provides no aid to Raytheon. The insurers are not contending that there have been subsequent developments in the litigation absolving them of an initial duty to defend. Rather, they are contending that they do not even have the initial duty to defend. Nor is Raytheon contending that subsequent developments have created a duty to defend. Massachusetts law clearly provides that resolution of the issue of coverage, at least initially, is to be based on the allegations of the third-party complaints, here the complaints in the Securities and ERISA actions.

Lastly, Raytheon relies on various district court cases, especially *Home Ins. Co. of Ill. v. Spectrum Info. Techs., Inc.,* 930 F.Supp. 825 (E.D.N.Y.1996), for the proposition that resolution of the duty to defend on the pleadings is premature. To the extent that these cases are contrary to Massachusetts law, we must follow the Supreme Judicial Court.

On the merits, we must construe the Federal insurance policy and apply it to the allegations of the complaints. In light of our conclusion that coverage is excluded under the Federal policy, we need not analyze the Axis exclusion. "The responsibility of construing the language of an insurance contract is a question of law for the trial judge, and then for the reviewing court." *Cody v. Conn. Gen. Life Ins. Co.,* 387 Mass. 142, 439 N.E.2d 234, 237 (1982). We thus must independently determine the construction of the policy. In this inquiry, "doubts about ambiguous insurance policy provisions are to be resolved against the insurance company." *J. D'Amico, Inc. v. City of Boston,* 345 Mass. 218, 186 N.E.2d 716, 721 (1962). But when the policy is "plain and free from ambiguity, we do not . . . construe them strictly against the insurer. Rather, we must construe the words of the policy in their usual and ordinary sense." *Barnstable County Mut. Fire Ins. Co. v. Lally,* 374 Mass. 602, 373 N.E.2d 966, 968 (1978).

The Federal policy provides an exclusion for:

> [A]ny Claim made against any Insured . . . based upon, arising from, or in consequence of any demand, suit or other proceeding pending . . . on or prior to [September 15, 2000], or the same or any substantially similar fact, circumstance or situation underlying or alleged therein.

J.A. at 32–33. The Federal policy is a "claims-made" policy, where liability for coverage is triggered by the filing of a claim during the policy period instead of the occurrence of an underlying event in the policy period. The policy defines a "claim" as including "a civil proceeding commenced by the service of a complaint or similar pleading . . . against any Insured for a Wrongful Act." J.A. at 37. Thus a claim for present purposes is equivalent to a complaint.

The language of the policy cannot reasonably be given the broadest possible construction, under which any overlapping fact between the two proceedings—for example, the identity of Raytheon as the defendant in the context of otherwise unrelated facts—would trigger the exclusion. We do not understand any party to contend otherwise. At the same time, complete identity between the lawsuits is plainly not required. Indeed, all parties agree that the two complaints need not be identical, and that differences in theories of recovery or the identity of the parties in the proceedings do not in and of themselves preclude exclusion. Beyond that, they disagree. The district court here construed "based upon . . . any substantially similar fact, circumstance or situation underlying or alleged" to exclude coverage when there are "any overlapping claims." The district court, however, did not make clear the degree of overlap required for the allegations in the complaint, instead finding only that Raytheon cannot "credibly argue that the core allegations of the prior litigation complaint and the ERISA complaint do not overlap" and that "a comparison of the complaints reveals numerous allegations of substantially similar facts, circumstances or situations."

Axis submits that "all that is required is for the ERISA litigation to contain 'any substantially similar fact, circumstance or situation' alleged in the Prior Litigation," though we understand this to mean any overlap in determinative facts. Br. of Axis at 20 (emphasis omitted). Federal appears to distance itself from this construction, stating that "whether a 'single overlapping fact or claim' would trigger the Exclusion is not a question the Court need answer," Br. of Federal at 18, but does not offer an alternative construction of the exclusion clause. For its part, Raytheon advocates that "the exclusion is triggered only when two *lawsuits* are 'the same' or 'substantially similar,' " or alternatively where "there is significant overlap between the lawsuits as a whole," Br. of Raytheon at 13, 14 (emphasis in original), apparently meaning that the two lawsuits must be virtually identical save for differences in the parties and theories of liability. *See id.* at 14–15 (purporting to cite cases articulating requirements of, *inter alia,* "allegations of 'virtually identical false statements;' " "the same underlying circumstance;" or " 'essentially the same set of facts' "). We think that the correct construction is somewhat different from the position of any of the parties.

Raytheon's construction, apparently relying on the "same or any substantially similar fact, circumstance or situation" language in the policy, is not warranted. While the exclusion clause uses the language "substantially similar," it refers to the subsequent "fact, circumstance or situation." The "substantially similar" language cannot by itself be read to refer to the "demand, suit, or other proceeding."

Raytheon argues alternatively that the second claim must be "based upon" the first. This is correct, and we must determine the meaning of the word "based" in this context. We do not agree with Raytheon's apparent construction of "based" to mean "virtually identical."

"Words in exclusionary clauses of insurance contracts should be construed 'in their usual and ordinary sense.' " *Bagley v. Monticello Ins. Co.,* 430 Mass. 454, 720 N.E.2d 813, 816 (1999) (quoting *Liquor Liab. Joint Underwriting Ass'n of Mass. v. Hermitage Ins. Co.,* 419 Mass. 316, 644 N.E.2d 964, 967 (1995)). In construing contracts courts often look to dictionaries for assistance in determining ordinary meaning. Reference to dictionaries in interpreting contracts of insurance is also appropriate. In particular, Massachusetts courts refer to dictionaries in interpreting insurance contracts.

Consulting the dictionary, the ordinary meaning of "based," used as a verb in this context, is "to use as a base or basis for . . . used with *on* or *upon,*" *Webster's Third New International Dictionary of the English Language* 180 (3d ed. 1961) ("Webster's Dictionary") (emphasis in original), or "to place on or upon a foundation or logical basis." *Oxford English Dictionary* 979 (2d ed.1989). Webster's Dictionary clarifies the usage in this context, explaining that "Base now usu[ally] applies to what underlies a belief, a system of thought, a judgment, a hope, and so on." *Webster's Dictionary* at 181. The dictionary definition of the word "based" here excludes situations in which the complaint in the second action does not draw substantial support from the allegations of the first complaint. Conversely, it does not require that the first action provide the sole support for the second. *Cf. MCI Telecomms. Corp. v. Am. Tel. & Tel. Co.*, 512 U.S. 218, 225, 114 S.Ct. 2223, 129 L.Ed.2d 182 (1994) ("modify" in its ordinary usage does not encompass fundamental change). We think that the policy thus requires the allegations in the second complaint find substantial support in the first complaint, i.e. that the allegations of the second complaint substantially overlap those of the first. Only with a substantial overlap can the first complaint be said to be a "foundation or logical basis" for the second. "Based" also suggests that the appropriate inquiry is whether the second complaint substantially overlaps the first with respect to relevant facts, without regard to whether the first complaint substantially overlaps the second.

Requiring a substantial but not complete overlap with the prior complaint also serves the policy behind such prior and pending litigation exclusion clauses. Most directly, prior and pending litigation exclusions "promote the giving of prompt notice and [ ] avoid stacking the limits of successive policies to cover essentially the same or very closely related claims." Kenneth S. Abraham, *Insurance Law and Regulation: Cases and Materials* 587 (4th ed. 2005). Prior and pending litigation exclusions thus combat the problem of adverse selection or "insuring the building already on fire"; that is, an insured who has previously been sued faces a greater risk of related litigation and has a corresponding incentive to seek insurance. John H. Mathias, Jr., et al., *Directors and Officers Liability: Prevention, Insurance and Indemnification* § 8.09 (2003) (internal quotations omitted); *see* George

L. Priest, *The Current Insurance Crisis and Modern Tort Law*, 96 Yale L.J. 1521, 1574 (1987). The insurance company's legitimate interest in combating the adverse selection problem is properly implicated when there is a real and substantial overlap with the complaint in the prior lawsuit, as opposed to an incidental or fortuitous relationship to the prior complaint.

Accordingly, we hold that the Federal exclusion, excluding any subsequent claim "based upon . . . the same or any substantially similar fact, circumstance or situation underlying or alleged" in a prior claim, applies when there is substantial overlap in the second complaint with the facts underlying or alleged in the first complaint.

Applying the policy as we have interpreted it to the allegations of the complaints, there is little doubt that there is substantial overlap in the allegations of the two complaints. Raytheon's counsel readily conceded at oral argument that "there is no question that the ERISA plaintiffs cut and pasted a lot of the factual allegations from the securities lawsuit."

As outlined previously, the ERISA complaint alleged important pre-October 12, 1999, misdeeds, including (1) Raytheon stock was overvalued due to cost overruns in defense related contracts; (2) RE & C improperly accounted for losses on major contracts; (3) RE & C prematurely recognized revenues on anticipated contracts; (4) RE & C improperly accelerated recognition of revenues on existing contracts; and (5) Raytheon failed to disclose material cost overruns and delays affecting projects related to the P–3 Orion aircraft. These allegations mirror the allegations of the Securities complaint. All four counts of the ERISA complaint recite these allegations by reference. As should be clear even from this brief summary, a substantial part of the operative facts alleged in the ERISA complaint appears in the Securities complaint. Thus these allegations substantially overlap with the prior allegations contained in the Securities complaint.

To be sure, not all of the facts alleged in the ERISA complaint are contained in the Securities complaint. In particular, most of the activities occurring after the Securities class cut-off date of October 12, 1999, do not appear in the Securities complaint. The ERISA plaintiffs allege, for example, that Raytheon shares continued to be an imprudent investment due to continuing accounting improprieties after October 12, 1999. They allege that "Defendants' misleading, inaccurate, and incomplete statements regarding the Company's fiscal health extended from 1998 through 1999, and beyond." J.A. at 195. Other post-October 12, 1999, conduct alleged includes the sale of the RE & C division to WGI and the consequent litigation with WGI and its shareholders, and SEC investigations into Raytheon and its executives. Raytheon correctly points out that, solely from a temporal perspective, the overlap constitutes one-sixth of the relevant period of the ERISA complaint. So too, some allegations pertaining exclusively to the elements of an ERISA lawsuit, such as communication with Plan beneficiaries by the fiduciary defendant, do not appear in the Securities complaint. Some of these non-overlapping facts are critical to the ERISA action—for example, the defendants' ERISA fiduciary status is a *sine qua non* of the ERISA action. But acknowledging that there are substantial areas of non-overlap does not defeat the fact here that there is substantial overlap between the two complaints.

Conclusion

We conclude that the Federal prior and pending litigation exclusion, excluding "any Claim made against any Insured . . . based upon, arising from, or in consequence of any demand, suit or other proceeding pending, or order, decree or judgment entered against any Insured . . ., or the same or any substantially similar fact, circumstance or situation underlying or alleged therein," is properly construed to exclude coverage if there is substantial overlap between allegations in the complaint of the claimed proceeding and allegations in the complaint of the prior proceeding. While we recognize that our interpretation will not cleanly resolve every case involving exclusionary policy language similar to that involved here, it easily resolves this case. There is clearly substantial overlap between the allegations in the ERISA complaint and the allegations in the Securities complaint. Coverage is therefore excluded. Accordingly, the judgment of the district court is affirmed.

It is so ordered.

NOTES AND QUESTIONS

1. *Impact of Relatedness.* Aside from the application of the "Prior and Pending Litigation" exclusion, why was it important whether the claims in the various actions in *Raytheon* were related?

2. *Substantially Similar?* If the various underlying actions in *Raytheon* had different plaintiffs, different legal theories of relief, and were related to different time periods, do you agree with the holding in *Raytheon* that the actions were "substantially similar?" Why or why not?

3. *Channeling Policy Language and the Whipsaw.* Most policies with "Prior and Pending Litigation" exclusions contain language that requires the earliest policy in which a related action was filed to cover all of the subsequent actions that are filed regardless of whether the subsequent lawsuits are filed during the policy period of the first action. What do you think the insurer on the risk in the first year in which a lawsuit is filed would say regarding the "relatedness" of another lawsuit that is filed after its policy period terminates?

E. INSURED VERSUS INSURED EXCLUSIONS

Another exclusion commonly included in claims-made policies, including D&O policies, is the "insured versus insured" exclusion. The rationale for the exclusion is similar to the "household" or "family" exclusion contained in auto policies. Insurers are attempting to exclude coverage for claims where insurers are concerned about the risk of collusion. The potential reach of such exclusions is, however, quite broad, and it can easily encompass claims where no real or plausible risk of collusion is present. Consequently, some courts look at the purpose of the exclusion, not just the words of the exclusion, when deciding whether it applies. Consider the next case.

INDIAN HARBOR INSURANCE COMPANY V. ZUCKER FOR LIQUIDATION TRUST OF CAPITOL BANCORP LTD.

860 F.3d 373 (6th Cir. 2017)

OPINION

SUTTON, CIRCUIT JUDGE.

Capitol Bancorp went bankrupt. After negotiations between Capitol's officers and the company's creditors during the bankruptcy process, Capitol created a Liquidation Trust to pursue the estate's legal claims. The Liquidation Trustee sued Capitol's officers for $18.8 million, alleging they breached their fiduciary duties to the company. Indian Harbor Insurance filed this lawsuit in response, seeking a declaratory judgment that the Trustee's lawsuit falls within the "insured-versus-insured" exclusion in Capitol's liability insurance policy. The district court agreed that the policy does not cover the Trustee's action, and so do we.

I.

A holding company incorporated in Michigan, Capitol Bancorp owned community banks in seventeen States. Joseph Reid founded Capitol and served as its chairman and chief executive officer. His daughter Cristin Reid served as president, her husband Brian English as general counsel.

The financial crisis was not good for Capitol. Many of its banks took large losses as customers stopped repaying their loans. The last time the company earned a profit was in 2007, and it accepted oversight by the Federal Reserve in 2009. In 2012, Capitol and its subsidiary, Financial Commerce Corporation, sought to shed some debts and to repay other creditors on reduced terms—in short to reorganize—under Chapter 11 of the Bankruptcy Code. With the bankruptcy filing, Capitol's assets became the property of the bankruptcy estate, and Capitol became the custodian of the estate, what Chapter 11 calls a "debtor in possession." 11 U.S.C. § 1101(1). Soon afterward, the United States Trustee appointed a creditors' committee to represent the interests of Capitol's unsecured creditors.

. . . .

The creditors and the debtor in possession . . . agreed to a liquidation plan that required Capitol to assign all of the company's causes of action to a Liquidating Trust, which could pursue those claims on behalf of creditors. The plan stipulated that the Reids had no liability for any conduct after they filed the bankruptcy petition, and limited any pre-petition liability to amounts recovered from Capitol's liability insurance policy. The liquidation plan also required the Reids to sue Indian Harbor, the company's Delaware-based insurer, if it denied coverage under the management liability policy.

Capitol took out a one-year management liability insurance policy from Indian Harbor in September 2011, a year or so before it filed the bankruptcy petition. The company twice extended the policy after the bankruptcy proceedings began. Under the insurance contract, Indian Harbor agreed to pay for any "Loss resulting from a Claim first made against the Insured Persons"—a group that included Capitol's directors, officers, and employees—"during the Policy Period . . . for a Wrongful Act." But the contract excluded from coverage "any claim made against an Insured Person . . . by, on behalf of, or in the name or right of, the Company or any Insured Person," except for derivative suits by independent shareholders and employment claims.

Many liability insurance contracts contain such insured-versus-insured exclusions. Not unlike a homeowners insurance policy that excludes coverage for a fire that the policyholder intentionally sets, these exclusions limit the management-liability insurance to claims by outsiders, prohibiting coverage for claims by people within the insured company. A company thus cannot hope to push the costs of mismanagement onto an insurance company just by suing (and perhaps collusively settling with) past officers who made bad business decisions.

In August 2014, the Liquidation Trustee, Clifford Zucker, sued the Reids for $18.8 million, alleging they breached their fiduciary duties to Capitol through a number of improper actions. . . .

Zucker notified Indian Harbor of the lawsuit against the Reids. Indian Harbor responded by filing this diversity action against Zucker and the Reids, seeking a declaratory judgment that it had no obligation to cover any damages from the lawsuit because the Trust's claims fell within the insured-versus-insured exclusion. The district court held that the exclusion applies. Zucker and the Reids appealed.

II.

In resolving this dispute, the terms of the contract are a good place to start. The insured-versus-insured exclusion applies to claims "by, on behalf of, or in the name or right of, the Company or any Insured Person" against an Insured Person. Consider a simple application of this exclusion. Had Capitol sued the Reids for mismanagement, that would be a claim "by" the

Company (an insured person) against its own officers (also insured persons). The exclusion would bar the claim, as both sides to this dispute agree.

Now consider today's fact pattern, one step removed from that example. The objects of the claim are the same (the officers) and so is the theory of liability (mismanagement). But the claimant is no longer the Company, which has assigned its rights to the Liquidation Trust. The outcome remains the same even so. As a voluntary assignee, the Trust stands in Capitol's shoes and possesses the same rights subject to the same defenses. Just as the exclusion covers a lawsuit "by" Capitol, it covers a lawsuit "by" the Trust "in the . . . right" of Capitol.

Not so, urge Zucker and the Reids. When Capitol and Indian Harbor formed the insurance contract, they argue, "the Company" referred to Capitol in its pre-bankruptcy form. But Capitol underwent a transformation when it filed for bankruptcy. All of its assets, including all causes of action, became property of the bankruptcy estate, 11 U.S.C. § 541(a)(1), and Capitol became a debtor in possession administering the estate for the benefit of the creditors. As Zucker and the Reids see it, a debtor in possession is legally distinct from "the [pre-bankruptcy] Company," making the insured-versus-insured exception inapplicable to Capitol or its assignee.

But this new-entity argument surely would not work *before* bankruptcy. Capitol could not have dodged the exclusion by transferring a mismanagement claim to a new company—call it Capitol II—for the purpose of filing a mismanagement claim against the Reids. No matter how legally distinct Capitol II might be, the claim would still be "by, on behalf of, or in the name or right of" Capitol.

The same conclusion applies to a claim filed *after* bankruptcy. Here too the voluntarily transferred claim would be filed "on behalf of" or "in . . . the right of" Capitol. The exclusion remains applicable by its terms.

. . . .

The relevant parties' actions are consistent with this reading of the contract. Capitol paid more than $3 million in total premiums to extend the policy—twice—after filing for bankruptcy.

The Bankruptcy Code does not alter this conclusion. It defines a Chapter 11 "debtor in possession" as the debtor, 11 U.S.C. § 1101(1), and defines "debtor" as "the person or municipality concerning which a case under this title has been commenced," *id.* § 101(13). "[T]he debtor in possession is the debtor, and the debtor is the person"—pre-bankruptcy Capitol—"that filed for bankruptcy." *Biltmore,* 572 F.3d at 671. The relevant bankruptcy provisions do not support Zucker and the Reids' contention that the debtor in possession and pre-bankruptcy company are necessarily distinct legal entities—at least for purposes of the insurance contract.

. . . .

Chapter 11 permits going concerns to continue operating during bankruptcy in order to maximize the property available to satisfy creditors and, where possible, to return the business to solvency in a reorganized form. The animating point is to keep the pre-bankruptcy company up and running. Rather than requiring an independent, court-appointed trustee to administer the bankruptcy estate for the benefit of the creditors, Chapter 11 gives the debtor in possession all the statutory powers and duties of a trustee. 11 U.S.C. § 1107(a). But there is one revealing exception: The debtor in possession need not investigate the debtor's financial condition or any improper conduct because "the debtor cannot be expected to inform on itself." *Norton* § 93:2; 11 U.S.C. § 1107(a). Zucker and the Reids do not come to grips with this distinction. Every case they invoke in support of their position involves a court-appointed trustee rather than an assignee from a Chapter 11 debtor in possession. If Capitol had successfully emerged from Chapter 11 bankruptcy, as Zucker's counsel (correctly) acknowledged at oral argument, it would once again be the same "Company" covered by the contract. How strange then to treat the debtor in possession as an entirely distinct entity for purposes of this insurance contract.

. . . .

It makes no difference that the bankruptcy court approved the plan transferring the bankruptcy estate's causes of action from Capitol to the Liquidation Trust. Zucker and the Reids may be right that court approval offers a safeguard against the collusive suits that insured-versus-insured exclusions seek to prevent. But that does not eliminate the practical and legal difference between an assignee and a court-appointed trustee that receives the right to sue on the estate's behalf by statute. The risk of collusion is surely higher when the insured individuals—the management of the debtor in possession—can negotiate and put conditions on a trustee's right to sue them. *In re R.J. Reynolds*, 315 B.R. 674, 680 (Bankr. W.D. Va. 2003). That a contractual term, like a statutory term, was designed to avoid certain problems does not mean that a fact-intensive search for that problem—here for collusion—must occur each time someone invokes the provision. And it does not mean that collusion must be found before the provision applies. We ask only whether "the Company" includes Capitol as debtor in possession. The contract itself, together with core principles of bankruptcy law, confirms that it does.

. . . .

For these reasons, we affirm.

DISSENT

BERNICE B. DONALD, dissenting.

I write separately to express my disagreement with the outcome of this case. The assigned trustee in this case should have the same right to be exempt from the insured-versus-insured exclusion as a court-appointed trustee. The plain language reading of the insurance contract in this case and Sixth Circuit precedent both support that finding. Because this decision makes it harder for companies to emerge from bankruptcy with a consensual plan of reorganization, I respectfully dissent.

"The primary intent of the development of the 'insured vs. insured' exclusion was to prevent collusive lawsuits in which an insured corporation would in essence 'force' its insurer to pay for the poor business decisions of its officers and directors by the corporation filing an action against its own officers and directors." Michael D. Sousa, *Making Sense of the Bramble-Filled Thicket: The "Insured vs. Insured" Exclusion in the Bankruptcy Context*, 23 EMORY BANKR. DEV. J. 365, 370 (2007). Many cases . . . . have held that court-appointed trustees are exempt from the insured-versus-insured exclusion because there is no risk of collusion since a court-appointed trustee is a completely independent entity. In fact, there is a split among "federal courts on the issue of whether a lawsuit against a corporation's former directors and officers brought by a debtor in possession, trustee, creditors' committee, or postconfirmation liquidating trustee triggers the 'insured vs. insured' exclusion in a directors and officers liability insurance policy." *Id.* Functionally, however, there is no distinction between an assigned trustee that a bankruptcy court has determined is independent and does not pose a risk of collusion, and one that is appointed by a bankruptcy court and is by nature of that appointment independent. As the majority correctly noted, there are several cases that have determined a trustee does not fall under the insured-versus-insured exclusion, but all of those cases involve a court-appointed trustee rather than an assigned trustee as we have in this case.

However, there has been a move towards an examination of the plain language of the insured-versus-insured exclusion which some courts have similarly found should not extend to successors or assigns. See *Alstrin v. St. Paul Mercury Insurance Co.*, 179 F.Supp.2d 376 (D. Del. 2002); *In re Molten Metal Technology*, 271 B.R. 711 (Bankr. D Mass 2002); *Zurich American Insurance Co. v. Boyes*, 2001 U.S. Dist. LEXIS 15123 (ND Tex 2001). The courts in each of these cases held that the plain language of the insured-versus-insured exclusion did not apply to claims by a trustee in bankruptcy or an estate representative, emphasizing that such claims "are not the same claims brought 'by' the Debtor under the exclusionary provision." *Alstrin*, 179 F.Supp.2d at 404. Specifically, the *Alstrin* court rejected the insurance company's argument that the insured-versus-insured exclusion applies to the estate representative because the company's estate and the company share the same identity. *Id.* Instead, the *Alstrin* court emphasized that the debtor's estate representative, by way of the debtor's estate, and the debtor are separate entities. Similar to *Alstrin,* the insured-versus-insured exception in *Molten Metals* excluded coverage for claims "brought by any Insured or by the Company." However, the *Molten Metals* court noted that "Company" was "expressly defined to mean MMT [the insurance corporation] and its subsidiaries. The definition includes no reference to successors or assigns of any nature." 271 B.R. at 725.

. . . .

If we look to the plain language of the insured-versus-insured exclusion in this case, we will find the same result. The relevant portion of the Insurance Policy provides,

> The Insurer shall not be liable to make any payment for Loss in connection with any claim made against an Insured Person . . . (G) by, on behalf of, or in the name or right of, the Company or any Insured Person. . . .

Insurance Policy. This is a common provision in director and officer insurance policies that excludes coverage for any claim made by an insured person against another insured person or the Company.

The lawsuit brought by the Liquidation Trustee against Capitol's officers was not made "by the Company or any Insured Person" nor is it suggested that the suit is an action on "behalf of an Insured Person." Thus, the only remaining provision of the insured-versus-insured exclusion left to potentially bar coverage for the lawsuit against Capitol's officers pertains to actions brought in the "name or right of the Company." Both the plain language of the insured-versus-insured exclusion and established precedent in this Circuit do not support the majority's interpretation that the insured-versus-insured exclusion prohibits the Liquidating Trustee's lawsuit against Capitol's officers.

First, the plain language of the policy defines the term "Company" as:

> [T]he parent Company [i.e., Capitol Bancorp Ltd.] and any Subsidiary created or acquired on or before the Inception Date set forth in item 2 of the Declarations or during the Policy Period, subject to General Conditions VI(D).

See Insurance Policy, § II(D). The term Company, therefore, only includes "Capitol Bancorp, its Subsidiaries, and 216 entities affiliated with Capitol Bancorp, including community banks, real estate holding companies, and trust companies." The plain meaning of the insured-versus-insured exclusion does not include a debtor-in-possession or other estate representative.[1] Therefore, if the Liquidating Trustee brings a suit on behalf of the debtor-in-possession, by the plain language of the insurance policy, it is not brought on behalf of the debtor company.

In fact, this Court has explained that a debtor company is not the same as a debtor-in-possession. In *Gordon Sel-Way v. United States*, this Court held that:

> In Chapter 11 bankruptcy, the debtor files a petition for bankruptcy, becomes a debtor in possession, and thus succeeds to a set of statutorily defined powers and duties. The debtor in possession is considered to be a separate legal entity from the debtor himself.

270 F.3d 280, 290 (6th Cir. 2001).

This Court also held that a bankruptcy estate and a debtor are separate legal entities. *Frank v. Mich. State Unemployment Agency*, 252 F.3d 852, 853 (6th Cir. 2001) (adopting district court opinion holding that debtor and estate were separate entities in the context of preference actions); *Mgmt. Inv'rs v. United Mine Workers of Am.*, 610 F.2d 384, 392 (6th Cir. 1979) (holding that the estate, a separate legal entity, must formally abandon a claim in order for the claim to revest in the debtor).

. . . .

Although this "new-entity" argument may seem unfair, this is precisely the reason that many companies file bankruptcy. Companies in bankruptcy are afforded certain rights in bankruptcy that they would not be afforded outside of bankruptcy, especially in the context of contracts.

. . . .

There is no question that the Liquidating Trust, and the Liquidation Trustee by association, are separate legal entities than the debtor company Capitol. This is one of the fundamental tenants of bankruptcy law.

. . . .

Although, as the majority suggests, the risk of collusion is surely higher when the insured individuals can negotiate and put conditions on a trustee's right to sue them, that did not happen in this case. The policy behind the insured-versus-insured exclusion (i.e. to prevent collusion between the directors and officers and the insured company) could be problematic if the trustee is not truly independent (as is intrinsically the case with a court-appointed trustee). However that only means that the independence of the trustee should be evaluated on a case-by-case basis.

---

[1] Further, it is a basic rule of insurance contracts that exclusion clauses in insurance policies are to be strictly construed against the insurer and in favor of the insured.

In fact, that is exactly what the bankruptcy court did here. The bankruptcy court determined that the bankruptcy plan, which was result of negotiations between all parties in which they agreed to transfer all potential claims against Capitol's officers to the Liquidation Trust to pursue on behalf of the creditors, was in good faith. Neither the bankruptcy court nor the district court found any evidence of collusion between the debtor company and the appointed Liquidation Trustee. Therefore, there is no reason that the assigned trustee in this case should trigger the insured-versus-insured exclusion. For those reasons, I respectfully dissent.

NOTES AND QUESTIONS

1. *Divided Courts.* The majority and dissenting opinions in the *Zucker* case represent the lay of the land regarding "insured versus insured" exclusions. The majority read the exclusion literally and applied it to conclude that it applied to the facts. The dissent, on the other hand, looked at the purposes of the exclusion and the bankruptcy laws and concluded that the exclusion should not apply. Courts across the country have divided between these two approaches. *Compare, e.g., Alstrin v. St. Paul Mercury Ins. Co.*, 179 F. Supp. 2d 376 (D. Del. 2002) ("insured versus insured" exclusion did not apply to bankrupt debtor's estate's claim against former directors and officers of the bankrupt company where there was no evidence of collusion in bringing the claims), *and In re Cent. Louisiana Grain Co-op., Inc.*, 467 B.R. 390 (Bankr. W.D. La. 2012) ("insured versus insured" exclusion did not apply to preclude coverage for claims under Louisiana law), *with In re R.J. Reynolds*, 315 B.R. 674, 682 (Bankr. W.D. Va. 2003) ("insured versus insured" exclusion applied to bankrupt estate's claims against former officers and directors). Which approach do you find more persuasive?

2. *Exception for Derivative Suits.* The "insured versus insured" exclusion typically contains an exception for shareholder derivative actions brought by shareholders of an institution against officers or directors of the company. *See* Barry R. Ostrager & Thomas R. Newman, Handbook on Insurance Coverage Disputes § 20.05[d] (18th ed. 2017). Why is there an exception for derivative actions?

F. DEFENSE AND SETTLEMENT OBLIGATIONS

CONTINENTAL CAS. CO. V. BOARD OF EDUC. OF CHARLES COUNTY

489 A.2d 536 (Md. 1985)

Opinion

RODOWSKY, JUDGE.

In this case the insurer and insured under a policy providing a form of directors' and officers' (D & O) liability insurance dispute the extent of the insurer's liability for counsel fees and expenses incurred by the insured in defense of a suit which alleged both covered and non-covered claims against the insured. The parties also dispute the liability of the insurer for the counsel fees and expenses incurred by the insured in prosecuting the instant action. We shall hold that fees and expenses which are reasonably related to the defense of a covered claim may ordinarily be allocated wholly to that covered claim. We shall also hold that the insurer is liable for the insured's fees and expenses in this case.

For a policy period of August 1, 1976, to August 1, 1979, Continental Casualty Company (CNA) issued to the Board of Education of Charles County, Maryland (the Board) a "Board of Education Liability Including School District Reimbursement Policy." The policy was issued with an optional broad form of coverage under which "Assureds" were "[a]ll persons who were, now are or shall be employed by the School District. . . ."

In the insuring clause of the basic policy CNA agreed:

> (a) With the Assureds that if, during the policy period any claim or claims are made against them . . . for a Wrongful Act occurring during the policy period, the Insurer will pay on behalf of . . . the Assureds . . . for all loss [sic] which the said Assureds or any of them shall become legally obligated to pay. . . .

"Wrongful Act" is defined in the policy to:

> [M]ean any actual or alleged errors or misstatement or misleading statement or act or omission or neglect or breach of duty by the Assureds in the discharge of their duties, individually or collectively, or any matter claimed against them solely by reason of their being or having been Assureds during this policy period.

"Loss" was defined to:

> [M]ean any amount which the Assured or School District are legally obligated to pay, including, but not limited to, any amounts which the School District may be required or permitted to pay as indemnity to an Assured, for a claim or claims made against an Assured for a Wrongful Act and shall include but not be limited to damages, judgments, settlements and costs, cost of investigation and defense of legal actions . . . claims or proceedings and appeals therefrom, costs of attachment or similar bonds, provided always, however, such subject of loss shall not include fines imposed by the law, or matters which shall be deemed uninsurable under the law pursuant to which this policy shall be construed.

The policy provisions relating to "Costs, Charges and Expenses," as amended by the "Liberalization Endorsement," read:

> (a) The Assureds and/or the School District shall select and retain legal counsel to represent them in the defense and appeal of any claim, suit, action or proceeding covered under this policy, but no fees, costs or expenses shall be incurred or settlements made, without the Insurer's consent, such consent not to be unreasonably withheld.
>
> (b) The Insurer may at its option and upon request, advance on behalf of an Assured, and/or the School District fees, costs and expenses which have been incurred in connection with claims made against an Assured, prior to disposition of such claims, provided always that, in the event it is finally established the Insurer has no liability hereunder, each agrees to repay to the Insurer, upon demand, all monies advanced on their behalf pursuant to this provision.

The Board's policy from CNA provides for a $1,000 retention as to "[e]ach loss" and a limit of liability of $3,000,000 which is the "[m]aximum annual aggregate."

As a result of an exclusion also added by the "Liberalization Endorsement," the policy does not cover any "Loss" resulting from breach of a construction contract.[2] Naturally, the litigation which spawned the subject case arose out of a construction contract.

On or about August 10, 1976, the Board entered into a contract with Iorio Construction Co., Inc. (Iorio) under which Iorio was to build a new high school in La Plata, Maryland. By letter dated August 29, 1979, the Board, acting through the Superintendent of Schools, gave notice that it was terminating the contract. That letter "enclosed a copy of the Architect's recommendation for termination . . . on the basis that [the Iorio] firm has failed to supply enough properly skilled workmen or proper materials to finish the project in a timely fashion."

. . . .

In October 1979 Iorio filed suit against the Board and others in the United States District Court for the District of Maryland. Iorio's claims sounded both in contract and in tort. . . .

---

2 As amended by the "Liberalization Endorsement," the exclusions section of the policy reads in relevant part:

> "IV. Exclusions
>
> (b) The Insurer shall not be liable to make any payment for loss in connection with any claim against the Assureds, and/or the School District. . . .
>
> > (6) For any amounts due, under the terms of any contractual obligation; however, except with respect to construction or demolition contracts this exclusion shall not apply to fees, costs and expenses of the investigation, defense or appeal of any claim or suit or arbitration or administrative proceeding resulting from failure to perform or breach of any contract."

CNA in early 1980 denied coverage.

On March 6, 1981, the Board, Runyon, Starkey, and Lavorgna sued CNA in the United States District Court for the District of Maryland for a declaratory judgment (the Declaratory Judgment Action). The plaintiffs sought a judicial determination that CNA was obligated for their expenses, including attorneys' fees, in defending Iorio's suit against them and also in the Declaratory Judgment Action.

The Board settled the Iorio suit in December 1982 so that the Declaratory Judgment Action has become a suit for damages and fees. There is no suggestion in the record that CNA has ever approved, or, after CNA took the position that there was no coverage, that CNA has been asked to approve, the defense conducted to the Iorio suit, the fees incurred by the Board or the settlement. In the course of proceedings in the Declaratory Judgment Action the federal court has concluded that certain claims in the Iorio suit were within the coverage of the CNA policy while other claims were not. Based on that preliminary legal ruling the Board has argued to the federal court that CNA was obligated to pay all of the legal fees and other expenses incurred by the Board in the Iorio suit while CNA has contended that an apportionment of those costs between covered and noncovered claims was required. At that point the federal court invoked the Maryland Uniform Certification of Questions of Law Act, Md.Code (1974, 1984 Repl.Vol.), §§ 12–601 to 609 of the Courts and Judicial Proceedings Article. The federal court has certified five questions to us, four of which deal with apportionment of litigation expenses between covered and non-covered claims. We shall state the precise questions and our answers to them in the course of analyzing the contentions of insurer and insured.

Review of the Iorio complaint is essential to an understanding of the issues raised in the litigation underlying the Declaratory Judgment Action. Iorio chose to divide its complaint into seven counts. The second and each succeeding count incorporate certain introductory allegations and all of the allegations of preceding counts. Counts I through III claim only against the Board and other governmental entities, but not against any individuals.

Count I alleges breach of the express construction contract and claims the difference between the contract price as "adjusted and fixed by the defendants" and the amount paid to Iorio. The difference is alleged to be $406,793. The second count seeks $298,313, allegedly representing the reasonable value of extras requested by the Board. Count III claims damages of $1,488,744, allegedly caused by delay attributable to the defendants. This count specifies sixteen aspects of the project as to which Iorio says it was impeded. These aspects range from an allegation that "the contract plans and specifications furnished required redesign" to an allegation that the defendants "interfered with local authorities in their inspection function to delay issuance of the temporary and permanent certificates of occupancy." Count IV claimed only against the architects. Count V was interpreted by the federal court to rest on *quantum meruit*. That count was apparently intended to be an alternative to counts I, II, and III. It claims the total of the amounts sought in each of those three counts.

In the sixth count Iorio sued only individuals. The contractor alleged that the defendant architects and officials of the Board had entered into a "corrupt agreement for the purpose of defrauding and injuring Iorio and in pursuance of their common scheme and conspiracy, caused and performed the acts complained of hereinabove." The *ad damnum* of count VI was $1,488,774. Because this is precisely the amount of the *ad damnum* in count III, it is fair to interpret the "acts complained of hereinabove" as referring to the acts of hindrance specified in count III. Thus, tortious acts of Assureds allegedly occurred at each stage of the project from design to occupancy. Count VII of the complaint sounds in tort against all defendants and seeks damages measured by the loss allegedly caused to Iorio through diminished bonding capacity resulting from the conduct of the defendants with respect to the project.

The federal court's interlocutory legal ruling is that CNA's policy afforded coverage with respect to counts VI and VII of Iorio's complaint. In count VI a claim is made against Assureds for a "Wrongful Act," and in count VII a claim is made against the Board and Assureds for a "Wrongful Act." The Board engaged counsel to defend and we infer that the Board is in effect indemnifying its three officials with respect to the costs of defense. The Board has become legally obligated to pay counsel and the litigation expenses. Those fees and costs allocable to counts VI and VII are a "Loss," as defined. CNA has promised to pay that "Loss." It has not. Thus we have a case of breach of contract by CNA.[8] The interrelated questions certified to us in effect ask what principles determine the proof of damages where the defense is to a suit making claims of "Wrongful Acts" and also making claims that are not of "Wrongful Acts."

The Board contends that CNA in effect breached an agreement to defend the entire Iorio suit so that the damages are measured by the cost of defending the entire suit. The Board's argument is an effort to bring this case under the rule of *Brohawn v. Transamerica Ins. Co.*, 276 Md. 396, 347 A.2d 842 (1975). That rule does not apply here.

---

[8] Under the policy "Loss" also includes the amount paid in settlement of a claim for a "Wrongful Act." The relief sought in the Declaratory Judgment Action by way of reimbursement specifically includes settlements. In the certified questions and in the briefs and arguments of the parties to this Court, however, the focus is exclusively on attorneys' fees and other litigation expenses. Consequently, this opinion addresses only fees and costs. We intimate no opinion on how the policy might operate, if at all, with respect to the settlement of the Iorio suit. Indeed, the record before us does not even indicate the terms of that settlement.

Brohawn involved a homeowner's policy which included "Comprehensive Personal Liability" coverage. There the insurer promised:

> To pay on behalf of the Insured all sums which the Insured shall become legally obligated to pay as damages because of bodily injury or property damage, and the *Company shall defend any suit against the Insured alleging such bodily injury* or property damage and seeking damages which are payable under the terms of this Section, *even if any of the allegations of the suit are groundless*. . . .

Id. at 400, 347 A.2d at 846 (italics in original).

The suit arose out of an altercation with the plaintiff who alleged, alternatively, that the insured's harm-causing conduct was either an act of negligence or an assault. Negligence was covered by the policy but assault was excluded. Coverage, as it related to the insurer's obligation to pay damages, would not be determined until the jury characterized the facts as assault or negligence or neither. With respect to the duty to defend, however, we said:

> Although the type of policy here considered is most often referred to as liability insurance, it is "litigation insurance" as well, protecting the insured from the expense of defending suits brought against him. . . . By clear and unequivocal language, [the insurer] has assumed the obligation of relieving its insured of the expense of defending an action alleging and seeking damages within the policy coverage.

Id. at 409–10, 347 A.2d at 851.

In order to give effect to the duty to defend where the allegations, even if groundless, present claims both within and without the policy coverage the rule in Maryland is that "the insurer still must defend if there is a *potentiality* that the claim could be covered by the policy." *Id.* at 408, 347 A.2d at 850 (italics in original).

In the case now before us the Board in effect equates Iorio's counts VI and VII with the negligence claim in *Brohawn*. Had Iorio's complaint gone to trial and a verdict and judgment been rendered based on count VI there would have been coverage (as to damages) under CNA's policy. Consequently, says the Board, that potentiality of coverage required CNA to defend the entire Iorio suit.

CNA on the other hand emphasizes that the subject policy is not a conventional liability policy. There is no "duty to defend" language; there is no reference to defense of groundless claims, and there is no conferral on the insurer of the right to select counsel and control the litigation. The Board counters by underscoring CNA's promise to pay fees and expenses in defending covered claims which the Board says is the substantial equivalent of a duty to defend.

The subject policy is a variation on a type of liability coverage initially offered to protect corporate directors and officers and now known as D & O. A form of D & O coverage is said to have been available through underwriters at Lloyd's since the 1940's, with the market for it having expanded rapidly in the mid-1960's. *See* Note, *Liability Insurance for Corporate Executives,* 80 Harv.L.Rev. 648 (1967). Policy forms have evolved and American companies have entered the field. As to D & O insurance generally, see J. Bishop, *The Law of Corporate Officers and Directors: Indemnification and Insurance* (1982 & 1984 Cum.Supp.) (ch. 8: "Directors' and Officers' Liability Insurance"); W. Knepper, *Liability of Corporate Officers and Directors* (3d ed. 1978) (ch. 20: "Liability Insurance") (Knepper); Hinsey, *The New Lloyd's Policy Form for Directors and Officers Liability Insurance-An Analysis,* 33 Bus.Law. 1961 (1978); and Johnston, *Corporate Indemnification and Liability Insurance for Officers and Directors,* 33 Bus.Law. 1993 (1978).

D & O coverage usually has two aspects. First it is intended to protect a corporation from its liability, either imposed by law or by a valid provision of the charter or by-laws, to indemnify officers and directors, including indemnification for legal fees and expenses in litigation. Such policies are also generally designed to protect officers, directors, and other covered corporate employees both from liability to third persons and as to litigation fees and expenses when claims are made that they have committed a covered wrongful act as an officer, director, or employee. In the instant case the insuring clause in CNA's basic policy, without the "Liberalization Endorsement," was structured in this manner.

Knepper, ¶ 20.06, at 628, advises that "[a] program of D & O insurance for school district board members and employees is also written. . . . Premiums are based on the number of students, number of board members, and litigation history of the school district." At 628 n. 45 Knepper supports the statement by citation to a newspaper article appearing in 1972, entitled " 'CNA Announces Entry in Growing D & O Field.' "

Knepper, ¶ 20.16, also describes the defense of actions under D & O policies:

> It has been noted that "costs, charges and expenses" includes attorneys' fees and other defense costs. Thus the insurer should be consulted when counsel are retained to defend threatened or pending litigation. Under D & O policies the insured must provide its defense, although the insurer may participate at its option and may have a voice in selection of defense counsel.

Provisions of the subject CNA policy relating to defense are substantially different from the duty to defend clause of a conventional liability policy.

Assureds and/or the Board, not CNA, select and retain defense counsel. "Loss," whether incurred by way of judgment, settlement, or defense costs, is charged against the policy limit without distinguishing between damages and legal fees. CNA has the option, but not the obligation, to advance expenses. CNA's consent, which is not unreasonably to be withheld, is to be obtained before expenses are incurred or settlements made. If CNA advances expenses under the subject policy and "it is finally established the Insurer has no liability" under the policy, then each recipient of advances agrees to repay CNA all monies advanced on his or her behalf.

Here it has been established that counts VI and VII of Iorio's complaint asserted "Wrongful Acts" so that there is liability of CNA for the cost of defense attributable to those counts. That is not the same as a breach of the contractual duty to defend the entire suit under a policy and under a state of facts like those presented in *Brohawn*. Consequently, the damages here are not measured, as a matter of law, by the reasonable cost of defending the entire Iorio suit. That brings us to the problem of apportionment and to the certified questions.

Question 1 is:

> Should the costs and expenses, including attorneys' fees, incurred by an insured under a policy of insurance, such as was written in this case, be apportioned between those counts of the suit against the insured for which there is insurance coverage and those counts for which there is no insurance coverage under the policy?

The answer is "Yes," as explained above.

Question 2 is the heart of the case. It asks:

> If such apportionment is required, what standard should the finder of fact apply in apportioning costs and expenses, including attorneys' fees?

CNA urges that the services and expenses must be "reasonably and directly related to" covered claims. The Board advocates a standard under which the service or expense must be "reasonably related and supportive of the defense of" covered claims.

The question really asks what standard measures the damages to which the Board is entitled for CNA's breach of its contract. These damages can be measured in relation to the Board's expectation interest. The Board is entitled to be put in as good a position as it would have occupied had CNA performed the contract. Counsel defending the Iorio suit could properly have billed CNA for all services and expenses reasonably related to the defense of counts VI and VII. Legal services and expenses are reasonably related to a covered count if they would have been rendered and incurred by reasonably competent counsel engaged to defend a suit against the

Board and Assureds arising out of the same factual background as did the Iorio suit but which alleged only the matters complained of in counts VI and VII of the Iorio complaint.

Application of a reasonable relationship standard, as we have defined it above, will depend upon the facts. Nevertheless, in order further to clarify application of that standard, some generalizations about anticipated proof in the Declaratory Judgment Action are appropriate. Undoubtedly much of the work of defense counsel in the Iorio suit was factual preparation. It would have embraced review of the records involving the project in the possession or control of the clients, of codefendants, and of Iorio, either by formal discovery or by cooperation of counsel. It would have included interviews and depositions of individuals involved in the project. It seems likely that most if not all of this kind of factual preparation is reasonably related to the defense of count VI. Count VI is no more than a tort theory applied to the same facts which are involved in count III where the underlying theory is either a breach by the owner of an express provision of the construction contract or a breach by the owner of a duty implied in law not to hinder the contractor's performance. Both the tort and contract theories take the factual investigator through the entire history of the project.

Preparation on the facts which may have gone beyond the history of the project and into subsequent jobs bid on or performed by Iorio, and which may have gone into the economic results to Iorio from jobs obtained or from jobs sought but not obtained, would be related if it were not excessively disproportionate to the risk of liability against the Board or Assureds on the theory of count VII.

To phrase our meaning of "reasonably related" in another way, we do not believe that CNA is entitled to an apportionment between tort and contract counts based simply on the fact that an item of legal service or expense would also be of use to counsel in defending a claim asserted under a contract count of the Iorio suit in addition to its use in defending a tort count. Having purchased this form of litigation insurance, the Board is entitled to the full benefit of its bargain. So long as an item of service or expense is reasonably related to defense of a covered claim, it may be apportioned wholly to the covered claim.

The unusual combination of the allegations of count VI with the fact that the Board, either justifiably or unjustifiably, terminated the construction contract bears on the reasonable relationship standard as applied to both legal and factual preparation by defense counsel. Count VI speaks of a conspiracy between Assureds and the architects to harm Iorio by impeding his performance of the construction contract. The Board now argues to us that the contract claims of the Iorio suit and count VI are legally tied together by the legal principles applicable to conspiracies to induce a breach of a contract. This Court stated the rules in *Edison Realty Co. v. Bauernschub,* 191 Md. 451, 461, 62 A.2d 354, 358 (1948):

> A fraudulent conspiracy, sufficient to serve as the basis for an action in a civil case, is the confederation of two or more persons to cheat and defraud, when the design has actually been executed by the confederates with resulting damage to their victim. Since a breach of contract is unlawful, it is unlawful for a third person knowingly to aid the maker of a contract in breaking it. If the maker combines with others to break the contract, their conduct is a conspiracy which entitles the other party to the contract to recover against the conspirators any damages he may sustain. . . . But where the loss to the complainant was not caused by any breach of legal or equitable duty, it is *damnum absque injuria* . . . . In this case the bill alleges a breach of contract, but there is no allegation of any specific act of fraud committed at the time of the execution of the contract, and no allegation of any specific act of conspiracy to break the contract. Consequently, the demurrers of the three co-defendants should be sustained.

It is not necessary for us on these certified questions, or for the federal court in the Declaratory Judgment Action, to determine whether the above principles would have been a legally valid defense to count VI of the Iorio complaint. If the proof in the Declaratory Judgment Action shows that counsel for the Board did in fact conceive of that legal theory as a defense to count VI while the Iorio suit was pending, and if the trier of fact in the Declaratory Judgment Action concludes that it was reasonable for counsel to pursue that theory of defense, then there may be a basis for a factual finding that legal research on Iorio's breach of contract theories is reasonably related to count VI. Otherwise, we are not able to speculate on a state of facts which would demonstrate a reasonable relationship between legal research, if any, directed to the liability aspects of the breach of contract legal theories and counts VI or VII. The theory of defense to count VI which the Board advances to us, if it were in fact pursued while the Iorio suit was pending, would be an additional basis for finding a reasonable relation between factual preparation of the total suit and count VI.

Finally, there are undoubtedly charges to the Board for the time of counsel which has been devoted to moving the Iorio case as a whole. This would include the preparation of motions and supporting memoranda, and the appearance of counsel before the federal court. Because the facts underlying count VI also underlie the contract claims it again seems likely that most if not all of the time of counsel devoted to motions practice will turn out to be work which it would have been reasonable for counsel to have done if the Iorio case had alleged only counts VI and VII.

Question 3 is:

> Which party (insurer or insured) bears the burden of establishing the apportionment of costs and expenses, including attorneys' fees, between the covered and non-covered claims pursuant to the standard discussed in question 2?

The insured has the burden of establishing that a given item of legal service or expense was reasonably related to the defense of counts VI and/or VII. The Board must prove its damages.

Question 4 is:

> If a division of costs and expenses, including attorneys' fees, pursuant to the standard discussed in question 2, cannot be accomplished, is the insured entitled to:
>
> (a) recovery of all costs and expenses, including attorneys' fees;
>
> (b) partial recovery of costs and expenses, including attorneys' fees; or
>
> (c) no recovery whatsoever of costs and expenses, including attorneys' fees?

If the insured is unable to present proof of any damages caused by the breach of contract, that is, is unable to show that it has become legally obligated to pay counsel fees and expenses which are reasonably related to the defense of counts VI and/or VII, as we have explained that relationship in the answer to question 2, then the insured is entitled only to nominal damages.

Question 5 asks:

> Is the insured entitled to recover from the insurer the costs and expenses, including attorneys' fees, incurred in the prosecution of the instant action?

Our answer is "Yes."

The general rule is that costs and expenses of litigation, other than the usual and ordinary Court costs, are not recoverable in an action for damages, nor are such costs even recoverable in a subsequent action; but where the wrongful acts of the defendant [have] involved the plaintiff in litigation with others, or placed him in such relations with others as make it necessary to incur expense to protect his interest, such costs and expenses should be treated as the legal consequences of the original wrongful act. *McGaw v. Acker, Merrall & Condit Co.*, 111 Md. 153, 160, 73 A. 731, 734 (1909).

In seeking to recover counsel fees and expenses reasonably related to the defense of covered claims in the Iorio litigation, the Board is seeking to have the general rule applied. The Board's claim in the Declaratory Judgment Action for counsel fees and expenses incurred in prosecuting the Declaratory Judgment Action does not fit within the rule as stated in *McGaw*. Nevertheless, this Court has sustained the award of counsel fees incurred by an insured in litigation with an insurer where the issue was whether the insurer was obligated to defend the insured against a claim asserted by a third party and where the insurer unsuccessfully maintained that it was not so obliged. The legal theory supporting this rule remains unrefined. *See Cohen v. American Home Assurance Co.*, 255 Md. 334, 363, 258 A.2d 225, 239 (1969) ("[W]hether one speaks in terms of [the insurer's] having authorized the expenditure by its failure to defend or whether one speaks in terms of the attorney's fees for the declaratory judgment action being a part of the damages sustained by the insured by [the insurer's] wrongful breach of the contract, we hold [the insurer] bound to pay the fees incurred by [the insured] in bringing the declaratory judgment action to establish that [the insurer] had not done that which it had agreed with her to do."). *Cohen* represents an exception to the general rule stated in *McGaw*, and the exception is now firmly established.

On certified question 5 CNA reiterates that the subject policy does not contain a duty to defend provision and points out that the Maryland cases holding an insurer obligated to pay counsel fees of the insured in the litigation between them involved policies with a duty to defend provision. On this phase of the instant case that distinction is meaningless. The cases between insurer and insured in which counsel fees of the insured were awarded as part of the relief to the insured were concerned primarily with which party, insurer or insured, would pay for the defense of the action brought against the insured by a third party. It makes no difference whether the duty to pay for the defense arises out of a promise to defend or whether it arises out of a promise to pay for "Loss," defined to include the cost of defense, when a claim is made against the insured for a "Wrongful Act."

HILCO CAPITAL, LP V. FEDERAL INS. CO.

978 A.2d 174 (Del. 2009)

Opinion

BERGER, JUSTICE:

This appeal involves an insurance coverage dispute that was resolved by a decision granting partial summary judgment to the insurer, followed by a jury verdict responding to three special interrogatories, also in favor of the insurer. Appellants argue that the trial court erred in holding that: (1) the insurer had no implied duty of good faith to consider a settlement of appellants' claims; and (2) the insurer's consent was required before the claims could be settled. In addition, appellants challenge several evidentiary rulings at trial as well as certain jury instructions. We find that, even if the trial court erred in some respects, the jury verdict in favor of the insurer was correct and must be affirmed.

FACTUAL AND PROCEDURAL BACKGROUND

Hilco Capital, LP and Congress Financial Corporation (collectively, Hilco) are financial institutions that made loans to Payless Cashways, Inc. In 2003, Hilco sued Payless's officers and directors (the Insureds), alleging that they had misrepresented the value and amount of Payless's inventory (the Barron Action). The Insureds had three layers of directors and officers liability coverage from three different insurers. National Union Fire Insurance Company of Pittsburgh, PA issued the primary policy, covering the first $10 million of exposure. Federal Insurance Company issued the first excess policy, covering the next $10 million of exposure, and Twin City Fire Insurance Company provided the third $10 million layer of coverage.

The parties to the Barron Action tried to settle their claim at an early mediation, but were unsuccessful. Discovery ended in October 2004, and trial was scheduled to begin on January 24, 2005. A second mediation took place on December 7, 2004. The parties, National Union, and their counsel attended. Federal's claims examiner, Mary Ann Alsnauer, talked with counsel for the Insureds, David Shay, about whether she should attend. Because both Shay and National Union valued the Barron Action claims at less than $10 million, and because Shay told Alsnauer that the defense team would rather try the case than settle for more than $10 million, it was agreed that Federal would not attend the mediation. Nonetheless, Alsnauer remained available to be contacted by telephone.

After a day-long mediation had achieved no resolution, the mediator proposed that the parties agree to arbitrate a single issue-whether any of the Insureds should have known that a Payless employee had falsified the company's inventory numbers. Under the mediator's proposal, National Union would pay Hilco $5 million immediately. If Hilco lost at the arbitration, Hilco would retain that payment, but receive nothing more. If Hilco won, it would receive the balance of National Union's policy (approximately $3.5 million) and approximately $7 million from Federal's policy.

The parties to the mediation agreed to the proposal, but that occurred at about 10 p.m. Eastern time, and Shay was unable to reach Alsnauer to determine whether Federal would agree. Rather than wait until the next morning, the parties eliminated the need for Federal's consent by agreeing that the Insureds would not be personally liable and that the Insureds would assign their rights in the Federal policy to Hilco. Under the Memorandum of Understanding (MOU) executed that evening, Hilco would be assured a recovery against National Union up to its policy limits (if the arbitrator ruled in Hilco's favor), and would have the right to proceed against Federal for the approximately $7 million, which was Hilco's agreed maximum recovery.

While the settlement was being finalized, Hilco asked Federal to consent to it. Alsnauer reviewed the proposal, as well as Shay's letter analyzing the risks, but concluded that the settlement was not acceptable. From a defense standpoint, she noted that the one question being presented to the arbitrator eliminated several important defenses and standards of proof that would have benefited the Insureds at a trial. From a settlement perspective, she thought that a "straight" settlement could be achieved at a lower amount. Alsnauer explained that, since Hilco had agreed to a range of $3.8–15.5 million,[1] Hilco probably would agree to an amount midway between the high and low amounts in order to avoid the risk of losing the arbitration. Such a result might not even reach Federal's layer of coverage.

A court-ordered settlement conference was set to take place on January 5, 2005. Alsnauer asked the parties to wait until after the settlement conference before signing the final MOU, but they did not. Alsnauer formally objected to the settlement when it was presented to the court on January 5, 2005. Months later, the Insureds arbitrated the one question presented in the MOU, and Hilco prevailed. National Union paid its policy limits, but Federal denied coverage on the ground that the Insureds breached the policy by settling their claims without Federal's consent.

Federal brought a declaratory action in Superior Court at the same time that Hilco sued in Missouri to collect on its judgment. The Missouri action was dismissed for lack of jurisdiction, so Hilco interposed its claim for payment as a counterclaim in this action. On cross motions for summary judgment, the trial court held that: 1) Federal had no duty to negotiate with the Insureds under Missouri's implied covenant of good faith and fair dealing; and 2) the consent-to-settlement provision in National Union's policy applied to Federal. The remaining issues-whether Federal unreasonably withheld its consent, and whether the settlement was reasonable and non-collusive-were tried to a jury. By special interrogatories, the jury found that: 1) the Insureds breached the policy before Federal made any decision whether to consent to the settlement; 2) Federal did not unreasonably withhold its consent to the settlement; and 3) Federal was not permitted to effectively associate in the negotiation of the settlement. This appeal followed.

DISCUSSION

Hilco argues that the trial court erred in both of its legal rulings on summary judgment. In addition, Hilco claims that the trial court erred or abused its discretion in: 1) instructing the jury that the question of whether Federal unreasonably withheld its consent is determined under a

[1] Originally, the low number was $5 million, but the parties negotiated that down to $3.8 million.

subjective rather than an objective standard; 2) excluding Hilco's expert testimony; 3) instructing the jury that the Insureds could breach the policy if they manifested an intent to settle before Federal had a chance to consent; 4) allowing the jury to consider the "effective association" issue; and 5) excluding correspondence between counsel for National Union and Federal concerning their differing views about the settlement.

We agree with Hilco that the trial court erred in its analysis of the covenant of good faith and fair dealing. The law in Missouri, as in Delaware, is that all contracts include an implied covenant of good faith and fair dealing. The trial court correctly stated the general principle that, "there can be no breach of the . . . covenant of good faith and fair dealing where the contract expressly permits the actions being challenged. . . ." But, the corollary is that, when a contract gives one party discretion, "it must not be exercised to deprive the other party of the benefit of the contractual relationship or evade the spirit of the bargain." Thus, despite the fact that the Participation Clause in the Federal policy gave Federal "sole discretion" whether to participate in the settlement of any claim, Federal still had to exercise that discretion consistent with its covenant of good faith and fair dealing.

The trial court granted Federal summary judgment on this issue without considering the record. It held that the Participation Clause precluded a claim for breach of the covenant of good faith and fair dealing. We conclude that summary judgment is appropriate, but for a different reason. Viewing the record in the light most favorable to Hilco, there are no issues of material fact in dispute and Federal is entitled to judgment as a matter of law.

The undisputed evidence is that Federal, National Union, and the Insureds all agreed that Federal should not attend the December 2004 mediation because it would send the wrong message about the defense team's assessment of their potential liability. Thus, there is no support for a claim that Federal breached the covenant by failing to attend the mediation. After the mediation participants agreed in principle to the "high-low, one issue" arbitration, it was they who refused to wait until the next day to discuss that proposal with Federal. Instead, they effectively cut Federal out of the process by agreeing that the Insureds would assign their rights to Hilco.

During the period between the execution of the MOU and the scheduled settlement conference, the parties to the MOU worked on finalizing the terms of their agreement. Viewing the facts in the light most favorable to Hilco, Federal "refused" to participate, and "insisted" that National Union offer its policy limits before Federal would join in the negotiations. Those facts, however, do not support a claim that Federal breached the covenant of good faith and fair dealing.

Federal was willing to negotiate, but it wanted to pursue a "straight" settlement. Such a settlement would require National Union's agreement to tender policy limits (unless the settlement amount was below National Union's policy limits, in which case Federal would have no economic interest). But National Union would not agree, because the MOU gave it a better deal. At worst, National Union would have to pay policy limits, and at best, National Union would have to pay approximately $3.8 million less than policy limits. Thus, Federal's only recourse with respect to negotiations was to present its position to the Missouri court at the settlement conference. The mediation participants mooted that effort by executing a definitive settlement agreement the day before the conference. In sum, there is no record support for a breach of good faith claim against Federal.

We affirm the second summary judgment ruling on the basis of the trial court's decision, correctly holding that Federal's policy incorporated the consent provision from the National Union policy. Not only does that result follow the language of the policy, but also it comports with the understanding of both parties to the contract. Hilco was not a party to the contract, and acquired its interest in the Federal policy with knowledge of the parties' interpretation of their contract. The intent of the contracting parties, not outsiders, controls the construction of the agreement.

The remaining issues relate to Federal's decision to withhold consent to the settlement. The jury found that Federal did not act unreasonably, but Hilco complains about certain evidentiary rulings as well as allegedly improper jury instructions. Regarding the evidentiary rulings, the trial court allowed Federal's expert, a D & O attorney, to testify that: (1) he had never encountered a high-low settlement like the one agreed to here; (2) it was totally contrary to custom and practice to negotiate such an agreement without the excess carrier's consent; and (3) Federal had no ability to negotiate after the parties agreed in principle to the mediation proposal. Hilco proffered another attorney, an expert in mediations, to rebut those opinions. The trial court excluded Hilco's expert, without explanation. In addition, the trial court excluded correspondence between attorneys for National Union and Federal that, according to Hilco, contained significant admissions concerning Federal's settlement strategy. Finally, the trial court allowed Shay to testify that Federal had a reasonable basis to withhold consent to the settlement.

Hilco also argues that three of the jury instructions were improper. First, Hilco contends that the trial court incorrectly instructed the jury to use a subjective, rather than an objective, standard in deciding whether Federal unreasonably withheld its consent to the settlement. Second, Hilco argues that there was no factual basis on which to instruct the jury that the Insureds could breach the Federal policy by orally agreeing to a settlement before Federal had the opportunity to grant or withhold its consent. Third,

Hilco argues that there was no factual basis on which to instruct the jury that the Insureds could breach the Federal policy by depriving Federal of the opportunity to "effectively associate" in the settlement.

We review the trial court's evidentiary rulings for abuse of discretion. If there is an abuse of discretion, we then must "consider whether the mistakes constituted significant prejudice so as to have denied [Hilco] a fair trial." The trial court acted well within its discretion in excluding the post-settlement correspondence between attorneys. It was both hearsay and irrelevant. Assuming without deciding that the trial court abused its discretion in making the remaining evidentiary rulings, we are satisfied that those rulings did not deny Hilco a fair trial.

Hilco's expert would have testified, in essence, that: 1) the mediation process and result were reasonable; 2) Federal was not deprived of opportunities to negotiate; and 3) the Barron Action would not have settled within National Union's policy limits. But those opinions were not critical to Hilco. Shay agreed that the mediation process and the result were in the best interest of the Insureds. Alsnauer agreed that Federal was free to attend the mediation, but declined. And both witnesses confirmed that Hilco was not willing to settle within National Union's policy limits. Thus, Hilco suffered little, if any, prejudice from the exclusion of its expert.

The same analysis applies to Shay's testimony that, as the attorney for the Insureds, he believed Federal had a reasonable basis to withhold consent to the settlement. Shay was the principal witness for Federal. He testified at length about the Barron Action-the evidence developed through discovery, the numerous claims and defenses, and the claimed damages. He believed it was more likely than not that the Insureds would win if the case went to trial and that Hilco had grossly overstated its damages. Shay also testified that he believed a "straight" settlement could have been negotiated for less than the $15.5 million "high" end of the high-low agreement. In light of this testimony, it was obvious that Shay thought Federal had a reasonable basis to withhold its consent. Thus, his testimony on that question did not deny Hilco a fair trial.

Hilco also complains about the jury instruction on Federal's withholding consent to the settlement. The policy's consent clause provides that the Insureds "shall not . . . enter into any settlement agreement . . . without the prior written consent of the Insurer. . . . The Insurer's consent shall not be unreasonably withheld . . ." The trial court instructed the jury:

> To show that [Federal] unreasonably withheld its consent to the settlement, the HILCO parties must first prove that [Federal's] consent to the settlement was, in fact, requested. If they do, then the HILCO parties must prove, based upon the totality of the facts and circumstances known to [Federal], that [Federal] did not have a reasonable basis for its decision to withhold consent to the

> settlement. It is not enough for the HILCO parties to show that the settlement offer was reasonable, or that other individuals or insurers might have consented to the settlement under the same circumstances.

Hilco argues that this instruction tells the jury to use a subjective standard, contrary to law. We review jury instructions *de novo*. The instruction need not be perfect, but is must "give a correct statement of the substance of the law and must be reasonably informative and not misleading."

. . . .

Here, the reasonableness of the amount of the settlement certainly would be a factor in considering whether Federal complied with its contractual obligation. But it is not the only factor. The trial court correctly instructed the jury to consider all the facts and circumstances in deciding whether Federal had a reasonable basis to withhold its consent. The instructions were not misleading and they did not allow the jury to use a subjective standard in deciding the reasonableness of Federal's decision.

Because the jury found that Federal had a reasonable basis to withhold consent, we need not address the two alternative grounds on which the jury found for Federal.

CONCLUSION

Based on the foregoing, the judgment of the Superior Court is hereby AFFIRMED.

NOTES AND QUESTIONS

1. *Duty to Defend?* Unlike occurrence-based policies, insurers typically do not have a duty to defend the policyholder under claims-made policies. Instead, the policyholder defends itself. Defense costs are covered "losses" to the extent the claims asserted against the policyholder are covered claims. Consequently, there often is an allocation of defense and settlement costs between covered and non-covered claims. If it is unclear whether defense costs were related solely to non-covered claims, then the insurer has an obligation to pay them. In such circumstances, what advice would you give to underlying defense counsel regarding the recording of time if you represented the policyholder? What if you represented the insurer and defense counsel was "panel counsel" for the insurer, which means it is approved by the insurer and regularly works for the insurer?

2. *Duty to Settle?* Similarly, unlike CGL policies, under claims-made policies, the insurer typically does not control settlement. The policyholder makes settlement decisions subject to the insurer's approval, which cannot unreasonably be withheld. What bases might an insurer that is not defending the policyholder have to withhold consent to a settlement?

G. PUBLIC POLICY ISSUES AND CLAIMS FOR RESTITUTIONARY RELIEF

LEVEL 3 COMMUNICATIONS, INC. V. FEDERAL INS. CO.

272 F.3d 908 (7th Cir. 2001)

Opinion

POSNER, CIRCUIT JUDGE.

This appeal comes in a diversity suit seeking damages from a pair of insurance companies (a primary carrier, Federal, and an excess carrier that's no longer a party) that refused to pay on a policy of directors' and officers' liability insurance, a "D & O" policy, as it's known. Despite its name, such a policy insures not only officers and directors themselves but also their corporation if, as happened here, the corporation indemnifies them for their liability. This is known as "company reimbursement coverage," as distinct from "direct" coverage of the directors and officers.

The district court granted summary judgment for Federal initially on the ground that one of the plaintiffs, Pompliano, in the suit against Level 3 (a securities-fraud suit brought by Pompliano and other shareholders of a corporation alleged to have been defrauded by Level 3) fell within the "insured versus insured" exclusion in the policy; Pompliano had been a director of one of Level 3's subsidiaries, and as a result was covered by Federal's policy. We held that Pompliano's status did not bar the entire claim by the insured, that instead his share of the settlement in the securities-fraud suit should be subtracted and Level 3 thus entitled, in the absence of other defenses by Federal, to recover the rest of the settlement from Federal under the D & O policy. *Level 3 Communications, Inc. v. Federal Ins. Co.*, 168 F.3d 956 (7th Cir.1999). On remand, the district court determined that the amount of the settlement had been $11.8 million, that it was a loss within the meaning of the policy, that $1.8 million of the settlement had gone to Pompliano, and that Federal was therefore liable to its insured, Level 3, for $10 million.

[In the policy, "loss" was defined as "the total amount which any insured person becomes legally obligated to pay on account of each claim and for all claims in each policy period . . . made against them for wrongful acts for which coverage applies, including, but not limited to, damages, judgments, settlements, costs and defense costs. Loss does not include . . . matters uninsurable under the law pursuant to which this coverage section is construed."]

Federal has appealed, arguing that the settlement, though an outlay by the insured, was not a "loss" within the meaning of the insurance policy, defined as "the total amount which any Insured Person becomes legally obligated to pay . . . including, but not limited to . . . settlements," because the relief sought in the suit against Level 3 was restitutionary in nature. The plaintiffs had sold shares in their corporation to Level 3 and charged that they had done so because of fraudulent representations that Level 3 had made. In effect, Level 3 was accused of having obtained the plaintiffs' company by false pretenses; and the plaintiffs' suit sought to rescind the transaction and recover their shares, or rather the monetary value of the shares because their company can no longer be reconstituted. It's as if, Federal argues, Level 3 had stolen cash from Pompliano and the other shareholders and had been forced to return it and were now asking the insurance company to pick up the tab. Federal continues that a D & O policy is designed to cover only losses that injure the insured, not ones that result from returning stolen property, and that if such an insurance policy did insure a thief against the cost to him of disgorging the proceeds of the theft it would be against public policy and so would be unenforceable. *Mortenson v. National Union Fire Ins. Co.*, 249 F.3d 667, 672 (7th Cir.2001); *Bank of the West v. Superior Court,* 2 Cal.4th 1254, 10 Cal.Rptr.2d 538, 833 P.2d 545, 554–55 (1992); *Central Dauphin School District v. American Casualty Co.*, 493 Pa. 254, 426 A.2d 94, 96 (1981). This ground for dismissing Level 3's suit was raised by Federal in the initial summary judgment proceedings, and it is in retrospect unfortunate that the district judge did not decide whether it had merit, as that would have avoided the need for two appeals to resolve Level 3's entire case.

The interpretive principle for which Federal contends that a "loss" within the meaning of an insurance contract does not include the restoration of an ill-gotten gain-is clearly right. The two cases on which Level 3 relies, *International Ins. Co. v. Johns*, 874 F.2d 1447, 1454–55 (11th Cir.1989), and *Limelight Productions, Inc. v. Limelite Studios, Inc.*, 60 F.3d 767, 769 (11th Cir.1995), are distinguishable, though *Limelight* only tenuously. The facts were similar to those in the present case, but the operative term in the insurance policy was "damages" rather than "loss," and so was broader. *In re Estate of Corriea*, 719 A.2d 1234, 1240–41 (D.C.App.1998), is similar.

As the interpretive principle controls this case, we need not consider the issue of enforceability, though the two issues are intertwined, since obviously an insurance policy wouldn't be presumed to have been drafted in such a way as to make it unenforceable.

It is true, as Level 3 emphasizes, that the plaintiffs in the underlying suit were not seeking either the return of the shares that Level 3 had allegedly winkled them out of or the value of the shares on the date they were purchased. They were seeking the difference between the value of the stock at the time of trial and the price they had received for the stock from Level 3. That is standard damages relief in a securities-fraud case. But it is restitutionary in character. It seeks to divest the defendant of the present value of the property obtained by fraud, minus the cost to the defendant of obtaining the property. In other words, it seeks to deprive the defendant of the net benefit of the unlawful act, the value of the unlawfully obtained stock minus the cost to the defendant of obtaining the stock. It is equivalent to seeking to impress a constructive trust on the property in favor of the rightful owner. How the claim or judgment order or settlement is worded is irrelevant. An insured incurs no loss within the meaning of the insurance contract by being compelled to return property that it had stolen, even if a more polite word than "stolen" is used to characterize the claim for the property's return.

We can imagine situations in which there would be a covered loss; this is important as showing that the D & O policy would not be rendered illusory by the acceptance of Federal's interpretation. An example would be a fraudulent statement by a corporate officer that inflated the price of the corporation's stock without conferring any measurable benefit on the corporation. Or suppose that unbeknownst to Level 3 the officer had stolen property for its benefit and, not knowing this, Level 3 defended against a suit seeking the return of the property and incurred heavy legal expenses in that defense. Those expenses would be a loss to the company not offset by any benefit to it, unlike the "expense" that consists simply of the value of the stolen property, a wash. All that the plaintiffs in the underlying suit obtained was the amount they received in settlement of their claim against Level 3, and that amount was part of Level 3's gain from its officers' misbehavior.

Level 3 acknowledges that if a judgment had been entered in the suit against it on the basis of a judicial determination that it had engaged in fraud, Federal would win; the policy so provides. It couples this acknowledgment with the inconsistent assertion that almost the entire purpose of D & O policies is to insure corporations and their officers and directors against claims of fraud. Pressed at argument concerning this inconsistency, it argued that the line runs between judgments and settlements. As long as the case is settled before entry of judgment, the insured is covered regardless of the nature of the claim against it. That can't be right. *Reliance Group Holdings, Inc. v. National Union Fire Ins. Co., supra*, 594 N.Y.S.2d at 25 ("determination of this appeal should not hinge on the circumstance that Reliance made restitution by way of settlement instead of in satisfaction of a judgment after trial"). It would mean, as Level 3's lawyer confirmed at argument, that if Level 3, seeing the handwriting on the wall, had agreed to pay the plaintiffs in the fraud suit all they were asking for (a very large amount-almost $70 million), which they surely would not have done had there been no evidence of fraud (no rational defendant settles a nuisance suit for the full amount demanded in the complaint, unless the amount is trivial), Federal would still be obligated to reimburse Level 3 for that amount. And that would enable Level 3 to retain the profit it had made from a fraud. In fact Level 3 settled with the plaintiffs in the fraud suit for the not inconsiderable amount of

$12 million after the trial had begun and much of the expense of defending the suit had therefore already been incurred. It is not surprising, therefore, that Level 3 has made no attempt to show that the fraud suit was groundless and the settlement merely an effort to avoid the expense of defending a nuisance suit.

If Level 3 *had* shown that the fraud suit was groundless, that there was no ill-gotten gain that insurance would enable it to keep, would the $12 million be a "loss" within the meaning of the policy? Federal argues no, that all that matters is that the payment by the insured for which reimbursement is sought be in respect of a claim of fraudulent appropriation. Level 3 denies this. We need not decide; and prudence is definitely the better part of valor here, since we can find no guidance on the point from cases or other materials.

The judgment is reversed with instructions to enter judgment for the defendant.

NOTE

1. *Level 3 Criticism*. The *Level 3* decision is subject to extensive criticism.[6]

First, as also noted by another legal scholar, the Seventh Circuit used provocative language such as "thief" and "stolen" to describe the policyholder and the amount paid to settle the claims even though it is standard business practice in the corporate world for companies to acquire other companies in exchange for stock and to do so for as little as possible. The fact that an acquired company may actually be worth more than the purchase price does not mean the buyer "stole" the company. Nonetheless, under the reasoning of the Seventh Circuit, any deal that turns out to be unfavorable for one of the parties could be characterized as a form of theft.

Second, the Seventh Circuit essentially held the policyholder would have to prove its conduct was not fraudulent in order to recover under a D&O policy even though the policyholder settled without an admission of liability or fault. Such a holding is simply wrong from a legal perspective because insurers bear the burden of proving that the conduct at issue falls within an exclusion that precludes coverage.

Third, in order to make an insurance coverage determination, a court is supposed to evaluate only: 1) the allegations in the underlying complaint (for the duty to defend) and the findings of fact (for indemnity if the case is tried), 2) the relevant policy language, 3) the purpose of the insurance, and 4) the rules of policy interpretation. The court should not be evaluating whether the amount of the settlement was a "nuisance" value settlement or an implicit admission of wrongdoing. Thus, the Seventh Circuit erred in *Level 3* by

[6] This Note is taken verbatim from Christopher C. French, *The Insurability of Claims for Restitution*, 18 U. Pa. J. Bus. L. 599, 631–633 (2016) (citations omitted).

analyzing whether, in the court's judgment, the settlement was fair to the underlying claimants or was an implicit admission of wrongdoing.

Fourth, when the *Level 3* decision is closely analyzed, one will note that the Seventh Circuit spent very little time actually discussing or analyzing: (1) the actual policy language at issue, which did not expressly exclude coverage for claims for restitution or (2) whether the insurer agreed to provide the coverage for the claims at issue under the terms of the policy in exchange for a premium. In fact, the underlying claims at issue in *Level 3* were fairly routine security law claims for which corporate managers specifically purchase D&O coverage and for which insurers readily accept premiums. [If the insurer expressly agreed to cover such claims but the insurer can successfully argue it is against public policy to cover such claims, does that mean the insurer sold illusory coverage? Would that be fraudulent? Some courts that have addressed the issue think so. *See, e.g., Alstrin v. St. Paul Mercury Ins. Co.*, 179 F. Supp. 2d 376, 396–98 (D. Del. 2002) ("Given that [the insurer's policy] explicitly covers securities fraud claims . . . If [such claims were not actually covered], there would be little or nothing left to that coverage. Particularly, in a D&O insurance policy, where securities fraud claims are among the most common claims filed against directors and officers, the effect of such an exclusion would be particularly devastating.").]

[Although not discussed in the case, D&O policies typically contain insuring agreement language worded as follows: "If during the policy period any claim or claims are made against the Insureds . . . for a Wrongful Act (as hereinafter defined) while acting in their individual or collective capacity as Directors or Officers, the Insurer will pay on behalf of the Insureds or any of them [100%] of all Loss (as hereinafter defined), which the Insureds or any of them shall become legally obligated to pay. . . ." *International Insurance Co. v. Alfred M. Johns*, 874 F.2d 1447, 1452 n.9 (11th Cir. 1989). "Wrongful Act" is often defined as: "Any actual or alleged error or misstatement or misleading statement or act or neglect or breach of duty by the Insureds while acting in their individual or collective capacities, or any matter not excluded by the terms and conditions of this policy claimed against them solely by reason of their being Directors or Officers of the Company." *Id.* "Loss" is defined as: "Any amount which the Insureds are legally obligated to pay for a claim or claims made against them for Wrongful Acts, and shall include but not be limited to damages, judgments, settlements and costs, costs of investigation . . . and defense of legal actions, claims or proceedings and appeals therefrom, cost of attachment or similar bonds; providing always, however, such subject of loss shall not include fines or penalties imposed by law, or matters which may be deemed uninsurable under the law pursuant to which this policy shall be construed." *Id.* Under such provisions, there can be little question that securities claims seeking to recover for allegedly inflated stock prices due to misstatements by a corporate manager are covered "losses" due to a "Wrongful Act."]

Finally, insurers do not need the judicial activism evidenced in the *Level 3* decision in order to avoid liability for claims for restitution because insurers draft the language contained in policies and they can and do expressly exclude coverage for such relief when they desire to do so. In short, because insurance policies are contracts of adhesion drafted by sophisticated insurers, the Seventh Circuit should have interpreted and applied the terms of the policy subject to the rules of policy interpretation instead of substituting its own view of justice.

J.P. MORGAN SECURITIES INC. V. VIGILANT INS. CO.

992 N.E.2d 1076 (N.Y. 2013)

OPINION OF THE COURT

GRAFFEO, J.

In this insurance dispute arising from the insured's monetary settlement of a Securities and Exchange Commission (SEC) proceeding and related private litigation predicated on the insured's violations of federal securities laws, we conclude that the insurers are not entitled to a CPLR 3211 dismissal of the insured's coverage claims. We therefore reverse and reinstate the insured's complaint.

In 2003, the SEC and other regulatory entities undertook an investigation of Bear Stearns & Co., Inc., a broker-dealer, and Bear Stearns Securities Corp., a clearing firm, for allegedly facilitating late trading and deceptive market timing on behalf of certain customers (predominately large hedge funds) for the purchase and sale of shares in mutual funds.[1] During the course of the investigation, the SEC notified Bear Stearns of its intention to commence a civil proceeding charging Bear Stearns with violations of federal securities laws and seeking injunctive relief and sanctions of $720 million. Bear Stearns disputed the proposed charges in a "Wells Submission" in which it claimed that, as a clearing broker that processed transactions initiated by others, it did not knowingly violate any law; its management did not facilitate the late trading or market timing; and it did not share in the profits or benefits from the late trading, from which it received only $16.9 million in commissions.

Nevertheless, Bear Stearns made a formal offer of settlement in November 2005. The SEC accepted the offer and in March 2006 it issued an "Order Instituting Administrative and Cease-and-Desist Proceedings, Making Findings, and Imposing Remedial Sanctions" (the SEC order). "Solely for

[1] Late trading is the practice of placing orders to buy, redeem or exchange mutual fund shares after the 4:00 p.m. close of trading, but receiving the price based on the net asset value set at the close of trading. The practice allows traders to obtain improper profits by using information obtained after the close of trading. Market timing involves the frequent buying and selling of shares of the same mutual fund or the buying or selling of mutual fund shares to exploit inefficiencies in mutual fund pricing. Although market timing is not per se improper, it can be deceptive if it induces a mutual fund to accept trades it otherwise would not accept under its own market timing policies.

the purpose of these proceedings" and "without admitting or denying the findings," Bear Stearns agreed to pay $160 million as "disgorgement" and $90 million as a civil penalty.[2] The agreed-upon $250 million payment was deposited in a fund to compensate any mutual fund investors who had been harmed by Bear Stearns' conduct. The SEC order provided that, "[t]o preserve the deterrent effect of the civil penalty," Bear Stearns agreed that it would not benefit from an offset in any related private litigation for sums distributed to those private litigants that were attributable to the $90 million penalty. The SEC order did not contain a similar restriction regarding the right to offset the $160 million disgorgement payment.

The SEC order also set forth detailed findings stating that, between 1999 and 2003, Bear Stearns "facilitated a substantial amount of late trading and deceptive market timing"; "knowingly or recklessly processed thousands of late trades"; "took no steps to alter [its] procedures or to implement effective measures to stop deceptive timing"; "took affirmative steps to hide from mutual funds the identity of customers that were known market timers by, for example, assigning multiple account numbers to customers"; and "knew or [was] reckless in not knowing" that its brokers' use of multiple account numbers for certain customers "would be used for market timing." Based on its role in supporting the late trading and market timing activities of its customers, the SEC found that Bear Stearns "willfully" violated section 17(a) of the Securities Act of 1933 (*see* 15 USC § 77q [a]); sections 10(b) and 15(c) of the Securities Exchange Act of 1934 (*see* 15 USC §§ 78j [b]; 78*o* [c]); and SEC Rules 10b–5 and 22c–1 (a) (*see* 17 CFR 240.10b–5, 270.22c–1 [a]).

Meanwhile, during the pendency of the SEC matter, Bear Stearns was named as a defendant in a number of private class action lawsuits brought by various mutual funds based on similar late trading and market timing allegations. Following the SEC settlement and the establishment of the $250 million fund, Bear Stearns settled the private actions for $14 million. According to Bear Stearns, it incurred $40 million in defense costs attributable to defending both the SEC proceeding and the private litigation.

Bear Stearns then sought indemnification from its insurers—defendants Vigilant Insurance Company, its primary carrier, and six excess carriers (collectively, the Insurers). It requested indemnity for three claims: the $160 million SEC disgorgement payment (less a $10 million self-insured retention); $40 million in defense costs; and the $14 million private settlement. Bear Stearns did not seek coverage for the $90 million SEC penalty.

---

[2] Defendants in SEC enforcement proceedings commonly consent to sanctions without admitting or denying guilt (*see* 6 Hazen, Treatise on the Law of Securities Regulation § 16.2[1][B] at 171 [6th ed. 2009]).

The primary professional liability policy, to which the excess policies follow form, provides that the Insurers are to "pay on behalf of [Bear Stearns] all Loss which [Bear Stearns] shall become legally obligated to pay as a result of any Claim . . . for any Wrongful Act of [Bear Stearns]." "Loss" is defined as:

> "(1) compensatory damages, multiplied damages, punitive damages where insurable by law, judgments, settlements, costs, charges and expenses or other sums [Bear Stearns] shall legally become obligated to pay as damages resulting from any Claim or Claim(s);
>
> "(2) costs, charges and expenses or other damages incurred in connection with any investigation by any governmental body or self-regulatory organization (SRO), provided however, Loss shall not include:
>
> > "(i) fines or penalties imposed by law; or . . .
> >
> > "(v) matters which are uninsurable under the law pursuant to which this policy shall be construed."

The term "Wrongful Act" under the policy means "any actual or alleged act, error, omission, misstatement, misleading statement, neglect or breach of duty by [Bear Stearns]." A "Claim" includes both private civil actions as well as investigations and proceedings initiated by governmental bodies or SROs. The Insurers had no separate duty to defend; rather, defense costs expended by Bear Stearns could be recouped if they fell within the definition of Loss. Finally, although the policy contains an exclusion for "deliberate, dishonest, fraudulent or criminal" acts or omissions, it provides that Bear Stearns would remain "protected under the terms of this policy" unless and until a "judgment or other final adjudication" established that Bear Stearns committed such acts or omissions.

After the Insurers denied coverage for all three claims, plaintiffs J.P. Morgan Securities Inc., J.P. Morgan Clearing Corp. and The Bear Stearns Companies LLC (collectively, Bear Stearns) commenced this breach of contract and declaratory judgment action against the Insurers. Bear Stearns asserted that its claims all fell within the definition of Loss and alleged that a substantial portion of the SEC disgorgement payment ($140 million) represented illicit profits obtained by its hedge fund customers rather than gains enjoyed by Bear Stearns itself. The Insurers moved to dismiss the complaint pursuant to CPLR 3211(a)(1) and (7) arguing, among other things, that Bear Stearns could not be indemnified for any portion of the SEC disgorgement payment as a matter of public policy.

Supreme Court denied the Insurers' dismissal motions, holding that it was unable to conclude, on the basis of the SEC order alone, that the $160 million disgorgement payment was "specifically linked" to Bear Stearns' improperly acquired funds, as opposed to profits that flowed to its customers (2010 N.Y. Slip Op. 33799[U], *10 [2010]). The Appellate Division reversed and dismissed the complaint in its entirety, holding that, as a matter of public policy, Bear Stearns could not seek recoupment of the $160 million disgorgement payment (91 A.D.3d 226, 936 N.Y.S.2d 102 [1st Dept.2011]). We granted Bear Stearns leave to appeal (19 N.Y.3d 806, 950 N.Y.S.2d 104, 973 N.E.2d 202 [2012]).

Bear Stearns submits that the Appellate Division erred in concluding, as a matter of law, that it could not pursue coverage under its policies for any of the $160 million SEC disgorgement payment. It acknowledges that it is reasonable to preclude an insured from obtaining indemnity for the disgorgement of its own ill-gotten gains, but contends that it was not unjustly enriched by at least $140 million of the disgorgement payment because that portion was attributable to the profits of its customers. In response, the Insurers do not earnestly dispute that the claims fall within the policy's definition of Loss. Rather, they posit that the Appellate Division correctly concluded, for public policy reasons, that Bear Stearns should not be entitled to seek indemnity for the $160 million disgorgement payment because Bear Stearns enabled its customers to make millions through its trading tactics. The Insurers also argue that there is a separately applicable public policy category that prohibits insurance coverage for intentionally-caused harm. Aside from these two public policy rationales, the Insurers also invoke two insurance policy exclusions, one applicable to all the Insurers and one limited to an excess carrier.

At the outset, the rules governing CPLR 3211 motions to dismiss are well established. In assessing the adequacy of a complaint under CPLR 3211(a)(7), the court must give the pleading a liberal construction, accept the facts alleged in the complaint to be true and afford the plaintiff "the benefit of every possible favorable inference." Whether the plaintiff "can ultimately establish its allegations is not part of the calculus in determining a motion to dismiss." And to prevail on a motion to dismiss pursuant to CPLR 3211(a)(1), the moving party (here, the Insurers) must establish that the documentary evidence "conclusively refutes" the plaintiff's allegations.

Analysis of the claims in this action begins with the basic principle that insurance contracts, like other agreements, will ordinarily be enforced as written. Freedom of contract "is deeply rooted in public policy." As a result, parties to an insurance arrangement may generally "contract as they wish and the courts will enforce their agreements without passing on the substance of them" (*Slayko v. Security Mut. Ins. Co.,* 774 N.E.2d 208 (N.Y. 2002) (explaining that courts "are reluctant to inhibit freedom of contract by finding insurance policy clauses violative of public policy").

Our cases, however, have recognized two situations in which a countervailing public policy will override the freedom to contract, thereby precluding enforcement of an insurance agreement. First, an insurer may not indemnify an insured for a punitive damages award, and a policy provision purporting to provide such coverage is unenforceable. The rationale underlying this public policy exception emphasizes that allowing coverage "would defeat the purpose of punitive damages, which is to punish and to deter others from acting similarly." Second, as a matter of public policy, an insured may not seek coverage when it engages in conduct "with the intent to cause injury." *Austro v. Niagara Mohawk Power Corp.,* 66 N.Y.2d 674, 676, 496 N.Y.S.2d 410, 487 N.E.2d 267 (1985) ("Indemnification agreements are unenforceable as violative of public policy only to the extent that they purport to indemnify a party for damages flowing from the intentional causation of injury.").

Relying on the findings in the SEC order, the Insurers claim that the latter public policy exception for intentional injury precludes coverage of any of Bear Stearns' claims. The Insurers note that the SEC order determined that Bear Stearns willfully violated numerous federal securities laws through its active facilitation of late trading and market timing activities on behalf of its hedge fund customers. But the public policy exception for intentionally harmful conduct is a narrow one, under which it must be established not only that the insured acted intentionally but, further, that it acted with the intent to harm or injure others (*see Public Serv. Mut. Ins. Co. v. Goldfarb,* 425 N.E.2d 810 (N.Y. 1981) ("Whether such coverage is permissible depends upon whether the insured, in committing his criminal act, intended to cause injury.")). On the limited record before us, we are unable to say, as a matter of law, that this public policy exception clearly bars Bear Stearns' coverage claims. The SEC order, while undoubtedly finding Bear Stearns' numerous securities laws violations to be willful, does not conclusively demonstrate that Bear Stearns also had the requisite intent to cause harm.[6]

The Insurers also maintain—and the Appellate Division agreed—that, on a separate public policy ground, Bear Stearns is not entitled to recover any portion of the $160 million SEC disgorgement payment. Although we have not considered the issue, other courts have held that the risk of being ordered to return ill-gotten gains—disgorgement—is not insurable. Some courts reached this conclusion because, as a matter of contract interpretive principles, the return of improperly acquired funds does not constitute a "loss" or "damages" within the meaning of insurance policies (*see e.g. Level 3 Communications, Inc. v. Federal Ins. Co.,* 272 F.3d 908, 910 (7th Cir.2001)

[6] Notably, the Insurers did not predicate their dismissal motions on the exclusion in the insurance policy for "deliberate, dishonest, fraudulent or criminal" acts or omissions. The parties apparently dispute whether Bear Stearns' conduct fell within the meaning of this language and, if so, whether the SEC order is a "judgment or other final adjudication"—a prerequisite for the application of the exclusion. We have no occasion to address these questions on this appeal.

(stating that "a 'loss' within the meaning of an insurance contract does not include the restoration of an ill-gotten gain"); *Vigilant Ins. Co. v. Credit Suisse First Boston Corp.*, 782 N.Y.S.2d 19 (1st Dept. 2004) (same)). Others have emphasized that public policy prohibits an insured from receiving indemnification for the disgorgement of its own illicit gains (*see Bank of the W. v. Superior Ct.*, 833 P.2d 545, 555 (Cal. 1992) ("Otherwise, the wrongdoer would retain the proceeds of his illegal acts, merely shifting his loss to an insurer.")).

Bear Stearns does not disagree with these principles, but urges that they do not prohibit coverage here since the bulk of the disgorgement payment—approximately $140 million—represented the improper profits acquired by third-party hedge fund customers, not revenue that Bear Stearns itself pocketed. Put differently, Bear Stearns alleges that much of the payment, although labeled disgorgement by the SEC, did not actually represent the disgorgement of its own profits. It submits that the rule precluding coverage for disgorgement should apply only where the insured requests coverage for the disgorgement of its own illicit gains. On the record before us, we agree with Bear Stearns that the Insurers are not entitled to dismissal of its coverage claim premised on the SEC disgorgement payment.

In the context of these dismissal motions, we must assume Bear Stearns' allegations to be true unless conclusively refuted by the relevant documentary evidence, in this case, the SEC order. Contrary to the Insurers' position, the SEC order does not establish that the $160 million disgorgement payment was predicated on moneys that Bear Stearns itself improperly earned as a result of its securities violations. Rather, the SEC order recites that Bear Stearns' misconduct enabled its "customers to generate hundreds of millions of dollars in profits." Hence, at this CPLR 3211 stage, the documentary evidence does not decisively repudiate Bear Stearns' allegation that the SEC disgorgement payment amount was calculated in large measure on the profits of others.

Moreover, the cases upon which the Insurers rely are distinguishable (*see e.g. Millennium Partners, L.P. v. Select Ins. Co.*, 889 N.Y.S.2d 575 (1st Dept. 2009), *appeal dismissed*, 927 N.E.2d 558 (N.Y. 2010); *Credit Suisse*, 782 N.Y.S.2d 19). In each, the insured was barred from obtaining coverage for SEC-ordered disgorgement because the SEC's findings "conclusively link[ed]" the disgorgement payment to improperly acquired funds in the hands of the insured. In other words, they directly implicated the policy rationale for precluding indemnity for disgorgement—to present the unjust enrichment of the insured by allowing it to, in effect, retain the ill-gotten gains by transferring the loss to its carrier. In this case, in contrast, Bear Stearns alleges that it is not pursuing recoupment for the turnover of its own improperly acquired profits and, therefore, it would not be unjustly enriched by securing indemnity. The Insurers have not identified a single precedent, from New York or otherwise, in which coverage was prohibited where, as Bear Stearns claims, the disgorgement payment was (at least in large part) linked to gains that went to others. Consequently, at this early juncture, we conclude that the Insurers are not entitled to dismissal of Bear Stearns' insurance claims related to the SEC disgorgement payment.

. . . .

In sum, although we certainly do not condone the late trading and market timing activities described in the SEC order, the Insurers have not met their heavy burden of establishing, as a matter of law on their CPLR 3211 dismissal motions, that Bear Stearns is barred from pursuing insurance coverage under its policies.

Accordingly, the order of the Appellate Division should be reversed, with costs, and defendants' motions to dismiss the complaint denied.

NOTES AND QUESTIONS

1. *Level 3 or J.P. Morgan?* Are the holdings in *Level 3* and *J.P. Morgan* reconcilable? Which case has the more compelling reasoning?

2. *Insurer Fraud?* Should insurers be allowed to sell insurance that expressly covers certain types of claims and then be allowed to argue it is against public policy to cover such claims? Should the insurer be required to refund the premiums if it does so? What if the policyholder has detrimentally relied upon the presence of insurance?

3. *State Legislatures Views of Public Policy*. Statutes and the Constitution are supposed to be the primary source of public policy, with courts making their own determinations when statutes and the Constitution fail to address an issue. *See, e.g.*, Restatement (Second) of Contracts, § 178(1) (1979) (A contract term is unenforceable "if legislation provides that it is unenforceable or the interest in its enforcement is clearly outweighed in the circumstances by a public policy against the enforcement of such terms."). In the area of allowing insurance for shareholder claims against corporate officers and directors, state legislatures have spoken. *See* Christopher C. French, *The Insurability of Claims for Restitution*, 18 U. Pa. J. Bus. L. 599, 615 (2016) ("[M]any states, including Delaware where over 50% of all publicly traded corporations and over 63% of the Fortune 500 are incorporated, have passed statutes that allow companies to indemnify corporate managers for many types of misconduct and to purchase insurance to cover the losses they are allowed to indemnify as well as the ones they are unable to indemnify.") (citations omitted); *see also* Tom Baker & Sean J. Griffith, Ensuring Corporate Misconduct: How Liability Insurance Undermines Shareholder Litigation 43–44 (2010).

4. *Differences Between CGL Policies and Claims-Made Policies.* Although the insurance industry unsuccessfully attempted to replace occurrence-based Commercial General Liability insurance with claims-made

Commercial General Liability insurance in the mid-1980s, insurers were successful in shifting policyholders to claims-made insurance for most newer lines of liability insurance, including D&O, Medical and Legal Malpractice, Employment Practices, Cyber Risk, E&O, and Environmental Liability insurance. As the above discussion reveals, the differences between occurrence-based insurance and claims-made insurance are extensive. This book touches upon just a few of the differences.

a. *Consequences of Late Notice*. Late notice is handled differently depending on whether the policy is occurrence-based or claims-made. Under occurrence-based policies, the insurer usually must prove that it was materially prejudiced by the policyholder providing late notice of a claim before the policyholder forfeits coverage. Under claims-made policies, a showing of prejudice is usually not required as a predicate to invalidating the coverage. Why is this so?

b. *Trigger Issues*. Occurrence-based insurance is triggered if an injury or damage occurs during the policy period. Under claims-made insurance, coverage typically is triggered if both the event giving rise to the injury occurs during the policy period (or after the retroactive date) and the claim is tendered during the policy period.

In addition, under occurrence-based insurance, multiple policy periods may be required to cover a claim if the injury occurs over multiple policy periods, as is common for certain types of toxic tort claims and environmental claims. On the other hand, claims-made insurance policies typically contain "channeling" language that purports to limit coverage for the injury to the first policy period during which the injury begins or a claim related to the injury is asserted against the policyholder.

c. *Duty to Defend and Settlement Obligations*. Unlike occurrence-based policies, insurers typically do not have a duty to defend the policyholder or the right to settle claims asserted against the policyholder under claims-made insurance. Instead, the policyholder defends itself and makes settlement decisions subject to the insurers' approval, which cannot unreasonably be withheld. Defense costs are covered "losses" to the extent the claims asserted against the policyholder are covered claims. Consequently, there is often an allocation of defense and settlement costs between covered and non-covered claims.

d. *What Constitutes a "Claim" That Must Be Reported?* There is a greater possibility of the policyholder getting "whipsawed" under claims-made insurance because the policyholder typically is required to report any events that are "reasonably likely" to result in a claim under claims-made insurance. If the policyholder reports such an event, the insurers in subsequent policy years typically will take the position that their policies do not cover any claims related to the event even if the claim is asserted against the policyholder for the first time during their subsequent policy periods. Conversely, the insurer in the policy period in which notice of the event was first given may take the position that no claim was asserted against the policyholder during its policy period so there is no coverage for the claim when a claim is asserted in a subsequent policy period.

e. *"Tail" Coverage: How Does One Go out of Business When Coverage Is Claims-Made?* If the policyholder has insured itself with claims-made coverage and now wishes to go out of business, does this mean the policyholder must continue to buy annual policies indefinitely into the future (or at least until the statute of limitations has reliably run)? The policyholder should anticipate that claims from today's activities might be filed many years in the future, thereby necessitating the need for some kind of coverage. The answer is that the insured wishing to go out of business purchases one policy to cover the years after business operations cease. This is called "Extended Reporting" or "Tail" coverage.

How is occurrence-based coverage different? Under occurrence-based insurance, the triggering event is the time at which the injury occurs, which ordinarily (but not always) is near the time of the loss-producing conduct, which is normally (but not always) prior to the cessation of the policyholder's business, and thus at a time when the policyholder still has insurance.

f. *The Perils of Making Changes*. This difference between the claims-made and occurrence-based coverage with respect to the triggering event creates additional problems when a policyholder switches from occurrence-based to claims-made insurance or switches between claims-made insurers in subsequent policy periods. When this happens, a gap in coverage might be created for claims asserted against the policyholder for the first time during the policy period of a subsequent insurer but which result from the policyholder's conduct during the occurrence-based policy period or a prior claims-made policy period. Although less common, the same problem can arise if the policyholder switches from claims-made insurance to occurrence-based insurance because an injury may predate the purchase of the occurrence-based insurance but not be asserted against the policyholder until the occurrence-based insurance commences, in which case both the claims-made insurer and the occurrence-based insurer likely would deny the claim.

g. *"Interrelated Wrongful Acts."* Under claims-made insurance, disputes often arise regarding whether the claims asserted in multiple lawsuits that span multiple policy periods are due to "Interrelated Wrongful Acts." This is less of problem with occurrence-based insurance because coverage under such policies focuses on when the injuries occur, not whether the same injury-causing acts caused multiple claims during multiple policy periods.

EXERCISE

1. You are the executive director of a local youth hockey organization. The organization has D&O insurance. One of the players in the organization is known to start fights, but the organization allows the player to continue playing because he is a star with a bright future in the game (including the prospect of a generous athletic scholarship when he is ready to go to college). During a game, the player beats up another player, which results in the other player getting a concussion. Should you notify the D&O carrier of the potential of a claim against the organization due to the organization's decision to allow the player to continue playing? Draft a 3-page memo that weighs the pros and cons of giving notice. In your memo, discuss how the organization might avoid being whipsawed by the D&O insurers if the injured player sues after the current policy expires but during a subsequent policy period.

CHAPTER FIVE

AUTOMOBILE INSURANCE

■ ■ ■

> *"Before the advent of motor vehicles, death or serious injury in accidents on the public highway was a rarity; now it is a commonplace. But the people are not more careless now than then; in fact they are more careful, because more fearful. The increase in accidents is due to the danger inherent in the operation of motor vehicles by and among people of average human frailty. It is not preventable by any practical means yet devised. But perhaps the resulting monetary loss may be spread over the motoring class most responsible therefor, partially for their own benefit but with some corresponding benefits to the non-motoring class least responsible. . . . A motor vehicle accident compensation act seems desirable if it can be made workable; but can it?"*
>
> — Ernest C. Carman, a "Member of the Minneapolis Bar," in *Is a Motor Vehicle Accident Compensation Act Advisable?*, 4 Minn. L. Rev. 1, 12–13 (1919)

Automobile accidents are a significant problem. Approximately 40,000 people are killed annually, and more than 3 million people are injured. Ensuring that the people injured or killed by automobiles, and their families, are compensated is the primary driver of insurance law in this area. Indeed, auto insurance is one of the areas of insurance law where public policy often overrides insurers' preferences regarding policy language.

In this chapter, we examine automobile insurance as it stands today, but it already is apparent that significant change will come in the relatively near future. Driverless, or "autonomous," vehicles have operated for millions of miles on our highways already. Although the technologies enabling cars and trucks to operate without a "driver's seat" in all settings are many years away, the transition to this remarkable world is inevitable. This promises enormous changes for the tort liability system as it relates to automobiles and for automobile insurance itself. Insurance regulators, the insurance industry, academics, and the tort bar are discussing how this new liability and victim compensation framework should be structured. We now turn, however, to the world as it exists today—before driverless cars.

As the Sample Policy in the next section reflects, auto insurance policies, like homeowners insurance policies, are hybrid policies that contain both first-party and third-party coverages. The policyholder's automobile is covered if it is damaged (the property coverage), and the policyholder's liabilities for injuries or damage the policyholder causes third parties are also covered (the liability coverage). In addition, if the policyholder is injured and the party responsible for causing the injuries is unknown, uninsured, or underinsured, then the automobile policy also provides compensation for the policyholder's injuries. In addition, the policy may include what is typically modest coverage for the insured's medical expenses resulting from injuries suffered in an auto accident (the "med-pay" coverage, sometimes called "Personal Injury Protection," or "PIP," benefit).

What follows is the 2017 version of ISO's Auto Policy, which is used by many automobile insurers in the United States. A number of companies use their own forms, and companies that operate in different states will typically use forms specially tailored for the requirements and rules of the particular state. The ISO policy form is likely to be accompanied by state-specific endorsements that adapt the general ISO form to the requirements of a particular state. Thus, it is important to read the policy that covers a specific claim. It also is important to read the statutory auto insurance laws because it is not unusual for policy language to be inconsistent with such laws, in which case the statutory law trumps the policy language.

I. SAMPLE AUTO POLICY

PERSONAL AUTO
PP 00 01 09 18

PERSONAL AUTO POLICY

AGREEMENT

In return for payment of the premium and subject to all the terms of this Policy, we agree with you as follows:

DEFINITIONS

A. Throughout this Policy, "you" and "your" refer to:

1. The named insured shown in the Declarations; and

2. The spouse if a resident of the same household.

If the spouse ceases to be a resident of the same household during the policy period or prior to the inception of this Policy, the spouse will be considered "you" and "your" under this Policy but only until the earlier of:

a. The end of 90 days following the spouse's change of residency;

b. The effective date of another policy listing the spouse as a named insured; or

c. The end of the policy period.

B. "We", "us" and "our" refer to the company providing this insurance.

C. For purposes of this Policy, a private passenger type auto, pickup or van shall be deemed to be owned by a person if leased:

1. Under a written agreement to that person; and

2. For a continuous period of at least six months.

Other words and phrases are defined. They are in quotation marks when used.

D. "Bodily injury" means bodily harm, sickness or disease, including death that results.

E. "Business" includes trade, profession or occupation.

F. "Family member" means a person related to you by blood, marriage or adoption who is a resident of your household. This includes a ward or foster child.

G. "Occupying" means:

1. In;

2. Upon; or

3. Getting in, on, out or off.

H. "Property damage" means physical injury to, destruction of or loss of use of tangible property.

I. "Trailer" means a vehicle designed to be pulled by a:

1. Private passenger auto; or

2. Pickup or van.

It also means a farm wagon or farm implement while towed by a vehicle listed in **1.** or **2.** above.

J. "Your covered auto" means:

1. Any vehicle shown in the Declarations;

2. A "newly acquired auto";

3. Any "trailer" you own; or

4. Any auto or "trailer" you do not own while used as a temporary substitute for any other vehicle described in this definition which is out of normal use because of its:

a. Breakdown;

b. Repair;

c. Servicing;

d. Loss; or

e. Destruction.

This provision **(J.4.)** does not apply to Coverage For Damage To Your Auto.

K. "Newly acquired auto":

1. "Newly acquired auto" means any of the following types of vehicles you become the owner of during the policy period:

a. A private passenger auto; or

b. A pickup or van, for which no other insurance policy provides coverage, that:

(1) Has a Gross Vehicle Weight Rating of 10,000 lbs. or less; and

(2) Is not used for the delivery or transportation of goods and materials unless such use is:

(a) Incidental to your "business" of installing, maintaining or repairing furnishings or equipment; or

(b) For farming or ranching.

2. Coverage for a "newly acquired auto" is provided as follows:

a. For any coverage provided in this Policy other than Coverage For Damage To Your Auto, a "newly acquired auto" will have the broadest coverage we now provide for any vehicle shown in the Declarations. However, for this coverage to apply, you must ask us to insure it within 14 days after you become the owner.

b. Collision Coverage for a "newly acquired auto" begins on the date you become the owner. However, for this coverage to apply, you must ask us to insure it within:

(1) 14 days after you become the owner, if the Declarations indicates that Collision Coverage applies to at least one auto. In this case, the "newly acquired auto" will have the broadest coverage we now provide for any auto shown in the Declarations.

(2) Four days after you become the owner, if the Declarations does not indicate that Collision Coverage applies to at least one auto. If you comply with the four-day requirement and a loss occurred before you asked us to insure the "newly acquired auto", a Collision deductible of $500 will apply.

c. Other Than Collision Coverage for a "newly acquired auto" begins on the date you become the owner. However, for this coverage to apply, you must ask us to insure it within:

(1) 14 days after you become the owner, if the Declarations indicates that Other Than Collision Coverage applies to at least one auto. In this case, the "newly acquired auto" will have the broadest coverage we now provide for any auto shown in the Declarations.

(2) Four days after you become the owner, if the Declarations does not indicate that Other Than Collision Coverage applies to at least one auto. If you comply with the four-day requirement and a loss occurred before you asked us to insure the "newly acquired auto", an Other Than Collision deductible of $500 will apply.

d. For all coverages addressed in Paragraphs **K.2.a., b.** and **c.,** if you first ask us to insure the "newly acquired auto" after the applicable time period has elapsed, coverage will begin on the day you first ask us to insure the "newly acquired auto".

L. "Transportation network platform" means an online-enabled application or digital network used to connect passengers with drivers using vehicles for the purpose of providing prearranged transportation services for compensation.

PART A – LIABILITY COVERAGE

INSURING AGREEMENT

A. We will pay damages for "bodily injury" or "property damage" for which any "insured" becomes legally responsible because of an auto accident. Damages include prejudgment interest awarded against the "insured". We will settle or defend, as we consider appropriate, any claim or suit asking for these damages. In addition to our limit of liability, we will pay all defense costs we incur. Our duty to settle or defend ends when our limit of liability for this coverage has been exhausted by payment of judgments or settlements. We have no duty to defend any suit or settle any claim for "bodily injury" or "property damage" not covered under this Policy.

B. "Insured" as used in this Part means:

1. You or any "family member" for the ownership, maintenance or use of any auto or "trailer".

2. Any person using "your covered auto".

3. For "your covered auto", any person or organization but only with respect to legal responsibility for acts or omissions of a person for whom coverage is afforded under this Part.

4. For any auto or "trailer", other than "your covered auto", any other person or organization but only with respect to legal responsibility for acts or omissions of you or any "family member" for whom coverage is afforded under this Part. This provision **(B.4.)** applies only if the person or organization does not own or hire the auto or "trailer".

SUPPLEMENTARY PAYMENTS

We will pay on behalf of an "insured":

1. Up to $250 for the cost of bail bonds required because of an accident, including related traffic law violations. The accident must result in "bodily injury" or "property damage" covered under this Policy.

2. Premiums on appeal bonds and bonds to release attachments in any suit we defend.
3. Interest accruing after a judgment is entered in any suit we defend. Our duty to pay interest ends when we offer to pay that part of the judgment which does not exceed our limit of liability for this coverage.
4. Up to $250 a day for loss of earnings, but not other income, because of attendance at hearings or trials at our request.
5. Other reasonable expenses incurred at our request.

These payments will not reduce the limit of liability.

EXCLUSIONS

A. We do not provide Liability Coverage for any "insured":

1. Who intentionally causes "bodily injury" or "property damage".

2. For "property damage" to property owned or being transported by that "insured".

3. For "property damage" to property:

a. Rented to;

b. Used by; or

c. In the care of;

that "insured".

This exclusion **(A.3.)** does not apply to "property damage" to a residence or private garage.

4. For "bodily injury" to an employee of that "insured" during the course of employment. This exclusion **(A.4.)** does not apply to "bodily injury" to a domestic employee unless workers' compensation benefits are required or available for that domestic employee.

5. For that "insured's" liability arising out of the ownership or operation of a vehicle while it is being used as a public or livery conveyance. This includes but is not limited to any period of time a vehicle is being used by any "insured" who is logged into a "transportation network platform" as a driver, whether or not a passenger is "occupying" the vehicle.

This exclusion **(A.5.)** does not apply to:

a. A share-the-expense car pool; or

b. The ownership or operation of a vehicle while it is being used for volunteer or charitable purposes.

6. While employed or otherwise engaged in the "business" of:

a. Selling;

b. Repairing;

c. Servicing;

d. Storing; or

e. Parking;

vehicles designed for use mainly on public highways. This includes road testing and delivery. This exclusion **(A.6.)** does not apply to the ownership, maintenance or use of "your covered auto" by:

(1) You;

(2) Any "family member"; or

(3) Any partner, agent or employee of you or any "family member".

7. Maintaining or using any vehicle while that "insured" is employed or otherwise engaged in any "business" (other than farming or ranching) not described in Exclusion **A.6.**

This exclusion **(A.7.)** does not apply to the maintenance or use of a:

a. Private passenger auto;

b. Pickup or van; or

c. "Trailer" used with a vehicle described in **a.** or **b.** above.

8. Using a vehicle without a reasonable belief that that "insured" is entitled to do so. This exclusion **(A.8.)** does not apply to a "family member" using "your covered auto" which is owned by you.

9. For "bodily injury" or "property damage" for which that "insured":

a. Is an insured under a nuclear energy liability policy; or

b. Would be an insured under a nuclear energy liability policy but for its termination upon exhaustion of its limit of liability.

A nuclear energy liability policy is a policy issued by any of the following or their successors:

(1) Nuclear Energy Liability Insurance Association;

(2) Mutual Atomic Energy Liability Underwriters; or

(3) Nuclear Insurance Association of Canada.

10. For the ownership, maintenance or use of "your covered auto" while:

a. Enrolled in a personal vehicle sharing program under the terms of a written agreement; and

b. Being used in connection with such personal vehicle sharing program by anyone other than you or any "family member".

B. We do not provide Liability Coverage for the ownership, maintenance or use of:

1. Any vehicle which:

a. Has fewer than four wheels; or

b. Is designed mainly for use off public roads.

This exclusion **(B.1.)** does not apply:

(1) While such vehicle is being used by an "insured" in a medical emergency;

(2) To any "trailer"; or

(3) To any non-owned golf cart.

2. Any vehicle, other than "your covered auto", which is:

a. Owned by you; or

b. Furnished or available for your regular use.

3. Any vehicle, other than "your covered auto", which is:

a. Owned by any "family member"; or

b. Furnished or available for the regular use of any "family member".

However, this exclusion **(B.3.)** does not apply to you while you are maintaining or "occupying" any vehicle which is:

(1) Owned by a "family member"; or

(2) Furnished or available for the regular use of a "family member".

4. Any vehicle, located inside a facility designed for racing, for the purpose of:

a. Participating or competing in; or

b. Practicing or preparing for;

any prearranged or organized:

(1) Racing or speed contest; or

(2) Driver skill training or driver skill event.

5. Any vehicle which is designed or can be used for flight.

LIMIT OF LIABILITY

A. The Limit Of Liability shown in the Declarations for each person for Bodily Injury Liability is our maximum limit of liability for all damages, including damages for care, loss of services or death, arising out of "bodily injury" sustained by any one person in any one auto accident. Subject to this limit for each person, the Limit Of Liability shown in the Declarations for each accident for Bodily Injury Liability is our maximum limit of liability for all damages for "bodily injury" resulting from any one auto accident.

The Limit Of Liability shown in the Declarations for each accident for Property Damage Liability is our maximum limit of liability for all "property damage" resulting from any one auto accident.

This is the most we will pay regardless of the number of:

1. "Insureds";

2. Claims made;

3. Vehicles or premiums shown in the Declarations; or

4. Vehicles involved in the auto accident.

B. No one will be entitled to receive duplicate payments for the same elements of loss under this coverage and:

1. Part **B** or Part **C** of this Policy; or

2. Any Underinsured Motorists Coverage provided by this Policy.

OUT OF STATE COVERAGE

If an auto accident to which this Policy applies occurs in any state or province other than the one in which "your covered auto" is principally garaged, we will interpret your policy for that accident as follows:

A. If the state or province has:

1. A financial responsibility or similar law specifying limits of liability for "bodily injury" or "property damage" higher than the limit shown in the Declarations, your policy will provide the higher specified limit.

2. A compulsory insurance or similar law requiring a nonresident to maintain insurance whenever the nonresident uses a vehicle in that state or province, your policy will provide at least the required minimum amounts and types of coverage.

B. No one will be entitled to duplicate payments for the same elements of loss.

FINANCIAL RESPONSIBILITY

When this Policy is certified as future proof of financial responsibility, this Policy shall comply with the law to the extent required.

OTHER INSURANCE

If there is other applicable liability insurance, we will pay only our share of the loss. Our share is the proportion that our limit of liability bears to the total of all applicable limits. However, any insurance we provide for a vehicle you do not own, including any vehicle while used as a temporary substitute for "your covered auto", shall be excess over any other collectible insurance except insurance written specifically to cover as excess over the limits of liability that apply in this Policy.

PART B – MEDICAL PAYMENTS COVERAGE

INSURING AGREEMENT

A. We will pay reasonable expenses incurred for necessary medical and funeral services because of "bodily injury":

1. Caused by an accident; and

2. Sustained by an "insured".

We will pay only those expenses incurred for services rendered within three years from the date of the accident.

B. "Insured" as used in this Part means:

1. You or any "family member":

a. While "occupying"; or

b. As a pedestrian when struck by;

a motor vehicle designed for use mainly on public roads or a trailer of any type.

2. Any other person while "occupying" "your covered auto".

EXCLUSIONS

We do not provide Medical Payments Coverage for any "insured" for "bodily injury":

1. Sustained while "occupying" any motorized vehicle having fewer than four wheels.

2. Sustained while "occupying" "your covered auto" when it is being used as a public or livery conveyance. This includes but is not limited to any period of time "your covered auto" is being used by any "insured" who is logged into a "transportation network platform" as a driver, whether or not a passenger is "occupying" the vehicle.

This exclusion **(2.)** does not apply:

a. To a share-the-expense car pool; or

b. While "your covered auto" is being used for volunteer or charitable purposes.

3. Sustained while "occupying" any vehicle located for use as a residence or premises.

4. Occurring during the course of employment if workers' compensation benefits are required or available for the "bodily injury".

5. Sustained while "occupying", or when struck by, any vehicle (other than "your covered auto") which is:

a. Owned by you; or

b. Furnished or available for your regular use.

6. Sustained while "occupying", or when struck by, any vehicle (other than "your covered auto") which is:

a. Owned by any "family member"; or

b. Furnished or available for the regular use of any "family member".

However, this exclusion **(6.)** does not apply to you.

7. Sustained while "occupying" a vehicle without a reasonable belief that that "insured" is entitled to do so. This exclusion **(7.)** does not apply to a "family member" using "your covered auto" which is owned by you.

8. Sustained while "occupying" a vehicle when it is being used in the "business" of an "insured". This exclusion **(8.)** does not apply to "bodily injury" sustained while "occupying" a:

a. Private passenger auto;

b. Pickup or van; or

c. "Trailer" used with a vehicle described in **a.** or **b.** above.

9. Caused by or as a consequence of:

a. Discharge of a nuclear weapon (even if accidental);

b. War (declared or undeclared);

c. Civil war;

d. Insurrection; or

e. Rebellion or revolution.

10. From or as a consequence of the following, whether controlled or uncontrolled or however caused:

a. Nuclear reaction;

b. Radiation; or

c. Radioactive contamination.

11. Sustained while "occupying" any vehicle located inside a facility designed for racing, for the purpose of:

a. Participating or competing in; or

b. Practicing or preparing for;

any prearranged or organized:

(1) Racing or speed contest; or

(2) Driver skill training or driver skill event.

12. Sustained while "occupying", or when struck by, "your covered auto" while:

a. Enrolled in a personal vehicle sharing program under the terms of a written agreement; and

b. Being used in connection with such personal vehicle sharing program by anyone other than you or any "family member".

13. Sustained while "occupying", or when struck by, any vehicle which is designed or can be used for flight.

LIMIT OF LIABILITY

A. The Limit Of Liability shown in the Declarations for this coverage is our maximum limit of liability for each person injured in any one accident. This is the most we will pay regardless of the number of:

1. "Insureds";

2. Claims made;

3. Vehicles or premiums shown in the Declarations; or

4. Vehicles involved in the accident.

B. No one will be entitled to receive duplicate payments for the same elements of loss under this coverage and:

1. Part **A** or Part **C** of this Policy; or

2. Any Underinsured Motorists Coverage provided by this Policy.

OTHER INSURANCE

If there is other applicable auto medical payments insurance, we will pay only our share of the loss. Our share is the proportion that our limit of liability bears to the total of all applicable limits. However, any insurance we provide with respect to a vehicle you do not own, including any vehicle while used as a temporary substitute for "your covered auto", shall be excess over any other collectible auto insurance providing payments for medical or funeral expenses.

PART C – UNINSURED MOTORISTS COVERAGE

INSURING AGREEMENT

A. We will pay compensatory damages which an "insured" is legally entitled to recover from the owner or operator of an "uninsured motor vehicle" because of "bodily injury":

1. Sustained by an "insured"; and

2. Caused by an accident.

The owner's or operator's liability for these damages must arise out of the ownership, maintenance or use of the "uninsured motor vehicle".

Any judgment for damages arising out of a suit brought without our written consent is not binding on us.

B. "Insured" as used in this Part means:

1. You or any "family member";

2. Any other person "occupying" "your covered auto"; or

3. Any person for damages that person is entitled to recover because of "bodily injury" to which this coverage applies sustained by a person described in **1.** or **2.** above.

C. "Uninsured motor vehicle" means a land motor vehicle or trailer of any type:

1. To which no bodily injury liability bond or policy applies at the time of the accident.

2. To which a bodily injury liability bond or policy applies at the time of the accident. In this case its limit for bodily injury liability must be less than the minimum limit for bodily injury liability specified by the financial responsibility law of the state in which "your covered auto" is principally garaged.

3. Which is a hit-and-run vehicle whose operator or owner cannot be identified and which hits:

a. You or any "family member";

b. A vehicle which you or any "family member" are "occupying"; or

c. "Your covered auto".

4. To which a bodily injury liability bond or policy applies at the time of the accident but the bonding or insuring company:

a. Denies coverage; or

b. Is or becomes insolvent.

However, "uninsured motor vehicle" does not include any vehicle or equipment:

(1) Owned by or furnished or available for the regular use of you or any "family member".

(2) Owned or operated by a self-insurer under any applicable motor vehicle law, except a self-insurer which is or becomes insolvent.

(3) Owned by any governmental unit or agency.

(4) Operated on rails or crawler treads.

(5) Designed mainly for use off public roads while not on public roads.

(6) While located for use as a residence or premises.

EXCLUSIONS

A. We do not provide Uninsured Motorists Coverage for "bodily injury" sustained:

1. By an "insured" while "occupying", or when struck by, any motor vehicle owned by that "insured" which is not insured for this coverage under this Policy. This includes a trailer of any type used with that vehicle.

2. By any "family member" while "occupying", or when struck by, any motor vehicle you own which is insured for this coverage on a primary basis under any other policy.

B. We do not provide Uninsured Motorists Coverage for "bodily injury" sustained by any "insured":

1. If that "insured" or the legal representative settles the "bodily injury" claim and such settlement prejudices our right to recover payment.
2. While "occupying" "your covered auto" when it is being used as a public or livery conveyance. This includes but is not limited to any period of time "your covered auto" is being used by any "insured" who is logged into a "transportation network platform" as a driver, whether or not a passenger is "occupying" the vehicle.

   This exclusion **(B.2.)** does not apply:

   a. To a share-the-expense car pool; or

   b. While "your covered auto" is being used for volunteer or charitable purposes.
3. Using a vehicle without a reasonable belief that that "insured" is entitled to do so. This exclusion **(B.3.)** does not apply to a "family member" using "your covered auto" which is owned by you.
4. While "occupying", or when struck by, "your covered auto" while:

   a. Enrolled in a personal vehicle sharing program under the terms of a written agreement; and

   b. Being used in connection with such personal vehicle sharing program by anyone other than you or any "family member".
5. While "occupying", or when struck by, any vehicle which is designed or can be used for flight.

C. This coverage shall not apply directly or indirectly to benefit any insurer or self-insurer under any of the following or similar law:

1. Workers' compensation law; or
2. Disability benefits law.

D. We do not provide Uninsured Motorists Coverage for punitive or exemplary damages.

LIMIT OF LIABILITY

A. The Limit Of Liability shown in the Declarations for each person for Uninsured Motorists Coverage is our maximum limit of liability for all damages, including damages for care, loss of services or death, arising out of "bodily injury" sustained by any one person in any one accident. Subject to this limit for each person, the Limit Of Liability shown in the Declarations for each accident for Uninsured Motorists Coverage is our maximum limit of liability for all damages for "bodily injury" resulting from any one accident.

This is the most we will pay regardless of the number of:

1. "Insureds";
2. Claims made;
3. Vehicles or premiums shown in the Declarations; or
4. Vehicles involved in the accident.

B. No one will be entitled to receive duplicate payments for the same elements of loss under this coverage and:

1. Part **A** or Part **B** of this Policy; or
2. Any Underinsured Motorists Coverage provided by this Policy.

C. We will not make a duplicate payment under this coverage for any element of loss for which payment has been made by or on behalf of persons or organizations who may be legally responsible.

D. We will not pay for any element of loss if a person is entitled to receive payment for the same element of loss under any of the following or similar law:

1. Workers' compensation law; or
2. Disability benefits law.

OTHER INSURANCE

If there is other applicable insurance available under one or more policies or provisions of coverage that is similar to the insurance provided under this Part of the Policy:

1. Any recovery for damages under all such policies or provisions of coverage may equal but not exceed the highest applicable limit for any one vehicle under any insurance providing coverage on either a primary or excess basis.
2. Any insurance we provide with respect to a vehicle you do not own, including any vehicle while used as a temporary substitute for "your covered auto", shall be excess over any collectible insurance providing such coverage on a primary basis.
3. If the coverage under this Policy is provided:

   a. On a primary basis, we will pay only our share of the loss that must be paid under insurance providing coverage on a primary basis. Our share is the proportion that our limit of liability bears to the total of all applicable limits of liability for coverage provided on a primary basis.

b. On an excess basis, we will pay only our share of the loss that must be paid under insurance providing coverage on an excess basis. Our share is the proportion that our limit of liability bears to the total of all applicable limits of liability for coverage provided on an excess basis.

ARBITRATION

A. If we and an "insured" do not agree:

1. Whether that "insured" is legally entitled to recover damages; or

2. As to the amount of damages which are recoverable by that "insured";

from the owner or operator of an "uninsured motor vehicle", then the matter may be arbitrated. However, disputes concerning coverage under this Part may not be arbitrated.

Both parties must agree to arbitration. If so agreed, each party will select an arbitrator. The two arbitrators will select a third. If they cannot agree within 30 days, either may request that selection be made by a judge of a court having jurisdiction.

B. Each party will:

1. Pay the expenses it incurs; and

2. Bear the expenses of the third arbitrator equally.

C. Unless both parties agree otherwise, arbitration will take place in the county in which the "insured" lives. Local rules of law as to procedure and evidence will apply. A decision agreed to by at least two of the arbitrators will be binding as to:

1. Whether the "insured" is legally entitled to recover damages; and

2. The amount of damages. This applies only if the amount does not exceed the minimum limit for bodily injury liability specified by the financial responsibility law of the state in which "your covered auto" is principally garaged. If the amount exceeds that limit, either party may demand the right to a trial. This demand must be made within 60 days of the arbitrators' decision. If this demand is not made, the amount of damages agreed to by the arbitrators will be binding.

PART D – COVERAGE FOR DAMAGE TO YOUR AUTO

INSURING AGREEMENT

A. We will pay for direct and accidental loss to "your covered auto" or any "non-owned auto", including its equipment, minus any applicable deductible shown in the Declarations. If loss to more than one "your covered auto" or "non-owned auto" results from the same "collision", only the highest applicable deductible will apply. We will pay for loss to "your covered auto" caused by:

1. Other than "collision" only if the Declarations indicates that Other Than Collision Coverage is provided for that auto.

2. "Collision" only if the Declarations indicates that Collision Coverage is provided for that auto.

If there is a loss to a "non-owned auto", we will provide the broadest coverage applicable to any "your covered auto" shown in the Declarations.

B. "Collision" means the upset of "your covered auto" or a "non-owned auto" or its impact with another vehicle or object.

Loss caused by the following is considered other than "collision":

1. Missiles or falling objects;

2. Fire;

3. Theft or larceny;

4. Explosion or earthquake;

5. Windstorm;

6. Hail, water or flood;

7. Malicious mischief or vandalism;

8. Riot or civil commotion;

9. Contact with bird or animal; or

10. Breakage of glass.

If breakage of glass is caused by a "collision", you may elect to have it considered a loss caused by "collision".

C. "Non-owned auto" means:

1. Any private passenger auto, pickup, van or "trailer" not owned by or furnished or available for the regular use of you or any "family member" while in the custody of or being operated by you or any "family member"; or

2. Any auto or "trailer" you do not own while used as a temporary substitute for "your covered auto" which is out of normal use because of its:
   a. Breakdown;
   b. Repair;
   c. Servicing;
   d. Loss; or
   e. Destruction.

D. "Custom equipment" means equipment, furnishings and parts in or upon any auto, other than:
   1. Original manufacturer equipment, furnishings or parts; or
   2. Any replacement of original manufacturer equipment, furnishings or parts with other equipment, furnishings or parts of like kind and quality.

   "Custom equipment" includes but is not limited to:
   a. Special carpeting or insulation;
   b. Furniture or bars;
   c. Height-extending roofs;
   d. Body, engine, exhaust or suspension enhancers;
   e. Winches, or anti-roll or anti-sway bars;
   f. Custom grilles, louvers, side pipes, hood scoops or spoilers;
   g. Custom wheels, tires or spinners;
   h. Custom chrome, murals, paintwork, decals or other graphics; or
   i. Caps, covers or bedliners.

   "Custom equipment" does not include electronic equipment that reproduces, receives or transmits audio, visual or data signals.

TRANSPORTATION EXPENSES

A. In addition, we will pay, without application of a deductible, up to a maximum of $900 for:
   1. Temporary transportation expenses not exceeding $30 per day incurred by you in the event of a loss to "your covered auto". We will pay for such expenses if the loss is caused by:
      a. Other than "collision" only if the Declarations indicates that Other Than Collision Coverage is provided for that auto.
      b. "Collision" only if the Declarations indicates that Collision Coverage is provided for that auto.
   2. Expenses for which you become legally responsible in the event of loss to a "non-owned auto". We will pay for such expenses if the loss is caused by:
      a. Other than "collision" only if the Declarations indicates that Other Than Collision Coverage is provided for any "your covered auto".
      b. "Collision" only if the Declarations indicates that Collision Coverage is provided for any "your covered auto".

   However, the most we will pay for any expenses for loss of use is $30 per day.

B. Subject to the provisions of Paragraph **A.**, if the loss is caused by:
   1. A total theft of "your covered auto" or a "non-owned auto", we will pay only expenses incurred during the period:
      a. Beginning 48 hours after the theft; and
      b. Ending when "your covered auto" or the "non-owned auto" is returned to use or we pay for its loss.
   2. Other than theft of a "your covered auto" or a "non-owned auto", we will pay only expenses beginning when the auto is withdrawn from use for more than 24 hours.

Our payment will be limited to that period of time reasonably required to repair or replace the "your covered auto" or the "non-owned auto".

EXCLUSIONS

We will not pay for:

1. Loss to "your covered auto" or any "non-owned auto" which occurs while it is being used as a public or livery conveyance. This includes but is not limited to any period of time "your covered auto" or any "non-owned auto" is being used by any person who is logged into a "transportation network platform" as a driver, whether or not a passenger is "occupying" the vehicle.

   This exclusion **(1.)** does not apply:
   a. To a share-the-expense car pool; or
   b. While "your covered auto" or any "non-owned auto" is being used for volunteer or charitable purposes.
2. Damage due and confined to:
   a. Wear and tear;
   b. Freezing;

c. Mechanical or electrical breakdown or failure; or

d. Road damage to tires.

This exclusion **(2.)** does not apply if the damage results from the total theft of "your covered auto" or any "non-owned auto".

3. Loss due to or as a consequence of:

a. Radioactive contamination;

b. Discharge of any nuclear weapon (even if accidental);

c. War (declared or undeclared);

d. Civil war;

e. Insurrection; or

f. Rebellion or revolution.

4. Loss to any electronic equipment that reproduces, receives or transmits audio, visual or data signals. This includes but is not limited to:

a. Radios and stereos;

b. Tape decks;

c. Compact disc systems;

d. Navigation systems;

e. Internet access systems;

f. Personal computers;

g. Video entertainment systems;

h. Telephones;

i. Televisions;

j. Two-way mobile radios;

k. Scanners; or

l. Citizens band radios.

This exclusion **(4.)** does not apply to electronic equipment that is permanently installed in "your covered auto" or any "non-owned auto".

5. Loss to tapes, records, discs or other media used with equipment described in Exclusion **4.**

6. A total loss to "your covered auto" or any "non-owned auto" due to destruction or confiscation by governmental or civil authorities.

This exclusion **(6.)** does not apply to the interests of Loss Payees in "your covered auto".

7. Loss to:

a. A "trailer", camper body or motor home, which is not shown in the Declarations; or

b. Facilities or equipment used with such "trailer", camper body or motor home. Facilities or equipment include but are not limited to:

(1) Cooking, dining, plumbing or refrigeration facilities;

(2) Awnings or cabanas; or

(3) Any other facilities or equipment used with a "trailer", camper body or motor home.

This exclusion **(7.)** does not apply to a:

a. "Trailer", and its facilities or equipment, which you do not own; or

b. "Trailer", camper body, or the facilities or equipment in or attached to the "trailer" or camper body, which you:

(1) Acquire during the policy period; and

(2) Ask us to insure within 14 days after you become the owner.

8. Loss to any "non-owned auto" when used by you or any "family member" without a reasonable belief that you or that "family member" are entitled to do so.

9. Loss to equipment designed or used for the detection or location of radar or laser.

10. Loss to any "custom equipment" in or upon "your covered auto" or any "non-owned auto".

This exclusion **(10.)** does not apply to the first $1,500 of "custom equipment" in or upon "your covered auto" or any "non-owned auto".

11. Loss to any "non-owned auto" being maintained or used by any person while employed or otherwise engaged in the "business" of:

a. Selling;

b. Repairing;

c. Servicing;

d. Storing; or

e. Parking;

vehicles designed for use on public highways. This includes road testing and delivery.

12. Loss to "your covered auto" or any "non-owned auto", located inside a facility designed for racing, for the purpose of:

a. Participating or competing in; or

b. Practicing or preparing for;

any prearranged or organized:

(1) Racing or speed contest; or

(2) Driver skill training or driver skill event.

13. Loss to, or loss of use of, a "non-owned auto" rented by:

a. You; or

b. Any "family member";

if a rental vehicle company is precluded from recovering such loss or loss of use, from you or that "family member", pursuant to the provisions of any applicable rental agreement or state law.

14. Loss to "your covered auto" which occurs while:

a. Enrolled in a personal vehicle sharing program under the terms of a written agreement; and

b. Being used in connection with such personal vehicle sharing program by anyone other than you or any "family member".

15. Loss to, or loss of use of, a "non-owned auto" used by:

a. You; or

b. Any "family member";

in connection with a personal vehicle sharing program if the provisions of such a personal vehicle sharing program preclude the recovery of such loss or loss of use, from you or that "family member", or if otherwise precluded by any state law.

16. Loss to any vehicle which is designed or can be used for flight.

LIMIT OF LIABILITY

A. Our limit of liability for loss will be the lesser of the:

1. Actual cash value of the stolen or damaged property; or

2. Amount necessary to repair or replace the property with other property of like kind and quality.

However, the most we will pay for loss to:

a. Any "non-owned auto" which is a trailer is $1,500.

b. Electronic equipment that reproduces, receives or transmits audio, visual or data signals, which is permanently installed in the auto in locations not used by the auto manufacturer for installation of such equipment, is $1,000.

c. "Custom equipment" in or upon "your covered auto" or any "non-owned auto" is $1,500.

B. An adjustment for depreciation and physical condition will be made in determining actual cash value in the event of a total loss.

C. If a repair or replacement results in better than like kind or quality, we will not pay for the amount of the betterment.

PAYMENT OF LOSS

We may pay for loss in money or repair or replace the damaged or stolen property. We may, at our expense, return any stolen property to:

1. You; or

2. The address shown in this Policy.

If we return stolen property we will pay for any damage resulting from the theft. We may keep all or part of the property at an agreed or appraised value.

If we pay for loss in money, our payment will include the applicable sales tax for the damaged or stolen property.

NO BENEFIT TO BAILEE

This insurance shall not directly or indirectly benefit any carrier or other bailee for hire.

OTHER SOURCES OF RECOVERY

If other sources of recovery also cover the loss, we will pay only our share of the loss. Our share is the proportion that our limit of liability bears to the total of all applicable limits. However, any insurance we provide with respect to a "non-owned auto" shall be excess over any other collectible source of recovery including, but not limited to:

1. Any coverage provided by the owner of the "non-owned auto".

2. Any other applicable physical damage insurance.

3. Any other source of recovery applicable to the loss.

APPRAISAL

A. If we and you do not agree on the amount of loss, either may demand an appraisal of the loss. In this event, each party will select a competent and impartial appraiser. The two appraisers will select an umpire. The appraisers will state separately the actual cash value and the amount of loss. If they fail to agree, they will submit their differences to the umpire. A decision agreed to by any two will be binding. Each party will:

1. Pay its chosen appraiser; and

2. Bear the expenses of the appraisal and umpire equally.

B. We do not waive any of our rights under this Policy by agreeing to an appraisal.

PART E – DUTIES AFTER AN ACCIDENT OR LOSS

We have no duty to provide coverage under this Policy if the failure to comply with the following duties is prejudicial to us:

A. We must be notified promptly of how, when and where the accident or loss happened. Notice should also include the names and addresses of any injured persons and of any witnesses.

B. A person seeking any coverage must:

   1. Cooperate with us in the investigation, settlement or defense of any claim or suit.

   2. Promptly send us copies of any notices or legal papers received in connection with the accident or loss.

   3. Submit, as often as we reasonably require:

      a. To physical exams by physicians we select. We will pay for these exams.

      b. To examination under oath and subscribe the same.

      c. To recorded statements.

   4. Authorize us to obtain:

      a. Medical reports; and

      b. Other pertinent records.

   5. Submit a proof of loss when required by us.

C. A person seeking Uninsured Motorists Coverage must also:

   1. Promptly notify the police if a hit-and-run driver is involved.

   2. Promptly send us copies of the legal papers if a suit is brought.

D. A person seeking Coverage For Damage To Your Auto must also:

   1. Take reasonable steps after loss to protect "your covered auto" or any "non-owned auto" and its equipment from further loss. We will pay reasonable expenses incurred to do this.

   2. Promptly notify the police if "your covered auto" or any "non-owned auto" is stolen.

   3. Permit us to inspect and appraise the damaged property before its repair or disposal.

PART F – GENERAL PROVISIONS

BANKRUPTCY

Bankruptcy or insolvency of the "insured" shall not relieve us of any obligations under this Policy.

CHANGES

A. This Policy contains all the agreements between you and us. Its terms may not be changed or waived except by endorsement issued by us.

B. If there is a change to the information used to develop the policy premium, we may adjust your premium. Changes during the policy term that may result in a premium increase or decrease include, but are not limited to, changes in:

   1. The number, type or use classification of insured vehicles;

   2. Operators using insured vehicles;

   3. The place of principal garaging of insured vehicles; or

   4. Coverage, deductible or limits.

If a change resulting from **A.** or **B.** requires a premium adjustment, we will make the premium adjustment in accordance with our manual rules.

C. If we make a change which broadens coverage under this edition of your policy without additional premium charge, that change will automatically apply to your policy as of the date we implement the change in your state. This paragraph **(C.)** does not apply to changes implemented with a general program revision that includes both broadenings and restrictions in coverage, whether that general program revision is implemented through introduction of:

   1. A subsequent edition of your policy; or

   2. An Amendatory Endorsement.

FRAUD

We do not provide coverage for any "insured" who has made fraudulent statements or engaged in fraudulent conduct in connection with any accident or loss for which coverage is sought under this Policy.

LEGAL ACTION AGAINST US

A. No legal action may be brought against us until there has been full compliance with all the terms of this Policy. In addition, under Part **A**, no legal action may be brought against us until:

   1. We agree in writing that the "insured" has an obligation to pay; or

   2. The amount of that obligation has been finally determined by judgment after trial.

B. No person or organization has any right under this Policy to bring us into any action to determine the liability of an "insured".

OUR RIGHT TO RECOVER PAYMENT

A. If we make a payment under this Policy and the person to or for whom payment was made has a right to recover damages from another, we shall be subrogated to that right. That person shall do:

1. Whatever is necessary to enable us to exercise our rights; and

2. Nothing after loss to prejudice them.

However, our rights in this paragraph **(A.)** do not apply under Part **D**, against any person using "your covered auto" with a reasonable belief that that person is entitled to do so.

B. If we make a payment under this Policy and the person to or for whom payment is made recovers damages from another, that person shall:

1. Hold in trust for us the proceeds of the recovery; and

2. Reimburse us to the extent of our payment.

POLICY PERIOD AND TERRITORY

A. This Policy applies only to accidents and losses which occur:

1. During the policy period as shown in the Declarations; and

2. Within the policy territory.

B. The policy territory is:

1. The United States of America, its territories or possessions;

2. Puerto Rico; or

3. Canada.

This Policy also applies to loss to, or accidents involving, "your covered auto" while being transported between their ports.

TERMINATION

A. Cancellation

This Policy may be cancelled during the policy period as follows:

1. The named insured shown in the Declarations may cancel by:

a. Returning this Policy to us; or

b. Giving us advance written notice of the date cancellation is to take effect.

2. We may cancel by mailing to the named insured shown in the Declarations at the address shown in this Policy:

a. At least 10 days' notice:

(1) If cancellation is for nonpayment of premium; or

(2) If notice is mailed during the first 60 days this Policy is in effect and this is not a renewal or continuation policy; or

b. At least 20 days' notice in all other cases.

3. After this Policy is in effect for 60 days, or if this is a renewal or continuation policy, we will cancel only:

a. For nonpayment of premium; or

b. If your driver's license or that of:

(1) Any driver who lives with you; or

(2) Any driver who customarily uses "your covered auto";

has been suspended or revoked. This must have occurred:

(a) During the policy period; or

(b) Since the last anniversary of the original effective date if the policy period is other than one year; or

c. If the Policy was obtained through material misrepresentation.

B. Nonrenewal

If we decide not to renew or continue this Policy, we will mail notice to the named insured shown in the Declarations at the address shown in this Policy. Notice will be mailed at least 20 days before the end of the policy period. Subject to this notice requirement, if the policy period is:

1. Less than six months, we will have the right not to renew or continue this Policy every six months, beginning six months after its original effective date.

2. Six months or longer, but less than one year, we will have the right not to renew or continue this Policy at the end of the policy period.

3. One year or longer, we will have the right not to renew or continue this Policy at each anniversary of its original effective date.

C. Automatic Termination

If we offer to renew or continue and you or your representative does not accept, this Policy will automatically terminate at the end of the current policy period. Failure to pay the required renewal or continuation premium when due shall mean that you have not accepted our offer.

If you obtain other insurance on "your covered auto", any similar insurance provided by this Policy will terminate as to that auto on the effective date of the other insurance.

D. Other Termination Provisions

1. We may deliver any notice instead of mailing it. Proof of mailing of any notice shall be sufficient proof of notice.
2. If this Policy is cancelled, you may be entitled to a premium refund. If so, we will send you the refund. The premium refund, if any, will be computed according to our manuals. However, making or offering to make the refund is not a condition of cancellation.
3. The effective date of cancellation stated in the notice shall become the end of the policy period.

TRANSFER OF YOUR INTEREST IN THIS POLICY

A. Your rights and duties under this Policy may not be assigned without our written consent. However, if a named insured shown in the Declarations dies, coverage will be provided for:

1. The surviving spouse if resident in the same household at the time of death. Coverage applies to the spouse as if a named insured shown in the Declarations; and
2. The legal representative of the deceased person as if a named insured shown in the Declarations. This applies only with respect to the representative's legal responsibility to maintain or use "your covered auto".

B. Coverage will only be provided until the end of the policy period.

TWO OR MORE AUTO POLICIES

If this Policy and any other auto insurance policy issued to you by us apply to the same accident, the maximum limit of our liability under all the policies shall not exceed the highest applicable limit of liability under any one policy.

Page 14 of 14 © Insurance Services Office, Inc., 2017 PP 00 01 09 18

NOTES AND QUESTIONS

1. *The Structure of the ISO Policy Form*. Generally speaking, automobile insurance policies have four principal coverages: liability, first-party medical payments, uninsured motorist, and first-party property. Underinsured motorist protection may be included within the uninsured motorist section, but it also frequently appears as an endorsement to the policy

itself. A definitions section is ordinarily the first section, although some policies have a very short "general definitions" section and then include definitions relating to the particular coverages within each coverage section. Some conditions are ordinarily included within the specific coverage sections, and then a general conditions section contains provisions that are applicable to all sections in the policy.

2. *The First-Party Property Coverage.* If an insured's vehicle is destroyed in an accident caused by the negligence of a third party, that third party (or the third party's liability insurer) pays for the insured's property damage. In many situations, however, the insured's car or truck may be damaged and no third party is responsible. An auto accident in which the insured is at fault is one obvious example. Hailstorms, falling trees, vandals, and thieves are other common perils, to name a few. The insured has an obvious interest in insuring owned property against these kinds of losses. Because it is so common to purchase vehicles with borrowed funds, the lender is certain to have a security interest in the vehicle, and the lender is likely to insist that the owner acquire and maintain insurance against such perils as well in order to protect the property that will be used to pay the insured's debt in the event of the insured's default on the loan.

In the first-party property coverage, the collision coverage and the comprehensive coverage address distinct perils. The coverages are meant to dovetail, and if a policyholder purchases both of them, then the policyholder is not likely to confront any unusual problems in having his or her loss covered by the insurer. The situation changes, of course, if only one (or neither) of the property coverages is purchased.

3. *What About Trailers?* Are things being hauled by an insured vehicle, such as a boat trailer, covered under the Sample Auto Policy?

II. COMPULSORY INSURANCE

ODUM V. NATIONWIDE MUTUAL INSURANCE CO.

401 S.E.2d 87, cert. denied, 407 S.E.2d 539 (N.C. 1991)

JOHNSON, JUDGE.

This action arises out of an auto accident which occurred on 16 June 1987 when a car driven by Robert McPhaul, husband of the insured, Arnetta McPhaul, crossed the center line and collided with a car driven by Clifton Oxendine. Mrs. McPhaul was a passenger in the car driven by Robert. Both Arnetta McPhaul and Clifton Oxendine died of injuries sustained in the wreck. Following Nationwide's denial of coverage, plaintiffs brought suit to collect under a motor vehicle liability insurance policy issued to Arnetta McPhaul.

. . . .

Nationwide answered plaintiffs' complaint and counterclaimed, alleging that Arnetta McPhaul made fraudulent and intentional misrepresentations on her insurance application which rendered the policy void ab initio. Nationwide moved for summary judgment on the ground that there was no genuine issue of material fact and the insurance policy was void ab initio as a matter of law. By judgment dated 8 December 1989, Judge Farmer denied Nationwide's motion for summary judgment and decreed that the insurance policy was in full effect and that defendant Nationwide was bound by the terms and conditions of the policy. Nationwide appeals.

The parties stipulate to the following facts:

Nationwide issued a motor vehicle liability insurance policy to Arnetta McPhaul for a 1979 Datsun owned by her. The stated policy limits for bodily injury liability were $50,000 each person and $100,000 each accident. As of the day of the accident, 16 June 1987, the premium charged on that policy was paid current. On that day, at about 6:30 a.m., Arnetta McPhaul was riding as a passenger in the Datsun which was driven by her husband, Robert. The Datsun collided with a vehicle operated by Clifton Oxendine. Both Arnetta McPhaul and Clifton Oxendine died as a result of their injuries.

In her application for insurance, Mrs. McPhaul represented that she was divorced, that she was the sole driver in her household and that no driver in her household had any convictions or motor vehicle offenses in the last five years. Her signature was witnessed by the Nationwide agent taking the application, who informed her that by law she was required to list her husband on the application if she was married and that her signature on the application was an attestation that the information on the application was true.

It is further stipulated that Vonzell McPhaul, Robert's brother, knew that as of 5 August 1986, Robert and Arnetta had been married for about nine years and that on 16 June 1987, the day of the accident, they were living together as man and wife; that the vehicle registered in Arnetta's name was a family vehicle which was often driven by Robert and that on the morning of the accident Robert was driving himself and Arnetta to work, as he regularly did. It is further stipulated that on 25 March 1985 Robert McPhaul was convicted of driving while impaired.

The parties stipulate that it is Nationwide's customary practice when writing automobile insurance policies to order driving records for all drivers listed on a new application and if the record should reveal a conviction for driving while impaired within five years of the date of the application, Nationwide automatically and without exception cedes the insurance risk to the reinsurance facility. Had Mrs. McPhaul listed Robert as her husband, Nationwide would have discovered his conviction and automatically ceded the insurance.

Finally, the parties stipulate that Nationwide was notified of the accident and subsequently conducted an investigation during which it became aware that the vehicle was operated by Robert McPhaul, husband of Arnetta McPhaul, and that having such knowledge, Nationwide tendered payment of $939.00 pursuant to the collision coverage provided to Arnetta McPhaul.

. . . .

Defendant Nationwide contends that the trial court erred in ruling that, despite Mrs. McPhaul's deliberate and material misrepresentations, the policy was not void ab initio but was in full effect. Nationwide argues in the alternative, that the misrepresentations render the policy void as to Mrs. McPhaul even though it is valid as to the injured third party. . . .

The issue on appeal is whether the insurer on an automobile liability policy can avoid liability after an injury has occurred on the ground that the policy was procured by the insured's deliberate and material misrepresentations on the application.

Neither party made a distinction in its arguments between the minimum mandatory coverage required by G.S. § 20–279.21(b)(2) (1989) (bodily injury: $25,000 per person, $50,000 per accident) and the larger amount of coverage under the liability policy at issue in this case ($50,000 per person, $100,000 per accident). Such a distinction is important to a proper resolution of this appeal.

First, Nationwide argues that G.S. § 58–3–10 applies to the automobile liability policy at issue and thus a material misrepresentation on an application form constitutes a defense to recovery under the policy. As to the statutory amount of coverage required by G.S. § 20–279.21, we disagree.

General Statutes § 58–3–10, adopted in 1901, falls within Chapter 58, Insurance, article 3, General Regulations for Insurance. As an earlier and more general statement of insurance law, it is superseded with respect to automobile liability insurance by Chapter 20, Motor Vehicles, specifically by article 9A, The Motor Vehicle Safety and Financial Responsibility Act of 1953, and article 13, The Vehicle Financial Responsibility Act of 1957. Chapter 20 represents a complete and comprehensive legislative scheme for the regulation of motor vehicles and as such, its insurance provisions regarding automobiles prevail over the more general insurance regulations of Chapter 58. The 1953 Act, found at G.S. §§ 20–279.1 to 20–279.39, applies to drivers whose licenses have been suspended and relates to the restoration of driver's licenses while the 1957 Act, found at G.S. §§ 20–309 to 20–319, applies to all motor vehicles owners and relates to vehicle registration. The two Acts are complementary and are to be construed in *pari materia* so as to harmonize them and give effect to both.

Chapter 20 requires, *inter alia*, the following with regard to liability insurance. No self-propelled motor vehicle shall be registered in this state unless the owner has financial responsibility as provided in article 13. G.S. § 20–309(a). Financial responsibility shall be a liability insurance policy or other approved form as defined in Chapter 20, article 9A. G.S. § 20–309(b). An owner's policy of liability insurance shall insure against loss from the liability imposed by law for damages arising out of the ownership, maintenance or use of the vehicle because of bodily injury, in the amounts of $25,000 per person, and $50,000 per accident, because of injury to or death of two or more persons in any one accident. G.S. § 20–279.21(b)(2). General Statutes § 20–279.21(f) expressly provides:

> Every motor vehicle liability policy shall be subject to the following provisions which need not be contained therein: (1) Except as hereinafter provided, the liability of the insurance carrier *with respect to the insurance required by this Article shall become absolute whenever injury or damage covered by said motor vehicle liability policy occurs*; said policy may not be canceled or annulled as to such liability by any agreement between the insurance carrier and the insured after the occurrence of the injury or damage; *no statement made by the insured* or on his behalf and no violation of said policy *shall defeat or void said policy* (emphasis added).

Although we can find no North Carolina case which deals specifically with the effect of G.S. § 20–279.21(f)(1) in a situation involving a misrepresentation made in the application for insurance, there are several North Carolina cases which have interpreted the impact of § 20–279.21(f)(1) on the liability of insurance carriers when an insured violates a provision of the policy. The seminal case is *Swain v. Insurance Co.*, 253 N.C. 120, 116 S.E.2d 482 (1960), where the insurance contract provided that the insured, in the event of suit against him, must forward immediately to the insurer "every demand, notice, summons or other process received by him" and must cooperate with the insurer in defending the suit. *Swain*, 253 N.C. at 127, 116 S.E.2d at 487. The insured violated this provision and the insurance company pleaded this violation as a defense to recovery under the policy by an injured third party who had obtained a default judgment against the insured. The Court found:

> The manifest purpose of the 1957 Act [is] to provide protection, within the required limits, to persons injured or damaged by the negligent operation of a motor vehicle; and, in respect of a "motor vehicle liability policy," to provide such protection notwithstanding violations of policy provisions by the owner

> subsequent to accidents on which such injured parties base their claim.

Swain, 253 N.C. at 126, 116 S.E.2d at 487. The Court further found that "to bar recovery from an insurer on account of such a policy violation would 'practically nullify the statute by making the enforcement of the rights of the person intended to be protected dependent upon the acts of the very person who caused the injury.' " *Id.*, quoting *Ott v. American Fidelity & Cas. Co.*, 161 S.C. 314, 159 S.E. 635 (1931). *Accord, Jones v. Ins. Co.*, 270 N.C. 454, 155 S.E.2d 118 (1967) (failure of insured to give notice of suit to insurer as required by policy is no defense against default judgment in favor of injured third party); *see also, Insurance Co. v. Roberts*, 261 N.C. 285, 134 S.E.2d 654 (1964) (primary purpose of compulsory motor vehicle liability insurance is to compensate innocent victims therefore no reason why injured third party's rights to recover from insurance carrier should depend upon whether the conduct of its insured was intentional or negligent). The *Swain* and *Jones* decisions specifically concerned violations of insurance policy provisions with regard to notice, the violation of which occurred after the injury had occurred and after the liability of the insurer had become absolute. These decisions were based upon the legislative purpose for mandatory vehicle liability insurance (to protect innocent victims) and the words of the statute ("the liability of the carrier . . . shall become absolute whenever injury . . . occurs . . . and no violation of said policy shall defeat or void said policy," G.S. § 20–279.21(f)(1)). We find that this analysis demands a similar result when the defense asserted is fraud in the application for insurance. Subsection (f)(1) of G.S. § 20–279.21, quoted above in part, provides that the insurer's liability becomes absolute whenever injury occurs, and "no statement made by the insured . . . shall defeat or void said policy." Every policy is subject to this provision whether it is expressly stated in the contract or not. G.S. § 20–279.21(f) ("Every motor vehicle liability policy shall be subject to the following provisions which need not be contained therein[.]"). This result is strengthened by the recognition that the legislature included at subsection (h) a provision by which insurers could recoup losses for which they became obligated solely by operation of the statute. Subsection (h) of G.S. § 20–279.21 states:

> Any motor vehicle liability policy may provide that the insured shall reimburse the insurance carrier for any payment the insurance carrier would not have been obligated to make under the terms of the policy except for the provision of this Article.

See, Insurance Co. v. Webb, 10 N.C. App. 672, 179 S.E.2d 803 (1971). We note that the insurance policy at issue in this case was not included in the record and defendant Nationwide has not pleaded this clause in any counterclaim for recoupment.

We find, however, that the holding above, that fraud in an application for motor vehicle liability insurance is not a defense to the insurer's liability once injury has occurred, applies only to the statutory minimum amount. In the case *sub judice*, the stated policy limit was greater than the statutory minimum and as to that amount, the above analysis does not apply.

The distinction between the mandatory amount of coverage required by statute (see G.S. § 20–279.21(b)(2)) and any amount in excess of that, is found in G.S. § 20–279.21(g):

> Any policy which grants the coverage required for a motor vehicle liability policy may also grant any lawful coverage in excess of or in addition to the coverage specified for a motor vehicle liability policy and such excess or additional coverage shall not be subject to the provision of this Article. With respect to a policy which grants such excess or additional coverage the term "motor vehicle liability policy" shall apply only to that part of the coverage which is required by this section.

The effect of this distinction was recognized in *Swain*, 253 N.C. at 127, 116 S.E.2d at 487–88. As explained in *Swain*, the 1957 Act changed the law with respect to the compulsory amount such that a violation of a policy provision was not a defense to liability of the insurer, but as to any amount in excess of that, a policy provision requiring notice to the insurer would be enforced as written and a violation was a valid and complete defense. The *Swain* Court pointed to *Muncie v. Ins. Co.*, 253 N.C. 74, 116 S.E.2d 474 (1960), as being a statement of the applicable law as to coverage "in excess of or in addition to the coverage specified for a motor vehicle liability policy." *Muncie* involved an accident which occurred prior to the effective date of the 1957 Act. An injured third party sued the insurer to collect on a judgment against the insured. The insurer plead as a defense the violation of a policy provision requiring the insured to give the insurer timely notice of the accident. The Court held that the constitutional guaranty of freedom of contract required that the policy provision be enforced as written. Thus, the violation of the notice provision in the policy by the insured was a complete defense both as to the insured and the injured third party.

We therefore hold that as to any coverage in excess of the statutory minimum, the insurer is not precluded by statute or public policy from asserting the defense of fraud. Such a defense, if successful, would insulate the insurer against liability as to both the insured, Arnetta McPhaul, and the injured third party, Mr. Oxendine. *Muncie*, 253 N.C. 74, 116 S.E.2d 474.

. . . .

In summary, we find that as to the mandatory amount of motor vehicle liability insurance coverage required by G.S. § 20–279.21, fraud in an application for insurance is not a defense to the insurer's liability once injury has occurred, but as to any amount of coverage in excess of the statutory minimum, fraud is a defense under common law or contract law principles.

Therefore, we modify the decision of the court below in that we affirm summary judgment for plaintiffs, finding the insurance policy valid, but only to the extent of the mandatory amount of coverage. As to the amount in excess, we find that there exist genuine issues of material fact.

We modify and affirm in part the judgment below, and remand for further proceedings not inconsistent with this opinion.

Modified and affirmed in part and remanded.

EAGLES and PARKER, JJ., concur.

NOTES AND QUESTIONS

1. *What Exactly Is North Carolina's Public Policy?* The court in *Odum* makes clear that the purpose of compulsory liability insurance is to protect third parties. To the extent of the statutory minimums, Nationwide cannot assert a fraud defense, and the rationale has to do with North Carolina's policy of protecting third parties. Why does this public policy "end" when amounts exceeding the statutory minimums are implicated? Is it the public policy of North Carolina to help accident victims as long as they are not helped "too much"?

2. *The Compulsory Liability Insurance Landscape.* Every state has a financial security requirement to operate a motor vehicle. In most states, every person registering a motor vehicle is required to purchase liability insurance in at least a specified minimum amount. The specified minimums are likely to be "bodily injury per person," "bodily injury per occurrence," and "property damage per occurrence." Thus, a person who purchases "25/50/10" in liability limits will have $50,000 in limits available to reimburse victims for bodily injury in any one accident, regardless of the number of people injured; however, the insurer will pay no single victim more than $25,000. The insured would have $10,000 in coverage available to pay for property damage caused by the insured.

What weaknesses do you see in this landscape? Despite the mandate, liability insurance is not purchased by everyone, and some policyholders allow their policies, once purchased, to lapse. In some accidents, the tortfeasor cannot be identified (e.g., a "hit and run"). The mandatory limits are low relative to the liabilities associated with the injuries and damage that occur in many accidents, and some estimates are that 90 percent of all policyholders purchase only the statutory minimums. In many states, the property damage minimum is $10,000. How many automobiles on the highways today are worth more than $10,000? How would you improve this system? As we move through the materials in this chapter, one of the themes is how the automobile accident compensation system has evolved to address these gaps.

3. *No-Pay, No-Play?* To encourage more people to purchase and maintain liability insurance, some states prohibit individuals who do not purchase it from suing other drivers for non-economic damages, such as pain and suffering. Is this a good idea? *See, e.g.*, Cal. Civ. Code § 3333.4(a); La. Rev. Stat. § 32:866(A)(1). If you like the idea, would you support taking away the victim's ability to sue the tortfeasor for *any* kind of loss if the victim has failed to purchase all of the mandated automobile coverages? *See, e.g.*, N.J. Stat. Ann. § 39:6A–4.5.

4. *Household Exclusions.* Insurers are concerned that family members will collude to create false automobile injury claims. To address that fear, insurers have created what is known as the "Household Exclusion" or "Family Exclusion," which purports to eliminate coverage for claims brought by one family member against another family member. The majority rule is that such exclusions violate the standard financial responsibility act or compulsory liability insurance laws, at least to the extent of statutorily prescribed minimums. *See, e.g., State Farm Mutual Automobile Insurance Co. v. Mastbaum*, 748 P.2d 1042, 1043 (Utah 1987); *Nation v. State Farm Insurance Co.*, 880 P.2d 877 (Okla. 1994).

5. *Fortuity, Compensating Victims, and Intentional Wrongs.* It should come as no surprise that automobile insurance, like other kinds of insurance, is meant to compensate for accidental, fortuitous losses. If an insured intentionally inflicts loss on another person, one would think that the intentional act exclusion would apply to eliminate the insured's liability insurance coverage. (Whether the insured acted intentionally so as to trigger the exclusion would involve issues similar to those that arise in connection with the intentional act exclusion in property coverage, which was discussed in Chapter 4.) Does the logic of *Odum*, however, extend to intentional torts? In other words, suppose the insured, while driving his insured car, takes offense at the behavior of a pedestrian and deliberately strikes the pedestrian with the vehicle, causing serious injury. If the pedestrian sues the insured for willful, wanton, reckless, and negligent behavior, must the insured's liability carrier provide coverage? *Compare State Farm Mutual Automobile Insurance Co. v. Wertz*, 540 N.W.2d 636 (S.D. 1995), *with State Farm Fire & Cas. Co. v. Tringali*, 686 F.2d 821 (9th Cir. 1982), *and Wheeler v. O'Connell*, 9 N.E.2d 544 (Mass. 1937).

If you are inclined to enforce the intentional act exclusion to deny coverage, does your analysis change if domestic abuse is involved? In *State Farm Mutual Automobile Insurance Co. v. Martin*, 660 A.2d 66 (Pa. Super. Ct. 1995), the insured, while intoxicated, drove to the rented home where his wife, from whom he was separated, was living, drove his truck into the rear of his wife's vehicle, drove across the lawn when his wife came out of the house and struck her, and then drove his truck into the wall of the house three times. Should other, well-behaved insureds, who belong to the same risk pool in which the insured in *Martin* belonged, contribute premiums to pay for these kinds of liabilities? Or, does the public policy favoring victim compensation trump the fortuity principle?

In a different twist on the fortuity issue, consider *Nygaard v. State Farm Insurance Co.*, 591 N.W.2d 738 (Minn. Ct. App. 1999), where the insured deliberately drove her car into the path of an 18-wheel tractor-trailer in a successful suicide attempt. The truck's driver was injured. Should the insured's liability insurer provide coverage on behalf of the decedent's estate for the benefit of the injured truck driver? Was there an "accident" in these circumstances? Whose perspective matters?

6. *The Rise and Fall of No-Fault Insurance. Will It Rise Again?* In the 1960s, high automobile liability insurance premiums nationwide caused about half the states to change their automobile accident compensation systems to what are called "no-fault" systems. Although the details varied from state to state, the architecture of no-fault looked like this: (1) accident victims with minor injuries (typically defined by dollars, i.e., below a monetary threshold) were prohibited from suing the tortfeasor in tort; (2) in exchange for the loss of the right to sue in tort, victims recovered first-party benefits from their own insurer without regard to fault. The theory was that the cost savings accrued by eliminating the costs associated with pursuing small claims in court would be reallocated to more robust—and more speedily paid—first-party benefits than an insured would receive if a claim were pursued in the tort system. Some state no-fault systems worked well, but many did not because the ability to bring a tort claim was not sufficiently constrained (for example, in New Jersey a tort claim could be pursued whenever an insured suffered a "soft-tissue injury"), while at the same time first-party benefits were significantly increased. These no-fault systems were "out of balance," and, naturally, premiums increased. Also, in some states, the monetary thresholds actually encouraged more medical care (and therefore expense) so that victims would qualify to bring a tort claim in court. Thus, in about half the states that embraced no-fault at one time, the statutes have been repealed or significantly modified. It may be that the proponents of no-fault will have the last laugh, however, because no-fault may be the most viable framework for the new world of driverless cars.

III. OMNIBUS COVERAGE

Under auto insurance, as evidenced by the compulsory liability insurance requirement, the principal interest protected is that of the auto accident victim, not the driver or owner of the auto. To that end, auto insurance policies typically have broad language regarding who is "insured," and courts' interpretation of that language is also typically broad.

ODOLECKI V. HARTFORD ACCIDENT & INDEMNITY CO.

264 A.2d 38 (N.J. 1970)

PROCTOR, J.

This case concerns the question of coverage under the omnibus clause of an automobile liability insurance policy. The policy was issued by the defendant, Hartford Accident & Indemnity Company (Hartford) to Mrs. Kathryn Zylka, and covered her automobile which was involved in a collision on July 7, 1964. The omnibus clause was of standard form and provided in pertinent part that coverage under the policy was extended to the named insured, her spouse, and "any person while using the automobile . . . provided the actual use of the automobile is by the named insured or such spouse or with the permission of either."

The facts are not in material dispute. Mrs. Zylka, the owner of the insured vehicle, gave her teenage son, Michael, general permission to use the car when he returned home from college for his summer vacation. She also told him not to let anyone else drive the car. This admonition was repeated on several occasions when he used the car. On the night of July 7, 1964, Michael was using the car for a social visit to a neighbor's house. While there he permitted his friend, the plaintiff, Douglas Odolecki, to borrow the car in order that the latter might pick up his girlfriend. On his way to a hospital where the girl worked, Odolecki was involved in an accident with another car which resulted in the filing of several personal injury actions against him.

After receiving notice of the accident, the defendant-insurer informed the plaintiff that he was not covered by the policy issued to Mrs. Zylka since he was not operating the vehicle with the "permission" of the named insured or her spouse as required by the policy. The plaintiff filed the present action to have himself declared an additional insured. Sitting without a jury, the trial court held that the Zylka policy did not cover the plaintiff as an additional insured because Mrs. Zylka had never given him permission to use the car, because she had expressly prohibited her son from giving permission to others to use the car, and because the use of the car was not within the use granted by Mrs. Zylka to her son. In denying plaintiff relief the trial judge relied principally on this Court's decision in *Baesler v. Globe Indemnity Co.,* 33 N.J. 148, 162 A.2d 854 (1960). Plaintiff appealed to the Appellate Division, and pending argument there, we granted certification on our own motion.

Baesler, upon which the trial court relied, is virtually identical with the present case. There, the named insured bought a car for the exclusive use of his nephew with the stipulation that the car not be used by others. Despite this admonition, the nephew permitted a friend to use the automobile for a social engagement, and while the friend was driving he had an accident in which his passenger was injured. The passenger recovered a judgment for personal injuries against the friend-driver, and the latter, claiming to be an additional insured, sued the insurer of the named insured to recover the amount of the judgment. In a four to three decision, this Court held that the plaintiff was not covered by the policy which the defendant had issued. The Court noted the general rule that, ordinarily, a permittee is not authorized to allow another to use an insured vehicle on the basis of his own permission to use it and that therefore there could be no coverage under the standard omnibus clause. *Id.* at 151, 162 A.2d 854. Since we adhered to this rule at that time, it followed, *a fortiori,* that when there was an express prohibition by the named insured, and no other countervailing factor, the second permittee could not claim a greater right than he could in the absence of such a prohibition. The plaintiff concedes that under *Baesler* he is not entitled to qualify as an additional insured, but he argues that our decisions since *Baesler* have eroded the holding in that case to the point where it no longer represents the law of this state. The validity of this contention depends upon an analysis of these post-*Baesler* decisions.

In the term of court following *Baesler,* we decided *Matits v. Nationwide Mutual Ins. Co.,* 33 N.J. 488, 166 A.2d 345 (1960). There we dealt with the related question of whether the original permittee was an additional insured when she substantially deviated from the scope of the named insured's permission. In that case the husband of the named insured lent his wife's car to a neighbor so that the latter could visit her sick mother in a nearby town. After the visit, the permittee drove in a direction away from the named insured's home and alternately visited two bars over a period of several hours. On the way home, she was involved in a collision with another car.

We were called upon to decide whether the permittee's deviation vitiated the named insured's initial permission so as to deprive her of coverage under the standard omnibus clause of the policy issued by the defendant insurer. The law of New Jersey pertaining to coverage when a permittee deviated from the scope of permission was then unclear. Other jurisdictions had adopted one of three views. The first is the liberal or "initial permission" rule which allows coverage if a person has permission to use the automobile irrespective of any deviations from the scope of permission so long as it remains in his possession. The second view, the moderate or "minor deviation" rule, allows coverage only where the deviation from the scope of the permissive use does not constitute a gross violation. Finally, the strict or "conversion" rule denies coverage for *any* deviation from the time, place, or purpose specified. For a discussion of these rules, *see generally* 7 Appleman, Insurance Law and Practice, §§ 4366, 4367, 4368, and cases cited therein.

In *Matits,* we adopted the initial permission rule. It was our view that the minor deviation and conversion rules, which made coverage turn on the scope of permission given in the first instance, rendered coverage uncertain, fostered unnecessary litigation, and did not comport with New Jersey's legislative policy of assuring an available fund for the innocent victims of automobile accidents. *See* Motor Vehicle Security-Responsibility Law, N.J.S.A. 39:6–23 to 60; Unsatisfied Claim and Judgment Fund Law, N.J.S.A. 39:6–61 to 91; Motor Vehicle Liability Security Fund Act, N.J.S.A. 39:6–92 to 104. Accordingly, we held that if a person is given permission to use a motor vehicle in the first instance, *any* subsequent use short of an unlawful taking while it remains in his possession, is a permissive use within the standard omnibus clause in an automobile liability insurance policy regardless of any restrictions given by the named insured. Therefore, the permittee was an additional insured under the policy issued by the defendant insurer.

In a dissenting opinion, Justice Hall contended that the minor deviation rule was the only sound approach to the problem. He expressed the belief, however, that the Court's adoption of the initial permission rule undermined the holding of *Baesler* since it rendered irrelevant any actions by a permittee subsequent to the grant of original permission. He reasoned that the majority's holding made it impossible for an insured to restrict a grant of permission, and therefore that the result in *Baesler* was irreconcilable with that in *Matits*.

Our holding in *Matits* has since been reaffirmed in *Small v. Schuncke,*[1] 42 N.J. 407, 201 A.2d 56 (1964) and *Selected Risks Insurance Co. v. Zullo,* 48 N.J. 362, 225 A.2d 570 (1966). Now we must decide whether initial permission is unrestrictable in terms of second permittees as well as in terms of scope of deviations.

We had already indicated in *Baesler* that in certain circumstances a prohibition of a loan to a second permittee could be ineffective regarding insurance coverage. There we noted that if, for example, a father gave his son the use of the family car for a social engagement and the son turned over the wheel to a fellow occupant despite his father's admonitions to the contrary, there might be coverage. 33 N.J. at 153–154, 162 A.2d 854. This dictum later became our holding in *Indemnity Ins. Co., etc. v. Metropolitan Cas. Ins. Co. of N. Y.,* 33 N.J. 507, 166 A.2d 355 (1960), decided the same day in *Matits*. There the named insured lent her car to an employee for the purpose of driving several customers on a business inspection. The employee was specifically instructed not to let anyone else drive the car. While returning from the inspection the employee allowed a passenger to drive and the car was involved in an accident. We held that the passenger-second permittee was covered since the car was being used for the purpose

[1] Interestingly, *Small* involved a second permittee as well as a deviation from the scope of permission. However, the insurer conceded that if the first permittee was covered under the omnibus clause at the time of collision, the second permittee was also covered. 42 N.J. at 412, 201 A.2d 56.

permitted by the named insured. Thus, it was possible for a second permittee to qualify as an additional insured notwithstanding the original permittee's violation of the named insured's instructions.

In *Matits*, and the subsequent cases in which we continued to follow the initial permission rule, we emphasized the importance of minimizing litigation of omnibus clause coverage. We were concerned with the continuing problem of determining factually the scope of permission given by the named insured. In order to alleviate the problem we adopted the rule that once permission was given to use a car on the highways, the person giving permission could not bar coverage by restricting the time, place, or purpose for which the car could be used. Clearly, the same kind of litigation results from a rule which inquires into the named insured's permission regarding the use of the car by persons other than his initial permittee. The question again depends upon the scope of the permission. Instead of what the named insured said regarding the time, place, and purpose of the permissive use, a court must examine what was said regarding other drivers. This kind of inquiry is precisely what we sought to avoid in *Matits*.

Thus, *Baesler* is not consistent with our announced policy of limiting litigation which turns on petty factual distinctions, particularly where these distinctions bear so little relationship to the subject of insurance coverage in the named insured's own mind. A named insured's admonitions to his permittee regarding the use of the vehicle by other drivers is rarely if ever intended to restrict the scope of insurance coverage. Moreover, as Chief Justice Weintraub pointed out in his dissent in *Baesler:* "A named insured untutored in law and fearful that his consent might lead to his own liability for damages in excess of the policy limits (indeed by statute in some jurisdictions he would be so liable) may well be tempted to invent a claim that he prohibited others to drive or to convert a precatory request into a binding prohibition." 33 N.J. at 159, 162 A.2d at 860–861. We add that the fear of insurance policy cancellations might well have the same effect.

A second and more important policy is that of assuring that all persons wrongfully injured have financially responsible persons to look to for damages. *Matits v. Nationwide Mutual Ins. Co., supra,* 33 N.J. at 495–496, 166 A.2d 345. In other words, a liability insurance contract is for the benefit of the public as well as for the benefit of the named or additional insured. The Legislature's desire to implement this policy is demonstrated by our financial responsibility laws cited above. In *Selected Risks Ins. Co. v. Zullo, supra,* we discussed the importance of these statutes and held that an insurer could not depart from the omnibus coverage described in N.J.S.A. 39:6–46(a) which contained substantially the same language we construed in *Matits. Id.* 48 N.J. 369, 225 A.2d 570. Thus, insurers were required to draw policies which conformed with the initial permission rule.

Although the above policy considerations would seem to dictate a departure from *Baesler,* we are urged that the language of the omnibus clause precludes coverage for a prohibited second permittee. More specifically, defendant argues that the words "provided the actual use of the automobile is by the named insured . . . or with [her] permission" could not include use by Odolecki since Mrs. Zylka had told her son not to let anyone else drive the car. We fail, however, to see the distinction between a case where a first permittee exceeds the scope of permission in terms of time, place, or purpose, and a case where he exceeds the scope of permission in terms of use of the vehicle by another. Once an owner voluntarily hands over the keys to his car, the extent of permission he actually grants is as irrelevant in the one case as in the other. And as *Matits* and its progeny indicate restrictions are irrelevant in scope cases. The spurious nature of this distinction was pointed out by Cohen & Cohen in their article, "Automobile Liability Insurance: Public Policy and the Omnibus Clause in New Jersey," 15 Rutgers L. Rev. 155, 168 (1961). We think that once the initial permission has been given by the named insured, coverage is fixed, barring theft or the like. There is no claim of such an unlawful taking in the present case.

Accordingly, we hold that plaintiff was an additional insured within the terms of the policy issued to Mrs. Zylka by the defendant insurer. *Baesler v. Globe Indemnity Co., supra,* is no longer the law of this state.

Reversed.

NOTES AND QUESTIONS

1. *Persons Insured.* The question of who is insured under the liability coverages of a personal automobile policy has many different dimensions. If the person claiming coverage is named in the appropriate space on the declaration page of the policy, then this person is a "named insured." Few problems arise with these designations, apart from mistaken designations and other misunderstandings. But there are two other important groups of people that may be covered, and the precise language of the policy needs to be consulted. The other groups may include, for example, relatives (a category that may be limited to relatives who reside in the named insured's household or who do not own a vehicle themselves), individuals listed as "additional insureds" on the declaration page (a category that may be limited to individuals who do not own a motor vehicle themselves), and individuals operating the vehicle with the permission or general consent of the named insured or the spouse of the named insured (or perhaps simply with the permission or consent of an "insured").

2. *Modern Trend.* Although the minor deviation rule is the majority rule, the modern trend has been to adopt the "initial permission" or liberal interpretation rule. *See, e.g., Commercial Union Insurance Co. v. Johnson,* 745 S.W.2d 589 (Ark. 1988) (citing authorities which have adopted and rejected the

position). That being said, it is important to examine the controlling authorities in any given jurisdiction, as nuances in these tests and how they are applied to particular fact settings are important. Moreover, the fact patterns raising the permission issue are virtually endless, and the energy spent in sorting out coverage in these cases is enormous. Thus, it is fair to ask whether there's a better way for insurance policies to define coverage for these cases. Consider the next case.

CLOSE V. EBERTZ

583 N.W.2d 794 (N.D. 1998)

SANDSTROM, JUSTICE.

American Economy Insurance Co. (American) appealed a summary judgment awarding Clifford Close $50,000 and Millie Close $10,000 in their garnishment action to collect insurance proceeds for personal injuries under an automobile liability policy issued to John Ebertz. We hold the entitlement exclusion under the policy excluding coverage to "any person" using an auto without a reasonable belief the person is entitled to do so applies to a "family member" of the insured. Because the Closes do not dispute the trial court's ruling John Ebertz's son, Dominic Ebertz, was driving the vehicle at the time of the accident without his father's express or implied permission, we further hold the policy provides no coverage. We reverse the summary judgment and remand for entry of summary judgment in favor of American.

I

On October 1, 1992, American issued an automobile policy to John Ebertz for a 1979 Ford van. On October 12, 1992, John Ebertz's 15-year-old son, Dominic Ebertz, skipped school, took the van, and went riding around Devils Lake with a friend while his father and stepmother were at work. Dominic Ebertz had no drivers license, and he and his friend returned the van to the home before his parents returned for lunch. The boys hid in the van until the parents returned to work.

The boys, with Dominic Ebertz at the wheel, continued driving around Devils Lake during the afternoon. When an off-duty police officer attempted to stop the boys, Dominic Ebertz fled. During the chase, Dominic Ebertz entered an intersection and collided with a vehicle driven by Randy Holtz. The collision caused the Ebertz van to veer into a vehicle driven by Clifford Close, which was approaching the intersection from the opposite direction. Clifford Close suffered serious injuries in the accident. Dominic Ebertz was charged with unauthorized use of the vehicle.

Clifford Close and his wife, Millie Close, sued Dominic Ebertz, John Ebertz, and Randy Holtz to collect damages for Clifford Close's personal injuries. Millie Close also sought damages for loss of consortium. The Closes alleged

John Ebertz was liable under the family car doctrine or under the doctrine of negligent entrustment. The court granted summary judgment dismissing John Ebertz, concluding neither doctrine applied because Dominic Ebertz was not using the van with his father's express or implied permission. The Closes and Randy Holtz reached a settlement agreement. The Closes were awarded a default judgment against Dominic Ebertz in the amount of $168,131.82.

The Closes then brought a garnishment action against John Ebertz's insurance company, American. American claimed the entitlement exclusion in the policy excluding coverage to "any person" using an auto without a reasonable belief the person is entitled to do so applied to "family members." Because Dominic Ebertz used the van without John Ebertz's express or implied permission, American asserted there was no coverage under the policy. The Closes did not challenge the trial court's earlier ruling Dominic Ebertz used the van without his father's permission, but argued the policy language was ambiguous and should be interpreted to provide coverage under the circumstances.

Both parties moved for summary judgment. The trial court concluded the "any person" language in the policy did not include "family members," and ruled the policy provided coverage. Judgment was entered against American awarding Clifford Close $50,000, the per person limit under the policy, and Millie Close an additional $10,000 on her loss of consortium claim.

. . . .

II

. . . .

A

John Ebertz's American automobile policy's "Part A-Liability Coverage" says:

> Insuring Agreement
>
> A. We will pay damages for "bodily injury" or "property damage" for which any "insured" becomes legally responsible because of an auto accident. . . .
>
> B. "Insured," as used in this Part, means:
>
> 1. You or any "family member" for the ownership, maintenance or use of any "auto" or "trailer."
> 2. Any person using "your covered auto."

A "family member" is defined in the policy as "a person related to you by blood, marriage or adoption who is a resident of your household. This includes a ward or foster child."

The policy contains nine exclusions, including the following:

> Exclusions
>
> A. We do not provide Liability Coverage for any person:
>
> * * *
>
> 8. Using an "auto" without a reasonable belief that person is entitled to do so.

The term "any person" is not defined in the policy. The trial court noted the undefined term "any person" is used both in the introductory Paragraph A to the Exclusions and in Paragraph B.2 of the "Insuring Agreement" defining an insured as "[a]ny person using 'your covered auto.' " The court reasoned the "undefined term 'any person' could reasonably be interpreted to mean any 'insured' or as simply a reference to the second category of insureds i.e. 'any person using your covered auto' as described in B-2 of the Insuring Agreement." The court further reasoned because "the provision can be reasonably interpreted in either way, it is ambiguous and must be interpreted . . . against [American], who could have eliminated the ambiguity through a more careful choice of terms. . . ." The court therefore held the exclusion of "any person" did not include a "family member," and ruled the American policy provided coverage for the Closes' injuries arising from the October 12, 1992, accident.

B

The interpretation of an insurance policy is a question of law, fully reviewable on appeal. This Court reviews the trial court's interpretation by independently construing and examining the insurance policy. We look first to the language of the insurance contract, and if the language is clear on its face, there is no room for construction. If coverage hinges on an undefined term, we apply the plain, ordinary meaning of the term in interpreting the contract. Although insurance policies are contracts of adhesion, and we will resolve ambiguities in favor of the insured when appropriate, we will not strain the definition to provide coverage for the insured.

The question whether an entitlement exclusion in an automobile policy applies to members of the family of the named insured has generated a fairly substantial amount of litigation. *See* Annot., *Application of Automobile Insurance "Entitlement" Exclusion to Family Member*, 25 A.L.R.5th 60 (1994). Construing policy language indistinguishable from the language at issue here, a minority of courts have determined the "any person" language of the exclusion does not include a "family member," and there is coverage under circumstances comparable to this case. The majority of courts, however, have concluded the "any person" language unambiguously includes a "family member," and there is no coverage under these circumstances.

The reasoning underlying the minority view is the phrases "any person" and "family member" in the policy define mutually exclusive classes, so an exclusion for "any person" does not include family members but means any person other than a family member. The minority view is also based on the conclusion the policy language is ambiguous and should be resolved against the insurer. Some minority-view courts also rely on the reasonable expectation of the insured that family members will be protected when operating a covered family vehicle even without permission, and conclude the family member's disobedience is a family matter to be dealt with internally.

The reasoning underlying the majority view is the term "any person" is unambiguous, with no technical or restricted definition in the policy, and should be given its common meaning to include any person, including a "family member." The majority-view courts reject arguments an ambiguity is created merely because one part of the policy establishes general coverage while the other part establishes specific exclusions. The majority reason policy exclusions should be logically construed to include the named insured and family members, those "persons" typically covered, because it would be pointless for the policy to exclude coverage for "persons" not covered by the policy in the first place. The majority also reason, while the entitlement exclusion does not contain an exception for the named insured or a "family member," certain other policy exclusions, while pertaining generally to "any person," contain specific exceptions for the named insured or any "family member." These courts have observed if the exclusion for nonpermissive use does not apply to the named insured or a family member, neither would any other policy exclusion, including the one for intentional torts, because all of the exclusions refer to "any person." The majority-view courts argue the minority view's reasonable expectations and public policy arguments merely create coverage the insured has not paid for and the insurer has not agreed to provide.

C

We believe the reasoning of the majority is sound, and we, therefore, hold the American policy excludes coverage for the Closes' injuries under the circumstances. Several considerations lead us to this conclusion.

First, the "Insuring Agreement" of the policy distinguishes between the named insured and family members, and any other person, to provide coverage for the named insured and family members while driving either the covered vehicle or a borrowed vehicle. The "Insuring Agreement" thus limits coverage for any other person to those instances in which the other person is driving a covered vehicle.

Second, there is nothing ambiguous about the phrase "any person" used in the American policy exclusions section. Because the phrase "any person" has no technical meaning and is not defined in the policy, we give the phrase its plain, ordinary meaning. "Any" is defined as "unlimited in amount, quantity, number, time, or extent." *Webster's Third New International Dictionary*, at p. 97 (1971). Thus, "any person" must be construed to mean all persons, including family members.

Third, there are nine exclusions listed in the American policy applicable to "any person." Exclusion A.6 states American will not provide liability coverage for "any person:"

> 6. While employed or otherwise engaged in the "business" of:
>
> a. selling;
>
> b. repairing;
>
> c. servicing;
>
> d. storing; or
>
> e. parking;
>
> vehicles designed for use mainly on public highways. This includes road testing and delivery. This exclusion (A.6.) does not apply to the ownership, maintenance or use of "your covered auto" by:
>
> a. you;
>
> b. any "family member"; or
>
> c. any partner, agent or employee of you or any "family member."

Obviously, if "any person" did not include family members, there would be no need to specifically except family members from exclusion A.6. The specific exception of family members from exclusion A.6, but not from exclusion A.8, strongly implies family members are included in exclusion A.8.

Fourth, if the exclusion for nonpermissive use does not apply to family members, none of the other eight exclusions would apply to family members because all exclusions apply to "any person." Adopting the minority view would arguably result in allowing coverage for insureds and their family members for intentional torts under exclusion A.1 of the American policy. There is a strong public policy in North Dakota precluding an insured from being indemnified for losses caused by the insured's intentional or willful conduct.

Finally, because the term "insured" under the "Insuring Agreement" is defined as including the named insured as well as any "family member" using "any 'auto,'" whether it is the covered auto or not, adopting the minority view would allow coverage for a car thief under his own policy or under the policy of a family member with whom he resides, not only when stealing the family car, but when stealing any car. This result is untenable and contrary to public policy.

The Closes rely on the dissenting opinion in [*Hartford Insurance Co. of the Midwest v.*] *Halt,* 646 N.Y.S.2d [589 (N.Y.App.Div. 1996)] at 596–97 (Callahan, J., dissenting), in which the New York Supreme Court, Appellate Division, Fourth Department, overruled its earlier decision in *Paychex, Inc. v. Covenant Ins. Co.*, 156 A.D.2d 936, 549 N.Y.S.2d 237 (4 Dept.1989), which had adopted the minority view. The dissent in *Halt,* 646 N.Y.S.2d at 596, focuses on "the many disputes caused by these provisions and the different resolutions in various jurisdictions" to support a conclusion of ambiguity. However, we are not persuaded disagreement among courts over the proper interpretation of an insurance policy automatically means there is ambiguity requiring coverage.

The dissent in *Halt,* 646 N.Y.S.2d at 597, also stresses the 1989 *Paychex* decision placed New York insurers on notice its policy was considered ambiguous, but the insurers did nothing to revise the policy language. While this argument may have some force in New York, it carries little weight in North Dakota. Indeed, this Court had never addressed the issue and the majority of courts have not followed the *Paychex* line of reasoning.

We conclude, as a matter of law, the entitlement exclusion to the American automobile policy excluding coverage to "any person" using an auto without a reasonable belief the person is entitled to do so applies to a "family member" of the insured. Because the Closes do not challenge the trial court's ruling Dominic Ebertz was driving the vehicle at the time of the accident without his father's express or implied permission, we conclude the insurance policy provides no coverage for the Closes' injuries resulting from the October 12, 1992, accident.

. . . .

IV

We reverse the summary judgment and remand for entry of summary judgment in favor of American.

NOTES AND QUESTIONS

1. *Implications.* In the policy in *Odolecki,* the named insured and household residents were covered, plus anyone using the vehicle with the permission of the named insured or the named insured's spouse. What does the "reasonable belief" exclusion accomplish in light of the coverage-granting provisions? Did the court in *Close* give insufficient attention to North Dakota's public policies as reflected in its requirement that all drivers have liability insurance or show financial responsibility as a condition to registering a vehicle? *See* N.D. Cent. Code § 26.1–41–02 (1995). Was the court too hasty in saying what is good for New York is not good for North Dakota?

2. *"Look, Ma—No Driver's License!"* If a person is operating a vehicle without a valid driver's license (either because the driver is underage or because the license has been suspended or revoked), is that person using the vehicle "without a reasonable belief that [he] is entitled to do so"? *See Craig v. Barnes*, 710 A.2d 258 (Me. 1998) (insured's fiancée, who owned vehicle but did not have a driver's license, lacked reasonable belief in entitlement to use vehicle, so there was no coverage); *Farm and City Insurance Co. v. Gilmore*, 539 N.W.2d 154 (Iowa 1995) (unlicensed teenager had reasonable belief that he was entitled to drive vehicle after being asked to do so by insured's brother who had lawful possession of vehicle, so there was coverage).

Some policies have exclusions for named insureds and permissive users who do not have a valid driver's license. In *Adams v. Thomas*, 729 So. 2d 1041 (La. 1999), the Supreme Court of Louisiana struck down the clause as contravening the state's statutory omnibus clause and the public policies of the state, which favor protecting accident victims. If your liability insurance premiums would decline if no coverage were extended to unlicensed drivers, would you support the exclusion?

If a member of the insured's household has a poor driving record (imagine a person with multiple DUI convictions, several prior accidents and moving violations, and/or some history of driving without a valid license), should the insurer be allowed to issue the policy with an endorsement that excludes coverage for a particular named person? Should the insurer be required to sell the coverage but be allowed to charge a higher premium?

3. *The Permittee's Permittee Revisited.* Is the "reasonable belief" exclusion to be applied to whomever is driving the car at the time of the accident? If a parent gives permission to a licensed child to drive the family car, and this child gives permission to an unlicensed sibling to drive the car, does the exclusion apply? What if the parent has told the licensed child not to let anyone else drive the car, but the second permittee, also a licensed driver, does not know this? In *Rutgers Casualty Co. v. Collins*, 730 A.2d 833 (N.J. 1999), the Supreme Court of New Jersey held that if the passenger had initial permission to drive, the reasonableness of the driver's belief was irrelevant in circumstances where the passenger had extended permission to the driver. Is this result supported by the policy text, or is it an effort to protect accident victims? For comparison, *see State Farm Mutual Automobile Insurance Co. v. Ragatz*, 571 N.W.2d 155 (S.D. 1997), where the court upheld the insurer's denial of coverage when the owner's son, who had permission to drive the car provided he did not let anyone else drive it, gave permission to a friend and roommate who was driving the car at the time of the accident.

4. *Problems of Liability Coverage While Driving a Rented Car.* The simple act of renting a car can raise a surprising number of complex insurance questions. The standard auto liability policy will provide coverage to the insured for liability incurred while driving a rented car. If the renter does not have insurance, the rental car company will provide it, albeit for a pricy fee. One major way rental car companies reduce their risk is to refuse to rent cars

to drivers under 25 years of age. Beyond the driver's liability, rental companies will have their own coverage, inasmuch as they are at risk of being sued whenever one of their cars is operated by a lessee. If you have rented a vehicle, you probably know that you are asked who will be driving the vehicle, and sometimes you are charged an extra fee for an additional driver. You are also probably aware that lessees sometimes let third parties drive rental cars without having obtained permission for this use from the rental car company. Should an insurer which issues a liability policy to an auto rental company be allowed to disclaim responsibility for a person operating a rented vehicle with the lessee's permission but in violation of the rental agreement between the lessee and the rental company?

5. *"Rentals—Oh, My. We Are Just Getting Started."* If the lessee commits in the rental agreement to comply with applicable laws, and then proceeds to drive the car while intoxicated (in violation of law) with the result that a third-party is injured, is this deviation from the scope of permission a "material" one which renders the loss outside the lessor's liability insurer's coverage? *See Liberty Mutual Insurance Co. v. Thomas*, 971 S.W.2d 244 (Ark. 1998) (coverage). What if the rental agreement has an exclusion for "driving while intoxicated"? *See Budget Rent-A-Car Systems, Inc. v. Ricardo*, 942 P.2d 507 (Haw. 1997) (coverage). What if the lessee agrees in the rental agreement not to drive the car in a particular location (e.g., a public road that is particularly dangerous), but the lessee violates this provision and injures a third party in a collision? *See Budget Rent-A-Car Systems, Inc. v. Coffin*, 922 P.2d 964 (Haw. 1996) (no coverage). Can you identify a principle which reconciles the cited cases?

IV. "USE" OF VEHICLE

The liability coverage provided under auto insurance typically only applies to the "use" of the vehicle. Consequently, questions often arise as to what constitutes the "use" of a vehicle. The next two cases are examples of how courts have addressed the issue.

MCNEILL V. MARYLAND INSURANCE GUARANTY ASSOCIATION

427 A.2d 1056 (Md. Ct. Spec. App. 1981)

LISS, JUDGE.

Appellee, Maryland Insurance Guaranty Association, filed a declaratory judgment action in the Superior Court of Baltimore City seeking a determination of automobile liability coverage under an insurance policy issued by the bankrupt Maryland Indemnity Insurance Company (hereinafter MIIC) to its policyholder, Evelyn Watkins. Appellant, Charlie McNeill, answered the bill for declaratory judgment, and the parties agreed to submit the case on a stipulated statement of facts. That statement reads as follows:

On September 2, 1975, Maryland Indemnity Insurance Company issued Policy No. A58318 to Evelyn Watkins for a 1968 Dodge Coronet, Serial No. WP46F8A2379106. That policy was in effect on December 12, 1975.

On December 12, 1975, Charlie McNeill could not start his motor vehicle; whereupon he requested his friend, Evelyn Watkins, to bring her car to his location so that he could "jump start" or "hot shot" his car. Evelyn Watkins authorized Edward Hill to take her car to the aid of Charlie McNeill and he did so.

Charlie McNeill connected the cables to the batteries of both cars and the Watkins car engine was running at all times, all at the explicit direction of Charlie McNeill. Charlie McNeill then took off one or more of the battery caps from the battery located in his vehicle. At this time, Edward Hill, who was not in any of the vehicles but was standing in the area as an observer, lit a match causing the battery in the McNeill vehicle to explode resulting in Charlie McNeill being seriously injured.

Negligence and the absence of contributory negligence are admitted and, therefore, are not at issue. The Maryland Insurance Guaranty Association, representing the bankrupt insurer Maryland Indemnity, has filed the Declaratory Judgment action seeking determination of whether coverage may be afforded on the above policy to the claimant McNeill.

At oral argument before this Court the panel of judges hearing this case inquired whether the jumper cables were connected to both cars at all times pertinent; i.e., whether the cables remained connected uninterruptedly from the time they were originally connected until the time the battery exploded. Counsel for the parties were unable to answer this question at argument. Several days later, however, a letter was received in which both parties stipulated that the answer to the query was "yes." Furthermore, the letter (signed by both parties) represented to the panel:

Counsel also wish to bring to the Panel's attention, a clarification on the role of the match in causing the battery to explode. Counsel would agree that the lighting of a match which has absolutely nothing to do with the use or operation of a motor vehicle caused the explosion and . . . it is further necessary to point out that the lighting of the match caused an explosion not in the Watkins car, but in McNeill's car. It was McNeill's battery that exploded and it was caused by a match.

Counsel, of course, disagree as to whether appellant's injuries given the factual situation in its totality, "arose out of . . . the use of the insured's vehicle."

We have accepted the added stipulation of the parties as an additional portion of the appellate record.[1]

The Watkins vehicle was covered by the aforementioned policy which provided in pertinent part:

> Coverage A—Bodily Injury Liability. . .
>
> To pay on behalf of the insured all sums which the insured shall become legally obligated to pay as damages because of:
>
> > A. bodily injury . . . arising out of the ownership, maintenance or use of the owned automobile. . . .

The trial judge, after consideration of the agreed statement of facts and memoranda of law submitted by the parties, held that the injury sustained by appellant did not arise out of the "ownership, maintenance or use" of the Watkins automobile and that MIIC was not liable to appellant under the terms of the Watkins policy. From this judgment, McNeill appeals.

The sole issue to be determined by this appeal is whether the injury sustained by the appellant was caused by an accident arising out of the "ownership, maintenance or use" of the Watkins vehicle.

The standard adopted by the Court of Appeals in the interpretation of provisions of an insurance policy where the disputed provision is susceptible to more than one construction is that the provision must be "liberally construed in order to promote . . . recovery for innocent victims of motor vehicle accidents." "Ownership, maintenance or use clauses" do not limit recovery solely to injuries that are caused by direct physical contact with the insured vehicle; nor is it necessary that the damages be directly sustained or inflicted by the operation of the motor vehicle.

Appellant contends that it is sufficient to establish liability and coverage where there is a substantial nexus between the injury sustained and the use of the motor vehicle as contemplated by the insurance carrier and the insured.

Appellee argues that an automobile liability policy which provides coverage for accidents arising out of the "use" of a covered vehicle does not insure the owner of the vehicle unless it is shown that there is a causal connection between the use of the automobile and the accident, or the creation of the condition which caused the accident.

The Court of Appeals, in *Frazier v. Unsatisfied Claim and Judgment Board*, 262 Md. 115, 277 A.2d 57 (1971) had before it a factual situation in

---

[1] In fairness to the trial court we point out that the judge did not have before him the additional facts elicited by the query of the panel on appeal. We, of course, cannot speculate as to whether the additional information would have affected the trial court's conclusion. We have concluded that we should not avail ourselves of the provisions of Maryland Rule 1071 which permits a remand to the trial court under these circumstances; rather, in the interest of judicial economy of time, we choose to dispose of the issue raised by this appeal.

which a child of five years was a passenger in the rear seat of an open convertible vehicle which was being operated by the child's mother. An unidentified vehicle proceeding in the opposite direction passed the convertible and a lighted firecracker was thrown from the unidentified vehicle into the rear seat of the convertible. Distracted by the occurrence, the mother lost control of her car and struck a tree, severely injuring her child. The trial court concluded as a matter of law that the injuries did not arise out of the ownership, maintenance and use of the unidentified automobile. In reversing the trial court, the Court of Appeals held:

> 8 Blashfield, Automobile Law & Practice § 317.1 at 5 6 (Lewis ed. 1966); 7 Appleman, Insurance Law & Practice § 4317 at 144 6 (1942) and an Annotation, 89 A.L.R.2d 150 would seem to support the proposition that whether an injury is or is not within the coverage provided by an automobile insurance policy may well turn on the question whether the use of an automobile is directly or merely incidentally causally connected with the injury, even though the automobile itself may not have proximately caused the injury. Compare, for example, *National Indemnity Co. v. Ewing*, 235 Md. 145, 200 A.2d 680 (1964) (recovery allowed plaintiff, who fell from insured's car, and was injured while being escorted back to car on foot) and *Mullen v. Hartford Accident & Indemnity Co.*, 287 Mass. 262, 191 N.E. 394 (1934) (injury sustained from slipping on oil leaking from car held to be within provisions of policy) *with Commercial Union Ins. Co. of New York v. Hall*, 246 F. Supp. 64 (E.D.S.C. 1965) (no liability to plaintiff, whose way was blocked by insured's car and was then assaulted by insured) and *Kraus v. Allstate Ins. Co.*, 258 F. Supp. 407 (W.D. Pa. 1966) aff'd 379 F.2d 443 (3d Cir. 1967) (insurer not liable to pedestrians when insured detonated dynamite in his car). [262 Md. at 118, 277 A.2d 57.]

. . . .

From our reading of the briefs submitted by the parties we find no appreciable dispute between the parties as to the applicable principles of law governing this case. Both sides concede that a causal relationship or connection must exist between an accident and the ownership, maintenance and use of the insured vehicle in order for coverage to be provided under the policy provision. They further agree that absent such a causal connection of relationship, recovery will be denied. The problem arises as to the application of the law to the facts of the instant case.

Appellee relies heavily upon *Plaxco v. United States Fidelity & Guaranty Co.*, 252 S.C. 437, 166 S.E.2d 799 (1969), where an action was also sought in declaratory relief. The issue in *Plaxco* was whether the use by an insured of his automobile battery to crank the engines of his airplane by connecting the batteries with jumper cables constituted a use of an automobile within the meaning of the automobile liability insurance policy providing coverage arising out of the ownership, maintenance or use of any automobile. In *Plaxco*, the plaintiff drove his automobile to the airport for the purpose of making a trip in his airplane. The plane battery was either dead or too weak to start the engine so he drove his automobile to the left wing and connected the batteries of the plane to the auto by use of a jumper cable. When this was done he entered the plane, started the engine and engaged the brakes and alighted to disconnect the jumper cables, leaving the airplane engine running. After the plaintiff disconnected one of the cables from the automobile battery, and while attempting to disconnect the other, the airplane brakes failed to hold and struck another aircraft. The court held that the accident did not result from the use of plaintiff's automobile, when it stated:

> The accident in question did not result from the use of plaintiff's automobile. The only connection between the automobile and the airplane was the use of the automobile battery to start the airplane engine. This purpose had been completed when the airplane moved forward, after the brakes failed to hold. We find nothing in the facts or circumstances to show a causal connection between the use of the automobile battery as a source of power to start the airplane engine and the subsequent forward movement of the airplane. As stated by the trial judge, "the power source was coincidental only." The facts show that the accident resulted from the use of the airplane and not the insured automobile.

[252 S.C. at 441, 166 S.E.2d 799.]

We conclude that the facts in *Plaxco* are distinguishable from the case at bar. The use of the Watkins vehicle was clearly a use which was or should have been contemplated and anticipated by the insurance carrier and the owner of the vehicle. It is not unusual that an insured might on occasion be required to use his vehicle to charge the battery of another vehicle. At the time the explosion took place, the Watkins vehicle was still being used in an activity permitted by her policy. The additional stipulation makes it clear that the Watkins vehicle was still attached by the jumper cables to McNeill's vehicle at the time Watkins' driver negligently threw the match. McNeill's activity in unscrewing the battery caps was entirely consistent with an effort to determine whether the battery had sufficient fluid and charge to permit McNeill's car to operate without being attached to the jumper cables. The lighting of the cigarette by Watkins' driver was not an intervening or independent cause, as was the failure of the airplane brakes in *Plaxco*. We conclude that this case on its facts is governed by *Merchants Co. v. Hartford Accident and Indemnity Co.*, 187 Miss. 301, 188 So. 571 (1939), where the Court held:

> In examining the cited cases, it will be observed that some of them proceed as if the automobile liability policy had expressly required that the injury for which the insurer could be held must be the proximate result of the use of the automobile truck. And if the policy here before us contained that express language, it might be that liability under the St. Paul Company policy in the present case would be denied on the ground that the proximate cause of the injury was the technically separable fact of the failure to remove the poles from the road. But we are in accord with the ruling expressed in *Panhandle Steel Products Co. v. Fidelity Union Cas. Co.* [Tex. Civ. App., 23 S.W.2d 799] . . . that an insurance contract such as we have here does not require that the injury must be the proximate result, in the strict legal sense of that term, of a negligent act which happened in the actual use or operation of the truck; and, on the other hand, we would not assent to a contention that the policy liability would extend to something distinctly remote, although within the line of causation.
>
> Our conclusion, under a policy such as is here before us, is that where a dangerous situation causing injury is one which arose out of or had its source in, the use or operation of the automobile, the chain of responsibility must be deemed to possess the requisite articulation with the use or operation until broken by the intervention of some event which has no direct or substantial relation to the use or operation,—which is to say, that the event which breaks the chain, and which, therefore, would exclude liability under the automobile policy, must be an event which bears no direct or substantial relation to the use or operation; and until an event of the latter nature transpires the liability under the policy exists.

[188 So. at 572.]

Appellee would, in effect, have us adopt the strict rules of direct and proximate cause in order to deny coverage. This, in light of the opinions by the Court of Appeals which we have cited, we decline to do. Under the facts in this case we conclude that there was a causal relationship between the use of the Watkins vehicle to start McNeill's automobile and that the explosion was caused by the careless throwing of the match by Watkins' driver which ignited the fumes released when the battery caps were unscrewed. We find that at the time this occurred the Watkins vehicle was being "used" as contemplated by the Watkins liability insurance policy.

Judgment reversed, costs to be paid by appellee.

FARM BUREAU MUTUAL INSURANCE CO. V. EVANS

637 P.2d 491 (Kan. Ct. App. 1981)

ABBOTT, JUDGE.

This is an appeal by two automobile liability insurance carriers from an order granting summary judgment against them holding that the respective policies issued by them provided coverage for the accident in question.

The determinative issue in this case is whether liability for bodily injury caused by the throwing of a lighted firecracker (M 80) from the rear of a parked station wagon "arose out of the use of an automobile" so as to be covered under the automobile liability insurance policies in issue.

On April 28, 1979, a going away party was being held for David and Karen Evans. The party was held in a large, open field. Several bonfires were going; keg beer was available. It started to rain and turn cold. Damon Rose (not a party to this action), at his wife's request, parked the Roses' station wagon so that the back seat was facing a bonfire. The Rose station wagon has three seats, the back one of which faces the rear of the station wagon. The tailgate was open. Mike Ehinger was sitting in the middle of the back seat facing the fire. Kathy Rose and Danny Ireland were beside him. It is alleged that Ehinger, with the aid of Rose and Ireland, lit an explosive device known as an M 80 and threw it out of the rear of the station wagon. It landed in a glass of beer held by Karen Evans. When it exploded, Karen Evans received extensive damage to her hand and a number of puncture wounds to her body from the shattered glass.

The Evanses are plaintiffs in a personal injury action brought against Kathy Rose, Mike Ehinger and Danny Ireland for Karen's personal injuries sustained as a result of the explosion. Farm Bureau Mutual Insurance Company, Inc., insures the Rose automobile and Farmers Insurance Company, Inc., insures an automobile owned by Mike Ehinger. Both policies provide coverage for bodily injury "arising out of the ownership, maintenance or use" of the insured vehicle.

The question before the trial court was whether the two policies provided coverage for Mike Ehinger, Danny Ireland and Kathy Rose, or any of them, with regard to claims made against them by the Evanses. The trial court determined that there was coverage because the automobile was being used as shelter, a reasonable incident of its use and one reasonably contemplated by the parties to the insurance contract.

The policy provision in question is mandated by the legislature. K.S.A.1980 Supp. 40 3107(b). As an automobile liability coverage clause, it is to be interpreted broadly to afford the greatest possible protection to the insured. In the case before us, the trial court found the vehicle was being "used" within the meaning of the coverage clause because of its use as a shelter.

But mere use of a vehicle, standing alone, is not sufficient to trigger coverage. Thus, even though the vehicle was being used within the meaning of the automobile liability policies, the question remains whether that use is so remote from the negligent act that it can be said there was no causal relationship between the use of the car and the injuries sustained.

Kansas has construed the word "use" in connection with automobile liability policies on three occasions: *Alliance Mutual Casualty Co. v. Boston Insurance Co.*, 196 Kan. 323, 411 P.2d 616 (1966); *Esfeld Trucking, Inc. v. Metropolitan Insurance Co.*, 193 Kan. 7, 392 P.2d 107 (1964); *United States Fidelity & Guar. Co. v. Farm Bureau Mut. Ins. Co.*, 2 Kan. App. 2d 580, 584 P.2d 1264. None of these cases is exactly in point, but language found in *Esfeld* indicates Kansas follows the majority rule that there must be some causal connection between the use of the insured vehicle and the injury. In *Esfeld*, the court stated: "In determining the coverage of a policy such as our present one a court must consider whether the injury sustained was a natural and reasonable incident or consequence of the use of the vehicle involved for the purposes shown by the declarations of the policy though not foreseen or expected." 193 Kan. at 11, 392 P.2d 107.

The general rule in other jurisdictions is that "arising out of the use" of a vehicle requires the finding of some causal connection or relation between the use of the vehicle and the injury. Stated another way, an injury does not arise out of the "use" of a vehicle within the meaning of the coverage clause of an automobile liability policy if it is caused by some intervening cause not identifiable with normal ownership, maintenance and use of the insured vehicle and the injury complained of. The provision, however, imparts a more liberal concept of a causation than "proximate cause" in its traditional, legal sense.

We need not decide whether a different result might be reached if the vehicle had been in motion at the time. Some courts have held that if a vehicle is moving and the speed of the car contributed to the impact of a thrown missile, such would be a sufficient causal connection. Likewise, the mere throwing of the contents of an ashtray or other trash normally found in a vehicle could constitute a use. The throwing of an explosive device from a car, however, has generally been held to be so remotely connected with the use of the vehicle that it is not causally related to the injury.

The use of the Roses' vehicle did not causally contribute to Karen's injuries anymore [sic] than it would have if one of the occupants under the facts present in this case had shot her with a firearm. The fact that the M 80 was lit inside the vehicle and the defendants might have had difficulty lighting it if no shelter had been available is so remote that it does not furnish the necessary causal relationship between the use of the car and her injuries. We see no more difference in the use of the vehicle here under the facts present than if the owner of the vehicle had been outside the car and in order to avoid the rain had held the device under the car or stood on the "leeward" side of it to light the device.

Having concluded the trial court erred in determining that the insurance policies in question provided coverage, we deem the remaining issues moot.

Reversed with directions to enter judgment for the insurance carriers on their motions for summary judgment.

NOTES AND QUESTIONS

1. *The Essence of the Coverage.* If an automobile is being driven when an accident occurs, does the loss automatically arise out of the "ownership, maintenance, or use" of the vehicle? What if the victim is standing on the bed of the insured's truck as the truck is slowly driven past a row of apple trees and the victim falls out of the truck while trying to reach for an apple? Does the answer change if the truck was stationary when the fall occurred? What if the insured fell from the truck because he had placed a stepladder in the truck's bed, failed to properly secure the ladder, and then fell off the ladder while reaching for the apple? *See Leverette v. Aetna Casualty & Surety Co.*, 276 S.E.2d 859 (Ga. Ct. App. 1981).

Generally speaking, people purchase a homeowners (or renters) policy to cover their general personal liabilities except for liabilities arising out of the use of automobiles, and automobile liability policies are purchased to provide insurance for the automobile-related risks. When the insured negligently operates the insured vehicle and crashes into another in a garden-variety automobile accident, the automobile is being "used" as an automobile. People, however, put their automobiles to many kinds of uses, some of them quite innovative, and the question often arises whether the loss arises out of the automobile's "ownership, maintenance, or use."

2. *Coverage and Non-Owned Automobiles.* Although liability coverage under standard automobile policies is limited to bodily injury or property damage "arising out of the ownership, maintenance or use" of the insured's automobile, note that coverage ordinarily is also extended to an insured's operation or use of a non-owned automobile but under somewhat narrower circumstances.

3. *Ownership, Maintenance, or Use?* Each term in the "ownership, maintenance, or use" coverage provision applies to distinct risks notwithstanding the possibility of overlap in some situations. The first two terms are narrower than the third and have produced less litigation than the term "use."

Note that both *McNeill* and *Evans* involve the liability coverages of the automobile policy. The "ownership, maintenance, or use" issue also arises in connection with the uninsured and underinsured coverages, which are discussed later in this chapter.

a. *Ownership*. One may be liable as an owner of an automobile under the common law "family purpose" doctrine or by virtue of an owner consent statute. *See* Dan B. Dobbs, The Law of Torts § 340 (2000). The term "ownership" in the policy applies to these situations as well as any other where mere ownership is the basis for imposing liability, vicarious or otherwise.

If the insured has sold his vehicle under a conditional sales agreement and retains title for security purposes until the last payment is made, is the insured the "owner" of the vehicle for insurance purposes? *See Beatty v. Western Pacific Insurance Co.*, 445 P.2d 325 (Wash. 1968). It is very common in recent years for people to lease vehicles for multi-year terms instead of purchasing the vehicle with borrowed funds and making payments on a promissory note. Standard policy language treats vehicles leased under long-term arrangements as the equivalent of owned vehicles.

b. *Maintenance*. The unqualified term "maintenance" applies to anyone who negligently injures a third party as a result of servicing, repairing, or otherwise maintaining the vehicle, but standard policies generally exclude coverage for those who are in the business of furnishing such services. Thus, your friendly auto mechanic does not get the benefit of your coverage when he negligently repairs your brakes. However, you or your friendly neighbor would be covered if either or both of you did so. If an insured is assaulted by third parties while changing a tire, do the insured's injuries arise out of the maintenance of the vehicle? *See Blish v. Atlanta Casualty Co.*, 736 So. 2d 1151 (Fla. 1999) (yes).

c. *Use*. The term "use," as illustrated in *McNeill* and *Evans*, has produced a substantial amount of litigation, as might be imagined given all that transpires in and around the automobile in our society.

Do you agree with the *McNeill* court that Hill was "using" Watkins' car when he lit the match that caused the battery in McNeill's car to explode? Would it be important to know whether the charging of the McNeill battery by the Watkins' car created the situation where an explosion could occur, i.e., whether the chemical process involved in charging a battery in this manner produces more combustible fumes than are otherwise emitted by a battery? Depending on the answer, would it have behooved one of the attorneys to make sure that information on the subject was introduced at trial or contained in the stipulation?

If McNeill was "using" Watkins' car, were Ehinger and his pals "using" the Rose vehicle in the *Evans* case? What is the difference?

4. *"Use" as a "Transportational Function."* Some courts ask whether the vehicle is being used in its "transportational function." The focus, then, is on whether the motor vehicle is being used "as a motor vehicle," to be

distinguished from being used as "a housing facility of sorts, as an advertising display (such as at a car dealership), as a foundation for construction equipment, as a mobile public library, or perhaps even when a car is on display in a museum." *McKenzie v. Auto Club Insurance Ass'n*, 580 N.W.2d 424 (Mich. 1998) (insured is non-fatally asphyxiated while sleeping in camper attached to pickup truck). But, do you agree that a vehicle is solely a device for getting from one place to another? Can it not also be used (and expected to be used) as a device for shelter (e.g., the so called "car campers")? Anyone who has spent time on a farm knows that farming vehicles are put to many different uses. If an insured uses a pickup truck to pull a rope that lifts a wooden platform via a pulley system, the rope breaks, and the platform falls on someone causing injury, does the loss "arise out of the use" of the truck? *See Lawver v. Boling*, 238 N.W.2d 514 (Wis. 1976). How would the court in *Evans* have decided the farm truck and the pulley case?

People also use vehicles to transport things, including pets. If a dog named Rover is being transported by a car and bites a passenger while the car is moving (or getting ready to move), does this injury arise out of the use of the vehicle? If the vehicle is stopped and parked while Rover rests inside it, a child opens the door and gets in the car, and Rover bites the child, does this injury arise out of the use of the vehicle? *See Keppler v. American Family Mutual Insurance Co.*, 588 N.W.2d 105 (Iowa 1999); *Farmers Union Cooperative Insurance Co. v. Allied Property and Casualty Insurance Co.*, 569 N.W.2d 436 (Neb. 1997).

5. *Vehicles and Firearms*. Cars and trucks are dangerous enough, but many people have demonstrated through the years that one can multiply risk exponentially by using a car and a gun at the same time. This has produced a large number of perplexing cases where the meaning of the term "use" was contested.

Can you reconcile the following two cases? In *Kohl v. Union Insurance Co.*, 731 P.2d 134 (Colo. 1986), a claimant bystander's injuries were held to be causally related to the insured defendant's use of his jeep. In *Kohl*, the accidental discharge of a rifle occurred while the insured was lifting the rifle out of the jeep's gun rack while the jeep was parked in preparation for unloading the rifle and safely storing it for the journey home from a hunting trip. In *Azar v. Employers Casualty Co.*, 495 P.2d 554 (Colo. 1972), the claimant passenger's injuries were held not to be causally related to defendant driver's use of the car in which both were riding while hunting rabbits. In *Azar*, the defendant stopped the car, prepared to fire his shotgun through the window, but changed his mind and accidentally discharged the gun while bringing it back into the car.

What about these two cases? In *Fidelity & Casualty Co. v. Lott*, 273 F.2d 500 (5th Cir. 1960), the insured was held to be "using" his car when he rested his rifle on the top of the car for better aim and fired. The bullet struck the curvature of the roof, deflected downward, and killed a passenger. But, in *Norgaard v. Nodak Mutual Insurance Co.*, 201 N.W.2d 871 (N.D. 1972), the insured was held not to be "using" his car when he used the roof as a gun rest, fired, and killed a passenger whom he did not see alighting from the car.

Some courts have attempted to articulate a test in car gunshot accidents which distinguishes a situation in which a vehicle is the mere "situs" of an accident from one in which the vehicle itself or permanent attachments to the vehicle causally contribute in some way to produce the injury. *See, e.g.*, *Thornton v. Allstate Insurance Co.*, 391 N.W.2d 320 (Mich. 1986). How helpful is this test? Do you think the cramped physical quarters of the car contributed significantly to the accident in *Azar*? Did the autos in *Lott* and *Norgaard* causally contribute in some way to produce the injuries?

6. *Vehicles as Launching Pads. Evans* puts the "car as launching pad" issue in play. Judge Abbott acknowledged, but did not address, the complication that would arise if the car had been in motion. Where objects, such as eggs or beer bottles, are thrown from a moving vehicle, does this constitute a "use" within the automobile liability coverage clause? *See National Am. Insurance Co. v. Insurance Co. of N. Am.*, 74 Cal. App. 3d 565 (1977). Should a distinction be made between throwing the "usual stuff" out of cars (such as apple cores, sticks, and trash) and tossing out inherently dangerous objects (such as fireworks)?

Should firing a gun (i.e., launching a bullet) from inside a vehicle be handled under the same principles? Given the recent increase in gun-related violence committed from inside moving vehicles (e.g., drive-by shootings), is it fair to suggest that these kinds of events involve "expected" uses of vehicles, at least for the purpose of insurance coverage? *See, e.g., State Farm Mutual Automobile Insurance Co. v. Bookert*, 523 S.E.2d 181 (S.C. 1999) (insured not entitled to UIM benefits for injuries from gunshots fired from a vehicle); *Farmers Texas County Mutual Insurance Co. v. Griffin*, 955 S.W.2d 81 (Tex. 1997) (victim of drive-by shooting did not allege "auto accident" within meaning of liability policy); *Lexie v. State Farm Mutual Automobile Insurance Co.*, 469 S.E.2d 61 (Va. 1996) (no causal connection between two separate drive-by shooting incidents and use of vehicles for purposes of UM coverage).

Should injuries suffered by the insured driver during a crime be covered? *See Bourne v. Farmers Insurance Exchange*, 534 N.W.2d 491 (Mich. 1995) (insurer not obligated to pay no-fault benefits to insured for injuries suffered during carjacking). In *Pemco Insurance Co. v. Schlea*, 817 P.2d 878 (Wash. Ct. App. 1991), the insured was abducted and raped in an automobile her assailant had taken from a co-worker. The majority held it did not arise out of the "use" of the vehicle because "[k]idnapping, assault, and rape are not motoring risks against which the parties intended to insure." *Id.* at 880. The dissent had a different view: "While using a vehicle as a means of transporting a victim and as a place to commit a rape is not either a 'reasonable,' or 'traditional' use of an automobile, it is . . . a use nonetheless." *Id.*

7. *Other Policy Forms.* Some motor vehicle policies use slightly different wording. They provide coverage for liability arising out of the "ownership, maintenance or use, including loading and unloading" of the vehicle. Does the

"loading and unloading" language really add anything to the word "use"? The "loading and unloading" language has produced some surprisingly broad legal interpretations under the comprehensive general liability and basic auto policies, and steps were taken in drafting the business version of the automobile policy to limit this language to activities more directly involved in the actual or immediate loading and unloading process.

If a passenger is bitten by the insured's dog as the passenger is getting out of the insured's car, does the injury arise out of the "unloading" of the vehicle? *See Hartford Accident & Indemnity Co. v. Civil Service Employees Insurance Co.*, 108 Cal. Rptr. 737 (Cal. Ct. App. 1973). Does it matter whether the dog was in the car at the time of the bite, as opposed to running across the lawn to meet his prey? If the former, is it customary to expect vehicles to be used to transport pets, which means the unloading issue need not even be reached? If the victim is already out of the car at the time of the bite, is the process of "unloading" already over, so that the insurance does not provide coverage? *See Shoreland Early Childhood Center v. Alexander*, 616 N.E.2d 274 (Ohio Ct. App. 1992).

8. *Other More or Less Common Situations.* As one might predict, the situations in which insureds become liable to third parties and a motor vehicle is somewhere in the picture are virtually infinite. Consider the following:

a. Do altercations between people who have just been involved in auto accidents "arise out of the ownership, maintenance, or use" of the vehicles? *See Foss v. Cignarella*, 482 A.2d 954 (N.J. Super. Ct. Law Div. 1984) (insured sideswiped plaintiff when passing on left by driving on median; plaintiff's vehicle bumped insured's as both stopped; insured emerged from vehicle in rage and stabbed plaintiff, who was still in car with window partially down); *see also Allstate Insurance Co. v. Gillespie*, 455 So. 2d 617 (Fla. Dist. Ct. App. 1984) (assault on insured, who was sitting in car, by person who was enraged by manner in which insured was driving; insured produced gun, which discharged and injured attacker, and attacker sued insured); *Morosini v. Citizens Insurance Co. of Am.*, 602 N.W.2d 828 (Mich. 1999) (insured's vehicle was struck from behind by another motorist in minor accident; when insured left his vehicle to inspect damage, other motorist assaulted and injured insured).

b. What if the victim falls from a moving vehicle while trying to resist the amorous advances of the driver? *See Chapman v. Allstate Insurance Co.*, 211 S.E.2d 876 (S.C. 1975).

c. If the insured accidentally slams the door on a passenger's hand, causing injury, is the loss covered? Are you entirely comfortable covering such claims if the victim is a member of the insured's family? *See Coletrain v. Coletrain*, 121 S.E.2d 89 (S.C. 1961).

d. The insured uses his covered vehicle to transport tools to an intersection. He stops the car and turns it off. He takes the tools out of the car and uses them to remove (i.e., steal) a stop sign at the intersection, which he places in his car along with the tools. He drives off with his loot. Later, a motorist is killed at the intersection because of the stop sign's removal. The heirs of the decedent bring a negligence action against the insured. Does the auto liability policy provide coverage for the death? *See Molitor v. Davidson*, 978 P.2d 294 (Kan. Ct. App. 1999). If the court adheres to the precedent of *Evans*, what result?

EXERCISE

1. On July 4, Howard asked Green to help him attempt to pull his boat and boat trailer across a beach by hauling it with Howard's car. Green lent Howard a nylon rope, two shackles, and a pulley. Green hitched the pulley to a telephone pole. Green stayed at the trailer with Spiro in order to help guide the boat and trailer in the proper direction at the time it was to be towed. Howard attached one shackle to the rear bumper of his car and the other shackle to the trailer, thereby attaching the line to both the car and the trailer. Howard started the car and began to go forward. At that time, Spiro and Green held onto the tongue of the trailer in order to guide it in the proper direction. When Howard started to move his car, the line tightened and, a few seconds later, slackened. The shackle attached to the rear bumper of his car broke and a fragment struck and fatally injured Paul, a lifeguard who was about 50 feet away. At no time did Green drive the car. Howard's boat and trailer were registered to him. The trailer was designed for use with a private passenger motor vehicle, and it was not being used during this incident for business purposes with another type of motor vehicle.

Assume that Green has an automobile policy in the form of the Sample Auto Policy at the beginning of this chapter. Write a 3-page memo regarding whether Green has any coverage under the policy if Paul's estate sues Green.

V. COLLISION VERSUS COMPREHENSIVE COVERAGE

In addition to the mandatory coverage for liability claims asserted against the policyholder, many purchasers of auto insurance buy coverage for damage to their own vehicle. Two types of property coverage are available to policyholders for their vehicles: collision and comprehensive.

Although there are some exceptions, collision coverage generally covers damage to the vehicle caused by the upset of the vehicle or impact between the vehicle and an object or another vehicle. Auto policies typically define the term "collision," and it is common for those definitions to define collision by reference to what it is not—by listing causes of damage that do not constitute a "collision," such as fire, windstorm, and theft. There are, however, some causes that intuitively seem like they should be treated as collisions, such as animals hitting the vehicle, but which are not covered by the terms defining collision coverage in some policies. Under the Sample Auto Policy at the beginning of this chapter, in addition to animals hitting the vehicle, what other causes are excluded from the definition of "collision"?

Comprehensive coverage, on the other hand, covers the non-collision causes of damage such as fire, windstorm, and theft. Why would someone buy only collision or only comprehensive coverage? Does it matter whether something foreseeable is excluded from the collision coverage if it is covered by the comprehensive coverage?

As you read the next two cases, consider whether you agree with the courts' analyses regarding whether the damage to the vehicles at issue was caused by a "collision."

MCKAY V. STATE FARM MUT. AUTO. INS. CO.

933 F. Supp. 635 (S.D. Texas 1995)

MEMORANDUM AND ORDER GRANTING SUMMARY JUDGMENT

HARMON, DISTRICT JUDGE.

Pending before the Court in the above referenced action seeking a declaratory judgment that Defendant State Farm Mutual Automobile Insurance Company breached an automobile insurance policy issued to Plaintiff Gillian M. McKay is Defendant's motion for summary judgment.

Plaintiff's policy provides in relevant part,

> PART D—COVERAGE FOR DAMAGE TO YOUR AUTO INSURING AGREEMENT
>
> A. We will pay for direct and accidental loss to *your covered auto,* including its equipment, less any applicable deductible shown in the declarations. However, we will pay for loss covered by *collision* only if the Declarations indicate that Collision Coverage (Coverage D2) is provided.
>
> B. *Collision* means the upset, or *collision* with another object *of your covered auto*. However, loss caused by the following are not considered *collision* and are covered only if the Declarations indicate that Coverage D1 is provided:
>
> 1. Missiles or falling objects;
> 2. Fire;
> 3. Theft or larceny;
> 4. Explosion or earthquake;
> 5. Windstorm;
> 6. Hail, water, or flood;

7. Malicious mischief or vandalism;

8. Riot or civil commotion;

9. Contact with bird or animal;

10. Breakage of glass.

If breakage of glass is caused by a collision or if loss is caused by contact with a bird or animal, you may elect to have it considered a loss caused by collision.

Plaintiff asserts claims for breach of contract. . . .

Plaintiff Gillian McKay purchased an automobile insurance policy containing comprehensive property damage coverage, but no collision coverage, for her Blazer. On March 24, 1995, when Plaintiff's son was driving the vehicle on a freeway at night in Houston, Texas, a man darted onto the freeway, and, although the driver swerved to attempt to avoid hitting the man, the Blazer and the man collided. The man, who was subsequently run over by two other vehicles and died at Ben Taub Hospital, was determined to have had a blood alcohol level of 0.148 around the time. Defendant states that it denied Plaintiff's subsequent property damage claim because Plaintiff did not have collision coverage and because it was not covered under the comprehensive coverage that she had purchased.

Plaintiff's original petition alleges that because the man who ran into the side of the Blazer is not an "object," there was no "collision" under the definition of the policy, which therefore unambiguously provides for coverage of "direct and accidental loss" to the damaged Blazer. Defendant moves for summary judgment. . . . First Defendant maintains that under the terms of the policy and the law in Texas, Plaintiff did not have collision coverage, the accident was a collision, and therefore Defendant is entitled to summary judgment as a matter of law. The policy defines "collision" as "the upset, or collision with another object of your covered auto." According to the Texas Supreme Court, in reviewing a policy with very similar language and adopting the definition of the Century Dictionary Cyclopedia, a collision is "[t]he meeting and mutual striking or clashing of two moving bodies, or of a moving body with a stationary one." *Providence Washington Insurance Co. v. Proffitt,* 150 Tex. 207, 239 S.W.2d 379, 382 (1951) (holding that the force of floodwaters against an automobile was a collision within the terms of the policy).

Plaintiff's complaint alternatively alleges that coverage exists under the policy for malicious mischief, vandalism, and contact with bird or animal, and that the intoxicated man's conduct constituted such. Plaintiff contends that to show that a defendant was motivated by malice, a plaintiff need not prove that the defendant acted with personal spite but only that the defendant committed negligent acts in reckless disregard of another's rights and with indifference to injury to that party. *Missouri Pacific R. Co.*

v. Lemon, 861 S.W.2d 501 (Tex.App.—Houston [14th Dist.] 1993, no writ). Plaintiff argues that the man who ran into the freeway and damaged the Blazer acted in a negligent manner and with reckless disregard for the welfare of the drivers on the freeway.

Defendant maintains that there is no coverage here under the exception for "contact with a bird or animal" because "in the language of the law, the word 'animal' is used to mean all animal life other than man and signifies an inferior or irrational sentient being, general, but not necessarily possessed of the power of self motivation." 4 Am.Jur.2d § 1 (1995). *See also Tate v. Ogg,* 170 Va. 95, 195 S.E. 496, 499 (1938) ("Viewed in its broadest sense, the word 'animal' in the language of the law is used in contra-distinction to a human being and signifies an inferior living creature, generally having the power of self-motion."); *Tillery v. Crook,* 297 S.W.2d 9, 13 (Ct.App.Mo.1957), Defendant further contends that because the policy couples animal with bird, the language means animal other than man.

Regarding Plaintiff's insistence that the pedestrian caused the damage to the Blazer by "malicious mischief" or vandalism, Defendant argues that vandalism or malicious mischief are intentional acts and there is no evidence that the pedestrian intended to damage McKay's car by running across the freeway late at night. Indeed the pedestrian's action does not constitute vandalism or malicious mischief, which has been defined as a "wanton, intentional act committed with the fixed purpose to damage or destroy property." *Imperial Casualty and Indemnity Company v. Terry,* 451 S.W.2d 303, 305 (Tex.Civ.App.—Tyler 1970).

. . . .

Plaintiff responds that Defendant is attempting to exclude coverage under the policy by claiming that she should have purchased another policy for collision insurance. The comprehensive policy states, "We will pay for direct and accidental loss. . . ." Defendant has the burden of proving that coverage in this instance should be excluded. Tex.Ins.Code Ann. art. 21.57 (Vernon 1981). To do so, Defendant must show, but has failed to do so, that a human being is an "object" but not an "animal" under the definition of "collision" in the policy and that Plaintiff's definition of "collision" in the policy and that Plaintiff's property damage was not the result of "contact" with an "animal." Neither "object" nor "animal" is defined in the policy. When a term in an insurance policy is not defined, the term will be given the meaning that an "ordinary person" would apply. She argues that to an ordinary person a person is not an object. The ordinary meaning of animal includes human beings. . . .

Plaintiff contends that Defendant never advised Plaintiff of its "strained interpretation" of the policy prior to the time of purchase, but instead advised her that any property loss would be covered under a "comprehensive" policy as long as she or her children, as listed drivers, were not at fault in an accident with another vehicle. She insists that there is no difference between a person running into the side of her vehicle and a deer doing the same, yet Defendant asserts that only the latter is covered.

Plaintiff maintains that Defendant has refused to accept her reasonable construction of her policy.

. . . .

After reviewing the record and the applicable law, this Court concludes that Defendant is entitled to summary judgment as a matter of law. Under the definition of "collision" embodied in the policy and the definition approved by the Texas Supreme Court in *Proffitt,* 239 S.W.2d at 382, cited frequently since, the accident between the moving Blazer and running man was a collision. Plaintiff's policy expressly excludes collisions from coverage unless there is a separate collision policy, which Plaintiff admits she did not have. Moreover a human being is an "object." Black's *Law Dictionary,* at 967, *citing Moore v. Union Mutual Fire Ins. Co.*, 112 Vt. 218, 22 A.2d 503, 505, defines "object" as, "Anything which comes within the cognizance or scrutiny of the senses, especially anything that tangible or visible." Furthermore, this Court's research has led it to concur with Defendant that the legal definition of animal excludes human beings. *See, e.g.,* Black's *Law Dictionary* at 80 (5th ed. West 1979) (defining "animal" as "Non-human, animate being which is endowed with the power of voluntary motion. Animal life other than man."), *citing Bernardine,* 44 N.Y.S.2d at 883. Despite creative arguments from Plaintiff, this Court concludes that a man darting across a freeway at night does not constitute malicious mischief or vandalism. There is no evidence that he intentionally damaged or destroyed Plaintiff's personal property in an act far more likely to endanger him than the speeding vehicles. Section 28.03 of the Texas Penal Code Ann. (Vernon's 1994), defines "criminal mischief" as follows:

> (a) A person commits an offense if, without the effective consent of the owner:
>
> > (1) he intentionally or knowingly damages or destroys the tangible property of the owner;
> >
> > (2) he intentionally or knowingly tampers with the tangible property of the owner and causes pecuniary loss or substantial inconvenience to the owner or a third person; or
> >
> > (3) he intentionally or knowingly makes markings, including inscriptions, slogans, drawing, or paintings, on the tangible property of the owner.

[Plaintiff's] reliance on Defendant's previous coverage when a deer ran into her vehicle is [also] inappropriate in that such an accident would fall under the "animal or bird" exception. Given the unlikelihood of such an occurrence, Plaintiff's statement in her affidavit that "State Farm never said before I purchased my 'comprehensive' automobile insurance coverage that State Farm would not pay for any accidental damage caused by a person running into my automobile" does not support a claim for fraud or misrepresentation, an intentional tort.

. . . .

[T]he Court ORDERS that Defendant's motion for summary judgment is GRANTED.

USAA COUNTY MUT. INS. CO. V. COOK

241 S.W.3d 93 (Tex. App. 2007)

OPINION

TERRY JENNINGS, JUSTICE.

Appellant, USAA County Mutual Insurance Company ("USAA"), challenges the trial court's judgment entered, after a jury trial, in favor of appellee, Hayden P. Cook, in Cook's suit for breach of contract. . . . USAA . . . contends that the trial court erred in denying its motion for directed verdict and, alternatively, its motion for judgment notwithstanding the verdict, "based on Mr. Cook's judicial admissions and the terms of the insurance policy" as "the accident was caused by a collision, a coverage not purchased by Mr. Cook"; the evidence is legally and factually insufficient to support the jury's finding that "the accident was the result of vandalism"; the trial court erred in admitting evidence of vandalism; and, because "no coverage was owed and no breach of contract established . . . as a matter of law."

. . . .

We affirm.

Factual and Procedural Background

At trial, Cook testified that after purchasing his 1998 Volkswagon Jetta in June 2004, he called USAA and purchased an insurance policy. . . . Cook paid $70.55 for a six-month term for "other than collision loss" coverage, with a $200 deductible.

Cook further testified that, while looking for a job in Washington, D.C., he and some friends took a break and he drove them to Atlanta, Georgia, to attend a baseball game. On October 8, 2004, on their way back to Washington, D.C., they stopped for lunch at a restaurant in Fayetteville, North Carolina, and Cook parallel parked his car approximately two feet from the rear of a very large sports utility vehicle ("SUV"). Cook and his friends then went into the restaurant and, about forty-five minutes later, they returned to find that Cook's car had been damaged. The hood was "bent up," there was damage to the grill, and the car had been pushed back fifteen feet, no longer in the parking spot where Cook had originally parked it. When he initially parallel parked his car, Cook put the transmission in park. The large SUV in the space immediately in front of his car faced the same direction, and another car was parked right in front of the SUV. Cook explained that the parking lot layout was extremely confined. On one side of the parked cars, there was a three-inch curb with grass, trees, and bushes. When Cook returned to his car, he found that the transmission to his car remained in park, but the car had still been moved back fifteen feet, roughly a full car length. The impact to the hood of the car showed that it was a "direct head-on collision" and not from the side. Only the front grill and hood of the car were damaged. The SUV previously parked in front of Cook's car was no longer there, but there was still a car in the space in front of where the SUV had been parked. A black mark on the top portion of the bumper of Cook's car indicated that the mark was made from a vehicle with a taller bumper, such as the SUV.

After Cook and his friends took note of the damage, they asked around for witnesses, but no one saw what caused the damage. The group of friends noticed video surveillance cameras near the restaurant, but learned that the cameras were only decoys. They called the local police department and, at the scene, told an officer what happened and that there were no witnesses to the incident.

After returning to Washington, D.C., Cook read his insurance policy. Part D of the policy states,

> A. We will pay for direct and accidental loss to **your covered auto,** including its equipment less any applicable deduction shown in the Declarations. However, we will pay for loss caused by **collision** only if the Declarations indicate that Collision Coverage is provided.
>
> B. **"Collision"** means the upset, or **collision** with another object of **your covered auto.** However, loss caused by the following are not considered **"collision"**:
>
> 1. Missiles or falling objects;
> 2. Fire;
> 3. Theft or larceny;
> 4. Explosion or earthquake;
> 5. Windstorm;
> 6. Hail, water or flood;
> 7. Malicious mischief or vandalism;
> 8. Riot or civil commotion;
> 9. Contact with bird or animal; or

10. Breakage of glass.

If breakage of glass is caused by a collision or if loss is caused by contact with a bird or animal, you may elect to have it considered a loss caused by **collision.**

The policy does not define the term "vandalism."

Based on his reading of the policy, Cook thought that the damage to his car was caused by "vandalism," and, on October 21, 2004, Cook called USAA to make a claim under the policy. Cook took his car to be inspected by Larry O'Hara, whom USAA had requested, and he estimated that it would cost $2,126.56 to repair the damage. USAA subsequently denied Cook's claim for damages on the ground that the damage to his automobile was not covered by the policy.

Tracy Huggins, a claims adjuster for USAA, testified that USAA denied the claim because "it was a collision loss and unfortunately, there was no collision coverage on the policy for this loss." Huggins explained that she tried to get all of the information available. In her view, Cook only told her the facts that he wanted her to know. For example, Cook did not tell her whether there were any passengers present in his car. Huggins noted that although most people call in their claim within one or two days of an incident, Cook waited approximately two weeks to report his claim.

Huggins further testified that Cook reported the loss as "vandalism" and that "vandalism is covered under comprehensive coverage." In her conversation with Cook, his "main point was that because the car was moved back 15 feet, it was obviously struck in a willful, intentional way." When Huggins asked Cook what caused the damage to the car, he told her, "I don't know." Huggins put Cook "on notice that [because] he didn't carry collision coverage on the policy, it didn't look like we were going to be able to issue payment for his damage." Cook "understood there was no collision [coverage] but he persisted on having it covered under comprehensive."

At the conclusion of the trial, the jury found that USAA failed to comply with the insurance policy, found that the failure to comply with the policy was not excused, and awarded actual damages to Cook in the amount of $1,926.56. . . .

Legal and Factual Sufficiency

In its first issue, USAA argues that the trial court erred in denying its motion for directed verdict and, alternatively, its motion for judgment notwithstanding the verdict, "based on Mr. Cook's judicial admissions and the terms of the insurance policy because the accident was caused by a collision, a coverage not purchased by Mr. Cook." In its third and fourth issues, USAA argues that the evidence is legally and factually insufficient to support the jury's finding that the damage to Cook's car was caused by vandalism and that USAA breached its policy because at most, "Cook offered evidence that his car was damaged and pushed back fifteen feet."

. . . .

Standard of Review

. . . .

Our review of the factual sufficiency of the evidence requires us to consider, weigh, and examine all of the evidence that supports or contradicts the jury's determination. We may set aside the verdict only if the evidence that supports the jury's finding is so contrary to the overwhelming weight of the evidence as to be clearly wrong or unjust.

Terms of the Policy

In its first issue, USAA contends that this case should have been "resolved on the policy coverages Mr. Cook, himself chose to purchase," asserting that in his answers to requests for admission, and at trial, Cook admitted that the damage was the result of a "collision" and that the policy issued by USAA did not provide collision coverage.

[T]he amended declarations page of the policy provides that Cook purchased coverage under "Part A—Liability" for "Bodily Injury" and "Property Damage." Cook also purchased coverage under "Part D—Damage to Your Auto" for "Other than Coll[ision] Loss," which contained a $200 deductible. Although the policy provides that USAA "will pay for direct and accidental loss to your covered auto, including its equipment less any applicable deduction shown in the Declarations," the policy does not further describe or define what constitutes an "other than collision loss."

In its briefing, USAA asserts that Cook could "treat the loss as either a collision or non-collision loss" only "if the loss resulted from damages caused by a bird or animal" and that the policy "did not permit an insured to treat vandalism as either vandalism or collision." USAA argues that "the policy, as a matter of law, quite simply said that vandalism was not a covered collision loss" and, if interpreted otherwise, "coverage would equally be owed for collisions involving missiles, falling objects, explosion, flood, or riot." USAA further argues that such an "interpretation of the insurance policy is patently absurd." In other words, the ten listed items, including vandalism, "were exclusions to collision coverage not grants of coverage." However, at oral argument, USAA abandoned this argument and conceded that a loss caused by vandalism would in fact be covered under Cook's policy. USAA also agreed that one could use a car to intentionally collide with another car to cause damage, resulting in an act of vandalism.

Cook did testify that he believed that the damage to his car was the result of a large SUV "colliding" with the front-end of his car. However, our examination of the insurance policy in question does not reveal that the terms "collision" and "vandalism" are mutually exclusive. It is undisputed that Cook did not purchase "collision" coverage, which the policy defines as "the upset, or collision with another object of your covered auto." However, the policy specifically provides that loss caused by "malicious mischief or vandalism" is not considered a "collision."

In its charge, the trial court instructed the jury that "vandalism" means "the willful or malicious destruction of public or private property" and that "malice" means "the intent, with or without cause, or reason, to commit an unlawful act that will result in injury to another or others." "Vandalism" is commonly defined as an "action involving deliberate destruction of or damage to public or private property." THE NEW OXFORD AMERICAN DICTIONARY 1868 (1st ed. 2001). "Collision" is defined as "an instance of one moving object or person striking violently against another." *Id.* at 336. In most instances, acts of vandalism involve causing an object, be it a baseball bat or a car, to collide with another object to deliberately cause damage. Thus, the real issue here is whether the damage to Cook's car was caused by a deliberate as opposed to a negligent act.

As discussed more fully below, Cook presented evidence that the damage caused to his car was the result of a willful or malicious act, not a negligent act. Accordingly, we hold that Cook's "judicial admissions and the terms of the insurance policy" do not establish, as a matter of law, that the damage to Cook's car resulted from a non-covered "collision" and not from "vandalism."

We overrule USAA's first issue.

Result of "Vandalism"

In its third and fourth issues, in support of its argument that the evidence is legally and factually insufficient to support the jury's finding that the damage to Cook's car was the result of vandalism, USAA asserts that Cook "could not confirm that the SUV he originally saw caused the collision, or that the car originally parked in front of the SUV was the same" and that the "police reported it as a hit and run." It also asserts that Cook's "evidence consisted o[f] his lone surmise, and a remarkably unreasonable surmise, that a person in a large, and presumably expensive, SUV, would intentionally ram his vehicle into [Cook's] Jetta for fun or sport." USAA also argues that because the "competing inferences" of a negligent hit-and-run and an act of intentional vandalism are "equal inferences," the jury's finding that USAA failed to comply with the insurance policy cannot survive a sufficiency challenge.

. . . .

Here, although there were no eyewitnesses to the incident in question, Cook presented evidence that upon entering the restaurant, he left the transmission in park; a large SUV was parallel parked approximately two feet in front of Cook's car, with the SUV's rear bumper facing Cook's front bumper; another car was parallel parked immediately in front of the SUV; and the parking lot was very confined. After returning to his car approximately forty-five minutes later, Cook observed that his car was moved fifteen feet from where he initially parked the car; the transmission was still in park; the front grill and hood of Cook's car were damaged, a black mark was above Cook's front bumper, a piece of plastic debris from Cook's car was on the ground; and the damage to Cook's car appeared to have resulted from a "head-on" impact. Also, Larry O'Hara, the USAA appraiser, told Cook that he did not feel that the damage to Cook's car was "accidental."

In the instant case . . . the jury could have reasonably concluded that, based on the dimensions of the parking lot, the driver of the SUV parallel parked immediately in front of Cook's car willfully or maliciously caused the damage to Cook's car by ramming the SUV into the car. Given the fact that Cook's car, with the parking brake activated, was physically moved approximately fifteen feet, no other conclusion appears reasonable. This evidence does not reveal "a single vehicular collision" that was the result of negligence, as USAA contends, but rather a deliberate act akin to road rage. As such, the occurrence of mere negligence or accident cannot be equally inferred. Accordingly, we hold that the evidence is legally and factually sufficient to support the jury's implied finding that the damage to Cook's car was the result of vandalism and its express finding that USAA failed to comply with the insurance policy.

We overrule USAA's third and fourth issues.

. . . .

Conclusion

We affirm the judgment of the trial court.

NOTES AND QUESTIONS

1. *A Drunk Person Is an Object, but Not an Animal?* In *McKay*, the court concluded a drunk person who runs into a vehicle is an object, but not an animal. Do you agree?

2. *Unknown Causes of Loss and Burdens of Proof.* In *Cook*, it was unknown what caused the damage to the policyholder's vehicle. The policyholder has the burden of proving a loss is covered. How, if at all, did the policyholder in *Cook* meet that burden?

3. *Difference Between Collision and Comprehensive.* As the *McKay* and *Cook* cases illustrate, the difference between collision and comprehensive coverage is not always a bright line. Indeed, in the *Cook* case, the "accident" arguably could be viewed both as a "collision" and as vandalism, which was

covered under the comprehensive coverage provisions. Is there a guiding principle one can use to determine when an event causing damage is covered by collision coverage versus comprehensive coverage? Are collisions always events that occur while the vehicle is in operation?

4. *Deductibles and Coverage.* Collision coverage typically is subject to a deductible, while comprehensive coverage often is not. Can you think of any good reasons why that is the case?

EXERCISE

1. Your car is stolen. Three days later, the police find the car crashed against a tree. Draft a 2-page memo analyzing whether the loss should be covered by the collision versus comprehensive coverage.

VI. UNINSURED AND UNDERINSURED MOTORIST COVERAGE

Uninsured motorist (often called "UM") coverage was developed by the insurance industry in the 1950s as a response to gaps in the traditional tort liability-compensation system. The hit-and-run driver is one obvious kind of gap. A post-accident financial responsibility system might keep uninsured drivers off the road, but such a system does little to help the victim of an uninsured driver's first accident. Charitable immunities have been substantially eroded through the years (sometimes only to the extent of the charity's liability insurance), but early on these immunities were problematic for some accident victims as well.

Initially, UM coverage was offered only in the amounts specified in the financial responsibility law of the state. However, through a series of evolutionary steps, UM coverage became more widespread. First, legislatures began to require that UM coverage be offered. Then, the coverage was deemed to be included unless the policyholder refused it in writing. Finally, in some states, UM coverage was a mandated part of the compulsory auto liability policy. Statutes typically require that coverage be provided or offered in an amount equal to the financial responsibility laws of the particular state, but some statutes require that an amount "at least" as high as that sum be provided or offered. *See, e.g.*, 1 Alan I. Widiss, Uninsured and Underinsured Motorist Insurance § 2.12, at 46–47 (rev. 2d ed. 1999).

Is uninsured motorist insurance first-party coverage or third-party coverage? The answer is first-party coverage because the policyholder looks directly to the insurer for reimbursement of the policyholder's own loss, i.e., for protection of the policyholder's own interest. But tort liability concepts determine the extent of the insurer's obligation to its insureds. This is because the insured must establish that an uninsured third-party was responsible for the insured's loss, meaning that the insured must establish the uninsured motorist's liability in tort. If the insurer can establish that no tort occurred or that it has a viable defense to the alleged tort, then the insured does not recover. In a sense, it is as if the insured purchases a contingent liability insurance policy for the benefit of some unknown third-party tortfeasor. If the third-party injures an insured and has no insurance, then the UM coverage will provide the coverage the tortfeasor might have (indeed, should have) purchased, but the proceeds are paid to the insured-victim.

Underinsured motorist insurance is a separate but related coverage. Usually called "UIM" insurance, it was developed in the 1980s as a complement to uninsured motorist coverage. Whereas UM coverage applies when the tortfeasor who injures the insured has no auto liability insurance at all or less than that legally required, UIM coverage applies when the tortfeasor carries enough insurance to meet any legal requirements but the amount is insufficient to pay the insured's full loss.

There are essentially two distinct models of UIM insurance. Under one approach, if the tortfeasor lacks sufficient liability insurance to reimburse the victim's loss, the victim can recover UIM benefits from the insured's own insurer measured by the difference between the insured's own higher liability limits and the tortfeasor's lower liability limits. Under this kind of UIM coverage, the insured who is injured by another driver is provided with coverage as though the insured were injured by a driver with liability limits equal to the insured's own. This kind of statute is not so much interested in fully compensating the insured for her own loss, but instead seeks to ensure that the victim-insured has available coverage at least as extensive as the victim's own liability insurance. The other approach to UIM coverage makes the amount of the insured's coverage (measured by, depending on the policy, either the liability limits or the UM limits) an add-on to the amount of the tortfeasor's liability coverage up to the amount of the insured's loss. The first approach operates as "gap-filling" coverage, whereas the second approach operates as "topping off" coverage. In either case, an insured with high limits who is injured by a tortfeasor with minimum liability limits will recover more than just the tortfeasor's liability limits. The basic idea is that the tortfeasor is "underinsured" and the insured's own insurer provides additional coverage to protect against the risk that the insured will be injured by an "underinsured" motorist. In most states, underinsured motorist protection is optional, although some states require the insured to opt out of the coverage.

A. ESTABLISHING THE LIABILITY OF THE TORTFEASOR

ALLSTATE INS. CO. V. BOYNTON

486 So. 2d 552 (Fla. 1986)

Opinion

EHRLICH, JUSTICE.

In this uninsured motorist case, Allstate Insurance Company seeks review of the decision of the District Court of Appeal, Fifth District, in *Boynton v. Allstate Insurance Co.,* 443 So.2d 427 (Fla. 5th DCA 1984). Acknowledging conflict with *Centennial Insurance Co. v. Wallace,* 330 So.2d 815 (Fla. 3d DCA), *cert. denied,* 341 So.2d 1087 (Fla.1976), the district court reversed a summary judgment that had been entered in favor of the uninsured motorist insurance carrier. We have jurisdiction pursuant to article V, section 3(b)(3), Florida Constitution.

We quash the district court's decision. We agree with the district court that a vehicle may be an "uninsured motor vehicle" under section 627.727(1), Florida Statutes (Supp.1978), even when it is covered by a liability insurance policy, if that policy does not provide coverage for the particular occurrence that caused plaintiff's damages. However, we also hold that the phrase "legally entitled to recover" in the context of section 627.727(1) does not encompass claims where the uninsured tortfeasor is immune from liability because of the Workers' Compensation Law, chapter 440; Florida Statutes.

In this case, the plaintiff, Richard Boynton, was employed by Sears, Roebuck & Company as an auto mechanic. While on the job, Boynton was struck and injured by a car on which his co-employee, James Luke, was working. The car was leased to Xerox Corporation and was left at the Sears Auto Center for repairs. Boynton first brought suit against Sears, Xerox, and their insurance carriers. He voluntarily dismissed his suit against Sears and its insurer because Sears was immune from tort suit under section 440.11, Florida Statutes.[2] The trial court granted summary

---

[2] 440.11 Exclusiveness of liability.—

(1) The liability of an employer prescribed in s. 440.10 shall be exclusive and in place of all other liability of such employer to any third-party tortfeasor and to the employee, the legal representative thereof, husband or wife, parents, dependents, next of kin, and anyone otherwise entitled to recover damages from such employer at law or in admiralty on account of such injury or death, except that if an employer fails to secure payment of compensation as required by this chapter, an injured employee, or the legal representative thereof in case death results from the injury, may elect to claim compensation under this chapter or to maintain an action at law or in admiralty for damages on account of such injury or death. In such action the defendant may not plead as a defense that the injury was caused by negligence of a fellow servant, that the employee assumed the risk of the employment, or that the injury was due to the

judgment in favor of Xerox and its insurer based on *Castillo v. Bickley,* 363 So.2d 792 (Fla.1978). That case held that an automobile owner, absent his own negligence, is not liable for the negligent operation of a vehicle left at a repair shop. Boynton then sought to recover damages from Luke's automobile liability insurance carrier, but that carrier denied coverage because of a provision in Luke's policy excluding injuries occurring during the pursuit of a business.

Boynton then amended his complaint to allege that Luke was an uninsured motorist and sought to recover under his own uninsured motorist policy with Allstate.[3] The trial court entered summary judgment in favor of Allstate. On appeal from this judgment, Boynton raised two issues:

> (1) Is a vehicle an uninsured vehicle when a policy of liability insurance covers it, but the policy does not provide coverage for the particular occurrence?
>
> (2) Is the insured "legally entitled to recover" from the operator of an uninsured motor vehicle when there is a statutory bar to an action against the operator, but for which bar, recovery would lie?

The Fifth District reversed. It held that in the context of the Florida uninsured motorist statute, a vehicle is an "uninsured vehicle" when a policy of liability insurance covers it, but the policy does not provide coverage for the particular occurrence and that an insured is "legally entitled to recover" from the operator of an uninsured motor vehicle when there is a statutory bar to an action against the operator, but for which bar, recovery would lie.

First Issue

Allstate asserts that the vehicle in question was not "uninsured" because Xerox had a liability insurance policy that would have provided coverage if Boynton had had a cause of action against Xerox. We reject this argument. The fact that an owner or operator of a motor vehicle has a liability insurance policy does not always mean that the vehicle is insured in the context of section 627.727(1). A vehicle is insured in this context only when

---

contributory negligence or comparative negligence of the employee. The same immunities from liability enjoyed by an employer shall extend as well to each employee of the employer when such employee is acting in furtherance of the employer's business and the injured employee is entitled to receive benefits under this chapter. Such fellow-employee immunities shall not be applicable to an employee who acts, with respect to a fellow employee, with willful and wanton disregard or unprovoked physical aggression or with gross negligence when such acts result in injury or death or such acts proximately cause such injury or death, nor shall such immunities be applicable to employees of the same employer when each is operating in the furtherance of the employer's business but they are assigned primarily to unrelated works within private or public employment.

[3] In Boynton's uninsured motorist policy, Allstate agreed that:

We will pay damages for bodily injury, sickness, death or disease which you are *legally entitled to recover from the owner or operator of an uninsured auto.* Injury must be caused by accident and arise out of the ownership, maintenance or use of an uninsured or underinsured auto. (Emphasis added).

the insurance in question is available to the injured plaintiff. It is undisputed that Xerox was without fault as a matter of law and that it could not be held responsible for Luke's negligence. That being the case, Xerox's liability insurance was not available to Boynton. In the context of Boynton's uninsured motorist claim, it cannot be said that this was an insured motor vehicle just because Xerox had liability insurance coverage.

Allstate next asserts that the vehicle in question was not "uninsured" because Luke also had a liability insurance policy. We likewise reject this contention. Luke's policy specifically excluded injuries occurring in the pursuit of a business. This exclusion is applicable to the facts of this case. Luke's policy, therefore, did not provide coverage for this particular occurrence.

An analogous situation is found in *American Fire & Casualty Co. v. Boyd,* 357 So.2d 768 (Fla. 1st DCA 1978). In that case, Boyd was injured in an automobile accident caused by the negligence of Hansen. Hansen had a liability policy which excluded coverage while traveling on military orders, which is what he was doing at the time of the accident. The district court correctly found that Hansen's automobile was "uninsured" in the context of Boyd's uninsured motorist policy and permitted him to recover uninsured motorist benefits. The district court reasoned:

Although Hansen had procured a policy of insurance, that policy afforded no coverage because of the exclusionary clause; and the mere fact that Hansen was in such a position as to cause to be invoked by his negligence the provisions of the Federal Tort Claims Act does not mean that he is thereby "insured" within the meaning of the statute.

Id. at 769. The availability of a collateral remedy, the Federal Tort Claims Act in *Hansen,* workers' compensation in this case, likewise does not render a vehicle "insured."

In the present case, we hold that in the context of Boynton's uninsured motorist policy, the motor vehicle which injured him was "uninsured." Xerox's policy afforded no coverage because Xerox was without fault as a matter of law. Luke's liability policy afforded no coverage because of the policy exclusion.[5]

---

[5] Allstate, citing *Reid v. State Farm Fire & Casualty Co.,* 352 So.2d 1172 (Fla.1977), asserts in its brief that a valid exclusion in a liability policy does not make a vehicle uninsured for uninsured motorist purposes. In *Reid,* we held that a vehicle cannot be both an insured and uninsured vehicle under the *same* policy. The present case is distinguishable because it involves separate policies. *Reid* is inapplicable.

Also, denial of coverage by Luke's carrier renders the vehicle uninsured within the express terms of Boynton's Allstate policy, which provides: "An uninsured auto is . . . [a] motor vehicle for which the insurer denies coverage. . . ."

Second Issue

Although the vehicle was technically uninsured as to respondents, section 627.727(1) and the policy endorsement still require the policyholder be "legally entitled to recover" from the owner or operator of the uninsured vehicle. The plain meaning of the requirement would appear to be that the insured must have a claim against the tortfeasor which could be reduced to judgment in a court of law. The district court, however, construes the phrase in more limited fashion:

The majority of courts which have construed the words "legally entitled to recover" have construed them to mean simply that the insured must be able to establish fault on the part of the uninsured motorist which gives rise to the damages and to prove the extent of the damages. See, *e.g., Winner v. Ratzlaff*, 211 Kan. 59, 505 P.2d 606 (1973), and cases cited in Anno., 73 A.L.R.3d 632, 649. Recovery may be had under this coverage when the claimant shows conduct on the part of the tortfeasor which would entitle claimant to recover damages, even though a defense available to the tortfeasor would defeat actual recovery.

Boynton v. Allstate, 443 So.2d 427, 430 (Fla. 5th DCA 1984). However, none of the cases cited in support of this interpretation were decided in the context of a statutory bar by a workers' compensation law.

For instance, in *Winner v. Ratzlaff* the issue was not even whether some statutory bar to recovery against the tortfeasor prevented recovery from the insurer, but rather whether the insured could sustain a direct action against his insurer. The insured had originally sued only the tortfeasor, but, after discovery revealed the defendant was uninsured, the insured added his UM carrier as a defendant. He then sought to dismiss the tortfeasor from the suit. The Kansas Supreme Court held it was error for the trial judge to have refused to dismiss the tortfeasor. The court reasoned that the Kansas uninsured motorist law had been enacted, in part, to avoid any requirement that a judgment be had against the tortfeasor before liability would arise against the UM carrier. In reaching this conclusion, the court discussed the phrase at issue here.

We construe the words "legally entitled to recover as damages" to mean simply that the insured must be able to establish fault on the part of the uninsured motorist which gives rise to the damages and to prove the extent of those damages. This would mean in a direct action against the insurer the insured has the burden of proving that the other motorist was uninsured, that the other motorist is legally liable for damage to the insured, and the amount of this liability. *In resisting the claim the insurer would have available to it, in addition to policy defenses compatible with the statute, the substantive defenses that would have been available to the uninsured motorist such as contributory negligence, etc.*

211 Kan. at 64, 505 P.2d at 610 (citation omitted, emphasis added). The district court was correct in noting that the insured need only show fault and damages, but neglected to note the qualification that the insurer has available all substantive defenses the tortfeasor could have raised.

The *Winner* court looked to the cogent observations of a commentator on UM law in reaching its conclusion. His explanation of the origins of UM coverage sheds light on the problem before us.

> The antecedent of the uninsured motorist endorsement . . . can be found in the unsatisfied judgment insurance first offered in about 1925 by the Utilities Indemnity Exchange. This insurance provided indemnification when the insured showed both (1) that he had reduced a claim to judgment and (2) that he was unable to collect the judgment from the negligent party. Such insurance was available from several companies during the years from 1925 until 1956. When the uninsured motorist coverage became generally available, the unsatisfied judgment insurance was abandoned. *It should be noted that the uninsured motorist endorsement—as proposed and subsequently issued—differed significantly from its predecessor in that it eliminated the requirement that the insured obtain a judgment against the uninsured motorist prior to recovering under his policy.*

A. Widiss, *A Guide to Uninsured Motorist Coverage* § 1.9 (1969) (emphasis added) (hereinafter cited as *Widiss*).

Uninsured motorist coverage therefore arose in the context of providing a less cumbersome method for an insured to receive payment from the party with the ultimate financial responsibility, the insurer. UM coverage, with its normal procedure of settling disputes through arbitration, would save both the insured and insurer the time and expense of a trial against the uninsured motorist, and would also help the insurer avoid the complications inherent in a trial where the interests of the tortfeasor and the insurer may not necessarily coincide.

None of this suggests that UM coverage was developed to expand the coverage previously provided by unsatisfied judgment insurance. Indeed, *Widiss* notes that "[t]he insurance industry conceived and developed the uninsured motorist endorsement in an attempt to forestall the enactment of state legislation directed at either creating compulsory insurance requirements or otherwise altering the character of the then-existing insurance market in order to deal with the hazard created by [financially irresponsible] uninsured motorists." *Widiss* at § 1.12. It seems unlikely that the companies would deliberately relinquish valid substantive defenses when it was wholly unnecessary to do so to achieve the goal of protecting against financially irresponsible motorists. Widiss also observes that in most states where UM coverage has been made mandatory subsequent to its development, the legislation has merely required a UM endorsement. While Florida's section 627.727 does go into some detail regarding UM coverage, the first sentence of the statute, containing the language at issue here, merely defines UM coverage in terms sufficient to identify it as such. This does not suggest any legislative intent to expand UM coverage beyond that contemplated by the insurance-industry-developed endorsement.

The legislature wisely enacted a scheme whereby a motorist may obtain a limited form of insurance coverage for the uninsured motorist, by requiring that every insurer doing business in this state offer and make available to its automobile liability policyholders UM coverage in an amount equal to the policyholder's automobile liability insurance. The policyholder pays an additional premium for such coverage. The uninsured motorist statute provides that coverage is "for the protection of persons insured thereunder who are legally entitled to recover damages from owners or operators of uninsured motor vehicles because of bodily injury." § 627.727(1). The UM coverage, in purpose and effect, provides a limited form of insurance coverage up to the applicable policy limits for the uninsured motorist. The carrier effectually stands in the uninsured motorist's shoes and can raise and assert any defense that the uninsured motorist could urge. In other words, UM coverage is a limited form of third party coverage inuring to the limited benefit of the tortfeasor to provide a source of financial responsibility if the policyholder is entitled under the law to recover from the tortfeasor. It is not first party coverage even though the policyholder pays for it. In first party coverage, such as medical, collision or theft insurance, fault is not an element. The insurance carrier pays even though the policyholder is totally at fault. With UM coverage, the carrier pays only if the tortfeasor would have to pay, if the claim were made directly against the tortfeasor.

One involved in an accident with an uninsured motorist can bring a common law action against the uninsured motorist, if he so desires. The uninsured motorist can of course defend and interpose any defense available to him at law including contributory negligence and the exclusiveness of worker's compensation. If the injured party recovers a judgment, he may endeavor to satisfy his judgment from the tortfeasor's assets. However, the insured motorist may opt to make claim against his UM carrier instead of suing the tortfeasor. In so doing he has a policy prerequisite, namely, proof that the tortfeasor is uninsured. The tortfeasor may be financially responsible, but if he is without insurance or has not complied with the self-insurance provisions of the statutes, the injured party may make claim against his UM carrier. The insurer is subrogated to any sum that it pays the policyholder under the UM coverage and may bring suit against the uninsured motorist to recover all sums it has paid its insured under the UM policy. The subrogation right would be frustrated if the insurer were forced to pay claims when it would be barred by a substantive defense from winning a judgment against a tortfeasor.

The district court and respondent dispute the argument that the case is controlled by the proposition that the insurer stands in the shoes of the tortfeasor. The court relied in part on *Sahloff v. Western Casualty & Surety Co.,* 45 Wis.2d 60, 171 N.W.2d 914 (1969), which held that the expiration of the statute of limitations which would bar an action against the tortfeasor did not bar an action against the insurer when the suit was brought before expiration of the statute of limitations for contract actions. From the portion of *Sahloff* quoted by the district court, it is clear the Wisconsin court relied heavily on the notion that the relationship between insurer and insured arises in contract, not tort. *See also Mendlein v. United States Fidelity & Guaranty Co.*, 277 So.2d 538 (Fla. 3d DCA 1973) (district court did not dispute assumption of all parties that contract statute of limitations controlled the UM claim at issue). Also, while substantive defenses are available to the insurer, *Winner,* a procedural defense such as a statute of limitations is not necessarily also available. However, the statute of limitations issue is not before us, and we reserve a decision on this for a later day. It is enough that we here find that the insurer has the tortfeasor's substantive defenses available, and we need not decide whether this is to the exclusion of some or all procedural defenses.

There is another reason for our decision here. Widiss writes, in the context of whether the insurer should be able to claim the protection of the tortfeasor's tort immunities:

> The issue raised by such immunities is whether, for purposes of the uninsured motorist coverage, the claimant is "legally entitled to recover" as contemplated in the endorsement. . . .
>
> Professor Prosser states that "such immunity does not mean that conduct which would amount to a tort on the part of other defendants is not equally tortious in character, but merely that for protection of the particular defendant or interests which he represents, he is given absolution from liability." [W. Prosser, *Law of Torts* 996 (3d ed. 1964).] Professor Prosser's language seems to suggest that the injured party *is* legally entitled to recover, but that the immunity involved absolves the defendant from liability. . . .
>
> Attempting to resolve this issue as a problem in semantics—that is, over whether the claimant is "legally entitled"—is not especially productive. . . . To the extent that there is a strong interest in protecting the insurance company's right of subrogation following the payment of a claim, there is a persuasive reason why the existence of an immunity from liability should mean that the insurer will not be liable under the policy.

> On the other hand, to the extent that the objective of providing indemnification is a stronger policy in this context, the technicality of whether the tortfeasor is immune from litigation assumes a much smaller degree of importance. It seems probable that in those states where the trend is to assure that a source of indemnification is available, the courts are likely to reject an argument as to the applicability of such tort immunities. However, it may not be appropriate to attempt to speak of all these immunities as an undivided group. For example, in a jurisdiction which affirms the importance of the interspousal immunity, the court might well be inclined to distinguish this type of case on the basis that the policy and goals underlying the establishment of this type of immunity are sufficiently important to warrant separate consideration and treatment.

Widiss at § 2.27 (footnotes deleted, emphasis in original). In Florida a source of indemnification for a worker injured by a co-worker driving an uninsured vehicle is already available, i.e. the benefits of the Workers' Compensation Law. Society's goal of protecting the worker under this circumstance has been achieved. We do not need to torture the meaning of a statute aimed at curing another ill entirely to provide a remedy where one has already been provided.

In addition, the immunity offered through workers' compensation exists not only to protect the employer in exchange for his provision of immediate, guaranteed benefits, but also to protect society by limiting the impact of a work-related injury to the remedy offered. Expanding UM coverage to cover the circumstance before us here would, as Judge Upchurch noted in his dissent in the district court, 443 So.2d at 433, create a large class of uninsured vehicles. The ensuing litigation would roil the waters in an area where the legislature has attempted to calm the seas. Absent a clear statement of intent from the legislature that it considers the benefits of broader UM coverage to outweigh the detriment, we will not disturb its clear and unambiguous statement that coverage exists only when the insured is legally entitled to recover from the tortfeasor.

Accordingly, the decision of the district court is quashed and remanded for further proceedings in accord herewith.

It is so ordered.

B. "HIT AND RUN" AND "MISS AND RUN" DRIVERS

LOWING V. ALLSTATE INSURANCE CO.

859 P.2d 724 (Ariz. 1993)

MARTONE, JUSTICE.

We are asked to decide whether an unidentified accident-causing motorist is "uninsured" within the meaning of the Uninsured Motorist Act, A.R.S. § 20–259.01, and thus whether an insurance policy that does not provide coverage for bodily injury caused by such motorists, unless physical contact occurred between the motorist and the insured, fails to comply with the statute. We answer both of these questions in the affirmative and therefore overrule our previous rulings to the contrary in *Balestrieri v. Hartford Accident & Indem. Ins. Co.*, 112 Ariz. 160, 540 P.2d 126 (1975) and *State Farm Mut. Auto. Ins. Co. v. Brudnock*, 151 Ariz. 268, 727 P.2d 321 (1986).

I. BACKGROUND

A. *Horvath v. Continental Casualty*

Lewis Horvath and three of his children sustained injuries when Horvath swerved his car to avoid another car attempting to pass a truck in a no-passing zone on a curve. Though Horvath's action prevented a head-on collision, he was forced off the road. The driver of the other car, whose identity remains unknown, did not stop.

Because Horvath's uninsured motorist insurance covers only those accidents caused by unknown motorists who actually "hit" the insured's vehicle, his insurance carrier, Continental Casualty, refused to cover Horvath's losses.[1] Horvath sued, seeking a declaration that the policy limitation is contrary to the requirements of A.R.S. § 20–259.01, Arizona's Uninsured Motorist Act, and thus void. The trial court granted Continental's motion to dismiss, and the court of appeals affirmed based on this court's holding in *Balestrieri* that such provisions are valid. We granted Horvath's petition for review.

---

[1] The policy reads, in relevant part:

> We pay damages which you or any other covered person are legally entitled to recover from the owner or operator of an uninsured or underinsured motor vehicle or boat because of bodily injury: 1. Sustained by you or any covered person; and 2. Caused by a motor vehicle or boat accident.

CNA's Universal Security Policy Deluxe, at 23 (Exhibit A to Complaint). Twenty-six pages later, in the definitions section of the policy, "uninsured motor vehicle or boat" is defined as:

> A land motor vehicle or boat or trailer of any type:
>
> * * *
>
> c. Which is a hit-and-run motor vehicle or boat whose operator or owner cannot be identified and which hits: (1) You or any covered person; (2) A motor vehicle which you or any covered person are occupying; or (3) Your motor vehicle or boat.

Id. at 49.

B. *Lowing v. Allstate Ins. Co.*

Paula Lowing sustained injuries when Salvatore Gentile, the owner and driver of the vehicle in which she was a passenger, swerved to avoid colliding with a vehicle that ran a stop sign. Gentile's car missed the other vehicle, but left the roadway and overturned. The other vehicle did not stop, and its driver was never identified. Gentile's uninsured motorist insurance carrier, Allstate, refused to cover Lowing's damages because its policy limits coverage to cases in which there is actual physical contact with the unknown accident-causing vehicle.[2] Gentile sued, seeking a declaration that the policy limitation is void under A.R.S. § 20–259.01. The trial court granted Allstate's motion for summary judgment and the court of appeals affirmed based on the *Balestrieri* line of cases. We granted Lowing's petition for review and consolidated it with the *Horvath* case.

II. ANALYSIS

A. Does A.R.S. § 20–259.01 require coverage of unidentified motorists?

The first question we must answer is one of statutory interpretation: does A.R.S. § 20–259.01 require coverage of unidentified motorists in addition to known motorists who are demonstrably uninsured? "The primary principle of statutory interpretation is to determine and give effect to legislative intent." *Wyatt v. Wehmueller*, 167 Ariz. 281, 284, 806 P.2d 870, 873 (1991). The best and most reliable index of a statute's meaning is its language. That language, where clear and unequivocal, controls the statute's meaning unless it leads to absurd or impossible results. Where, instead, the statute's language is subject to different interpretations, the court is free to consult other sources of legislative intent such as the statute's context, historical background, consequences, spirit and purpose. Section 20–259.01(A) states:

> No automobile liability or motor vehicle liability policy . . . shall be delivered or issued for delivery in this state . . . unless coverage is provided in the policy . . . for the protection of persons insured who are legally entitled to recover damages from owners or operators of uninsured motor vehicles because of bodily injury. . . .

In *Balestrieri*, we upheld a physical contact requirement against a public policy challenge based on what the court perceived to be the "plain language" of § 20–259.01. We reasoned that the statute requires coverage of injuries caused by "uninsured motorists" and that "uninsured" means those motorists we know are uninsured, not unidentified motorists who may or may not be uninsured. 112 Ariz. at 163, 540 P.2d at 129. Therefore, the statute does not require coverage of damages caused by any

[2] The insurance policy defines an "uninsured auto" as, inter alia, "[a] hit and run motor vehicle which causes bodily injury to a person insured by physical contact with the insured or with the vehicle occupied by that person. The identity of the operator and owner of the vehicle must be unknown."

unidentified accident-causing motorist, whether "hit and run" or "miss and run." *Id.*

In reality, however, we cannot apply the "plain language" of the statute because we cannot know which unidentified motorists are uninsured and which are not. We must instead presume either that unidentified motorists are insured or that they are uninsured. If we presume the former, some persons injured by uninsured motorists will go uncompensated. If we presume the latter, some persons injured by insured motorists will recover from their uninsured motorist insurance carrier. Neither situation is contemplated by the literal language of the statute. The statute does not address the unidentified motorist issue. It is therefore ambiguous, and we must consult other sources to determine which of the two interpretations is more in line with legislative intent.

The purpose of § 20–259.01 is, broadly speaking, to "close the gap in protection under the Safety Responsibility Act, A.R.S. § 28–1101 et seq.", *Calvert v. Farmers Ins. Co. of Arizona*, 144 Ariz. 291, 294, 697 P.2d 684, 687 (1985), and protect people who are injured by financially irresponsible motorists, *id.* at 295, 697 P.2d at 688. Section 20–259.01 is remedial in nature and should be liberally construed in order to effectuate its purpose. *Id.* at 294, 697 P.2d at 687. Exclusions and limitations on coverage are generally invalid unless contemplated by the statute. *Id.*

Interpreting the statute to require coverage of damages caused by unidentified motorists advances its protective goal; interpreting it in a way that does not require such coverage frustrates that goal. It is unlikely that the legislature intended to protect the injured person from an uninsured motorist responsible enough to stop and be identified but not from a motorist, insured or not, irresponsible enough to cause an accident and then flee.

In *Porter v. Empire Fire and Marine Ins. Co.*, 106 Ariz. 274, 475 P.2d 258 (1970), we held that an insured who recovers less than the statutory minimum amount of coverage from a negligent motorist because the negligent driver's liability insurance is split among multiple claimants may recover the balance (i.e., up to the statutory minimum) from his or her uninsured motorist coverage. The rationale of the case was that, although the negligent motorist purchased some liability insurance, he or she is functionally uninsured as to the injured person because insurance is not available up to the minimum amount required by statute. Because the Uninsured Motorist Act was designed to make available to all persons injured by negligent motorists a certain minimum amount of compensation, the motorist was uninsured within the meaning of the act.

Likewise, unidentified motorists are functionally uninsured as to the persons they injure because they have no insurance that is in fact available and collectible. In *Balestrieri*, we attempted to reconcile our holding with

Porter by noting that "in both [cases] the injured party maintains the burden of establishing the fact that the negligent motorist was uninsured." 112 Ariz. at 163–64, 540 P.2d at 129–30. But an insured will never know, and can never prove, whether an unidentified negligent motorist is insured. What is important in the two cases is not which party has the burden of proof, but who is considered uninsured. In *Porter* an insured motorist with too little insurance to compensate an injured party up to the minimum statutory limits is considered uninsured. When we held in *Balestrieri* that an unidentified motorist is presumed to be insured until the plaintiff proves otherwise, we departed from the spirit of the earlier case.[3]

Thus, interpreting "owners or operators of uninsured motor vehicles" to include unidentified motorists is consistent with the general purpose of the statute, and with this court's construction of the statute. But there is more. [The court reviewed the history of A.R.S. § 20–259.01 and concluded that "the legislature specifically intended the statute to include the unidentified motorist."]

. . . .

We thus hold that an unidentified accident-causing motorist is an "owner or operator of an uninsured motor vehicle" within the meaning of § 20–259.01, and that the statute requires every automobile liability policy delivered or issued for delivery in Arizona to provide coverage for bodily injury caused by such motorists.

B. Is the physical contact requirement void as against public policy?

The policies at issue in this case do provide coverage for some unidentified accident-causing drivers: those that actually "hit" or have "physical contact" with the insured or the vehicle occupied by the insured. Having concluded that § 20–259.01 requires coverage of damages caused by unidentified motorists, the question becomes whether the contact limitation violates the statute. We conclude that it does. Exceptions to coverage are not generally permitted unless expressly allowed by statute. The physical contact requirement, by arbitrarily excluding a class of people from coverage, directly conflicts with what we have determined to be the

[3] One might argue that, if we apply the rationale of *Porter* to the instant case, we would have to hold that the person injured by an unidentified driver can only recover from his or her insurer up to the minimum amount required by the financial responsibility act even if he or she had purchased greater uninsured motorist protection. This is not the case, however. In *Porter* the negligent motorist did in fact have insurance; the only problem was that it was split between several claimants. Had the court allowed the plaintiff in that case to recover up to the limits of his uninsured motorist coverage (which might, after all, have been over the statutory minimum) it would have turned uninsured motorist coverage into a form of underinsured motorist coverage. It makes sense that we refused to do so. In the instant case, however, the same rationale does not apply. From the viewpoint of the injured party, the unidentified accident-causing motorist is wholly uninsured and the injured party should be able to recover up to the limits of his or her uninsured motorist coverage.

public policy of protecting people who are injured by financially irresponsible motorists.

The physical contact requirement flows from the language of the policy—not the language of our statute, and is wholly unrelated to the question of being "uninsured in fact." Our knowledge of the "insured" status of a hit and run driver is no better than our knowledge of the "insured" status of a miss and run driver. In either case, the unknown motorist is uninsured as to the injured party—there is no coverage available. The whole purpose of uninsured and underinsured motorist coverage is to allow a prudent person to protect himself or herself against the universe of risks. To exclude miss and run drivers from the definition frustrates the purpose of the statute.

Commentators agree that the physical contact requirement was created by insurance companies to prevent fraudulent claims by insureds who negligently damage their vehicles and invent a "phantom" vehicle in an attempt to recover from their insurer. The contact requirement, however, is both too broad and too narrow to accomplish this goal. *See DeMello v. First Ins. Co. of Hawaii*, 55 Haw. 519, 523 P.2d 304, 310 (1974). As one commentator noted, if twenty witnesses will swear that an accident occurred as claimed by the injured insured, it is simply arbitrary to deny coverage in the absence of physical contact under the rubric of fraud prevention. *Brown v. Progressive Mut. Ins. Co.*, 249 So. 2d 429, 430 (Fla. 1971). Conversely, if there are no witnesses to an insured's own negligence, he or she can easily claim physical contact when there was none, and create the evidence to corroborate such a claim. *See Anderson v. State Farm Mut. Auto. Insurance Co.*, 133 Ariz. 464, 470, 652 P.2d 537, 543 (1982) (Feldman, J., concurring).

We therefore conclude that the physical contact requirement of the policies is not an authorized exception to the coverage required by the statute. It is therefore void as against public policy.

C. Stare Decisis

We have dealt with the merits of the issue as though this were a case of first impression. Of course it is not. In *Balestrieri*, we upheld the physical contact requirement, and have since refused two invitations to overrule that case.

. . . .

. . . While we should and do pay appropriate homage to precedent, we also realize that we are not prisoners of the past. In this case, there are compelling reasons to overrule precedent. . . . We conclude that this is another instance in which a departure from precedent is warranted.

. . . [B]y overruling *Balestrieri* we return to the policy expressed in *Porter* of evaluating the status of the financially irresponsible motorist from the viewpoint of the injured insured. [Further,] the facts of these cases demonstrate that the *Balestrieri* interpretation is unjust. As one commentator noted:

> An alert, athletic pedestrian who barely manages to avoid contact with such a car by leaping through a plate glass window receives the unkindest cuts of all for his efforts, but cannot qualify. Snubbed, too, is the driver who miraculously manages to steer his car off the highway and thus avoid a collision with an oncoming vehicle traveling in the wrong lane, but in so doing effects a rather abrupt stop against an unyielding bridge abutment.

McGlynn v. Safeco Insurance Co. of America, 216 Mont. 379, 701 P.2d 735, 739 (1985) (quoting 55 Ill. Bar J. 143, 147 (1966)). In contrast, a less alert pedestrian or driver would recover. Finally, by overruling *Balestrieri* we join the view of a leading commentator in the field. See Alan I. Widiss, 1 Uninsured and Underinsured Motorist Insurance § 9.7 at 484–85 (2d ed. 1990). In short, although we have a healthy respect for stare decisis, we will not be bound by a rule with nothing more than precedent to recommend it. See *Streitweiser v. Middlesex Mut. Assurance Co.*, 219 Conn. 371, 593 A.2d 498 (1991) (court overruled prior precedent and held that the Connecticut uninsured motorist statute requires coverage of damages caused by unidentified motorists).

. . . .

IV. CONCLUSION

We hold that unidentified accident-causing drivers are uninsured within the meaning of A.R.S. § 20–259.01. Therefore, insurers issuing automobile liability policies within this state must provide coverage for damages caused by these drivers. Physical contact requirements, by restricting coverage to only those unidentified drivers who actually hit the insured, are in conflict with the statute and are void. By so holding, we overrule our prior decisions to the contrary. The memorandum decision of the court of appeals in *Lowing* is vacated. That part of the memorandum decision in *Horvath* that relates to the physical contact requirement is vacated. In both cases the judgments of the superior court are reversed and the cases are remanded to the superior court for proceedings consistent with this opinion.

C. STACKING OF LIMITS

TAFT V. CERWONKA

433 A.2d 215 (R.I. 1981)

OPINION

MURRAY, JUSTICE.

The plaintiffs, Earl W. Taft and his wife, Marian F. Taft, brought this civil action to recover for the alleged wrongful death of their daughter, Beverly A. Taft (Beverly), alleging that the negligence of the defendant Eric A. Cerwonka (Cerwonka) in operating a motor vehicle was the proximate cause of their daughter's death. Because the defendant Cerwonka, and the defendant Richard A. Miller (Miller), the owner of the vehicle, were uninsured at the time of the fatal mishap, the plaintiffs also filed a complaint against their insurer, Allstate Insurance Company (Allstate) under the uninsured-motorist provisions of their policy. Prior to trial, the two suits were consolidated.

The facts giving rise to this action are as follows. In the fall of 1976, Beverly, a ninth-grade student at Winman Junior High School, lived at home with her parents in the Potowomut section of Warwick. Beverly's friend, Lauren Cesana (Lauren), who attended Tollgate High School, also lived at home with her parents in that same section of the city. At approximately 6:30 p. m. on the evening of November 2, 1976, Lauren walked from her home to the Taft residence to meet Beverly. Approximately thirty minutes after Lauren's arrival, Beverly and Lauren left the Taft residence and walked to Angelo's, a neighborhood variety store which, according to Lauren, was a gathering place for local youths. After another half-hour or forty-five minutes had elapsed, Beverly and Lauren decided to visit some friends. Because the home of the friends they desired to visit was not within walking distance and because neither Beverly nor Lauren had a driver's license, they decided to look for someone to offer them a ride.

A few minutes after the girls' decision, along came defendant Cerwonka driving a 1965 Buick Skylark that was owned by his roommate, defendant Miller. According to Lauren, who was an acquaintance of Cerwonka, he parked the car and went into Angelo's to purchase a soda. Before he entered Angelo's, Cerwonka offered a ride to Lauren and Beverly and they accepted.

It is not disputed that shortly after the trio left Angelo's and proceeded up Ives Road, Cerwonka lost control of the vehicle; as a result, it left the road, first striking a guy wire attached to a utility pole and immediately thereafter striking the pole itself. Beverly, who was seated next to the front-seat passenger door, died as a result of the injuries she sustained in the collision.

Prior to trial, plaintiffs moved for partial summary judgment on the issue of whether they would be able to "stack" the uninsured-motorist coverage provided for each automobile on the one policy underwritten by defendant Allstate. Such motion was granted by a justice of the Superior Court. The matter then proceeded to trial in the Superior Court. After all parties had rested, defendant Allstate moved for a directed verdict, stating "that if there is a verdict for the plaintiff, and I see no reason why at this juncture that the verdict for the plaintiff should not be entered, that the jury be instructed and directed that the verdict should be the minimum verdict of five thousand dollars * * *." The trial justice denied this motion and then gave his instructions to the jury, which returned a verdict in favor of plaintiffs in the sum of $33,000. Subsequently, Allstate moved for a new trial on the issue of damages, and it also moved the court to enter judgment against it in the amount of $10,000, the amount it contended was the limit of its liability under the policy issued to plaintiffs. The trial justice's denial of these motions and his entry of judgment in the amount of $20,000 (the aggregate limits of Allstate's liability) against defendant Allstate forms the basis of its present appeal.

I

In passing upon defendant's contention, we are called upon to determine an issue of first impression in this jurisdiction. That issue is whether plaintiffs should be permitted to "stack" the uninsured-motorist coverage provided for each of the two automobiles insured by Allstate.

Because the fact situations in "stacking" cases tend to be similar and because the Rhode Island uninsured-motorist statute is typical of those in other jurisdictions, decisions of other courts that have confronted this issue merit analysis here. In those jurisdictions where intra-policy stacking has been allowed,[3] courts have advanced one or more of three general theories in support of their decisions. *See* Comment, *Intra-Policy Stacking of Uninsured Motorist and Medical Payments Coverage: To Be or Not To Be*, 22 S. D. L. Rev. 349 (1977). One theory advanced is the theory that the applicable provisions of the insurance contract are ambiguous and that such ambiguities are to be resolved against the insurer. For example, in *Jeffries v. Stewart*, 159 Ind.App. 701, 309 N.E.2d 448 (1974), the Supreme Court of Indiana found an ambiguity in that the separability clause and the limits-of-liability clause conflicted with each other. The court resolved the ambiguity in favor of the insured and allowed him to stack the limits of liability. *See Id.* at 709, 309 N.E.2d at 453.

[3] Intra-policy stacking is the aggregation of the limits of liability for uninsured-motorist coverage of each car covered in one policy, whereas inter-policy stacking involves the aggregation of coverage under more than one policy.

Another theory cited in support of stacking is that the particular jurisdiction's uninsured-motorist statute requires such a result. Representative of this class of cases is *Tucker v. Government Employees Insurance Co.*, 288 So.2d 238 (Fla.1974). In that case, the Supreme Court of Florida held that their uninsured-motorist statute, Fla.Stat.Ann. s 627.727 (West 1977) "does not disclose any statutory basis for a 'stacking' exclusion in a policy combining auto liability coverage for two or more automobiles of the named insured with uninsured motorist coverage included." *Id.* at 241.[4] Another court in *Holloway v. Nationwide Mutual Insurance Co.*, 376 So.2d 690 (Ala.1979), held that the jurisdiction's uninsured-motorist statute mandated stacking for the primary insured.

A final theory is the double-premiums theory, under which courts have held that the payment of separate premiums for uninsured-motorist coverage for each vehicle covered by the policy entitles the insured to stack the limits of liability for each insured vehicle of the policy. A recent case espousing this view is *Kemp v. Allstate Insurance Co., Mont.*, 601 P.2d 20 (1979).

In the jurisdictions where intra-policy stacking has not been allowed, courts have attempted to discredit each of the above theories. In *Grimes v. Concord General Mutual Insurance Co.*, N.H., 422 A.2d 1312 (1980) the Supreme Court of New Hampshire discarded the double-premium theory, stating:

> Neither can we agree, with confidence that the plaintiff is paying an extra premium without receiving something in return. When an insured owns two vehicles that are constantly available for use, not only by him, but by members of his family and others, the risk that someone operating one of those vehicles will be involved in an accident with an uninsured motorist is obviously greater than if only one vehicle were available for use. Consequently, an insurance carrier's exposure to that risk may be enhanced. Other courts have recognized that the second premium paid on the second car does afford some extra protection that otherwise would not exist.

(Citations omitted.) *Id.* 422 A.2d at 1315. The court went on to hold that their uninsured-motorist statute did not require intra-policy stacking.

We note that the Grimes case is part of a significant minority of authority. *See Hampton v. Allstate Insurance Co.*, 126 Ariz. 403, 616 P.2d 78 (1980); *Sharples v. General Casualty Co. of Illinois*, 85 Ill.App.3d 899, 41 Ill.Dec. 176, 407 N.E.2d 674 (1980); *Pettid v. Edwards*, 195 Neb. 713, 240 N.W.2d

---

[4] We note here that the legislature in the State of Florida has since passed antistacking legislation. See Fla.Stat.Ann. s 627.4132 (West 1977).

344 (1976).[6] However, the clear trend of late has been in favor of stacking. We find the reasoning of the courts in the mainstream of this trend to be the more logical and equitable of the two approaches.

It is not disputed that plaintiffs paid two separate premiums for uninsured-motorist coverage; nevertheless, Allstate contends that to allow stacking is to render a "tortured" construction of the policy and of our uninsured-motorist statute. To give credence to Allstate's contentions, however, would defeat the reasonable expectations of a policyholder. "It is reasonable to expect the same coverage where comparable premium dollars are paid to insure the same two cars, for convenience, under a single policy. A combination coverage should not be the predicate for an exclusion of coverage. Such a result would allow a simple change in form to defeat the insured's reasonable expectation, as well as the substance of law." (citation omitted.) *Allstate Insurance Co. v. Maglish*, 94 Nev. 699, 703, 586 P.2d 313, 315 (1978). Indeed if plaintiffs had insured their automobiles under two separate policies and had paid uninsured-motorist premiums for each car, they would be entitled to $20,000 in uninsured-motorist coverage from Allstate. Under these circumstances we find persuasive the statement of dissenting Justice Douglas of the Supreme Court of New Hampshire in *Grimes v. Concord General Mutual Insurance Co.*, N.H., 422 A.2d at 1317, that "(i)t is an anomaly that if the same two premiums were paid to two different companies, we would permit inter-policy stacking of 'as many uninsured motorist policies as are applicable to him, up to his total damages,' *Courtemanche v. Lumbermens Mut. Cas. Co.*, 118 N.H. 168, 173, 385 A.2d 105, 108 (1978), but because the two different coverages were both purchased from the same insurer, we do not." (Emphasis in original.) Other cases have reflected the same view, e. g., *Traveler's Insurance Co. v. Pac*, 337 So.2d 397 (Fla.App.1976); *Breaux v. Government Employees Insurance Co.*, 373 So.2d 1335 (La.App.1979); *Allstate Insurance Co. v. Maglish*, 94 Nev. 699, 586 P.2d 313 (1978).

We hold therefore that under the circumstances of this case where plaintiffs have paid two separate premiums providing each vehicle with uninsured-motorist coverage, they are entitled to recover under the uninsured-motorist provisions of the policy sums found legally recoverable up to the aggregate sum of the motor vehicles so insured. Accord, *Kemp v. Allstate Insurance Co., Mont.*, 601 P.2d 20, 24 (1979). We are careful to limit our holding on this issue to cases factually similar to the one at bar, for we foresee and rue the day when our reasoning may be twisted to achieve an absurd result. For example, what is the result to be if a plaintiff was injured while riding in an automobile which was insured as only one

[6] For a compendium of earlier cases denying stacking, *see* Comment, *Intra-Policy Stacking of Uninsured Motorist and Medical Payments Coverages: To Be or Not To Be*, 22 S.D.L.Rev. 349, 351 n. 10 (1977).

of a fleet of cars? We defer decision on this and related issues until a case with the appropriate factual setting presents itself for review.

. . . .

Accordingly, the defendant's appeal is denied and dismissed. The judgment appealed from is affirmed, and the case is remanded to the Superior Court.

NOTES AND QUESTIONS

1. *The Meaning of "Stacking."* The term "stacking" appears in a number of different contexts in insurance law. Generally speaking, the term is used to refer to the application of two or more policies, or two or more coverages within a policy, to a particular event. Also, sometimes the term is used to refer to the application of consecutive policies to an occurrence that continues through multiple policy periods. This latter issue is discussed in Chapter 4, Section I.C. The term "inter-policy stacking" refers to the application of two or more policies to a single event, and the term "intra-policy stacking" refers to the application of two or more coverages within a single policy.

2. *Is Stacking Good or Bad?* The short answer is "it depends on your perspective." In some contexts, anti-stacking rules or policy provisions promote the principle of indemnity, which furthers the notion that one who suffers a loss should not recover more than the loss. Absent a no-stacking rule, it is possible that multiple coverages could be combined and result in the payment of proceeds greater than the amount of the loss, which raises moral hazard concerns. Chapter 5, Section VII.B in this book discusses "other insurance" clauses. One of the purposes of these clauses is to prevent policyholders from recovering more than the amount of the loss when multiple policies apply to a loss. Thus, other insurance clauses can be understood as "anti-inter-policy stacking" provisions. Yet, from a different perspective, when a policyholder's loss exceeds the combined limits of coverage and the indemnity principle is inoperative, allowing stacking has the advantage of promoting fuller compensation, which is especially important for third-party victims of accidental loss.

3. *UM & UIM Insurance.* The *Taft* case is representative of the large number of stacking disputes that have arisen in the context of uninsured and underinsured motorist insurance. Essentially, stacking multiplies the uninsured and underinsured limits by the number of vehicles insured, which has the effect of increasing protection for the policyholder in the event the policyholder is in an accident with an uninsured or underinsured motorist. Of course, when coverage multiplies, premiums should be expected to increase. If a policyholder prefers reduced coverage and a lower premium, should the policyholder be able to purchase a policy with an anti-stacking provision in it? If the policyholder suffers a loss greater than the combined potentially applicable limits but the policyholder received a premium reduction because the policy has an anti-stacking provision, should the policyholder be allowed to

argue that the anti-stacking provision violates public policy and should not be enforced?

If premiums are calculated based on how many vehicles one owns or if a premium is charged for each vehicle, a notion of "restitutionary equity"—if the policyholder paid a premium, then the policyholder ought to get coverage—arguably kicks in and cuts against anti-stacking provisions. This argument has been influential to some courts in situations where the insured's loss exceeds the benefits paid due to enforcement of an anti-stacking provision.

4. *Examples of Complexities.* Virtually every state has at least the equivalent of a few volumes of its reports filled with cases sorting out the complexities of UM and UIM coverage. For a taste of the complexities, assume that the automobiles of *A*, who has the uninsured and underinsured motorist coverages set out in the Sample Auto Policy, and *B*, who is the negligent cause, collide.

a. If *B* has a personal liability policy that covers his negligent acts in general but no automobile liability policy, is *B* uninsured? *See State Farm Mutual Automobile Insurance Co. v. Taylor*, 725 P.2d 821 (Mont. 1986).

b. If *B* has an applicable auto liability policy but the insurer is insolvent and in receivership, is *B* uninsured?

c. What if *A* is not carrying collision coverage under his policy and *B* has no insurance? Can *A* collect for the physical damage to his car caused by *B* under *A*'s uninsured motorist coverage?

d. If *A*'s underinsured motorist coverage is in the amount of $100,000 for bodily injury to one person and *B* has $15,000 in liability coverage which is available to pay for *A*'s injuries, assuming *B*'s coverage complies with the applicable state law and that *A*'s damages for bodily injury were $110,000, how much can *A* collect from his own insurance company?

e. Assume further in (d) that there was a pedestrian injured and the pedestrian was entitled to a portion of *B*'s insurance so that *A* received only $5,000 from *B*'s liability insurer. How much can *A* now collect from his own insurer? *See American States Insurance Co. v. Estate of Tollari*, 362 N.W.2d 519 (Iowa 1985).

5. *The Hit-and-Run Conundrum.* "Several state statutes require that the insured's vehicle have a 'physical contact' with the hit-and-run driver. Other state statutes reject the physical contact requirement. A third group of state statutes require that uninsured motorist coverages provide protection for the victims of hit-and-run drivers, but the statutes do not specifically require or proscribe physical contact as a prerequisite to coverage. In these states, courts have been asked to interpret the statutes, and the courts have reached divergent results. Courts in a narrow majority of states have declared that the statutes do not require physical contact, and policies that require such contact are contrary to the statute and are void as against public policy. In many other

states, courts have declined to follow this reasoning and have upheld policies in which the insurer has limited uninsured motorist coverage to situations where the physical contact is evident." Robert H. Jerry, II & Douglas R. Richmond, Understanding Insurance Law § 135[b][4], at 962 (5th ed. 2012).

If you were a legislator, would you support a statute that required hit-and-run UM coverage in the absence of physical contact, provided the insured has at least one disinterested witness willing to substantiate the insured's version of the accident? In *Hamric v. Doe*, 499 S.E.2d 619 (W. Va. 1997), the Supreme Court of West Virginia interpreted that state's statute, which requires a physical contact (*see* W. Va. Code § 33–6–31(e)(iii) (Supp. 2000)), as being satisfied if independent, disinterested third-party testimony showed that the vehicle would have struck the insured but for the insured's evasive action. Even if this answer makes sense, is it appropriate for a court to fashion it, as opposed to leaving the issue to the legislature?

6. *Other Kinds of Impacts*. In the following situations, assume the insured has uninsured motorist coverage and that the insured suffers bodily injury in the described incidents. Is the insured covered?

a. The insured hits a piece of vehicular debris lying in the roadway (such as a tire fragment, a muffler, etc.) and has an accident as a result of this contact. *See Theis v. Midwest Security Insurance Co.*, 606 N.W.2d 162 (Wis. 2000) (truck leaf spring); *State Farm Mutual Automobile Insurance Co. v. Norman*, 446 S.E.2d 720 (W. Va. 1994) (semi-truck tire); *Allstate Insurance Co. v. Killakey*, 580 N.E.2d 399 (N.Y. 1991) (tire and rim). What if the debris is non-vehicular (such as, for example, a barrel that has fallen off the back of a truck or a piece of ice)? In either case, is it essential that the insured (or some disinterested party) see the debris fall off some other vehicle? Is the case easier if the debris falls off the vehicle and is still in motion at the time of the impact with the victim's car? *See Dehnel v. State Farm Mutual Automobile Insurance Co.*, 604 N.W.2d 575 (Wis. Ct. App. 1999) (ice); *Government Employees Insurance Co. v. Goldschlager*, 355 N.Y.S.2d 9 (N.Y. App. Div. 1974) (detached wheel). In *Bauer v. Government Employees Insurance Co.*, 61 F. Supp. 2d 514 (E.D. La. 1999), the court made an "Erie guess" at Mississippi law: "Mississippi law does not allow recovery under a UM policy for contact with debris in the roadway unless there is a 'complete, proximate, direct and timely relationship' between an unidentified vehicle and the injury to the insured." 61 F. Supp. 2d at 519. Does this test clear the air?

b. An unknown motorist's vehicle kicks up a piece of debris (like a rock or fragment of a car) and propels it through the insured's windshield, causing an accident. *Compare Hill v. Citizens Insurance Co.*, 403 N.W.2d 147 (Mich. Ct. App. 1986), *with Masler v. State Farm Mutual Automobile Insurance Co.*, 894 S.W.2d 633 (Ky. 1995). Should a distinction be drawn between an object which was a piece of the unidentified vehicle or which was projected by that vehicle and an object which originates from an occupant of the unidentified vehicle? *See Wills v. State Farm Insurance Co.*, 564 N.W.2d 488 (Mich. Ct. App. 1997) (answering question posed in affirmative). Is the case easier if the unknown motorist hits a second car, which in turn is propelled into the insured's car? See *Hoyle v. Carroll*, 646 S.W.2d 161 (Tenn. 1983).

c. An uninsured motorist is driving a car on an interstate highway, runs out of gas, leaves his vehicle, and starts walking to a gas station; the path he chooses to walk, however, is the middle of a traffic lane. The insured swerves to miss the uninsured pedestrian but loses control and is seriously injured in the ensuing accident. Does the accident "arise out of the use" of the uninsured motorist's automobile? *See Aryainejad v. Economy Fire & Casualty Co.*, 663 N.E.2d 1107 (Ill. App. Ct. 1996).

d. Insured, a bicycle commuter, is injured when a passing truck grazes a bag strapped to the rear carrier of the bicycle he is riding. *See General Accident Insurance Co. v. Gladstone*, 687 N.Y.S.2d 830 (N.Y. App. Div. 1999).

Can a principle be articulated that provides consistent results across all of these situations?

7. *Residual Markets.* As the caselaw and auto statutes make clear, there is a clear public policy in favor of making sure vehicles on the roads are insured. There are some drivers, however, that insurers view as such high risks that insurers simply will not insure them voluntarily. To ensure that such drivers still have the ability to drive, states have created residual markets to provide insurance to them. The most common type is an "assigned risk plan," which is used in 42 states and the District of Columbia. Under assigned risk plans, drivers who are unable to procure insurance on the private insurance market are randomly assigned to insurers proportionally based upon each insurer's premium volume in the state. The premium rates for such coverage typically are higher than the premium rates in the private insurance market, but the rates are often still subsidized because the private market rates for these drivers would be much higher if insurers had a choice regarding whether to insure them. Residual markets are criticized because they allow people to drive who the private insurance market has determined, from an actuarial perspective, perhaps should not be driving.

8. *Occupancy.* Another key phrase in most uninsured motorist policies connects insureds to the coverage through the concept of "occupancy." In the Sample Auto Policy in the beginning of this chapter, the term "insured" includes "[a]ny other person 'occupying' 'your covered auto.' " Note that the same phrase appears in the Medical Payments Coverage (Part B) and that the named insured and "family members" are covered while "occupying" a motor vehicle or while in the status of a pedestrian. Is someone "occupying" a vehicle when she is getting out of it? *See Olsen v. Farm Bureau Insurance Co. of Neb.*, 609 N.W.2d 664 (Neb. 2000) (yes). When a child is crossing the traffic lanes en

route to getting on a school bus, is the student "occupying" the bus? *See Newman v. Erie Insurance Exchange*, 507 S.E.2d 348 (Va. 1998) (no, but student was "using" the bus). Is it necessary to be in physical contact with a vehicle to be occupying it? *See Tropf v. American Family Mutual Insurance Co.*, 558 N.W.2d 158 (Iowa 1997) (yes; insured, who had exited insured vehicle after it was involved in two-car crash and then was injured when lunging out of path of another vehicle, was not occupying the insured vehicle at time of injury).

VII. ADDITIONAL INSURER DEFENSES

No insurer undertakes to provide coverage to an insured under all circumstances, and we have already encountered a number of limitations in standard policy language on insurers' obligations. In this subsection, we explore two additional bases that insurers sometimes assert when contesting their responsibility for auto insurance claims. These two defenses are taken up in this chapter—before we move to property insurance—because they also apply to other kinds of liability insurance. First, we will examine the duty to cooperate, and then we will turn our attention to "other insurance" clauses.

A. DUTY TO COOPERATE

RAMOS V. NORTHWESTERN MUT. INS. CO.

336 So. 2d 71 (Fla. 1976)

ROBERTS, JUSTICE.

. . . .

The controlling question in the cause certified to us by the District Court involves whether or not an automobile insurance carrier may still be permitted to avoid liability pursuant to a provision in its contract requiring the insured to give his cooperation in connection with any claim of which the carrier would have responsibility under the contract notwithstanding recent developments in the law. These recent developments referred to include Florida's Financial Responsibility Act,[1] provisions contained in Florida Automobile Reparations Reform Act, and decisions of this Court including *Shingleton v. Bussey,* 223 So. 2d 713 (Fla. 1969).

---

1 Section 324.011, Florida Statutes, announcing the purpose of the Financial Responsibility Act provides:

> It is the intent of this chapter to recognize the existing rights of all to own motor vehicles and to operate them on the public streets and highways of this state when such rights are used with due consideration for others; to promote safety, and provide financial security by such owners and operators whose responsibility it is to recompense others for injury to person or property caused by the operation of a motor vehicle, so it is required herein that the owner and operator of a motor vehicle involved in an accident shall respond for such damages and show proof of financial ability to respond for damages in future accidents as a requisite to his future exercise of such privileges.

Petitioner Mercedes Ramos sued Lawrence Williams and Respondent Northwestern Mutual Insurance Company for damages in connection with injuries suffered in an auto accident in which Williams was allegedly negligent. Northwestern admitted the issuance of the policy of automobile liability insurance to Williams, but alleged as an affirmative defense that the policy did not provide coverage in this case because the accident was not reported by him to his insurer nor did he cooperate with the insurer as required by the terms of the policy. The trial judge granted Northwestern's motion to sever the trial on the coverage issue from the original claim relating to liability and damages. In the underlying tort action, a jury returned a verdict for Ramos and awarded her damages against Williams in the amount of $52,037.

After a non-jury trial on the insurance coverage issues, the trial court entered a judgment in favor of Northwestern, finding no coverage because of the insured's failure to cooperate. Specifically, the trial court found that "NORTHWESTERN received notice of the accident from plaintiff's counsel on December 29, 1969. However, WILLIAMS never contacted NORTHWESTERN, failed to report the accident, failed to notify NORTHWESTERN of his apparent changes of address and, despite efforts of NORTHWESTERN *and* plaintiff's counsel, was never located." Further, the trial court found that Williams "breached the terms of the policy issued by NORTHWESTERN because of his total failure to cooperate. *Further, the breach was material and substantially prejudiced NORTHWESTERN.*" (Emphasis original.) The trial court's conclusions of law continued as follows:

> It is, therefore, the opinion and judgment of this Court that WILLIAMS was not entitled to coverage under the policy and that NORTHWESTERN was correct in its denial of coverage. The plaintiff relies in part upon the case of *American Fire and Casualty Company v. Collura,* Fla.[App.] 1964, 163 So. 2d 784. Such reliance, however, is misplaced because there the insured notified his carrier of the accident and his whereabouts were known to all parties throughout the proceedings. Further, in considering the issue of cooperation in that case the Second District Court of Appeal stated at page 788:
>
>> In considering the issue of breach of a cooperation clause in an insurance policy, it must always be borne in mind that in order for the company to avoid liability by reason of the insured's breach, the company must show that it has exercised diligence and good faith in bringing about the cooperation of the insured, and that it has in good faith complied with the terms and conditions of the policy. *On the other hand the insured is bound to cooperate with his insurer* and to abide, both in letter and in spirit, with the terms of the

> contract; or he should *at least* be held to reasonably strict compliance with the terms thereof.
>
> Here, not only did NORTHWESTERN exercise diligence in attempting to locate WILLIAMS but, also, was precluded by WILLIAMS' concealment from "bringing about" his cooperation. Moreover, WILLIAMS totally disregarded his own responsibility in the premises. [Emphases supplied]

Plaintiff appealed to the District Court of Appeal, Third District, which affirmed the judgment of the trial court although expressly stating that it did so in reliance on past precedent. The District Court opined that the plaintiff made a persuasive argument and but for precedent and this Court's ruling in *Hoffman v. Jones,* 280 So. 2d 431 (Fla. 1973), wherein this Court stated that District Courts should not change law as a matter of public policy, the District Court would have been inclined to reverse the trial court's judgment. Relative to existing precedent, the District Court stated:

> Under existing Florida law, we conclude that the trial judge's order should be affirmed. *American Fire and Casualty Company v. Vliet,* 148 Fla. 568, 4 So. 2d 862; *American Fire and Casualty Company v. Collura,* Fla. App. 1964, 163 So. 2d 784; *Bordettsky v. Hertz Corporation,* Fla. App. 1965, 171 So. 2d 174; Anno. 60 A.L.R.2d 1146. However, the appellant has made a persuasive argument that because of the modern trend of requiring that motorists carry insurance [§ 627.733, Fla. Stat.; 7 Am. Jur. 2d, Automobile Insurance, §§ 4, 6] insurance carriers are real parties in interest in automobile accident litigation. *Stecher v. Pomeroy,* Fla. 1971, 253 So. 2d 421; *Godshall v. Unigard Insurance Company,* Fla. 1973, 281 So. 2d 499; *Allred v. Chittenden Pool Supply Inc.,* Fla. 1974, 298 So. 2d 361. That, because of the mandatory requirements of the no fault insurance act adopted in recent years in Florida, these older decisions should be ignored and the law should be changed as a matter of public policy and a carrier should suffer the responsibility of finding its insured and, if it could not, it should then be required to respond for any damages within the limits of its policy to the injured innocent party and be left to its remedy by seeking indemnification from its insured.

The District Court concluded that it would certify the matter to this Court as one passing upon a question of great public interest in that it determines that, notwithstanding recent developments in the law, an automobile insurance carrier may still be permitted to avoid liability pursuant to a provision in its contract requiring the insured to give his cooperation in connection with any claim of which the carrier would have responsibility under the contract.

Respondent, Insurance Company, suggests in line with past precedent of this Court and other Florida Appellate Courts, that where an insured has a contractual duty to cooperate with the insurer and there is undisputed evidence that the insured failed to cooperate, thereby breaching his contractual obligation to the substantial prejudice of the insurer in that the insurer was (1) unable to confirm that the vehicle listed was the one involved in the accident, (2) unable to determine the liability situation, (3) unable to determine if there were any passengers in the vehicle in order to obtain their version of the intersectional accident and the existence of injuries inasmuch as the police report indicated no visible injuries, and (4) unable to obtain the insured's cooperation in the defense of the case, an automobile insurance carrier may still be permitted to avoid liability based upon lack of cooperation. Respondent posits that neither Florida Statutes nor recent Florida decisions have abrogated the insured's duty to cooperate. Sub judice, the trial court found that the insured failed completely to cooperate with Northwestern Mutual and found that this breach of the terms of the insurance policy was material and substantially prejudiced Northwestern Mutual. Restating the findings and conclusions of the trial court, the District Court affirmed the final judgment denying coverage.

In light of current public policy as reflected by *Shingleton v. Bussey, supra,* and its progeny, petitioner requests that this Court recede from the Florida decisions which stand for the proposition that an insurer may deny coverage and avoid payment of compensation to the victim of the insured's tort where the insured has been guilty of lack of cooperation which is material and is of such a nature as would substantially prejudice the rights of the insurer, where the insurer has exercised diligence and good faith in seeking to bring about the cooperation of the insured, and where the insurer has in good faith complied with the terms and conditions of the policy.

Relating to petitioner's assertion that the financial responsibility law renders obsolete the defense of prejudicial non-cooperation, the District Court of Appeal, Third District, in *Atlantic National Insurance Co. v. Johnson,* 178 So. 2d 733 (Fla. App. 3, 1965), held that the financial responsibility law does not preclude the insurer from raising the defense of failure to give notice to the insurer for a period of seventeen months after the accident at which time Allstate, the insurer of the other vehicle involved in the accident, notified it.

We are not unmindful of the decisions cited by petitioner, but we adhere to the general philosophy of the precedent set out in *American Fire and Casualty Co. v. Vliet, supra; American Fire and Casualty Co. v. Collura, supra;* and *Bordettsky v. Hertz Corporation, supra. American Universal*

Insurance Co. v. Stotsberry, 116 So. 2d 482 (Fla. App. 3, 1959), *Barnes v. Pennsylvania Threshermen & Farmers' Mutual Casualty Insurance Co.,* 146 So. 2d 119 (Fla. App. 3, 1962), *cert. den.* 153 So. 2d 305 (Fla. 1963). We do not feel that the compulsory insurance law or third party beneficiary concept are sufficient justification to recede from that reasoning.

This Court in *American Fire and Casualty Co. v. Vliet, supra,* emphasized that to constitute the breach of a policy, the lack of cooperation must be material and the insurance company must show that it was substantially prejudiced in the particular case by failure to cooperate. Furthermore, as is stated in *Collura, supra,* the insurer must show that it has exercised diligence and good faith in bringing about the cooperation of its insured and must show that it has complied in good faith with the terms of the policy.

Not every failure to cooperate will release the insurance company. Only that failure which constitutes a material breach and substantially prejudices the rights of the insurer in defense of the cause will release the insurer of its obligation to pay. The question of whether the failure to cooperate is so substantially prejudicial as to release the insurance company of its obligation is ordinarily a question of fact, but under some circumstances, particularly where the facts are admitted, it may well be a question of law.

Accordingly, the decision of the District Court is affirmed and the writ is discharged.

It is so ordered.

NOTES AND QUESTIONS

1. *Duty or Condition or Both?* In contract law, express conditions to a party's duties must be strictly satisfied absent some kind of "policing" or regulatory principle that softens the effect of the general rule. An example of a softening principle is that if enforcement of the express condition will produce disproportionate forfeiture, then the condition will not be enforced. Also, another basic principle of contract law is that when contract language is ambiguous, the default is to interpret the language as a duty rather than a condition. This is because the performance of duties is constructively conditioned on the other party's performance of its duty, and the constructive condition architecture only requires that the condition be substantially satisfied, instead of strictly satisfied. This, too, is a softening principle. *See* Restatement (Second) of Contracts § 227 (standards for interpreting event as condition or duty); § 229 (excuse of condition to prevent disproportionate forfeiture); § 237 (a party's remaining duties are conditioned on absence of uncured material failure to perform by other party); § 241 (circumstances used to determine whether a failure of performance is material).

Insurers would prefer to treat the duty to cooperate (and the duty to give timely notice, etc.) as an express condition to the insurer's duty to pay proceeds in order to take advantage of the strict satisfaction principle of contract law. In other words, insurers would prefer an analysis under which the insurer's duty to defend or indemnify is expressly conditioned on the policyholder's cooperation. If the cooperation is not forthcoming, the nonoccurrence of the condition has the effect of suspending, and ultimately discharging, the insurer's duty. The usual treatment, however, considers the policyholder's cooperation as a duty the policyholder owes the insurer. If the policyholder breaches this duty in a material way, then, under a traditional contract analysis of dependent obligations, it follows that the insurer can suspend its performance. Was the petitioner in *Ramos* urging a repeal of these widely accepted principles of contract law?

2. *Restatement of the Law of Liability Insurance.* The Restatement recognizes a policyholder has a duty to cooperate with its insurer, but the Restatement follows the majority rule in requiring the insurer to prove the insurer has been prejudiced by the breach of the duty without taking a position regarding the level of prejudice that must occur to cause a forfeiture of coverage:

§ 30 Consequences of the Breach of the Duty to Cooperate

(1) An insured's breach of the duty to cooperate relieves an insurer of its obligations under an insurance policy only if the insurer demonstrates that the failure caused or will cause prejudice to the insurer. . . .

3. *The Substantial Prejudice Standard.* Similar to the prejudice requirement for the successful assertion of the late notice defense, an insurer attempting to defeat coverage on the basis of the policyholder's alleged failure to cooperate has the burden of proving it was materially and substantially prejudiced by the lack of cooperation. Does that mean the insurer must show that it would have won the case if the policyholder had cooperated? In most jurisdictions, it does not. *See, e.g., State Farm Mut. Auto. Ins. Co. v. Davies*, 310 S.E.2d 167 (Va. 1983) (rejecting a standard that would require the insurer to prove it would have won at trial if the policyholder had cooperated; instead, the court only required the insurer to prove there would have been a material dispute of fact for a jury to resolve had the policyholder cooperated). Because the standard of "material and substantial prejudice" is so imprecise, it often is difficult to predict the likely success of the defense.

4. *Direct Action Statutes.* The fact that the liability insurer agrees to provide a defense and to pay damages on behalf of the policyholder does not make the insurer a real party in interest to the tort action in most states. Notable exceptions are those few states which have a direct action statute. In these states, the plaintiff can sue the tortfeasor's insurer directly and in the insurer's name. *See, e.g.*, La. Rev. Stat. Ann. § 22:655 (West 1995); Wis. Stat. Ann. § 632.24 (West 1995). Other states have rejected the idea of a judicially-created direct action procedure. *See, e.g., White v. Goodville Mutual Casualty Co.*, 596 P.2d 1229 (Kan. 1979). Why should the insurer care whether it is a

named party in the underlying tort action brought by the plaintiff-victim? As a general rule, the fact that the policyholder carries liability insurance is irrelevant to the merits of the tort action and therefore inadmissible. The mere mention of it before a jury by either plaintiff or defendant might be considered prejudicial and may result in a mistrial. *See Deschaine v. Deschaine*, 140 A.2d 746 (Me. 1958); *Terry v. Plateau Electric Cooperative*, 825 S.W.2d 418 (Tenn. Ct. App. 1992). Is it not true, however, that liability insurance is so widespread that jurors know, whether the insurer's name is mentioned or not, that an insurer is very likely in the background? Does a direct action procedure make more sense in tort actions arising out of automobile accidents?

5. *Between Rocks and Hard Places*. The fact that the liability insurer may have a defense because the policyholder has failed in some way to abide by the terms of the contract can present some real dilemmas for the insurer. There are, however, several options. One is for the insurer to attempt to resolve the issue of whether it owes a duty to defend or indemnify by bringing a declaratory judgment action. If this option is pursued and the issue is resolved before the trial of the tort action is commenced, then the insurer will know whether it has a coverage obligation. In the meantime, what should the insurer do? As time passes, evidence may disappear, witnesses' memories may fade, and, in general, the defense of the tort case may suffer. Thus, should the insurer provide a defense pending the outcome of the declaratory judgment proceeding? What if the trial of the tort case is nearing and preparation is imperative, or what if the tort case is actually called for trial? The insurer has essentially two alternatives: either defend or refuse to defend. Which is better? If it chooses to defend, how can it protect itself against a claim of waiver or estoppel regarding the policy defense?

Another option is for the insurer to forego an action for declaratory judgment and to confront the basic issue of coverage outright by telling the insured coverage either will or will not be provided. Again, is there any way to preserve the policy defense issue where the insurer chooses to defend? What options are available to the insured in this situation?

6. *Insurer's Control, Insured's Cooperation, and Conflicting Objectives*. If the policyholder objects to the manner in which the insurer is exercising its right to control the defense, has the policyholder breached its duty to cooperate? If the policyholder believes that the insurer is taking too few depositions to prepare an adequate defense, does the policyholder breach the duty to cooperate if it requests more depositions be taken? What if a demand is made for more depositions, instead of a request? What if the issue is one of trial strategy? Suppose the policyholder is concerned about the damage to his or her reputation resulting from media publicity of a long trial and is objecting to the insurer's "let's-grind-down-the-plaintiff" approach to the case. What are the policyholder's options? Can the insurer ignore the policyholder's requests and conduct the litigation as it sees fit? If the insurer withdraws from the defense on the ground that the policyholder has breached the duty to cooperate, what risks does the insurer run? What if the insurer's assessment of the policyholder's cooperation, or lack thereof, is later found to be wrong?

MILLER V. SHUGART

316 N.W.2d 729 (Minn. 1982)

Opinion

SIMONETT, JUSTICE.

While Milbank Mutual Insurance Company was litigating whether it had coverage for both the insured car owner and the driver, the insured owner and the driver settled with the injured plaintiff and confessed judgment for a stipulated sum. After the coverage question was decided adversely to Milbank, plaintiff commenced a garnishment action against Milbank to collect on the judgment. Milbank appeals from an order in the garnishment proceeding granting plaintiff summary judgment to collect from Milbank on defendants' confessed judgment to the extent of the policy limits plus interest. Finding that Milbank must indemnify, we affirm plaintiff's recovery of the policy limits but reverse the ruling on interest.

Plaintiff Lynette Miller was injured in an automobile accident on June 19, 1976, when a car owned by defendant Barbara Locoshonas and driven by defendant Mark Shugart, in which Lynette was a passenger, struck a tree. Locoshonas had an auto liability policy with Milbank. Milbank, however, contended Shugart, the driver of the car, was not an agent of the owner and thus not covered under the policy. To determine this coverage question, Milbank, shortly after the accident, commenced a declaratory judgment action. Milbank provided separate counsel at its expense to represent the insured and the driver.

On January 8, 1979, judgment was entered in the declaratory judgment action adjudging that Milbank's policy afforded coverage to both Locoshonas and Shugart. On January 31, 1979, plaintiff Lynette Miller commenced her personal injury action against Locoshonas and Shugart. In April 1979, Milbank appealed the declaratory judgment decision to this court, and in April 1980, we summarily affirmed.

Twice while the appeal was pending, counsel for Locoshonas and Shugart advised Milbank they were negotiating a settlement with plaintiff's attorney and invited Milbank to participate in the negotiations. Milbank refused, pointing out it could not do so while the coverage question was unresolved.

In September 1979, plaintiff and the two defendants signed a stipulation for settlement of plaintiff's claims in which defendants confessed judgment in the amount of $100,000, which was twice the limit of Milbank's policy. The stipulated judgment further provided that it could be collected only from proceeds of any applicable insurance with no personal liability to defendants. Milbank was advised of the stipulation. Judgment on the stipulation was entered on November 15, 1979.

In May 1980, following this court's summary affirmance on the coverage issue, plaintiff Miller served a garnishment summons on Milbank. Milbank interposed an answer to the supplemental complaint setting out the history of the litigation and alleging that the confession of judgment was in violation of its policy and that Milbank was thus not bound by the judgment. Plaintiff then moved for summary judgment in her favor for $50,000, the policy limits, plus interest and costs. Milbank countered with its own motion for summary judgment, claiming defendants had breached the cooperation clause of the policy, that garnishment did not lie, and that the confessed judgment was invalid. The trial court granted plaintiff's motion, adjudging plaintiff was entitled to recover the $50,000 limits plus interest on $100,000.

Three main issues present themselves: (1) Does garnishment lie, (2) may Milbank avoid responsibility for the confessed judgment, and (3) if Milbank is bound by the judgment, must it also pay interest on the entire $100,000?

I.

Milbank says there has never been a trial on the merits, that the purported judgment, insofar as it is concerned, is still an "unliquidated tort claim," and that, consequently, the sum due plaintiff is not "due absolutely," and so garnishment does not lie. Minn.Stat. § 571.43 (1980). Milbank overlooks, however, that as between plaintiff and the defendants the tort claim has been liquidated and reduced to a judgment. So long as this has occurred, the basis for garnishment exists. *Northwestern National Bank of Bloomington-Richfield v. Hilton & Associates*, 271 Minn. 564, 136 N.W.2d 646 (1965).

What Milbank is really saying is that the judgment does not liquidate the claim because it obligates the defendants to pay nothing. While it is true that defendants need not pay anything, it is also true that the judgment effectively liquidates defendants' personal liability. We hold, therefore, that plaintiff may seek to collect on that judgment in a garnishment proceeding against the insurer.

II.

The next question is whether the judgment stipulated to by the plaintiff and the defendant insureds is the kind of liability the insurer has agreed under its policy to pay. This involves an inquiry into whether the judgment is the product of fraud or collusion perpetrated on the insurer and whether the judgment reflects a reasonable and prudent settlement.

A.

We first must deal with a threshold issue. Milbank argues the indemnity agreement of its policy has been voided because the insureds breached their duty under the policy to cooperate.[1] We disagree.

Under the auto liability policy, Milbank has a duty to defend and indemnify its insureds, and the insureds have a reciprocal duty to cooperate with their insurer in the management of the claim. Plaintiff contends that defendants were relieved from their duty to cooperate because Milbank breached its duty to defend. We would put the issue differently. Milbank has never abandoned its insureds nor, by seeking a determination of its coverage, has it repudiated its policy obligations. Milbank had a right to determine if its policy afforded coverage for the accident claim, and here Milbank did exactly as we suggested in *Prahm v. Rupp Construction Co.*, 277 N.W.2d 389, 391 (1979), where we said a conflict of interest might be avoided by bringing a declaratory judgment action on the coverage issue prior to trial. This is the route Milbank followed, appropriately providing another set of attorneys to defend the insureds in the declaratory judgment action.

On the other hand, while Milbank did not abandon its insureds neither did it accept responsibility for the insureds' liability exposure. What we have, then, is a question of how should the respective rights and duties of the parties to an insurance contract be enforced during the time period that application of the insurance contract itself is being questioned. Viewed in this context, Milbank's position, really, is that it has a superior right to have the coverage question resolved *before* the plaintiff's personal injury action is disposed of either by trial or settlement. It is unlikely plaintiff could have forced defendants to trial before the coverage issue was decided. Put this way, the question becomes: Did the insureds breach their duty to cooperate by not waiting to settle until after the policy coverage had been decided? In our view, the insureds did not have to wait and, therefore, did not breach their duty to cooperate.

While the defendant insureds have a duty to cooperate with the insurer, they also have a right to protect themselves against plaintiff's claim. The attorneys hired by Milbank to represent them owe their allegiance to their clients, the insureds, to best represent their interests. If, as here, the insureds are offered a settlement that effectively relieves them of any personal liability, at a time when their insurance coverage is in doubt, surely it cannot be said that it is not in their best interest to accept the

---

[1] The insurance policy provides in pertinent part:

"The insured shall cooperate with the company and, upon the company's request, assist in making settlements * * *. The insured shall not, except at his own cost, voluntarily make any payment, assume any obligation or incur any expense other than for first aid for others at the time of the accident."

A breach of the cooperation clause must be a substantial and material breach which prejudices the insurer. *Juvland v. Plaisance*, 255 Minn. 262, 96 N.W.2d 537 (1959).

offer. Nor, do we think, can the insurer who is disputing coverage compel the insureds to forego a settlement which is in their best interests.

On the facts of this case we hold, therefore, that the insureds did not breach their duty to cooperate with the insurer, which was then contesting coverage, by settling directly with the plaintiff.

B.

The next issue is whether Milbank may avoid the stipulated judgment on the grounds of fraud or collusion. We hold as a matter of law that the judgment was not obtained by fraud or collusion.

We start with the general proposition that a money judgment confessed to by an insured is not binding on the insurer if obtained through fraud or collusion. *Coblentz v. American Security Co. of New York*, 416 F.2d 1059 (5th Cir. 1969); *cf. Spencer v. Hawkeye Security Ins. Co.*, 216 N.W.2d 406 (Iowa 1974). In this case, however, Milbank has not made any showing of fraud or collusion. In its answer to the supplemental complaint, Milbank has neither pleaded fraud or collusion nor pleaded facts for such a defense. *See* Rules of Civil Procedure, Rule 9.02 ("In all averments of fraud or mistake, the circumstances constituting fraud or mistake shall be stated with particularity.") Neither, in opposing plaintiff's motion for summary judgment, has Milbank submitted affidavits or other evidence to make out any fact issue of fraud or collusion. Rules of Civil Procedure, Rule 56.05.

As we understand Milbank's argument, it is that the fraud and collusion consist of the defendant insureds settling the claims over Milbank's objections and contrary to the insurer's best interests, and in confessing judgment for a sum twice the amount of the policy limits. This conduct, however, need be neither fraudulent nor collusive. As we have just held, the defendant insureds had a right to make a settlement relieving them of liability. They also advised Milbank of what they were doing. Moreover, they waited to settle until after the district court had found coverage to exist. We see nothing improper in defendants' conduct. Nor is there anything wrong with the insureds' confessing judgment in an amount double the policy limits, since plaintiff, in her motion for summary judgment, has recognized Milbank's coverage is only $50,000 and seeks to recover no more than that sum from Milbank. . . .

This is not to say that Milbank's position is enviable. As the trial court observed, it had "serious doubts about the propriety of the procedure whereby the insurer is placed in a 'no-win' situation as was done here." If the insurer ignores the "invitation" to participate in the settlement negotiations, it may run the risk of being required to pay, even within its policy limits, an inflated judgment. On the other hand, if the insurer decides to participate in the settlement discussions, ordinarily it can hardly do so meaningfully without abandoning its policy defense. Nevertheless, it seems to us, if a risk is to be borne, it is better to have the insurer who makes the decision to contest coverage bear the risk. Of course, the insurer escapes the risk if it should be successful on the coverage issue, and, in that event, it is plaintiff who loses.

We hold, as a matter of law, on the showing made on plaintiff's motion for summary judgment, that the stipulated judgment against the defendant insureds was not obtained by fraud or collusion.

C.

Although having found that the stipulated judgment is untainted by fraud or collusion, our inquiry is not at an end. It seems to us there must also be a showing that the settlement on which the stipulated judgment is based was reasonable and prudent.

The settlement stipulation recites that defendants confess judgment in favor of plaintiff in the amount of $100,000 "upon the condition that plaintiff agree that her judgment may be satisfied only from liability insurance policies in force at the time * * * and that this judgment is not satisfiable nor may it be a lien upon any other assets of defendants * * *." Defendants agreed judgment could be entered *ex parte* adjudging the driver Shugart negligent although the parties further agreed, somewhat inconsistently, that the stipulation "does not constitute an admission by either defendant of his or her negligence," and it was also agreed the stipulation and judgment could not be used as an admission by the defendants in any other lawsuit.

Plainly, the "judgment" does not purport to be an adjudication on the merits; it only reflects the settlement agreement. It is also evident that, in arriving at the settlement terms, the defendants would have been quite willing to agree to anything as long as plaintiff promised them full immunity. The effect of the settlement was to substitute the claimant for the insureds in a claim against the insurer. Thus, on this appeal we see only the plaintiff claimant and the defendants' insurer in dispute, with the insureds taking a passive, disinterested role. Moreover, it is a misnomer for the parties to call plaintiff's judgment a "confessed" judgment. If this were truly a confessed judgment or even a default judgment, it is doubtful that it could stand.[6] It seems more accurate to refer to the judgment as a judgment on a stipulation.

In these circumstances, while the judgment is binding and valid as between the stipulating parties, it is not conclusive on the insurer. The burden of proof is on the claimant, the plaintiff judgment creditor, to show that the

6 Strictly speaking, a confessed judgment applies to debts, not unliquidated tort claims, and, to be valid, it must comply with the provisions of Minn.Stat. § 548.22 (1980), which requires a verified statement by the defendant debtor setting out facts concisely showing the sum confessed is justly due or to become due. None of this was, or could have been, done here. A confessed judgment, it is worth noting, is valid between the parties but voidable as to third parties, such as other creditors, entitled to attack it. *Hackney v. Wolloston*, 73 Minn. 114, 75 N.W. 1037 (1878).

settlement is reasonable and prudent. The test as to whether the settlement is reasonable and prudent is what a reasonably prudent person in the position of the defendant would have settled for on the merits of plaintiff's claim. This involves a consideration of the facts bearing on the liability and damage aspects of plaintiff's claim, as well as the risks of going to trial. This can be compared with the somewhat analogous situation in which a joint tortfeasor seeking consideration from a co-tort-feasor must prove the settlement made was reasonable. *See, e.g., Samuelson v. Chicago, Rock Island & Pacific R. Co.*, 287 Minn. 264, 178 N.W.2d 620 (1970).

. . . .

This leaves us with the question of what to do in this case. The trial court granted plaintiff summary judgment against Milbank for its policy limits of $50,000. The question is whether the record shows, as a matter of law, that the stipulated judgment, to the extent of $50,000, was reasonable and prudent. Not much proof was submitted to the trial court on this issue at the hearing on the motions for summary judgment. Nonetheless, it does appear, without dispute, that this was a one-car accident, with the plaintiff as passenger, in which the car left the road and hit a tree. As to damages, the settlement stipulation recites, and it is undisputed by Milbank, that plaintiff suffered "severe and disfiguring personal injuries," that no-fault benefits in excess of $20,000 were paid and that the no-fault benefits were likely to total $35,000 or more. The trial court states in its memo that Mr. Forsythe, retained by Milbank to represent the insureds, had reviewed the liability and damage aspects of the claim and had concluded "there was a substantial likelihood that ultimately judgment would be entered against his clients * * * for more than any possible insurance coverage * * *." On this showing, not disputed, we conclude the trial court did not err in granting summary judgment in favor of plaintiff and against Milbank to the extent of $50,000.

. . . .

Plaintiff's stipulated judgment was not conclusive on the insurer until the insurer had an opportunity to litigate the issues of whether it was bound by the judgment.[7]

---

[7] The "no action" clause in Milbank's policy reads:

> "No action shall lie against the company unless, as a condition precedent thereto, the insured shall have fully complied with all the terms of this policy, nor shall an action lie under the liability coverage *until the amount of the insured's obligation to pay shall have been fully determined either by judgment against the insured after actual trial or by written agreement by the insured, the claimant and the company*."

(emphasis added). This "no action" clause does not prevent the insureds from entering into the settlement stipulation with plaintiff, *see Butler Brothers v. American Fidelity Co.*, 120 Minn. 157, 139 N.W. 355 (1913). Since the stipulated judgment did not require the insured to pay anything, it was not until the summary judgment of March 25, 1981, that anyone's liability to pay was determined and only then would interest start running.

. . . .

We hold that the trial court's order for summary judgment in favor of plaintiff and against Milbank in the amount of $50,000 is affirmed; that Milbank is liable for interest accruing on its $50,000 judgment entered in the garnishment proceeding from March 25, 1981. . . .

NOTES AND QUESTIONS

1. *Cooperation?* How did the court in *Miller* reach the conclusion that a policyholder satisfied the duty to cooperate even though it allowed a confessed judgment to be entered against it for an amount that is twice the policy limits and the underlying claimant can only execute on the judgment against the policy? Do you think the ruling is fair?

When coverage is in doubt or the plaintiff is asserting claims in excess of the policy limits, the policyholder is in a difficult spot. In a doubtful coverage case, the insurer may offer to defend under a reservation of rights, but if the policyholder accepts this offer, the policyholder surrenders control of the defense to the insurer in circumstances where the policyholder lacks an assurance that the insurer will cover any adverse judgment. If the plaintiff's claim exceeds the policy limits, the policyholder is giving up control of the defense in circumstances where the policyholder will be personally liable for any excess judgment beyond the policy limits—and perhaps all of the judgment if coverage is also in doubt.

To deal with this difficulty, courts in most states (and the legislature in at least one state—Missouri) have approved a procedure where the policyholder enters into an agreement with the plaintiff under which the policyholder consents to a judgment being entered against it in the underlying action (often with no admission of fault or liability), the policyholder might pay something to the plaintiff (although often nothing is paid), the policyholder assigns its rights against the insurer to the plaintiff, and the plaintiff promises not to pursue claims against or garnish the policyholder's personal assets. The plaintiff is also assigned the policyholder's rights to any bad faith claims that the policyholder might have against the insurer. As the defendant/policyholder, this eliminates the risk that the policyholder's personal assets will be needed to pay an excess or non-covered judgment to the plaintiff, thereby solving the difficulty mentioned above. For the plaintiff (especially when suing a policyholder who has essentially no assets other than the liability policy), this arrangement settles the liability issue and leaves the plaintiff with the need to establish that the policy provides coverage to the policyholder for plaintiff's injuries, which is accomplished in a lawsuit against the insurer. Ordinarily, this consent judgment is subject to a court's approval, where reasonableness of the stipulated amount in the agreed judgment is evaluated. Do you agree that these arrangements are a fair balancing of the competing interests of insurer and insured? *See* Douglas R. Richmond, *The Consent Judgment Quandary of Insurance Law*, 48 Tort Trial & Ins. L. J. 537 (2013).

2. *The Standard for Enforcing Confessed Judgments*. The standard the *Miller* court applied to determine whether the confessed judgment was enforceable is fairly common. It is a 2-part test: 1) was there "fraud or collusion" between the underlying claimant and the policyholder in entering the agreement, and 2) was the settlement amount "reasonable and prudent" from the policyholder's perspective? The insurer has the burden of proof on the first part, while the underlying claimant has the burden of proof on the second part.

3. *Heads the Insurer Loses and Tails the Policyholder Wins*. What did the insurer do wrong in *Miller*? It provided a defense subject to a reservation of rights and it sought declaratory relief that it did not have a defense or indemnity obligation to the policyholder, yet it was held liable for the full amount of its policy limits even though it did not consent to the settlement and no trial was conducted.

4. *Restatement of the Law of Liability Insurance and Unilateral Settlements*. The Restatement also recognizes that a policyholder may unilaterally settle when an insurer is defending an action subject to a reservation of rights, but the insurer refuses to settle the underlying case:

> **§ 27 Remedies for Breach of the Duty to Make Reasonable Settlement Decisions**
>
> . . . .
>
> (2) When an insurer has breached the duty to make reasonable settlement decisions, the insured may settle the action without the insurer's consent and without violating the duty to cooperate or other restrictions on the insured's settlement rights contained in the policy if:
>
> (a) The insurer receives all information reasonably necessary to evaluate the legal action and has a reasonable amount of time to do so;
>
> (b) The insurer is given a reasonable opportunity to participate, and is kept reasonably informed of developments, in the settlement process;
>
> (c) The insured makes a reasonable effort to obtain the insurer's consent or approval of the settlement, including by providing the insurer with a reasonable amount of time to evaluate all the terms of the settlement agreement; and
>
> (d) The settlement agreed to by the insured is one that a reasonable person who bears the sole financial responsibility for the full amount of the potential covered judgment would make.

5. *No Action Clauses*. The "no action" clause at issue in *Miller* is common in most types of liability policies, including CGL and auto insurance. "No action" clauses purport to allow the policyholder to recover under policies only if the insurer agrees in writing to the settlement or there is a trial on the merits wherein a judgment is entered against the policyholder. How did the *Miller* court get around this policy language? Was the court's reasoning persuasive?

EXERCISE

1. Draft a 1-page memo that sets forth various strategies an insurer could employ in a case like *Miller* to avoid being liable for a confessed judgment.

B. OTHER INSURANCE

Once a policy has been triggered and the insurer's other defenses to coverage have been overcome by the policyholder, insurers still may not concede that payment is due under their policies. This is because insurers have a number of policy provisions that purport to shift responsibility for payment to other insurers. Some of the most common cost-shifting provisions are known as "other insurance" clauses. "Other insurance" clauses appear in many types of liability insurance policies, including auto insurance, and they purport to require any other triggered policies to pay before, or in combination with, the policy at issue. Indeed, it is fairly unusual today if a liability policy does not contain an "other insurance" clause. Consequently, if all of the triggered policies contain clauses that purport to shift liability to another insurer, does any insurer have to pay? The next case is an example of one court addressing such clauses.

CARRIERS INS. CO. V. AMERICAN POLICYHOLDERS' INS. CO.

404 A.2d 216 (Me. 1979)

DELAHANTY, JUSTICE.

This action was brought in the Superior Court, Kennebec County, by the plaintiff, Carriers Insurance Company (Carriers), seeking contribution from the defendant, American Policyholders' Insurance Co. (American). The parties joined issue upon whether and to what extent American was required to contribute to a settlement made by the plaintiff. Upon an agreed statement of facts, the presiding Justice found for Carriers, and American has appealed. We deny the appeal.

During April of 1963, Cummings Bros. (Cummings) entered into a contractual agreement with Merrill's Rental Service, Inc. (Merrill's) whereby it leased certain motor vehicles from Merrill's. Pursuant to the lease and for Cummings' benefit, Merrill's agreed to provide insurance coverage—both personal injury and property damage—for its vehicles while they were being operated by Cummings' employees. In 1971, this personal injury liability coverage which Merrill's obtained through Carriers stood at approximately $3,000,000 with $500,000 of property damage coverage. In the meantime, Cummings independently procured $250,000 of liability insurance through the defendant, American.

In March of 1972, one of Cummings' employees, while negligently driving a vehicle leased from Merrill's, collided with a Lincoln Continental killing the driver and extensively damaging his automobile. Carriers, acting in good faith and in the best interests of its insured, settled a wrongful death claim for $200,000 and a property damage claim for approximately $8,000. . . . Thereafter, Carriers instituted the present action and received a judgment against the defendant for approximately $104,000. Both Carriers and American had "other insurance" clauses in their insurance policies. Carriers' contract stated:

> OTHER INSURANCE
>
> If there is other insurance against an occurrence covered by this policy, the insurance afforded by this policy shall be deemed excess insurance over and above the applicable limits of all such other insurance.

(emphasis supplied.)

American's policy contained an endorsement specifically covering "hired automobiles" which provided:

> OTHER INSURANCE
>
> This insurance shall be excess insurance over any other valid and collectible insurance for Bodily Injury Liability, for Property Damage Liability and for Automobile Medical Payments.

(emphasis supplied.)

Faced with these competing clauses, the presiding Justice disregarded them as "mutually repugnant." American assigns this as error and insists that its clause should be given preference over Carriers'.

I.

We begin our discussion by acknowledging the utter confusion that pervades the entire realm of "other insurance" clauses. Originating in the property insurance field, these clauses were designed to prevent fraudulent claims induced by overinsuring. With automobiles, however, the fear of death or injury was in itself sufficient to deter specious accidents. The original purpose of other insurance clauses has little relevance, therefore, to automobile liability insurance other than to limit, reduce, or avoid an insurer's loss in those cases where there is multiple coverage. *See* Comment, *"Other Insurance" Clauses: The Lamb Weston Doctrine*, 47 Or. L. Rev. 430 (1968); Note, *Concurrent Coverage in Automobile Liability Insurance*, 65 Colum. L. Rev. 319 (1965). However, these clauses violate no public policy and in the absence of a statute to the contrary they will be given effect, even if the insured is unaware of the existence of the other insurance. 8 D. Blashfield, Automobile Law and Practice § 345.10 (3rd ed. 1966).

There are three basic types of other insurance clauses which regulate how liability is to be divided when multiple coverage exists. The first, a "pro rata" clause, limits the liability of an insurer to a proportion of the total loss. The second, an "escape" clause, seeks to avoid all liability. The third, an "excess" clause, the provision used in the present case, provides that the insurance will only be excess. *See* 8 J. Appleman, Insurance Law and Practice § 4911 (Cum. Supp. 1973); 7 Am. Jur. 2d Automobile Insurance §§ 200–202 (2d ed. 1963).

No problems arise as long as only one policy contains an other insurance clause since the particular provision can be given effect as written. Complications and conflicts occur where more than one applicable policy contains an other insurance clause. In that situation, the court is faced with a battle of the clauses.

In the case at bar, each policy, in virtually identical language, states that it will be excess over any other valid and collectible insurance. Any attempt at a literal reconciliation of the clauses involves hopeless circular reasoning. One clause cannot be given effect as "excess" unless the other is considered "primary." Since both claim to be excess, neither could operate as primary and hence neither could take effect as excess. Taken to its *reductio ad absurdum* conclusion, even though each insurer concedes that its policy would have covered the loss in the absence of the other, where there is double coverage both would escape liability, a result which neither party advocates. As well stated in *State Farm Mutual Insurance Co. v. Travelers Insurance Co.*, 184 So. 2d 750, 753 54 (La. App. 1966) (TATE, J., concurring):

> Indeed, there is actually no way by logic or word sense to reconcile two such clauses, where each policy by itself can apply as a primary insurer, but where the clause in each policy nevertheless attempts to make its own liability secondary to that of any other policy issued by a similar primary insurer: For then the primary and (attempted) secondary liability of each policy chase the other through infinity, something like trying to answer the question: Which came first, the chicken or the egg?

Faced with this logical logjam, a number of different and conflicting methods have at various times been used to determine which policy is primary and hence which should bear the brunt of the loss. Thus, it has been stated that the primary policy is the one: covering the tortfeasor; issued prior in time; insuring the vehicle's owner; whose policy covered the particular loss more specifically; or whose other insurance clause is written in more general terms.

Seizing on one of these approaches, American argues that Carriers' policy should be construed as primary based upon minute differences in the language of the excess insurance clauses. We prefer not to engage in such semantic microscopy. "It [merely] encourages the continuing draftsmanship battle by which insurers seek still more specific policy terms, and the end is not in sight." Note, *Concurrent Coverage in Automobile Liability Insurance, supra* at 322. Fairly read, each insurer, through its excess clause, seeks to place the initial loss on any other applicable insurance, saving for itself a role as secondary insurer.

As an alternative argument, American asserts that the intent of the underlying parties should be given effect. Merrill's, for valuable consideration, contractually agreed to insure Cummings. Merrill's' insurance should therefore be considered primary.

We disagree.

American's argument would be well taken were this suit simply one for breach of contract between Cummings and Merrill's. We fail, however, to see the relevance in this case of the lease agreement to which the insurers were neither parties nor beneficiaries. The only appropriate considerations are the two insurance policies through which the respective insurers and insureds manifested their contractual intent. An examination of the policies issued is the single criteria for analyzing an insurer's obligations which can neither be enlarged nor diminished beyond the terms employed. A determination of the primary insurer must turn, therefore, upon a construction of the insurance contracts and not upon a collateral agreement between an insured and a third party.

We perceive no methodology which is neither arbitrary nor utterly mechanical by which we could rationally resolve the enigma of which policy should be given effect over the other. Both clauses attempt to occupy the same legal status. Any construction this Court renders should attempt to maintain this status quo. This goal can be achieved only by abandoning the search for the mythical "primary" insurer and insisting instead that both insurers share in the loss. Such an approach best carries out the intent of the insurers which was to reduce or limit their liability.

There are additional benefits to adopting this rule. It would introduce certainty and uniformity into the insurance industry, discourage litigation between insurers, and enable underwriters to predict the losses of the insurers more accurately. Note, *Conflicts Between "Other Insurance" Clauses in Automobile Liability Insurance Policies*, 20 Hastings L.J. 1292, 1304 (1969). We hold that where there are conflicting excess insurance clause provisions they are to be disregarded as mutually repugnant thus rendering applicable the general coverage of each policy. This, we note, is the clear majority rule.

II.

Having found that both policies are to be considered "primary," we are brought to the question of how should the liability be prorated where the total loss does not exceed the limits of either policy. American argues that the loss should be prorated according to the policy limits. Because Carriers provided \$2,990,000 of coverage compared to only \$250,000 for American, appellant contends that Carriers should bear close to ninety percent of the settlement cost. Carriers, on the other hand, argues that the loss should be shared equally between the insurers, the approach adopted by the presiding Justice.

There are three basic methods of proration. The majority rule, the one urged upon by appellant, prorates liability according to the limits contained in each policy. The next, which is seldom followed, prorates on the basis of the premiums paid to each insurer. Finally, there is a minority but growing number of courts which prorate the loss equally up to the limits of the lower policy, the approach adopted by the court below.

Each method is grounded on the premises, often unarticulated, that on equitable principles the loss should be shared among the insurers either on the basis of the risk that they have undertaken or the benefit they have received. In its clearest expression, the majority rule has been justified on the theory that the burden imposed on each insurer is generally proportional to the benefit which he received, since the size of the premium is most always directly related to the size of the policy.

Lamb Weston, Inc. v. Oregon Automobile Insurance Company, [346 P.2d 643, 647 (Or. 1959)]. On precisely these grounds, the majority rule has been criticized since "[i]t is commonly known that the cost of liability insurance does not increase proportionately with the policy limits." Once minimum coverage has been obtained, significant supplemental coverage can be provided at only a modest increase in cost.

On the other hand, if the majority rule is less equitable than that minority approach which apportions on the basis of premiums received, it has the advantage of facile application. Unless the multiple policies cover the identical risks, there would be too many variables affecting the premiums to permit them to serve as a benchmark for an equitable adjustment.

The minority rule adopted by the presiding Justice utilizes the best aspects of both approaches without the limitations. Like the majority rule, it is easy to administer. It would simply require each company to contribute equally until the limits of the smaller policy were exhausted, with any remaining portion of the loss then being paid from the larger policy up to its limits.

Unlike the majority rule, this Solomon like approach comports with a most basic sense of justice. *See* Exodus, ch. 21, par. 35 ("When one man's ox hurts another's ox so badly that it dies, they shall sell the live ox and divide this money as well as the dead animal they shall divide equally between them.") Moreover, the majority rule unfairly discriminates against the larger policy by apportioning the loss in proportion to the respective policy limits, utterly forgetting that both insurers, by their contracts, have in fact agreed to cover a loss up to the limits of the lesser policy. Until that point is reached, the majority rule amounts to no more than an unacceptable subsidy from the high coverage to the low coverage carrier. We are in complete accord with the presiding Justice when he adopted the persuasive opinion of Judge Doyle in *Ruan Transport Corp. v. Truck Rentals, Inc., supra* note 7 at 696.

The majority method of prorating operates inequitably in its differentiating treatment of the high loss and low loss insurer. In return for a greater premium the insurer providing higher coverage has undertaken to protect the insured against accidents involving high losses. Yet because of this undertaking to protect against high loss the larger insurer is in an unfavorable position vis à vis the other insurer even in cases of low loss, since under the majority method of prorating the insurer affording the greater maximum coverage pays the greater segment of any loss incurred, regardless of the amount of the loss. This seems inequitable since both insurers have equally undertaken to insure against the low loss accident.

The majority rule would hardly encourage an insurer from increasing its coverage where it is aware that there is a lesser policy. It would increase the insurer's potential liability not only in the high risk situation which the additional premiums are presumably meant to recompense, but it would have the untoward effect of increasing liability in the more likely to occur low risk situation. Carried to its extreme, it would further increase the cost of additional insurance thereby reducing the likelihood that an insured would choose such coverage. The Court would be reluctant to adopt a rule which would seemingly have little social utility.

For all of the aforesaid reasons, the presiding Justice correctly prorated the loss between Carriers and American.

Accordingly, the entry shall be:

Appeal denied.

Judgment affirmed.

NOTES AND QUESTIONS

1. *Types of Clauses in Different Types of Insurance.* The "other insurance" clause is not the sole province of liability insurance. They exist in other lines of insurance too, as insurers seek to coordinate the coverage they provide with that of other insurers that cover the same risk. The court in *Carriers* identified the three principle categories of "other insurance" clauses. Some courts and commentators recognize a fourth—the "excess-escape" clause, which, as the name suggests, combines the features of excess and escape clauses. Under this provision, the insurer is liable only in excess of other available insurance, but it has no liability if the other insurance is equal to or in excess of its own limits. There are also many "tailor-made" variations on these categories, which appear when insurers have specific coordination objectives in mind with respect to particular risks. For example, some property

insurance policies have a variation on the "escape" clause, which states that if there is other insurance on the property described in the policy, and if the insurer does not consent to such other insurance, then the policy is void. Generally speaking, in order to constitute "other insurance" so as to void a property insurance policy by operation of such an "escape" clause, the "other insurance" must cover the same risks, the same property, and the same interests as those covered by the policy containing the "escape" provision. *See* David B. Harrison, Annotation, *What Constitutes "Other Insurance" Within Meaning of Insurance Policy Provisions Prohibiting Insured From Obtaining Other Insurance on Same Property*, 7 A.L.R.4th 494 (1981). Health insurance policies also contain the equivalent of "other insurance" clauses, but they are typically labeled "coordination of benefit" (or "COB") clauses. For an exhaustive survey of "other insurance" clauses and how they operate, *see* Douglas R. Richmond, *Issues and Problems in "Other Insurance," Multiple Insurance, and Self-Insurance*, 22 Pepp. L. Rev. 1373 (1995). *See also* Susan Randall, *Coordinating Liability Insurance*, 1995 Wis. L. Rev. 1339, 1360–65.

2. *Majority View?* The *Carriers* case describes the majority position when mutually repugnant "other insurance" clauses exist in the different applicable policies as prorating the loss based upon the various triggered policies' limits, but that is not accurate today. The majority approach today uses the *Carriers*' approach, which is to equally prorate the loss among the triggered policies regardless of the policies' limits. Once a policy's limits are exhausted, however, the policy's obligation to pay terminates and any excess amount allocated to that policy is reallocated to the non-exhausted policies. *See* Christopher C. French, *The "Non-Cumulation, Clause": an "Other Insurance Clause" by Another Name*, 60 U. Kan. L. Rev. 375, 407 (2012). Escape clauses have, in general, been met with judicial hostility and often are simply unenforced, although much depends on the nature of the risk and other circumstances. *See, e.g., CSE Insurance Group v. Northbrook Property and Casualty Co.*, 23 Cal. App. 4th 1839 (1994); *Connecticut Indemnity Co. v. Cordasco*, 535 A.2d 631, 633 (Pa. Super. Ct. 1987). Are there reasons to treat escape clauses differently from excess clauses in conflict situations? Does the nature of the insured risk matter? What if, for example, two policies have escape clauses, but one insures a building against fire damage and the other insures crops against hail damage?

3. *Property Loss Versus Liability to Third Parties.* In property insurance, "other insurance" clauses have an obvious connection to the principle of indemnity, in that they prevent the policyholder from recovering multiple times for the same loss. The issue in *Carriers* concerned overlapping liability coverages. In that context, "other insurance" clauses are not designed to prevent net gain because the policies themselves merely agree to pay for losses caused by the insured to a third party. Since the third party is not entitled to collect more than her loss from the policyholder, there is no danger that the liability insurer or insurers will have to pay an amount that would result in a net gain by the third party. On the other hand, "other insurance" clauses in liability policies can have the effect of reducing the insurers'

obligations to something less than full recovery by the third party. This is especially true where effect is given to an "escape" clause. This can also happen in property insurance if the policy limits of all of the policies are less than the value of the property and one or more of these policies has an "escape" clause, which is a reason courts generally are hostile to them.

4. *The Matter of "Layering."* The prototype "other insurance" case involves two insurers providing overlapping coverage at the same level (or in the same "layer"). It is important to distinguish this from the situation where the coverage from multiple insurers is designed to apply in layers. For example, the policyholder might purchase a policy from Insurer A for "layer one," covering all losses up to $500,000. Then, a second policy might be purchased from Insurer B for "layer two" in the amount of $2 million. In the trade, Insurer A would be referred to as the "primary" carrier, and B would be called the "first level excess" carrier. If a loss is under $500,000, then it is entirely the responsibility of Insurer A. If the loss exceeds $500,000, Insurer B pays for any loss exceeding $500,000 and up to the policy limits of $2 million. Thus, for example, if the loss were $1.5 million, Insurer A would pay $500,000 of the loss and Insurer B would pay $1 million of the loss. Large corporations (e.g., of the Fortune 500 variety) are likely to structure their coverages in multiple layers, with a first excess, second excess, third excess, and perhaps other carriers. To complicate things further, the policyholder might have several insurers participating concurrently in one (or more) of the excess levels. It is also likely that such a company will have a large self-insured retention, which functions as a large deductible.

An "umbrella policy," purchased by many individuals, is primarily designed to provide excess coverage over the primary coverage provided by the homeowners and the automobile policies. Umbrella policies also commonly provide some additional primary coverage for certain types of claims (e.g., personal liability coverages) that typically are not covered under the underlying auto and homeowners policies. Umbrella policies are sometimes called "true excess" policies, however, to underscore the intent that they operate in a different layer than the primary coverages to the extent there is primary coverage for the claims at issue. *See, e.g., Bosco v. Bauermeister*, 571 N.W.2d 509 (Mich. 1997) (employer's auto policy, which contained excess clause, was not excess over umbrella policies, which were "true excess" policies).

5. *Life Insurance.* Life insurers rarely, if ever, resort to "other insurance" clauses, as reflected by the dearth of cases on the subject. *See* West's American Digest System Key No. "217K2444 Other Insurance." Of the relatively few cases on the subject, many of them are older cases involving burial insurance or industrial life insurance. Life insurers tend to address the matter by making inquiries in the application process and limiting the amount sold accordingly to ensure the policyholder is not so over-insured that a moral hazard arises.

6. *Self-Insurance as "Other Insurance."* If a firm chooses to self-insure instead of purchasing liability insurance, should the self-insured retention be treated as "other insurance" for the purpose of offsetting a liability insurer's responsibility? On the general issue of whether self-insured retentions constitute "insurance," most courts have answered the question in the negative. *See, e.g.*, *St. John's Regional Health Center v. American Casualty Co.*, 980 F.2d 1222 (8th Cir. 1992); *Hillsborough County Hospital & Welfare Board v. Taylor*, 546 So. 2d 1055 (Fla. 1989). The reason for this is simple—no insurance (i.e., self-insurance) is not a type of insurance, and if there is no insurance, then a loss certainly is not covered by it.

7. *Restatement of the Law of Liability Insurance.* The Restatement adopts the approach of the court in *Carriers*. Specifically, if multiple triggered policies contain irreconcilable "other insurance" clauses, then the clauses are mutually repugnant and the loss is divided pro rata among the triggered policies until the limits of the insurance for each policy are exhausted:

§ 40 Indemnification from Multiple Policies: The General Rule

Comment:

. . . .

d. When an allocation term in one policy cannot be harmonized with an allocation rule in another. Some allocation provisions contained in overlapping, concurrently issued policies simply cannot be harmonized with each other. In such cases, if the allocation terms were read literally the result would be no coverage for the insured, violating the principle that an insured should not be worse off as a result of being the beneficiary of multiple policies. Courts confronted with such conflicting allocation terms typically hold such terms to be repugnant, irreconcilable, or simply in violation of public policy and therefore unenforceable. In place of those conflicting terms the courts apply an equitable remedy, which usually entails some form of pro rata allocation among insurers. This Section follows that rule as well.

CHAPTER SIX

PROPERTY INSURANCE

■ ■ ■

"People who live in glass houses should take out insurance."

— Unknown

Modern property insurance originated in England after the Great Fire of London in 1666 substantially destroyed the city. Benjamin Franklin pushed the idea of property insurance against the risk of fire in the American colonies. Over time, fire insurers recognized a market to insure other kinds of risks (e.g., wind, storm, hail, etc.) and began selling separate property policies that covered such risks. In the 1940s and 1950s, insurers began bundling coverages for multiple perils together in a single policy that became known as a "multi-peril" policy. Because these multi-peril policies grew out of single-risk coverage, they were "specified risk" policies, meaning that only the perils specifically included in the policies were covered. Insurers subsequently began to sell "all risk" policies, which covered any damage to covered property regardless of the cause, leaving it to the language in the exclusions to cut back on the broad coverage provisions.

Today, there are many kinds of property insurance policies, including homeowners, renters, commercial property, inland marine, boiler and machinery, and crime insurance. Other kinds of property policies provide temporally limited coverage while, for example, the property is being transported or used in a unique way (such as when an art masterpiece is loaned to another museum for display). For most American households, the largest asset (with the possible exception in some households of retirement plans) is typically the home, with an automobile probably coming in second. Homeowners insurance is the insurance purchased by consumers to protect their homes, along with personal property, and this coverage is bundled with personal liability insurance for non-vehicular risks. Commercial property insurance similarly covers property owned by business entities, but it also can cover the revenue stream of the business if the policyholder elects to purchase such coverage.

Although this chapter will provide a sample of some of the issues that arise under standard homeowners and commercial property insurance, the general principles discussed in this chapter are relevant to all kinds of property insurance. To begin, we will take a closer look at a standard form homeowners policy.

I. SAMPLE HOMEOWNERS INSURANCE POLICY

As you read the Sample Homeowners Insurance Policy that is reproduced below, consider its complexity. It contains multiple sections that set forth the coverage provided for real and personal property damage, a section that sets forth the liability coverages, multiple sections that set forth definitions and exclusions, and multiple "Conditions" sections. Does the Sample Homeowners Policy provide "all risk" coverage, named-peril coverage, or a combination of both?

HOMEOWNERS
HO 00 03 05 11

HOMEOWNERS 3 – SPECIAL FORM

AGREEMENT

We will provide the insurance described in this policy in return for the premium and compliance with all applicable provisions of this policy.

DEFINITIONS

A. In this policy, "you" and "your" refer to the "named insured" shown in the Declarations and the spouse if a resident of the same household. "We", "us" and "our" refer to the Company providing this insurance.

B. In addition, certain words and phrases are defined as follows:

1. "Aircraft Liability", "Hovercraft Liability", "Motor Vehicle Liability" and "Watercraft Liability", subject to the provisions in **b.** below, mean the following:

a. Liability for "bodily injury" or "property damage" arising out of the:

(1) Ownership of such vehicle or craft by an "insured";

(2) Maintenance, occupancy, operation, use, loading or unloading of such vehicle or craft by any person;

(3) Entrustment of such vehicle or craft by an "insured" to any person;

(4) Failure to supervise or negligent supervision of any person involving such vehicle or craft by an "insured"; or

(5) Vicarious liability, whether or not imposed by law, for the actions of a child or minor involving such vehicle or craft.

b. For the purpose of this definition:

(1) Aircraft means any contrivance used or designed for flight except model or hobby aircraft not used or designed to carry people or cargo;

(2) Hovercraft means a self-propelled motorized ground effect vehicle and includes, but is not limited to, flarecraft and air cushion vehicles;

(3) Watercraft means a craft principally designed to be propelled on or in water by wind, engine power or electric motor; and

(4) Motor vehicle means a "motor vehicle" as defined in **7.** below.

2. "Bodily injury" means bodily harm, sickness or disease, including required care, loss of services and death that results.

3. "Business" means:

a. A trade, profession or occupation engaged in on a full-time, part-time or occasional basis; or

b. Any other activity engaged in for money or other compensation, except the following:

(1) One or more activities, not described in **(2)** through **(4)** below, for which no "insured" receives more than $2,000 in total compensation for the 12 months before the beginning of the policy period;

(2) Volunteer activities for which no money is received other than payment for expenses incurred to perform the activity;

(3) Providing home day care services for which no compensation is received, other than the mutual exchange of such services; or

(4) The rendering of home day care services to a relative of an "insured".

4. "Employee" means an employee of an "insured", or an employee leased to an "insured" by a labor leasing firm under an agreement between an "insured" and the labor leasing firm, whose duties are other than those performed by a "residence employee".

5. "Insured" means:

a. You and residents of your household who are:

(1) Your relatives; or

(2) Other persons under the age of 21 and in your care or the care of a resident of your household who is your relative;

b. A student enrolled in school full-time, as defined by the school, who was a resident of your household before moving out to attend school, provided the student is under the age of:

(1) 24 and your relative; or

(2) 21 and in your care or the care of a resident of your household who is your relative; or

c. Under Section **II:**

(1) With respect to animals or watercraft to which this policy applies, any person or organization legally responsible for these animals or watercraft which are owned by you or any person described in **5.a.** or **b.** "Insured" does not mean a person or organization using or having custody of these animals or watercraft in the course of any "business" or without consent of the owner; or

(2) With respect to a "motor vehicle" to which this policy applies:

(a) Persons while engaged in your employ or that of any person described in **5.a.** or **b.**; or

(b) Other persons using the vehicle on an "insured location" with your consent.

Under both Sections **I** and **II**, when the word an immediately precedes the word "insured", the words an "insured" together mean one or more "insureds".

6. "Insured location" means:

a. The "residence premises";

b. The part of other premises, other structures and grounds used by you as a residence; and

(1) Which is shown in the Declarations; or

(2) Which is acquired by you during the policy period for your use as a residence;

c. Any premises used by you in connection with a premises described in **a.** and **b.** above;

d. Any part of a premises:

(1) Not owned by an "insured"; and

(2) Where an "insured" is temporarily residing;

e. Vacant land, other than farm land, owned by or rented to an "insured";

f. Land owned by or rented to an "insured" on which a one-, two-, three- or four-family dwelling is being built as a residence for an "insured";

g. Individual or family cemetery plots or burial vaults of an "insured"; or

h. Any part of a premises occasionally rented to an "insured" for other than "business" use.

7. "Motor vehicle" means:

a. A self-propelled land or amphibious vehicle; or

b. Any trailer or semitrailer which is being carried on, towed by or hitched for towing by a vehicle described in **a.** above.

8. "Occurrence" means an accident, including continuous or repeated exposure to substantially the same general harmful conditions, which results, during the policy period, in:

a. "Bodily injury"; or

b. "Property damage".

9. "Property damage" means physical injury to, destruction of, or loss of use of tangible property.

10. "Residence employee" means:

a. An employee of an "insured", or an employee leased to an "insured" by a labor leasing firm, under an agreement between an "insured" and the labor leasing firm, whose duties are related to the maintenance or use of the "residence premises", including household or domestic services; or

b. One who performs similar duties elsewhere not related to the "business" of an "insured".

A "residence employee" does not include a temporary employee who is furnished to an "insured" to substitute for a permanent "residence employee" on leave or to meet seasonal or short-term workload conditions.

11. "Residence premises" means:

a. The one-family dwelling where you reside;

b. The two-, three- or four-family dwelling where you reside in at least one of the family units; or

c. That part of any other building where you reside;

and which is shown as the "residence premises" in the Declarations.

"Residence premises" also includes other structures and grounds at that location.

SECTION I – PROPERTY COVERAGES

A. Coverage A – Dwelling

1. We cover:
   a. The dwelling on the "residence premises" shown in the Declarations, including structures attached to the dwelling; and
   b. Materials and supplies located on or next to the "residence premises" used to construct, alter or repair the dwelling or other structures on the "residence premises".
2. We do not cover land, including land on which the dwelling is located.

B. Coverage B – Other Structures

1. We cover other structures on the "residence premises" set apart from the dwelling by clear space. This includes structures connected to the dwelling by only a fence, utility line, or similar connection.
2. We do not cover:
   a. Land, including land on which the other structures are located;
   b. Other structures rented or held for rental to any person not a tenant of the dwelling, unless used solely as a private garage;
   c. Other structures from which any "business" is conducted; or
   d. Other structures used to store "business" property. However, we do cover a structure that contains "business" property solely owned by an "insured" or a tenant of the dwelling, provided that "business" property does not include gaseous or liquid fuel, other than fuel in a permanently installed fuel tank of a vehicle or craft parked or stored in the structure.
3. The limit of liability for this coverage will not be more than 10% of the limit of liability that applies to Coverage **A**. Use of this coverage does not reduce the Coverage **A** limit of liability.

C. Coverage C – Personal Property

1. **Covered Property**

   We cover personal property owned or used by an "insured" while it is anywhere in the world. After a loss and at your request, we will cover personal property owned by:

   a. Others while the property is on the part of the "residence premises" occupied by an "insured"; or
   b. A guest or a "residence employee", while the property is in any residence occupied by an "insured".

2. **Limit For Property At Other Locations**

   a. Other Residences

   Our limit of liability for personal property usually located at an "insured's" residence, other than the "residence premises", is 10% of the limit of liability for Coverage **C**, or $1,000, whichever is greater. However, this limitation does not apply to personal property:

   (1) Moved from the "residence premises" because it is:
   (a) Being repaired, renovated or rebuilt; and
   (b) Not fit to live in or store property in; or

   (2) In a newly acquired principal residence for 30 days from the time you begin to move the property there.

   b. Self-storage Facilities

   Our limit of liability for personal property owned or used by an "insured" and located in a self-storage facility is 10% of the limit of liability for Coverage **C**, or $1,000, whichever is greater. However, this limitation does not apply to personal property:

   (1) Moved from the "residence premises" because it is:
   (a) Being repaired, renovated or rebuilt; and
   (b) Not fit to live in or store property in; or

   (2) Usually located in an "insured's" residence, other than the "residence premises".

3. **Special Limits Of Liability**

The special limit for each category shown below is the total limit for each loss for all property in that category. These special limits do not increase the Coverage **C** limit of liability.

a. $200 on money, bank notes, bullion, gold other than goldware, silver other than silverware, platinum other than platinumware, coins, medals, scrip, stored value cards and smart cards.

b. $1,500 on securities, accounts, deeds, evidences of debt, letters of credit, notes other than bank notes, manuscripts, personal records, passports, tickets and stamps. This dollar limit applies to these categories regardless of the medium (such as paper or computer software) on which the material exists.

This limit includes the cost to research, replace or restore the information from the lost or damaged material.

c. $1,500 on watercraft of all types, including their trailers, furnishings, equipment and outboard engines or motors.

d. $1,500 on trailers or semitrailers not used with watercraft of all types.

e. $1,500 for loss by theft of jewelry, watches, furs, precious and semiprecious stones.

f. $2,500 for loss by theft of firearms and related equipment.

g. $2,500 for loss by theft of silverware, silver-plated ware, goldware, gold-plated ware, platinumware, platinum-plated ware and pewterware. This includes flatware, hollowware, tea sets, trays and trophies made of or including silver, gold or pewter.

h. $2,500 on property, on the "residence premises", used primarily for "business" purposes.

i. $1,500 on property, away from the "residence premises", used primarily for "business" purposes. However, this limit does not apply to antennas, tapes, wires, records, disks or other media that are:

(1) Used with electronic equipment that reproduces, receives or transmits audio, visual or data signals; and

(2) In or upon a "motor vehicle".

j. $1,500 on portable electronic equipment that:

(1) Reproduces, receives or transmits audio, visual or data signals;

(2) Is designed to be operated by more than one power source, one of which is a "motor vehicle's" electrical system; and

(3) Is in or upon a "motor vehicle".

k. $250 for antennas, tapes, wires, records, disks or other media that are:

(1) Used with electronic equipment that reproduces, receives or transmits audio, visual or data signals; and

(2) In or upon a "motor vehicle".

4. **Property Not Covered**

We do not cover:

a. Articles separately described and specifically insured, regardless of the limit for which they are insured, in this or other insurance;

b. Animals, birds or fish;

c. "Motor vehicles".

This includes a "motor vehicle's" equipment and parts. However, this Paragraph **4.c.** does not apply to:

(1) Portable electronic equipment that:

(a) Reproduces, receives or transmits audio, visual or data signals; and

(b) Is designed so that it may be operated from a power source other than a "motor vehicle's" electrical system.

(2) "Motor vehicles" not required to be registered for use on public roads or property which are:

(a) Used solely to service a residence; or

(b) Designed to assist the handicapped;

d. Aircraft, meaning any contrivance used or designed for flight, including any parts whether or not attached to the aircraft.

We do cover model or hobby aircraft not used or designed to carry people or cargo;

e. Hovercraft and parts. Hovercraft means a self-propelled motorized ground effect vehicle and includes, but is not limited to, flarecraft and air cushion vehicles;

f. Property of roomers, boarders and other tenants, except property of roomers and boarders related to an "insured";

g. Property in an apartment regularly rented or held for rental to others by an "insured", except as provided in **E.10.** Landlord's Furnishings under Section **I** – Property Coverages;

h. Property rented or held for rental to others off the "residence premises";

i. "Business" data, including such data stored in:

(1) Books of account, drawings or other paper records; or

(2) Computers and related equipment.

We do cover the cost of blank recording or storage media and of prerecorded computer programs available on the retail market;

j. Credit cards, electronic fund transfer cards or access devices used solely for deposit, withdrawal or transfer of funds except as provided in **E.6.** Credit Card, Electronic Fund Transfer Card Or Access Device, Forgery And Counterfeit Money under Section **I** – Property Coverages; or

k. Water or steam.

D. Coverage D – Loss Of Use

The limit of liability for Coverage **D** is the total limit for the coverages in **1.** Additional Living Expense, **2.** Fair Rental Value and **3.** Civil Authority Prohibits Use below.

1. Additional Living Expense

If a loss covered under Section **I** makes that part of the "residence premises" where you reside not fit to live in, we cover any necessary increase in living expenses incurred by you so that your household can maintain its normal standard of living.

Payment will be for the shortest time required to repair or replace the damage or, if you permanently relocate, the shortest time required for your household to settle elsewhere.

2. Fair Rental Value

If a loss covered under Section **I** makes that part of the "residence premises" rented to others or held for rental by you not fit to live in, we cover the fair rental value of such premises less any expenses that do not continue while it is not fit to live in.

Payment will be for the shortest time required to repair or replace such premises.

3. Civil Authority Prohibits Use

If a civil authority prohibits you from use of the "residence premises" as a result of direct damage to neighboring premises by a Peril Insured Against, we cover the loss as provided in **1.** Additional Living Expense and **2.** Fair Rental Value above for no more than two weeks.

4. Loss Or Expense Not Covered

We do not cover loss or expense due to cancellation of a lease or agreement.

The periods of time under **1.** Additional Living Expense, **2.** Fair Rental Value and **3.** Civil Authority Prohibits Use above are not limited by expiration of this policy.

E. Additional Coverages

1. Debris Removal

a. We will pay your reasonable expense for the removal of:

(1) Debris of covered property if a Peril Insured Against that applies to the damaged property causes the loss; or

(2) Ash, dust or particles from a volcanic eruption that has caused direct loss to a building or property contained in a building.

This expense is included in the limit of liability that applies to the damaged property. If the amount to be paid for the actual damage to the property plus the debris removal expense is more than the limit of liability for the damaged property, an additional 5% of that limit is available for such expense.

b. We will also pay your reasonable expense, up to $1,000, for the removal from the "residence premises" of:

(1) Your trees felled by the peril of Windstorm or Hail or Weight of Ice, Snow or Sleet; or

(2) A neighbor's trees felled by a Peril Insured Against under Coverage **C**;

provided the trees:

(3) Damage a covered structure; or

(4) Do not damage a covered structure, but:

(a) Block a driveway on the "residence premises" which prevents a "motor vehicle", that is registered for use on public roads or property, from entering or leaving the "residence premises"; or

(b) Block a ramp or other fixture designed to assist a handicapped person to enter or leave the dwelling building.

The $1,000 limit is the most we will pay in any one loss, regardless of the number of fallen trees. No more than $500 of this limit will be paid for the removal of any one tree.

This coverage is additional insurance.

2. Reasonable Repairs

a. We will pay the reasonable cost incurred by you for the necessary measures taken solely to protect covered property that is damaged by a Peril Insured Against from further damage.

b. If the measures taken involve repair to other damaged property, we will only pay if that property is covered under this policy and the damage is caused by a Peril Insured Against. This coverage does not:

(1) Increase the limit of liability that applies to the covered property; or

(2) Relieve you of your duties, in case of a loss to covered property, described in **C.4.** under Section **I** – Conditions.

3. Trees, Shrubs And Other Plants

We cover trees, shrubs, plants or lawns, on the "residence premises", for loss caused by the following Perils Insured Against:

a. Fire or Lightning;

b. Explosion;

c. Riot or Civil Commotion;

d. Aircraft;

e. Vehicles not owned or operated by a resident of the "residence premises";

f. Vandalism or Malicious Mischief; or

g. Theft.

We will pay up to 5% of the limit of liability that applies to the dwelling for all trees, shrubs, plants or lawns. No more than $500 of this limit will be paid for any one tree, shrub or plant. We do not cover property grown for "business" purposes.

This coverage is additional insurance.

4. Fire Department Service Charge

We will pay up to $500 for your liability assumed by contract or agreement for fire department charges incurred when the fire department is called to save or protect covered property from a Peril Insured Against. We do not cover fire department service charges if the property is located within the limits of the city, municipality or protection district furnishing the fire department response.

This coverage is additional insurance. No deductible applies to this coverage.

5. Property Removed

We insure covered property against direct loss from any cause while being removed from a premises endangered by a Peril Insured Against and for no more than 30 days while removed.

This coverage does not change the limit of liability that applies to the property being removed.

6. Credit Card, Electronic Fund Transfer Card Or Access Device, Forgery And Counterfeit Money

a. We will pay up to $500 for:

(1) The legal obligation of an "insured" to pay because of the theft or unauthorized use of credit cards issued to or registered in an "insured's" name;

(2) Loss resulting from theft or unauthorized use of an electronic fund transfer card or access device used for deposit, withdrawal or transfer of funds, issued to or registered in an "insured's" name;

(3) Loss to an "insured" caused by forgery or alteration of any check or negotiable instrument; and

(4) Loss to an "insured" through acceptance in good faith of counterfeit United States or Canadian paper currency.

All loss resulting from a series of acts committed by any one person or in which any one person is concerned or implicated is considered to be one loss.

This coverage is additional insurance. No deductible applies to this coverage.

b. We do not cover:

(1) Use of a credit card, electronic fund transfer card or access device:

(a) By a resident of your household;

(b) By a person who has been entrusted with either type of card or access device; or

(c) If an "insured" has not complied with all terms and conditions under which the cards are issued or the devices accessed; or

(2) Loss arising out of "business" use or dishonesty of an "insured".

c. If the coverage in **a.** above applies, the following defense provisions also apply:

(1) We may investigate and settle any claim or suit that we decide is appropriate. Our duty to defend a claim or suit ends when the amount we pay for the loss equals our limit of liability.

(2) If a suit is brought against an "insured" for liability under **a.(1)** or **(2)** above, we will provide a defense at our expense by counsel of our choice.

(3) We have the option to defend at our expense an "insured" or an "insured's" bank against any suit for the enforcement of payment under **a.(3)** above.

7. Loss Assessment

a. We will pay up to $1,000 for your share of loss assessment charged during the policy period against you, as owner or tenant of the "residence premises", by a corporation or association of property owners. The assessment must be made as a result of direct loss to property, owned by all members collectively, of the type that would be covered by this policy if owned by you, caused by a Peril Insured Against under Coverage **A**, other than:

(1) Earthquake; or

(2) Land shock waves or tremors before, during or after a volcanic eruption.

The limit of $1,000 is the most we will pay with respect to any one loss, regardless of the number of assessments. We will only apply one deductible, per unit, to the total amount of any one loss to the property described above, regardless of the number of assessments.

b. We do not cover assessments charged against you or a corporation or association of property owners by any governmental body.

c. Paragraph **Q.** Policy Period under Section **I** – Conditions does not apply to this coverage.

This coverage is additional insurance.

8. Collapse

a. The coverage provided under this Additional Coverage – Collapse applies only to an abrupt collapse.

b. For the purpose of this Additional Coverage – Collapse, abrupt collapse means an abrupt falling down or caving in of a building or any part of a building with the result that the building or part of the building cannot be occupied for its intended purpose.

c. This Additional Coverage – Collapse does not apply to:

(1) A building or any part of a building that is in danger of falling down or caving in;

(2) A part of a building that is standing, even if it has separated from another part of the building; or

(3) A building or any part of a building that is standing, even if it shows evidence of cracking, bulging, sagging, bending, leaning, settling, shrinkage or expansion.

d. We insure for direct physical loss to covered property involving abrupt collapse of a building or any part of a building if such collapse was caused by one or more of the following:

(1) The Perils Insured Against named under Coverage **C;**

(2) Decay, of a building or any part of a building, that is hidden from view, unless the presence of such decay is known to an "insured" prior to collapse;

(3) Insect or vermin damage, to a building or any part of a building, that is hidden from view, unless the presence of such damage is known to an "insured" prior to collapse;

(4) Weight of contents, equipment, animals or people;

(5) Weight of rain which collects on a roof; or

(6) Use of defective material or methods in construction, remodeling or renovation if the collapse occurs during the course of the construction, remodeling or renovation.

e. Loss to an awning, fence, patio, deck, pavement, swimming pool, underground pipe, flue, drain, cesspool, septic tank, foundation, retaining wall, bulkhead, pier, wharf or dock is not included under **d.(2)** through **(6)** above, unless the loss is a direct result of the collapse of a building or any part of a building.

f. This coverage does not increase the limit of liability that applies to the damaged covered property.

9. Glass Or Safety Glazing Material

a. We cover:

(1) The breakage of glass or safety glazing material which is part of a covered building, storm door or storm window;

(2) The breakage of glass or safety glazing material which is part of a covered building, storm door or storm window when caused directly by earth movement; and

(3) The direct physical loss to covered property caused solely by the pieces, fragments or splinters of broken glass or safety glazing material which is part of a building, storm door or storm window.

b. This coverage does not include loss:

(1) To covered property which results because the glass or safety glazing material has been broken, except as provided in **a.(3)** above; or

(2) On the "residence premises" if the dwelling has been vacant for more than 60 consecutive days immediately before the loss, except when the breakage results directly from earth movement as provided in **a.(2)** above. A dwelling being constructed is not considered vacant.

c. This coverage does not increase the limit of liability that applies to the damaged property.

10. Landlord's Furnishings

We will pay up to $2,500 for your appliances, carpeting and other household furnishings, in each apartment on the "residence premises" regularly rented or held for rental to others by an "insured", for loss caused by a Peril Insured Against in Coverage **C**, other than Theft.

This limit is the most we will pay in any one loss regardless of the number of appliances, carpeting or other household furnishings involved in the loss.

This coverage does not increase the limit of liability applying to the damaged property.

11. Ordinance Or Law

a. You may use up to 10% of the limit of liability that applies to Coverage **A** for the increased costs you incur due to the enforcement of any ordinance or law which requires or regulates:

(1) The construction, demolition, remodeling, renovation or repair of that part of a covered building or other structure damaged by a Peril Insured Against;

(2) The demolition and reconstruction of the undamaged part of a covered building or other structure, when that building or other structure must be totally demolished because of damage by a Peril Insured Against to another part of that covered building or other structure; or

(3) The remodeling, removal or replacement of the portion of the undamaged part of a covered building or other structure necessary to complete the remodeling, repair or replacement of that part of the covered building or other structure damaged by a Peril Insured Against.

b. You may use all or part of this ordinance or law coverage to pay for the increased costs you incur to remove debris resulting from the construction, demolition, remodeling, renovation, repair or replacement of property as stated in **a.** above.

c. We do not cover:

(1) The loss in value to any covered building or other structure due to the requirements of any ordinance or law; or

(2) The costs to comply with any ordinance or law which requires any "insured" or others to test for, monitor, clean up, remove, contain, treat, detoxify or neutralize, or in any way respond to, or assess the effects of, pollutants in or on any covered building or other structure.

Pollutants means any solid, liquid, gaseous or thermal irritant or contaminant, including smoke, vapor, soot, fumes, acids, alkalis, chemicals and waste. Waste includes materials to be recycled, reconditioned or reclaimed.

This coverage is additional insurance.

12. Grave Markers

We will pay up to $5,000 for grave markers, including mausoleums, on or away from the "residence premises" for loss caused by a Peril Insured Against under Coverage **C.**

This coverage does not increase the limits of liability that apply to the damaged covered property.

SECTION I – PERILS INSURED AGAINST

A. Coverage A – Dwelling And Coverage B – Other Structures

1. We insure against direct physical loss to property described in Coverages **A** and **B.**

2. We do not insure, however, for loss:

a. Excluded under Section **I** – Exclusions;

b. Involving collapse, including any of the following conditions of property or any part of the property:

(1) An abrupt falling down or caving in;

(2) Loss of structural integrity, including separation of parts of the property or property in danger of falling down or caving in; or

(3) Any cracking, bulging, sagging, bending, leaning, settling, shrinkage or expansion as such condition relates to **(1)** or **(2)** above;

except as provided in **E.8.** Collapse under Section **I** – Property Coverages; or

c. Caused by:

(1) Freezing of a plumbing, heating, air conditioning or automatic fire protective sprinkler system or of a household appliance, or by discharge, leakage or overflow from within the system or appliance caused by freezing. This provision does not apply if you have used reasonable care to:

(a) Maintain heat in the building; or

(b) Shut off the water supply and drain all systems and appliances of water.

However, if the building is protected by an automatic fire protective sprinkler system, you must use reasonable care to continue the water supply and maintain heat in the building for coverage to apply.

For purposes of this provision, a plumbing system or household appliance does not include a sump, sump pump or related equipment or a roof drain, gutter, downspout or similar fixtures or equipment;

(2) Freezing, thawing, pressure or weight of water or ice, whether driven by wind or not, to a:

(a) Fence, pavement, patio or swimming pool;

(b) Footing, foundation, bulkhead, wall, or any other structure or device that supports all or part of a building, or other structure;

(c) Retaining wall or bulkhead that does not support all or part of a building or other structure; or

(d) Pier, wharf or dock;

(3) Theft in or to a dwelling under construction, or of materials and supplies for use in the construction until the dwelling is finished and occupied;

(4) Vandalism and malicious mischief, and any ensuing loss caused by any intentional and wrongful act committed in the course of the vandalism or malicious mischief, if the dwelling has been vacant for more than 60 consecutive days immediately before the loss. A dwelling being constructed is not considered vacant;

(5) Mold, fungus or wet rot. However, we do insure for loss caused by mold, fungus or wet rot that is hidden within the walls or ceilings or beneath the floors or above the ceilings of a structure if such loss results from the accidental discharge or overflow of water or steam from within:

(a) A plumbing, heating, air conditioning or automatic fire protective sprinkler system, or a household appliance, on the "residence premises"; or

(b) A storm drain, or water, steam or sewer pipes, off the "residence premises".

For purposes of this provision, a plumbing system or household appliance does not include a sump, sump pump or related equipment or a roof drain, gutter, downspout or similar fixtures or equipment; or

(6) Any of the following:

(a) Wear and tear, marring, deterioration;

(b) Mechanical breakdown, latent defect, inherent vice or any quality in property that causes it to damage or destroy itself;

(c) Smog, rust or other corrosion, or dry rot;

(d) Smoke from agricultural smudging or industrial operations;

(e) Discharge, dispersal, seepage, migration, release or escape of pollutants unless the discharge, dispersal, seepage, migration, release or escape is itself caused by a Peril Insured Against named under Coverage **C.**

Pollutants means any solid, liquid, gaseous or thermal irritant or contaminant, including smoke, vapor, soot, fumes, acids, alkalis, chemicals and waste. Waste includes materials to be recycled, reconditioned or reclaimed;

(f) Settling, shrinking, bulging or expansion, including resultant cracking, of bulkheads, pavements, patios, footings, foundations, walls, floors, roofs or ceilings;

(g) Birds, rodents or insects;

(h) Nesting or infestation, or discharge or release of waste products or secretions, by any animals; or

(i) Animals owned or kept by an "insured".

Exception To c.(6)

Unless the loss is otherwise excluded, we cover loss to property covered under Coverage **A** or **B** resulting from an accidental discharge or overflow of water or steam from within a:

(i) Storm drain, or water, steam or sewer pipe, off the "residence premises"; or

(ii) Plumbing, heating, air conditioning or automatic fire protective sprinkler system or household appliance on the "residence premises". This includes the cost to tear out and replace any part of a building, or other structure, on the "residence premises", but only when necessary to repair the system or appliance. However, such tear out and replacement coverage only applies to other structures if the water or steam causes actual damage to a building on the "residence premises".

We do not cover loss to the system or appliance from which this water or steam escaped.

For purposes of this provision, a plumbing system or household appliance does not include a sump, sump pump or related equipment or a roof drain, gutter, downspout or similar fixtures or equipment.

Section **I** – Exclusion **A.3.** Water, Paragraphs **a.** and **c.** that apply to surface water and water below the surface of the ground do not apply to loss by water covered under **c.(5)** and **(6)** above.

Under **2.b.** and **c.** above, any ensuing loss to property described in Coverages **A** and **B** not precluded by any other provision in this policy is covered.

B. Coverage C – Personal Property

We insure for direct physical loss to the property described in Coverage **C** caused by any of the following perils unless the loss is excluded in Section **I** – Exclusions.

1. Fire Or Lightning

2. Windstorm Or Hail

This peril includes loss to watercraft of all types and their trailers, furnishings, equipment, and outboard engines or motors, only while inside a fully enclosed building.

This peril does not include loss to the property contained in a building caused by rain, snow, sleet, sand or dust unless the direct force of wind or hail damages the building causing an opening in a roof or wall and the rain, snow, sleet, sand or dust enters through this opening.

3. **Explosion**
4. **Riot Or Civil Commotion**
5. **Aircraft**

   This peril includes self-propelled missiles and spacecraft.
6. **Vehicles**
7. **Smoke**

   This peril means sudden and accidental damage from smoke, including the emission or puffback of smoke, soot, fumes or vapors from a boiler, furnace or related equipment.

   This peril does not include loss caused by smoke from agricultural smudging or industrial operations.
8. **Vandalism Or Malicious Mischief**
9. **Theft**

   a. This peril includes attempted theft and loss of property from a known place when it is likely that the property has been stolen.

   b. This peril does not include loss caused by theft:

   (1) Committed by an "insured";

   (2) In or to a dwelling under construction, or of materials and supplies for use in the construction until the dwelling is finished and occupied;

   (3) From that part of a "residence premises" rented by an "insured" to someone other than another "insured"; or

   (4) That occurs off the "residence premises" of:

   (a) Trailers, semitrailers and campers;

   (b) Watercraft of all types, and their furnishings, equipment and outboard engines or motors; or

   (c) Property while at any other residence owned by, rented to, or occupied by an "insured", except while an "insured" is temporarily living there. Property of an "insured" who is a student is covered while at the residence the student occupies to attend school as long as the student has been there at any time during the 90 days immediately before the loss.

10. **Falling Objects**

    This peril does not include loss to property contained in a building unless the roof or an outside wall of the building is first damaged by a falling object. Damage to the falling object itself is not included.
11. **Weight Of Ice, Snow Or Sleet**

    This peril means weight of ice, snow or sleet which causes damage to property contained in a building.
12. **Accidental Discharge Or Overflow Of Water Or Steam**

    a. This peril means accidental discharge or overflow of water or steam from within a plumbing, heating, air conditioning or automatic fire protective sprinkler system or from within a household appliance.

    b. This peril does not include loss:

    (1) To the system or appliance from which the water or steam escaped;

    (2) Caused by or resulting from freezing except as provided in Peril Insured Against **14.** Freezing;

    (3) On the "residence premises" caused by accidental discharge or overflow which occurs off the "residence premises"; or

    (4) Caused by mold, fungus or wet rot unless hidden within the walls or ceilings or beneath the floors or above the ceilings of a structure.

    c. In this peril, a plumbing system or household appliance does not include a sump, sump pump or related equipment or a roof drain, gutter, downspout or similar fixtures or equipment.

    d. Section **I** – Exclusion **A.3.** Water, Paragraphs **a.** and **c.** that apply to surface water and water below the surface of the ground do not apply to loss by water covered under this peril.
13. **Sudden And Accidental Tearing Apart, Cracking, Burning Or Bulging**

    This peril means sudden and accidental tearing apart, cracking, burning or bulging of a steam or hot water heating system, an air conditioning or automatic fire protective sprinkler system, or an appliance for heating water.

    We do not cover loss caused by or resulting from freezing under this peril.

14. Freezing

a. This peril means freezing of a plumbing, heating, air conditioning or automatic fire protective sprinkler system or of a household appliance, but only if you have used reasonable care to:

(1) Maintain heat in the building; or

(2) Shut off the water supply and drain all systems and appliances of water.

However, if the building is protected by an automatic fire protective sprinkler system, you must use reasonable care to continue the water supply and maintain heat in the building for coverage to apply.

b. In this peril, a plumbing system or household appliance does not include a sump, sump pump or related equipment or a roof drain, gutter, downspout or similar fixtures or equipment.

15. Sudden And Accidental Damage From Artificially Generated Electrical Current

This peril does not include loss to tubes, transistors, electronic components or circuitry that is a part of appliances, fixtures, computers, home entertainment units or other types of electronic apparatus.

16. Volcanic Eruption

This peril does not include loss caused by earthquake, land shock waves or tremors.

SECTION I – EXCLUSIONS

A. We do not insure for loss caused directly or indirectly by any of the following. Such loss is excluded regardless of any other cause or event contributing concurrently or in any sequence to the loss. These exclusions apply whether or not the loss event results in widespread damage or affects a substantial area.

1. Ordinance Or Law

Ordinance Or Law means any ordinance or law:

a. Requiring or regulating the construction, demolition, remodeling, renovation or repair of property, including removal of any resulting debris. This Exclusion **A.1.a.** does not apply to the amount of coverage that may be provided for in **E.11.** Ordinance Or Law under Section **I** – Property Coverages;

b. The requirements of which result in a loss in value to property; or

c. Requiring any "insured" or others to test for, monitor, clean up, remove, contain, treat, detoxify or neutralize, or in any way respond to, or assess the effects of, pollutants.

Pollutants means any solid, liquid, gaseous or thermal irritant or contaminant, including smoke, vapor, soot, fumes, acids, alkalis, chemicals and waste. Waste includes materials to be recycled, reconditioned or reclaimed.

This Exclusion **A.1.** applies whether or not the property has been physically damaged.

2. Earth Movement

Earth Movement means:

a. Earthquake, including land shock waves or tremors before, during or after a volcanic eruption;

b. Landslide, mudslide or mudflow;

c. Subsidence or sinkhole; or

d. Any other earth movement including earth sinking, rising or shifting.

This Exclusion **A.2.** applies regardless of whether any of the above, in **A.2.a.** through **A.2.d.,** is caused by an act of nature or is otherwise caused.

However, direct loss by fire, explosion or theft resulting from any of the above, in **A.2.a.** through **A.2.d.,** is covered.

3. Water

This means:

a. Flood, surface water, waves, including tidal wave and tsunami, tides, tidal water, overflow of any body of water, or spray from any of these, all whether or not driven by wind, including storm surge;

b. Water which:

(1) Backs up through sewers or drains; or

(2) Overflows or is otherwise discharged from a sump, sump pump or related equipment;

c. Water below the surface of the ground, including water which exerts pressure on, or seeps, leaks or flows through a building, sidewalk, driveway, patio, foundation, swimming pool or other structure; or

d. Waterborne material carried or otherwise moved by any of the water referred to in **A.3.a.** through **A.3.c.** of this exclusion.

This Exclusion **A.3.** applies regardless of whether any of the above, in **A.3.a.** through **A.3.d.,** is caused by an act of nature or is otherwise caused.

This Exclusion **A.3.** applies to, but is not limited to, escape, overflow or discharge, for any reason, of water or waterborne material from a dam, levee, seawall or any other boundary or containment system.

However, direct loss by fire, explosion or theft resulting from any of the above, in **A.3.a.** through **A.3.d.,** is covered.

4. Power Failure

Power Failure means the failure of power or other utility service if the failure takes place off the "residence premises". But if the failure results in a loss, from a Peril Insured Against on the "residence premises", we will pay for the loss caused by that peril.

5. Neglect

Neglect means neglect of an "insured" to use all reasonable means to save and preserve property at and after the time of a loss.

6. War

War includes the following and any consequence of any of the following:

a. Undeclared war, civil war, insurrection, rebellion or revolution;

b. Warlike act by a military force or military personnel; or

c. Destruction, seizure or use for a military purpose.

Discharge of a nuclear weapon will be deemed a warlike act even if accidental.

7. Nuclear Hazard

This Exclusion **A.7.** pertains to Nuclear Hazard to the extent set forth in **N.** Nuclear Hazard Clause under Section **I** – Conditions.

8. Intentional Loss

Intentional Loss means any loss arising out of any act an "insured" commits or conspires to commit with the intent to cause a loss.

In the event of such loss, no "insured" is entitled to coverage, even "insureds" who did not commit or conspire to commit the act causing the loss.

9. Governmental Action

Governmental Action means the destruction, confiscation or seizure of property described in Coverage **A, B** or **C** by order of any governmental or public authority.

This exclusion does not apply to such acts ordered by any governmental or public authority that are taken at the time of a fire to prevent its spread, if the loss caused by fire would be covered under this policy.

B. We do not insure for loss to property described in Coverages **A** and **B** caused by any of the following. However, any ensuing loss to property described in Coverages **A** and **B** not precluded by any other provision in this policy is covered.

1. Weather conditions. However, this exclusion only applies if weather conditions contribute in any way with a cause or event excluded in **A.** above to produce the loss.

2. Acts or decisions, including the failure to act or decide, of any person, group, organization or governmental body.

3. Faulty, inadequate or defective:

a. Planning, zoning, development, surveying, siting;

b. Design, specifications, workmanship, repair, construction, renovation, remodeling, grading, compaction;

c. Materials used in repair, construction, renovation or remodeling; or

d. Maintenance;

of part or all of any property whether on or off the "residence premises".

SECTION I – CONDITIONS

A. Insurable Interest And Limit Of Liability

Even if more than one person has an insurable interest in the property covered, we will not be liable in any one loss:

1. To an "insured" for more than the amount of such "insured's" interest at the time of loss; or

2. For more than the applicable limit of liability.

B. Deductible

Unless otherwise noted in this policy, the following deductible provision applies:

With respect to any one loss:

1. Subject to the applicable limit of liability, we will pay only that part of the total of all loss payable that exceeds the deductible amount shown in the Declarations.

2. If two or more deductibles under this policy apply to the loss, only the highest deductible amount will apply.

C. Duties After Loss

In case of a loss to covered property, we have no duty to provide coverage under this policy if the failure to comply with the following duties is prejudicial to us. These duties must be performed either by you, an "insured" seeking coverage, or a representative of either:

1. Give prompt notice to us or our agent;
2. Notify the police in case of loss by theft;
3. Notify the credit card or electronic fund transfer card or access device company in case of loss as provided for in **E.6.** Credit Card, Electronic Fund Transfer Card Or Access Device, Forgery And Counterfeit Money under Section I – Property Coverages;
4. Protect the property from further damage. If repairs to the property are required, you must:
   - **a.** Make reasonable and necessary repairs to protect the property; and
   - **b.** Keep an accurate record of repair expenses;
5. Cooperate with us in the investigation of a claim;
6. Prepare an inventory of damaged personal property showing the quantity, description, actual cash value and amount of loss. Attach all bills, receipts and related documents that justify the figures in the inventory;
7. As often as we reasonably require:
   - **a.** Show the damaged property;
   - **b.** Provide us with records and documents we request and permit us to make copies; and
   - **c.** Submit to examination under oath, while not in the presence of another "insured", and sign the same;
8. Send to us, within 60 days after our request, your signed, sworn proof of loss which sets forth, to the best of your knowledge and belief:
   - **a.** The time and cause of loss;
   - **b.** The interests of all "insureds" and all others in the property involved and all liens on the property;
   - **c.** Other insurance which may cover the loss;
   - **d.** Changes in title or occupancy of the property during the term of the policy;
   - **e.** Specifications of damaged buildings and detailed repair estimates;
   - **f.** The inventory of damaged personal property described in **6.** above;
   - **g.** Receipts for additional living expenses incurred and records that support the fair rental value loss; and
   - **h.** Evidence or affidavit that supports a claim under **E.6.** Credit Card, Electronic Fund Transfer Card Or Access Device, Forgery And Counterfeit Money under Section **I** – Property Coverages, stating the amount and cause of loss.

D. Loss Settlement

In this Condition **D.**, the terms "cost to repair or replace" and "replacement cost" do not include the increased costs incurred to comply with the enforcement of any ordinance or law, except to the extent that coverage for these increased costs is provided in **E.11.** Ordinance Or Law under Section **I** – Property Coverages. Covered property losses are settled as follows:

1. Property of the following types:
   - **a.** Personal property;
   - **b.** Awnings, carpeting, household appliances, outdoor antennas and outdoor equipment, whether or not attached to buildings;
   - **c.** Structures that are not buildings; and
   - **d.** Grave markers, including mausoleums;

   at actual cash value at the time of loss but not more than the amount required to repair or replace.
2. Buildings covered under Coverage **A** or **B** at replacement cost without deduction for depreciation, subject to the following:
   - **a.** If, at the time of loss, the amount of insurance in this policy on the damaged building is 80% or more of the full replacement cost of the building immediately before the loss, we will pay the cost to repair or replace, without deduction for depreciation, but not more than the least of the following amounts:
     - **(1)** The limit of liability under this policy that applies to the building;
     - **(2)** The replacement cost of that part of the building damaged with material of like kind and quality and for like use; or
     - **(3)** The necessary amount actually spent to repair or replace the damaged building.

     If the building is rebuilt at a new premises, the cost described in **(2)** above is limited to the cost which would have been incurred if the building had been built at the original premises.

b. If, at the time of loss, the amount of insurance in this policy on the damaged building is less than 80% of the full replacement cost of the building immediately before the loss, we will pay the greater of the following amounts, but not more than the limit of liability under this policy that applies to the building:

(1) The actual cash value of that part of the building damaged; or

(2) That proportion of the cost to repair or replace, without deduction for depreciation, that part of the building damaged, which the total amount of insurance in this policy on the damaged building bears to 80% of the replacement cost of the building.

c. To determine the amount of insurance required to equal 80% of the full replacement cost of the building immediately before the loss, do not include the value of:

(1) Excavations, footings, foundations, piers, or any other structures or devices that support all or part of the building, which are below the undersurface of the lowest basement floor;

(2) Those supports described in **(1)** above which are below the surface of the ground inside the foundation walls, if there is no basement; and

(3) Underground flues, pipes, wiring and drains.

d. We will pay no more than the actual cash value of the damage until actual repair or replacement is complete. Once actual repair or replacement is complete, we will settle the loss as noted in **2.a.** and **b.** above.

However, if the cost to repair or replace the damage is both:

(1) Less than 5% of the amount of insurance in this policy on the building; and

(2) Less than $2,500;

we will settle the loss as noted in **2.a.** and **b.** above whether or not actual repair or replacement is complete.

e. You may disregard the replacement cost loss settlement provisions and make claim under this policy for loss to buildings on an actual cash value basis. You may then make claim for any additional liability according to the provisions of this Condition **D.** Loss Settlement, provided you notify us, within 180 days after the date of loss, of your intent to repair or replace the damaged building.

E. Loss To A Pair Or Set

In case of loss to a pair or set we may elect to:

1. Repair or replace any part to restore the pair or set to its value before the loss; or

2. Pay the difference between actual cash value of the property before and after the loss.

F. Appraisal

If you and we fail to agree on the amount of loss, either may demand an appraisal of the loss. In this event, each party will choose a competent and impartial appraiser within 20 days after receiving a written request from the other. The two appraisers will choose an umpire. If they cannot agree upon an umpire within 15 days, you or we may request that the choice be made by a judge of a court of record in the state where the "residence premises" is located. The appraisers will separately set the amount of loss. If the appraisers submit a written report of an agreement to us, the amount agreed upon will be the amount of loss. If they fail to agree, they will submit their differences to the umpire. A decision agreed to by any two will set the amount of loss.

Each party will:

1. Pay its own appraiser; and

2. Bear the other expenses of the appraisal and umpire equally.

G. Other Insurance And Service Agreement

If a loss covered by this policy is also covered by:

1. Other insurance, we will pay only the proportion of the loss that the limit of liability that applies under this policy bears to the total amount of insurance covering the loss; or

2. A service agreement, this insurance is excess over any amounts payable under any such agreement. Service agreement means a service plan, property restoration plan, home warranty or other similar service warranty agreement, even if it is characterized as insurance.

H. Suit Against Us

No action can be brought against us unless there has been full compliance with all of the terms under Section **I** of this policy and the action is started within two years after the date of loss.

I. Our Option

If we give you written notice within 30 days after we receive your signed, sworn proof of loss, we may repair or replace any part of the damaged property with material or property of like kind and quality.

J. Loss Payment

We will adjust all losses with you. We will pay you unless some other person is named in the policy or is legally entitled to receive payment. Loss will be payable 60 days after we receive your proof of loss and:

1. Reach an agreement with you;

2. There is an entry of a final judgment; or

3. There is a filing of an appraisal award with us.

K. Abandonment Of Property

We need not accept any property abandoned by an "insured".

L. Mortgage Clause

1. If a mortgagee is named in this policy, any loss payable under Coverage **A** or **B** will be paid to the mortgagee and you, as interests appear. If more than one mortgagee is named, the order of payment will be the same as the order of precedence of the mortgages.

2. If we deny your claim, that denial will not apply to a valid claim of the mortgagee, if the mortgagee:

a. Notifies us of any change in ownership, occupancy or substantial change in risk of which the mortgagee is aware;

b. Pays any premium due under this policy on demand if you have neglected to pay the premium; and

c. Submits a signed, sworn statement of loss within 60 days after receiving notice from us of your failure to do so. Paragraphs **F.** Appraisal, **H.** Suit Against Us and **J.** Loss Payment under Section **I** – Conditions also apply to the mortgagee.

3. If we decide to cancel or not to renew this policy, the mortgagee will be notified at least 10 days before the date cancellation or nonrenewal takes effect.

4. If we pay the mortgagee for any loss and deny payment to you:

a. We are subrogated to all the rights of the mortgagee granted under the mortgage on the property; or

b. At our option, we may pay to the mortgagee the whole principal on the mortgage plus any accrued interest. In this event, we will receive a full assignment and transfer of the mortgage and all securities held as collateral to the mortgage debt.

5. Subrogation will not impair the right of the mortgagee to recover the full amount of the mortgagee's claim.

M. No Benefit To Bailee

We will not recognize any assignment or grant any coverage that benefits a person or organization holding, storing or moving property for a fee regardless of any other provision of this policy.

N. Nuclear Hazard Clause

1. "Nuclear Hazard" means any nuclear reaction, radiation, or radioactive contamination, all whether controlled or uncontrolled or however caused, or any consequence of any of these.

2. Loss caused by the nuclear hazard will not be considered loss caused by fire, explosion, or smoke, whether these perils are specifically named in or otherwise included within the Perils Insured Against.

3. This policy does not apply under Section **I** to loss caused directly or indirectly by nuclear hazard, except that direct loss by fire resulting from the nuclear hazard is covered.

O. Recovered Property

If you or we recover any property for which we have made payment under this policy, you or we will notify the other of the recovery. At your option, the property will be returned to or retained by you or it will become our property. If the recovered property is returned to or retained by you, the loss payment will be adjusted based on the amount you received for the recovered property.

P. Volcanic Eruption Period

One or more volcanic eruptions that occur within a 72-hour period will be considered as one volcanic eruption.

Q. Policy Period

This policy applies only to loss which occurs during the policy period.

R. Concealment Or Fraud

We provide coverage to no "insureds" under this policy if, whether before or after a loss, an "insured" has:

1. Intentionally concealed or misrepresented any material fact or circumstance;
2. Engaged in fraudulent conduct; or
3. Made false statements;

relating to this insurance.

S. Loss Payable Clause

If the Declarations shows a loss payee for certain listed insured personal property, the definition of "insured" is changed to include that loss payee with respect to that property.

If we decide to cancel or not renew this policy, that loss payee will be notified in writing.

SECTION II – LIABILITY COVERAGES

A. Coverage E – Personal Liability

If a claim is made or a suit is brought against an "insured" for damages because of "bodily injury" or "property damage" caused by an "occurrence" to which this coverage applies, we will:

1. Pay up to our limit of liability for the damages for which an "insured" is legally liable. Damages include prejudgment interest awarded against an "insured"; and
2. Provide a defense at our expense by counsel of our choice, even if the suit is groundless, false or fraudulent. We may investigate and settle any claim or suit that we decide is appropriate. Our duty to settle or defend ends when our limit of liability for the "occurrence" has been exhausted by payment of a judgment or settlement.

B. Coverage F – Medical Payments To Others

We will pay the necessary medical expenses that are incurred or medically ascertained within three years from the date of an accident causing "bodily injury". Medical expenses means reasonable charges for medical, surgical, x-ray, dental, ambulance, hospital, professional nursing, prosthetic devices and funeral services. This coverage does not apply to you or regular residents of your household except "residence employees". As to others, this coverage applies only:

1. To a person on the "insured location" with the permission of an "insured"; or
2. To a person off the "insured location", if the "bodily injury":
   a. Arises out of a condition on the "insured location" or the ways immediately adjoining;
   b. Is caused by the activities of an "insured";
   c. Is caused by a "residence employee" in the course of the "residence employee's" employment by an "insured"; or
   d. Is caused by an animal owned by or in the care of an "insured".

SECTION II – EXCLUSIONS

A. "Motor Vehicle Liability"

1. Coverages **E** and **F** do not apply to any "motor vehicle liability" if, at the time and place of an "occurrence", the involved "motor vehicle":
   a. Is registered for use on public roads or property;
   b. Is not registered for use on public roads or property, but such registration is required by a law, or regulation issued by a government agency, for it to be used at the place of the "occurrence"; or
   c. Is being:
      (1) Operated in, or practicing for, any prearranged or organized race, speed contest or other competition;
      (2) Rented to others;
      (3) Used to carry persons or cargo for a charge; or
      (4) Used for any "business" purpose except for a motorized golf cart while on a golfing facility.
2. If Exclusion **A.1.** does not apply, there is still no coverage for "motor vehicle liability", unless the "motor vehicle" is:
   a. In dead storage on an "insured location";
   b. Used solely to service a residence;
   c. Designed to assist the handicapped and, at the time of an "occurrence", it is:
      (1) Being used to assist a handicapped person; or
      (2) Parked on an "insured location";
   d. Designed for recreational use off public roads and:
      (1) Not owned by an "insured"; or

(2) Owned by an "insured" provided the "occurrence" takes place:

(a) On an "insured location" as defined in Definition **B.6.a., b., d., e.** or **h.**; or

(b) Off an "insured location" and the "motor vehicle" is:

(i) Designed as a toy vehicle for use by children under seven years of age;

(ii) Powered by one or more batteries; and

(iii) Not built or modified after manufacture to exceed a speed of five miles per hour on level ground;

e. A motorized golf cart that is owned by an "insured", designed to carry up to four persons, not built or modified after manufacture to exceed a speed of 25 miles per hour on level ground and, at the time of an "occurrence", is within the legal boundaries of:

(1) A golfing facility and is parked or stored there, or being used by an "insured" to:

(a) Play the game of golf or for other recreational or leisure activity allowed by the facility;

(b) Travel to or from an area where "motor vehicles" or golf carts are parked or stored; or

(c) Cross public roads at designated points to access other parts of the golfing facility; or

(2) A private residential community, including its public roads upon which a motorized golf cart can legally travel, which is subject to the authority of a property owners association and contains an "insured's" residence.

B. "Watercraft Liability"

1. Coverages **E** and **F** do not apply to any "watercraft liability" if, at the time of an "occurrence", the involved watercraft is being:

a. Operated in, or practicing for, any prearranged or organized race, speed contest or other competition. This exclusion does not apply to a sailing vessel or a predicted log cruise;

b. Rented to others;

c. Used to carry persons or cargo for a charge; or

d. Used for any "business" purpose.

2. If Exclusion **B.1.** does not apply, there is still no coverage for "watercraft liability" unless, at the time of the "occurrence", the watercraft:

a. Is stored;

b. Is a sailing vessel, with or without auxiliary power, that is:

(1) Less than 26 feet in overall length; or

(2) 26 feet or more in overall length and not owned by or rented to an "insured"; or

c. Is not a sailing vessel and is powered by:

(1) An inboard or inboard-outdrive engine or motor, including those that power a water jet pump, of:

(a) 50 horsepower or less and not owned by an "insured"; or

(b) More than 50 horsepower and not owned by or rented to an "insured"; or

(2) One or more outboard engines or motors with:

(a) 25 total horsepower or less;

(b) More than 25 horsepower if the outboard engine or motor is not owned by an "insured";

(c) More than 25 horsepower if the outboard engine or motor is owned by an "insured" who acquired it during the policy period; or

(d) More than 25 horsepower if the outboard engine or motor is owned by an "insured" who acquired it before the policy period, but only if:

(i) You declare them at policy inception; or

(ii) Your intent to insure them is reported to us in writing within 45 days after you acquire them.

The coverages in **(c)** and **(d)** above apply for the policy period.

Horsepower means the maximum power rating assigned to the engine or motor by the manufacturer.

C. "Aircraft Liability"

This policy does not cover "aircraft liability".

D. "Hovercraft Liability"

This policy does not cover "hovercraft liability".

E. **Coverage E – Personal Liability And Coverage F – Medical Payments To Others**

Coverages **E** and **F** do not apply to the following:

1. **Expected Or Intended Injury**

"Bodily injury" or "property damage" which is expected or intended by an "insured", even if the resulting "bodily injury" or "property damage":

a. Is of a different kind, quality or degree than initially expected or intended; or

b. Is sustained by a different person, entity or property than initially expected or intended.

However, this Exclusion **E.1.** does not apply to "bodily injury" or "property damage" resulting from the use of reasonable force by an "insured" to protect persons or property;

2. **"Business"**

a. "Bodily injury" or "property damage" arising out of or in connection with a "business" conducted from an "insured location" or engaged in by an "insured", whether or not the "business" is owned or operated by an "insured" or employs an "insured".

This Exclusion **E.2.** applies but is not limited to an act or omission, regardless of its nature or circumstance, involving a service or duty rendered, promised, owed, or implied to be provided because of the nature of the "business".

b. This Exclusion **E.2.** does not apply to:

(1) The rental or holding for rental of an "insured location";

(a) On an occasional basis if used only as a residence;

(b) In part for use only as a residence, unless a single-family unit is intended for use by the occupying family to lodge more than two roomers or boarders; or

(c) In part, as an office, school, studio or private garage; and

(2) An "insured" under the age of 21 years involved in a part-time or occasional, self-employed "business" with no employees;

3. **Professional Services**

"Bodily injury" or "property damage" arising out of the rendering of or failure to render professional services;

4. **"Insured's" Premises Not An "Insured Location"**

"Bodily injury" or "property damage" arising out of a premises:

a. Owned by an "insured";

b. Rented to an "insured"; or

c. Rented to others by an "insured";

that is not an "insured location";

5. **War**

"Bodily injury" or "property damage" caused directly or indirectly by war, including the following and any consequence of any of the following:

a. Undeclared war, civil war, insurrection, rebellion or revolution;

b. Warlike act by a military force or military personnel; or

c. Destruction, seizure or use for a military purpose.

Discharge of a nuclear weapon will be deemed a warlike act even if accidental;

6. **Communicable Disease**

"Bodily injury" or "property damage" which arises out of the transmission of a communicable disease by an "insured";

7. **Sexual Molestation, Corporal Punishment Or Physical Or Mental Abuse**

"Bodily injury" or "property damage" arising out of sexual molestation, corporal punishment or physical or mental abuse; or

8. **Controlled Substance**

"Bodily injury" or "property damage" arising out of the use, sale, manufacture, delivery, transfer or possession by any person of a Controlled Substance as defined by the Federal Food and Drug Law at 21 U.S.C.A. Sections 811 and 812. Controlled Substances include but are not limited to cocaine, LSD, marijuana and all narcotic drugs. However, this exclusion does not apply to the legitimate use of prescription drugs by a person following the lawful orders of a licensed health care professional.

Exclusions **A.** "Motor Vehicle Liability", **B.** "Watercraft Liability", **C.** "Aircraft Liability", **D.** "Hovercraft Liability" and **E.4.** "Insured's" Premises Not An "Insured Location" do not apply to "bodily injury" to a "residence employee" arising out of and in the course of the "residence employee's" employment by an "insured".

F. Coverage E – Personal Liability

Coverage **E** does not apply to:

1. Liability:

a. For any loss assessment charged against you as a member of an association, corporation or community of property owners, except as provided in **D.** Loss Assessment under Section **II** – Additional Coverages;

b. Under any contract or agreement entered into by an "insured". However, this exclusion does not apply to written contracts:

(1) That directly relate to the ownership, maintenance or use of an "insured location"; or

(2) Where the liability of others is assumed by you prior to an "occurrence";

unless excluded in **a.** above or elsewhere in this policy;

2. "Property damage" to property owned by an "insured". This includes costs or expenses incurred by an "insured" or others to repair, replace, enhance, restore or maintain such property to prevent injury to a person or damage to property of others, whether on or away from an "insured location";

3. "Property damage" to property rented to, occupied or used by or in the care of an "insured". This exclusion does not apply to "property damage" caused by fire, smoke or explosion;

4. "Bodily injury" to any person eligible to receive any benefits voluntarily provided or required to be provided by an "insured" under any:

a. Workers' compensation law;

b. Non-occupational disability law; or

c. Occupational disease law;

5. "Bodily injury" or "property damage" for which an "insured" under this policy:

a. Is also an insured under a nuclear energy liability policy issued by the:

(1) Nuclear Energy Liability Insurance Association;

(2) Mutual Atomic Energy Liability Underwriters;

(3) Nuclear Insurance Association of Canada;

or any of their successors; or

b. Would be an insured under such a policy but for the exhaustion of its limit of liability; or

6. "Bodily injury" to you or an "insured" as defined under Definition **5.a.** or **b.**

This exclusion also applies to any claim made or suit brought against you or an "insured" to:

a. Repay; or

b. Share damages with;

another person who may be obligated to pay damages because of "bodily injury" to an "insured".

G. Coverage F – Medical Payments To Others

Coverage **F** does not apply to "bodily injury":

1. To a "residence employee" if the "bodily injury":

a. Occurs off the "insured location"; and

b. Does not arise out of or in the course of the "residence employee's" employment by an "insured";

2. To any person eligible to receive benefits voluntarily provided or required to be provided under any:

a. Workers' compensation law;

b. Non-occupational disability law; or

c. Occupational disease law;

3. From any:

a. Nuclear reaction;

b. Nuclear radiation; or

c. Radioactive contamination;

all whether controlled or uncontrolled or however caused; or

d. Any consequence of any of these; or

4. To any person, other than a "residence employee" of an "insured", regularly residing on any part of the "insured location".

SECTION II – ADDITIONAL COVERAGES

We cover the following in addition to the limits of liability:

A. Claim Expenses

We pay:

1. Expenses we incur and costs taxed against an "insured" in any suit we defend;

2. Premiums on bonds required in a suit we defend, but not for bond amounts more than the Coverage **E** limit of liability. We need not apply for or furnish any bond;

3. Reasonable expenses incurred by an "insured" at our request, including actual loss of earnings (but not loss of other income) up to $250 per day, for assisting us in the investigation or defense of a claim or suit; and
4. Interest on the entire judgment which accrues after entry of the judgment and before we pay or tender, or deposit in court that part of the judgment which does not exceed the limit of liability that applies.

B. First Aid Expenses

We will pay expenses for first aid to others incurred by an "insured" for "bodily injury" covered under this policy. We will not pay for first aid to an "insured".

C. Damage To Property Of Others

1. We will pay, at replacement cost, up to $1,000 per "occurrence" for "property damage" to property of others caused by an "insured".
2. We will not pay for "property damage":
   a. To the extent of any amount recoverable under Section **I**;
   b. Caused intentionally by an "insured" who is 13 years of age or older;
   c. To property owned by an "insured";
   d. To property owned by or rented to a tenant of an "insured" or a resident in your household; or
   e. Arising out of:
      (1) A "business" engaged in by an "insured";
      (2) Any act or omission in connection with a premises owned, rented or controlled by an "insured", other than the "insured location"; or
      (3) The ownership, maintenance, occupancy, operation, use, loading or unloading of aircraft, hovercraft, watercraft or "motor vehicles".

      This Exclusion **e.(3)** does not apply to a "motor vehicle" that:
      (a) Is designed for recreational use off public roads;
      (b) Is not owned by an "insured"; and
      (c) At the time of the "occurrence", is not required by law, or regulation issued by a government agency, to have been registered for it to be used on public roads or property.

D. Loss Assessment

1. We will pay up to $1,000 for your share of loss assessment charged against you, as owner or tenant of the "residence premises", during the policy period by a corporation or association of property owners, when the assessment is made as a result of:
   a. "Bodily injury" or "property damage" not excluded from coverage under Section **II** – Exclusions; or
   b. Liability for an act of a director, officer or trustee in the capacity as a director, officer or trustee, provided such person:
      (1) Is elected by the members of a corporation or association of property owners; and
      (2) Serves without deriving any income from the exercise of duties which are solely on behalf of a corporation or association of property owners.
2. Paragraph **I.** Policy Period under Section **II** – Conditions does not apply to this Loss Assessment Coverage.
3. Regardless of the number of assessments, the limit of $1,000 is the most we will pay for loss arising out of:
   a. One accident, including continuous or repeated exposure to substantially the same general harmful condition; or
   b. A covered act of a director, officer or trustee. An act involving more than one director, officer or trustee is considered to be a single act.
4. We do not cover assessments charged against you or a corporation or association of property owners by any governmental body.

SECTION II – CONDITIONS

A. Limit Of Liability

Our total liability under Coverage **E** for all damages resulting from any one "occurrence" will not be more than the Coverage **E** Limit Of Liability shown in the Declarations. This limit is the same regardless of the number of "insureds", claims made or persons injured. All "bodily injury" and "property damage" resulting from any one accident or from continuous or repeated exposure to substantially the same general harmful conditions shall be considered to be the result of one "occurrence".

Our total liability under Coverage **F** for all medical expense payable for "bodily injury" to one person as the result of one accident will not be more than the Coverage **F** Limit Of Liability shown in the Declarations.

B. Severability Of Insurance

This insurance applies separately to each "insured". This condition will not increase our limit of liability for any one "occurrence".

C. Duties After "Occurrence"

In case of an "occurrence", you or another "insured" will perform the following duties that apply. We have no duty to provide coverage under this policy if your failure to comply with the following duties is prejudicial to us. You will help us by seeing that these duties are performed:

1. Give written notice to us or our agent as soon as is practical, which sets forth:
   a. The identity of the policy and the "named insured" shown in the Declarations;
   b. Reasonably available information on the time, place and circumstances of the "occurrence"; and
   c. Names and addresses of any claimants and witnesses;
2. Cooperate with us in the investigation, settlement or defense of any claim or suit;
3. Promptly forward to us every notice, demand, summons or other process relating to the "occurrence";
4. At our request, help us:
   a. To make settlement;
   b. To enforce any right of contribution or indemnity against any person or organization who may be liable to an "insured";
   c. With the conduct of suits and attend hearings and trials; and
   d. To secure and give evidence and obtain the attendance of witnesses;
5. With respect to **C.** Damage To Property Of Others under Section **II** – Additional Coverages, submit to us within 60 days after the loss a sworn statement of loss and show the damaged property, if in an "insured's" control;
6. No "insured" shall, except at such "insured's" own cost, voluntarily make payment, assume obligation or incur expense other than for first aid to others at the time of the "bodily injury".

D. Duties Of An Injured Person – Coverage F – Medical Payments To Others

1. The injured person or someone acting for the injured person will:
   a. Give us written proof of claim, under oath if required, as soon as is practical; and
   b. Authorize us to obtain copies of medical reports and records.
2. The injured person will submit to a physical exam by a doctor of our choice when and as often as we reasonably require.

E. Payment Of Claim – Coverage F – Medical Payments To Others

Payment under this coverage is not an admission of liability by an "insured" or us.

F. Suit Against Us

1. No action can be brought against us unless there has been full compliance with all of the terms under this Section **II.**
2. No one will have the right to join us as a party to any action against an "insured".
3. Also, no action with respect to Coverage **E** can be brought against us until the obligation of such "insured" has been determined by final judgment or agreement signed by us.

G. Bankruptcy Of An "Insured"

Bankruptcy or insolvency of an "insured" will not relieve us of our obligations under this policy.

H. Other Insurance

This insurance is excess over other valid and collectible insurance except insurance written specifically to cover as excess over the limits of liability that apply in this policy.

I. Policy Period

This policy applies only to "bodily injury" or "property damage" which occurs during the policy period.

J. Concealment Or Fraud

We do not provide coverage to an "insured" who, whether before or after a loss, has:

1. Intentionally concealed or misrepresented any material fact or circumstance;
2. Engaged in fraudulent conduct; or
3. Made false statements;

relating to this insurance.

SECTIONS I AND II – CONDITIONS

A. Liberalization Clause

If we make a change which broadens coverage under this edition of our policy without additional premium charge, that change will automatically apply to your insurance as of the date we implement the change in your state, provided that this implementation date falls within 60 days prior to or during the policy period stated in the Declarations.

This Liberalization Clause does not apply to changes implemented with a general program revision that includes both broadenings and restrictions in coverage, whether that general program revision is implemented through introduction of:

1. A subsequent edition of this policy; or

2. An amendatory endorsement.

B. Waiver Or Change Of Policy Provisions

A waiver or change of a provision of this policy must be in writing by us to be valid. Our request for an appraisal or examination will not waive any of our rights.

C. Cancellation

1. You may cancel this policy at any time by returning it to us or by letting us know in writing of the date cancellation is to take effect.

2. We may cancel this policy only for the reasons stated below by letting you know in writing of the date cancellation takes effect. This cancellation notice may be delivered to you, or mailed to you at your mailing address shown in the Declarations. Proof of mailing will be sufficient proof of notice.

a. When you have not paid the premium, we may cancel at any time by letting you know at least 10 days before the date cancellation takes effect.

b. When this policy has been in effect for less than 60 days and is not a renewal with us, we may cancel for any reason by letting you know at least 10 days before the date cancellation takes effect.

c. When this policy has been in effect for 60 days or more, or at any time if it is a renewal with us, we may cancel:

(1) If there has been a material misrepresentation of fact which if known to us would have caused us not to issue the policy; or

(2) If the risk has changed substantially since the policy was issued.

This can be done by letting you know at least 30 days before the date cancellation takes effect.

d. When this policy is written for a period of more than one year, we may cancel for any reason at anniversary by letting you know at least 30 days before the date cancellation takes effect.

3. When this policy is canceled, the premium for the period from the date of cancellation to the expiration date will be refunded pro rata.

4. If the return premium is not refunded with the notice of cancellation or when this policy is returned to us, we will refund it within a reasonable time after the date cancellation takes effect.

D. Nonrenewal

We may elect not to renew this policy. We may do so by delivering to you, or mailing to you at your mailing address shown in the Declarations, written notice at least 30 days before the expiration date of this policy. Proof of mailing will be sufficient proof of notice.

E. Assignment

Assignment of this policy will not be valid unless we give our written consent.

F. Subrogation

An "insured" may waive in writing before a loss all rights of recovery against any person. If not waived, we may require an assignment of rights of recovery for a loss to the extent that payment is made by us.

If an assignment is sought, an "insured" must sign and deliver all related papers and cooperate with us.

Subrogation does not apply to Coverage **F** or Paragraph **C.** Damage To Property Of Others under Section **II** – Additional Coverages.

G. Death

If any person named in the Declarations or the spouse, if a resident of the same household, dies, the following apply:

1. We insure the legal representative of the deceased but only with respect to the premises and property of the deceased covered under the policy at the time of death; and

2. "Insured" includes:

a. An "insured" who is a member of your household at the time of your death, but only while a resident of the "residence premises"; and

b. With respect to your property, the person having proper temporary custody of the property until appointment and qualification of a legal representative.

NOTES AND QUESTIONS

1. *Reading the Policy*. For dwellings and other structures, the Sample Homeowners Policy expressly covers: a) bodily injuries; b) mold, fungus or wet rot; c) wear and tear; or d) direct physical loss?

2. *Liabilities Unrelated to the Insured Home*. Does the Sample Homeowners Policy cover the policyholder's liabilities for property damage and

bodily injuries the policyholder causes that are unrelated to the policyholder's insured home?

3. *All Risk Coverage?* Does the Sample Homeowners Policy provide all risk coverage?

4. *Is Land Covered?* If a home is destroyed by a fire or a landslide, as examples, is the cost to restore the land and landscaping covered under the Sample Homeowners Policy?

5. *Termites.* Is termite damage covered under the Sample Homeowners Policy?

II. PHYSICAL LOSS

In order to recover under a property policy, whether a homeowners policy or a commercial property policy, there must be a "direct physical loss." Is "direct physical loss" the same thing as "property damage" under CGL policies that was discussed in Chapter 4? Consider the next case.

BOARD OF EDUCATION OF TOWNSHIP HIGH SCHOOL DIST. NO. 211 V. INTERNATIONAL INSURANCE CO.

720 N.E.2d 622 (Ill. App. Ct. 1999)

Opinion

Plaintiff, the Board of Education of Township High School District No. 211, filed a declaratory judgment action against defendant, International Insurance Company, seeking a determination of coverage under two property insurance policies for asbestos-related property damage in three of plaintiffs high schools. The trial court granted summary judgment for defendant. Plaintiff filed this timely appeal. We reverse and remand.

Facts

Defendant sold plaintiff two property insurance policies that provided coverage from April 1, 1981, to March 31, 1986, for "all risks of physical loss or damage" to the five high schools operated by plaintiff. In 1983, plaintiff hired Arcon Associates, an architectural firm, to inspect the schools for the presence of "friable" asbestos, *i.e.,* asbestos that can be crumbled by hand. Richard Kumnick, an employee of Arcon, discovered friable asbestos in three of the schools. Kumnick opined that the asbestos-containing building materials (ACBMs) were releasing harmful fibers into the air and that ordinary activities such as sweeping and dusting were "reentraining," or making airborne again, previously released fibers.

Kumnick further opined that the Asbestos Abatement Act (105 ILCS 105/1 *et seq.* (West 1994)) required the removal of the ACBMs. The Asbestos Abatement Act provides for "the identification, containment or removal of those asbestos materials that constitute a significant health hazard * * * to students, school personnel, parents and visitors to such schools * * *." 105 ILCS 105/2 (West 1994).

Plaintiff notified Kumnick that it had decided to remove all ACBMs from its schools. According to Kumnick, plaintiff incurred over $2.6 million in asbestos removal and restoration costs between June 1984 and July 1986. To date, plaintiff has incurred about $18 million in asbestos removal and restoration costs.

Plaintiff made claim upon defendant for coverage under the two property insurance policies. Defendant denied the claim.

Plaintiff filed this declaratory judgement action against defendant, seeking a declaration that the policies cover the damage resulting from the presence of friable asbestos and toxic asbestos fibers in its schools. The trial court granted summary judgment for defendant, finding that the presence of asbestos in the school buildings did not constitute property damage covered by the policies. Plaintiff filed this timely appeal.

Analysis

In determining whether summary judgment for defendant is proper, the two property insurance policies at issue must be construed. The construction of insurance policies is a matter of law subject to *de novo* review. The construction of the policies is to give effect to the intent of the parties as expressed in their agreement. If the terms of the policies are unambiguous, they must be given their plain and ordinary meaning. If the terms of the policies are capable of more than one meaning, they are construed strictly against the insurer.

The two policies provide, in part, that defendant agrees to indemnify plaintiff for "all risks of physical loss or damage to all real or personal property of every kind and description wherever located occurring during the period of this insurance."

Defendant contends that the presence of friable ACBMs and asbestos fibers in plaintiff's schools does not constitute physical loss or damage to property covered under the property insurance policies at issue. In support, defendant cites a New Mexico Supreme Court case, *Leafland Group-II, Montgomery Towers Ltd. Partnership v. Insurance Co.,* 118 N.M. 281, 881 P.2d 26 (1994). Leafland purchased an apartment complex, Montgomery Towers, in 1983. After purchasing the property, Leafland bought a comprehensive insurance policy from Insurance Company of North America (INA) that provided both property coverage and liability coverage for the subject property. *Leafland,* 118 N.M. at 282, 881 P.2d at 27. Leafland subsequently discovered that asbestos had been used in the construction of Montgomery Towers and that the presence of the asbestos had diminished the value of the property by $1,750,000. *Leafland,* 118 N.M. at 282, 881 P.2d at 27. Leafland made a claim under the insurance policy, but INA refused to pay for the property's diminished value. *Leafland,* 118 N.M. at 282, 881 P.2d at 27.

The New Mexico Supreme Court held that the policy, which insured against "direct loss or damage," did not cover the diminution in value of the apartment complex caused by the presence of asbestos installed during construction. The court stated that there was "no event that happened during the time the policy was in effect that caused direct loss or damage" to the property. *Leafland,* 118 N.M. at 282, 881 P.2d at 28.

Leafland is factually inapposite to the present case because the all-risk policies at issue here contain no language limiting their coverage to "direct loss or damage" to plaintiff's buildings. Further, unlike Leafland, which sought coverage for the diminution in value of the property that occurred prior to the policy period, plaintiff here seeks coverage for the removal of ACBMs in its buildings that were in a friable condition and emitting toxic fibers during the policy period.

Our supreme court has spoken to this issue in *United States Fidelity & Guaranty Co. v. Wilkin Insulation Co.,* 144 Ill.2d 64, 161 Ill.Dec. 280, 578 N.E.2d 926 (1991). In *Wilkin,* school districts and building owners sued Wilkin and others of the "asbestos industry." *Wilkin,* 144 Ill.2d at 69, 161 Ill.Dec. 280, 578 N.E.2d 926. The plaintiffs prayed for reimbursement of incurred asbestos abatement costs. *Wilkin,* 144 Ill.2d at 69, 161 Ill.Dec. 280, 578 N.E.2d 926. Wilkin sought defense and indemnification from United States Fidelity & Guaranty Co. (USF & G), which had issued a comprehensive general liability policy to Wilkin. *Wilkin,* 144 Ill.2d at 69–70, 161 Ill.Dec. 280, 578 N.E.2d 926. Under that policy, USF & G agreed to defend and provide coverage for Wilkin in any action seeking damages on account of "property damage" caused by an "occurrence." *Wilkin,* 144 Ill.2d at 70, 161 Ill.Dec. 280, 578 N.E.2d 926. USF & G's policy defined property damage as:

> 1) physical injury to or destruction of tangible property, which occurs during the policy period, including the loss of use thereof at any time resulting therefrom.

Wilkin, 144 Ill.2d at 75, 161 Ill.Dec. 280, 578 N.E.2d 926.

USF & G then brought an action for declaratory judgment that it had no duty to defend or indemnify Wilkin under that policy. *Wilkin,* 144 Ill.2d at 70, 161 Ill.Dec. 280, 578 N.E.2d 926. USF & G argued that the underlying complaints did not allege physical damage to tangible property and that the presence of asbestos-containing products resulted only in economic loss in diminished market values of the buildings. *Wilkin,* 144 Ill.2d at 75, 161 Ill.Dec. 280, 578 N.E.2d 926.

After the trial court granted summary judgment for USF & G and the appellate court reversed (*Wilkin,* 144 Ill.2d at 72, 161 Ill.Dec. 280, 578

N.E.2d 926), our supreme court held that asbestos fiber contamination constitutes physical injury to tangible property, including buildings and their contents, and further noted that it had so held in an earlier case. *Wilkin,* 144 Ill.2d at 75, 161 Ill.Dec. 280, 578 N.E.2d 926, citing *Board of Education v. A, C & S, Inc.,* 131 Ill.2d 428, 137 Ill.Dec. 635, 546 N.E.2d 580 (1989). *Wilkin* quoted from its holding in *A, C & S*:

> [I]t would be incongruous to argue there is no damage to other property when a harmful element exists throughout a building or an area of a building which by law must be corrected . . . . The view that asbestos fibers may contaminate a building sufficiently to allege damage to property has been recently adopted in a number of cases. . . . The essence of the allegations [of the complaints] is that the buildings have been contaminated by asbestos to the point where corrective action, under the law, must be taken. Thus, the buildings have been damaged.

Wilkin, 144 Ill.2d at 75–76, 161 Ill.Dec. 280, 578 N.E.2d 926, *quoting A, C & S,* 131 Ill.2d at 446–49, 137 Ill.Dec. 635, 546 N.E.2d 580.

Here, defendant contends *Wilkin* is distinguishable because *Wilkin* involved a third-party liability policy providing coverage for damage to the property of others, whereas this case involves first-party property insurance policies providing coverage for damage to one's own property. Defendant cites California case law holding that a third-party liability policy generally insures against a broader spectrum of risk than a first-party property insurance policy. *See Garvey v. State Farm Fire and Casualty Co.,* 48 Cal.3d 395, 770 P.2d 704, 257 Cal.Rptr. 292 (1989); *Montrose Chemical Corp. of California v. Admiral Insurance Co.,* 10 Cal.4th 645, 42 Cal.Rptr.2d 324, 913 P.2d 878 (1995). Defendant submits that the term "property damage," as used in the third-party liability policy in *Wilkin,* is so broad that it does not necessarily require *physical* loss or damage to property as is required under the first-party property insurance policies here.

A close examination of *Wilkin* is instructive and belies defendant's argument. "Property damage" in the liability policy in *Wilkin* is defined as "*physical* injury to or destruction of tangible property." *Wilkin,* 144 Ill.2d at 75, 161 Ill.Dec. 280, 578 N.E.2d 926. The *Wilkin* court held that asbestos fiber contamination, if proved, constitutes physical injury to property and therefore meets the liability policy's definition of property damage. *Wilkin,* 144 Ill.2d at 75–76, 161 Ill.Dec. 280, 578 N.E.2d 926; accord, *United States Gypsum Co. v. Admiral Insurance Co.,* 268 Ill.App.3d 598, 205 Ill.Dec. 619, 643 N.E.2d 1226 (1994). Here, the property insurance policies provide a definition of property damage virtually identical to the one used in *Wilkin:* "physical loss or damage to all real * * * property." Pursuant to *Wilkin,* the asbestos fiber contamination in plaintiff's schools meets such a definition of property damage. Thus, *Wilkin* applies here to defeat summary judgment for defendant.

Next, defendant contends plaintiff failed to provide sufficient "factual proof" of asbestos fiber contamination to withstand its motion for summary judgment. We disagree. The nonmoving party in a summary judgment case is not required to prove his case but must only present some factual basis to support his claim.

Plaintiff presented such a factual basis through the affidavit of Richard Kumnick, who stated that he had examined plaintiff's high schools and discovered friable ACBMs that were releasing asbestos fibers into the air. Kumnick further opined that the asbestos fibers from the friable ACBMs were recirculating throughout the buildings even into areas not containing asbestos installations. In Kumnick's opinion, the friable ACBMs constituted a "significant health hazard to occupants, and therefore had to be removed . . . pursuant to the Illinois Asbestos Abatement Act." Kumnick's testimony was sufficient to provide a factual basis to support plaintiff's claim of asbestos fiber contamination in its schools.

Of note, during oral argument on this case, defendant argued that plaintiff had engaged in *wholesale* removal of asbestos, even asbestos that was not friable or releasing toxic fibers. Defendant contended that, at most, its policies provide coverage only for the removal of friable asbestos and resulting fibers. *Wilkin, A, C & S* and *Gypsum* define asbestos property damage as asbestos materials actively releasing toxic fibers, or asbestos materials posing a risk of future fiber release through age, friability, or repeated contact. Thus, the policies at issue here, which indemnify plaintiff for "all risks of physical loss or damage to all real or personal property," would not cover the removal of asbestos or ACBMs that were not releasing toxic fibers or that were not at any risk for future fiber release. The issue of whether plaintiff removed such noncovered asbestos is a factual one inappropriate for resolution by summary judgment.

Next, defendant contends coverage was never triggered because no physical loss or damage occurred during the period the policies were in effect. In support, defendant again cites *Leafland. Leafland* held that the use of asbestos in the construction of the subject property had caused that property to diminish in value long before Leafland purchased the property or procured the insurance policy. In other words, the diminution in property value was discovered, but not caused, during the time the policy was in effect. *Leafland,* 118 N.M. at 284, 881 P.2d at 29. Therefore, the New Mexico Supreme Court held that Leafland could not claim coverage for diminution in property value under the policy. *Leafland,* 118 N.M. at 284, 881 P.2d at 29.

Here, defendant asserts that the use of the asbestos similarly predates the issuance of the policies and that, pursuant to *Leafland,* plaintiff cannot claim coverage under the policies. We disagree.

Leafland sought coverage for the diminution in value that occurred prior to the time the policy was in effect, whereas in the present case plaintiff seeks coverage for asbestos removal costs allegedly incurred during the policy period. Therefore, *Leafland* is factually inapposite. We find more persuasive an Illinois case, *Gypsum,* which held:

> Property damage . . ., whether from the presence of airborne [asbestos] fibers or settled fibers subject to reentrainment, occurs over a span of time and cannot be linked to or confined to different policy periods. The difficulty in determining precisely when the damage occurred or in following its progress or proliferation is further exacerbated by the interchangeable nature of the fibers and that their release occurs on a continuing basis. The precise amount of airborne released fibers and grounded fibers that could be reentrained changes on a continuing basis. The burden of proving exactly when property damage occurred would be virtually impossible.

Gypsum, 268 Ill.App.3d at 645–46, 205 Ill.Dec. 619, 643 N.E.2d 1226.

Gypsum held that "claims seeking coverage for property damage caused by asbestos fiber release are prototypes for the appropriate application of the equitable continuous trigger." *Gypsum,* 268 Ill.App.3d at 645, 205 Ill.Dec. 619, 643 N.E.2d 1226. Under the equitable continuous trigger:

> [P]roperty damage is deemed to have 'occurred' continuously for a fixed period (the "trigger period"), and every insurer on the risk at any time during that trigger period is jointly and severally liable to the extent of their policy limits, the entire loss being equitably allocated among the insurers.

Gypsum, 268 Ill.App.3d at 644, 205 Ill.Dec. 619, 643 N.E.2d 1226, *quoting Sentinel Insurance Co. v. First Insurance Co. of Hawaii, Ltd.*, 76 Hawai'i 277, 298, 875 P.2d 894, 915 (1994).

In the present case, the trigger period for coverage purposes begins with the installation of the friable, fiber-releasing asbestos materials and ends when those asbestos materials are removed or contained. See *Gypsum,* 268 Ill.App.3d at 645–46, 205 Ill.Dec. 619, 643 N.E.2d 1226. Plaintiff has established, through the affidavit of Richard Kumnick, that friable, fiber-releasing ACBMs were present in its schools since at least 1983. The property insurance policies were in effect at that time; therefore, coverage was triggered.

Defendant argues that it should not have to pay for asbestos removal costs incurred after the policies expired. Defendant's argument is flawed, as the proper focus of the analysis should be on the trigger period, not the policy period. Under the equitable continuous trigger, the asbestos property damage is deemed an ongoing, continuous process triggering every policy, including defendant's, in effect during the period beginning with the installation of the friable, fiber-releasing asbestos materials and ending when those materials are removed or contained.

We recognize that *Gypsum* involved the construction of third-party liability insurance policies, whereas the present case involves the construction of first-party property insurance policies. However, as discussed above, the liability policies in *Gypsum* and the property insurance policies here each provide coverage for asbestos-related property damage occurring during the respective policy periods. *Gypsum* adopted the equitable continuous trigger to determine the timing of the asbestos damage for coverage purposes; we find the *Gypsum* analysis compelling and applicable in the present case.

For the foregoing reasons, we reverse the trial court's order granting summary judgment for defendant and remand for further proceedings.

Reversed and remanded.

NOTES AND QUESTIONS

1. *What Is "Physical Loss"?* What was the "physical loss" in *Board of Education*? Was it different from "property damage" under CGL policies? Asbestos was intentionally installed in the buildings due to its fire-retardant properties. Did the mere presence of asbestos in a building become a "physical loss" when it was discovered? If not, what was the triggering event that would change the presence of asbestos into a "physical loss"?

2. *Loss of Use as "Physical Loss or Damage."* Similar to the *Board of Education* decision, other courts also have held that property that is unusable or uninhabitable due to some condition at the property can constitute "physical loss or damage." *See, e.g., Motorists Mut. Ins. Co. v. Hardinger*, 131 F. App'x 823, 826 (3d Cir. 2005) (presence of e-coli bacteria in a well that supplied water to an insured house could constitute physical loss or damage to the house if it made the house useless or uninhabitable even though the well itself was not covered by the policy); *Oregon Shakespeare Festival Ass'n v. Great Am. Ins. Co.*, 2016 WL 3267247, at *7 (D. Or. June 7, 2016) (cancellation of theater event due to wildfire smoke was covered because "the infiltration of smoke into the interior of the theater is a covered 'physical loss of or damage to property' "); *Gregory Packaging, Inc. v. Travelers Prop. Cas. Co. of Am.*, 2014 WL 6675934, at *6 (D. N.J. Nov. 25, 2014) (business interruption caused by "ammonia discharge inflicted 'direct physical loss of or damage to' . . . facility . . . because the ammonia physically rendered the facility unusable for a period of time").

3. *Incorporation of Dangerous Materials and Construction Defects.* Chapter 4 discussed how the presence of a defective product or workmanship can be a covered "occurrence" under CGL policies where the defect causes

damage to something else. Under the *Board of Education* decision, does the asbestos present in a building need to damage something in order for the cost of its removal to be covered? Not necessarily. For example, in *Pepsico, Inc. v. Winterthur International America Co.*, 24 A.D. 3d 743 (N.Y. App. Div. 2005), the court held the presence of a non-injurious ingredient in Pepsi that caused an "off-taste" constituted "physical damage." The key to the holding was that the ingredient seriously impaired the product's function and value.

4. *Cyber Risks.* Does the loss of data on a computer or computer system constitute a "physical loss?" The case law is mixed. *Compare Wakefern Food Corp. v. Liberty Mutual Fire Insurance Co.*, 968 A.2d 724 (N.J. Super. Ct. App. Div. 2009) (food spoilage at a supermarket as a result of a power failure caused by hacking was "physical damage"), *and NMS Services, Inc. v. The Hartford*, 119 S.W.3d 16 (Tex. App. 2003) (destruction of data stored on a computer due to hacking constituted "physical loss"), *with Ward Gen. Ins. Servs, Inc. v. The Employers Fire Ins. Co.*, 114 Cal. App. 4th 548 (2003) (loss of data was not a "physical loss" because data was not viewed as tangible property). In recent years, insurers have attempted to "clarify" the issue under many traditional "all risk" property policies by expressly excluding coverage for lost data, and insurers now offer to sell policyholders a separate policy that specifically covers cyber losses.

5. *Trigger, Allocation, and Number of "Losses"/"Occurrences."* The issues of trigger, allocation, and number of "occurrences" or "losses" also arise under property policies. Courts treat the issues very similarly to CGL policies, with some variation. For example, in property insurance, more courts apply a manifestation trigger than under CGL policies. *See, e.g., Prudential-LMI Comm. Ins. v. Superior Court,* 798 P.2d 1230 (Cal. 1990) (applying manifestation trigger to continuous property damage under a property policy). Why do you suppose this is so? In addition, many property policies cover "losses," as opposed to "occurrences." In many cases, however, the analysis of the number of "losses" is treated the same as or similarly to the number of "occurrences" issue arising under CGL policies. Numerous courts have reasoned, sometimes applying policy language designed to unify multiple events into one loss or occurrence, that multiple injuries arising from a single injury-causing situation constitute a single loss.

III. CONCURRENT CAUSATION

When a "physical loss" occurs, there are often many causes of it. Some of those causes may be covered under property policies, while others may be excluded. The situation where multiple covered and excluded causes combine to produce a loss is known as "concurrent causation." Although the common definition of "concurrent" implies a degree of temporal simultaneity, courts and commentators have routinely used the term "concurrent" to refer to sequential chains of events; independent, unrelated events acting in conjunction; and even events that undoubtedly operated in succession. *See* Mark M. Bell, *A Concurrent Mess and a Call for Clarity in First-Party Property Insurance Coverage Analysis*, 18 Conn. Ins. L. J. 73, 74 (2011). Whether a loss is covered in a concurrent causation situation is a question that arises frequently in property insurance disputes.

The possible approaches to deciding concurrent causation cases range from finding coverage whenever a covered cause contributes to a loss without regard to the presence of excluded causes in the mix, finding no coverage whenever an excluded cause contributes to a loss without regard to the presence of covered causes in the mix, and engaging in some kind of evaluation designed to identify the most important or dominant cause in the mix and have coverage turn on whether that cause is covered or excluded. Insurers, in an effort to simplify the analysis and direct the answers toward pro-insurer outcomes, commonly add "anti-concurrent causation" exclusions to their policies. Anti-concurrent causation exclusions purport to exclude coverage for losses caused in any part by an excluded peril as per this representative language: "This policy does not insure loss or damage caused directly or indirectly by any Peril excluded. . . ."[1]

Adding further complexity to the problem is the fact that many property policies also contain "ensuing loss" clauses. The following language is a common example of such a clause: "We insure for all risks of physical loss to the property described in Coverage A except for loss caused by [listing 6 excluded perils]. . . . Any ensuing loss from items 1 through 6 not excluded is covered."[2] Typically, the term "ensuing loss" is not defined in the policies. Courts have struggled with this clause, and the results in the ensuing loss cases are "inconsistent and unpredictable." *See* Christopher C. French, *The "Ensuing Loss" Clause in Insurance Policies: The Forgotten and Misunderstood Antidote to Anti-Concurrent Causation Exclusions*, 13 Nev. L. J. 215, 255 (2012).

A. EFFICIENT PROXIMATE CAUSE

Some states apply an "efficient proximate cause" test to the concurrent causation problem. Although similarities exist, the test should not be confused with the tort law concept of proximate cause. Under the insurance test, the coverage determination is not based on an analysis of the anti-concurrent causation language or an ensuing loss clause. Instead, the analysis focuses on whether the initial peril that started the causation chain of events, or the predominant peril that dominated the causes working in conjunction, that led to the loss was a covered or an excluded peril. Of course, the initial cause may not be the predominant one, and

---

1 *Blaine Constr. Corp. v. Ins. Co. of N. Am.*, 171 F.3d 343, 346 (6th Cir. 1999).

2 *Roberts v. State Farm Fire & Cas. Co.*, 705 P.2d 1335, 1336 (Ariz. 1985). *See also Blaine Constr. Corp.*, 171 F.3d at 346.

exactly what approach a court is following may be difficult to discern. What version of the test does the court in the next case adopt?

GARVEY V. STATE FARM FIRE & CASUALTY CO.

770 P.2d 704 (Cal. 1989)

Opinion

We granted review to consider the Court of Appeal's reversal of a directed verdict of coverage in favor of Jack and Rita Garvey (hereafter plaintiffs). We sought to resolve some of the confusion that has arisen regarding insurance coverage under the "all risk" section of a homeowner's insurance policy when loss to an insured's property can be attributed to two causes, one of which is a nonexcluded peril, and the other an excluded peril.

In recent years, some courts have misinterpreted and misapplied our decisions in *Sabella v. Wisler* (1963) 59 Cal.2d 21 [27 Cal.Rptr. 689, 377 P.2d 889], and *State Farm Mut. Auto. Ins. Co. v. Partridge* (1973) 10 Cal.3d 94 [109 Cal.Rptr. 811, 514 P.2d 123]. In so doing, they have allowed coverage in first party property damage cases under our holding in *Partridge* by inappropriately using the *Partridge* concurrent causation approach as an alternative to *Sabella's* efficient proximate cause analysis.

This extension of the analysis in *Partridge*, a third party liability case, allows coverage under a first party property insurance policy whenever a covered peril is a concurrent proximate cause of the loss, without regard to the application of specific policy exclusion clauses. Such reasoning ignores the criteria set forth in Insurance Code sections 530 and 532, the relevant analysis in *Sabella* and the important distinction between property loss coverage under a first party property policy and tort liability coverage under a third party liability insurance policy. Indeed, because a covered peril usually can be asserted to exist somewhere in the chain of causation in cases involving multiple causes, applying the *Partridge* approach to coverage in first party cases effectively nullifies policy exclusions in "all risk" homeowner's property loss policies, thereby essentially abrogating the limiting terms of insurance contracts in such cases. We cannot believe *Partridge* intended such a sweeping result in first party property loss cases. To the contrary, as we explain below, we must put *Partridge* in its proper perspective, i.e., that decision should be utilized only in liability cases in which true concurrent causes, each originating from an independent act of negligence, simultaneously join together to produce injury. Therefore, as will appear, we conclude this case should be remanded to the Court of Appeal with directions to remand to the trial court for a jury determination of causation pursuant to *Sabella*.

I.

Facts

Plaintiffs bought their house in the mid-1970's. In 1977, plaintiffs purchased from State Farm Fire and Casualty Company (hereafter defendant) an "all risk" homeowner's policy of insurance which was in effect at all times relevant. Section I of the policy in question provided coverage for "all risks of physical loss to the property covered" except as otherwise excluded or limited. Losses excluded by this portion of the policy included those "caused by, resulting from, contributed to or aggravated by any earth movement, including but not limited to earthquake, volcanic eruption, landslide, mudflow, earth sinking, rising or shifting," and losses caused "by . . . settling, cracking, shrinkage, bulging or expansion of pavements, patios, foundations, walls, floors, roofs or ceilings . . . ."

In August 1978, plaintiffs noticed that a house addition, built in the early 1960's, had begun to pull away from the main structure. They also discovered damage to a deck and garden wall. There ensued numerous phone calls, letters, meetings and investigations as plaintiffs tried to determine from defendant whether the damage was covered by their homeowner's property insurance policy.

In October 1979, after receiving from its counsel an opinion that the loss was not covered, defendant notified plaintiffs by letter that the "policy excludes coverage for the loss herein. Normally, such a denial of coverage would leave you to your remedies. However, because the company wishes to resolve the coverage issue in an atmosphere free from extraneous matters such as bad-faith and class action issues, the company is prepared to advance you the claimed sum of $ 11,550 subject to a reservation of rights as authorized by *Johansen v. CSAA*, 15 Cal.3d 9 . . . ." Under the agreement proposed, defendant would make the advance and file a declaratory relief action on the issue of coverage; plaintiffs would pay back the advance if the court ruled in defendant's favor, would waive "any claim of consequential or punitive damages arising out of any allegation of bad-faith, mental distress, oppression, fraud or insurance-related tort," and would not "institute any class-action against defendant on account of the facts and issues involved in this loss and claim."

After refusing to sign the foregoing agreement, plaintiffs sued, claiming that although their policy excluded coverage for losses caused or aggravated by earth movement, it implicitly provided coverage for losses caused by contractor negligence because negligence was not a specifically excluded peril under the policy. Plaintiffs also argued that defendant denied their claim before adequately investigating the damage to the structure, and that subsequent investigations were undertaken merely to confirm the original denial. In addition, plaintiffs asserted, defendant's denial of coverage constituted a breach of the implied covenant of good faith and fair dealing and violated various provisions of the Insurance Code. Plaintiffs sought as relief (i) policy benefits, (ii) general damages for economic detriment and emotional distress, and (iii) punitive damages.

Defendant rested on the 12th day of trial, and the court granted a directed verdict for plaintiffs on the coverage issue. The court informed the parties it was following the decisions in *Partridge* and *Sabella*, and that plaintiffs were covered under the policy because negligent construction, a covered risk, was a concurrent proximate cause of the damage. Specifically, the trial court stated: "[The Supreme Court] told me in *Sabella* that negligent construction can be a proximate cause. They told me in *Partridge* there may be coverage whenever an insured risk constitutes simply a concurrent proximate cause of the injuries. Now, to me that is crystal clear, putting those two causes together, that if negligent construction is a concurrent proximate cause of the loss, there is coverage." The court continued, "The key witness for the defense, Mr. Nelson, conceded in his testimony, as I heard it and understood it, that the negligent construction was a cause of the room falling away. He did not use the word 'proximate.' He said a causative factor at one time. I don't recall the exact language when he answered a question. In substance, that it was a cause on another occasion. As a matter of law, based upon the evidence, it was a proximate cause."

The jury subsequently found defendant liable for $47,000 in policy benefits and general damages, and $1 million in punitive damages. The court denied defendant's motions for judgment notwithstanding the verdict and for a new trial, and declined to issue a remittitur with respect to the punitive damages award. The court entered judgment in accordance with the verdict. Defendant appealed, and the Court of Appeal reversed the judgment in a divided opinion. . . .

II.

Discussion

A. Development of Multiple Causation Insurance Coverage Analyses

1. The efficient proximate cause standard

Our courts have long struggled to enunciate principles that determine whether coverage exists when excluded and covered perils interact to cause a loss. Initially, the courts attempted to reconcile section 530 (which provides for coverage when a peril insured against was the "proximate cause" of loss) with section 532 (which provides, that "If a peril is specifically excepted in a contract of insurance, and there is a loss which would not have occurred but for such peril, such loss is thereby excepted [from coverage] even though the immediate cause of the loss was a peril which was not excepted").

In our 1963 *Sabella* decision, we faced a difficult property loss coverage question arising after a building contractor constructed a house on uncompacted fill and negligently installed a sewer line; negligent installation was a covered peril. Eventually, the sewer line ruptured causing water to saturate the ground surrounding the insureds' house, resulting in subsidence, an excluded peril. The insureds brought a first party action against their insurer, seeking recovery for property loss under their homeowner's property policy.

The trial court found the loss was not covered because subsidence was a specifically excluded peril under the policy. The insureds appealed this ruling and we reversed.

On its face, section 532 would have precluded coverage because the loss would not have occurred "but for" the excluded peril of subsidence. We recognized, however, that such a result would be absurd because it would deny coverage even though an insured peril "proximately" caused the loss simply because a subsequent, excepted peril was also part of the chain of causation. We reasoned that sections 530 and 532 were not intended to deny coverage for losses whenever "an excepted peril operated to any extent in the chain of causation so that the resulting harm would not have occurred 'but for' the excepted peril's operation . . . ." (*Sabella,* 59 Cal.2d at 33.) Rather, we explained that when section 532 is read along with section 530, the "but for" clause of section 532 necessarily refers to a "proximate cause" of the loss, and the "immediate cause" refers to the cause most immediate in time to the damage.

Thus, *Sabella* held that: " '[In] determining whether a loss is within an exception in a policy, where there is a concurrence of different causes, the efficient cause—the one that sets others in motion—is the cause to which the loss is to be attributed, though the other causes may follow it, and operate more immediately in producing the disaster.' " (59 Cal.2d at 31–32, *quoting* from Couch on Insurance (1930) § 1466; Houser & Kent, *Concurrent Causation in First-Party Insurance Claims: Consumers Cannot Afford Concurrent Causation* (1986) Tort & Ins. L.J. 573, 575.)

Furthermore, in characterizing the "but for" clause of section 532 as referring to the efficient proximate cause of the loss, we impliedly recognized that coverage would not exist if the covered risk was simply a remote cause of the loss, or if an excluded risk was the efficient proximate (meaning predominant) cause of the loss. On the other hand, the fact that an excluded risk contributed to the loss would not preclude coverage if such a risk was a remote cause of the loss. We relied heavily in *Sabella* on our earlier decision in *Brooks v. Metropolitan Life Ins. Co.* (1945) 27 Cal.2d 305 [163 P.2d 689], in which recovery was allowed on a homeowner's policy insuring against death by accidental means. In *Brooks*, the insured, who was suffering from incurable cancer, an excluded peril, died in a fire. We held, "recovery may be had even though a diseased or infirm condition appears to actually contribute to cause the death if the accident sets in progress the chain of events leading directly to death, or if it is the prime or moving cause." (Id., at 309–310.) *Brooks* thus defined efficient proximate cause in the first party loss context as the "prime or moving cause."

The Court of Appeal here replaced the *Sabella* term "efficient proximate cause" with the term "moving cause." *Sabella* defined "efficient proximate cause" alternatively as the "one that sets others in motion" and as "the predominating or moving efficient cause." We use the term "efficient proximate cause" (meaning predominating cause) when referring to the *Sabella* analysis because we believe the phrase "moving cause" can be misconstrued to deny coverage erroneously, particularly when it is understood literally to mean the "triggering" cause. Indeed, we believe misinterpretation of the *Sabella* definition of "efficient proximate cause" has added to the confusion in the courts and, in part, is responsible for the erroneous application of *Partridge* to first-party property loss cases.

By relying on *Brooks,* and construing sections 530 and 532, *Sabella,* sets forth a workable rule of coverage that provides a fair result within the reasonable expectations of both the insured and the insurer whenever there exists a causal or dependent relationship between covered and excluded perils. In multiple cause cases, a proximate cause analysis, focusing on the efficient proximate cause, could be employed to determine whether or not the insured was covered for the loss under the property portion of the homeowner's insurance policy. . . .

2. The doctrine of concurrent causation

In 1973, we were faced with a third party tort liability situation that presented a "novel question of insurance coverage" and did not fit the *Sabella* analysis because no single peril could be labeled the predominant cause of the loss. In *Partridge,* the insured was covered under both an automobile liability policy and a homeowner's liability policy with comprehensive personal liability coverage. (The latter liability policy excluded losses "arising out of the use" of a motor vehicle.) The insured, after filing the trigger mechanism of his pistol to create a "hair-trigger" action (such negligence was a covered risk under the homeowner's property policy), hunted jackrabbits at night from his vehicle. As he drove over rough terrain while waving the gun in his hand (negligent driving was an excluded risk under homeowner's liability policy), the gun fired and injured a passenger.

First party property coverage issues were not involved. The case concerned the personal liability of the insured who was sued by his injured passenger. Both policies were issued by the same insurer, which conceded the accident was covered under the automobile liability policy. The parties, however, disputed whether coverage was also afforded under the homeowner's liability policy, which excluded coverage for injuries "arising out of the use of motor vehicles." As in *Sabella,* we relied on *Brooks* to find coverage under the homeowner's policy. In analyzing the liability coverage, we explicitly recognized, "the 'efficient cause' language [of *Sabella*] is not very helpful, for here both causes were independent of each other: the filing of the trigger did not 'cause' the careless driving, nor vice versa. Both, however, caused the injury . . . . If committed by separate individuals, both actors would be joint tortfeasors fully liable for the resulting injuries. Moreover, the fact that both acts were committed by a single person does not alter their nature as concurrent proximate causes." We concluded by stating, "Although there may be some question whether either of the two causes in the instant case can be properly characterized as the " 'prime,' 'moving' or 'efficient' cause of the accident we believe that coverage under a liability insurance policy is equally available to an insured whenever an insured risk constitutes simply a concurrent proximate cause of the injuries."

Because *Partridge* dealt with causation in the context of third party liability insurance, we did not address, nor did we contemplate, the application of our decision to the determination of coverage in the first party property insurance context. Indeed, *Partridge* asserted only that the "concurrent cause" standard was "consistent with Insurance Code sections 530 and 532, as authoritatively construed in *Sabella v. Wisler* . . . ."

Furthermore, *Partridge* never considered in what manner concurrent causation could apply in the first party property insurance context. Rather, by recognizing in *Partridge* the "novel question" of liability coverage presented because two separate acts of negligence simultaneously joined together to cause an injury, we also impliedly recognized the limited scope of our holding. We did not extend our holding to first party property insurance cases. Accordingly, we should not apply the decision to such cases merely because it appears to simplify the coverage analysis.

B. The Distinction Between Liability and Property Insurance

. . . .

First-and third party coverage is today typically provided in a single policy, and under both types of coverage, once the insured shows that an event falls within the scope of basic coverage under the policy, the burden is on the insurer to prove a claim is specifically excluded. Moreover, exclusionary clauses are interpreted narrowly, whereas clauses identifying coverage are interpreted broadly.

The scope of coverage and the operation of the exclusion clauses, however, are different in the separate policy portions and should be treated as such. As one commentator has recently stated: "Liability and corresponding coverage under a third party insurance policy must be carefully distinguished from the coverage analysis applied in a first party property contract. Property insurance, unlike liability insurance, is unconcerned with establishing negligence or otherwise assessing tort liability." (Bragg,

Concurrent Causation and the Art of Policy Drafting: New Perils for Property Insurers (1985) 20 Forum 385, 386.)

For these reasons it is important to separate the causation analysis necessary in a first party property loss case from that which must be undertaken in a third party tort liability case. The following quotation summarizes the distinction that must be drawn: "Property insurance . . . is an agreement, a contract, in which the insurer agrees to indemnify the insured in the event that the insured property suffers a covered loss. Coverage, in turn, is commonly provided by reference to causation, e.g., 'loss caused by . . .' certain enumerated perils. The term 'perils' in traditional property insurance parlance refers to fortuitous, active, physical forces such as lightning, wind, and explosion, which bring about the loss. Thus, the 'cause' of loss in the context of a property insurance contract is totally different from that in a liability policy. This distinction is critical to the resolution of losses involving multiple causes. Frequently property losses occur which involve more than one peril that might be considered legally significant. If one of the causes (perils) arguably falls within the coverage grant—commonly either because it is specifically insured (as in a named peril policy) or not specifically excepted or excluded (as in an "all risks" policy)—disputes over coverage can arise. The task becomes one of identifying the most important cause of the loss and attributing the loss to that cause." (Bragg, *supra*, 20 Forum at pp. 386–387). On the other hand, the right to coverage in the third party liability insurance context draws on traditional tort concepts of fault, proximate cause and duty. This liability analysis differs substantially from the coverage analysis in the property insurance context, which draws on the relationship between perils that are either covered or excluded in the contract. In liability insurance, by insuring for personal liability, and agreeing to cover the insured for his own negligence, the insurer agrees to cover the insured for a broader spectrum of risks. In order to further demonstrate the differences between property loss and liability coverage, we compare two sections of a typical homeowner's policy—the all-risk property loss coverage section of the policy in this case and the personal liability section at issue in *Partridge*.

Each policy section is governed by separate exclusions. For example, the all-risk first party property loss coverage section in this case provides for coverage against "all risk of physical loss" except: losses "caused by . . . settling cracking, shrinkage, bulging or expansion of pavements, patios, foundations, walls, floors, roofs or ceilings . . . ."

In comparison, in *Partridge*, "The coverage clause of the 'Personal Liability' section of the 'Homeowner's Policy' provides in relevant part: 'This Company agrees to pay on behalf of the Insured all sums which the Insured shall become legally obligated to pay as damages because of bodily injury or property damage, to which this insurance applies, caused by an occurrence.' . . . ." Moreover, "[the] applicable exclusionary clause reads: 'This policy does not apply: 1. Under Coverage E—Personal Liability . . . (a) To Bodily Injury or Property Damage Arising Out of the Ownership, Maintenance, Operation, Use, Loading or Unloading of: . . . (2) Any Motor Vehicle Owned or Operated By, or Rented or Loaned to, any Insured . . . .' "

As the two provisions cited above illustrate, under the all-risk first party property policy, because generally "all risk of physical loss" is covered, the exclusions become the limitation on loss coverage. Under the liability portion of the policy, on the other hand, the focus is, at least initially, on the insured's legal obligation to pay for injury or damage arising out of an "occurrence."

In the property insurance context, the insurer and the insured can tailor the policy according to the selection of insured and excluded risks and, in the process, determine the corresponding premium to meet the economic needs of the insured. On the other hand, if the insurer is expected to cover claims that are outside the scope of the first party property loss policy, an "all risk" policy would become an "all loss" policy. (Friedman, *Concurrent Causation: The Coverage Trap* (1985) 86 Best's Rev.: Prop./Casualty 50, 58.) In most instances, the insured can point to some arguably covered contributing factor. As we shall discuss, if the rule in *Partridge* were extended to first party cases, the presence of such a cause, no matter how minor, would give rise to coverage.

Finally, . . . the reasonable expectations of the insurer and the insured in the first party property loss portion of a homeowner's policy—as manifested in the distribution of risks, the proportionate premiums charged and the coverage for all risks except those specifically excluded—cannot reasonably include an expectation of coverage in property loss cases in which the efficient proximate cause of the loss is an activity expressly excluded under the policy. Indeed, if we were to approve of the trial court's directed verdict, we would be requiring ordinary insureds to bear the expense of increased premiums necessitated by the erroneous expansion of their insurers' potential liabilities.

. . . .

E. The Trial Court Erred in Directing the Verdict

Finally, because we believe the *Partridge* analysis should be limited to third party liability cases, we cannot sustain the directed verdict in this case. Plaintiffs argue the directed verdict was proper because there was no evidence of sufficient substantiality to support a determination other than the following: the included risk of negligent construction and the excluded risk of earth movement in the form of soil creep, if any, were independent, concurrent proximate causes of the loss plaintiffs sustained to their property.

We disagree. . . . The record discloses that the experts were in marked disagreement as to the causes of plaintiffs' damages. For example, Mr. Nelson, the defense expert, testified: "There was settlement and creep. The room addition moved away from the house and was caused by—probably caused by settlement and creep." Plaintiffs' expert, Mr. Hillebrandt testified to the contrary. To the question, "Was what happened to the room addition in August 1978 related to any respect to soil creep, in your opinion?" Hillebrandt replied, "In my opinion, it didn't. And the reason is because the actual breaking—the footing of the support beam was actually on a level surface. It was on a level fill surface that had been placed behind the rock wall, and the whole hillside may have been creeping, but this was just one part of it, and it was a level surface." At another point during the trial, however, Hillebrandt testified that the damage to the deck was caused by the following: "In this case, the footing [of the retaining wall] was not deep enough, so consequently, when the creep forces at the surface caused this downhill movement, the footing just went along for the ride."

This case presents a classic *Sabella* situation. Coverage should be determined by a jury under an efficient proximate cause analysis. Accordingly, bearing in mind the facts here, we conclude the question of causation is for the jury to decide.

If the earth movement was the efficient proximate cause of the loss, then coverage would be denied under *Sabella.* On the other hand, if negligence was the efficient proximate cause of the loss, then coverage exists under *Sabella.* These issues were jury questions because sufficient evidence was introduced to support both possibilities.

The judgment of the Court of Appeal is affirmed with directions to remand the cause to the trial court for further proceedings consistent with the opinion of this court.

NOTES AND QUESTIONS

1. *Third-Party Versus First-Party Insurance.* In *Garvey*, the court made a distinction between the test applied to third-party insurance (i.e., liability insurance) and first-party insurance (e.g., property insurance) with respect to when losses caused by concurrent causes were covered. What was the court's reasoning behind making the distinction? Was the court's reasoning persuasive?

2. *Initial Cause Versus Predominant Cause?* In *Garvey*, in applying the efficient proximate cause test, the California Supreme Court noted that some courts had interpreted the test to require the factfinder to determine the predominant cause of the loss, while other courts require the factfinder to determine the initial cause of the chain of events that led to the loss. Which version of the test did the California Supreme Court adopt in *Garvey*? For cases employing the initial cause version of the test, *see Graham v. Public Employers Mut. Ins. Co.*, 656 P.2d 1077 (Wash. 1983) (remanding the case for the

factfinder to determine whether Mt. St. Helens' eruption was an "explosion," a covered peril, that set in motion the chain of events leading to mudflows, an excluded peril, that ultimately destroyed the policyholder's home); *McDonald v. State Farm Fire & Casualty Co.*, 837 P.2d 1000 (Wash. 1992) (applying the initial cause version of the efficient proximate cause test); *Vision One, LLC v. Phila. Indem. Ins. Co.*, 276 P.3d 300 (Wash. 2012) (noting that the efficient proximate cause test is employed for the benefit of policyholders when the initial cause of a loss in the chain of causation is a covered peril).

3. *Initial Versus Predominant Cause (Part II).* Does it make a difference which version of the efficient proximate cause test is used? For example, under homeowners insurance, including the Sample Homeowners Insurance Policy at the beginning of this chapter, damage caused by wind is covered while damage caused by flooding is excluded. If you are a homeowner whose house begins to be damaged by high winds and then is completely destroyed down to the foundation slab by the storm surge, would coverage be available under the initial efficient proximate cause test? Would coverage be available under the predominant efficient proximate cause test?

4. *Consistent with Contra Proferentem?* Is the use of the efficient proximate cause test consistent with *contra proferentem*? Stated differently, does the policy language unambiguously dictate that courts apply the efficient proximate cause test in concurrent causation situations? If not, what is the basis for its application?

5. *Mixing Tort Law and Contract Law?* Is it appropriate to apply tort causation principles to insurance contract claims? Some judges do not think so. For example, nearly seventy years ago in his dissent in *Standard Oil Company of New Jersey v. United States*, 340 U.S. 54 (1950), Justice Frankfurter cogently explained why incorporating tort causation principles into contractual insurance disputes was inappropriate in his view:

> Unlike obligations flowing from duties imposed upon people willy-nilly, an insurance policy is a voluntary undertaking by which obligations are voluntarily assumed. Therefore the subtleties and sophistries of tort liability for negligence are not to be applied in construing the covenants of a policy. It is one thing for the law to impose liability by its own notions of responsibility, and quite another to construe the scope of engagements brought and paid for. . . . The law does not play an unreal metaphysical game of trying to find a single isolatable factor as the sole responsibility to which is to be attributed a loss against which insurance has been bought. As a matter of experience and reason such losses are invariably the resultant of a combination of factors.

Id. at 66 (Frankfurter, J., dissenting).

Similarly, nearly ninety years ago in *Palsgraf v. Long Island Railroad Company*, 162 N.E. 99 (N.Y. 1928), Judge Andrews recognized, in one of the most famous dissents of all time, that the idea that a single cause in a causation chain of events is *the* "proximate cause" of an accident is a fiction:

> These two words have never been given an inclusive definition. What is a cause in a legal sense, still more what is a proximate cause, depend[s] in each case upon many considerations. . . . Any philosophical doctrine of causation does not help us. . . . You may speak of a chain, or, if you please, a net. An analogy is of little aid. Each cause brings about future events. Without each the future would not be the same. Each is proximate in the sense it is essential. But that is not what we mean by the word. Nor[,] on the other hand[,] do we mean sole cause. There is no such thing. . . . What we . . . mean by the word "proximate" is that, because of convenience, [because] of public policy, [because] of a rough sense of justice, the law arbitrarily declines to trace a series of events beyond a certain point. This is not logic. It is practical politics. . . . It is all a question of expediency. There are no fixed rules to govern our judgment. . . . This is rather rhetoric than law. There is[,] in truth[,] little to guide us other than common sense.

Id. at 103–04 (Andrews, J., dissenting).

EXERCISE

1. Under the facts discussed in Note 3, draft a 2-page memo in which you argue there would be coverage for the destroyed home under the initial efficient proximate cause test but not under the predominant efficient proximate cause test.

B. ENSUING LOSS CLAUSES

At 5:12 a.m. on Wednesday, April 18, 1906, "a deafening rumble filled the air" in San Francisco as "buildings swayed" and then crumbled to the ground.[3] A massive earthquake had struck, but the real catastrophe was still to come. The earthquake caused gas-fed fires to erupt, which were magnified by the fire department's ill-fated attempts to stop the spreading blaze by using dynamite to create areas where the fire could not pass, which are known as firebreaks. With water mains broken, firefighters could not stop the inferno, and the largest city west of the Mississippi River was destroyed in three days. Thousands of people were killed and most of the residents were left homeless. The damage caused by the earthquake and fire cost billions in today's dollars.

At that time, most property policies in the U.S. covered losses caused by fire, but also contained an "anti-concurrent causation" exclusion that barred coverage for losses caused "directly or indirectly" by earthquakes.

[3] This introductory section is taken verbatim from Christopher C. French, *The "Ensuing Loss" Clause in Insurance Policies: The Forgotten and Misunderstood Antidote to Anti-Concurrent Causation Exclusions*, 13 Nev. L. J. 215, 216–18 (2012) (citations omitted).

Not surprisingly, when the massive loss claims were presented, many insurers refused to pay. They argued the losses were not covered because the earthquake set in motion the chain of events that led to the fires and destruction. The highest courts that heard the cases, the Supreme Court of California and the Ninth Circuit, held the losses were covered notwithstanding the anti-concurrent causation language contained in the earthquake exclusion.

In the wake of these decisions, the California legislature enacted a set of statutes designed to prevent insurers from disclaiming coverage for fire damage that followed an earthquake. In response, insurers created a policy provision known as the "ensuing loss" clause, which specified that losses that follow both an earthquake and a fire are covered even if the policy excludes coverage for losses caused by earthquakes. As the coverage provided under property insurance was expanded to cover losses caused by other perils in addition to fire, broader versions of the ensuing loss clause were adopted to encompass all covered perils even though such policies also often contain anti-concurrent causation exclusions. Thus, although originally created for the specific context of earthquakes and fires, the ensuing loss clause came to ensure that losses caused at least in part by a covered peril remain covered under property policies even if an excluded peril also played a role in causing the loss.

Today, the ensuing loss clause is found in various types of property policies, including homeowners policies, but many of these policies also contain anti-concurrent causation exclusions. For a descent into the mysteries of the ensuing loss clause, consider the next case.

ROBERTS V. STATE FARM FIRE & CASUALTY CO.

705 P.2d 1335 (Ariz. 1985)

Opinion

Donald R. Roberts and his wife Elsie (hereinafter Roberts) brought an action against their insurer, State Farm Fire and Casualty (hereinafter State Farm), for damages to their home allegedly covered by their insurance policy. The trial court found that Roberts' policy did not cover the type of damage complained of and granted State Farm's motion for summary judgment. The Court of Appeals affirmed the trial court's decision, and Roberts petitioned this court for review. We have jurisdiction.

We address only one issue:

> Does an insurance policy that excludes damage done by insects cover, through an "ensuing loss" provision, damage done after the insects are exterminated by the leakage of honey from their hive?

FACTS

In late May of 1980, Roberts began finding live honeybees inside their home. A few days after this discovery, Roberts noticed that a swarm of the insects had formed on their roof. Apparently the bees had made their way through the roof and were constructing a hive in Roberts' attic. A beekeeper was consulted but due to the inaccessible location of the hive, he could not extract the queen and thereby draw off the swarm. Instead, he recommended extermination.

A few days after the bees were dispatched, Roberts noticed honey dripping into their dining room. At first, this drip confined itself to one location, but gradually it began to spread and eventually encompassed the entire room. Apparently, after the bees were exterminated, the hive began to leak.

Roberts contacted their insurer, State Farm, and a representative told them to get estimates. Eventually, however, State Farm denied coverage, claiming that the damage was caused by insects and specifically excluded from Roberts' policy.

ENSUING LOSS

The relevant portion of Roberts' policy read as follows:

> We insure for all risks of physical loss to the property described in Coverage A except for loss caused by:
>
> . . . .
>
> 6. wear and tear; marring; deterioration; inherent vice; latent defect; mechanical breakdown; rust; mold; wet or dry rot; contamination; smog; smoke from agricultural smudging or industrial operations; settling, cracking, shrinking, bulging, or expansion of pavements, patios, foundations, walls, floors, roofs or ceilings; birds, vermin, rodents, insects or domestic animals. . . . Any ensuing loss from items 1 through 6 not excluded is covered.

State Farm contends that the damage to Roberts' home was due to insects and clearly excluded from coverage by the terms of the policy. Roberts, on the other hand, maintain that the loss was not due to insects, but due to the absence of insects. They claim that after the bees were exterminated the hive began to melt and only then did the honey seepage begin. They therefore conclude that this was an "ensuing loss" from insects covered through the ensuing loss provision of their policy. They concede that the actual damage done by the bees themselves, i.e., the cost of tearing out hive and accompanying repairs is not covered. They dispute, however, that the damage to their dining room is not covered.

In their petition for review, Roberts argue that the terms of their policy are ambiguous and as such should be construed against their insurer. State Farm responds, claiming that Roberts have never raised this argument before nor pointed to which term "they feel to be ambiguous." State Farm does not inform us as to what conclusions we are to draw from this assertion. We gather, however, State Farm wishes to raise a waiver argument: those arguments not raised in the trial court are waived if raised for the first time on appeal from a summary judgment. *See Crook v. Anderson*, 115 Ariz. 402, 403–04, 565 P.2d 908, 909–10 (App.1977).

We disagree with what we take to be State Farm's assertion. Throughout this litigation Roberts have proposed definitions for the word "ensue" and have cited cases dealing with ambiguous policies. In their motion for partial summary judgment, Roberts stated "[i]f the Court somehow finds that the policy is ambiguous, it must apply [the] well established rule that in the event of ambiguity, an insurance policy is to be construed in favor of the insured and against the insurer (citations omitted)." Roberts did not waive their ambiguity argument.

. . . .

With this law in mind, we return to Roberts' policy. We note that the term "ensuing loss" is nowhere defined in the policy. Both parties have agreed, however, that the word "ensuing" means "to take place afterward . . . to follow as a chance, likely, or necessary consequence: RESULT . . . to follow in chronological succession." *See Roberts v. State Farm*, 146 Ariz. at 302, 705 P.2d at 1353; Webster's Third New International Dictionary, 756 (1969) (definition of the word "ensue"). We note that this definition of "ensue" is not without precedent. *See Aetna Insurance Co. v. Getchell Steel Treating Co.*, 395 F.2d 12, 16 (8th Cir.1968) ("to follow as a chance, likely or necessary consequence: to take place afterwards"). Both parties have also agreed on the meaning of certain other language within the policy: both agree that bees are insects and both agree that a loss occurred. With these agreements in mind, we focus on the disputed provision. In shortened form, it reads:

> We insure for all risks of physical loss to the property . . . except for loss caused by:
>
> . . . .
>
> 6. . . . [bees] . . . .
>
> Any . . . loss [taking place afterward or following as a chance, likely, or necessary consequence] from . . . [bees] . . . not excluded is covered.

We do not believe this language is ambiguous. It cannot be construed in more than one sense. The plain import of this language is that the loss, due to honey seepage, is an ensuing loss and is covered by the policy, unless one of the other various exclusions applies. Unless, for example, the honey seepage caused "marring" or "settling" or any one of the numerous other exclusions. It was error for the trial court to dismiss Roberts' suit.

Opinion of the Court of Appeals is vacated. Reversed and remanded for further proceedings consistent with this opinion.

NOTES AND QUESTIONS

1. *Sophistry and Abuse?* In a letter written shortly before his death, John Adams opined, "Abuse of words has been the great instrument of sophistry and chicanery, of party, faction and division of society." Was the court's argument in *Roberts* mere sophistry? If losses caused by bees were excluded from coverage, how were losses caused by bees' honey covered?

2. *Different Interpretations of Ensuing Loss Clauses.* One interpretation of ensuing loss clauses is that if a loss results from a covered peril, then there is coverage even if the covered peril was caused by an excluded peril. The 1906 San Francisco Fire losses are classic examples of that interpretation—the fire, a covered peril, was caused by an earthquake, an excluded peril.

In some versions of this interpretation, there must be a "separate and independent" covered cause of the loss in order for coverage to be reinstated. For example, in *Weeks v. Co-Operative Ins. Companies*, 817 A.2d 292 (N.H. 2003), the court instituted and explained this requirement:

> 'We interpret the ensuing loss provision to apply to the situation where there is a 'peril,' i.e., a hazard or occurrence which causes a loss or injury, *separate* and *independent* but resulting from the original excluded peril, and this new peril is not an excluded one, from which loss ensues.' Thus, the exception to the exclusion operates to restore coverage if the damage ensues from a covered cause of loss. . . . Accordingly, coverage will be reinstated under the exception to the exclusion when an excluded risk sets into motion a chain of causation which leads to a covered cause of loss. In that case, the policy insures against damage directly caused by the ensuing covered cause of loss.

Id. at 296 (quoting *Acme Galvanizing v. Fireman's Fund Ins.*, 221 Cal. App.3d 170, 179 (1990)). Does the phrase "separate and independent" appear anywhere in the policy language? If not, on what basis have courts created this version of the test?

Another interpretation of the ensuing loss clause is based upon the insurance policy interpretation rule of *contra proferentem*. Under this approach, where the policy language is not completely clear as to when coverage should be reinstated, any time a loss follows (i.e., ensues from) a covered peril, coverage exists. *See, e.g., Blaine Constr. Corp. v. Ins. Co. of N. Am.*, 171 F.3d 343, 349–50, 354 (6th Cir. 1999) (explaining under Tennessee law, despite faulty workmanship exclusion, coverage for loss caused by faulty workmanship was reinstated under the ensuing loss exception because the exclusion was ambiguous); *Lake Charles Harbor & Terminal Dist. v. Imperial Cas. & Indem. Co.*, 857 F.2d 286, 287, 289 (5th Cir. 1988) (explaining under Louisiana law, exclusion in all-risk inland marine policy for mechanical breakdowns "unless an insured peril ensues" did not exclude coverage for catastrophic damage to insured's shiploader after worn out cable on shiploader snapped because such damage was an ensuing loss).

3. *Consistent Application?* Which, if any, of the foregoing interpretations of ensuing loss clauses allows for courts to reach consistent and predictable results?

C. ANTI-CONCURRENT CAUSATION EXCLUSIONS

As discussed above, some courts apply ensuing loss clauses and the efficient proximate cause test with little, or no, regard for the presence of anti-concurrent causation exclusions. Does that mean such exclusions are unenforceable? Consider the next two cases.

BOZEK V. ERIE INS. GROUP

46 N.E.3d 362 (Ill. App. Ct. 2015)

Opinion

Following cross-motions for summary judgment concerning coverage for damage to an in-ground swimming pool, the trial court granted judgment to defendant, Erie Insurance Group. The court found that, as a matter of law, the insurance policy's anticoncurrent-causation clause operated to preclude coverage because two events, one covered under the policy (a failed pressure-relief valve) and one excluded under the policy (hydrostatic pressure), contributed to a single loss (the lifting of the pool out of the ground). The anticoncurrent-causation clause read: "We do not pay for loss resulting directly or indirectly from any of the following, even if other events or happenings contributed concurrently, or in sequence, to the loss."

In the trial court (as on appeal), the plaintiffs, Marek and Bozena Bozek, argued that the anticoncurrent-causation clause does not apply to the underlying facts. They posited that a reasonable definition of "in sequence" is "subsequent to." Therefore, the anticoncurrent-causation clause would mean that, if a covered cause happened *subsequent to* the excluded cause, there would be no coverage. Here, according to the Bozeks, the covered cause, the failure of the pressure-relief valve, happened *prior to* the excluded cause, the hydrostatic pressure. As such, in the Bozeks' view, the anticoncurrent-causation clause did not apply.

The trial court rejected the Bozeks' interpretation of "in sequence" and its function in the anticoncurrent-causation clause. We interpret the anticoncurrent-causation clause *de novo*, and we determine that, while the trial court reached the correct result, given the underlying facts, it focused on the wrong portion of the clause. In this fact pattern, the two causes at issue, the failed valve and the hydrostatic pressure, "contributed concurrently" to the loss. The failed valve and the hydrostatic pressure did not "contribute[ ] * * * in sequence" to the loss, as put forth by the Bozeks. We do not look to the point in time that each cause *came into existence*. We look to the point in time that it *contributed* to the loss. The term "concurrently" contains no ambiguity, and, as each cause contributed concurrently, the anticoncurrent-causation clause precludes coverage for the loss.

Alternatively, the Bozeks hint that, even if the anticoncurrent-causation clause must be read to preclude coverage, we should find anticoncurrent-causation clauses to be against public policy. The Bozeks have not sufficiently briefed that question, and, so, we leave its resolution to a future court. We affirm.

I. BACKGROUND

Following a rain storm, the Bozeks incurred damage to their in-ground swimming pool. The Bozeks had a homeowner's insurance policy with Erie, which provided $89,000 in coverage for damage to the pool. The Bozeks reported the loss to Erie. Erie sent a company, Engineering Systems, Inc. (ESI), to investigate the loss.

ESI's report stated:

> "On June 27, 2013[,] the pool at the subject address heaved out of the ground. ESI was retained to determine the cause of the distress in the pool. The following provides a summary of ESI's opinions.
>
> Weather Conditions
>
> According to unofficial weather records in the location of this property, it rained approximately 3.5 inches in five days prior to the event. This amount is nearly the average (4 inches) for the entire typical month of July. It rained nearly 2.5 inches in the 48 hours before the incident occurred.
>
> Cause of Distress
>
> The amount of rain that occurred can result in saturated soils that produce significant uplift hydrostatic pressures. The weight of the water in the pool must exceed the uplift forces of the water pressure in the soil for the pool to remain in place. However in the subject incident the pool had been emptied to clean debris making it susceptible to uplift.
>
> In-ground pools are provided with a method to balance uplift in the event of the pool being emptied. Pools utilize pressure relief valves to prevent this uplift. In the event that the pool is empty, the relief valve allows ground water to enter into the pool to counterbalance the uplift of the ground hydrostatic pressure. The water was not clear enough at the time of the site inspection to

> see if there was a pressure relief valve. However, the owner stated that there was a pressure relief valve.
>
> The pool lifted upward because the ground water pressure pushed the pool upward because the pressure relief did not function properly.
>
> <u>Damages</u>
>
> The in-ground pool was damaged to the point that it must be replaced in its entirety. The heaving of the pool also damaged the concrete slab around the pool. The concrete slab will also need to be replaced."

Erie denied coverage, stating that cause(s) of distress were excluded under the policy. The relevant portions of the policy stated:

> "*We do not pay for loss resulting directly or indirectly from any of the following, even if other events or happenings contributed concurrently, or in sequence, to the loss*:
>
> * * *
>
> 3. by freezing thawing, pressure or weight of water or ice, whether driven by wind or not, to a fence, pavement, patio, deck, swimming pool, foundation, retaining wall, bulkhead, pier, wharf[,] or dock.
>
> * * *
>
> 5. * * * by
>
> * * *
>
> (b) mechanical breakdown, deterioration, wear and tear, marring, inherent vice, latent defect, tree roots, rust, smog, wet or dry rot, mold, fungus or spores;
>
> * * *
>
> 9. by water damage, meaning:
>
> * * *
>
> (c) water below the surface on the ground. This includes water which exerts pressure on, or flows seeps or leaks through any part of a building or other structure, including sidewalks, driveways, foundations, pavements, patios, swimming pools or decks." (Emphasis added).

The emphasized introductory sentence of the exclusion section set forth above is known as an anticoncurrent-causation clause. It is the root of the instant controversy.

The Bozeks filed a complaint for declaratory judgment. They alleged that Erie improperly denied coverage. They conceded that hydrostatic pressure was an excluded cause (under either paragraph 3 or paragraph 9 of the exclusion section). However, they argued that Erie did not establish that the failure of the pressure-relief valve was an excluded cause. Specifically, the Bozeks asserted in subsequent filings that Erie did not establish that the failure of the pressure-relief valve qualified as an excluded "mechanical breakdown" under paragraph 5 of the exclusion section. In the Bozeks' view, the anticoncurrent-causation clause dictated that, because the failure of the pressure-relief valve, a covered event, preceded the increase in hydrostatic pressure, an excluded event, the loss was covered.

In support of their position, the Bozeks pointed to the anticoncurrent-causation clause's use of the phrase, *in sequence*: "We do not pay for loss resulting directly or indirectly from any of the following, even if other events or happenings contributed concurrently, or *in sequence*, to the loss." (Emphasis added). The Bozeks posited that a reasonable definition of "in sequence" is "subsequent to."[1]

Therefore, the anticoncurrent-causation clause meant that, if a covered cause (*i.e.*, "other events or happenings") happened *subsequent to* an excluded cause, there would be no coverage. Here, however, the covered cause, the failure of the pressure-relief valve, happened *prior to* the excluded cause, the hydrostatic pressure. As such, the anticoncurrent-causation clause did not apply. The Bozeks then argued that, in the absence of an *applicable* anticoncurrent-causation clause, they could not be divested of coverage for the loss, associated with the covered failure of the pressure-relief valve, simply because an excluded cause later occurred (citing *Corban v. United Services Automobile Ass'n*, 2008–IA–00645–SCT (Miss. 2009), 20 So. 3d 601, and *Robichaux v. Nationwide Mutual Fire Insurance Co.*, 2010–CA–00109–SCT (Miss. 2011), 81 So. 3d 1030.

The parties filed cross-motions for summary judgment. The Bozeks argued as set forth above. Erie argued that, even if the court were to accept that the failure of the pressure-relief valve was covered under the policy, the anticoncurrent-causation clause precluded coverage. Erie posited that the phrase "in sequence" meant "one after the other." However, because the policy did not specify which cause must come after the other (or which cause must come first), *any* sequence of events involving an excluded cause would preclude coverage. The use of the words "concurrently" and "in

[1] The Bozeks quote dictionary definitions of "sequence" to be: "(1) The state of being sequent or following; a following or coming of one thing after another; succession; (2) A particular order of succession or following; an arrangement; order; (3) A continuous or related series of things following in a certain order or succession; [or] (4) Result; consequence; sequel." Webster's Unabridged Dictionary (2d ed. 1983). We see that a definition of "sequence" is the "state of being sequent," which in turn means "1: CONSECUTIVE, SUCCEEDING[; or] 2: CONSEQUENT, RESULTANT." Merriam-Webster Dictionary, http://www.merriam-webster.com/dictionary/sequent (last visited Nov. 17, 2015).

sequence" avoids coverage where two events occur at the same time or one after the other. Where an excluded cause is *a* cause, there is no coverage.

Erie cited many cases discussing policies with anticoncurrent-causation clauses. Most relevant was *South Carolina Farm Bureau Mutual Insurance Co. v. Durham*, 380 S.C. 506, 671 S.E.2d 610, 613 (S.C. 2009). In *Durham*, the insureds emptied their pool in order to clean it. Within two or three days, the pool " 'floated' " out above the foundation (*id.* at 611), because, as here, underground hydrostatic pressure pushed against the pool without release or countervailing pressure from inside the pool. The insurance company denied coverage, because the policy did not cover damage due to hydrostatic pressure. The policy also contained an anticoncurrent-causation clause: " 'We do not insure for loss caused directly or indirectly by any of the following. Such loss is excluded regardless of any other cause or event contributing concurrently or in any sequence to the loss.' " *Id.* at 612.

The *Durham* court affirmed the denial of coverage. *Id.* at 613. It recognized that, *absent* an anticoncurrent-causation clause, an argument could be made that the draining of the pool was the "but for" cause, allowing for coverage despite the additional, excluded cause of hydrostatic pressure. *Id.* However, the court held that the anticoncurrent-causation clause precluded coverage. *Id.* It unambiguously stated that it excluded loss caused by hydrostatic pressure, even if another cause, such as draining the pool, contributed in any sequence to the loss. *Id.* The anticoncurrent-causation clause required that, where an excluded cause was *a* cause, there was no coverage. *Id.*

Erie acknowledged that, unlike the instant policy, the policy in *Durham* prefaced the word "sequence" with the word "any": " 'Such loss is excluded regardless of any other cause or event contributing concurrently or in *any* sequence to the loss.' " (Emphasis added). *Id.* at 612. Erie contended, however, that the instant policy's lack of the word "any" was a distinction without a difference. The word "any" in *Durham* was superfluous. Like the *Durham* policy's use of the words "concurrently" and "in any sequence," the instant policy's use of the words "concurrently" and "in sequence" avoids coverage where two events occur at the same time or one after the other. Where an excluded cause is *a* cause, there is no coverage.

The trial court granted summary judgment to Erie and denied summary judgment to the Bozeks. It acknowledged that a question of fact remained as to whether the failure of the pressure-relief valve was a covered cause or was excluded as a mechanical failure. However, even if, for the purposes of summary judgment, the court categorized the failure of the pressure-relief valve as a covered cause, the anticoncurrent-causation clause precluded coverage as a matter of law. The court accepted Erie's reading of the policy that any sequence of events involving an excluded clause would preclude coverage. "[T]he only fair reading I could give it was to read it as in *any* sequence." (Emphasis added). Where an excluded cause is *a* cause, the court found, there is no coverage. Here, there was no question that hydrostatic pressure was an excluded cause. Therefore, there was no coverage. This appeal followed.

II. ANALYSIS

The Bozeks appeal the trial court's summary judgment rulings.

. . . .

Specifically, the Bozeks raise two issues: (1) whether the failure of the pressure-relief valve is a covered cause; and (2) whether the anticoncurrent-causation clause precludes coverage. First, the Bozeks argue that, because Erie did not meet its burden to show that the failure of the pressure-relief valve was an excluded mechanical breakdown, it must be considered a covered event. Second, they argue that, because the covered event happened first, the anticoncurrent-causation clause does not apply to divest them of coverage. They contend that the court erred in that it essentially inserted an additional word, "any," in interpreting the anticoncurrent-causation clause. The Bozeks need to prevail on both issues in order to establish coverage as a matter of law, whereas Erie need prevail on only one issue to show that coverage should be denied as a matter of law. Because we hold that, even if the failure of the pressure-relief valve is a covered cause, the anticoncurrent-causation clause precludes coverage as a matter of law, we address only that issue.

. . . .

We begin by discussing the origin of anticoncurrent-causation clauses. Insurance companies started putting anticoncurrent-causation clauses in their policies in response to concurrent-causation controversies. Concurrent-causation controversies arise where more than one cause contributes to a loss, some of which are covered and some of which are excluded. *See, e.g.*, Peter Nash Swisher, *Causation Requirements in Tort and Insurance Law Practice: Demystifying Some Legal Causation "Riddles,"* 43 Tort Trial & Ins. Prac. L.J. 1, 26 (2007). Many coverage cases have sought to determine, in the absence of specific policy language, exactly how substantial or sufficient a given causal nexus needs to be in order to provide coverage. *Id.* at 31. There are four basic stops on the causal spectrum of insurance coverage: (1) most broadly, but-for or minimally sufficient causation, providing coverage if *a* covered cause contributes to the loss, regardless of its dominance or order in a chain of events; (2) in the middle, efficient or dominant proximate causation, providing coverage "if a risk of loss that is specifically insured against in the insurance policy sets in motion, in an unbroken causal sequence, the events that cause the ultimate loss, even though the immediate cause in the chain of causation is an excluded cause," or if it is simply the dominant cause; (3) more narrowly, immediate causation, providing coverage only where the covered cause is the last, immediate cause in the chain of causation; and (4) most narrowly, regardless of order, if any excluded cause contributes to the loss, there is no coverage. *Id.* at 22–27 (grouping together categories three and four).

The immediate-cause rule is the traditional insurance rule. *Id.* at 22. However, in practice, the immediate-cause rule can result in claim denials that are contrary to the intent and reasonable expectations of the contracting parties. *Id.* at 24. As such, the majority of jurisdictions now favor the middle-ground, efficient-or-dominant-proximate-cause rule. *Id.* at 23–24. Only a minority of jurisdictions favor the broad, but-for-causation rule. See, *e.g., Durham*, 671 S.E.2d at 613. Indeed, it appears that Illinois favors the efficient-or-dominant-proximate-cause rule in the absence of contrary language in the policy. See, *e.g., American Economy Insurance Co. v. Holabird & Root*, 382 Ill. App. 3d 1017, 1035, 886 N.E.2d 1166, 320 Ill. Dec. 97 (2008) (the court did not apply the "proximate cause" rule where the policy expressly provided coverage for loss "arising out of" the covered cause, thus invoking but-for causation).

Of course, the policy itself may determine the requisite causal nexus. *Id.* Just as policies may specify but-for causation, they may also specify a more conservative causation rule. Swisher, *supra*, at 27. On the extreme of specifying narrow coverage, many policies include anticoncurrent-causation clauses. *Id.* at 27–28. The purpose of anticoncurrent-causation clauses is to avoid application of the general rule that there is coverage so long as the efficient or dominant cause is covered. *Id.* When an anticoncurrent-causation clause can be applied to the facts underlying the claim, there is no coverage if even one contributing cause is an excluded event. *Id.* at 27. The Insurance Services Office, an advisory organization, set forth in its 1990 homeowners' property insurance form this example of a standard anticoncurrent-causation clause:

> "We do not insure for loss caused directly or indirectly by any of the following. Such loss is excluded regardless of any other cause or event contributing concurrently or in *any* sequence to the loss." (Emphasis added).

Id. (quoting Insurance Services Office, Homeowners Policy-Broad Form (HO 00 03 04 91) (1990)).

The Bozeks argue that the instant anticoncurrent-causation clause's omission of the word "any" changes the meaning of the clause. Again, the clause states: "We do not pay for loss resulting directly or indirectly from any of the following, even if other events or happenings contributed concurrently, or *in sequence*, to the loss." (Emphasis added).

The Bozeks focus on the phrase, "in sequence." However, this is the wrong portion of the clause upon which to focus. Erie added to this misunderstanding by arguing that the use of the words "concurrently" and "in sequence" avoids coverage where two events, one covered and one excluded, *occur* at the same time or one after the other. Erie should have stated that the use of the words "concurrently" and "in sequence" avoids coverage where two events, one covered and one excluded, *contribute to the loss* at the same time or one after the other.

When two perils converge at the same point in time, contemporaneously and operating in conjunction, there is a "concurrent" cause or event. *Corban*, 2008–IA–00645–SCT, ¶ 36 (Miss. 2009), 20 So. 3d 601. The sentence structure in the instant anticoncurrent causation clause is consistent with this proposition of law. "Concurrently" is an adverb that modifies "contribute[ ]." Likewise, the term "in sequence" functions in the sentence as the adverb "sequentially" and also modifies "contribute[ ]." As such, as far as any sort of order, sequence, or timing is concerned, we look to the point in time that the cause contributed to the loss, not the point in time that the cause came into existence. Here, we do not look at the point in time that the valve failed; we look at the point in time that the failed valve contributed to the loss. The failed valve and the hydrostatic pressure contributed concurrently to the loss.

. . . .

Without a separate loss, the Bozeks' interpretation of the anticoncurrent-causation clause would lead to an untenable result. *See United States Fire*, 312 Ill. App. 3d at 155. Again, the Bozeks contend that they are entitled to coverage for the loss caused by the failed pressure-release valve, stating that coverage for that loss vested and cannot be undone by a subsequent excluded event. However, the Bozeks' position begs the question, *what loss*? The failed pressure valve did not cause any loss *until* it converged with the excluded event. Put another way, prior to the excluded event, there was no loss for which coverage could conceivably vest. The Bozeks want coverage for the uplifted pool and damaged concrete. Neither of these physical losses occurred until the hydrostatic pressure acted upon the sides of the pool. Like the water pushed in by the wind in *Corban* and the storm surge in *Robichaux*, the uplift of the pool resulted from the *convergence* of two causes, the hydrostatic pressure and the valve's failure to relieve that pressure. The two causes "contributed concurrently" to the loss. Thus, the anticoncurrent-causation clause plainly precludes coverage.

Under the Bozeks' interpretation, when the first event is covered and it sets into motion a chain of events that leads to a loss, the loss is covered, even if later events in the chain are excluded. In actuality, this is a restatement of the efficient-proximate-cause rule, *i.e.*, "if a risk of loss that is specifically insured against in the insurance policy sets in motion, in an unbroken causal sequence, the events that cause the ultimate loss, even though the last immediate cause in the chain of causation is an excluded cause." Swisher, *supra*, at 24. We leave for another court to determine whether the use of the phrase "in sequence," as opposed to "in *any* sequence," when applicable to the underlying fact pattern, so neuters the anticoncurrent-causation clause as to transform it into a statement of the efficient-proximate-cause rule, the very rule that a typical effective anticoncurrent-causation clause is written to avoid.

We have concluded that, here, application of the anticoncurrent-causation clause precludes coverage as a matter of law. We turn to the Bozeks' alternative argument. Ultimately, however, we determine that it is forfeited due to insufficient briefing.

The Bozeks hint that, in general, Illinois courts should hold anticoncurrent-causation clauses to be unenforceable as against public policy. Their public policy argument reads:

> Not surprisingly, [anticoncurrent-causation clauses] have been rejected by several other state courts because of their oppressive use to defeat the paying insureds' reasonable expectations of coverage. *See, e.g., Wright v. Safeco Ins. Co. of America*, 124 Wn. App. 263, 109 P.3d 1 (Wash. Ct. App. 2004); *West. Nat'l Mut. Ins. Co. v. Univ. of North Dakota*, 2002 ND 63, 643 N.W.2d 4 (N.D. 2003); *West Virginia Fire & Cas. Co. v. Mathews*, 209 W. Va. 107, 543 S.E.2d 664 (W. Va. 2001); *Garvey v. State Farm Fire & Cas. Co.*, 48 Cal. 3d 395, 257 Cal. Rptr. 292, 770 P.2d 704 (Cal. 1989). As the Complaint at issue alleged: "Illinois law has never formally recognized anticoncurrent causation clauses on public policy grounds," and this Honorable Court could dispose of almost all issues by finding the anticoncurrent causation provision at issue to be unenforceable.

The cases cited by the Bozeks are off-point. *Wright v. Safeco Insurance Co. of America*, 124 Wn. App. 263, 109 P.3d 1 (Wash. Ct. App. 2004), *West Virginia Fire & Casualty Co. v. Mathews*, 209 W. Va. 107, 543 S.E.2d 664 (W.Va. 2000), and *Garvey v. State Farm Fire & Casualty Co.*, 48 Cal. 3d 395, 257 Cal. Rptr. 292, 770 P.2d 704 (Cal. 1989), merely discuss the efficient-proximate-cause rule, without reference to a competing anticoncurrent-causation clause. *Western National Mutual Insurance Co. v. University of North Dakota*, 2002 ND 63, ¶ 20, 643 N.W.2d 4, 13, holds that, where a state statutorily adopts the efficient proximate cause rule, insurance companies may not contract around it with an anticoncurrent-causation clause. The Bozeks have not cited any such statute in Illinois. Notifying the court of a potential issue and citing a handful of cases but without discussion is not the same as briefing and arguing an issue. Ill. S. Ct. R. 341(h)(7) (eff. Feb. 6, 2013). The Bozeks have inappropriately placed the burden of research and argument on the court in informing us that we "could" find the anticoncurrent-causation clause to be unenforceable. Only a minority of jurisdictions have found anticoncurrent-causation clauses to be unenforceable. *See, e.g., Boazova v. Safety Insurance Co.*, 462 Mass. 346, 968 N.E.2d 385, 394 (Mass. 2012). The majority of jurisdictions have rejected public policy challenges. *Id*. This is simply too complex an issue to address essentially *sua sponte*. The Bozeks have forfeited any public policy argument by virtue of insufficient briefing.

We have chosen to publish this decision, because there are no other reported cases in Illinois addressing anticoncurrent-causation clauses. However, we intend for a narrow application of this decision. We have touched upon, but not decided, many issues, such as: (1) whether efficient or dominant proximate cause is the default requisite causal nexus in the absence of contrary policy language; (2) whether the use of the phrase, "in sequence," as opposed to, "in *any* sequence," when applicable to the underlying facts, transforms an anticoncurrent-causation clause into a statement of the efficient-proximate-cause rule; and (3) whether public policy renders anticoncurrent-causation clauses unenforceable. We leave the resolution of these issues for future courts.

III. CONCLUSION

For the aforementioned reasons, we affirm the trial court's judgment.

NOTES AND QUESTIONS

1. *Ambiguity?* In *Bozek*, the court stated the insurer had misinterpreted the anti-concurrent causation exclusion to mean something different than both the court's interpretation and the policyholder's. Does that mean the language was ambiguous? If not, does that mean that only the court's interpretation was "reasonable"?

2. *Insufficient Briefing?* The *Bozek* court held the policyholder had forfeited the right to argue that anti-concurrent causation exclusions should not be enforced on public policy grounds because the policyholder's briefing of the argument was "insufficient." The court did not cite any authorities to support the conclusion that a party waives its right to have an argument addressed when the court finds the party "insufficiently" briefed the argument. Was the court's assertion of the "insufficient briefing" waiver doctrine, if it can be called that, simply the court's way of avoiding an argument for which it did not have an adequate response?

In its opinion, the *Bozek* court distinguished the next case, *Corban v. United Servs. Auto. Ass'n*, 20 So.3d 601 (Miss. 2009). As you read the case, consider whether the *Bozek* court's treatment of *Corban* is persuasive.

CORBAN V. UNITED SERVS. AUTO. ASS'N

20 So. 3d 601 (Miss. 2009)

En Banc

RANDOLPH, JUSTICE FOR THE COURT:

Dr. Magruder S. and Margaret Corban ("Corbans") incurred losses caused by physical damage to their Long Beach, Mississippi, residence during Hurricane Katrina on August 29, 2005. The Corbans had purchased a homeowner's policy and a flood policy from United Services Automobile Association Insurance Agency ("USAA"), both of which were in force at the time the losses were suffered.

The Corbans notified USAA of their claim for losses. USAA adjusters inspected the property and obtained an engineering report for an opinion as to whether the losses were caused by "wind damage. . . versus flood damage." Subsequently, USAA informed the Corbans that the majority of the physical damage to their property was the result of flooding and that payment for losses caused by flood, an excluded peril in the homeowner's policy, would not be made under that policy.

Dissatisfied with USAA's decision, the Corbans filed suit. After answering the Complaint, USAA filed a "Motion for Partial Summary Judgment." Subsequently, the Corbans filed a "Motion for Partial Summary Judgment." The competing motions focused on the ambiguity, *vel non,* of the "water damage" exclusion and the "anticoncurrent cause" ("ACC") clause contained in the homeowner's policy, *inter alia.* The Corbans further asserted that if the policy language was determined to be unambiguous, then the provisions, when read together, were contrary to Mississippi public policy.

Following a hearing, the Circuit Court of Harrison County, Mississippi, First Judicial District, entered an "Order Granting Partial Summary Judgment to [USAA] and Denying Partial Summary Judgment to [the Corbans] Regarding Anticoncurrent Causation Clause and Storm Surge Issues (With Findings of Fact and Conclusions of Law)." The circuit judge found that "storm surge" is an "excluded peril" within the "water damage definition of the subject policy"; that the "water damage" exclusion and ACC clause are "unambiguous"; and that, although expressing a contrary interpretation of the policy language, "the anticoncurrent causation clause will be applied herein as interpreted by the United States Fifth Circuit Court of Appeals, thereby barring coverage under the homeowner's policy for any damage caused by water as defined in the policy or caused concurrently or sequentially by wind and water in combination." The Corbans sought an interlocutory appeal of these rulings, which this Court granted.

FACTS

The Corbans had resided on East Beach Boulevard, Long Beach, Mississippi, several hundred feet from the Mississippi Gulf Coast, since 1988. The subject property was insured by two policies, a homeowner's policy and a flood policy, each procured from USAA. The insured property included a two-story dwelling, multi-car garage, guest cottage, gazebo, and potting shed, among other structures. Significant damage was wrought upon the Corbans' real and personal property during Hurricane Katrina, causing significant losses. The Corbans filed a claim seeking indemnity for their losses, in the amount of $ 1,607,926.

USAA assigned Chris Sims and Joe Howell to adjust the Corbans' claim. According to Howell, Sims retained an engineer to inspect the property because "[w]e were using engineers on large, significant losses to help determine whether there was wind damage . . . versus flood damage." Paul R. William, P.E., and Jim D. Wiethorn, P.E., of Haag Engineering Company ("Haag") inspected the property. Howell testified that no engineering report was necessary for a flood-policy claim as "it's obviously total flood damage in excess of the [flood] policy limit . . . ."

In October 2005, the Corbans received $250,000, the limit of liability for loss to the dwelling under the flood policy. Thereafter, the Corbans received an additional $100,000, the limit of liability for loss to contents under the flood policy. The Corbans also received $4,000 under the homeowner's policy for loss of jewelry, watches, furs, and silverware, and $1,900 under the homeowner's policy for refrigerated food losses.

In early 2006, Howell received the Haag report, which attributed all damage to "the first story living area to flooding and wave wash." After receiving the report, Howell inspected the property. Howell "determined what was to be paid on the wind loss[,]" relying on the Haag report and "[m]y observations of the loss and looking at the house and the damage that presented itself." Howell attributed none of the first-floor damage to wind, concluding that payment to the Corbans was limited to "replac[ing] the cottage roof and . . . replac[ing] the roof and some fascia repair and paint around the main house[,]" as well as for power washing and a "repair allowance" on the gazebo and the potting shed.[4]

In January 2006, the Corbans received $39,971.91 under "Coverage A—Dwelling" and "Coverage B—Other Structures" of the homeowner's policy for losses USAA attributed to wind damage. The Corbans also received $16,955.38 under the homeowner's policy for additional living expenses incurred. In February 2006, USAA issued a letter to the Corbans, stating that, based upon the Haag report, "[i]t was determined that the majority of the damage to your home was the result of flooding. Unfortunately, flood is

---

[4] Experts subsequently employed by the Corbans contend that the home and other structures were destroyed by wind before the "storm surge" arrived.

an excluded peril in your HO-3 Homeowners Policy and payment cannot be made for these damages." The Corbans finally received a payment of $21,077 under the homeowner's policy for personal property insured under a "personal articles floater." Thus, the Corbans received a total of $433,903.77 ($350,000 under the flood policy and $83,903.77 under the homeowner's policy), leaving $1,174,022.23 in claimed losses unsatisfied.

The Corbans filed suit based on a variety of contract and tort theories.

. . . .

USAA later filed a "Motion for Partial Summary Judgment," asserting, *inter alia,* that:

> (1) Storm surge is flood and is an excluded peril under the water damage exclusion.
>
> (2) The [Corbans] are judicially estopped from denying that the insured structures and contents were damaged by flood at least to the extent of the amount paid under the flood insurance policy. . . .

The Corbans then filed a "Motion for Partial Summary Judgment," maintaining that the ACC clause in the policy should be invalidated as ambiguous and contrary to Mississippi public policy, such that "Plaintiffs are entitled to judgment as a matter of law . . . ." USAA responded that "the ACC clause contained in [the] policy is unambiguous and should be enforced as written."

. . . .

The circuit judge found "storm surge" to be within the "water damage definition . . . and . . ., therefore, an excluded peril." The circuit judge further found that the "water damage" exclusion and ACC clause were "unambiguous." Finally, the circuit judge concluded that "the anticoncurrent causation clause will be applied herein as interpreted by the United States Fifth Circuit Court of Appeals, thereby barring coverage under the homeowner's policy for any damage caused by water as defined in the policy or caused concurrently or sequentially by wind and water in combination."

The Corbans' "Petition for Interlocutory Appeal" followed entry of the aforementioned order, and was granted by this Court.

ISSUES

. . . .

[T]his Court . . . will consider . . . the following issues:

> (1) Whether the circuit court erred in finding that "storm surge" is included in the "water damage" exclusion.

(2) Whether the circuit court erred in finding that the ACC clause is applicable in the case *sub judice*.

(3) Which party bears the burden of proof.

ANALYSIS

. . . .

In Mississippi, insurance policies:

> [A]re contracts, and as such, they are to be enforced according to their provisions. When parties to a contract make mutual promises (barring some defense or condition which excuses performance), they are entitled to the benefit of their bargain. Thus, insurance companies must be able to rely on their statements of coverage, exclusions, disclaimers, definitions, and other provisions, in order to receive the benefit of their bargain and to ensure that rates have been properly calculated.

Noxubee County, 883 So. 2d at 1166 (citations omitted).

The substantive contract law of this state likewise has been clearly declared by this Court to include the following concepts:

> [I]f a contract is clear and unambiguous, then it must be interpreted as written. . . . If a contract contains ambiguous or unclear language, then ambiguities must be resolved in favor of the non-drafting party. Ambiguities exist when a policy can be logically interpreted in two or more ways, where one logical interpretation provides for coverage. However, ambiguities do not exist simply because two parties disagree over the interpretation of a policy. Exclusions and limitations on coverage are also construed in favor of the insured. Language in exclusionary clauses must be "clear and unmistakable," as those clauses are strictly interpreted.

United States Fid. & Guar. Co. v. Martin, 998 So. 2d 956, 963 (Miss. 2008) (internal citations omitted). *See also Frazier v. N. Miss. Shopping Ctr., Inc.,* 458 So. 2d 1051, 1054 (Miss. 1984) ("[a] construction leading to an absurd, harsh or unreasonable result in a contract should be avoided unless the terms are express and free of doubt.").

It is undisputed that the policy provides "all-risk" coverage as to "Coverage A—Dwelling" and "Coverage B—Other Structures," such that "direct physical loss" caused by any risk (i.e., peril(s)) not expressly excluded is covered. USAA concedes that "[t]his means that all risks to the structures are covered, other than those risks specifically excluded from coverage." It is likewise undisputed that the policy provides only "named-perils" coverage as to "Coverage C—Personal Property," such that only "direct physical loss" caused by a listed peril is covered, unless such *loss* is expressly excluded. The Corbans concede that the policy provides only "named perils" coverage as to "Coverage C—Personal Property." Finally, it is undisputed that the provision excluding "water damage" loss, which includes the ACC clause, excludes loss, not perils.

Regarding pertinent coverage and exclusions, there is no dispute that under Coverages A, B, and C, any loss caused by wind is covered, while any loss caused by "water damage," as defined, is excluded.

. . . .

1. Whether the circuit court erred in finding that "storm surge" is included in the "water damage" exclusion.

The policy expressly excludes, in pertinent part, "[w]ater damage, meaning: (1) flood, surface water, waves, tidal water, overflow of a body of water, or spray from any of these, whether or not driven by wind . . . ." The Corbans maintain that "storm surge" is a covered peril because "[t]he policy itself defines 'water damage' and purposely does not include storm surge within that definition." USAA responds that "storm surge" is obviously an "excluded peril" under the "water damage" exclusion.

The circuit court ruled that:

> All of the sources reviewed by this [c]ourt refer to storm surge as ocean or lake water being pushed by or affected by wind causing the water to rise and move toward or onto shore. Many of these sources refer to this surge as combining with the normal tides or as causing a rising of sea level. Certainly by these definitions, storm surge could be considered surface water, waves, tidal water, or even overflow of a body of water. Storm surge is included in the policy terminology delineating the meaning of "water damage" by virtue of its definition. [*Leonard*] and [*Tuepker*], and cases cited therein also found that "storm surge" is included in such a definition. The lack of the words "storm surge" do[es] not either render the provision ambiguous or provide coverage for storm surge.

"Storm surge is a phenomenon associated with hurricanes. Atmospheric conditions and wind forces combine to force tidal waters ashore and temporarily inundate areas of normally dry land." *Leonard v. Nationwide Mut. Ins. Co.,* 438 F. Supp. 2d 684, 692 (S.D. Miss. 2006). In *Leonard* and *Tuepker,* both the United States district court and the Fifth Circuit found that "storm surge" was included within comparable "water damage" exclusions. *See Tuepker,* 507 F.3d at 353; *Leonard,* 499 F.3d at 436–38; *Leonard,* 438 F. Supp. 2d at 693; *Tuepker v. State Farm Fire & Cas. Co.,* 2006 U.S. Dist. LEXIS 34710, 2006 WL 1442489, at *3 (S.D. Miss. 2006) (affirmed in part; reversed in part and remanded by *Tuepker,* 507 F.3d at 346).

In *Leonard,* the Fifth Circuit held that:

> Courts have interpreted water-damage exclusions like the one found in the Leonards' policy to encompass the peril of wind-driven inundation by water, or storm surge for ages. Mississippi courts have upheld such exclusions before and after Hurricane Katrina. . . . Further, this court's most recent consideration of the term "flood" also supports Nationwide's contention that the term is unambiguous and has a concrete meaning, whether or not used in the context of an insurance policy. *See Vanderbrook v. Unitrin Preferred Ins. Co. (In re Katrina Canal Breaches Litig.),* 495 F.3d 191, 2007 U.S. App. LEXIS 18349, 2007 WL 2200004, at *16–18 (5th Cir. 2007) . . . . No decision of this court or any other of which we are aware endorses the Leonards' view that storm surge is a unique meteorological phenomenon not contemplated by water-damages exclusions like Nationwide's. . . .
>
> The phrase "storm surge" is little more than a synonym for a "tidal wave" or wind-driven flood, both of which are excluded perils. The omission of the specific term "storm surge" does not create ambiguity in the policy regarding coverage available in a hurricane and does not entitle the Leonards to recovery for their flood-induced damages.

Leonard, 499 F.3d at 437–38 (footnotes omitted).

We affirm the circuit court's ruling that "storm surge" is contained unambiguously within the "water damage" exclusion. This Court finds that "storm surge" is plainly encompassed within the "flood" or "overflow of a body of water" portions of the "water damage" definition, and no other "logical interpretation" exists. *Martin,* 998 So. 2d at 963.

2. Whether the circuit court erred in finding that the ACC clause is applicable in the case *sub judice.*

A.

The circuit judge first stated that "[a] plain common sense reading of the policy, without resort to legal jargon or theories, would seem to be the proper means to interpret provisions in an insurance policy that average citizens are expected to read and understand." The circuit judge then deemed the "water damage" exclusion and ACC clause to be "unambiguous," observing that:

> Using the simple rules learned in middle school or high school English classes, the exclusion provides that it does not cover a loss caused by water damage. The second sentence refers to "[s]uch loss" being excluded even if in combination with or in any sequence to other causes. The term "[s]uch loss" can only refer to the loss caused by water damage mentioned in the first sentence

> of the exclusion. It is that loss and that loss only that is excluded by the plain language of the provision. The remainder of the second sentence goes on to elaborate on the exclusion by providing that the water damage is excluded no matter what other causes exist and whether the water damage occurs first, last, or simultaneously with some other cause. This simple, basic interpretation of the language used and sentence structure used bars coverage for water damage and only the water damage, whether occurring alone or in any order with another cause.

. . . .

That ruling set the stage for this appeal, i.e., a fair reading and interpretation of the policy in issue by this Court.

The ACC clause reads:

> **SECTION I—EXCLUSIONS**
>
> 1. We do not insure for *loss* caused directly or indirectly by any of the following. Such *loss* is *excluded regardless of any other cause or event contributing concurrently or in any sequence to the loss.*

(emphasis added). The terms "loss," "concurrently," and "in any sequence" are pertinent to our inquiry. The policy lends limited assistance to this endeavor, as it fails to define those terms. Thus, "those words are afforded their ordinary and popular meaning." *Noxubee County*, 883 So. 2d at 1165. Additionally, the use of these terms elsewhere in the policy can assist our inquiry. *See Martin*, 998 So. 2d at 963 (citing *J&W Foods Corp.*, 723 So. 2d at 552) ("[a] policy must be considered as a whole, with all relevant clauses together.").

"Loss"

We first observe that the parties and trial court in this proceeding, as well as other courts in cases cited, have conflated the terms "loss" and "damage." A "loss" is incurred by an insured and typically, but not always, follows "damage" to his or her property.

"Property damage" is defined within the policy as "physical damage to, or destruction of tangible property, including loss of use of this property." The policy does not cover or exclude "damage," but rather covers or excludes "loss," and it is to "loss" that the deductible is applied.

With "loss" undefined in the policy, we look for its "ordinary and popular meaning." *Noxubee County,* 883 So. 2d at 1165. Elsewhere, "loss" has been defined as "1. An act or instance of losing. 2. One that is lost. 3. Injury or suffering caused by losing or by being lost." Webster's II New College Dictionary 647 (3d ed. 2001). *See also* Bryan A. Garner, *A Dictionary of Modern Legal Usage,* 538 (2d ed. 1995) (to "lose" is "to suffer the deprivation of; to part with."); Black's Law Dictionary 54 (4th ed. 1968) ("actual loss" is defined as "[o]ne resulting from the real and substantial destruction of the property insured.").

Based upon policy usage and the "ordinary and popular meaning," *Noxubee County,* 883 So. 2d at 1165, we find that loss occurs at that point in time when the insured suffers deprivation of, physical damage to, or destruction of the property insured. This determination is likewise consistent with "Loss Settlement" provisions of the homeowner's policy, which grant USAA the option of settling "[c]overed property losses" by paying the insured "the *cost* to repair or restore the property to the condition it was in *just before the loss.*" *See* Appendix (emphasis added). . . .

No reasonable person can seriously dispute that if a loss occurs, caused by either a covered peril (wind) or an excluded peril (water), that particular loss is not changed by any subsequent cause or event. Nor can the loss be excluded after it has been suffered, as the right to be indemnified for a loss caused by a covered peril attaches at that point in time when the insured suffers deprivation of, physical damage to, or destruction of the property insured. An insurer cannot avoid its obligation to indemnify the insured based upon an event which occurs subsequent to the covered loss.

The insured's right to be indemnified for a covered loss vests at time of loss. Once the duty to indemnify arises, it cannot be extinguished by a successive cause or event. *See Bland v. Bland,* 629 So. 2d 582, 589 (Miss. 1993) ("[b]enefits *vest* under a casualty policy when the event occurs . . . .") (emphasis added); *Pitts v. Am. Sec. Life Ins. Co.,* 931 F.2d 351, 358 (5th Cir. 1991) ("[s]ince the policy . . . was in full force at the time Pitts was injured, his benefits under the policy *vested.*") (emphasis added). The same principle applies in reverse. In the case of a loss caused by an excluded peril, that particular loss is not changed by any subsequent covered peril or event. Nor can that excluded loss become a covered loss, after it has been suffered.

"Loss to property can consist of *many losses* because property can consist of *many elements,* and 'loss' need *not* refer *only* to the *totality of the damage* and in fact *should not when different forces have caused different damage.*" Appleman on Insurance § 192.03[H] (2009) (emphasis added). The subject homeowner's policy insures "for direct, physical loss" to property. Following the policy language and the principles enumerated herein, the Corbans are entitled to recover for all covered "direct, physical loss[es]" to the property,[20] not otherwise excluded.

"Concurrently"

A hurricane includes a number of weather conditions, elements, and/or forces, at times acting dependently, at other times independently.

[20] Under Coverages A, B, and C, the "Perils Insured Against" section of the homeowner's policy provides coverage "for direct, physical *loss to the property* . . . ." (Emphasis added).

USAA argues that this policy excludes losses caused by perils which may coexist. We examine the policy to determine if this assertion is supported by its language. Before that determination can be made, we must render a fair reading and interpretation of the express language "concurrently."

The term "concurrently" is defined as "1. Occurring at the same time. 2. Operating in conjunction. 3. Meeting or tending to meet at the same point: Convergent." Webster's II New College Dictionary at 234. *See also* Black's Law Dictionary at 363 (defining "concurrent" as "[r]unning together; . . . acting in conjunction; . . . contributing to the same event; contemporaneous").

Thus, the exclusion applies only in the event that the perils act in conjunction, as an indivisible force, occurring at the same time, to cause direct physical damage resulting in loss. In that event, we accept the Fifth Circuit's interpretation of Mississippi law, and would apply the ACC clause to exclude coverage.

However, the facts presented in the case *sub judice* do not reveal a claim by either party that an "indivisible" force (wind and flood), occurring at the same time, caused direct physical damage resulting in simultaneous loss to the property. Based upon the record as it now stands, and as presented by both parties, the subject perils acted in sequence, not concurrently, i.e., at different times, causing different damage, resulting in separate losses. It is only when the two perils converge at the same point in time, contemporaneously and operating in conjunction, that there is a "concurrent" cause or event. If the wind peril causes damage resulting in a loss either before or after the water peril ("flood") causes damage resulting in a loss, the losses are *not* "concurrent." Only if it can be proven that the perils (wind and flood) contemporaneously converged, operating in conjunction to cause loss, that the "concurrent" provision will apply. In that circumstance, the policy clearly excludes coverage.

"In Any Sequence"

This Court interprets the term "in any sequence" to mean "sequentially." The term "sequentially" is defined as "1. Forming or marked by a sequence, as of notes or units." Webster's II New College Dictionary at 1008. *See also* Garner, *A Dictionary of Modern Legal Usage* at 795 (" '[s]equential' means 'forming a sequence or consequence.' ").

"If a contract contains ambiguous or unclear language, then ambiguities must be resolved in favor of the non-drafting party. . . . Exclusions and limitations on coverage are also construed in favor of the insured. Language in exclusionary clauses must be 'clear and unmistakable,' as those clauses are strictly interpreted." *Martin,* 998 So. 2d at 963. Relatedly:

> Where the policy is subject to two interpretations, equally reasonable, that which gives the greater indemnity to the insured

> will prevail. If one construction, looking to the other provisions of the policy, and to its general object and scope, would lead to an unreasonable result, such construction must be abandoned, and that construction adopted which will be more consistent with reason. In all cases the policy must be liberally construed in favor of the insured, in order to accomplish the purpose of the insurance.

Southern Home Ins. Co. v. Wall, 156 Miss. 865, 127 So. 298, 299 (1930).

The term "in any sequence" is contained within an exclusionary clause for "water damage" losses. The term is undefined in the policy. As "loss occurs at that point in time when the insured suffers deprivation of, physical damage to, or destruction of the property insured[,]" this term cannot be used to devest an insured's right of indemnity for a covered loss, as such an interpretation conflicts with other provisions of the USAA policy. For instance, "Section I—Conditions" regarding "Insurable Interest and Limit of Liability" provides that, "in any one loss," USAA will not be liable "for more than the amount of the *insured's interest at the time of loss* . . . ." *See* Appendix (emphasis added). Moreover, "Section I—Conditions" regarding "Loss Settlement" states that USAA has the option of paying "the *cost to repair or restore* the *property to* the *condition* it was in *just before the loss*." *Id.* (emphasis added). Additionally, the "Replacement Cost Coverage—Personal Property" section states that "*[r]eplacement cost* means the *cost, at the time of loss* . . . ." *Id.* (emphasis added). Finally, the "Loss Settlement" provision within the "Special Coverage on Jewelry, Watches, Furs and Silverware" section provides that "[t]he *value* of the covered property . . . will be *set at* the *time of loss or damage*[,]" and that USAA has the option of paying "*the cost to repair or restore the property to the condition it was in just before the loss*." *See id.* (emphasis added).

These provisions irreconcilably conflict with the "in any sequence" language, thereby creating an ambiguity. Our precedent requires this Court to construe an "equally reasonable" interpretation in favor of the nondrafting, insured party (the Corbans). *Wall,* 127 So. at 299. Therefore, this Court concludes that the "in any sequence" language in the policy may not be used to devest the insureds of their right to be indemnified for covered losses. *See Martin,* 998 So. 2d at 963; *Wall,* 127 So. at 300 (if "[t]he two clauses of the policy are so conflicting that they cannot stand together—one must give way to the other; and, under the principles stated, the provision most favorable to the insured must be upheld.").

B.

As aptly stated by the circuit judge, "simple rules learned in middle school or high school English classes" dictate that the ACC clause applies only to losses caused by "water damage." As such, with respect to the "water damage" exclusion, based upon the factual scenario presented to this Court, we conclude that the ACC clause should be read as follows:

SECTION I—EXCLUSIONS

> 1. We do not insure for *loss* caused directly or indirectly by [water damage]. Such loss [from water damage] is excluded regardless of any other cause or event [wind damage] contributing concurrently or in any sequence to the loss [from water damage].

(emphasis added).

In assessing the applicability, *vel non,* of the ACC clause, we reiterate that different perils from a hurricane generally, but not without exception, result in separate damage and loss. The policy establishes a duty to indemnify for covered "direct physical losses" under Coverages A, B, and C. The ACC clause applies only if and when covered and excluded perils contemporaneously converge, operating in conjunction, to cause damage resulting in loss to the insured property. If the insured property is separately damaged by a covered or excluded peril, the ACC clause is inapplicable. If damage is caused by a covered peril, the insured is entitled to indemnification for the covered loss, as the insured's right to recover for the loss has vested. Conversely, if the damage is caused by an excluded peril, the insured is not entitled to indemnification for that uncovered loss.

Based on the evidence thus far presented, the same loss with multiple causes is not at issue here. Thus, a finder of fact must determine what losses, if any, were caused by wind, and what losses, if any, were caused by flood. If the property suffered damage from wind, and separately was damaged by flood, the insured is entitled to be compensated for those losses caused by wind. Any loss caused by "[flood] damage" is excluded. If the property first suffers damage from wind, resulting in a loss, whether additional "[flood] damage" occurs is of no consequence, as the insured has suffered a compensable wind-damage loss. Conversely, if the property first suffers damage from flood, resulting in a loss, and then wind damage occurs, the insured can only recover for losses attributable to wind.

. . . .

We conclude that the ACC clause has no application for losses caused by wind peril. An insurer may not abrogate its duty to indemnify for such loss by the occurrence of a subsequent, excluded cause or event, a position advanced by amicus Nationwide. According to Nationwide, the loss occurred in the same event, which they contend was the hurricane. Nationwide unconvincingly posits that loss is not determined until the hurricane is over.

Nationwide contends that any loss which the "storm surge" would have caused anyway is excluded. Such an interpretation fails to consider the common understanding of "loss," and would avoid payment for covered "losses," an unreasonable result. Such an interpretation is contradicted by the principle that all "[e]xclusions and limitations on coverage are . . . construed in favor of the insured." *Martin,* 998 So. 2d at 963.

The parties to this action agree that the ACC clause has no application to different losses caused by different perils. This Court finds that within the context of this case, under Coverages A, B, and C, any loss caused by damages resulting from wind is a covered loss, while any loss caused by damages resulting from the "storm surge" is an excluded loss. Applying the "ordinary and popular meaning[,]"*Noxubee County,* 883 So. 2d at 1165, of the terms "loss," "concurrently," and "in any sequence," the ACC clause is inapplicable. We are in accord with the district judge in *Dickinson,* who stated:

> *It is clear to me that storm surge flooding cannot be a cause (directly or indirectly) of damage that occurs before the storm surge flooding reaches the insured property, i.e. before the excluded peril of flooding occurs. . . .*
>
> *Wind damage that precedes the arrival of the storm surge and damage that happens after the storm surge arrives are separate losses from separate causes, and not concurrent causes or sequential causes of the same loss*[.] . . .
>
> *Wind damage that precedes flood damage happens in a sequence of events, but the wind damage is not caused, directly or indirectly, by storm surge flooding, and the damage done by the wind is therefore not a part of "the loss" the ACC refers to.* Since the ACC does not apply to this separate wind damage, the wind damage is a covered loss. The insurance benefits that apply to this covered loss vest in the insured at the time the loss occurs. Wind and flood were separate and not concurrent causes of damage to the insured property, and the wind damage that precedes the storm surge does not contribute, sequentially or concurrently, to "the [excluded] loss" caused by storm surge flooding and referred to by the ACC.

Dickinson, 2008 U.S. Dist. LEXIS 34354, 2008 WL 1913957, at *2–4 (emphasis added).

After a thorough examination of Mississippi case law, the evidence presented to date in this case, the briefs of the parties and amici, and the USAA policy at issue, this Court declares the ACC clause inapplicable. We respectfully reject the proposition that, under the subject ACC clause, "*indivisible*[23] *damage caused by both* excluded perils and covered perils or other causes is not covered." *Tuepker,* 507 F.3d at 354 (emphasis added).

. . . .

[23] The term "indivisible" is found nowhere in the subject homeowner's policy.

We conclude that the circuit judge correctly interpreted the ACC clause, but then erred in applying the Fifth Circuit's "*Erie-guess*" regarding its application. The ACC clause is inapplicable here. All "direct physical losses" under Coverages A, B, and C which are caused by wind are covered. All "direct physical losses" under Coverages A, B, and C which are caused by "[flood] damage" are excluded. Any "[flood] damage" losses to which a covered peril (in this case, wind) "contribut[ed] concurrently" are excluded. As this presents issues of fact for jury determination, we next consider the applicable burden of proof.

3. Which party bears the burden of proof.

The parties agree that the subject policy provides "all-risk" coverage as to "Coverage A—Dwelling" and "Coverage B—Other Structures." "The purpose of an 'All-Risk' policy is to insure losses when the cause of the loss is unknown or the specific risk was not explicitly contemplated by either party." Lee R. Russ & Thomas F. Segalla, 7 Couch on Insurance § 101:7 (3d ed. 2007). Under such coverage, "the insured has the initial burden to prove that the loss occurred." *Id.* Thereafter, the burden shifts to the insurer, as "[i]n an all-risk . . . policy where an exclusion is specifically pleaded as an affirmative defense the burden of proving such affirmative defense is upon the insurer . . . ." *Lunday v. Lititz Mut. Ins. Co.*, 276 So. 2d 696, 698 (Miss. 1973). *See also Morrison Grain Co. v. Utica Mut. Ins. Co.*, 632 F.2d 424, 430 (5th Cir. 1980) ("[i]t would seem to be inconsistent with the broad protective purposes of 'all risks' insurance to impose on the insured . . . the burden of proving the precise cause of the loss or damage.").

. . . .

This Court finds that with respect to the "all-risk" coverage of "Coverage A—Dwelling" and "Coverage B—Other Structures," the Corbans are required to prove a "direct, physical loss to property described." Thereafter, USAA assumes the burden to prove, by a preponderance of the evidence, that the causes of the losses are excluded by the policy, in this case, "[flood] damage." USAA is obliged to indemnify the Corbans for all losses under "Coverage A—Dwelling" and "Coverage B—Other Structures" which USAA cannot establish, by a preponderance of the evidence, to have been *caused* or *concurrently contributed to* by "[flood] damage." "Contributed to" comes into play only when "[flood] damage" is a cause or event *contributing concurrently* to the loss. Pursuant to the policy language, only if proof of a "concurrent" cause is presented to a jury for consideration would the jury receive an instruction including the policy phrase "contributing concurrently." Likewise, striking the proper balance, under "Coverage C—Personal Property," the plaintiff must prove that the loss was caused by a peril insured against, not "caused or contributed to." Upon proper instruction, these determinations are for a jury.

. . . .

CONCLUSION

Accordingly, the circuit court did not err in ruling that "storm surge" is included in the "water damage" exclusion. However, the circuit court erred in holding that the ACC clause is applicable in the case *sub judice*. Therefore, the "Order Granting Partial Summary Judgment to [USAA] and Denying Partial Summary Judgment to [the Corbans] Regarding Anticoncurrent Causation Clause and Storm Surge Issues (With Findings of Fact and Conclusions of Law)" is affirmed in part and reversed in part, and this case is remanded for further proceedings consistent with this opinion. Moreover, as there are questions of fact for jury resolution, we set forth the burden of proof borne by each party under Coverages A, B, and C.

NOTES AND QUESTIONS

1. *Ambiguity.* The *Corban* court found the anti-concurrent causation exclusion ambiguous. What exactly was the ambiguity? Was the court's analysis persuasive?

2. *Wind Versus Water Damage.* The *Corban* court's approach requires a factfinder to determine how much damage was caused by wind versus how much by water. Is that possible in situations where the home is no longer there? What type of evidence can the parties marshal to prove wind versus water damage?

3. *Burden of Proof.* Under an "all risk" homeowners policy, the policyholder simply has the burden of proving that a "physical injury" or "property damage" caused a loss. The burden of proof then shifts to the insurer to prove an exclusion applies. If the policy is a named-peril policy, however, then the policyholder has the burden of proving the loss was caused by the named peril.

4. *Is Impartiality Possible?* If the case is being tried to a jury comprised of homeowners in an area destroyed by a hurricane, is it realistic to believe a jury might find in favor of an insurer? "More than 6,600 lawsuits were filed in federal court in New Orleans in connection with Hurricane Katrina. In Mississippi, one insurer involved in the Hurricane Katrina litigation filed a motion to transfer the lawsuits out of Mississippi on the basis of a survey that showed that 49% of the people in southern Mississippi 'believe that insurance executives are on the same level as child molesters.' " Christopher C. French, *The Role of the Profit Imperative in Risk Management*, 17 U. Pa. J. Bus. L. 1081, 1133 (2015) (*citing* Jay M. Feinman, Delay, Deny, Defend: Why Insurance Companies Don't Pay Claims and What You Can Do About It 145–47 (2010), and Benick, *The Flood After the Storm: The Hurricane Katrina Homeowners' Insurance Litigation*, 4 Bus. L. Brief (Am. U.) 51 (Fall 2007)). What can an insurer do to ensure it receives a fair trial in front of an impartial factfinder?

5. *Public Policy and the Enforceability of Anti-Concurrent Causation Exclusions.* Both the *Corban* and *Bozek* courts declined to address the issue of

whether anti-concurrent causation exclusions violate public policy, but the *Bozek* court noted the majority of the courts that have considered the issue have concluded such exclusions do not violate public policy. That does not mean, however, that such exclusions are enforceable in all states. For example, some courts have held anti-concurrent causation exclusions are unenforceable if the application of them leads to results inconsistent with the results dictated by the efficient proximate cause doctrine. *See, e.g., Murray v. State Farm Fire and Cas. Co.*, 509 S.E.2d 1 (W. Va. 1998); *Safeco Ins. Co. of America v. Hirschmann*, 773 P.2d 413 (Wash. 1989); *Howell v. State Farm Fire & Casualty Co.*, 218 Cal. App. 3d 1446 (1990).

6. *The National Flood Insurance Program (NFIP).* "Flooding is the most common catastrophe in America and the world, accounting for approximately 90% of all catastrophic losses annually. For the past thirty years in America, floods have on average caused more than $8 billion in damages annually, and most of the damage is uninsured. Hurricanes Katrina and Sandy alone caused over $160 billion in damage." Christopher C. French, *Insuring Floods: The Most Common and Devastating Natural Catastrophes in America*, 60 Vill. L. Rev. 53, 53 (2015). The reason most flood losses are uninsured is because damage caused by flooding is excluded from coverage under homeowners insurance. Thus, for areas prone to flooding, whether from water associated with hurricanes or otherwise, the homeowner must purchase a separate policy sold by private insurers such as USAA in the *Corban* case. Although sold by private insurers, flood policies are actually underwritten by the National Flood Insurance Program (NFIP) and claims are paid by the NFIP, not the private insurer who sold and administers the policy. *See id.* at 65–67. The NFIP is fraught with problems. The coverage provided under it is poor (a maximum of $250,000 with exclusions for areas such as basements and landscaping), there are low participation rates in it (7% of homeowners), and it repeatedly is insolvent (currently a $24 billion deficit). *Id.* at 68–69. Attempts to reform the NFIP have been met with political resistance.

7. *Insurer Conflicts of Interest.* For the American homeowners who have flood insurance and homeowners insurance (about 10% of the Hurricane Katrina victims, 50% of Hurricane Sandy victims, and 7% of homeowners nationwide), the wind versus water issue arises every time a hurricane hits because homeowners insurance excludes coverage for flood damage while NFIP policies only cover water damage. The private insurers who administer the NFIP policies have "a financial incentive to claim that most, if not all, of a concurrently caused loss is due to water. Doing so ensures that the federal government, instead of the homeowners insurer, will pay for the loss." Christopher C. French, *Hurricanes, Fraud And Insurance: The Supreme Court Weighs In But Does Not Wade Into The Concurrent Causation Conundrum In State Farm Fire And Casualty Company v. Rigsby*, 165 U. Pa. L. Rev. Online 99, 100 (2017) (citations omitted). In 2016, the conflict of interest this situation creates was before the U.S. Supreme Court in *State Farm Fire and Casualty Company v. United States ex rel. Rigsby*, 137 S. Ct. 436 (2016). In *Rigsby*, the insurer's claims handlers alleged they were instructed to fraudulently shift

losses that should be covered by the private homeowners insurance to the NFIP program. Although the Supreme Court did not substantively address the concurrent causation problem, the Court affirmed a jury award of $3.7 million, which included a treble damages award and attorneys' fees, under the False Claims Act (FCA), which imposes civil liability on any entity who "knowingly presents . . . a false or fraudulent claim for payment or approval" to the federal government. *Rigsby*, 794 F.3d 457, 465 (5th Cir. 2015), *aff'd*, 137 S. Ct. 436 (2016).

EXERCISE

1. Draft a 3-page memo in which you compare and contrast the analysis of the *Bozek* and *Corban* decisions regarding the enforceability of anti-concurrent causation exclusions and then argue which court's reasoning is the most persuasive and why.

IV. PROOFS OF LOSS AND EXAMINATIONS UNDER OATH

Property policies typically require the policyholder to submit a sworn "proof of loss" within a certain period of time before an insurer's obligation to pay becomes due. The proof of loss requirement is similar to the notice requirement under liability policies. By requiring the policyholder to timely submit a sworn proof of loss, the insurer ensures that it will be able to conduct a timely investigation of the claim and that the policyholder swears the loss occurred and the value of the loss.

As part of its investigation of a loss, insurers also can require policyholders to submit to an "examination under oath," which is similar to a deposition in that the policyholder swears to tell the truth and a court reporter records the policyholder's answers to the insurer's questions. Unlike depositions, however, no rules of civil procedure control the attorneys' conduct. This leaves both insurers and policyholders ample room for "creative" lawyering.

The next two cases are examples of common issues that arise related to proofs of loss and examinations under oath.

SIRAVO V. GREAT AM. INS. CO.

410 A.2d 116 (R.I. 1980)

WEISBERGER, JUSTICE.

[The insured's home was completely destroyed by fire. She sued her insurers in federal district court on two fire insurance policies, which had been issued to her in conformity with the forms specified by state statutes. The insurers had three defenses: the insured's arson; the insured's misrepresentation of the extent of loss; and the insured's failure to timely file a sworn proof of loss. A general jury verdict was entered for the insurers, and plaintiff appealed. The First Circuit found that all but one of plaintiff's grounds for appeal lacked merit, but that this one ground turned on a question of law that the First Circuit concluded should be answered by the Supreme Court of Rhode Island.]

The United States Court of Appeals for the First Circuit . . . has certified to us the following question of law:

> Does an insured's late filing of the sworn proof of loss, which under the standard form of fire insurance policy, R.I. Gen. Laws § 27–5–3, he is supposed to render within sixty (60) days after the loss, bar the insured's recovery under the policy in the absence of the company's proving prejudice stemming from the insured's failure to comply with the time limits contained in said proof of loss provision?

. . . .

The plaintiff relies on *Pickering v. American Employers Insurance Co.*, 109 R.I. 143, 282 A.2d 584 (1971) to argue that her failure to file the proof of loss within sixty days should not bar recovery unless defendants are able to demonstrate that they were thereby prejudiced. In *Pickering*, the plaintiff sought recovery on her automobile liability insurance policy for injuries caused by an uninsured motorist. Among the defenses raised by the insurer was the plaintiff's failure to comply with three provisions included in the policy. Those provisions declared that the giving of notice of a loss and the filing of a sworn written proof of claim should be done "as soon as practicable," while copies of legal process served in the uninsured motorist's suit were to be forwarded to the insurer "immediately."

In *Pickering*, we defined the term "notice" to include such items as the furnishing of a proof of claim and a copy of the summons and complaint. We then held that an insurer could not rely on any of the so called "notice" provisions of its policy unless it could demonstrate that it had been prejudiced by the lack of notice. . . .

. . . .

Although both notice and proof of loss provisions serve a broad common purpose of informing an insurer of the loss for which a claim is made, the two are distinct. The sole purpose of a notice of loss provision is to afford the insurer a seasonable opportunity for investigation to protect its interests. The purpose of a proof of loss, on the other hand, is to afford the insurer an adequate opportunity to protect its interests by facilitating its investigation.

We believe, however, that the distinction does not warrant a refusal to extend *Pickering* to proof of loss provisions. *Pickering* required that an automobile insurer show prejudice resulting from an untimely notice of loss. Such prejudice would result from an insurer's inability to conduct any investigation until the time that notice of loss is provided. Without notice of loss, an insurer can conduct no investigation at all. In contrast, an insured's untimely compliance with a proof of loss provision may adversely affect the adequacy, but not the existence, of an insurer's opportunity to investigate a claim. The Supreme Court of Wisconsin has noted, "There is no great hurry there [to furnish a proof of loss], such as there is when loss occurs and the insurer must be notified so that it may proceed . . . ." *Britz v. American Insurance Co. of Newark, N.J.*, 2 Wis. 2d 192, 202, 86 N.W.2d 18, 23 (1957). We therefore conclude that logic and reason impel a showing of prejudice, even more forcefully, before a declaration of forfeiture may be based upon an insured's untimely compliance with a proof of loss provision. For this purpose, we analogize a proof of loss provision to the so called group of "notice" provisions at issue in *Pickering*.

. . . .

We therefore apply the *Pickering* rule and hold that an insurer cannot rely on an insured's failure to submit a timely proof of loss under the standard form of fire insurance policy in order to defeat recovery unless the insurer can demonstrate that it has been prejudiced by the late filing.

We thus answer the question certified to us in the negative.

NOTES AND QUESTIONS

1. *Timing of Proofs of Loss*. Property insurance policies typically require that the policyholder submit, within a specified number of days (often 60 days) after the loss, a written document, typically on a form provided by the insurer, that sets forth considerable detail about the policyholder's loss and claim. *See, e.g.*, Sample Homeowners Policy, Conditions, § C.8.

2. *Life Insurance*. In life insurance, a beneficiary will submit to the insurer a "proof of death." This simple form will be accompanied by a copy (usually certified) of the death certificate and perhaps some other documentation establishing the entitlement of the beneficiary to the proceeds. Normally, the only time limit for submitting a proof of death is whatever statute of limitations applies to contract actions in the particular locale. Proving a loss in life insurance rarely raises complex issues. Indeed, few events are more unambiguous than death. There are, however, situations in which the content of the proof of death may be quite significant. If, for example, a claim is made for accidental death benefits in circumstances where the presence of an "accidental" cause is not obvious, the evidence contained in the proof of death will be very important. Also, if the insured's death is sought to be proved circumstantially (i.e., through absence or disappearance) instead of directly (i.e., through the existence of a dead body), the content of the proof of death will be important. Some policies attempt to deal with the issue through a provision for proof of death based on unexplained absence. In the absence of a controlling policy provision or a controlling statute, death might be

established by invoking the common law presumption. Ordinarily, the test to invoke the presumption requires the claimant to allege and prove an unexplained absence for seven years, a diligent unsuccessful search for the *cestui que vie*, and circumstances justifying the conclusion that death is the probable reason for the absence, such as the individual's failure to communicate with those persons most likely to hear from him. *See Malone v. Reliastar Life Ins. Co.*, 558 F.3d 683 (7th Cir. 2009) (applying Indiana law); *Borzage v. Metropolitan Life Insurance Co.*, 270 A.2d 688 (Conn. Cir. Ct. 1970).

3. *Does Compliance with Proof of Loss Requirements Ever Matter?* As *Siravo* suggests, a prejudice requirement is typically imposed by courts in situations where the insurer seeks to deny coverage for noncompliance with a proof of loss requirement. *See also National Union Fire Insurance Co. v. Federal Deposit Insurance Corp.*, 957 P.2d 357 (Kan. 1998). If the proof of loss is deficient on its face, should the insurer be required to notify the policyholder of the deficiency and give the policyholder an opportunity to correct it? *See Tennessee Farmers Mutual Insurance Co. v. Wheeler*, 341 S.E.2d 898 (Ga. Ct. App. 1986). Also, many courts have held that the policyholder need only "substantially comply" with the proof of loss requirement. *See, e.g., Hartford Fire Insurance Co. v. Himelfarb*, 736 A.2d 295 (Md. 1999); *Allstate Insurance Co. v. Charity*, 496 S.E.2d 430 (Va. 1998). Plus, there is the possibility that the insurer might waive or be estopped from asserting the requirement. *See Cotton States Mutual Insurance Co. v. Walker*, 500 S.E.2d 487 (Ga. Ct. App. 1998) (insurer's agent allegedly told policyholder's spouse that proof of loss needed to be redone, that detailed information had to be provided, and that she "didn't have to be in any big hurry"). After all of this, what is left of the proof of loss requirement?

4. *Proof of Loss Forms and the NFIP.* Unlike the common law in most states, which requires that the insurer prove it was prejudiced by a late or deficient submission of a proof of loss in order for a forfeiture of coverage to result, under the NFIP, "the requirement to submit a proof of loss form in accordance with the terms of NFIP policy is strictly enforced by courts." Christopher C. French, *Insuring Floods: The Most Common and Devastating Natural Catastrophes in America*, 60 Vill. L. Rev. 53, 68 (2015) (*citing Shuford v. Fidelity Nat'l Prop. & Cas. Ins. Co.*, 508 F.3d 1337, 1342 (11th Cir. 2007)).

5. *False Swearing.* Many property insurance policies contain a clause that provides the policy is void if the policyholder willfully conceals or misrepresents a material fact concerning a loss. Absent a statute to the contrary, no separate requirement exists that requires the insurer to show prejudice from the false swearing. Obviously, one place where false swearing is likely to occur is in the proof of loss. False swearing can arise, however, in any aspect of post-loss investigation and processing of the claim. *See Fine v. Bellefonte Underwriters Insurance Co.*, 725 F.2d 179 (2d Cir.), *cert. denied*, 469 U.S. 874 (1984); *Longobardi v. Chubb Insurance Co.*, 582 A.2d 1257 (N.J. 1990). The false swearing defense should be distinguished from a defense that the insured has failed to cooperate by, for example, failing to produce relevant

documents. In the latter situation, prejudice from the noncooperation may be required. *See King v. Federal Insurance Co.*, 788 F. Supp. 506 (D. Kan. 1992).

6. *Exaggeration or False Swearing?* What if the policyholder makes a good faith overvaluation of the amount of his or her claim? Everyone thinks his or her property is worth more than it really is, right? At some point, an exaggerated valuation becomes false swearing, but the line is not easy to draw. *See Auto-Owners Insurance Co. v. Hansen Housing, Inc.*, 604 N.W.2d 504 (S.D. 2000); *Nagel Taylor Automotive Supplies, Inc. v. Aetna Casualty & Surety Co.*, 402 N.E.2d 302 (Ill. App. Ct. 1980). Some states have passed so called "anti-technicality statutes" to avoid the problem of distinguishing between deliberately false statements on a proof of loss and an innocent misstatement. Under these statutes, the misrepresentation or false statement made in a proof of loss has no effect unless the insurer proves that the false statements were made fraudulently, and the insurer was misled. *See* Tex. Ins. Code Ann., art. 21.19 (West 1981).

GOLDMAN V. STATE FARM FIRE GEN. INS. CO.

660 So. 2d 300 (Fla. Dist. Ct. App. 1995)

Opinion

RIVKIND, LEONARD, ASSOCIATE JUDGE.

Appellants, plaintiffs below, appeal from a final summary judgment entered in favor of appellee, defendant below, in an action for the breach of an insurance policy. This appeal presents issues arising from a condition in the insurance contract which required each insured to submit to examinations under oath while not in the presence of any other insured. Although motions for summary judgments are reviewed with special scrutiny and a jury determination is generally favored, we have nonetheless concluded that the entry of summary judgment was correct. The facts material to the instant appeal follow.

I.

In June 1992, appellee issued a homeowners/tenants insurance policy to appellants which included personal property and contents coverage. The appellants' residence was burglarized on October 8, 1992, and they submitted a sworn proof of loss setting forth their claim under the policy. Appellee then began investigating appellants' claim and the circumstances surrounding the loss. On December 30, 1992, as part of its investigation, appellee demanded in writing that both appellants submit to an examination under oath as well as produce certain documents and records. Such demand was made pursuant to a policy condition requiring the insured to submit to an examination under oath. In a section entitled "Suits Against Us," the policy expressly provides that "no action shall be brought unless there has been compliance with the policy provisions."

The examinations under oath were initially scheduled for January 14, 1993, but were rescheduled at the request of appellants' counsel. There is no genuine factual dispute that appellants were aware of appellee's request that they submit to examinations under oath at a mutually convenient time and place as contemplated by the policy.

On January 19, 1993, appellants filed suit against appellee for breach of the insurance contract, maintaining that although they had complied with all conditions precedent necessary to entitle them to recovery under the insurance policy, appellee had refused to pay their claim. On the same date that suit was filed, appellants' attorney wrote to appellee's counsel suggesting that the sworn statements be renoticed as depositions in accordance with the Florida Rules of Civil Procedure.[3] Appellee, by letter dated March 1, 1993, renewed its requests for appellants to submit to examinations under oath.

On March 30, 1993, appellee moved for summary judgment on its affirmative defenses of noncompliance with the policy provisions arguing that appellants' failure to submit to examinations under oath prior to filing suit constituted a material breach of the policy terms as well as a failure to satisfy a condition precedent to filing suit on the insurance policy. In support of its motion, appellee submitted affidavits to the effect that it had been unable to complete its investigation due to appellants' failure to submit to an examination under oath; that appellee had neither made payment of the loss nor denied the claim due to its inability to complete its investigation; and that appellants had commenced their legal action against appellee prior to the taking of the examination under oath.

In opposition to the motion for summary judgment, appellants in their opposing affidavits stated that they had complied with the requests of appellee in regard to their claim under the insurance policy to the best of their ability and that, at no time, had they refused to submit to a sworn statement under oath by appellee.

On January 5, 1994, the trial judge granted appellee's motion for summary judgment finding as follows:

> 1. The contractual requirement for an insured to submit to examination under oath is a valid and binding provision, with which an insured must comply before bringing suit against the insurer on the policy.

---

[3] Although appellants claim appellee was subsequently able to depose them under oath, the policy does not expressly provide that depositions may be substituted for examinations under oath as appellants suggest. Instead, the policy requires separate examinations under oath for each insured. The trial judge declined to equate depositions with examinations under oath noting that "there is a big difference between taking a sworn statement under the provisions of this contract and taking of a deposition. It's a horse of another color." Each insured was deposed in the other's presence.

2. The Plaintiffs failed to appear for examinations under oath prior to filing suit, despite written requests by State Farm.

3. The Plaintiffs' failure to submit to examinations under oath prior to filing their lawsuit is a material breach of the insurance contract which will relieve the insurer of its obligation to pay under the policy.

On March 9, 1994, final judgment was entered for appellee on the breach of contract claim. Appellants have appealed from the final judgment.

II.

Appellants argue on appeal that summary judgment was improper because genuine issues of material fact existed as to whether appellants' failure to submit to the examination was material and whether such failure resulted in substantial prejudice to appellee. Because a finding of prejudice is not essential to a resolution of the legal issues raised in this case, we find that appellants have failed to establish the existence of any genuine issue of material fact which would preclude the entry of summary judgment. . . .

III.

An insured's refusal to comply with a demand for an examination under oath is a willful and material breach of an insurance contract which precludes the insured from recovery under the policy. Other jurisdictions have similarly interpreted the examination under oath requirement of an insurance policy, holding that failure to submit to examination under oath is a material breach of the policy terms and a condition precedent to an insured's right to recover and/or bring suit under the policy. *See, e.g., Pervis v. State Farm Fire & Cas. Co.*, 901 F.2d 944 (11th Cir.), *cert. denied,* 498 U.S. 899, 111 S.Ct. 255, 112 L.Ed.2d 213 (1990) (policy provision requiring the insured to take an examination under oath was a condition precedent to suit and that noncompliance constituted a material breach justifying the entry of summary judgment); *Fineberg v. State Farm Fire & Cas. Co.,* 113 N.C.App. 545, 438 S.E.2d 754, *review denied,* 336 N.C. 315, 445 S.E.2d 395 (1994) (failure to comply with insurance policy condition of submission to examination under oath bars recovery under policy as well as the right to bring suit under policy); *Watson v. National Sur. Corp.,* 468 N.W.2d 448 (Iowa 1991); *see also* 5A J. Appleman & J. Appleman, *Insurance Law & Practice* § 3549, at 549–50 (1970) (citing jurisdictions which hold that failure to submit to an examination under oath constitutes material breach and is a defense to an action on the policy); 13A G. Couch, *Couch on Insurance 2d* § 49A:361, at 759 (M. Rhodes rev. ed. 1982); 44 Am.Jur.2d *Insurance* § 1364, at 290–91, § 1366 at 294 (1982); Christopher Vaeth, Annotation, *Requirement Under Property Insurance Policy That Insured Submit To Examination Under Oath As To Loss,* 16 A.L.R.5th 412 (1993).

In analogous cases, where the terms of the insurance policy require that the insured submit to other types of examinations, such as independent medical examinations, Florida courts have held that the insured's willful refusal to submit to such examinations constitutes a material breach which bars recovery. *See Griffin v. Stonewall Ins. Co.*, 346 So.2d 97 (Fla. 3d DCA 1977); *DeFerrari v. Government Employees Ins. Co.*, 613 So.2d 101 (Fla. 3d DCA), *review denied,* 620 So.2d 760 (Fla.1993); *Allstate Ins. Co. v. Graham,* 541 So.2d 160 (Fla. 2d DCA 1989); *Tindall v. Allstate Ins. Co.,* 472 So.2d 1291 (Fla. 2d DCA 1985), *review denied,* 484 So.2d 10 (Fla.1986).

The determinative issue in this case is whether the policy provision requiring the insured to submit to a sworn examination outside the presence of the other insured is a condition precedent to filing suit. A substantial line of cases supports the rule that an insurer need not show prejudice when the insured breaches a condition precedent to suit. *See United States Fidelity & Guar. Co. v. Wigginton,* 964 F.2d 487 (5th Cir.1992) (fire policy was rendered void by insured's failure to submit to examination under oath, regardless of whether insurer was prejudiced where an examination clause was a condition precedent); *Bolivar County Bd. of Supervisors v. Forum Ins. Co.,* 779 F.2d 1081 (5th Cir.1986) (no showing of prejudice necessary when provision is condition precedent); *Reliance Ins. Co. v. County Line Place, Inc.,* 692 F.Supp. 694 (S.D.Miss.1988) (no showing of prejudice necessary when notice provision is condition precedent); *Bankers Ins. Co. v. Macias,* 475 So.2d 1216 (Fla.1985) (in cases involving the breach of a condition precedent, the burden is on the insured to show a lack of prejudice); *DeFerrari,* 613 So.2d at 101 (Fla. 3d DCA 1993) (prejudice is not at issue when an insured refuses to submit to an examination because the examination is a condition precedent to coverage); *Wolverine Ins. Co. v. Sorrough,* 122 Ga.App. 556, 177 S.E.2d 819 (1970) (insured's noncompliance with condition precedent precluded recovery notwithstanding lack of showing of prejudice by insurer).

On the other hand, if the provision is a cooperation clause, the burden would be on the insurer to demonstrate substantial prejudice before a breach would preclude recovery under the policy. *See Macias,* 475 So.2d at 1216 (Fla.1985) (failure to cooperate is a condition subsequent and it is proper to place the burden of showing prejudice on the insurer); *Bontempo v. State Farm Mut. Auto. Ins. Co.,* 604 So.2d 28 (Fla. 4th DCA 1992); *Ramos v. Northwestern Mut. Ins. Co.,* 336 So.2d 71 (Fla.1976) (an insurer may not avoid liability under its policy by merely showing the violation of a clause requiring "assistance and cooperation" of the insured without a further showing of how this violation prejudiced the insurer); *American Fire & Cas. Co. v. Collura,* 163 So.2d 784 (Fla. 2d DCA), *cert. denied,* 171 So.2d 389 (Fla.1964); *American Fire & Cas. Co. v. Vliet,* 148 Fla. 568, 4 So.2d 862

(Fla.1941); *United States Fidelity & Guar. v. Snite,* 106 Fla. 702, 143 So. 615 (Fla.1932). . . .

We conclude that the policy provisions requiring appellants to submit to examinations under oath are conditions precedent to suit rather than cooperation clauses. *See Fineberg,* 438 S.E.2d at 754 (compliance with a condition in a fire insurance policy, such as the examination under oath provision, is a condition precedent to suing on a fire policy); *Pervis,* 901 F.2d at 946 (construing requirement that insured submit to examination under oath as condition precedent to suit); *Watson,* 468 N.W.2d at 448. *Cf. Thompson v. West Virginia Essential Property Ins. Ass'n.,* 186 W.Va. 84, 411 S.E.2d 27 (1991) (policy language made compliance with an examination under oath provision a condition precedent to recovery rather than to suit); *Puckett v. State Farm General Ins. Co.,* 444 S.E.2d 523 (S.C.1994).

Notwithstanding appellants' affidavits to the contrary, the giving of recorded statements or the taking of depositions with both sides present does not constitute substantial compliance with the policy conditions. *See Pervis,* 901 F.2d at 946 (recorded statements insured gave to insurer did not satisfy insured's obligation under policy to submit to "examination under oath" before filing action to recover policy proceeds); *Archie v. State Farm Fire & Cas. Co.,* 813 F.Supp. 1208, 1213 (S.D.Miss.1992) (insured's agreement to sit for deposition following suit did not satisfy spirit of insurance policy mandating examinations under oath). *Cf. Thompson,* 411 S.E.2d at 27; *Farm Bureau Town & Country Ins. Co. of Missouri v. Crain,* 731 S.W.2d 866 (Mo.App.1987) (factual question whether insured's initial refusal to answer questions during examination under oath was repaired by subsequent deposition).

We are unpersuaded that appellee's post-suit deposition of appellants obviated any prejudice to appellee. The policy does not provide that depositions may be substituted for examinations under oath as appellants suggest. Rather, depositions and examinations under oath serve vastly different purposes. First, the obligation to sit for an examination under oath is contractual rather than arising out of the rules of civil procedure. Second, an insured's counsel plays a different role during examinations under oath than during depositions. Third, examinations under oath are taken before litigation to augment the insurer's investigation of the claim while a deposition is not part of the claim investigation process. Fourth, an insured has a duty to volunteer information related to the claim during an examination under oath in accordance with the policy while he would have no such obligation in a deposition. Finally, the insurer has the right to examine insured independently in sworn examinations while it would have no parallel right to do so under the Florida Rules of Civil Procedure. *See Ferrigno v. Yoder,* 495 So.2d 886 (Fla. 2d DCA 1986), *review denied sub nom. Suncoast Insurers, Inc. v. Ferrigno,* 504 So.2d 768 (Fla.1987) (trial court abused its discretion when precluding plaintiffs from attending each other's depositions).

Furthermore, since the insurance policy clearly requires compliance with all of its requirements in order for appellants to bring this action, appellants' failure to comply with any one of the conditions as a matter of law would be sufficient grounds for upholding the lower court's order.

Since forfeitures are not favored, this court has considered the possibility of remanding the case with directions that appellants submit to an examination under oath. However, we decline to exercise this option since any belated compliance by appellants more than two (2) years subsequent to the loss and the commencement of suit would satisfy neither the spirit nor intent of the policy conditions at issue. *See Watson v. National Sur. Corp.*, 468 N.W.2d 448 (Iowa 1991) (insured's belated offers to submit to examinations under oath were not substantial compliance with questioning-under-oath provision of fire policy since insurer needed evidence at time of investigation when facts were more easily recalled and before crucial evidence was destroyed or became otherwise unavailable); *Pervis*, 901 F.2d at 948 (insured's offer came too late to be considered); *Azeem v. Colonial Assurance Co.*, 96 A.D.2d 123, 468 N.Y.S.2d 248, 250 (1983) (insured's willingness to submit to examination under oath almost one and a half years after the first scheduled examination and two years after the fire does not satisfy contractual obligation of cooperation).

We, therefore, hold that the policy provision at issue is a condition precedent to suit and that appellants' noncompliance precludes an action on the policy regardless of a showing of prejudice by the insurer.

AFFIRMED.

NOTES AND QUESTIONS

1. *No Prejudice Requirement.* Under *Goldman*, the insurer was not required to prove it was prejudiced by the policyholder's failure to submit to an examination under oath. This holding is different than the requirement that an insurer prove prejudice in most circumstances where the policyholder fails to satisfy policy requirements, such as late notice and failure to cooperate. Not all courts have agreed with *Goldman*. Some courts have required the insurer to prove it was prejudiced by the failure of the policyholder to submit to an examination under oath. *See, e.g.*, *Miles v. Great N. Ins. Co.*, 656 F. Supp. 2d 218, 222 (D. Mass. 2009) ("When an insurer investigates a claim of loss, the insured has a duty to cooperate by submitting to an examination under oath and producing documents relevant to the claimed loss. The insurer may not deny the claim for failure to cooperate, however, unless it makes 'an affirmative showing of actual prejudice resulting from the failure.' "). In fact, it is questionable whether *Goldman* even remains good law in Florida because the *Goldman* court relied upon older cases in which the courts held the failure to submit to an independent medical exam barred recovery. In 2014, the

Florida Supreme Court held an insurer must prove prejudice due to an insured's failure to submit to an independent medical exam before uninsured motorist benefits were forfeited. *See State Farm Mut. Auto. Ins. Co. v. Curran*, 135 So. 3d 1071 (Fla. 2014). It remains to be determined whether the *Curran* court's holding is limited to just uninsured motorist claims or applies more broadly to other types of claims.

2. *Examination Under Oath Versus Deposition*. The *Goldman* court stated depositions and examinations under oath are different exercises that serve different purposes. How so?

3. *Purpose of Examination Under Oath*. What should an insurer try to accomplish when it takes an examination under oath?

4. *Attorneys' Role During Examination Under Oath*. The *Goldman* court notes examinations under oath are not subject to the relevant rules of civil procedure and that attorneys' roles in them are different. Does that mean an attorney who is defending a witness who is being examined under oath can "coach" the witness by supplying answers to questions? Can she object to questions and then instruct the witness not to answer them for non-privileged reasons?

V. SUBROGATION

Subrogation is an equitable remedy with its roots in the English Court of Chancery. It arises by operation of law, although it can also be created by statute or by contract. With the merger of law and equity now well established, it is common to refer to subrogation that arises, other than by statute or contract, as "common law subrogation" or "common law equitable subrogation." A subrogation right arises when one party pays the debt of another as a result of some kind of legal compulsion. Assuming all the circumstances necessary to assert an equitable right are present, the person paying the debt (the subrogee) succeeds to the rights the debtor (the subrogor) may have against third parties. In the property insurance context, for example, suppose an insurer pays a policyholder's fire loss. The fire, however, was caused by a negligent third party who should be held liable for the loss. In that circumstance, the insurer has a common law subrogation right and claim against the third party who caused the fire. In addition to a common law subrogation right, most insurance policies contain express subrogation provisions that set forth the insurer's subrogation right.

Three issues that frequently arise with respect to subrogation will be addressed in this subchapter: 1) an insurer's subrogation right against a policyholder who has prejudiced the insurer's subrogation claim, 2) an insurer's subrogation right against a policyholder when the insurer is obligated to cover a loss that otherwise would not be covered due to the policyholder's conduct, and 3) an insurer's subrogation right against the policyholder's tenant in the landlord/tenant context.

A. POLICYHOLDER'S PREJUDICE OF INSURER'S SUBROGATION RIGHT

TATE V. SECURA INSURANCE

587 N.E.2d 665 (Ind. 1992)

Opinion

DICKSON, JUSTICE.

Plaintiff-appellant Thomas Tate seeks transfer to this Court following the decision of the Court of Appeals affirming summary judgment for Secura Insurance, A Mutual Company, the defendant-appellee, as to the interpretation to be given an automobile insurance policy providing underinsured motorists coverage.

Background

Tate was seriously injured as he was providing assistance to a car stalled in the parking lane of an Indianapolis street when it was struck by a vehicle operated by an intoxicated driver. Tate settled with the driver's insurance company for $50,000, the maximum payable under the driver's bodily injury liability coverage. With alleged preliminary medical expenses already in excess of $60,000, past and future income losses, permanent impairment, and the possibility of future amputation, Tate claimed that the reasonable value of his total damages was in excess of $100,000 and asserted a claim under the underinsured motorists provision of his own automobile insurance policy with Secura, which denied the claim. Tate's law suit for breach of contract ensued, resulting in summary judgment in favor of Secura, and the Court of Appeals affirmed. We now grant Tate's petition for transfer.

Secura contends, and we agree, that the summary judgment should be affirmed if the trial court was correct upon any one of the of the following potentially dispositive issues:

. . . .

3. whether Tate's claim is precluded for failure to obtain Secura's consent to his settlement with the underinsured driver.

. . . .

Analysis

3. Failure to Obtain Secura's Settlement Consent

Secura contends that Tate is estopped from recovery because he did not obtain Secura's consent to his settlement with the tortfeasor. Secura argues that Tate's settlement operated to destroy its subrogation rights against the tortfeasor, thereby breaching the policy contract, which includes the following pertinent provisions:

> B. Exclusions [included as an additional provision applicable only to the uninsured and underinsured coverages]
>
> We do not cover *bodily injury* to a person:
>
> * * * * * *
>
> 2. If that person or the legal representative of that person makes settlement without our written consent.
>
> * * * * * *
>
> F. Our Recovery Rights [included in Part IV-General Provisions]
>
> If we make a payment under this policy, we are entitled to all the rights of recovery that the person or organization to or for whom payment was made has against another. That person or organization must:
>
> 1. Sign and deliver to us any legal papers relating to that recovery.
>
> 2. Do whatever else is necessary to help us exercise those rights and
>
> 3. Do nothing after the accident, occurrence or *loss* to harm our rights.
>
> If a person to or for whom we have made payment under this policy also recovers from another, that person shall:
>
> 1. Hold the amount recovered in trust for us and
>
> 2. Reimburse us to the extent of our payment.

Record at 11, 17. In exchange for payment of the tortfeasor's liability coverage limits of $50,000, Tate executed a covenant not to sue promising to forever refrain from bringing suit against the tortfeasor on account of any and all claims resulting from the accident. Record at 386.

The applicable principles supporting Secura's contention are succinctly stated in *Allstate Ins. Co. v. Meek* (1986), Ind.App., 489 N.E.2d 530, 533:

> In summary, an insured who destroys the insurer's contractual subrogation rights breaches the insurance contract and, as a result, extinguishes his right of action on the policy. An insured destroys the insurer's contractual subrogation right by releasing the tortfeasor prior to settling with the insurer because it is that very settlement which enables the insurer to protect its subrogation right by giving notice thereof to the tortfeasor.

However, where the insurer has given notice to the tortfeasor of its payment and the tortfeasor thereafter makes settlement and obtains a release, it will not be a defense as against the insurer in enforcing its rights as subrogee. Similarly, the rule does not apply where the doctrines of waiver and estoppel are available.

Tate argues that Secura has waived any subrogation rights and is estopped from asserting any claimed violation thereof because Secura was fully apprised of Tate's claim negotiations and proposed settlement, and yet never objected or raised any issue of intended subrogation. Secura does not specifically address this argument.

Beginning within a few days after the December 20, 1986, accident, numerous communications occurred between Tate's counsel and Secura's adjuster. By January 17, 1987, Secura knew of Tate's intention to present an underinsured motorists coverage claim. By a letter to the adjuster dated March 30, 1987, Tate's attorney again indicated that such a claim would be made as soon as Tate's medical condition stabilized, and enclosed a copy of a letter to the tortfeasor's insurer offering to settle Tate's claims for payment of the applicable $50,000 liability limits. On April 13, 1987, Tate's counsel informed Secura's adjuster that a settlement had been concluded on April 9, 1987, for the tortfeasor's policy limits, and expressing the intent to make a "formal demand" for settlement pursuant to the underinsured motorist coverage as soon as further information was known regarding Tate's medical progress. At no time did Secura object to Tate's negotiations with the tortfeasor's insurer nor assert any right to consent to any resulting settlement. Tate executed the covenant not to sue on April 21, 1987. In a letter dated April 27, 1987, Secura denied Tate's underinsured motorists coverage claim asserting as the sole grounds provision D-1 (Reductions in the Amounts Payable) because Tate's underinsured motorists coverage limits were the same as the tortfeasor's bodily injury liability limits. As discussed in Issue 1 above, the language of Secura's underinsured motorists coverage does not permit it to deny the claim for this reason.

The term "estoppel" has a meaning distinct from "waiver," but is often used synonymously with "implied waiver."

> Technically, there is a distinction between "waiver" and "estoppel." A waiver is an intentional relinquishment of a known right and is a voluntary act, while the elements of estoppel are the misleading of a party entitled to rely on the acts or statements in question and a consequent change of position to his detriment. But in the law of insurance, the distinction between "estoppel" and "implied waiver" is not easy to preserve, and, quite commonly, in insurance cases, the courts have found it unnecessary or inadvisable to make a distinction between them and have used the terms interchangeably.

We find nothing in the alleged facts to indicate that Secura expressly manifested an intentional relinquishment of its subrogation rights. Mere silence or inaction on the part of an insurer is not sufficient to constitute an express waiver. At issue is whether estoppel or implied waiver may apply. In the absence of resulting prejudice, there is no estoppel or implied waiver.

For this reason, we find no estoppel or implied waiver from Secura's conduct in failing to include in its April 27, 1987, denial letter any assertion or reservation of its contractual rights to consent to settlement and to subrogation. By this time, Tate had already negotiated his settlement with the tortfeasor and signed the covenant not to sue. Tate suffered no prejudice from Secura's letter of April 27.

The remaining related question is whether an estoppel may arise from Secura's failure to act between January 17, 1987, and April 9, 1987, notwithstanding its knowledge of Tate's negotiations seeking settlement for the tortfeasor's liability coverage limits. The facts in this case are similar to those in *Fincher,* 428 N.E.2d 1386, which involved a claim for uninsured motorists coverage denied on grounds that the insured had already covenanted not to sue the tortfeasor and had thereby destroyed the insurer's subrogation rights.

Acknowledging the general rule that recovery by an insured is barred when, before receiving payment from his own insurer, the insured settles with or releases the alleged tortfeasor, *Fincher* nevertheless applied [implied] waiver and estoppel, finding that under the evidence the trial court properly found that the insurer had waived, or was estopped to assert, its right of subrogation.

> [A]n insurer "cannot sit down and hold its hands and purse and thereafter escape liability for fulfillment of its contract by reason of the insured's effort, after fair notice, to recoup his loss by litigation against a wrongdoer."

428 N.E.2d at 1390 (quoting with approval from *Powers v. Calvert Fire Ins. Co.* (1950), 216 S.C. 309, 316, 57 S.E.2d 638, 642).

We conclude that genuine issues of fact exist relating to whether Secura's silence notwithstanding knowledge of Tate's ongoing negotiations operated to mislead Tate, whether Tate was entitled to rely on Secura's said conduct, and whether Tate suffered a consequent change of position to his detriment. Secura is not entitled to summary judgment on this issue.

Conclusion

The opinion of the Court of Appeals is vacated, the order of summary judgment is reversed, and this cause is remanded to the trial court for further proceedings.

NOTES AND QUESTIONS

1. *Prejudice of Subrogation Claim. Tate* sets forth many of the basic rules regarding subrogation with respect to insurers and policyholders. Does the policyholder or insurer have the burden of proof with respect to the issue of whether the insurer's subrogation claim has been prejudiced?

2. *Waiver and Estoppel Regarding Insurer's Subrogation Rights.* In *Tate*, the policyholder was arguing that the insurer had implicitly waived its subrogation rights or should be estopped from denying coverage on the grounds that its subrogation rights had been prejudiced because the insurer was aware the policyholder intended to settle with the tortfeasor, but the insurer failed to object to the settlement. In that situation, does the policyholder or the insurer have the burden of proving the policyholder detrimentally relied upon the insurer's conduct?

3. *Contractual Right Versus Common Law Right.* In addition to a contractual subrogation right based upon policy provisions, insurers have a common law subrogation right. *See, e.g., Gibbs v. Hawaiian Eugenia Corp.*, 966 F.2d 101, 105–06 (2d Cir. 1992) (*citing* 16 Couch on Insurance 2d §§ 61:4, 61:18 and 61:20 (Rev. ed. 1983)). Was the insurer's subrogation right in *Tate* premised upon language in the insurance policy or the common law? Does it make a difference legally?

4. *Release of Subrogation Claim Before or After a Loss Occurs.* One of the most powerful defenses against a claim is an allegation backed by facts that the claim has already been released, i.e., has already been settled. When this idea is combined with the principle that defenses that are good against a subrogor are generally good against a subrogee, we encounter the possibility that a policyholder might suffer damage caused by a tortfeasor, receive compensation from the tortfeasor, give the tortfeasor a release, and then seek compensation from the insurer for remaining loss. What has happened is that the policyholder, in releasing the tortfeasor, has compromised the insurer's subrogation right because the tortfeasor will assert the defense of the release, which is good against the subrogor-policyholder if the policyholder were to seek more compensation from the tortfeasor, against the subrogee-insurer. A defendant typically demands a release from a plaintiff when the parties settle a claim. Providing such a release prejudices an insurer's subrogation right unless the defendant-tortfeasor was aware of the insurance (why does this exception exist?); thus, courts generally treat the release as a breach of the policyholder's obligation not to prejudice the insurer's subrogation right. *See, e.g., Ins. Co. of N. Am. v. Abiouness*, 313 S.E.2d 663 (Va. 1984) (policyholder who released claims against a contractor for defective workmanship after defects were discovered forfeited coverage because it prejudiced insurer's subrogation right); *Allied Mut. Ins. Co. v. Heiken*, 675 N.W.2d 820 (Iowa 2004) (policyholder did not forfeit coverage when providing a release to another party where the other party was aware of the insurer's subrogation claim before the release was provided).

On the other hand, if a policyholder releases its claims against another party *before* a loss has occurred, then the policyholder does not forfeit coverage even though the insurer's subrogation right has been prejudiced under the principal rationale that many standard form contracts contain waivers or limits of liability, and the policyholder should not lose insurance coverage simply due to the existence of such a provision. Why should the timing of the loss in relation to the timing of the release make a difference on the question of whether the insurer has a subrogation right? *See, e.g.*, *Blume v. Evans Fur Co.*, 466 N.E.2d 1366 (Ill. App. Ct. 1984) (limit of liability contained in bailor agreement was binding on insurer); *Great N. Oil Co. v. St. Paul Fire & Marine Ins. Co.*, 189 N.W.2d 204 (Minn. 1971) (policyholder's release of contractor before work was performed was binding on insurer).

B. MORTGAGES

Virtually all mortgage loans related to the purchase of real estate contain provisions giving the lender a security interest in the property being mortgaged. The mortgage loan agreement also requires the purchaser of the property to insure the property in an amount adequate to cover the mortgage amount and that the insurance procured contain a provision expressly covering the lender. *See, e.g.*, Sample Homeowners Insurance, Condition L. The lender then becomes an additional insured under the policy. In the event the insured property is destroyed, the net effect of the insurance policy and mortgage agreement is that the lender is paid the amount of the mortgage first, and any remaining insurance proceeds are paid to the policyholder. What happens if the policyholder's conduct is a breach of the terms of the policy or voids the policy? Does the insurer still have to pay the lender? Does the insurer have any rights against its policyholder?

NORTHWEST FARM BUREAU INSURANCE COMPANY V. ALTHAUSER

750 P.2d 1166 (Or. Ct. App. 1988)

Opinion

JOSEPH, CHIEF JUDGE.

This is a foreclosure action. Northwest Farm Bureau Insurance (plaintiff) issued the Althausers (defendants) a homeowners' insurance contract which included fire insurance coverage and mortgagee protection. After a fire, plaintiff paid the mortgagees. Plaintiff claims that it is subrogated to the mortgagees' rights, because its contract with defendants was made void by defendants' material misrepresentations concerning the fire loss. The trial court entered a summary judgment of foreclosure, and defendants appeal. We affirm.

Defendants owned a house which was subject to two mortgages. Plaintiff's policy provided that any fire loss would be payable to mortgagees named in the policy to the extent of their interests. The policy also provided that the mortgagee's interest was protected even if the mortgagor breached the policy.[2] In 1981, a fire severely damaged the house. In accordance with the policy, plaintiff paid the first mortgagee the full value of its mortgage, and the mortgagee assigned the mortgage to plaintiff. The remainder of the structural damage insurance proceeds was paid to the second mortgagee.

The insurance policy also provided coverage for personal property. Before the present action was filed, defendants sued plaintiff to recover their personal property losses. Plaintiff denied liability on two grounds: arson and material misrepresentation. The jury found that defendants did not commit arson but that they did "breach the insurance contract by knowingly misrepresenting or concealing a material fact relating to [the loss claim]." Judgment was entered for plaintiff.

Plaintiff then filed this action, asserting, *inter alia,* that it is equitably subrogated to both mortgages and seeking to foreclose both, because defendants had not made any mortgage payments since the fire.

"Subrogation is the substitution of another person in place of the creditor to whose rights he succeeds in relation to the debt, and gives to the substitute all of the rights [and remedies] of the party for whom he is substituted." *United States F. & G. Co. v. Bramwell,* 108 Or. 261, 277, 217 P. 332 (1923); *see Maine Bonding v. Centennial Ins. Co.*, 298 Or. 514, 693 P.2d 1296 (1985). Subrogation extends to "every instance in which one party is required to pay a debt for which another is primarily answerable." *United States F. & G. Co. v. Bramwell, supra,* 108 Or. at 277, 217 P. 332. The purpose of subrogation is to impose the financial consequences of a loss on the party "primarily responsible" for the loss. *Maine Bonding v. Centennial Ins. Co., supra,* 298 Or. at 521 n. 4, 693 P.2d 1296.

Before the fire, defendants were "primarily responsible" for the mortgage debts. The insurance contract required that, after the fire, plaintiff pay the

---

2 The policy provides, in part:

"14. MORTGAGEE. Loss shall be payable to mortgagees named in the coverage summary to the extent of their interest and in the order of precedence.

"We will:

"a. Protect the mortgagee's interest in insured property in the case of breach of warranty, increase in hazard, change of ownership, or foreclosure if the mortgagee has no knowledge of these conditions * * *.

"* * * * *

"The mortgagee will:

"* * * * *

"d. Give us the right of recovery against any party liable for loss * * *.

"e. After a loss, permit us to satisfy the mortgage requirements and receive full transfer of the mortgage."

See ORS 743.639(2).

mortgagees, and it did so. If defendants remained primarily responsible for the mortgage debts after the fire, plaintiff is subrogated to the rights of the mortgagees, because it paid debts for which defendants were primarily responsible.

Defendants contend, essentially, that the fire made plaintiff primarily responsible for the debt, because the insurance contract required it to pay in the event of fire. Defendants argue that, if they were still responsible for the debt after the fire, they will have paid for fire insurance but will not have benefitted from it. They are not entitled to the benefits of the insurance, because they made material misrepresentations in connection with the policy. By statute, a fire insurance policy must contain a provision voiding the policy if there have been material misrepresentations by the insureds. ORS 743.612. The jury in the previous case brought by defendants determined that they had made material misrepresentations. The effect of that was to void the entire policy as between plaintiff and defendants. ORS 743.612. The mortgagees' interest was protected, even though defendants' conduct had voided the policy as to themselves.

Because the misrepresentations voided the policy, plaintiff's payments to the mortgagees did not, as defendants contend, satisfy defendants' obligation on the mortgages. Rather, the payments satisfied a separate and distinct duty that plaintiff owed the mortgagees under the insurance contract.

"[W]here one has been compelled to pay a debt which ought to have been paid by another, he is entitled to exercise all of the remedies which the creditor possesses against that other * * *." *United States F. & G. Co. v. Bramwell, supra*, 108 Or. at 277, 217 P. 332.

Defendants "ought to have" paid the mortgage debts, even after the fire, because their insurance was void. Because plaintiff was compelled to pay the debt by its separate duty to the mortgagees, it is entitled to the mortgagees' remedies.

Affirmed.

NOTES AND QUESTIONS

1. *No Subrogation Right Against Policyholder*. The general rule is that an insurer does not have a subrogation right against the policyholder even if the loss was the policyholder's fault. *See* John F. Dobbyn & Christopher C. French, Insurance Law In A Nutshell 424 (5th ed. 2016); Robert H. Jerry II & Douglas R. Richmond, Understanding Insurance Law 725–28 (5th ed. 2012). Why is that the basic rule?

In *Althauser*, the court discussed an exception to the general rule that an insurer cannot bring a subrogation claim against its policyholder—situations where the insurer is required under the policy language to pay a loss to the mortgagee even though the insurer has a valid defense to the claim if it were brought by the policyholder. In that circumstance, why does the insurer have a subrogation right against the policyholder?

2. *Innocent Co-Insureds.* What if the insurer has a valid defense to a claim on the basis that one of the insureds intentionally caused the loss? For example, Section I, Exclusion A.8 of the Sample Homeowners Policy at the beginning of this chapter provides:

> We do not insure for loss caused directly or indirectly by any of the following: . . . 8. "Intentional Loss." Intentional Loss means any loss arising out of any act an "insured" commits or conspires to commit with the intent to cause a loss. In the event of such loss, no "insured" is entitled to coverage, even "insureds" who did not commit or conspire to commit the act causing the loss.

In a situation where an estranged spouse burns down the couple's house and the insurer pays off the mortgage pursuant to the mortgage clause in the policy, does the insurer have a subrogation claim against the spouse who had nothing to do with the arson due to the "intentional loss" exclusion? Some courts will enforce "intentional loss" exclusions that purport to apply to innocent co-insureds, but in most states the exclusion will not be enforced against innocent co-insureds. *See, e.g.*, Jerry & Richmond, Understanding Insurance Law, *supra*, at 425–26 (noting that five states have adopted The National Association of Insurance Commissioners' model statute regarding innocent co-insureds, and at least 36 other states have their own statutes).

C. TENANTS

What about tenants? If a tenant accidentally burns down a house the tenant is renting, can the landlord who owns the property and has homeowners insurance pay the owner's loss and then exercise its subrogation right against the tenant?

SAFECO INS. COMPANIES V. WEISGERBER

767 P.2d 271 (Idaho 1989)

Opinion

HUNTLEY, JUSTICE.

Safeco Insurance Companies (Safeco) brought a subrogation action against Chris Weisgerber to recover amounts paid to Stanley and Anita LaFrenz on account of a fire allegedly caused by the negligence of Chris Weisgerber, the tenant in a residence rented to him by the LaFrenzes. Weisgerber moved for summary judgment upon the ground that a landlord's insurer has no right of subrogation against a negligent tenant. The district court granted summary judgment to defendant. Safeco appeals. We affirm.

I.

On December 23, 1983, a home owned by the LaFrenzes and rented to Weisgerber was damaged by fire. The LaFrenzes possessed a general homeowner's policy issued by Safeco. Following the fire Safeco paid $28,762.08 for repairs to the house and replacement or compensation for personal property damaged or destroyed in the fire.

The parties to the rental agreement do not dispute the fact that they never mentioned the question of insuring the premises against loss by fire during any discussions or negotiations regarding the rental agreement. Weisgerber had a renter's policy with Farm Bureau Insurance which included insurance for his own personal property. Weisgerber states that he did not obtain fire insurance on the real property because the landlords never requested that he do so and he did not feel it was his responsibility to obtain such insurance.

On June 11, 1982, Weisgerber signed the rental agreement. Paragraph 5(b) of the agreement required Weisgerber to maintain the premises in a good state and condition of repair, "damage by . . . fire excepted."

II.

The issue presented on appeal is whether the trial court erred in granting summary judgment to Weisgerber upon the basis that an insurance carrier for a landlord has no right of subrogation against a tenant to recover for damages to leased premises caused by the negligence of the tenant.

The question of whether a landlord's insurer has a cause of action by way of subrogation against a negligent tenant is an issue of first impression in the state of Idaho. Decisions from other jurisdictions which have considered the question overwhelmingly embrace the view, relied upon by the district court in awarding summary judgment to Weisgerber, that the landlord/homeowner obtains insurance that is held for the benefit of both landlord and tenant, thereby giving the tenant the status of a co-insured, absent an express agreement to the contrary.[1]

III.

In *Pendlebury v. Western Casualty & Surety Co.,* 89 Idaho 456, 406 P.2d 129 (1965), this Court held a fire insurance carrier cannot maintain a subrogation action against its insured for loss of the insured premises due to the insured's negligence.

The following cases, most of which are discussed in more detail, *infra,* have held that the tenant has the status of a coinsured with the landlord, absent an express agreement to the contrary. *Sutton v. Jondahl,* 532 P.2d 478

[1] Only the Arkansas Supreme Court is of the view that the tenant is liable for negligence which caused a premises fire in a subrogation action by the homeowner's insurer, absent an express agreement to the contrary. *Page v. Scott,* 263 Ark. 684, 567 S.W.2d 101 (1978).

(Okla.App.1975); *Cascade Trailer Court v. Jim Beeson, et al.,* 50 Wash.App. 678, 749 P.2d 761 (1988) (rev. denied May 31, 1988); [(other citations omitted).]

One cogent rationale for concluding that a tenant is a coinsured of the landlord is expressed in *Sutton v. Jondahl, supra.*

> This principle is derived from a recognition of a rational reality, namely, that both landlord and tenant have an insurable interest in the rented premises—the former owns the fee and the latter has a possessory interest. Here the landlords (Suttons) purchased the fire insurance from Central Mutual Insurance Company to protect such interests in the property against loss from fire. This is not uncommon. And as a matter of sound business practice, the premium paid had to be considered in establishing the rent rate on the rental unit. Such premium was chargeable against the rent as an overhead or operating expense. And of course it follows then that the tenant actually paid the premium as part of the monthly rental. . . . To suggest the fire insurance does not extend to the insurance interest of an occupying tenant is to ignore the realities of urban apartment dwelling and single-family dwelling renting.
>
> Prospective tenants ordinarily rely upon the owner of the dwelling to provide fire protection for the realty (as distinguished from personal property) absent an express agreement otherwise. Certainly it would not likely occur to a reasonably prudent tenant that the premises were without fire insurance protection or if there was such protection it did not inure to his benefit and that he would need to take out another fire policy to protect himself from any loss during his occupancy. Perhaps this comes about because the companies themselves have accepted coverage of a tenant as a natural thing. Otherwise their insurance salesmen would have long ago made such need a matter of common knowledge by promoting the sale to tenants of a second fire insurance policy to cover the real estate.

Sutton, supra, 532 P.2d 478.

In *Cascade Trailer Court v. Jim Beeson, et al., supra,* 749 P.2d 761, the court affirmed the decision of the trial court granting summary judgment to the tenants and holding that the tenants were implied coinsureds with the landlord under the landlord's fire policy, thus defeating the subrogation claim against them. The court responded to the criticism of the *Sutton* rationale . . . as follows:

> We are not persuaded by Cascade's general arguments attacking the rationale of *Sutton v. Jondahl,* 532 P.2d 478 (Okla.Ct.App.1975). Whether rent covers all of a landlord's expenses, including insurance premiums, is not the critical

> question. Rather, the issue concerns the parties' reasonable expectations. Where the landlord has secured fire insurance covering the leased premises, the tenant can reasonably expect the insurance to cover him as well, unless the parties have specifically agreed otherwise. Why?—because the tenant is in privity of contract with the landlord, and he has a property interest in the premises the insurance protects.

The rule barring subrogation against a tenant by the insurer of the landlord applies with equal force to fire damage caused by the tenant's negligence [even if the tenant agrees in the lease to pay for damage it negligently causes]. *Cascade Trailer Court v. Jim Beeson, et al., supra; McGinnis ex rel. C.I.E. Service Corp. v. LaShelle, supra. . . .*

[T]he court in *Cascade Trailer Court v. Jim Beeson, et al., supra* stated:

> We hold that the fact that the disputed lease provided the tenants would not negligently destroy the premises does not indicate the parties intended to limit the benefit of the insurance to the landlord. A tenant could sign the written lease at issue and reasonably never contemplate that if the premises were destroyed by a fire he negligently caused, his landlord's insurer could collect damages from him. We adopt the reasonable expectations rationale of the Sutton line of cases and hold Cascade is presumed to carry its insurance for the tenant's benefit because the lease did not contain an express provision to the contrary.

Cascade, supra, 749 P.2d 761.

The rental agreement (paragraph 5(b)) in the instant action provided in pertinent part that the tenant was required to:

> Maintain premises and furnishings in a good state and condition with reasonable wear and tear, damage by the elements and fire excepted, and to pay for repairs to the property made necessary by damage resulting from the negligence of Tenants.

When a tenant agrees to maintain the property in a good state and condition with "damage by fire excepted," a landlord should reasonably be expected to bear the burdens associated with damage by fire and insure against that eventuality. A lease provision requiring a tenant to return property in good condition, with damage by fire excepted, prohibits subrogation against that tenant by a landlord's insurer for fire damage caused by a tenant's negligence.

Since subrogation is an equitable doctrine, equity principles apply in determining its availability. In *Aetna Ins. Co. v. Craftwall of Idaho, Inc.,* Case No. 82–3073 (D.C. Idaho, 1983) [reversed and remanded at 757 F.2d 1030 (9th Cir.1985)], Judge Ryan opined:

> Consequently, it is the opinion of this court that there are strong public policy reasons for denying a landlord's insurance carrier a subrogation action against a negligent tenant, and that absent an agreement between the landlord and the tenant to the contrary, when a landlord insures the premises which are rented to third parties, the third parties are coinsureds for purposes of subrogation.

Judge Ryan also quoted from R. Keeton *Insurance Law,* § 4.4(b) at 210 (1971).

> Probably it is undesirable, from the point of view of public interest, that the risk of loss from a fire negligently caused by a lessee be upon the lessee rather than the lessor's insurer.

Equity prevents recovery from a tenant who leaves herself unprotected by insurance under circumstances in which she reasonably expected coverage from the landlord's policy. Denial of a right to subrogation in this instance prevents windfalls to insurers, prevents the double-insuring of property and places the risk where it was intended to be, on the landlords's insurance carrier which has collected premiums to cover the loss insured against.

Affirmed.

NOTES AND QUESTIONS

1. *Majority Rule. Weisgerber* represents the majority rule. In the absence of a lease provision that expressly requires the tenant to procure insurance for the dwelling, the homeowner's insurer cannot bring a subrogation claim against a tenant who negligently causes a loss. This rule saves the tenant the expense and hassle of procuring property insurance for a leased space. Of course, as was the case in *Weisgerber*, a tenant still may want to purchase renter's insurance to cover personal property.

2. *Subrogation Under Liability Policies and the "Made Whole" Rule.* Insurers also have subrogation rights under liability policies, typically pursuant to express policy provisions and under the common law. Most courts have adopted the "made whole" rule, which requires that the insurer can only recover in subrogation after the policyholder has been fully compensated for her loss. *See* John F. Dobbyn & Christopher C. French, Insurance Law In A Nutshell 423 (5th ed. 2016); Robert H. Jerry II & Douglas R. Richmond, Understanding Insurance Law 654 (5th ed. 2012).

3. *Workers' Compensation.* Under workers' compensation, which is governed by statutes, in many states the insurer that pays a workers' compensation claim for an injury caused by a third-party tortfeasor gets paid first from any recoveries from the tortfeasor, which is the exact opposite of the "made whole" rule. *See generally* Arthur Larson, Larson's Workers Compensation § 117.01[1].

4. *Health Insurance.* You may have noticed when visiting a physician or hospital that the intake form asks you whether the reason for your visit involves an accident. Now that you have studied the materials in this chapter, do you understand the reason this question is frequently asked? In recent years, health insurers have asserted subrogation claims much more aggressively. When someone goes to a physician or the hospital, normally the person presents their health insurance card. But, if the reason for the visit is an accident, then the costs of the visit might be covered by an automobile, workers' compensation, homeowners, or commercial liability policy, either on a first-party or a third-party basis. Health insurers have strong incentives to reduce their own claims costs by shifting payment responsibility to these other potential payors, and subrogation is an important tool to accomplish that.

EXERCISE

1. The *Weisgerber* court held that notions of "equity" prevent an insurer from bringing a subrogation claim against a negligent tenant. A public policy argument can be made that it would be better to place the risk of loss, and the incentive to buy insurance, on the tenant instead of the homeowner. Draft a 1-page memo that makes the argument that public policy favors placing the risk of loss, and the responsibility to procure insurance, on the tenant.

VI. BUSINESS INTERRUPTION INSURANCE

Another type of insurance commonly sold as part of a commercial property policy is "Business Interruption Insurance." Business interruption insurance is intended to replace a policyholder's lost revenues when its business operations are interrupted due to a covered peril. As such, it is a very important part of a business's portfolio of coverage. Although the proceeds are paid for lost income, the nexus to property is that the lost income results from the destruction of property the insured owns upon which the insured's business depends. Indeed, in many situations, the value of a destroyed physical plant is not a businessperson's greatest concern. Rather, it is the inability to produce income while the plant is out of commission: this can easily be the most significant financial loss.

Business interruption losses caused by natural and unnatural disasters are enormous.[4] For example, the business interruption losses associated with the 9/11 terrorist attack have been estimated to exceed $10 billion. Hurricane Katrina caused more than $45 billion in damage. The governors of New York and New Jersey estimated that Hurricane Sandy caused more than $60 billion in damages. Many businesses impacted by such disasters never recover. Indeed, the United States Department of

[4] The remainder of this introductory section was taken verbatim from Christopher C. French, *The Aftermath of Catastrophes: Valuing Business Interruption Insurance Losses*, 30 Ga. St. U. L. Rev. 461, 463–64, 469–70 (2014) (citations omitted).

Labor has estimated that 40% of businesses never reopen after experiencing a disaster. Of those that do, at least 25% fail within two years.

The genealogy of business interruption insurance begins over two hundred years ago and has its roots in insurance that was issued to protect property owners' rental income. Because property insurance historically did not protect against lost rent, separate coverage had to be purchased. Originally, such insurance was referred to as "use and occupancy" insurance. In the 1930s, the name evolved to business interruption insurance, and in the 1980s, the Insurance Services Office (ISO) coined the term "business income insurance" when it issued a new policy form for business interruption insurance.

As many courts and commentators have stated, the purpose of business interruption insurance is to return the policyholder to the position it would have occupied if the disaster had not occurred:

> The purpose of business interruption insurance is to protect the insured against losses that occur when its operations are unexpectedly interrupted, and to place it in the position it would have occupied if the interruption had not occurred.

The modern forms of business interruption insurance, which cover net profits plus continuing expenses, such as payroll and taxes, were introduced in the mid-1920s. There currently are two common business interruption policy forms: 1) Gross Earnings and 2) Business Income. Gross Earnings forms calculate business interruption losses from the top down, which means the business interruption loss is the total amount the policyholder would have earned if not for the interruption of its operations less the costs or expenses the policyholder did not incur due to the interruption in its business (i.e., the variable costs it saved because its operations were suspended). Business Income forms calculate business interruption losses from the bottom up, which means the business interruption loss is the net income the policyholder would have earned if not for the interruption plus the policyholder's continuing fixed expenses, such as payroll and taxes. In theory, the amount of a business interruption loss should be the same under the two policy forms.

Sometimes business interruption insurance disputes involve the question of whether a claim is covered, but more frequently such disputes involve valuation of business interruption claims. This is because the calculation of loss is based upon answers to questions that are frequently speculative. For example, how long should it take the policyholder to rebuild and resume its operations after the initial interruption? How much money would the policyholder have made if not for the interruption? Would the policyholder's business have increased *or decreased* if not for the interruption? Consider how these issues are treated in the following cases.

A. PERIOD OF RESTORATION

DUANE READE, INC. V. ST. PAUL FIRE AND MARINE INS. CO.

411 F.3d 384 (2d Cir. 2005)

Opinion

JOHN M. WALKER, JR., CHIEF JUDGE.

This case involves an insurance dispute arising from the destruction of the World Trade Center by terrorists on September 11, 2001 ("9/11"). Plaintiff-appellee Duane Reade, Inc. ("Duane Reade"), which up until that day had operated its most profitable drugstore in the main concourse of the World Trade Center ("WTC"), filed this action against its insurer defendant-appellant St. Paul Fire & Marine Insurance Co. ("St. Paul"), seeking, *inter alia,* a declaratory judgment that its recovery for business interruption losses caused by the store's destruction will continue until the entire WTC complex is rebuilt. St. Paul countered that Duane Reade's business interruption coverage terminated 21 months after 9/11, the time St. Paul claims was reasonably necessary for Duane Reade to relocate its store to a new location and resume operations.

The United States District Court for the Southern District of New York (Jed S. Rakoff, *Judge*), issued a decision declaring, in part, that Duane Reade's recovery of business interruption losses would continue for the hypothesized time it would take for Duane Reade to rebuild its store and that "[o]nce Duane Reade could resume functionally equivalent operations in the location where its WTC store once stood, the [recovery for business interruption losses] would be at an end." *Duane Reade, Inc. v. St. Paul Fire & Marine Ins. Co.,* 279 F.Supp.2d 235, 239 (S.D.N.Y.2003) ("*Duane Reade II*"). For the following reasons, we modify the district court's judgment to, *inter alia,* (1) eliminate any reference to "the location where [the] WTC store once stood," and (2) change "functionally equivalent operations" to "operations." *Id.* The judgment of the district court, as modified, is AFFIRMED.

BACKGROUND

The relevant facts are straightforward and undisputed. Duane Reade owns and operates more than 200 drugstores in and around New York City, including 124 in Manhattan. Prior to 9/11, its single most profitable store occupied leased premises on the main concourse of the WTC. On 9/11, Duane Reade was insured under a $150 million property insurance policy written by St. Paul that covered (1) losses caused by damage or destruction to "Real and Personal Property," defined as all of Duane Reade's own property as well as any other property in Duane Reade's "care, custody, or control" or for which Duane Reade was legally liable; (2) several specified coverages, referred to as "Time Element" coverages, that indemnify Duane Reade for losses that arise initially from damage or destruction to Real and Personal Property, but which increase with the passage of time; and (3) certain "Extensions of Coverage" and supplemental coverages.

At issue in this appeal is the Time Element coverage for business interruption ("BI"), which indemnifies Duane Reade for lost earnings and expenses if Duane Reade's business is partially or totally interrupted as a result of a covered property damage. The parties dispute the measure of time during which Duane Reade may recover for BI losses stemming from the destruction of the WTC store. The relevant valuation provision, entitled "PERIOD OF RESTORATION AND/OR INDEMNITY," provides that recovery of BI losses "shall not exceed such length of time as would be required with the exercise of due diligence and dispatch to rebuild, repair, or replace such property that has been destroyed or damaged" (the "Restoration Period").

St. Paul asserts that it began to adjust Duane Reade's claim soon after 9/11 and has already paid Duane Reade for all of its property damage and business interruption losses. As to the latter, it paid $9.8 million to cover 9 months of lost profits "to locate, furnish and open a new drug store," and an additional 12 months of profits to compensate for the lowered profits Duane Reade is likely to receive once its store reopens.

Duane Reade, not surprisingly, takes a different position: it rejects the premise underlying St. Paul's calculations that coverage for business interruption losses extended only until Duane Reade could relocate its WTC store to an alternative location. Duane Reade therefore filed an action for breach of contract and a declaratory judgment in which it asserted that:

> [T]he Restoration Period consists of the actual time period that would, or will, be required to restore Duane Reade's operations to the kind, quality, and level which existed at the WTC Store prior to the terrorist attacks and that such Restoration Period is coterminous with the time necessary to rebuild the complex which will replace the World Trade Center.

. . . .

[T]he district court . . . issued a declaratory judgment construing the policy's business interruption coverage. *Duane Reade II,* 279 F.Supp.2d at 235. The district court rejected as overly restrictive St. Paul's position that the "the period of restoration should last only so long as it would take Duane Reade to build a 'replacement' store somewhere in the vicinity of the former World Trade Center." *Id.* at 238 n. 4. In the district court's view, "such an interpretation would . . . be unreasonable, [because] it finds no support in the plain language of the Policy and . . . it would render superfluous the other clauses requiring mitigation of damages." *Id.*

But the district court also rejected as "untenable" Duane Reade's expansive reading "that the Restoration Period must be coterminous with the time actually required to rebuild the entire complex that will replace the World Trade Center." *Id.* at 239. Instead, the district court held, the proper reading of the policy fell somewhere in between the parties' views, such that the Restoration Period was to be measured by the "hypothetical or constructive (as opposed to actual) time frame for rebuilding . . . the WTC store itself, not the entire complex that once surrounded it," and that the Restoration Period would end "[o]nce Duane Reade could resume functionally equivalent operations in the location where its WTC store once stood." *Id.* (internal citation omitted).

Following a bench trial to resolve other issues and the entry of final judgment, St. Paul filed this appeal challenging the district court's declaration.

DISCUSSION

St. Paul's primary contentions on appeal are that (1) the district court erred in tying the "hypothesized time" of the Restoration Period to the time required to rebuild Duane Reade's store "at the location where its WTC store stood"; and (2) the Restoration Period continues until Duane Reade resumes "functionally equivalent" operations. We agree and modify the district court's declaration accordingly.

St. Paul also argues that . . . (5) the district court's declaration was internally inconsistent because it tied the duration of the BI coverage to both the rebuilding of Duane Reade's store and Duane Reade's resumption of operations; and (6) Duane Reade's asserted BI losses are barred in any event because they result from the elimination of a consumer market in the area of the World Trade Center, a peril expressly excluded under the policy. Each of these arguments is meritless.

. . . .

IV. *The Period of Restoration*

With the underbrush thus cleared, we turn to the subject of the principle dispute on this appeal: the district court's declaration of the scope of Duane Reade's BI coverage,[1] which it determined primarily by construing the policy's Restoration Period clause. The district court held, in relevant part,

> On their face, the Restoration Period clauses envision a hypothetical or constructive (as opposed to actual) time frame for

---

[1] The policy's business interruption clause provides coverage for:

The interest of [Duane Reade] in loss of earning (business interruption), including ordinary payroll, continuing expenses, loss of royalties and bonus programs as a result of an interruption of [Duane Reade]'s business (either partial or total) if such interruption is a result of a peril, not excluded under this policy, causing direct physical loss or damage to any Real or Personal Property whether insured or not . . . including but not limited to loss or damage to . . . property of [Duane Reade], . . . and property of customers . . . .

> rebuilding, as evidenced, for example, by their use of the subjunctive "would." Moreover, what is to be hypothesized is the time it would take to rebuild, repair, or replace the WTC store itself, not the entire complex that once surrounded it. Once Duane Reade could resume functionally equivalent operations in the location where its WTC store once stood, the [Restoration Period] would be at an end. Any losses continuing beyond that point would be addressed by the "Extended Recovery Period" provision in the Policy, not by the [Restoration Period] clause.

Duane Reade II, 279 F.Supp.2d at 239 (internal citations omitted). St. Paul argues that the district court erred by (1) extending the Restoration Period to when Duane Reade resumes operations that are "functionally equivalent" to its pre-9/11 operations; and (2) declaring that the length of the Restoration Period is tied to rebuilding a store at the specific WTC site where Duane Reade's store was located. We discuss each of these issues in turn.

A. *"Functionally Equivalent Operations"*

St. Paul contends that the district court's declaration that the Restoration Period ends at the point Duane Reade "could resume functionally equivalent operations" effectively rewrites the policy by superseding and enlarging upon the more limited coverage provided by the policy's Extended Recovery Period clause. We agree.

The Restoration Period clause establishes that BI coverage lasts only for the reasonable amount of time it would take Duane Reade "exercis[ing] . . . due diligence and dispatch to rebuild, repair, or replace such property that has been destroyed or damaged." Courts have consistently construed this or similar language as entitling the insured to continue to recover its lost profits until it can build a reasonably equivalent store in a reasonably equivalent location. *See, e.g.,* Lee R. Russ, 12 *Couch on Insurance* §§ 183:55, 185:7 (3d ed. 1998 & Supp.2003); *Beautytuft, Inc. v. Factory Ins. Ass'n,* 431 F.2d 1122, 1128 (6th Cir.1970) (holding that insured's resumption of partial operations in inferior, temporary premises did not terminate business interruption coverage); *see also Anchor Toy Corp. v. Am. Eagle Fire Ins. Co.,* 4 Misc.2d 364, 155 N.Y.S.2d 600, 603 (N.Y.Sup.Ct.1956) (holding that insured was entitled to modernize premises upon rebuilding). The rationale behind such holdings has generally been that insureds would lack any incentive to resume partial operations in temporary locations or under other inferior circumstances in order to mitigate damages if such actions would terminate their BI coverage. *See Couch on Insurance* §§ 183:55, 185:7. By contrast, we have found no case ruling that an insured is entitled to BI coverage until it can resume "functionally equivalent operations."

The fact that the district court incorporated novel terminology in order to determine the scope of coverage under such unusual circumstances is not, in and of itself, what proves fatal. Rather, it is that the novel terminology the district court chose conflicts with the coverage provided by the Extended Recovery Period clause, which provides:

> This policy is extended to cover the Actual Loss Sustained by [Duane Reade] resulting from interruption of business for such additional length of time as would be required with the exercise of due diligence and dispatch to restore [Duane Reade]'s business to the condition that would have existed had no loss occurred, commencing with the [later] of the following dates:
>
> a) the date on which liability of [St. Paul] of loss resulting from interruption of business would terminate if the [Extended Recovery Period] clause had not been attached to this policy or
>
> b) the date on which repair, replacement, or rebuilding of such part of the property as has been damaged is actually replaced, but in no event for more than twelve months from said later commencement date.

The purpose of the Extended Recovery Period is to provide additional coverage for the likely event that Duane Reade will continue to suffer losses due to its business interruption after it reopens the WTC store. The Extended Recovery Period guarantees Duane Reade its pre-9/11 profits until the earlier of when Duane Reade can restore business at its WTC store to the condition it would have been in had the WTC not been destroyed or twelve months after the Restoration Period ends.

Although the district court plainly recognized the relationship between the Restoration Period and the Extended Recovery Period, *see Duane Reade II*, 279 F.Supp.2d at 239 ("Any losses continuing beyond th[e] point [that Duane Reade could resume functionally equivalent operations] would be addressed by the 'Extended Recovery Period' provision in the Policy, not by the Restoration Period clause.") (internal citation omitted), its use of "functionally equivalent" to enhance the level of operations that will terminate the Restoration Period leaves no room for the Extended Recovery Period to operate. If Duane Reade achieves functionally equivalent operations within twelve months of resuming operations, the Restoration Period will terminate, but the Extended Recovery Period will not be triggered because Duane Reade will already have met the criteria for terminating that coverage. More important, if Duane Reade requires more than twelve months to achieve functionally equivalent operations, it will continue to receive business interruption coverage after the Extended Recovery Period coverage expires. As a result, the district court not only rendered the Extended Recovery Period provision superfluous, it nullified the express time constraints the parties agreed to place on such recovery, thereby effectively rewriting the policy to increase Duane Reade's coverage.

Because the district court's interpretation of the Restoration Period cannot be reconciled with the policy's other provisions, particularly the Extended Recovery Period, it must be modified to eliminate "functionally equivalent" to define the type of operations that will terminate the Restoration Period.

B. *Tying Restoration to the Site of the WTC Store*

The district court held that the Restoration Period was necessarily tied to a hypothesized rebuilding of Duane Reade's store at its former site at the WTC. Both parties construe this ruling as extending the Restoration Period to include, at a minimum, the time it would take to build the WTC building in which Duane Reade's store would be located. We need not decide whether this interpretation is correct because, in any event, we conclude that the district court erred in tying the Restoration Period to the specific site of Duane Reade's former store at the WTC.

Duane Reade defends the district court's site-specific reading of the Restoration Period by asserting that the parties intended to protect Duane Reade's interest in the specific location of its valuable WTC store. As evidence of this intent, Duane Reade points to the BI clause's coverage for damage to "Real or Personal Property whether insured or not, including . . . property of others." Duane Reade characterizes this language as creating "Contingent Business Interruption" coverage that reimburses Duane Reade for BI losses that are caused by damage to property that is not owned by Duane Reade but upon which its business depends, *i.e.*, the WTC building in which Duane Reade's store was located. Duane Reade also relies on a policy provision entitled "Attraction Properties," which provides:

> This policy is extended to cover the Actual Loss Sustained by [Duane Reade] directly resulting from the interruption of [Duane Reade]'s operation caused by damage to or destruction of Real or Personal property at Attraction Properties.
>
> Attraction Properties are defined as properties within on[e] statute mile of [Duane Reade]'s location, not operated by [Duane Reade], which attract potential customers to [Duane Reade]'s location.

Duane Reade contends that the inclusion in the policy of these two coverages establishes site-specific coverage for BI losses Duane Reade suffers as a result of damage to property owned by third parties. We disagree with Duane Reade's reasoning.

Even if we assume that the St. Paul policy provides coverage for business interruption losses caused by damage to properties owned by others but upon which Duane Reade's business depends, Duane Reade did not file a claim for losses under either of these coverages following the destruction of the WTC. In addition, neither coverage alters or affects the critical language of the Restoration Period setting forth the mechanism for determining the duration of coverage. We conclude, therefore, that neither of these two coverages has any bearing on this case.

The primary flaw in Duane Reade's claim that the parties specifically intended to provide BI coverage until Duane Reade could resume operations at the site of its former WTC store, however, is that the St. Paul policy is a general one covering all 200 Duane Reade stores. It makes no reference to the WTC store or, for that matter, *any* specific property other than Duane Reade's main headquarters, which is listed on the policy's declarations page. This omission distinguishes this case from those cases, relied upon by Duane Reade, in which the court tied the length of business interruption coverage to the rebuilding and/or replacing of the specific property that was the subject of the insurance policy.

. . . .

By contrast, the physical premises of the WTC building in which Duane Reade's store was located was not the subject of the St. Paul policy. Nor was the WTC even mentioned by name, as might be expected had the parties intended to single out the WTC store in a policy that covered all of Duane Reade's 200 stores. Instead, the declarations page lists only Duane Reade's corporate address, and no specific property is referred to in the BI clause, which omits even generic terms for location, such as "premises," "site," or "building." Thus nothing in the BI clause supports Duane Reade's claim that it provides site-specific coverage for its WTC store.

Our interpretation of the Restoration Period is consistent with the only case we have found that addresses the length of a restoration period in the context of leased premises that are contained within a larger building, *Streamline Capital, L.L.C. v. Hartford Casualty Insurance Co.,* No. 02 CIV. 8123(NRB), 2003 WL 22004888 (S.D.N.Y. Aug 25, 2003). In *Streamline,* offices that the insured, a computer facilities management company, had leased in the WTC were destroyed on 9/11. Judge Buchwald rejected the insured's argument that the restoration period for its BI coverage extended until the WTC was rebuilt. Distinguishing cases like *Anchor Toy,* the district court held,

> Given that "premises" in the phrase "property at the described premises" [in the policy's restoration period clause] means plaintiff's office suite, the only reasonable construction of the word "property" [in that same phrase] is [that it means] the plaintiff's own personal property-computers, desks, chairs, etc. This interpretation is logical, given that the Policy's Business Income coverage states: "We will pay for the actual loss of Business Income you sustain due to the necessary suspension of your 'operations' during the 'period of restoration.' " That the business

> income coverage only applies to the suspension of the plaintiff's "operations" indicates that it is dependent only on replacing what is necessary to resume those operations-namely, the plaintiff's personal property, not a specific office at a specific location.

Id. at *9.

We agree with Judge Buchwald's reasoning and find it equally applicable to the present case. As in *Streamline,* the St. Paul policy says nothing about the specific location of the interrupted business. It simply provides coverage until Duane Reade can "repair, rebuild, or replace" the property that was damaged and resume operations. Also in line with *Streamline,* the damaged property is the property Duane Reade had located in the premises it leased from the WTC.

Doubtless, if awaiting the rebuilding of the WTC and moving Duane Reade's WTC store to a new location were roughly equivalent tasks, the BI coverage would extend to whichever task Duane Reade, in its discretion, chose to do. The rebuilding of the WTC, however, will be a herculean undertaking far exceeding the rebuilding of a Duane Reade store in an existing building, or even in an as-yet-to-be built Manhattan office building, and involving numerous and complex contingencies over which neither Duane Reade nor St. Paul has any control. Under these circumstances, it would be entirely unreasonable to interpret the Restoration Period to include the time it would take for Duane Reade to resume operations in a store located at its former site where that site was neither the subject of the insurance policy nor expressly provided for in the calculus set forth in the Restoration Period. *See Streamline,* 2003 WL 22004888, at *9–*10 ("It is wholly unreasonable to think that the period of restoration should be tied to the rebuilding of real property over which neither the insured nor the insurer had any control, instead of tying it to a process that the plaintiff controlled: the acquisition of replacement office space and the installation of the plaintiff's personal property in that space."); *Roundabout Theatre Co.,* 751 N.Y.S.2d at 7–8 (rejecting plaintiff's claim that the Restoration Period extended until damage that occurred on the street and prevented access to theater was repaired because "the insured obviously has no duty to repair a third party's property"); *Anchor Toy,* 155 N.Y.S.2d at 603 (holding that while insured was entitled to modernize its new building, "[d]oubtless if an extraordinary additional time would be required to include improvements or innovations these would not be included."); *see also Cong. Bar & Res., Inc. v. Transamerica Ins. Co.,* 42 Wis.2d 56, 165 N.W.2d 409 (1969) (holding that restoration beyond what is reasonably necessary to restore the premises to its previous condition, such as demolition or reconstruction, are irrelevant and cannot be used to extend the period of compensation). In light of the foregoing, we conclude that the district court erred in holding that the St. Paul policy indemnifies Duane Reade for BI losses until the interrupted business can be resumed at the same location.

. . . .

In sum, we hold that the St. Paul policy does not provide BI coverage until Duane Reade can resume operations in a store located at its former WTC site. Instead, coverage extends only for the hypothetical time it would reasonably take Duane Reade to "repair, rebuild, or replace" its WTC store at a suitable location. To be sure, there are few if any locations in New York City comparable to the WTC, and Duane Reade will most likely not be able to recreate the profit stream it once enjoyed there. But any discrepancies between the new building and the WTC in terms of benefits and advantages are exclusively accounted for under the Leasehold Interest clause.

We therefore modify the district court's construction of. . . . the Restoration Period in order to effectuate the policy's separate treatment of loss due to business interruption and losses due to the cancellation of a leasehold. To that end, we eliminate the district court's restriction of location, *i.e.*, rebuilding the WTC store at its former site, as well as its emphasis on "rebuilding," despite the BI clause's broader reference to "repair[ing], rebuild[ing], or replac[ing]," which together impermissibly extended Duane Reade's BI coverage to include injury caused by Duane Reade's loss of the WTC leasehold.

V. The "Loss of Market" Exclusion

Finally, St. Paul renews the argument it made in the district court that Duane Reade's losses are excluded under the policy because they would have occurred in any event as a result of the disappearance of the local consumer market that ensued from the destruction of the WTC. The provision relied on by St. Paul excludes "loss or damage caused by . . . delay or loss of market."

. . . .

Put simply, whether Duane Reade's BI losses can be attributed in whole or in part to a loss of market in the WTC vicinity has no bearing in this case. . . . St. Paul has already acknowledged that Duane Reade has suffered a loss due to BI and has paid Duane Reade some $9.8 million for these losses. Because there is no dispute that Duane Reade suffered a BI loss, St. Paul's assertion that the "loss of market" exclusion applies to Duane Reade's claim creates, at most, a factual issue concerning the amount of loss Duane Reade may recover. Such factual issues are properly the subject of the appraisal proceeding.

CONCLUSION

For the foregoing reasons, we modify the district court's declaration to read as follows:

> On their face, the Restoration Period clauses envision a hypothetical or constructive (as opposed to actual) time frame for rebuilding, *repairing, or replacing,* as evidenced, for example, by their use of the subjunctive "would." Moreover, what is to be hypothesized is the time it would take to rebuild, repair, or replace the *functional equivalent of the store Duane Reade lost,* not the *WTC* complex that once surrounded it. Once Duane Reade could resume operations in *a permanent location reasonably equivalent to the site of its former store at the WTC,* the Restoration Period would be at an end. Any losses continuing beyond that point would be addressed by the "Extended Recovery Period" provision in the Policy, not by the Restoration Period clause.

(modifications italicized).

The judgment of the district court as modified by this opinion is AFFIRMED.

NOTES AND QUESTIONS

1. *Made Whole?* Will Duane Reade be made whole for its business interruption loss under the Second Circuit's ruling?

2. *Business Interruption/Time Element Coverage.* Business interruption insurance is also often referred to as "time element" coverage because the time period associated with the business interruption is part of the damage calculation. There are a number of elements to a business interruption claim that must be satisfied for coverage to be triggered: 1) there must be "physical loss or damage" to property covered by the policy, 2) the cause of the "physical loss or damage" must be a covered peril, and 3) there must be an interruption of the policyholder's business. What constitutes "physical loss or damage" is currently being litigated in the context of COVID-19 business interruption losses, which insurers generally contend are not covered by business interruption insurance because, insurers argue, such losses are not caused by "physical loss or damage." For a discussion of the arguments for and against coverage for COVID-19 business interruption losses, *see* Christopher C. French, *COVID-19 Business Interruption Insurance Losses: The Cases For And Against Coverage*, 27 Conn. Ins. L. J. 1 (2020).

3. *Loss of Market Exclusion.* Although not substantively addressed by the Second Circuit in *Duane Reade*, business interruption insurance typically contains a "loss of market" exclusion that specifies that the insurance does not cover purely economic losses caused by market disruptions unrelated to a covered peril. For example, if a business loses its customers due to another business taking its share of the market such that the company begins shutting

down production for periods of time to adjust to lower demand for its products, business interruption insurance does not cover such "losses." Following disasters such as Hurricane Katrina and 9/11, some insurers, based upon the argument that there was no longer any demand for the policyholder's products or services in the area of the disaster, attempted with little success to rely upon the market loss exclusion to deny coverage.

4. *Contingent Business Interruption Coverage*. Policyholders can also purchase contingent business interruption coverage to insure against business interruptions caused by an important supplier being unable to supply a necessary product due to a covered peril impacting the supplier or an important customer being unable to purchase the policyholder's product due to a covered peril impacting the customer. It is important to note that the interruption of supplies or purchases must be due to physical damage to the supplier's or customer's property as a result of a covered peril.

5. *Loss of Utilities*. Business interruption insurance also typically covers business interruptions caused by a loss of utility services, such as gas or electricity, necessary to operate the policyholder's business. Again, the utility provider must suffer physical damage of a type covered by the policy in order to trigger coverage.

6. *Period of Interruption*. As reflected by the *Duane Reade* case, the length of time used to measure the loss can have a significant impact on the size of the claim. The policy language typically defines the period of interruption as the earlier of: 1) the actual date business operations resumed or 2) when, "with the exercise of due diligence and dispatch," business operations could have been restored. As in the *Duane Reade* case, in situations where the policyholder's business is located in, for example, a mall or is otherwise dependent upon a nearby attraction, the damage formula does not actually replace the policyholder's lost revenue between the time of interruption and resumption of operations by the mall or nearby attraction.

7. *Extended Recovery Period*. For many types of business, the policyholder's revenue stream will not return to the same amount immediately upon resumption of business operations after an interruption. Customers frequently find replacement suppliers and do not return to do business with the policyholder, it takes time to create inventory to sell, etc. Consequently, it is common for policyholders to purchase business interruption coverage for what is called an "Extended Recovery Period." The extended recovery period, commonly 90 days or another specified period of time, allows for business interruption coverage to extend beyond the date business operations resume.

B. VALUATION OF BUSINESS INTERRUPTION CLAIMS

The valuation of business interruption claims is a fertile source of conflict between insurers and policyholders. Determining lost income is inherently speculative to some extent, and situations where accountants (often called "forensic accountants" in this setting) disagree are common.

Although there are many minor variations in the wording used in business interruption policies because insurers often have their own policy forms that they prefer to use, all such forms are drafted by insurers. . . .[5] One common version of the insuring agreement language found in Gross Earnings policy forms provides:

> [The insurer] shall be liable for the ACTUAL LOSS SUSTAINED by insured resulting directly from such interruption of business, but not exceeding the reduction in gross earnings less charges and expenses which do not necessarily continue during the interruption. . . .

In short, the policyholder is entitled to recover its lost gross earnings less saved variable expenses. This is a top down approach where the calculation starts with lost gross earnings and then deducts the variable expenses that were not incurred due to the interruption of operations.

Another common version of the insuring agreement language used in Business Income policy forms is worded as follows:

> [The insurer] will pay an insured during its period of suspended business operation the "(i) Net Income (Net Profit or Loss before income taxes) that would have been earned or incurred if no physical loss or damage had occurred. . .; and (ii) Continuing normal operating expenses incurred, including payroll[.]"

In short, the policyholder is entitled to recover its net profits plus fixed continuing expenses. This is a bottom up approach where the calculation starts with net profits and then adds continuing fixed expenses. Theoretically, the amount should be the same under Gross Earnings and Business Income forms.

The loss valuation provisions are commonly worded as follows:

> In determining the amount of gross earnings covered hereunder for the purposes of ascertaining the amount of loss sustained, *due consideration shall be given to the experience of the business before the date of the damage or destruction and to the probable experience thereafter had no loss occurred.*

Notably, the term "gross earnings" is not defined in the policies. Also, this language clearly contemplates doing a projection regarding the business's "probable experience" if the loss had not occurred.

Another version of the valuation language that also is often used provides:

---

[5] The remainder of this introductory section was taken verbatim from Christopher C. French, *The Aftermath of Catastrophes: Valuing Business Interruption Insurance Losses*, 30 Ga. St. U. L. Rev. 461, 470–72 (2014) (citations omitted).

> We'll cover your actual loss of earnings and extra expenses incurred because of necessary or potential interruption of business . . . . *In figuring earnings, we'll weigh the performance of your business before the loss and what its performance probably would have been afterwards had no loss occurred.*

Again, the language contemplates that an analysis will be conducted regarding what the policyholder's hypothetical "performance probably would have been" if no loss had occurred.

Consider how the courts in the following two cases grappled with the valuation of business interruption losses under the applicable policy language.

CATLIN SYNDICATE LTD. V. IMPERIAL PALACE OF MISSISSIPPI, INC.

600 F.3d 511 (5th Cir. 2010)

Opinion

Insurer Catlin Syndicate and casino operator Imperial Palace disagree about how to determine loss under the business-interruption provision of the insurance policy that Catlin issued to Imperial Palace. Catlin argues that the business-interruption provision unambiguously indicates that only historical sales figures should be considered when determining loss. Imperial Palace argues that the provision is ambiguous, and therefore sales figures after reopening should also be taken into account.

We addressed the definition of "loss" under a materially identical business-interruption provision in *Finger Furniture Co. v. Commonwealth Insurance Co.*, 404 F.3d 312 (5th Cir.2005). *Finger Furniture* does not control this case because it dealt with a question of Texas law, while this case deals with a question of Mississippi law. However, there is no significant difference between Texas and Mississippi law on this issue. Accordingly, we find that Mississippi courts would apply the law in the same way as Texas courts, and we AFFIRM.

Facts

Hurricane Katrina damaged Imperial Palace, forcing it to shut down for several months. When Imperial Palace reopened, its revenues were much greater than before the hurricane; many nearby casinos remained closed, and people who wanted to gamble had few choices. Imperial Palace submitted a claim to its insurers, including Catlin. Catlin agreed to pay the claim, but the parties disputed Imperial Palace's losses. Imperial Palace stated that its losses were approximately $165 million, while Catlin believed the losses were closer to $65 million. The largest discrepancy was in the amount of business-interruption loss: Imperial Palace put this amount at about $80 million, while Catlin put it at about $6.5 million. This discrepancy resulted from the parties' different interpretations of the policy's business-interruption provision, which states, in pertinent part:

> Experience of the business—In determining the amount of the Time Element loss as insured against by this policy, due consideration shall be given to experience of the business before the loss and the probable experience thereafter had no loss occurred.

Catlin filed a complaint in federal district court, seeking declaratory relief. Imperial Palace counterclaimed for breach of contract and negligence, among other claims. The parties filed cross-motions for summary judgment. Catlin argued that under the business-interruption provision, Imperial Palace's recovery should be based on net profits Imperial Palace would probably have earned if Hurricane Katrina had not struck the Mississippi Gulf Coast and damaged its facilities. Thus, Catlin stated that Imperial Palace's loss should be determined by looking solely at pre-hurricane sales. Imperial Palace argued that the correct hypothetical was not one in which Hurricane Katrina did not strike at all; it was one in which Hurricane Katrina struck but did not damage Imperial Palace's facilities. Accordingly, Imperial Palace averred that its recovery should be based in part on the amount it actually earned when it reopened after Katrina.

After considering the parties' arguments, the district court denied Imperial Palace's motion in its entirety, and granted Catlin's motion "to the extent that Catlin [sought] a partial summary judgment that [Imperial Palace's] profits upon reopening after Hurricane Katrina should not be taken into account to determine what [Imperial Palace] would have experienced had the storm not occurred." *Catlin Syndicate Ltd. v. Imperial Palace of Miss., Inc.,* No. 1:08–CV–97, 2008 WL 5235888, at *1, *8 (S.D.Miss. Dec. 15, 2008). We granted leave to appeal the district court's interlocutory order solely as to this ruling.

Analysis

In *Finger Furniture,* a tropical storm caused Finger's stores to close for one to two days. 404 F.3d at 313. A week after reopening, Finger slashed prices, and sales soared. *Id.* Finger filed a claim for lost sales under the business-interruption provision of its insurance contract with Commonwealth. *Id.* The business-interruption provision stated, in pertinent part:

> In determining the amount of gross earnings covered hereunder for the purposes of ascertaining the amount of loss sustained, due consideration shall be given to the experience of the business before the date of the damage or destruction and to the probable experience thereafter had no loss occurred.

Id. at 314.

Commonwealth denied the claim, arguing that Finger's increased sales the following week made up for the sales that it did not make while closed. *Id.* at 314. Commonwealth filed a declaratory judgment action. *Id.* at 313. The district court granted Finger's motion for summary judgment, and Commonwealth appealed. *Id.*

In affirming, we explained that the proper method for determining loss under the business-interruption provision was to look at sales before the interruption rather than sales after the interruption. *Id.* at 314. We noted that "the policy requires due consideration of the business's experience before the date of the loss and the business's probable experience had the loss not occurred," and that this language should be interpreted as meaning "that a business-interruption loss will be based on historical sales figures." *Id.* We stated that "[h]istorical sales figures reflect a business's experience before the date of the damage or destruction and predict a company's probable experience had the loss not occurred," and that "[t]he strongest and most reliable evidence of what a business would have done had the catastrophe not occurred is what it had been doing in the period just before the interruption." *Id.*

We declined to consider post-interruption sales, noting that "the business-loss provision says nothing about taking into account actual post-damage sales to determine what the insured would have experienced had the storm not occurred." *Id.* Further, we stated that "[t]he contract language does not suggest that the insurer can look prospectively to what occurred after the loss to determine whether its insured incurred a business-interruption loss." *Id.*

The language in the business-interruption provision of Imperial Palace's insurance policy with Catlin mirrors the language in *Finger Furniture,* with one minor distinction. In *Finger Furniture,* the provision said, "In determining the amount of . . . loss . . ., due consideration shall be given to the experience of the business before the . . . *damage or destruction* and to the probable experience thereafter had no loss occurred." Here, the provision says, "In determining the amount of the . . . loss . . ., due consideration shall be given to experience of the business before the *loss* and the probable experience thereafter had no loss occurred." Imperial Palace urges us to distinguish *Finger Furniture* on this basis. But this is a distinction without a difference; in the context of these business-interruption provisions, the terms "damage or destruction" and "loss" are functionally equivalent. Indeed, in common usage "damage" and "destruction" are two definitions of "loss." RANDOM HOUSE WEBSTER'S UNABRIDGED DICTIONARY 1137 (2d ed. 2001). Likewise, "loss" is a synonym for "damage." *Id.* at 504.

In addition, Imperial Palace tries to distinguish *Finger Furniture* on its facts. In *Finger Furniture,* the insurer argued that post-storm sales should be taken into account to show that the insured did not actually incur any losses. Here, the insured—not the insurer—argues that post-hurricane sales should be taken into account to show that losses were much greater than pre-hurricane figures would indicate. But our determination in *Finger Furniture,* like our determination here, was based on a legal analysis of the business-interruption provision and did not depend on the facts that Imperial Palace highlights. The language in the two provisions is materially identical, so the analysis is the same despite the factual dissimilarities.

Imperial Palace also argues that *Finger Furniture* is distinguishable because a "favorable conditions clause" might have existed in that case, but none exists in the instant case. A favorable conditions clause prohibits consideration of post-loss business increases when determining the amount of business-interruption losses. If a favorable conditions clause existed in *Finger Furniture,* it did not impact the analysis. Accordingly, it is not a valid basis on which to distinguish *Finger Furniture* from the instant case.

Finally, Imperial Palace argues that Catlin's interpretation of the business-interruption provision conflates the term "loss" with the idea of an "occurrence." In this case, Hurricane Katrina was the "occurrence," which inflicted "losses" on many victims, one of which was Imperial Palace. Imperial Palace asserts that Catlin asks us to interpret the business-interruption provision in such a way that the phrase "had no loss occurred" morphs into "had no occurrence occurred." Imperial Palace argues that instead, we should disentangle the loss from the occurrence and determine loss based on a hypothetical in which Hurricane Katrina hit Mississippi, damaged all of Imperial Palace's competitors, but left Imperial Palace intact: the occurrence occurred, but the loss did not. While we agree with Imperial Palace that the loss is distinct from the occurrence—at least in theory—we also believe that the two are inextricably intertwined under the language of the business-interruption provision. Without language in the policy instructing us to do so, we decline to interpret the business-interruption provision in such a way that the loss caused by Hurricane Katrina can be distinguished from the occurrence of Hurricane Katrina itself.

Because "loss" and "damage or destruction" are equivalent terms, the business-interruption provision in *Finger Furniture* is materially identical to the provision in this case, and our interpretation of the provision in *Finger Furniture* guides us now. *Finger Furniture* tells us "that a business-interruption loss will be based on historical sales figures," and that we should not "look prospectively to what occurred after the loss." 404 F.3d at 314. Thus, in the business-interruption provision at hand, only historical sales figures should be considered when determining loss, and sales figures after reopening should not be taken into account.

Finger Furniture does not control this case because it dealt with a question of Texas law, while this case deals with a question of Mississippi law. However, there is no material difference between Texas and Mississippi law on this issue. *Compare Puckett v. U.S. Fire Ins. Co.*, 678 S.W.2d 936, 938 (Tex.1984) ("When there is no ambiguity [in an insurance contract], it is the court's duty to give the words used their plain meaning."), *with Martin*, 998 So.2d at 963 ("[I]f [an insurance policy] is clear and unambiguous, then it must be interpreted as written."). Accordingly, we find that Mississippi courts would apply the law in the same way as Texas courts.

Conclusion

We AFFIRM.

BERK-COHEN ASSOCIATES, LLC V. LANDMARK AMERICAN INS. CO.

2009 WL 2777163 (E.D. La. Aug. 27, 2009)

Opinion

Before the Court are several motions for partial summary judgment . . . by defendant, Landmark American Insurance Co. (Landmark). For the following reasons, defendant's motion to limit plaintiffs' business loss is DENIED. . . .

Background

Plaintiff Berk-Cohen Associates, LLC (Berk-Cohen) owns a sixty-six building apartment complex. The complex consists of more than 700 apartments and is known as Forest Isle Apartments. Plaintiff Manhattan Management Co. (Manhattan Management) manages the apartment complex under the terms of a management agreement entered into with plaintiff Berk-Cohen. As part of its managerial responsibilities, Manhattan Management obtained two policies of insurance from Landmark. The first, Policy No. LHD340608, covered the Forest Isle Apartments between April 25, 2005 and April 25, 2006. The second, Policy No. LHD346361, covered the Forest Isle Apartments between April 25, 2006 and April 25, 2007. Each policy provided insurance coverage for physical damage to the Forest Isle Apartments as well as lost rental value resulting from such damage. In addition, each policy provided insurance coverage for other properties Berk-Cohen owned, including apartment complexes in New Jersey and New York. Both plaintiff Berk-Cohen and plaintiff Manhattan Management are named insureds on each policy.

As a result of a series of unfortunate events, the Forest Isle Apartments were severely damaged. In August 2005, two weeks before Hurricane Katrina, a tornado struck the apartments. Landmark paid $846,262.00 to cover the physical damage to the buildings. Before any repairs were made,

Hurricane Katrina decimated the greater New Orleans area. Landmark paid $19,349,197.00 for new damages to the buildings. In May 2006, a fire broke out in ten apartments still under repair from Hurricane Katrina. Landmark paid $609,186.00 for the fire damage. And lastly, in October 2006, a vehicle struck a transformer causing a temporary power outage. Landmark paid $60,703.00 to fix the transformer. Repair and rehabilitation of the Forest Isle Apartments began immediately after Hurricane Katrina and, despite the setbacks caused by the fire and transformer incidents, were completed roughly two years later, in September 2007.

On August 28, 2007, plaintiff Berk-Cohen sued Landmark in state court. On the same day, plaintiff Manhattan Management also sued Landmark in state court. Landmark removed both suits to this Court in accordance with 28 U.S.C. §§ 1332, 1441 and 1446, and the Court consolidated them. The allegations made by Berk-Cohen and Manhattan Management in each of their respective complaints are generally the same. Both plaintiffs allege "losses in business income due to windstorm and other non-flood damages to the Forest Isle Apartment Complex." The derivation of Berk-Cohen's and Manhattan Management's lost business income, however, is different. Berk-Cohen claims business income losses relating to rental revenue received from the Forest Isle Apartments. Manhattan Management claims lost income stemming from a management fee granted under the Management Agreement. Berk-Cohen also claims additional losses relating to a ten percent management fee owed to Manhattan Management under the Management Agreement for overseeing "repair, restoration and rehabilitation" of the Forest Isle Apartments.

Analysis

Insurance Policy Interpretation

The Court has diversity jurisdiction over this matter under 28 U.S.C. § 1332, and Louisiana state law applies to the insurance contract at issue. Under Louisiana law, an insurance policy is a contract that constitutes the law between the parties, and it must be interpreted in accordance with the general rules of contract interpretation set forth in the Louisiana Civil Code. The extent of insurance coverage is determined by the parties' intent as reflected by words in the policy. If the policy wording is clear, and it expresses the intent of the parties, the agreement must be enforced as written. La. Civ.Code art.2046; *Pareti,* 536 So.2d at 420. The policy must be construed as a whole, and one portion should not be construed separately at the expense of disregarding another. *Pareti,* 536 So.2d at 420. If an ambiguity exists, the ambiguity must be construed in favor of the party seeking coverage. *Id.* The Court may not alter the terms of the policy under the guise of contract interpretation when the language of the policy is unambiguous. *Id.*

Lost Business Income

A. Berk-Cohen

The first of the issues defendant presents arises out of Berk-Cohen's claim for business income lost from its inability to rent apartments in the wake of Hurricane Katrina. Plaintiff claims that its total business income loss exceeds the policy limits of $4,647,286, and it seeks the maximum recoverable under the policy. Defendant, on the other hand, contends that Berk-Cohen's business income loss is less than the policy limit. The difference in the two parties' figures stems from the manner in which each calculates business income loss. Berk-Cohen's calculations account for a post-Katrina increase in occupancy rate from 91.4 percent to 100 percent and an additional up-tick in rental price. Specifically, Berk-Cohen claims that the housing shortage after Hurricane Katrina caused an increase in demand for apartments in the New Orleans area and consequently, an increase in the rental market value of the Forest Isle Apartments by more than 40 percent. Defendant's calculations, on the other hand, rely solely on pre-Katrina occupancy rates and rental prices.

The purpose of a business income loss provision is to indemnify insureds for lost income resulting from those events covered by their insurance policy. Whether market changes are appropriate considerations in calculating lost business income depends upon the language of the policy itself. When a provision in an insurance policy is found to be ambiguous, it "is construed against the insurer in favor of coverage." *Arctic Slope Regional Corp. v. Affiliated FM Ins. Co.,* 564 F.3d 707, 709–10 (5th Cir.2009)(quoting *Sher v. Lafayette Ins. Co.*, 988 So.2d 186, 193 (La.2008)); *see also Herbert v. Webre,* 982 So.2d 770, 774 (La.2008).

The operative language of the Landmark Insurance Policy defines business income as "a) Net Income (Net Profits or Loss before income taxes) that would have been earned or incurred; and b) continuing normal operating expenses incurred, including payroll." (R. Doc. 19, Ex. A and B). The Landmark Insurance Policy further states how business income loss will be determined:

> 3. Loss Determination
>
> a. The amount of Business Income loss will be determined based on:
>
> (1) The Net Income of the business before the direct physical loss or damage occurred;
>
> (2) The likely Net Income of the business if no physical loss or damage had occurred, but not including any Net Income that would likely have been earned as a result of an increase in the volume of business due to favorable

business conditions caused by the impact of the Covered Cause of Loss on customers or on other businesses;

(3) The operating expenses, including payroll expenses, necessary to resume "operations" with the same quality of service that existed just before the direct physical loss or damage; and

(4) Other relevant sources of information, including:

(a) Your financial records and accounting procedures;

(b) Bills, invoices and other vouchers; and

(c) Deeds, liens or contracts.

Landmark's policy language has not been construed by the Fifth Circuit or any other appellate court. The Fifth Circuit has analyzed the language of a business income loss provision in *Finger Furniture Co. Inc. v. Commonwealth Ins. Co.*, 404 F.3d 312 (5th Cir.2005). In that case, the policy provided:

> In determining the amount of gross earnings covered hereunder for the purposes of ascertaining the amount of loss sustained, due consideration shall be given to the experience of the business before the date of the damage or destruction and to the probable experience thereafter had no loss occurred.

Finger Furniture, 404 F.3d at 314. The *Finger Furniture* plaintiff conducted an inventory sale at its furniture store one week after Tropical Storm Allison, which had previously closed the store for two days. In its claim for business income loss, the furniture store attempted to use profits from the post-storm sale as documenting actual business lost. The Fifth Circuit construed the policy language to preclude the use of post-damage market data. *Id.* In doing so, the court found that a business's historical sales figures are the best indicator of probable future success. *Id.* The holding set forth by the Fifth Circuit in *Finger Furniture* reflects the Court's understanding of what contracting parties would likely expect regarding policy coverage, *ex ante*. The insured could not say that a storm did not occur to recover business income loss and simultaneously calculate such loss on the basis that the storm did, in fact, occur and generate greater market demand. *Id.* As the Fourth Circuit stated in a case with a similar factual context, "had the hurricane not occurred, . . . neither would the specifically claimed earnings source have come into being." *Prudential LMI v. Colleton Enterprises, Inc.*, No. 91–1757, 1992 WL 252507, at *4.

Berk-Cohen presents no evidence that the occupancy rate at Forest Isle Apartment Complex would have increased in the absence of the effects Hurricane Katrina had on the area in which it competes for business. Nor does plaintiff present evidence that an increase of rental value would have occurred without the housing shortage resulting from the storm. Instead, Berk-Cohen focuses on the language of paragraph 3(a)(2).

The first clause of Paragraph 3(a)(2) ("[t]he likely Net Income of the business if no physical loss or damage had occurred . . ."), is a familiar one. It roughly mirrors the language of both the *Finger Furniture* and *Prudential LMI* business income loss provisions. If the Landmark policy stopped there, *Finger Furniture* would control. It does not, however. The conjunctive phrase beginning "but not" sheds further light on the scope of the intended coverage. This clause explains what is not covered by the first clause, *i.e.*, which type of projected income the insured cannot use to prove his business income loss. The insured cannot prove business income using evidence of "likely Net Income . . . earned as a result of an increase in the *volume* of business . . . caused by the impact of *the Covered Cause of Loss*." Berk-Cohen argues that the exclusion applies to increases in business due only to "the Covered Cause of Loss" requires a different result than that reached in *Finger Furniture*.

Specifically, Berk-Cohen argues that evidence of favorable business conditions caused by flooding escape the exclusionary wording in paragraph 3(a)(2) because flooding was not the Covered Cause of Loss from which the Forest Isle property sustained covered damage. Landmark's policy language is different from that of the policies analyzed in *Finger Furniture* and *Prudential LMI* in both a unique and a significant way. The second clause of paragraph 3(a)(2) explicitly refers to "the Covered Cause of Loss" under the policy. "Covered Cause of Loss" is a term defined within the policy itself. The provision is instructive, however, because it differentiates between those favorable business conditions created by the type of loss triggering coverage by the Landmark Policy and those that are not. The policy excludes only favorable business conditions caused by the same cause of loss for which the insured is invoking coverage under the policy. *Finger Furniture* and *Prudential LMI* contained no such language. The *expressio unius est exclusion alterius* principle of construction—"the expression of one thing implies the exclusion of the other"—instructs that the explicit removal of favorable market conditions resulting from "the Covered Cause of Loss" from the business income calculation implies that those market conditions resulting from non-covered causes of losses are permissible.

Landmark argues that flood is covered under the policy, so that favorable business conditions due to flooding are foreclosed as a source of lost business income. Landmark makes this argument because the policy covers multiple properties and the policy contains flood coverage endorsements covering flood damage to properties in certain flood zones. Landmark's argument is rejected because the policy excludes changed business conditions caused by *the* Covered Cause of Loss, not *a* Covered

Cause of Loss. The use of the definite article "the" restricts the covered loss to the one that triggered the coverage at the insured property at issue.

Landmark ultimately concedes that flood is not a Covered Cause of Loss at Forest Isle Apartments. But, defendant argues that allowing recovery for favorable business conditions resulting from flood when the policy precludes recovery for actual flood damage is "an absurd conclusion." The flood exclusion is property-specific, relieving Landmark of obligation to cover property for flood damage because of its particular location and presumably the risk it poses of being flooded. Berk-Cohen did not seek to recover for flood damage at the Forest Isle location. Landmark got the benefit of its flood exclusion. Landmark's policy illustrates an intent to prevent the insured from benefitting from the same cause of loss for which it invoked coverage. Further, Landmark's interpretation would render the second clause in paragraph 3(a)(2) superfluous. It would make no sense for the drafters of the Landmark Policy to include language in paragraph 3(a)(2) that explicitly excludes favorable business conditions resulting from the Covered Cause of Loss, if the drafters intended to also exclude favorable business conditions resulting from losses not covered under the policy, such as those resulting from flood. The Court must interpret the Landmark Policy as to give meaning to all of its various provisions. *See* La. Civ.Code art. 2049 ("A provision susceptible of different meanings must be interpreted with a meaning that renders it effective and not with one that renders it ineffective.").

Lastly, Landmark argues that the policy covers physical loss resulting from the hurricane as a unitary storm resulting in both wind and flood damage, and therefore the distinction between wind and flood is of no import. Though distilling the cause of damage may be difficult at times, the Landmark Policy wording specifically references "the Covered Cause of Loss" and subsequently differentiates between wind and flood damage. The Court will not treat wind and flood damage as the same when the policy itself does not do so.

The Court finds the Landmark Policy allows Berk-Cohen to recover for favorable market conditions resulting from flooding. It should come as no surprise that seemingly disparate coverages would result when a single policy attempts to account for the range of risks attributable to properties in diverse geographic locations. The parties appear to have contemplated different business income coverages for each property covered under policy when they incorporated both clauses of paragraph 3(a)(2) into the policy, and referred to "the Covered Cause of Loss" in the second clause. For the foregoing reasons, the Court DENIES defendant's motion for partial summary judgment precluding Berk-Cohen's use of changed market conditions as evidence of future business income.

NOTES AND QUESTIONS

1. *"Probable Experience Thereafter"?* What did the *Catlin* court interpret this policy language to mean? Was the court's interpretation persuasive?

Is the damages formula for business interruption losses unambiguous? How do you determine what a party's "probable experience" in the future will be if it is not based upon the party's past experience? If it is based upon past experience, then what is the point of the language that says a party's "probable experience" in the future will also be considered? How are changes in the economic climate, such as a recession, addressed in the formula?

2. *Finger Furniture.* Both the *Catlin* and *Berk-Cohen* courts addressed the Fifth Circuit's decision in *Finger Furniture Co. Inc. v. Commonwealth Ins. Co.*, 404 F.3d 312 (5th Cir. 2005). How did the courts reconcile their holdings with *Finger Furniture*?

3. *Flood Versus Wind.* If flood is an excluded peril, how did the policyholder in *Berk-Cohen* recover for its business interruption in light of the fact that business interruption coverage only applies if the interruption is due to a covered peril?

4. *Reasonable Certainty.* Damages must be proven to a reasonable degree of certainty. *See, e.g.*, Lee R. Russ & Thomas F. Segalla, Couch on Insurance § 175:64 (3d ed. 2005) ("[T]here can be no recovery where the loss cannot be determined within reasonable certainty."). In light of the fact that what a business would have earned if the catastrophe had not occurred is inherently speculative, how can a party prove a speculative amount to a reasonable certainty?

5. *Daily Loss Value.* "During the annual policy renewal process, a policyholder provides a business interruption loss projection to the insurer's underwriters that is based upon the policyholder's current budget, revenue, and cost data that the insurer then uses to: (1) evaluate the insured risk, (2) calculate a daily loss value, and (3) in part, establish the amount of the premium." Christopher C. French, *The Aftermath of Catastrophes: Valuing Business Interruption Insurance Losses*, 30 Ga. St. U. L. Rev. 461, 511 (2014) (citation omitted). Instead of the amorphous loss valuation language used in business interruption insurance that has resulted in numerous disputes, would it make more sense to use the "daily loss" value for business interruption losses that the parties agreed to during the underwriting process and which is used to calculate the policy's premium?

EXERCISE

1. Draft a 2-page memo that analyzes the pros and cons of using a "daily loss" value for valuing business interruption losses instead of basing such calculations on the current policy language.

CHAPTER SEVEN

LIFE INSURANCE

■ ■ ■

"A full-time student with no siblings or parents who might be affected by his premature death, Harry Potter doesn't have a need for life insurance."

— David Woods

The first mutual aid arrangements that resemble life insurance are found in the practices of a number of early societies (going as far back as the ancient Egyptians) that provided the services for, or paid the expenses of, burying the dead and caring for the deceased's family members. The first enduring effort to market life insurance did not emerge until 1706, and the first life insurance company (or "assurance society") was formed in England in 1762. Today, life insurance is one of the most important and widely purchased insurance products in the world. In 2015, life insurance premiums in the U.S. totaled $552 billion, and global premiums exceeded $2.5 trillion. *See* Insurance Information Institute, 2017 Insurance Fact Book, pp. 1–2.

"Life insurance is essentially a contract to make specific payments upon the death of the person whose life is insured. The cast of characters involved in a policy of life insurance other than the insurer includes (a) the owner of the policy, who has the power to name or change the beneficiary, the right to assign the policy (under certain conditions), the ability to cash it in for its surrender value, or use it as collateral in obtaining a loan, and the obligation to pay the premiums; (b) the person whose life is the subject of the policy (also known as the cestui que vie); and (c) the beneficiary to whom the proceeds are paid. One person might occupy all three positions by naming his estate as beneficiary; or each of the three positions may be held by a separate party." John F. Dobbyn & Christopher C. French, Insurance Law In A Nutshell 8–9 (5th ed. 2016).

There are two basic types of life insurance: life insurance with a savings component (e.g., universal and whole life insurance) and term life insurance. Life insurance with a savings component, such as whole life insurance, is "intended to run for the entire life of the insured individual, with proceeds to be paid upon his or her death. Part of the premium goes to cover the cost of the death benefit and part of it goes to savings on a tax-deferred basis. Typically, the percentage of the premium put towards savings will increase as the insured gets older in age, although the premium payment paid by the policyholder remains constant. The amount of the accumulated savings value of the policy is the 'cash surrender value' of the policy, which the owner of the policy can receive if the policy is cancelled or lapses due to the non-payment of premiums. The possibility of a cash surrender value is generally available at any time after the policy has been in force for two or three years and prior to the death of the insured. In view of the accumulation of the cash surrender value, as well as the certainty of ultimate payment in some form, whole-life insurance involves a substantial element of investment, as well as insurance." *Id.* at 9–10.

Term life insurance is intended "to last only for the specified term (one month, ten years, twenty years), and payment of the specified amount of proceeds occurs only if the insured dies within the term. There is generally no provision for payment of a cash surrender value upon surrender or lapse of the policy. Because the insured person may not die during the policy period, it is uncertain that the insurer will be obliged to pay anything in proceeds whatsoever. Consequently, this form of life insurance does not carry with it an element of investment." *Id.* at 10.

Life insurance is often sold as group insurance or provided as an employee fringe benefit for a base amount with an option to purchase additional coverage. If life insurance is obtained as a fringe benefit through employment, it is subject to ERISA (the Employee Retirement Income Security Act of 1974), which varies some of the state common law rules that otherwise apply when the insurance is sold by private companies to individuals outside the employment setting. In fact, whenever insurance is provided as a fringe benefit in employment, it is vitally important to think "ERISA" and ask "how might ERISA apply." ERISA will be discussed more fully in Chapter 9.

I. INSURABLE INTEREST

The use of insurance as a subterfuge for gambling first emerged in marine insurance in England in the seventeenth century.[1] English marine insurers of this era did not require the policyholder to demonstrate ownership in or any legal relationship to a ship or cargo being insured, and this enabled policyholders to place wagers or bets on whether an insured vessel or cargo would successfully complete a voyage. This became enough of a problem—imagine the temptation to help a ship or cargo disappear in order to collect the insurance proceeds—that Parliament in 1746 passed a statute requiring, as a prerequisite to the validity of a policy of marine insurance, that the policyholder have an "interest" in the property being insured. With gaming practices in property insurance being prohibited, the use of insurance to make a bet spread to life insurance.

---

[1] This Introductory section is from Robert H. Jerry II & Douglas R. Richmond, Understanding Insurance Law 255–58 (5th ed. 2012).

Popular accounts of the period describe the practice of purchasing insurance on the lives of those being tried for capital crimes. These policies constituted naked wagers on whether the accused would ultimately be convicted and executed for the alleged offense. A related practice was the purchase of insurance on the lives of famous, elderly persons; the premium would be a function of what was known about the person's health, including any recent illnesses. Insuring a life in which one has no interest creates a temptation to bring the insured's life to an early end, but the greater concern in eighteenth-century England was the practice of wagering. Thus, when England's Parliament enacted an insurable interest statute for life insurance in 1774, the articulated concern in the statute was gaming, not the risk that the insured's life might be destroyed. The 1774 statute prohibited issuing insurance on "the life or lives of any person or persons, or any other event or events whatsoever, wherein the person or persons for whose use, benefit, or on whose account such policy or policies shall be made, shall have no interest, or by way of gaming or wagering." [The Life Assurance Act of 1774, 14 Geo. 3, c. 48 (Eng.).] Like the 1746 Act, the effect of the 1774 Act was to prohibit judicial enforcement of policies issued without satisfying the insurable interest requirement. . . .

In the United States, the insurable interest doctrine was first adopted by courts, although many state legislatures later enacted insurable interest statutes. These statutes are typically written in broad language, leaving considerable room for judicial interpretation. . . .

The purposes of the insurable interest requirement remain those that prompted the doctrine's creation: (1) discouraging the practice of using insurance as a device for gambling or wagering; and (2) removing the incentive for the procurer of the insurance to destroy the subject matter of the insurance, whether it be a life or an item of property. Of these two purposes, the more important is the second. Because gambling is not perceived, in and of itself, to be a terrible evil, the reason for disallowing insurance policies to serve as disguised wagers is the incentive such contracts create to destroy the insured property or life. Thus, increased moral hazard is the reason most often given to justify the insurable interest requirement, but it is not uncommon to find courts, when asked to decide whether an insurable interest exists in a particular insurance transaction, inquiring into whether the insurance contract in question functions as a wager.

MUTUAL SAVINGS LIFE INSURANCE CO. V. NOAH

282 So.2d 271 (Ala. 1973)

HEFLIN, CHIEF JUSTICE.

This is a declaratory judgment action in equity in which the appellee-complainant, Donald R. Noah, alleges in his bill of complaint that he is the named beneficiary in three policies of insurance issued by the appellant-respondent, Mutual Savings Life Insurance Company; that the life of William L. Noah, the brother of the appellee-complainant, was insured under each of these policies; that the insured died by drowning in the City of Galveston, Texas, while the policies were in force; and that the appellant-respondent insurance company refused to pay the amounts due under any of said policies (except that a partial payment [of $434.66] was made on [the burial policy]). The bill seeks a decree construing the policies and declaring the rights of the appellee-complainant and the obligations of the appellant-respondent insurer thereunder, and ultimately that the court declare that the insurer is obligated to pay the death benefits and the balance of the burial benefits prescribed under one of the policies, plus the accidental death benefits provided in all three.

Copies of the three policies were attached as Exhibits A, B and C, respectively, to the bill. . . . Exhibit A provides for a death benefit of $1,500 and double that sum in case of accidental death, amounting to $3,000. It is provided therein that William L. Noah, who the evidence shows met death by drowning in or near Galveston, Texas, on September 13, 1971, is named therein as the insured and the appellee-complainant is named as the primary beneficiary. The policy bears date of February 15, 1971, which under the evidence is to be taken as the date of issuance. Exhibit B shows a policy with the same date of issuance and the same terms and beneficiary as that contained in Exhibit A, except that the ordinary death benefit is $1,000 and the accidental death benefit is in double that amount, $2,000. Each of the two policies is characterized as a "Twenty Pay Life Insurance Policy." Exhibit C is entitled a "Burial Insurance Policy," and provides that the insurer will furnish described funeral services, including, among other things, a casket, if the death of the insured, William L. Noah, should occur within the State of Alabama and within 35 miles of an authorized funeral director. There is the further provision that if the insured's death occurs outside the State of Alabama or more than 35 miles from an authorized funeral director, the company agreed to pay to the beneficiary (Donald) one-half of the retail value of the policy as a cash payment. Since the retail value of the policy is $600, the cash payment to the beneficiary for a death outside the State would be $300. However, there is a further provision that in a case of accidental death the company would pay an additional amount equal to one-third of the retail value, which in this case would be an additional sum of $200, meaning a total cash payment of $500. The date of issuance was February 15, 1971, the same date as the other two policies.

The evidence shows that the beneficiary, Donald R. Noah, by written instrument dated September 16, 1971, declared that he became indebted to Kilgore Funeral Home, Pell City, Alabama, for funeral services and supplies for the burial of William I. Noah in the amount of $434.66, and he thereby assigned unto said funeral firm that amount out of the proceeds of the said burial policy, authorizing Mutual Savings Life Insurance Company to make its check payable to said firm for the assigned amount and directing it to pay the remainder of the proceeds of the policy to the beneficiary, Donald R. Noah. If this burial policy is held to be effective, unquestionably the obligation of the insurer has been partially discharged up to the amount of $434.66, and the insurer owes the beneficiary the unpaid balance of the maximum benefit of $500 due thereunder, viz., $65.34 with interest thereon.

The respondent in its answer and the amendment thereto denies liability under the policies on the ground that the complainant and beneficiary obtained the policies of insurance on his brother's life and that he had no insurable interest which would entitle him to recover, and also on the ground that the policies had lapsed for non-payment of premium.

The trial court rendered a judgment in favor of the appellee-complainant and against the appellant-respondent on all three policies in the total amount of $5,065.34, consisting of $5,000 under the life policies (Exhibits A & B), and $65.34 under the burial policy (Exhibit C), with interest from October 6, 1971, specified as the date the appellant-respondent denies liability.

The most divisive issue with which this court is faced is presented by appellant-respondent's contention that Donald R. Noah has no insurable interest in the life of the insured, and that each of the three policies was invalid by reason thereof. It may be well to note at the outset that this court holds the burial policy not to be subject to the insurable interest requirement. The public policy grounds for requiring an insurable interest, which are discussed below, are not applicable to a burial policy wherein the benefits are substantially restricted to providing burial services. For this reason, it is the named insured in such a policy who is in reality the recipient of the insurance benefits, not the named beneficiary. *Jordan's Mutual Aid Association v. Edwards*, 232 Ala. 80, 166 So. 780. But, even if it could be said that the burial policy is subject to the insurable interest requirement, this court holds, for the reasons stated below, that Donald R. Noah did have an insurable interest in William's life.

Under the evidence the two life policies were procured or "taken out" (an expression used in our cases) by the beneficiary, and thus the long-established rule that the insurance is invalid unless the beneficiary has an "insurable interest" in the life of the insured applies. This rule is to the effect that a person has an unlimited insurable interest in his own life and may designate any person as his beneficiary so long as the insurance was procured or taken out by the insured and the premiums paid by him, but one taking out a policy of insurance for his own benefit, on the life of another person, must have an insurable interest in the continuance of the life of such insured. Tit. 28A, § 316, Code of Alabama, 1940 (Recomp. 1958).[1]

Several reasons have been assigned as the basis for the insurable interest requirement, both of which are grounded upon public policy considerations: a policy taken out by one for his own benefit on the life of another, in whom he has no insurable interest is, in substance, a wagering contract; and such a policy may hold out a temptation to the beneficiary to hasten by improper means the death of the insured.

Certain blood relationships have been held sufficient, in and of themselves to negate the supposition that the beneficiary would take out such a policy for the purpose of wagering on the insured's death, or that such a policy would entice the beneficiary to take the insured's life, and in such cases the relationship alone is said to create an insurable interest. This is true notwithstanding the fact that the beneficiary may have no reasonable expectation of pecuniary advantage through the continued life of the insured or consequent loss by reason of his death, which would otherwise be required in order to find an insurable interest.

The relationship of husband and wife has been held to be sufficiently close to give either an insurable interest in the life of the other. *Jennings v. Jennings*, 250 Ala. 130, 33 So. 2d 251. The parent-child relationship has been accorded the same status as that given to husband and wife in *Jennings*.

On the other hand, the following relationships have been held not to create an insurable interest on the basis of such relationship alone. Cousin and cousin, beneficiary has no interest in the life of the wife of his wife's brother, aunt and niece, aunt-in-law and niece, niece and uncle.

The specific issue presented in the case under review is whether one has an insurable interest in the life of his brother by virtue of the relationship alone. While realizing that this issue is one of first impression in Alabama, and that other jurisdictions are in conflict on this matter, a review of the holdings of other states has convinced this court that the vast majority[2] and best reasoned holdings support the proposition that the brother-brother relationship will, in and of itself, support an insurable interest.

---

1 Although the Insurance Code, i.e., Title 28A, became effective after all relevant times for purposes of the instant case, this court is of the opinion that the result obtained in the instant case would not be altered by the application of section 316, which provides as follows:

> § 316. Insurable interest; personal insurance.—(1) Insurable interest with reference to personal insurance is an interest based upon a reasonable expectation of pecuniary advantage through the continued life, health or bodily safety of another person and consequent loss by reason of his death or disability, or a substantial interest engendered by love and affection in the case of individuals closely related by blood or by law.

2 This court's research has disclosed that of the nineteen jurisdictions which have written to this issue, fourteen have stated that one has an insurable interest in the life of his brother by virtue of the relationship alone.

. . . .

The reason most often assigned as the basis of a holding that such relationship will, in and of itself, support an insurable interest is that the natural love and affection prevailing between the two and the expectation that one will render the other aid in time of need is sufficient to overcome any wagering contract argument, as well as any impulse to hasten the death of the insured. . . .

Perhaps the facts of the instant case tend to contradict the closeness and mutual love and affection which the above holdings attribute to the brother-brother relationship, but this court does not write for this case alone. The holding of this court today will govern all future cases, not just the exceptional one where the natural love and affection common to the brother-brother relationship may be missing.

In view of the foregoing it is the conclusion of this court that the brother-brother relationship will, standing alone, support an insurable interest.

This court has reviewed the holdings of various other jurisdictions[3] which are contra to the decision announced by this court today, and finds that the rationale underlying these cases is that one would take out an insurance policy on the life of his brother for the purpose of gambling on the time of his death, or would, by virtue of such policy, be induced to take the life of his brother for a price, which is not, in the opinion of this court, substantiated by the common experience of mankind.

. . . .

Accordingly, this court holds that the insurance company is obligated to pay Donald Noah, in addition to the amount due under the life insurance policies, the balance due on the burial policy being the sum of $65.34, with interest from September 16, 1971.

Affirmed.

JONES, JUSTICE (dissenting).

I must disagree with the majority holding that one has an insurable interest in the life of his brother (or sister) on the basis of their relationship alone. The public policy which provides the "insurable interest" requirement has its roots in two related, yet independent, principles. Absent insurable interest such contracts have been discredited for two reasons. One is that they are wagering contracts and the other is that they

[3] For cases holding that the relationship of brother-brother does not constitute an insurable interest, *see Lord v. Dall*, 12 Mass. 115, 7 Am. Dec. 38 (1815); *Lewis v. Phoenix Mut. Life Ins. Co.*, 39 Conn. 100 (1872); *Miller v. Travelers' Ins. Co.*, 81 Ind. App. 618, 144 N.E. 554 (1924); *Abernathy v. Springfield Mut. Ass'n*, 284 S.W. 198 (Mo. App. 1926); *Gulf Life Ins. Co. v. Davis*, 52 Ga. App. 464, 183 S.E. 640 (1936); *Dieterle v. Standard Life Ins. Co.*, 119 S.W.2d 440 (Mo. App. 1938); *Williams v. Northeast Mut. Ins. Ass'n*, 72 S.W.2d 166 (Mo. App. 1934); *Masonic Ben. Ass'n of Central Illinois v. Bunch*, 109 Mo. 560, 19 S.W. 25 (1892).

may be an inducement to homicide. It is not necessary that both reasons exist at the same time or to any given policy. While each might considerably influence the other, these two public policy principles are mutually exclusive and not interdependent.

This brings us to the question whether the relationship of brother and brother (and, incidentally, brother and sister or sister and sister) is such a relationship that it in itself creates an insurable interest. We know that the relationship of husband and wife constitutes such a relationship per se, *Jennings v. Jennings,* 250 Ala. 130, 33 So. 2d 251; and while I do not find that this Court has been specifically called upon to decide whether in every case the relationship of parent and child, or child and parent, in and of itself, with a presumption that is not even rebuttable, gives rise to an insurable interest in either, the overwhelming weight of authority is that this relationship is sufficient to constitute an insurable interest by one in the life of the other (44 C.J.S. Insurance § 204, at 907). But is the relationship of brothers in the same category, or does it depend upon the circumstances of the particular case?

. . . .

In any case, I think that the relationship alone is not sufficient, that the rule requiring something other than the relation is the sound one and I would so hold. This is based on the rationale that there is but one test for insurable interest—that of a pecuniary interest or some reasonable expectation of monetary benefit from the continuance of the insured's life; and within certain blood or affinity relationships this pecuniary interest or benefit is conclusively presumed. Such relationships are that of husband and wife, parent and child, grandparent and grandchild, and under certain conditions loco parentis relationships. This "conclusive presumption" rule with respect to these relationships does not violate the public policy necessitating insurable interest aimed at preventing homicide and wager contracts. While an extension of this rule to the brother relationship might be permissible as to the homicide aspect, to so extend this rule would facilitate the violation of the second evil which the aforementioned public policy seeks to prevent; vis., wager contracts.

Having adopted the above view, I would hold that the line must be drawn short of the brother relationship, and that insurable interest in such cases should depend upon a pecuniary benefit, or advantage to be gained from the continued life of the insured, which cannot be conclusively presumed, but is subject to proof.

My dissent is limited to the holding of the majority with respect to the insurable interest feature of the life insurance policies, and in all other respects, I concur.

NOTES AND QUESTIONS

1. *Does It Matter Who Buys a Life Insurance Policy? (Yes).* Insurable interest requirements for life insurance can be divided into two general categories based on who takes out the insurance. As indicated in *Noah*, every competent person has an insurable interest in his or her own life and may take out a policy of life insurance thereon, designating whomever the person chooses as beneficiary. There is no requirement that the beneficiary have an insurable interest.

The second category consists of policies taken out by a person on another's life. Here, as a general rule, the benefits must be payable to: (1) the person whose life is insured or to his or her personal representative, or (2) a person who is closely related to the insured person by blood, marriage, or adoption, or who has an economic interest in having the insured person's life continue.

2. *Timing.* The insurable interest requirement in life insurance must be satisfied at the time the policy is purchased, as opposed to when the insured person dies. Is this adequate to satisfy the goals of the insurable interest requirement?

3. *Statutory Sources of the Insurable Interest Doctrine.* Some states have statutes that set forth the test for insurable interest. The familial relationship test for insurable interest, which appears in the Alabama statute at issue in *Noah*, is rather amorphous. Nonetheless, a number of states have statutes similar to the Alabama statute set out in footnote 1 of *Noah* and, of course, these statutes just leave the problem for the courts. Other states have adopted statutes that are more restrictive. Many statutes specifically make reference to the economic interest test.

Compare the insurable interest statutes of Alabama, New York, and California:

a. *McKinney's Insurance Law (New York) § 3205*

§ 3205. Insurable interest in the person; consent required; exceptions

(a) In this section:

(1) The term, "insurable interest" means:

(A) in the case of persons closely related by blood or by law, a substantial interest engendered by love and affection;

(B) in the case of other persons, a lawful and substantial economic interest in the continued life, health or bodily safety of the person insured, as distinguished from an interest which would arise only by, or would be enhanced in value by, the death, disablement or injury of the insured.

(2) The term "contract of insurance upon the person" includes any policy of life insurance and any policy of accident and health insurance.

(3) The term "person insured" means the natural person, or persons, whose life, health or bodily safety is insured.

(b) (1) Any person of lawful age may on his own initiative procure or effect a contract of insurance upon his own person for the benefit of any person, firm, association or corporation. Nothing herein shall be deemed to prohibit the immediate transfer or assignment of a contract so procured or effectuated.

(2) No person shall procure or cause to be procured, directly or by assignment or otherwise any contract of insurance upon the person of another unless the benefits under such contract are payable to the person insured or his personal representatives, or to a person having, at the time when such contract is made, an insurable interest in the person insured.

(3) Notwithstanding the provisions of paragraphs one and two of this subsection, a Type B charitable, educational or religious corporation formed pursuant to paragraph (b) of section two hundred one of the not-for-profit corporation law, or its agent, may procure or cause to be procured, directly or by assignment or otherwise, a contract of life insurance upon the person of another and may designate itself or cause to have itself designated as the beneficiary of such contract.

(4) If the beneficiary, assignee or other payee under any contract made in violation of this subsection receives from the insurer any benefits thereunder accruing upon the death, disablement or injury of the person insured, the person insured or his executor or administrator may maintain an action to recover such benefits from the person receiving them.

(c) No contract of insurance upon the person, except a policy of group life insurance, group or blanket accident and health insurance, or family insurance, as defined in this chapter, shall be made or effectuated unless at or before the making of such contract the person insured, being of lawful age or competent to contract therefor, applies for or consents in writing to the making of the contract, except in the following cases:

(1) A wife or a husband may effectuate insurance upon the person of the other.

(2) Any person having an insurable interest in the life of a minor under the age of fourteen years and six months or any person upon whom such minor is dependent for support and maintenance, may effectuate a contract of insurance upon the life of such minor, in an amount which shall not exceed the limits specified in section three thousand two hundred seven of this article.

. . . .

b. *West's Annotated California Insurance Code*

§ 10110. Insurable interest

Every person has an insurable interest in the life and health of:

(a) Himself.

(b) Any person on whom he depends wholly or in part for education or support.

(c) Any person under a legal obligation to him for the payment of money or respecting property or services, of which death or illness might delay or prevent the performance.

(d) Any person upon whose life any estate or interest vested in him depends.

4. *Waiver and Estoppel Reprise.* As with property insurance, courts divide over whether insurers can be barred by waiver or estoppel from asserting a lack of insurable interest, but most courts hold that these doctrines do not bar insurers from asserting lack of insurable interest. *See Beard v. American Agency Life Insurance Co.*, 550 A.2d 677 (Md. 1988) (doctrines of waiver and estoppel cannot bar insurers from raising insurable interest defense); *Cundiff v. Cain*, 707 So. 2d 187 (Miss. 1998) (insurer was estopped from avoiding payment to estate, which had standing to raise question of insurable interest); Phoebe Carter, Annotation, *Estoppel of, or Waiver by, Issuer of Life Insurance Policy to Assert Defense of Lack of Insurable Interest*, 86 A.L.R.4th 828 (1991). If a life insurer has actual or constructive knowledge that there is no insurable interest at the inception of the policy but is not barred by estoppel or waiver from raising the defense, are there other legal remedies available to the policyholder or beneficiary (assuming the beneficiary has an insurable interest at the time of loss)?

5. *Economic Interest in the Life of Another Person.* When a familial relationship supporting an insurable interest is nonexistent, an economic interest may suffice. Thus, a partner can have an insurable interest in the life of his or her partners, an employer can have an insurable interest in the life of a key employee, and a creditor can have an insurable interest in the life of a debtor. A particularly important use of life insurance is to fund buy-out arrangements that enable a surviving business partner to continue the business and purchase the interest of the heirs of a deceased partner. But it is incorrect to say that the mere existence of some kind of economic relationship automatically gives rise to an insurable interest. If the economic arrangement appears to be a subterfuge, courts are often persuaded not to recognize the interest. Moreover, even when an economic relationship creates an insurable interest, it does not follow that the insurable interest is unlimited.

6. *Insurable Interest Requirement in Property Insurance.* Property insurance also has an insurable interest requirement. It differs from the insurable interest requirement in life insurance in at least three respects.

One, the requirement must be satisfied at the time of loss, instead of at the time the insurance is procured. *See* Robert H. Jerry II & Douglas R. Richmond, Understanding Insurance Law 283 (5th ed. 2012).

Two, the test for satisfying the insurable interest requirement is different. As the property rules have developed, and sometimes these are enshrined in statutes as well, the policyholder must meet either a "legal interest" test or a "factual expectancy" test in order to insure property. The legal interest test can be met in a variety of ways. For example, any kind of legal title—fee simple, a remainder right, a life estate, etc.—meets the legal interest test. A contract right to property, such as the right a secured creditor has to foreclose against property in the event of a debtor's default, also satisfies the legal interest test. A person who has entered into a contract of sale to acquire the title to property at a future date does not have legal title today, he but does have "equitable title," which represents the right to receive the property in the future. Any kind of equitable title is sufficient to support an insurable interest under the legal interest test. Likewise, if a person would have legal liability in the event property was destroyed, that person has an insurable interest under the legal interest test.

Under the factual expectancy test, the question is whether the policyholder would suffer an economic loss by virtue of the destruction of the property, or would receive an economic benefit by virtue of the continued existence of the property. Often, a legal interest exists along with a factual expectancy, but the factual expectancy does not depend on the existence of a legal interest. Can you imagine a situation in which this would be the case? Have you ever possessed stolen property? If you unwittingly purchased stolen property, how would you describe your "interest" in that property? Did you ever possess a car that you treated as your own but which was titled in the name of someone else (like a parent)?

The factual expectancy test has greater ascendancy in the case law, and it also appears in many state statutes. As between the legal interest test and factual expectancy test, which test does a better job of furthering the purposes of the insurable interest doctrine?

Three, the insurance payout at the time of loss is limited to the value of the policyholder's insurable interest. *See, e.g., Gossett v. Farmers Ins. Co. of Washington*, 948 P.2d 1264, 1273 (Wash. 1997) (en banc) ("[A]n insured with a partial interest in the property can generally recover only to the extent of that interest.") (citing *City of Carlsbad v. Northwestern Nat'l Ins. Co.*, 463 P.2d 32 (N.M. 1970)). Thus, for example, assume the policy has a limit of liability of $100,000 and the property was totally destroyed. If the policyholder's insurable interest in the property was only $10,000 despite paying premiums for $100,000 of coverage, then the policyholder would only receive $10,000.

7. *Standing to Challenge the Lack of an Insurable Interest*. In property insurance, whether a party other than the insurer has standing to challenge the lack of insurable interest is not likely to arise. Because third parties typically lack an interest in the proceeds of property insurance, there is

nothing to be gained by arguing that the policyholder lacked an insurable interest in the insured property. In life insurance, the situation can be different. Beneficiaries might wish to claim, for example, that the owner of the policy (e.g., an employer) lacks an insurable interest in the life of the CQV (e.g., an employee) and that the proceeds should therefore be paid to a beneficiary. Of the jurisdictions addressing the question, most have held that only the insurer has standing to challenge the validity of a policy on the basis of lack of insurable interest. *See, e.g., Ryan v. Tickle*, 316 N.W.2d 580 (Neb. 1982); *Secor v. Pioneer Foundary Co.*, 173 N.W.2d 780 (Mich. Ct. App. 1969). Is the majority rule supported by sound policy considerations?

Some jurisdictions have altered this rule somewhat by permitting an action against a person without an insurable interest who has received the life insurance benefits from the insurer. In some states, this has been accomplished by statute, and courts have modified the standing rules in others. *See Cundiff v. Cain*, 707 So.2d 187 (Miss. 1998) (estate of insured, who was owner of life insurance policy procured by beneficiary forging insured's signature on application, had standing to raise question of insurable interest). If you were asked to draft a statute producing this result, who would you permit to bring the action and to whom would you distribute the proceeds?

II. INCONTESTABILITY

ALLSTATE LIFE INS. CO. V. MILLER

424 F.3d 1113 (11th Cir. 2005)

Opinion

BARKETT, CIRCUIT JUDGE:

In this diversity insurance case, Appellant Allstate Life Insurance Company ("Allstate") appeals the summary judgment order granting to appellees Steve Miller and Nicholas Demetro ("the beneficiaries") the proceeds of a life insurance policy on the life of John Miller. Allstate argued below that the life insurance policy insuring the life of John Miller should be rescinded or declared void, alleging that the policy was obtained through the use of an imposter in Miller's place during the initial required medical examination. The district court rejected Allstate's attempts to rescind or void the life insurance policy at issue because: (i) the policy contained a clause-required by Florida statute-that rendered the policy incontestable after it was in force for two years during the life of the insured; and (ii) more than two years had passed since the policy was issued. Because we agree with the district court that Florida law recognizes no implied "imposter" exception to the two-year statutory incontestability period, summary judgment was properly granted and we affirm.

BACKGROUND

The Allstate life insurance policy on which this case centers went into effect on September 20, 2000, insuring the life of John Miller. The policy stated that if the insured died while the policy was in force, Allstate would pay a death benefit to the policy beneficiaries upon receiving proof of death. As required by Fla. Stat. § 627.455, the policy further provided that it would become incontestable after remaining in force during the lifetime of the insured for a period of two years from its effective date.[1] On October 4, 2002, John Miller requested that the beneficiaries of the policy be changed, and named Steve Miller and Nicholas Demetro as beneficiaries. John Miller died on April 20, 2003—more than two years after the policy went into effect. The beneficiaries accordingly filed statements seeking to collect benefits under the policy.

Rather than disburse the benefits, Allstate sought a declaratory judgment that the policy was void ab initio, alleging that the policy application was completed using fraudulent information and that an imposter had appeared at the medical exam initially required by the insurance company in the place of John Miller. Allstate's complaint averred that this was the only possible conclusion that could be drawn from discrepancies between statements made on the policy application and the health of the individual examined before the policy was issued, as compared with the health conditions which ultimately led to John Miller's death. In response, the beneficiaries counter-claimed, alleging breach of contract based on Allstate's failure to pay benefits upon proof of death in accordance with the insurance policy's terms.

Although the district court permitted Allstate to engage in discovery to establish the factual predicate for its imposter argument, the district court ultimately granted the beneficiaries' motion for summary judgment, holding that because Allstate's claim was made after two years from the date of the policy's issue, it was barred by the policy's incontestability clause. The district court reasoned that Florida precedent has interpreted incontestability clauses as absolute bars to efforts by the insurer to rescind the policy after two years for any other reason than the articulated exceptions in the statute. Though Florida courts have not expressly rejected an insurer's attempt to bring an imposter-based fraud claim after the policy becomes incontestable, the district court found there to be no material difference between Allstate's imposter defense and the defenses of fraud and misrepresentation that Florida courts have expressly rejected

[1] The text of the policy's incontestability clause reads: "This contract shall be incontestable after it has been in force during the lifetime of the insured for a period of two years from its start date except for nonpayment of premiums and expect as to provisions relative to benefits in event of disability and as to provisions which grant additional insurance specifically against death by accident or accidental death."

once the two-year contestability period has expired. Allstate timely appealed.

. . . .

DISCUSSION

Florida law requires that "[e]very insurance contract shall provide that the policy shall be incontestable after it has been in force during the lifetime of the insured for a period of 2 years from its date of issue . . . ." Fla. Stat. § 627.455. Excepted from this statutory incontestability period are challenges based upon "nonpayment of premiums and . . . at the option of the insurer, [challenges] as to provisions relative to benefits in event of disability and as to provisions which grant additional insurance specifically against death by accident or accidental means." *Id.*

The Florida Supreme Court has explained that incontestability clauses, such as the one contained in § 627.455, are "in the nature of, and serve[ ] a similar purpose as, a statute of limitations." *Prudential Ins. Co. of Am. v. Prescott,* 130 Fla. 11, 176 So. 875, 878 (1937). As such, while incontestability clauses "recognize[ ] fraud and all other defenses, [they] provide[ ] a reasonable time in which they may be, but beyond which they cannot be, established." *Id.* The incontestability clause thus works to the mutual advantage of the insurer and the insured, "giv[ing] the insured a guaranty against expensive litigation to defeat his policy after the lapse of the time specified, and at the same time giv[ing] the company a reasonable time and opportunity to ascertain whether the [insurance] contract should remain in force." *Id.*

Accordingly, just as Florida courts would dismiss an otherwise-valid action once the statute of limitations on that claim had run, Florida's appellate courts have uniformly held that once the incontestability clause becomes effective, insurers are barred from attempting to rescind or cancel the insurance policy based on allegations that the insured engaged in fraud or misrepresentation. *See Kaufman v. Mut. of Omaha Ins. Co.*, 681 So.2d 747, 750–53 (Fla.Dist.Ct.App.1996) (rejecting insurer's attempt to rescind policy, based in part on insured's non-disclosure of preexisting conditions, where "the insurer's attempted rescission of the policy occurred over two years after the policy was issued, and consequently the attempted recision was legally ineffective"); *Prudential Ins. Co. of Am. v. Rhodriquez,* 285 So.2d 689, 690 (Fla.Dist.Ct.App.1973) (holding that insurer was not entitled to cancel or rescind insurance policies based upon insured's misrepresentations as to health and medical history because the policies became incontestable after they were in effect for two years); *Great S. Life Ins. Co. v. Porcaro,* 869 So.2d 585, 587 (Fla.Dist.Ct.App.2004), *review denied* 884 So.2d 23 (Fla.2004) ("Pursuant to [Fla. Stat. § 627.455], a reinstatement [of an insurance policy] is incontestable on the ground of fraud after it has been in force, during the lifetime of the insured, for a period of two years."); *Allstate Life Ins. Co. v. Fox,* 700 So.2d 49, 49–50 (Fla.Dist.Ct.App.1997) ("The [incontestability] clause required by statute prevents the insurer from raising as a defense to payment of a claim, any misrepresentations a decedent made in the policy application when that decedent survives at least two years from the date the policy is issued."); *DiFranco v. Nat'l Found. Life Ins. Co.,* 551 So.2d 535, 536 (Fla.Dist.Ct.App.1989) ("the incontestability clause of the subject insurance policy, as required by [Florida statute], clearly precludes the defendant from raising the affirmative defense that the plaintiffs failed to fully and completely disclose the prior medical treatment and history of the plaintiff"); *see also, Bankers Sec. Life Ins. Soc. v. Kane,* 885 F.2d 820, 821–22 (11th Cir.1989) (refusing to create any court-created exception to the Florida incontestability statute and holding that the statutory incontestability clause barred efforts to rescind a policy based on alleged fraudulent misrepresentations made by the insured); *Reliance Life Ins. Co. v. Everglades Disc. Co.,* 204 F.2d 937, 942 (5th Cir.1953) (suggesting that Florida insurers lose the defense of fraud upon expiration of the statutory contestability period).

Under these cases, while an insurer may assert an imposter claim (or any number of other grounds) to rescind or void an insurance policy before the incontestability clause goes into effect, § 627.455 prevents an insurer from doing so once the policy has been in effect for two years during the life of the insured, except on the three grounds enumerated in the statute.[3] Accordingly, we find Allstate's arguments to the contrary unpersuasive.

First, Allstate argues that it is not contesting the policy in a manner prohibited by § 627.455 because its suit is based upon a claim that the policy is void ab initio. Specifically, Allstate claims that its lack of knowledge as to John Miller's true medical condition meant that there was no meeting of the minds and no actual contract. However, Florida courts have already rejected claims by an insurer who sought to rescind an insurance policy because it would not have agreed to issue the policy had it known the true facts of the insured's medical history. *See Rhodriquez,* 285 So.2d at 689–90; *see also, Home Life Ins. Co. v. Regueira,* 313 So.2d 438, 439 (Fla.Dist.Ct.App.1975) (explaining that where an insurer's claim relates to the validity of the insurance policy, that claim is barred by an incontestability clause).

Second, Allstate relies on the "weight of authority in other jurisdictions" to argue that we should recognize an imposter exception to the

[3] While the decisions of Florida's appellate courts compel this conclusion, we note that it is also supported by the canons of statutory construction. Specifically, where the legislature has included certain exceptions to the two-year incontestability rule, the doctrine of *expressio unis est exclusio alterius* counsels against judicial recognition of additional exceptions. *See, e.g., Grenitz v. Tomlian,* 858 So.2d 999, 1002 (Fla.2003). While Allstate argues the policy wisdom of the resulting absence of an imposter exception to the incontestability clause, Allstate's complaint is properly directed to the Florida legislature-not this court.

incontestability period. However, in diversity cases we are required to adhere to the decisions of the Florida appellate courts absent some persuasive indication that the Florida Supreme Court would decide the issue otherwise. *Ernie Haire Ford, Inc. v. Ford Motor Co.*, 260 F.3d 1285, 1290 (11th Cir.2001). As discussed above, the Florida appellate courts have uniformly and expressly held that the § 627.455 incontestability clause bars an insurer from rescinding or contesting the policy based on alleged fraudulent misrepresentations the insured made in the policy application. We can discern no indication that the Florida Supreme Court would disagree. While Allstate argues that its so-called "imposter defense" is different in kind from the sorts of fraud and misrepresentation that Florida's appellate courts have rejected as a basis for obviating the statutory incontestability clause, we agree with the district court that the "imposter defense" is merely a species of fraud, indistinguishable from the use of an imposter for incontestability purposes. *Cf. Bradford Trust Co. v. Tex. Am. Bank-Houston*, 790 F.2d 407, 410 (5th Cir.1986) (characterizing imposter scheme as species of fraud).

Finally, Allstate would have us rely on *Fioretti v. Massachusetts General Life Insurance Co.*, 892 F.Supp. 1492 (S.D.Fla.1993), which distinguished an imposter defense from the fraudulent misrepresentations addressed by the Florida appellate courts. However, this court determined on appeal that it was New Jersey law which governed the insurance policy at issue. *See Fioretti*, 53 F.3d 1228, 1236 (11th Cir.1995). Moreover, after *Fioretti*, the Fourth District Court of Appeal decided *Great Southern Life Insurance Co. v. Porcaro*, 869 So.2d 585 (Fla.Dist.Ct.App.2004). In *Porcaro*, the insured mysteriously disappeared. The insurer continued to accept premium payments, and more than two years after the policy was issued the representative of his estate obtained a probate court judgment declaring the insured to be dead. *Id.* at 586. The insurer refused to pay the policy proceeds, citing evidence that the insured *was not in fact dead*, but rather had fraudulently absconded in order to avoid prosecution. The trial court entered judgment for the estate in the amount of the policy, holding that the insurer was precluded from contesting the policy because of failure to do so within the two-year contestability window. *See id.* While the appeals court reversed and remanded because of a material issue of fact as to whether the insured died before the policy had been in effect for two years, its decision recognized that were a jury to determine that the insured lived for two years from the date the policy issued, the statutory incontestability clause would bar any defense of fraud based on the circumstances of the insured's disappearance. *See id.* at 587. If claims of potential fraud as to the fact of an insured's death-a fact most central to a life insurance contract-are subject to the statutory incontestability clause, Allstate's imposter claims cannot obviate § 627.455 based on their importance in the contractual scheme. Furthermore, even if it could be argued that the alleged fraud in *Porcaro* prevented a meeting of the minds, as noted earlier, this rationale has been rejected by Florida courts. *See Rhodriquez*, 285 So.2d at 689 (holding that statutory incontestability clause barred insurer's claim that had it known insured's true condition, it would not have agreed to issue the policy).

Because we agree with the district court that the statutory incontestability clause bars Allstate's efforts in this case to void the policy, we hold that summary judgment was properly granted.

AFFIRMED.

NOTES AND QUESTIONS

1. *Imposter Defense.* The imposter defense typically is successfully asserted only in the limited circumstance where the person allegedly insured under the life insurance policy is not the person who applied to be insured under the policy at the time of the policy's procurement (e.g., a person purportedly buys a life insurance policy covering his own life, but the life actually insured is another person's). *Compare, e.g., Amex Life Insurance Co. v. Superior Court*, 930 P.2d 1264 (Cal. 1997) (policy was incontestable even though an imposter took the medical exam on behalf of the HIV positive person whose life was being insured), *and North American Co. for Life and Health Insurance v. Rypins*, 29 F. Supp. 2d 619 (N.D. Cal. 1998) (policy was incontestable even though the insured's signature was forged by the beneficiary on a reinstatement authorization form), *with Fioretti v. Mass. Gen. Life Ins. Co.*, 53 F.3d 1228 (11th Cir. 1995) (the incontestability clause did not apply where a person applying for life insurance used another person's name).

2. *Statutory Mandates.* Most states require life insurance contracts to contain an incontestability clause. This requirement may apply to group contracts as well as individual contracts. Some states also require that prescribed incontestability clauses appear in accident, disability, and health insurance contracts. It is not uncommon, however, to find statutes permitting insurers to except disability and accidental death benefits in life insurance contracts from the operation of such a clause. *See generally* Dale Joseph Gilsinger, Annotation, *Construction of Incontestable Clause Applicable to Disability Insurance*, 67 A.L.R.5th 513 (1999).

3. *Standard Text.* The standard incontestability clause reads as follows: "This policy shall be incontestable after it has been in force during the lifetime of the insured, for a period of two years from the issue date, except for nonpayment of premiums." Note that if the *cestui que vie* dies within the two-year period, this particular clause permits the insurer to contest the validity of the policy beyond the two-year period.

Earlier versions of the clause did not contain this feature, and it was held that the insurer lost the right to contest the policy after two years regardless of when the death occurred. *See, e.g., Monahan v. Metropolitan Life Ins. Co.*, 119 N.E. 68 (Ill. 1918). This was true even though the death occurred so close to the end of the two-year period that it was not possible for the insurer to learn of it or bring an action to rescind before the two years expired. Under this rule, if there was any doubt about the validity of the policy, an astute claimant could wait until the two years expired, assuming this would not breach some other time limitation, and thereby preclude the insurer's defenses.

Some insurers continued to use the earlier version as a result of some courts holding that the new version made the equitable remedy of rescission unavailable to the insurer. The reasoning behind these decisions was that because the insurer could defend at any time against claims on the policy, the insurer had an adequate remedy at law and the rescission remedy was therefore unavailable. By omitting the phrase "during the lifetime of the insured," the insurer preserved the right to the equitable remedy. *Massachusetts Mutual Life Insurance Co. v. Goodelman*, 160 F. Supp. 510 (E.D.N.Y. 1958). Under modern rules of civil procedure and with the merger of law and equity, there is little reason today for insurers to continue to use the earlier version.

4. *Calculating the Duration of the Incontestability Period.* The language "after it has been in force" can give rise to disputes regarding the date from which the two years is to be measured. Does this mean the date of issue stated in the policy, or could it be some other date? For example, if the policy has a "delivered while in good health" clause, could it be argued that the incontestability period does not begin to run until the policy is delivered, regardless of the date of issue? Or, if the insurer uses a conditional receipt in a jurisdiction that treats this as creating temporary coverage, does the temporary coverage period count as part of the incontestability period?

5. *To Which Defenses Does the Clause Apply?* The incontestability clause was designed to preclude an insurer from raising certain defenses after the stated time period has elapsed. Which defenses are subject to the clause? The clause generally is viewed as applying to "defenses based on misrepresentations where the policy is not affirmatively repudiated within the incontestable period, at least when the misrepresentations are not such as to render the entire policy void ab initio under the law of the jurisdiction." Steven Plitt, et. al., 17 Couch on Ins. § 240:67 (2017).

What about the defense of fraud? If an applicant for insurance deliberately misrepresents his health status and the insurer fails to catch the falsehood within two years, should the insurer be foreclosed from contesting the policy? If the answer is "yes," then what kinds of incentives does this create for dishonest individuals who learn that they suffer from a terminal or disabling illness? In many cases, courts have held the insurer's defense of fraud is subject to the incontestability clause. *See, e.g., Bankers Security Life Insurance Society v. Kane*, 885 F.2d 820 (11th Cir. 1989) (applying Florida law); *Perry v. Bankers Life and Casualty Co.*, 362 S.W.2d 213 (Tex. Civ. App. 1962); *see also Paul Revere Life Insurance Co. v. Fima*, 105 F.3d 490 (9th Cir. 1997) (applying California law to disability policy).

What if the statute mandating the incontestability clause does not specifically mention fraud and the insurer has a policy provision excepting fraud from the scope of the clause? Courts have not answered this question consistently. In *Protective Life Insurance Co. v. Sullivan*, 682 N.E.2d 624 (Mass. 1997), the court held that the insurer could not rescind the policy for fraud after passage of the two-year incontestability period in circumstances where the insured knew, but failed to disclose, he was HIV positive at the time of application. The fact the insurance policy, a form approved by the state insurance department, provided the policy was contestable for fraud at any time, did not matter. The Massachusetts incontestability statute was held to prohibit an insurer from enforcing a fraud exception in the policy. *Id.* at 627–28. In *New England Mutual Life Insurance Co. v. Doe*, 710 N.E.2d 1060 (N.Y. 1999), the court held that once the incontestability period had passed, a disability insurer could not deny coverage by claiming that the applicant, who was being treated for HIV, falsely stated at the time of the application that he was not receiving any medical treatment. But, unlike in *Sullivan*, the insurer had not reserved a right to contest the policy for fraud at any time. In light of that omission, the court stated "[a] carrier may, compatibly with the incontestability clause, protect itself by including a provision in its incontestability clause creating an exception for 'fraudulent misstatements.' " *Id.* at 1063. Should insurers be allowed to include a fraud exception to the incontestability clause? Should they be allowed to do so if the premium charged for the coverage is reduced? On what basis might one argue that fraud differs from negligent misrepresentation?

6. *Coverage Versus Validity*. Most jurisdictions have held that incontestability clauses do not affect the scope of coverage, but instead, they only apply to defenses relating to the policy's validity. This principle, however, is easier to state than to apply. The problem is that it is not always easy to distinguish coverage provisions to which the clause does not apply from other provisions that give rise to defenses or grounds for avoidance and should be preempted by the clause.

This issue has arisen most prominently in cases involving eligibility requirements for group life insurance. For a list of cases categorized by holdings, *see Bonitz v. Travelers Insurance Co.*, 372 N.E.2d 254 (Mass. 1978). For some courts, the standard applied is whether the condition or situation which would give rise to a defense or grounds for avoidance was discoverable. The emphasis is put on the insurer's obligation to investigate on pain of being denied a defense on the basis that the insured did not meet the eligibility requirements. The cases addressing the issue are almost evenly divided in their results. *See* Robert H. Jerry, II & Douglas R. Richmond, Understanding Insurance Law § 104B (5th ed. 2012).

7. *Other Exceptions to Incontestability*. There are some other areas where courts have held that the policy's validity remains contestable notwithstanding the incontestability clause. For example, it has been held that the incontestability clause does not bar a defense or grounds for avoidance where there is no insurable interest, *Carter v. Continental Life Insurance Co.*, 115 F.2d 947 (D.C. Cir. 1940), and where the policy was procured with intent to murder the *cestui que vie*, *Henderson v. Life Insurance Co. of Va.*, 179 S.E.

680 (S.C. 1935). If policies are contestable on these grounds, then why not on the basis of the applicant's fraud? Is there a principled distinction between a defense or a ground for avoidance that is based on a theory that the policy was void *ab initio* as compared to a theory that the policy is merely voidable?

EXERCISE

1. Ace Manufacturing Company has a work force of 85 employees. The leaders of the employee association ask the chief executive officer to provide a group life insurance plan as a fringe benefit. To help employee morale and loyalty, the CEO agrees. Ace purchases a group plan from Reliable Insurance Company providing $100,000 in life insurance coverage to each employee. To be eligible for the insurance, the employee must be a full-time employee, which is defined as anyone who is employed and actually works at least 35 hours per week. Ace signs up the interested employees and sends the list of covered employees, plus the premium, every month.

The CEO has a part-time assistant who works 20 hours per week, on average. The assistant prefers this arrangement because of responsibilities at home, and the assistant completes all the needed work with this part-time schedule. As a reward for the assistant's loyalty, the CEO signs the assistant up for the insurance and continues to list the assistant as a covered employee on the monthly reports for three years. The premium is continuously paid during this period.

At the end of the third year, the assistant tragically dies in an automobile accident. The beneficiaries fill out a claim form seeking the $100,000 in proceeds. Ace denies the claim on the ground that the assistant was a part-time employee and therefore ineligible for the insurance.

Write a 3-page memo evaluating Ace's defense and opining on the validity of the beneficiaries' claim.

III. ASSIGNABILITY AND CHANGING BENEFICIARIES

Does the insurable interest requirement limit the ability of a person whose life is insured to transfer the policy only to other persons who have an insurable interest in the person's life? There are relatively few cases involving insurance law decided by the Supreme Court of the United States, but *Grigsby v. Russell*, 222 U.S. 149 (1911) is one of the classics.

Also, what steps must be taken to change the beneficiary under a life insurance policy? Is it enough for the owner of the policy to simply express an intention to make the change before dying? *Lemke v. Schwarz*, 286 N.W.2d 693 (Minn. 1979) addresses those questions.

GRIGSBY V. RUSSELL

222 U.S. 149 (1911)

Opinion

MR. JUSTICES HOLMES delivered the opinion of the court:

This is a bill of interpleader brought by an insurance company to determine whether a policy of insurance issued to John C. Burchard, now deceased, upon his life, shall be paid to his administrators or to an assignee, the company having turned the amount into court. The material facts are that after he had paid two premiums and a third was overdue, Burchard, being in want and needing money for a surgical operation, asked Dr. Grigsby to buy the policy, and sold it to him in consideration of $100 and Grigsby's undertaking to pay the premiums due or to become due; and that Grigsby had no interest in the life of the assured. The circuit court of appeals, in deference to some intimations of this court, held the assignment valid only to the extent of the money actually given for it and the premiums subsequently paid. ___ L.R.A. ___, 94 C. C. A. 61, 168 Fed. 577.

Of course, the ground suggested for denying the validity of an assignment to a person having no interest in the life insured is the public policy that refuses to allow insurance to be taken out by such persons in the first place. A contract of insurance upon a life in which the insured has no interest is a pure wager that gives the insured a sinister counter interest in having the life come to an end. And although that counter interest always exists, as early was emphasized for England in the famous case of Wainewright (Janus Weathercock), the chance that in some cases it may prove a sufficient motive for crime is greatly enhanced if the whole world of the unscrupulous are free to bet on what life they choose. The very meaning of an insurable interest is an interest in having the life continue, and so one that is opposed to crime. And what, perhaps, is more important, the existence of such an interest makes a roughly selected class of persons who, by their general relations with the person whose life is insured, are less likely than criminals at large to attempt to compass his death.

But when the question arises upon an assignment, it is assumed that the objection to the insurance as a wager is out of the case. In the present instance the policy was perfectly good. There was a faint suggestion in argument that it had become void by the failure of Burchard to pay the third premium *ad diem*, and that when Grisby paid, he was making a new contract. But a condition in a policy that it shall be void if premiums are not paid when due means only that it shall be voidable at the option of the company. Knickerbocker L. Ins. Co. v. Norton, 96 U. S. 234, 24 L. ed. 689; Oakes v. Manufacturers' F. & M. Ins. Co. 135 Mass. 248. The company waived the breach, if there was one, and the original contract with Burchard remained on foot. No question as to the character of that contract is before us. It has been performed and the money is in court. But this being so, not only does the objection to wagers disappear, but also the principle of public policy referred to, at least, in its most convincing form. The danger that might arise from a general license to all to insure whom they like does not exist. Obviously it is a very different thing from granting such a general license, to allow the holder of a valid insurance upon his own life to transfer it to one whom he, the party most concerned, is not afraid to trust. The law has no universal cynic fear of the temptation opened by a pecuniary benefit accruing upon a death. It shows no prejudice against remainders after life estates, even by the rule in Shelley's Case. Indeed, the ground of the objection to life insurance without interest in the earlier English cases was not the temptation to murder, but the fact that such wagers came to be regarded as a mischievous kind of gaming. Stat. 14 George III., chap. 48.

On the other hand, life insurance has become in our days one of the best recognized forms of investment and self-compelled saving. So far as reasonable safety permits, it is desirable to give to life policies the ordinary characteristics of property. This is recognized by the bankruptcy law, § 70, which provides that unless the cash surrender value of a policy like the one before us is secured to the trustee within thirty days after it has been stated, the policy shall pass to the trustee as assets. Of course the trustee may have no interest in the bankrupt's life. To deny the right to sell except to persons having such an interest is to diminish appreciably the value of the contract in the owner's hands. The collateral difficulty that arose from regarding life insurance as a contract of indemnity only (Godsall v. Boldero, 9 East, 72), long has disappeared (Phoenix Mut. L. Ins. Co. v. Bailey, 13 Wall. 616, 20 L. ed. 501). And cases in which a person having an interest lends himself to one without any, as a cloak to what is, in its inception, a wager, have no similarity to those where an honest contract is sold in good faith.

Coming to the authorities in this court, it is true that there are intimations in favor of the result come to by the circuit court of appeals. But the case in which the strongest of them occur was one of the type just referred to, the policy having been taken out for the purpose of allowing a stranger association to pay the premiums and receive the greater part of the benefit, and having been assigned to it at once. Warnock v. Davis, 104 U. S. 775, 26 L. ed. 924. On the other hand, it has been decided that a valid policy is not avoided by the cessation of the insurable interest, even as against the insurer, unless so provided by the policy itself. Connecticut Mut. L. Ins. Co. v. Schaefer, 94 U. S. 457, 24 L. ed. 251. And expressions more or less in favor of the doctrine that we adopt are to be found also in Aetna L. Ins. Co. v. France, 94 U. S. 561, 24 L. ed. 287; Mutual L. Ins. Co. v. Armstrong, 117 U. S. 591, 29 L. ed. 997, 6 Sup. Ct. Rep. 877. It is enough to say that while the court below might hesitate to decide against the language of *Warnock v. Davis*, there has been no decision that precludes us from exercising our own judgment upon this much debated point. It is at least satisfactory to learn from the decision below that in Tennessee, where this assignment was made, although there has been much division of opinion, the supreme court of that state came to the conclusion that we adopt, in an unreported case, *Lewis v. Edwards*, December 14, 1903. The law in England and the preponderance of decisions in our state courts are on the same side.

Some reference was made to a clause in the policy that 'any claim against the company, arising under any assignment of the policy, shall be subject to proof on interest.' But it rightly was assumed below that if there was no rule of law to that effect, and the company saw fit to pay, the clause did not diminish the rights of Grigsby, as against the administrators of Burchard's estate.

Decree reversed.

LEMKE V. SCHWARZ

286 N.W.2d 693 (Minn. 1979)

KELLY, JUSTICE.

This is an appeal from a judgment entered in the District Court of St. Louis County. The district court, after a full hearing, ruled that by reason of her status as named beneficiary, defendant, Bernadine Schwarz, was entitled to the entire proceeds of two insurance policies in the name of her deceased husband. Judgment was entered accordingly, and plaintiffs appealed. We reverse.

At the time of his death, decedent was the named insured under the terms of two life insurance policies which listed defendant as the beneficiary. Both policies provided that the insured could from time to time designate a change of beneficiary by filing a written request with the company.

Shortly before his death on September 8, 1975, the insured wrote a letter, entirely in his own handwriting, to his daughter, Debora, one of the plaintiffs herein. The letter was dated September 7, 1975, and postmarked the following day. The letter read in part as follows:

> ". . . [T]here are a few things that I want you to know & I want you to keep because of legal matters that might arise in the near future. I should have kept a copy of this letter, but I haven't & so it's up to you. Hang on to this because sometimes it takes a long time for things to develop & then you may need some evidence & this letter should be a part of a record."

Decedent then set forth the following provision between quotation marks:

> "I hereby decree & make it known to all persons that whatever are my possessions—material things such as shall be known by my wife Bernie Schwarz to be things as housewares, painting and misc. items that I contributed to our household, let it be known

> that my daughters Debora Schwarz & Denise Lemke (Schwarz) have the right to share and share alike in these items and that my wife Bernie Schwarz, has not one right to withhold these items."
>
> "Also let it be known that I also bequeath to my two daughters, Debora & Denise, all other assets that I have at the time of my death. These assets namely would be to the best of my knowledge at this writing a life insurance policy with Goodwill Industries in the amount of $5,000—a Retirement Benefit with the National Health and Welfare Association—all my retirement benefits plus a death benefit of two years of my salary. Also at the time of this writing & date I have been informed by my brother-in-law Omer Larson, that I am the benefactor of at least $5,000 from the estate of my late, father, Walter Schwarz. This also should be considered a part of my estate & divided equally between my two daughters."

At the conclusion of these provisions, it stated:

> "All parts enclosed under the sign of 'marks are to be known as my last will & testament.' Let no one contest my last wishes."

Thereafter, insured concluded this letter as follows:

> "Share nothing with Bernie [defendant] because she has not been willing to share her life with me.
>
> I love you,
>
> Daddy"

This letter did not reach Debora until after she had returned from her father's funeral. After receipt of that letter, plaintiffs retained legal counsel and notified the respective insurance companies, indicating their belief that the insured had intended them to be the beneficiaries on the insurance policies and demanding that no payment be made to anyone until an appropriate resolution had been reached. Both insurance companies subsequently paid the proceeds of the insurance policies to the plaintiffs' attorney to be held in trust pending the resolution of this matter. The insurance companies are not parties to this action.

The district court made no findings respecting the legal effect of the letter which insured sent to his daughter, Debora, nor did it make a finding as to insured's intent in drafting the letter. The court merely ruled that, as the named beneficiary, defendant was entitled to the entire proceeds of both insurance policies.

On this appeal, plaintiffs do not argue that decedent's letter to his daughter constituted a valid will. They do contend, however, that the letter was effective to change the beneficiary on the two policies in question from decedent's wife, Bernadine, the named beneficiary, to decedent's daughters, the plaintiffs herein. We agree.

This court has, in our prior decisions, made it clear that a change of beneficiary may properly be effected in spite of the failure of the insured to comply with each and every policy requirement. *Pabst v. Hesse*, 286 Minn. 33, 173 N.W.2d 925 (1970); *Brown v. Agin*, 260 Minn. 104, 109 N.W.2d 147 (1961). In *Brown v. Agin, supra,* speaking to this issue, we reasoned as follows (260 Minn. 109, 109 N.W.2d 150):

> . . . Such provisions are for the protection of the insurer, and where, as here, the insurance company has deposited the proceeds of the policy to be paid in accordance with the order of the court, it has waived any defense it might have to the claim of either party.

We therefore determined that in cases such as these equitable principles should control. We additionally adopted a two-pronged test as a guideline for future determinations:

> . . . (1) whether the insured intended to change the beneficiary and (2) whether he took affirmative action or otherwise did substantially all that he could do to demonstrate that intention without regard to whether he complied with the change-of-beneficiary provisions in the policy.

260 Minn. 109, 109 N.W.2d 151.

In order to utilize the above test, a close examination of the facts before us becomes necessary. Here, the insured had been married three times. At the time of his death, he had been married to defendant for a little more than a year. There was testimony that during the last 6 months of their marriage the relationship between defendant and the insured became progressively worse, to the extent that at one point defendant left her husband and remained separated from him for a period of a week. On the evening prior to his death, defendant informed the insured of her intent to leave him. It was sometime subsequent to this that the insured wrote the letter in question.

Defendant claims that the insured's act of sending the letter to his daughter neither evidences an intent to change beneficiaries nor constitutes a substantial effort to demonstrate that intent. We disagree. The language of the letter expresses the insured's clear and unambiguous intent that his daughters rather than his wife receive the entire proceeds of the policies. It is also apparent that the insured expected and fully intended the letter to have legal significance.[1]

Defendant maintains that even assuming that the insured had the requisite intent, his subsequent acts were not sufficient to effect the change claimed by the plaintiffs. Defendant suggests that had the insured

---

[1] "Hang on to this because sometimes it takes a long time for things to develop & then you may need some evidence & this letter should be a part of a record."

simultaneously written to his employer or to the insurer or even sent them copies of the original letter, the policy provisions may have been satisfied. It is undisputed that the insured could have changed his mind several times regarding the choice of beneficiary on the life insurance policies. There seems to be, however, little, if any, distinction between writing a letter to the insurer of the change and making an unequivocal statement of such intent in a letter to another, so long as the insurer, for whose benefit the notice requirements exist, is not thereby prejudiced.

Many courts that have required relatively strict compliance with the policy formalities have reasoned that this best effectuates the original intent of the parties and insures that the insured ". . . unequivocally desired to make that change, and that he did not at some time thereafter abandon his purpose by failing to take affirmative steps to carry out his intent." *Allen v. Abrahamson,* 12 Wash. App. 103, 107, 529 P.2d 469, 471 (1974). We do not find this reasoning persuasive. We hold that where an insured has clearly and unambiguously demonstrated an intent to change the beneficiary on a life insurance policy, this intent should be given effect unless prejudice to the insurer would result. If there exists any confusion as to the insured's intent or conflicting expressions of intent, then the named beneficiary should be entitled to the proceeds. This will avoid the practical difficulties which have troubled some courts.

In the instant case, the trial court made no findings of fact regarding the insured's mental state. However, because the letter written by the insured constitutes the primary evidence on this issue, this court is as able as the trial court to make the ultimate determination.

As we have already stated, we believe that the insured intended to substitute his daughters as beneficiaries on his insurance policies in place of his wife. In addition, we find that the insured made affirmative efforts to effect this change and under the circumstances substantially complied with the relevant policy provisions. For the foregoing reasons, we reverse the judgment of the trial court and hold that the plaintiffs are entitled to the proceeds of both policies.

Reversed.

NOTES AND QUESTIONS

1. *Types of Interests in Life Insurance.* There are a number of interests or rights in contracts of life insurance that may be held by different persons or entities. The three main persons or entities, aside from the insurer, are the *owner* of the policy, the *beneficiary*, and the person whose life is insured, or *cestui que vie* (or simply "CQV"). The earliest forms of life insurance were contracts taken out by the beneficiary on the life of the *cestui que vie*; consequently, the beneficiary held all the ownership rights. Today, the *cestui que vie* most often applies for, and therefore owns, the policy on her own life.

Where a person takes out a policy on her own life and makes another the beneficiary, the ownership rights are held by the *cestui que vie* unless otherwise alienated. The beneficiary may be entitled to the proceeds on the death of the *cestui que vie*, but the owner, in the meantime, may change the beneficiary, surrender the policy for any cash value, borrow against the cash surrender value or on the security of the policy, assign the policy in whole or in part, and exercise any other rights under the contract. Thus, the owner has the power to alienate or convey any number of distinct rights or interests to various persons or entities.

2. *Modern Policy Forms and the Right to Change Beneficiary.* Modern policy forms require policyholders to designate beneficiaries and reserve the right to change beneficiaries. But where that right is waived or otherwise foreclosed under the contract, the beneficiary has a vested right to the proceeds upon death, subject to the policy being maintained in force. *See Morton v. United States*, 457 F.2d 750 (4th Cir. 1972).

3. *Attempts to Change Beneficiary.* Should courts require that attempts to change beneficiaries meet the exact conditions set out in the policy? Should the subject be approached with the same sanctity as that of wills? The substantial compliance rule with the two-pronged test set out in *Lemke* is the approach favored by a majority of jurisdictions today. *See, e.g., Engelman v. Connecticut General Life Insurance Co.*, 690 A.2d 882 (Conn. 1997); *IDS Life Insurance Co. v. Estate of Groshong*, 736 P.2d 1301 (Idaho 1987).

Attempts to change a life insurance beneficiary by will have been held void where the policy, as most policies do today, sets out specific procedures for making beneficiary changes that do not authorize change by such a method. *See, e.g., McCarthy v. Aetna Life Insurance Co.*, 704 N.E.2d 557 (N.Y. 1998); *Stone v. Stephens*, 99 N.E.2d 766 (Ohio 1951). Is the rationale of these decisions undermined if the jurisdiction adheres to the "substantial compliance" rule outlined in *Lemke*? *See Rindlaub v. Travelers Insurance Co.*, 196 N.E.2d 602 (Ohio Ct. App. 1962). Note that a will, like a life insurance contract, is not operative until the *cestui que vie* dies. Consequently, at the moment of death, the original beneficiary is entitled to the proceeds so that the will cannot operate simultaneously to change the beneficiary. This may be a more formidable reason for voiding testamentary attempts to change a beneficiary. Some courts have adhered to this reasoning in holding that such an attempt is inherently ineffective. *See Cook v. Cook*, 111 P.2d 322 (Cal. 1941).

Lemke involved a writing. Should oral statements ever be deemed sufficient by themselves (i.e., without a writing) to change a beneficiary under the substantial compliance rule? *Compare DeCeglia v. Estate of Colletti*, 625 A.2d 590 (N.J. Super. Ct. App. Div. 1993) (insured's oral statements did not accomplish a beneficiary change), *with Bell v. Parker*, 563 So.2d 594 (Miss. 1990) (insured's oral request for change of beneficiary constituted substantial compliance with policy terms requiring request for change to be in writing).

4. *Effect of Divorce.* The general rule is that a divorce decree or settlement agreement does not, in and of itself, automatically terminate a

spouse's rights as a named beneficiary of a life insurance policy. Instead, courts look for—and drafters of such decrees and agreements must be careful to insert—language which clearly manifests an intention to terminate a beneficiary's interest. As one court explained it, the "manifestation can take the form of either an express renunciation of the expectancy as beneficiary or other language which unmistakenly evidences an intent to waive the expectancy." *Christensen v. Sabad*, 773 P.2d 538, 540 (Colo. 1989) (holding that marital property separation agreement lacked sufficiently clear language to extinguish respondent's expectancy). *See also Ohran v. Sierra Health and Life Insurance Co.*, 895 P.2d 1321 (Nev. 1995) (divorce decree did not contain explicit language needed to divest former husband of rights as designated life insurance beneficiary). Thus, with sufficiently clear language, a beneficiary's interest may be effectively terminated by an agreement or court order, and this is true even where there is no reservation in the policy of the right to change the beneficiary or, if there is a right to do so, the beneficiary is never actually changed or is not changed in accordance with the policy provisions after the divorce. *See, e.g., Napper v. Schmeh*, 773 P.2d 531 (Colo. 1989) (en banc); *Beneficial Life Insurance Co. v. Stoddard*, 516 P.2d 187 (Idaho 1973); *Larsen v. Northwestern National Life Insurance Co.*, 463 N.W.2d 777 (Minn. Ct. App. 1990). Likewise, the policy owner's right to change a beneficiary may be limited by a divorce decree, property settlement, or other contractual agreement. *See Holt v. Holt*, 995 S.W.2d 68 (Tenn. 1999).

Careful thought needs to be given to how the obligation under any one of these devices may be enforced if there is a breach. In that event, is the contempt power of the court available, or may the court impose a constructive trust or order any unauthorized beneficiary change set aside? Or, is the remedy one for damages only? *See* Annotation, *Divorce: Provision in Decree that One Party Obtain or Maintain Life Insurance for Benefit of Other Party or Child*, 59 A.L.R.3d 9 (1974) (particularly §§ 18–20, which discuss remedies for enforcement).

5. *Statutory Changes in Common Law Rule Regarding Effect of Divorce.* In recent years, some states have adopted statutes that affect the rights of the owner of a life insurance policy and the beneficiary upon divorce. These statutes, in effect, treat the beneficiary-spouse as having predeceased the owner-spouse unless steps are taken at the time of divorce or otherwise to counteract the statutes. *See, e.g.*, Mich. Comp. Laws Ann. § 552.101 (West 1988); Ohio Rev. Code Ann. § 1339.63 (Anderson 1993); Okla. Stat. Ann. tit. 15, § 178 (West 1993 & Supp. 2000); Tex. Fam. Code §§ 7.005 (West 1998). This paucity in legislation has begun to change, however, because the Uniform Probate Code was amended in 1990 to contain a provision that automatically revokes a life insurance spousal beneficiary designation upon divorce unless the insurance policy, a court order, or an agreement of the parties precludes such a change. The effect of the revocation is to treat the situation as if the former beneficiary-spouse disclaimed the policy benefits. *See* Uniform Probate Code § 2–804(b) and (d), 8 U.L.A. 23–24 (Supp. 2000). This means that a contingent beneficiary or, in the absence of such, the estate of the owner-

spouse, would be entitled to the benefits. The life insurance industry was not in favor of including this provision in the UPC. Can you think of any good reasons for their opposition?

6. *Terminal Illnesses, "Viatical Settlements," and Accelerated Benefits.* As a result of *Grigsby* allowing for the transfer of life insurance policies, during the early 1980s, largely stemming from the onset of the AIDS epidemic, some individuals started businesses that offer to provide immediate cash payments to terminally ill owners of life insurance policies in an amount less than the expected death benefit in exchange for an assignment of the right to the policy proceeds. Depending on the insured's life expectancy, the cash payment might range anywhere from fifty to eighty percent of the expected death benefit. The market ebbed somewhat in the mid-1980s. Observers attributed this to unanticipated medical developments which extended the life expectancies of terminally ill AIDS patients, which reduced the profits of assignees of the policies.

Since the 1980s, it has become much more common for insurers to include a provision in life insurance policies allowing, under certain conditions, a terminally ill insured to receive a percentage of the policy's benefits prior to death. Eligibility for accelerated benefits is typically triggered by a medical condition that limits the insured's life expectancy to two or fewer years, a condition requiring extraordinary medical intervention (e.g., through an organ transplant or continuous life support), a condition requiring lifetime institutionalization of the insured, or specified illnesses or conditions that have one or more of these characteristics.

Since the 1990s, the market for buying life insurance policies has seen significant growth, particularly with respect to older insureds who no longer need life insurance to protect against economic loss, so they are solicited to assign their policies to an investor rather than to allow the policy to lapse. *See* Barry A. Wilkinson, *New Market Ripe for Fraud,* Best's Review-Life/Health Insurance Edition, Oct 1, 1999, at 86. The purchase prices are based upon the life expectancies of the insureds, which are based upon the insured's health and age. Why should state insurance commissioners be concerned about viatical settlements?

In 1993, the National Association of Insurance Commissioners promulgated the Viatical Settlements Model Act which regulates any viatical settlement business in an enacting state by requiring that the business be licensed and settlement contracts approved by the insurance regulator. The model was amended substantially in 1998, 2001, and again in 2007. *See* NAIC, Viatical Settlements Model Act, Model Laws, Regulations & Guidelines (2009). The Act requires certain disclosures regarding benefit calculations and ordinarily regulates the amount of proceeds payable to the *cestui que vie* through a formula that references a stated percentage of the person's income at the time of disability or by resort to a schedule of benefits based on the nature of the disability. In addition, the regulator has the power to examine the financial aspects of the business.

7. *STOLI.* In the early 2000s, a controversial practice known as stranger-owned life insurance (STOLI) emerged. In a STOLI arrangement, an individual (typically an elderly person) procures insurance on his own life and subsequently assigns the policy to a third party after the incontestability period has run. The insured receives an up-front cash payment from an investor to pay the premium. In exchange, the insured promises to sell the policy to the investor in the future. The cash payment to pay the premium is a non-recourse loan, so the insured can procure the policy at virtually no cost to himself. The insured also assumes the role as a grantor on a life insurance trust (called an "ILIT," or individual life insurance trust, which is a very important and useful tool in estate planning) that is used to apply for the policy, and the insured understands that if he survives the contestability period, the policy will be sold to investors for a sum that will pay the loan and accrued interest, leaving a profit that he and the investor group will divide. Few question that insureds should be allowed to sell life insurance policies they no longer need in a secondary market, but STOLI arrangements create insurance coverage far removed from the purposes for which life insurance is ordinarily purchased, and lead to the moral hazard concerns that the insurable interest rules are meant to avoid.

The emergence of the STOLI market led the National Conference of Insurance Legislators to propose another model act, titled the "Life Settlements Model Act." This 2007 model, which was re-approved by NCOIL in 2014, takes a more aggressive stance regarding the regulation of STOLI transactions than the Viatical Settlements Model Act. As of 2020, 43 states had adopted legislation that regulates life settlements. For more discussion of viatical arrangements and state regulation of them, *see* Miriam R. Albert, *Selling Death Short: The Regulatory and Policy Implications of Viatical Settlements*, 61 Alb. L. Rev. 1013 (1998).

EXERCISE

1. Draft a 5-page memo that addresses the arguments in favor of and against viatical settlements.

IV. DISQUALIFICATION OF BENEFICIARIES

PRUDENTIAL INS. CO. OF AM. V. ATHMER

178 F.3d 473 (7th Cir. 1999)

POSNER, CHIEF JUDGE.

A pair of insurance companies brought this interpleader action to determine who should receive the proceeds of two life insurance policies owned by a man who was murdered by his wife. The contenders are the victim's natural daughter, and the murderess's natural son and sister. Upon stipulated facts, the district judge rendered judgment for the latter two, and the daughter appeals.

Kevin Spann, a soldier in the U.S. Army, was the insured. Prudential had issued him a life insurance policy pursuant to the Servicemen's Group Life Insurance Act of 1965 (SGLI), 38 U.S.C. §§ 1965 et seq., for $200,000 in 1992 when he was stationed in Germany. The policy named Spann's wife, Gina Spann, as primary beneficiary and Gina's natural son, Steven Hill, as contingent or secondary beneficiary. Steven was 13 and had been living with Kevin and Gina throughout the eleven years of their marriage. The other policy, which was for $100,000, had been issued in 1994, also in Germany, by Boston Mutual. This policy also named Gina as primary beneficiary, but it named her sister, Betty Jo Pierce, rather than Steven, as the contingent beneficiary, and it was not issued under SGLI. Neither policy mentioned Chrystal Athmer, Kevin Spann's natural daughter. He had never lived with her or even acknowledged the relationship, which was established by DNA testing after his death. In his will Spann devised his estate to Steven, describing him as "my son."

At the time of his death in 1997, Spann was a permanent resident of Illinois but was stationed in Georgia. His wife had him murdered there by her 18-year-old lover and three of his 16-year old pals. She pleaded guilty to the murder and was sentenced to life in prison without parole plus five additional years (as the district judge judiciously put it, "the State of Georgia even tacked an additional five years onto that already lengthy sentence"). She no longer has custody of her son. In fact, as Steven's lawyer explained without contradiction, "the whole family is estranged from her. The sister [Betty Jo Pierce] didn't have anything to do with her. They've been trying to get Kevin away from her for years. Gina is somewhere else." The sister is Steven's legal guardian, and has instituted a proceeding to adopt him; neither was complicit in Kevin Spann's murder. Gina is conceded to be disqualified from taking anything under the life insurance policies. The question is whether Steven and his aunt are also disqualified. The district judge held not.

. . . .

The principle that no person shall be permitted to benefit from the consequences of his or her wrongdoing has long been applied to disqualify murderers from inheriting from their victims, whether the route of inheritance is a will, an intestacy statute, or a life insurance policy. It is undoubtedly an implicit provision of the Servicemen's Group Life Insurance Act of 1965, and it disqualifies Gina Spann from receiving any of the proceeds of Kevin's SGLI policy, even though she is the primary beneficiary named in it.

The usual consequence when a primary beneficiary disclaims or is forced to disclaim an interest under an insurance policy, will, pension plan, or other such instrument is that the contingent beneficiary takes in the place of the primary one. And this is the approach that a majority of courts take when the beneficiary is disqualified by reason of having murdered his benefactor. We take it, although the case law is sparse, that if the contingent beneficiary is himself a wrongdoer and his wrongdoing contributed to the death of his benefactor, as where the contingent beneficiary is the accomplice of the primary beneficiary in the benefactor's murder, the same rule that disqualifies the primary beneficiary disqualifies the contingent beneficiary. *In re Estate of Vallerius*, 259 Ill.App.3d 350, 196 Ill.Dec. 341, 629 N.E.2d 1185, 1188 (Ill.App.1996).

But this leaves the case in which the primary beneficiary may derive an indirect benefit if the contingent beneficiary (assumed to be completely innocent) is allowed to obtain the benefits. *Estate of Vallerius* is the plainest illustration: the grandchildren murdered their grandmother, who had left her estate to their (innocent) mother, who died, having devised her estate, now including the grandmother's money, to her children—the murderers. They were, of course, barred from taking under their mother's will. Subtler cases of indirect benefit can be imagined. Suppose that Steven Hill (the murderess's son and victim's stepson) were an adult and he promised that he would use the life insurance proceeds to pay for his mother's lawyer or to buy her books or other goods that the prison would allow her to receive. Or suppose that Steven needed an expensive operation that Kevin could not or would not pay for and Gina killed Kevin so that the proceeds of his life insurance could be used to pay for the operation; or that Gina had been given a short prison sentence and Kevin had promised to support her in style out of the life insurance proceeds when she was released. The lawyer for Steven and Betty Jo argued to us that the fulfillment of such a promise would be barred by the "murdering heir" rule itself, but that is not correct. The rule forbids the murderer to take under the will or other instrument; it does not impress on the benefits a kind of reverse constructive trust placing them forever beyond the murderer's reach.

These cases can be multiplied indefinitely. Some states have decided that the best way to deal with them and make utterly certain that the murderer does not profit from his crime is to disqualify all the murderer's relatives, except his or her children if they are also the victim's children. *E.g.*, Ga. Stat. 53–4–64(c); *Crawford v. Coleman*, 726 S.W.2d 9 (Tex.1987). Under that rule, Steven and Betty Jo would be disqualified. We need not decide whether that is or should be the federal common law rule governing murders by beneficiaries of Servicemen's Group Life Insurance policies, because Chrystal, the daughter, the party who would benefit from such a rule, does not advocate a uniform federal rule. She argues for the rule of the insured's domicile, here Illinois. Steven and Betty Jo argue for a uniform federal rule, not a borrowed state rule—a uniform rule that does not cut out the murderer's bloodline, that instead requires proof that the murderer will in fact benefit if the contingent beneficiary is allowed to take in the murderer's place. We could turn the tables on Steven and Betty Jo and say, yes, we agree with you that a uniform federal rule is desirable, but we don't like your rule; we like the rule that would entitle the natural daughter to a victory in this suit. But we do not reverse judgments in civil cases on the basis of grounds not argued by the appellant at any stage of the litigation—grounds, therefore, that the appellee had no opportunity to meet.

The life insurance policy issued by Boston Mutual was not issued under the aegis of the Servicemen's Group Life Insurance Act, and so federal common law is not in the picture. The choice of law rule of the forum state, that is, Illinois, must therefore be used to determine which jurisdiction shall supply the rule of decision. In the case of life insurance, that rule picks the law of the state where the insured was domiciled when the policy was applied for, hence in this case Illinois, unless some other state has a more significant relationship. That at any rate is the rule of the Second Restatement, *see* section 192 (and note that comment b to that section confirms Kevin Spann's status as an Illinois domiciliary), which Illinois follows. But one could argue, consistent with the principle—which is a principle of Illinois law—that the law of the place of the tort is the presumptive or default rule of choice of law in tort cases, that the law of Georgia should govern this case instead. For it was a tort, namely the wrongful death that Gina Spann inflicted on her husband, that is the basis for refusing to enforce the contract as written. Georgia has the paramount interest in deciding whether to refuse to enforce a contract as a means of increasing the punishment for a murder committed in Georgia. But just to show how complicated choice of law analysis can be, we point out that arguably what is at stake in "murdering heir" cases is donative intent rather than deterrence. Deterrence of murdering heirs is a legitimate concern, given the number of murders by spouses and children (more than 1,000 in 1997, *see* FBI, Uniform Crime Reports for the United States 1997 21 (1998) (tab.2.12)), but could be achieved by imposing on the murderer a fine equal to the amount he inherited from his victim. Even so, the victim would not have made the murderer his heir (or the beneficiary of his life insurance policy) had he known what the future held. And if this is the important thing it would point us back toward Illinois.

Neither side argues for the application of German law. Although that is where the contracts were made, the parties to the contracts had only the most adventitious connection to Germany and it is highly doubtful that they contemplated the application of German law to any dispute under the policy that might arise. The choice is thus between Illinois and Georgia.

Both states have "slayer statutes," but they are not the same. The Illinois statute forbids the murderer to "receive any property, benefit or other interest by reason of the death [of the murderer's victim], whether as heir, legatee, beneficiary . . . or in any other capacity," and provides that if the murderer is disqualified, the property, etc. shall "pass as if the person causing the death died before the decedent." 755 ILCS 5/2–6. Judicial interpretation has established that the statute is applicable to life insurance. Georgia has a statute that deals expressly with murder by the beneficiary of a life insurance policy, and provides that in such a case the property goes to the secondary beneficiary if one is named in the policy. Ga.Code Ann. § 33–25–13. So the Illinois statute defines "benefit" broadly enough to encompass cases of indirect benefit such as we posited earlier, while the Georgia statute, read literally, allows no room for such consideration. This creates a tension with Georgia's will statute, which, as noted earlier, absolutely excludes the murderer's family, provided there is no blood relationship between them and the victim.

Kevin Spann's daughter pitches her appeal with regard to both policies on cases interpreting the Illinois statute, and since those cases do not carry the day for her, we have no need to delve into Georgia case law, and anyway we cannot find any relevant cases. The daughter relies primarily on a case in which an Illinois court refused to allow the children of a convicted murderess to take under the victim's will. *In re Estate of Mueller*, 275 Ill.App.3d 128, 211 Ill.Dec. 657, 655 N.E.2d 1040 (Ill.App.1995). As in this case, the victim was the murderess's husband and the children were hers, not his. But Chrystal has missed the real significance of *Estate of Mueller*. What it shows is that Illinois does not cut off the murderess's bloodline regardless of circumstances. The court thought it important that the murderess had already been released from prison and had custody of one of her children (the other was an adult) and that the marriage had been a sham and the children had not lived with her husband. *Id.* at 1043, 1046. It was quite likely in these circumstances that the murderess would benefit if her husband's bequest went to the children; indeed, it was almost certain so far as the bequest to the younger child was concerned, since she was living with her murderous mom.

Estate of Mueller suggests that Illinois "murdering heir" case law requires the trial court to make a factual determination whether allowing a relative of the murderer to take in the place of the murderer is likely to confer a significant benefit on him. *Estate of Vallerius*, discussed earlier, is consistent with that approach, and we cannot find any contrary precedent in Illinois. Which is not to say that it is necessarily the best approach. Rejected by many states, it requires an inherently speculative judgment about the future and an investigation of family relations quite likely to be of Faulknerian opacity, but it is Illinois's approach and we are bound by it. It is the approach followed by the district judge, and, as should be apparent from the stipulated facts sketched at the outset of this opinion, the conclusion he reached cannot be adjudged clearly erroneous. It is exceedingly unlikely that Gina Spann will ever benefit significantly from the proceeds of her husband's life insurance policies in the hands of her son and her sister.

But we do not think the judge was right to place any weight on the tenuousness of Chrystal's claim to any place in her father's affections. The question of indirect benefit to the murderer is the focus of inquiry under Illinois law as we understand it and it is unaffected by the victim's affection for the person who will take under the will or the insurance policy if the named beneficiary is disqualified. The "person" could be the state under an escheat statute, so far as anything to do with the policy behind Illinois's murdering-heir rule is concerned. But we do not think the judge's decision would have been different had he ignored the affective dimensions of Chrystal's relationship with her father; his emphasis was quite properly on the remoteness of Gina's prospects of ever deriving any benefit from the life insurance policies.

AFFIRMED.

NOTES AND QUESTIONS

1. *Right Decision?* Why did Chrystal, the victim's natural daughter, not receive the life insurance proceeds? Do you agree with the decision? Why or why not?

2. *The Applicable Test.* What test did Judge Posner apply in *Athmer* to determine whether relatives of the murderer could recover as beneficiaries?

CARTER V. CARTER

88 So. 2d 153 (Fla. 1956)

THORNAL, JUSTICE.

[Hunter J. Carter, Jr. was shot and killed by his wife, Ruby J. Carter. Hunter's life was insured by the Equitable Life Assurance Society of the United States under a group policy, and Ruby was named as beneficiary. Ruby was tried on a charge of second degree murder, and was acquitted. She earlier had pled guilty to the charge of manslaughter, but was allowed to withdraw the plea to go to trial on the murder charge, which turned out to be good judgment on her part. The Equitable filed an interpleader action against Ruby, Hunter's father, and Hunter's estate to determine who was entitled to the proceeds. Ruby claimed entitlement to the proceeds under the reasoning that her acquittal established that "the killing was clearly not felonious." The father claimed that Ruby was disqualified and that he as a "surviving parent" was designated by the policy as the successive beneficiary. The administratrix of the estate claimed that Ruby was a surviving, albeit disqualified beneficiary who held the proceeds in trust for the benefit of the estate. Ruby moved for summary judgment, and the trial judge denied her motion, decreeing that the "issues will be made up to determine by a *preponderance of the evidence* whether the claimant wife feloniously killed her husband." Ruby sought review of this order by petition for certiorari.

On review, the court rejected Ruby's position that the acquittal established her right to proceeds.]

[W]e conclude the initial aspect of our problem by adhering to the rule that since a wrongdoer will not be permitted to profit by his own wrong, the beneficiary of a life insurance policy will not be permitted to receive the proceeds of a policy on the life of one whom he unlawfully and intentionally killed.

By the order under review, the trial judge decreed that the issues in this cause would be decided by a "preponderance of the evidence". The petitioner insists that the verdict of acquittal in her trial on the charge of second degree murder is admissible in this civil action to preclude any consideration of her guilt in the homicide of her husband. This court is committed to the rule that the verdict and judgment in a criminal proceeding are not admissible in a civil proceeding as evidence of the guilt or innocence of a party to the civil cause. The rule is not without some exceptions, for example, under Section 731.31, Florida Statutes, F.S.A., where the ultimate fact of conviction of murder is a condition precedent to denying inheritance to one entitled to inherit. The instant case, however, is not within any of the exceptions and we agree with the trial judge that the verdict and judgment acquitting the petitioner in the criminal action is not admissible in evidence in this case.

The respondents on the other hand contend that the felonious nature of the killing was established by the petitioner's plea of guilty to manslaughter which was withdrawn in the criminal case. Consistent with the rule that the judgment of acquittal is not admissible, we do not feel that the plea of guilty to manslaughter, which was withdrawn, is admissible as evidence against the petitioner in this civil action. It could hardly be fairly contended that a defendant in a criminal proceeding should be charged with the pleadings on some obviously tactical maneuver on the criminal side of the court and at the same time be denied the benefit of the judgment and verdict in her favor. The issues in this civil case, as the trial judge ruled, should be decided on the basis of the preponderance of the evidence produced in this case entirely exclusive of the record in the criminal proceeding. This likewise has been the rule in similar cases in other courts.

The record before us reveals nothing at all with reference to the facts that produced the homicide. However, if at the trial a preponderance of the evidence should establish the fact that the homicide was intentional and unlawful in nature and therefore was without the purifying effect of excuse or justification, the petitioner insofar as this cause is concerned would be confronted by the rule heretofore announced that a person will not be permitted to profit by his own wrong. If, however, the evidence preponderates in favor of justification or excuse, an example of which would be self-defense, accident or insanity, then there would be no area for the application of the rule that would prevent her recovery. The burden of proof in the first instance will rest on the party who alleges that the killing was intentional and unlawful. The order of the Chancellor provided that a preponderance of the evidence would govern whether the claimant-wife "feloniously killed" her husband. By the expression "feloniously killed" in this particular type of situation, we understand the Chancellor to have reference to an "unlawful and intentional" killing. As so construed, we find no objection to the use of the word "feloniously". It is altogether appropriate to permit the establishment of these facts by a preponderance of the evidence which is the degree of proof required in civil cases, for the perfectly obvious reason that in a criminal proceeding, which imposes upon the State the burden of proving guilt beyond a reasonable doubt, a jury, being conscious that it is the custodian of the life and liberty of an accused is often apt to emphasize in its thinking extraneous facts and circumstances that are allowed to mitigate the severe penalties of the criminal law. These misplaced emphases cannot be permitted to influence the decision in a civil proceeding where the rights of the parties are evaluated in an entirely different atmosphere undisturbed by those invisible and intangible cross-currents that we all know oftentimes subconsciously influence the judgment of the criminal court jury.

Finally, we are confronted with a decision as to the ultimate recipient of the proceeds of the insurance money here involved in the event that it should be determined that the petitioner is not entitled thereto. The trial judge decided that the father of the deceased should receive the proceeds, there being no surviving children, and the father being next in order of designated priority. The respondent, Clara Brown, as administratrix of the estate of the deceased, claims the proceeds and the petitioner says that even though she is precluded from receiving the insurance as a designated beneficiary, nevertheless, if the money goes to the estate then she is entitled to receive it as a beneficiary of her husband's estate.

Although the problem is not without difficulty, we are of the view that the trial judge again ruled correctly. . . .

. . . .

There is sound reason for this position [i.e., that "the beneficiary next in priority to the excluded beneficiary should receive the proceeds of the policy in preference to the estate of the deceased"]. Although obviously not a will, the beneficiary clause of a life insurance policy is in some measure analogous in principle to the disposition of one's estate by will. It is usually ambulatory. It is almost always donative, and in a sense it is testamentary in character in that payment is customarily contingent upon the death of the insured. In view of the nature of the beneficiary clause, it would appear to be appropriate in construing it to endeavor to give effect to the intent of the insured if it is possible to do so without doing violence to the expressed language of the policy.

Some of the writers have undertaken to resolve the problem by declaring that the primary beneficiary becomes the trustee of a constructive trust and holds the proceeds for the use and benefit of the beneficiary next in priority. We think it unnecessary to complicate the problem with involved trust principles. It is perfectly clear that it was the intent of this decedent that if his widow could not receive the insurance, then it would go to his parents in the event that he had no children. While in this case we cannot conclude that the petitioner would be relegated to a status of one civilly dead, we can with safety conclude that when the policy provided for the distribution of the proceeds to various contingent beneficiaries if there was no designated beneficiary "surviving at the death" of the insured, the language was intended to mean a beneficiary entitled to receive the proceeds. Undoubtedly, the deceased never contemplated that he would be killed by his wife, if he was. Certainly, if he had so contemplated, he would not have encouraged the act by establishing a reward in the form of a policy of insurance on his life.

We must assume that the word "beneficiary" as used in a life insurance policy comprehends beneficiary in its broadest legal aspect and in that sense it necessarily must be considered as having reference to the survival of a beneficiary eligible to take. Admittedly, there are those who apply a rule of strict construction to such provisions and by so doing arrive at the conclusion that the words "beneficiary surviving at the death" of the insured mean just exactly that, without the implication of the additional inference of an eligible beneficiary and that if the designated beneficiary survives but becomes ineligible by operation of law then the members of the various successive classes are prevented from taking because of the "survival" of the designated beneficiary. Under this rule the proceeds of the policy would go to the estate of the deceased. . . .

We prefer to adhere to what we consider to be the better rule which is the one that appears to give effect to the intent of the insured by paying the proceeds to the beneficiary first in priority who is eligible under the law to receive the money. In this case it would be the respondent, Hunter J. Carter, Sr., in the event the petitioner is found to be disqualified. This would be so because in the absence of an express provision of the insurance policy, the insurance company itself is not to be relieved of the obligation to pay the amount which it contracted to pay merely because of the alleged wrongdoing of a particular beneficiary.

. . . .

For the reasons hereinabove stated, the prayer of the petition for certiorari is hereby—

Denied.

NOTES AND QUESTIONS

1. *General Principles.* That a beneficiary who slays the *cestui que vie* should not be allowed to benefit from the wrongful act is well settled. "It would be a reproach to the jurisprudence of the country, if one could recover insurance money payable on the death of a party whose life he had feloniously taken." *Mutual Life Insurance Co. v. Armstrong*, 117 U.S. 591, 600 (1886). Most states have addressed the issue statutorily. Set forth below is a model statute on the issue that has been adopted in many states.

UNIFORM PROBATE CODE § 2–803

8 U.L.A. 20 (Supp. 2000)

§ 2–803. Effect of Homicide on Intestate Succession, Wills, Trusts, Joint Assets, Life Insurance, and Beneficiary Designations.

(a) [Definitions.] In this section:

(1) "Disposition or appointment of property" includes a transfer of an item of property or any other benefit to a beneficiary designated in a governing instrument.

(2) "Governing instrument" means a governing instrument executed by the decedent.

(3) "Revocable," with respect to a disposition, appointment, provision, or nomination, means one under which the decedent, at the time of or immediately before death, was alone empowered, by law or under the governing instrument, to cancel the designation in favor of the killer, whether or not the decedent was then empowered to designate himself [or herself] in place of his [or her] killer and or the decedent then had capacity to exercise the power.

(b) [Forfeiture of Statutory Benefits.] . . . .

(c) [Revocation of Benefits Under Governing Instrument.] The felonious and intentional killing of the decedent:

(1) revokes any revocable (i) disposition or appointment of property made by the decedent to the killer in a governing instrument, ...

(2) . . . .

(d) [Effect of Severance.] . . . .

(e) [Effect of Revocation.] Provisions of a governing instrument are given effect as if the killer disclaimed all provisions revoked by this section . . . .

(f) [Wrongful Acquisition of Property.] A wrongful acquisition of property or interest by a killer not covered by this section must be treated in accordance with the principle that a killer cannot profit from his [or her] wrong.

(g) [Felonious and Intentional Killing; How Determined.] After all right to appeal has been exhausted, a judgment of conviction establishing criminal accountability for the felonious and intentional killing of the decedent conclusively establishes the convicted individual as the decedent's killer for purposes of this section. In the absence of a conviction, the court, upon the petition of an interested person, must determine whether, under the preponderance of evidence standard, the individual would be found criminally accountable for the felonious and intentional killing of the decedent. If the court determines that, under that standard, the individual would be found criminally accountable for the felonious and intentional killing of the decedent, the determination conclusively establishes that individual as the decedent's killer for purposes of this section.

(h) [Protection of Payors and Other Third Parties.] . . . .

(i) [Protection of Bona Fide Purchasers; Personal Liability of Recipient.] . . . .

2. *Who Is Disqualified?* One of the questions that arises is who receives the proceeds when the beneficiary is disqualified? Obviously, the slayer should be disqualified. But should this also disqualify everyone who would inherit through the slayer but for the slayer's disqualification? This is the rule in some states, but it is not in other states.

Carter raises a slightly different question: whether the slaying beneficiary could *directly* benefit from the proceeds by inheriting through the estate. That she thought there was some chance of winning this argument had something to do with the then-applicable Florida statute relating to disqualification of heirs: "Any person convicted of murder of a decedent shall not be permitted to inherit from the decedent or to take any portion of his estate as a legatee or devisee." Fla. Stat. Ann. § 731.31. The Florida statute did not pertain to life insurance beneficiaries, as many state statutes now do (like the Uniform Probate Code provision set forth above). What weaknesses do you see in the Florida statute, and how would you propose to fix it?

3. *The Intent of the CQV.* If the *cestui que vie* designates primary and contingent beneficiaries, and if the primary beneficiary slays the *cestui que vie* in circumstances where the contingent beneficiary is innocent, should the contingent beneficiary receive the proceeds? Or should the slaying beneficiary hold the proceeds in constructive trust for the *cestui que vie's* estate, which means that the proceeds will be distributed in accordance with the *cestui que vie's* will or the laws of intestate succession? Does your answer change if the slayer was also the owner of the policy and the one who designated the beneficiaries? Should the dominant consideration be making sure the slayer does not benefit, or should it be trying to determine what the deceased *cestui que vie* would have wanted?

If the primary beneficiary predeceases the insured, it is clear that the contingent beneficiaries recover. Thus, is the right answer to treat the slayer as predeceasing the insured? If the slayer is disqualified but is not treated as predeceasing the insured, then the slayer presumably holds the proceeds in constructive trust for someone, and some courts have held that this person is the estate of the insured. *See, e.g.*, *Webb v. Voirol*, 773 F.2d 208, 212 (8th Cir. 1985) (applying Missouri law); *Crawford v. Coleman*, 726 S.W.2d 9 (Tex. 1987).

To make matters more complicated, what if the slayer commits suicide after murdering the insured? Or what if the slayer lays a fatal wound upon the insured before committing suicide, but the insured does not finally succumb until after the slayer's death? To get a glimpse of the complexities that can arise in the murder-suicide situation, *see Diep v. Rivas*, 745 A.2d 1098 (Md. 2000) (policy entitled siblings of victim's husband, the slayer who then committed suicide, to benefits, and the slayer rule did not bar siblings from recovery). It is worth noting that *Diep* involved an accidental death policy, and that the disqualification rules do not change for that very similar product.

4. *The Intent of the Slayer*. If the slayer purchases insurance on the *cestui que vie* with a simultaneous, and necessarily undisclosed, intent to slay the *cestui que vie*, and if the slayer successfully implements the plan, the accepted rule is that the policy is void *ab initio*. *See New England Mutual Life Insurance Co. v. Null*, 605 F.2d 421 (8th Cir. 1979) (applying Missouri law); *Chute v. Old American Insurance Co.*, 629 P.2d 734 (Kan. Ct. App. 1981). Why should this be so? Why not have the slayer hold the proceeds in constructive trust for the benefit of the deceased insured's estate? What does this rule have to do with concealment?

5. *The Role of Interpleader*. Obviously, interpleader is important to insurers in these kinds of cases. Note that interpleader is not costless. Courts can award the insurer the costs of the interpleader action out of the "stake," i.e., the proceeds of the policy deposited in court, and the successful defendant's litigation expenses will offset some of the proceeds.

When the insurer is discharged pursuant to a judgment in the interpleader, the insurer's contractual obligations under the insurance contract are fulfilled. Does this mean that the contract is "discharged" for all purposes? If the policy has provisions relevant to beneficiary's rights, do these continue to be relevant if the contract itself has been discharged? Presumably, if the insurance policy is discharged and no longer controlling, the court's decision on who is entitled to the proceeds will be based on "equitable principles" in the absence of a statute requiring a different standard. Is "doing equity" the better approach regardless?

6. *Criminal Versus Civil Proceedings*. If the slayer in *Carter* had been convicted of murdering her husband, would she have been at liberty to argue in the interpleader action that the criminal conviction was incorrect? Should a guilty plea be treated the same as a conviction after there has been a full trial? *See State Farm Fire and Casualty Co. v. Fullerton*, 118 F.3d 374 (5th Cir. 1997)

(in context of intentional act exclusion in liability policy, the court treated the guilty plea as dispositive).

If a slaying beneficiary is acquitted in a criminal proceeding, it does not follow that the slaying beneficiary is entitled to the proceeds. A slaying beneficiary might be found to have caused the death of the CQV by a preponderance of the evidence, and is thereby disqualified from receiving the proceeds, in circumstances where the slaying was not established beyond a reasonable doubt.

7. *A Duty to Investigate?* If the insured perishes in circumstances where the primary beneficiary is a suspect, is the insurer obligated to conduct an independent investigation of the circumstances of the insured's death in order to determine who is entitled to the proceeds? If the insurer is notified that the primary beneficiary is being investigated for possible involvement in the insured's death, can the insurer discharge its obligations by making payment to the primary beneficiary? *See Harper v. Prudential Insurance Co.*, 662 P.2d 1264 (Kan. 1983). Can the insurer withhold paying proceeds if the insured has simply died under "suspicious circumstances"? These are difficult questions for the insurer, and the guidance in the case law is imperfect because the facts of individual cases run across the board. It is commonly said that the insurer has a duty to act reasonably in paying the policy proceeds. *See Lunsford v. Western States Life Insurance*, 908 P.2d 79, 86 (Colo. 1995) (en banc). Filing an interpleader is one option for an insurer, but can filing an interpleader too quickly constitute a breach of this duty?

CHAPTER EIGHT

DISABILITY INSURANCE

■ ■ ■

"Two-thirds of Americans who work in the private sector lack disability insurance, even though most workers say missing work for three months or more because of sickness or injury would cause 'financial hardship,' a new survey finds."

— Ann Carrns, *Most Workers Lack Disability Insurance, Survey Finds*, New York Times, May 1, 2012

Most people are surprised to learn that, according to data available through the Social Security Administration,[1] the risk of a worker becoming disabled is greater than dying at every age until reaching normal retirement age (i.e., the age at which a worker is entitled to receive full Social Security benefits). Moreover, a 20-year-old has more than a one-in-four probability of becoming disabled before reaching that age, whereas the probability of dying is less than one-in-eight. Yet, the U.S. market for individual disability insurance is a relatively small one given the importance of the risk, and it is certainly small when compared to the market for life insurance.

A number of reasons contribute to this. First, in 1954, Congress added a disability benefit to the Social Security retirement program, and in 2014, over nine million workers and nearly two million of their dependents received benefits under this program, totaling over $141 billion dollars.[2] The per-worker and per-family benefits are not robust, as nearly half of recipients under age 40 have family income below 150 percent of the federal poverty level.[3] But the availability of these benefits has reduced the public's interest in acquiring private disability insurance. Second, people who are hurt while working can recover under the no-fault workers compensation system. In 2013, approximately $32 billion in wage loss

[1] J. Maleh & T. Bosley, *Actuarial Note: Disability and Death Probability Tables for Insured Workers Born in 1999*, Social Security Administration, Office of the Chief Actuary, Oct. 2016, available at https://www.ssa.gov/OACT/NOTES/ran6/ (visited May 19, 2020).

[2] Social Security Administration, *Annual Statistical Supplement to the Social Security Bulletin*, 2015, p. 17 (bulletin available at https://www.ssa.gov/policy/docs/statcomps/supplement/2015/index.html (visited May 19, 2020).

[3] *See* Social Security Administration, *Fact Sheet: Individuals Who Receive Social Security Disability Insurance Benefits, by Age Group*, available at https://www.ssa.gov/news/press/factsheets/ss-customer/age-group-dib.pdf (visited May 19, 2020).

compensation was paid to workers and their survivors under federal and state workers' compensation programs.[4] Third, approximately 33 percent of private industry workers participate in long-term disability insurance plans (and 39 percent participate in short-term plans, defined as plans covering periods of less than six months).[5] Fourth, the number of insurers selling the product is small because moral hazard and adverse selection concerns weigh heavily in this area of insurance. People most likely to suffer disabling injuries are those most interested in purchasing such insurance. Plus, when people are paid to not work, there is tendency among some benefit recipients to not want to get well enough to go back to work. It is not a coincidence that disability insurance claims have increased during every economic downturn in U.S. history. Insurers attempt to combat these problems in a number of ways, including by providing only a percentage of a disabled person's income (commonly 60 percent of after-tax income).

What constitutes a disability that triggers insurance coverage? The next case is an example of a court addressing the issue.

SHAPIRO V. BERKSHIRE LIFE INS. CO.

212 F.3d 121 (2d Cir. 2000)

JACOBS, CIRCUIT JUDGE:

Paul Shapiro, a licensed dentist, brought this diversity action against Berkshire Life Insurance Co. ("Berkshire") contesting Berkshire's denial of his claim for total disability benefits. Berkshire appeals from the judgment of the United States District Court for the Southern District of New York (Schwartz, J.) awarding summary judgment in Shapiro's favor on his claim for total disability benefits against Berkshire. Shapiro cross-appeals the court's grant of summary judgment in favor of Berkshire on his claim under § 349 of the New York General Business Law. We affirm.

BACKGROUND

A. *The Insurance Contracts*

On November 1, 1990, Berkshire issued a Disability Income Insurance Policy, which provided a monthly $3,100 benefit in the event of Shapiro's total disability (the "1990 policy"). On November 1, 1995, Berkshire issued

---

[4] *See* note 2, *supra*, at https://www.ssa.gov/policy/docs/statcomps/supplement/2015/workerscomp.html (visited May 19, 2020).

[5] Kristen Monaco, *Disability Insurance Plans: Trends in Employee Access and Employer Costs, Beyond the Numbers*, Feb. 2015, available at https://www.bls.gov/opub/btn/volume-4/disability-insurance-plans.htm (visited May 19, 2020).

a second, identical policy, which provided Shapiro an additional $1,000 monthly benefit (the "1995 policy").[1]

The policies define "total disability" as "the inability to perform the material and substantial duties of your occupation," and "your occupation" is limited to "the occupation you are engaged in immediately preceding the onset of disability." In another clause, the policies also provide benefits for residual disability, and define it: "Residual disability means that due to injury or sickness you are unable: (1) to do one or more of the substantial and material duties of your business or profession; or (2) to perform your duties for the length of time that they usually require." The insured is ineligible for residual disability benefits unless he has suffered a 20 percent drop in income as a result of the disability.

B. *Shapiro's Responsibilities*

Shapiro has been a licensed dentist since 1981. In 1988, he opened his own practice called Park South Dental. In that office, patients were treated by Shapiro as well as by another full-time dentist, a periodontist and an orthodontist employed by Shapiro. Shapiro also owns North Hill Dental, a one-dentist office at which Shapiro treated patients only rarely. Shapiro is also the 44 percent owner and President of Sharraty Properties, Inc. ("Sharraty"), a for-profit corporation he founded with his brother-in-law, Dr. Monte Ezratty, to provide dental assistants, receptionists and clerical personnel for their offices.

Shapiro testified that before the onset of his disability he worked four or five days a week for a total of 40 to 45 hours. In 1995, the year before he became disabled, Shapiro saw nine to eleven patients a day, and performed an average of 275 procedures per month.

In addition to this dentistry work, Shapiro also spent between one and a half and four hours per week attending to various administrative and managerial duties related to Park South Dental, North Hill Dental and Sharraty. Shapiro's non-dentistry responsibilities included, inter alia, personnel decisions, staff evaluations, staff meetings, consultations with his office manager on major equipment purchases and difficult billing disputes, troubleshooting the computer, and insurance and health plan proposal reviews.

C. *Shapiro's Disability & Berkshire's Denial of His Claim*

In December 1995, Shapiro concluded that progressive skeletal illnesses (osteoarthritis and spondylosis of the elbow, neck and other joints) had left him medically unable to perform "chair dentistry," which is the sum of procedures involved in treating dental patients in the dentist's chair. Shapiro stopped treating patients on January 30, 1996. The parties agree

[1] The 1990 policy and the 1995 policy will be referenced collectively as the "policies" or the "insurance contracts."

that this event marked the "onset of [Shapiro's] disability" within the meaning of the insurance contracts.

On March 26, 1996, Shapiro filed his claim for total disability benefits. Berkshire investigated the claim, agreed that Shapiro was unable to perform chair dentistry, and undertook to pay total disability benefits for a limited time only, while Shapiro recovered from arm surgery, after which time, benefits could be paid only under the "residual disability" provisions of the policies. Berkshire's coverage position was that Shapiro's occupation immediately preceding the onset of his disability was as an administrator and manager of his various dental practices as well as a practitioner of chair dentistry; because the disability did not prevent Shapiro from doing his administrative or managerial work, Berkshire reasoned, Shapiro did not satisfy the policies' definition of total disability: "the inability to perform the material and substantial duties of your occupation."

D. *Procedural History*

Shapiro brought this diversity action against Berkshire, alleging, inter alia, breach of contract and deceptive business conduct in violation of § 349 of the General Business Law of New York. The parties cross-moved for summary judgment. The district court granted summary judgment in favor of Shapiro on his breach of contract claim. As to the § 349 claim, the court concluded there was no violation and granted summary judgment in favor of Berkshire. Berkshire appeals and Shapiro cross-appeals.

DISCUSSION

The substantive law of New York controls this diversity case. We review a district court's grant of summary judgment de novo, construing the evidence in the light most favorable to and drawing all reasonable inferences in favor of the non-moving party.

A. *The Contract Claim*

Under New York law, Shapiro bears the burden of proving that he is totally disabled within the meaning of the policies. The definition of total disability in Berkshire's policies tracks the standard articulated by the New York courts: "[A] claimant is 'totally disabled' when he or she is no longer able to perform the 'material' and 'substantial' responsibilities of his or her job." *Klein v. National Life of Vt.*, 7 F.Supp.2d 223, 227 (E.D.N.Y.1998) (Trager, J.) (citing, inter alia, *McGrail v. Equitable Life Assurance Soc'y*, 292 N.Y. 419, 425–26, 55 N.E.2d 483 (1944)). The coverage question entails a "fact-oriented, functional approach that look[s] to the professional activities in which the insured was regularly engaged at the time of the onset of the insured's disability." Id.

After reviewing the record, we conclude that the district court properly granted summary judgment in Shapiro's favor on the breach of contract claim because in the relevant period Shapiro's occupation was that of a dentist. It is uncontested that he spent the vast majority of his time performing chair dentistry. Viewing the evidence in the light most favorable to Berkshire, Shapiro's administrative duties consumed no more than four of his forty working hours per week: 90 percent of his time was spent fixing the teeth of patients and 10 percent on non-dentistry duties. He saw several patients every day, four or five days a week. His office manager described his schedule as being "booked every day" with patients. Shapiro was thus regularly engaged in chair dentistry at the time of the onset of his disability. His administrative work was incidental to his material and substantial duties as a full-time dentist. *See Brumer v. National Life of Vt.*, 874 F.Supp. 60, 64 (E.D.N.Y.1995) (Trager, J.) ("[W]ere one able to find that the plaintiff's managerial activities were peripheral or incidental when considered in light of the medical or surgical tasks he performed, the court would have to find that he did not have a separate occupation as a medical administrator."), *aff'd sub nom., Brumer v. Paul Revere Life Ins. Co.*, 133 F.3d 906 (2d Cir.1998) (unpublished summary order).

Berkshire relies primarily on *Klein* and *Brumer*, and argues that Shapiro, like the two podiatrist partners in those cases, is not entitled to total disability benefits because of his continued ability to perform administrative duties. On the whole, however, *Klein* and *Brumer* support Shapiro's argument, because the plaintiff in neither case could make a credible claim of being a full-time podiatrist. Klein spent (at most) 24 percent of his time performing (or assisting with) a total of 251 surgeries in the thirteen months preceding his disability. *See Klein*, 7 F.Supp.2d at 229–30. The bulk of his time was spent operating and managing his six podiatric clinics. Brumer performed no podiatric surgery in the year preceding the onset of his disability, because (for all but the final eight weeks of that year) his podiatry license was suspended. *See Brumer*, 874 F.Supp. at 61–62. Thus Klein and Brumer were predominantly administrators and managers. *See, e.g., Klein*, 7 F.Supp.2d at 227 ("[T]he record is clear that [immediately preceding onset of disability] plaintiff was predominantly engaged in operating and managing his podiatric clinics while practicing, at most, a minimal amount of podiatric surgery.").

In the period relevant to this claim, Shapiro devoted 90 percent of his full-time working hours to treating patients, and performed 275 procedures per month. Berkshire emphasizes, however, that the onset of Shapiro's disability caused no change in the gross revenues of his three businesses. We reject this argument for three reasons:

(i) It is well-settled in New York that "occupational disability policies are designed to indemnify against loss of capacity to work, not against loss of income." *Blasbalg v. Massachusetts Cas. Ins. Co.*, 962 F.Supp. 362, 368 (E.D.N.Y.1997). "[R]ecovery will not, therefore, be precluded even if plaintiff were to earn a larger income from his new occupation." *Id.*

(ii) Although earnings may have some bearing on the question of a policyholder's capacity to work, the appropriate inquiry in this case concerns net income of the individual, rather than his gross revenue (much less the gross revenue of his business). An individual whose sole occupation had been the practice of chair dentistry could suffer total disability without losing a cent of gross revenue simply by hiring a substitute dentist to treat his patients. Here, the record evidence shows that Shapiro's net income decreased following the onset of his disability. This fact thus tends to support Shapiro's argument that he was, in fact, a dentist.

(iii) The stability of gross revenues cited by Berkshire does not tend to refute the idea that Shapiro was a full-time dentist because Shapiro in fact hired a dentist to replace himself.

. . . .

At some point, a medical entrepreneur's administrative and managerial responsibilities may well become the material and substantial duties of the insured's occupation. But we need not decide where to fix that point in order to resolve this appeal. Immediately preceding the onset of his disability, Paul Shapiro was a dentist. Because his disability prevents him from performing the material and substantial duties of that occupation, he is entitled to total disability benefits under the insurance contracts.

. . . .

[In an omitted part of the opinion, the court upheld the summary judgment for the insurer on the policyholder's claim that Berkshire engaged in deceptive conduct in violation of Section 349 of the General Business Law.]

CONCLUSION

For the foregoing reasons, the judgment is affirmed.

NOTES AND QUESTIONS

1. *The Nature and Purpose of the Coverage.* If a worker or business owner is suddenly disabled, what kinds of economic dislocations would you expect that person to suffer? The answers provide insight into the purposes—and limitations—of disability insurance. Disability insurance is designed to protect against loss of income due to illness or injury. Some policies limit coverage to disability from accidental injuries, but the more common forms, and the customary coverage with group programs, cover disability from both illness and accidents. The coverage may be short-term (a typical "short-term period" is six months) or long-term, meaning that the policy provides benefits for what is essentially permanent impairment. The payment of benefits under a long-term policy typically must be preceded by the expiration of a waiting

period (called an "elimination period" or "qualification period") that may range from thirty days to two years, although a six-month period is common. If a range of possible waiting periods is offered, the cost of the policy will go down as the length of the period increases. Life insurance policies often include a provision that waives the insured's obligation to make future premium payments if he becomes disabled. In fact, this is how disability insurance first originated. Not surprisingly, most disability policies also have waiver of premium provisions.

2. *Policy Language Matters.* There are two basic kinds of disability coverage, occupational and general, although occupational coverage is more commonly encountered. Note that each defines disability by reference to a person's capacity to do work, not by reference to the person's loss of income. Should it be otherwise? Within these general categories, subtle variations in policy language are common, and the differences matter a lot in specific cases. In *Mossa v. Provident Life and Casualty Insurance Co.*, 36 F. Supp. 2d 524 (E.D.N.Y. 1999), the policy defined "total disability" as "that due to Injuries or Sickness: 1) you are not able to engage in any gainful occupation in which you might reasonably be expected to engage because of education, training, or experience; and 2) you are receiving care by a Physician which is appropriate for the condition causing the disability." If this policy language had applied in *Shapiro*, would the case have been decided the same way?

3. *What Is an "Occupation," Anyway?* If Shapiro had been a part of a dental clinic with ten dentists who divided the administrative work among themselves, and if, despite his disability, he had undertaken, with no loss of income, 100 percent of the administrative work while his colleagues were engaged 100 percent in chair dentistry, would this court have still found Shapiro to be totally disabled? What would be the answer under the *Mossa* policy? *See Dym v. Provident Life and Accident Insurance Co.*, 19 F. Supp. 2d 1147 (S.D. Cal. 1998) (policyholder does not suffer from "total disability" if he can perform one of the significant duties of his occupation).

If a law professor loses her voice, is she disabled from her "occupation"? What if she is able to move into a full-time research position? Or do full-time work, with no loss of income, in the admissions office? Is a concert pianist disabled if she can earn a reasonable income as a piano teacher but nowhere near the income commanded prior to a disabling accident? What if the policyholder cannot instruct but can earn a modest living as a salesperson in a music store or as a piano tuner? Is it the amount of money, the nature of the work, or both, which is to be compared to the former situation?

4. *More on Determining the Existence of a Disability.* Some disability policies state that the policyholder is not totally disabled if she is receiving any income from any business activity. In what circumstances might this present a special problem for a policyholder? Some policies create "presumptions" of total disability if certain kinds of disabilities are incurred, such as loss of sight in both eyes, loss of use of both hands or both feet (or one hand and one foot), or loss of hearing in both ears. If the policyholder fits within one of these

presumptions, benefits are payable even if the policyholder is able to continue to work and does not need continuing medical treatment. What is the point of having such presumptions?

5. *Partial Versus Total Disability*. Most disability policies are total disability policies, but some policies do cover partial disability. The following clause is an example:

> B. Partial Disability. When, as the result of injury and commencing while this policy is in force or immediately following a period of total disability for which indemnity is payable under Paragraph A of this Part, the Insured is continuously disabled and prevented from performing one or more of the important duties of his occupation, the Company will pay forty per cent of the Monthly Indemnity stated in the Schedule for the period of such disability, not to exceed three consecutive months as the result of any one accident.

The case in which this clause appeared was *Dittmar v. Continental Casualty Co.*, 150 A.2d 666 (N.J. 1959). What phrases in this clause are magnets for possible litigation?

One way to deal with the problems associated with determining whether the policyholder is partially disabled is for the insurer to tier the coverage. The policyholder who is partially disabled is treated as totally disabled for a specific period of time (e.g., two years), but thereafter the insurer provides coverage only for total disability. *See, e.g., Ryan v. ITT Life Insurance Corp.*, 450 N.W.2d 126 (Minn. 1990) (occupational coverage for five years, followed by general disability coverage).

As noted, however, most disability policies do not cover anything less than a total disability (either occupational or general). This sets most disability insurance apart from the disability benefits available under state workers' compensation systems, where much energy is expended attempting to calculate the degree of disability in individual cases. *See, e.g.*, Alaska Code § 23.30.190, § 23.30.200 (Michie Supp. 1997); Ariz. Rev. Stat. Ann. § 23–1044 (1995); Ala. Code § 25–5–57 (1992). On the other hand, the typical disability policy puts the partially disabled person in an "either-or" predicament that is not without some risk—either the policyholder is totally disabled or is "not-at-all disabled."

6. *Other Facets of the Typical Disability Policy*. The amount of the policyholder's monthly benefit is typically the lesser of a percentage of the policyholder's income (usually 60 to 80 percent) or a specified dollar amount. Disability payments are not subject to federal income tax if the individual policyholder pays the premium, but if the employer pays for the coverage as a fringe benefit, the benefit is taxable income to the employee. It is common for policies to have "coordination of benefit" provisions so that the coverages of multiple policies cannot be stacked. It is also common for policies to link the definition of disability to the policyholder's continued receipt of medical care for the disabling condition.

7. *Pre-Existing Condition Clauses.* Disability policies typically have "pre-existing condition" clauses. The language of these clauses varies, but the general effect is to deny coverage for any disability that occurs as a result of a condition that existed at the time the application was filed (or policy issued) or perhaps during a period of time prior to the issuance of the policy. A less common provision excludes coverage for any disability that arises during a period of time (e.g., up to two years) after the application for the policy. A near-consensus exists that pre-existing condition clauses are problematic in health insurance. Why are pre-existing conditions not viewed the same way in the disability insurance context?

8. *Factual Versus Social or Legal Disability.* Being disabled by an illness or an accident is called a "factual" disability to distinguish it from other kinds of disability. For example, in *Gates v. Prudential Insurance Co.*, 270 N.Y.S. 282 (N.Y. App. Div. 1934), the policyholder was declared a "typhoid carrier," meaning that he was not ill with typhoid or physically impaired from working in any respect, but he carried the typhoid bacilli and was for that reason banned by state statute from his occupation of milking cows and handling milk. Indeed, he would not have known he was a carrier but for laboratory tests that showed the condition. The court concluded that "[w]hen public good with regard to the safety of others steps in and puts a limitation upon his activities, the disability resulting is social in its nature rather than physical," and that the policyholder was not disabled within the meaning of the policy. *Id.* at 286–87. This reasoning was followed in *Dang v. Northwestern Mutual Life Insurance Co.*, 960 F. Supp. 215 (D. Neb. 1997), where a surgeon, who was discovered to be a hepatitis B virus carrier, was banned from certain surgical procedures without a patient's informed consent. The court held that he was not totally or partially disabled under the terms of the policy, given that he remained physically able to perform these duties. *Id.* at 218. Why should the policyholders in these cases be treated differently than a policyholder whose virus is manifested in a present disabling illness?

If the policy requires that the policyholder be disabled by accident or illness, it should be obvious that a policyholder who is "disabled" from working due to revocation of a professional license or being imprisoned for a crime is not entitled to monthly benefits. When this kind of "legal" disability commingles with an accident or illness, however, the question is more difficult. *See, e.g., Massachusetts Mutual Life Insurance Co. v. Millstein*, 129 F.3d 688 (2d Cir. 1997) (attorney claimed he was disabled by attention deficit disorder, conduct disorder, and chemical dependency; held, policyholder's loss of income was caused not by disability but by loss of license to practice on account of illegal use of client funds); *BLH v. Northwestern Mutual Life Insurance Co.*, 92 F. Supp. 2d 910 (D. Minn. 2000) (fact questions as to whether doctor's sexual disorder rendered him disabled precluded summary judgment); *Goomar v. Centennial Life Insurance Co.*, 855 F. Supp. 319 (S.D. Cal. 1994), *aff'd*, 76 F.3d 1059 (9th Cir. 1996) (even if insured doctor was seeing astral beings because of psychological disorder when license was revoked due to molestation of patients allegedly caused by disorder, doctor was not totally disabled); *Holzer* *v. MBL Life Assurance Corp.*, 1999 WL 649004, at *1 (S.D.N.Y. Aug. 25, 1999) (a material question of fact existed regarding whether an anesthesiologist who surrendered license due to opioid dependence was disabled due to an addiction problem).

Suppose the policyholder is disabled by an accident, starts receiving monthly disability benefits, and he is then convicted of a crime and incarcerated. Does the imprisonment act as a superseding legal disability that cuts off the policyholder's right to benefits, under the reasoning that the policy protects against lost income and the policyholder cannot earn income while in prison? *See Weissman v. First Unum Life Insurance Co.*, 44 F. Supp. 2d 512 (S.D.N.Y. 1999). What if the order is reversed—the policyholder is incarcerated and then suffers what would have been a disabling illness? *See Allmerica Financial Life Insurance and Annuity Co. v. Llewellyn*, 139 F.3d 664 (9th Cir. 1997) (chiropractor's license is revoked and he subsequently becomes mentally ill). Why does it not violate public policy for convicted felons to receive disability payments while in prison? If you were the insurance commissioner, would you approve a form that contained a provision eliminating coverage in the event of the policyholder's incarceration for a felony? *See Ohio National Life Assurance Corp. v. Crampton*, 53 F.3d 328 (4th Cir. 1995).

HELLER V. EQUITABLE LIFE ASSUR. SOC. OF U.S.

833 F.2d 1253 (7th Cir. 1987)

Opinion

COFFEY, CIRCUIT JUDGE.

The Equitable Life Assurance Society, defendant-appellant, appeals from the order of the district court entering a declaratory judgment in favor of Dr. Stanley Heller, plaintiff-appellee, for the defendant's alleged breach of a disability income insurance contract. The district court found that Dr. Heller was entitled to receive $5,880 per month from Equitable on the insurance contract from March 21, 1984, through February 5, 1986, and thereafter for the time period Dr. Heller was totally disabled. . . . We affirm in part, reverse in part, and remand for further proceedings consistent with this opinion.

I.

Dr. Stanley Heller, a physician, is licensed to practice medicine in the state of Illinois. Dr. Heller is a board-certified physician in the field of Cardiovascular Diseases and specializes in invasive cardiology. He was also the Director of the Cardiovascular Catheterization Laboratory at St. Joseph's Hospital, Chicago.

In early 1983 Dr. Heller met with Paul Berlin, an agent for The Equitable Life Assurance Society (Equitable) to discuss simplifying his existing professional disability insurance coverage, for at the time he was insured under six or seven different policies issued by at least two different companies. After evaluating Dr. Heller's existing policies, Mr. Berlin informed Dr. Heller that if he decided to purchase the Equitable disability income policy as offered ($7,000 monthly), he would be required to cancel his other disability policies.[3] At the time Dr. Heller applied for disability coverage in March of 1983, he represented on the application that he had no other disability coverage as he intended to cancel his other disability policy at the time Equitable's coverage took effect. Equitable's policy, issued the following month in April of 1983, provided that Dr. Heller would be paid the sum of $7,000 per month, after a 90-day elimination period, if and when he became totally disabled as defined in the policy. Dr. Heller, with the payment of an added premium, contracted for additional $1,200-per-month coverage while totally disabled under the policy for a period limited to one year with the same 90-day elimination period incorporated therein. Dr. Heller testified that he directed his office manager to cancel all his other disability policies when the Equitable policy became effective, and "to the best of [his] knowledge," she cancelled the policies. . . .

During the latter quarter of 1983 Dr. Heller developed a painful and crippling condition in his left wrist and hand diagnosed as carpal tunnel syndrome. Dr. Heller testified that as he experienced the debilitating symptoms of the condition in his left wrist and into his hand, he was prevented from practicing in his specialty as an invasive cardiologist after March 20, 1984. Dr. Heller applied for benefit payments on his Equitable disability income policy in late March 1984. The policy issued to Dr. Heller defined "total disability" as follows:

> Total disability means the complete inability of the Insured, because of injury or sickness, to engage in the Insured's regular occupation, . . . provided, however, the total disability will not be considered to exist for any period during which the Insured is not under the regular care and attendance of a physician,. . . .

Dr. Heller claimed that because he was unable to engage in his profession as an invasive cardiologist as a result of the carpal tunnel syndrome condition, and because he was under the regular care of a physician and had made timely premium payments, he was entitled to disability benefits under the policy. Initially, Equitable made payments pursuant to the disability income provisions, but terminated these payments after May 5, 1985, because he (Dr. Heller) refused to undergo carpal tunnel surgery

---

[3] Equitable sets the amount of disability coverage available to an insured after considering, *inter alia*, the insured's income and the existence of other disability insurance. In order to prevent over-insuring, insurance companies demand that the applicant disclose all other coverage. Dr. Heller's income was $200,000 per year, and in the absence of other disability insurance he would have been eligible for a monthly disability payment of $8,400 to $8,700 on the basic policy. Dr. Heller made application for only $7,000-per-month coverage on the basic policy, representing on the application that he carried no other disability insurance. In addition to the basic $7,000-per-month payment, he also carried an excess coverage as referred to above.

upon Equitable's insistence. As a result of Equitable's refusal to continue payments under the contract, Dr. Heller initiated the present action.

Following a trial to the court, the trial judge found that if Dr. Heller were to undergo surgery to decompress the median nerve in his left wrist, he might very well be relieved of the carpal tunnel syndrome condition, thus allowing him to return to his practice. After reviewing Equitable's disability policy, the trial judge determined that Dr. Heller was not required to submit to elective surgery because Equitable failed to include the surgery requirement in its professional disability contract. . . .

On appeal Equitable argues that because Dr. Heller refused to submit to surgery to relieve the debilitating and limiting effects of his carpal tunnel syndrome condition, the trial court erred in finding Dr. Heller to be totally disabled under the terms of the policy. . . .

II.

Illinois law controls this case as Equitable issued the policy to Dr. Heller in Illinois, the state where Dr. Heller resided and practiced medicine. Our research reveals, and both parties agree, that the Illinois courts have not directly addressed the question of whether a disability income policy providing that the claimant must be "under the regular care and attendance of a physician" requires an insured to submit to surgical treatment for the condition causing the total disability in order to receive benefits. Thus, we rely on the traditional principles of insurance and contract law, long recognized by the Illinois courts as an appropriate basis for resolving whether the clause conditions coverage on the insured's undergoing surgery. . . .

A reading of the Equitable disability policy discloses that it fails to set forth any requirement or limitation of coverage requiring an insured to submit to surgery for treatment of the condition causing the total disability. The policy provides coverage where (1) the insured is prevented from engaging in his or her regular occupation because of sickness or injury and is totally disabled; and (2) that the insured be under "the regular care and attendance of a physician." Equitable does not dispute that Dr. Heller is presently unable to practice as an invasive cardiologist but argues that his failure to submit to surgery for his disabling condition as recommended[9] requires a finding by the Court that he is no longer "under the regular care and attendance of a physician." Therefore, Equitable asserts that Dr. Heller is no longer entitled to disability income benefits.

We reject Equitable's arguments because the language in the policy stating that the claimant must be "under the regular care and attendance of a physician" clearly does not include surgical procedures. Although the policy

[9] Dr. Heller was examined by and consulted with a number of doctors, and at least two recommended surgery.

does not define the parameters of the clause "under the regular care and attendance of a physician," we refuse to add to and construe the policy beyond its clear and obvious language, to require the insured to submit to surgery, if and when surgery is recommended by the physician "rendering regular care and [in] attendance." The language is clear on its face to the average citizen and even more so to a member of the medical profession. We are convinced that under Illinois law the clause "under the regular care and attendance" means just what it says, namely, that the insured is obligated to periodically consult and be examined by his or her treating physician at intervals to be determined by the physician. Clearly the language does not condition disability payments on the insured's undergoing surgery if recommended by the physician rendering "regular care and [in] attendance." We refuse to indulge in judicial activism and condition coverage under the contract on the insured's undergoing surgery, when the insurer failed to provide such a conditional clause in the policy.

The clause, "under the regular care and attendance of a physician," was not intended to allow the insurer to scrutinize, determine, and direct the method of treatment the claimant receives. We are convinced that the purpose of the clause requiring the insured to be "under the regular care and attendance of a physician" is to determine that the claimant is actually disabled, is not malingering, and to prevent fraudulent claims.

The insurance industry by its very nature offers insurance coverage on a non-negotiable basis, and consumers are unable to participate in the drafting of the language or the terms of the policy. Case law and fairness require that ambiguities in insurance policies be construed against the drafter of the policy, the insurance company.

In the absence of a clear, unequivocal and specific contractual requirement that the insured is obligated to undergo surgery to attempt to minimize his disability, we refuse to order the same. To hold otherwise and to impose such a requirement would, in effect, enlarge the terms of the policy beyond those clearly defined in the policy agreed to by the parties. Thus, under the terms of this disability policy, Dr. Heller is not required to undergo surgery for treatment of his carpal tunnel syndrome condition before he receives disability income payments.

. . . .

Lastly, Equitable argues that the "principle of fairness and good faith, a policy of motivating persons to correct rather than accept physical disabilities," necessitates that an insured suffering from causes that disabled him, avail himself of all reasonable means and remedies to relieve his disability, including surgery. Once again, we reject Equitable's argument. The record clearly establishes that Dr. Heller acted in good faith. Initially, Dr. Heller properly reported his disability to Equitable and consulted with and remained under the regular care of his physician as required under the policy. Further, at Equitable's request, Dr. Heller acquiesced to an examination performed by two specialists selected by Equitable, one a hand surgeon and the other a neurologist, at the Mayo Clinic in Rochester, Minnesota. Additionally, there is nothing in the record to establish that Dr. Heller failed to provide Equitable with any and/or all supplemental information required. The record further demonstrates that after Dr. Heller's condition was diagnosed and before he filed a claim for disability payments, Dr. Heller was forced to reduce his case load beginning in December 1983 to March 1984, and thereafter was forced to withdraw from practice.[12] The trial court found that Dr. Heller fulfilled his obligations under the policy; we agree and hold that Dr. Heller did all that was required of him under the terms of the Equitable disability policy.

However, Equitable insists that the insured, as a party to an insurance contract, has a good faith "duty to cure his disability if he can do so without reasonable risk and pain to himself." Equitable ignores the fact that many insureds like the plaintiff-appellee, choose not to undergo surgery because of the accompanying risks of infection, transfusion (hepatitis), bleeding, motor enervation of the median nerve, adhesions, scar tissue, possible anesthetic shock, trauma, anxiety, and even reoccurrence of the carpal tunnel syndrome condition. We are convinced that under Illinois law an insured is not required to undergo these risks in the absence of a specific contractual requirement. Furthermore, it seems very evident that because of these risks and other risks in the majority of surgical procedures, courts have wisely adopted the doctrine of informed consent.

Although we might not choose to follow the same course of conduct and path of reasoning as Dr. Heller,[14] there is no moral, much less legal obligation or compelling reason, to second guess an insured's, and in this case Dr. Heller's, decision to forgo surgery. The insurance company seeking to condition coverage on its insureds' acquiescence to undergo surgery to minimize the extent of their disabilities, as well as the financial loss to the insurer, need only incorporate a specific requirement to that effect in the policy, and we would not hesitate to enforce the same. On the other hand, insurers who fail to include this express surgical contractual requirement, and who refuse to cover an insured after entering into a binding and enforceable agreement after accepting substantial premiums, in circumstances such as those before us, cause problems not only for the insured, but for the insurance industry as well. Insurance companies, members of a service industry, must recognize that, like their insureds, they have corresponding duties and obligations under the policy and must conduct themselves accordingly instead of attempting to rely on the courts

[12] It is significant to point out that Dr. Heller received treatment for his carpal tunnel syndrome condition. Dr. Loughran, an orthopedic surgeon at St. Joseph Hospital, injected a steroid into Dr. Heller's wrist, attempting to minimize the disability and allow him to return to practice.

[14] We note that Dr. Heller has apparently abandoned his profession as a surgeon to pursue a new career in law.

to correct their own deficiencies in underwriting and/or careless policy drafting.

. . . .

The judgment of the district court is affirmed in part and reversed in part, and the case is remanded to the district court for further proceedings consistent with this opinion.

NOTES AND QUESTIONS

1. *A Duty to Mitigate?* In *Heller*, the Seventh Circuit concluded the policyholder was not required to submit to surgery as a condition to continued coverage under the disability policy. What about the duty to mitigate? Should a policy provision requiring a policyholder to submit to surgery if it would minimize the insurer's payments under the policy be enforceable? Should there be a distinction between "major" and "minor" surgery?

2. *Moral Hazard Concerns.* Does the holding in *Heller* create concerns about moral hazard? If so, what are they, and how could they be addressed?

3. *Other Occupations.* If a person is disabled for purposes of her current occupation, should she be able to work in another occupation and still collect disability payments? For example, in *Heller*, the policyholder, a doctor, was planning to become an attorney. Should a doctor be able to collect disability insurance money even though he is now working as an attorney? *See, e.g.*, *Moots v. Bankers Life Co.*, 707 P.2d 1083 (Kan. 1985) (policyholder was allowed to collect disability insurance proceeds for back injury despite working as a bus driver even though the policy expressly precluded coverage if the policyholder engaged in "any occupation, work or employment").

4. *Post-Heller.* In the wake of *Heller* and other cases like it, insurers changed the policy language in commonly used forms. Instead of, or in addition to, the "regular care" requirement, the more recent policies require that the policyholder receive "appropriate care." Thus, in *Paul Revere Life Ins. Co. v. DiBari*, 2010 WL 4876054, at *1 (D. Conn. Nov. 19, 2010), the court held that the insurer did have the right to condition the receipt of benefits on the policyholder undergoing corrective surgery. The policyholder was a dentist who developed carpal tunnel syndrome and became unable to practice dentistry. When DiBari refused to undergo surgery as a condition of receiving benefits, his benefits were terminated. The court noted that both the treating physicians and the insurer's consultants agreed that the surgery was not risky, had a high rate of success, and was medically appropriate. The court in *DiBari* said that the dentist was not compelled to get the surgery, but that he needed to do so if he wanted to receive disability insurance benefits. If the dentist needs income to support his family and has no other independent income or wealth, is it fair to say that he has a choice? What if he could not undergo surgery on account of his religious convictions?

CHAPTER NINE

REGULATION OF INSURANCE

■ ■ ■

"During the financial crisis, the collapse of America's largest insurance conglomerate, the American International Group, along with the failure of a host of its bond insurers, suggested that the insurance industry was not necessarily a stable, staid keeper of our rainy day funds. Insurance is a global business, with huge firms writing not just life and home insurance policies, but entering into more exotic lines of business. . . . But the American insurance regulation system has long been focused on the local market and the protection of policyholders, instead of the global market and the stability of insurance firms. . . . [A] stronger federal role in insurance regulation, something that the largest insurance companies probably would like to see, makes sense."

— David Zaring, Assistant Professor at the Wharton School of Business, University of Pennsylvania, *It is Time to Rethink Insurance Regulation*, New York Times, Jan. 22, 2014

For most of the twentieth century, the proposition that the insurance industry should be regulated was not questioned. Rather, the only question was who should regulate it, i.e., whether regulation should occur at the federal or state level of government. Today, some of the assumptions about the proper mix of regulation and free competition in the business of insurance continue to be questioned, particularly with respect to commercial lines and health care.

Why should any industry be regulated? The classic rationales for regulation possibly relevant to the insurance industry include restraining excessive competition, compensating for inadequate information, remedying unequal bargaining power, and implementing paternalism (i.e., regulation is required to override irrational decisions of market participants). Which of these are plausible justifications for regulating the business of insurance? Promoting and preserving the solvency of insurers is sometimes mentioned as the most important goal of insurance regulation. This is clearly related to the rationale of restraining excessive competition, but regulation for solvency goals has more expansive implications than simply regulating excessive competition.

Sometimes, regulation is justified on the ground of producing desirable social outcomes that the market will not achieve if it is left to its own devices. Does this explain why health insurance, to take a prominent example, not only is heavily regulated but also has a significant government presence as an insurance provider and financier (most notably, Medicaid and Medicare)? How successfully would an unregulated market provide health insurance, especially for the elderly? The poor, by definition, cannot afford to buy insurance (and other goods and services), but the poor rarely have lots of assets that need insurance protection. But is access to health care, which in America is provided through health insurance, something different, thereby justifying regulation of the product that provides it?

I. THE HISTORY OF INSURANCE REGULATION

With a couple of notable exceptions that will be discussed, one of the most striking characteristics of the insurance business is the extent to which it has escaped significant federal regulation. Indeed, the business of insurance is easily the largest—and is arguably the last—major U.S. industry to be predominantly regulated by the states. To understand how this happened, one must take a quick look at the history of the industry.

In the early years of the colonies, insurance on domestic risks was normally placed with British underwriters. Consequently, there was not much of an insurance business to regulate. Slowly but surely, however, the American insurance industry emerged and began to grow. During the last years of the colonial period, insurance offices opened in Philadelphia, New York, and other port cities. The first fire insurance company was established in Philadelphia in 1752, and the first American insurance corporation was chartered in 1792. Seventeen more companies were chartered by 1803.

During this early period, the little regulation that existed primarily occurred through the restrictions placed on insurers in specific corporate charters granted by state legislatures. From the beginning, colonial and state governments did not completely ignore the fledgling industry because they understood the industry's tax revenue potential, so there was a desire to tax insurers and their agents in this early time period. Early in the nineteenth century, general incorporation statutes were enacted, and the practice of granting specific charters for insurance companies fell into disuse. But many states, at the same time general incorporation legislation was passed, also passed legislation governing the establishment of insurance companies. These statutes imposed requirements similar to those contained in a typical insurer's corporate charter. Insurers were required to make periodic reports to a state official, avoid certain kinds of investments, and maintain certain minimum levels of capitalization and reserves. States often imposed more onerous burdens on out-of-state insurers.

Insurance companies generally viewed the developing patchwork system of state regulation as burdensome, and by the 1860s, insurers were urging Congress to adopt national standards that would make insurers federal institutions analogous to banks. As part of the effort to encourage the federal government to take over the function of insurance regulation, a number of New York insurance companies set up a case they hoped would invalidate the system of state regulation. Paul, a Virginia resident, was appointed by these companies as their agent. He applied for a Virginia license, but he refused to deposit bonds with the state treasurer as required by state law. Paul was not granted a license, but he proceeded to sell a policy of insurance to a Virginia resident anyway, and he was convicted of violating the Virginia licensing statute. The Virginia Supreme Court affirmed his conviction. Paul challenged his conviction in the U. S. Supreme Court on the grounds that Virginia's stricter requirements for foreign insurers violated the Privileges and Immunities Clause of the United States Constitution, that the federal commerce power allowed for the regulation of insurers, and that this regulatory power resided exclusively with the federal government.

In 1869, the Supreme Court rejected Paul's arguments, thereby dashing the hopes of the insurers who were interested in promoting federal regulation. The Court held in *Paul v. Virginia*, 75 U.S. (8 Wall.) 168 (1869), that a corporation is not a citizen within the meaning of the Privileges and Immunities Clause. More importantly, the Court held that "issuing a policy of insurance is not a transaction of commerce," which was tantamount to placing the business of insurance outside the constitutional authority of Congress. Under this ruling, to which the Court adhered for seventy-five years, individual states retained the authority to regulate insurance companies.

The insurance industry grew with the rest of the country. As the insurance business became bigger and more complex, the public urged more rigorous state regulation. By 1900, most states had some kind of licensing procedure for companies and agents, but abuses in the life insurance industry attracted the public's attention. These practices included the payment of excessively large commissions to agents, the making of false representations about future dividends, the waste of company assets on lobbying activities and the inability of many companies to account for related expenditures, nepotism in the hiring of insurance company employees, and other practices where company officials abused their positions for personal gain. It was not coincidental that populist fervor at the turn of the century was hostile to combinations of capital and restraints of trade, and insurance companies bore their fair share of public disdain.

These pressures culminated in an investigation by a committee of the New York state legislature. Chaired by Senator William W. Armstrong, this committee became known as the "Armstrong Committee." In 1906, the Committee issued a lengthy report on insurer abuses, and the Committee's many recommendations led to the enactment of remedial legislation in New York. Some of the changes in New York law included requiring detailed year-end reporting by insurers, ordering the allocation of policy dividends to policyholders, limiting the amount of new business insurers could write each year, and imposing strict regulations on agent commissions. New York's initiatives were influential in other states, and by 1919, thirty-six states had separate insurance departments vested with the exclusive task of administering state regulatory statutes.

By 1930, legislatures in most states gave these relatively new insurance departments greater authority to collect information from insurers and enhanced responsibilities to preserve insurer solvency. The departments were likewise authorized to review insurers' business decisions on reserve levels, valuation of assets, and investments. In addition, regulators were given some authority over policy forms and unfair trade practices, such as rebating, misrepresentation, twisting, and discrimination. By 1944, state insurance regulation was relatively comprehensive in all areas but ratemaking, even if it was not always particularly aggressive.

In the early 1940s, the Attorney General of Missouri, frustrated with the ineffectiveness of state ratemaking regulation and hoping to encourage federal involvement, sought a determination in federal court that the business of insurance constituted interstate commerce subject to the antitrust laws. He obtained an indictment against the South-Eastern Underwriters Association, an association of 198 stock fire insurance companies in six states, its officers, and its member companies. The indictment charged the defendants with violating the Sherman Act by agreeing to fix rates and boycotting non-members. The district court dismissed the indictment on the authority of the Supreme Court's decision in *Paul*, ruling that insurance was not interstate commerce. In 1944, however, the U.S. Supreme Court reversed the dismissal in *United States v. South-Eastern Underwriters Association*, 322 U.S. 533 (1944). In a four to three decision, the Court overruled the longstanding precedent of *Paul* and held that insurance transactions were subject to federal regulation under the Commerce Clause. This ruling removed the constitutional impediment to federal regulation of the insurance industry.

Ironically, by 1944, the insurance industry preferred the generally lax state regulatory system. Moreover, the industry was concerned that federal antitrust laws might be applied in a way that prohibited the pooling of actuarial data, a practice central to the ratemaking process. For other reasons, too, the industry feared both the potential havoc that federal antitrust regulation might create and the uncertainties inherent in substituting federal for state regulation. The industry also was realistic that the Court's holding in *SEUA* regarding the scope of the Commerce Clause would not be overturned. Therefore, the industry rallied behind legislation proposed by the National Association of Insurance Commissioners (NAIC) to limit the impact of the *SEUA* decision. (The NAIC, as the name suggests, was and remains an association of the leaders of state insurance departments who, under the auspices of the association, work together to propose model legislation and regulation, share information, and otherwise provide a unifying force to state regulatory efforts. The impact of the NAIC is discussed in more detail in the next subsection.). Congress enacted this proposal, and the resulting statute is known as the McCarran-Ferguson Act, 15 U.S.C. §§ 1011 et seq.

II. STATE REGULATION OF INSURANCE THROUGH THE McCARRAN-FERGUSON ACT

In Section 1 of the McCarran-Ferguson Act, Congress stated the underlying policy of the statute as one favoring state regulation of the insurance business:

> Congress declares that the continued regulation and taxation by the several States of the business of insurance is in the public interest, and that silence on the part of the Congress shall not be construed to impose any barrier to the regulation or taxation of such business by the several States.

If one takes the foregoing preamble at face value, Congress stated a clear preference for state regulation of the insurance business, and accordingly threw the full weight of its authority behind state regulatory systems. The rationale for this preference—aside from responding to lobbying by the industry, which combined their advocacy with that of state regulators with a stake in preserving their existence—involved supporting state regulation because of the states' closer proximity to the problems needing regulation and concerns over the effect of supplanting existing structures of state regulation with untested, yet-to-be-devised federal structures.

The operative language of the McCarran-Ferguson Act appears in section 2:

> (a) The business of insurance, and every person engaged therein, shall be subject to the laws of the several States which relate to the regulation or taxation of such business.
>
> (b) No Act of Congress shall be construed to invalidate, impair, or supersede any law enacted by any State for the purpose of regulating the business of insurance, or which imposes a fee or tax upon such business, unless such Act specifically relates to the business of insurance: Provided, That after June 30, 1948, [the Sherman Act of 1890, the Clayton Act of 1914, and the Federal

> Trade Commission Act of 1914] shall be applicable to the business of insurance to the extent that such business is not regulated by State law.

Notably, the states' exclusive power to regulate only applies to "the business of insurance." Is "the business of insurance" the same thing as the "insurance business"? As will be discussed in more detail in Section III.B of this chapter, the U.S. Supreme Court has answered that question "no." Indeed, the Supreme Court has created a test to apply to determine whether a law relates to "the business of insurance" that has resulted in a fairly narrow interpretation of the phrase.

Section 3(b) of the of the McCarran Ferguson Act states that the Sherman Act still applies to some insurer activities regardless of whatever regulation the states might enact:

> Nothing contained in this chapter shall render the said Sherman Act inapplicable to any agreement to boycott, coerce, or intimidate, or act of boycott, coercion, or intimidation.

In 1993, the meaning of "boycott" used in this section of the McCarran-Ferguson Act was addressed by the U.S. Supreme Court in *Hartford Fire Ins. Co. v. California*, 509 U.S. 764 (1993). That case will be addressed in Section III.A of this chapter.

Finally, Section 4 of the McCarran-Ferguson Act maintains the supremacy of three labor statutes: "Nothing contained in this chapter shall be construed to affect in any manner the application to the business of insurance of the . . . National Labor Relations Act, or . . . the Fair Labor Standards Act of 1938, or . . . the Merchant Marine Act, 1920." Whatever the motives underlying the McCarran-Ferguson Act, its significance was unmistakable. As the Supreme Court soon explained in 1946:

> Obviously Congress' purpose was broadly to give support to the existing and future state systems for regulating and taxing the business of insurance. . . . Its purpose was evidently to throw the whole weight of its power behind the state systems.

Prudential Insurance Co. v. Benjamin, 328 U.S. 408, 429–30 (1946).

In essence, the McCarran-Ferguson Act gave supremacy to state regulation of the business of insurance to the extent the states chose to occupy the regulatory field. Accordingly, shortly after the McCarran-Ferguson Act was passed, state insurance commissioners and representatives of the industry collaborated in an effort to draft and propose state legislation to occupy the areas vacated by the federal government to the extent the states chose to regulate. The NAIC, with the input of industry representatives, began by drafting model rate regulation and unfair trade practices statutes. The model ratemaking legislation reflected the beliefs that concerted ratemaking was essential to insurer solvency and that such joint activity should proceed under state supervision. By 1950, some form of rate regulation had been adopted in every state.

The states were somewhat slower to enact unfair trade practices legislation. In the mid-1950s, the Federal Trade Commission initiated inquiries into unsavory practices in the advertising of accident and health insurance. Concern about possible federal intervention encouraged the states to act, and, by 1963, unfair trade practices statutes were adopted in all of the states. This legislation, as enacted in most states, empowered the state insurance commissioners to issue cease and desist orders for misrepresentations and false advertising, defamation, boycotts, coercion, and intimidation, issuing false financial statements, providing stock options and advisory board contracts, and unfairly discriminating in life insurance, annuities, accident, and health insurance, and rebating commissions.

The process repeated itself in the 1960s and early 1970s when public concern over automobile insurance rates led to a Department of Transportation inquiry. With the prospect of federal intervention looming, a majority of the states enacted some kind of no-fault automobile insurance statute. In about half of these states, the statutory changes reformed the tort system with respect to compensation of victims of auto accidents.

Since the 1970s, efforts to shift more regulatory responsibility to the federal government arose from time to time, typically prompted by consumer advocates and, more recently, by some insurers frustrated with the difficulties of dealing with up to fifty different regulatory authorities. None of these initiatives has progressed very far, with two notable exceptions. One, in 1974, when Congress enacted significant pension regulation, it also included (perhaps inadvertently) insurance provided as a fringe benefit in the employer-employee relationship within the ambit of the statutory regulatory scheme (and all other employee benefits). The relevant statute is known as "ERISA," which refers to the Employee Retirement Income Security Act of 1974 (ERISA), 29 U.S.C. § 1001 et seq. Two, the federal government has had a significant presence in and influence upon health insurance markets ever since the enactment of Medicare in 1965. This federal role has expanded incrementally since then, up to and through the 2010 enactment of the Patient Protection and Affordable Care Act (Affordable Care Act), 42 U.S.C. § 18001 et seq. As of mid-2020, whether the federal-state relationships established in the ACA will be modified by congressional action is unsettled, and likely will remain unsettled as long as neither party controls both houses of Congress.

A. THE STRUCTURE OF STATE REGULATION

Because each state separately regulates the business of insurance, the statutory law of each state is the starting point for understanding the legislative regulatory framework. The sheer volume of this statutory law precludes a detailed discussion in a single volume, let alone a chapter like this, but a number of generalizations are possible.

All states have some sort of office that is charged with the duty of administering the state's regulatory insurance laws. In most states, the office is called the "Department of Insurance," and the official who heads the Department is usually called the "Insurance Commissioner." In about two-thirds of the states, the department is a separate regulatory entity. In the other states, the insurance agency is a part of some other state department, such as a "Department of Insurance and Banking" or a "Corporation Commission." In a majority of the states, the commissioner is appointed by, and serves at the pleasure of, the governor. In about half of the remaining states, the commissioner is appointed by some other governmental entity, and in the other half, the commissioner is elected by the voting public.

The department of insurance (or whatever it might be called) exercises authority delegated to it by the legislature. Thus, general principles of administrative law are important to understanding state regulation of insurance. The primary responsibility of the insurance commissioner (or other head of the department) is to protect the public, and to that end, the authority of the commissioner is usually stated broadly. As an implementer of law, the commissioner makes "law" by administering and applying a statute because doing so inevitably requires an interpretation of the statute's substance and the creation of procedural rules for the implementation of the substantive standards. As administrative lawyers know well, the substantive and procedural rules generated in the administrative process have a tangible effect on the conduct of regulated parties.

Given that the insurance business is regulated by fifty different state agencies, it would be reasonable to predict utter disarray and chaos in this industry. Such a prediction, surprisingly enough, misses the mark, with one possible exception: when compared to state commercial legislation, state insurance legislation is disorganized. There is nothing in state insurance law equivalent to the unifying influence of, for example, the Uniform Commercial Code. In fact, few states have insurance "codes" in the ordinary sense of the term. Most state insurance "codes" are a hodgepodge of many independently drafted and enacted provisions. In fact, one insurance law professor once described state insurance statutes a few decades ago as a "rubbish heap without parallel in the law making of modern man." Spencer L. Kimball, *Unfinished Business in Insurance*

Regulation, 1969 Wis. L. Rev. 1019. Today, Professor Kimball's observation is arguably an overstatement given the unifying influence of the efforts of the NAIC, but one cannot seriously argue that state insurance statutes are generally well organized.

But, when one gets past the organizational disarray, a surprising degree of uniformity exists across the states. This is due primarily to two factors. First, many states have enacted model acts promulgated by the NAIC, and this has resulted in substantial uniformity in many state statutes as they apply to particular regulatory topics. The NAIC is an association of the chief insurance regulatory officials of the fifty states, the District of Columbia, and the territories. It was organized in 1871, shortly after the Supreme Court's decision in *Paul* made it clear that the states had the exclusive authority to regulate the insurance business. The NAIC, through its staff and various committees currently headquartered in Kansas City, Missouri, proposes model laws and regulations for possible adoption by the states, studies problems of insurance regulation, gathers and distributes information on regulatory matters, and maintains financial data for the purpose of detecting insurer insolvency at an early stage. Most proceedings of the NAIC's meetings, including committee meetings, are published, and now much (but not all) of the NAIC's materials (including model acts and regulations) are available to the public online. The NAIC has no legal authority, but it does provide a significant coordinating influence on the regulation of the insurance industry by the several states.

Second, and perhaps more important, the purposes and objectives of state regulation are virtually identical in every state. As stated above, many state insurance statutes are similar in both content and wording. But the objectives of state governmental regulation, as articulated somewhere in most states' insurance codes, are essentially the same everywhere. In most formulations, the goals of state regulation have four distinct aspects: (1) ensuring that consumers are charged fair and reasonable prices for insurance products, (2) protecting the solvency of insurers, (3) preventing unfair practices and overreaching by insurers, and (4) guaranteeing the availability of coverage to the public. To a large extent, these objectives overlap. For example, in regulating rates, the first and second objectives overlap: it is important not only that a fair price be charged for the risk assumed but also that a sufficiently high price be charged to maintain insurers' solvency. Similarly, the first and third objectives overlap: unfair prices may be related to an unfair practice of discriminating against particular groups.

Yet, to some extent, the articulated state regulatory objectives are contradictory. For example, the second and fourth objectives are sometimes difficult to achieve simultaneously: charging a premium sufficiently high to maintain adequate reserves may result in coverage being unaffordable to certain segments of the population. To some extent, the first and third objectives are also inconsistent: eliminating discrimination in insurance rating is potentially at odds with setting a fair or reasonable rate, given that insurance rates should be a function of risk. An unbounded effort to categorize and subdivide risks in search of the fair rate for everyone likely would eventually lead to prohibitively expensive rates for certain classes of people or no insurance would even be sold to them.

B. SOLVENCY REGULATION AND GUARANTY ASSOCIATIONS

The modern era of solvency regulation dates to the 1960s, when a wave of insurer insolvencies developed primarily among companies writing substandard auto insurance. In the wake of these insolvencies, the NAIC proposed model statutes to create guaranty associations. These statutes create an association of insurers to satisfy the obligations of insolvent insurers through assessments on insurers doing business in the state. In effect, these statutes create a safety net for policyholders who happen to purchase insurance from a financially unstable insurer.

Guaranty associations are directed primarily at protecting smaller policyholders, such as individual consumers, rather than larger corporations. The statutes that provide recovery from guaranty funds commonly treat such guaranty associations as sources of recovery of last resort, which means any other insurance the policyholder has must be exhausted before the guaranty association is required to pay anything. Further, although many states use lower amounts, under the NAIC's Post-Assessment Property and Liability Insurance Guaranty Association Model Act (1987), policyholders that have a net worth in excess of $50 million cannot recover from guaranty associations. In addition, the per-claim recovery from guaranty associations is limited to $300,000 in most states.

Another important aspect of solvency regulation is statutes that provide for periodic examinations of insurers and audits of their annual reports. By investigating detailed accounting information submitted by insurers, state regulators, working with the NAIC, seek to determine whether insurers doing business in the state have the financial ability to meet their commitments. The examination audit statutes dovetail with the licensing statutes: state regulators will only license an insurer to do business in the state if it appears that the insurer is a financially stable institution. The financial requirements for insurers to obtain a license vary greatly in the different states.

Several other kinds of statutes have as a predominant purpose the protection and furtherance of insurer solvency. For example, all states have statutes prescribing the kinds of investments insurers are allowed to make. Similar statutes regulate the methods by which insurer assets are valued so that a true picture of the insurer's financial health is available. All states have statutes that require insurers to create, as a liability on their balance sheets, a "reserve" thought adequate to provide a fund to meet policy obligations as they are incurred. Most states have adopted statutes or regulations that regulate insurer holding company systems. This is intended to ensure that those who control or seek to acquire control of insurers will not manage the companies in a manner contrary to the interests of policyholders.

C. REGULATION OF INSURER TRADE PRACTICES

The special relationship between insurer and insured was explored in Chapter 3. As one would expect, much early statutory law and judicial case law were directed toward equalizing the relationship between insurer and policyholder. Initially, specific problems were often met with specific solutions. For example, in the nineteenth century, some states enacted statutes providing that no condition in an application for insurance would be valid unless specifically stated in the policy itself. These statutes were designed to prevent insurers from relying on obscure conditions outside the text of the policy that purported to relieve the insurer of liability in certain circumstances. Throughout most of the nineteenth century, it was assumed that a policyholder who stopped paying premium payments under a whole life insurance policy forfeited any equity he had previously accumulated. But statutes enacted in many states in the late nineteenth and early twentieth centuries required the insurer to provide some sort of minimum cash surrender value in the event the policyholder defaulted after the policy was in force for a specified period of time. The old rule of contract law that allowed a party to void a contract upon the other party's breach of a warranty provision regardless of the provision's materiality worked great hardship on many policyholders. Thus, statutes enacted in many states beginning in the early twentieth century declared that no policy would be voided for breach of warranty unless the fact warranted was material or was intentionally misrepresented.

As noted earlier, under the impetus of the McCarran-Ferguson Act, state legislatures took steps to regulate the bargaining relationship between the insurer and the applicant in the late 1940s and early 1950s, thereby preempting a federal regulatory role. Each state enacted statutes to prohibit such practices as false or misleading advertising, misrepresentation of a competitor's product, and failing to pay valid claims. Most of these statutes authorize the state insurance commissioner to commence an investigation into alleged unfair trade practices and to issue cease and desist orders where such practices are occurring. An example of such as statute is Pennsylvania's Unfair Insurance Practices Act (40 Pa.C.S.A. § 1171.5(a)(10)), which was discussed in Chapter 3.

In recent years, legislative efforts to combat overreaching and unfairness in the marketplace have taken the form of increasing the availability of, and access to, information. For example, much attention has been given to making more information available about the price of insurance at the point of sale. One important source of information for consumers in the insurance business is advertising. Advertising, by making consumers aware of available products and the alternatives, both promotes distribution of coverage and enhances product competition. Inaccurate advertising, however, has an equal potential for frustrating the public interest by encouraging unnecessary and incorrect purchases. Thus, much modern regulation can fairly be described as "truth in advertising" regulation. Under the reasoning that a consumer who understands his or her rights and obligations under a contract is less likely to be the victim of sharp practices and is more likely to purchase a useful product, statutes in some states mandate minimum standards for language used in policies, often using "reading ease tests" to determine whether the policy's language is sufficiently "plain." Insurance commissioners usually have the express authority to disapprove forms that are obscure, misleading, or unclear.

Most statutes on insurer overreaching are aimed at the marketing practices of insurers and their agents. Claims processing is regulated by statutes that assess penalties for delays in paying claims. Also, a number of states have statutes that impose penalties against an insurance company that refuses to pay a claim, forces the policyholder to sue the insurer to recover, and subsequently loses the policyholder's suit. All states have some procedure by which the insurance department can receive consumer complaints. Some legitimate complaints will fall within an area where the department has the authority to investigate and give relief.

Generally, data regarding insurers' claims practices and the bases of complaints asserted against insurers with respect to claims payment practices is collected by state insurance commissioners, but it ordinarily is not publicly available. One would think that making such data public would help consumers select insurers and would deter insurer misconduct. Insurers contend, and insurance regulators apparently agree, that such information should be kept confidential because it contains private policyholder information. One would think that the information could be aggregated and shared with the public without disclosing the identities of specific policyholders. So, why is it not? Perhaps the answer to that question can be found in the next section.

For a general discussion of disclosure of information regarding insurers and their claims practices, *see* Daniel Schwarcz, *Transparently Opaque: Understanding the Lack of Transparency in Insurance Consumer Protection*, 61 UCLA L. Rev. 394 (2014).

D. REGULATION OF COVERAGE

States regulate the insurance coverage provided by insurers in a number of ways. The most direct kind of coverage regulation seeks to increase the amount of coverage that policyholders possess by mandating that consumers purchase insurance. For example, all states have financial responsibility statutes for owners of automobiles, and these statutes effectively require owners of automobiles to have liability insurance to pay for losses they cause. The public policy underlying these statutes is to ensure that adequate funds will exist to reimburse individuals who suffer physical injury or economic loss in most automobile accidents.

Legislatures also sometimes specify the content of insurance policies, and this has obvious effects on coverage. For example, some statutes in some states prohibit insurers from offsetting increased Social Security benefits in group disability income policies. In a majority of states, statutes now limit insurers' use of genetic information to make risk or premium classifications in health insurance, and sometimes in life and disability insurance, as well.

States also regulate coverage by prescribing rules for access to insurance. For example, all states have some kind of "residual market plan" through which automobile insurance is sold to people unable to obtain insurance in the voluntary market. The most common mechanism in the states is the "assigned risk" plan, under which insurers doing business in a state are required to insure some portion of otherwise uninsurable risks.

Finally, state insurance commissioners are empowered to review and approve policy forms. In doing so, they can reject terms that are "unfair," "ambiguous," "unreasonable," and/or "contrary to public policy." *See, e.g.*, Ala. Code § 27–14–9 (2016); Ga. Code Ann. § 33–24–10 (2016); Neb. Rev. Stat. § 44–7513 (2016). But the gap between the theoretical value of form review and actual practice is a wide one. First, although each new or revised form must go through regulatory review, the sheer number of policy forms and their individual complexity, when combined with the limited staffing available to conduct these reviews, means that full and close review is impossible. This is not to say that forms are never disapproved, but the mere fact that a form has been approved does not guarantee its clarity or even its actual compliance with the requirements of state law. Second, form review tends to focus on a limited range of issues. For example, insurance department review "generally focuses on making sure that insurers cannot cancel or refuse to renew policies without providing adequate notice and on ensuring that policies meet minimum readability requirements, based on the length of words and sentences rather than the overall complexity or comprehensibility." Christopher C. French, *Understanding Insurance Policies as Non-Contracts: An Alternative*

Approach to Drafting and Construing These Unique Financial Instruments, 89 Temp. L. Rev. 535, 552–53 (2017). Third, during the review process, "insurers are represented by attorneys, and the state regulators are typically former employees of insurers (who will return to work for insurers after serving as regulators)." *Id.* This is the well-known phenomenon of "regulatory capture," which means "the regulation of an industry is dominated by the industry itself such that the industry is actually regulated for its own benefit." *Id.* The upshot of the reality of form review is that "[s]tate insurance regulators, despite express statutory authority to do so, generally do not exercise their power to reject policy language that could be considered unfair, ambiguous, unreasonable, or contrary to public policy," and "do not rigorously scrutinize or police policy language." *Id.*

E. REGULATION OF "EXCESSIVE" AND "DISCRIMINATORY" RATES

The current methods of rate regulation in the states are quite diverse, and therefore they defy easy generalization. Not every line of insurance is subject to the same kind of regulation, and different states approach the task in different ways. Prescription of rates by the state regulator is uncommon. It is more typical for insurers to file proposed rates with the insurance department, which must approve them before they can be used. The "prior approval" approach usually has a mechanism under which a filed rate becomes effective unless the department disapproves the rate within a specified period of time. The "file and use" approach allows the insurer to use the filed rate, unless the insurance department takes steps to disapprove the rate within a specified period of time. These two methods are sometimes combined in what is commonly called "flex rating." Under flex rating, insurers can file and use their rates, provided they are within a specified range, but any rate changes outside the range must receive the department's prior approval. The "open competition" method relies upon market forces to set rates, although the insurance department can take steps to intercede in appropriate circumstances. Rate regulation is closely connected to solvency regulation, to be sure, but other state statutes also seek to promote and preserve insurer solvency.

Most states have enacted statutes that require insurance departments to assure that insurance rates are not "excessive, inadequate, or unfairly discriminatory." Rates are rarely challenged for being too low. Rather, rates typically are only challenged when they are perceived as "excessive" or "discriminatory."

How does one determine whether a premium rate is "excessive"? For example, if a person is a reckless driver routinely involved in accidents but has not yet been required to surrender his driver's license, is an insurer charging an "excessive" rate if it charges this person triple the amount it charges safe drivers who have not had any accidents?

1. Excessive Rates

STATE EX REL. COMM'R OF INS. V. N.C. RATE BUREAU (IN RE FILING DATED JANUARY 3, 2014 BY N.C. RATE BUREAU)

791 S.E.2d 211 (N.C. 2016)

Opinion

MCCULLOUGH, JUDGE.

The North Carolina Rate Bureau ("Bureau") appeals from order entered by the North Carolina Commissioner of Insurance ("Commissioner") that rejected the Bureau's filed rate increases and imposed alternative rate changes. For the following reasons, we affirm the Commissioner's order.

I. Background

On 3 January 2014, the North Carolina Department of Insurance ("Department") received the Bureau's filing for revised homeowners' insurance rates and revised homeowners' insurance territory definitions (the "filing"). In the filing, the Bureau sought approval of an overall statewide average rate level change of +25.6%, with the filed rates varying between the newly defined territories.

Broken down into categories, the filing included the following statewide rate increases: 24.8% for owners, 54.9% for tenants, and 50.0% for condominiums. The Bureau requested that the filed rates be applied to all new and renewal policies becoming effective on or after 1 August 2014.

. . . .

The matter came on for public hearing in Raleigh before Commissioner Wayne Goodwin on 20 October 2014. The hearing continued on 21, 27, 28, 29, 30, and 31 October 2014 and 3, 5, 6, 11, and 12 November 2014. During the hearing, over fifty exhibits of prefiled testimony and documentary evidence and over two thousand pages of live testimony were offered for consideration.

The Commissioner issued his order on . . . 13 January 2015. . . . In the order, the Commissioner . . . determined the Bureau failed to meet its burden of proof regarding its filed rate increases and, therefore, disapproved the filed rates. Instead of the Bureau's filed rates that resulted in an overall statewide average rate level change of +25.6%, the Commissioner ordered rates that resulted in an overall statewide average rate level change of 0%. In reaching the 0% change, the Commissioner ordered rate increases for tenants and condominiums and decreases for owners. The ordered rates were to be effective 1 June 2015.

The Bureau filed notice of appeal from the Commissioner's order on 16 January 2015.

II. Discussion

On appeal, the Bureau seeks to have the Commissioner's order declared null and void so that its filed rates and territory definitions become effective by operation of law.

. . . .

The Bureau further asserts that there are too many issues with the Commissioner's order to address each issue on appeal; therefore, the Bureau asserts the following arguments challenging specific components of the ordered rates: (1) the Commissioner erred as a matter of law by ordering an underwriting profit provision that fails to meet legal and constitutional standards; (2) the Commissioner erred by rejecting the reinsurance provision filed by the Bureau and by selecting a provision that is unsupported by material and substantial evidence. . . .

. . . .

Standard of Review

Just as the Commissioner's review of the Bureau's filing is governed by statute, so is this Court's review of the Commissioner's order. Concerning judicial review of rates and classifications, ... "Any order or decision of the Commissioner, if supported by substantial evidence, shall be presumed to be correct and proper. . . ." N.C. Gen. Stat. § 58–2–80 (2015). After an order or decision of the Commissioner is appealed to this Court,

> So far as necessary to the decision and where presented, the court shall decide all relevant questions of law, interpret constitutional and statutory provisions, and determine the meaning and applicability of the terms of any action of the Commissioner. The court may affirm or reverse the decision of the Commissioner, declare the same null and void, or remand the case for further proceedings; or it may reverse or modify the decision if the substantial rights of the appellants have been prejudiced because the Commissioner's findings, inferences, conclusions or decisions are:
>
> (1) In violation of constitutional provisions, or
>
> (2) In excess of statutory authority or jurisdiction of the Commissioner, or
>
> (3) Made upon unlawful proceedings, or
>
> (4) Affected by other errors of law, or
>
> (5) Unsupported by material and substantial evidence in view of the entire record as submitted, or
>
> (6) Arbitrary or capricious.

N.C. Gen. Stat. § 58–2–90(b) (2015). This Court has further explained that,

> When reviewing an order by the Commission, this Court must examine the whole record and determine whether the Commissioner's conclusions of law are supported by material and substantial evidence. The whole record test requires the reviewing court to consider the record evidence supporting the Commissioner's order, to also consider the record evidence contradicting the Commissioner's findings, and to determine if the Commissioner's decision had a rational basis in the material and substantial evidence offered. Substantial evidence is such relevant evidence as a reasonable mind might accept as adequate to support a conclusion. It is more than a scintilla or a permissible inference.
>
> The Commissioner determines the weight and sufficiency of the evidence presented during the hearing, including the credibility of any witnesses. It is not our function to substitute our judgment for that of the Commissioner when the evidence is conflicting. Instead, the Commissioner's order is presumed correct if it is supported by substantial evidence. The order must conform to the guidelines set out in [N.C. Gen. Stat.] § 58–36–10[.]
>
> . . . .
>
> As long as the Commissioner's order meets the criteria of [N.C. Gen. Stat.] § 58–36–10 and is supported by material and substantial evidence, the order should be upheld.

State ex rel. Comm'r of Ins. v. N.C. Rate Bureau, 160 N.C. App. 416, 420–21, 586 S.E.2d 470, 472–73 (2003) ("2001 Auto") (internal quotation marks, citations, and alterations omitted), *aff'd per curiam on those issues raised in the dissent*, 358 N.C. 539, 597 S.E.2d 128 (2004). Relevant to this appeal, the following standards apply to the making and use of property insurance rates:

> (1) Rates or loss costs shall not be excessive, inadequate or unfairly discriminatory.
>
> (2) Due consideration shall be given to actual loss and expense experience within this State for the most recent three-year period for which that information is available; to prospective loss and expense experience within this State; to the hazards of conflagration and catastrophe; to a reasonable margin for underwriting profit and to contingencies; to dividends, savings, or unabsorbed premium deposits allowed or returned by insurers to their policyholders, members, or subscribers; to investment income earned or realized by insurers from their unearned premium, loss, and loss expense reserve funds generated from

> business within this State; to past and prospective expenses specially applicable to this State; and to all other relevant factors within this State: Provided, however, that countrywide expense and loss experience and other countrywide data may be considered only where credible North Carolina experience or data is not available.
>
> . . . .

N.C. Gen. Stat. § 58–36–10 (2015).

1. Underwriting Profit

In the Bureau's first challenge to the Commissioner's order, the Bureau claims the underwriting profit provision adopted by the Commissioner violates applicable legal and constitutional standards. We disagree.

Our courts have long recognized the requirement that the Commissioner set rates to allow insurers to earn "a fair and reasonable profit" after the payment of losses and operating expenses. *See In re N.C. Fire Ins. Rating Bureau*, 275 N.C. 15, 34, 165 S.E.2d 207, 220 (1969) ("1967 Fire") (explaining "that the premium [must] be fixed at a level which will enable the insuring company . . . (1) to pay the losses which will be incurred during the life of the policies to be issued under such rates, (2) to pay other operating expenses, and (3) to retain a 'fair and reasonable profit' and no more"). "An insurance company's total profit is derived from two distinct parts of the insurance business—(1) profit earned by the insurance operations and (2) profits earned by investing capital and surplus funds." *2001 Auto*, 160 N.C. App. at 421, 586 S.E.2d at 473. Yet, in North Carolina, the total profit is not considered in determining whether rates allow insurers to earn a fair and reasonable profit; only the profit from the insurance operations is considered.

> The profit from insurance operations includes both the underwriting profit and investment income from policyholder-supplied funds. The underwriting profit can be defined as the difference between insurance premiums collected and the amount the company pays out for losses and expenses. Policyholder-supplied funds are the amount of premiums paid to the insurance company. Policyholder-supplied funds are usually invested during the insurance coverage period.

2001 Auto, 160 N.C. App. at 421–22, 586 S.E.2d at 473. Although underwriting profit is a component of the profit earned by the insurance operations, which must be sufficient to allow insurers to earn fair and reasonable profit, there are no requirements specific to underwriting profit. . . .

In this case, the filing included an underwriting profit of 10.5% of premium. Upon review, the Commissioner rejected the Bureau's underwriting profit provision in favor of an underwriting profit of 5.2% of premium. As stated above, the Bureau now claims this was error.

The Bureau's argument that the Commissioner's underwriting profit provision violates legal and constitutional standards is founded on its assertion that a "fair and reasonable profit" must be equal to and determined using the cost of equity (also known as the "cost of capital" or the "cost of equity capital"). . . .

Upon review of the cases cited by the Bureau, we are not convinced the cost of equity is a constitutionally mandated standard, as the Bureau asserts. Thus, we affirm the Commissioner's rejection of the filed underwriting profit provision.

The Bureau argues North Carolina law has long defined a "fair and reasonable profit" as the level of profit demanded by the investment market on business ventures of comparable risk, which the Bureau equates to the cost of equity. . . .

[O]ur Supreme Court has acknowledged that, "[i]n North Carolina, there is no prescribed methodology for calculating the return on profits (profit methodology), and [it] has specifically recognized that creativity is acceptable within the parameters of the applicable statutes." *State ex rel. Comm'r of Ins. v. N.C. Rate Bureau*, 350 N.C. 539, 542, 516 S.E.2d 150, 152 (1999) ("1996 Auto"). "The Commissioner is considered an expert in the field of insurance and his reliance on various methods of analysis of the profit to which the insurance companies are entitled lies entirely within his discretion." *State ex rel. Comm'r of Ins. v. N.C. Rate Bureau*, 124 N.C. App. 674, 687, 478 S.E.2d 794, 803 (1996) ("1994 Auto") (internal quotation marks and citation omitted), *disc. rev. denied*, 346 N.C. 184, 486 S.E.2d 217 (1997). Accordingly, we hold the Commissioner did not violate any constitutionally mandated standard in refusing to accept the Bureau's cost of equity profit methodology. . . .

. . . .

2. Net Cost of Reinsurance

The Bureau next argues the Commissioner erred in determining the net cost of reinsurance to be included in rates, which the Commissioner addressed in findings 375 through 454.

Reinsurance is insurance purchased by primary insurers from other insurance companies, or reinsurers, to mitigate the risk of large payouts in excess of what a primary insurer could bear in the event of catastrophic losses. It does so by spreading the risk between primary insurers and reinsurers. Reinsurers are willing to accept portions of the risk associated with potential catastrophic losses in exchange for a share of the premiums paid by the insureds. Primary insurers, in turn, pass the expense of reinsurance to the insureds by including the net cost of reinsurance in the rates. A large portion of the exposure to catastrophic losses in North Carolina is due to hurricanes.

In this case, the Bureau's filing included a provision for a net cost of reinsurance of 17.5% of premium. . . .

. . . .

Upon review of the evidence concerning net cost of reinsurance in this case, the Commissioner rejected the Bureau's filed net cost of reinsurance of 17.5% of premium and ordered a net cost of reinsurance of 10% of premium. The Bureau now contends the Commissioner erred in doing so.

At the outset, it is apparent from the Commissioner's order that the Commissioner fully considered the evidence on the net cost of reinsurance, as the Commissioner summarized both the Bureau's and the Department's cases and explained his reasons for rejecting the Bureau's filed net cost of reinsurance provision and adopting the 10% provision. Despite the Commissioner's detailed order, the Bureau claims the Commissioner erred.

The Bureau first challenges the Commissioner's rejection of the filed net cost of reinsurance provision. The Bureau contends the filed net cost of reinsurance provision based on the "procedure" developed by Appel, which the Bureau now refers to as an "economic model," was reasonable and supported by the evidence.

The Commissioner's rejection is concisely explained in the following findings:

> 446. . . . Basically what the Commissioner was presented with in regards to the net cost of reinsurance was a hypothetical model, poorly documented, that was developed by an economist with no discernible background in reinsurance other than vague associations with other professionals who may have some reinsurance experience. Although market information was produced on rebuttal to support model input, the model does not reflect the significant price decreases in the market over the past couple of years because the model is not market-based. Moreover, the reinsurance model utilizes the AIR WSST model to estimate losses; however, the scientific underpinnings of the WSST are debatable and the WSST results in significantly higher losses than the STD model, which produced losses in this filing that the Commissioner has already found excessive.
>
> 447. Given all of the issues . . ., and the fact that the proposed net cost of reinsurance represents 22.1% of the base rate for Owners, the Commissioner can only conclude that the Bureau has not met its burden of proof with regards to the reinsurance component of the indicated rates. . . .

. . . .

> 453. Thus, based on the foregoing, the Commissioner finds that the Bureau's proposed net cost of reinsurance is excessive and will result in excessive rates.

Although the Bureau acknowledges that the Commissioner has discretion in weighing the evidence, the Bureau contends the Commissioner abused his discretion in this case by disregarding evidence. . . .

. . . .

Upon review of the Commissioner's findings and the evidence, we hold the Commissioner did not abuse his discretion.

. . . .

[W]e are hesitant to say that the Commissioner erred in disregarding the data where, on appeal, the Bureau has failed to direct this Court to any concrete evidence indicating what portion of [one insurer's] data was not reinsurance to guard against the risk of catastrophe losses. Moreover, as found by the Commissioner in finding 451 and argued by the Department on appeal, our Supreme Court has recognized that "the loss experience data of a single carrier in this State does not establish the 'composite' of loss experience of all the carriers, which the establishment of the Bureau was intended to create." *Foremost Ins. Co., Inc. v. Ingram*, 292 N.C. 244, 249, 232 S.E.2d 414, 418 (1977). This seems to hold particularly true where the single carrier . . . in the present case offers homeowners' insurance extensively, but exclusively, in North Carolina. While the Bureau claims this makes [the insurer] "uniquely reflective" of a single hypothetical company operating in North Carolina, both Bureau and Department witnesses acknowledged that many insurers in North Carolina are multi-state and multi-line carriers. Department witness Schwartz explained that he did not believe the Bureau's calculation took into account that "the aggregate company in North Carolina . . . writes other lines of insurance in North Carolina, and writes business in other states, and has a substantial premium base and surplus amount which would allow for a higher retention." Based on this evidence, we cannot hold the Commissioner abused his discretion in disregarding the [one insurer's] data as illustrative of reinsurance for the entire state.

. . . .

Even if the countrywide data was properly considered, the Bureau contends the Commissioner acted arbitrarily in selecting the 10% net cost of reinsurance provision from the data. Again, we disagree. While 10% may not be an exact calculation, Schwartz's recommendation and the Commissioner's selection of 10% for the net cost of reinsurance was based on a reasoned analysis with a rational basis in the evidence. Specifically, the data relied on by Schwartz shows that, for the years included, the net cost of reinsurance as a percent of direct earned premium ranges from an average of 4.6% on a calendar year basis to a maximum of 10.1% on a calendar year basis, and from an average of 7.8% on an accident year basis and to a maximum of 15.9% on an accident year basis. Schwartz used that data to recommend a range of 5% to 16%, considering both the accident year and calendar year bases. Schwartz then selected a 10% net cost of reinsurance from the middle of the range. Upon review, it is clear that Schwartz's analysis was well reasoned and constitutes material and substantial evidence. Furthermore, it supports the Commissioner's findings and conclusions. Thus, the Commissioner's selection of the 10% net cost of reinsurance was not arbitrary.

. . . .

III. Conclusion

Upon a full review of the Commissioner's order, we hold the order reflects a careful, thoughtful, and thorough consideration of the evidence. The evidence in the record supports the Commissioner's critical findings and ultimate conclusions. This Court will not second guess the Commissioner's determinations as to the credibility of the witnesses or the weight to be given their testimony. Therefore, the order of the Commissioner is affirmed.

AFFIRMED.

NOTES AND QUESTIONS

1. *Allowable Profit Margin*. What is the acceptable premium rate that insurers are allowed to charge? How is the rate determined? What type of evidence did the state insurance department introduce to the state insurance commissioner, who is charged with determining appropriate premium rates?

2. *Standard of Review*. If an insurer appeals the premium rates allowed by a state insurance commissioner, what is the judicial standard of review?

3. *Few Excessive Rate Cases*. There are few reported cases regarding challenges to state insurance commissioners' rulings regarding premium rates. Having read the *N.C. Rate Bureau* case, why do you think that is so?

2. Discriminatory Rates

The very heart of risk classification, and the premiums insurers charge that is based on risk classification, is discrimination. Insurers intentionally discriminate against actual and potential policyholders. Insurers discriminate against some risky people by refusing to insure them or charging them higher premiums, and many policyholders generally want insurers to discriminate against risky people so that they do not have to subsidize the losses associated with riskier people's conduct through higher premiums. Indeed, Progressive Auto Insurance Company, for example, has television commercials in which it tells potential customers that they do not need to worry about "rate suckers" if they do business with Progressive, presumably meaning that Progressive policyholders do not subsidize the premium rates of other higher-risk policyholders because Progressive either rejects such people as customers or charges them more. If that type of "discrimination" were prohibited, then how could an insurance market work? Is there a difference between having rates that *discriminate* and having *discriminatory* rates? Consider the next case.

FLEISHER V. PHOENIX LIFE INS. CO.

18 F. Supp. 3d 456 (S.D.N.Y. 2014)

MCMAHON, DISTRICT JUDGE:

Plaintiffs Martin Fleisher ("Fleisher"), as Trustee of the Michael Moss Irrevocable Life Insurance Trust II, and Jonathan Berck ("Berck," and, together with Fleisher, "Plaintiffs"), as Trustee of the John L. Loeb, Jr. Insurance Trust, initiated this class action against Defendant Phoenix Life Insurance Company ("Phoenix"). The only remaining claim (Count One) alleges that Phoenix breached the terms of certain insurance policies owned by the Trusts.

Both the Plaintiffs and the Defendant move for partial summary judgment on liability for Fleisher's claim pursuant to Rule 56 of the Federal Rules of Civil Procedure. For the reasons discussed below, the Defendant's motion is granted in part and denied in part, and the Plaintiffs' motion is denied in its entirety.

BACKGROUND

A. The Parties

Plaintiff Fleisher is the trustee of the Michael Moss Irrevocable Life Insurance Trust II. Plaintiff Berck is the trustee of the John L. Loeb, Jr. Insurance Trust. These two trusts own life insurance policies issued by Defendant Phoenix. *See* Pl. 56.1 Statement at ¶ 2.

Plaintiff Fleisher brings his breach of contract claim on behalf of a class. The Court previously certified a class consisting of:

> All owners of flexible-premium "universal life" insurance policies issued by Phoenix Life Insurance Company that were subjected to the Cost of Insurance rate increase announced by Phoenix on or about November 1, 2011 (excluding defendant Phoenix, its officers and directors, members of their immediate families, and the heirs, successors or assigns of any of the foregoing).

We have come to refer to this class as the "2011 Class" . . . .

B. The PAUL Policies

Plaintiff Fleisher and the members of the 2011 Class own (or owned) "substantively identical" Phoenix Accumulator Universal Life ("PAUL") insurance policies.

. . . .

Traditional whole life insurance policies require payment of a fixed monthly premium. The cost of life insurance for any insured increases over time as the insured ages and becomes more likely to die. In order to spread out this insurance cost into fixed monthly premium payments, the premium charged earlier in the life of the insured must be greater than the actual insurance cost, and the premium charged later in life must be less than the actual insurance cost. The amount of early year premiums paid in excess of actual insurance costs goes into a cash reserve that accumulates in value (the "policy value"). This policy value functions like a savings account. When the insurance cost exceeds the fixed monthly premium later in life, the policy value is used to supplement the fixed premium in order to cover the total actual insurance cost.

During the life of the insured, the policyholder may choose to cash out his accumulated policy value by "surrendering" the policy. Though surrender causes the policyholder to lose life insurance protection, he is able to withdraw the balance of the policy value in cash, subject to any surrender charges specified in the contract.

Universal life insurance is similar to traditional whole life insurance but with a central distinguishing feature—the policyholder is not required to pay a fixed monthly premium.

Under the terms of these "flexible premium" PAUL policies, a policyholder must pay a Minimum Initial Premium, which is specified in his contract. This amount covers his up-front costs. Any amount in excess of the Minimum Initial Premium that the insured chooses to pay is deposited into his savings account—his "Policy Value," on which Phoenix pays interest.

Thereafter, the policyholder has options. The only requirement is that he must pay enough each month to cover the monthly insurance expenses (referred in the policy as the "Monthly Deduction"). If he fails to do that, the policy will lapse.

Otherwise, the policyholder has flexibility to determine the amount and timing of his premium payments. He may choose to make monthly payments equal to the Monthly Deduction and nothing more—rather like buying a term life insurance policy. If the policyholder chooses to pay this minimum amount every month, his Policy Value will never increase above zero. Such a policyholder would not be utilizing the savings component of his policy.

Alternatively, a policyholder can pay an amount in excess of the minimum Monthly Deduction. The excess payment will be added to his Policy Value.

. . . .

In sum, it is entirely up to the policyholder whether to utilize the savings (or "Cash Accumulation") feature of his policy. He may choose to pay the minimum Monthly Deduction each month, or he may take advantage of the option to pay excess premiums, to build up his Policy Value, and to use the accumulated Policy Value to cover his Monthly Deductions. He may maintain a high Policy Value, a low Policy Value, or no Policy Value at all. . . . These are truly "flexible premium" policies.

C. Computation of the Monthly COI Charge

One of the insurance charges included in the Monthly Deduction is the "Cost of Insurance" ("COI") charge. The COI charge represents Phoenix's risk of paying the death benefit (the policy's "Face Amount") to the policy's beneficiary upon the death of the insured. The policyholder's payment of COI charges to cover Phoenix's risk is the policy's insurance component.

The policy sets forth a formula for calculating the monthly COI charge. The formula is this: Monthly COI Charge = COI Rate × Net Amount at Risk.

. . . .

The policy does not contain a simple, straightforward definition of the "COI rate," as it does for the other terms used. Instead, Section 9 of the policy—entitled "Policy Value"—explains how to calculate something called the "Cost of Insurance Charge."

. . . .

"Paragraph B" explains how to calculate the COI Charge (which the policy defines as "the charge for the Net Amount at Risk") for "a specific Policy Month." A "Policy Month" is defined as "the period from one Monthly Calculation Date up to, but not including, the next Monthly Calculation Date." In simpler terms, a Policy Month is any month during which the policy is in force. Paragraph B states:

> The Cost of Insurance Charge for a specific Policy Month is the charge for the Net Amount at Risk. The charge for the Net Amount at Risk is an amount equal to the per dollar cost of insurance rate for that month multiplied by the Net Amount at Risk, and such rates will be based on our expectations of future mortality, persistency, investment earnings, expense experience, capital and reserve requirements, and tax assumptions. The Maximum Monthly Rates at any Age are shown in Section 2. . . .

This lawsuit is about the meaning of this paragraph.

To establish the COI Charge for any particular Policy Month, Phoenix multiplies the "per dollar *cost of insurance rate for that month*" by the NAR (Total Face Amount less Policy Value). *Id.* (emphasis added). . . . In any succeeding month, the COI rate may be adjusted in accordance with the terms of Paragraph B before calculating the COI Charge.

The policy says that "such rates" (*i.e.,* the COI rates for any Policy Month) will be based on Phoenix's "expectations" about six identified factors: future mortality, persistency, investment earnings, expense experience, capital and reserve requirements, and tax assumptions. . . .

Phoenix is not required to calculate a new COI rate every month. The company starts with the initial COI rate in force on the Policy Date and "review[s] [its] COI rates periodically, and may re-determine Cost of Insurance rates at such time . . ."

The COI rate is also subject to certain maximum rates set forth in the policy, which vary in accordance with the age of the insured.

One of the breach of contract allegations in this lawsuit is that, in calculating a COI rate adjustment in 2011 (the "2011 COI Rate Adjustment") for some (but not all) of the PAUL policies, Phoenix violated the contract by using factors in its calculation of the "cost of insurance rate for that month" that are impermissible under the terms of the policy. Whether plaintiffs are correct about that turns on the correct interpretation of Paragraph B.

D. The 2011 COI Rate Adjustment

In November 2011, Phoenix announced that it was imposing the 2011 COI Rate Adjustment; it changed the COI rates for some (but not all) of the PAUL policies, including those held by Fleisher and the members of the 2011 Class. The company sent letters to the affected policyholders to tell them that the 2011 COI Rate Adjustment would take effect on their next policy anniversaries. The members of the 2011 Class are those policyholders whose COI rates increased.

It is undisputed that, in setting a new "cost of insurance rate for that month," Phoenix took Policy Values into consideration. Phoenix admits that it "analyzed funding ratios . . . in the process of defining the class" that would be subject to the 2011 COI Rate Adjustment. A policy's funding ratio is equal to the Policy Value divided by the Total Face Amount. Essentially, Phoenix determined which policies had low funding ratios (and thus, lower Policy Values)—*i.e.,* it determined which policies were not being used as investment vehicles, which made them less remunerative to Phoenix—and then identified groups of policies that more or less matched the policies with low funding ratios (PAUL series IIIA policies with insureds age 68 or older and face amounts of $1 million or more, and PAUL series IIIB/C policies with insureds age 65 or older and face amounts of $1 million or more) and subjected these groups to the 2011 COI Rate Adjustment.

Fleisher argues that Policy Value (or funding ratio, which derives from Policy Value) is not among the factors that can be taken into consideration in adjusting COI rates for months after the Policy Date, because it is not one of the six factors enumerated in Paragraph B.

. . . .

Fleisher [also] argues that the rate adjustment breached the contract because (1) Phoenix "unfairly" discriminated within a class of insureds by applying the rate adjustment to only a subset of PAUL policies, and (2) Phoenix designed the rate adjustment to recoup prior losses, not to restore prospective profitability.

. . . .

DISCUSSION

. . . .

IV. An Issue of Fact Remains as to Whether Phoenix Unfairly Discriminated Within a Class of Insureds.

. . . Fleisher contends that the 2011 COI Rate Adjustment "discriminate[d] unfairly within any class of insureds," in violation of the policy terms. This allegation cannot be resolved on a motion for summary judgment.

Fleisher contends that Phoenix violated this provision of the contract by imposing the 2011 COI Rate Adjustment only on two groups of PAUL policyholders: PAUL series IIIA policies with insureds age 68 or older and face amounts of $1 million or more, and PAUL series IIIB/C policies with insureds age 65 or older and face amounts of $1 million or more. The question is whether Phoenix "discriminate[d] unfairly within any class of insureds" by subdividing the PAUL policies based on age and face amount, and then imposing the 2011 COI Rate Adjustment on only the two subsets.

Though the policy does nothing to elucidate the meaning of "discriminate unfairly within any class of insureds," the Court is guided by a nearly identical provision in New York Insurance Law, which states:

> No life insurance company doing business in this state . . . shall . . . make or permit any *unfair discrimination between individuals of the same class and of equal expectation of life,* in the amount or payment or return of premiums, or rates charged for policies of life insurance or annuity contracts, or in the dividends or other benefits payable thereon, or in any of the terms and conditions thereof. . .

N.Y. Ins. Law. § 4224(a)(1) (emphasis added). Thus, the interpretation of this policy provision should track the statutory definition of what constitutes "unfair discrimination:" it is discrimination that does not have a proper underwriting basis. New York deems discrimination to be "fair" as long as the insurance company's differential treatment of insureds is appropriate under generally accepted actuarial standards.

The leading New York General Counsel Opinion interpreting § 4224(a)(1) states:

> The language of N.Y. Ins. Law § 4224(a)(1) is clear that only UNFAIR discrimination is prohibited. All types of discrimination are not prohibited. All risk classification necessarily involves discrimination, with each person paying according to the risk he or she represents. Classifying and pricing risks is the very essence of insurance. . . .
>
> An insurer is free to impose any appropriate rules for classifying, selecting, and pricing risks that it believes are required based on sound underwriting practices and in accordance with accepted insurance and actuarial principles, provided such rules are not contrary to law.

Thus, an insurance company does not unfairly discriminate within a class of insureds "when differential treatment has a *proper underwriting basis.*"

So imposing the 2011 COI Rate Adjustment on the classes of insureds identified will not be deemed "unfair" as long as it can be justified under accepted actuarial principles.

There is a genuine issue of material fact concerning whether what Phoenix did can be justified under accepted actuarial principles. Phoenix's expert claims that the company's classifications of policies based on age and face amount met the requirements of the official guidance of the Actuarial Standards Board—the Actuarial Standards of Practice ("ASOP"). Fleisher's expert disagrees.

Intuitively, it seems obvious that age would be an appropriate way to classify insureds in the life insurance context—the older a person is, the higher his risk of death. However, it is not so apparent that face value is an appropriate way to classify insureds; this factor is not clearly tied to life expectancy, and it seems more closely associated with profitability. The parties' experts disagree about whether face amount and profitability are appropriate classification considerations under accepted actuarial standards.

The text of ASOP 2 (the actuarial principle cited by Phoenix) does not clearly resolve the factual dispute. With respect to "Policy Classes," the rule states:

> Policies will usually be grouped into classes for purposes of determining nonguaranteed charges or benefits. The

determination policy may include a definition of the policy classes to be used. If the policy classes have not been defined in the determination policy, the actuary should establish policy classes considering criteria such as the following:

a. the similarity of the policy types;

b. the structure of policy factors and nonguaranteed charges or benefits;

c. the similarity of anticipated experience factors;

d. the time period over which the policies were issued; and

e. the underwriting and marketing characteristics of the policies.

Actuarial Standard of Practice No. 2, Nonguaranteed Charges or Benefits for Life Insurance Policies and Annuity Contracts, at § 3.4 (Actuarial Standards Board, March 2013). This language offers only general guidance and does not settle the issue of whether it is appropriate under actuarial standards to classify insureds based on their age and face amounts. Given the experts' differing opinions regarding the relevant actuarial standards, an issue of fact remains.

. . .

The Court thus denies the parties' cross motions for summary judgment on this breach of contract claim.

. . . .

NOTES AND QUESTIONS

1. *Unfair Discrimination?* Almost every state prohibits "unfair discrimination." Yet, it is not clear in many states what constitutes "unfair discrimination." As reflected by the *Fleisher* case, however, most courts would agree that there must be an actuarially sound basis for discriminating among policyholders for such discrimination to be fair. Beyond that, states do not necessarily agree regarding what constitutes "unfair discrimination."

Instead of relying on courts to create definitions of "unfair discrimination" through the common law, some states codify the prohibition against "unfair discrimination" and then define the term. Consider, as an example, Arkansas' statute, Ark. Code Ann. § 23–66–206, which defines "unfair discrimination" as follows:

(14) "Unfair discrimination" means:

(A) Making or permitting any unfair discrimination between individuals of the same class and equal expectation of life in the rates charged for any contract of life insurance or of life annuity or in the dividends or other benefits payable thereon, or in any other of the terms and conditions of such a contract;

(B) Making or permitting any unfair discrimination between individuals of the same class and of essentially the same hazard in the amount of premium policy fees or rates charged for any policy or contract of accident and health insurance, or in the benefits payable thereunder, or in any of the terms or conditions of the contract, or in any other manner whatever;

(C) Making or permitting any unfair discrimination between individuals or risks of the same class and of essentially the same hazards by refusing to issue, refusing to renew, cancelling, or limiting the amount of insurance coverage on a property or casualty risk because of the geographic location of the risk unless:

(i) The refusal, cancellation, or limitation is for a business purpose that is not a mere pretext for unfair discrimination; or

(ii) The refusal, cancellation, or limitation is required by law or regulatory mandate;

(D) Making or permitting any unfair discrimination between individuals or risks of the same class and of essentially the same hazards by refusing to issue, refusing to renew, cancelling, or limiting the amount of insurance coverage on a residential property risk or on the personal property contained therein because of the age of the residential property unless:

(i) The refusal, cancellation, or limitation is for a business purpose that is not a mere pretext for unfair discrimination; or

(ii) The refusal, cancellation, or limitation is required by law or regulatory mandate;

(E) Refusing to insure, refusing to continue to insure, or limiting the amount of coverage available to an individual because of the marital status of the individual. However, nothing in this subdivision (14)(E) shall prohibit an insurer from taking marital status into account for the purpose of defining persons eligible for dependent benefits;

(F) Terminating or modifying coverage or refusing to issue or refusing to renew any policy or contract of insurance solely because the applicant or insured or any employee of either is mentally or physically impaired. However, this subdivision (14)(F) shall not be interpreted to modify any other provision of law relating to the termination, modification, issuance, or renewal of any insurance policy or contract; and

(G) (i) Refusing to insure or continue to insure an individual or risks solely because of the individual's race, color, creed, national origin, citizenship, status as a victim of domestic abuse, or sex.

. . . .

2. *Gender Discrimination in Insurance.* The average life expectancy at birth in the United States is longer for females than males. Suppose an insurer offers a life insurance product which charges older applicants more than younger ones (based on a table that sets a higher premium for each additional year of an applicant's age) but makes no distinction based on the applicant's sex. Would you expect more men or more women to purchase the product? How would the insurer's risk pool be affected if a competing insurer decided to offer the same product except that women would pay slightly less (at each age) than men to account for the average advantage women enjoy in longevity?

Under the logic of two U.S. Supreme Court cases, it is a violation of Title VII of the Civil Rights Act of 1964, 42 U.S.C. § 2000e 2(a)(1), for an employer to provide its employees any kind of insurance benefit, including life insurance or a retirement plan, unless identical benefits are provided to both men and women and unless contributions, if any, are the same for both sexes. *See Los Angeles Department of Water & Power v. Manhart*, 435 U.S. 702 (1978); *Arizona Governing Committee v. Norris*, 463 U.S. 1073 (1983). Thus, unless the practice is specifically prohibited by state law, or unless the insurance coverage is provided as a fringe benefit in the employment setting where Title VII will apply, insurers may permissibly charge men and women different prices for the same coverage. Is this unfairly discriminatory?

The evidence shows that young male drivers have many more injury-producing and damage-causing accidents than young female drivers (although this gap has been closing in recent years). Should young men pay more for auto insurance than young women, or should young men and young women pay the same? Why not use the frequency of injury-producing and damage-causing accidents to set auto insurance premiums instead of sex and age? For more discussion, *see* Robert H. Jerry II & Douglas R. Richmond, Understanding Insurance Law § 24[a] (5th ed. 2012).

Telematics is changing—some may say, disrupting—the automobile insurance market. With the advent of low-cost devices that can record details about driving distances, speeds, braking, g-forces during cornering, hours of operation, and virtually anything else about a driver's behavior, insurers now have the capability of inexpensively tailoring rates to fit an individual's particular risk profile. Is it unfairly discriminatory *not* to require the use of this technology? Do you have privacy concerns with the collection of this data? Should those who want privacy (i.e., to exercise an option not to use these devices) be required to pay more for their auto insurance?

3. *Race, Religion and Sex.* Current data show that white people, on average, enjoy longevity advantages over most minority groups. Should insurers be allowed to distinguish among individuals in the pricing of insurance based on the individual's race?

What about religion? If the evidence showed that Baptists have shorter average life spans than non-Baptists (we are aware of no data ever collected on this question), would it be appropriate for insurers to charge Baptists more for life insurance? Are your answers to these questions consistent with your answers to the questions posed with respect to insurance distinctions based on the individual's sex?

These questions demonstrate that insurance law reflects, in many respects, the broader values of our society. It is now well-settled in the law that using race as a basis for charging people different prices for the same insurance coverage is unacceptable. But, as of 2017, sex discrimination does not get the same level of scrutiny as race discrimination, and this disparateness is reflected in more tolerance for sex-based distinctions in insurance.

4. *"Redlining."* Redlining refers to the practice of drawing "red lines" around certain geographic areas on a map and then declining to sell products or services in that location. For example, a bank might decide that residents of a particular area are poor risks for repayment of loans and, therefore, it might decide not to make loans to anyone in that area. If an insurer is concerned that properties in a particular geographic area present particularly high risks, the insurer might "redline" that area. If redlining has the effect of denying insurance coverage to disproportionate numbers of members of racial and ethnic minority groups, should the practice be allowed? If the practice is disallowed, can insurers be effectively prevented from achieving the same result by declining to designate agents to service particular areas, by charging higher prices for properties in certain areas, or by making discriminatory use of property inspections? Exactly what is wrong with insurers charging higher prices to higher-risk insureds? *See* William E. Murray, Note, *Homeowners Insurance Redlining: The Inadequacy of Federal Remedies and the Future of the Property Insurance War*, 4 Conn. Ins. L. J. 735 (1998).

5. *Genetic Classifications.* Suppose A applies for a policy of life insurance. A review of A's ancestry shows that A's parents and grandparents had a history of premature death due to heart disease. Suppose further that the evidence shows that A is more likely than other persons whose ancestors had no history of heart disease to die prematurely. B also applies for life insurance. B is identically situated to A except that B has no indications or family history of heart disease. Should an insurer be allowed to charge A more for life insurance than Applicant B? Does your answer change if the product is health insurance?

In 2003, the Human Genome Initiative, the massive research project coordinated by the National Institute for Health, completed the construction of a map of the human genome, the chromosomal material (i.e., DNA) where human genes reside and which defines many individual physical characteristics. The project identified many genes that correlate with diseases such as Huntington's disease, sickle cell anemia, and cystic fibrosis, and new discoveries are being announced regularly. If a genetic marker were discovered for certain kinds of heart disease and an inexpensive test were devised to identify the gene, should insurers be allowed to use the test for the purpose of charging those who have the gene higher premiums for life, disability, and health insurance? Scholarly commentaries on this subject are voluminous. For a survey of the arguments for and against allowing insurers to use genetic information, *see* Mark A. Hall, *Insurers' Use of Genetic Information*, 37 Jurimetrics J. 13 (1996).

6. *Credit Scores*. By some estimates, approximately 95 percent of auto insurers and 85 percent of homeowners insurers use credit scores to determine the premium amount to charge policyholders in states where this kind of underwriting is allowed. Some insurers calculate a "credit-based insurance score" that uses some, but not all, of the factors on which a regular credit score is based. Some states prohibit the use of credit scores in underwriting, some allow it in only specified lines of insurance, and other states allow it to be used in any line of insurance. *See Credit-Based Insurance Scores: How and Insurance Company Can Use Your Credit to Determine Your Premium*, Nat'l Ass'n Ins. Commissioners (June 2012), http://www.naic.org/documents/consumer_alert_credit_based_insurance_scores.htm. Is it fair for an insurer to calculate the policyholder's premium based on the past record of timely paying bills, how much debt the policyholder has, how long the policyholder has had lines of credit, whether the policyholder recently has applied for new credit, and the types of credit the policyholder has? Is this "unfairly discriminatory"? If "big data" shows that these factors correlate with a policyholder's likely claims history, is it fair for the insurer to use them? In auto insurance, is it fairer to use a factor like age or sex?

7. *Price Optimization*. Price optimization is a term generally used to refer to an insurer's practice of charging different policyholders different prices based on non-risk-related factors. This controversial practice is used, by some estimates, by about a quarter of all insurance companies and nearly half of all large companies. The most common example of price optimization involves an insurer giving a policyholder a discount if the policyholder threatens to change companies for some reason or is identified in "big data" as having browsed websites looking for better rates—whereas another policyholder with similar risk characteristics whose possible "disloyalty" to the company is not supported by any data would not be given the discount. In other words, many companies reward loyal customers with discounts, special offers, etc. But in insurance, if you are loyal to the company, your premium may be higher.

As of 2020, regulators in twenty states have prohibited or restricted the use of price optimization products—most under the reasoning that this practice is unfairly discriminatory. If you were the insurance commissioner, would you prohibit price optimization?

F. THE LIMITS OF STATE REGULATION

Generally speaking, the McCarran-Ferguson Act gives state insurance statutes supremacy over federal laws, but this statement is subject to significant qualification. The McCarran-Ferguson Act does not give the states supremacy over all activities of insurance companies. Rather, it allows states to regulate activities of insurers that are within the "business of insurance." What constitutes the "business of insurance" will be explored further in the next part of this chapter. If an activity is not within the "business of insurance," then the activity is subject to the full reach of Congress's authority under the Commerce Clause. Thus, many activities of insurers are subject to "paramount federal regulation" if the "business of insurance" is not involved. *See Securities and Exchange Commission v. National Securities, Inc.*, 393 U.S. 453, 459–60 (1969). For example, insurance companies must comply with federal tax laws, many of the filing and disclosure requirements of the securities laws, and federal labor laws. Moreover, Congress's decision in the McCarran-Ferguson Act to give state statutes primacy over Congress's exercise of its commerce power does not limit the applicability of the Equal Protection Clause. *See Metropolitan Life Insurance Co. v. Ward*, 470 U.S. 869 (1985).

III. FEDERAL REGULATION OF INSURANCE

A. THE MEANING OF "BOYCOTT"

As discussed in Chapter 4, there are two types of liability insurance policies—occurrence-based and claims-made. As reflected in some of the cases covered in that chapter, occurrence-based policies cover long-tail claims, such as asbestos and environmental claims, for injuries or damage that may manifest years after the relevant policy period, provided some injury or damage occurred during the policy period. In the 1980s and 1990s, insurers faced hundreds of billions of dollars of liabilities for long-tail asbestos and environmental claims under CGL policies. Consequently, insurers wanted to switch policyholders to claims-made CGL policies to create more certainty regarding insurers' liability for long-tail claims (i.e., insurers wanted to limit their liability for such claims). The *Hartford Fire Insurance* case is the product of the insurers' attempt to move CGL policyholders from occurrence-based coverage to claims-made coverage.

HARTFORD FIRE INS. CO. V. CALIFORNIA

509 U.S. 764 (1993)

Opinion

Justice Souter announced the judgment of the Court and delivered the opinion of the Court with respect to Parts I, II-A, III, and IV, and an opinion concurring in the judgment with respect to Part II-B.

The Sherman Act makes every contract, combination, or conspiracy in unreasonable restraint of interstate or foreign commerce illegal. 26 Stat. 209, as amended, 15 U.S.C. § 1. These consolidated cases present questions about the application of that Act to the insurance industry, both here and abroad. The plaintiffs (respondents here) allege that both domestic and foreign defendants (petitioners here) violated the Sherman Act by engaging in various conspiracies to affect the American insurance market. A group of domestic defendants argues that the McCarran-Ferguson Act, 59 Stat. 33, as amended, 15 U.S.C. § 1011 *et seq.*, precludes application of the Sherman Act to the conduct alleged; a group of foreign defendants argues that the principle of international comity requires the District Court to refrain from exercising jurisdiction over certain claims against it. We hold that most of the domestic defendants' alleged conduct is not immunized from antitrust liability by the McCarran-Ferguson Act, and that, even assuming it applies, the principle of international comity does not preclude District Court jurisdiction over the foreign conduct alleged.

I.

The two petitions before us stem from consolidated litigation comprising the complaints of 19 States and many private plaintiffs alleging that the defendants, members of the insurance industry, conspired in violation of § 1 of the Sherman Act to restrict the terms of coverage of commercial general liability (CGL) insurance available in the United States. Because the cases come to us on motions to dismiss, we take the allegations of the complaints as true.[2]

A.

According to the complaints, the object of the conspiracies was to force certain primary insurers (insurers who sell insurance directly to consumers) to change the terms of their standard CGL insurance policies to conform with the policies the defendant insurers wanted to sell. The defendants wanted four changes.

First, CGL insurance has traditionally been sold in the United States on an "occurrence" basis, through a policy obligating the insurer "to pay or defend claims, whenever made, resulting from an accident or 'injurious exposure to conditions' that occurred during the [specific time] period the policy was in effect." In place of this traditional "occurrence" trigger of coverage, the defendants wanted a "claims-made" trigger, obligating the insurer to pay or defend only those claims made during the policy period. Such a policy has the distinct advantage for the insurer that when the policy period ends without a claim having been made, the insurer can be certain that the policy will not expose it to any further liability.

Second, the defendants wanted the "claims-made" policy to have a "retroactive date" provision, which would further restrict coverage to claims based on incidents that occurred after a certain date. Such a

[2] Following the lower courts and the parties, see *In re Insurance Antitrust Litigation,* 938 F.2d 919, 924, 925 (CA9 1991), we will treat the complaint filed by California as representative of the claims of Alabama, Arizona, California, Massachusetts, New York, West Virginia, and Wisconsin, and the complaint filed by Connecticut as representative of the claims of Alaska, Colorado, Connecticut, Louisiana, Maryland, Michigan, Minnesota, Montana, New Jersey, Ohio, Pennsylvania, and Washington. . . .

provision eliminates the risk that an insurer, by issuing a claims-made policy, would assume liability arising from incidents that occurred before the policy's effective date, but remained undiscovered or caused no immediate harm. Third, CGL insurance has traditionally covered "sudden and accidental" pollution; the defendants wanted to eliminate that coverage. Finally, CGL insurance has traditionally provided that the insurer would bear the legal costs of defending covered claims against the insured without regard to the policy's stated limits of coverage; the defendants wanted legal defense costs to be counted against the stated limits (providing a "legal defense cost cap").

To understand how the defendants are alleged to have pressured the targeted primary insurers to make these changes, one must be aware of two important features of the insurance industry. First, most primary insurers rely on certain outside support services for the type of insurance coverage they wish to sell. Defendant Insurance Services Office, Inc. (ISO), an association of approximately 1,400 domestic property and casualty insurers (including the primary insurer defendants, Hartford Fire Insurance Company, Allstate Insurance Company, CIGNA Corporation, and Aetna Casualty and Surety Company), is the almost exclusive source of support services in this country for CGL insurance. ISO develops standard policy forms and files or lodges them with each State's insurance regulators; most CGL insurance written in the United States is written on these forms. All of the "traditional" features of CGL insurance relevant to this litigation were embodied in the ISO standard CGL insurance form that had been in use since 1973 (1973 ISO CGL form). For each of its standard policy forms, ISO also supplies actuarial and rating information: it collects, aggregates, interprets, and distributes data on the premiums charged, claims filed and paid, and defense costs expended with respect to each form, and on the basis of this data it predicts future loss trends and calculates advisory premium rates. Most ISO members cannot afford to continue to use a form if ISO withdraws these support services.

Second, primary insurers themselves usually purchase insurance to cover a portion of the risk they assume from the consumer. This so-called "reinsurance" may serve at least two purposes, protecting the primary insurer from catastrophic loss, and allowing the primary insurer to sell more insurance than its own financial capacity might otherwise permit. Thus, "[t]he availability of reinsurance affects the ability and willingness of primary insurers to provide insurance to their customers." Insurers who sell reinsurance themselves often purchase insurance to cover part of the risk they assume from the primary insurer; such "retrocessional reinsurance" does for reinsurers what reinsurance does for primary insurers. Many of the defendants here are reinsurers or reinsurance brokers, or play some other specialized role in the reinsurance business;

defendant Reinsurance Association of America (RAA) is a trade association of domestic reinsurers.

B.

The prehistory of events claimed to give rise to liability starts in 1977, when ISO began the process of revising its 1973 CGL form. For the first time, it proposed two CGL forms (1984 ISO CGL forms), one the traditional "occurrence" type, the other "with a new 'claims-made' trigger." The "claims-made" form did not have a retroactive date provision, however, and both 1984 forms covered " 'sudden and accidental' pollution" damage and provided for unlimited coverage of legal defense costs by the insurer. Within the ISO, defendant Hartford Fire Insurance Company objected to the proposed 1984 forms; it desired elimination of the "occurrence" form, a retroactive date provision on the "claims-made" form, elimination of sudden and accidental pollution coverage, and a legal defense cost cap. Defendant Allstate Insurance Company also expressed its desire for a retroactive date provision on the "claims-made" form. Majorities in the relevant ISO committees, however, supported the proposed 1984 CGL forms and rejected the changes proposed by Hartford and Allstate. In December 1983, the ISO Board of Directors approved the proposed 1984 forms, and ISO filed or lodged the forms with state regulators in March 1984.

Dissatisfied with this state of affairs, the defendants began to take other steps to force a change in the terms of coverage of CGL insurance generally available, steps that, the plaintiffs allege, implemented a series of conspiracies in violation of § 1 of the Sherman Act. The plaintiffs recount these steps as a number of separate episodes corresponding to different claims for relief in their complaints; because it will become important to distinguish among these counts and the acts and defendants associated with them, we will note these correspondences.

The first four Claims for Relief in the California Complaint and the Second Claim for Relief in the Connecticut Complaint charge the four domestic primary insurer defendants and varying groups of domestic and foreign reinsurers, brokers, and associations with conspiracies to manipulate the ISO CGL forms. In March 1984, primary insurer Hartford persuaded General Reinsurance Corporation (General Re), the largest American reinsurer, to take steps either to procure desired changes in the ISO CGL forms, or "failing that, [to] 'derail' the entire ISO CGL forms program." General Re took up the matter with its trade association, RAA, which created a special committee that met and agreed to "boycott" the 1984 ISO CGL forms unless a retroactive-date provision was added to the claims-made form, and a pollution exclusion and defense cost cap were added to both forms. RAA then sent a letter to ISO "announc[ing] that its members would not provide reinsurance for coverages written on the 1984 CGL forms," and Hartford and General Re enlisted a domestic reinsurance broker to give a speech to the ISO Board of Directors, in which he stated that no reinsurers would "break ranks" to reinsure the 1984 ISO CGL forms.

The four primary insurer defendants (Hartford, Aetna, CIGNA, and Allstate) also encouraged key actors in the London reinsurance market, an important provider of reinsurance for North American risks, to withhold reinsurance for coverages written on the 1984 ISO CGL forms. As a consequence, many London-based underwriters, syndicates, brokers, and reinsurance companies informed ISO of their intention to withhold reinsurance on the 1984 forms, and at least some of them told ISO that they would withhold reinsurance until ISO incorporated all four desired changes into the ISO CGL forms.

For the first time ever, ISO invited representatives of the domestic and foreign reinsurance markets to speak at an ISO Executive Committee meeting. At that meeting, the reinsurers "presented their agreed upon positions that there would be changes in the CGL forms or no reinsurance." The ISO Executive Committee then voted to include a retroactive-date provision in the claims-made form, and to exclude all pollution coverage from both new forms. (But it neither eliminated the occurrence form, nor added a legal defense cost cap.) The 1984 ISO CGL forms were then withdrawn from the marketplace, and replaced with forms (1986 ISO CGL forms) containing the new provisions. After ISO got regulatory approval of the 1986 forms in most States where approval was needed, it eliminated its support services for the 1973 CGL form, thus rendering it impossible for most ISO members to continue to use the form.

. . . .

C

Nineteen States and a number of private plaintiffs filed 36 complaints against the insurers involved in this course of events, charging that the conspiracies described above violated § 1 of the Sherman Act, 15 U.S.C. § 1. After the actions had been consolidated for litigation in the Northern District of California, the defendants moved to dismiss for failure to state a cause of action, or, in the alternative, for summary judgment. The District Court granted the motions to dismiss. *In re Insurance Antitrust Litigation,* 723 F.Supp. 464 (1989). It held that the conduct alleged fell within the grant of antitrust immunity contained in § 2(b) of the McCarran-Ferguson Act, 15 U.S.C. § 1012(b), because it amounted to "the business of insurance" and was "regulated by State Law" within the meaning of that section; none of the conduct, in the District Court's view, amounted to a "boycott" within the meaning of the § 3(b) exception to that grant of immunity. 15 U.S.C. § 1013(b). . . .

The Court of Appeals reversed. *In re Insurance Antitrust Litigation,* 938 F.2d 919 (CA9 1991). Although it held the conduct involved to be "the business of insurance" within the meaning of § 2(b), it concluded that the defendants could not claim McCarran-Ferguson Act antitrust immunity for two independent reasons. First, it held, the foreign reinsurers were beyond the regulatory jurisdiction of the States; because their activities could not be "regulated by State Law" within the meaning of § 2(b), they did not fall within that section's grant of immunity. Although the domestic insurers were "regulated by State Law," the court held, they forfeited their § 2(b) exemption when they conspired with the nonexempt foreign reinsurers. Second, the Court of Appeals held that, even if the conduct alleged fell within the scope of § 2(b), it also fell within the § 3(b) exception for "act[s] of boycott, coercion, or intimidation."

. . . .

We granted certiorari in No. 91–1111 to address two narrow questions about the scope of McCarran-Ferguson Act antitrust immunity. . . . We now affirm in part, reverse in part, and remand.

. . . .

[JUSTICE SCALIA delivered the Court's opinion with respect to the following part.]

Determining proper application of § 3(b) of the McCarran-Ferguson Act to the present cases requires precise definition of the word "boycott."[1] It is a relatively new word, little more than a century old. It was first used in 1880, to describe the collective action taken against Captain Charles Boycott, an English agent managing various estates in Ireland. The Land League, an Irish organization formed the previous year, had demanded that landlords reduce their rents and had urged tenants to avoid dealing with those who failed to do so. Boycott did not bend to the demand and instead ordered evictions. In retaliation, the tenants "sen[t] Captain Boycott to Coventry in a very thorough manner." J. McCarthy, England Under Gladstone 108 (1886). "The population of the region for miles round resolved not to have anything to do with him, and, as far as they could prevent it, not to allow anyone else to have anything to do with him. . . . [T]he awful sentence of excommunication could hardly have rendered him more helplessly alone for a time. No one would work for him; no one would supply him with food." *Id.,* at 108–109; see also H. Laidler, Boycotts and the Labor Struggle 23–27 (1968). Thus, the verb made from the unfortunate Captain's name has had from the outset the meaning it continues to carry today. To "boycott" means "[t]o combine in refusing to hold relations of any kind, social or commercial, public or private, with (a

[1] Section 3(b) of the McCarran-Ferguson Act, 15 U.S.C. § 1013(b), provides:

"Nothing contained in this Act shall render the said Sherman Act inapplicable to any agreement to boycott, coerce, or intimidate, or act of boycott, coercion, or intimidation."

neighbour), on account of political or other differences, so as to punish him for the position he has taken up, or coerce him into abandoning it." 2 Oxford English Dictionary 468 (2d ed. 1989).

Petitioners have suggested that a boycott ordinarily requires "an absolute refusal to deal on any terms," which was concededly not the case here. We think not. As the definition just recited provides, the refusal may be imposed "to punish [the target] for the position he has taken up, or *coerce him into abandoning it.*" The refusal to deal may, in other words, be *conditional,* offering its target the incentive of renewed dealing if and when he mends his ways. This is often the case—and indeed seems to have been the case with the original Boycott boycott. . . .

It is, however, important—and crucial in the present cases—to distinguish between a conditional boycott and a concerted agreement to seek particular terms in particular transactions. A concerted agreement to terms (a "cartelization") is "a way of obtaining and exercising market power by concertedly exacting terms like those which a monopolist might exact." L. Sullivan, Law of Antitrust 257 (1977). The parties to such an agreement (the members of a cartel) are not engaging in a boycott, because:

> They are not coercing anyone, at least in the usual sense of that word; they are merely (though concertedly) saying "*we will deal with you only on the following trade terms.*"
>
> . . . Indeed, if a concerted agreement, say, to include a security deposit in all contracts is a "boycott" because it excludes all buyers who won't agree to it, then by parity of reasoning every price fixing agreement would be a boycott also. The use of the single concept, boycott, to cover agreements so varied in nature can only add to confusion.

Ibid. (emphasis added).

Thus, if Captain Boycott's tenants had agreed among themselves that they would refuse to renew their leases unless he reduced his rents, that would have been a concerted agreement on the terms of the leases, but not a boycott. The tenants, of course, did more than that; they refused to engage in other, unrelated transactions with Boycott—*e.g.,* selling him food—unless he agreed to their terms on rents. It is this expansion of the refusal to deal beyond the targeted transaction that gives great coercive force to a commercial boycott: unrelated transactions are used as leverage to achieve the terms desired.

. . . .

Of course as far as the Sherman Act (outside the exempted insurance field) is concerned, concerted agreements on contract terms are as unlawful as boycotts. . . . These sorts of concerted actions, similar to what is alleged to have occurred here, are not properly characterized as "boycotts," and the word does not appear in the opinions. In fact, in the 65 years between the coining of the word and enactment of the McCarran-Ferguson Act in 1945, "boycott" appears in only seven opinions of this Court involving commercial (nonlabor) antitrust matters, and *not once* is it used as Justice SOUTER uses it—to describe a concerted refusal to engage in particular transactions until the terms of those transactions are agreeable.

. . . .

The one case in which we have found an activity to constitute a "boycott" within the meaning of the McCarran-Ferguson Act is *St. Paul Fire & Marine Ins. Co. v. Barry,* 438 U.S. 531, 98 S.Ct. 2923, 57 L.Ed.2d 932 (1978). There the plaintiffs were licensed physicians and their patients, and the defendant (St. Paul) was a malpractice insurer that had refused to renew the physicians' policies on an "occurrence" basis, but insisted upon a "claims made" basis. The allegation was that, at the instance of St. Paul, the three other malpractice insurers in the State had collectively refused to write insurance for St. Paul's customers, thus forcing them to accept St. Paul's renewal terms. Unsurprisingly, we held the allegation sufficient to state a cause of action. The insisted-upon condition of the boycott (not being a former St. Paul policyholder) was "artificial": it bore no relationship (or an "artificial" relationship) to the proposed contracts of insurance that the physicians wished to conclude with St. Paul's competitors.

. . . .

Under the test set forth above, there are sufficient allegations of a "boycott" to sustain the relevant counts of complaint against a motion to dismiss. For example, the complaints allege that some of the defendant reinsurers threatened to "withdra[w] entirely from the business of reinsuring primary U.S. insurers who wrote on the occurrence form." Construed most favorably to respondents, that allegation claims that primary insurers who wrote insurance on disfavored forms would be refused all reinsurance, *even* as to risks written on *other forms.* If that were the case, the reinsurers might have been engaging in a boycott—they would, that is, unless the primary insurers' other business were relevant to the proposed reinsurance contract (for example, if the reinsurer bears greater risk where the primary insurer engages in riskier businesses). *Cf.* Gonye, Underwriting the Reinsured, in Reinsurance 439, 463–466 (R. Strain ed. 1980); 2 R. Reinarz, J. Schloss, G. Patrik, & P. Kensicki, Reinsurance Practices 21–23 (1990) (same). Other allegations in the complaints could be similarly construed. For example, the complaints also allege that the reinsurers "threatened a boycott of North American CGL risks," not just CGL risks containing dissatisfactory terms, that "the foreign and domestic reinsurer representatives presented their agreed upon positions that there would be changes in the CGL forms or no reinsurance," that some of the defendant insurers and reinsurers told "groups of insurance brokers and agents . . . that a reinsurance boycott, and thus loss of income to the agents and brokers who would be unable to find available markets for their customers, would ensue if the [revised] ISO forms were not approved."

Many other allegations in the complaints describe conduct that may amount to a boycott if the plaintiffs can prove certain additional facts. For example, General Re, the largest American reinsurer, is alleged to have "agreed to either coerce ISO to adopt [the defendants'] demands or, failing that, 'derail' the entire CGL forms program." If this means that General Re intended to withhold all reinsurance on all CGL forms—even forms having no objectionable terms—that might amount to a "boycott." Also, General Re and several other domestic reinsurers are alleged to have "agreed to boycott the 1984 ISO forms unless a retroactive date was added to the claims-made form, and a pollution exclusion and a defense cost cap were added to both [the occurrence and claims made] forms." Liberally construed, this allegation may mean that the defendants had linked their demands so that they would continue to refuse to do business on *either* form until *both* were changed to their liking. Again, that might amount to a boycott. "[A] complaint should not be dismissed unless 'it appears beyond doubt that the plaintiff can prove no set of facts in support of his claim which would entitle him to relief.' "

[Consequently, the Court of Appeals' ruling is affirmed in part and reversed in part.]

NOTES AND QUESTIONS

1. *What Happened on Remand?* The case settled on remand. Today, although ISO offers a claims-made CGL policy form, occurrence-based CGL policies still dominate the market. As discussed in Chapter 4, claims-made policy forms are used, however, in many other lines of liability insurance, and it is the dominant policy form used in many new lines of insurance.

2. *What Concerted Actions Are Allowed?* What concerted actions constitute a "boycott," which is disallowed under the McCarran-Ferguson Act, and what concerted actions are allowed? For example, is ISO allowed to require insurers to be members of ISO in order to gain access to claims data? Can ISO require insurers to use ISO's policy forms?

3. *Repeal of McCarran-Ferguson Act?* Why should insurers be immune from the antitrust prohibitions of the Sherman Act? One of the justifications for such immunity is that insurers need to be able to share claims data in order to be able to accurately price insurance, which in turn is necessary to ensure insurer solvency. Is that justification still true today in the age of the Internet and "Big Data"?

Although insurers compete on premium price in many lines of insurance, they often all use the same or very similar policy forms. What are the arguments in favor of and against allowing insurers to sell the same policy form?

EXERCISE

1. Draft a 2-page memo that sets forth the argument for the repeal of the McCarran-Ferguson Act.

B. GROUP INSURANCE PLANS AND ERISA

Many types of insurance, such as health insurance, life insurance, and disability insurance, are provided by employers to their employees as fringe benefits. There are three primary reasons for this: 1) subject to some limitations, these benefits are excluded from the employee's taxable income, which means an additional "dollar of fringe benefit" is worth more to the employee than an additional dollar of salary, which is taxable; 2) if the employee pays any portion of the premium, the premium amounts paid can be, at the employee's option, directly offset from taxable income, which reduces the amount of income taxes that the employee will pay; and 3) group insurance provided through employment is less expensive per unit of coverage due to the administrative cost savings associated with managing large plans and the minimization of adverse selection concerns resulting from the risk pooling impact when large numbers of insureds are combined for purposes of coverage. A fourth consideration is not related to insurance, per se, but providing fringe benefits to employees has benefits to the employer in terms of employee satisfaction and loyalty.

Unlike most questions of insurance law, which are governed by state law as discussed earlier in this chapter, employer-provided insurance as a fringe benefit in the employment setting creates one of the few exceptions where insurance is subject to federal law too. Whenever insurance is provided to an employee as a fringe benefit, it is necessary to consider the implications of a federal statute known as the Employment Retirement Income Security Act of 1974 (ERISA). ERISA has a number of aspects that create variations on the substance or impact of state insurance law. In this subchapter, two aspects will be explored: 1) the preemptive effect of ERISA on state insurance laws, and what that means for certain state insurance law claims; and 2) challenging denials of coverage under insurance plans governed by ERISA.

1. ERISA Preemption

PILOT LIFE INS. CO. V. DEDEAUX

481 U.S. 41 (1987)

O'CONNOR, J., delivered the opinion for a unanimous Court.

This case presents the question whether the Employee Retirement Income Security Act of 1974 (ERISA), 88 Stat. 829, as amended, 29 U.S.C. § 1001 *et seq.,* pre-empts state common law tort and contract actions asserting improper processing of a claim for benefits under an insured employee benefit plan.

I.

In March 1975, in Gulfport, Mississippi, respondent Everate W. Dedeaux injured his back in an accident related to his employment for Entex, Inc. (Entex). Entex had at this time a long term disability employee benefit plan established by purchasing a group insurance policy from petitioner, Pilot Life Insurance Co. (Pilot Life). Entex collected and matched its employees' contributions to the plan and forwarded those funds to Pilot Life; the employer also provided forms to its employees for processing disability claims, and forwarded completed forms to Pilot Life. Pilot Life bore the responsibility of determining who would receive disability benefits. Although Dedeaux sought permanent disability benefits following the 1975 accident, Pilot Life terminated his benefits after two years. During the following three years Dedeaux's benefits were reinstated and terminated by Pilot Life several times.

In 1980, Dedeaux instituted a diversity action against Pilot Life in the United States District Court for the Southern District of Mississippi. Dedeaux's complaint contained three counts: "Tortious Breach of Contract"; "Breach of Fiduciary Duties"; and "Fraud in the Inducement." App. 18–23. Dedeaux sought "[d]amages for failure to provide benefits under the insurance policy in a sum to be determined at the time of trial," "[g]eneral damages for mental and emotional distress and other incidental damages in the sum of $250,000.00," and "[p]unitive and exemplary damages in the sum of $500,000.00." *Id.,* at 23–24. Dedeaux did not assert any of the several causes of action available to him under ERISA. . . .

At the close of discovery, Pilot Life moved for summary judgment, arguing that ERISA pre-empted Dedeaux's common law claim for failure to pay benefits on the group insurance policy. The District Court granted Pilot Life summary judgment, finding all Dedeaux's claims pre-empted. App. to Pet. Cert. 16a.

The Court of Appeals for the Fifth Circuit reversed, primarily on the basis of this Court's decision in *Metropolitan Life Ins. Co. v. Massachusetts,* 471 U.S. 724, 105 S.Ct. 2380, 85 L.Ed.2d 728 (1985). See 770 F.2d 1311 (1985).

We granted certiorari, 478 U.S. 1004, 106 S.Ct. 3293, 92 L.Ed.2d 708 (1986), and now reverse.

II.

In ERISA, Congress set out to:

> "protect . . . participants in employee benefit plans and their beneficiaries, by requiring the disclosure and reporting to participants and beneficiaries of financial and other information with respect thereto, by establishing standards of conduct, responsibility, and obligation for fiduciaries of employee benefit plans, and by providing for appropriate remedies, sanctions, and ready access to the Federal courts." § 2, as set forth in 29 U.S.C. § 1001(b).

ERISA comprehensively regulates, among other things, employee welfare benefit plans that, "through the purchase of insurance or otherwise," provide medical, surgical, or hospital care, or benefits in the event of sickness, accident, disability, or death. § 3(1), 29 U.S.C. § 1002(1).

Congress capped off the massive undertaking of ERISA with three provisions relating to the pre-emptive effect of the federal legislation:

> "Except as provided in subsection (b) of this section [the saving clause], the provisions of this subchapter and subchapter III of this chapter shall supersede any and all State laws insofar as they may now or hereafter relate to any employee benefit plan. . . ." § 514(a), as set forth in 29 U.S.C. § 1144(a) (pre-emption clause).
>
> "Except as provided in subparagraph (B) [the deemer clause], nothing in this subchapter shall be construed to exempt or relieve any person from any law of any State which regulates insurance, banking, or securities." § 514(b)(2)(A), as set forth in 29 U.S.C. § 1144(b)(2)(A) (saving clause).
>
> "Neither an employee benefit plan . . . nor any trust established under such a plan, shall be deemed to be an insurance company or other insurer, bank, trust company, or investment company or to be engaged in the business of insurance or banking for purposes of any law of any State purporting to regulate insurance companies, insurance contracts, banks, trust companies, or investment companies." § 514(b)(2)(B), 29 U.S.C. § 1144(b)(2)(B) (deemer clause).

To summarize the pure mechanics of the provisions quoted above: If a state law "relate[s] to . . . employee benefit plan[s]," it is pre-empted. § 514(a). The saving clause excepts from the pre-emption clause laws that "regulat[e] insurance." § 514(b)(2)(A). The deemer clause makes clear that a state law that "purport[s] to regulate insurance" cannot deem an employee benefit plan to be an insurance company. § 514(b)(2)(B).

"[T]he question whether a certain state action is pre-empted by federal law is one of congressional intent. " 'The purpose of Congress is the ultimate touchstone.' " " *Allis-Chalmers Corp. v. Lueck,* 471 U.S. 202, 208, 105 S.Ct. 1904, 1909, 85 L.Ed.2d 206 (1985), quoting *Malone v. White Motor Corp.,* 435 U.S. 497, 504, 98 S.Ct. 1185, 1189, 55 L.Ed.2d 443 (1978), quoting *Retail Clerks v. Schermerhorn,* 375 U.S. 96, 103, 84 S.Ct. 219, 222, 11 L.Ed.2d 179 (1963). We have observed in the past that the express pre-emption provisions of ERISA are deliberately expansive, and designed to "establish pension plan regulation as exclusively a federal concern." *Alessi v. Raybestos-Manhattan, Inc.,* 451 U.S. 504, 523, 101 S.Ct. 1895, 1906, 68 L.Ed.2d 402 (1981). As we explained in *Shaw v. Delta Air Lines, Inc.,* 463 U.S. 85, 98, 103 S.Ct. 2890, 2900, 77 L.Ed.2d 490 (1983):

> The bill that became ERISA originally contained a limited pre-emption clause, applicable only to state laws relating to the specific subjects covered by ERISA. The Conference Committee rejected those provisions in favor of the present language, and indicated that section's pre-emptive scope was as broad as its language. *See* H.R.Conf.Rep. No. 93–1280, p. 383 (1974); S.Conf.Rep. No. 93–1090, p. 383 (1974).

The House and Senate sponsors emphasized both the breadth and importance of the pre-emption provisions. Representative Dent described the "reservation to Federal authority [of] the sole power to regulate the field of employee benefit plans" as ERISA's "crowning achievement." 120 Cong.Rec. 29197 (1974). Senator Williams said:

> It should be stressed that with the narrow exceptions specified in the bill, the substantive and enforcement provisions of the conference substitute are intended to preempt the field for Federal regulations, thus eliminating the threat of conflicting or inconsistent State and local regulation of employee benefit plans. This principle is intended to apply in its broadest sense to all actions of State or local governments, or any instrumentality thereof, which have the force or effect of law.

Id., at 29933. *See also Shaw v. Delta Air Lines, Inc., supra,* at 99–100, n. 20, 103 S.Ct., at 2901, n. 20 (describing remarks of Sen. Javits).

In *Metropolitan Life,* this Court, noting that the pre-emption and saving clauses "perhaps are not a model of legislative drafting," 471 U.S., at 739, 105 S.Ct., at 2389, interpreted these clauses in relation to a Massachusetts statute that required minimum mental health care benefits to be provided Massachusetts residents covered by general health insurance policies. The appellants in *Metropolitan Life* argued that the state statute, as applied to insurance policies purchased by employee health care plans regulated by ERISA, was pre-empted.

The Court concluded, first, that the Massachusetts statute did "relate to . . . employee benefit plan[s]," thus placing the state statute within the broad sweep of the pre-emption clause, § 514(a). *Metropolitan Life, supra,* at 739, 105 S.Ct., at 2389. However, the Court held that, because the state statute was one that "regulate[d] insurance," the saving clause prevented the state law from being pre-empted. In determining whether the Massachusetts statute regulated insurance, the Court was guided by case law interpreting the phrase "business of insurance" in the McCarran-Ferguson Act, 59 Stat. 33, as amended, 15 U.S.C. § 1011 *et seq.*

Given the "statutory complexity" of ERISA's three pre-emption provisions, *Metropolitan Life, supra,* at 740, 105 S.Ct., at 2389, as well as the wide variety of state statutory and decisional law arguably affected by the federal pre-emption provisions, it is not surprising that we are again called on to interpret these provisions.

III.

There is no dispute that the common law causes of action asserted in Dedeaux's complaint "relate to" an employee benefit plan and therefore fall under ERISA's express pre-emption clause, § 514(a). In both *Metropolitan Life, supra,* and *Shaw v. Delta Air Lines, Inc., supra,* 463 U.S., at 96–100, 103 S.Ct., at 2899–2901, we noted the expansive sweep of the pre-emption clause. In both cases "[t]he phrase 'relate to' was given its broad common-sense meaning, such that a state law 'relate[s] to' a benefit plan 'in the normal sense of the phrase, if it has a connection with or reference to such a plan.'" *Metropolitan Life, supra,* 471 U.S., at 739, 105 S.Ct., at 2389, quoting *Shaw v. Delta Air Lines, supra,* 463 U.S., at 97, 103 S.Ct., at 2900. In particular we have emphasized that the pre-emption clause is not limited to "state laws specifically designed to affect employee benefit plans." *Shaw v. Delta Air Lines, supra,* at 98, 103 S.Ct., at 2900. The common law causes of action raised in Dedeaux's complaint, each based on alleged improper processing of a claim for benefits under an employee benefit plan, undoubtedly meet the criteria for pre-emption under § 514(a).

Unless these common law causes of action fall under an exception to § 514(a), therefore, they are expressly pre-empted. Although Dedeaux's complaint pleaded several state common law causes of action, before this Court Dedeaux has described only one of the three counts-called "tortious breach of contract" in the complaint, and "the Mississippi law of bad faith" in respondent's brief-as protected from the pre-emptive effect of § 514(a).

The Mississippi law of bad faith, Dedeaux argues, is a law "which regulates insurance," and thus is saved from pre-emption by § 514(b)(2)(A).[1]

In *Metropolitan Life,* we were guided by several considerations in determining whether a state law falls under the saving clause. First, we took what guidance was available from a "common-sense view" of the language of the saving clause itself. 471 U.S., at 740, 105 S.Ct., at 2389. Second, we made use of the case law interpreting the phrase "business of insurance" under the McCarran-Ferguson Act, 15 U.S.C. § 1011 *et seq.,* in interpreting the saving clause.[2] Three criteria have been used to determine whether a practice falls under the "business of insurance" for purposes of the McCarran-Ferguson Act:

> *[F]irst,* whether the practice has the effect of transferring or spreading a policyholder's risk; *second,* whether the practice is an integral part of the policy relationship between the insurer and the insured; and *third,* whether the practice is limited to entities within the insurance industry. *Union Labor Life Ins. Co. v. Pireno,* 458 U.S. 119, 129, 102 S.Ct. 3002, 3009, 73 L.Ed.2d 647 (1982) (emphasis in original).

In the present case, the considerations weighed in *Metropolitan Life* argue against the assertion that the Mississippi law of bad faith is a state law that "regulates insurance."

As early as 1915 the Mississippi Supreme Court had recognized that punitive damages were available in a contract case when "the act or omission constituting the breach of the contract amounts also to the commission of a tort." *See Hood v. Moffett,* 109 Miss. 757, 767, 69 So. 664, 666 (1915) (involving a physician's breach of a contract to attend to a woman at her approaching "accouchement"). In *American Railway Express Co. v. Bailey,* 142 Miss. 622, 631, 107 So. 761, 763 (1926), a case involving a failure of a finance company to deliver to the plaintiff the correct amount of money cabled to the plaintiff through the finance company's offices, the Mississippi Supreme Court explained that punitive damages could be available when the breach of contract was "attended by some intentional wrong, insult, abuse, or gross negligence, which amounts to an independent tort." In *Standard Life Insurance Co. v. Veal,* 354 So.2d 239 (1977), the Mississippi Supreme Court, citing *D.L. Fair Lumber Co. v. Weems,* 196 Miss. 201, 16 So.2d 770 (1944) (breach of contract was accompanied by "the breaking down and destruction of another's fence"), *American Railway*

[1] Decisional law that "regulates insurance" may fall under the saving clause. The saving clause, § 514(b)(2)(A), covers "any law of any State." For purposes of § 514, "[t]he term 'State law' includes all laws, decisions, rules, regulations, or other State action having the effect of law, of any State." 29 U.S.C. §§ 1144(c)(1) and (2).

[2] The McCarran-Ferguson Act provides, in relevant part: "The business of insurance, and every person engaged therein, shall be subject to the laws of the several States which relate to the regulation or taxation of such business." 15 U.S.C. § 1012(a).

Express Co. v. Bailey, supra, and *Hood v. Moffett, supra,* upheld an award of punitive damages against a defendant insurance company for failure to pay on a credit life policy. Since *Veal,* the Mississippi Supreme Court has considered a large number of cases in which plaintiffs have sought punitive damages from insurance companies for failure to pay a claim under an insurance contract, and in a great many of these cases the court has used the identical formulation, first stated in *Bailey,* of what must "attend" the breach of contract in order for punitive damages to be recoverable. Recently the Mississippi Supreme Court stated that "[w]e have come to term an insurance carrier which refuses to pay a claim when there is no reasonably arguable basis to deny it as acting in 'bad faith,' and a lawsuit based upon such an arbitrary refusal as a 'bad faith' cause of action." *Blue Cross & Blue Shield of Mississippi, Inc. v. Campbell,* 466 So.2d 833, 842 (Miss. 1984).

Certainly a common-sense understanding of the phrase "regulates insurance" does not support the argument that the Mississippi law of bad faith falls under the saving clause. A common-sense view of the word "regulates" would lead to the conclusion that in order to regulate insurance, a law must not just have an impact on the insurance industry, but must be specifically directed toward that industry. Even though the Mississippi Supreme Court has identified its law of bad faith with the insurance industry, the roots of this law are firmly planted in the general principles of Mississippi tort and contract law. Any breach of contract, and not merely breach of an insurance contract, may lead to liability for punitive damages under Mississippi law.

Neither do the McCarran-Ferguson Act factors support the assertion that the Mississippi law of bad faith "regulates insurance." Unlike the mandated-benefits law at issue in *Metropolitan Life,* the Mississippi common law of bad faith does not effect a spreading of policyholder risk. The state common law of bad faith may be said to concern "the policy relationship between the insurer and the insured." The connection to the insurer-insured relationship is attenuated at best, however. In contrast to the mandated-benefits law in *Metropolitan Life,* the common law of bad faith does not define the terms of the relationship between the insurer and the insured; it declares only that, whatever terms have been agreed upon in the insurance contract, a breach of that contract may in certain circumstances allow the policyholder to obtain punitive damages. The state common law of bad faith is therefore no more "integral" to the insurer-insured relationship than any State's general contract law is integral to a contract made in that State. Finally, as we have just noted, Mississippi's law of bad faith, even if associated with the insurance industry, has developed from general principles of tort and contract law available in any Mississippi breach of contract case. Cf. *Hart v. Orion Ins. Co.,* 453 F.2d 1358 (CA10 1971) (general state arbitration statutes do not regulate the business of insurance under the McCarran-Ferguson Act); *Hamilton Life*

Ins. Co. v. Republic National Life Ins. Co., 408 F.2d 606 (CA2 1969) (same). Accordingly, the Mississippi common law of bad faith at most meets one of the three criteria used to identify the "business of insurance" under the McCarran-Ferguson Act, and used in *Metropolitan Life* to identify laws that "regulat[e] insurance" under the saving clause.

In the present case, moreover, we are obliged in interpreting the saving clause to consider not only the factors by which we were guided in *Metropolitan Life,* but also the role of the saving clause in ERISA as a whole. On numerous occasions we have noted that " " "[i]n expounding a statute, we must not be guided by a single sentence or member of a sentence, but look to the provisions of the whole law, and to its object and policy." " " *Kelly v. Robinson,* 479 U.S. 36, 43, 107 S.Ct. 353, 358, 93 L.Ed.2d 216 (1986), quoting *Offshore Logistics, Inc. v. Tallentire,* 477 U.S. 207, 221, 106 S.Ct. 2485, 2493, 91 L.Ed.2d 174 (1986) (quoting *Mastro Plastics Corp. v. NLRB,* 350 U.S. 270, 285, 76 S.Ct. 349, 359, 100 L.Ed. 309 (1956) (in turn quoting *United States v. Heirs of Boisdoré,* 8 How. 113, 122, 12 L.Ed. 1009 (1849))). Because in this case, the state cause of action seeks remedies for the improper processing of a claim for benefits under an ERISA-regulated plan, our understanding of the saving clause must be informed by the legislative intent concerning the civil enforcement provisions provided by ERISA § 502(a), 29 U.S.C. § 1132(a).

. . . . The conclusion that § 502(a) was intended to be exclusive is supported, first, by the language and structure of the civil enforcement provisions, and second, by legislative history in which Congress declared that the pre-emptive force of § 502(a) was modeled on the exclusive remedy provided by § 301 of the Labor Management Relations Act, 1947 (LMRA), 61 Stat. 156, 29 U.S.C. § 185.

The civil enforcement scheme of § 502(a) is one of the essential tools for accomplishing the stated purposes of ERISA.[3] The civil enforcement

---

[3] Section 502(a), as set forth in 29 U.S.C. § 1132(a), provides:

"A civil action may be brought—

(1) by a participant or beneficiary—

(A) for the relief provided for in subsection (c) of this section [concerning requests to the administrator for information], or

(B) to recover benefits due to him under the terms of his plan, to enforce his rights under the terms of the plan, or to clarify his rights to future benefits under the terms of the plan;

(2) by the Secretary, or by a participant, beneficiary or fiduciary for appropriate relief under section 1109 of this title [breach of fiduciary duty];

(3) by a participant, beneficiary, or fiduciary (A) to enjoin any act or practice which violates any provision of this subchapter or the terms of the plan, or (B) to obtain other appropriate equitable relief (i) to redress such violations or (ii) to enforce any provisions of this subchapter or the terms of the plan;

(4) by the Secretary, or by a participant, or beneficiary for appropriate relief in the case of a violation of 1025(c) of this title [information to be furnished to participants];

scheme is sandwiched between two other ERISA provisions relevant to enforcement of ERISA and to the processing of a claim for benefits under an employee benefit plan. Section 501, 29 U.S.C. § 1131, authorizes criminal penalties for violations of the reporting and disclosure provisions of ERISA. Section 503, 29 U.S.C. § 1133, requires every employee benefit plan to comply with Department of Labor regulations on giving notice to any participant or beneficiary whose claim for benefits has been denied, and affording a reasonable opportunity for review of the decision denying the claim. Under the civil enforcement provisions of § 502(a), a plan participant or beneficiary may sue to recover benefits due under the plan, to enforce the participant's rights under the plan, or to clarify rights to future benefits. Relief may take the form of accrued benefits due, a declaratory judgment on entitlement to benefits, or an injunction against a plan administrator's improper refusal to pay benefits. A participant or beneficiary may also bring a cause of action for breach of fiduciary duty, and under this cause of action may seek removal of the fiduciary. §§ 502(a)(2), 409. In an action under these civil enforcement provisions, the court in its discretion may allow an award of attorney's fees to either party. § 502(g). See *Massachusetts Mutual Life Ins. Co. v. Russell,* 473 U.S. 134, 147, 105 S.Ct. 3085, 3092–3093, 87 L.Ed.2d 96 (1985). In *Russell,* we concluded that ERISA's breach of fiduciary duty provision, § 409(a), 29 U.S.C. § 1109(a), provided no express authority for an award of punitive damages to a beneficiary. Moreover, we declined to find an implied cause of action for punitive damages in that section, noting that " '[t]he presumption that a remedy was deliberately omitted from a statute is strongest when Congress has enacted a comprehensive legislative scheme including an integrated system of procedures for enforcement.' " *Russell, supra,* at 147, 105 S.Ct., at 3093, quoting *Northwest Airlines, Inc. v. Transport Workers,* 451 U.S. 77, 97, 101 S.Ct. 1571, 1583, 67 L.Ed.2d 750 (1981). Our examination of these provisions made us "reluctant to tamper with an enforcement scheme crafted with such evident care as the one in ERISA." *Russell, supra,* 473 U.S., at 147, 105 S.Ct., at 3093.

In sum, the detailed provisions of § 502(a) set forth a comprehensive civil enforcement scheme that represents a careful balancing of the need for prompt and fair claims settlement procedures against the public interest in encouraging the formation of employee benefit plans. The policy choices reflected in the inclusion of certain remedies and the exclusion of others under the federal scheme would be completely undermined if ERISA-plan participants and beneficiaries were free to obtain remedies under state law that Congress rejected in ERISA. "The six carefully integrated civil

(5) except as otherwise provided in subsection (b) of this subsection, by the Secretary (A) to enjoin any act or practice which violates any provision of this subchapter, or (B) to obtain other appropriate equitable relief (i) to redress such violation or (ii) to enforce any provision of this subchapter;

(6) by the Secretary to collect any civil penalty under subsection (i) of this section."

enforcement provisions found in § 502(a) of the statute as finally enacted . . . provide strong evidence that Congress did *not* intend to authorize other remedies that it simply forgot to incorporate expressly." *Russell, supra,* at 146, 105 S.Ct., at 3092 (emphasis in original).

The deliberate care with which ERISA's civil enforcement remedies were drafted and the balancing of policies embodied in its choice of remedies argue strongly for the conclusion that ERISA's civil enforcement remedies were intended to be exclusive. This conclusion is fully confirmed by the legislative history of the civil enforcement provision. The legislative history demonstrates that the pre-emptive force of § 502(a) was modeled after § 301 of the LMRA.

The Conference Report on ERISA describing the civil enforcement provisions of § 502(a) says:

> Under the conference agreement, civil actions may be brought by a participant or beneficiary to recover benefits due under the plan, to clarify rights to receive future benefits under the plan, and for relief from breach of fiduciary responsibility. . . . [W]ith respect to suits to enforce benefit rights under the plan or to recover benefits under the plan which do not involve application of the title I provisions, they may be brought not only in U.S. district courts but also in State courts of competent jurisdiction. *All such actions in Federal or State courts are to be regarded as arising under the laws of the United States in similar fashion to those brought under section 301 of the Labor-Management Relations Act of 1947.*

H.R.Conf.Rep. No. 93–1280, p. 327 (1974), U.S.Code Cong. & Admin.News 1974, pp. 4639, 5107 (emphasis added).

Congress was well aware that the powerful pre-emptive force of § 301 of the LMRA displaced all state actions for violation of contracts between an employer and a labor organization, even when the state action purported to authorize a remedy unavailable under the federal provision. Section 301 pre-empts any "state-law claim [whose resolution] is substantially dependent upon the analysis of the terms of an agreement made between the parties in a labor contract." *Allis-Chalmers Corp. v. Lueck,* 471 U.S., at 220, 105 S.Ct., at 1916. . . . Congress' specific reference to § 301 of the LMRA to describe the civil enforcement scheme of ERISA makes clear its intention that all suits brought by beneficiaries or participants asserting improper processing of claims under ERISA-regulated plans be treated as federal questions governed by § 502(a). *See also* H.R.Rep. No. 93–533, p. 12 (1973), U.S.Code Cong. & Admin.News 1974, p. 4639, reprinted in 2 Senate Committee on Labor and Public Welfare, Legislative History of ERISA, 94th Cong., 2d Sess., 2359 (Comm. Print 1976) ("The uniformity of decision which the Act is designed to foster will help administrators, fiduciaries and participants to predict the legality of proposed actions without the necessity of reference to varying state laws"); 120 Cong.Rec. 29933 (1974) (remarks of Sen. Williams) (suits involving claims for benefits "will be regarded as arising under the laws of the United States, in similar fashion to those brought under section 301 of the Labor Management Relations Act"); *id.*, at 29942 (remarks of Sen. Javits) ("[i]t is also intended that a body of Federal substantive law will be developed by the courts to deal with issues involving rights and obligations under private welfare and pension plans"). The expectations that a federal common law of rights and obligations under ERISA-regulated plans would develop, indeed, the entire comparison of ERISA's § 502(a) to § 301 of the LMRA, would make little sense if the remedies available to ERISA participants and beneficiaries under § 502(a) could be supplemented or supplanted by varying state laws.

. . . .

Considering the common-sense understanding of the saving clause, the McCarran-Ferguson Act factors defining the business of insurance, and, most importantly, the clear expression of congressional intent that ERISA's civil enforcement scheme be exclusive, we conclude that Dedeaux's state law suit asserting improper processing of a claim for benefits under an ERISA-regulated plan is not saved by § 514(b)(2)(A), and therefore is pre-empted by § 514(a). Accordingly, the judgment of the Court of Appeals is

Reversed.

AETNA HEALTH INC. V. DAVILA

542 U.S. 200 (2004)

Opinion

JUSTICE THOMAS delivered the opinion of the Court.

In these consolidated cases, two individuals sued their respective health maintenance organizations (HMOs) for alleged failures to exercise ordinary care in the handling of coverage decisions, in violation of a duty imposed by the Texas Health Care Liability Act (THCLA), Tex. Civ. Prac. & Rem.Code Ann. §§ 88.001–88.003 (West 2004 Supp. Pamphlet). We granted certiorari to decide whether the individuals' causes of action are completely pre-empted by the "interlocking, interrelated, and interdependent remedial scheme," *Massachusetts Mut. Life Ins. Co. v. Russell,* 473 U.S. 134, 146, 105 S.Ct. 3085, 87 L.Ed.2d 96 (1985), found at § 502(a) of the Employee Retirement Income Security Act of 1974 (ERISA), 88 Stat. 891, as amended, 29 U.S.C. § 1132(a) *et seq*. 540 U.S. 981, 124 S.Ct. 462, 463, 157 L.Ed.2d 370 (2003). We hold that the causes of action are completely pre-empted and hence removable from state to federal court. The Court of Appeals, having reached a contrary conclusion, is reversed.

I.

A.

Respondent Juan Davila is a participant, and respondent Ruby Calad is a beneficiary, in ERISA-regulated employee benefit plans. Their respective plan sponsors had entered into agreements with petitioners, Aetna Health Inc. and CIGNA HealthCare of Texas, Inc., to administer the plans. Under Davila's plan, for instance, Aetna reviews requests for coverage and pays providers, such as doctors, hospitals, and nursing homes, which perform covered services for members; under Calad's plan sponsor's agreement, CIGNA is responsible for plan benefits and coverage decisions.

Respondents both suffered injuries allegedly arising from Aetna's and CIGNA's decisions not to provide coverage for certain treatment and services recommended by respondents' treating physicians. Davila's treating physician prescribed Vioxx to remedy Davila's arthritis pain, but Aetna refused to pay for it. Davila did not appeal or contest this decision, nor did he purchase Vioxx with his own resources and seek reimbursement. Instead, Davila began taking Naprosyn, from which he allegedly suffered a severe reaction that required extensive treatment and hospitalization. Calad underwent surgery, and although her treating physician recommended an extended hospital stay, a CIGNA discharge nurse determined that Calad did not meet the plan's criteria for a continued hospital stay. CIGNA consequently denied coverage for the extended hospital stay. Calad experienced postsurgery complications forcing her to return to the hospital. She alleges that these complications would not have occurred had CIGNA approved coverage for a longer hospital stay.

Respondents brought separate suits in Texas state court against petitioners. Invoking THCLA § 88.002(a), respondents argued that petitioners' refusal to cover the requested services violated their "duty to exercise ordinary care when making health care treatment decisions," and that these refusals "proximately caused" their injuries. *Ibid.* Petitioners removed the cases to Federal District Courts, arguing that respondents' causes of action fit within the scope of, and were therefore completely pre-empted by, ERISA § 502(a). The respective District Courts agreed, and declined to remand the cases to state court. Because respondents refused to amend their complaints to bring explicit ERISA claims, the District Courts dismissed the complaints with prejudice.

B.

Both Davila and Calad appealed the refusals to remand to state court. The United States Court of Appeals for the Fifth Circuit consolidated their cases with several others raising similar issues. The Court of Appeals recognized that state causes of action that "duplicat[e] or fal[l] within the scope of an ERISA § 502(a) remedy" are completely pre-empted and hence removable to federal court. *Roark v. Humana, Inc.*, 307 F.3d 298, 305

(2002) (internal quotation marks omitted). After examining the causes of action available under § 502(a), the Court of Appeals determined that respondents' claims could possibly fall under only two: § 502(a)(1)(B), which provides a cause of action for the recovery of wrongfully denied benefits, and § 502(a)(2), which allows suit against a plan fiduciary for breaches of fiduciary duty to the plan.

Analyzing § 502(a)(2) first, the Court of Appeals concluded that, under *Pegram v. Herdrich,* 530 U.S. 211, 120 S.Ct. 2143, 147 L.Ed.2d 164 (2000), the decisions for which petitioners were being sued were "mixed eligibility and treatment decisions" and hence were not fiduciary in nature. 307 F.3d, at 307–308. The Court of Appeals next determined that respondents' claims did not fall within § 502(a)(1)(B)'s scope. It found significant that respondents "assert tort claims," while § 502(a)(1)(B) "creates a cause of action for breach of contract," *id.,* at 309, and also that respondents "are not seeking reimbursement for benefits denied them," but rather request "tort damages" arising from "an external, statutorily imposed duty of 'ordinary care,' " *ibid.* From *Rush Prudential HMO, Inc. v. Moran,* 536 U.S. 355, 122 S.Ct. 2151, 153 L.Ed.2d 375 (2002), the Court of Appeals derived the principle that complete pre-emption is limited to situations in which "States . . . duplicate the causes of action listed in ERISA § 502(a)," and concluded that "[b]ecause the THCLA does not provide an action for collecting benefits," it fell outside the scope of § 502(a)(1)(B). 307 F.3d, at 310–311.

II.

. . . .

B.

Congress enacted ERISA to "protect . . . the interests of participants in employee benefit plans and their beneficiaries" by setting out substantive regulatory requirements for employee benefit plans and to "provid[e] for appropriate remedies, sanctions, and ready access to the Federal courts." 29 U.S.C. § 1001(b). The purpose of ERISA is to provide a uniform regulatory regime over employee benefit plans. To this end, ERISA includes expansive pre-emption provisions, see ERISA § 514, 29 U.S.C. § 1144, which are intended to ensure that employee benefit plan regulation would be "exclusively a federal concern." *Alessi v. Raybestos-Manhattan, Inc.,* 451 U.S. 504, 523, 101 S.Ct. 1895, 68 L.Ed.2d 402 (1981).

ERISA's "comprehensive legislative scheme" includes "an integrated system of procedures for enforcement." *Russell,* 473 U.S., at 147, 105 S.Ct. 3085 (internal quotation marks omitted). This integrated enforcement mechanism, ERISA § 502(a), 29 U.S.C. § 1132(a), is a distinctive feature of ERISA, and essential to accomplish Congress' purpose of creating a comprehensive statute for the regulation of employee benefit plans. As the

Court said in *Pilot Life Ins. Co. v. Dedeaux,* 481 U.S. 41, 107 S.Ct. 1549, 95 L.Ed.2d 39 (1987):

> [T]he detailed provisions of § 502(a) set forth a comprehensive civil enforcement scheme that represents a careful balancing of the need for prompt and fair claims settlement procedures against the public interest in encouraging the formation of employee benefit plans. The policy choices reflected in the inclusion of certain remedies and the exclusion of others under the federal scheme would be completely undermined if ERISA-plan participants and beneficiaries were free to obtain remedies under state law that Congress rejected in ERISA. 'The six carefully integrated civil enforcement provisions found in § 502(a) of the statute as finally enacted . . . provide strong evidence that Congress did *not* intend to authorize other remedies that it simply forgot to incorporate expressly.'

Id., at 54, 107 S.Ct. 1549 (quoting *Russell, supra,* at 146, 105 S.Ct. 3085). Therefore, any state-law cause of action that duplicates, supplements, or supplants the ERISA civil enforcement remedy conflicts with the clear congressional intent to make the ERISA remedy exclusive and is therefore pre-empted. *See* 481 U.S., at 54–56, 107 S.Ct. 1549; see also *Ingersoll-Rand Co. v. McClendon,* 498 U.S. 133, 143–145, 111 S.Ct. 478, 112 L.Ed.2d 474 (1990).

The pre-emptive force of ERISA § 502(a) is still stronger. In *Metropolitan Life Ins. Co. v. Taylor,* 481 U.S. 58, 65–66, 107 S.Ct. 1542, 95 L.Ed.2d 55 (1987), the Court determined that the similarity of the language used in the Labor Management Relations Act, 1947 (LMRA), and ERISA, combined with the "clear intention" of Congress "to make § 502(a)(1)(B) suits brought by participants or beneficiaries federal questions for the purposes of federal court jurisdiction in like manner as § 301 of the LMRA," established that ERISA § 502(a)(1)(B)'s pre-emptive force mirrored the pre-emptive force of LMRA § 301. Since LMRA § 301 converts state causes of action into federal ones for purposes of determining the propriety of removal, so too does ERISA § 502(a)(1)(B). Thus, the ERISA civil enforcement mechanism is one of those provisions with such "extraordinary pre-emptive power" that it "converts an ordinary state common law complaint into one stating a federal claim for purposes of the well-pleaded complaint rule." *Metropolitan Life,* 481 U.S., at 65–66, 107 S.Ct. 1542. Hence, "causes of action within the scope of the civil enforcement provisions of § 502(a) [are] removable to federal court." *Id.,* at 66, 107 S.Ct. 1542.

III.

A.

ERISA § 502(a)(1)(B) provides:

> A civil action may be brought—(1) by a participant or beneficiary—. . . (B) to recover benefits due to him under the terms of his plan, to enforce his rights under the terms of the plan, or to clarify his rights to future benefits under the terms of the plan.

29 U.S.C. § 1132(a)(1)(B).

This provision is relatively straightforward. If a participant or beneficiary believes that benefits promised to him under the terms of the plan are not provided, he can bring suit seeking provision of those benefits. A participant or beneficiary can also bring suit generically to "enforce his rights" under the plan, or to clarify any of his rights to future benefits. Any dispute over the precise terms of the plan is resolved by a court under a *de novo* review standard, unless the terms of the plan "giv[e] the administrator or fiduciary discretionary authority to determine eligibility for benefits or to construe the terms of the plan." *Firestone Tire & Rubber Co. v. Bruch,* 489 U.S. 101, 115, 109 S.Ct. 948, 103 L.Ed.2d 80 (1989).

It follows that if an individual brings suit complaining of a denial of coverage for medical care, where the individual is entitled to such coverage only because of the terms of an ERISA-regulated employee benefit plan, and where no legal duty (state or federal) independent of ERISA or the plan terms is violated, then the suit falls "within the scope of" ERISA § 502(a)(1)(B). *Metropolitan Life, supra,* at 66, 107 S.Ct. 1542. In other words, if an individual, at some point in time, could have brought his claim under ERISA § 502(a)(1)(B), and where there is no other independent legal duty that is implicated by a defendant's actions, then the individual's cause of action is completely pre-empted by ERISA § 502(a)(1)(B).

To determine whether respondents' causes of action fall "within the scope" of ERISA § 502(a)(1)(B), we must examine respondents' complaints, the statute on which their claims are based (the THCLA), and the various plan documents. Davila alleges that Aetna provides health coverage under his employer's health benefits plan. Davila also alleges that after his primary care physician prescribed Vioxx, Aetna refused to pay for it. The only action complained of was Aetna's refusal to approve payment for Davila's Vioxx prescription. Further, the only relationship Aetna had with Davila was its partial administration of Davila's employer's benefit plan.

Similarly, Calad alleges that she receives, as her husband's beneficiary under an ERISA-regulated benefit plan, health coverage from CIGNA. She alleges that she was informed by CIGNA, upon admittance into a hospital for major surgery, that she would be authorized to stay for only one day.

She also alleges that CIGNA, acting through a discharge nurse, refused to authorize more than a single day despite the advice and recommendation of her treating physician. Calad contests only CIGNA's decision to refuse coverage for her hospital stay. And, as in Davila's case, the only connection between Calad and CIGNA is CIGNA's administration of portions of Calad's ERISA-regulated benefit plan.

It is clear, then, that respondents complain only about denials of coverage promised under the terms of ERISA-regulated employee benefit plans. Upon the denial of benefits, respondents could have paid for the treatment themselves and then sought reimbursement through a § 502(a)(1)(B) action, or sought a preliminary injunction, *see Pryzbowski v. U.S. Healthcare, Inc.,* 245 F.3d 266, 274 (C.A.3 2001) (giving examples where federal courts have issued such preliminary injunctions).

Respondents contend, however, that the complained-of actions violate legal duties that arise independently of ERISA or the terms of the employee benefit plans at issue in these cases. Both respondents brought suit specifically under the THCLA, alleging that petitioners "controlled, influenced, participated in and made decisions which affected the quality of the diagnosis, care, and treatment provided" in a manner that violated "the duty of ordinary care set forth in §§ 88.001 and 88.002." Respondents contend that this duty of ordinary care is an independent legal duty. They analogize to this Court's decisions interpreting LMRA § 301, 29 U.S.C. § 185, with particular focus on *Caterpillar Inc. v. Williams,* 482 U.S. 386, 107 S.Ct. 2425, 96 L.Ed.2d 318 (1987) (suit for breach of individual employment contract, even if defendant's action also constituted a breach of an entirely separate collective-bargaining agreement, not pre-empted by LMRA § 301). Because this duty of ordinary care arises independently of any duty imposed by ERISA or the plan terms, the argument goes, any civil action to enforce this duty is not within the scope of the ERISA civil enforcement mechanism.

The duties imposed by the THCLA in the context of these cases, however, do not arise independently of ERISA or the plan terms. The THCLA does impose a duty on managed care entities to "exercise ordinary care when making health care treatment decisions," and makes them liable for damages proximately caused by failures to abide by that duty. § 88.002(a). However, if a managed care entity correctly concluded that, under the terms of the relevant plan, a particular treatment was not covered, the managed care entity's denial of coverage would not be a proximate cause of any injuries arising from the denial. Rather, the failure of the plan itself to cover the requested treatment would be the proximate cause.[3] More

[3] To take a clear example, if the terms of the health care plan specifically exclude from coverage the cost of an appendectomy, then any injuries caused by the refusal to cover the appendectomy are properly attributed to the terms of the plan itself, not the managed care entity that applied those terms.

significantly, the THCLA clearly states that "[t]he standards in Subsections (a) and (b) create no obligation on the part of the health insurance carrier, health maintenance organization, or other managed care entity to provide to an insured or enrollee treatment which is not covered by the health care plan of the entity." § 88.002(d). Hence, a managed care entity could not be subject to liability under the THCLA if it denied coverage for any treatment not covered by the health care plan that it was administering.

Thus, interpretation of the terms of respondents' benefit plans forms an essential part of their THCLA claim, and THCLA liability would exist here only because of petitioners' administration of ERISA-regulated benefit plans. Petitioners' potential liability under the THCLA in these cases, then, derives entirely from the particular rights and obligations established by the benefit plans. So, unlike the state-law claims in *Caterpillar, supra,* respondents' THCLA causes of action are not entirely independent of the federally regulated contract itself. *Cf. Allis-Chalmers Corp. v. Lueck,* 471 U.S. 202, 217, 105 S.Ct. 1904, 85 L.Ed.2d 206 (1985) (state-law tort of bad-faith handling of insurance claim pre-empted by LMRA § 301, since the "duties imposed and rights established through the state tort . . . derive[d] from the rights and obligations established by the contract"); *Steelworkers v. Rawson,* 495 U.S. 362, 371, 110 S.Ct. 1904, 109 L.Ed.2d 362 (1990) (state-law tort action brought due to alleged negligence in the inspection of a mine was pre-empted, as the duty to inspect the mine arose solely out of the collective-bargaining agreement).

Hence, respondents bring suit only to rectify a wrongful denial of benefits promised under ERISA-regulated plans, and do not attempt to remedy any violation of a legal duty independent of ERISA. We hold that respondents' state causes of action fall "within the scope of" ERISA § 502(a)(1)(B), *Metropolitan Life,* 481 U.S., at 66, 107 S.Ct. 1542, and are therefore completely pre-empted by ERISA § 502 and removable to federal district court.

B.

The Court of Appeals came to a contrary conclusion for several reasons, all of them erroneous. First, the Court of Appeals found significant that respondents "assert a tort claim for tort damages" rather than "a contract claim for contract damages," and that respondents "are not seeking reimbursement for benefits denied them." 307 F.3d, at 309. But, distinguishing between pre-empted and non-pre-empted claims based on the particular label affixed to them would "elevate form over substance and allow parties to evade" the pre-emptive scope of ERISA simply "by relabeling their contract claims as claims for tortious breach of contract." *Allis-Chalmers, supra,* at 211, 105 S.Ct. 1904. Nor can the mere fact that the state cause of action attempts to authorize remedies beyond those authorized by ERISA § 502(a) put the cause of action outside the scope of the ERISA civil enforcement mechanism. In *Pilot Life, Metropolitan Life,* and *Ingersoll-Rand,* the plaintiffs all brought state claims that were labeled either tort or tort-like. See *Pilot Life,* 481 U.S., at 43, 107 S.Ct. 1549 (suit for, *inter alia,* " 'Tortious Breach of Contract' "); *Metropolitan Life, supra,* at 61–62, 107 S.Ct. 1542 (suit requesting damages for "mental anguish caused by breach of [the] contract"); *Ingersoll-Rand,* 498 U.S., at 136, 111 S.Ct. 478 (suit brought under various tort and contract theories). And, the plaintiffs in these three cases all sought remedies beyond those authorized under ERISA. *See Pilot Life, supra,* at 43, 107 S.Ct. 1549 (compensatory and punitive damages); *Metropolitan Life, supra,* at 61, 107 S.Ct. 1542 (mental anguish); *Ingersoll-Rand, supra,* at 136, 111 S.Ct. 478 (punitive damages, mental anguish). And, in all these cases, the plaintiffs' claims were pre-empted. The limited remedies available under ERISA are an inherent part of the "careful balancing" between ensuring fair and prompt enforcement of rights under a plan and the encouragement of the creation of such plans. *Pilot Life, supra,* at 55, 107 S.Ct. 1549.

Second, the Court of Appeals believed that "the wording of [respondents'] plans is immaterial" to their claims, as "they invoke an external, statutorily imposed duty of 'ordinary care.' " 307 F.3d, at 309. But as we have already discussed, the wording of the plans is certainly material to their state causes of action, and the duty of "ordinary care" that the THCLA creates is not external to their rights under their respective plans.

Ultimately, the Court of Appeals rested its decision on one line from *Rush Prudential.* There, we described our holding in *Ingersoll-Rand* as follows: "[W]hile state law duplicated the elements of a claim available under ERISA, it converted the remedy from an equitable one under § 1132(a)(3) (available exclusively in federal district courts) into a legal one for money damages (available in a state tribunal)." 536 U.S., at 379, 122 S.Ct. 2151. The point of this sentence was to describe why the state cause of action in *Ingersoll-Rand* was pre-empted by ERISA § 502(a): It was pre-empted because it attempted to convert an equitable remedy into a legal remedy. Nowhere in *Rush Prudential* did we suggest that the pre-emptive force of ERISA § 502(a) is limited to the situation in which a state cause of action precisely duplicates a cause of action under ERISA § 502(a).

Nor would it be consistent with our precedent to conclude that only strictly duplicative state causes of action are pre-empted. Frequently, in order to receive exemplary damages on a state claim, a plaintiff must prove facts beyond the bare minimum necessary to establish entitlement to an award. *Cf. Allis-Chalmers, supra,* at 217, 105 S.Ct. 1904 (bad-faith refusal to honor a claim needed to be proved in order to recover exemplary damages). In order to recover for mental anguish, for instance, the plaintiffs in *Ingersoll-Rand* and *Metropolitan Life* would presumably have had to prove the existence of mental anguish; there is no such element in an ordinary suit brought under ERISA § 502(a)(1)(B). *See Ingersoll-Rand, supra,* at 136, 111 S.Ct. 478; *Metropolitan Life, supra,* at 61, 107 S.Ct. 1542. This did not save these state causes of action from pre-emption. Congress' intent to make the ERISA civil enforcement mechanism exclusive would be undermined if state causes of action that supplement the ERISA § 502(a) remedies were permitted, even if the elements of the state cause of action did not precisely duplicate the elements of an ERISA claim.

C.

Respondents also argue—for the first time in their brief to this Court—that the THCLA is a law that regulates insurance, and hence that ERISA § 514(b)(2)(A) saves their causes of action from pre-emption (and thereby from complete pre-emption).[5] This argument is unavailing. The existence of a comprehensive remedial scheme can demonstrate an "overpowering federal policy" that determines the interpretation of a statutory provision designed to save state law from being pre-empted. *Rush Prudential,* 536 U.S., at 375, 122 S.Ct. 2151. ERISA's civil enforcement provision is one such example.

As this Court stated in *Pilot Life,* "our understanding of [§ 514(b)(2)(A)] must be informed by the legislative intent concerning the civil enforcement provisions provided by ERISA § 502(a), 29 U.S.C. § 1132(a)." 481 U.S., at 52, 107 S.Ct. 1549. The Court concluded that "[t]he policy choices reflected in the inclusion of certain remedies and the exclusion of others under the federal scheme would be completely undermined if ERISA-plan participants and beneficiaries were free to obtain remedies under state law that Congress rejected in ERISA." *Id.,* at 54, 107 S.Ct. 1549. The Court then held, based on

> [T]he common-sense understanding of the saving clause, the McCarran-Ferguson Act factors defining the business of insurance, and, *most importantly,* the clear expression of congressional intent that ERISA's civil enforcement scheme be exclusive, . . . that [the plaintiff's] state law suit asserting improper processing of a claim for benefits under an ERISA-regulated plan is not saved by § 514(b)(2)(A).

Id., at 57, 107 S.Ct. 1549 (emphasis added).

Pilot Life's reasoning applies here with full force. Allowing respondents to proceed with their state-law suits would "pose an obstacle to the purposes and objectives of Congress." *Id.,* at 52, 107 S.Ct. 1549. As this Court has recognized in both *Rush Prudential* and *Pilot Life,* ERISA § 514(b)(2)(A) must be interpreted in light of the congressional intent to create an exclusive federal remedy in ERISA § 502(a). Under ordinary principles of

[5] ERISA § 514(b)(2)(A), 29 U.S.C. § 1144(b)(2)(A), reads, as relevant: "[N]othing in this subchapter shall be construed to exempt or relieve any person from any law of any State which regulates insurance, banking, or securities."

conflict pre-emption, then, even a state law that can arguably be characterized as "regulating insurance" will be pre-empted if it provides a separate vehicle to assert a claim for benefits outside of, or in addition to, ERISA's remedial scheme.

. . . .

V.

We hold that respondents' causes of action, brought to remedy only the denial of benefits under ERISA-regulated benefit plans, fall within the scope of, and are completely pre-empted by, ERISA § 502(a)(1)(B), and thus removable to federal district court. The judgment of the Court of Appeals is reversed, and the cases are remanded for further proceedings consistent with this opinion.

It is so ordered.

JUSTICE GINSBURG, with whom JUSTICE BREYER joins, concurring.

The Court today holds that the claims respondents asserted under Texas law are totally preempted by § 502(a) of the Employee Retirement Income Security Act of 1974 (ERISA or Act), 29 U.S.C. § 1132(a). That decision is consistent with our governing case law on ERISA's preemptive scope. I therefore join the Court's opinion. But, with greater enthusiasm, as indicated by my dissenting opinion in *Great-West Life & Annuity Ins. Co. v. Knudson,* 534 U.S. 204, 122 S.Ct. 708, 151 L.Ed.2d 635 (2002), I also join "the rising judicial chorus urging that Congress and [this] Court revisit what is an unjust and increasingly tangled ERISA regime." *DiFelice v. Aetna U.S. Healthcare,* 346 F.3d 442, 453 (C.A.3 2003) (Becker, J., concurring).

Because the Court has coupled an encompassing interpretation of ERISA's preemptive force with a cramped construction of the "equitable relief" allowable under § 502(a)(3), a "regulatory vacuum" exists: "[V]irtually all state law remedies are preempted but very few federal substitutes are provided." *Id.,* at 456, 457 (internal quotation marks omitted).

A series of the Court's decisions has yielded a host of situations in which persons adversely affected by ERISA-proscribed wrongdoing cannot gain make-whole relief. First, in *Massachusetts Mut. Life Ins. Co. v. Russell,* 473 U.S. 134, 105 S.Ct. 3085, 87 L.Ed.2d 96 (1985), the Court stated, in dicta: "[T]here is a stark absence—in [ERISA] itself and in its legislative history—of any reference to an intention to authorize the recovery of extracontractual damages" for consequential injuries. *Id.,* at 148, 105 S.Ct. 3085. Then, in *Mertens v. Hewitt Associates,* 508 U.S. 248, 113 S.Ct. 2063, 124 L.Ed.2d 161 (1993), the Court held that § 502(a)(3)'s term " 'equitable relief' . . . refer[s] to those categories of relief that were *typically* available in equity (such as injunction, mandamus, and restitution, but not compensatory damages)." *Id.,* at 256, 113 S.Ct. 2063 (emphasis in original).

Most recently, in *Great-West,* the Court ruled that, as "§ 502(a)(3), by its terms, only allows for *equitable* relief," the provision excludes "the imposition of personal liability . . . for a contractual obligation to pay money." 534 U.S., at 221, 122 S.Ct. 708 (emphasis in original).

As the array of lower court cases and opinions documents, *see, e.g., DiFelice; Cicio v. Does,* 321 F.3d 83 (C.A.2 2003), cert. pending *sub nom. Vytra Healthcare v. Cicio,* No. 03–69 [Reporter's Note: See post, 542 U.S. 933, 124 S.Ct. 2902], 72 USLW 3093 (2003), fresh consideration of the availability of consequential damages under § 502(a)(3) is plainly in order. *See* 321 F.3d, at 106, 107 (Calabresi, J., dissenting in part) ("gaping wound" caused by the breadth of preemption and limited remedies under ERISA, as interpreted by this Court, will not be healed until the Court "start[s] over" or Congress "wipe[s] the slate clean"); *DiFelice,* 346 F.3d, at 467 ("The vital thing . . . is that either Congress or the Court act quickly, because the current situation is plainly untenable."); Langbein, What ERISA Means by "Equitable": The Supreme Court's Trail of Error in *Russell, Mertens,* and *Great-West,* 103 Colum. L.Rev. 1317, 1365 (2003) ("The Supreme Court needs to . . . realign ERISA remedy law with the trust remedial tradition that Congress intended [when it provided in § 502(a)(3) for] 'appropriate equitable relief.' ").

. . . .

NOTES AND QUESTIONS

1. *Bad Faith Claims and the Insurer-Policyholder Relationship Under Metropolitan Life.* Do you agree with the majority's analysis of the application of the three-prong *Metropolitan Life* standard used to determine whether state insurance laws have been preempted in *Pilot Life*? Specifically, is the majority's conclusion in *Pilot Life* that the payment of insurance claims is not "an integral part of the policy relationship between the insurer and insured" correct? Assuming that bad faith breach of contract claims in Mississippi generally are only viable in the context of wrongful denials of insurance claims, do you agree with the majority's conclusion in *Pilot Life* that the assertion of bad faith claims in Mississippi are not "limited to entities within the insurance industry?"

2. *Different Damages Rules for Employer-Provided Group Insurance and Individual Insurance.* The damage remedies for a denial of coverage under ERISA do not include punitive damages, emotional distress damages, or consequential damages even if the denial of coverage would constitute "bad faith" under state law. Attorneys' fees are available under ERISA, however, in the court's discretion. In contrast, under many states' insurance laws, reasonably foreseeable consequential damages, including attorney's fees, emotional distress damages, and even punitive damages may be available for a bad faith denial of coverage.

3. *Standard of Review*. Under ERISA, denials of benefits are reviewed *de novo* unless the benefit plan gives the administrator or fiduciary discretionary authority to determine the eligibility of benefits or to construe the terms of the plan. *See Firestone Tire & Rubber Co. v. Bruch*, 489 U.S. 101, 115 (1989). When discretion is reserved, which it commonly is, the standard of review is abuse of discretion. The effect of the abuse of discretion standard of review is that *contra proferentem* and the reasonable expectations doctrine effectively do not apply to the construction of policy language. In addition, before a beneficiary under a group plan can seek judicial review of a denial of coverage, the beneficiary must exhaust all internal review processes that the plan provides unless doing so demonstrably would be futile. *See, e.g., Davenport v. Harry N. Abrams, Inc.*, 249 F.3d 130, 133 (2d Cir. 2001). Nor are jury trials available under ERISA. *See, e.g., Muller v. First Unum Life Ins. Co.*, 341 F.3d 119, 124 (2d Cir. 2003).

In contrast, under state laws that apply to individual insurance policies, the interpretation of insurance policy language is a question of law that is reviewed *de novo* on appeal. And, of course, *contra proferentem* and the reasonable expectations doctrine apply to such interpretations. To the extent there are any material facts in dispute relevant to the interpretation of the policy language, a jury trial may be conducted. *See* Chapter 2, Section V.

4. *Preservation of Claims for Breaches of "Independent Duties."* One exception to ERISA preemption of state law claims involves claims that arise due to a duty independent of the insurance plan itself. One of the most notable examples of such duties and claims related to a breach thereof are malpractice claims. Thus, if a doctor negligently performs a surgery, for example, ERISA does not preempt the malpractice claim against the doctor.

5. *Negative Impact of ERISA on Consumers*. The manner in which ERISA has been interpreted by courts has resulted in consumers receiving less protection in insurance disputes than under most states' laws. It is unlikely that Congress intended this result, given the fact that ERISA was enacted to expand employees' benefits rights. From a purely insurance coverage perspective (i.e., not considering availability, cost, or convenience), individuals in many situations would be better off buying individual insurance policies rather than participating in employer-provided group plans.

EXERCISE

1. Draft a 3-page memo explaining why the *Pilot Life* case was wrongly decided.

2. Changing Benefit Plans and Judicial Review

McGANN v. H & H MUSIC CO.

946 F.2d 401 (5th Cir. 1991)

Opinion

GARWOOD, CIRCUIT JUDGE:

Plaintiff-appellant John McGann (McGann) filed this suit under section 510 of the Employee Retirement Income Security Act of 1974, Pub.L. No. 93–406, 88 Stat. 832 (29 U.S.C. §§ 1001–1461) (ERISA), against defendants-appellees H & H Music Company (H & H Music), Brook Mays Music Company (Brook Mays) and General American Life Insurance Company (General American) (collectively defendants) claiming that they discriminated against McGann, an employee of H & H Music, by reducing benefits available to H & H Music's group medical plan beneficiaries for treatment for acquired immune deficiency syndrome (AIDS) and related illnesses. The district court granted defendants' motion for summary judgment on the ground that an employer has an absolute right to alter the terms of medical coverage available to plan beneficiaries. 742 F.Supp. 392. We affirm.

FACTS AND PROCEEDINGS BELOW

McGann, an employee of H & H Music, discovered that he was afflicted with AIDS in December 1987. Soon thereafter, McGann submitted his first claims for reimbursement under H & H Music's group medical plan, provided through Brook Mays, the plan administrator, and issued by General American, the plan insurer, and informed his employer that he had AIDS. McGann met with officials of H & H Music in March 1988, at which time they discussed McGann's illness. Before the change in the terms of the plan, it provided for lifetime medical benefits of up to $1,000,000 to all employees.

In July 1988, H & H Music informed its employees that, effective August 1, 1988, changes would be made in their medical coverage. These changes included, but were not limited to, limitation of benefits payable for AIDS-related claims to a lifetime maximum of $5,000.[1] No limitation was placed on any other catastrophic illness. H & H Music became self-insured under the new plan and General American became the plan's administrator. By January 1990, McGann had exhausted the $5,000 limit on coverage for his illness.

[1] Other changes included increased individual and family deductibles, elimination of coverage for chemical dependency treatment, adoption of a preferred provider plan and increased contribution requirements.

In August 1989, McGann sued H & H Music, Brook Mays and General American under section 510 of ERISA, which provides, in part, as follows:

> It shall be unlawful for any person to discharge, fine, suspend, expel, discipline, or discriminate against a participant or beneficiary for exercising any right to which he is entitled under the provisions of an employee benefit plan, . . . or for the purpose of interfering with the attainment of any right to which such participant may become entitled under the plan . . . .

29 U.S.C. § 1140.

McGann claimed that defendants discriminated against him in violation of both prohibitions of section 510. He claimed that the provision limiting coverage for AIDS-related expenses was directed specifically at him in retaliation for exercising his rights under the medical plan and for the purpose of interfering with his attainment of a right to which he may become entitled under the plan.

Defendants, conceding the factual allegations of McGann's complaint, moved for summary judgment. These factual allegations include no assertion that the reduction of AIDS benefits was intended to deny benefits to McGann for any reason which would not be applicable to other beneficiaries who might then or thereafter have AIDS, but rather that the reduction was prompted by the knowledge of McGann's illness, and that McGann was the only beneficiary then known to have AIDS.[4] On June 26, 1990, the district court granted defendants' motion on the ground that they had an absolute right to alter the terms of the plan, regardless of their intent in making the alterations. The district court also held that even if the issue of discriminatory motive were relevant, summary judgment would still be proper because the defendants' motive was to ensure the future existence of the plan and not specifically to retaliate against McGann or to interfere with his exercise of future rights under the plan.

DISCUSSION

McGann contends that defendants violated both clauses of section 510 by discriminating against him for two purposes: (1) "for exercising any right to which [the beneficiary] is entitled," and (2) "for the purpose of interfering with the attainment of any right to which such participant may become entitled." In order to preclude summary judgment in defendants' favor, McGann must make a showing sufficient to establish the existence of a genuine issue of material fact with respect to each material element on

[4] We assume, for purposes of this appeal that the defendants' knowledge of McGann's illness was a motivating factor in their decision to reduce coverage for AIDS-related expenses, that this knowledge was obtained either through McGann's filing of claims or his meetings with defendants, and that McGann was the only plan beneficiary then known to have AIDS.

which he would carry the burden of proof at trial. *Celotex Corp. v. Catrett,* 477 U.S. 317, 106 S.Ct. 2548, 2552, 91 L.Ed.2d 265 (1986).

At trial, McGann would bear the burden of proving the existence of defendants' specific discriminatory intent as an essential element of either of his claims. *Kimbro v. Atlantic Richfield Co.,* 889 F.2d 869, 881 (9th Cir.1989) (employee must prove employer's specific intent to retaliate for employee's exercise of rights under plan), *cert. denied,* 498 U.S. 814, 111 S.Ct. 53, 112 L.Ed.2d 28 (1990); *Clark v. Resistoflex Co., a Div. of Unidynamics Corp.*, 854 F.2d 762, 770 (5th Cir.1988) (employee must prove specific intent to interfere with employee's pension rights); *Dister v. Continental Group, Inc.*, 859 F.2d 1108, 1111 (2d Cir.1988) (section 510 claimant must prove specific intent to engage in activity prohibited by section 510); *Gavalik v. Continental Can Co.*, 812 F.2d 834, 851 (3d Cir.) (claimant must prove specific intent to violate ERISA), *cert. denied,* 484 U.S. 979, 108 S.Ct. 495, 98 L.Ed.2d 492 (1987). Thus, in order to survive summary judgment McGann must make a showing sufficient to establish that a genuine issue exists as to defendants' specific intent to retaliate against McGann for filing claims for AIDS-related treatment or to interfere with McGann's attainment of any right to which he may have become entitled.

Although we assume there was a connection between the benefits reduction and either McGann's filing of claims or his revelations about his illness, there is nothing in the record to suggest that defendants' motivation was other than as they asserted, namely to avoid the expense of paying for AIDS treatment (if not, indeed, also for other treatment), no more for McGann than for any other present or future plan beneficiary who might suffer from AIDS. McGann concedes that the reduction in AIDS benefits will apply equally to all employees filing AIDS-related claims and that the effect of the reduction will not necessarily be felt only by him. He fails to allege that the coverage reduction was otherwise specifically intended to deny him particularly medical coverage except "in effect." He does not challenge defendants' assertion that their purpose in reducing AIDS benefits was to reduce costs.

Furthermore, McGann has failed to adduce evidence of the existence of "any right to which [he] may become entitled under the plan." The right referred to in the second clause of section 510 is not simply any right to which an employee may conceivably become entitled, but rather any right to which an employee may become entitled pursuant to an existing, enforceable obligation assumed by the employer. "Congress viewed [section 510] as a crucial part of ERISA because, without it, employers would be able to circumvent the provision of *promised* benefits." *Ingersoll-Rand Co. v. McClendon,* 498 U.S. 133, 111 S.Ct. 478, 485, 112 L.Ed.2d 474 (1990) (emphasis added).

McGann's allegations show no *promised* benefit, for there is nothing to indicate that defendants ever promised that the $1,000,000 coverage limit was permanent. The H & H Music plan expressly provides: "Termination or Amendment of Plan: The Plan Sponsor may terminate or amend the Plan at any time or terminate any benefit under the Plan at any time." There is no allegation or evidence that any oral or written representations were made to McGann that the $1,000,000 coverage limit would never be lowered. Defendants broke no promise to McGann. The continued availability of the $1,000,000 limit was not a right to which McGann may have become entitled for the purposes of section 510. To adopt McGann's contrary construction of this portion of section 510 would mean that an employer could not effectively reserve the right to amend a medical plan to reduce benefits respecting subsequently incurred medical expenses, as H & H Music did here, because such an amendment would obviously have as a purpose preventing participants from attaining the right to such future benefits as they otherwise might do under the existing plan absent the amendment. But this is plainly not the law, and ERISA does not require such "vesting" of the right to a continued level of the same medical benefits once those are ever included in a welfare plan. *See Moore v. Metropolitan Life Insurance Co.*, 856 F.2d 488, 492 (2d Cir.1988).

McGann appears to contend that the reduction in AIDS benefits alone supports an inference of specific intent to retaliate against him or to interfere with his future exercise of rights under the plan. McGann characterizes as evidence of an individualized intent to discriminate the fact that AIDS was the only catastrophic illness to which the $5,000 limit was applied and the fact that McGann was the only employee known to have AIDS. He contends that if defendants reduced AIDS coverage because they learned of McGann's illness through his exercising of his rights under the plan by filing claims, the coverage reduction therefore could be "retaliation" for McGann's filing of the claims.[6] Under McGann's theory, any reduction in employee benefits would be impermissibly discriminatory if motivated by a desire to avoid the anticipated costs of continuing to provide coverage for a particular beneficiary. McGann would find an implied promise not to discriminate for this purpose; it is the breaking of this promise that McGann appears to contend constitutes interference with a future entitlement.

McGann cites only one case in which a court has ruled that a change in the terms and conditions of an employee-benefits plan could constitute illegal discrimination under section 510. *Vogel v. Independence Federal Sav. Bank,* 728 F.Supp. 1210 (D.Md.1990). In *Vogel,* however, the plan change at issue resulted in the plaintiff and only the plaintiff being excluded from

[6] We assume that discovery of McGann's condition-and realization of the attendant, long-term costs of caring for McGann-did in fact prompt defendants to reconsider the $1,000,000 limit with respect to AIDS-related expenses and to reduce the limit for future such expenses to $5,000.

coverage. McGann asserts that the *Vogel* court rejected the defendant's contention that mere termination of benefits could not constitute unlawful discrimination under section 510, but in fact the court rejected this claim not because it found that mere termination of coverage could constitute discrimination under section 510, but rather because the termination at issue affected only the beneficiary. *Id.* at 1225. Nothing in *Vogel* suggests that the change there had the potential to then or thereafter exclude any present or possible future plan beneficiary other than the plaintiff. *Vogel* therefore provides no support for the proposition that the alteration or termination of a medical plan could alone sustain a section 510 claim. Without necessarily approving of the holding in *Vogel,* we note that it is inapplicable to the instant case. The post-August 1, 1988 $5,000 AIDS coverage limit applies to any and all employees.

McGann effectively contends that section 510 was intended to prohibit any discrimination in the alteration of an employee benefits plan that results in an identifiable employee or group of employees being treated differently from other employees. The First Circuit rejected a somewhat similar contention in *Aronson v. Servus Rubber, Div. of Chromalloy,* 730 F.2d 12 (1st Cir.), *cert. denied,* 469 U.S. 1017, 105 S.Ct. 431, 83 L.Ed.2d 357 (1984). In *Aronson,* an employer eliminated a profit sharing plan with respect to employees at only one of two plants. The disenfranchised employees sued their employer under section 510, claiming that partial termination of the plan with respect to employees at one plant and not at the other constituted illegal discrimination. The court rejected the employees' discrimination claim, stating in part:

> [Section 510] relates to discriminatory conduct directed against individuals, not to actions involving the plan in general. The problem is with the word 'discriminate.' An overly literal interpretation of this section would make illegal any partial termination, since such terminations obviously interfere with the attainment of benefits by the terminated group, and, indeed, are expressly intended so to interfere. . . . This is not to say that a plan could not be discriminatorily modified, intentionally benefitting, or injuring, certain identified employees or a certain group of employees, but a partial termination cannot constitute discrimination per se. A termination that cuts along independently established lines-here separate divisions-and that has a readily apparent business justification, demonstrates no invidious intent.

Id. at 16 (citation omitted).

The Supreme Court has observed in dictum: "ERISA does not mandate that employers provide any particular benefits, and does not itself proscribe discrimination in the provision of employee benefits." *Shaw v. Delta Air*

Lines, Inc., 463 U.S. 85, 103 S.Ct. 2890, 2897, 77 L.Ed.2d 490 (1983). To interpret "discrimination" broadly to include defendants' conduct would clearly conflict with Congress's intent that employers remain free to create, modify and terminate the terms and conditions of employee benefits plans without governmental interference.

. . . .

As persuasively explained by the Second Circuit, the policy of allowing employers freedom to amend or eliminate employee benefits is particularly compelling with respect to medical plans:

> With regard to an employer's right to change medical plans, Congress evidenced its recognition of the need for flexibility in rejecting the automatic vesting of welfare plans. Automatic vesting was rejected because the costs of such plans are subject to fluctuating and unpredictable variables. Actuarial decisions concerning fixed annuities are based on fairly stable data, and vesting is appropriate. In contrast, medical insurance must take account of inflation, changes in medical practice and technology, and increases in the costs of treatment independent of inflation. These unstable variables prevent accurate predictions of future needs and costs.

Moore v. Metropolitan Life Ins. Co., 856 F.2d 488, 492 (2d Cir.1988) (*Metropolitan Life*).

In *Metropolitan Life,* the court rejected an ERISA claim by retirees that their employer could not change the level of their medical benefits without their consent. The court stated that limiting an employer's right to change medical plans increased the risk of "decreas[ing] protection for future employees and retirees." *Id.* at 492; *see also Reynolds Metals*, 740 F.2d at 457 ("judicial interference into the establishment of pension plan provisions . . . would serve only to discourage employers from creating voluntarily pension plans") (footnote omitted).

McGann's claim cannot be reconciled with the well-settled principle that Congress did not intend that ERISA circumscribe employers' control over the content of benefits plans they offered to their employees. McGann interprets section 510 to prevent an employer from reducing or eliminating coverage for a particular illness in response to the escalating costs of covering an employee suffering from that illness. Such an interpretation would, in effect, change the terms of H & H Music's plan. Instead of making the $1,000,000 limit available for medical expenses on an as-incurred basis only as long as the limit remained in effect, the policy would make the limit *permanently* available for all medical expenses as they might thereafter be incurred because of a single event, such as the contracting of AIDS. Under McGann's theory, defendants would be effectively proscribed from reducing coverage for AIDS once McGann had contracted that illness and filed claims for AIDS-related expenses. If a federal court could prevent an employer from reducing an employee's coverage limits for AIDS treatment once that employee contracted AIDS, the boundaries of judicial involvement in the creation, alteration or termination of ERISA plans would be sorely tested.

As noted, McGann has failed to adduce any evidence of defendants' specific intent to engage in conduct proscribed by section 510. A party against whom summary judgment is ordered cannot raise a fact issue simply by stating a cause of action where defendants' state of mind is a material element. *Clark,* 854 F.2d at 771. " 'There must be some indication that he can produce the requisite quantum of evidence to enable him to reach the jury with his claim.' " *Id.* at 771 (quoting *Hahn v. Sargent,* 523 F.2d 461, 468 (1st Cir.1975), *cert. denied,* 425 U.S. 904, 96 S.Ct. 1495, 47 L.Ed.2d 754 (1976)).

Proof of defendants' specific intent to discriminate among plan beneficiaries on grounds not proscribed by section 510 does not enable McGann to avoid summary judgment. ERISA does not broadly prevent an employer from "discriminating" in the creation, alteration or termination of employee benefits plans; thus, evidence of such intentional discrimination cannot alone sustain a claim under section 510. That section does not prohibit welfare plan discrimination between or among categories of diseases. Section 510 does not mandate that if some, or most, or virtually all catastrophic illnesses are covered, AIDS (or any other particular catastrophic illness) must be among them. It does not prohibit an employer from electing not to cover or continue to cover AIDS, while covering or continuing to cover other catastrophic illnesses, even though the employer's decision in this respect may stem from some "prejudice" against AIDS or its victims generally. The same, of course, is true of any other disease and its victims. That sort of "discrimination" is simply not addressed by section 510. Under section 510, the asserted discrimination is illegal only if it is motivated by a desire to retaliate against an employee or to deprive an employee of an existing right to which he may become entitled. The district court's decision to grant summary judgment to defendants therefore was proper. Its judgment is accordingly

AFFIRMED.

NOTES AND QUESTIONS

1. *The Law Today.* The holding of *McGann* remains good law today—employers can modify benefit plans under ERISA so long as they reserve the right to do so and the changes are not intended to discriminate against a specific employee.

2. *State or Federal Regulation?* Now that you have considered both the states' and the federal government's approach to the regulation of insurance,

which is better—state or federal regulation? Which approach favors consumers versus insurers? What are the advantages and disadvantages of each approach? *See generally* Robert H. Jerry, II and Douglas R. Richmond, Understanding Insurance Law § 23A[a] (5th ed. 2012).

EXERCISE

1. Draft a 3-page memo analyzing whether ERISA would allow a law firm to change its 401(k) plan on New Year's Eve, effective January 1, so that the law firm no longer needs to provide a contribution to employees' savings plans.

CHAPTER TEN

PUBLIC POLICY

■ ■ ■

"[Relying on public policy in a case is akin to riding] a very unruly horse, and when once you get astride it you never know where it will carry you. It may lead you from the sound law. It is never argued at all but when other points fail."

— *Richardson v. Mellish*, 130 Eng. Rep. 294, 303 (1824)

Public policy is relevant to all areas of law, of course, but in some areas of law, it is fair to say that public policy carries more weight, or at least does so more obviously. For example, as noted in the opening chapter of this book, public policy plays a more significant role in insurance law than other areas of contract law. This derives largely from the fact that individuals and families depend on insurance, which in some lines (like life insurance and long-term care insurance) are long-term contracts, for their most basic financial needs (or to protect against the risk of having these needs). This does not mean that an ordinary commercial contract to buy and sell carrots to make soup is unimportant, but what is at stake with respect to a promise to sell a crop of carrots is much less than what is at stake with a contract of life, disability, or health insurance. Similarly, for a business, some of the insurance products it buys are necessary for the entrepreneur to even take the risk associated with *creating* the business, which is a set of higher stakes than a contract to buy input goods that are otherwise available elsewhere in the market if the seller does not perform.

Public policy also explains important features of key aspects of insurance law. For example, in the area of auto insurance, the public policy that favors compensating victims is the reason auto liability insurance is compulsory. It also is the reason that numerous exclusions and other provisions in auto insurance policies purporting to limit or eliminate coverage have not been enforced by courts or have been overridden by legislation. Public policy is what ultimately underlies the insurable interest requirement in life insurance and property insurance. As explored in Chapter 7, this requirement is designed to prevent wagering (essentially gambling) on people's lives or on whether property will continue to exist, which helps break the potential tie between insurance and an incentive to kill people or intentionally destroy property. The strict liability version of *contra proferentem* and the doctrine of reasonable expectations are manifestations of the public policy of protecting consumers because the balance of power between insurers and policyholders leans very heavily in insurers' favor in almost every aspect of the insurance relationship, ranging from the drafting and sale of policies to the defense and settlement of claims. When insurance law allows for the award of extra-contractual damages for breach of the duty to settle, bad faith denial of claims, or bad faith claims handling, public policy concerns unique to insurance are operative.

In this final chapter, we will examine the competing public policy interests at stake in insurance in a few areas: insuring crimes, insuring punitive damages, and situations where the policyholder is forced to make gruesome choices in order to preserve an entitlement to insurance proceeds. Although public policy arguments are often viewed as a last-ditch effort to override contract language in a garden-variety contract dispute, it is unwise to view them in such a limited manner in the context of insurance. As you read the following cases, keep in mind that legislatures, not courts, are the primary source of public policy. That being said, on what bases did the courts make their findings regarding the dominant public policy in these cases?

I. CRIMINAL ACTS

MINNESOTA FIRE AND CAS. CO. V. GREENFIELD

855 A.2d 854 (Pa. 2004)

OPINION ANNOUNCING THE JUDGMENT OF THE COURT

JUSTICE NEWMAN.

We must decide today whether an insurance company owes a duty to defend or indemnify a homeowner for the wrongful death of his houseguest occasioned by his selling heroin to her. For the reasons that follow, we affirm the holding of the Superior Court, albeit on different grounds, that no such obligation exists.

FACTS AND PROCEDURAL HISTORY

At 8 p.m. on February 9, 1998, eighteen year-old Angela Smith (Smith) arrived at the home of Michael J. Greenfield (Greenfield) at 600 North Third Street, in Wormleysburg, hoping to obtain some heroin from him. Another young woman, Brook Broadwater (Broadwater), was with Smith. When they arrived, Greenfield had been drinking Mad Dog beer and was under the influence of marijuana and heroin.

Greenfield was no stranger to the use of heroin, having lost consciousness three times from it in the past. He was using heroin on a daily basis. He had used heroin with Smith before, and she, too, had become unconscious twice from it. Greenfield had sold heroin to Smith on other occasions and was arrested in 1995 for possession of marijuana. Greenfield acknowledged that he sold drugs out of his house "occasionally;" for the most part, he sold "mostly just weed" and "didn't really sell heroin to too many people."

In exchange for some marijuana and a small sum of money, Greenfield provided Smith with a bag of heroin, which was labeled "Suicide." At approximately 8:20 p.m., Smith voluntarily injected herself with the heroin. From that time until 10 p.m., Smith lay in a chair and communicated only when directly addressed. Greenfield put out some blankets for her, and she went to sleep on the floor. Greenfield left with Broadwater, returning to the house approximately 10:45 p.m. Smith remained in the residence, and when Greenfield awoke around 6:30 a.m., he found Smith still on the floor. When he left for work, he told Smith to lock the door if she left, and Smith groggily responded.

When Greenfield came home from work later that day, he found Smith dead on the floor where he had left her that morning. Greenfield knew that she was dead because "she was pale and not breathing." Autopsy results showed that Smith died from a heroin overdose. Greenfield called a friend, Robert Rollins (Rollins), who came to his residence. Wearing gloves because he "didn't want to touch" Smith's dead body, Greenfield, with his friend, took the body and put it in a vehicle owned by Greenfield. They drove around the area, and then dumped the body in York County near the Yellow Breeches Creek. Greenfield then contacted the police and concocted a story to the effect that he had simply found a body near the creek. Rollins initially told the same story, but recanted and told the truth. The men were arrested later that same day.

Greenfield was charged criminally for the outcome of the death of Smith; he pled guilty and was sentenced on counts of involuntary manslaughter, abuse of a corpse, and unlawful delivery of heroin. During the guilty plea colloquy, counsel stated that the maximum penalty on the felony charge (unlawful delivery of Schedule I controlled substance) is five years and $15,000.00; for the misdemeanor one (involuntary manslaughter), it is five years and fine; and for the misdemeanor two (abuse of corpse), it is two years and fine. . . .

Greenfield obtained a homeowner's policy (the Policy) from Minnesota Fire and Casualty Company (Insurance Company) when he purchased his residence. This was the Policy in place when Smith died, and it provided as follows:

> Section II, Coverage E—Personal Liability
>
> If a claim is made or a suit is brought against an insured for damages because of bodily injury or property damage caused by an occurrence to which this coverage applies, we will:
>
> 1. pay up to our limit of liability for the damages for which the insured is legally liable; and

> 2. provide a defense at our expense by counsel of our choice, even if the suit is groundless, false or fraudulent. We may investigate and settle any claim or suit that we decide is appropriate. Our duty to settle or defend ends when the amount we pay for damages resulting from the occurrence equals our limit of liability.

The Policy defines "occurrence" as "an accident, including exposure to conditions, which results, during the policy period, in: a. bodily injury; or b. property damage." "Bodily injury" is "bodily harm, sickness or disease, including required care, loss of services and death that result." *Id.* However, the Policy excludes coverage for bodily injury "which is expected or intended by the insured." Bodily injury "arising out of business pursuits of an insured" is also excluded. *Id.* "Business" is defined as a "trade, profession or occupation."

On June 10, 1999, Sharon L. Smith and Arlin C. Smith, the parents of Smith, filed wrongful death and survival actions against Greenfield in the Court of Common Pleas of Cumberland County (trial court), individually and on behalf of all the other beneficiaries of the Estate of Angela C. Smith, as administrators of that Estate. . . .

The Insurance Company filed a Declaratory Judgment Action in the trial court, claiming . . . that it had no legal obligation to defend or indemnify Greenfield on the ground that public policy bars the insurance coverage asserted.

On March 14, 2001, the trial court ruled on the parties' Cross-Motions for Summary Judgment, which sought summary judgment regarding a duty of the Insurance Company to defend and indemnify Greenfield in the wrongful death and survival action. . . . [T]he trial court ordered the Insurance Company to defend the case and sustain any ultimate liability. The court cited *United Services Automobile Association v. Elitzky,* 358 Pa.Super. 362, 517 A.2d 982 (1986), *petition for allowance of appeal denied,* 515 Pa, 600, 601, 528 A.2d 957 (1987), which involved a homeowner's insurance policy with an exclusionary clause identical to the one presently before the Court; i.e., it did not cover liability for bodily injury "which is expected or intended by the insured." In *Elitzky,* the court stated that "the exclusionary clause applies only when the insured intends to cause a harm. Insurance coverage is not excluded because the insured's actions are intentional unless he also intended the resultant damage." *Id.* at 987. Relying on that, the trial court in the case *sub judice* found that although the Complaint alleged an intentional act by Greenfield, i.e., supplying heroin to Smith, there were no averments alleging or reasonably inferring that Greenfield expected or intended to cause her death. . . .

The Superior Court reversed and determined that [at least one] factor[ ] precluded coverage: . . . public policy. The court noted "compelling public policy reasons" to deny coverage, for, "[i]n effect, the courts are being asked to help provide insurance for heroin dealers. . . . [T]he legislature . . . has already determined the inherent danger of heroin. . . . It should not be the public policy . . . to insure the sale of such a . . . dangerous and illegal narcotic. . . ."

. . . .

Greenfield filed a Petition for Allowance of Appeal with this Court. . . . For the reasons that follow, we determine that although the Superior Court erred in expanding the inferred intent doctrine, it reached the correct result in determining that public policy precludes the Insurance Company from any duty to defend or indemnify Greenfield.

DISCUSSION

. . . .

Based on our analysis, we conclude that the trial court erred as a matter of law when it found that the Insurance Company is required to defend Greenfield and when it held that public policy does not prohibit insurance coverage for the death of Smith. . . . We agree with the result that the Superior Court reached in reversing the trial court [, and] we affirm only that part of its holding that determines that public policy precludes coverage under the Policy.

. . . .

The question concerning whether Greenfield "expected or intended" Smith to die when he provided her with heroin is certainly difficult to answer. . . .

When this Court first considered the effect of a similar exclusionary clause in a homeowner's policy, we stated that "the vast majority of courts which have considered such a provision [an exclusionary clause] have reached the conclusion that before the insurer may validly disclaim liability, it must be shown that the insured intended by his act to produce the damage which did in fact occur." *Eisenman v. Hornberger,* 438 Pa. 46, 264 A.2d 673–74 (1970) (internal citations omitted). We emphasized in that case the difference between intending an act and intending a result.[8] In *Eisenman,* we held that the exclusionary clause did not preclude coverage for damages caused by a house fire during the course of a burglary. Further, we found that although the perpetrators intended to burglarize the house, they did not anticipate or plan the resulting house fire occasioned by their use of matches to light their way in the dark.

The trial court found that "the facts averred support Smiths' allegation that the death of Angela Smith was caused by Greenfield's negligence." It is in

[8] We stated that "the question is not whether the dropping of the matches was an 'intentional act,' but rather whether the resulting property damage was 'intentionally caused' by the insured." *Eisenman,* 264 A.2d at 674.

the context of this jurisprudential background that the Superior Court extended and applied the doctrine of inferred intent, presumably for the reason that it was unable to establish actual intent, given the absence of allegations that Greenfield expected or intended Smith to lose consciousness or die. The earlier ruling of the Superior Court in *Elitzky,* which involved an identical exclusionary clause, was consistent with our articulation of the standard in *Eisenman.* "An insured will only be covered if he causes a harm of a generally different type than that which he set out to cause." *Elitzky,* 517 A.2d at 988. The harm that occurred in the case *sub judice* is exactly the type of evil inherent in the use of heroin. Sometimes, users are fortunate and suffer no ill effects; other times, they lose consciousness; in the worst of all scenarios, they die.

. . . .

We cannot know with certainty what Greenfield's state of mind was, a fact neither necessary to nor dispositive of our decision. We do ratify existing principles of our jurisprudence. . . .

Having said that, however, the Superior Court's determination that the Insurance Company is not required to defend or indemnify under the Policy is correct. . . . [T]he court based its determination on the "compelling public policy reasons for denying a claim such as this [where, i]n effect, the courts are being asked to help provide insurance for heroin dealers." The court reiterated that heroin is a Schedule I controlled substance, and that its sale and possession for use or delivery are illegal. The court cited the many reasons for the illegality of heroin, including its "inherent harm . . . [and] not only the harm caused to society in terms of costs and quality of life, but the real and devastating harm done to the user."

In *Eisenman,* we rejected an argument that allowing recovery pursuant to an insurance policy where property damage arose out of the commission of a crime by the insured would contravene public policy. We did so for two reasons: (1) the insurance contract itself did not contain a "violation of law" clause; and (2) our analysis that "under the facts of this case, we are not confronted with any overriding public policy which would preclude recovery."

Our decision in that case determined that an insurance company was required to indemnify against losses caused by a carelessly lit match that was dropped when teenagers were burglarizing a home. We supported our holding on two bases: (1) the widely accepted principle that "before the insurer may validly disclaim liability, it must be shown that the insured intended by his act to produce the damage which did in fact occur[;]" and (2) the absence of any "overriding public policy" to preclude recovery.

Using our analysis in the case at bar, and providing further refinement of our thirty-four year-old holding in *Eisenman,* we find that recovery is precluded for damages that arise out of an insured's criminal acts regarding a Schedule I substance, as a matter of overriding public policy. Therefore, in situations when an insured commits a criminal act, with respect to a Schedule I controlled substance, and unintended or unexpected injuries or losses occur as a result, whether by accident or negligence, public policy will not allow coverage under the contract of insurance.

However, in cases that do not involve a criminal act by an insured with respect to a Schedule I controlled substance, our decision in *Eisenman,* reiterating the test traditionally required for an insurer to disclaim liability; i.e. the insurer must prove that the insured intended by his act to produce the damage which did actually occur, retains its validity.

The Court in *Eisenman* was distressed at the lack of a violation of law clause in the insurance policy there.[12] It is obvious that a homeowner's policy is not designed to protect a drug dealer from personal liability for supplying heroin that results in the death of his house guest. "Only dominant public policy" justifies the invalidating of a contract on the basis of public policy, and one such indication of that policy is "statutory enactments." If the explicit criminalization of use or possession or sale of drugs that have a high potential for abuse, no currently accepted medical use in the United States, and lack of accepted safety for use under medical supervision does not manifest convincing proof of public interest, what would? While we were "loath to insert [a 'violation of law'] clause for the greater protection of the insurer" in *Eisenman,* public policy demands that we do so now and in every case where a loss has arisen from the insured's commission of a crime involving the sale, use, or possession of a Schedule I controlled substance. *Id.* at 675.

. . . .

"Only in the clearest cases, therefore, may a court make an alleged public policy the basis of judicial decision." Regardless of whether the insurance contract listed the possession, use and sale of heroin as an exclusion, the fact is that the legislature has criminalized the conduct that resulted in the damages in the instant matter. This exemplifies the clearest of cases.

. . . .

Our Commonwealth, from the legislature to the Secretary of Health, has made its policy on the illegality of heroin abundantly clear: "heroin has a high potential for abuse, has no accepted medical use within the United States, and . . . is unsafe for use even under medical supervision."

---

[12] The dissent wrongly casts the majority into the role of a "super-scrivener," based on our holding that damages arising from an insured's criminal acts are excluded, even when the specific crimes are not listed by name in the policy. This view fails to recognize that it is the **legislature** that has acted as scrivener, by criminalizing specific acts, one of which is the possession, use, or sale of heroin. Although the Insurance Company may reap a benefit from our holding, this alone cannot allow the Court to lend its efforts to require reimbursement for damages arising out of the conduct of a policyholder that our legislature has defined as illegal. [emphasis in original].

Given this clear enunciation of public policy regarding Schedule I controlled substances, we find that the Insurance Company is not required to defend or indemnify against damages arising out of its insured's criminal acts where the voluntary participation of the victim in an illegal heroin-transaction caused her death.

CONCLUSION

The public policy in our Commonwealth, as articulated by the legislature, is clear: possession, sale, and use of heroin are illegal. Public policy does not allow recovery under an insurance contract where a willing and frequent participant in this type of criminalized activity dies as a result. This is true regardless of whether the victim intended to die or whether the criminal intended the death, for we will not countenance the turning of illegal activities regarding Schedule I controlled substances into money-making occasions. Although we reject the reasoning of the Superior Court that extended the doctrine of inferred intent to general liability policies, we affirm the Order of the Superior Court based on its articulation of public policy.

. . . .

CHIEF JUSTICE CAPPY, dissenting.

Because I cannot agree with the majority's decision to rewrite the insurance policy at issue, I must respectfully dissent.

We are not here confronted with the question of whether an insurer may enforce an exclusion which excludes from coverage damages arising out of the sale of heroin or any other illegal drug. Rather, at issue is whether this court may insert, via the invocation of public policy, such an exclusion into an insurance policy. The majority finds that this court may rewrite the contract on the basis that an insured should be precluded from receiving coverage where damages result from the insured's criminal act.

In my opinion, this court should not rewrite the contract for the insurance company. The Minnesota Fire and Casualty Company drafted the insurance policy. It is beyond cavil that it was capable of writing an exclusion which would exempt from coverage damages arising out of the sale of illegal narcotics, and yet it did not do so. Arguably, this was a failing on the part of the insurance company. Yet, is it the role of this court to act as super-scrivener, correcting the apparent errors in business judgment committed by insurers? With all due respect to the majority, I submit that this is not a proper role for this body.

Furthermore, I am concerned about the potential sweeping reach of the majority's decision and have grave concerns about its application to future cases. While the majority purports to limit its public policy exception to situations in which an insured engages in illegal activity regarding Schedule I controlled substances, its underlying rationale for creating that limited exception could easily be extended to create exceptions for other illegal acts. Indeed, the majority suggests in a footnote that this court should not require an insurance company to reimburse a policyholder for damages arising from *any* "conduct . . . that our legislature has defined as illegal." I am uneasy about this court issuing such a broad and amorphous pronouncement.

For the foregoing reasons, I respectfully dissent.

NOTES AND QUESTIONS

1. *Public Policy Against Criminal Conduct.* The *Greenfield* decision is not anomalous. Many courts have held it is against public policy to allow insurance to cover criminal conduct. *See, e.g., Bohrer v. Church Mut. Ins. Co.*, 965 P.2d 1258, 1262 (Colo. 1998) ("[I]t is contrary to public policy to insure against liability arising directly against the insured from intentional or willful wrongs, including the results and penalties of the insured's own criminal acts."); *Everglades Marina, Inc. v. Am. E. Dev. Corp.*, 374 So. 2d 517, 519 (Fla. 1979) ("[P]ublic policy precludes recovery under an insurance policy when the insured has committed a criminal act with known and necessary consequences."); *Goldsmith v. Green*, 47 So. 3d 637, 641 (La. Ct. App. 2010) ("[N]o reasonable policyholder would expect for his own intentional criminal acts to be insured. . . ."); *Perreault v. Maine Bonding & Cas. Co.*, 568 A.2d 1100, 1102 (Me. 1990) (denial of coverage was "in accord with the general rule that insurance to indemnify an insured against his or her own violation of criminal statutes is against public policy and, therefore, void").

Yet, the well-settled rule is that basic life insurance benefits should not be denied the insured's beneficiaries simply because the insured dies while committing a crime. Why should this be so? What does the concept of fortuity mean in these cases?

2. *The Legislature Has Spoken?* In *Greenfield*, the Supreme Court of Pennsylvania stated, "The public policy in our Commonwealth, as articulated by the legislature, is clear: possession, sale, and use of heroin are illegal. Public policy does not allow recovery under an insurance contract where a willing and frequent participant in this type of criminalized activity dies as a result." The *Greenfield* court did not cite or quote anything from the legislature in which the legislature said anything about allowing insurance to cover the victims of crimes. Nevertheless, does the holding in the case mean it is against public policy in Pennsylvania to allow insurance to cover any kind of crimes, or does the holding only apply to crimes that result in death? Does the holding only apply to "frequent participants" in criminal activity? What about reckless driving that results in a death? The driver could be charged with manslaughter. Does that mean there would not be any coverage to compensate the victim's family? What if the person killed by the reckless driver is a single parent with two young children? Are you comfortable arguing the children should receive nothing even though the driver has an insurance policy that does not exclude the claim?

3. *Competing Public Policies.* Deterring crimes is not the only public policy at issue in *Greenfield.* There are also the public policies that favor compensating injured parties and enforcing contracts as written. If Greenfield were in jail and were otherwise judgment proof, what chance of a monetary recovery for the wrongful death of their child do the Smiths have? As discussed in Chapter 4, insurers commonly put criminal acts exclusions in policies, but the insurance policy at issue in *Greenfield* did not contain this kind of exclusion. Justice Cappy argues in his dissent that courts should not rewrite policies for the benefit of insurers. Do you agree?

4. *Restatement of the Law of Liability Insurance.* While acknowledging that public policy can override policy language, the Restatement generally allows for liability insurance to cover criminal acts:

> **§ 45 Insurance of Liabilities Involving Aggravated Fault**
>
> . . . .
>
> (2) Except as barred by legislation or judicially declared public policy, a term in a liability insurance policy providing coverage for civil liability arising out of aggravated fault is enforceable, including civil liability for: criminal acts, expected or intentionally caused harm, fraud, or other conduct involving aggravated fault.

II. PUNITIVE DAMAGES

NORTHWESTERN NAT. CAS. CO. V. MCNULTY

307 F.2d 432 (5th Cir. 1962)

Opinion

WISDOM, CIRCUIT JUDGE.

This case presents the question of the liability of an insurance company, under an automobile accident liability policy, for punitive damages in a judgment against the insured. We hold that under Florida law public policy prohibits insurance against liability for punitive damages.

The Northwestern National Casualty Company issued a family combination automobile policy for $50,000 to the defendant, Walter S. Smith, in Virginia where Smith resides. The accident giving rise to the suit occurred in Florida. Smith, a drunken driver, traveling at eighty miles an hour or faster, weaving from side to side of the road, tried to pass the automobile the plaintiff, Edward McNulty, was driving. He made the attempt where it was impossible to pass or he completely lost control of his car. Smith's car smashed into the rear of McNulty's car. Without stopping to render aid, Smith fled the scene of the accident. He was arrested twelve miles down the highway when his car ran out of gas. McNulty suffered severe injuries including permanent damage to his brain.

McNulty sued Smith in a Florida state court. The complaint prayed for compensatory and punitive damages. The insurer's attorneys undertook the defense of the suit. They notified Smith that 'there is always a possibility that the amount recovered, if any, could be in excess of (the insurance) coverage' and informed him that he had 'the right . . . to employ an attorney to represent (him) for this possible excess', but added, 'please understand that you are not required to go to this expense as we will defend this case under the provisions of your insurance policy'. After investigating the facts, they concluded, as they later wrote Smith after the trial, the 'facts in this case were very bad and about the worst case we have ever had on the question of liability.' The attorneys advised the insured that they planned to admit liability for compensatory damages but not for punitive damages. They did not inform the insured at any time before the trial that the insurance company disclaimed liability for the payment of punitive damages, if any should be included in the judgment.

The jury returned a verdict in favor of the plaintiff in the amount of $57,500, representing $37,500 in compensatory damages and $20,000 in punitive damages. McNulty, joined by Smith, then brought this ancillary garnishment action in the District Court for the Southern District of Florida to recover on the liability policy up to $50,000. The district court granted summary judgment for the plaintiff. The insurer appeals from that part of the judgment holding punitive damages recoverable.

I.

Under the terms of the policy, the insured agreed:

> To pay on behalf of the insured all sums which the insured shall become legally obligated to pay as damages because of:
>
> > A. Bodily injury, sickness or disease, including death resulting therefrom, hereinafter called "bodily injury" sustained by any person;
> >
> > B. injury to or destruction of property, including loss of use thereof, thereinafter called "property damage" . . . .

The policy excludes claims for "bodily injury or property damage caused intentionally by or at the direction of the insured."

The insurance company's first defense is that the language of the contract does not cover punitive damages. The appellant argues that a claim for punitive damages is not one for "bodily injury"; by definition punitive damages go beyond compensation for bodily injury. The appellant argues also that the "wilful, reckless, or wantonly negligent conduct" of the defendant, necessary under Florida law as a predicate for the award of punitive damages, is equivalent to intentional wrong; the insurance contract expressly excludes 'damage caused intentionally'. We find it unnecessary to construe the contract; we hold that should a policy provide specifically for such coverage, it would contravene public policy.

II.

The force of public policy on insurance covering punitive damages depends on the nature or character of punitive damages. The character of punitive damages—as compensation for the plaintiff or as punishment of the defendant and deterrence to others—depends on the function such damages serves.

A. In this case the law of Florida and the law of Virginia are interrelated. The legal relations, rights, and liabilities between McNulty and Smith arising out of the automobile accident are governed by the law of Florida, where the accident occurred. The rights and obligations under the insurance contract between Smith and the appellant are governed by the law of Virginia, where the contract was made and issued, where Smith resides, and where, at the time it was made the contract might be expected to have its more important effects. McNulty, after obtaining his judgment against Smith, succeeded to Smith's rights against the appellant on the insurance contract. Since this is a suit on the contract, Virginia law governs the question whether an insurance policy against punitive damages contravenes public policy. Virginia cases reflect the same view of punitive damages as Florida cases,[5] but no Virginia court has passed on whether an insurer may be liable for such damages. In seeking to ascertain what the Virginia policy would be, however, we must look to the law imposing the punitive damages to determine their character. This brings us back to Florida, where the accident occurred, where the action was brought and the damages awarded, and where the punitory and deterrent effects of the punitive damages awarded in this case would have their greatest impact.

Florida cases follow the orthodox theory that punitive damages are punitory and a deterrent. The first case in Florida to discuss this subject was *Smith v. Bagwell*, 19 Fla. 117, 121 (1882). In that decision the court's description of punitive damages might be interpreted as indicating that in Florida such damages are partly compensatory. The court said: 'Compensatory damages are such as arise from actual and indirect pecuniary loss, mental suffering, value of time, actual expenses, and to these may be added bodily pain and suffering. Exemplary, vindictive or punitory damages are such as blend together the interests of society and of the aggrieved individual, and are not only a recompense to the sufferer but a punishment to the offender and an example to the community.' The support this decision gives to a compensatory theory of punitive damages is undercut by two other factors. First, in spite of the quoted statement,

[5] The Virginia cases reflect the view that punitive damages are not given as the plaintiff's due, but are given for the protection of the public, as punishment to the defendant, and as a warning and example to deter him and others from committing like offenses. . . .

throughout its opinion the court emphasized that punitive damages are assessed against the defendant to punish the offender and act as an example and warning to the community. Second, the question before the court in *Smith v. Bagwell* was whether the allowance of punitive damages in a case where the defendant was subject to criminal sanctions contravened the constitutional protection against double jeopardy. When this point has been raised some courts have avoided the difficult constitutional question whether the civil penalty violates prohibition against double jeopardy by treating punitive damages as compensatory or retributive; the payment is to the injured person, not to the state.

Later Florida cases base punitive damages on punishment rather than compensation. Thus, in *Winn & Lovett Grocery Co. v. Archer*, 126 Fla. 308, 171 So. 214, 221 (1936) the court limited the statement in Smith v. Bagwell, which the court said authorized 'vindictive damages' for an assault and battery committed under aggravating circumstances 'because the circumstances of aggravation attending the injury have increased the injury.' The court said: 'Damages known as exemplary or punitive damages (smart money) are altogether of a different character than vindictive damages. . . . Exemplary or punitive damages are therefore damages ultra compensation, and are authorized to be inflicted when the wrong done partakes of a criminal character, though not punishable as an offense against the state, or consists of aggravated misconduct or a lawless act. . . .' Similarly, in *Dr. P. Phillips & Sons, Inc. v. Kilgore*, 152 Fla. 578, 582, 12 So.2d 465, 467 (1943) the court again said: 'Punitive or exemplary damages is an amount allowed over and above actual or compensatory damages. Its allowance depends on malice, moral turpitude, wantonness, or the outrageousness of the tort and is awarded as a deterrent to others inclined to commit a like offense.'

. . . .

The Florida characterization of punitive damages as a penalty, imposed as a means of punishing the defendant in order to deter him and others from antisocial conduct, and to no significant extent compensation, conforms with the most widely accepted basis for punitive damages in other American jurisdictions. Only a few jurisdictions recognize punitive damages as compensatory: Connecticut, Michigan, and New Hampshire. In Connecticut punitive damages are viewed as primarily compensatory. They are awarded, however, only in cases of extreme culpability and are limited to the plaintiff's demonstrable litigation expenses. In a few other states punitive damages are not accepted at all, except as allowed by statute in certain situations: Illinois, Louisiana (following the civil law rejection of the doctrine), Massachusetts, Nebraska, and Washington.

. . . .

C. The argument that insurance against punitive damages would contravene public policy is sometimes said to rest on the doctrine that 'no one shall be permitted to take advantage of his own wrong.' Mr. Justice Cardozo in *Messersmith v. American Fidelity Co.*, 232 N.Y. 161, 133 N.E. 432, 19 A.L.R. 876 (1921). That doctrine is not necessarily applicable to cases of automobile liability insurance covering punitive damages. In such cases the public policy against coverage is not so much to prevent encouragement of wrong-doing by obstructing the hopes of profit; it is rather to make effective the discouragement of wrong-doing by the imposition of punishment. Where a person is able to insure himself against punishment he gains a freedom of misconduct inconsistent with the establishment of sanctions against such misconduct. It is not disputed that insurance against criminal fines or penalties would be void as violative of public policy. The same public policy should invalidate any contract of insurance against the civil punishment that punitive damages represent.

The policy considerations in a state where, as in Florida and Virginia, punitive damages are awarded for punishment and deterrence, would seem to require that the damages rest ultimately as well nominally on the party actually responsible for the wrong. If that person were permitted to shift the burden to an insurance company, punitive damages would serve no useful purpose. Such damages do not compensate the plaintiff for his injury, since compensatory damages already have made the plaintiff whole. And there is no point in punishing the insurance company; it has done no wrong. In actual fact, of course, and considering the extent to which the public is insured, the burden would ultimately come to rest not on the insurance companies but on the public, since the added liability to the insurance companies would be passed along to the premium payers. Society would then be punishing itself for the wrong committed by the insured.

There are substantial practical difficulties, bearing on public policy, in allowing insurance against punitive damages. (1) It would produce a serious conflict of interest between the insurer and the insured in settlement negotiations and in trial tactics. There was a conflict of interest in this case when the insurer refused an offer of settlement for $35,000, again when the insurer said nothing to the insured before trial about punitive damages, and still again when the insurer elected to concede liability for compensatory damages. (2) There would be a conflict between the rule that in assessing punitive damages evidence of the financial standing of the defendant may be considered by the jury and the rule against referring to the defendant's insurance in the presence of the jury. (3) Fantastic results would be possible having no relation to making the injured party whole. Thus in *Edwards v. Nulsen*, 1941, 347 Mo. 1077, 152 S.W.2d 28, the court approved actual damages of one dollar and punitive damages of $25,000; in *Livesey v. Stock*, 1929, 208 Cal. 315, 281 P. 70, there were actual damages of $750 and punitive damages of $10,000. One of these cases was a suit for libel and one for battery but they point up the unrealities of jury verdicts when juries go beyond compensatory damages either by directly awarding punitive damages or by awarding a lump-sum verdict including an x-factor representing the jury's sense of retribution and estimate of the amount needed to punish and deter. Such verdicts are justifiable only if the man who pays is the wrongdoer.

There is an argument for regarding the punitory theory of punitive damages as anachronistic in cases where, historically, exemplary damages represent nonpecuniary losses such as injured feelings, damaged reputation, humiliation, shame, pain and suffering (in certain states). In these cases it can be said that liability insurance is for the injured party, and that the insurance carrier should be liable for such losses. At the other end of the scale, there is an argument that the law should not favor punitive damages: there is enough of a punitive element in a tort system of liability based on fault. In an early, able decision Justice Foster, for the New Hampshire Supreme Court, argued that the 'true rule, simple and just, is to keep the civil and criminal process and practice distinct and separate'. He denounced punitive damages as 'a monstrous heresy . . . an unhealthy excrescence, deforming the symmetry of the body of the law.' *Fay v. Parker*, 53 N.H. 342, 382 (1873). But a hundred years ago Judge Foster did not drive down highways dodging drunken drivers weaving in and out of traffic at a hundred miles an hour.

Considering the theory of punitive damages as punitory and as a deterrent and accepting as common knowledge the fact that death and injury by automobile is a problem far from solved by traffic regulations and criminal prosecutions, it appears to us that there are especially strong public policy reasons for not allowing socially irresponsible automobile drivers to escape the element of personal punishment in punitive damages when they are guilty of reckless slaughter or maiming on the highway. It is no answer to say, society imposes criminal sanctions to deter wrongdoers; that it is enough when a civil offender, through insurance, pays what he is adjudged to owe. A criminal conviction and payment of a fine to the state may be atonement to society for the offender. But it may not have a sufficient effect on the conduct of others to make the public policy in favor of punitive damages useful and effective. So, at least, seems to be the policy of Florida and Virginia. To make that policy useful and effective the delinquent driver must not be allowed to receive a windfall at the expense of the purchasers of insurance, transferring his responsibility for punitive damages to the very people—the driving public—to whom he is a menace. We are sympathetic with the innocent victim here; perhaps there is no such thing as money damages making him whole. But his interest in receiving non-compensatory damages is small compared with the public interest in lessening the toll of injury and death on the highways; and there is such a thing as a state policy to punish and deter by making the wrongdoer pay.

. . . .

The judgment is affirmed as to the compensatory damages and reversed as to the punitive damages, without prejudice to the appellees' bringing any other actions against the appellants.

LAZENBY V. UNIVERSAL UNDERWRITERS INS. CO.

383 S.W.2d 1 (Tenn. 1964)

Opinion

DYER, JUSTICE.

Frances Jean Lazenby, a minor, by next friend, Mary Frances Lazenby, were the complainants below and Universal Underwriters Insurance Company was the defendant below and will be referred to herein as complainant and defendant, respectively.

Complainant, in the Circuit Court of Shelby County, secured a judgment against Norman Frank Crutchfield in the total amount of $4,000.79, of which $1,087.00 represented punitive damages, as a result of personal injuries sustained by complainant in an automobile accident due to the negligence of said Norman Frank Crutchfield. Crutchfield was driving his vehicle in an intoxicated condition. Defendant is the insurance carrier on the Crutchfield car and has paid the amount of the compensatory damages but has failed and refused, under their insurance contract, to pay the amount awarded as punitive damages. The suit in the case at bar was filed to secure judgment against defendant for the punitive damages. The Chancellor found for complainant and defendant has appealed to this Court since the cause was heard on agreed stipulation of facts.

The provision of the policy under which defendant would be liable, if liable, is as follows:

> Coverage A—*Bodily Injury Liability* To pay on behalf of the insured all sums which the insured shall become legally obligated to pay as damages because of bodily injury, sickness or disease, including death at anytime resulting therefrom sustained by any person caused by accident and arising out of ownership, maintenance or use of the automobile.

In argument before the bar of this Court and in the excellent briefs filed there is raised one question simple to state, but difficult to answer, to wit: In Tennessee, as a matter of public policy, is an automobile liability insurance carrier required to pay punitive damages assessed against their assured, as the result of an automobile accident. It should be kept in mind the issue here is not the liability of the assured defendant to pay punitive damages, only the liability of his insurance carrier to pay them.

In support of his position Counsel for defendant cites and principally relies upon the case of *Northwestern National Casualty Company v. McNulty*, 307 F.2d 432 (5 C.C.A. 1962). This case arose in the State of Florida on an insurance policy made and issued in the State of Virginia. Counsel for defendant states, in his brief, that his position in this cause is well set forth by Judge Wisdom in the McNulty case as follows:

> The argument that insurance against punitive damages would contravene public policy is sometimes said to rest on the doctrine that "no one shall be permitted to take advantage of his own wrong." Mr. Justice Cardozo in *Messersmith v. American Fidelity Co.*, 232 N.Y. 161, 133 N.E. 432, 19 A.L.R. 876 (1921). That doctrine is not necessarily applicable to cases of automobile liability insurance covering punitive damages. In such cases the public policy against coverage is not so much to prevent encouragement of wrong-doing by obstructing the hopes of profit; it is rather to make effective the discouragement of wrong-doing by the imposition of punishment. When a person is able to insure himself against punishment he gains a freedom of misconduct inconsistent with the establishment of sanctions against such misconduct. It is not disputed that insurance against criminal fines or penalties would be void as violative of public policy. The same public policy should invalidate any contract of insurance against the civil punishment that punitive damages represent.

Northwestern National Casualty Co. v. McNulty, supra.

In the *McNulty* case Judge Wisdom wrote the opinion for the majority. Judge Gewin wrote a separate specially concurring opinion. Judge Wisdom further states in his opinion as follows:

> Considering the theory of punitive damages as punitory and as a deterrent and accepting as common knowledge the fact that death and injury by automobile is a problem far from solved by traffic regulations and criminal prosecutions, it appears to us that there are especially strong public policy reasons for not allowing socially irresponsible automobile drivers to escape the element of personal punishment in punitive damages when they are guilty of reckless slaughter or maiming on the highway. It is no answer to say, society imposes criminal sanctions to deter wrongdoers; that it is enough when a civil offender, through insurance, pays what he is adjudged to owe. A criminal conviction and payment of a fine to the state may be atonement to society for the offender. But it may not have a sufficient effect on the conduct of others to make the public policy in favor of punitive damages useful and effective. So, at least, seems to be the policy of Florida and Virginia. To make that policy useful and effective the delinquent driver must not be

> allowed to receive a windfall at the expense of the purchasers of insurance, transferring his responsibility for punitive damages to the very people—the driving public—to whom he is a menace. We are sympathetic with the innocent victim here; perhaps there is no such thing as money damages making him whole. But his interest in receiving non-compensatory damages is small compared with the public interest in lessening the toll of injury and death on the highways; and there is such a thing as a state policy to punish and deter by making the wrongdoer pay.

Northwestern National Casualty Company v. McNulty, supra.

Judge Gewin in his separate specially concurring opinion states as follows:

> The more appropriate basis upon which to hold that public policy prohibits insurance against liability is the nature of the conduct of the wrongdoer—not the nature of the damages awarded. If the defendant acted willfully, intentionally, maliciously or fraudulently, coverage should be denied; because, in such circumstances, he should not be able to avoid punishment by shifting the penalty to an insurance carrier. I doubt that such protection is ever afforded by insurance, because the companies who are experience in such matters and who write the contracts, expressly exclude such conduct from the protection afforded by the policy. . . .
>
> All of us are concerned with the high death toll and personal injuries occurring on the highways, but I am somewhat skeptical that the prohibition of insurance against liability for punitive damages will accomplish the results expected by the majority. There is no certain measuring stick to determine the effectiveness with which the law operates in a given field, but all the states have rather strict criminal laws relating to the operation of motor vehicles. If the criminal penalties provided by such statutes fail to deter the wrongdoers, I seriously doubt that closing the market to insurance coverage will do so. As a matter of fact, if is my judgment that the opposite result will follow. . . .
>
> It is also quite apparent that my brothers of the majority are looking at this question from one direction only—from the point of view of the nature of the wrong which caused the injury. What about the injured party? Implicit in the entire field of tort liability and insurance law is the concept of furnishing some protection to those who are injured. Public policy is involved here to a greater extent. What will society do with the thousands who are injured daily and to some of whom punitive damages are awarded.

Northwestern National Casualty Co. v. McNulty, supra.

The holding of the court in the *McNulty* case is based first on the finding, in Florida and Virginia, that the dominant purpose of punitive damages is not as compensation for a plaintiff, but rather as punishment for a defendant, and as a deterrence to him and others from repetition of the wrongful conduct. Then the Court accepts, as common knowledge, that death and injuries are wrought daily on our roads and streets and it is and should be the public policy of the State to establish sanctions against socially irresponsible drivers causing or contributing to such conditions. That the allowance of punitive damages against these drivers is one of the sanctions against such conduct. Then to allow one to insure himself against this punishment, which in effect transfers the penalty to the premium paying public, is inconsistent with the establishment of the sanctions and violative of the public policy of the State.

The doctrine of punitive damages is well established in Tennessee although there have been several judicial statements challenging the efficacy and soundness of the doctrine. Such damages are allowed, after an award for compensatory damages, in negligence cases when there has been some willful misconduct, or entire want of care which would raise the presumption of a conscious indifference to consequences. In such cases the interest of society and of the agreed individual are blended and such damages are allowed as punishment for such conduct and as an example or warning to the one so guilty, and others, in order to deter them from committing like offenses in the future. Such damages are not based so much upon the nature and extent of the injury as they are upon the oppression of the party who does the injury.

Although the dominant purpose for the allowance of punitive damages in Tennessee is similar to Florida and Virginia, as found by the Fifth Circuit Court in the *McNulty* case, we do not reach the same conclusion as the Fifth Circuit on the public policy issue for the following reasons.

FIRST. We accept, as common knowledge, the fact death and injuries on our highways and streets is a very serious problem and such is a matter of great public concern. We further accept, as common knowledge, socially irresponsible drivers, who by their actions in operation of motor vehicles, could be liable for punitive damages are a great part of this problem. We, however, are not able to agree the closing of the insurance market, on the payment of punitive damages, to such drivers would necessarily accomplish the result of deterring them in their wrongful conduct. This State, in regard to the proper operation of motor vehicles, has a great many detailed criminal sanctions, which apparently have not deterred this slaughter on our highways and streets. Then to say the closing of the insurance market, in the payment of punitive damages, would act to deter guilty drivers would in our opinion contain some element of speculation.

SECOND. The language in the insurance policy in the case at bar, which is similar to many types of liability policies, has been construed by most courts, as a matter of interpretation of the language of a policy, to cover both compensatory and punitive damages. Since most courts have so construed this language in the policy, we think the average policy holder reading this language would expect to be protected against all claims, not intentionally inflicted.

THIRD. There is often a fine line between simple negligence and negligence upon which an award for punitive damages can be made.

Public policy is the present concept of public welfare or general good. Public policy is practically synonymous with public good and unless the private contract is in terms of such a character as to tend to harm or injure the public good, public interest on public welfare or to violate the Constitution, laws, common or statutory, or judicial decisions of the State, it is not violative of public policy nor void on that account.

The insurance contract in the case at bar is a private contract between defendant and their assured, Norman Frank Crutchfield, which when construed as written would be held to protect him against claims for both compensatory and punitive damages. Then to hold assured, as a matter of public policy, is not protected by the policy on a claim for punitive damages would have the effect to partially void the contract. We do not think such should be done except in a clear case, and the reasons advanced do not make such a clear case.

We recognize there are many factors, pro and con, involved in this matter that have not been discussed in this opinion; such as the possible affect on insurance rates paid by the public and the possible conflict of interest between the insurance company and their assured at the trial. We have weighed a great many such factors and suffice to say we do not think they are determinative of the matter.

Judgment affirmed.

NOTES AND QUESTIONS

1. *McNulty Versus Lazenby*. The *McNulty* and *Lazenby* decisions are the grandparents of the two schools of thought on the issue of insuring punitive damages. Which decision did you find more persuasive?

2. *Level of Wrongdoing*. Liability for intentionally inflicted injuries generally is already excluded pursuant to the intentional act exclusion, except for injuries covered under the Personal and Advertising Liability coverage provisions. Thus, in most cases where the plaintiff's injuries were intentionally caused by the policyholder, no coverage exists, including coverage for punitive damages. But punitive damages can be awarded in situations that fall outside the reach of the intentional act exclusion. As the *Lazenby* court noted, punitive damages can be awarded for a variety of misconduct ranging from situations

where the party recklessly, intentionally, or egregiously causes harm to situations where the conduct is only slightly more blameworthy than negligence. Indeed, a number of states allow the award of punitive damages for liability vicariously imposed. One approach to the issue of insuring punitive damages would be to look at the nature of the specific conduct at issue instead of making a blanket rule that punitive damages are or are not allowed to be covered by insurance as a matter of public policy. What are the pros and cons of such an approach?

3. *Why Not Expressly Exclude Punitive Damages?* If insurers do not want to cover punitive damages, then why not expressly exclude such damages from coverage with clear policy language instead of relying upon public policy arguments once claims are asserted? This is not a new idea. In 1977, ISO attempted to insert a punitive damages exclusion into liability policies, but insurers rejected the proposal. *See, e.g.*, Alan I. Widiss, *Liability Insurance Coverage for Punitive Damages? Discerning Answers to the Conundrum Created by Disputes Involving Conflicting Public Policies, Pragmatic Considerations and Political Actions*, 39 Vill. L. Rev. 455, 488 (1994). Why would insurers want to allow policies to cover punitive damages claims under the express terms of the policies they sell but then argue that such coverage should not be allowed as a matter of public policy when claims are tendered?

Professor Tom Baker commented on this apparent inconsistency with these thoughtful observations:

> The agreements do not distinguish among kinds of damages. . . . Indeed, there is little dispute that, on their face, most primary general and automobile policies provide coverage for punitive damages. . . . It takes some familiarity with insurance practice to fully appreciate the irony of insurance companies relying upon public policy arguments to avoid paying claims otherwise covered by their policies. The irony comes from the steadfast complaints of insurance interests about judges who 'rewrite' insurance policies to provide coverage that the insurance companies did not sell. According to the same logic, a judge who refused to enforce an insurance company's promise to pay a punitive damages claim would be 'rewriting' the policy to take away coverage that the policyholder bought.

Tom Baker, *Reconsidering Insurance for Punitive Damages*, 1998 Wis. L. Rev. 101, 115, 124, n.78 (1998).

Where liability insurance policies specifically exclude punitive damages, some courts have enforced the exclusions. *See, e.g.*, *Rummel v. St. Paul Surplus Lines Ins. Co.*, 945 P.2d 985 (N.M. 1997); *Cassel v. Schacht*, 683 P.2d 294 (Ariz. 1984).

4. *Is McNulty Still Good Law?* The *McNulty* decision effectively has been overruled under Virginia law by statute. *See* Va. Code Ann. § 38.2–227 (West) ("It is not against the public policy of the Commonwealth for any person to purchase insurance providing coverage for punitive damages arising out of

the death or injury of any person as the result of negligence, including willful and wanton negligence, but excluding intentional acts. This section declares existing policy."). Under Florida law, punitive damages are insurable for liability imposed vicariously on the policyholder. *See U.S. Concrete Pipe Co. v. Bould*, 437 So. 2d 1061, 1064 (Fla. 1983) ("Florida public policy does not preclude insurance coverage of punitive damages when the insured himself is not personally at fault, but is merely vicariously liable for another's wrong.").

5. *Majority Rule*. Courts are split on the question of whether punitive damages should be allowed to be insured as a matter of public policy. Although courts in many states have concluded it is against public policy to allow insurance to cover punitive damages, the majority rule is that public policy does not forbid insuring such damages. Thus, in most states, unless the insurance policy at issue expressly excludes coverage for punitive damages, they are covered. In addition, in many states, even if punitive damages are not allowed to be covered if liability is imposed directly on the policyholder, if the policyholder's liability is vicarious, then such damages can be covered. *See* Peter J. Kalis, Thomas M. Reiter & James R. Segerdahl, Policyholder's Guide to the Law of Insurance Coverage § 5.04, Chart 5–2 (1st ed. 1997 & Supp. 2020).

6. *What About Uninsured Drivers?* One of the topics examined in Chapter 5 involved the unique nature of uninsured (and underinsured) motorist insurance as first-party coverage where the amount of the insurer's obligation is defined by third-party concepts. When a policyholder is entitled to punitive damages against an uninsured or underinsured motorist, should the policyholder be entitled to collect such damages from the uninsured or underinsured motorist insurer?

III. GRUESOME CHOICES

MARTIN V. ALLIANZ LIFE INS. CO. OF NORTH AMERICA

573 N.W.2d 823 (N.D. 1998)

Opinion

VANDEWALLE, CHIEF JUSTICE.

Donald D. Martin appealed from a Judgment entered after the Cass County District Court granted Defendant's Motion for Summary Judgment. We affirm.

I

On October 5, 1995, Donald D. Martin was involved in a serious motor vehicle collision in Tennessee. Initially, Martin was treated at the University of Tennessee Memorial Hospital. His most serious injury was a severe fracture dislocation of his lower left leg. Dr. David Reath, a Tennessee physician, noted in his medical report "[Martin] does have a chance at limb salvage although certainly ankle function will be severely decreased."

At the end of October, Martin was transported by air ambulance to Dakota Heartland Hospital in Fargo. After weeks at Dakota Heartland, a local nursing home, and the Dakota Rehab Unit, Martin was discharged to his home in mid January. Throughout the initial hospitalization and rehabilitation, the viability of Martin's lower left leg was in question.

Martin was readmitted to the hospital at the end of February. He underwent two surgeries and was discharged to nursing home care. On April 18, 1996, 196 days after the initial injury, Martin's lower left leg was amputated.

Martin owned a group Accidental Death and Dismemberment Insurance policy offered through his membership in the American Legion. The group insurance policy was underwritten by Allianz Life Insurance Company of North America, the Legionnaire Insurance Trust, the A.G.I.A., Inc., and the Life Insurance Company of North America (collectively, Allianz). The Allianz policy included the following provisions:

> **WHEN BENEFITS ARE PAYABLE:**
>
> Allianz Life will pay benefits when all of the following conditions have been met:
>
> > (1) The Member or Insured Dependent sustained an accidental bodily injury while his insurance under the Group Policy was effective.
> >
> > (2) The injury, directly and independently of all other causes, resulted in a Covered Loss.
> >
> > (3) *The Covered Loss occurred within 90 days after the injury was sustained.*
>
> **COVERED LOSSES AND AMOUNT PAYABLE:**
>
> The Principal Sum applicable to the Member and to each Insured Dependent is shown in the Schedule. When benefits are payable, Allianz Life will pay the percentage of the applicable Principal Sum for a Covered Loss as indicated below.

Covered loss	Percentage of Principal Sum Payable
* * *	
loss of one limb	50%
* * *	

> If an insured person sustains more than one Covered Loss as a result of any one accident, the total amount payable for all Covered Losses shall never exceed his Principal Sum.
>
> *Loss of a limb means severance at or above the wrist or ankle.* Loss of sight means total and irrecoverable loss of sight.

(bold retained, emphases added).

Martin filed a claim for accidental injury disability benefits. Allianz denied coverage because the severance of Martin's lower left leg did not occur within the 90 day period in the insurance contract.

Martin filed this action, claiming breach of contract and bad faith. Allianz and Martin each filed motions for summary judgment. The district court found Martin's leg was not physically separated above the ankle until long after the 90-day limitation expired and granted Allianz's Motion for Summary Judgment.

II

On appeal, Martin claims the meaning of the word "severance" is ambiguous and should be interpreted to provide coverage because his leg was "functionally severed" following the collision. Martin also argues the 90-day contract limitation period is unreasonable and the district court erred in dismissing his bad faith claim. . . .

A. *Ambiguity of "Severance"*

. . . .

A "covered loss" under the Allianz policy includes "loss of a limb." "Loss of a limb means *severance at or above* the wrist or ankle." (Emphasis added). Martin claims the term "severance" is ambiguous because it could mean "physical severance" or "functional severance." A contract term is ambiguous when it can have at least two alternative meanings. *Kief Farmers,* 534 N.W.2d at 32. In the present case Martin's argument "jumps the gun" on contract interpretation by suggesting an ambiguity exists, and should be resolved in his favor, without first looking to the plain meaning of the term "severance." *Walle Mut. Ins. Co. v. Sweeney,* 419 N.W.2d 176, 178 (N.D.1988) (interpreting Chapter 9–07, N.D.C.C., as requiring other rules of interpretation to fail before ambiguities are held against the drafter, N.D.C.C. § 9–07–19). "[M]ost courts agree [ ] the phrase 'severance at or above' contemplates substantially complete physical, as contrasted with functional, loss of a member." J.L. Isham, Annotation, *Accident Insurance: What is "Loss" of a Body Member,* 51 A.L.R.4th 156, 164.

Neither "physical" nor "functional" appears in the Allianz insurance contract. We will not add these words to the contract to create an ambiguity because they do not define, but rather modify, the true contract term, "severance." Adding words to a contract in order to create an ambiguity violates the purpose of contract interpretation. *Cf. Kief Farmers,* 534 N.W.2d at 36 (refusing to rewrite an insurance contract to exclude coverage). An action for reformation is the appropriate legal vehicle for the judicial redrafting of a contract. *Ell v. Ell,* 295 N.W.2d 143 (N.D.1980). *Cf. Link,* 386 N.W.2d at 900 (refusing to strain the insurance contract language or create an ambiguity merely to side with the insured).

Where a term is undefined in the contract we usually look to its clear, ordinary meaning. . . . The ordinary meaning is the definition a non law-trained person would attach to the term. "Severance" is defined as "[t]he act or process of severing . . . [t]he condition of being severed . . . [s]eparation; partition." *The American Heritage College Dictionary* 1248 (3d ed.1997). "Sever" means "[t]o set or keep apart; divide or separate . . . [t]o cut off (a part) from a whole. . . ." *Id.* We believe the term severance means what it says; that is, where a member is separated or taken apart from the rest of the body. The "functional severance" or immobility of Martin's leg following the collision is not within the plain meaning of severance and does not invoke the Allianz dismemberment coverage.

In this case, the "plain meaning" and the "complex" or "legal meaning" of the word "severance" are in agreement. Most courts hold the term severance is unambiguous. *See, e.g., Travelers Ins. Co. v. Burchett,* 841 F.2d 155, 157 (6th Cir.1988) (holding the term "severance" is unambiguous and means actual physical severance), *Reid v. Life Ins. Co. of N. Am., Inc.,* 718 F.2d 677, 680–82 (4th Cir.1983) (holding severance clearly and unambiguously requires an actual cutting off of the member at the place indicated), *Cornellier v. American Casualty Co.,* 389 F.2d 641, 643 (2d Cir.1968) (noting most courts have found provisions using the term severance to be unambiguous).

. . . .

In the present case Martin was covered by a group policy with the title "ACCIDENTAL DEATH & DISMEMBERMENT INSURANCE." To conclude the definition of "severance" is somehow broader than the main "dismemberment" title would turn the typical insurance contract on its head. From our observations it is typical for the initial portions of an insurance contract to describe in broad terms the coverage provided with the limitations appearing later, in the "small print." This Court construes insurance policies as a whole to give meaning to each word and phrase. Thus, we would ordinarily consider insurance contract titles as descriptive of the coverage provided. A "DEATH AND DISMEMBERMENT INSURANCE" title describes a policy providing coverage in case the insured dies or loses a member of his body. Neither happened here within the 90-day limitation period.

Under North Dakota law, "[a]n agreement which is essentially a 'contract of adhesion' should be examined with special scrutiny by the courts to assure [ ] it is not applied in an unfair or unconscionable manner against the party who did not participate in its drafting." *Farmers Union Grain Terminal Ass'n v. Nelson,* 223 N.W.2d 494, 497 (N.D.1974). Although we give adhesion contracts "special scrutiny" that does not mean we will strike out a term in the contract in order to provide coverage for the insured. Denying coverage on the basis of a contract term may appear unduly harsh, but straining the language of an insurance policy to favor the insured would do greater harm to the public interest by creating uncertainty in an otherwise unambiguous contract.

We conclude the district court was correct in granting summary judgment in favor of Allianz because "severance" of Martin's leg did not occur within the 90-day limitation period.

B. *Unreasonableness of 90-Day Limitation*

Martin argues the 90-day contract limitation period is unreasonable and against public policy because it requires the insured to choose between losing a savable limb or taking the insurance proceeds. There is authority holding similar limitation periods unenforceable. *Strickland v. Gulf Life Ins. Co.,* 240 Ga. 723, 242 S.E.2d 148, 149, 152 (1978) (reversing so the trial court can fully consider public policy issues and framing the issue as a "gruesome choice" between collecting insurance proceeds or cutting off ones leg). However, the vast majority of cases have upheld such limitation periods when challenged as unreasonable, unconscionable, or against public policy. *See Hawes v. Kansas Farm Bureau,* 238 Kan. 404, 710 P.2d 1312, 1316–17 (1985) (citing 17 cases holding 90-day limitations periods not unconscionable and 2 cases holding such provisions invalid on public policy grounds), and Laurent B. Frantz, Annotation, *Validity and Construction of Provision in Accident Insurance Policy Limiting Coverage For Death or Loss of Member to Death or Loss Occurring Within Specified Period After Accident,* 39 A.L.R.3d 1311, 1313 (noting similar limitation clauses have been uniformly upheld when attacked as unreasonable, unconscionable, or against public policy).

In *Cornellier v. American Casualty Co.,* the plaintiff made a similar public policy argument. 389 F.2d at 642. In that case the plaintiff was struck by a vehicle and suffered severe injuries to his left leg. *Id.* The American Casualty insurance contract contained a 90-day limitation period. *Id.* The plaintiff's leg was amputated over 90 days after the accident. *Id.* Interpreting Vermont state law in a federal diversity case, the court noted:

> In ruling on this question, we must keep in mind [ ] a court's power to invalidate contractual provisions as offensive to public policy is not exercised in every case in which the contract may seem to operate harshly on one of the parties. As a general rule, parties to a contract are bound by its provisions and an insured is entitled only to the coverage for which he contracted; it is not the function

> of a court to rewrite insurance policies so as to provide coverage which the court might have considered more equitable. Thus, the question is not whether the 90-day limitation in the present case results in a hardship to the plaintiff, but whether that provision is so unreasonable [ ] it must be held contrary to the public interest and void.

Id. at 644.

In *Johnson v. Peterbilt of Fargo, Inc.,* 438 N.W.2d 162, 163–164 (N.D.1989) we said:

> Public policy, with respect to contract provisions, is a principle of law whereby a contract provision will not be enforced if it has a tendency to be injurious to the public or against the public good. *Ness v. Fargo,* 64 N.D. 231, 251 N.W. 843 (1933). Whether a particular provision is against public policy is generally provided for by statute or by the State Constitution. However, when a contract provision is inconsistent with fair and honorable dealing, contrary to sound policy and offensive to good morals, courts have the authority to declare the provision void as against public policy.

But when a court is faced with deciding whether a contract is against public policy, it must be mindful of the right of individuals, in this case an association, the American Legion, to enter into a contract. *Id.* at 164. Although agreements will not be enforced if they are injurious to the public or against the public good, if this matter is one for which a public policy should be announced, the legislative branch is much better suited than the courts to set the public policy of the State. *See Downtowner, Inc. v. Acrometal Products, Inc.,* 347 N.W.2d 118, 124 (N.D.1984) (noting the legislature "can do studies, gather evidence, hold hearings, and come to a decision" and "broad public policy issues are best handled by legislatures with their comprehensive machinery for public input and debate" (citations and quotations omitted)).

We do not believe the 90-day limitation period is so unreasonable as to be contrary to the public interest of North Dakota. While the limitation period may appear to present the insured with the "gruesome choice" of collecting the insurance proceeds or cutting off his leg, the nature of death and dismemberment insurance is to provide coverage in gruesome situations.

Citing *Strickland,* 242 S.E.2d at 152, Martin claims today's medical advancements make a 90-day limitation period unreasonable because there is a greater possibility of saving the limb. While medical science has advanced, the advancement does not immediately change the terms of a contract. If policy holders prefer a longer limitation period than 90 days, the competitive insurance market is better positioned than are the courts to react to advancements in medical science.

We are not willing to head down the slippery slope of holding a 90-day limitation unreasonable. Such a conclusion begs the question: What is reasonable? 91 days? 92 days? 100? "[T]here has always been and there always will be those who will die [or are dismembered] on the 89th day following the injury and those who will die [or are dismembered] on the 91st day following an injury." *Hawes,* 710 P.2d at 1318. Whether or not the 90-day limitation is a number arbitrarily selected by the insurer, a court-picked number would be just as arbitrary and defeat the expectations of contracting parties.

The district court correctly granted summary judgment because Martin's leg was not severed within the 90-day limitation period.

. . . .

NOTES AND QUESTIONS

1. *What Public Policy Was at Issue?* Did the *Martin* court rely upon public policy to reach its holding? If so, what exactly was the public policy?

The *Martin* court's opinion does not discuss whether Martin was aware he was insured under the American Legion group policy or, if he knew this, whether he was aware of the 90-day provision in the policy's coverage during the months after his accident and before his leg was amputated. Accidental death and dismemberment coverage sometimes attaches to people in unexpected ways, such as through possession or use of a credit card, membership in an organization (as was the case in *Martin*), or an offer (which would need to be accepted) from a bank or other financial institution to an account holder. Is it relevant whether Martin knew about the coverage and understood it? Before you answer, consider the next note.

2. *Life or Death?* Amputation is gruesome enough, but the issue confronted in *Martin* can arise in other situations. Suppose Grandma, who is insured under a $1 million policy of accidental death insurance, with family members as beneficiaries and containing a 90-day provision like that in *Martin,* is severely injured in an auto accident. Grandma is in a non-vegetative coma, and she is connected to a life support machine that makes it possible for her to breathe. Although the prospects for recovery are slim, doctors say there is nevertheless hope for her survival. As day 90 approaches, she remains in the coma, and the doctors' slim hopes for recovery are waning. Yet on days 88 and 89, Grandma's body, although struggling, refuses to give up. What are the public policy implications of this scenario? Should insurance policy language be allowed to be a factor into the family's decision, in combination with the advice of the physicians, whether to remove life support?

If you answer the last question "no," how much time should be allowed after the 90 days to make the decision about life support? Is there any reasoned way for an insurer to know whether the family member beneficiaries have had enough time to decide before attempting to enforce a time limit for recovery? Note that Grandma is going to die eventually from some cause. Thus, the longer she survives, the more likely it is that her death will not be caused by the accident, but it will instead be due to something else. Does this help explain the logic of the 90-day clause, and does this matter to the public policy analysis? For Americans, generally, the odds that a person will die due to an illness, rather than an accident or some other cause unrelated to illness, are overwhelming. According to the Center for Disease Control, in 2014, 5.2% of all deaths in America were caused by accidents and approximately 93% resulted from illness. *See* Center for Disease Control, National Vital Statistics Reports, Vol. 65, No. 5, June 30, 2016 (updated June 1, 2017), at 9.

Does this discussion help explain why accidental death insurance appears to be very inexpensive relative to life insurance? Does this fact have any public policy implications of its own?

3. *Public Policy, Auto Insurance, and Accident Insurance.* As discussed in Chapter 5, auto insurance is mandatory in every state so that injured parties have a source of money from which to recover in the event they are injured by another driver in an auto accident. Why should compensating victims of car crashes under an auto policy be of greater importance than compensating a person who loses a limb as a result of an auto accident under a personal Accidental Death and Dismemberment Insurance policy?

4. *Majority Rule. Martin* represents the majority rule. Most courts have enforced time restrictions set forth in policies regarding the time limit for recovering for lost limbs or other body parts. However, there are cases, such as *Strickland v. Gulf Life Ins. Co.*, 242 S.E.2d 148 (Ga. 1978), which the *Martin* court cited, wherein courts have refused to enforce such provisions on public policy grounds in the absence of a showing of the reasonableness of the time period used in the policy. In remanding the case for an evidentiary hearing regarding the purpose of the time limitation and its reasonableness, the *Strickland* court indicated that a relevant factor in the analysis would be whether the policyholder had a choice regarding the time limitation contained in the policy.

On the other hand, the *Martin* court, in quoting another decision upon which it relied, stated, the "insured is entitled only to the coverage for which he contracted; it is not the function of a court to rewrite insurance policies so as to provide coverage which the court might have considered more equitable." Having now spent a semester studying insurance law, do policyholders have a choice regarding the policy provisions that set forth the length of time in which to decide whether to amputate a limb? If a court will not rewrite insurance policies to provide "more equitable" provisions for the policyholder, then who will? Who else could come to policyholders' rescue?

EXERCISE

1. Draft a 2-page memo that makes the pro and con arguments for courts using public policy as the basis for ignoring or rewriting policy language. Please be sure to use as many examples as you can from the cases covered this semester to support your arguments.

INDEX

References are to Pages